D1569782

Comic Book PRICE GUIDE 2010

Maggie Thompson • Brent Frankenhoff • Peter Bickford

© 2010 by Krause Publications, a division of F+W Media, Inc.

Includes issue information © 2010 F+W Media, Inc., and Human Computing.

Published by

krause publications

A division of F+W Media, Inc.

700 East State Street • Iola, WI 54990-0001
715-445-2214 • 888-457-2873
www.krausebooks.com

Our toll-free number to place an order is (800) 258-0929
or visit our online bookstore at *http://shop.collect.com*.

All rights reserved. No portion of this publication may be reproduced or transmitted in any form or by any means, electronic or mechanical, including photocopy, recording, or any information storage and retrieval system, without permission in writing from the publisher, except by a reviewer who may quote brief passages in a critical article or review to be printed in a magazine or newspaper, or electronically transmitted on radio, television, or the Internet.

Library of Congress Control Number: 2010924835
ISBN-13: 978-1-4402-1399-1
ISBN-10: 1-4402-1399-2

Edited by:
Brent Frankenhoff
Maggie Thompson

Designed by:
Stacy Bloch
Sandi Carpenter
Shawn Williams
Heidi Zastrow

Product names, logos, and images used herein are depicted for the sole purpose of identification and are the intellectual property of their respective manufacturers.

Printed in the United States of America

Contents

COMICS! COMICS! COMICS!

Thanks, first to you, for buying this book — an evolution of our annual ***Comic Book Checklist and Price Guide*** and ***Comics Values Annual*** — and also to the many people who helped us put this book together. As ever, there are so many of them to thank that we're bound to miss a few. To anyone who should be thanked but isn't (you know who you are): We're sorry, and you know we couldn't have done this without you.

First and foremost, without the copious contributions of ***ComicBase*** developer Peter Bickford, this book simply wouldn't exist. While his research has often paralleled our own, he has also obtained information to which we didn't have access, just as our information has added many titles to his computerized comics database program. This book, which has evolved from our long-running ***Comic Book Checklist and Price Guide*** series, contains a number of fresh updates obtained through various sources, including many of ComicBase's users.

That brings us to the publishers and individual creators who provided copies of their titles, so that we could maintain a database based on actually published material. We thank them all and encourage others to do the same.

Thanks also to the readers of our other price guides (***Comic Book Checklist and Price Guide, The Standard Catalog of Comic Books***, and ***Comics Values Annual***) who have been providing additional data on their favorite titles.

Thanks go, as well, to our own behind-the-scenes people, including: Tammy Kuhnle and Steve Duberstein, computer services; Sandi Carpenter and Stacy Bloch in our book production department; graphic designers Heidi Zastrow and Shawn Williams; and the entire antiques and collectibles division at Krause Publications.

Most of all, we acknowledge the work of Don Thompson, who nursed this project through the last 11 years of his life. We miss you, Don.

And, again, we thank you all.

Maggie Thompson
Brent Frankenhoff
Iola, Wisconsin
April 8, 2010

SAVE YOUR COMICS!

We see it all the time: Rare and valuable comics, going for pennies on the dollar in estate sales. Or rotting away, stuffed in corners in wet basements.

Because most people don't know what they have, whether their comics are rare and valuable — or whether they're plentiful and worth less (though not worthless). And because most people don't know how best to take care of the comics they have.

But you won't have that problem — ***The Comic Book Price Guide*** is here to help.

We're the people behind ***Comics Buyer's Guide***, the world's longest-running magazine about comics. Started in 1971, it's been published continuously and passed the 1,650-issue mark near the end of 2008. We've maintained a price guide database since the early 1980s — and, in the early 1990s, we published the first edition of an annual ***Checklist*** as both a price guide and a collectors' utility for comics published after 1961.

Since then, we've added to the line with the mammoth ***CBG Standard Catalog of Comic Books***, which includes everything that's in this volume plus story titles, circulation figures, and comics from the 1930s, 1940s, and 1950s. Of course, that's a monster of a book — the latest print edition was 1,624 pages and a DVD-ROM edition is now available with more than 3,500 "virtual" pages in full color — so the ***Comic Book Price Guide*** was developed as a more portable reference for comics buyers and sellers. It's an evolution of our ***Checklist and Price Guide*** and ***Comics Values Annual*** — but it's still intended to function in a number of fashions.

There's more than one way to use it.

You can use it as a "have" list, in which you maintain an inventory of the comics you're collecting.

You can use it as a guide to show prices you can expect to pay for items, if you look for them in comics shops throughout the country, online, or at conventions. The prices

NEAR MINT

(Abbreviated **NM**)

This is a nearly perfect comic book.

Its cover shows barely perceptible signs of wear. Its spine is tight, and its cover has only minor loss of luster and only minor printing defects. Some discoloration is acceptable in older comics — as are signs of aging.

Near Mint prices are what are listed in this guide.

[The term for this grade is the same one used for CGC's 9.4 grade.]

Our illustrated grading guide can be found on Page 15!

listed are arrived at by surveying comics shops, online sales, convention sales, auctions, and mail-order houses.

With that information, our price guide reflects what a smart person with those choices would be willing to pay for a given issue.

You can use it as a guide for value, when you're buying or trading items.

And you can carry it with you in your comics storage box, because it's sized to fit in a comics box.

Condition is vital.

Whether you're buying or selling comic books, one of the most important factors in setting the price is the condition of the material.

A scuffed, torn "reading copy" (that is, one that is suitable for reading but not for getting high prices at resale) will bring only a fraction of the price of a copy of the same issue which looks as though it has just come off the newsstand.

Picky collectors will even go through all the copies on a newsstand so as to buy the one in best condition. [Even a so-called "newsstand mint" copy of *Fantastic Four* #1 may have what is called "Marvel chipping" (a frayed right edge), since many of those early-'60s issues were badly cut by the printer.]

On the other hand, beat-up copies can provide bargains for collectors whose primary focus is reading the comic-book story. The same goes for reprints of comics which would otherwise be hard to find.

In fact, you may find prices on poor-condition copies even lower than the prices in this guide, depending on the attitude of the seller. It's a good time to get into collecting comics for the fun of it.

A major change in the comics-collecting world, CGC grading, has meant a huge jump in prices for certain hotly collected issues in almost-perfect condition. The third-party graders of Certified Guaranty Company evaluate the condition of submitted copies and then encapsulate the graded issue in a labeled container. Because of the independent nature of the process and the reliability of the evaluating team, confidence in buying such items has meant a premium over the standard price in that condition.

More information on the company can be found in the pages ahead.

Visit our website at www.cbgxtra.com!

Answers for readers who are NEW TO COMICS!

Readers have been kind enough to ask many questions about our price guide. To help you make the best use of this volume, we're answering many of them here (and we're answering questions you didn't ask, too, in an attempt to provide more information than you can possibly use).

Why do we need a price guide at all?

We've spent nearly 30 years developing a guide so that buyers and sellers of back issues will have help knowing what a consumer with various buying choices can expect to pay, if he's looking — for example — for that issue that will complete his run of the two DC series of *Shade the Changing Man*. The collector will find that even the highest-priced issue in the best condition probably won't cost more than about $4 — and that's the sort of information that can motivate a casual reader to become a collector.

Moreover, we try to provide helpful information to people who purchase it in order to have a (yes) guide to buying comics. Pricing information is just *part* of what we offer. In fact, we are increasingly intrigued by the more detailed information you'll find in this book, including character appearances and publishing anomalies.

Why can't I find a title in your list?

We're working constantly to expand the listings themselves and increase the information on those we already provide. Check out what we have included, and — if you have something we're not listing — please let us know the details!

We need to know the information as given in the indicia of the issue (that's the tiny print, usually on the first few pages, that gives the publishing information): the full title, the number, and the issue month and year — and the U.S. price given on the cover. If there's a significant event (an origin, a birth, a death, *etc.)*, please include that, too.

We're also always on the lookout for creator information as it appears in the issue, along with story titles and any other bits of data that we can add to our database. That database doesn't just produce this book, but other price guides as well and is shared with ComicBase, a software package for comics inventory management.

Check, too, on whether you're looking up the title as it appears in the indicia. For example, we list *Vampire Lestat*, not *Anne Rice's The Vampire Lestat*; we list *Mack Bolan: The Executioner,* not *Don Pendleton's Mack Bolan: The Executioner.* Many Marvel titles have adjectives.

What's in this book?

This price guide began as a quarterly update of activity in comics published since 1961, as reflected in prices comics shops were likely to charge. Moreover, the focus was pretty much limited to Silver Age super-hero titles — in fact, Silver Age super-hero titles *that were being published when the price guide began*. This meant that such titles as *OMAC*, a title that starred a super-hero but was not still being published by 1983, didn't get listed in that earliest edition. It also meant that so-called "funny animal" titles, "war" titles, and the like were not included.

However, once the listings were begun (not by ***Comics Buyer's Guide*** staff, incidentally; the material was started for another publication), Don Thompson took over the compilation. From that point, every effort was made to include every issue of every comic book received in the office. However, since the entries were not on a database and had to be compressed to fit the space available, annotation, dates, and original prices were not usually part of the listing. On the other hand (and because of Don's care, once he took over the project), material which was often overlooked by other reference publishers has been listed from the beginning in the ***CBG*** listings. *Concrete* and *Teenage Mutant Ninja Turtles,* for example, were first listed in ***CBG***'s price listings.

In the years since, we've expanded our focus even further, adding in the hundreds of titles published in the 1930s, '40s, and '50s, as well as many lesser-known titles of the Silver Age and beyond. Our cooperative agreement with *ComicBase* has led to the inclusion of hundreds of new titles and issues, as well as a wealth of variant editions.

And we continue to fill in remaining information whenever we get it.

What are the "Golden Age" and the "Silver Age?"

Comic-book collectors divide the history of comics into the "Golden Age" and the "Silver Age." "Golden Age" indicates the first era of comic-book production — the '30s and '40s. It was a time of incredible creation in the field, when such characters as Superman and Batman first appeared.

"Silver Age" is used to indicate a period of comic-book production of slightly less (nostalgic?) luster than that of the Golden Age. It is usually considered to have begun with the publication of the first revival of a '40s super-hero: the appearance of The Flash in *Showcase* #4 (Oct 1956).

There are additional comics ages, but discussion of those is beyond the scope of this piece.

This guide lists #8 and #10. Where's #9?

We haven't seen a copy and can't verify its existence. There was a time when comics collectors could safely assume that issue numbers would run in normal sequence, when no numbers were skipped and when there were no special numbers to confuse completists. That's not the case any more. What we need from those who want to help add to our information is confirmation that an item has *actually been published.*

In the case of multiple variants of a given issue, if they have the same value, they're lumped together in one listing here. For example, the multiple variants of a given Image issue, designated as 1/A, 1/B, 1/C, and so on, could appear as 1/A-1/E in our listings.

So do you own all these comics?

No. Many publishers and collectors have helped us over the years by sending photocopies of indicia, records of publication, annotations, and the like — all of which has permitted us to provide collectors with more information every year. What *ComicBase* and we cannot do — and *do* not do — is pull information from other price guides or from announcements of what is *scheduled* for publication. The former would not be proper; the latter leads to errors — the sort of errors that have been known to become imbedded in some price guides' information files.

Every effort has been made to make the notations consistent, but this list has more than 150,000 individual issues coordinated between *ComicBase* and ***CBG***, so this can be an arduous task.

Why do some of your listings say (first series), (second series), etc., while others have (Vol. 1), (Vol. 2), and so on? Is there a difference?

Although publishers may begin a series again at #1, they often don't update the volume number in the indicia, which leads to the (first series) and (second series) notations. If the volume number changes (and it's a clear change, as in the case of Marvel's "Heroes Reborn" and "Heroes Return" title restarts), that is what differentiates the series.

On the other hand, when the volume number changes each year (as was the case with some Golden Age and early Silver Age material) but the series number is ongoing in sequence (Vol. 2, #21), then we don't note that change.

Marvel's return to original numbering for *Fantastic Four* and *Amazing Spider-Man* in mid-2003 caused both titles' later listings, beginning with #500 for each, to revert to the respective title's first volume. To help show where the issues from later volumes of those series fall in sequences, we've added parenthetical notations to the original numbers like this: 1 (442).

I've heard some of my squarebound comics referred to variously as "bookshelf format," "prestige format," and "Dark Knight format." What's the difference?

Various formats — usually reserved for special projects (mini-series and one-shots) — have different names, depending on the publisher. We use the term "prestige format" generically to indicate a fancier package than the average comic book. Marvel refers to some titles in upscale formats as "bookshelf format," whereas DC initially solicited some of its titles in the format of *Batman: The Dark Knight* as "Dark Knight format." Details of fancy formats can be widely varied.

I tried to sell my comics to a retailer, but he wouldn't even offer me 10% of the prices you list. Is he trying to cheat me? Are your prices wrong?

Remember, our prices are based on what an informed collector with some choices is willing to pay for a comic book, not necessarily what a shop is charging or paying for that comic book. A shop has huge overhead and needs to tailor its stock to match the interest shown by its customers.

If no one locally is buying comics starring Muggy-Doo, Boy Cat, it doesn't matter that *Muggy-Doo, Boy Cat* is bringing high prices elsewhere in the country.

Comics listed at their original prices may be showing no movement in most comics shops. In such cases, a retailer won't usually be interested in devoting store space to such titles, no matter ***how*** nice they are or ***how*** much you're discounting them. We've seen dealers being more selective than ever in what they will buy in recent years.

I'm a publisher, and I'd be willing to buy a hundred copies of my first issue at the price you list. I get calls from all over America from would-be buyers who would pay 10 times the price you give here for out-of-print issues of my comics. What's going on?

A publisher like you hears from faithful fans across the nation. A comics shop deals with a market of one community or smaller. You're dealing with a narrow, focused market of aficionados of your product who are looking for the specific issues they're missing. And with more and more online offerings, those fans find it easier to seek you out. As a result, a publisher who has back issues for sale may get higher prices than readers will find in this checklist. It doesn't mean you're ripping off fans; it means fans looking to buy that material are competing within a nationwide pool; the Internet may eventually put everyone in the same pool.

***Can I just order the back-issue comics I want from* Comics Buyer's Guide?**

This price guide is just that: a guide to the average back-issue prices comics shops are likely to charge their customers.

We maintain no back-issue stock for sale; we leave that to retailers who specialize in back issues. (Start with your local shops. You'll be able to check out the variety of material available and take a look in advance at what you're buying.)

Comics Buyer's Guide itself is the magazine of the comic-book field. As such, it carries ads from retailers across the country. You can check those ads for specific back issues that you're looking for. You can even take out a "wanted" ad to locate particular items, if that appeals to you. Subscription and advertising information can be found at ***www.cbgxtra.com***.

What are "cover variants"?

These occur when publishers try to increase "collectibility" of and interest in a title by releasing an issue with an assortment of covers. This is in hopes that completists will want to buy multiple copies, instead of just one. (The practice even spread to publications like *TV Guide*.)

So how are these performing as "rare" back issues? So far: poorly. Prices may rise at the time of release, but they usually fall again relatively quickly.

What's the first thing to do when I find a bunch of old comics?

If you've found a box of old comics in the attic and wonder what to do next, the first thing to do is find out what you've got. The same goes when you're looking for what you want to buy.

Here are some basics: Look at the copyright dates; if there are multiple dates, look at the *last* date. (If they're before 1950, chances are the comics are considered "Golden Age." Comics from the mid-1950s and later are Silver Age or more recent.)

Almost all comics are collected and identified by title and issue number. Look at the indicia, the fine print on the inside front page or inside front cover. That's what you'll use to find a specific issue in this or any other price guide. You'll want to check the issue title as given there — and the issue number.

What's the second thing to look at when I find a bunch of old comics?

Evaluate the condition of the copies. What does the comic book look like? Check the grading guide pages of our price guide to get a feel for the shape your comics are in. If they're beaten up, enjoy them for reading but don't expect to get a lot of money for them.

For this reason, many beginning collectors focus on exactly such poor issues, getting the pleasure of reading without making a heavy investment.

What's next for comic-book collecting?

The Internet has gained in its importance to collectors, e-mail is connecting collectors around the world, and third-party grading services have led to incredible price variations in some back issues, and computers are permitting collectors, as well as retailers, to monitor what they've got, what condition it's in, and what they want to buy.

So it'll help my collecting to have a computer?

You bet. If you have a home computer, you'll find it increases your sources for buying and selling. (And *ComicBase* can help in your inventory.)

Our website, *www.cbgxtra.com*, is a fun and friendly forum for new and longtime collectors to discuss all aspects of comics. But, it's not the only comics-related website out there. Surf the Web to find more!

PRICING!

Traditionally, comics price guides have relied solely on those "in-the-know" — advisors with recent experience in buying or selling comics.

While it's a method tried by most pricing publications at one time or another over the years, its shortcomings are readily apparent.

Advisor information sometimes tended to be anecdotal, speaking in broad terms about entire lines rather than in specifics about particular issues in certain grades.

Price guides often received advice in the form of spoken or written reports, rather than spreadsheets or other electronic formats likelier to deal in numerical detail.

And, too often, critics charged, advisors — most of whom were also retailers themselves — provided the prices they would have *liked* to have sold comics at, rather than the prices that they had *actually* sold comics at.

Wishful thinking (plus a simple business desire not to devalue their inventory) on behalf of advisors therefore tended to drive pricing in many guides up, up, up — even when prices were clearly falling for thousands of comic books.

The ***Comic Book Price Guide*** determines a single Near Mint price for each comic book through research by parties with no vested interest in seeing prices increase. Additionally, sales of CGC-graded copies are also analyzed, with the current sales ratios for non-encapsulated comics applied to the CGC prices to determine how the market is reacting.

Ungraded-copy price research

This volume includes a Near Mint price for the comic books listed herein. The prices are the result of a combined effort by Human Computing, producers of ***ComicBase***, and the staff of ***Comics Buyer's Guide***.

Human Computing has set more than 2 million prices for comic books over the years. It's investigated every title at least once, usually multiple times over the years, rechecking whenever a new trend surfaces. Convention sales, mail-order sales, and shop prices throughout the United States are gathered on a continual basis.

Comics Buyer's Guide has used many of the same methods, including making reference to the largest sortable database of actual online transactions ever assembled in comics.

Since 2000, the ***Comics Buyer's Guide*** staff has downloaded hundreds of thousands of completed transactions from such Internet sources as eBay and Heritage Comic Auctions, including auctions involving comic books graded by CGC. These transactions have been used to inform, rather than set, the prices for "unslabbed" comics seen herein.

The highest price isn't always right. Our philosophy isn't to publish the highest prices we can find to make people feel better about their collections, but rather to publish the prices that smart collectors shopping at a variety of retail, convention, and online venues are likely to find.

If you're in a remote area with only

one shop or the Internet to rely on, the prices you're likely to find will be higher. Likewise, a comic book with some pedigree — having come from a famous collection — may also sell for more.

We've included a handy multiplier table at to help determine prices in the other grades. Note that **one size does not necessarily fit all when it comes to these ratios.** Most Very Fine books fetch a third less than their Near Mint equivalents — but some very rare books fetch more, and some newer ones bring less.

To find prices for other grades for comic books **not graded by CGC, multiply our listed NM prices by:**

Mint: 150%	F-: 30%
NM/M:125%	VG/F: 25%
NM+: 110%	VG+: 23%
NM-: 90%	**Very Good: 20%**
VF/NM: 83%	VG-: 17%
VF+: 75%	G+: 14%
Very Fine: 66.6%	**Good: 12.5%**
VF-: 55%	G-: 11%
F/VF: 48%	FR/G: 10%
F+: 40%	**Fair: 8%**
Fine: 33.3%	**Poor: 2%**

CGC-graded prices

Simply toughening grading standards and raising NM prices to reflect the high prices CGC-slabbed comics fetch is not a solution. From our observations, we can say that it is not generally the case that the high CGC prices have exerted upward influence on identical unslabbed copies. Rather, two separate markets have developed with two separate sets of valuations, one for slabbed books and the other for their unslabbed counterparts.

In general, a Near Mint unslabbed comic book is fetching about what a slabbed VF/VF+ issue is bringing!

You can estimate CGC prices through the ratios at the bottom of this page to help determine prices in the other grades.

"CGC" and "slabbed" comics

CGC became part of the comics collector's lexicon in 2000, when what is now known as the Certified Guaranty Company began serving the comic-book field. Today, **CGC grading** is widely used by online buyers and sellers to provide a standard on which both can agree.

Info is available on the website, ***www.CGCcomics.com***, and by calling (877) NM-COMIC. There are several levels of service.

Graders do not determine a value; they identify defects and place a grade on the comic book. This lets online buyers purchase items evaluated by a common standard — and identifies for buyer and seller such matters as whether issues have been restored.

If you plan to buy a CGC-graded comic book:

First, yes: You ***can*** remove the comic book from the sealed container. If you retain the container and paperwork with the comic book, CGC even offers a discount on re-encapsulation.

The observed price ratio for **CGC-graded comics published after 1990** is...

1	2	4	10
9.6 NM+	9.8 NM/M	9.9 M	10.0 M

The observed price ratio for **CGC-graded comics published before 1990** is...

1	2	4	10	20	50
2.0 G	4.0 VG	6.0 F	8.0 VF	9.0 VF/NM	9.4 NM

CONDITION!

Why are comics from the 1940s, 1950s, and 1960s generally considered sound investment material, when comics from last Wednesday aren't?

Part of that is because comics are literally living things — they were once trees, after all — and their natural inclination over the years is to decompose.

So even if the number of copies around to begin with can be determined, there's a mortality factor at work, meaning comics in great shape are going to be harder and harder to find over time. Even if they haven't been loved to death through multiple readings and spine folds, comics are still going to try to turn yellow and brittle.

Collectors can slow that process with **storage devices**, ranging from the very expensive to the makeshift. The most common archival storage solution involves products made from **Mylar**, a transparent chemically inert substance.

Much more common are bags made from plastic, most commonly polypropylene, of varying thicknesses and backing boards with coated surfaces.

In general, the cheaper the method, the less protection it tends to afford.

Also, just as in real estate, it's important to remember location, location, location. Storing comics in a damp basement without a dehumidifier will result in rusted staples and musty books. A hot attic will age paper more rapidly. A cool, dry storage area away from direct sunlight (which will fade color from covers and cause paper to brown) is the best choice. Choose a location that's comfortable for you as well as your comics and you'll both enjoy the collecting experience all the more.

Communicating the condition of your comics to buyers — and understanding what condition sellers' comics are in — requires knowing a few simple terms.

For the last few decades, back-issue comic books have been sold with a designation indicating their condition. The eight grades recognized by the **Comic Book Price Guide**, ***Comics Buyer's Guide***, and ***ComicBase*** appear on pages 15-18, along with aids to help you see what each condition basically allows.

The grades:

Mint • Near Mint
Very Fine • Fine
Very Good • Good
Fair • Poor

The terms seen above have universal acceptance, even if different price guides — and, indeed, individual collectors and dealers — may not fully agree when it comes to what the attributes a comic book in each grade should have.

Half-grades (Very Fine + or Very Good -, for example) can be applied when a comic book narrowly misses the next grade.

Comic Book Grading Guide

When comics are compared with the Comic Book Grading Guide, it's easy to see there are many comics which fall between categories in something of an infinite gradation. For example, a "Fair" condition comic book (which falls between "Good" and "Poor") may have a soiled, slightly damaged cover, a badly rolled spine, cover flaking, corners gone, tears, and the like. It is an issue with multiple problems but it is intact — and some collectors enjoy collecting in this grade for the fun of it. Tape may be present and is always considered a defect.

The condition of a comic book is a vital factor in determining its price.

MINT

(Abbreviated **M, Mt**)

This is a perfect comic book. Its cover has full luster, with edges sharp and pages like new. There are no signs of wear or aging. It is not imperfectly printed or off-center. "Mint" means just what it says.

Mint prices are 150% of the Near Mint prices listed in this guide.
[The term for this grade is the same one used for CGC's 10.0 grade.]

NEAR MINT

(Abbreviated **NM**)

This is a nearly perfect comic book.
Its cover shows barely perceptible signs of wear. Its spine is tight, and its cover has only minor loss of luster and only minor printing defects. Some discoloration is acceptable in older comics — as are signs of aging.

Near Mint prices are what are listed in this guide.
[The term for this grade is the same one used for CGC's 9.4 grade.]

VERY FINE

(Abbreviated **VF**)

This is a nice comic book with beginning signs of wear. There can be slight creases and wrinkles at the staples, but it is a flat, clean issue with definite signs of being read a few times. There is some loss of the original gloss, but it is in general an attractive comic book.

Very Fine prices are 66.6% of the Near Mint prices listed in this guide.
[The term for this grade is the same one used for CGC's 8.0 grade.]

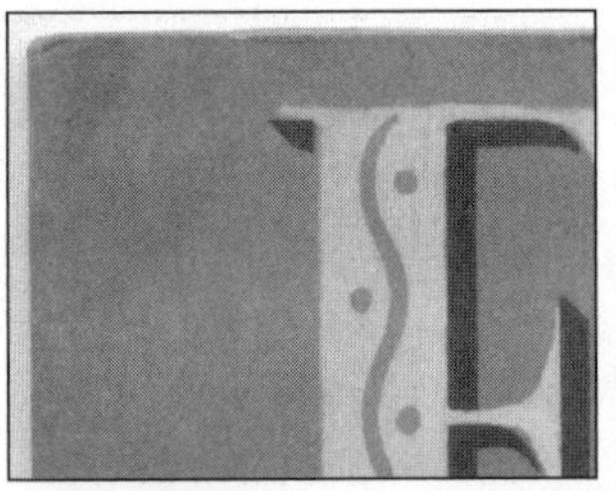

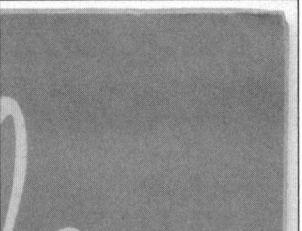

FINE

(Abbreviated **F, Fn**)

This comic book's cover is worn but flat and clean with no defacement. There is usually no cover writing or tape repair. Stress lines around the staples and more rounded corners are permitted. It is a good-looking issue at first glance.

Fine prices are 33.3% of the Near Mint prices listed in this guide.
[The term for this grade is the same one used for CGC's 6.0 grade.]

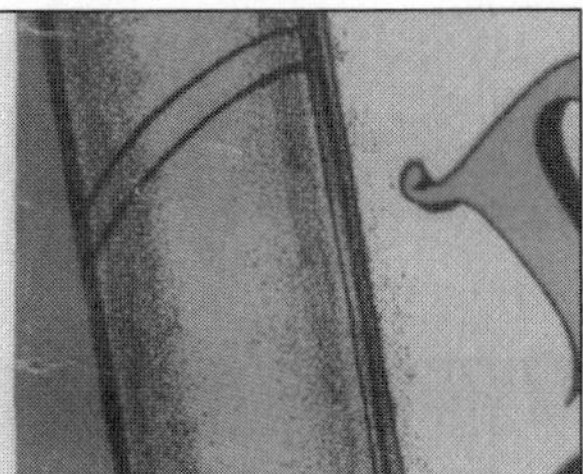

VERY GOOD

(Abbreviated **VG, VGd**)

Most of the original gloss is gone from this well-read issue.
There are minor markings, discoloration, and/or heavier stress lines around the staples and spine. The cover may have minor tears and/or corner creases, and spine-rolling is permissible.

Very Good prices are 20% of the Near Mint prices listed in this guide.
[The term for this grade is the same one used for CGC's 4.0 grade.]

GOOD

(Abbreviated **G, Gd**)

This is a very worn comic book with nothing missing.
Creases, minor tears, rolled spine, and cover flaking are permissible. Older Golden Age comic books often come in this condition.

Good prices are 12.5% of the Near Mint prices listed in this guide.
[The term for this grade is the same one used for CGC's 2.0 grade.]

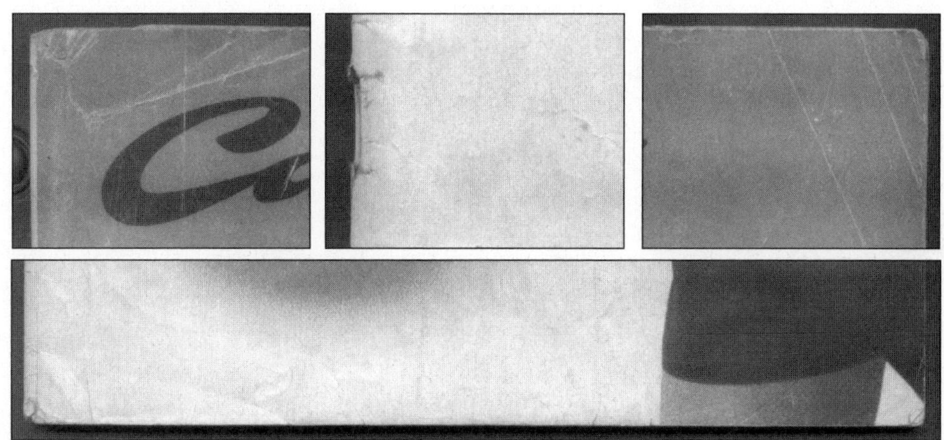

FAIR

(Abbreviated **FA, Fr**)

This comic book has multiple problems but is structurally intact.
Copies may have a soiled, slightly damaged cover, a badly rolled spine, cover flaking, corners gone, and tears. Tape may be present and is always considered a defect.

Fair prices are 8% of the Near Mint prices listed in this guide.
[The term for this grade is the same one used for CGC's 1.0 grade.]

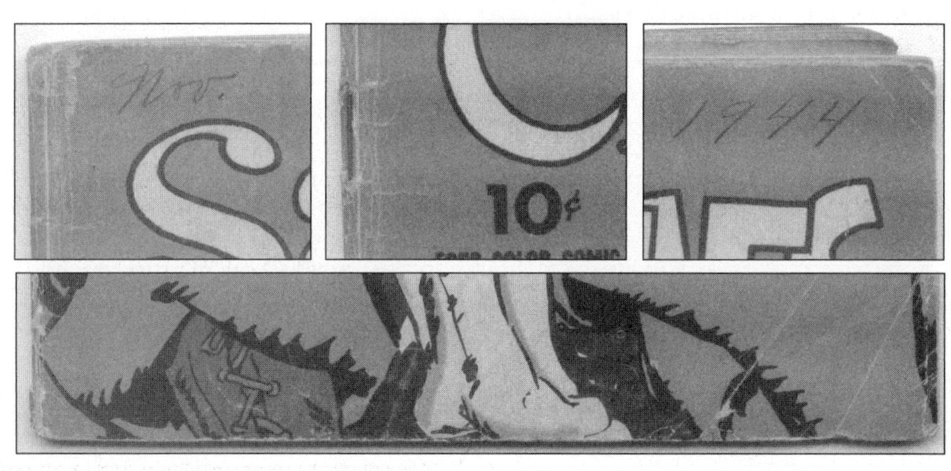

POOR

(Abbreviated **P, Pr**)

This issue is damaged and generally considered unsuitable for collecting.
While the copy may still contain some readable stories, major defects get in the way. Copies may be in the process of disintegrating and may do so with even light handling.

Poor prices are 2% of the Near Mint prices listed in this guide.
[The term for this grade is the same one used for CGC's 0.5 grade.]

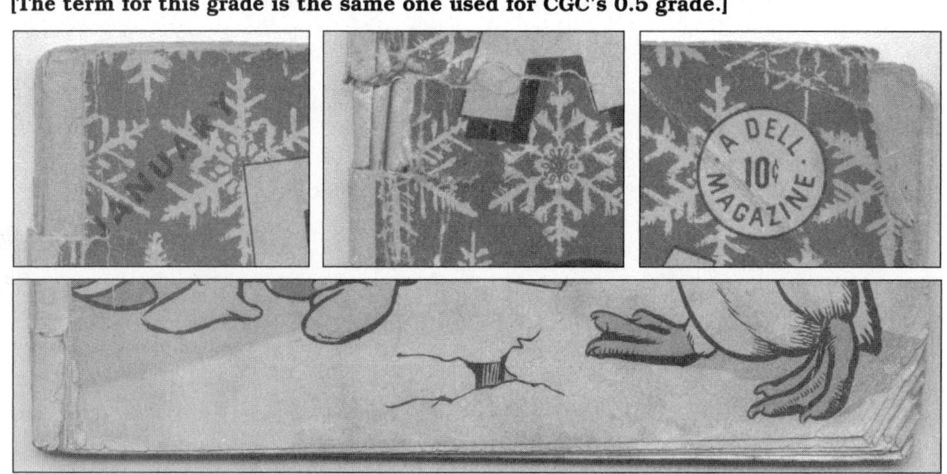

Guide to Defects

Theoretically, given a set of grading rules, determining the condition of a comic book should be simple. But flaws vary from item to item, and it can be difficult to pin one label on a particular issue — as with a sharp issue with a coupon removed. Another problem lies in grading historically significant vs. run-of-the-mill issues.

The examples shown here represent specific defects listed. These defects need to be taken into account when grading, but should *not* be the sole determinant of a comic's grade.

(For example, the comics with stamped arrival date, off-center staple are *not* in Mint condition aside from those defects.)

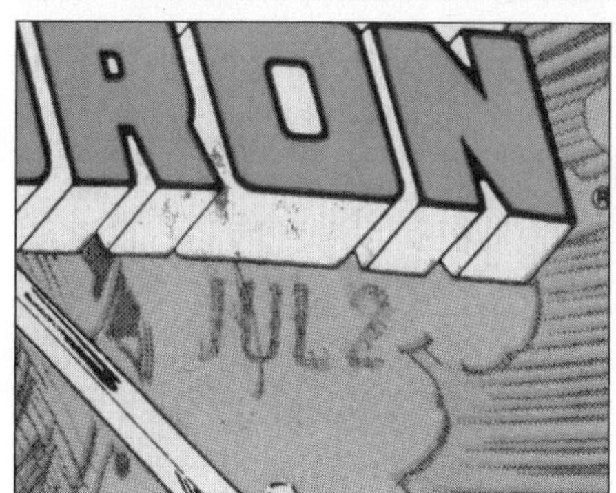

Stamped arrival date and off-center cover and off-center stapling.

Minor defects. Some will not call it "Mint"; some will.

Writing defacing cover.

Marking can include filling in light areas or childish scribbling. Usually no better than "Good."

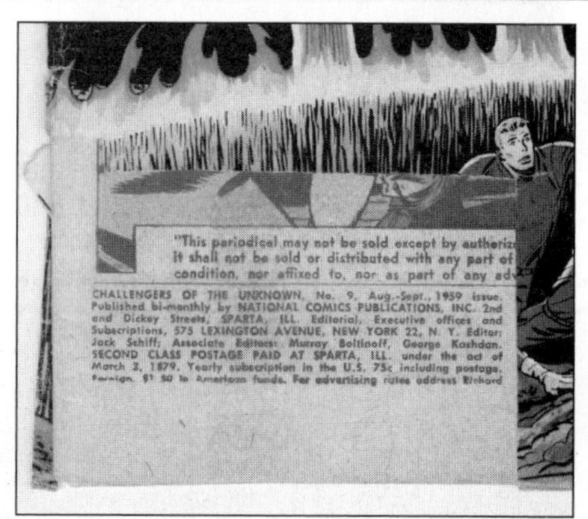

Clipped coupon.

A square or rectangular piece deliberately removed from the front or back cover or one of the interior pages.

No better than "Fair."

Subscription crease.
Comic books sent by mail were often folded down the middle, leaving a permanent crease. Definitely no better than "Very Good"; probably no better than "Good."

Water damage.
Varies from simple page-warping to staining shown here behind and on the logo. Less damage than this could be "Good"; this is no better than "Fair."

Missing pages and other material.
Ask before taking a comic book out of its bag, but most sellers should allow you to carefully flip through a comic book, looking for such items as clipped coupons from interior pages, scribbling on interior pages, a missing center section, or such lost extra material as trading cards or 3-D glasses.

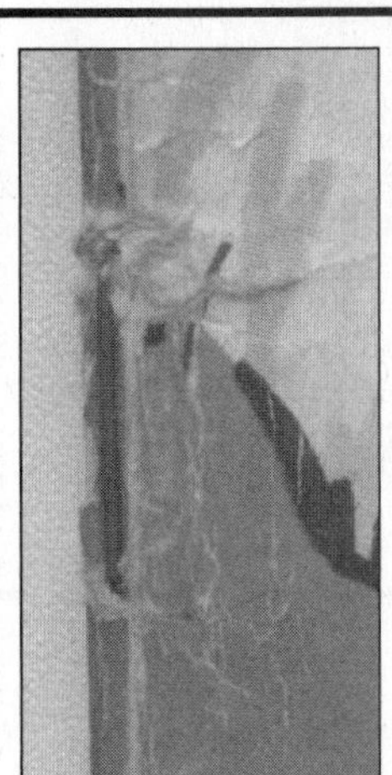

Rusty staple.
Caused by dampness during storage, rust stains around staples may be minor — or more apparent. No better than "Very Good."

Chunk missing.
Sizable piece missing from the cover (front or back). No better than "Fair."

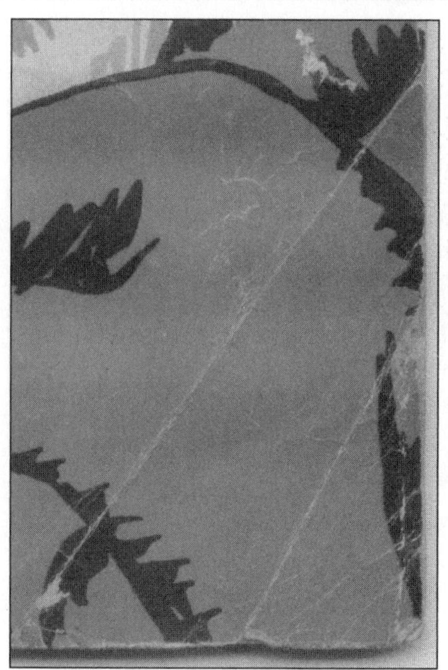

Multiple folds and wrinkles.
No better than "Fair" condition.

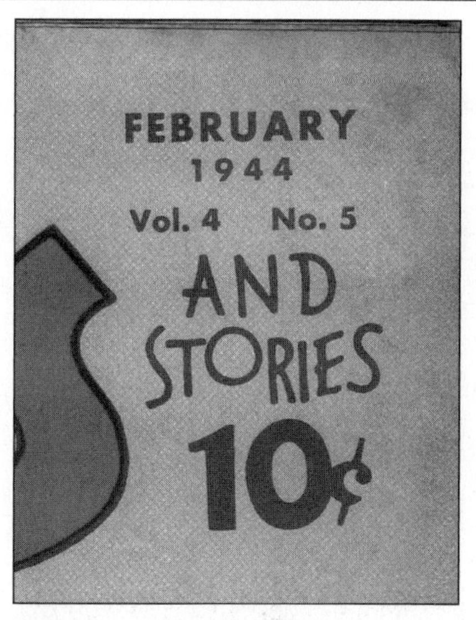

Stains.
Can vary widely, depending on cause. These look like dirt — but food, grease, and the like also stain. No better than "Good."

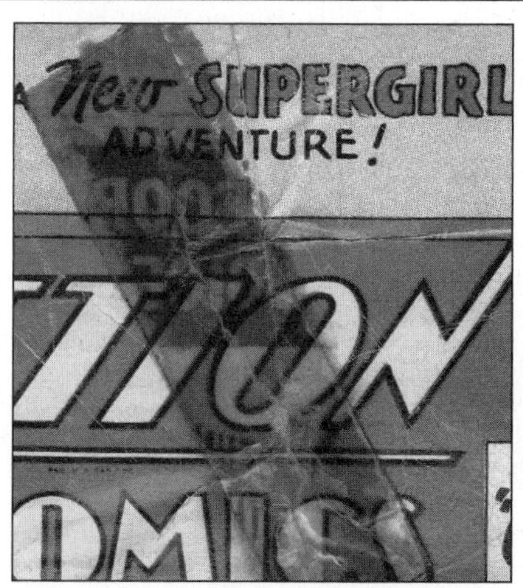

Tape.
This extreme example of tape damage is used to show ***why*** tape shouldn't be used on a comic book — or ***any*** book — for repairs. ***All*** tape (even so-called "magic" tape) ages badly — as does rubber cement. Use of tape usually means "Fair," at best.

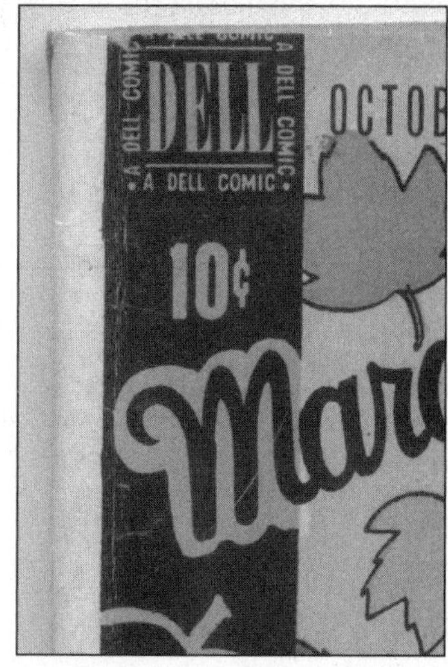

Rolled Spine.
Caused by folding back each page while reading — rather than opening the issue flat. Repeated folding permanently bent the spine. ***May*** be corrected, but the issue is no better than "Very Good."

The Key

What's in the Price Guide

- Most English-language **comic books published and offered for sale in North America since 1935** for which we've been able to confirm existence. (This includes, for example, reprints of Fleetway's British comics that the publisher repackaged for the American market.)
- Many English-language **giveaway comic books** published in North America.
- Many English-language **graphic novels** published in North America, hardcover and softcover, whose existence we've been able to confirm.
- Listings for hundreds of variant editions along with identifiers of same.
- Grouped listings for consecutive issues of a title that share the same value. For example, if issues #1 through #10 of a title are valued at $1 each, the listing will be: 1-10 .... $1.00

What's not in the Price Guide

- Comic books released close to press time. With new comics released each week, we had to take a snapshot of our database at a certain point to begin the production process.
- Hardcover and softcover reprints of issues within a series.
- Comic books whose existence we have not been able to confirm.
- Comics in languages other than English.
- Comics not published in North America.
- Paperback or hardcover reprints of comic strips not published in the dimensions of a comic book; *e.g.*, Fawcett *Peanuts* reprints.

Finding a title

The real, legal name of any comic book appears in its **indicia**, a block of small print usually found on the first inside page of most comics. **It does not necessarily match what's on the cover**; publishers have been known to relabel a single (or several) issues within a series for a stunt, while never *really* changing the names of their series.

We alphabetize titles as if there were no spaces in their names. Numbers are spelled out. Leading articles (a, an, and the) are dropped.

Drop proper names

Many titles have the name of one of their creators or the owner of a studio in their proper titles, such as *Kurt Busiek's Astro City*. In most cases, we have listed these comics in this manner: *Astro City (Kurt Busiek's...)*.

There are a handful of cases where the series has only ever been identified by the name of a creator or studio, and in those few cases, such as *Walt Disney's Comics & Stories*, we've left the title alone.

Multiple series, same name

When a publisher has used the same name for a series more than once, such as in the case of *Amazing Spider-Man* Vol. 1 and *Amazing Spider-Man* Vol. 2, we list those different titles in order of release with some indicator to differentiate them from each other. We generally, but not always, run them uninterrupted in order of their release.

When two or more publishers have published distinct and unrelated series with the same name, we generally run them in chronological order of release. This is a change from earlier editions, which sorted those titles alphabetically by publisher name.

When a series changes publishers but does not interrupt its numbering, we tend to print them as separate listings but in consecutive chronological order.

A-1 Comics

Life's Romances, 1944

0 .... 200.00
1 .... 100.00
2-4 .... 50.00
5-9 .... 40.00
10-12 .... 34.00
13 .... 135.00
nn 40.00
15 .... 34.00

A1 True Life Bikini Confidential

Atomeka

1 .... 7.00

A1 (Vol. 1)

Atomeka, 1989

1 .... 6.00
2 .... 10.00
3-4 .... 6.00
5 .... 8.00
6 .... 9.00
6/A 10.00
7 .... 8.00

A1 (Vol. 2)

Marvel, 1992

1-4 .... 6.00

A', A

Viz

1 .... 16.00

Aam-Ka-Jutsu

E.C. McGilvray III

1 .... 3.00

Aardwolf

Aardwolf, 1994

1-2 .... 3.00

Aaron Strips

Image, 1997

1-6 .... 3.00

Abadazad

CrossGen, 2004

1 .... 5.00
1/2nd 4.00
2 .... 3.00
3 .... 4.00
3/2nd 3.00

Abbie an' Slats

United Feature, 1948

1 .... 70.00
2 .... 45.00
3-4 .... 40.00

Abbott and Costello

St. John, 1948

1 .... 385.00
2 .... 200.00
3-9 .... 125.00
10 .... 140.00
11-20 .... 80.00
21-30 .... 55.00
31-40 .... 42.00
3D 1 .... 275.00

Abbott & Costello

Charlton, 1968

1 .... 30.00
2-3 .... 20.00
4-10 .... 14.00
11-22 .... 12.00

ABC: A To Z - Greyshirt and Cobweb

DC, 2006

1 .... 4.00

ABC: A To Z - Terra Obscura and Splash Brannigan

DC, 2006

1 .... 4.00

ABC: A To Z - Tom Strong and Jack B. Quick

DC, 2005

1 .... 4.00

ABC: A To Z - Top 10 and Teams

DC, 2006

1 .... 4.00

A.B.C. Warriors

Fleetway-Quality, 1990

1-8 .... 2.00

ABC Warriors: Khronicles of Khaos

Fleetway-Quality

1-4 .... 3.00

Abe Sapien Drums of the Dead

Dark Horse, 1998

1 .... 3.00

Abiding Perdition

APComics, 2005

1 .... 3.00
1/A-1/D 4.00
2 .... 3.00
2/A-2/B 4.00

A. Bizarro

DC, 1999

1-4 .... 3.00

A-Bomb

Antarctic, 1993

1-16 .... 3.00

Abominations

Marvel, 1996

1-3 .... 2.00

A-1 Comics

Abe Sapien Drums of the Dead

A-Bomb

Accident Man

Ace Comics

Action Comics

Action Planet Comics

Adam-12

Above & Below: Two Tales of the American Frontier

Drawn & Quarterly, 2004

1 .... 10.00

Abraham Lincoln Life Story

Dell, 1958

1 .... 16.00

Abraham Stone (Epic)

Marvel, 1995

1-2 .... 7.00

Absolute Vertigo

DC, 1995

1 .... 4.00

Absolute Zero

Antarctic, 1995

1 .... 4.00
2-6 .... 3.00

Absurd Art of J.J. Grandville

Tome

1 .... 3.00

Abyss

Dark Horse, 1989

1-2 .... 3.00

AC Annual

AC

1 .... 4.00
2 .... 5.00
3-4 .... 4.00
2005 .... 5.00

Accelerate

DC, 2000

1-4 .... 3.00

Accidental Death, An

Fantagraphics, 1993

nn 4.00

Accident Man

Dark Horse, 1993

1-3 .... 3.00

Acclaim Adventure Zone

Acclaim, 1997

1-3 .... 5.00

Ace

Harrier

1 .... 2.00

Ace Comics

McKay, 1937

1 .... 2,100.00
2 .... 700.00
3 .... 465.00
4 .... 400.00
5-10 .... 365.00
11 .... 425.00
12-14 .... 245.00
15-20 .... 200.00
21-25 .... 175.00
26 .... 725.00
27-30 .... 180.00
31-36 .... 150.00
37-40 .... 135.00
41-59 .... 105.00
60-79 .... 95.00
80-90 .... 80.00
91-99 .... 68.00
100 .... 85.00
101-119 .... 60.00
120-143 .... 54.00
144-145 .... 80.00
146-148 .... 70.00
149-151 .... 60.00

Ace Comics Presents

Ace, 1987

1-4 .... 2.00

Ace McCoy

Avalon

1-3 .... 3.00

Ace of Spades

ZuZupetal

1 .... 3.00

5Aces

Eclipse, 1988

1-5 .... 3.00

Aces High

E.C., 1955

1 .... 120.00
2 .... 90.00
3-5 .... 75.00

Aces High (RCP)

RCP, 1999

1-5 .... 3.00
Ann 1 .... 14.00

ACG Christmas Special

Avalon

1 .... 3.00

ACG's Civil War

Avalon, 1995

1 .... 3.00

ACG's Halloween Special

Avalon

1 .... 3.00

Achilles Storm: Dark Secret

Brainstorm, 1997

1-2 .... 3.00

Achilles Storm/Razmataz

Aja Blu, 1990

1-4 .... 2.00

Acid Bath Case

Kitchen Sink

1 .... 5.00

Ack the Barbarian

Innovation, 1987

1 .... 2.00

Acme

Fandom House, 1987

1-7 .... 3.00
8 .... 2.00
9 .... 3.00

Acme Novelty Library

Fantagraphics, 1993

1 .... 10.00
1/2nd 4.00
2 .... 7.00
2/2nd-4/2nd 5.00
5-6 .... 4.00
7 .... 7.00
8-12 .... 5.00
13 .... 4.00
14 .... 11.00
15 .... 10.00
16 .... 16.00

Acolyte

Mad Monkey, 1993

1 .... 4.00

Action Comics

DC, 1938

0 .... 3.00
1 .... 330,000.00
☛1st Superman
1/2nd 18.00
1/3rd 14.00
1/4th 6.00
1/5th 5.00
1/Ashcan 20,000.00
2 .... 29,250.00
3 .... 19,000.00
4-5 .... 10,600.00
6 .... 15,400.00
7 .... 15,500.00
8-9 .... 6,650.00
10 .... 8,200.00
11-12 .... 4,150.00
13 .... 6,175.00
14 .... 3,825.00
15 .... 6,175.00
16 .... 3,125.00
17 .... 4,350.00
18 .... 3,825.00
19 .... 4,050.00
20 .... 3,825.00
21-22 .... 2,600.00
23 .... 7,300.00
☛1st Luthor
24-25 .... 2,475.00
26 .... 2,060.00
27-30 .... 1,700.00
31-32 .... 2,600.00
33 .... 7,300.00
☛1st Mr. America
34-35 .... 2,475.00
36 .... 2,060.00
37-40 .... 1,700.00
41 .... 1,050.00
42 .... 2,600.00
☛1st Vigilante
43-46 .... 980.00
47 .... 1,300.00
☛1st Luthor cover
48-52 .... 980.00
53 .... 850.00
54-60 .... 710.00
61-63 .... 630.00
64 .... 750.00
65-70 .... 630.00
71-99 .... 580.00
100 .... 600.00
101 .... 1,200.00
☛A-Bomb cover
102-126 .... 525.00
127 .... 600.00
128-150 .... 525.00
151-157 .... 480.00
158 .... 750.00
☛Superman origin
159-161 .... 450.00
162 .... 500.00
163-180 .... 385.00
181-201 .... 340.00
202-220 .... 290.00
221-240 .... 240.00
241 .... 250.00
242 .... 1,200.00
☛1st Brainiac
243-251 .... 185.00
252 .... 1,200.00
☛1st Supergirl
253 .... 425.00
254 .... 325.00
255 .... 225.00
256-261 .... 100.00
262 .... 90.00
263 .... 100.00
264-266 .... 80.00
267 .... 650.00
☛1st Colossal Boy
268-270 .... 80.00
271-275 .... 65.00
276 .... 125.00
☛Legion app.
277-284 .... 60.00
285 .... 100.00
☛Legion app.
286-294 .... 60.00
295 .... 90.00
296 .... 65.00
297 .... 90.00
298-299 .... 60.00
300-316 .... 50.00
317-324 .... 40.00

Adam Strange

AD Police

Adventure Comics

Adventure Into Mystery

All comics prices listed are for NEAR MINT condition.

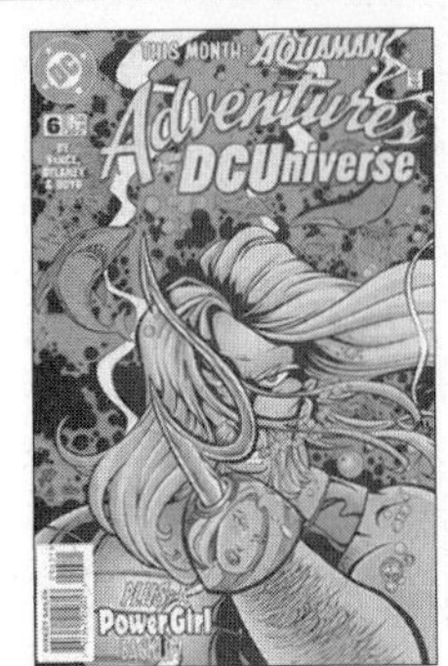

Adventures in the DC Universe

Adventures in the Rifle Brigade

Adventures into the Unknown

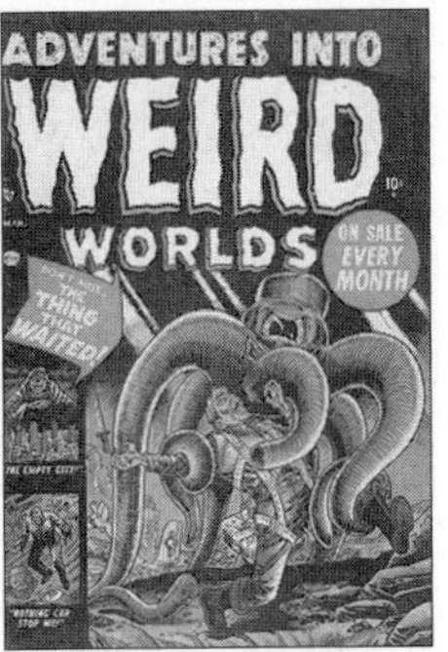

Adventures Into Weird Worlds

Issue	Price
325	50.00
326-333	40.00
334	60.00
335-338	40.00
339	70.00
340-346	40.00
347	50.00
348-362	40.00
363-373	30.00
374-387	20.00
388	25.00
389-399	20.00
400	40.00
401-406	17.00
407	15.00
408	20.00
409	15.00
410-411	13.00
412-415	12.00
416-418	11.00
419	14.00
420-422	11.00
423-424	10.00
425	19.00
426	10.00
427-436	8.00
437	29.00
☛Giant-size issue	
438-439	8.00
440	25.00
☛1st Grell Green Arrow	
441	12.00
442	8.00
443	26.00
☛Giant-size issue	
444-454	7.00
455-465	6.00
466	7.00
467-481	5.00
481/Whitman	10.00
482	5.00
482/Whitman	10.00
483	5.00
483/Whitman	10.00
484	5.00
484/Whitman	10.00
485	8.00
485/Whitman	10.00
486	5.00
486/Whitman	10.00
487	5.00
487/Whitman	10.00
488	5.00
488/Whitman	10.00
489	5.00
489/Whitman	10.00
490	5.00
490/Whitman	10.00
491	5.00
491/Whitman	10.00
492	5.00
492/Whitman	10.00
493	5.00
493/Whitman	10.00
494	5.00
494/Whitman	10.00
495	5.00
495/Whitman	10.00
496	5.00
496/Whitman	10.00
497	5.00
497/Whitman	10.00
498	5.00
498/Whitman	10.00
499	5.00
499/Whitman	10.00
500	5.00
500/Whitman	10.00
501	5.00
501/Whitman	10.00
502	5.00
502/Whitman	10.00
503	5.00
503/Whitman	10.00
504	4.00
504/Whitman	8.00
505	4.00
505/Whitman	8.00
506	4.00
506/Whitman	8.00
507	4.00
507/Whitman	8.00
508	4.00
508/Whitman	8.00
509-544	4.00
545-566	3.00
567-597	2.00
598	15.00
☛1st Checkmate	
599	2.00
600	5.00
601-659	2.00
660	3.00
661	2.00
662	4.00
662/2nd-682	2.00
683	3.00
683/2nd	2.00
684	3.00
684/2nd-685	2.00
685/2nd-685/3rd	1.00
686-687	2.00
687/CS	3.00
688-695	2.00
695/Variant	3.00
696-699	2.00
700	3.00
700/Platinum	5.00
701-769	2.00
770	4.00
771-774	2.00
775	5.00
775/2nd	4.00
776-799	2.00

800 .... 4.00
801-810 .... 2.00
811 .... 5.00
812 .... 8.00
812/2nd 2.00
813 .... 4.00
814-817 .... 3.00
818 .... 4.00
819-825 .... 3.00
826 .... 5.00
☛Inf. Crisis tie
827-828 .... 3.00
829 .... 6.00
829/Variant 3.00
830 .... 4.00
831-843 .... 3.00
844 .... 6.00
845 .... 5.00
846-849 .... 3.00
850 .... 4.00
851-857 .... 3.00
858 .... 4.00
859-862 .... 3.00
863-875 .... 4.00
1000000 .... 1.00
Ann 1 .... 4.00
Ann 2-6 .... 3.00
Ann 7 .... 4.00
Ann 8 .... 3.00
Ann 9 .... 4.00
Anl 10-11/A 5.00

A.C.T.I.O.N. Force (Lightning)

Lightning, 1987

1 .... 2.00

Action Girl Comics

Slave Labor, 1994

1 .... 4.00
1/2nd-14 .... 3.00
15-19 .... 4.00

Action Planet Comics

Action Planet, 1997

1-3 .... 4.00
Ashcan 1 .... 2.00
GS 1 .... 6.00

Actions Speak (Sergio Aragonés)

Dark Horse, 2001

1-6 .... 3.00

Actual Confessions

Atlas, 1952

13-14 .... 80.00

Actual Romances

Atlas, 1949

1-2 .... 125.00

Ada Lee

NBM

1 .... 10.00

A.D.A.M.

The Toy Man

1 .... 3.00
Ashcan 1 .... 1.00

Adam-12

Gold Key, 1973

1 .... 20.00
2 .... 15.00
3-5 .... 12.00
6-10 .... 10.00

Adam and Eve A.D.

Bam, 1985

1-10 .... 2.00

Adam Bomb Comics

Blue Monkey, 1999

1 .... 2.00

Adam Strange

DC, 1990

1-3 .... 4.00

Adam Strange (2nd Series)

DC, 2004

1 .... 10.00
2-3 .... 6.00
4-6 .... 5.00
7 .... 7.00
8 .... 8.00

Addam Omega

Antarctic, 1997

1-4 .... 3.00

Addams Family

Gold Key, 1974

1 .... 60.00
2-3 .... 35.00

Addams Family Episode Guide

Comic Chronicles

1 .... 6.00

Adele & The Beast

NBM, 1990

1 .... 10.00

Adolescent Radioactive Black Belt Hamsters

Eclipse, 1986

1 .... 2.00
1/Gold 3.00
1/2nd-9 .... 2.00

Adolescent Radioactive Black Belt Hamsters Classics

Parody, 1992

1-5 .... 3.00

Adventures of Captain America

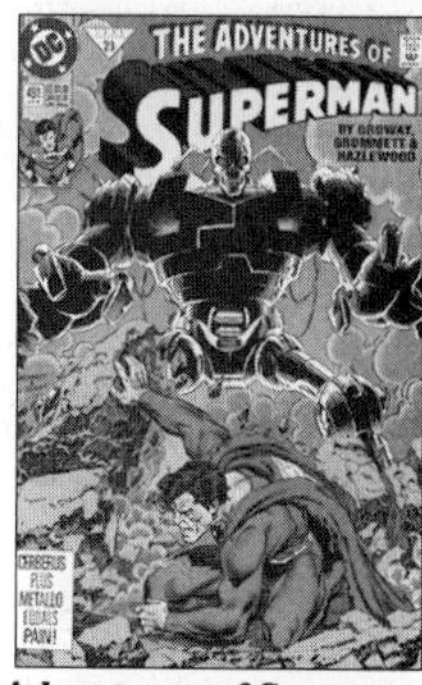

Adventures of Superman

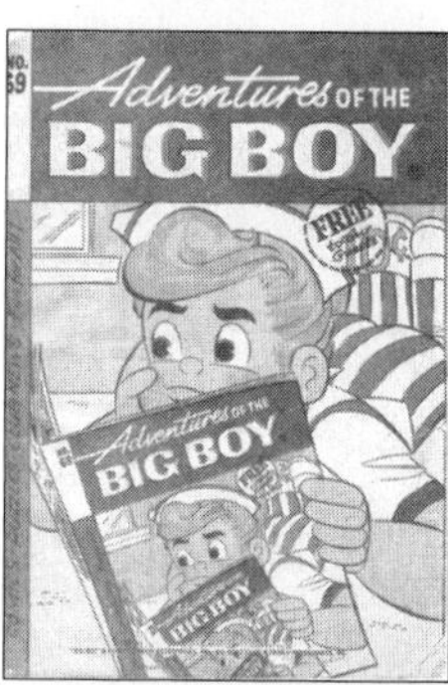

Adventures of the Big Boy

Adventures of the Fly

Adventures of the Jaguar

Adventures of the Mask

Adventures of the Super Mario Bros.

Adventures of the Vital-Man

Adolescent Radioactive Black Belt Hamsters in 3-D

Eclipse, 1986

1-4 .... 3.00

Adolescent Radioactive Black Belt Hamsters: Lost and Alone in New York

Parody

1 .... 3.00

Adolescent Radioactive Black Belt Hamsters Massacre the Japanese Invasion

Eclipse, 1989

1 .... 3.00

Adolescent Radioactive Black Belt Hamsters: The Lost Treasures

Parody

1 .... 3.00

AD Police

Viz, 1994

1 .... 15.00
1/2nd 13.00

Adrenalynn

Image, 1999

14 .... 3.00

Adult Action Fantasy Featuring: Tawny's Tales

Louisiana Leisure

1-2 .... 3.00

Adults Only! Comic Magazine

Inkwell, 1979

1-3 .... 3.00

Advanced Dungeons & Dragons

DC, 1988

1-36 .... 2.00
Ann 1 .... 3.00

Adventure Comics

DC, 1938

32 .... 2,800.00
33-35 .... 1,450.00
36-39 .... 1,275.00
40 .... 36,000.00
☛1st Sandman
41 .... 4,700.00
42 .... 5,500.00
43 .... 3,200.00
44 .... 5,500.00
45 .... 2,800.00
46-47 .... 4,200.00
48 .... 22,000.00
☛1st Hourman
49-50 .... 1,950.00
51 .... 2,630.00
☛Sandman cover
52 .... 1,600.00
☛1st Kirk Manhunter
53-59 .... 1,450.00
60 .... 2,500.00
61 .... 10,750.00
☛1st Starman
62-65 .... 1,300.00
66 .... 1,800.00
67-68 .... 1,300.00
69 .... 1,650.00
70-71 .... 1,275.00
72 .... 13,200.00
☛1st Kirby Sandman
73 .... 11,500.00
☛1st Kirby Manhunter
74-80 .... 1,500.00
81-91 .... 925.00
92-99 .... 700.00
100 .... 800.00
101-102 .... 700.00
103 .... 2,400.00
☛Super-heroes start
104 .... 850.00
105-110 .... 525.00
111-120 .... 450.00
121-126 .... 390.00
127 .... 450.00
128 .... 400.00
129-130 .... 375.00
131-149 .... 340.00
150-151 .... 425.00
152 .... 310.00
153 .... 425.00
154 .... 310.00
155 .... 425.00
156 .... 310.00
157 .... 425.00
158 .... 310.00
159 .... 425.00
160 .... 310.00
161 .... 425.00
162 .... 310.00
163 .... 425.00
164-169 .... 310.00
170-180 .... 255.00
181-199 .... 235.00
200 .... 350.00
201-209 .... 260.00
210 .... 2,400.00
☛1st Krypto
211-220 .... 200.00
221-246 .... 170.00
247 .... 4,400.00
☛1st Legion
248-255 .... 130.00
256 .... 525.00
257-259 .... 125.00
260 .... 500.00

☛Aquaman origin
261-266 .... 80.00
267 .... 740.00
☛2nd Legion
268 .... 80.00
269 .... 225.00
☛1st Aqualad
270 .... 80.00
271 .... 225.00
☛Lex Luthor origin
272-274 .... 65.00
275 .... 145.00
276-280 .... 65.00
281 .... 60.00
282 .... 95.00
283 .... 100.00
284 .... 60.00
285-286 .... 110.00
287-289 .... 60.00
290 .... 100.00
291-292 .... 45.00
293 .... 100.00
294 .... 90.00
☛1st Mon-El Legion
295-298 .... 45.00
299 .... 55.00
300 .... 200.00
☛Legion
301 .... 70.00
302-305 .... 55.00
306-323 .... 45.00
324-339 .... 40.00
340 .... 45.00
341-345 .... 40.00
346 .... 60.00
347-350 .... 40.00
☛1st White Witch
351-352 .... 50.00
353-355 .... 35.00
356 .... 30.00
357 .... 60.00
358-366 .... 30.00
367-372 .... 25.00
373 .... 22.00
374 .... 30.00
375-377 .... 22.00
378 .... 45.00
379-380 .... 22.00
381 .... 60.00
☛Supergirl starts
382-389 .... 22.00
390 .... 30.00
391-400 .... 22.00
401-402 .... 21.00
403 .... 50.00
404-415 .... 20.00
416 .... 18.00
417-427 .... 13.00
428 .... 28.00
☛1st Black Orchid
429-430 .... 15.00
431 .... 28.00
☛Aparo Spectre
432-433 ....15.00
434-435 ....12.00
436-441 ....10.00
442-447 ....6.00
448-458 ....5.00
459-460 ....4.00
461 ....6.00
462 ....7.00
463-479 ....4.00
480-503 ....3.00

Adventure Comics (2nd Series)

DC, 1998

1 ....2.00
GS 1 ....5.00

Adventure Into Mystery

Atlas, 1956

1 ....160.00
2 ....115.00
3 ....95.00
4-6 ....85.00
7-8 ....75.00

Adventure is My Career

Street & Smith, 1945

1 ....60.00

Adventure of the Copper Beeches

Tome

1 ....3.00

Adventure of the Naval Treaty

Caliber

1 ....4.00

Adventurers (Aircel)

Aircel

1-2 ....2.00

Adventurers (Book 1)

Adventure, 1986

0-10 ....2.00

Adventurers (Book 2)

Adventure, 1987

0-10 ....2.00

Adventurers (Book 3)

Adventure, 1989

1-6 ....2.00

Adventures

St. John, 1949

1 ....130.00
2 ....100.00

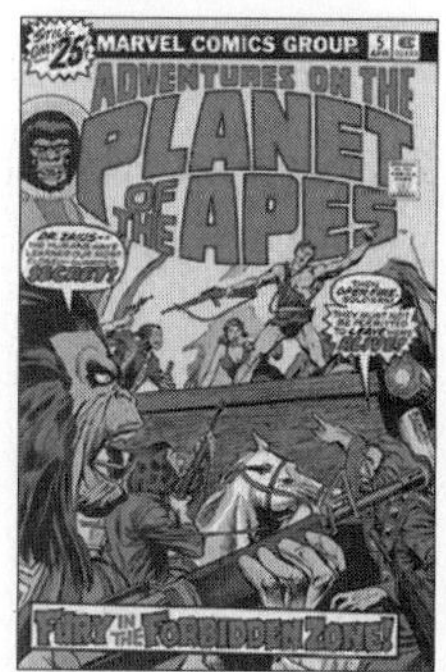

Adventures On the Planet of the Apes

Aeon Flux

After Apocalypse

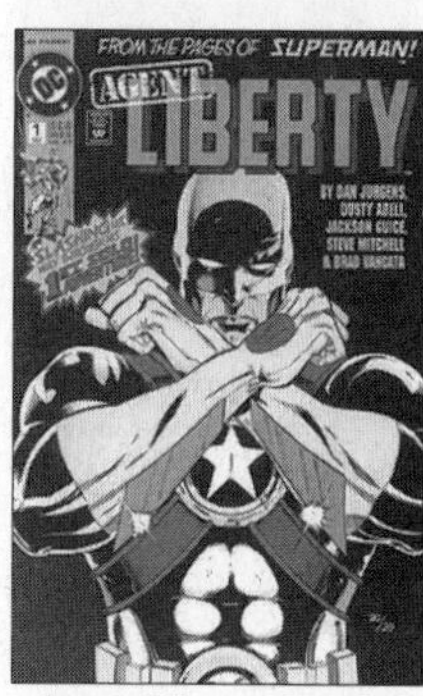

Agent Liberty Special

Agents of Law

Agent Three Zero

Agent Unknown

Agent X

Adventures of Bio Boy
Speakeasy Comics, 2005

1 .... 3.00

Adventures of Ozzie and Harriet
DC, 1949

1 .... 600.00
2 .... 285.00
3-5 .... 230.00

Adventures @ eBay
eBay, 2000

1 .... 1.00

Adventures for Boys
Bailey, 1955

1 .... 28.00

Adventures in Reading Starring: The Amazing Spider-Man
Marvel, 1990

1 .... 1.00
1/A-1/B 2.00

Adventures in the DC Universe
DC, 1997

1 .... 3.00
2-19 .... 2.00
Ann 1 .... 4.00

Adventures in the Mystwood
Blackthorne, 1986

1 .... 2.00

Adventures in the Rifle Brigade
DC, 2000

1-3 .... 3.00

Adventures in the Rifle Brigade: Operation Bollock
DC, 2001

1-3 .... 3.00

Adventures in 3-D
Harvey, 1953

1 .... 55.00
2 .... 38.00

Adventures Into Darkness
Standard, 1952

5 .... 215.00
6-9 .... 130.00
10-12 .... 110.00
13 .... 125.00
14 .... 100.00

Adventures Into Terror
Atlas, 1950

1 (#43) 400.00
2 (#44) 240.00
3-4 .... 160.00
5 .... 165.00
6 .... 145.00
7 .... 300.00
8 .... 145.00
9-10 .... 125.00
11-20 .... 110.00
21-31 .... 90.00

Adventures into the Unknown
ACG, 1948

1 .... 1,400.00
2 .... 600.00
3 .... 580.00
4-5 .... 350.00
6-7 .... 225.00
8-10 .... 175.00
11-15 .... 140.00
16-26 .... 120.00
27 .... 135.00
28-30 .... 120.00
31-40 .... 90.00
41-50 .... 80.00
51 .... 225.00
☛3-D covers start
52-58 .... 190.00
59 .... 85.00
60-62 .... 70.00
63-70 .... 45.00
71-90 .... 38.00
91-99 .... 32.00
100 .... 36.00
101-120 .... 28.00
121-140 .... 26.00
141-160 .... 24.00
161-174 .... 18.00

Adventures into the Unknown
A-Plus, 1990

1-4 .... 3.00

Adventures Into Weird Worlds
Atlas, 1952

1 .... 285.00
2 .... 175.00
3-5 .... 140.00
6-10 .... 125.00
11-20 .... 100.00
21-30 .... 85.00

Adventures in Wonderland
Lev Gleason, 1955

1 .... 140.00
2 .... 100.00
3-5 .... 65.00

Adventures Made in America
Rip Off

0-6 .... 3.00

Adventures of Aaron
Chiasmus, 1995
1-2 .... 3.00

Adventures of Aaron (2nd Series)
Image, 1997
1-100 .... 3.00

Adventures of Adam & Bryon
American Mule, 1998
1 .... 3.00

Adventures of Alan Ladd
DC, 1949
1 .... 450.00
2 .... 325.00
3-5 .... 235.00
6-9 .... 180.00

Adventures of a Lesbian College School Girl
NBM
1 .... 9.00

Adventures of Alice
Pentagon, 1945
1 .... 40.00
2-3 .... 28.00

Adventures of Bagboy and Checkout Girl
Acetelyne, 2002
Ashcan 1 .... 1.00

Adventures of Baron Munchausen
Now, 1989
1-4 .... 2.00

Adventures of Barry Ween, Boy Genius
Image, 1999
1-3 .... 3.00

Adventures of Barry Ween, Boy Genius 2.0
Oni, 2000
1-3 .... 3.00

Adventures of Barry Ween, Boy Genius 3: Monkey Tales
Oni, 2001
1-6 .... 3.00

Adventures of Bayou Billy
Archie, 1989
1-5 .... 1.00

Adventures of Bob Hope
DC, 1950
1 .... 900.00
2 .... 500.00
3-4 .... 450.00
5-6 .... 250.00
7-8 .... 200.00
9-10 .... 150.00
11-15 .... 125.00
16-20 .... 90.00
21-31 .... 85.00
32 .... 70.00
33-50 .... 55.00
51-60 .... 40.00
61-70 .... 35.00
71-80 .... 30.00
81-90 .... 25.00
91-105 .... 15.00
106-109 .... 25.00

Adventures of B.O.C.
Invasion, 1986
1-3 .... 2.00

Adventures of Browser & Sequoia
SaberCat, 1999
1 .... 3.00
2 .... 2.00

Adventures of Captain America
Marvel, 1991
1-4 .... 5.00

Adventures of Captain Jack
Fantagraphics, 1986
1-12 .... 2.00

Adventures of Captain Nemo
Rip Off
1 .... 3.00

Adventures of Chrissie Claus
Hero, 1991
1-2 .... 3.00

Adventures of Chuk the Barbaric
White Wolf, 1987
1-2 .... 2.00

Adventures of Cyclops and Phoenix
Marvel, 1994
1-4 .... 3.00

Adventures of Dean Martin & Jerry Lewis
DC, 1952
1 .... 550.00
2 .... 275.00
3-10 .... 140.00
11-19 .... 90.00
20-30 .... 75.00
31-40 .... 55.00

Age of Bronze

Age of Reptiles

Aggie Mack

Agony Acres

Aida-Zee

Airboy

Airboy Meets the Prowler

Airboy versus the Airmaidens

Adventures of Dr. Graves
A-Plus

1 .... 3.00

Adventures of Dolo Romy
DÙlo Blue

1 .... 3.00

Adventures of Doris Nelson, Atomic Housewife
Jake Comics, 1996

1 .... 3.00

Adventures of Edgar Mudd and Elaine
Wet Earth

1 .... 4.00

Adventures of Evil & Malice
Image, 1999

1-3 .... 4.00

Adventures of Felix the Cat
Harvey, 1992

1 .... 2.00

Adventures of Ford Fairlane
DC, 1990

1-4 .... 2.00

Adventures of Homer Ghost
Atlas, 1957

1 .... 35.00
2 .... 30.00

Adventures of Jerry Lewis
DC, 1957

41 .... 40.00
42-50 .... 36.00
51-60 .... 34.00
61-80 .... 28.00
81-91 .... 25.00
92 .... 30.00
93-96 .... 25.00
97 .... 35.00
98-100 .... 25.00
101 .... 32.00
102 .... 55.00
☛Beatles app.
103-104 .... 32.00
105 .... 40.00
106-116 .... 14.00
117 .... 20.00
118-119 .... 14.00
120-124 .... 12.00

Adventures of Jo-Joy
W.T. Grant, 1945

1 .... 12.00
2-9 .... 10.00

Adventures of Kelly Belle: Peril on the High Seas
Atlantis, 1996

1 .... 3.00

Adventures of Kool-Aid Man
Marvel, 1983

1 .... 1.00
5 .... 1.00

Adventures of Liberal Man
Political, 1996

1-8 .... 3.00

Adventures of Luther Arkwright (Valkyrie)
Valkyrie, 1987

1-10 .... 3.00

Adventures of Luther Arkwright
Dark Horse, 1990

1 .... 3.00
2-9 .... 2.00

Adventures of Mark Tyme
John Spencer & Co.

1-2 .... 2.00

Adventures of MGM's Lassie
Western Publishing, 1949

1 .... 200.00

Adventures of Mighty Mouse (1st Series)
St. John, 1952

2 .... 125.00
3 .... 85.00
4-5 .... 65.00
6-10 .... 52.00
11-18 .... 38.00

Adventures of Mighty Mouse (2nd Series)
Literary Enterprises, 1955

126 .... 40.00
127-130 .... 34.00
131-140 .... 32.00
141-150 .... 30.00
151-160 .... 26.00

Adventures of Mighty Mouse
Gold Key, 1979

166-172 .... 4.00

Adventures of Mr. Pyridine
Fantagraphics

1 .... 3.00

Adventures of Misty

Forbidden Fruit, 1991

1-12 .... 3.00

Adventures of Monkey

Womp, 1995

1-4 .... 2.00

Adventures of Oat Willie

Austintatious Comics, 1987

1 .... 3.00

Adventures of Pinky Lee

Atlas, 1955

1 .... 145.00
2-5 .... 85.00

Adventures of Pioneer Pete

Pioneer Chicken

1 .... 2.00

Adventures of Quik Bunny

Marvel, 1984

1 .... 3.00

Adventures of Rex the Wonder Dog

DC, 1952

1 .... 675.00
2 .... 350.00
3 .... 275.00
4-5 .... 235.00
6-10 .... 175.00
11 .... 190.00
12-15 .... 115.00
16-20 .... 100.00
21-30 .... 70.00
31-40 .... 42.00
41-46 .... 34.00

Adventures of Rheumy Peepers & Chunky Highlights

Oni, 1999

1 .... 3.00

Adventures of Rick Raygun

Stop Dragon, 1986

1-5 .... 2.00

Adventures of Riggin' Bill

Remington Morse

1 .... 35.00

Adventures of Robin Hood

Gold Key, 1974

1 .... 8.00
2 .... 5.00
3-7 .... 4.00

Adventures of Roma

Forbidden Fruit, 1993

1 .... 4.00

Adventures of Snake Plissken

Marvel, 1997

1 .... 3.00

Adventures of Spencer Spook

Ace, 1986

1-6 .... 2.00

Adventures of Spider-Man

Marvel, 1996

1-12 .... 2.00

Adventures of Stickboy

Stinky Armadillo

1 .... 1.00

Adventures of Superboy

DC, 1991

19-22 .... 2.00

Adventures of Superman

DC, 1987

0-2 .... 3.00
425 .... 4.00
426 .... 3.00
427-443 .... 2.00
444-462 .... 2.00
463 .... 3.00
464-465 .... 2.00
466 .... 3.00
467-479 .... 2.00
480 .... 3.00
481-495 .... 2.00
496 .... 3.00
496/2nd 2.00
497 .... 3.00
497/2nd 2.00
498 .... 3.00
498/2nd 2.00
499 .... 5.00
500 .... 3.00
500/CS 4.00
500/Silver 10.00
501-505 .... 2.00
505/Variant 3.00
506-549 .... 2.00
550 .... 4.00
551-599 .... 2.00
600 .... 4.00
601-623 .... 2.00
624 .... 5.00
625 .... 4.00
625/2nd 3.00
626 .... 2.00
627 .... 3.00
628-635 .... 3.00
636 .... 5.00
☛Identity Crisis tie
637 .... 4.00
638 .... 3.00
639 .... 5.00
640-641 .... 4.00

Air Fighters Classics

Airlock

Airman

Air Raiders

Airwaves

A.K.A. Goldfish

Akiko

Akira

642 .... 6.00
643 .... 12.00
643/2nd-648 .... 3.00
649 .... 10.00
1000000 .... 2.00
Ann 1 .... 4.00
Ann 2-Ann 6 .... 3.00
Ann 7 .... 4.00
Ann 8 .... 3.00
Ann 9 .... 4.00

Adventures of Superman (Magazine)
DC
1-3 .... 2.00

Adventures of Tad Martin
Caliber
1 .... 3.00

Adventures of the Big Boy
WEBS Group, 1956
1-1/East 750.00
2-2/East 295.00
3-3/East 125.00
4-4/East 90.00
5-5/East 75.00
6-7 .... 50.00
8-10/East 45.00
11-15 .... 30.00
16-20 .... 24.00
21-25 .... 16.00
26-30/East 12.00
31-40 .... 10.00
41-50/East 6.00
51 .... 5.00
52 .... 8.00
53-100 .... 5.00
101-150/East 4.00
151-300 .... 3.00
301-500 .... 2.00
501-521 .... 1.00

Adventures of the Big Boy (Paragon)
Paragon, 1976
1-34 .... 2.00
35-75 .... 1.00

Adventures of the Fly
Archie, 1959
1 .... 220.00
2 .... 140.00
3 .... 100.00
4-5 .... 80.00
6-17 .... 70.00
18-26 .... 40.00
27-31 .... 30.00

Adventures of the Jaguar
Archie, 1961
1 .... 125.00
2 .... 75.00
3 .... 50.00
4-5 .... 40.00
6-10 .... 30.00
11-15 .... 22.00

Adventures of the Little Green Dinosaur
Last Gasp
1-2 .... 5.00

Adventures of the Mad Hunda Day Day
Thaumaturge, 1995
1 .... 2.00

Adventures of the Mask
Dark Horse, 1996
1-12 .... 3.00
Special 1 .... 1.00

Adventures of the Outsiders
DC, 1986
33-46 .... 1.00

Adventures of Theown
Pyramid, 1986
1-3 .... 2.00

Adventures of the Screamer Brothers
Superstar, 1990
1-3 .... 2.00

Adventures of the Screamer Brothers (Vol. 2)
Superstar, 1991
1-3 .... 2.00

Adventures of the Super Mario Bros.
Valiant, 1991
1 .... 4.00
2-9 .... 3.00

Adventures of the Thing
Marvel, 1992
1-4 .... 2.00

Adventures of the Vital-Man
Budgie, 1991
1-4 .... 2.00

Adventures of the X-Men
Marvel, 1996
1-12 .... 2.00

Adventures of Tintin
Mammoth
1 .... 10.00
1/2nd-22 .... 9.00

Adventures on Space Station Freedom
Tadcorps
1 .... 3.00

Adventures on the Fringe
Fantagraphics, 1992

1-5 .... 2.00

Adventures On the Planet of the Apes
Marvel, 1975

1 .... 9.00
2-5 .... 4.00
5/30¢ 20.00
6 .... 4.00
6/30¢ 20.00
7 .... 4.00
7/30¢ 20.00
8-11 .... 4.00

Adventure Strip Digest
WCG, 1994

1-4 .... 3.00

Adventurous Uncle Scrooge McDuck
Gladstone, 1998

1-2 .... 3.00

Aeon Flux
Dark Horse, 2005

1-4 .... 3.00

Aeon Focus
Aeon, 1994

1-5 .... 3.00

Aertimisan: War of Souls
Almagest, 1997

1-2 .... 3.00

Aesop's Desecrated Morals
Magnecom

1 .... 3.00

Aesop's Fables
Fantagraphics, 1991

1-3 .... 3.00

Aeternus
Brick, 1997

1 .... 3.00

Aetos the Eagle
Orphan Underground, 1994

1-2 .... 3.00
2/Ash 2.00

Aetos the Eagle (Vol. 2)
Ground Zero, 1997

1-3 .... 3.00

Affable Tales for Your Imaginaton
Lee Roy Brown, 1987

1 .... 3.00

After Apocalypse
Paragraphics, 1987

1 .... 2.00

After Dark
Millennium

1 .... 3.00

Aftermath
Pinnacle, 1986

1 .... 2.00

Aftermath (Chaos)
Chaos, 2000

1 .... 3.00
1/A-Ash 1 .... 0.00

After/Shock: Bulletins from Ground Zero
Last Gasp

1 .... 2.00

After the Rain
NBM, 1999

1 .... 13.00

Against Blackshard: 3-D: The Saga of Sketch, the Royal Artist
Sirius

1 .... 2.00

Agency
Image, 2001

Ashcan 1 .... 3.00
Ashcan 1/Gold 5.00
1/A-5 .... 3.00
6 .... 5.00

Agent
Marvel

1 .... 10.00

Agent "00" Soul
Twist Records

1 .... 5.00

Agent America
Awesome

Ashcan 1 .... 5.00

Agent Liberty Special
DC, 1991

1 .... 2.00

Agents
Image, 2003

1-6 .... 3.00

Agents of Atlas
Marvel, 2006

1-6 .... 3.00

Agents of Law
Dark Horse, 1995

1-6 .... 3.00

Agent 13: The Midnight Avenger
TSR

1 .... 8.00

Alarming Adventures

Alex

Alf

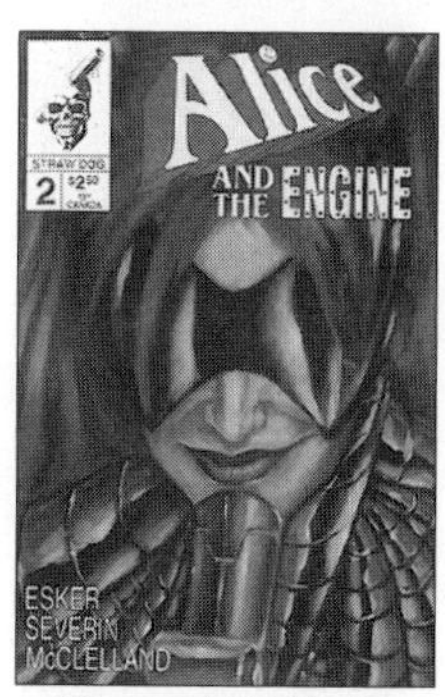

Alice and the Engine

Alice in Blunderland

Alice in Lost World

Alien 3

Alien Fire

Agent Three Zero
Galaxinovels

1 .... 4.00

Agent Three Zero: The Blue Sultan's Quest/ Blue Sultan-Galaxi Fact Files
Galaxinovels

1-4 .... 3.00

Agent Unknown
Renegade, 1987

1-3 .... 2.00

Agent X
Marvel, 2002

1-6 .... 2.00
7-15 .... 3.00

Age of Apocalypse: The Chosen
Marvel

1 .... 3.00

Age of Bronze
Image, 1998

1 .... 4.00
2-7 .... 3.00
8-25 .... 4.00
Special 1 .... 3.00
Special 2 .... 4.00

Age of Heroes
Halloween, 1996

1-4 .... 3.00
5 .... 4.00
Special 1 .... 5.00
Special 2 .... 7.00

Age of Heroes: Wex
Image, 1998

1 .... 3.00

Age of Innocence: The Rebirth of Iron Man
Marvel

1 .... 3.00

Age of Reptiles
Dark Horse, 1993

1-4 .... 3.00

Age of Reptiles: The Hunt
Dark Horse, 1996

1-5 .... 3.00

Aggie Mack
Superior, 1948

1 .... 165.00
2-3 .... 85.00
4 .... 95.00
5-8 .... 85.00

Agony Acres
AA2, 1995

1-5 .... 3.00

Ahlea
Radio, 1997

1-2 .... 3.00

Aida-Zee
Nate Butler

1 .... 2.00

Aiden McKain Chronicles: Battle for Earth
Digital Webbing, 2005

1 .... 3.00
1/Incentive 10.00

AIDS Awareness
Chaos City, 1993

1 .... 3.00

Aim (Vol. 2)
Cryptic

1 .... 2.00

Air Ace (Vol. 2)
Street & Smith, 1944

1-6 .... 60.00
7 .... 110.00
8 .... 65.00
9-12 .... 60.00

Air Ace (Vol. 3)
Street & Smith, 1946

1 .... 50.00

Airboy
Eclipse, 1986

1-9 .... 2.00
10-32 .... 1.00
33-49 .... 2.00
50 .... 5.00

Airboy Comics (Vol. 2)
Hillman, 1945

11 .... 400.00
12 .... 275.00

Airboy Comics (Vol. 3)
Hillman, 1946

1-8 .... 225.00
9 .... 250.00
10-12 .... 225.00

Airboy Comics (Vol. 4)
Hillman, 1947

1-11 .... 175.00
12 .... 160.00

Airboy Comics (Vol. 5)
Hillman, 1948

1-9 .... 125.00
10 .... 150.00
11-12 .... 125.00

Airboy Comics (Vol. 6)
Hillman, 1949

1-12 .... 100.00

Airboy Comics (Vol. 7)
Hillman, 1950

1-12 .... 90.00

Airboy Comics (Vol. 8)
Hillman, 1951

1 .... 90.00
2-12 .... 85.00

Airboy Comics (Vol. 9)
Hillman, 1952

1-12 .... 80.00

Airboy Comics (Vol. 10)
Hillman, 1953

1-4 .... 80.00

Airboy Meets the Prowler
Eclipse, 1987

1 .... 2.00

Airboy-Mr. Monster Special
Eclipse, 1987

1 .... 2.00

Airboy versus the Airmaidens
Eclipse, 1988

1 .... 2.00

Air Fighters Classics
Eclipse, 1987

1-7 .... 4.00

Air Fighters Comics (Vol. 1)
Hillman, 1941

1 .... 1,500.00
2 .... 2,200.00
3 .... 1,100.00
4 .... 700.00
5 .... 600.00
6 .... 685.00
7 .... 640.00
8-12 .... 500.00

Air Fighters Comics (Vol. 2)
Hillman, 1943

1 .... 500.00
2 .... 650.00
3-9 .... 425.00
10 .... 450.00

Airfighters Meet Sgt. Strike Special
Eclipse, 1988

1 .... 2.00

Airlock
Eclectus, 1990

1-3 .... 3.00

Airmaidens Special
Eclipse, 1987

1 .... 2.00

Airman
Malibu, 1993

1 .... 2.00

Airmen
Mansion, 1995

1 .... 3.00

Air Raiders
Marvel, 1987

1-5 .... 1.00

Airshell
-Ism, 2005

1 .... 4.00

Airtight Garage
Marvel, 1993

1-4 .... 3.00

Air War Stories
Dell, 1964

1 .... 22.00
2-8 .... 14.00

Airwaves
Caliber, 1991

1-4 .... 3.00

Ai Yori Aoshi
Tokyopop, 2004

1-11 .... 10.00

A.K.A. Goldfish
Caliber, 1994

1-3 .... 4.00
4 .... 3.00
5 .... 4.00

Akiko
Sirius, 1996

1 .... 6.00
2 .... 5.00
3-10 .... 4.00
11-49 .... 3.00
50 .... 4.00
51-Ash 1 .... 3.00

Akiko on the Planet Smoo
Sirius, 1995

1 .... 5.00
1/HC 20.00
1/2nd 4.00
Fan ed. 1/A 3.00

Akiko on the Planet Smoo: The Color Edition
Sirius, 2000

1 .... 5.00

Alien Nation

Alien Resurrection

All-American Comics

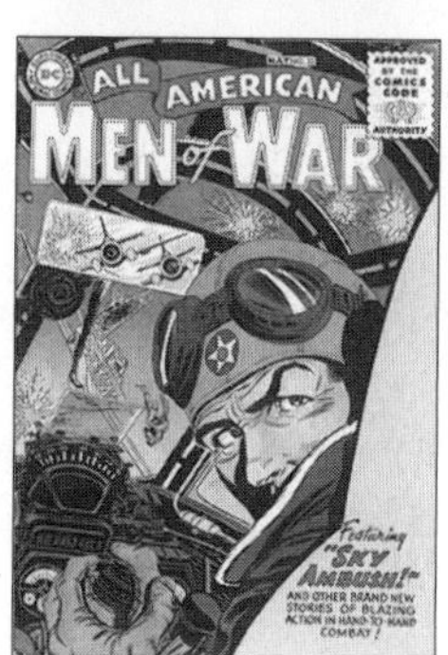

All-American Men of War

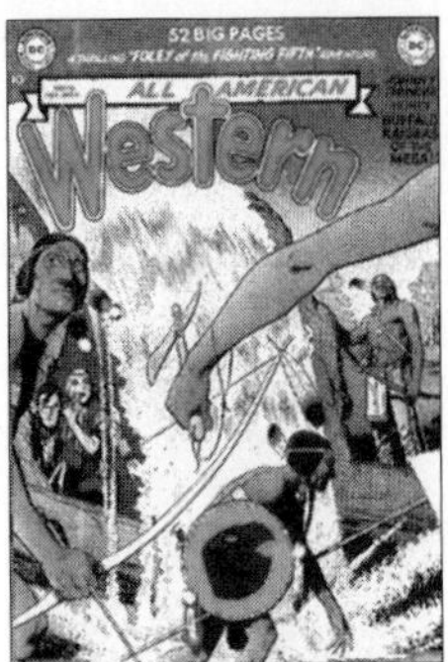

All-American Western

Allegra

Alley Cat

Alley Oop Adventures

Akira

Marvel, 1988

1 .... 8.00
1/2nd 4.00
2 .... 5.00
2/2nd 4.00
3 .... 5.00
4-33 .... 4.00
34-38 .... 7.00

A*K*Q*J

Fantagraphics, 1991

1 .... 3.00

Aladdin (Conquest)

Conquest, 1993

0 .... 3.00

Aladdin

Marvel, 1994

1-11 .... 2.00

Alamo

Antarctic, 2004

1 .... 5.00

Alarming Adventures

Harvey, 1962

1 .... 40.00
2 .... 25.00
3 .... 20.00

Alarming Tales

Harvey, 1957

1 .... 110.00
2 .... 65.00
3-4 .... 50.00
5-6 .... 40.00

Albedo (1st Series)

Thoughts & Images, 1984

0 .... 8.00
0/A 30.00
0/B 15.00
0/2nd 5.00
0/3rd-0/4th 3.00
1 .... 14.00
1/A-1/2nd 10.00
2 .... 250.00
☛1st Usagi Yojimbo
3 .... 10.00
4-5 .... 4.00
6-8 .... 3.00
9-14 .... 2.00

Albedo (2nd Series)

Antarctic, 1991

1 .... 4.00
2-10 .... 3.00
Special 1 .... 4.00

Albedo (3rd Series)

Antarctic, 1994

1-4 .... 3.00

Albedo (4th Series)

Antarctic, 1996

1-2 .... 3.00

Albedo (5th Series)

Antarctic, 2002

1 .... 5.00

Albino Spider of Dajette

Verotik, 1997

1 .... 3.00
2-0 .... 3.00

Albion

DC, 2005

1-6 .... 3.00

Alec Dear

Mediocre Concepts, 1996

1 .... 2.00

Alec: Love and Beerglasses

Escape

1 .... 4.00

Aleister Arcane

Idea & Design Works, 2004

1-3 .... 4.00

Alex

Fantagraphics, 1994

1-6 .... 3.00

Alexis (Vol. 2)

Fantagraphics, 1995

1-5 .... 3.00

Alf

Marvel, 1988

1 .... 2.00
2-49 .... 1.00
50-Spring 1 .... 2.00

Alf Comics Magazine

Marvel, 1988

1-2 .... 2.00

Alias:

Now, 1990

1-5 .... 2.00

Alias

Marvel, 2001

1 .... 4.00
2-28 .... 3.00

Ali-Baba: Scourge of the Desert

Gauntlet

1 .... 4.00

Alice
Ziff-Davis, 1951
10 .... 125.00
11 .... 75.00

Alice and the Engine
Straw Dog
1-3 .... 3.00

Alice in Blunderland
Industrial Services
1 .... 100.00

Alice in Lost World
Radio, 2001
1-4 .... 3.00

Alien 3
Dark Horse, 1992
1-3 .... 3.00

Alien Ducklings
Blackthorne, 1986
1-4 .... 2.00

Alien Encounters (Fantaco)
Fantaco, 1980
1 .... 2.00

Alien Encounters (Eclipse)
Eclipse, 1965
1-14 .... 2.00

Alien Fire
Kitchen Sink, 1987
1-3 .... 2.00

Alien Fire: Pass in Thunder
Kitchen Sink, 1995
1 .... 7.00

Alien Hero
Zen, 1999
1 .... 9.00

Alien Legion (Vol. 1)
Marvel, 1984
1-20 .... 2.00

Alien Legion (Vol. 2)
Marvel, 1987
1-18 .... 2.00

Alien Legion: A Grey Day to Die
Marvel
1 .... 7.00

Alien Legion: Binary Deep
Marvel, 1993
1 .... 4.00

Alien Legion: Jugger Grimrod
Marvel, 1992
1 .... 6.00

Alien Legion: One Planet at a Time
Marvel, 1993
1-3 .... 5.00

Alien Legion: On the Edge
Marvel, 1990
1-3 .... 5.00

Alien Legion: Tenants of Hell
Marvel, 1991
1-2 .... 5.00

Alien Nation
DC, 1988
1 .... 3.00

Alien Nation: A Breed Apart
Adventure, 1990
1-4 .... 3.00

Alien Nation: The Firstcomers
Adventure, 1991
1-4 .... 3.00

Alien Nation: The Lost Episode
Malibu, 1992
1 .... 5.00

Alien Nation: The Public Enemy
Adventure, 1991
1-4 .... 3.00

Alien Nation: The Skin Trade
Adventure, 1991
1-4 .... 3.00

Alien Nation: The Spartans
Adventure, 1990
1-4 .... 3.00

Alien Resurrection
Dark Horse, 1997
1-2 .... 3.00

Aliens
Gold Key, 1982
1 .... 12.00
2 .... 5.00

Aliens (Vol. 1)
Dark Horse, 1988
1 .... 5.00
1/2nd 3.00
1/3rd-1/5th 2.00
1/6th 2.00
2 .... 4.00
2/2nd 3.00
2/3rd-2/4th 2.00
3 .... 3.00

All Famous Crime Stories

All-Famous Police Cases

All-Flash

All Funny Comics

All Good Comics

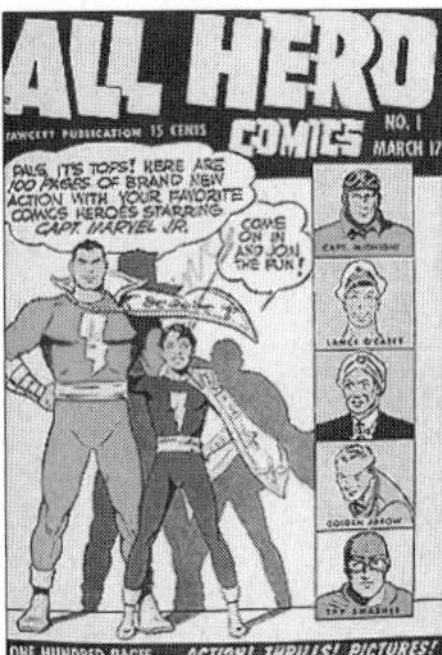

All Hero Comics

All Hitler Comics

All Humor Comics

3/2nd-3/3rd 2.00
4 .... 3.00
4/2nd 2.00
5 .... 3.00
5/2nd 2.00
6 .... 3.00
6/2nd 2.00

Aliens (Vol. 2)
Dark Horse, 1989

1-4 .... 3.00

Aliens: Alchemy
Dark Horse, 1997

1-3 .... 3.00

Aliens: Apocalypse: The Destroying Angels
Dark Horse, 1999

1-4 .... 3.00

Aliens: Berserker
Dark Horse, 1995

1-4 .... 3.00

Aliens: Colonial Marines
Dark Horse, 1993

1-10 .... 3.00

Aliens: Earth Angel
Dark Horse, 1994

1 .... 3.00

Aliens: Earth War
Dark Horse, 1990

1-4 .... 3.00

Alien Sex/Monster Lust
Fantagraphics, 1992

1 .... 3.00

Aliens: Genocide
Dark Horse, 1991

1-4 .... 3.00

Aliens: Glass Corridor
Dark Horse, 1998

1 .... 3.00

Aliens: Havoc
Dark Horse, 1997

1 .... 3.00
2 .... 4.00

Aliens: Hive
Dark Horse, 1992

1-4 .... 3.00

Aliens: Kidnapped
Dark Horse, 1997

1-3 .... 3.00

Aliens: Labyrinth
Dark Horse, 1993

1-4 .... 3.00

Aliens: Lovesick
Dark Horse, 1996

1 .... 3.00

Aliens (Magazine) (Vol. 1)
Dark Horse, 1991

1-5 .... 4.00
6-17 .... 3.00

Aliens (Magazine) (Vol. 2)
Dark Horse, 1992

1-22 .... 3.00

Aliens: Mondo Heat
Dark Horse, 1996

1 .... 3.00

Aliens: Mondo Pest
Dark Horse, 1995

1 .... 3.00

Aliens: Music of the Spears
Dark Horse, 1994

1-4 .... 3.00

Aliens: Newt's Tale
Dark Horse, 1992

1-2 .... 5.00

Aliens: Pig
Dark Horse, 1997

1 .... 3.00

Aliens/Predator: The Deadliest of the Species
Dark Horse, 1993

1 .... 3.00
1/Ltd 4.00
2-12 .... 3.00

Aliens: Purge
Dark Horse, 1997

1 .... 3.00

Aliens: Rogue
Dark Horse, 1993

1-4 .... 3.00

Aliens: Sacrifice
Dark Horse, 1993

1 .... 5.00

Aliens: Salvation
Dark Horse, 1993

1 .... 5.00

Aliens: Salvation and Sacrifice
Dark Horse, 2001

1 .... 13.00

Aliens: Special
Dark Horse, 1997

1 .... 3.00

Aliens: Stalker
Dark Horse, 1998

1 .... 3.00

Aliens: Stronghold

Dark Horse, 1994

1-4 .... 3.00

Aliens: Survival

Dark Horse, 1998

1-3 .... 3.00

Aliens vs. Predator

Dark Horse, 1990

0 .... 5.00
1 .... 4.00
1/2nd 3.00
2 .... 4.00
2/2nd-4/2nd 3.00
Ann 1 .... 5.00

Aliens vs. Predator: Booty

Dark Horse, 1996

1 .... 3.00

Aliens vs. Predator: Duel

Dark Horse, 1995

1-2 .... 3.00

Aliens vs. Predator: Eternal

Dark Horse, 1998

1-4 .... 3.00

Aliens vs. Predator vs. The Terminator

Dark Horse, 2000

1-4 .... 3.00

Aliens vs. Predator: War

Dark Horse, 1995

0-4 .... 3.00

Aliens vs. Predator: Xenogenesis

Dark Horse, 1999

1-4 .... 3.00

Aliens: Wraith

Dark Horse, 1998

1 .... 3.00

Aliens: Xenogenesis

Dark Horse, 1999

1-4 .... 3.00

Alien: The Illustrated Story

HM Communications

1 .... 5.00

Alien Worlds

Pacific, 1982

1 .... 3.00
2-3D 1 .... 2.00

Alien Worlds (Blackthorne)

Blackthorne

1 .... 6.00

Alison Dare, Little Miss Adventures

Oni, 2000

1 .... 5.00

Alister the Slayer

Midnight, 1995

1 .... 3.00

Alizarin's Journal

Avatar, 1999

1 .... 4.00

Allagash Incident

Tundra, 1993

1 .... 3.00

All-American Comics

DC, 1939

1 .... 5,700.00
2 .... 2,000.00
3 .... 1,400.00
4-5 .... 1,250.00
6-7 .... 980.00
8 .... 1,800.00
9-10 .... 950.00
11 .... 1,025.00
12-15 .... 950.00
16 .... 72,000.00
☛1st Green Lantern
17 .... 15,600.00
☛2nd Green Lantern
18 .... 8,800.00
19 .... 13,800.00
☛1st Atom
20 .... 4,850.00
21-23 .... 2,000.00
24 .... 2,200.00
☛1st Mid-Nite, Sargon
25 .... 8,300.00
☛Dr. Mid-Nite origin
26 .... 3,000.00
☛Sargon origin
27 .... 3,500.00
28-30 .... 1,250.00
31-40 .... 1,040.00
41-50 .... 785.00
51-60 .... 675.00
61 .... 4,400.00
☛1st Solomon Grundy
62-70 .... 600.00
71-88 .... 550.00
89 .... 1,200.00
☛1st Harlequin
90 .... 775.00
91-99 .... 525.00
100 .... 850.00
101 .... 1,000.00
☛Scarce
102 .... 1,650.00
☛Scarce

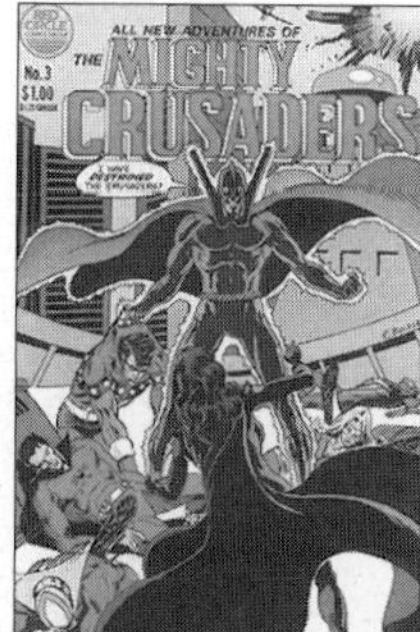

All New Adventures of the Mighty Crusaders

All-New Comics

All New Underground Comix

All-Select Comics

All-Star Comics

All-Star Squadron

All Surprise

All Suspense

All-American Comics (2nd Series)

DC, 1999

1 .... 2.00

All-American Men of War

DC, 1952

0 (127) 900.00
1 (128) 500.00
2 .... 360.00
3 .... 295.00
4-5 .... 260.00
6-10 .... 235.00
11-18 .... 210.00
19-28 .... 165.00
29 .... 190.00
30 .... 165.00
31-40 .... 130.00
41-50 .... 100.00
51-60 .... 80.00
61-65 .... 70.00
66 .... 80.00
67 .... 130.00
68-80 .... 70.00
81 .... 50.00
82 .... 135.00
83-90 .... 50.00
91-100 .... 35.00
101-110 .... 24.00
111-117 .... 20.00

All-American Western

DC, 1948

103 .... 375.00
104 .... 265.00
105-110 .... 225.00
111-120 .... 165.00
121-126 .... 110.00

All Detective

Avalon

1 .... 3.00

Allegra

Image, 1996

1-4 .... 3.00

Alley Cat

Image, 1999

1-1/B 3.00
2-Ashcan 1/E 3.00

Alley Cat Lingerie Edition

Image, 1999

1 .... 5.00

Alley Cat vs. Lady Pendragon

Image, 2000

1-1/A 3.00

Alley Oop (Standard)

Standard, 1947

10 .... 135.00
11-18 .... 110.00

Alley Oop (Argo)

Argo, 1955

1 .... 125.00
2-3 .... 85.00

Alley Oop

Dell, 1962

1 .... 40.00
2 .... 26.00

Alley Oop (Dragon Lady)

Dragon Lady

1 .... 6.00
2 .... 7.00
3 .... 8.00

Alley Oop Adventures

Antarctic, 1998

1-3 .... 3.00

Alley Oop Quarterly

Antarctic, 1999

1-3 .... 3.00

All-Famous Crime

Star Publications, 1950

4 .... 185.00
5 .... 135.00
8 .... 125.00
9 .... 175.00
10 .... 115.00

All Famous Crime Stories

Fox, 1949

1 .... 300.00

All-Famous Police Cases

Star Publications, 1952

6 .... 100.00
7-8 .... 85.00
9-16 .... 75.00

All-Flash

DC, 1941

1 .... 12,500.00
☛Flash origin
2 .... 2,400.00
3-4 .... 1,600.00
5-10 .... 1,100.00
11-15 .... 850.00
16-20 .... 800.00
21-32 .... 625.00

All for Love (Vol. 1)

Prize, 1957

1 .... 40.00
2 .... 25.00
3-6 .... 20.00

All for Love (Vol. 2)

Prize, 1958

1 .... 28.00
2-5/A 18.00

All for Love (Vol. 3)
Prize, 1959

1 .... 20.00
1/A-4 .... 16.00

All Funny Comics
DC, 1943

1 .... 275.00
2 .... 125.00
3-10 .... 80.00
11-13 .... 70.00
14 .... 55.00
15 .... 70.00
16 .... 175.00
17 .... 55.00
18-19 .... 70.00
20-23 .... 55.00

All Girls School Meets All Boys School
Angel

1 .... 3.00

All Good Comics
Fox, 1946

1 .... 120.00

All Good
St. John, 1949

1 .... 475.00

All Great Jungle Adventures
Fox, 1949

1 .... 350.00

All Hallow's Eve
Innovation

1 .... 5.00

All Hero Comics
Fawcett, 1943

1 .... 1,050.00

All Hitler Comics
Paragon

1 .... 5.00

All Humor Comics
Quality, 1946

1 .... 130.00
2 .... 70.00
3 .... 40.00
4-5 .... 34.00
6-10 .... 26.00
11-17 .... 22.00

Alliance
Image, 1995

1-3/A 3.00

All New Adventures of the Mighty Crusaders
Archie, 1983

1-3 .... 1.00

All-New Atom
DC, 2006

1-7 .... 3.00

All New Collectors' Edition
DC, 1977

C-53 .... 26.00
☛Rudolph
C-54 .... 12.00
☛Supes v. Wonder Woman
C-55 .... 15.00
☛Legion
C-56 .... 40.00
☛Superman vs. Ali
C-56/Whitman 35.00
C-58 .... 12.00
☛Supes vs. Shazam
C-60 .... 20.00
☛Rudolph's Summer
C-62 .... 12.00
☛Superman movie

All-New Comics
Harvey, 1943

1 .... 2,200.00
2 .... 750.00
3 .... 550.00
4 .... 425.00
5-11 .... 485.00
12-14 .... 385.00
15 .... 540.00

All New Exiles
Malibu, 1995

0 .... 2.00
0/Variant-1 .... 2.00
2-4 .... 2.00
5 .... 3.00
6-11 .... 2.00

All New Official Handbook of the Marvel Universe A to Z
Marvel, 2006

1-12 .... 4.00

All-New Tenchi Muyo Part 1
Viz, 2002

1-5 .... 3.00

All-New Tenchi Muyo Part 2
Viz, 2002

1-5 .... 3.00

All New Underground Comix
Last Gasp, 1973

1 .... 5.00
2-5 .... 3.00

All-Out War
DC, 1979

1-6 .... 3.00

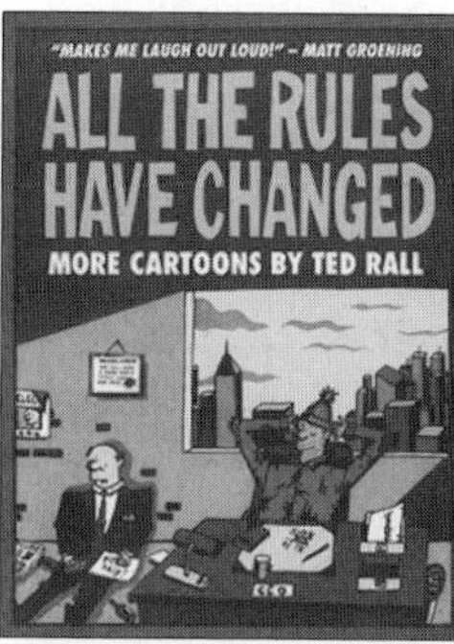

All the Rules Have Changed

All the Wrong Places

All-Thrill Comics

All-Time Sports Comics

All True Crime

Ally

Alone in the Shade Special

Alphabet

All Picture Adventures

St. John, 1952

1 .... 175.00
2 .... 250.00

All-Select Comics

Timely, 1943

1 .... 11,000.00
2 .... 3,300.00
3 .... 1,750.00
4-5 .... 1,400.00
6-10 .... 1,250.00
11 .... 1,650.00

All Shook Up

Rip Off, 1990

1 .... 4.00

All Star Batman and Robin Boy Wonder

DC, 2005

1/Batman-1/Robin 5.00
1/Special 4.00
1/RRP 150.00
2/Miller-2/Lee 4.00
3 .... 3.00

All-Star Comics

DC, 1940

1 .... 10,000.00
2 .... 3,500.00
3 .... 25,000.00
☛1st JSA
4 .... 3,000.00
5 .... 2,800.00
☛1st Hawkgirl
6-7 .... 1,800.00
8 .... 16,000.00
☛1st Wonder Woman
9-11 .... 1,600.00
12-15 .... 1,400.00
16-25 .... 1,200.00
26-32 .... 900.00
33 .... 1,800.00
☛Grundy appearance
34-35 .... 900.00
36 .... 1,300.00
☛Batman, Supes app.
37 .... 900.00
38 .... 975.00
☛Black Canary starts
39-49 .... 900.00
50 .... 975.00
☛Frazetta art
51-56 .... 900.00
57 .... 1,200.00
☛25-year hiatus starts
58 .... 12.00
☛1st Power Girl
59-61 .... 6.00
62 .... 8.00
63 .... 6.00
64-65 .... 7.00
66 .... 8.00
67-68 .... 6.00
69 .... 10.00
70-73 .... 6.00
74 .... 8.00

All Star Comics (2nd Series)

DC, 1999

1 .... 3.00
2 .... 3.00
GS 1 .... 5.00

All-Star Index

Eclipse, 1987

1 .... 2.00

All-Star Squadron

DC, 1981

1 .... 4.00
2-10 .... 2.00
11-14 .... 1.00
15-46 .... 1.00
47 .... 3.00
48-67 .... 1.00
Ann 1 .... 2.00
Ann 2-3 .... 1.00

All-Star Superman

DC, 2006

1-10 .... 3.00

All-Star Western (1st Series)

DC, 1951

58 .... 325.00
59-60 .... 150.00
61-63 .... 160.00
64-66 .... 125.00
67 .... 170.00
☛Johnny Thunder starts
68-70 .... 125.00
71-80 .... 85.00
81-98 .... 60.00
99 .... 65.00
100 .... 60.00
101-107 .... 50.00
108 .... 100.00
109-119 .... 50.00

All-Star Western (2nd Series)

DC, 1970

1 .... 30.00
2-3 .... 15.00
4-5 .... 14.00
6-9 .... 9.00
10 .... 260.00
☛1st Jonah Hex
11 .... 75.00

All Surprise

Timely, 1943

1 .... 150.00
2 .... 80.00
3-5 .... 60.00
6-12 .... 48.00

All Suspense

Avalon, 1998

1 .... 3.00

All Teen

Timely, 1947

20 .... 200.00

All the Rules Have Changed

Rip Off

1 .... 10.00

All the Wrong Places

Laszlo

1 .... 3.00

All-Thrill Comics

Mansion

845 .... 3.00

All-Time Sports Comics

Hillman, 1949

4 .... 125.00
5-7 .... 90.00

All Top Comics

Fox, 1946

1 .... 110.00
2 .... 60.00
3-7 .... 45.00
8 .... 1,550.00
9-10 .... 800.00
11-13 .... 700.00
14 .... 825.00
15-17 .... 700.00
18 .... 450.00

All True Crime

Leading, 1948

26 .... 125.00
27-29 .... 85.00
30-40 .... 60.00
41-51 .... 48.00
52 .... 55.00

All Western Winners

Timely, 1948

2 .... 450.00
3 .... 250.00
4 .... 225.00

All-Winners Comics (1st Series)

Timely, 1941

1 .... 16,000.00
☛Cap America starts
2 .... 5,200.00
3 .... 3,150.00
4 .... 3,100.00
5-6 .... 2,300.00
7-10 .... 1,950.00
11-18 .... 1,350.00
19 .... 3,350.00
☛All-Winner Squad org.
21 .... 3,500.00
☛Scarce

All-Winners Comics (2nd Series)

Timely, 1948

1 .... 2,150.00

Ally

Ally-Winsor, 1995

1-3 .... 3.00

Almuric

Dark Horse, 1991

1 .... 11.00

Alone in the Dark

Image, 2002

1-2 .... 5.00

Alone in the Shade Special

Alchemy

1 .... 2.00

Alpha and Omega

Spire, 1978

1 .... 5.00

Alphabet

Dark Visions, 1993

1 .... 3.00

Alpha Centurion Special

DC, 1996

1 .... 3.00

Alpha Flight (1st Series)

Marvel, 1983

1 .... 5.00
☛1st Marrina, Puck
2-10 .... 4.00
11-19 .... 3.00
20-24 .... 2.00
25-27 .... 1.00
28 .... 3.00
29-32 .... 2.00
33 .... 6.00
☛Wolverine appears
34 .... 3.00
35-45 .... 2.00
46 .... 3.00
47 .... 4.00
☛1st Jim Lee at Marvel
48-53 .... 2.00
54 .... 3.00
55-56 .... 2.00
57-74 .... 1.00
75-105 .... 2.00
106 .... 3.00
☛Northstar outed
106/2nd-130 .... 2.00
Ann 1 .... 4.00
Ann 2 .... 1.00
Special 1 .... 3.00

Alpha Centurion Special

Alpha Flight Special

Alpha Track

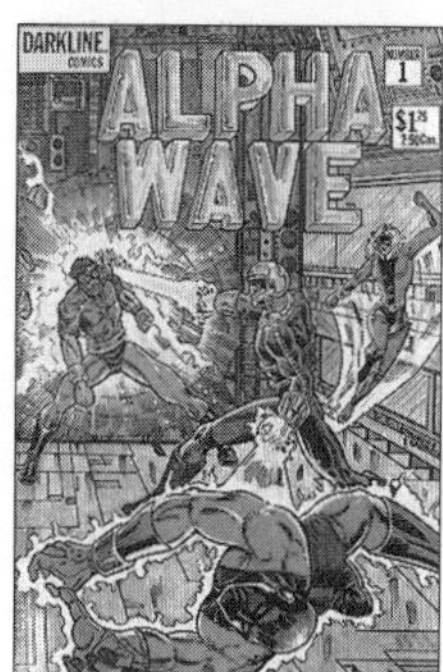

Alpha Wave

Altered Image

Alter Ego

Alternate Heroes

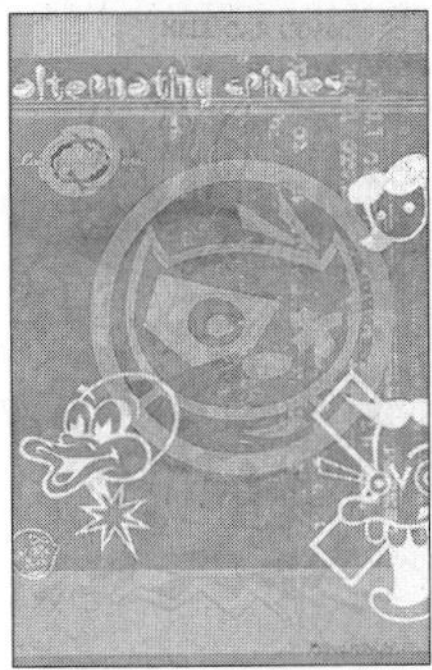

Alternating Crimes

Alpha Flight (2nd Series)
Marvel, 1997

1....3.00
2-20....2.00
Ann 1998....4.00

Alpha Flight (3rd Series)
Marvel, 2004

1-12....3.00

Alpha Flight: In the Beginning
Marvel, 1997

-1....2.00

Alpha Flight Special
Marvel, 1991

1-4....2.00

Alpha Illustrated
Alpha Productions, 1994

0....1.00
1....4.00

Alpha Korps
Diversity, 1996

1....3.00
Ashcan 1....1.00

Alpha Team Omega
Fantasy Graphics, 1983

1....1.00

Alpha Track
Fantasy General, 1985

1-2....2.00

Alpha Wave
Darkline

1....2.00

Altered Image
Image, 1998

1-3....3.00

Altered Realities
Altered Reality

1....2.00

Alter Ego
First, 1986

1-4....2.00

Alternate Existance
Dragonmaster, 1982

1-2....2.00

Alternate Heroes
Prelude

1....2.00

Alternating Crimes
Alternating Crimes, 1996

1-2....3.00

Alternation
Image, 2004

1-4....3.00

Alternative Comics
Revolutionary, 1994

1....3.00

Alternity
Navigator, 1992

1....3.00

Alvar Mayor: Death and Silver
4Winds

1....9.00

Alvin
Dell, 1962

1....25.00
2....18.00
3-10....15.00
11-20....12.00
21-28....8.00

Alvin and the Chipmunks
Harvey, 1992

1-5....2.00

A Man Called Kev
DC, 2006

1-5....3.00

Amanda and Gunn
Image, 1997

1-4....3.00

Amazing Adult Fantasy
Marvel, 1961

7....600.00
8....475.00
9-13....425.00
13/2nd....3.00
14....525.00

Amazing Adventure
Marvel, 1988

1....5.00

Amazing Adventure Funnies
Centaur, 1940

1....1,200.00
2....750.00

Amazing Adventures (1st Series)
Ziff-Davis, 1950

1....450.00
2-6....225.00

Amazing Adventures (2nd Series)
Marvel, 1961

1....900.00
2....525.00
3-6....425.00

Amazing Adventures (3rd Series)
Marvel, 1970

1....30.00

2-3 .... 20.00
4-5 .... 14.00
6 .... 20.00
7 .... 14.00
8 .... 22.00
9-10 .... 20.00
11 .... 150.00
☛1st blue Beast
12-13 .... 30.00
14 .... 25.00
15-17 .... 20.00
18 .... 14.00
19-25 .... 5.00
26-28 .... 4.00
29 .... 5.00
30-36 .... 3.00
36/30¢ 20.00
37-37/30¢ 8.00
38-39 .... 3.00

Amazing Adventures (4th Series)
Marvel, 1979
1 .... 3.00
2-14 .... 2.00

Amazing Adventures of Ace International
Starhead, 1993
1 .... 3.00

Amazing Adventures of Frank and Jolly (Alan Groening's...)
Press This
1-10 .... 2.00

Amazing Adventures of Professor Jones
Antarctic, 1996
1-4 .... 3.00

Amazing Adventures of The Escapist (Michael Chabon Presents The)
Dark Horse, 2004
1-6 .... 9.00
7 .... 10.00
8 .... 9.00

Amazing Adventures of the JLA
DC, 2006
1 .... 4.00

Amazing Chan and the Chan Clan
Gold Key, 1973
1 .... 14.00
2-4 .... 9.00

Amazing Comics (Timely)
Timely, 1944
1 .... 1,600.00

Amazing Comics (Avalon)
Avalon
1-3 .... 3.00

Amazing Comics Premieres
Amazing, 1987
1-5 .... 2.00

Amazing Cynicalman
Eclipse
1 .... 3.00

Amazing Detective Cases
Atlas, 1950
3 .... 145.00
4-6 .... 85.00
7-10 .... 75.00
11 .... 120.00
12-14 .... 90.00

Amazing Fantasy
Marvel, 1962
15 .... 32,000.00
☛1st Spider-Man
15/2nd 5.00
16-18 .... 5.00

Amazing Fantasy (2nd Series)
Marvel, 2004
1 .... 4.00
2-14 .... 3.00
15 .... 4.00
16-20 .... 3.00

Amazing Heroes Swimsuit Special
Fantagraphics, 1990
Ann 1990 .... 6.00
Ann 1991 .... 8.00
Ann 1992 .... 10.00
4 .... 4.00
5 .... 5.00

Amazing High Adventure
Marvel, 1984
1-5 .... 3.00

Amazing Joy Buzzards
Image, 2005
1-4 .... 3.00

Amazing Joy Buzzards (Vol. 2)
Image, 2005
1-5 .... 3.00

Amazing-Man Comics
Centaur, 1939
5 .... 11,000.00

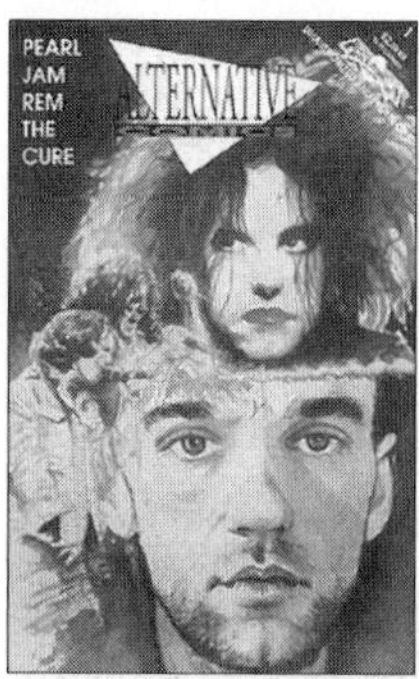

Alternative Comics

Alternity

Alvin

Alvin and the Chipmunks

Amanda and Gunn

Amazing Adult Fantasy

Amazing Adventure Funnies

Amazing Chan and the Chan Clan

6 .... 2,200.00
7 .... 1,425.00
8-9 .... 1,100.00
10-11 .... 950.00
12-13 .... 900.00
14 .... 850.00
15-20 .... 800.00
21-24 .... 750.00
25-26 .... 800.00

Amazing Mysteries
Atlas, 1949

32 .... 500.00
33 .... 210.00
34-35 .... 105.00

Amazing Mystery Funnies
Centaur, 1938

1 .... 2,400.00
2 .... 1,250.00
3 .... 700.00
4 .... 575.00
5-10 .... 525.00
11 .... 2,200.00
12 .... 850.00
13-15 .... 500.00
16 .... 1,000.00
17-18 .... 500.00
19 .... 600.00
20 .... 500.00
21-24 .... 600.00

Amazing Scarlet Spider
Marvel, 1995

1-2 .... 2.00

Amazing Screw-On Head
Dark Horse, 2002

1-1/2nd 3.00

Amazing Spider-Girl
Marvel, 2006

0 .... 2.00
1-4 .... 3.00

Amazing Spider-Man
Marvel, 1963

-1 .... 3.00
1 .... 27,000.00
☛1st Chameleon
1/Golden 200.00
2 .... 3,400.00
☛1st Vulture
3 .... 4,600.00
☛1st Dr. Octopus
4 .... 2,300.00
☛1st Sandman
5 .... 2,500.00
☛Dr. Doom app.
6 .... 1,650.00
☛1st Lizard
7 .... 1,100.00
8 .... 800.00
9 .... 1,025.00
☛1st Electro
10 .... 990.00
11 .... 1,900.00
12 .... 825.00
13 .... 1,200.00
☛1st Mysterio
14 .... 2,050.00
☛1st Green Goblin
15 .... 1,800.00
☛1st Kraven
16-17 .... 800.00
☛2nd Green Goblin
18 .... 510.00
☛1st Ned Leeds
19 .... 460.00
20-21 .... 510.00
22 .... 425.00
23 .... 510.00
24-25 .... 500.00
26 .... 550.00
27 .... 500.00
28 .... 450.00
29-30 .... 240.00
31 .... 325.00
32 .... 175.00
33 .... 140.00
34 .... 240.00
35-36 .... 225.00
37 .... 250.00
38 .... 195.00
39 .... 350.00
☛1st Romita Spidey
40 .... 375.00
☛Goblin origin
41 .... 300.00
☛1st Rhino
42 .... 185.00
☛1st view of MJ
43 .... 120.00
44 .... 175.00
45 .... 115.00
46 .... 250.00
☛1st Shocker
47 .... 105.00
48 .... 120.00
49 .... 125.00
50 .... 625.00
☛Spidey quits
51 .... 200.00
52 .... 150.00
53 .... 105.00
54-55 .... 110.00
56 .... 90.00
57 .... 80.00
58 .... 100.00
59 .... 70.00
60 .... 105.00
61 .... 72.00
62 .... 75.00
63 .... 160.00
☛vs. both Vultures
64 .... 60.00
65 .... 55.00

66 .... 80.00
☛1st Randy
67-68 .... 60.00
69 .... 75.00
70-71 .... 70.00
72 .... 85.00
73 .... 50.00
74 .... 80.00
75-77 .... 65.00
78 .... 70.00
79-80 .... 60.00
81 .... 55.00
82-83 .... 50.00
84-85 .... 55.00
86 .... 60.00
87 .... 75.00
88 .... 60.00
89 .... 70.00
90 .... 75.00
91 .... 50.00
92 .... 62.00
93 .... 80.00
94 .... 65.00
95 .... 52.00
96 .... 85.00
97 .... 72.00
98 .... 80.00
99 .... 60.00
100 .... 100.00
101 .... 130.00
101/2nd 3.00
102 .... 105.00
☛Morbius origin
103 .... 50.00
104 .... 90.00
105 .... 25.00
106 .... 40.00
107-108 .... 27.00
109-110 .... 30.00
111 .... 34.00
112 .... 30.00
113 .... 35.00
114 .... 50.00
115 .... 33.00
116 .... 22.00
117 .... 25.00
118 .... 22.00
☛vs. Hulk
119-120 .... 50.00
☛vs. Hulk
121 .... 150.00
☛Gwen Stacy dies
122 .... 150.00
☛Green Goblin dies
123 .... 35.00
124 .... 42.00
125 .... 30.00
126 .... 18.00
127 .... 25.00
128 .... 20.00
129 .... 225.00
☛1st Punisher
130 .... 20.00
131 .... 25.00
☛Uncle Doc Ock
132 .... 22.00
133 .... 16.00
134 .... 28.00
☛2nd Punisher
135 .... 45.00
136 .... 60.00
☛Harry as Goblin II
137 .... 25.00
138 .... 15.00
139 .... 19.00
140 .... 17.00
141 .... 15.00
142 .... 18.00
143 .... 15.00
144 .... 17.00
145-146 .... 15.00
147 .... 14.00
148 .... 25.00
149 .... 27.00
☛Spider-clone dies
150 .... 16.00
151 .... 24.00
152 .... 11.00
153-154 .... 10.00
155 .... 12.00
155/30¢ 20.00
156 .... 12.00
156/30¢ 20.00
157 .... 12.00
157/30¢ 40.00
158 .... 10.00
158/30¢ 20.00
159 .... 11.00
☛vs. Doc Ock
159/30¢ 20.00
160 .... 9.00
161 .... 12.00
162 .... 11.00
163 .... 10.00
164 .... 12.00
165-166/Whitman 9.00
167-168/Whitman 7.00
169-169/Whitman 10.00
169/35¢ 15.00
170-170/Whitman 7.00
170/35¢ 15.00
171-171/Whitman 7.00
171/35¢ 15.00
172-172/Whitman 8.00
172/35¢ 15.00
173 .... 25.00
173/Whitman 18.00
173/35¢ 25.00
174-175/Whitman 10.00
176-177 .... 12.00
☛1st Hamilton Goblin
178-180/Whitman 11.00
181-181/Whitman 9.00
182 .... 8.00

Amazing Comics Premieres

Amazing Detective Cases

Amazing Fantasy

Amazing High Adventure

Amazing-Man Comics

Amazing Mystery Funnies

Amazing Spider-Girl

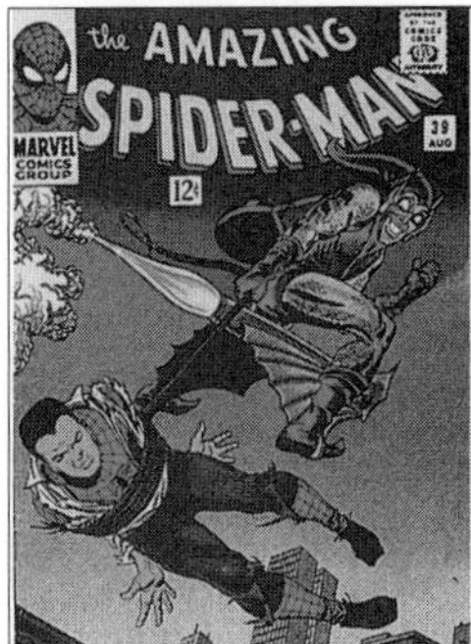

Amazing Spider-Man

183-183/Whitman 7.00
184 .... 8.00
184/Whitman 6.00
185-185/Whitman 7.00
186-187/Whitman 8.00
188-188/Whitman 7.00
189-189/Whitman 6.00
190 .... 7.00
191-193 .... 6.00
194 .... 21.00
☛1st Black Cat
195 .... 10.00
196-198 .... 6.00
199 .... 7.00
200 .... 10.00
201 .... 9.00
202 .... 7.00
203 .... 6.00
204 .... 8.00
205-206 .... 6.00
207 .... 5.00
208-211 .... 6.00
212-218 .... 5.00
219-220 .... 6.00
221-222 .... 4.00
223 .... 5.00
224-225 .... 4.00
226 .... 7.00
227 .... 6.00
228 .... 4.00
229 .... 11.00
230-232 .... 6.00
233 .... 4.00
234 .... 6.00
235 .... 4.00
236-237 .... 5.00
238 .... 22.00
☛1st Hobgoblin
239 .... 10.00
240 .... 5.00
241 .... 4.00
242 .... 5.00
243 .... 6.00
244-245 .... 5.00
246-248 .... 4.00
249 .... 5.00
250-251 .... 6.00
252 .... 10.00
☛1st black costume
253-254 .... 5.00
255-258 .... 4.00
259-263 .... 5.00
264-265 .... 4.00
265/2nd 2.00
266-267 .... 3.00
268-270 .... 4.00
271 .... 5.00
272-273 .... 4.00
274-276 .... 5.00
277-279 .... 4.00
280-284 .... 5.00
285 .... 6.00
286 .... 4.00
287 .... 5.00
288-289 .... 6.00
290-293 .... 5.00
294-295 .... 6.00
296 .... 5.00
297 .... 6.00
298 .... 16.00
☛McFarlane starts
299 .... 9.00
☛Venom cameo
300 .... 35.00
☛1st Venom
301 .... 6.00
302 .... 4.00
303 .... 5.00
304-307 .... 4.00
308 .... 5.00
309 .... 4.00
310-313 .... 5.00
314 .... 4.00
315-316 .... 5.00
317-318 .... 6.00
319 .... 5.00
320 .... 3.00
321 .... 4.00
322 .... 5.00
323 .... 3.00
324 .... 5.00
325-327 .... 4.00
328 .... 5.00
329 .... 4.00
330-343 .... 3.00
344 .... 4.00
☛1st Cletus Kassidy
345-347 .... 3.00
348-353 .... 2.00
354 .... 3.00
355-357 .... 2.00
358 .... 6.00
359 .... 2.00
360 .... 3.00
361 .... 6.00
☛1st Carnage
361/2nd 2.00
362 .... 25.00
☛2nd Carnage
362/2nd 2.00
363 .... 4.00
364 .... 3.00
365 .... 4.00
366-369 .... 2.00
370 .... 3.00
371-373 .... 2.00
374 .... 3.00
375 .... 5.00
376 .... 4.00
377 .... 3.00
378 .... 4.00
379 .... 5.00
380 .... 3.00
381 .... 4.00

382-388 .... 3.00
388/Variant 2.00
389-394 .... 3.00
394/Variant 4.00
395-397 .... 3.00
398-399 .... 3.00
400 .... 5.00
☛no overlay
☛gray overlay
400/Gray-400/White 30.00
☛white overlay
401-418 .... 2.00
419 .... 2.00
420-421 .... 2.00
422-424 .... 2.00
425-432 .... 2.00
432/Variant 5.00
433-441 .... 2.00
500 .... 5.00
501 .... 4.00
502 .... 3.00
503-509 .... 2.00
509/DirCut 7.00
☛Director's Cut
510 .... 4.00
511 .... 3.00
512 .... 5.00
513 .... 3.00
514-520 .... 2.00
521-525 .... 3.00
526 .... 3.00
527 .... 3.00
528 .... 3.00
529 .... 20.00
529/2nd 6.00
529/3rd 5.00
530 .... 8.00
531-532 .... 6.00
533 .... 4.00
534-536 .... 4.00
537 .... 3.00
538 .... 6.00
539 .... 10.00
540-541 .... 5.00
542-544 .... 3.00
545 .... 4.00
546 .... 4.00
547-549 .... 3.00
550 .... 3.00
551 .... 3.00
552 .... 3.00
553 .... 3.00
554-555 .... 3.00
556-560 .... 3.00
Aim Giveaway 1 .... 4.00
Aim Giveaway 2 .... 2.00
Ann 1 .... 700.00
☛1st Sinister Six
Ann 2 .... 550.00
Ann 3 .... 140.00
Ann 4 .... 90.00
Ann 5 .... 75.00
Ann 5/2nd 3.00
Ann 6-7 .... 35.00
Ann 8-9 .... 22.00
Ann 10-2 .... 8.00
Ann 13 .... 7.00
Ann 14 .... 6.00
Ann 15 .... 7.00
Ann 16 .... 5.00
Ann 17-21 .... 4.00
☛Spidey marries
Ann 21/Direc-22 .... 5.00
Ann 23-25 .... 3.00
Ann 26 .... 4.00
Ann 27-28 .... 3.00
Ann 1996 .... 4.00
Ann 1997 .... 3.00
Ashcan 1 .... 1.00

Amazing Spider-Man (Vol. 2)

Marvel, 1999

1 (442) 7.00
1/DF Romita 12.00
1/DF Lee 35.00
1/Dynamic 5.00
1/Autographed 10.00
1/Authentix 8.00
1/Sunburst 18.00
2 (443)-2/Kubert 3.00
3 (444) 2.00
4 (445)-11 (452) 2.00
12 (453) 3.00
13 (454)-17 (458) 2.00
18 (459)-19 (460) 3.00
20 (461) 5.00
21 (462)-24 (465) 2.00
25 (466) 3.00
25/Speckle 4.00
26 (467)-29 (470) 2.00
30 (471) 5.00
☛Straczynski starts
31 (472) 3.00
32 (473)-33 (474) 4.00
34 (475) 5.00
35 (476) 4.00
36 (477) 9.00
☛9/11 issue
37 (478)-39 (480) 3.00
40 (481) 2.00
41 (482) 4.00
42 (483)-43 (484) 3.00
44 (485)-45 (486) 2.00
46 (487)-49 (490) 2.00
50 (491) 6.00
51 (492)-56 (497) 2.00
57 (498)-58 (499) 3.00
Ann 1999-2000 .... 4.00
Ann 2001 .... 3.00

Amazing World of Superman

Amazing X-Men

Amazon Tales

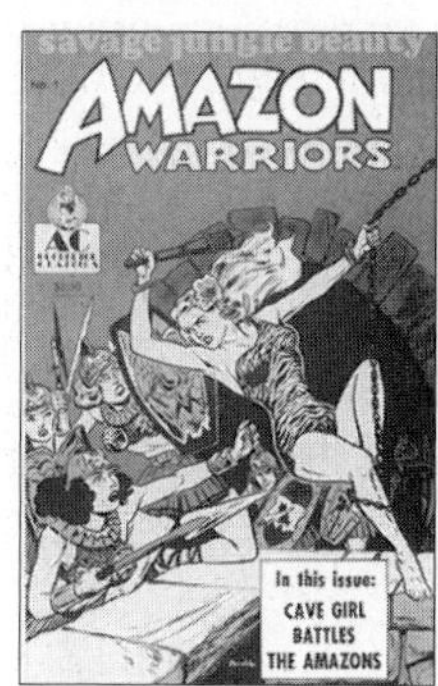

Amazon Warriors

Ambush Bug

Amelia Rules

American Air Forces

American Century

Amazing Spider-Man 30th Anniversary Poster Magazine
Marvel
1 ....4.00

Amazing Spider-Man Giveaways
Marvel, 1977
1 ....4.00
2-3 ....4.00
4 ....6.00
5-11 ....4.00

Amazing Spider-Man: Hooky
Marvel
1 ....9.00

Amazing Spider-Man (Public Service Series)
Marvel, 1990
1 ....3.00
1/2nd 2.00
2 ....3.00
2/2nd 2.00
3 ....3.00
3/2nd 2.00
4 ....3.00
4/2nd 2.00

Amazing Spider-Man: Soul of the Hunter
Marvel, 1992
1 ....6.00

Amazing Spider-Man Super Special
Marvel, 1995
1 ....4.00

Amazing Spider-Man: The Birth of a Super Hero!
Marvel, 1969
1 ....2.00

Amazing Strip
Antarctic, 1994
1-10 ....3.00

Amazing Wahzoo
Solson, 1986
1 ....2.00

Amazing Willie Mays
Famous Funnies, 1954
1 ....500.00

Amazing World of Superman
DC, 1973
1 ....4.00

Amazing X-Men
Marvel, 1995
1-4 ....2.00

Amazon
DC, 1996
1 ....2.00

Amazon Attack 3-D
3-D Zone, 1990
1 ....4.00

Amazons
Fantagraphics
1 ....3.00

Amazon Tales
Fantaco
1-3 ....3.00

Amazon
Comico, 1989
1-3 ....2.00

Amazon Warriors
AC, 1989
1 ....3.00

Amazon Woman (1st Series)
Fantaco, 1994
1-2 ....3.00

Amazon Woman (2nd Series)
Fantaco, 1994
1-4 ....3.00

Amber: Nine Princes in Amber (Roger Zelazny's...)
DC, 1996
1-3 ....7.00

Amber: The Guns of Avalon (Roger Zelazny's...)
DC, 1996
1-3 ....7.00

Ambush Bug
DC, 1985
1-4 ....1.00

Ambush Bug Nothing Special
DC, 1992
1 ....3.00

Ambush Bug Stocking Stuffer
DC, 1986
1 ....1.00

Amelia Rules
Renaissance, 2001
1-11 ....3.00

America's Greatest Comics (AC)
AC, 2005
1-13 ....7.00

America in Action
Dell, 1942

1 .... 100.00
2 .... 75.00

America Menaced!
Vital, 1950

1 .... 175.00

American
Dark Horse, 1987

1-8 .... 2.00
Special 1 .... 2.00

American Air Forces
Wise, 1944

1 .... 100.00
2 .... 115.00
3-4 .... 60.00

American Book
Dark Horse, 1988

1 .... 6.00

American Century
DC, 2001

1-27 .... 3.00

American Flagg
First, 1983

1 .... 3.00
2-13 .... 2.00
14-45 .... 1.00
46-Special 1 .... 2.00

American Flagg (Howard Chaykin's...)
First, 1988

1-12 .... 2.00

American Flyer
Last Gasp

1-2 .... 4.00

American Freak: A Tale of the Un-Men
DC, 1994

1-5 .... 2.00

American Heroes
Personality

1 .... 3.00

American Library
David McKay, 1944

1 .... 160.00
2 .... 125.00
3-6 .... 60.00

American: Lost in America
Dark Horse, 1992

1-4 .... 3.00

American Primitive
3-D Zone

1 .... 3.00

American Splendor
DC, 2006

1-2 .... 3.00
3-4 .... 20.00

American Splendor
Pekar, 1976

1 .... 65.00
2 .... 30.00
3-5 .... 20.00
6-10 .... 15.00
11-13 .... 10.00
14 .... 18.00
15 .... 8.00
16 .... 4.00
17 .... 8.00

American Splendor: Bedtime Stories
Dark Horse, 2000

1 .... 4.00

American Splendor: Comic-Con Comics
Dark Horse, 1996

1 .... 3.00

American Splendor: Music Comics
Dark Horse, 1997

1 .... 3.00

American Splendor: Odds & Ends
Dark Horse, 1997

1 .... 3.00

American Splendor: On the Job
Dark Horse, 1997

1 .... 3.00

American Splendor: Portrait of the Author in his Declining Years
Dark Horse, 2001

1 .... 4.00

American Splendor: Terminal
Dark Horse, 1999

1 .... 3.00

American Splendor: Transatlantic Comics
Dark Horse, 1998

1 .... 3.00

American Splendor: Unsung Hero
Dark Horse, 2002

1-3 .... 4.00

American Flagg

American Flyer

American Splendor

Anarchy Comics

Anarky

Ancient Joe

Andy Devine Western

Angela

American Splendor: Windfall
Dark Horse, 1995

1-2 ....4.00

American Splendor Special: A Step Out of the Nest
Dark Horse, 1994

1 ....3.00

American Tail, An: Fievel Goes West
Marvel, 1992

1-3 ....1.00

American Virgin
DC, 2006

1-15 ....3.00

American Way
DC, 2006

1-8 ....3.00

American Woman
Antarctic, 1998

1-2 ....3.00

America's Best Comics
America's Best, 2001

Special 1 ....7.00

America's Best Comics
Nedor, 1942

1 ....1,600.00
2 ....850.00
3 ....600.00
4-6 ....440.00
7 ....575.00
8-10 ....400.00
11-20 ....360.00
21-24 ....325.00
25-31 ....265.00

America's Best Comics Preview
America's Best, 1999

1 ....2.00

America's Best Comics Sketchbook
DC

1 ....6.00

America's Best TV Comics
ABC TV, 1967

1 ....95.00

America's Biggest Comics Book
Wise, 1944

1 ....275.00

America's Greatest Comics
Fawcett, 1941

1 ....1,900.00
2 ....900.00
3 ....675.00
4-5 ....500.00
6-8 ....450.00

America vs. the Justice Society
DC, 1985

1 ....2.00
2-4 ....1.00

Americomics
AC, 1983

1-Special 1 ....2.00

Amethyst
DC, 1985

1-Special 1 ....1.00

Amethyst
DC, 1987

1-4 ....1.00

Amethyst, Princess of Gemworld
DC, 1983

1 ....1.00
1/75 cent 5.00
2 ....1.00
2/75 cent 5.00
3 ....1.00
4 ....1.00
5 ....1.00
6 ....1.00
7 ....1.00
8-10 ....1.00
11 ....1.00
12 ....1.00
Ann 1 ....1.00

A Midnight Opera
Tokyopop, 2005

1 ....10.00

Ammo Armageddon
Atomeka

1 ....5.00

Amnesia
NBM

1 ....10.00

Amora (Gray Morrow's...)
Fantagraphics, 1991

1 ....3.00

Amusing Stories
Renegade, 1987

1 ....2.00

Amy Papuda
Northstar

1-2 ....3.00

Amy Racecar Color Special
El Capitan, 1997

1 ....3.00
2 ....4.00

Anal Intruders from Uranus
Fantagraphics, 2005
1-2 .... 4.00

Anarchy Comics
Last Gasp
1-4 .... 3.00

Anarky
DC, 1997
1-4 .... 3.00

Anarky
DC, 1999
1-8 .... 3.00

Anchors Andrews
St. John, 1953
1 .... 85.00
2-4 .... 40.00

Ancient Joe
Dark Horse, 2001
1-3 .... 4.00

Andromeda (Andromeda)
Andromeda, 1995
1-2 .... 3.00

Andromeda (Silver Snail)
Silver Snail, 1977
1-6 .... 2.00

Andy Devine Western
Fawcett, 1950
1 .... 325.00
2 .... 225.00

Andy Panda (Walter Lantz...)
Dell, 1952
16-20 .... 13.00
21-30 .... 11.00
31-56 .... 9.00

Andy Panda
Gold Key, 1973
1 .... 4.00
2-4 .... 3.00
5-23 .... 2.00

A-Next
Marvel, 1998
1-12 .... 2.00

Angel (1st Series)
Dell, 1955
2-16 .... 9.00

Angel (2nd Series)
Dark Horse, 1999
1-17/Variant 3.00

Angel (3rd Series)
Dark Horse, 2001
1-4/Variant 3.00

Angela
Image, 1994
1-1/B 4.00
2-3 .... 3.00

Angel: After the Fall
Idea & Design Works, 2007
1 .... 12.00
2 .... 5.00

Angela/Glory: Rage of Angels
Image, 1996
1/A-1/B 3.00

Angel and the Ape
DC, 1968
1 .... 40.00
2 .... 20.00
3-7 .... 15.00

Angel and the Ape
DC, 1991
1-4 .... 1.00

Angel and the Ape
DC, 2001
1-4 .... 3.00

Angel: Auld Lang Syne
Idea & Design Works, 2006
1 .... 4.00
2 .... 4.00

Angel Dust Neo Manga One Shot
ADV Manga, 2007
1 .... 11.00

Angel Fire
Crusade, 1997
1/A-1/C 3.00
2-3 .... 3.00

Angel Girl
Angel, 1997
0 .... 3.00
0/Nude 5.00

Angel Girl: Before the Wings
Angel, 1997
1 .... 3.00

Angel Girl Vs. Vampire Girls
Angel
1 .... 3.00
1/Nude 10.00

Angelic Layer
Tokyopop, 2002
1 .... 10.00
2-5 .... 0.00

Angel and the Ape

Angel Fire

Angelic Layer

Angel Love

All comics prices listed are for NEAR MINT condition.

Angel of Death

Angels of Destruction

Anima

Animal Comics

Angel Love
DC, 1986
1-Special 1 .... 1.00

Angel: Masks
Idea & Design Works, 2006
1 .... 7.00

Angel of Death
Innovation
1-4 .... 2.00

Angel: Old Friends
Idea & Design Works, 2005
1-5 .... 4.00

Angel: Old Friends Cover Gallery
Idea & Design Works, 2006
1 .... 4.00

Angels 750
Antarctic, 2004
1-5 .... 3.00

Angel Sanctuary
Tokyopop, 2004
1-10 .... 10.00

Angel Scriptbook
Idea & Design Works, 2006
1-7 .... 4.00

Angels of Destruction
Malibu, 1996
1 .... 3.00

Angel Spotlight: Connor
Idea & Design Works, 2006
1 .... 4.00

Angel Spotlight: Doyle
Idea & Design Works, 2006
1 .... 4.00

Angel Spotlight: Gunn
Idea & Design Works, 2006
1 .... 4.00

Angel Spotlight: Illyria
Idea & Design Works, 2006
1 .... 4.00

Angel Spotlight: Wesley
Idea & Design Works, 2006
1 .... 4.00

Angel Stomp Future (Warren Ellis'...)
Avatar, 2005
1 .... 4.00

Angel: The Curse
Idea & Design Works, 2005
1-5 .... 4.00

Angel: The Curse Cover Gallery
Idea & Design Works, 2006
1 .... 4.00

Angeltown
DC, 2005
1-5 .... 3.00

Anger Grrrl
Blatant, 1999
1 .... 3.00

Angryman
Caliber
1-3 .... 3.00

Angryman (2nd Series)
Iconografix
1-3 .... 3.00

Angry Shadows
Innovation, 1989
1 .... 5.00

Anima
DC, 1994
0-15 .... 2.00

Animal Antics (Movietown's...)
DC, 1946
1 .... 350.00
2 .... 175.00
3-4 .... 120.00
5-10 .... 100.00
11-20 .... 80.00
21-30 .... 58.00
31-40 .... 46.00
41-51 .... 40.00

Animal Comics
Dell, 1942
1 .... 900.00
2 .... 450.00
3 .... 340.00
4 .... 150.00
5 .... 300.00
6-7 .... 135.00
☛War bonds cover
8-10 .... 225.00
11-15 .... 170.00
16-20 .... 130.00
21-25 .... 105.00
26-30 .... 80.00

Animal Confidential
Dark Horse, 1992
1 .... 2.00

Animal Fables
E.C., 1946
1 .... 250.00
2 .... 175.00
3-7 .... 150.00

Animal Fair
Fawcett, 1946
1 .... 200.00
2-9 .... 100.00

Animal Man
DC, 1988

1 .... 4.00
2 .... 3.00
3-49 .... 2.00
50 .... 3.00
51-55 .... 2.00
56 .... 4.00
57-89 .... 2.00
Ann 1 .... 4.00

Animal Mystic
Cry for Dawn, 1994

1 .... 10.00
1/Ltd. 10.00
1/2nd 5.00
2 .... 7.00
2/2nd 4.00
3 .... 5.00
3/2nd 3.00
4-4/Ltd. 5.00
4/2nd 4.00

Animal Mystic Water Wars
Sirius, 1996

1-4 .... 3.00

Animal Rights Comics
Stabur

1 .... 3.00

Animal Weirdness
Cozmic

1 .... 3.00

Animaniacs
DC, 1994

1 .... 3.00
2-59 .... 2.00
Holiday 1 .... 3.00

Animated Comics
E.C., 1947

1 .... 400.00

Animated Funny Comic Tunes
U.S.A., 1944

16 .... 75.00
17 .... 60.00
18-23 .... 55.00

Animated Movie-Tunes
Margood, 1945

1-2 .... 130.00

Animation Comics
Viz

1-4 .... 4.00

Animax
Marvel, 1986

1-4 .... 1.00

Animerica Extra
Viz, 1998

1-2 .... 5.00

Animerica Extra (Vol. 2)
Viz, 1999

1-12 .... 5.00

Animerica Extra (Vol. 3)
Viz, 2000

1-12 .... 5.00

Animerica Extra (Vol. 4)
Viz, 2001

1-12 .... 5.00

Animerica Extra (Vol. 5)
Viz, 2002

1-12 .... 5.00

Animerica Extra (Vol. 6)
Viz, 2003

1 .... 5.00

Animism
Centurion, 1987

1 .... 2.00

Anita Blake: Vampire Hunter: Guilty Pleasures
Marvel, 2006

1 .... 12.00
2 .... 7.00
3 .... 5.00

Aniverse
Weebee, 1987

1-2 .... 2.00

Annex
Marvel, 1994

1-4 .... 2.00

Annex
Chalk Outlines Studios, 1999

1 .... 4.00

Annie
Marvel, 1982

1 .... 1.00
1/Special 5.00
2 .... 1.00

Annie Oakley
Timely, 1948

1 .... 300.00
2 .... 165.00
3-4 .... 125.00
5 .... 90.00
6-9 .... 65.00
10-11 .... 60.00

Annie Oakley and Tagg
Dell, 1955

4-10 .... 60.00
11-18 .... 45.00

Animal Confidential

Animal Fables

Animal Man

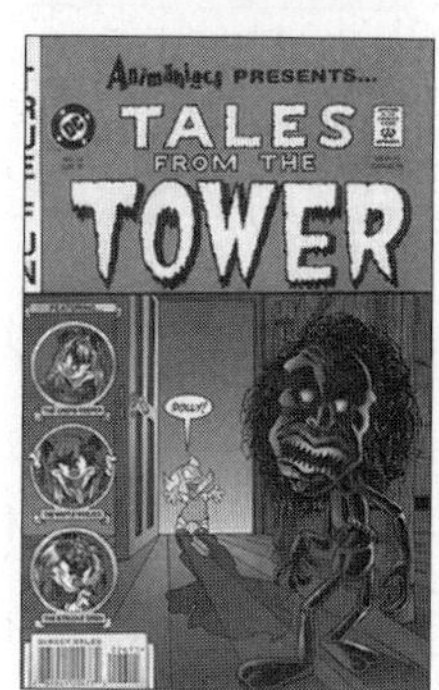

Animaniacs

Animated Movie-Tunes

Annie

Annie Oakley and Tagg

Anthro

Anti-Hitler Comics

Annie Oakley and Tagg (2nd Series)
Gold Key, 1965

1 .... 40.00

Annie Sprinkle Is Miss Timed
Rip Off, 1991

1-4 .... 3.00

Annihilation
Marvel, 2006

1 .... 3.00
2 .... 3.00
4-5 .... 3.00

Annihilation: Nova
Marvel, 2006

1-4 .... 3.00

Annihilation Prologue
Marvel, 2006

1 .... 4.00

Annihilation: Ronan the Accuser
Marvel, 2006

3-85 .... 3.00

Annihilation: Silver Surfer
Marvel, 2006

1-4 .... 3.00

Annihilation: Super-Skrull
Marvel, 2006

1-4 .... 3.00

Annihilation: The Nova Corps Files
Marvel, 2006

1 .... 4.00

Anomalies
Abnormal Fun, 2000

1 .... 3.00

Anomaly
Bud Plant, 1972

1 .... 8.00
2-4 .... 5.00

Anomaly (Brass Ring)
Brass Ring, 2000

1-2 .... 4.00

Another Day
Raised Brow, 1995

1-2 .... 3.00

Ant
Arcana, 2004

1 .... 10.00
1/Red foil 35.00
2 .... 5.00
3 .... 5.00
3/Variant 6.00

Ant (Vol. 2)
Image, 2005

1 .... 5.00
1/Sketch 3.00
1/RRP 20.00
1/Conv 15.00
2-9 .... 3.00

Antabuse
High Drive

1-2 .... 3.00

Antarctic Press Jam 1996
Antarctic, 1996

1 .... 3.00

Antares Circle
Antarctic

1-2 .... 2.00

Ant Boy
Steeldragon, 1988

1-2 .... 2.00

Ant Farm
Gallant, 1998

1-2 .... 3.00

Anthro
DC, 1968

1 .... 50.00
2-6 .... 20.00

Anticipator
Fantasy, 1996

1 .... 2.00

Antietam: The Fiery Trail
Heritage Collection, 1997

1 .... 4.00

Anti-Hitler Comics
New England

1-2 .... 3.00

Anti-Social
Helpless Anger

1 .... 2.00
2-4 .... 3.00

Anti Social for the Disabled
Helpless Anger

1 .... 5.00

Anti Social Jr.
Helpless Anger

1 .... 2.00

Ant-Man's Big Christmas
Marvel, 2000

1 .... 6.00

Anton's Drekbook
Fantagraphics, 1991

1 .... 3.00

Anubis
Super Crew

1 .... 3.00

Anubis (2nd Series)
Super Crew
1 .... 3.00

Anything but Monday
Anything But Monday, 1988
1-2 .... 2.00

Anything Goes!
Fantagraphics, 1986
1-6 .... 2.00

A-OK
Antarctic, 1992
1-4 .... 3.00

Apache Dick
Eternity, 1990
1-4 .... 2.00

Apache Kid
Atlas, 1950
53 (1) 200.00
2 .... 100.00
3-5 .... 65.00
6-10 .... 55.00
11-19 .... 45.00

Apache Skies
Marvel, 2002
1-4 .... 3.00

Apache Trail
Steinway, 1957
1 .... 58.00
2-4 .... 36.00

Apathy Kat
Express, 1995
1-4 .... 3.00

Ape
Catalan
1 .... 11.00

Ape City
Adventure, 1990
1-4 .... 3.00

Ape Nation
Adventure, 1991
1 .... 3.00
1/Ltd. 4.00
2-4 .... 2.00

Ape Omnibus
Ape Entertainment, 2004
1-2 .... 6.00

Apex
Aztec
1 .... 2.00

Apex Project
Stellar, 1990
1-2 .... 1.00

Aphrodisia
Fantagraphics, 1995
1-2 .... 3.00

Aphrodite IX
Image, 2000
0 .... 2.00
0/2nd 6.00
0/A-0/B 9.00
0/C-0/H 4.00
1/A 4.00
1/B-1/D 3.00
1/E-1/F 5.00
1/G-1/H 4.00
1/I-J 5.00
2 .... 2.00
2/A-2/K 3.00
3 .... 2.00
4 .... 4.00
4/A 5.00
Ashcan 1 .... 6.00
Ashcan 1/Ltd. 5.00

Apocalypse
Apocalypse, 1991
1-7 .... 4.00

Apocalypse Nerd
Dark Horse, 2005
1-5 .... 3.00

Apollo Smile
Mixx, 1998
1 .... 4.00
2 .... 3.00

Apparition
Caliber, 1996
1-5 .... 3.00

Apparition: Abandoned
Caliber, 1995
1 .... 4.00

Apparition: Visitations
Caliber, 1995
1 .... 4.00

Apple, P.I.
Parrot Communications, 1996
1 .... 1.00

Appleseed Book 1
Eclipse, 1988
1 .... 7.00
2-3 .... 5.00
4-5 .... 4.00

Appleseed Book 2
Eclipse, 1989
1 .... 5.00
2-5 .... 4.00

Appleseed Book 3
Eclipse, 1989
1-5 .... 4.00

A-OK

Apache Trail

Ape City

Ape Nation

Aphrodite IX

Appleseed Book 1

Aquaman Secret Files

Arcade

Appleseed Book 4
Eclipse, 1991

1-4 ... 4.00

Appleseed Databook
Dark Horse, 1994

1-2 ... 4.00

Approved Comics
St. John, 1954

1 ... 60.00
2 ... 90.00
3-4 ... 58.00
5 ... 60.00
6 ... 65.00
7 ... 60.00
8 ... 58.00
9 ... 65.00
10-12 ... 75.00

April Horrors
Rip Off, 1993

1 ... 3.00

Aquablue
Dark Horse, 1989

1 ... 7.00

Aquablue: The Blue Planet
Dark Horse, 1990

1 ... 9.00

Aqua Knight
Viz, 2000

1 ... 3.00
2-6 ... 4.00

Aqua Knight Part 2
Viz, 2000

1-5 ... 4.00

Aqua Knight Part 3
Viz, 2001

1-5 ... 4.00

Aquaman (1st Series)
DC, 1962

1 ... 900.00
2 ... 275.00
3-5 ... 150.00
6-10 ... 90.00
11 ... 125.00
☛1st Mera
12-17 ... 75.00
18 ... 90.00
☛Weds Mera
19-28 ... 60.00
29 ... 75.00
☛1st Ocean Master
30 ... 50.00
31 ... 45.00
32 ... 50.00
33-34 ... 45.00
35-41 ... 40.00
42-43 ... 30.00
44-46 ... 25.00
47 ... 40.00
48-49 ... 25.00
50 ... 75.00
51 ... 50.00
52 ... 40.00
53-58 ... 20.00
59-60 ... 10.00
61-62 ... 10.00
63 ... 10.00

Aquaman (2nd Series)
DC, 1986

1 ... 3.00
2 ... 3.00
3 ... 3.00
4 ... 3.00
Special 1 ... 2.00

Aquaman (3rd Series)
DC, 1989

1-5 ... 1.00
Special 1 ... 2.00

Aquaman (4th Series)
DC, 1991

1 ... 2.00
2-13 ... 1.00

Aquaman (5th Series)
DC, 1994

0-2 ... 3.00
3-70 ... 2.00
71-75 ... 3.00
1000000 ... 2.00
Ann 1 ... 4.00
Ann 2 ... 3.00
Ann 3 ... 4.00
Ann 4-5 ... 3.00

Aquaman (6th Series)
DC, 2003

1-14 ... 3.00
15 ... 12.00
☛Old costume back
16-17 ... 6.00
18-47 ... 3.00

Aquaman Secret Files
DC, 1998

1-2 ... 5.00

Aquaman: Time and Tide
DC, 1993

1-4 ... 2.00

Aquarium
CPM Manga, 2000

1/A-6 ... 3.00

Arabian Nights on the World of Magic: The Gathering

Acclaim, 1995

1-2 ... 3.00

Arachnophobia

Disney

1 ... 3.00

Aragonès 3-D

3-D Zone

1 ... 5.00

Araknis

Mushroom, 1995

0-6 ... 3.00

Arak Son of Thunder

DC, 1981

1 ... 1.00
2-50 ... 1.00
Ann 1 ... 2.00

Aramis

Comics Interview

1-3 ... 2.00

Arana: Heart of the Spider

Marvel, 2005

1 ... 3.00
1/Incentive ... 7.00
2-12 ... 3.00

Arc (Vol. 2)

Arts Industria, 1994

1 ... 3.00

Arcade

Print Mint, 1975

1 ... 10.00
2-3 ... 8.00
4-6 ... 7.00
7 ... 5.00

Arcana

DC, 1994

Ann 1 ... 4.00

Arcana

Tokyopop, 2005

1-3 ... 10.00

Arcana (Wells & Clark)

Wells & Clark, 1995

1-3 ... 3.00
4-10 ... 2.00

Arcane

Arcane

1 ... 2.00
2 ... 10.00

Arcane (2nd Series)

Graphik

1 ... 1.00

Arcanum

Image, 1997

½ ... 3.00
½/Gold ... 5.00
1-8 ... 3.00

Archaic

Fenickx Productions, 2003

1-5 ... 3.00

Archangel

Marvel, 1996

1 ... 3.00

Archangels: The Saga

Eternal, 1996

1-8 ... 3.00

Archard's Agents

CrossGen, 2003

1-3 ... 3.00

Archenemies

Dark Horse, 2006

1-4 ... 3.00

Archer & Armstrong

Valiant, 1992

0 ... 4.00
0/Gold ... 25.00
1 ... 4.00
2 ... 3.00
3-7 ... 2.00
8 ... 3.00
9 ... 2.00
10-21 ... 1.00
22 ... 2.00
23-25 ... 1.00
26 ... 5.00

Archie

Archie, 1942

1 ... 12,200.00
2 ... 3,325.00
3 ... 2,175.00
4 ... 1,100.00
5 ... 1,000.00
6 ... 740.00
7-9 ... 660.00
10 ... 585.00
11-15 ... 475.00
16-20 ... 400.00
21-24 ... 325.00
25-30 ... 275.00
31-35 ... 220.00
36-40 ... 175.00
41-50 ... 125.00
51-60 ... 110.00
61-70 ... 70.00
71-80 ... 56.00
81-90 ... 44.00
91-99 ... 34.00
100 ... 55.00
101-120 ... 22.00
121-140 ... 16.00
141-150 ... 13.00

Arcanum

Archangel

Archie

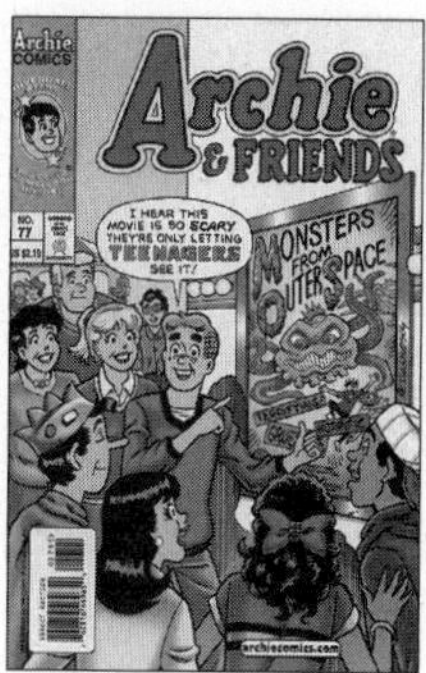

Archie and Friends

Archie at Riverdale High

Archie Digest Magazine

Archie Giant Series Magazine

Arcomics Premiere

151-180 ....9.00
181-200 ....5.00
201-250 ....3.00
251-599 ....2.00
Ann 1 ....1,350.00
Ann 2 ....660.00
Ann 3 ....475.00
Ann 4 ....345.00
Ann 5 ....285.00
Ann 6 ....180.00
Ann 7 ....160.00
Ann 8 ....135.00
Ann 9 ....120.00
Ann 10 ....110.00
Ann 11 ....70.00
Ann 12 ....60.00
Ann 13 ....58.00
Ann 14-15 ....50.00
Ann 16-17 ....26.00
Ann 18-19 ....22.00
Ann 20 ....14.00
Ann 21-22 ....9.00
Ann 23-26 ....8.00

Archie All Canadian Digest

Archie, 1996

1 ....2.00

Archie and Friends

Archie, 1992

1 ....3.00
2-129 ....2.00

Archie and Me

Archie, 1964

1 ....125.00
2 ....75.00
3 ....45.00
4-5 ....34.00
6-10 ....20.00
11-20 ....12.00
21-30 ....8.00
31-40 ....6.00
41-50 ....4.00
51-80 ....3.00
81-100 ....2.00
101-161 ....1.00

Archie Annual Digest Magazine

Archie, 1995

66-68 ....2.00

Archie... Archie Andrews, Where Are You? Digest Magazine

Archie, 1977

1 ....5.00
2-10 ....3.00
11-117 ....2.00

Archie As Pureheart the Powerful

Archie, 1966

1 ....55.00
2 ....35.00
3-6 ....25.00

Archie at Riverdale High

Archie, 1972

1 ....42.00
2 ....22.00
3-5 ....16.00
6-10 ....11.00
11-20 ....8.00
21-30 ....5.00
31-40 ....4.00
41-60 ....3.00
61-100 ....2.00
101-114 ....1.00

Archie Comics Presents the Love Showdown Collection

Archie, 1994

1 ....5.00

Archie Digest Magazine

Archie, 1973

1 ....26.00
2 ....10.00
3-5 ....6.00
6-10 ....4.00
11-20 ....3.00
21-244 ....2.00

Archie Giant Series Magazine

Archie, 1954

1 ....750.00
2 ....475.00
3-4 ....325.00
5-6 ....275.00
7-8 ....200.00
9-10 ....185.00
11 ....140.00
12 ....125.00
13 ....140.00
14-15 ....110.00
16 ....125.00
17 ....110.00
18 ....125.00
19 ....110.00
20 ....100.00
21 ....85.00
22 ....60.00
23 ....80.00
24-25 ....60.00
26 ....80.00
27 ....60.00
28 ....80.00
29-30 ....60.00
31-141 ....40.00
142 ....45.00
143-160 ....20.00
161-180 ....12.00
181-200 ....10.00
201-220 ....8.00
221-250 ....6.00

251 .... 4.00
452-550 .... 3.00
551-632 .... 2.00

Archie Meets the Punisher

Marvel, 1994

1 .... 3.00

Archie's Christmas Stocking (2nd Series)

Archie, 1994

1 .... 3.00
2-7 .... 2.00

Archie's Date Book

Spire

1 .... 4.00

Archie's Double Digest Magazine

Archie, 1982

1 .... 6.00
2-10 .... 4.00
11-138 .... 3.00
139-196 .... 4.00

Archie's Family Album

Spire, 1978

1 .... 4.00

Archie's Girls Betty & Veronica

Archie, 1950

1 .... 1,400.00
2 .... 675.00
3 .... 485.00
4-5 .... 375.00
6-10 .... 285.00
11-19 .... 225.00
20-29 .... 165.00
30-39 .... 115.00
40-50 .... 85.00
51-60 .... 55.00
61-70 .... 45.00
71-90 .... 32.00
91-110 .... 24.00
111-140 .... 16.00
141-160 .... 13.00
161-180 .... 10.00
181-200 .... 7.00
201-250 .... 5.00
251-319 .... 3.00
320 .... 8.00
321 .... 4.00
322-347 .... 3.00
Ann 1 .... 525.00
Ann 2 .... 325.00
Ann 3-4 .... 265.00
Ann 5 .... 250.00
Ann 6 .... 175.00
Ann 7 .... 150.00
Ann 8 .... 100.00

Archie's Holiday Fun Digest Magazine

Archie, 1997

1-10 .... 2.00
11-12 .... 3.00

Archie's Jokebook Magazine

Archie, 1953

nn 600.00
2 .... 375.00
3 .... 275.00
15 .... 165.00
16-20 .... 135.00
21-30 .... 100.00
31-40 .... 75.00
41 .... 135.00
42-43 .... 65.00
44-48 .... 70.00
49-60 .... 35.00
61-70 .... 24.00
71-80 .... 16.00
81-90 .... 12.00
91-100 .... 8.00
101-120 .... 5.00
121-150 .... 3.00
151-200 .... 2.00
201-288 .... 1.00

Archie's Love Scene

Spire, 1973

1 .... 5.00

Archie's Madhouse

Archie, 1959

1 .... 175.00
2 .... 95.00
3 .... 68.00
4-5 .... 50.00
6-10 .... 38.00
11-15 .... 26.00
16-20 .... 23.00
21 .... 18.00
22 .... 100.00
23-25 .... 18.00
26-30 .... 14.00
31-40 .... 9.00
41-50 .... 6.00
51-66 .... 4.00
Ann 1 .... 65.00
Ann 2 .... 25.00
Ann 3 .... 15.00
Ann 4-6 .... 10.00

Archie's Mechanics

Archie, 1954

1 .... 45.00
2 .... 35.00
3 .... 30.00

Archie's Mysteries

Archie, 2003

25-34 .... 2.00

Arctic Comics

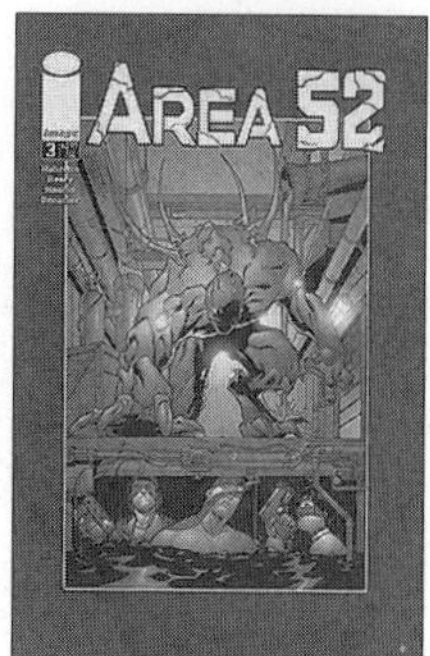

Area 52

Area 88

Argus

Aria

Arion the Immortal

Aristocratic X-Traterrestrial Time-Traveling Thieves

A.R.M.

Archie's Pal Jughead
Archie, 1949

1 .... 2,000.00
2 .... 675.00
3 .... 350.00
4-5 .... 230.00
6-10 .... 150.00
11-15 .... 95.00
16-20 .... 85.00
21-30 .... 55.00
31-40 .... 38.00
41-60 .... 22.00
61-80 .... 16.00
81-100 .... 10.00
101-120 .... 7.00
121-126 .... 5.00
Ann 1 .... 650.00
Ann 2 .... 350.00
Ann 3 .... 145.00
Ann 4 .... 85.00
Ann 5 .... 65.00
Ann 6-8 .... 45.00

Archie's Pal Jughead Comics
Archie, 1993

46-193 .... 2.00

Archie's Pals 'n' Gals
Archie, 1952

1 .... 575.00
2 .... 290.00
3 .... 215.00
4-5 .... 185.00
6-7 .... 135.00
8-10 .... 80.00
11-20 .... 45.00
21-28 .... 22.00
29 .... 45.00
30 .... 22.00
31-40 .... 13.00
41-50 .... 9.00
51-70 .... 7.00
71-81 .... 5.00
82-100 .... 4.00
101-150 .... 3.00
151-224 .... 2.00

Archie's Pals 'n' Gals Double Digest
Archie, 1995

1 .... 4.00
2-76 .... 3.00
77-129 .... 4.00

Archie's R/C Racers
Archie, 1989

1-10 .... 2.00

Archie's Rival Reggie
Archie, 1950

1 .... 740.00
2 .... 375.00
3 .... 225.00
4 .... 200.00
5 .... 175.00
6-7 .... 140.00
8-10 .... 125.00
11-12 .... 85.00
13-14 .... 80.00

Archie's Spring Break
Archie, 1996

1-5 .... 3.00

Archie's Story & Game Digest Magazine
Archie, 1995

32-39 .... 2.00

Archie's Super-Hero Special
Archie, 1979

1-2 .... 3.00

Archie's Super Teens
Archie, 1994

1-4 .... 3.00

Archie's TV Laugh-Out
Archie, 1969

1 .... 42.00
2 .... 24.00
3-5 .... 16.00
6 .... 12.00
7 .... 22.00
8-10 .... 12.00
11-20 .... 9.00
21-30 .... 7.00
31-40 .... 6.00
41-60 .... 4.00
61-106 .... 3.00

Archie's Vacation Special
Archie, 1994

1-8 .... 3.00

Archie's Weird Mysteries
Archie, 2000

1-24 .... 2.00
Ashcan 1 .... 1.00

Archie 3000
Archie, 1989

1 .... 3.00
2-5 .... 2.00
6-16 .... 1.00

Arcomics Premiere
Arcomics, 1993

1 .... 3.00

Arctic Comics
Nick Burns

1 .... 1.00

Area 52
Image, 2001

1-4 .... 3.00

Area 88
Eclipse, 1987

1 .... 4.00
1/2nd 2.00
2 .... 3.00
2/2nd-42 .... 2.00

Areala: Angel of War
Antarctic, 1998

1-4 .... 3.00

Arena
Alchemy

1 .... 2.00

Ares
Marvel, 2006

1-5 .... 3.00

Argonauts
Eternity, 1988

1-4 .... 2.00

Argonauts: System Crash
Alpha Productions

1-2 .... 3.00

Argon Zark!
Arclight, 1997

1 .... 7.00

Argus
DC, 1995

1-6 .... 2.00

Aria
Image, 1998

1-7 .... 3.00
Ashcan 1 .... 4.00

Aria: A Midwinter's Dream
Image, 2002

1 .... 5.00

Aria Angela
Image, 2000

1-2 .... 3.00

Aria Angela Blanc & Noir
Image, 2000

1 .... 3.00

Aria Blanc & Noir
Image, 1999

1-2 .... 3.00

Aria (manga)
ADV Manga, 2004

1 .... 10.00

Ariane & Bluebeard
Eclipse, 1989

1 .... 4.00

Arianne
Slave Labor, 1991

1 .... 5.00
2 .... 3.00

Arianne (Moonstone)
Moonstone, 1995

1 .... 5.00

Aria Summer's Spell
Image, 2002

1-2 .... 3.00

Aria: The Soul Market
Image, 2001

1-6 .... 3.00

Aria: The Uses of Enchantment
Image, 2003

1-4 .... 3.00

Arik Khan (A+)
A-Plus

1-2 .... 3.00

Arik Khan (Andromeda)
Andromeda, 1977

1-3 .... 2.00

Arion, Lord of Atlantis
DC, 1982

1-13 .... 1.00

Arion the Immortal
DC, 1992

1-6 .... 2.00

Aristocats
Gold Key, 1971

1 .... 4.00

Aristocratic X-Traterrestrial Time-Traveling Thieves
Comics Interview, 1987

1-12 .... 2.00

Aristocratic X-Traterrestrial Time-Traveling Thieves Micro-Series
Comics Interview, 1986

1-1/2nd 2.00

Aristokittens
Gold Key, 1973

1 .... 16.00
2 .... 10.00
3-5 .... 8.00
6-9 .... 6.00

Arizona: A Simple Horror
London Night, 1998

1-3 .... 3.00

Arizona Kid
Atlas, 1951

1 .... 100.00

Armadillo Comics

Armageddonquest

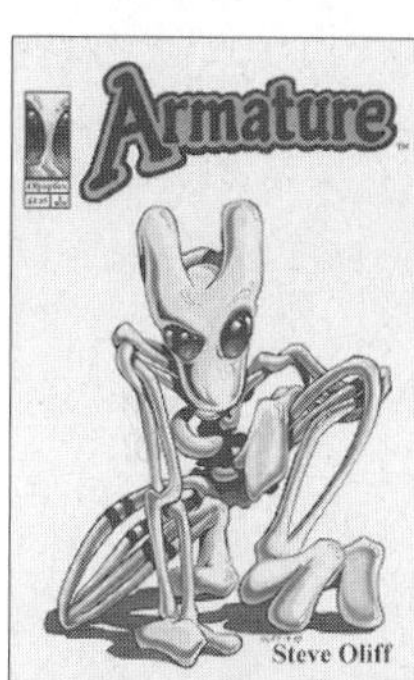

Armature

Armitage

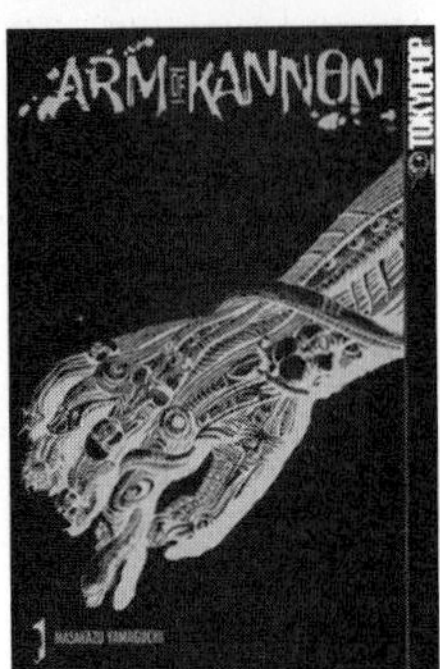

Arm of Kannon

Armor

Armored Trooper Votoms

Armorines

2-4 .... 60.00
5-6 .... 50.00

Arizona: Wild at Heart
London Night, 1998
1 .... 3.00

Arkaga
Image, 1997
1-2 .... 3.00

Ark Angels
Tokyopop, 2005
1 .... 10.00

Arkanium
Dreamwave, 2002
1-5 .... 3.00

Arkeology
Valkyrie, 1989
1 .... 2.00

Arkham Asylum Living Hell
DC, 2003
1-6 .... 3.00

Arlington Hammer in: Get Me to the Church on Time
One Shot
1 .... 3.00

A.R.M.
Adventure, 1990
1-3 .... 3.00

Armadillo Comics
Rip Off, 1969
1-2 .... 3.00

Armageddon
Last Gasp
1-2 .... 3.00

Armageddon (Chaos)
Chaos, 1999
1-4 .... 3.00

Armageddon 2001
DC, 1991
1-2 .... 2.00

Armageddon: Inferno
DC, 1992
1-4 .... 1.00

Armageddon: The Alien Agenda
DC, 1991
1-4 .... 1.00

Armageddon Factor
AC, 1987
1-3 .... 2.00

Armageddon Factor: The Conclusion
AC, 1990
1 .... 4.00

Armageddon Patrol: The Shot
Alchemy Texts, 1998
1 .... 3.00

Armageddonquest
Starhead, 1984
1-2 .... 4.00

Armageddon Rising
Millennium, 1997
1 .... 5.00

Armageddon Squad
Haze
1 .... 2.00

Armature
Olyoptics, 1996
1-2 .... 3.00

Armed and Dangerous (Acclaim)
Acclaim, 1996
1-4 .... 3.00
Special 1 .... 3.00

Armed & Dangerous: Hell's Slaughterhouse
Acclaim, 1996
1-4 .... 3.00

Armed & Dangerous
Kitchen Sink, 1995
1 .... 10.00

Armen Deep & Bug Boy
Dilemma, 1995
2 .... 3.00

Armitage
Fleetway-Quality
1-2 .... 3.00

Arm of Kannon
Tokyopop, 2004
1-7 .... 10.00

Armor
Continuity, 1985
4-13 .... 2.00

Armor (2nd Series)
Continuity, 1993
1-6 .... 3.00

Armored Trooper Votoms
CPM, 1996
1-2 .... 3.00

Armorines
Valiant, 1993
0/Gold 25.00

0 .... 1.00
0/StandAlone 30.00
1/VVSS 40.00
1-8 .... 1.00
9-11 .... 2.00
12 .... 4.00

Armorines (Vol. 2)
Acclaim, 1999
1-4 .... 4.00

Armorquest
Alias, 2005
0-2 .... 3.00

Armor X
Image, 2005
1-4 .... 3.00

Arm's Length
Third Wind, 2000
1 .... 4.00

Army and Navy Comics
Street & Smith, 1941
1 .... 325.00
2 .... 175.00
3-4 .... 125.00
5 .... 275.00

Army Ants
Michael T. Desing
8 .... 3.00

Army Attack
Charlton, 1964
1 .... 20.00
2-47 .... 15.00

Army at War
DC, 1978
1 .... 10.00

Army of Darkness
Dark Horse, 1992
1 .... 12.00
2-3 .... 9.00

Army of Darkness: Ashes 2 Ashes
Devil's Due, 2004
1/A-Bk 1/HC 0.00
1 .... 10.00
1/Incentive 5.00
1/Photo 4.00
1/Silvestri 3.00
1/Sketch 11.00
1/DirCut 7.00
1/Templesmith 3.00
2 .... 4.00
2/B&W 5.00
2/Photo 3.00
2/Land 3.00
2/Isanove 4.00
3 .... 3.00
4 .... 4.00
4/Garza 3.00

Army of Darkness: Shop Til You Drop (Dead)
Devil's Due, 2005
1 .... 3.00
1/Ebas 4.00
1/Isanove 3.00
1/Lee 4.00
1/Rivera 3.00
1/Glow 35.00
2 .... 3.00
2/Variant 8.00
2/DF 15.00
3-4 .... 3.00

Army Surplus Komikz Featuring: Cutey Bunny
Quagmire, 1985
1-5 .... 3.00

Army War Heroes
Charlton, 1963
1 .... 20.00
2 .... 10.00
3-5 .... 8.00
6-19 .... 6.00
20-21 .... 4.00
22 .... 6.00
23-38 .... 4.00

Aromatic Bitters
Tokyopop, 2004
1 .... 10.00

Around the World Under the Sea
Dell, 1966
1 .... 20.00

Arrgh!
Marvel, 1974
1 .... 15.00
2 .... 4.00
3-5 .... 3.00

Arrow
Centaur, 1940
1 .... 2,000.00
2 .... 950.00
3 .... 800.00

Arrow
Malibu, 1992
1 .... 2.00

Arrow Anthology
Arrow, 1997
1-5 .... 4.00

Arrowhead
Atlas, 1954
1 .... 100.00
2-4 .... 60.00

Arrowman
Parody
1 .... 3.00

Army of Darkness

Army War Heroes

Arrow Anthology

Arrow Spotlight

Arsenal

Arsenic Lullaby

Artesia

Artesia Afield

Arrowsmith
DC, 2003
1-6 .... 3.00

Arrowsmith/Astro City
DC, 2004
1 .... 3.00

Arrow Spotlight
Arrow, 1998
1 .... 3.00

Arsenal
DC, 1998
1-4 .... 3.00

Arsenal Special
DC, 1996
1 .... 3.00

Arsenic Lullaby
A. Silent, 1998
1-20 .... 3.00

Arsinoe
Fantagraphics, 2005
1-4 .... 4.00

Art & Beauty Magazine
Kitchen Sink, 2003
1-2 .... 5.00

Artbabe (Vol. 2)
Fantagraphics, 1997
1-4 .... 3.00

Art D'Ecco
Fantagraphics, 1990
1-4 .... 3.00

Artemis: Requiem
DC, 1996
1-6 .... 2.00

Artesia
Sirius, 1999
1-6 .... 3.00

Artesia Afield
Sirius, 2000
1-6 .... 3.00

Artesia Afire
Archaia Studios Press, 2003
1-6 .... 4.00

Arthur King of Britain
Tome, 1993
1-4 .... 3.00
5 .... 4.00

Arthur Sex
Aircel, 1991
1-8 .... 3.00

Artillery One-Shot
Red Bullet, 1995
1 .... 3.00

Art in Shambles
Max Hopper
1 .... 3.00

Artistic Comics
Golden Gate, 1973
0 .... 10.00

Artistic Comics
Kitchen Sink, 1995
1-1/2nd 3.00

Artistic Licentiousness
Starhead, 1994
1-3 .... 3.00

Art of Abrams
Lightning, 1996
1 .... 4.00

Art of Aubrey Beardsley
Tome
1 .... 3.00

Art of Heath Robinson
Tome
1 .... 3.00

Art of Homage Studios
Image, 1993
1 .... 6.00

Art of Jay Anacleto
Image, 2002
1 .... 6.00

Art of Marvel Comics
Marvel, 2004
1-2 .... 30.00

Art of Moebius
Marvel
1 .... 15.00

Art of Mucha
Tome, 1992
1 .... 3.00

Art of Pulp Fiction
A-List, 1998
1 .... 3.00

Art of Spanking
NBM
1 .... 18.00

Art of the Witchblade
Image, 2006
1 .... 3.00

Art of Usagi Yojimbo
Radio, 1997
1-2 .... 4.00

Art of Walter Simonson
DC
1 .... 20.00

Art of Wrightson
Side Show, 1996
1 .... 10.00

Art School Superstars
Fantagraphics
1 .... 3.00

Artxilla Tasty Treats 2005
Image, 2005
0 .... 7.00

Ascension
Image, 1997
0 .... 3.00
0/Gold 4.00
0/Ltd. 6.00
½ 4.00
1-1/A 3.00
1/B-1/D 4.00
2 .... 3.00
2/A-2/Gold 4.00
3-22 .... 3.00
Ashcan 1 .... 4.00

Ash
Event, 1994
0-0/C 4.00
½ 3.00
½/Ltd.-½/Platinum 4.00
1 .... 3.00
1/A 4.00
1/B-6/A 3.00

Ash/22 Brides
Event, 1996
1-2 .... 3.00

Ash: Cinder & Smoke
Event, 1997
1-6 .... 3.00

Ashen Victor
Viz, 1997
1-4 .... 3.00

Ashes
Caliber
1-5 .... 3.00

Ash Files
Event, 1997
1 .... 3.00

Ash: Fire and Crossfire
Event, 1999
1 .... 3.00
1/A 5.00
2 .... 3.00

Ashley Dust
Knight, 1994
1-3 .... 3.00

Ashpile
Side Show
1 .... 9.00

Ash: The Fire Within
Event, 1996
1-2 .... 3.00

Askani'son
Marvel, 1996
1-4 .... 3.00

Sort of Homecoming, A
Alternative, 2004
1-3 .... 4.00

Aspen Extended Edition
Aspen, 2004
1 .... 8.00
1/Conv. 15.00

Aspen
Aspen, 2003
1 .... 7.00
1/Variant 12.00
1/Conv. 10.00
2 .... 4.00
2/Variant 6.00
2/Conv. 10.00
3 .... 6.00
3/Variant 8.00
3/Conv. 10.00

Aspen Seasons: Spring 2005
Aspen, 2005
0 .... 3.00

Aspen Sketchbook
Aspen, 2003
1 .... 3.00

Asrial vs. Cheetah
Antarctic, 1996
1-2 .... 3.00

Assassin
Arcana, 2003
1 .... 3.00

Assassination of Malcolm X
Zone
1 .... 3.00

Assassinette
Pocket Change, 1994
1-7 .... 3.00

Assassinette Hardcore!
Pocket Change, 1995
1-2 .... 3.00

Assassins
DC, 1996
1 .... 2.00

Assassin School
APComics, 2003
0-1 .... 3.00

Assassin School (Vol. 2)
APComics, 2003
1 .... 5.00
2-6 .... 4.00

Arthur King of Britain

Artistic Licentiousness

Ascension

Assassinette

Assassins Inc.

Aster

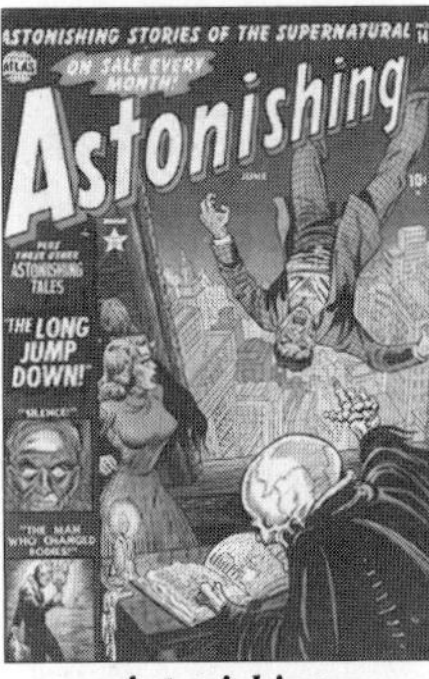

Astonishing

Astonishing Tales

Assassins Inc.
Silverline
1-2 ....2.00

Assembly
Antarctic, 2003
1 ....3.00
2 ....4.00
3-4 ....3.00

Aster
Express, 1994
0-4 ....3.00
Ashcan 1 ....1.00

Aster: The Last Celestial Knight
Express, 1995
1 ....4.00

Astonish!
Wehner
1 ....2.00

Astonishing
Atlas, 1951
3 ....675.00
4-6 ....465.00
7-10 ....225.00
11-20 ....200.00
21-24 ....160.00
25-29 ....135.00
30 ....175.00
31-40 ....125.00
41-63 ....85.00

Astonishing Excitement
All-Jonh
501-502 ....3.00
503 ....4.00

Astonishing Spider-Man
Marvel
1-32 ....4.00

Astonishing Tales
Marvel, 1970
1 ....40.00
2-5 ....20.00
6 ....12.00
7-8 ....15.00
9 ....10.00
10 ....20.00
11 ....10.00
12 ....30.00
☛Man-Thing story
13-20 ....10.00
21 ....25.00
22 ....10.00
23 ....15.00
24 ....10.00
25 ....25.00
☛1st Deathlok
26 ....10.00
27-29 ....7.00
30-32 ....5.00
33 ....10.00
34 ....6.00
35 ....7.00
☛Low distribution
35/30¢ 20.00
☛Low distribution
36-36/30¢ 10.00

Astonishing X-Men
Marvel, 1995
1-3 ....6.00
4 ....8.00

Astonishing X-Men
Marvel, 1999
1 ....5.00
2-3 ....3.00

Astonishing X-Men
Marvel, 2004
1 ....8.00
☛Whedon starts
1/Cassaday-1/DirCut 45.00
1/Dynamic 8.00
2 ....16.00
3 ....4.00
4 ....8.00
4/Variant 25.00
☛Colossus cover
5 ....8.00
6 ....5.00
7 ....4.00
8-10 ....3.00
10/Variant 5.00
11-19 ....3.00

Astounding Space Thrills
Day 1, 1998
1-3 ....3.00

Astounding Space Thrills: The Comic Book
Image, 2000
1-4 ....3.00
GS 1 ....5.00

Astrider Hugo
Radio, 2000
1-2 ....4.00

Astro Boy
Gold Key, 1965
1 ....265.00

Astro Boy
Dark Horse, 2002
1-23 ....10.00

Astro City: A Visitor's Guide
DC, 2004
1 ....6.00

Astro City Local Heroes
DC, 2003
1-5 ....3.00

Astro City: Samaritan Special
DC, 2006

1 .... 4.00

Astro City Special
DC, 2004

1 .... 4.00

Astro City: The Dark Age
DC, 2005

1-4 .... 3.00

Astro City
Image, 1995

1 .... 5.00
2-6 .... 3.00

Astro City
Image, 1996

½-½/Direct 3.00
1 .... 4.00
1/3D 5.00
2-22 .... 3.00

AstroComics
Harvey

1 .... 3.00

Astronauts in Trouble: Space 1959
AiT, 2000

1 .... 3.00

Astrothrill
Cheeky, 1999

1 .... 13.00

Asylum
Maximum, 1995

1-13 .... 3.00

Asylum
Millennium

1-2 .... 3.00
3 .... 5.00

Asylum
New Comics

1-2 .... 2.00

Atari Force
DC, 1984

1-20 .... 1.00
Special 1 .... 2.00

A-Team
Marvel, 1984

1 .... 2.00
2 .... 2.00
3 .... 2.00

Atheist
Image, 206

1-3 .... 4.00

Athena
Antarctic, 1995

0-14 .... 3.00

Athena Inc. Agents Roster
Image, 2002

1 .... 6.00

Athena Inc. The Beginning
Image, 2001

1 .... 6.00

Athena Inc. The Manhunter Project
Image, 2002

1-1/A 3.00
2/A-5/B 3.00
6/A-6/B 5.00
Ashcan 1 .... 1.00

Atlantis Chronicles
DC, 1990

1-7 .... 3.00

@Large
Tokyopop, 2003

1-3 .... 10.00

Atlas
Dark Horse, 1994

1-4 .... 3.00

Atlas (Avatar)
Avatar, 2002

1/A-1/F 4.00
1/G 6.00

Atom
DC, 1962

1 .... 750.00
2 .... 300.00
3 .... 225.00
4-5 .... 175.00
6 .... 125.00
7 .... 250.00
☛Hawkman app.
8 .... 125.00
9 .... 90.00
10-13 .... 85.00
14 .... 95.00
☛Hawkman app.
15 .... 85.00
16-17 .... 45.00
18 .... 50.00
19 .... 45.00
20 .... 60.00
21-23 .... 35.00
24 .... 40.00
25 .... 50.00
26-28 .... 35.00
29 .... 100.00
30 .... 55.00
31 .... 48.00
32 .... 35.00
33 .... 40.00
34-35 .... 35.00
36-37 .... 45.00
38 .... 30.00
Special 1-2 .... 3.00

Astonishing X-Men

Astounding Space Thrills

AstroComics

Atlas

Atoman

Atom and Hawkman

Atomic Age

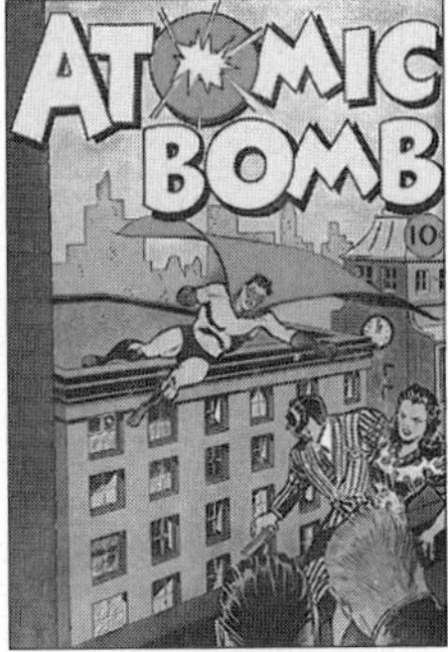
Atomic Bomb

Atom-Age Combat
St. John, 1952

1 .... 225.00
2 .... 140.00
3 .... 100.00
4 .... 125.00
5 .... 100.00

Atom-Age Combat
St. John, 1958

1 .... 85.00
2-3 .... 60.00

Atoman
Spark, 1946

1 .... 265.00
2 .... 175.00

Atom and Hawkman
DC, 1968

39-41 .... 30.00
42 .... 35.00
43-45 .... 30.00

Atom Ant
Gold Key, 1966

1 .... 85.00

Atomic Age
Marvel, 1990

1-4 .... 5.00

Atomic Age Truckstop Waitress
Fantagraphics, 1991

1 .... 2.00

Atomic Bomb
Jay Burtis, 1945

1 .... 750.00

Atomic City Tales
Kitchen Sink, 1996

1-3 .... 3.00
Special 1 .... 3.00

Atomic Comics
Green, 1946

1 .... 750.00
2 .... 400.00
3-4 .... 275.00

Atomic Man
Blackthorne, 1986

1-3 .... 2.00

Atomic Mouse
Charlton, 1953

1 .... 150.00
2 .... 75.00
3-5 .... 50.00
6-10 .... 35.00
11-20 .... 25.00
21-25 .... 18.00
26 .... 45.00
27-29 .... 18.00
30-50 .... 15.00
51-54 .... 13.00

Atomic Mouse
Charlton, 1984

10 .... 5.00
11-13 .... 3.00

Atomic Mouse
A+, 1990

1-3 .... 3.00

Atomicow
Vision, 1990

1 .... 3.00

Atomic Rabbit & Friends
Avalon

1 .... 3.00

Atomics
AAA Pop, 2000

1-11 .... 3.00
12-15 .... 4.00

Atomic Spy Cases
Avon, 1950

1 .... 175.00

Atomic Thunderbolt
Regor, 1946

1 .... 325.00

Atomic Toybox
Image, 1999

1-1/B 3.00

Atomic War!
Ace, 1952

1 .... 600.00
2-4 .... 375.00

Atomika
Speakeasy Comics, 2005

1-3 .... 3.00
4/Turner 5.00
4/Buzz 3.00
4/Jay 4.00
4/Rupps 3.00

Atomik Angels
Crusade, 1996

1 .... 3.00
1/Variant 4.00
2-3 .... 3.00
3/Variant 4.00
4-Special 1 .... 3.00

Atom the Atomic Cat
Avalon

1 .... 3.00

Atomz Man and Super Seeker
Atomz

1 .... 1.00

Attack
Youthful, 1952

1 .... 165.00
2-4 .... 85.00
5 .... 65.00
6-9 .... 55.00

Attack
Trojan, 1953

5 .... 35.00

Attack
Charlton, 1958

54 .... 24.00
55-60 .... 10.00
1 .... 25.00
2 .... 15.00
3-4 .... 12.00

Attack
Charlton, 1971

1 .... 7.00
2-3 .... 4.00
4-30 .... 3.00
31-48 .... 2.00

Attack!
Spire, 1975

1 .... 5.00

Attack of the Amazon Girls
Fantaco

1 .... 5.00

Attack of the Mutant Monsters
A-Plus

1 .... 3.00

Attack on Planet Mars
Avon, 1951

1 .... 750.00

At the Seams
Alternative, 1997

1 .... 3.00

Attitude
NBM, 2004

1-3 .... 14.00

Attitude Lad
Slave Labor

1 .... 3.00

Attractive Forces
NBM

1 .... 10.00

Attu
4Winds, 1989

1-2 .... 10.00

Augie Doggie
Gold Key, 1963

1 .... 45.00

August
Arrow

1-3 .... 3.00

Aurora Comic Scenes
Aurora, 1974

181 .... 30.00
☛Tarzan minicomic
182 .... 28.00
☛Spider-Man mini
183 .... 27.00
☛Tonto minicomic
184 .... 30.00
☛Hulk minicomic
185 .... 28.00
☛Superman mini
186 .... 27.00
☛Superboy mini
187 .... 26.00
☛Batman minicomic
188 .... 25.00
☛Lone Ranger mini
192 .... 27.00
☛Capt. America mini
193 .... 30.00
☛Robin minicomic

Authentic Police Cases
St. John, 1948

1 .... 285.00
2 .... 165.00
3 .... 290.00
4-5 .... 165.00
6 .... 300.00
7-15 .... 135.00
16-23 .... 85.00
24-28 .... 175.00
29-30 .... 75.00
31-32 .... 60.00
33-38 .... 65.00

Authority
DC, 1999

1 .... 5.00
2-3 .... 4.00
4-29 .... 3.00
Ann 2000 .... 4.00

Authority
DC, 2003

0-14 .... 3.00

Authority
DC, 2006

1 .... 3.00

Authority: Kev
DC, 2002

nn 5.00

Authority/Lobo Christmas Special
DC, 2003

1 .... 5.00

Authority/Lobo: Spring Break Massacre
DC, 2005

0 .... 5.00

Authority: The Magnificent Kevin
DC, 2005

1-5 .... 3.00

Atomic Comics

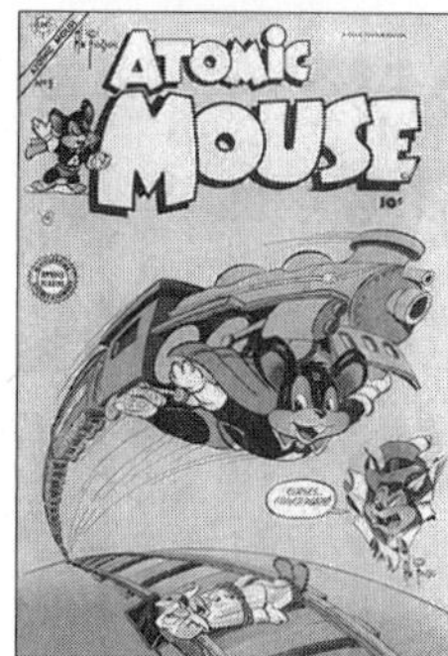

Atomic Mouse

Atomic Thunderbolt

Aurora Comic Scenes

Authentic Police Cases

Automaton

Avalon

Avatar

Authority: More Kev
DC, 2004

1-4 .... 3.00

Authority: Revolution
DC, 2004

1-12 .... 3.00

Authority: Scorched Earth
DC, 2003

1 .... 5.00

Automatic Kafka
WildStorm, 2002

1-9 .... 3.00

Automaton
Image, 1998

1-3 .... 3.00

Autumn
Caliber, 1995

1-3 .... 3.00

Autumn Adventures
Disney

1 .... 3.00

Autumn...Earth
Acid Rain

1 .... 3.00

Avalon
Harrier, 1986

1-14 .... 2.00

Avant Guard: Heroes at the Future's Edge
Day One, 1994

1-3 .... 3.00

Avataars: Covenant of the Shield
Marvel, 2000

1-3 .... 3.00

Avatar
DC

1-3 .... 4.00

Avelon
Drawbridge, 1997

1-11 .... 3.00

Avengeblade
Maximum, 96

1-2 .... 3.00

Avengelyne
Maximum, 1995

1-1/A 3.00
1/Gold-1/Variant 4.00
2-3/B 3.00
Ashcan 1 .... 4.00

Avengelyne
Maximum, 1996

0-½ 3.00
½/Platinum 4.00
1-1/Variant 3.00
2-2/A 4.00
2/B 5.00
3-15 .... 3.00

Avengelyne
Awesome, 1999

1 .... 3.00

Avengelyne Armageddon
Maximum, 1996

1-3 .... 3.00

Avengelyne Bible
Maximum, 1996

1 .... 4.00

Avengelyne: Dark Depths
Avatar, 2001

½-½/B 5.00
½/C 3.00
1-1/D 4.00
1/E 6.00
2-2/C 4.00

Avengelyne: Deadly Sins
Maximum, 1996

1 .... 3.00
1/Variant 4.00
2 .... 3.00

Avengelyne/Glory
Maximum, 1995

1-1/Variant 4.00

Avengelyne/Glory: The Godyssey
Maximum, 1996

1-1/Variant 3.00

Avengelyne: Power
Maximum, 1995

1/A-3 .... 3.00

Avengelyne-Prophet
Maximum, 1996

1-2 .... 3.00

Avengelyne Swimsuit
Maximum, 1995

1-1/D 3.00

Avengelyne/Warrior Nun Areala
Maximum, 1996

1/A-1/B 3.00

Avenger
AC, 1996

Ashcan 0 .... 6.00

Avengers
Marvel, 1963

0 .... 3.00
1 .... 4,200.00
☛1st Avengers
1.5 .... 3.00
2 .... 935.00
3 .... 750.00
4 .... 1,450.00

☛Cap. America joins
4/Golden 40.00
5 .... 350.00
6 .... 390.00
7 .... 460.00
8 .... 275.00
9 .... 225.00
☛1st Wonder Man
10 .... 180.00
☛1st Hercules
11 .... 275.00
☛Spider-Man app.
12 .... 115.00
13-14 .... 150.00
15 .... 100.00
16 .... 125.00
17 .... 115.00
18 .... 100.00
19 .... 150.00
20 .... 80.00
21-22 .... 70.00
23 .... 75.00
24 .... 70.00
25 .... 95.00
26 .... 65.00
27 .... 70.00
28-30 .... 50.00
31 .... 43.00
32 .... 37.00
33 .... 50.00
34 .... 55.00
35 .... 50.00
36 .... 35.00
37 .... 40.00
38 .... 43.00
39-41 .... 40.00
42 .... 50.00
43 .... 45.00
44 .... 40.00
45 .... 50.00
46 .... 30.00
47-48 .... 37.00
49 .... 32.00
50 .... 30.00
51 .... 40.00
52 .... 41.00
53 .... 60.00
☛X-Men app.
54-55 .... 30.00
56 .... 50.00
57 .... 110.00
☛1st Vision
58 .... 65.00
59-60 .... 40.00
61-66 .... 30.00
67 .... 45.00
68 .... 27.00
69-70 .... 30.00
71 .... 50.00
☛1st Invaders
72-73 .... 30.00
74-76 .... 25.00
77 .... 20.00
78 .... 25.00
79-81 .... 23.00
82 .... 26.00
83 .... 36.00
☛1st Valkyrie
84 .... 23.00
85-86 .... 25.00
87 .... 40.00
88 .... 25.00
88/2nd 2.00
89 .... 20.00
90-91 .... 22.00
92 .... 26.00
93 .... 120.00
☛Double-size
94 .... 35.00
95 .... 38.00
96 .... 35.00
97-98 .... 26.00
99 .... 30.00
100 .... 55.00
☛Knight gets sword
101 .... 18.00
102 .... 16.00
103 .... 40.00
☛Sentinels
104 .... 20.00
105 .... 18.00
106 .... 17.00
107 .... 20.00
108 .... 12.00
109 .... 18.00
110 .... 25.00
111 .... 22.00
112 .... 25.00
113 .... 11.00
114 .... 15.00
115 .... 13.00
116 .... 27.00
☛Defenders War
117 .... 20.00
118 .... 24.00
119 .... 15.00
120 .... 14.00
121 .... 10.00
122 .... 13.00
123 .... 9.00
124 .... 12.00
125 .... 20.00
126 .... 18.00
127-129 .... 12.00
130 .... 15.00
131 .... 12.00
132 .... 10.00
133 .... 8.00
134-135 .... 10.00
136-137 .... 8.00
138-140 .... 7.00
141 .... 10.00
142-145 .... 8.00
146 .... 10.00

Avengeblade

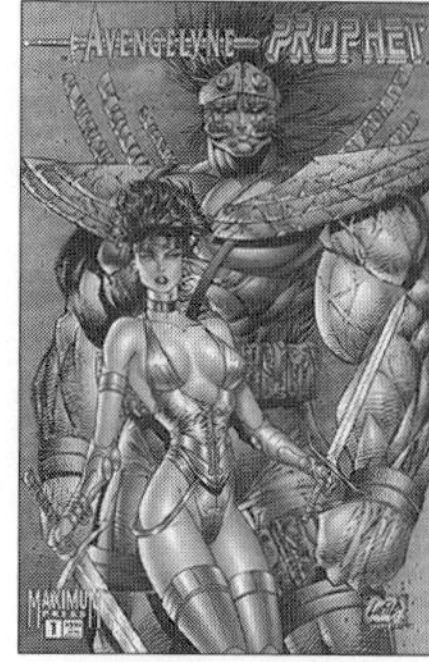

Avengelyne-Prophet

Avengers

Avengers Forever

Avengers Spotlight

Avengers Universe

Avengers West Coast

Avigon

Issue	Price
146/30¢	18.00
147	7.00
147/30¢	15.00
148	12.00
148/30¢	18.00
149	6.00
149/30¢	15.00
150	7.00
150/30¢	15.00
151	7.00
152-155	6.00
156	9.00
156/Whitman	8.00
157-157/Whitman	6.00
158	8.00
158/Whitman	6.00
159	8.00
159/Whitman-160/Whitman	6.00
160/35¢	15.00
161	7.00
161/Whitman	6.00
161/35¢	15.00
162-162/Whitman	8.00
162/35¢-163	15.00
163/Whitman	6.00
163/35¢-164	15.00
164/Whitman	6.00
164/35¢	15.00
165-166/Whitman	6.00
167	5.00
168	7.00
169-170	4.00
171	6.00
171/Whitman-174/Whitman	4.00
175	5.00
175/Whitman-180/Whitman	4.00
181	5.00
182	4.00
183	6.00
183/Whitman	5.00
184	6.00
185	7.00
186	5.00
187-189	6.00
190	4.00
191-195	5.00
196	7.00
197-199	5.00
200	9.00
☛Double-size	
201-218	3.00
219-224	2.00
225	3.00
226-249	2.00
250	3.00
251-262	2.00
263	3.00
264-349	2.00
350	3.00
351-359	1.00
360	3.00
361-362	1.00
363	3.00
364-365	1.00
366	4.00
☛Foil cover	
367-368	1.00
369	3.00
370-374	1.00
375	2.00
375/Collector's	3.00
376-379	2.00
379/Double	3.00
380	2.00
380/Double	3.00
381	2.00
381/Double	3.00
382	2.00
382/Double	3.00
383-399	2.00
400	4.00
401-402	3.00
Ann 1	125.00
Ann 2	120.00
Ann 3-4	22.00
Ann 5	25.00
Ann 6	7.00
Ann 7	12.00
Ann 8-9	8.00
Ann 10	9.00
Ann 11-16	4.00
Ann 17-23	3.00

Avengers

Marvel, 1996

Issue	Price
1 (403)-1/A	3.00
2 (404)-11 (413)	2.00
12 (414)	3.00
13 (415)	2.00

Avengers (Vol. 3)

Marvel, 1998

Issue	Price
0	2.00
1 (416)	4.00
1/Chromium	6.00
1/RoughCut-1/Variant	4.00
2 (417)-5 (420)	3.00
6 (421)-11 (426)	2.00
12 (427)	3.00
12/Dynamic	12.00
12/White	5.00
13 (428)-16 (431)	2.00
16/A	4.00
17 (432)-24 (439)	2.00
25 (440)	3.00
26 (441)	2.00
27 (442)	3.00
28 (443)-33 (448)	2.00
34 (449)	3.00
35 (450)-47 (462)	2.00
48 (463)	4.00
49 (464)	2.00
50 (465)	3.00
51 (466)-80 (495)	2.00

81 (496)-82 (497) 3.00
83 (498)-84 (499) 2.00
500 ..... 12.00
☛Disassembled
500/DirCut 18.00
501 ..... 5.00
☛Disassembled
502 ..... 7.00
☛Hawkeye dies
503 ..... 4.00
Ann 1998 ..... 3.00
Ann 1999-2000 ..... 4.00
Ann 2001 ..... 3.00

Avengers and Power Pack Assemble!
Marvel, 2006
1-4 ..... 3.00

Avengers Casebook
Marvel, 1999
1999 ..... 3.00

Avengers: Celestial Quest
Marvel, 2001
1-7 ..... 3.00
8 ..... 4.00

Avengers: Death Trap, the Vault
Marvel, 1991
1 ..... 10.00

Avengers: Earth's Mightiest Heroes
Marvel, 2004
1-8 ..... 4.00

Avengers: Earth's Mightiest Heroes II
Marvel, 2007
1-4 ..... 4.00

Avengers Finale
Marvel, 2005
1 ..... 4.00

Avengers Forever
Marvel, 1998
1 ..... 3.00
1/WF 5.00
2-12 ..... 3.00

Avengers (TV)
Gold Key, 1968
1 ..... 125.00
1/Variant 200.00

Avengers Icons: The Vision
Marvel, 2002
1-4 ..... 3.00

Avengers Infinity
Marvel, 2000
1 ..... 3.00
1/Dynamic 4.00
2-4 ..... 3.00

Avengers/JLA
DC, 2003
2 ..... 7.00
4 ..... 6.00

Avengers Legends
Marvel, 2003
1 ..... 25.00
2 ..... 20.00
3 ..... 17.00

Avengers: Living Legends
Marvel, 2004
1 ..... 20.00

Avengers Log
Marvel, 1994
1 ..... 2.00

Avengers Next
Marvel, 2007
1-5 ..... 3.00

Avengers Spotlight
Marvel, 1989
21-40 ..... 1.00

Avengers Strike File
Marvel, 1994
1 ..... 2.00

Avengers: The Crossing
Marvel, 1995
1 ..... 5.00

Avengers: The Terminatrix Objective
Marvel, 1993
1 ..... 3.00
2-4 ..... 1.00

Avengers: The Ultron Imperative
Marvel, 2001
1 ..... 6.00

Avengers/Thunderbolts
Marvel, 2004
1-6 ..... 3.00

Avengers: Timeslide
Marvel, 1996
1 ..... 5.00

Avengers Two: Wonder Man & Beast
Marvel, 2000
1-3 ..... 3.00

Avengers/Ultraforce
Marvel, 1995
1 ..... 4.00

Avengers: Ultron Unleashed
Marvel, 1999
1 ..... 4.00

A-V in 3-D

Awakening Comics

Awesome Holiday Special

Awesome Preview

Axel Pressbutton

Axis Mundi

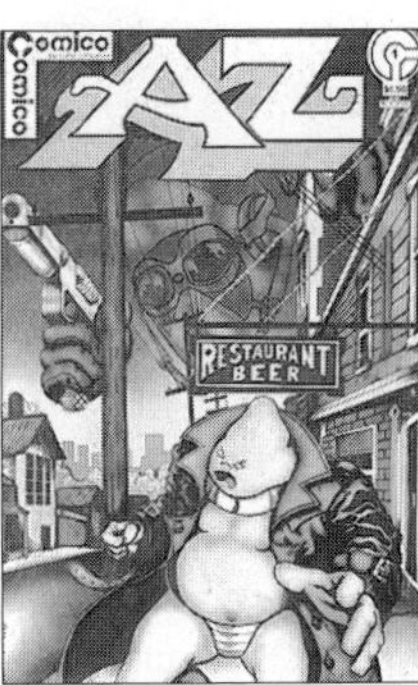

Az

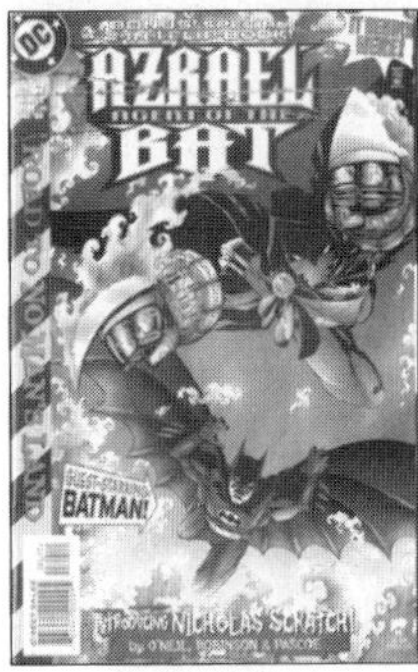

Azrael

Avengers: United They Stand
Marvel, 1999

1 .... 3.00
2-7 .... 2.00

Avengers Universe
Marvel, 2000

1-6 .... 3.00

Avengers Unplugged
Marvel, 1995

1-6 .... 1.00

Avengers West Coast
Marvel, 1989

47-55 .... 1.00
56 .... 8.00
☛Psycho Scarlet Witch
57-74 .... 1.00
75 .... 2.00
76-102 .... 1.00
Ann 4-7 .... 2.00
Ann 8 .... 3.00

Avengers/X-Men: Bloodties
Marvel, 1995

1 .... 16.00

Avenue D
Fantagraphics

1 .... 4.00

Avenue X
Purple Spiral, 1992

1-3 .... 3.00

Aviation Cadets
Street & Smith

1 .... 125.00

Avigon
Image, 2000

1 .... 6.00

A-V in 3-D
Aardvark-Vanaheim, 1984

1 .... 3.00

Awakening
Image, 1997

1-4 .... 3.00

Awakening Comics
Awakening Comics, 1997

1-2 .... 4.00
3-4 .... 3.00

Awakening Comics 1999
Awakening Comics, 1999

1 .... 4.00

Awesome Adventures
Awesome, 1999

1/A-1/B 3.00

Awesome Holiday Special
Awesome, 1997

1 .... 3.00

Awesome Man
Astonish, 2002

1 .... 3.00
2 .... 4.00

Awesome Preview
Awesome, 1997

1 .... 1.00

Awful Oscar
Timely, 1949

11-12 .... 40.00

Awkward
Slave Labor

1 .... 5.00

Awkward Universe
Slave Labor, 1995

1 .... 10.00

Axa
Eclipse, 1987

1-2 .... 2.00

Axa
Ken Pierce, 1981

1-GN 1 .... 6.00

Axed Files
Express, 1995

1 .... 3.00

Axel Pressbutton
Eclipse, 1984

1-6 .... 2.00

Axiom
Icon Creations, 94

1 .... 3.00

Axis Alpha
Axis, 1994

1 .... 3.00

Axis Mundi
Amaze Ink, 1996

2 .... 3.00

Az
Comico, 1983

1-2 .... 2.00

Azrach
Dark Horse, 1996

nn 7.00

Azrael
DC, 1995

1 .... 3.00
2-46 .... 2.00
47 .... 4.00
47/Ltd 6.00
48-68 .... 2.00
69-74 .... 3.00
75 .... 4.00
76-100 .... 3.00
1000000 .... 3.00
Ann 1 .... 4.00
Ann 2 .... 3.00
Ann 3 .... 4.00

Azrael/Ash
DC, 1997

1 .... 5.00

Azrael Plus
DC, 1996

1 .... 3.00

Aztec Ace
Eclipse, 1984

1 .... 3.00
2-15 .... 2.00

Aztec Anthropomorphic Amazons
Antarctic, 1994

1 .... 3.00

Aztec of the City
El Salto, 1993

1 .... 2.00

Aztec of the City
El Salto, 1996

1-2 .... 3.00

Aztek: The Ultimate Man
DC, 1996

1-10 .... 2.00

Azumanga Daioh
ADV Manga, 2003

1-4 .... 10.00

Babe
Dark Horse, 1994

1-4 .... 3.00

Babe 2
Dark Horse, 1995

1-2 .... 3.00

Babe, Darling of the Hills
Feature Publications, 1948

1 .... 85.00
2 .... 60.00
3-11 .... 50.00

Babe Ruth Sports Comics
Harvey, 1949

1 .... 240.00
2 .... 150.00
3 .... 125.00
4-11 .... 120.00

Babes of Broadway
Broadway, 1996

1 .... 3.00

Babewatch
Express, 1995

1-1/A 3.00

Baby Angel X
Brainstorm, 1995

1 .... 3.00

Baby Huey Digest
Harvey, 1992

1 .... 2.00

Baby Huey in 3-D
Blackthorne, 1998

1 .... 3.00

Baby Huey The Baby Giant
Harvey, 1956

1 .... 175.00
2 .... 90.00
3 .... 50.00
4-5 .... 36.00
6-10 .... 20.00
11-20 .... 15.00
21-30 .... 12.00
31-40 .... 9.00
41-50 .... 6.00
51-70 .... 4.00
71-99 .... 3.00
100-102 .... 1.00

Baby Huey
Harvey, 1991

1-9 .... 1.00

Babylon 5
DC, 1995

1 .... 5.00
2-4 .... 4.00
5-11 .... 3.00

Babylon 5: In Valen's Name
DC, 1998

1 .... 4.00
2-3 .... 3.00

Babylon Crush
Boneyard, 1995

1-Xmas 1 .... 3.00

Baby's First Deadpool Book
Marvel, 1998

1 .... 3.00

Baby Snoots
Gold Key, 1970

1 .... 12.00
2 .... 10.00
3 .... 8.00
4-12 .... 6.00
13-22 .... 5.00

Baby Surprise in My Pocket Magazine
Burghley

1-2 .... 3.00

Baby, You're Really Something!
Fantagraphics, 1990

1 .... 3.00

Bacchus
Harrier, 1988

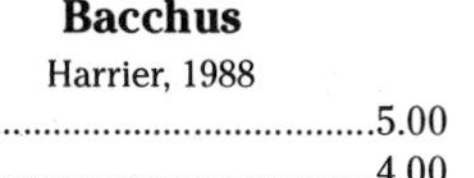

1 .... 5.00
2 .... 4.00

Aztec Ace

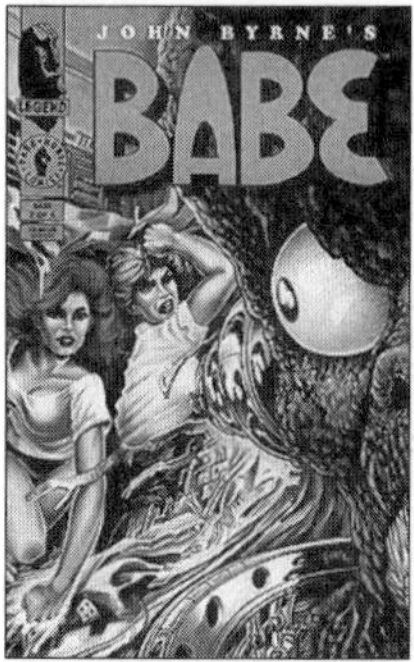

Babe

Baby Huey The Baby Giant

Babylon 5

Bacchus Color Special

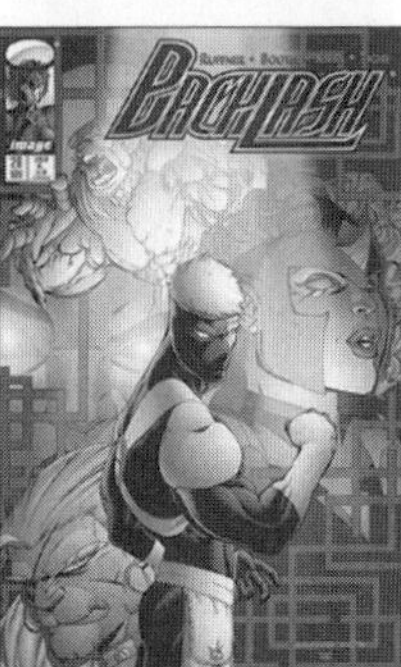

Backlash

Back to the Future

Bad Company

Bacchus
Eddie Campbell, 1995

1 .... 6.00
1/2nd 3.00
2-5 .... 4.00
6-60 .... 3.00

Bacchus Color Special
Dark Horse, 1995

1 .... 3.00

Bachelor Father
Dell, 1962

2 .... 50.00

Back Down the Line
Eclipse

1 .... 9.00

Backlash
Image, 1994

1-32 .... 3.00

Backlash & Taboo's African Holiday
DC, 1999

1 .... 6.00

Backlash/Spider-Man
Image, 1996

1-2 .... 3.00

Backpack Marvels: Avengers
Marvel, 2001

1 .... 7.00

Backpack Marvels: Spider-Man
Marvel, 2000

1 .... 7.00

Backpack Marvels: X-Men
Marvel, 2000

1-2 .... 7.00

Back-To-Back Horror Special
Timbuktu, 1989

1 .... 2.00

Back to the Future
Harvey, 1991

1-4 .... 2.00
Special 1 .... 1.00

Back to the Future: Forward to the Future
Harvey, 1992

1-3 .... 2.00

Bad Apples
High Impact, 1997

1-2 .... 3.00

Bad Art Collection
Slave Labor, 1996

1 .... 2.00

Badaxe
Adventure

1-3 .... 1.00

Bad Boy
Oni, 1997

1 .... 5.00

Bad Comics
Cat-Head

1 .... 3.00

Bad Company
Fleetway-Quality

1-19 .... 2.00

Bade Biker & Orson
Mirage, 1986

1-4 .... 2.00

Bad Eggs
Acclaim, 1996

1-8 .... 3.00

Badge
Vanguard, 1981

1 .... 3.00

Badger
Capital, 1983

1 .... 5.00
2-5 .... 3.00
6-49 .... 2.00
50 .... 4.00
51 .... 2.00
52-54 .... 3.00
55-70 .... 2.00

Badger
First, 1991

1 .... 5.00

Badger
Image, 1997

1-11 .... 3.00

Badger Goes Berserk
First, 1989

1-4 .... 2.00

Badger: Shattered Mirror
Dark Horse, 1994

1-4 .... 3.00

Badger: Zen Pop Funny-Animal Version
Dark Horse, 1994

1-2 .... 3.00

Bad Girls
DC, 2003

1-5 .... 3.00

Bad Girls (Bill Ward's...)
Forbidden Fruit

1 .... 2.00

Bad Girls of Blackout
Blackout, 1995

0-Ann 1 .... 4.00

Bad Hair Day
Slab-O-Concrete
1 .... 1.00

Bad Ideas
Image, 2004
1-2 .... 6.00

Bad Kitty
Chaos, 2001
1-3 .... 3.00

Bad Kitty: Mischief Night
Chaos, 2001
1-3 .... 3.00

Badlands
Dark Horse, 1991
1-6 .... 3.00

Bad Luck
Hero
1 .... 4.00

Bad Luck and Rick Dees Sentinel of Justice
King Comics, 1994
1 .... 3.00

Bad Meat
Fantagraphics, 1991
1-2 .... 2.00

Bad News
Fantagraphics
3 .... 4.00

Bad Planet
Image, 2005
1 .... 3.00

Badrock
Image, 1995
1-3 .... 2.00
Ann 1 .... 3.00

Badrock & Company
Image, 1994
1-Special 1 .... 3.00

Badrock/Wolverine
Image, 1996
1/A-1/D 5.00

Baffling Mysteries
Ace, 1951
5 .... 225.00
6-15 .... 165.00
16-19 .... 150.00
20 .... 165.00
21-24 .... 150.00
25-26 .... 135.00

Bakers
Kyle Baker Publishing, 2005
1 .... 3.00

Bakersfield Kountry Comics
Last Gasp, 1973
1 .... 2.00

Bakers Meet Jingle Belle
Dark Horse, 2007
1 .... 3.00

Baker Street
Caliber, 1989
1-10 .... 3.00

Baker Street Graffiti
Caliber
1 .... 3.00

Baker Street Sketchbook
Caliber
1 .... 4.00

Balance of Power
Mu, 1990
1-4 .... 3.00

Balder the Brave
Marvel, 1985
1-4 .... 1.00

Ballad of Halo Jones
Fleetway-Quality, 1987
1-12 .... 2.00

Ballad of Utopia
Black Daze, 2000
1-8 .... 3.00

Ball and Chain
DC, 1999
1-4 .... 3.00

Ballast
Active Images, 2005
0 .... 4.00

Ballistic
Image, 1995
1-3 .... 3.00

Ballistic Action
Image, 1996
1 .... 3.00

Ballistic Imagery
Image, 1996
1-2 .... 3.00

Ballistic Studios Swimsuit Special
Image, 1995
1 .... 3.00

Ballistic/Wolverine
Top Cow, 1997
1 .... 4.00

Balloonatiks
Best, 1991
1 .... 3.00

Badger

Badlands

Baffling Mysteries

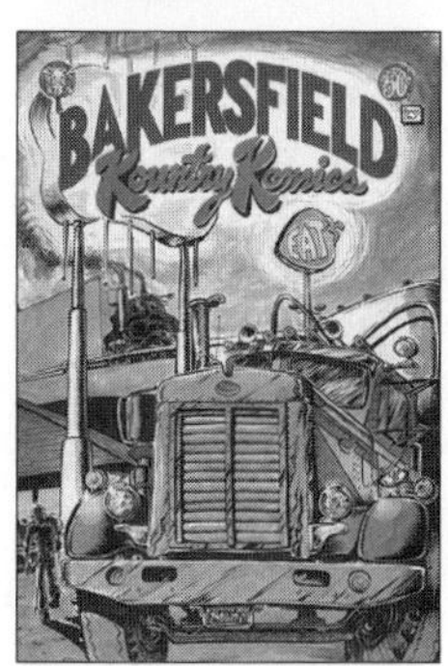

Bakersfield Kountry Comics

Baker Street

Balder the Brave

Ballistic

Balloon Vendor Comix

Balloon Vendor Comix
Rip Off, 1971
1 .... 4.00

Baloo & Little Britches
Gold Key, 1968
1 .... 25.00

Bambeano Boy
Moordam, 1998
1 .... 3.00

Bambi
Dell, 1956
3 .... 30.00
3/A 50.00

Bambi
Whitman
1 .... 3.00

Bambi and Her Friends
Friendly, 1991
1-9 .... 3.00
SE 1 .... 4.00

Bambi in Heat
Friendly
1-3 .... 3.00

Bambi the Hunter
Friendly, 1992
1-5 .... 3.00

Bamm-Bamm and Pebbles Flintstone
Gold Key, 1964
1 .... 75.00

Banana Fish
Tokyopop, 2004
1-7 .... 16.00
8-10 .... 10.00

Banana Splits
Gold Key, 1969
1 .... 30.00
2 .... 18.00
3-5 .... 14.00
6-8 .... 12.00

Banana Sundays
Oni, 2005
1-4 .... 3.00

Bandy Man
Caliber, 1996
1-3 .... 3.00

Bang Gang
Fantagraphics
1 .... 3.00

Bangs and the Gang
Shhwinng, 1994
1 .... 3.00

Banished Knights
Image, 2001
1 .... 7.00
1/A-2/B 3.00

Banzai Girl
Sirius, 2002
1-4 .... 3.00
Ann 1 .... 4.00

Baobab
Fantagraphics, 2005
1-2 .... 8.00

Baoh
Viz, 1995
1 .... 4.00
2-8 .... 3.00

Barabbas
Slave Labor, 1985
1-2 .... 2.00

Barbarian Comics
California, 1972
1-3 .... 3.00

Barbarians
Atlas-Seaboard, 1975
1 .... 8.00

Barbarians
Avalon
1-2 .... 3.00

Barbarians and Beauties
AC, 1990
1 .... 3.00

Barbaric Tales
Pyramid
1-2 .... 2.00

Barbarienne
Fantagraphics, 1992
1-3 .... 3.00
4-10 .... 4.00

Barbarienne
Harrier, 1987
1-8 .... 2.00

Barbie
Marvel, 1991
1-1/A 3.00
2-63 .... 2.00

Barbie & Baby Sister Kelly
Marvel, 1995
1 .... 8.00

Barbie and Ken
Dell, 1962
1 .... 200.00
2-4 .... 150.00
5 .... 165.00

Barbie Fashion
Marvel, 1991
1-1/A 3.00
2-55 .... 2.00

Barbi Twins Adventures
Topps, 1995
1 .... 3.00

Barb Wire
Dark Horse, 1994
1-9 .... 3.00

Barb Wire: Ace of Spades
Dark Horse, 1996
1-4 .... 3.00

Barb Wire Comics Magazine Special
Dark Horse, 1996
1 .... 4.00

Barb Wire Movie Special
Dark Horse, 1996
1 .... 4.00

Bar Crawl of the Damned
Mortco, 1997
1 .... 3.00

Barefootz Funnies
Kitchen Sink, 1975
1 .... 3.00
2-3 .... 2.00

Barefootz The Comix Book Stories
Renegade
1 .... 3.00

Barf
Revolutionary, 1990
1 .... 2.00
2-3 .... 3.00

Barker
Quality, 1946
1 .... 125.00
2-10 .... 75.00
11-15 .... 50.00

Barney and Betty Rubble
Charlton, 1973
1 .... 15.00
2 .... 10.00
3-11 .... 6.00
12-23 .... 5.00

Barney Bear Home Plate
Barbour
1 .... 2.00

Barney Bear Lost and Found
Spire
1 .... 2.00

Barney the Invisible Turtle
Amazing
1 .... 2.00

Barnyard Comics
Animated, 1944
1 .... 125.00
2 .... 65.00
3-5 .... 42.00
6-10 .... 32.00
11-12 .... 24.00
13-15 .... 42.00
16 .... 24.00
17 .... 42.00
18-20 .... 75.00
21 .... 42.00
22 .... 75.00
23 .... 42.00
24-25 .... 75.00
26-27 .... 42.00
28 .... 24.00
29 .... 42.00
30-31 .... 22.00

Barr Girls
Antarctic
1 .... 3.00

Barron Storey's Watch Annual
Vanguard
1 .... 6.00

Barry Windsor-Smith: Storyteller
Dark Horse, 1996
1-9 .... 5.00

Bar Sinister
Windjammer, 1995
1-4 .... 3.00

Bartman
Bongo, 1993
1 .... 4.00
2-6 .... 3.00

Basara
Viz, 2003
1-27 .... 10.00

Baseball Classics
Personality
1-3 .... 3.00

Baseball Comics
Kitchen Sink, 1991
1 .... 4.00
2 .... 3.00

Baseball Comics
Personality
1-2 .... 3.00

Baseball Greats
Dark Horse, 1992
1-3 .... 3.00

Baseball Hall of Shame in 3-D
Blackthorne
1 .... 3.00

Baseball Heroes
Fawcett, 1952
1 .... 500.00

Baseball Legends
Revolutionary, 1992
1-19 .... 3.00

Barbarians and Beauties

Barbie

Barb Wire

Bar Crawl of the Damned

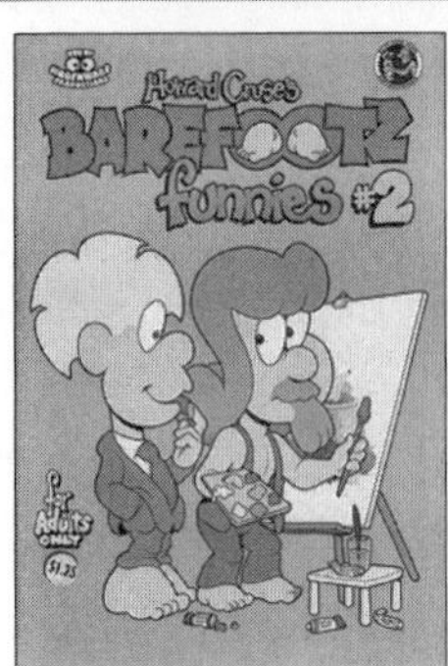

Barefootz Funnies

Barney and Betty Rubble

Barnyard Comics

Bartman

Baseball's Greatest Heroes
Magnum, 1991

1-2 .... 3.00

Baseball Sluggers
Personality

1-4 .... 3.00

Baseball Superstars Comics
Revolutionary, 1991

1-20 .... 3.00

Baseball Thrills 3-D
3-D Zone

1 .... 3.00

Basically Strange
John C., 1982

1 .... 4.00

Bastard
Viz, 2001

1-15 .... 4.00

Bastard Samurai
Image, 2002

1-3 .... 3.00

Bastard Tales
Baboon Books, 1998

1-2 .... 3.00

Bat
Apple, 1994

1 .... 3.00

Batbabe
Spoof

2 .... 3.00

Batch
Caliber

1 .... 3.00

Batgirl
DC, 2000

1 .... 4.00
1/2nd 3.00
2-5 .... 4.00
6-73 .... 3.00
Ann 1 .... 4.00

Batgirl Adventures
DC, 1998

1 .... 4.00

Batgirl Secret Files and Origins
DC, 2002

1 .... 5.00

Batgirl Special
DC, 1988

1 .... 3.00

Batgirl: Year One
DC, 2003

1-9 .... 3.00

Bathing Machine
C&T, 1987

1 .... 3.00
2-3 .... 2.00

Bathroom Girls
Modern, 1997

1-2 .... 3.00

Bat Lash
DC, 1968

1 .... 25.00
2-7 .... 15.00

Batman
DC, 1940

0 .... 3.00
1 .... 80,000.00
☛1st Catwoman
2 .... 15,000.00
3 .... 9,750.00
4 .... 7,500.00
5 .... 5,500.00
☛1st Batmobile
6-7 .... 4,500.00
8 .... 4,000.00
9 .... 3,750.00
10 .... 7,500.00
11 .... 4,750.00
12 .... 2,900.00
☛1st Batcave
13-14 .... 2,775.00
15 .... 2,625.00
16 .... 4,600.00
☛1st Alfred
17-20 .... 1,650.00
21-22 .... 1,275.00
23 .... 2,000.00
24 .... 1,275.00
25 .... 2,050.00
26-30 .... 1,275.00
31-36 .... 950.00
37 .... 1,200.00
38 .... 1,000.00
39 .... 950.00
40 .... 1,140.00
41-43 .... 760.00
44 .... 1,080.00
45-46 .... 760.00
47 .... 3,000.00
☛Batman origin
48 .... 965.00
49 .... 1,350.00
☛1st Mad Hatter
50-51 .... 690.00
52 .... 850.00
53-54 .... 690.00
55 .... 850.00
56-57 .... 690.00
58 .... 750.00
59-61 .... 690.00
62 .... 1,250.00
☛Catwoman origin
63 .... 575.00

64 ..... 515.00
65 ..... 575.00
66 ..... 660.00
☛vs. Joker
67-68 ..... 515.00
69 ..... 575.00
70-72 ..... 515.00
73 ..... 660.00
74 ..... 550.00
75-77 ..... 500.00
78 ..... 585.00
79-80 ..... 500.00
81 ..... 485.00
82-83 ..... 435.00
84 ..... 485.00
85-90 ..... 435.00
91-99 ..... 400.00
100 ..... 2,000.00
☛Anniversary issue
101-104 ..... 400.00
105 ..... 490.00
106-109 ..... 400.00
110 ..... 425.00
111-120 ..... 290.00
121 ..... 375.00
☛1st Mr. Freeze
122 ..... 225.00
123 ..... 220.00
124-126 ..... 195.00
127 ..... 240.00
☛vs. Joker
128 ..... 195.00
129 ..... 250.00
☛Robin origin
130 ..... 195.00
131 ..... 145.00
132-135 ..... 130.00
136 ..... 215.00
☛vs. Joker
137-145 ..... 140.00
146-147 ..... 110.00
148 ..... 140.00
☛vs. Joker
149-150 ..... 110.00
151 ..... 90.00
152 ..... 100.00
153 ..... 125.00
154 ..... 85.00
155 ..... 300.00
☛1st SA Penguin
156-164 ..... 85.00
165 ..... 130.00
166-168 ..... 85.00
169 ..... 90.00
170 ..... 85.00
171 ..... 450.00
☛1st SA Riddler
172 ..... 125.00
173-175 ..... 75.00
176 ..... 85.00
177 ..... 75.00
178 ..... 85.00
179 ..... 120.00
☛vs. Riddler
180 ..... 60.00
181 ..... 175.00
☛1st Poison Ivy
182-185 ..... 60.00
186 ..... 70.00
187 ..... 65.00
188 ..... 40.00
189 ..... 250.00
☛1st SA Scarecrow
190 ..... 45.00
191 ..... 40.00
192 ..... 60.00
193 ..... 70.00
194 ..... 80.00
195-196 ..... 40.00
197 ..... 100.00
☛Catwoman app.
198 ..... 85.00
199 ..... 40.00
200 ..... 100.00
☛Robin origin
201-202 ..... 35.00
203-204 ..... 30.00
205 ..... 40.00
206 ..... 30.00
207-208 ..... 50.00
209-212 ..... 30.00
213 ..... 45.00
214-217 ..... 30.00
218 ..... 70.00
☛Giant-size
219 ..... 50.00
220-221 ..... 30.00
222 ..... 75.00
223 ..... 40.00
224-226 ..... 30.00
227 ..... 50.00
228 ..... 40.00
229-231 ..... 30.00
232 ..... 350.00
☛1st Ra's al Ghul
233 ..... 30.00
234 ..... 115.00
☛1st SA Two-Face
235 ..... 17.00
236 ..... 25.00
237 ..... 75.00
☛1st Reaper
238 ..... 65.00
☛100 pages
239-240 ..... 17.00
241 ..... 30.00
242 ..... 17.00
243 ..... 70.00
☛vs. Ra's al Ghul
244 ..... 65.00
☛vs. Ra's al Ghul
245 ..... 70.00
246-247 ..... 15.00
248 ..... 20.00

Batgirl

Bat Lash

Batman

Batman and the Outsiders

Batman Beyond

Batman Plus

Batman Secret Files

Batman Versus Predator

249-250	15.00
251	60.00
☛vs. Joker	
252	14.00
253	26.00
254-255	32.00
256-258	35.00
259-261	32.00
262-263	15.00
264-266	9.00
267-285	8.00
286	12.00
☛vs. Joker	
287-290	9.00
291	12.00
292-294	9.00
295-299	8.00
300	15.00
301-306	7.00
306/Whitman	14.00
307	7.00
307/Whitman	14.00
308	7.00
308/Whitman	14.00
309-311	7.00
311/Whitman	20.00
312	7.00
312/Whitman	14.00
313	7.00
313/Whitman	14.00
314	7.00
314/Whitman	14.00
315	7.00
315/Whitman	14.00
316	7.00
316/Whitman	14.00
317	7.00
317/Whitman	17.00
318	7.00
318/Whitman	17.00
319	7.00
319/Whitman	17.00
320	7.00
320/Whitman	14.00
321-331	7.00
332	8.00
333-352	7.00
353	5.00
354-356	7.00
357	9.00
358-367	7.00
368	8.00
369-370	6.00
371-399	5.00
400	10.00
401-403	4.00
404	5.00
405	6.00
406-408	5.00
409-416	3.00
417	5.00
418-420	4.00
421-425	3.00
426-427	6.00
427/Direct	4.00
428	6.00
429	4.00
430	3.00
431-435	2.00
436	3.00
436/2nd	1.00
437-441	2.00
442	3.00
443-456	2.00
457	3.00
457/Direct	4.00
457/2nd-486	2.00
487	1.00
488-492	3.00
492/Silver	5.00
492/2nd	2.00
493	3.00
494-496	2.00
497	3.00
497/2nd-500	2.00
500/CS	4.00
501-515	2.00
515/Variant	4.00
516-530	2.00
530/Variant	3.00
531	2.00
531/Variant	3.00
532	2.00
532/Variant	3.00
533-535	2.00
535/Variant	4.00
536-549	2.00
550	3.00
550/Variant	4.00
551-562	2.00
563-564	3.00
565-599	2.00
600	4.00
601-607	2.00
608	5.00
☛Jim Lee begins	
608/2nd	2.00
608/Dynamic	25.00
608/Retailer ed	500.00
608/NYPost	5.00
609	4.00
☛vs. Superman	
610-619/2nd	3.00
620-629	2.00
630	3.00
631-632	2.00
633	3.00
634	6.00
635	15.00
☛Red Hood	
636-637	12.00
638	11.00
638/2nd	6.00
639	16.00

640-641 .... 6.00
642-650 .... 3.00
651 .... 6.00
652-671 .... 3.00
1000000 .... 4.00
Ann 1 .... 540.00
Ann 1/2nd 6.00
Ann 2 .... 275.00
Ann 3 .... 215.00
Ann 4-5 .... 110.00
Ann 6-7 .... 85.00
Ann 8 .... 7.00
Ann 9-11 .... 6.00
Ann 12-13 .... 5.00
Ann 14-15 .... 3.00
Ann 15/2nd 2.00
Ann 15/Silver/3 .... 4.00
Ann 16-18 .... 3.00
Ann 19 .... 4.00
Ann 20 .... 3.00
Ann 21 .... 4.00
Ann 22-23 .... 3.00
Ann 24 .... 4.00
Ann 25 .... 12.00
GS 1-2 .... 5.00
GS 3 .... 6.00

Batman Adventures

DC, 1992

1 .... 3.00
1/Silver 4.00
2-7 .... 2.00
7/CS 3.00
8-24 .... 2.00
25 .... 3.00
26-36 .... 2.00
Ann 1 .... 3.00
Ann 2 .... 4.00
Holiday 1 .... 3.00

Batman Adventures

DC, 2003

1-17 .... 2.00

Batman Adventures: Mad Love

DC, 1994

1 .... 8.00
1/2nd 6.00

Batman Adventures: The Lost Years

DC, 1998

1-5 .... 2.00

Batman/Aliens

Dark Horse, 1997

1-2 .... 5.00

Batman/Aliens II TP

DC, 2003

1 .... 15.00

Batman/Aliens II

DC-Dark Horse, 2003

1-3 .... 6.00

Batman Allies Secret Files 2005

DC, 2005

0 .... 5.00

Batman and Other DC Classics

DC, 1989

1 .... 2.00

Batman and Robin Adventures

DC, 1995

1 .... 3.00
2-24 .... 2.00
25 .... 3.00
Ann 1-2 .... 4.00

Batman and Robin Adventures: Sub-Zero

DC, 1998

1 .... 4.00

Batman and Robin: The Official Adaptation of the Warner Bros. Motion Picture

DC, 1997

1 .... 6.00

Batman & Superman Adventures: World's Finest

DC, 1997

1 .... 7.00

Batman and Superman: World's Finest

DC, 1999

1 .... 3.00
2-10 .... 2.00

Batman and the Mad Monk

DC, 2006

1-5 .... 4.00

Batman and the Monster Men

DC, 2006

1-5 .... 3.00
6 .... 4.00

Batman and the Outsiders

DC, 1983

1 .... 3.00
2-32 .... 2.00
Ann 1 .... 3.00
Ann 2 .... 2.00

Batman: Arkham Asylum - Tales of Madness

DC, 1998

1 .... 3.00

Bat Masterson

Bat-Thing

Battle

Battle Angel Alita Part 1

Battle Attack

Battleaxes

Battle Cry

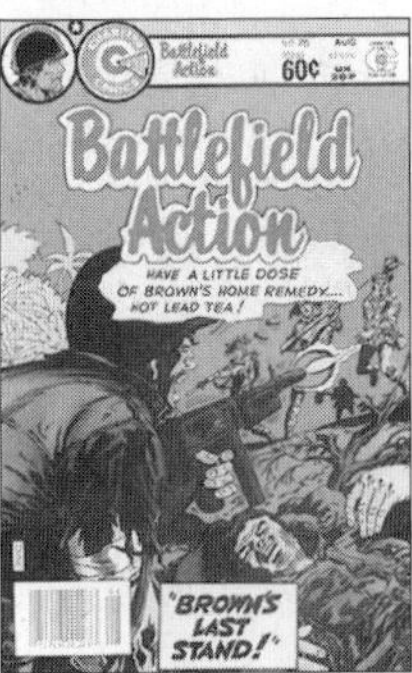

Battlefield Action

Batman: Arrow, Ring and Bat
DC, 2003

1 .... 20.00

Batman: A Word to the Wise
DC

1 .... 1.00

Batman: Bane
DC, 1997

1 .... 5.00

Batman: Bane of the Demon
DC, 1998

1-4 .... 2.00

Batman: Batgirl
DC, 1997

1 .... 5.00

Batman: Batgirl
DC, 1998

1 .... 2.00

Batman Begins Movie Adaptation
DC, 2005

0 .... 7.00

Batman Beyond
DC, 1999

1 .... 3.00
2-6 .... 2.00

Batman Beyond
DC, 1999

1 .... 3.00
2-24 .... 2.00

Batman Beyond: Return of the Joker
DC, 2001

1 .... 3.00

Batman Beyond Special Origin Issue
DC, 1999

1 .... 1.00

Batman Black and White
DC, 1996

1 .... 4.00
2-4 .... 3.00

Batman: Blackgate
DC, 1997

1 .... 4.00

Batman: Blackgate, Isle of Men
DC, 1998

1 .... 3.00

Batman: Book of the Dead
DC, 1999

1-2 .... 5.00

Batman: Bullock's Law
DC, 1999

1 .... 5.00

Batman/Captain America
DC, 1996

1 .... 6.00

Batman: Castle of the Bat
DC, 1994

1 .... 6.00

Batman: Catwoman Defiant
DC, 1992

1 .... 5.00

Batman/Catwoman: Trail of the Gun
DC, 2004

1-2 .... 6.00

Batman Chronicles
DC, 1995

1-12 .... 4.00
13-23 .... 3.00

Batman Chronicles Gallery
DC, 1997

1 .... 4.00

Batman Chronicles: The Gauntlet
DC, 1997

1 .... 5.00

Batman: City of Light
DC, 2003

1-8 .... 3.00

Batman Confidential
DC, 2007

1-30 .... 3.00

Batman/Danger Girl
DC, 2005

1 .... 5.00

Batman/Daredevil
DC, 2000

1 .... 6.00

Batman: Dark Allegiances
DC, 1996

1 .... 6.00

Batman: Dark Detective
DC, 2005

1-6 .... 3.00

Batman: The Dark Knight Adventures
DC

1 .... 8.00

Batman: Dark Knight Gallery
DC, 1996

1 .... 4.00

Batman: Dark Knight of the Round Table
DC, 1999

1-2 .... 5.00

Batman: Dark Victory
DC, 1999

0 .... 1.00
1 .... 5.00
2-13 .... 3.00

Batman: Day of Judgment
DC, 1999

1 .... 4.00

Batman: Death and the Maidens
DC, 2003

1-9 .... 3.00

Batman/Deathblow: After the Fire
DC, 2002

1-3 .... 6.00

Batman: Death of Innocents
DC, 1996

1 .... 4.00

Batman/Demon
DC, 1996

1 .... 5.00

Batman/Demon: A Tragedy
DC, 2000

1 .... 6.00

Batman: DOA
DC, 2000

1 .... 7.00

Batman: Dreamland
DC, 2000

1 .... 6.00

Batman: Ego
DC, 2000

1 .... 7.00

Batman Family
DC, 1975

1 .... 16.00
2 .... 10.00
3-6 .... 8.00
7-8 .... 6.00
9-12 .... 7.00
13-16 .... 5.00
17-19 .... 7.00
20 .... 8.00

Batman: Family
DC, 2002

1-8 .... 3.00

Batman Forever: The Official Comic Adaptation of the Warner Bros. Motion Picture
DC, 1995

1 .... 4.00
1/Prestige 6.00

Batman: Fortunate Son
DC

1 .... 25.00

Batman: Full Circle
DC, 1991

1 .... 6.00

Batman Gallery
DC

1 .... 3.00

Batman: GCPD
DC, 1996

1-4 .... 2.00

Batman: Ghosts
DC, 1995

1 .... 5.00

Batman: Gordon of Gotham
DC, 1998

1-4 .... 2.00

Batman: Gordon's Law
DC, 1996

1-4 .... 2.00

Batman: Gotham Adventures
DC, 1998

1-10 .... 3.00
11-60 .... 2.00

Batman: Gotham By Gaslight
DC, 1989

1 .... 4.00

Batman Gotham City Secret Files
DC, 2000

1 .... 5.00

Batman: Gotham County Line
DC, 2005

1-3 .... 6.00

Batman: Gotham Knights
DC, 2000

1 .... 4.00
2-54 .... 3.00
55 .... 4.00
56-74 .... 3.00

Battlefront

Battleground

Battle of the Planets

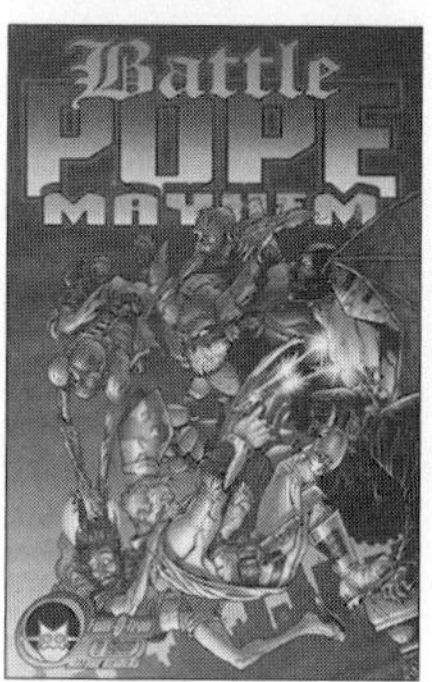

BattlePope

Battletide

Beach High

Bearfax Funnies

Beast Boy

Batman: Gotham Noir
DC, 2001
1 .... 7.00

Batman/Green Arrow: The Poison Tomorrow
DC, 1992
1 .... 6.00

Batman/Grendel
DC, 1993
1-2 .... 6.00

Batman/Grendel
DC, 1996
1-2 .... 5.00

Batman: Harley & Ivy
DC, 2004
1-3 .... 3.00

Batman: Harley Quinn
DC, 1999
1 .... 12.00
1/2nd 6.00

Batman: Haunted Gotham
DC, 2000
1-4 .... 5.00

Batman: Haunted Knight
DC
1 .... 13.00
1/2nd 15.00

Batman/Hellboy/Starman
DC, 1999
1 .... 3.00
2 .... 3.00

Batman: Hollywood Knight
DC, 2001
1-3 .... 3.00

Batman: Holy Terror
DC, 1991
1 .... 5.00

Batman/Houdini: The Devil's Workshop
DC
1 .... 5.00

Batman/Huntress: Cry for Blood
DC, 2000
1-6 .... 3.00

Batman: Hush Double Feature
DC, 2003
1 .... 5.00

Batman: I, Joker
DC, 1998
1 .... 5.00

Batman: In Darkest Knight
DC, 1994
1 .... 5.00

Batman: Jekyll and Hyde
DC, 2005
1-5 .... 3.00

Batman: Joker's Apprentice
DC, 1999
1 .... 4.00

Batman/Joker: Switch
DC, 2003
1 .... 13.00

Batman: Joker Time
DC, 2000
1-3 .... 5.00

Batman: Journey into Knight
DC, 2005
1-12 .... 3.00

Batman/Judge Dredd: Die Laughing
DC, 1998
1-2 .... 5.00

Batman/Judge Dredd: Judgment on Gotham
DC
1 .... 6.00

Batman/Judge Dredd: The Ultimate Riddle
DC
1 .... 5.00

Batman/Judge Dredd: Vendetta in Gotham
DC, 1993
1 .... 6.00

Batman: League of Batmen
DC, 2001
1-2 .... 6.00

Batman: Legends of the Dark Knight
DC, 1989
1-15 .... 3.00
16 .... 4.00
17-20 .... 3.00
21-26 .... 2.00
27 .... 3.00
28-49 .... 2.00
50 .... 4.00
51-64 .... 2.00
0 .... 3.00
65-99 .... 2.00
100 .... 5.00
101-119 .... 2.00
120 .... 4.00
121-157 .... 2.00

158-198 .... 3.00
200 .... 5.00
201-213 .... 3.00
Ann 1 .... 5.00
Ann 2-Ann 5 .... 4.00
Ann 6 .... 3.00
Ann 7 .... 4.00
Special 1 .... 7.00

Batman: Legends of the Dark Knight: Jazz
DC, 1995
1-3 .... 3.00

Batman: Madness a Legends of the Dark Knight Halloween Special
DC, 1994
1 .... 5.00

Batman: Manbat
DC, 1995
1-3 .... 5.00

Batman: Mask of the Phantasm-The Animated Movie
DC, 1993
1 .... 3.00
1/Prestige-1/Video 5.00

Batman: Masque
DC, 1997
1 .... 7.00

Batman: Master of the Future
DC, 1991
1 .... 6.00

Batman: Mr. Freeze
DC, 1997
1 .... 5.00

Batman: Mitefall
DC, 1995
1 .... 5.00

Batman: Nevermore
DC, 2003
1-5 .... 3.00

Batman/Nightwing: Bloodborne
DC, 2002
1 .... 6.00

Batman: No Law and a New Order
DC
1 .... 6.00

Batman: No Man's Land
DC, 1999
0 .... 5.00
1 .... 3.00
1/Variant 4.00
2-4 .... 3.00

Batman: No Man's Land Gallery
DC, 1999
1 .... 4.00

Batman: No Man's Land Secret Files
DC, 1999
1 .... 5.00

Batman: Nosferatu
DC, 1999
1 .... 6.00

Batman of Arkham
DC
1 .... 6.00

Batman: Order of the Beasts
DC, 2004
1 .... 6.00

Batman: Orpheus Rising
DC, 2001
1-5 .... 3.00

Batman: Our Worlds at War
DC, 2001
1 .... 3.00

Batman: Outlaws
DC, 2000
1-3 .... 5.00

Batman: Penguin Triumphant
DC, 1992
1 .... 5.00

Batman/Phantom Stranger
DC, 1997
1 .... 5.00

Batman Plus
DC, 1997
1 .... 3.00

Batman: Poison Ivy
DC, 1997
1 .... 5.00

Batman/Poison Ivy: Cast Shadows
DC, 2004
1 .... 7.00

Batman/Predator III
DC, 1997
1-4 .... 2.00

Batman: Prodigal
DC
1 .... 15.00

Beast Warriors of Shaolin

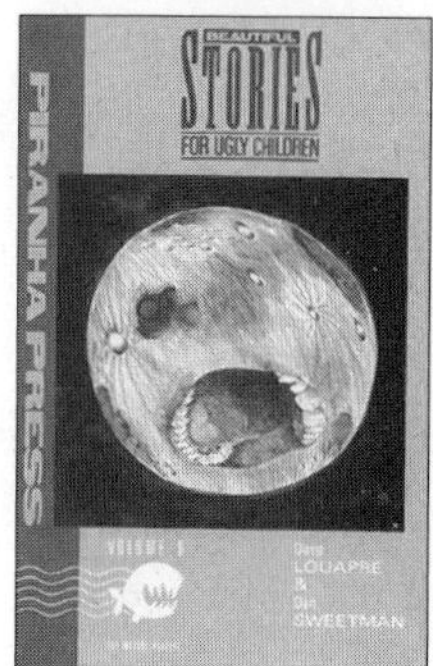

Beautiful Stories for Ugly Children

Beelzelvis

Beethoven

Beetlejuice in the Neitherworld

Behold 3-D

Bella Donna

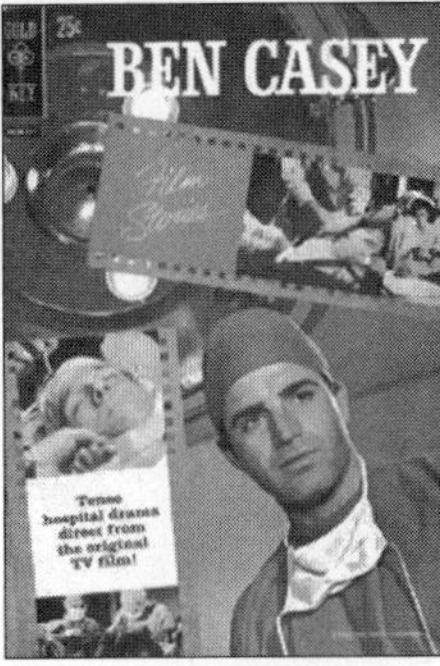

Ben Casey Film Stories

Batman/Punisher: Lake of Fire
DC, 1994
1 .... 5.00

Batman: Reign of Terror
DC, 1999
1 .... 5.00

Batman Returns: The Official Comic Adaptation of the Warner Bros. Motion Picture
DC, 1992
1 .... 4.00
1/Prestige 6.00

Batman: Riddler: The Riddle Factory
DC
1 .... 5.00

Batman: Roomful of Strangers
DC, 2004
1 .... 6.00

Batman: Run, Riddler, Run
DC, 1992
1-3 .... 5.00

Batman/Scarecrow 3-D
DC, 1998
1 .... 4.00
1/Variant 8.00

Batman/Scarface: A Psychodrama
DC, 2001
1 .... 6.00

Batman: Scar of the Bat
DC
1 .... 5.00

Batman: Scottish Connection
DC, 1998
1 .... 6.00

Batman Secret Files
DC, 1997
1 .... 5.00

Batman: Secrets
DC, 2006
1-5 .... 3.00

Batman: Seduction of the Gun
DC, 1993
1 .... 4.00

Batman: Shadow of the Bat
DC, 1992
0-1 .... 3.00
2-34 .... 3.00
35 .... 4.00
35/Variant 3.00
36-79 .... 2.00
80-80/Ltd. 5.00
81-82 .... 2.00
83 .... 9.00
84-93 .... 2.00
1000000 .... 3.00
94 .... 2.00
Ann 1-3 .... 4.00
Ann 4 .... 3.00
Ann 5 .... 4.00

Batman-Spawn: War Devil
DC, 1994
1 .... 5.00

Batman Special
DC, 1984
1 .... 3.00

Batman/Spider-Man
DC, 1997
1 .... 5.00

Batman: Spoiler/Huntress: Blunt Trauma
DC, 1998
1-4 .... 3.00

Batman Strikes
DC, 2004
1-29 .... 2.00

Batman/Superman/ Wonder Woman Trinity
DC, 2003
1 .... 9.00
2 .... 8.00
3 .... 7.00

Batman/Superman World's Finest TP
DC, 2003
1 .... 20.00

Batman: Sword of Azrael
DC, 1992
1 .... 4.00
1/Silver 2.00
2 .... 3.00
2/Silver 2.00
3 .... 3.00
3/Silver 2.00
4 .... 3.00
4/Silver 2.00

Batman/Tarzan: Claws Of The Cat-Woman
Dark Horse, 1999
1-4 .... 3.00

Batman: Tenses
DC, 2003
1-2 .... 7.00

Batman: Terror
DC, 2003

1 .... 13.00

Batman: The Abduction
DC, 1998

1 .... 6.00

Batman: The Ankh
DC, 2002

1-2 .... 6.00

Batman: The Blue, the Grey, and the Bat
DC, 1992

1 .... 6.00

Batman: The Book of Shadows
DC

1 .... 6.00

Batman: The Cult
DC, 1988

1 .... 5.00
2-4 .... 4.00

Batman: The Dark Knight
DC, 1986

1 .... 25.00
☛Frank Miller series
1/2nd 7.00
1/3rd 5.00
2 .... 9.00
2/2nd-2/3rd 3.00
3 .... 6.00
3/2nd 3.00
4 .... 5.00

Batman: The Doom that Came to Gotham
DC, 2000

1-3 .... 5.00

Batman: The Hill
DC, 2000

1 .... 3.00

Batman: The Killing Joke
DC, 1988

1 .... 7.00
☛Alan Moore, Brian Bolland
1/2nd 6.00
1/3rd-1/8th 5.00

Batman: The Long Halloween
DC, 1996

1 .... 9.00
2 .... 7.00
3 .... 6.00
4-6 .... 5.00
7-12 .... 4.00
13 .... 6.00

Batman: The Man Who Laughs
DC, 2005

1 .... 7.00

Batman: The Official Comic Adaptation of the Warner Bros. Motion Picture
DC, 1989

1 .... 3.00
1/Prestige 5.00

Batman/The Spirit
DC, 2007

1 .... 5.00

Batman: The 10-Cent Adventure
DC, 2002

1 .... 1.00

Batman: The Ultimate Evil
DC

1-2 .... 6.00

Batman 3-D
DC, 1990

1 .... 10.00

Batman: Thrillkiller
DC

1 .... 13.00

Batman: Toyman
DC, 1998

1-4 .... 2.00

Batman: Turning Points
DC, 2001

1-5 .... 3.00

Batman: Two-Face: Crime and Punishment
DC

1 .... 5.00

Batman: Two Faces
DC, 1998

1 .... 5.00
1/Ltd. 10.00

Batman: Two-Face Strikes Twice
DC, 1993

1-2 .... 5.00

Batman: Vengeance of Bane II
DC

1 .... 4.00

Batman: Vengeance of Bane Special
DC, 1993

1 .... 4.00

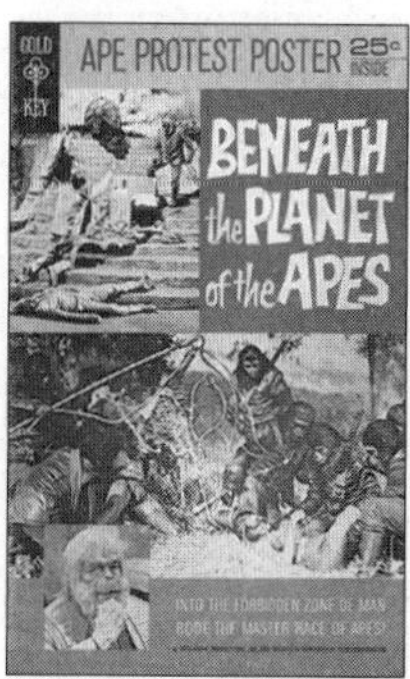

Beneath the Planet of the Apes

Benzine

Beowulf

Berlin

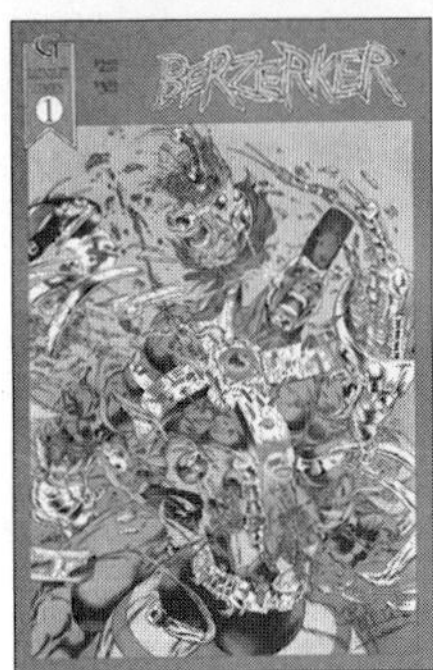
Berzerker

Berzerkers

Best of Dork Tower

Best of Furrlough

Batman Versus Predator

DC, 1991

1 ....3.00
1/Prestige Batm-1/Prestige Pred... 5.00
2 ....3.00
2/Prestige 5.00
3 ....3.00
3/Prestige 5.00

Batman versus Predator II: Bloodmatch

DC, 1994

1-4 ....3.00

Batman vs. the Incredible Hulk

DC, 1981

1 ....3.00
1/2nd 4.00

Batman Villains Secret Files

DC, 1998

1 ....5.00

Batman Villains Secret Files 2005

DC, 2005

0 ....5.00

Batman: War On Crime

DC, 1999

1 ....10.00

Batman/Wildcat

DC, 1997

1-3 ....2.00

Batman: Year 100

DC, 2006

1-4 ....6.00

Bat

Adventure, 1992

1 ....3.00

Bat Masterson

Dell, 1960

2 ....55.00
3-9 ....40.00

Bat Men

Avalon

1 ....3.00

Bats, Cats & Cadillacs

Now, 1990

1-2 ....2.00

Bat-Thing

DC, 1997

1 ....2.00

Battle

Atlas, 1951

1 ....175.00
2 ....100.00
3 ....75.00
4-10 ....54.00
11-20 ....45.00
21 ....58.00
22 ....42.00
23 ....58.00
24-30 ....42.00
31-50 ....32.00
51-63 ....26.00
64-66 ....45.00
67-68 ....55.00
69-70 ....45.00

Battle Action

Atlas, 1952

1 ....150.00
2 ....80.00
3-10 ....48.00
11-15 ....44.00
16-30 ....40.00

Battle Angel Alita Part 1

Viz, 1992

1-3 ....4.00
4-9 ....3.00

Battle Angel Alita Part 2

Viz, 1993

1-7 ....3.00

Battle Angel Alita Part 3

Viz, 1993

1-13 ....3.00

Battle Angel Alita Part 4

Viz, 1994

1-7 ....3.00

Battle Angel Alita Part 5

Viz, 1995

1-7 ....3.00

Battle Angel Alita Part 6

Viz, 1996

1-8 ....3.00

Battle Angel Alita Part 7

Viz, 1996

1-8 ....3.00

Battle Angel Alita Part 8

Viz, 1997

1-9 ....3.00

Battle Angel Alita: Last Order Part 1

Viz, 2002

1-6 ....3.00

Battle Armor

Eternity, 1988

1-3 ....2.00

Battle Attack

Stanmor, 1954

1 ....60.00
2 ....50.00
3 ....40.00
4-8 ....30.00

Battle Axe
Comics Interview

1 .... 3.00

Battleaxes
DC, 2000

1-4 .... 3.00

Battle Axis
Intrepid, 1993

1 .... 3.00

Battle Beasts
Blackthorne, 1988

1-4 .... 2.00

Battle Binder Plus
Antarctic, 1994

1-6 .... 3.00

Battle Chasers
Image, 1998

1-1/Wraparound 5.00
1/Holochrome 17.00
1/Gold 14.00
1/2nd 3.00
2 .... 4.00
2/Dynamic 5.00
2/B 6.00
3 .... 4.00
4/A-8 .... 3.00
9 .... 4.00
Ashcan 1 .... 5.00
Ashcan 1/Gold 7.00
Deluxe 1 .... 25.00

Battle Classics
DC, 1978

1 .... 4.00

Battle Cry
Stanmor, 1952

1 .... 65.00
2 .... 42.00
3-10 .... 28.00
11-20 .... 24.00

Battlefield
Atlas, 1952

1 .... 110.00
2 .... 60.00
3-5 .... 58.00
6-11 .... 44.00

Battlefield Action
Charlton, 1957

16 .... 28.00
17 .... 13.00
18-20 .... 10.00
21-30 .... 9.00
31-40 .... 7.00
41-50 .... 6.00
51-62 .... 5.00
63-89 .... 3.00

Battle for a Three Dimensional World
3-D Cosmic, 1982

1 .... 3.00

Battleforce
Blackthorne, 1987

1-2 .... 2.00

Battlefront
Marvel, 1952

1 .... 130.00
2 .... 75.00
3-5 .... 55.00
6-10 .... 42.00
11-20 .... 34.00
21-30 .... 28.00
31-48 .... 22.00

Battle Girlz
Antarctic, 2002

1-2 .... 3.00

Battle Gods: Warriors of the Chaak
Dark Horse, 1990

1-4 .... 3.00

Battleground
Marvel, 1954

1 .... 90.00
2 .... 50.00
3-5 .... 35.00
6-8 .... 24.00
9 .... 32.00
10 .... 24.00
11-12 .... 20.00
13 .... 32.00
14 .... 35.00
15-17 .... 20.00
18 .... 32.00
19-20 .... 20.00

Battleground Earth
Best

1-4 .... 3.00

Battle Group Peiper
Tome

1 .... 3.00

Battle Hymn
Image, 2005

1-5 .... 3.00

Battle of the Planets
Gold Key, 1979

1 .... 20.00
2 .... 15.00
3-6 .... 12.00
7 .... 30.00
8-10 .... 20.00

Battle of the Planets Artbook
Image, 2003

1 .... 5.00
☛Alex Ross art

Best of Horror and Science Fiction

Best of the West

Betti Cozmo

Betty

Betty and Veronica

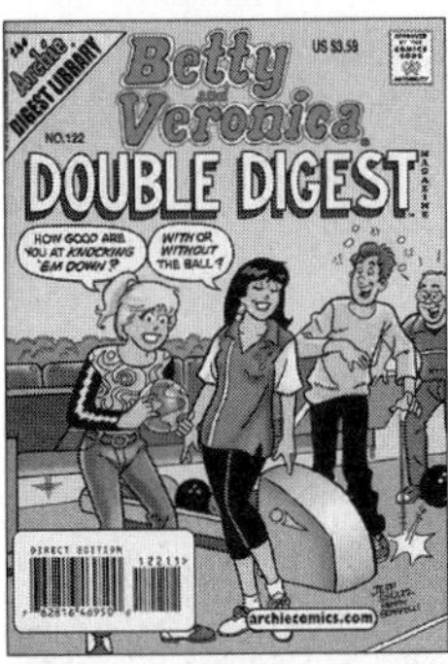

Betty and Veronica Double Digest

Betty and Veronica Spectacular

Betty Boop 3-D

Battle of the Planets
Image, 2002

½ 3.00
½/Gold 5.00
1/A-7 .... 3.00
7/A 5.00
8-11 .... 3.00
12 .... 5.00

Battle of the Planets: Jason
Image, 2003

1 .... 5.00

Battle of the Planets: Manga
Image, 2003

1-3 .... 3.00

Battle of the Planets: Mark
Image, 2003

1 .... 5.00

Battle of the Planets: Princess
Image, 2004

1-6 .... 3.00

Battle of the Planets/ Thundercats
Image, 2003

1-1/A 5.00

Battle of the Planets/ Witchblade
Image, 2003

1 .... 6.00

Battle of the Ultra-Brothers
Viz

1-5 .... 5.00

BattlePope
Funk-O-Tron, 2000

1 .... 3.00
2-3 .... 3.00
4 .... 3.00
5 .... 5.00
6-7 .... 3.00
8-9 .... 3.00
10 .... 5.00
11-13 .... 4.00

Battle Pope
Funk-O-Tron, 2006

1 .... 5.00
2 .... 4.00
3 .... 4.00
4-6 .... 3.00
7-9 .... 3.00
11 .... 5.00

Battle Pope Color
Image, 2005

1-8 .... 3.00
9-12 .... 4.00

Battler Britton
DC, 2006

1-5 .... 3.00

Battle Report
Farrell, 1952

1 .... 54.00

Battle Royale
Tokyopop, 2003

1 .... 16.00
2-14 .... 10.00

Battlestar Galactica 1999 Tour Book
Realm, 1999

1/A-1/B 3.00
1/C 7.00

Battlestar Galactica: Apollo's Journey
Maximum, 1996

1-3 .... 3.00

Battlestar Galactica: Eve of Destruction Prelude
Realm, 1999

nn 4.00

Battlestar Galactica: Journey's End
Maximum, 1996

1-4 .... 3.00

Battlestar Galactica
Marvel, 1979

1-1/Whitman 4.00
1/2nd 5.00
2-10 .... 3.00
11 .... 2.00

Battlestar Galactica
Maximum, 1995

1-Special 1 .... 3.00

Battlestar Galactica
Realm, 1997

1/A-5 .... 3.00

Battlestar Galactica: Search for Sanctuary
Realm, 1998

1 .... 3.00
Special 1 .... 4.00

Battlestar Galactica: Season III
Realm, 1999

1 .... 3.00
1/A-3/A 5.00
3/B 3.00
3/Conv. 5.00

Battlestar Galactica: Starbuck
Maximum, 1995

1-3 .... 3.00

Battlestar Galactica: The Compendium
Maximum, 1997

1 ... 3.00

Battlestar Galactica: The Enemy Within
Maximum, 1995

1-3/Variant ... 3.00

Battlestone
Image, 1994

1-2 ... 3.00

Battle Stories
Fawcett, 1952

1 ... 75.00
2 ... 45.00
3-11 ... 24.00

BattleTech
Malibu, 1995

0 ... 3.00

Battletech
Blackthorne, 1988

1-6 ... 2.00

BattleTech: Fallout
Malibu, 1994

1-4 ... 3.00

Battletech in 3-D
Blackthorne, 1988

1 ... 3.00

Battletide
Marvel, 1992

1-4 ... 2.00

Battletide II
Marvel, 1993

1 ... 3.00
2-4 ... 2.00

Battle to the Death
Imperial, 1987

1-3 ... 2.00

Battle Vixens
Tokyopop, 2004

1 ... 10.00

Battlezones: Dream Team 2
Malibu, 1996

1 ... 4.00

Battron
NEC, 1992

1-2 ... 3.00

Battron's 4 Queens: Guns, Babes & Intrigue
Commode

1 ... 4.00

Bay City Jive
DC, 2001

1-3 ... 3.00

Baywatch Comic Stories
Acclaim

1-4 ... 5.00

Bazooka Jules
Com.x, 2001

1-JE2 ... 3.00

Beach High
Big, 1997

1 ... 3.00

Beach Party
Eternity

1 ... 3.00

Beagle Boys
Gold Key, 1964

1 ... 22.00
2-5 ... 16.00
6-10 ... 12.00
11-20 ... 8.00
21-30 ... 6.00
31-40 ... 4.00
41-47 ... 3.00

Beagle Boys versus Uncle Scrooge
Whitman, 1979

1 ... 6.00
2 ... 5.00
3-7 ... 4.00
8-12 ... 3.00

Beany and Cecil
Dell, 1962

1 ... 75.00
2-5 ... 60.00

Bear
Slave Labor, 2003

1-10 ... 3.00

Bearers of the Blade Special
Image, 2006

1 ... 3.00

Bearfax Funnies
Treasure

1 ... 3.00

Bearskin: A Grimm Tale
Thecomic.Com

1 ... 2.00

Beast
Marvel, 1997

1-3 ... 3.00

Beast Boy
DC, 2000

1-4 ... 3.00

B.E.A.S.T.I.E.S.
Axis, 1994

1 ... 2.00

Beware Terror Tales

Bewitched

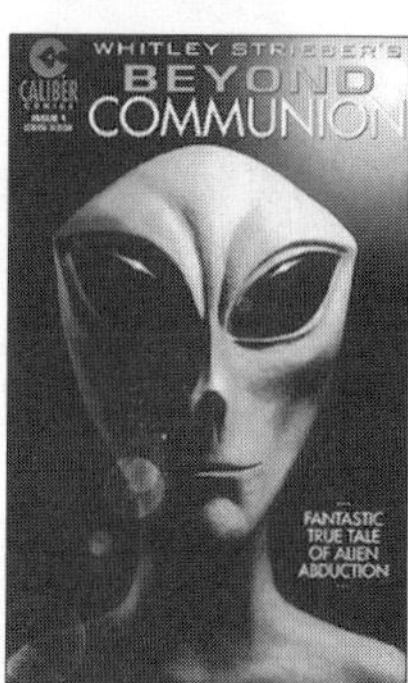

Beyond Communion

Beyond Mars

Beyond the Grave

Big

Big Blown Baby

Big Bruisers

Beast Warriors of Shaolin
Pied Piper, 1987

1-3 .... 2.00

Beatles
Dell, 1964

1 .... 440.00

Beatles Experience
Revolutionary, 1991

1-8 .... 3.00

Beatles
Personality

1 .... 5.00
1/Ltd. 8.00
2 .... 4.00

Beatles vs. The Rolling Stones
Celebrity, 1992

1 .... 3.00

Beatrix
Vision, 1997

1-2 .... 3.00

Beauties & Barbarians
AC

1 .... 2.00

Beautiful People
Slave Labor, 1994

1 .... 5.00

Beautiful Stories for Ugly Children
DC, 1989

1-30 .... 3.00

Beauty and the Beast
Disney

1 .... 3.00
1/Direct 5.00

Beauty and the Beast
Disney, 1994

1-13 .... 2.00
Holiday 1 .... 5.00

Beauty and the Beast
Innovation, 1993

1 .... 3.00
1/CS 4.00
2-6 .... 3.00

Beauty and the Beast
Marvel, 1984

1 .... 3.00
2-4 .... 2.00

Beauty and the Beast: Night of Beauty
First, 1990

1 .... 6.00

Beauty and the Beast: Portrait of Love
First, 1989

1 .... 6.00

Beauty and the Beast
Dark Horse

1 .... 5.00

Beauty Is the Beast
Viz, 2005

1 .... 9.00

Beauty of the Beasts
Mu, 1991

1-3 .... 3.00

Beavis & Butt-Head
Marvel, 1994

1 .... 3.00
1/2nd 2.00
2-5 .... 3.00
6-28 .... 2.00

Beck & Caul Investigations
Caliber, 1994

1-5 .... 3.00
Ann 1 .... 4.00

Beck: Mongolian Chop Squad
Tokyopop, 2005

1-10 .... 10.00

Bedlam!
Eclipse, 1985

1-2 .... 2.00

Bedlam
Image, 2006

1 .... 5.00

Bedlam
Chaos, 2000

1-1/Variant 3.00

Beelzelvis
Slave Labor, 1994

1 .... 3.00

Beep Beep
Dell, 1960

4-9 .... 24.00
10-14 .... 16.00

Beep Beep Road Runner
Gold Key, 1966

1 .... 50.00
2-5 .... 30.00
6-15 .... 15.00
16-40 .... 10.00
41-59 .... 8.00
60-79 .... 6.00
80-90 .... 3.00
91-92 .... 12.00
93 .... 17.00
94-101 .... 3.00
102-105 .... 12.00

Beer & Roaming in Las Vegas

Slave Labor, 1998

1 .... 3.00
Ashcan 1 .... 1.00

Beer Nutz

Tundra

1 .... 3.00
2-3 .... 2.00

Beethoven

Harvey, 1994

1-3 .... 2.00

Beetle Bailey

Dell, 1956

5-10 .... 24.00
11-20 .... 18.00
21-30 .... 14.00
31-40 .... 10.00
41-50 .... 8.00
51-60 .... 7.00
61-70 .... 6.00
71-100 .... 4.00
101-132 .... 3.00

Beetle Bailey

Harvey, 1992

1-GS 2 .... 2.00

Beetle Bailey Big Book

Harvey, 1992

1 .... 0.00
2 .... 2.00

Beetlejuice

Harvey, 1991

1-2 .... 2.00

Beetlejuice: Elliot Mess and the Unwashables

Harvey, 1992

1-3 .... 2.00

Beetlejuice Holiday Special

Harvey, 1992

1 .... 2.00

Beetlejuice in the Neitherworld

Harvey, 1991

1-2 .... 2.00

Beet the Vandel Buster

Viz, 2004

1-10 .... 8.00

Before the Fantastic Four: Ben Grimm and Logan

Marvel, 2000

1-3 .... 3.00

Before the FF: Reed Richards

Marvel, 2000

1-3 .... 3.00

Before the FF: The Storms

Marvel, 2000

1-3 .... 3.00

Behold 3-D

Edge Group

1 .... 4.00

Believe in Yourself Productions

Believe in Yourself Productions

1/Ashcan-1/Ltd. 1.00

Belladonna

Avatar, 2004

0/Preview 6.00
0/Conv 5.00
1 .... 4.00
1/Foil 8.00
1/Platinum 10.00
1/Wraparound 5.00
2 .... 4.00
2/Platinum 10.00
2/Premium 8.00
2/Wraparound 5.00
3 .... 4.00
3/Platinum 10.00
3/Premium 8.00
3/Wraparound 5.00
4 .... 4.00

Bella Donna

Pinnacle

1 .... 2.00

Belly Button

Fantagraphics, 2004

1-2 .... 5.00

Ben Casey Film Stories

Gold Key, 1962

1 .... 55.00

Beneath the Planet of the Apes

Gold Key, 1970

1 .... 35.00

Benzango Obscuro

Starhead

1 .... 3.00

Benzine

Antarctic, 2000

1-7 .... 5.00

Beowulf

DC, 1975

1 .... 5.00
2 .... 3.00
3-6 .... 2.00

Big Chief Wahoo

Big Edsel Band

Big Hair Productions

Big Monster Fight

Big Numbers

Big Shot

Big Town

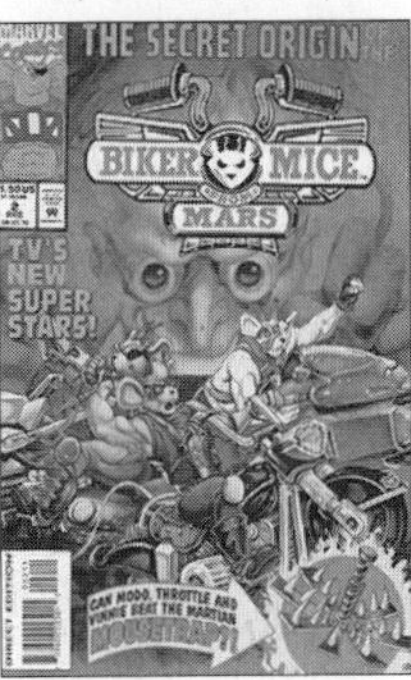

Biker Mice from Mars

Beowulf
Comic.Com, 1999
1-3 .... 5.00

Beowulf
Speakeasy Comics, 2005
1-4 .... 3.00

Berlin
Drawn & Quarterly, 1996
1-8 .... 3.00
10-12 .... 4.00

Bernie Wrightson, Master of the Macabre
Pacific, 1983
1-5 .... 3.00

Berserk
Dark Horse, 2003
1-10 .... 14.00

Berzerker
Gauntlet, 1993
1-6 .... 3.00

Berzerkers
Image, 1995
1-3 .... 3.00

Best Cellars
Out of the Cellar
1 .... 3.00

Best from Boys' Life Comics
Gilberton, 1957
1 .... 60.00
2 .... 40.00
3 .... 35.00
4 .... 40.00
5-6 .... 35.00

Best of Barron Storey's W.A.T.C.H. Magazine
Vanguard, 1993
1 .... 3.00

Best of Dark Horse Presents
Dark Horse, 1989
1 .... 6.00
2-3 .... 9.00

Best of DC
DC, 1979
1 .... 5.00
2-70 .... 4.00

Best of Dennis the Menace
Hallden Publications, 1959
1 .... 100.00
2-5 .... 65.00

Best of Donald Duck and Uncle Scrooge
Gold Key, 1964
1-2 .... 50.00

Best of Dork Tower
Dork Storm, 2001
1 .... 2.00

Best of Furrlough
Antarctic, 1995
1-2 .... 4.00

Best of Gold Digger
Antarctic, 1999
Ann 1 .... 3.00

Best of Horror and Science Fiction
Webster
1 .... 2.00

Best of Marvel Comics
Marvel, 1987
1 .... 20.00

Best of Northstar
Northstar, 1992
1 .... 2.00

Best of the Brave and the Bold
DC, 1988
1-6 .... 3.00

Best of the British Invasion
Revolutionary, 1993
1-2 .... 3.00

Best of the West
Magazine Enterprises, 1951
1 .... 265.00
2 .... 125.00
3-5 .... 110.00
6-12 .... 85.00

Best of the West
AC, 2005
1 .... 7.00
2-3 .... 5.00
4-32 .... 6.00
33-69 .... 7.00

Best of Tribune Co.
Dragon Lady, 1985
1-4 .... 3.00

Best of 2000 A.D.
Fleetway-Quality, 1985
1 .... 5.00
2-5 .... 4.00
6-20 .... 3.00
21-119 .... 2.00
Special 1-2 .... 4.00

Best of Uncle Scrooge & Donald Duck
Gold Key, 1968
1 .... 45.00

Best of Walt Disney Comics
Western, 1974
1 .... 15.00
2-4 .... 12.00

Best Romance
Standard, 1952

5-7 .... 50.00

Beta Sexus
Fantagraphics, 1994

1-2 .... 3.00

Betta: Time Warrior
Immortal

1-3 .... 3.00

Betti Cozmo
Antarctic, 1999

1-2 .... 3.00

Bettie Page Comics
Dark Horse, 1996

1 .... 4.00

Bettie Page Comics: Spicy Adventure
Dark Horse, 1997

1 .... 3.00

Bettie Page: Queen of the Nile
Dark Horse, 1999

1-3 .... 3.00

Betty
Archie, 1992

1 .... 4.00
2-161 .... 2.00
162-178 .... 3.00

Betty & Me
Archie, 1965

1 .... 65.00
2 .... 40.00
3-5 .... 24.00
6-10 .... 15.00
11-20 .... 10.00
21-30 .... 7.00
31-40 .... 6.00
41-50 .... 5.00
51-60 .... 4.00
61-70 .... 3.00
71-200 .... 2.00

Betty and Veronica
Archie, 1987

1 .... 6.00
2-3 .... 4.00
4-20 .... 3.00
21-223 .... 2.00

Betty & Veronica Annual Digest Magazine
Archie, 1995

12-16 .... 2.00

Betty and Veronica Comics Digest
Archie, 1982

1 .... 9.00
2-3 .... 5.00
4-10 .... 4.00
11-43 .... 3.00

Betty and Veronica Digest Magazine
Archie, 1990

44-50 .... 3.00
51-192 .... 2.00

Betty and Veronica Double Digest
Archie, 1987

1 .... 8.00
2-3 .... 5.00
4-10 .... 4.00
11-108 .... 3.00
109-168 .... 4.00

Betty and Veronica Spectacular
Archie, 1992

1 .... 4.00
2-5 .... 3.00
6-87 .... 2.00

Betty & Veronica Summer Fun
Archie, 1994

1-4 .... 3.00
5-6 .... 2.00

Betty Boop 3-D
Blackthorne, 1986

1 .... 3.00

Betty Boop's Big Break
First, 1990

1 .... 6.00

Betty in Bondage: Betty Mae
Shunga

1 .... 7.00

Betty in Bondage
Shunga, 1994

1-8 .... 3.00
Ann 1-3 .... 6.00

Betty Page 3-D Comics
3-D Zone

1 .... 4.00

Betty Page 3-D Picture Book
3-D Zone

1 .... 4.00

Betty Page Captured Jungle Girl 3-D
3-D Zone, 1990

1 .... 4.00

Betty Pages
Pure Imagination, 1989

1 .... 6.00
1/2nd-9 .... 5.00

Bill Barnes Comics

Billi 99

Billy Cole

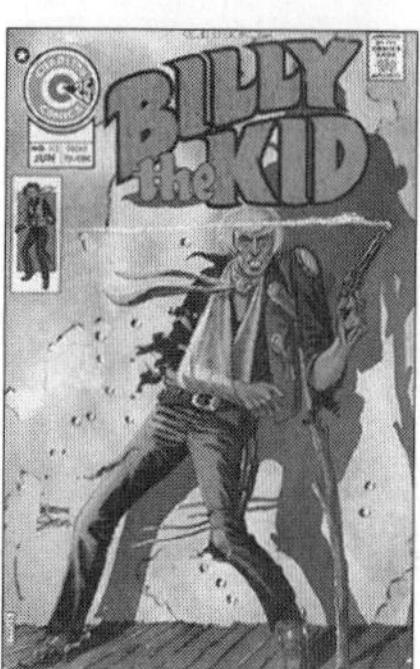

Billy the Kid

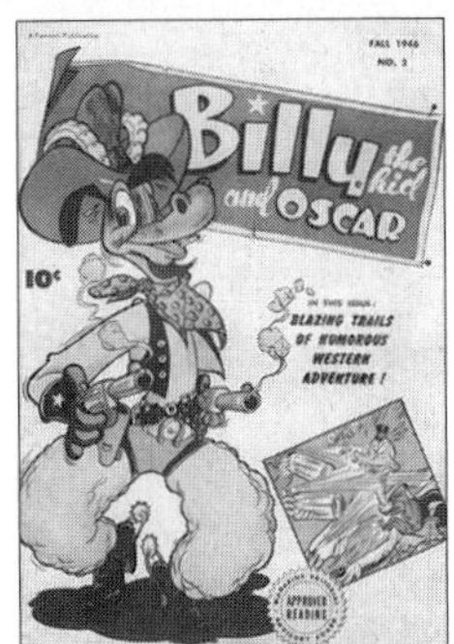
Billy the Kid and Oscar

Binky

Bio 90

Bio-Booster Armor Guyver

Betty Page: The 50's Rage
Illustration, 1993
1/A-2/B 3.00

Betty's Diary
Archie, 1986
1 ....4.00
2-5 ....3.00
6-40 ....2.00

Betty's Digest Magazine
Archie, 1996
1-2 ....2.00

Between the Sheets
Tokyopop, 2003
1 ....10.00

Beverly Hillbillies
Dell, 1963
1 ....60.00
2 ....38.00
3 ....28.00
4-5 ....24.00
6-10 ....18.00
11-17 ....15.00
18-21 ....12.00

Beware
Youthful, 1952
10 ....180.00
11-12 ....90.00

Beware
Trojan, 1953
13 (1) 400.00
14 (2) 250.00
15 (3)-16 (4) 200.00
5-13 ....175.00
14-15 ....150.00

Beware
Marvel, 1973
1 ....8.00
2-8 ....5.00

Beware Terror Tales
Fawcett, 1952
1 ....350.00
2 ....220.00
3-7 ....165.00
8 ....175.00

Beware the Creeper
DC, 1968
1 ....45.00
2-5 ....32.00
6 ....55.00

Beware the Creeper
DC, 2003
1-5 ....3.00

Bewitched
Dell, 1965
1 ....85.00
2 ....50.00
3-10 ....40.00
11-14 ....30.00

Beyblade
Viz, 2004
1-10 ....8.00

Beyond
Ace, 1950
1 ....265.00
2 ....175.00
3 ....120.00
4-10 ....110.00
11-20 ....85.00
21-30 ....80.00

Beyond!
Marvel, 2006
1-6 ....3.00

Beyond
Blue, 1996
1 ....3.00

Beyond Avalon
Image, 2005
1 ....3.00
2-3 ....4.00

Beyond Communion
Caliber
2 ....0.00
1 ....3.00

Beyond Mars
Blackthorne, 1989
1-5 ....2.00

Beyond the Grave
Charlton, 1975
1 ....7.00
2-3 ....4.00
4-17 ....3.00

Bicentennial Gross-Outs
Yentzer and Gonif, 1976
1 ....3.00

Biff Bang Pow!
Paisano, 1992
3 ....0.00
1-2 ....3.00

Big
Dark Horse, 1989
1 ....3.00

Big All-American Comic Book
DC, 1944
1 ....6,500.00

Big Ass Comics
Rip Off, 1969
1 ....50.00
1/2nd 24.00
1/3rd-1/4th 10.00
1/5th-1/6th 6.00
2 ....25.00
2/2nd 15.00

Big Bad Blood of Dracula
Apple
1-2 .... 3.00

Big Bang Comics: Round Table of America
Image, 2004
1 .... 4.00

Big Bang Comics
Caliber, 1994
0 .... 4.00
1-4 .... 3.00

Big Bang Comics
Image, 1996
1-22 .... 3.00
23 .... 4.00
24-26 .... 3.00
27-35 .... 4.00

Big Bang Presents: Ultiman Family
Image, 2005
1 .... 4.00

Big Bang
Zoo Arsonist
1 .... 3.00

Big Bang Summer Special
Image, 2003
1 .... 5.00

Big Black Kiss
Vortex, 1989
1-3 .... 4.00

Big Black Thing (Colin Upton's...)
Upton
1 .... 3.00

Big Blown Baby
Dark Horse, 1996
1-4 .... 3.00

Big Blue Couch Comix
Couch
1 .... 2.00

Big Boob Bondage
Antarctic, 1997
1 .... 3.00

Big Bruisers
Image, 1996
1 .... 4.00

Big Chief Wahoo
Eastern Color, 1942
1 .... 230.00
2 .... 125.00
3-5 .... 95.00
6-7 .... 65.00

Big Crap Scare
Fireman
1 .... 3.00

Big Daddy Danger
DC, 2002
1-9 .... 3.00

Big Dog Funnies
Rip Off, 1992
1 .... 3.00

Big Edsel Band
Ace
1 .... 2.00

Bigfoot
Idea & Design Works, 2005
1-4 .... 4.00

Big Funnies
Radio, 2001
1-8 .... 4.00

Bigger
Free Lunch, 1998
1 .... 4.00

Bigger: Will Rison & the Devil's Concubine
Free Lunch, 1998
1-4 .... 3.00

Bigg Time
DC
1 .... 15.00

Big Guy and Rusty the Boy Robot
Dark Horse, 1995
1-2 .... 10.00

Big Hair Productions
Image, 2000
1-2 .... 4.00

Big Lou
Side Show
1 .... 3.00

Big Monster Fight
Kidgang Comics
0-1 .... 3.00

Big Mouth
Starhead, 1996
1-7 .... 3.00

Big Numbers
Mad Love, 1990
1-2 .... 6.00

Big O Part 1
Viz, 2002
1-5 .... 4.00

Big O Part 2
Viz, 2002
1-4 .... 4.00

Big O Part 3
Viz, 2002
1-4 .... 4.00

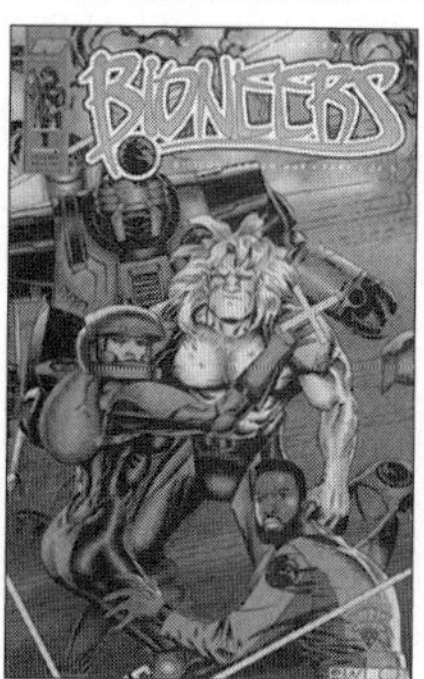

Bioneers

Birds of Prey

Birthright

Birth Rite

Bishop

Bizarre 3-D Zone

Bizarre Adventures

Bizarre Heroes

Big O Part 4
Viz, 2003
1-4 .... 4.00

Big Prize
Eternity, 1985
1-2 .... 2.00

Big Questions
Drawn & Quarterly, 2005
7 .... 5.00

Big Shot
Columbia, 1940
1 .... 1,000.00
2 .... 475.00
3 .... 385.00
4-5 .... 335.00
6-10 .... 275.00
11-13 .... 225.00
14 .... 300.00
15 .... 340.00
16-20 .... 160.00
21-27 .... 135.00
28 .... 185.00
29-30 .... 135.00
31-40 .... 110.00
41-49 .... 95.00
50-60 .... 85.00
61-70 .... 65.00
71-80 .... 55.00
81-104 .... 48.00

Big 3
Fox, 1940
1 .... 1,400.00
2 .... 650.00
3-5 .... 450.00
6-7 .... 375.00

Big Time
Delta, 1996
1-3 .... 2.00

Big Top
Toby, 1951
1 .... 50.00
2 .... 36.00

Big Top Bondage
Fantagraphics
1 .... 3.00

Big Town
DC, 1951
1 .... 500.00
2 .... 250.00
3 .... 185.00
4-5 .... 140.00
6-10 .... 110.00
11-20 .... 75.00
21-30 .... 65.00
31-50 .... 50.00

Big Town
Marvel, 2001
1-4 .... 4.00

Big Valley
Dell, 1966
1 .... 40.00
2-6 .... 25.00

Bijou Funnies
Kitchen Sink, 1968
1 .... 85.00
1/2nd-2 .... 30.00
3 .... 25.00
3/2nd 15.00
3/3rd 10.00
4 .... 25.00
5 .... 20.00
6-8 .... 18.00
8/2nd 4.00

Biker Mice from Mars
Marvel, 1993
1-3 .... 2.00

Bikini Assassin Team
Catfish
1 .... 3.00

Bikini Battle 3-D
3-D Zone
1 .... 4.00

Bill & Ted's Bogus Journey
Marvel, 1991
1 .... 3.00

Bill & Ted's Excellent Adventure Movie Adaptation
DC
1 .... 2.00

Bill & Ted's Excellent Comic Book
Marvel, 1991
1-12 .... 2.00

Bill Barnes Comics
Street & Smith, 1940
1 .... 525.00
2 .... 275.00
3-5 .... 200.00
6-12 .... 175.00

Bill Battle One-Man Army
Fawcett, 1952
1-4 .... 80.00

Bill Boyd Western
Fawcett, 1950
1 .... 250.00
2-6 .... 200.00
7-23 .... 100.00

Bill, the Galactic Hero
Topps, 1994
1-3 .... 5.00

Billi 99
Dark Horse
1-4 .... 4.00

Bill the Bull: Burnt Cain
Boneyard, 1992

1-3 ... 5.00

Bill the Bull: One Shot, One Bourbon, One Beer
Boneyard, 1994

1-2 ... 3.00

Bill the Clown
Slave Labor, 1992

1-1/2nd ... 3.00

Bill the Clown: Comedy Isn't Pretty
Slave Labor, 1992

1 ... 3.00

Bill the Clown: Death & Clown White
Slave Labor, 1993

1 ... 3.00

Billy Boy The Sick Little Fat Kid
Asylum, 2001

1 ... 3.00

Billy Buckskin
Atlas, 1955

1 ... 85.00

2 ... 55.00

3 ... 60.00

Billy Cole
Cult, 1994

1-4 ... 3.00

Billy Dogma
Modern, 1997

1-3 ... 3.00

Billy Joe Van Helsing: Redneck Vampire Hunter
Alpha

1 ... 3.00

Billy Nguyen, Private Eye
Attitude, 1988

1-3 ... 2.00

Billy Nguyen, Private Eye
Caliber

1 ... 3.00

Billy Ray Cyrus
Marvel Music

1 ... 6.00

Billy the Kid
Charlton, 1957

9 ... 58.00

10 ... 35.00

11 ... 40.00

12 ... 30.00

13 ... 40.00

14 ... 30.00

15-16 ... 40.00

17-19 ... 30.00

20-22 ... 35.00

23 ... 20.00

24-26 ... 35.00

27-30 ... 20.00

31-40 ... 14.00

41-50 ... 8.00

51-60 ... 7.00

61-70 ... 5.00

71-100 ... 4.00

101-153 ... 3.00

Billy the Kid Adventure Magazine
Toby, 1950

1 ... 175.00

2 ... 80.00

3-10 ... 75.00

11-20 ... 48.00

21-30 ... 36.00

Billy the Kid and Oscar
Fawcett, 1945

1 ... 75.00

2-3 ... 55.00

Billy the Kid's Old-Timey Oddities
Dark Horse, 2005

1-4 ... 3.00

Billy West
Standard, 1949

1 ... 60.00

2 ... 40.00

3-6 ... 28.00

7-8 ... 30.00

9 ... 28.00

B1N4RY
APComics, 2004

0-2 ... 4.00

3 ... 5.00

3/Sketch ... 6.00

4 ... 4.00

Binky
DC, 1970

72-75 ... 7.00

76-81 ... 6.00

82 ... 3.00

Binky's Buddies
DC, 1969

1 ... 26.00

2 ... 16.00

3 ... 12.00

4-12 ... 10.00

Bio 90
Bullet, 1992

1 ... 3.00

Bio-Booster Armor Guyver
Viz, 1993

1-5 ... 4.00

6-12 ... 3.00

Black and White Comics

Black Angel

Black Axe

Black Canary

Black Cat Comics

Black Cobra

Black Condor

Black Cross Special

Bio-Booster Armor Guyver Part 2
Viz, 1994

1-6 .... 3.00

Bio-Booster Armor Guyver Part 3
Viz, 1995

1-7 .... 3.00

Bio-Booster Armor Guyver Part 4
Viz, 1995

1-6 .... 3.00

Bio-Booster Armor Guyver Part 5
Viz, 1996

1-7 .... 3.00

Bio-Booster Armor Guyver Part 6
Viz, 1996

1-6 .... 3.00

Biologic Show
Fantagraphics, 1994

0-1 .... 3.00

Bioneers
Mirage, 1994

1-3 .... 3.00

Bionic Dog
Hugo Rex

1 .... 3.00

Bionicle
DC, 2001

1-9 .... 2.00

Bionic Woman
Charlton, 1977

1 .... 14.00
2-5 .... 6.00

Bionix
Maximum, 1996

1 .... 3.00

Bird
Entertainment, 1987

1 .... 2.00

Birdland
Fantagraphics, 1990

1-3 .... 2.00

Birdland (Vol. 2)
Fantagraphics, 1994

1 .... 3.00

Birds of Prey
DC, 1999

1 .... 4.00
2-7 .... 3.00
8 .... 12.00
☛Nightwing app.
9-75 .... 3.00
76 .... 15.00
☛1st Black Alice
77-99 .... 3.00
100 .... 4.00
101 .... 3.00

Birds of Prey: Batgirl
DC, 1998

1 .... 3.00

Birds of Prey: Catwoman
DC, 2003

1-2 .... 6.00

Birds of Prey: Manhunt
DC, 1996

1-4 .... 2.00

Birds of Prey: Revolution
DC, 1997

1 .... 3.00

Birds of Prey: Secret Files 2003
DC, 2003

1 .... 5.00

Birds of Prey: The Ravens
DC, 1998

1 .... 2.00

Birds of Prey: Wolves
DC, 1997

1 .... 3.00

Birth Caul
Eddie Campbell, 1999

1 .... 6.00

Birthday Boy
Beetlebomb

1-4 .... 3.00

Birthday Boy
Beetlebomb

1 .... 3.00

Birthday Riots
NBM

1 .... 15.00

Birthright
Fantagraphics, 1990

1-3 .... 3.00

Birthright
TSR

1 .... 2.00

Birth Rite
Congress

1-4 .... 3.00

Bishop
Marvel, 1994

1 .... 4.00
2-4 .... 3.00

Bishop The Last X-Man
Marvel, 1999
1 .... 3.00
2-11 .... 2.00
12 .... 3.00
13-16 .... 2.00

Bishop: Xse
Marvel, 1998
1-3 .... 3.00

Bisley's Scrapbook
Atomeka
1 .... 3.00

Bitch in Heat
Fantagraphics, 1997
1-14 .... 3.00

Bite Club
DC, 2004
1 .... 3.00
2 .... 4.00
3-6 .... 3.00

Bite Club: Vampire Crime Unit
DC, 2006
1-5 .... 3.00

Bits and Pieces
Mortified, 1994
1 .... 3.00

Bitter Cake
Tin Cup
1 .... 2.00

Bizarre 3-D Zone
Blackthorne, 1986
1-5 .... 2.00

Bizarre Adventures
Marvel, 1981
25-26 .... 3.00
27 .... 4.00
28 .... 5.00
29-34 .... 3.00

Bizarre Fantasy
Flashback, 1995
0 .... 3.00
1-2 .... 3.00

Bizarre Heroes
Kitchen Sink, 1990
1 .... 3.00

Bizarre Heroes
Fiasco, 1994
0-17 .... 3.00

Bizarre Sex
Kitchen Sink, 1972
1 .... 15.00
2 .... 9.00
3 .... 7.00
4 .... 5.00
4/2nd-4/3rd 4.00
5-8 .... 5.00
9 .... 18.00

Bizzarian
Ironcat, 2000
1-8 .... 3.00

B. Krigstein Sampler, A
Independent
1 .... 3.00

Blab!
Kitchen Sink, 1995
8 .... 17.00
9 .... 19.00
10-16 .... 20.00

Black & White
Image, 1994
1-3 .... 2.00

Black & White
Image, 1996
1 .... 3.00
Ashcan 1 .... 1.00

Black & White
Viz, 1999
1-3 .... 3.00

Black and White Bondage
Verotik
1 .... 5.00

Black and White Comics
Apex Novelties
1 .... 4.00

Black and White Theater
Double M, 1996
1-2 .... 3.00

Black Angel
Verotik, 1996
1 .... 10.00

Black Axe
Marvel, 1993
1-7 .... 2.00

Blackball Comics
Blackball, 1994
1 .... 3.00

Black Book
Eclipse, 1985
1 .... 2.00

Black Bow
Artline
1 .... 3.00

Blackburne Covenant
Dark Horse, 2003
1-4 .... 3.00

Black Canary
DC, 1991
1-4 .... 3.00

Black Diamond

Black Diamond Western

Black Fury

Black Goliath

Black Heart Billy

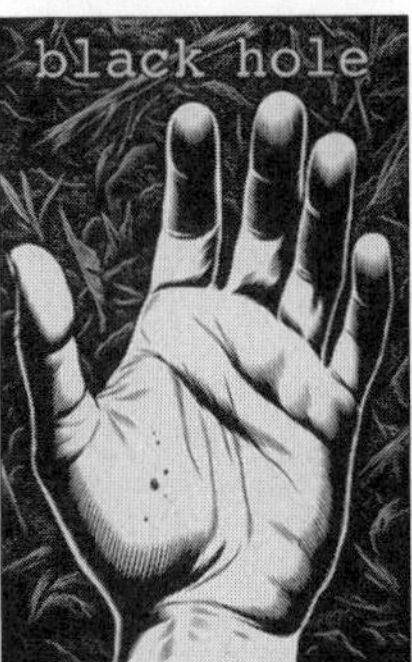

Black Hole

Blackmask

Black Mist

Black Canary
DC, 1993
1-12 .... 2.00

Black Canary/Oracle: Birds of Prey
DC, 1996
1 .... 4.00

Black Cat Comics
Harvey, 1946
1 .... 450.00
2 .... 275.00
3-5 .... 220.00
6-8 .... 175.00
9 .... 225.00
10-20 .... 135.00
21-29 .... 100.00
30 .... 150.00
31 .... 130.00
32-42 .... 125.00
43 .... 75.00
44-50 .... 125.00
51 .... 165.00
52-62 .... 54.00
63 .... 80.00
64-65 .... 75.00

Black Cat (The Origins)
Lorne-Harvey
1 .... 4.00

Black Cat The War Years
Recollections
1 .... 1.00

Black Cauldron
Scholastic
1 .... 4.00

Black Cobra
Ajax, 1954
1 .... 185.00
2 .... 120.00
3 .... 100.00

Black Condor
DC, 1992
1 .... 2.00
2-12 .... 1.00

Black Cross: Dirty Work
Dark Horse, 1997
1 .... 3.00

Black Cross Special
Dark Horse, 1988
1 .... 3.00
1/2nd 2.00

Black Diamond
AC, 1983
1-5 .... 2.00

Black Diamond Effect
Black Diamond Effect, 1991
1-7 .... 3.00

Black Diamond Western
Lev Gleason, 1949
9 .... 100.00
10 .... 70.00
11-12 .... 58.00
13-15 .... 45.00
16-28 .... 50.00
29-50 .... 30.00
51-52 .... 65.00
53-60 .... 24.00

Black Dragon
Marvel, 1985
1-4 .... 3.00
5-6 .... 2.00

Black Flag
Image, 1994
1 .... 2.00

Black Flag
Maximum, 1995
0-4/B 3.00

Black Forest
Image, 2003
1 .... 10.00

Black Fury
Charlton, 1955
1 .... 36.00
2 .... 18.00
3 .... 14.00
4-5 .... 10.00
6-15 .... 9.00
16-18 .... 30.00
19-30 .... 6.00
31-57 .... 5.00

Black Goliath
Marvel, 1976
1 .... 11.00
2 .... 5.00
2/30¢ 20.00
3 .... 4.00
3/30¢ 20.00
4 .... 4.00
4/30¢ 20.00
5 .... 4.00

Black Harvest
Devil's Due, 2005
1-6 .... 3.00

Blackhawk
DC, 1944
9 .... 2,600.00
10 .... 1,100.00
11 .... 900.00
12-15 .... 800.00
16-20 .... 525.00
21-25 .... 460.00
26-30 .... 400.00
31-35 .... 350.00
36-40 .... 300.00
41-49 .... 225.00

50 .... 200.00
51-60 .... 165.00
61-70 .... 145.00
71 .... 200.00
☛Blackhawk origin
72-80 .... 130.00
81-86 .... 125.00
87-92 .... 120.00
93 .... 135.00
94-99 .... 110.00
100 .... 140.00
101-107 .... 105.00
108 .... 325.00
☛1st DC issue
109 .... 130.00
110-117 .... 110.00
118 .... 135.00
119-130 .... 85.00
131-140 .... 65.00
141-149 .... 50.00
150-163 .... 48.00
164 .... 60.00
165-166 .... 48.00
167-180 .... 22.00
181-200 .... 16.00
201-227 .... 15.00
228 .... 30.00
229-243 .... 15.00
244-260 .... 4.00
261-273 .... 3.00

Blackhawk
DC, 1988
1-3 .... 4.00

Blackhawk
DC, 1989
1-6 .... 2.00
7 .... 3.00
8-16 .... 2.00
Ann 1 .... 3.00
Special 1 .... 4.00

Black Heart: Assassin
Iguana
1 .... 3.00

Black Heart Billy
Slave Labor, 2000
1-2 .... 3.00

Black Hole
Kitchen Sink, 1995
1-5 .... 4.00
6-10 .... 5.00

Black Hole
Whitman, 1980
1-4 .... 2.00

Black Hood
M.L.J., 1943
9 .... 650.00
10 .... 375.00
11 .... 275.00
12-18 .... 240.00
19 .... 315.00

Black Hood
DC, 1991
1-12 .... 1.00
Ann 1 .... 2.00

Black Hood
Archie, 1983
1 .... 3.00
2-3 .... 2.00

Blackjack
Dark Angel, 1996
1-4 .... 3.00
Special 1 .... 4.00

Blackjack
Dark Angel, 1997
1-2 .... 3.00

Black Jack
Charlton, 1957
20 .... 40.00
21 .... 25.00
22-23 .... 35.00
24-26 .... 45.00
27 .... 25.00
28 .... 45.00
29-30 .... 25.00

Black Jack
Viz, 1999
1 .... 4.00
Special 1 .... 3.00

Black Kiss
Vortex, 1988
1 .... 3.00
1/2nd-1/3rd 2.00
2 .... 3.00
2/2nd-12 .... 2.00

Black Knight
Toby, 1953
1 .... 150.00

Black Knight
Atlas, 1955
1 .... 575.00
2 .... 375.00
3-5 .... 285.00

Black Knight
Marvel, 1990
1-4 .... 2.00

Black Knight: Exodus
Marvel, 1996
1 .... 3.00

Black Lamb
DC, 1996
1-6 .... 3.00

Blacklight
Image, 2005
1-2 .... 3.00

Blackmoon

Black Ops

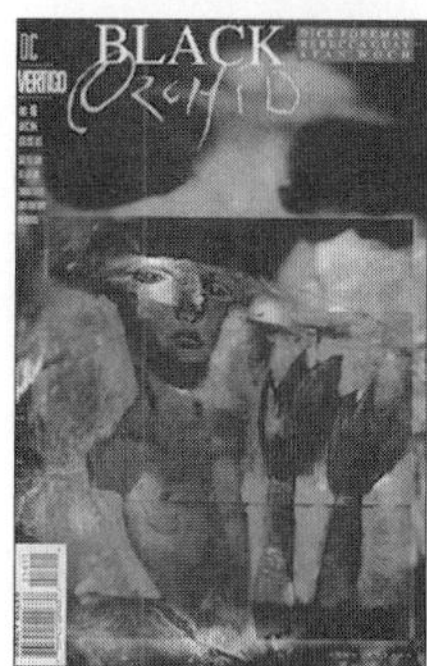

Black Orchid

Black Panther

Black Phantom

Black Rider

Black Scorpion

Blackstar

Black Lightning
DC, 1977

1 .... 10.00
2-11 .... 5.00

Black Lightning
DC, 1995

1 .... 3.00
2-5 .... 2.00
6 .... 3.00
7-13 .... 2.00

Black Lion The Bantu Warrior
Heroes from the Hood, 1997

1 .... 3.00

Black Magic
Prize, 1950

1 .... 640.00
2 .... 340.00
3 .... 250.00
4-6 .... 200.00

Black Magic
Prize, 1951

1 .... 165.00
2-12 .... 140.00

Black Magic
Prize, 1952

1-6 .... 125.00

Black Magic
Prize, 1953

1-2 .... 140.00
3 .... 300.00
4 .... 200.00
5 .... 160.00
6 .... 50.00

Black Magic
Prize, 1954

1 .... 50.00
2-3 .... 45.00

Black Magic
Prize, 1957

1-6 .... 36.00

Black Magic
Prize, 1958

1-6 .... 32.00

Black Magic
Prize, 1961

1-5 .... 30.00

Black Magic
DC, 1973

1 .... 15.00
2-9 .... 7.00

Black Magic
Eclipse, 1990

1 .... 4.00
2-4 .... 3.00

Blackmask
DC, 2000

1-3 .... 5.00

Blackmask
Eastern, 1988

1-3 .... 2.00

Black Mist
Caliber, 1994

1-4 .... 3.00

Black Mist: Blood of Kali
Caliber, 1998

1-3 .... 3.00

Blackmoon
U.S.Comics, 1985

1-3 .... 2.00

Black Ops
Image, 1996

1-5/B 3.00

Black Orchid
DC, 1993

1 .... 3.00
1/Platinum 5.00
2-22 .... 2.00
Ann 1 .... 4.00

Black Orchid
DC, 1988

1 .... 6.00
☛1st U.S. Gaiman
2-3 .... 5.00

Black Panther
Marvel, 1977

1 .... 12.00
2 .... 7.00
3-4 .... 5.00
4/35¢ 15.00
5 .... 5.00
5/35¢ 15.00
6-10 .... 5.00
11-15 .... 4.00

Black Panther
Marvel, 1998

1 .... 5.00
1/Variant 7.00
2/A-2/B 4.00
3-62 .... 3.00

Black Panther
Marvel, 1988

1-4 .... 2.00

Black Panther
Marvel, 2005

1 .... 6.00
1/2nd 4.00
1/Ribic 20.00
2-17 .... 3.00
18 .... 4.00
19-20 .... 3.00
21 .... 14.00

22 ... 6.00
23-41 ... 5.00

Black Panther: Panther's Prey

Marvel, 1991

1-4 ... 5.00

Black Pearl

Dark Horse, 1996

1 ... 4.00
2-5 ... 3.00

Black Phantom

AC

1-3 ... 3.00

Black Phantom

Magazine Enterprises, 1954

1 ... 250.00

Black Raven

ArtEffect Entertainment, 1998

1 ... 3.00

Black Rider

Atlas, 1950

8 ... 260.00
9 ... 125.00
10 ... 155.00
11-14 ... 95.00
15-19 ... 80.00
20 ... 90.00
21-27 ... 75.00

Black Rider Rides Again!

Atlas, 1957

1 ... 70.00

Black Sabbath

Rock-It, 1994

1 ... 4.00

Black Scorpion

Special Studio

1-3 ... 3.00

Black September

Malibu, 1993

Infinity ... 2.00

Blackstar

Imperial, 1987

1-2 ... 2.00

Blackstone, the Magician Detective Fights Crime

EC, 1947

1 ... 440.00

Blackstone, Master Magician Comics

Vital, 1946

1 ... 250.00
2-3 ... 175.00

Black Sun

WildStorm, 2002

1/A ... 0.00
1-6 ... 3.00

Black Sun: X-Men

Marvel, 2000

1 ... 3.00
1/A ... 6.00
2-5 ... 3.00

Black Swan Comics

M.L.J., 1945

1 ... 450.00

Black Terror

Visual Editions, 1942

1 ... 1,850.00
2 ... 725.00
3 ... 500.00
4-5 ... 425.00
6-10 ... 365.00
11-20 ... 300.00
21 ... 315.00
22-27 ... 275.00

Black Terror

Eclipse, 1989

1 ... 5.00
2 ... 5.00
3 ... 5.00

Blackthorne's 3 in 1

Blackthorne, 1986

1-2 ... 2.00

Blackthorne's Harvey Flip Book

Blackthorne

1 ... 2.00

Black Tide

Image, 2001

1/A-4 ... 3.00

Black Tide

Avatar, 2003

1-10 ... 3.00

Black Web

Inks

1-2 ... 3.00

Black Widow

Marvel, 1999

1 ... 4.00
2-3 ... 3.00

Black Widow

Marvel, 2001

1-3 ... 3.00

Black Widow

Marvel, 2004

1-6 ... 3.00

Black Widow: Pale Little Spider

Marvel, 2002

1-3 ... 3.00

Black Swan Comics

Black Web

Blackwulf

Blade of Shuriken

Blade of the Immortal

Blanche Goes to Hollywood

Blanche Goes to New York

Blast Corps

Black Widow: Things They Say About Her
Marvel, 2005
1-2 .... 3.00

Black Widow 2
Marvel, 2005
1-6 .... 3.00

Black Widow: Web of Intrigue
Marvel, 1999
1 .... 4.00

Blackwulf
Marvel, 1994
1 .... 3.00
2-10 .... 2.00

Black Zeppelin
Renegade, 1985
1-5 .... 2.00

Blade
Buccaneer, 1989
1-2 .... 2.00

Blade
Marvel, 1997
1 .... 2.00

Blade
Marvel, 1998
1 .... 4.00

Blade
Marvel, 1998
1-4 .... 3.00

Blade
Marvel, 1998
1-6 .... 4.00

Blade
Marvel, 2006
1-4 .... 3.00

Blade of Heaven
Tokyopop, 2005
1-8 .... 10.00

Blade of Kumori
Devil's Due, 2005
1-5 .... 3.00

Blade of Shuriken
Eternity, 1987
1-5 .... 2.00

Blade of the Immortal
Dark Horse, 1996
1 .... 4.00
2-8 .... 3.00
9-11 .... 4.00
12-33 .... 3.00
34 .... 4.00
35 .... 3.00
36-38 .... 4.00
39-99 .... 3.00
100 .... 6.00
101-121 .... 3.00

Blade Runner
Marvel, 1982
1 .... 2.00
2 .... 1.00

Blade: Sins of the Father
Marvel, 1998
1 .... 6.00

Bladesmen
Blue Comet
0-2 .... 2.00

Blade: The Vampire-Hunter
Marvel, 1994
1 .... 3.00
2-10 .... 2.00

Blade: Vampire Hunter
Marvel, 1999
1 .... 4.00
2-6 .... 3.00

Blade 2: Movie Adaptation
Marvel, 2002
1 .... 6.00

Blair Which?
Dark Horse, 1999
1 .... 3.00

Blair Witch Chronicles
Oni, 2000
1-4 .... 3.00

Blair Witch: Dark Testaments
Image, 2000
1 .... 3.00

Blair Witch Project
Oni, 1999
1 .... 5.00
1/2nd 3.00

Blame!
Tokyopop, 2005
1-10 .... 10.00

Blanche Goes to Hollywood
Dark Horse
1 .... 3.00

Blanche Goes to New York
Dark Horse, 1992
1 .... 3.00

Blarney
Discovery
1 .... 3.00

Blast!
John Brown, 1991
1-7 .... 4.00

Blast Corps
Dark Horse, 1998
1 .... 3.00

Blasters Special
DC, 1989
1 .... 2.00

Blast-Off
Harvey, 1965
1 .... 28.00

Blaze
Marvel, 1994
1 .... 3.00
2-12 .... 2.00

Blaze Carson
Marvel, 1948
1 .... 125.00
2 .... 90.00
3-5 .... 85.00

Blaze: Legacy of Blood
Marvel, 1993
1-4 .... 2.00

Blaze of Glory
Marvel, 2000
1-4 .... 3.00

Blaze The Wonder Collie
Marvel, 1949
2-3 .... 100.00

Blazin' Barrels
Tokyopop, 2005
1-3 .... 10.00

Blazing Battle Tales
Seaboard, 1975
1 .... 3.00

Blazing Combat
Warren, 1965
1 .... 90.00
2-3 .... 30.00
4 .... 40.00
Ann 1 .... 45.00

Blazing Combat
Apple, 1993
1-2 .... 5.00

Blazing Combat: World War I and World War II
Apple, 1994
1-2 .... 4.00

Blazing Comics
Enwil, 1944
1 .... 300.00
2-5 .... 150.00

Blazing Comics
Enwil, 1955
5-6 .... 100.00

Blazing Foxholes
Fantagraphics, 1994
1-3 .... 3.00

Blazing Sixguns
Avon, 1952
1 .... 100.00

Blazing West
ACG, 1948
1 .... 85.00
2 .... 48.00
3-5 .... 36.00
6-10 .... 30.00
11-13 .... 24.00
14 .... 58.00
15 .... 30.00
16-17 .... 24.00
18-20 .... 22.00
21-22 .... 20.00

Blazing Western
AC
1 .... 3.00

Blazing Western
Avalon, 1997
1 .... 3.00

Bleach
Viz, 2004
1-26 .... 8.00

Bleat
Slave Labor, 1995
1 .... 3.00

Bleeding Heart
Fantagraphics, 1991
1-5 .... 3.00

Blessed Pope Pius X and the Confraternity of Christian Doctrine
George A. Pflaum
1 .... 3.00

Blindside
Image, 1996
1 .... 1.00
1/A-1/B 3.00
2-7 .... 1.00

Blink
Marvel, 2001
1-4 .... 3.00

Blip
Marvel, 1983
1-7 .... 1.00

Blip
Bardic, 1998
1 .... 1.00

Blip and the C.C.A.D.S.
Amazing
1-2 .... 2.00

Blasters Special

Blast-Off

Blaze

Blaze of Glory

Blazing West

Blindside

Blink

Blite

Bliss Alley
Image, 1997

1-2 .... 3.00

Blite
Fantagraphics

1 .... 2.00

Blitz
Nightwynd

1-4 .... 3.00

Blitzkrieg
DC, 1976

1 .... 16.00
2 .... 8.00
3-5 .... 6.00

Blockade
Heritage Collection

1 .... 10.00

Blokhedz
Image, 2003

1-2 .... 3.00

Blonde
Fantagraphics

1-3 .... 3.00

Blonde Addiction
Blitzweasel

1-4 .... 3.00

Blonde Avenger
Blitz Weasel, 1993

1-8 .... 4.00

Blonde Avenger: Crossover Crazzeee
Blitzweasel

1 .... 4.00

Blonde Avenger
Fantagraphics, 1993

1-4 .... 3.00

Blonde Avenger Monthly
Blitzweasel, 1996

1 .... 4.00
2-6 .... 3.00

Blonde Avenger One-Shot Special: The Spying Game
Blitzweasel, 1996

1 .... 3.00

Blonde: Bondage Palace
Fantagraphics, 1994

1-5 .... 3.00

Blonde Phantom
Timely, 1946

12 .... 1,075.00
13 .... 665.00
14-15 .... 590.00
16 .... 700.00
17-22 .... 500.00

Blondie Comics
David McKay, 1947

1 .... 245.00
2 .... 100.00
3-5 .... 75.00
6-10 .... 45.00
11-16 .... 30.00
17-20 .... 22.00
21-50 .... 16.00
51-80 .... 12.00
81-99 .... 9.00
100 .... 10.00
101-124 .... 8.00
125 .... 9.00
126-130 .... 8.00
131-140 .... 7.00
141-167 .... 8.00
168-180 .... 5.00
181-200 .... 4.00
201-222 .... 3.00

Blood
Fantaco

1 .... 4.00

Blood and Glory
Marvel

1-3 .... 6.00

Blood & Kisses
Fantaco

1 .... 3.00
2 .... 4.00

Blood & Roses Adventures
Knight, 1995

1 .... 3.00

Blood & Roses: Future Past Tense
Sky, 1993

1 .... 2.00
1/Ashcan-1/Gold 3.00
2 .... 2.00

Blood & Roses: Search for the Time-Stone
Sky, 1994

1-2 .... 3.00

Blood & Roses Special
Knight, 1996

1 .... 3.00

Blood and Shadows
DC

1-4 .... 6.00

Blood and Thunder
Conquest

1 .... 3.00

Blood & Water
Slave Labor, 1991

1 .... 3.00

Blood and Water
DC, 2003

1-5 .... 3.00

Blood: A Tale
Marvel, 1987

1-4 .... 3.00

Blood: A Tale
DC, 1996

1-4 .... 3.00

Bloodbath
DC, 1993

1-2 .... 4.00

Blood Bounty
Highland

1 .... 2.00

Bloodbrothers
Eternity

1-4 .... 2.00

Bloodchilde
Millennium, 1994

1-4 .... 3.00

Blood Club
Kitchen Sink

2 .... 6.00

Bloodfang
Epitaph, 1996

0-1 .... 3.00

Blood Feast
Eternity

1-2/Variant 3.00

Blood Feast: The Screenplay
Eternity

1 .... 5.00

Bloodfire
Lightning, 1993

0-1/Variant 4.00
2-12 .... 3.00

Bloodfire/Hellina
Lightning, 1995

1 .... 3.00
1/Nude 4.00
1/Platinum 3.00

Blood Gothic
Fantaco

1-2 .... 5.00

Bloodhound
DC, 2004

1-10 .... 3.00

Bloodhunter
Brainstorm, 1996

1 .... 3.00

Blood is the Harvest
Catechetical Guild, 1950

1 .... 750.00

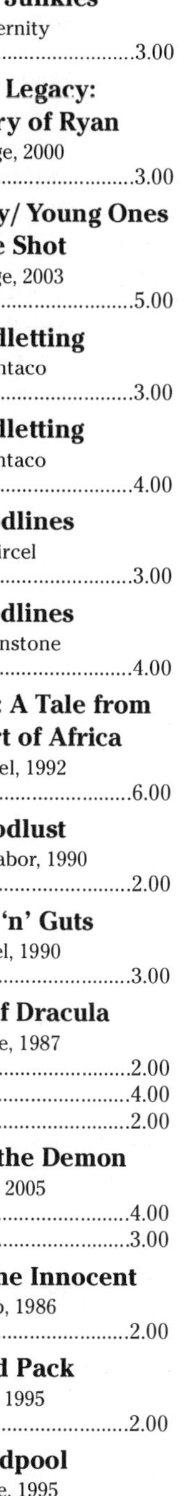

Blood Is the Harvest
Eclipse, 1992

1-4 .... 3.00

Blood Junkies
Eternity

1-2 .... 3.00

Blood Legacy: The Story of Ryan
Image, 2000

1-4 .... 3.00

Blood Legacy/ Young Ones One Shot
Image, 2003

1 .... 5.00

Bloodletting
Fantaco

1 .... 3.00

Bloodletting
Fantaco

1-2 .... 4.00

Bloodlines
Aircel

1-7 .... 3.00

Bloodlines
Moonstone

1 .... 4.00

Bloodlines: A Tale from the Heart of Africa
Marvel, 1992

1 .... 6.00

Bloodlust
Slave Labor, 1990

1 .... 2.00

Blood 'n' Guts
Aircel, 1990

1-4 .... 3.00

Blood of Dracula
Apple, 1987

1-14 .... 2.00
15 .... 4.00
16-20 .... 2.00

Blood of the Demon
DC, 2005

1 .... 4.00
2-17 .... 3.00

Blood of the Innocent
Warp, 1986

1-4 .... 2.00

Blood Pack
DC, 1995

1-4 .... 2.00

Bloodpool
Image, 1995

1-4 .... 3.00
Special 1 .... 4.00

Blitzkrieg

Blonde Phantom

Blondie Comics

Blood and Glory

Bloodfang

Blood is the Harvest

Blood Reign

Bloodseed

Blood Reign
Fathom, 1991

1-8 .... 3.00

Bloodscent
Comico, 1988

1 .... 2.00

Bloodseed
Marvel, 1993

1-2 .... 2.00

Bloodshed
Damage!, 1994

1-3 .... 3.00
Ashcan 1 .... 2.00

Bloodshot
Valiant, 1993

0/VVSS 25.00
0/PlatError 750.00
0 .... 3.00
0/Gold 25.00
1 .... 2.00
2-6 .... 1.00
6/VVSS 50.00
7-15 .... 1.00
16 .... 2.00
17-24 .... 1.00
25-37 .... 2.00
38-43 .... 3.00
44-47 .... 4.00
48-49 .... 5.00
50 .... 6.00
51 .... 10.00
YB 1-2 .... 5.00

Bloodshot
Acclaim, 1997

1-16 .... 3.00
Ashcan 1 .... 1.00

Bloodstone
Marvel, 2001

1-4 .... 3.00

Bloodstream
Image, 2004

1-4 .... 3.00

Bloodstrike
Image, 1993

1 .... 3.00
2-12 .... 2.00
13-24 .... 3.00
25 .... 2.00

Bloodstrike Assassin
Image, 1995

0-4 .... 3.00

Bloodsucker
Fantagraphics

1 .... 3.00

Blood Sword
Jademan, 1988

1-51 .... 2.00

Blood Sword Dynasty
Jademan, 1989

1-29 .... 1.00

Blood Syndicate
DC, 1993

1 .... 2.00
1/CS 3.00
2-9 .... 2.00
10 .... 3.00
11-24 .... 2.00
25 .... 3.00
26-27 .... 2.00
28 .... 3.00
29 .... 1.00
30-32 .... 3.00
33 .... 1.00
34 .... 3.00
35 .... 4.00

Bloodthirst: Terminus Option
Alpha Productions

1-2 .... 3.00

Bloodthirst: The Nightfall Conspiracy
Alpha

1-2 .... 3.00

Bloodthirsty Pirate Tales
Black Swan, 1995

1-8 .... 3.00

Blood Ties
Full Moon, 1991

1 .... 2.00

Bloodwing
Eternity, 1988

1-6 .... 2.00

Bloodwulf
Image, 1995

1-Summer 1 .... 3.00

Bloody Bones & Blackeyed Peas
Galaxy

1 .... 1.00

Bloodyhot
Parody

1 .... 3.00

Bloody Mary
DC, 1996

1-4 .... 2.00

Bloody Mary: Lady Liberty
DC, 1997

1-4 .... 3.00

Bloody School
Curtis Comic

1 .... 3.00

Blowjob
Fantagraphics, 2001

1 ..... 10.00
2-5 ..... 7.00
6-10 ..... 5.00
11-23 ..... 4.00

Blue
Image, 1999

1-2 ..... 3.00

Bluebeard
Slave Labor, 1993

1-3 ..... 3.00

Blue Beetle
Fox, 1939

1 ..... 2,750.00
2 ..... 950.00
3 ..... 700.00
4 ..... 475.00
5 ..... 425.00
6 ..... 390.00
7-8 ..... 350.00
9-15 ..... 325.00
16-20 ..... 275.00
21-27 ..... 200.00
28-30 ..... 175.00
31-40 ..... 165.00
41-45 ..... 140.00
46 ..... 150.00
47 ..... 800.00
48-50 ..... 625.00
51-54 ..... 510.00
55-57 ..... 485.00
58-60 ..... 100.00

Blue Beetle
Charlton, 1964

1 ..... 45.00
2 ..... 30.00
3-5 ..... 20.00

Blue Beetle
Charlton, 1965

50-54 ..... 27.00
1 ..... 60.00
2 ..... 40.00
3-5 ..... 27.00

Blue Beetle
Modern, 1977

1-3 ..... 5.00

Blue Beetle
DC, 1986

1-24 ..... 1.00

Blue Beetle
DC, 2006

1 ..... 6.00
1/2nd 4.00
2-10 ..... 3.00

Blue Block
Kitchen Sink

1 ..... 3.00

Blue Bolt
Novelty, 1940

1 ..... 2,900.00
2 ..... 1,400.00
3 ..... 1,100.00
4 ..... 805.00
5 ..... 950.00
6-12 ..... 800.00

Blue Bolt
Novelty, 1941

1 ..... 250.00
2 ..... 180.00
3-6 ..... 150.00
7-12 ..... 115.00

Blue Bolt
Novelty, 1942

1 ..... 100.00
2-12 ..... 85.00

Blue Bolt
Novelty, 1943

1 ..... 90.00
2-12 ..... 60.00

Blue Bolt
Novelty, 1944

1-8 ..... 45.00

Blue Bolt
Novelty, 1945

1-10 ..... 38.00

Blue Bolt
Novelty, 1946

1-12 ..... 32.00

Blue Bolt
Premium, 1947

1-12 ..... 32.00

Blue Bolt
Premium, 1948

1-9 ..... 32.00

Blue Bolt
Premium, 1949

1-2 ..... 32.00

Blue Bolt
Star Publications, 1949

102-104 ..... 160.00
105 ..... 325.00
106-119 ..... 250.00

Blue Bulleteer
AC, 1989

1 ..... 3.00

Blue Circle
REWL Publications, 1944

1 ..... 160.00
2 ..... 105.00
3 ..... 130.00
4-6 ..... 85.00

Bloodshot

Blood Sword Dynasty

Blood Syndicate

Blue

Blue Circle

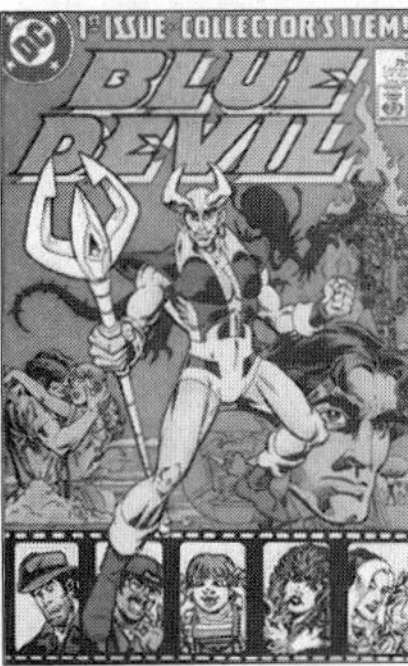

Blue Devil

Blue Ribbon Comics

B-Movie Presents

Blue Devil
DC, 1984

1-31 .... 1.00
Ann 1 .... 2.00

Blue Hole
Christine Shields

1 .... 3.00

Blue Ice
Martyr, 1992

1-2 .... 3.00

Blue Lily
Dark Horse, 1993

1-4 .... 4.00

Blue Loco
Kitchen Sink, 1997

1 .... 6.00

Blue Monday: Absolute Beginners
Oni, 2001

1-4 .... 3.00

Blue Monday: Lovecats
Oni, 2002

1 .... 3.00

Blue Monday: Painted Moon
Oni, 2004

1-4 .... 3.00

Blue Monday: The Kids Are Alright
Oni, 2000

1-3 .... 3.00

Blue Moon
Mu, 1992

1-5 .... 3.00

Blue Moon
Aeon, 1994

1 .... 3.00

Blue Notebook
NBM

1 .... 14.00

Blue Ribbon Comics
M.L.J., 1939

1 .... 2,200.00
2 .... 900.00
3-4 .... 600.00
5-8 .... 440.00
9 .... 1,850.00
10-13 .... 650.00
14-22 .... 550.00

Blue Ribbon Comics
Archie, 1983

1 .... 3.00
2-14 .... 2.00

B-Movie Presents
B-Movie

1-4 .... 2.00

BMW Films: The Hire
Dark Horse, 2004

1-4 .... 3.00

Board of Superheros
Not Available

1 .... 1.00

Bobby Benson's B-Bar-B Riders
Magazine Enterprises, 1950

1 .... 250.00
2 .... 95.00
3-5 .... 75.00
6-8 .... 65.00
9 .... 90.00
10 .... 65.00
11 .... 90.00
12 .... 60.00
13 .... 90.00
14-15 .... 75.00
16 .... 70.00
17-19 .... 60.00
20 .... 75.00

Bobby Benson's B-Bar-B Riders
AC, 1990

1 .... 3.00

Bobby Ruckers
Art

1 .... 3.00

Bobby Sherman
Charlton, 1972

1 .... 15.00
2-7 .... 10.00

Bob Colt
Fawcett, 1950

1 .... 225.00
2 .... 150.00
3-5 .... 110.00
6-10 .... 90.00

Bob, the Galactic Bum
DC, 1995

1-4 .... 2.00

Bob Marley, Tale of the Tuff Gong
Marvel

1-3 .... 6.00

Bobobo-bo Bo-bobo
Viz, 2005

1 .... 8.00

"Bob's" Favorite Comics
Rip Off

1-1/3rd 3.00

Bob Steele Western
Fawcett, 1950
1 .... 400.00
2-10 .... 200.00

Bob Steele Western
AC, 1990
1 .... 3.00

Bob Swift
Fawcett, 1951
1 .... 30.00
2-5 .... 20.00

Body Bags
Dark Horse, 1996
1 .... 4.00
2-Ashcan 1 .... 3.00

Body Bags: Father's Day
Image, 2005
1-2 .... 6.00

Body Count
Aircel
1-4 .... 2.00

Bodycount
Image, 1996
1-4 .... 3.00

Body Doubles
DC, 1999
1-4 .... 3.00

Body Doubles (Villains)
DC, 1998
1 .... 2.00

Bodyguard
Aircel, 1990
1-3 .... 3.00

Body Heat
NBM
1-2 .... 12.00

Body Paint
Fantagraphics, 1995
1-4 .... 3.00

Body Swap
Roger Mason
1 .... 3.00

Boffo in Hell
Neatly Chiseled Features
1 .... 3.00

Boffo Laffs
Paragraphics
1 .... 3.00
2-5 .... 2.00

Boffy the Vampire Layer
Fantagraphics, 2000
1-3 .... 3.00

Bogie Man
Fat Man, 1989
1-4 .... 3.00

Bogie Man: Chinatoon
Atomeka
1-4 .... 3.00

Bogie Man: The Manhattan Project
Tundra, 1992
1 .... 5.00

Bog Swamp Demon
Hall of Heroes, 1996
1-1/Variant 3.00
1/Commem 5.00
2-4 .... 3.00

Bohos
Image, 1998
1-3 .... 3.00

Bo Jackson vs. Michael Jordan
Celebrity
1-2 .... 3.00

Bold Adventure
Pacific, 1983
1-3 .... 2.00

Bolt and Starforce Six
AC, 1984
1 .... 2.00

Bolt Special
AC
1 .... 2.00

Bomarc
Nightwynd
1-3 .... 3.00

Bomba The Jungle Boy
DC, 1967
1 .... 16.00
2-7 .... 8.00

Bombast
Topps, 1993
1 .... 3.00

Bombastic
Screaming Dodo, 1996
1-5 .... 3.00

Bomber Comics
Elliott, 1944
1 .... 400.00
2 .... 275.00
3 .... 225.00
4 .... 250.00

Bomb Queen
Image, 2006
1-4 .... 4.00

Bomb Queen
Image, 2006
1-3 .... 4.00

Board of Superheros

Body Bags

Body Doubles

Boffo in Hell

Boffo Laffs

Bohos

Bolt and Starforce Six

Bombast

Bomb Queen vs. Blacklight
Image, 2006

1 .... 4.00

Bonafide
Bonafide, 1994

0-0/2nd 4.00

Bonanza
Gold Key, 1962

1 .... 110.00
2 .... 75.00
3-5 .... 50.00
6-10 .... 32.00
11-20 .... 22.00
21-30 .... 15.00
31-37 .... 12.00

Bondage Confessions
Fantagraphics, 1998

1-4 .... 3.00

Bondage Fairies
Antarctic, 1994

1 .... 4.00
1/2nd-1/4th 3.00
2 .... 4.00
2/2nd-6/2nd 3.00

Bondage Fairies Extreme
Fantagraphics, 1999

1-15 .... 4.00

Bondage Girls at War
Fantagraphics, 1996

1-6 .... 3.00

Bone
Cartoon Books, 1991

1 .... 80.00
1/2nd 8.00
1/3rd-1/9th 3.00
2 .... 45.00
2/2nd 6.00
2/3rd-2/8th 3.00
3 .... 25.00
3/2nd-3/8th 3.00
4 .... 16.00
4/2nd-4/6th 3.00
5 .... 12.00
5/2nd-5/7th 3.00
6 .... 7.00
6/2nd-6/6th 3.00
7 .... 7.00
7/2nd-7/5th 3.00
8 .... 7.00
8/2nd-8/7th 3.00
9 .... 4.00
9/2nd-9/4th 3.00
10 .... 4.00
10/2nd-10/3rd 3.00
11 .... 4.00
11/2nd 3.00
12 .... 4.00
12/2nd-12/3rd 3.00
13 .... 4.00
13/2nd 3.00
13.5-13.5/Gold 4.00
14-55 .... 3.00
Special 1 .... 2.00

Bone
Image, 1993

1-20 .... 3.00

Bone Sourcebook
Image, 1995

1/A-1/B 2.00

Bonerest
Image, 2005

1-8 .... 3.00

Bones
Malibu, 1987

1-4 .... 2.00

Bone Saw
Tundra

1 .... 15.00

Boneshaker
Caliber, 1994

1 .... 4.00

Boneyard
NBM, 2001

1-28 .... 3.00

Boneyard Press 1993 Tourbook
Boneyard

1 .... 2.00

Bongo Special Edition
Bongo

1 .... 20.00

Boof
Iconografix

1 .... 3.00

Boof
Image, 1994

1-6 .... 2.00

Boof and the Bruise Crew
Image, 1994

1-6 .... 2.00

Boogeyman
Dark Horse, 1998

1-4 .... 3.00

Boogieman
Rion

1 .... 2.00

Book
Dreamsmith, 1998

1-2 .... 4.00

Book of Angels
Caliber, 1997

1 .... 4.00

Book of Ballads and Sagas
Green Man, 1996
1-2 .... 3.00
3-4 .... 4.00

Book of Fate
DC, 1997
1-9 .... 2.00
10-12 .... 3.00

Book of Lost Souls
Marvel, 2005
1-6 .... 3.00

Book of Night
Dark Horse, 1987
1 .... 3.00
2-3 .... 2.00

Book of Shadows
Image, 2006
1-2 .... 4.00

Book of Spells
Double Edge, 1994
1-4 .... 2.00

Book of the Damned: A Hellraiser Companion
Marvel, 1991
1-4 .... 5.00

Book of the Dead
Marvel, 1993
1-4 .... 2.00

Book of the SubGenius
Simon & Schuster
1 .... 11.00

Book of the Tarot
Caliber
1 .... 4.00

Book of Thoth
Circle, 1995
1 .... 3.00

Book on the Edge of Forever
Fantagraphics, 1994
1 .... 7.00

Books of Doom
Marvel, 2006
1-6 .... 3.00

Books of Faerie
DC, 1997
1-3 .... 3.00

Books of Faerie: Auberon's Tale
DC, 1998
1-3 .... 3.00

Books of Faerie: Molly's Story
DC, 1999
1-4 .... 3.00

Books of Lore: Special Edition
Peregrine Entertainment, 1997
1 .... 3.00
1/Ltd. 5.00
2 .... 3.00

Books of Lore: Storyteller
Peregrine Entertainment
1 .... 3.00

Books of Lore: The Kaynin Gambit
Peregrine Entertainment, 1998
0-Ashcan 1 .... 3.00

Books of Magic
DC, 1990
1-4 .... 4.00

Books of Magic
DC, 1993
1 .... 3.00
1/Silver 4.00
2-75 .... 3.00
Ann 1-3 .... 4.00

Books of Magick: Life During Wartime
DC, 2004
1-15 .... 3.00

Boom Boom
Aeon, 1994
1-4 .... 3.00

Boondoggle
Knight, 1995
1-Special 1 .... 3.00

Boondoggle
Caliber, 1997
1-2 .... 3.00

Booster Gold
DC, 1986
1 .... 3.00
2-25 .... 1.00

Booster Gold
DC, 2007
0 .... 3.00
1 .... 6.00
2-27 .... 3.00

Boots of the Oppressor
Northstar, 1993
1 .... 3.00

Borderguard
Eternity, 1987
1-2 .... 2.00

Borderline
Kardia, 1992
1 .... 2.00

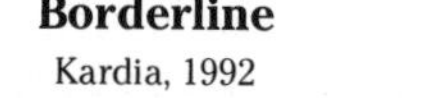

Bomber Comics

Bonanza

Bone

Boneyard

Booster Gold

Boots of the Oppressor

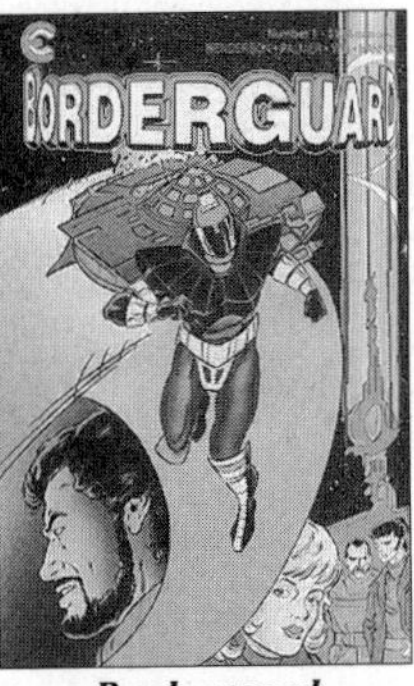

Borderguard

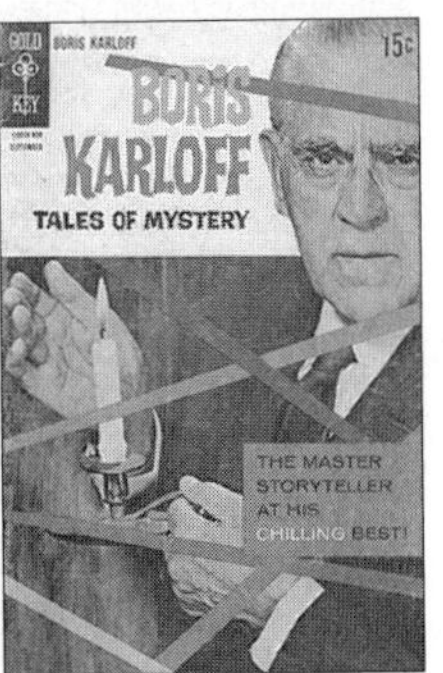

Boris Karloff Tales of Mystery

Border Patrol

P.L., 1951

1 ....50.00

Border Worlds

Kitchen Sink, 1986

1-7/A 2.00

Border Worlds

Kitchen Sink

1 ....2.00

Boris' Adventure Magazine

Nicotat, 1988

1 ....2.00
2-4 ....3.00

Boris Karloff Tales of Mystery

Gold Key, 1962

3 ....27.00
4-5 ....25.00
6-8 ....20.00
9 ....25.00
☛Wood art
10 ....15.00
11 ....22.00
12 ....15.00
13-14 ....12.00
15 ....15.00
16-20 ....12.00
21 ....18.00
22-30 ....10.00
31-40 ....9.00
41-50 ....8.00
51-59 ....6.00
60-74 ....5.00
75-79 ....3.00
80 ....7.00
☛Giant ish; scarce
81 ....6.00
☛Giant ish; scarce
82 ....5.00
☛Giant ish; scarce
83 ....6.00
☛Giant ish; scarce
84 ....5.00
☛Giant ish; scarce
85 ....6.00
☛Giant ish; scarce
86-97 ....3.00

Boris Karloff Thriller

Gold Key, 1962

1 ....75.00
2 ....55.00

Boris the Bear

Dark Horse, 1986

1 ....3.00
1/2nd-2 ....2.00
3-6 ....3.00
7-29 ....2.00
30-34 ....3.00

Boris the Bear Instant Color Classics

Dark Horse, 1987

1-3 ....2.00

Born

Marvel, 2003

1 ....5.00
2-4 ....4.00

Born Again

Spire

1 ....4.00

Born to Kill

Aircel, 1991

1-3 ....3.00

Boston Blackie: Blackout

Moonstone

0 ....6.00

Boston Bombers

Caliber, 1990

1-6 ....3.00
Special 1 ....4.00

Boudoir

Akbar

1 ....3.00

Boulevard of Broken Dreams

Fantagraphics

1 ....4.00

Bouncer

Fox, 1944

10 ....165.00
11 ....140.00
12-14 ....110.00

Bound and Gagged

Iconografix

1 ....3.00

Bound in Darkness: Infinity Issue

CFD

1 ....3.00

Bounty

Caliber, 1991

1-3 ....3.00

Bounty of Zone-Z

Sunset Strips

1 ....3.00

Bowie Butane

Mike Murdock, 1995

1 ....2.00

Box

Fantagraphics, 1991

1-6 ....2.00

Boxboy

Slave Labor, 1993

1-2 ....1.00

Box Office Poison
Antarctic, 1996
0........4.00
1........8.00
2........5.00
3-4........4.00
5-20........3.00
SS 1........5.00

Box Office Poison: Kolor Karnival
Antarctic, 1999
1........4.00

Boy and His 'Bot, A
Now, 1987
1........2.00

Boy Comics
Lev Gleason, 1942
3........1,500.00
4........1,100.00
5........575.00
6........950.00
☛Iron Jaw origin
7........620.00
8........515.00
9........450.00
10........615.00
11-14........350.00
15........400.00
16........225.00
17........250.00
18-20........200.00
21-25........140.00
26-29........130.00
30........200.00
☛Crimebuster origin
31-40........58.00
41-50........42.00
51-62........30.00
63-80........27.00
81-100........24.00
101-119........22.00

Boy Commandos
DC, 1942
1........4,500.00
2........1,500.00
3........1,000.00
4-6........500.00
7-10........275.00
11-22........190.00
23........220.00
24-30........150.00
31-35........135.00
36........195.00

Boy Commandos
DC, 1973
1........8.00
2........5.00

Boy Explorers Comics
Harvey, 1946
1........350.00
2........250.00

Boy Loves Girl
Lev Gleason, 1952
25........40.00
26-33........30.00
34-42........25.00
43........40.00
44-50........20.00
51-57........15.00

Boy Meets Girl
Lev Gleason, 1950
1........150.00
2-6........100.00
7-18........80.00
19-24........60.00

Boys
DC, 2006
1-6........3.00

Boys
Dynamite, 2007
7-40........3.00

Boys Be ...
Tokyopop, 2004
1-7........10.00

Boys Over Flowers
Viz, 2003
1-34........10.00

Boys' Ranch
Harvey, 1950
1........385.00
2........260.00
3........230.00
4........200.00
5-6........110.00

Bozo
Dell, 1951
2........85.00
3........45.00
4-7........38.00

Bozo
Dell, 1962
1........60.00
2-3........35.00
4........28.00

Bozo the Clown in 3-D
Blackthorne
1-2........3.00

Bozo: The World's Most Famous Clown
Innovation
1........6.00

Bozz Chronicles
Marvel, 1985
1-6........2.00

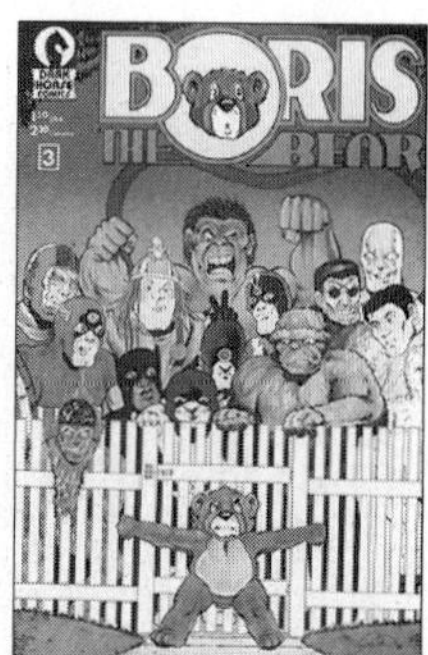

Boris the Bear

Box

Box Office Poison

Boy Comics

Boy Explorers Comics

Brain Boy

Brain Capers

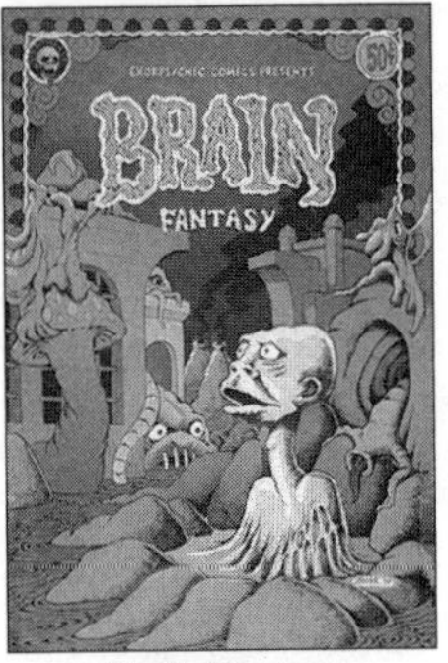
Brain Fantasy

BPRD: A Plague of Frogs
Dark Horse, 2004
1-5 ....3.00

BPRD: Dark Waters
Dark Horse, 2003
1 ....3.00

BPRD: Hollow Earth
Dark Horse, 2002
1-3 ....3.00

BPRD: Night Train
Dark Horse, 2003
1 ....3.00

BPRD: Soul of Venice
Dark Horse, 2003
1 ....3.00

BPRD: The Black Flame
Dark Horse, 2005
1-6 ....3.00

BPRD: The Dead
Dark Horse, 2004
1-5 ....3.00

BPRD: There's Something Under my Bed
Dark Horse, 2003
1 ....3.00

BPRD: The Universal Machine
Dark Horse, 2006
1-5 ....3.00

Bradleys
Fantagraphics, 1999
1-4 ....3.00

Brady Bunch
Dell, 1970
1 ....45.00
2 ....30.00

Bragade
Parody, 1993
1 ....3.00

Brainbanx
DC, 1997
1-6 ....3.00

Brain Bat 3-D
3-D Zone, 1992
1 ....4.00

Brain Boy
Dell, 1962
2 ....65.00
3 ....50.00
4-6 ....45.00

Brain Capers
Fantagraphics
1 ....4.00

Brainchild
Minneapolis College of Art and Design
2 ....1.00

Brain Fantasy
Last Gasp, 1972
1 ....3.00

Brainglo
Psi Comics
1 ....2.00

Brain
Magazine Enterprises, 1956
1 ....45.00
2-3 ....30.00
4-7 ....26.00

Brain
I.W., 1958
1 ....12.00
2-10 ....9.00
11-18 ....8.00

Braintrust Komicks
Spoon, 1993
1 ....3.00

Brand New York
Mean, 1997
1-2 ....4.00

Brass
Image, 1996
1 ....3.00
1/Deluxe 5.00
2-3 ....3.00

Brass
DC, 2000
1-6 ....3.00

Brath
CrossGen, 2003
1-14 ....3.00

Bratpack
King Hell, 1990
1-5 ....3.00

Brat Pack/Maximortal Super Special
King Hell, 1996
1 ....3.00

Brats Bizarre
Marvel, 1994
1-4 ....3.00

Brave and the Bold
DC, 1955
1 ....3,000.00
2 ....1,500.00
3 ....700.00
4-5 ....650.00
6-10 ....500.00
11-22 ....400.00
23 ....500.00

☛Vik. Prince origin
24 .... 350.00
25 .... 500.00
☛1st Suicide Squad
26 .... 325.00
27 .... 330.00
28 .... 5,000.00
☛1st JLA
29 .... 2,000.00
30 .... 1,750.00
31 .... 350.00
32-33 .... 200.00
34 .... 1,750.00
☛1st SA Hawkman
35-36 .... 400.00
37 .... 250.00
38-39 .... 225.00
40-41 .... 140.00
42 .... 300.00
43 .... 350.00
☛Hawkman origin
44 .... 260.00
45-49 .... 60.00
50 .... 175.00
51 .... 225.00
52 .... 125.00
53 .... 75.00
54 .... 350.00
☛1st Teen Titans
55-56 .... 45.00
57 .... 150.00
☛1st Metamorpho
58 .... 65.00
59 .... 80.00
60 .... 100.00
☛1st Wonder Girl
61 .... 125.00
☛Starman origin
62 .... 100.00
☛1st SA Wildcat
63 .... 40.00
64 .... 60.00
65-66 .... 22.00
67 .... 65.00
☛Batman starts
68 .... 80.00
☛Batman Hulk parody
69-73 .... 50.00
74 .... 40.00
75 .... 60.00
76 .... 50.00
77-78 .... 40.00
79 .... 75.00
☛Batman, Deadman
80-82 .... 50.00
83 .... 60.00
84 .... 50.00
85 .... 60.00
☛N. Adams GA
86 .... 50.00
87 .... 26.00
88-90 .... 20.00
91-92 .... 18.00
93 .... 30.00
94 .... 18.00
95 .... 24.00
96-98 .... 15.00
99 .... 22.00
100 .... 30.00
101-102 .... 15.00
103-110 .... 12.00
111-114 .... 18.00
115 .... 22.00
116-118 .... 18.00
119-126 .... 7.00
127-128 .... 6.00
129-130 .... 11.00
131 .... 6.00
132 .... 4.00
133 .... 5.00
134-140 .... 4.00
141 .... 10.00
142-145 .... 4.00
145/Whitman 8.00
146 .... 4.00
146/Whitman 8.00
147 .... 4.00
147/Whitman 8.00
148-149 .... 4.00
149/Whitman 8.00
150 .... 4.00
150/Whitman 12.00
151 .... 4.00
151/Whitman 8.00
152 .... 4.00
152/Whitman 8.00
153 .... 4.00
153/Whitman 20.00
154 .... 4.00
154/Whitman 8.00
155 .... 4.00
155/Whitman 8.00
156 .... 4.00
156/Whitman 8.00
157 .... 4.00
157/Whitman 8.00
158 .... 4.00
158/Whitman 8.00
159 .... 4.00
159/Whitman 8.00
160 .... 4.00
160/Whitman 8.00
161 .... 4.00
161/Whitman 8.00
162 .... 4.00
162/Whitman 8.00
163 .... 4.00
163/Whitman 8.00
164 .... 4.00
164/Whitman 8.00
165 .... 4.00
165/Whitman 8.00
166-179 .... 4.00
180-190 .... 3.00

Brave and the Bold

Bravura Preview Book

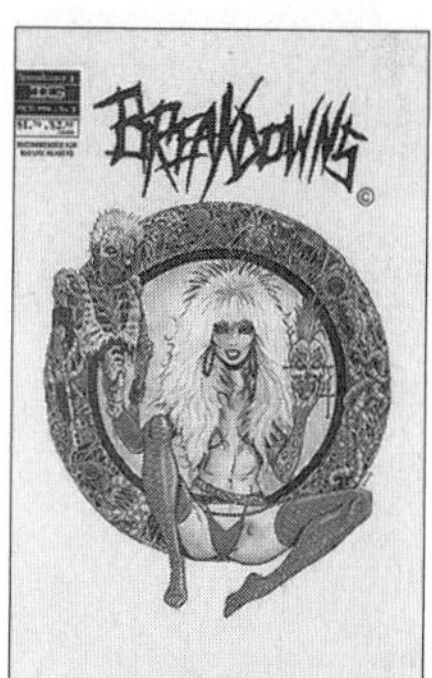

Breakdowns

Breakfast After Noon

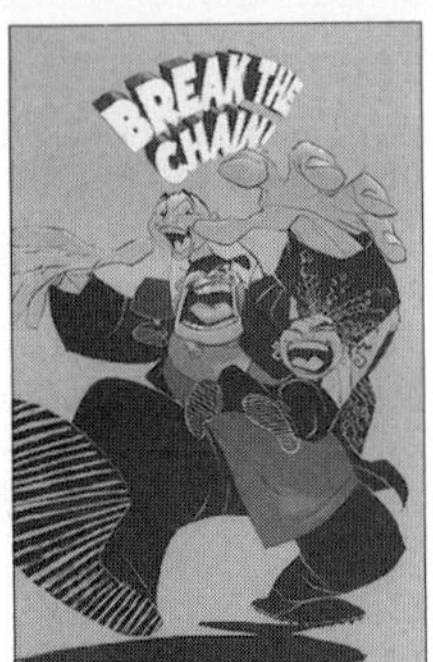

Break the Chain

Break-Thru

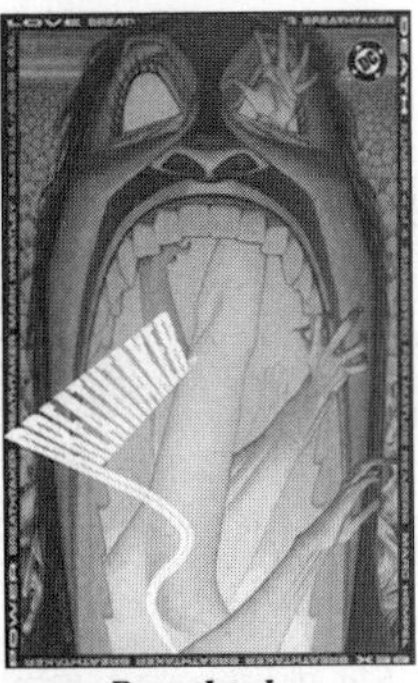
Breathtaker

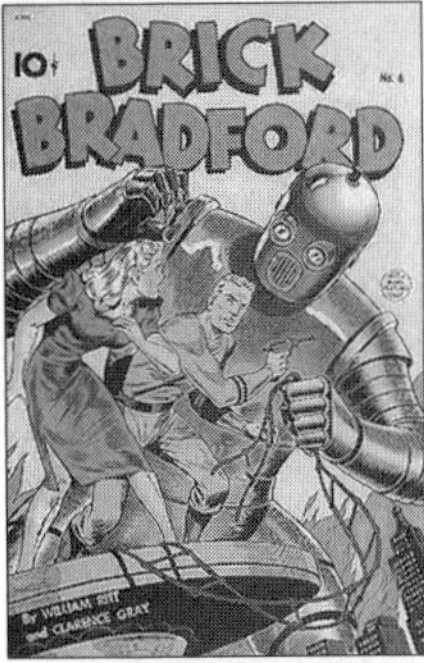

Brick Bradford

191 .... 8.00
192-196 .... 3.00
197 .... 4.00
198-199 .... 3.00
200 .... 7.00
Ann 1 .... 6.00

Brave and the Bold
DC, 1991

1 .... 3.00
2-6 .... 2.00

Brave and the Bold
DC, 2006

1-35 .... 3.00

Brave Old World
DC, 2000

1-4 .... 3.00

Bravestarr in 3-D
Blackthorne

1-2 .... 3.00

Bravo for Adventure
Dragon Lady

1 .... 6.00

Bravura Preview Book
Malibu, 1993

0 .... 3.00
1-2 .... 2.00

Breach
DC, 2005

1-2 .... 3.00
3 .... 5.00
☛Inf. Crisis tie
4-11 .... 3.00

Bread & Circuses
Moe, 1995

1 .... 3.00

Breakdown
Devil's Due, 2004

1/A-1/C 0.00
1 .... 4.00
1/Variant 5.00
2 .... 4.00
2/Variant 5.00
3-6 .... 3.00

Breakdowns
Infinity, 1986

1 .... 2.00

Breakfast After Noon
Oni, 2000

1-6 .... 3.00

Breakneck Blvd.
Motion, 1994

0-2 .... 3.00

Breakneck Blvd.
Slave Labor, 1995

1-6 .... 3.00

Break the Chain
Marvel Music

1 .... 7.00

Break-Thru
Malibu, 1993

1 .... 3.00
1/Ltd 4.00
2 .... 3.00

Breathtaker
DC, 1990

1-4 .... 5.00

'Breed
Malibu, 1994

1-6 .... 3.00

'Breed II
Malibu, 1994

1-6 .... 3.00

Breeder// certain.revolutions
Visceral

1 .... 1.00

Brenda Lee's Life Story
Dell, 1962

1 .... 50.00

Brenda Starr
Superior, 1947

13 .... 550.00
14 .... 500.00
3-4 .... 425.00
5-12 .... 350.00

Brenda Starr
Charlton, 1955

13-15 .... 85.00

Brenda Starr
Avalon

1-2 .... 3.00

Brenda Starr Cut-Outs and Coloring Book
Blackthorne

1 .... 7.00

Brenda Starr Reporter
Dell, 1963

1 .... 150.00

Brick Bradford
Standard, 1948

5-6 .... 120.00
7-8 .... 75.00

Brickman
Harrier

1 .... 2.00

Bride's Diary
Ajax, 1955

4 .... 18.00
5-7 .... 15.00
8-10 .... 12.00

Brides in Love
Charlton, 1956

1 .... 60.00
2 .... 35.00
3-10 .... 24.00
11-30 .... 18.00
31-45 .... 12.00

Bride's Secrets
Ajax, 1954

1 .... 48.00
2 .... 28.00
3-6 .... 18.00
7-10 .... 12.00
11-19 .... 10.00

Bridgman's Constructive Anatomy
A-List, 1998

1-4 .... 3.00

Brigade
Image, 1992

1-1/Gold 2.00
2-2/Gold 4.00
3-4 .... 2.00

Brigade
Image, 1993

0-2 .... 2.00
2/A 3.00
3-11 .... 2.00
12-22 .... 3.00
25-26 .... 2.00
27 .... 3.00

Brigade
Awesome, 2000

1 .... 3.00

Brigade Sourcebook
Image, 1994

1 .... 3.00

Brik Hauss
Blackthorne, 1987

1 .... 2.00

Brilliant Boy
Circus, 1997

1-5 .... 3.00

Brinke of Destruction
High-Top, 1995

1 .... 3.00
1/CS 7.00
2-3 .... 3.00
Special 1 .... 7.00

Brinke of Destruction
BV Books

1 .... 3.00

Brinke of Disaster
High-Top, 1996

1 .... 2.00

Brinke of Eternity
Chaos, 1994

1 .... 3.00

Brit
Image, 2003

1 .... 5.00

Brit-Cit Babes
Fleetway-Quality

1 .... 6.00

Brit/Cold Death One Shot
Image, 2004

1 .... 5.00

Brit: Red, White, Black & Blue One-Shot
Image, 2004

1 .... 5.00

Broadway Babes
Avalon

1 .... 3.00

Broadway Video Special Collectors Edition
Broadway, 1995

1 .... 1.00

Brodie's Law
Studio G, 2004

1-5 .... 3.00

Broid
Eternity, 1990

1 .... 3.00
2-4 .... 2.00

Broken Axis
Antarctic

1 .... 3.00

Broken Fender
Top Shelf Productions, 1997

1-2 .... 3.00

Broken Halo: Is There Nothing Sacred?
Broken Halos, 1998

2 .... 3.00
2/Nude 5.00

Broken Heroes
Sirius, 1998

1-12 .... 3.00

Broncho Bill
Standard, 1948

5 .... 135.00
6 .... 85.00
7-16 .... 50.00

Bronte's Infernal Angria
Headless Shakespeare Press, 2005

1 .... 4.00

Bronx
Eternity

1-3 .... 3.00

Brickman

Brilliant Boy

Broid

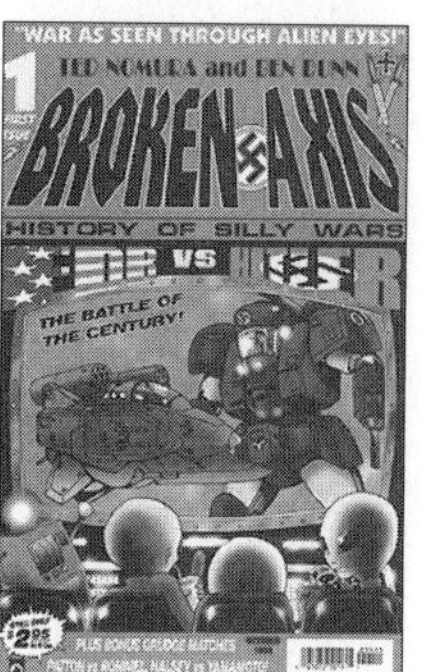

Broken Axis

Broken Fender

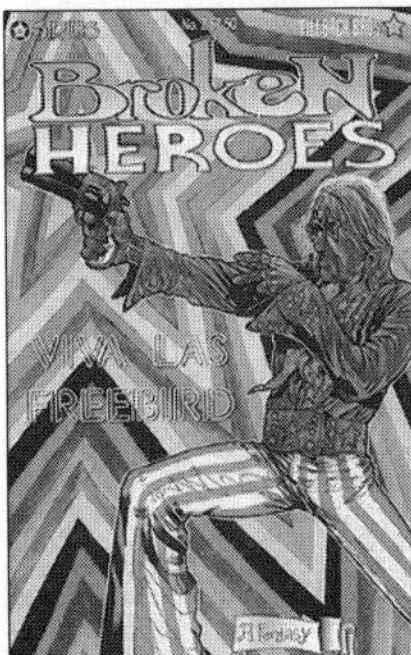
Broken Heroes

Brothers of the Spear

Bruce Lee

Brood Trouble in the Big Easy
Marvel, 1993
1 ....7.00

Brooklyn Dreams
DC, 1994
1-4 ....5.00

Brother Billy The Pain From Plains
Marvel, 1979
1 ....20.00

Brother Destiny
Mecca, 2004
1-3 ....3.00

Brotherhood
Marvel, 2001
1-9 ....2.00

Brotherman
Big City
1-8 ....2.00

Brother Man: Dictator of Discipline
Big City, 1996
11 ....3.00

Brother Power, the Geek
DC, 1968
1 ....45.00
2 ....20.00

Brothers, Hang in There
Spire
1 ....3.00

Brothers of the Spear
Gold Key, 1972
1 ....20.00
2 ....10.00
3-5 ....6.00
6-17 ....4.00
18 ....3.00

Bruce Gentry
Superior, 1948
1 ....350.00
2-8 ....180.00

Bruce Lee
Malibu, 1994
1-6 ....3.00

Bruce Wayne: Agent of S.H.I.E.L.D.
Marvel, 1996
1 ....2.00

Bru-Hed
Schism, 1993
1-4 ....3.00

Bru-Hed's Breathtaking Beauties
Schism, 1995
1 ....3.00

Bru-Hed's Bunnies, Baddies & Buddies
Schism
1 ....3.00

Bru-Hed's Guide to Gettin' Girls Now!
Schism
1-2 ....3.00

Bruiser
Anthem, 1994
1 ....2.00

Bruiser
Mythic
1-2 ....3.00

Brunner's Beauties
Fantagraphics
1 ....5.00

Brusel
NBM
1 ....20.00

Brute
Atlas-Seaboard, 1975
1 ....7.00
2-3 ....5.00

Brute Force
Marvel, 1990
1-4 ....1.00

B-Sides
Marvel, 2002
1 ....4.00
2-3 ....3.00

B-36
Paradise Valley
1-2 ....3.00

B'Tx
Tokyopop, 2006
1 ....10.00

Bubblegum Crisis: Grand Mal
Dark Horse, 1994
1-4 ....3.00

Buccaneers
Quality, 1950
19 ....320.00
20-21 ....240.00
22-23 ....185.00
24-26 ....160.00
27 ....180.00

Buce N Gar
Rak
1-3 ....2.00

Buckaroo Banzai
Marvel, 1984

1-2 .... 1.00

Buck Godot, Zap Gun For Hire
Palliard, 1993

1 .... 4.00
2-8 .... 3.00

Buck Jones
Dell, 1951

2 .... 50.00
3-8 .... 35.00

Buck Rogers
Eastern Color, 1940

1 .... 1,950.00
2 .... 850.00
3-4 .... 700.00
5-6 .... 625.00

Buck Rogers
Gold Key, 1964

1 .... 36.00
2 .... 5.00
3-4 .... 4.00
5-16 .... 3.00

Buck Rogers Comics Module
TSR

1-9 .... 3.00

Bucky O'Hare
Continuity, 1991

1 .... 3.00
2-5 .... 2.00

Buddha on the Road
Aeon, 1996

1-6 .... 3.00

Buffalo Bill
Youthful, 1950

2 .... 65.00
3-9 .... 50.00

Buffalo Bill Jr.
Dell, 1958

7-13 .... 30.00

Buffalo Bill Jr.
Gold Key, 1965

1 .... 30.00

Buffalo Bill Picture Stories
Street & Smith, 1949

1 .... 75.00
2 .... 60.00

Buffalo Wings
Antarctic, 1993

1-2 .... 3.00

Buffy the Vampire Slayer
Dark Horse, 1998

½ 4.00
½/Gold 8.00
½/Platinum 10.00
1 .... 5.00
1/A 10.00
1/B 5.00
1/Gold-1/Variant 10.00
1/2nd-2 .... 4.00
2/Variant-3/Variant 5.00
4-20 .... 4.00
20/Variant-49/Variant 3.00
50-50/Variant 4.00
51-63 .... 3.00
Ann 1999 .... 6.00

Buffy the Vampire Slayer: Angel
Dark Horse, 1999

1-1/Variant 4.00
2-3/Variant 3.00

Buffy the Vampire Slayer: Chaos Bleeds
Dark Horse, 2003

1 .... 3.00

Buffy the Vampire Slayer: Food Chain
Dark Horse

1 .... 17.00

Buffy the Vampire Slayer: Giles
Dark Horse, 2000

1-1/Variant 3.00

Buffy the Vampire Slayer: Haunted
Dark Horse, 2001

1-4 .... 3.00

Buffy the Vampire Slayer: Jonathan
Dark Horse, 2001

1 .... 3.00
1/Gold 10.00
1/Platinum 20.00

Buffy The Vampire Slayer: Lost and Found
Dark Horse, 2002

1 .... 3.00

Buffy the Vampire Slayer: Lover's Walk
Dark Horse, 2001

1 .... 3.00

Buffy The Vampire Slayer: Oz
Dark Horse, 2001

1-3 .... 3.00

Buffy the Vampire Slayer: Reunion
Dark Horse, 2002

1 .... 4.00

Buccaneers

Buckaroo Banzai

Buffalo Bill Picture Stories

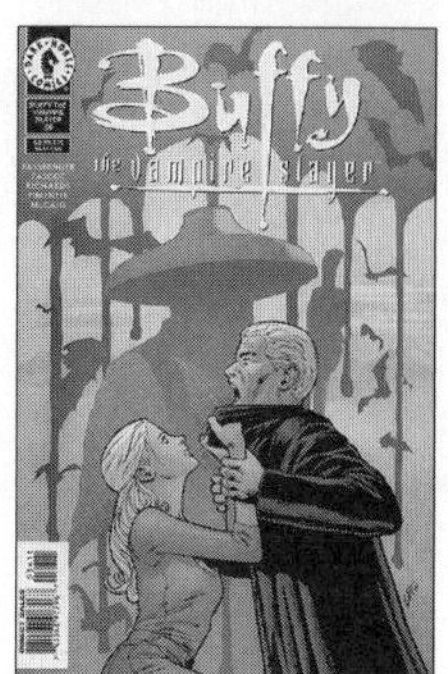

Buffy the Vampire Slayer

Bugboy

Bug-Hunters

Bugs Bunny and Porky Pig

Bulletman

Buffy the Vampire Slayer: Ring of Fire

Dark Horse, 2000

1 .... 10.00

Buffy the Vampire Slayer: Season Eight

Dark Horse, 2007

1 .... 15.00
2 .... 6.00
3 .... 4.00
4-30 .... 3.00

Buffy the Vampire Slayer: Spike and Dru

Dark Horse, 1999

1-3 .... 3.00

Buffy the Vampire Slayer, Tales of the Slayers

Dark Horse, 2001

1-1 .... 4.00

Buffy The Vampire Slayer: The Dust Waltz

Dark Horse, 1998

1 .... 10.00

Buffy the Vampire Slayer: The Origin

Dark Horse, 1999

1 .... 4.00
1/Ltd. 15.00
2-3 .... 3.00

Buffy the Vampire Slayer: Willow & Tara

Dark Horse, 2001

1 .... 5.00

Buffy the Vampire Slayer: Willow & Tara: Wilderness

Dark Horse, 2002

1-2 .... 3.00

Bug

Marvel, 1997

1 .... 3.00

Bug

Planet-X

1 .... 2.00

Bug & Stump

Aaargh!, 1993

1-9 .... 3.00

Bugboy

Image, 1998

1 .... 4.00

B.U.G.G.'s

Acetylene Comics, 2001

1-2 .... 2.00

B.U.G.G.'s (Vol. 2)

Acetylene Comics, 2001

1 .... 2.00
1/A 3.00
2 .... 2.00
3-4 .... 3.00

Bughouse

Ajax, 1954

1 .... 75.00
2 .... 50.00
3-4 .... 45.00

Bughouse (Cat-Head)

Cat-Head, 1994

1-5 .... 3.00

Bug-Hunters

Trident

1 .... 6.00

Bugnut

Comicosley, 1999

1 .... 3.00

Bugs Bunny

Dell, 1952

28-40 .... 35.00
41-60 .... 25.00
61-80 .... 20.00
81-85 .... 15.00

Bugs Bunny

Gold Key, 1962

86-101 .... 7.00
102-150 .... 6.00
151-200 .... 5.00
201-212 .... 3.00
213-245 .... 2.00

Bugs Bunny

DC, 1990

1-3 .... 2.00

Bugs Bunny and Porky Pig

Dell, 1965

1 .... 26.00

Bugs Bunny!

Burghley

1-2 .... 3.00

Bugs Bunny Monthly

DC

1-3 .... 2.00

Bugs Bunny's Christmas Funnies

Dell, 1950

1 .... 115.00
2 .... 75.00
3-5 .... 65.00
6-9 .... 55.00

Bugs Bunny's County Fair
Dell, 1957
1 .... 125.00

Bugs Bunny's Halloween Parade
Dell, 1953
1 .... 75.00
2 .... 65.00

Bugs Bunny's Trick 'n' Treat Halloween Fun
Dell, 1955
3-4 .... 65.00

Bugs Bunny's Vacation Funnies
Dell, 1951
1 .... 150.00
2 .... 120.00
3 .... 100.00
4-9 .... 80.00

Bugs Bunny Winter Fun
Gold Key, 1967
1 .... 30.00

Bug's Gift, A
Discovery
1 .... 2.00

Bugtown
Aeon, 2004
1-6 .... 3.00

Bug Wars
Avalon Communications, 1998
1 .... 3.00

Building
DC, 2000
1 .... 10.00

Buja's Diary
NBM, 2005
1 .... 20.00

Bulldog
Five Star
1 .... 3.00

Bulldog Drummond
Moonstone
0 .... 5.00

Bullet Crow, Fowl of Fortune
Eclipse
1-2 .... 2.00

Bulletman
Fawcett, 1941
1 .... 2,250.00
2 .... 975.00
3 .... 700.00
4-5 .... 625.00
6-10 .... 500.00
11-16 .... 375.00

Bullet Points
Marvel, 2007
1-4 .... 3.00

Bulletproof
Known Associates
1 .... 4.00

Bulletproof Comics
Wet Paint Graphics, 1999
1-3 .... 2.00

Bulletproof Monk
Image, 1998
1-3 .... 3.00

Bulletproof Monk: Tales of the Bulletproof Monk
Image, 2003
1 .... 3.00

Bullets and Bracelets
Marvel, 1996
1 .... 2.00

Bullseye Greatest Hits
Marvel, 2004
1-5 .... 3.00

Bulls-Eye
Mainline, 1954
1 .... 500.00
2 .... 400.00
3 .... 300.00
4-7 .... 250.00

Bullwinkle
Dell, 1962
1 .... 100.00

Bullwinkle and Rocky
Gold Key, 1962
1 .... 90.00
2 .... 68.00
3 .... 45.00
4-5 .... 40.00
6-11 .... 28.00
12 .... 14.00
13 .... 20.00
14 .... 16.00
15-20 .... 10.00
21-25 .... 8.00

Bullwinkle and Rocky
Charlton, 1970
1 .... 30.00
2 .... 18.00
3 .... 15.00
4-7 .... 12.00

Bullwinkle and Rocky
Marvel, 1987
1-9 .... 2.00

Bullwinkle & Rocky
Blackthorne, 1987
1-3D 1 .... 3.00

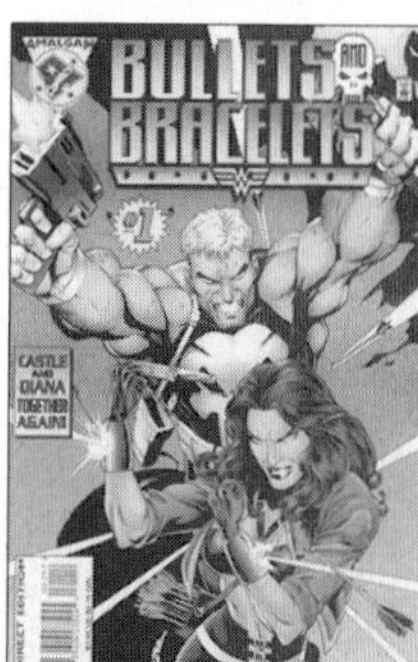

Bullets and Bracelets

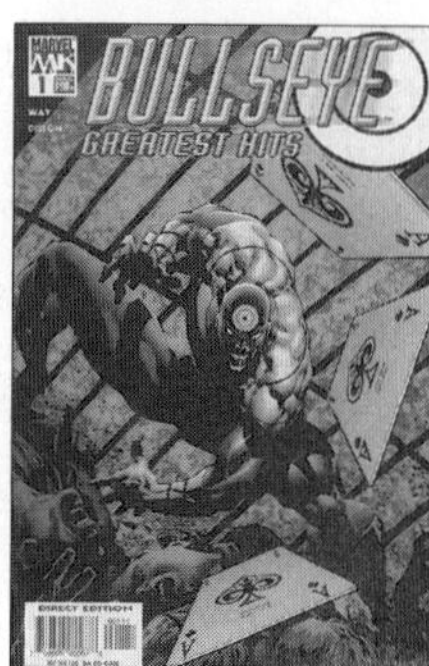

Bullseye Greatest Hits

Bumbercomix

Burrito

Bushido

Bushido Blade of Zatoichi Walrus

Buster Brown of the Safety Patrol

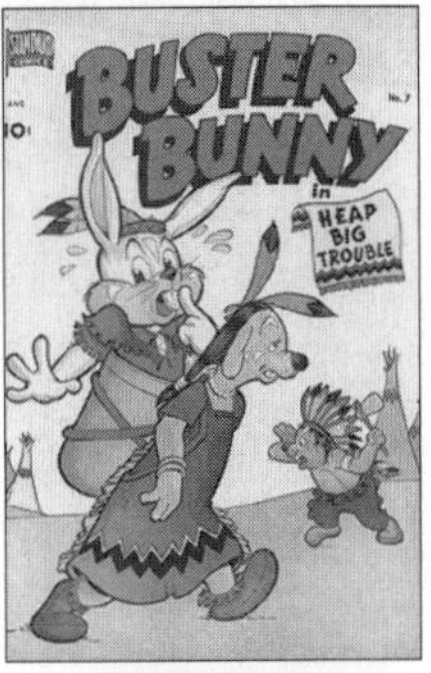

Buster Bunny

Bullwinkle for President in 3-D
Blackthorne, 1987

1 ....3.00

Bullwinkle Mother Moose Nursery Pomes
Dell, 1962

1 ....85.00

Bumbercomix
Starhead

1 ....1.00

Bumperboy Loses His Marbles
Adhouse Books, 2005

1 ....8.00

Bunny
Harvey, 1966

1 ....50.00
2-20 ....30.00
21 ....15.00

Bunny Town
Radio, 2002

1 ....3.00

Burger Bomb
Funny Book Institute, 1999

1-3 ....3.00

Burglar Bill
Image, 2005

1-4 ....3.00

Burglar Bill
Trident

1 ....2.00

Burial of the Rats
Roger Corman's Cosmic Comics, 1995

1-3 ....3.00

Buried Terror
NEC, 1995

1 ....3.00

Buried Treasure
Pure Imagination

1-3 ....6.00

Buried Treasure
Caliber

1-4 ....3.00

Burke's Law
Dell, 1964

1 ....24.00
2-3 ....20.00

Burrito
Accent!, 1995

1-5 ....3.00

Bushido
Eternity, 1988

1-4 ....2.00

Bushido Blade of Zatoichi Walrus
Solson, 1987

1-2 ....2.00

Bushwhacked
Fantagraphics

1 ....3.00

Buster
Crisis

1-2 ....3.00

Buster Brown Comic Book
Buster Brown

1 ....115.00
2 ....80.00
3-5 ....55.00
6-10 ....36.00
11-20 ....26.00
21-24 ....20.00
25 ....35.00
26-28 ....20.00
29-37 ....35.00
38-39 ....16.00
40-41 ....35.00
42-43 ....20.00

Buster Brown of the Safety Patrol
Custom

1 ....22.00

Buster Bunny
Standard, 1949

1 ....40.00
2 ....22.00
3-5 ....16.00
6-16 ....15.00

Buster Crabbe
Lev Gleason, 1953

1 ....125.00
2-4 ....110.00

Buster Crabbe
Famous Funnies, 1951

1 ....250.00
2-3 ....210.00
4 ....150.00
5-8 ....105.00
9 ....90.00
10-12 ....60.00

Buster the Amazing Bear
Ursus, 1992

1-5 ....3.00

Bustline Combat
Fantagraphics, 1999

1 ....3.00

Butcher
DC, 1990

1 ....3.00
2-5 ....2.00

Butcher Knight
Image, 2000

1...3.00

Butt Biscuit
Fantagraphics, 1992

1-3...2.00

Butterscotch
Fantagraphics

1-3...3.00

Button Man: The Killing Game
Kitchen Sink, 1995

1...16.00

Buz Sawyer
Standard, 1948

1...125.00
2...75.00
3...50.00

Buz Sawyer Quarterly
Dragon Lady, 1986

1-3...6.00

Buzz
Kitchen Sink, 1990

1-3...3.00

Buzz
Marvel, 2000

1-3...3.00

Buzz and Colonel Toad
Belmont, 1998

1-3...3.00

Buzzard
Cat-Head, 1990

1-11...3.00
12-20...4.00

Buzzboy
Skydog, 1998

1-4...3.00

Buzz Buzz Comics Magazine
Horse

1...5.00

Buzzy
DC, 1944

1...125.00
2...65.00
3...48.00
4-5...40.00
6-10...35.00
11-20...30.00
21-30...22.00
31-40...16.00
41-50...13.00
51-77...9.00

BVC
Fleetway-Quality

1-17...2.00

By Bizarre Hands
Dark Horse, 1994

1-3...3.00

By Bizarre Hands (Joe Lansdale's)
Avatar, 2004

1...4.00
1/Red foil...10.00
1/Wraparound...5.00
2...4.00
2/Red foil...8.00
2/Wraparound...5.00
3...4.00
3/Red foil...8.00
3/Wraparound...5.00
4...4.00
4/Red foil...8.00
4/Wraparound...5.00
5...4.00
5/Red foil...8.00
5/Wraparound...5.00
6...4.00
6/Red foil...8.00
6/Wraparound...5.00

By the Time I Get to Wagga Wagga
Harrier

1...2.00

C-23
Image, 1998

1...5.00
1/Ashcan...4.00
2...3.00
2/Variant...2.00
3-8...3.00
8/Variant...4.00

Cabbot: Bloodhunter
Maximum, 1997

1...3.00

Cabinet of Dr. Caligari
Monster, 1992

1-3...2.00

Cable
Marvel, 1993

-1...2.00
1...4.00
2-10...3.00
11-16...2.00
16/Variant...4.00
17-24...2.00
25...4.00
26-49...2.00
50...3.00
51-74...2.00
75...5.00
76-99...2.00
100...4.00
101-107...2.00
Ann 1998...3.00
Ann 1999...4.00

Buster the Amazing Bear

Buz Sawyer

Buzzy

Cable

Caffeine

Cage

Caliber Spotlight

California Girls

Cable: Blood and Metal
Marvel, 1992

1 .... 4.00
2 .... 3.00

Cable/Deadpool
Marvel, 2004

1 .... 4.00
2-50 .... 3.00

Cable: Second Genesis
Marvel, 1999

1 .... 4.00

Cable TV
Parody

1 .... 3.00

Cadavera
Monster

1-2 .... 2.00

Cadence of the Dirge
Gothic

1 .... 3.00

Cadet Gray of West Point
Dell, 1958

1 .... 75.00

Cadillacs & Dinosaurs
Marvel, 1990

1-6 .... 3.00
3D 1 .... 4.00

Cadillacs & Dinosaurs
Kitchen Sink, 1993

1 .... 4.00

Cadillacs & Dinosaurs
Topps, 1994

1-10 .... 3.00

Caffeine
Slave Labor, 1996

1-10 .... 3.00

Cage
Marvel, 1992

1 .... 3.00
2-20 .... 1.00

Cage
Marvel, 2002

1 .... 4.00
2-5 .... 3.00

Caged Heat 3000
Roger Corman's Cosmic Comics, 1996

1-3 .... 3.00

Cages
Tundra, 1993

1 .... 5.00
2-9 .... 4.00
10 .... 5.00

Cain
Harris, 1993

1-2 .... 3.00

Calculated Risk
Genesis, 1990

1 .... 2.00

Caliber Christmas, A
Caliber

1 .... 4.00

Caliber Christmas, A
Caliber, 1998

1 .... 6.00

Caliber Core
Caliber

0 .... 3.00
Ashcan 1 .... 1.00

Caliber Presents
Caliber, 1989

1 .... 15.00
☛1st Crow
2-7 .... 3.00
8 .... 2.00
9-24 .... 3.00

Caliber Presents: Cinderella on Fire
Caliber, 1994

1 .... 3.00

Caliber Presents: Generator Comics
Caliber

1 .... 3.00

Caliber Presents: Hybrid Stories
Caliber

1 .... 3.00

Caliber Presents: Petit Mal
Caliber

1 .... 3.00

Caliber Presents: Romantic Tales
Caliber, 1995

1 .... 3.00

Caliber Presents: Sepulcher Opus
Caliber, 1993

1 .... 3.00

Caliber Presents: Something Inside
Caliber

1 .... 4.00

Caliber Presents: Sub-Atomic Shock
Caliber

1 .... 3.00

Caliber Spotlight
Caliber, 1995
1 .... 3.00

Calibrations
Caliber
1-5 .... 1.00

Calibrations
Caliber, 1996
1-5 .... 1.00

California Comics
California, 1977
1 .... 5.00
2-3 .... 4.00

California Girls
Eclipse, 1987
1-8 .... 2.00

California Raisins in 3-D
Blackthorne, 1987
1-5 .... 3.00

Caligari 2050
Monster, 1992
1-3 .... 2.00

Caligari 2050: Another Sleepless Night
Caliber, 1993
1 .... 4.00

Call
Marvel, 2003
1-4 .... 2.00

Called From Darkness
Anarchy
1-1/2nd 3.00

Calling All Boys
Parents' Magazine Institute, 1946
1 .... 60.00
2 .... 28.00
3 .... 18.00
4-9 .... 15.00
10 .... 30.00
11 .... 15.00
12 .... 35.00
13 .... 30.00
14-17 .... 15.00

Calling All Girls
Parents' Magazine Institute, 1941
1 .... 100.00
2 .... 95.00
3 .... 90.00
4 .... 85.00
5 .... 80.00
6 .... 75.00
7 .... 70.00
8 .... 65.00
9 .... 60.00
10-13 .... 50.00
14-16 .... 45.00
17-19 .... 40.00
20-22 .... 35.00
23-26 .... 30.00
27-39 .... 25.00
40-43 .... 20.00

Calling All Kids
Parents' Magazine Institute, 1946
1 .... 55.00
2 .... 25.00
3 .... 18.00
4-10 .... 14.00
11-26 .... 12.00

Call Me Princess
CPM, 1999
1-6 .... 3.00

Call of Duty: The Brotherhood
Marvel, 2002
1-6 .... 2.00

Call of Duty: The Precinct
Marvel, 2002
1-5 .... 2.00

Call of Duty: The Wagon
Marvel, 2002
1-4 .... 2.00

Calvin and the Colonel
Dell, 1962
2 .... 25.00

Cambion
Slave Labor, 1995
1-3 .... 3.00

Cambion
Moonstone
3-5 .... 3.00

Camelot Eternal
Caliber
1-8 .... 3.00

Camelot 3000
DC, 1982
1 .... 3.00
2-12 .... 2.00

Camera Comics
U.S. Camera, 1944
1 .... 250.00
2 .... 140.00
3 .... 125.00
4-6 .... 100.00
7-11 .... 90.00

Camp Candy
Marvel, 1990
1-7 .... 1.00

Camp Comics
Dell, 1942
1 .... 500.00
2 .... 450.00
3 .... 400.00

Calling All Boys

Call Me Princess

Camelot Eternal

Camera Comics

Camp Candy

Camp Comics

Campus Loves

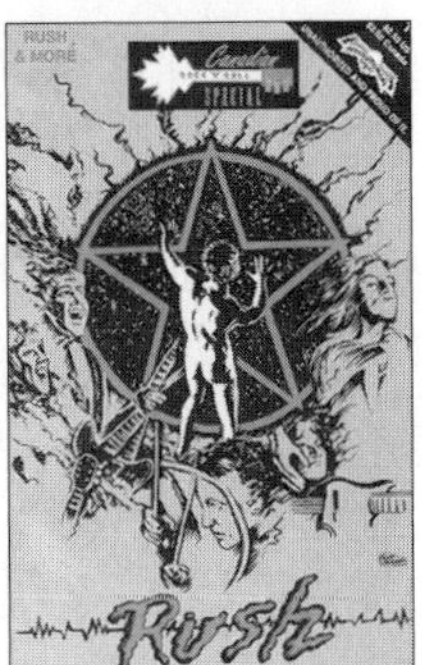

Canadian Rock Special

Campfire Stories
Global, 1992

1 .... 2.00

Camping with Bigfoot
Slave Labor, 1995

1 .... 3.00

Camp Runamuck
Dell, 1966

1 .... 40.00

Campus Loves
Quality, 1949

1 .... 300.00
2 .... 165.00
3-4 .... 125.00
5 .... 100.00

Campus Romances
Avon, 1949

1 .... 120.00
2-3 .... 85.00

Canadian Comics Cavalcade
Artworx

1 .... 2.00

Canadian Ninja
Quebec

1 .... 2.00

Canadian Rock Special
Revolutionary, 1994

1 .... 3.00

Cancer: The Crab Boy
Sabre's Edge

1-5 .... 3.00

Candidate Goddess
Tokyopop, 2004

1-2 .... 10.00

Candide Revealed
Fantagraphics

1 .... 2.00

Candy
Quality, 1944

1 .... 340.00
2 .... 215.00
3 .... 185.00

Candy
Comic Magazines, 1947

1 .... 100.00
2 .... 55.00
3-5 .... 36.00
6-10 .... 26.00
11-20 .... 22.00
21-30 .... 18.00
31-39 .... 15.00
40-50 .... 14.00
51-64 .... 12.00

Candyappleblack
Good Intentions Paving, 2004

1-7 .... 4.00

Cannibalis
Raging Rhino

1 .... 3.00

Cannon
Fantagraphics, 1991

1-8 .... 3.00

Cannon Busters
Devil's Due, 2004

0 .... 15.00
1 .... 3.00
1/Variant 4.00
2 .... 3.00
2/Variant 4.00

Cannon God Exaxxion
Dark Horse, 2001

1-8 .... 3.00
9-14 .... 4.00
15-20 .... 3.00

Cannon Hawke: Dawn of War (Michael Turner's)
Aspen, 2004

1 .... 6.00

Canteen Kate
St. John, 1952

1 .... 350.00
2-3 .... 300.00

Canyon Comics Presents
Grand Canyon Association, 1995

1-2 .... 2.00

Cape City
Dimension X

1-3 .... 3.00

Caper
DC, 2003

1-12 .... 3.00

Capes
Image, 2003

1-3 .... 4.00

Capital Capers Presents
BLT, 1994

1-2 .... 3.00

Cap'n Oatmeal
All American

1 .... 2.00

Cap'n Quick & a Foozle
Eclipse, 1984

1-3 .... 2.00

Captain Action
Karl Art

0 .... 2.00

Captain Action

DC, 1968

Issue	Price
1	45.00
2-4	35.00
5	20.00

Captain Aero Comics

Continental, 1941

Issue	Price
1	1,600.00
2	850.00
3-5	725.00
6-7	675.00
8	325.00
9-10	265.00
11-13	225.00
14-17	190.00
21-26	165.00

Captain Africa

African Prince Productions, 1992

Issue	Price
1	3.00

Captain America

Marvel, 1968

Issue	Price
100	210.00
101	55.00
102-108	35.00
109	45.00
☛Origin retold	
109/2nd	3.00
110	75.00
☛Steranko begins	
111	65.00
112	50.00
113	60.00
☛Avengers app.	
114-116	30.00
117	95.00
☛1st Falcon	
118-124	25.00
125-127	20.00
128-130	15.00
131-132	18.00
133	15.00
134-136	18.00
137	35.00
138	30.00
139-146	25.00
147	18.00
148	16.00
149	15.00
150	25.00
151-153	15.00
154-155	25.00
156	20.00
157-162	10.00
163-164	12.00
165-167	10.00
168	15.00
169	10.00
170	12.00
171-172	10.00
173	15.00
174	12.00
175-176	10.00
177-183	8.00
184-187	5.00
188	8.00
189-196	6.00
196/30¢	20.00
197	5.00
197/30¢	20.00
198	6.00
198/30¢	20.00
199	5.00
199/30¢	20.00
200	6.00
200/30¢	20.00
201	6.00
202	4.00
203	5.00
204-205	4.00
206-206/Whitman	5.00
207-207/Whitman	4.00
208-209/Whitman	5.00
210-210/Whitman	4.00
210/35¢	15.00
211-211/Whitman	4.00
211/35¢	15.00
212-212/Whitman	4.00
212/35¢	15.00
213-213/Whitman	4.00
213/35¢	15.00
214-214/Whitman	4.00
214/35¢	15.00
215-233/Whitman	4.00
234	6.00
235-240	4.00
241	8.00
242-255	4.00
256-271	2.00
272	3.00
273-275	2.00
276	4.00
277-281	2.00
282	3.00
282/2nd-283	2.00
284	3.00
285	2.00
286-288	3.00
289-297	2.00
298	3.00
299-331	2.00
332	3.00
333-349	2.00
350	3.00
351-382	2.00
383	3.00
384-399	2.00
400	3.00
401-420	2.00
420/CS	3.00
421-424	2.00
425	3.00
425/Variant	4.00
426-443	2.00

Cannon

Capital Capers Presents

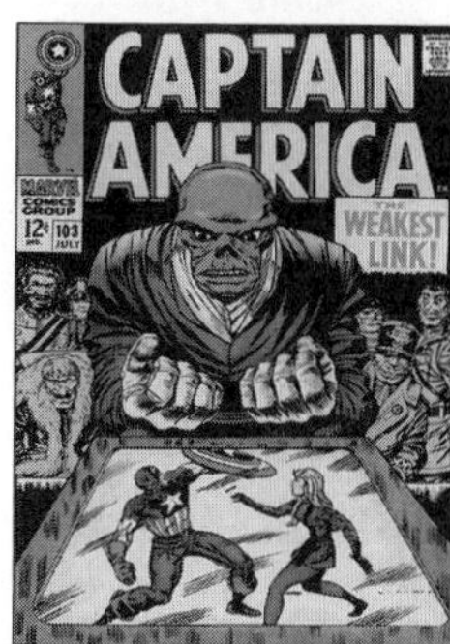

Captain America

Captain America Comics

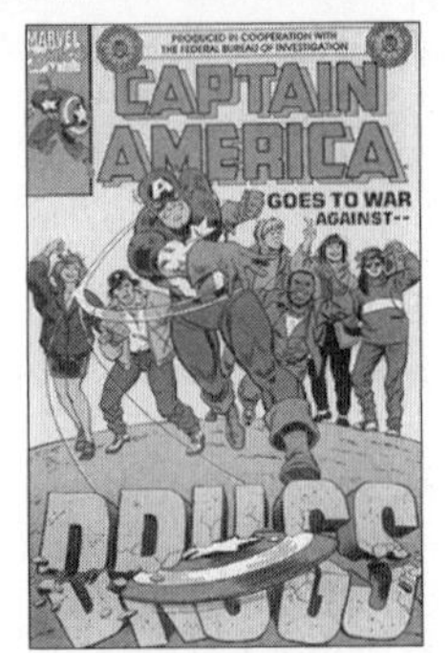

Captain America Goes to War Against Drugs

Captain Battle

Captain Battle Comics

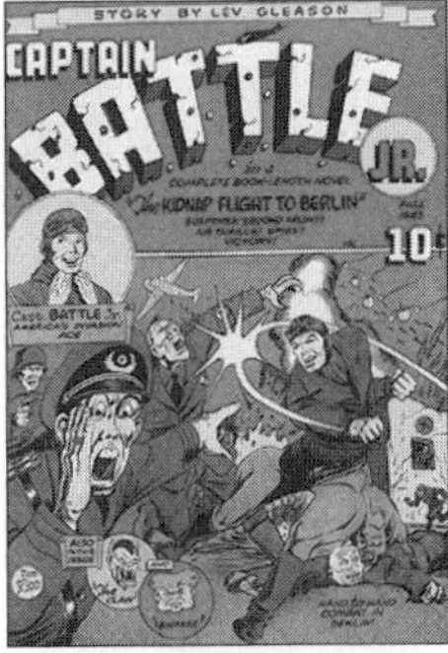

Captain Battle Jr.

444 .... 3.00
445-447 .... 2.00
448 .... 3.00
449-454 .... 2.00
Ann 1 .... 35.00
Ann 2 .... 20.00
Ann 3-4 .... 8.00
Ann 5-7 .... 3.00
Ann 8 .... 12.00
☛Wolverine app.
Ann 9-13 .... 3.00
Ashcan 1 .... 1.00
Special 1-2 .... 4.00

Captain America
Marvel, 1995

1 .... 3.00
1/Flag 4.00
1/Conv 25.00
2-13 .... 2.00
Ashcan 1-Ashcan 1/A 1.00

Captain America
Marvel, 1998

1 .... 4.00
1/Sunburst 5.00
2 .... 3.00
2/Variant 4.00
3-12 .... 2.00
12/Ltd. 6.00
13-17 .... 2.00
18 .... 3.00
19-24 .... 2.00
25 .... 3.00
26-49 .... 2.00
50 .... 6.00
Ann 1998-2000 .... 4.00
Ann 2001 .... 3.00

Captain America
Marvel, 2002

1 .... 4.00
2-32 .... 3.00

Captain America
Marvel, 2005

1 .... 8.00
2-3 .... 5.00
4-5 .... 3.00
6 .... 7.00
6/Variant 5.00
7 .... 3.00
8 .... 5.00
9-21 .... 3.00
22-24 .... 5.00
25-25/Variant 15.00
25/2nd 5.00
26-50 .... 3.00

Captain America and the Campbell Kids
Marvel, 1980

1 .... 3.00

Captain America & The Falcon
Marvel, 2004

1-5 .... 3.00
6 .... 4.00
☛Avengers Disassembled
7-14 .... 3.00

Captain America Battlebook
Marvel, 1998

1 .... 4.00

Captain America Comics
Marvel, 1941

1 .... 80,000.00
2 .... 20,000.00
3 .... 10,000.00
4 .... 6,500.00
5 .... 5,500.00
6 .... 4,750.00
7 .... 5,500.00
8 .... 4,000.00
9-10 .... 3,600.00
11-12 .... 3,100.00
13 .... 3,275.00
14-15 .... 3,100.00
16 .... 3,600.00
17 .... 2,585.00
18-20 .... 2,075.00
21-22 .... 1,850.00
22/A 12,000.00
☛GS issue
23-25 .... 1,850.00
26-30 .... 1,650.00
31-35 .... 1,385.00
36 .... 1,650.00
37 .... 1,550.00
38-40 .... 1,285.00
41-58 .... 1,175.00
59 .... 2,650.00
☛Cap origin
60 .... 1,175.00
61 .... 1,850.00
62-65 .... 1,075.00
66 .... 1,400.00
67-70 .... 1,175.00
71-73 .... 1,025.00
74 .... 4,350.00
☛Cap Weird Tales
75 .... 2,750.00
76-78 .... 875.00

Captain America: Dead Man Running
Marvel, 2002

1-3 .... 3.00

Captain America: Deathlok Lives!
Marvel

1 .... 5.00

Captain America: Drug War

Marvel, 1993

1 .... 2.00

Captain America Goes to War Against Drugs

Marvel, 1990

1 .... 1.00

Captain America: Medusa Effect

Marvel, 1994

1 .... 3.00

Captain America/Nick Fury: Blood Truce

Marvel, 1995

1 .... 6.00

Captain America/Nick Fury: The Otherworld War

Marvel, 2001

1 .... 7.00

Captain America: Sentinel of Liberty

Marvel, 1988

1 .... 2.00
1/Variant 3.00
2-5 .... 2.00
6 .... 3.00
7-11 .... 2.00
12 .... 3.00

Captain America 65th Anniversary Special

Marvel, 2006

1 .... 4.00

Captain America: The Legend

Marvel, 1996

1 .... 4.00

Captain America: The Movie Special

Marvel, 1992

1 .... 4.00

Captain America: What Price Glory

Marvel, 2003

1-4 .... 3.00

Captain & The Kids

United Feature, 1947

1 .... 100.00
2 .... 75.00
3 .... 50.00
4-6 .... 45.00
7-9 .... 40.00
10-12 .... 35.00
13-16 .... 30.00
17-19 .... 25.00
20-24 .... 20.00
25-29 .... 15.00
30-32 .... 12.00

Captain Armadillo: The Adventure Begins

Staton Graphics, 1989

1 .... 2.00

Captain Atom

Nationwide, 1950

1 .... 325.00
2 .... 165.00
3-5 .... 150.00
6-7 .... 125.00

Captain Atom

Charlton, 1965

78 .... 40.00
79-85 .... 25.00
86-89 .... 20.00

Captain Atom

Modern, 1977

83-85 .... 5.00

Captain Atom

DC, 1987

1-49 .... 1.00
50 .... 2.00
51-57 .... 1.00
Ann 1-2 .... 2.00

Captain Atom: Armageddon

DC, 2005

1-9 .... 3.00

Captain Awareness: Assault on Campus

2-D Graphics

1 .... 4.00

Captain Battle

Picture Scoop, 1942

3 .... 550.00
4-5 .... 450.00

Captain Battle Comics

New Friday, 1941

1 .... 1,250.00
2 .... 750.00

Captain Battle Jr.

Lev Gleason, 1943

1 .... 925.00
2 .... 700.00

Captain Britain

Marvel UK, 1985

1 .... 3.00
2-14 .... 2.00

Captain Canuck

Comely, 1975

1 .... 3.00
2-14 .... 2.00

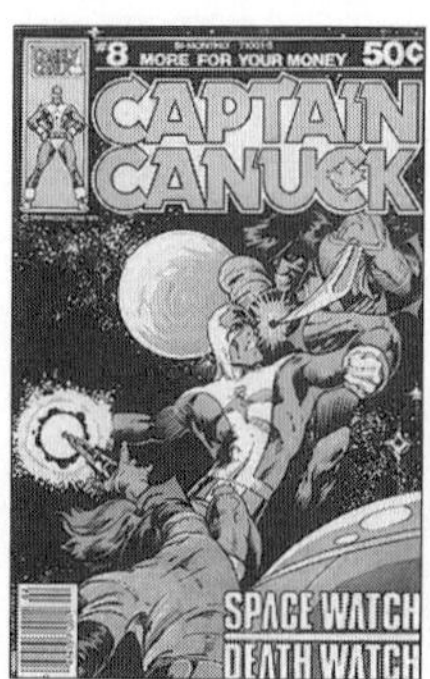

Captain Canuck

Captain Canuck Reborn

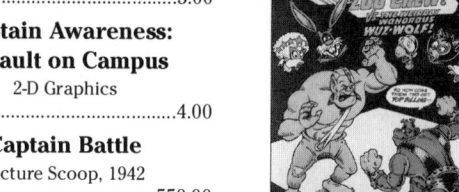

Captain Carrot and His Amazing Zoo Crew

Captain Easy

All comics prices listed are for NEAR MINT condition.

Captain Eo 3-D

Captain Fearless Comics

Captain Flight Comics

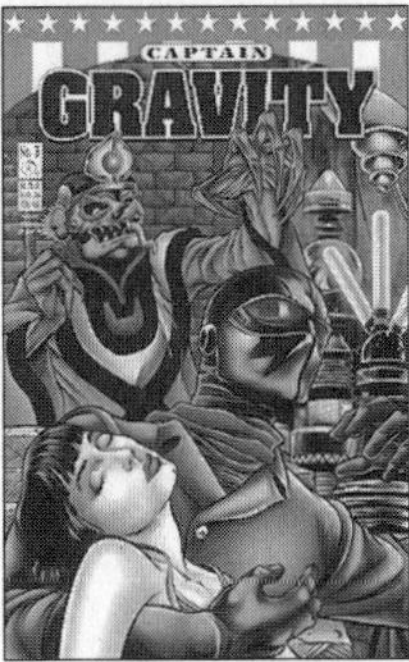

Captain Gravity

Captain Canuck First Summer Special
Comely, 1980

1 ....2.00

Captain Canuck Reborn
Semple, 1993

0 ....2.00
1-3 ....3.00

Captain Carrot and His Amazing Zoo Crew
DC, 1982

1 ....2.00
2-20 ....1.00

Captain Confederacy
Steeldragon, 1987

1-Special 2..2.00

Captain Confederacy
Marvel, 1991

1-4 ....2.00

Captain Cosmos, the Last Starveyor
Ybor City

1 ....3.00

Captain Crafty
Conception, 1994

1-2 ....3.00
2.5 ....1.00

Captain Crafty Color Spectacular
Conception, 1996

1-2 ....3.00

Captain Crusader
TPI, 1990

1 ....1.00

Captain Cult
Hammac

1 ....2.00

Captain Dingleberry
Slave Labor, 1998

1-6 ....3.00

Captain D's Adventure Magazine
Paragon, 1983

1-6 ....1.00

Captain Easy
Standard, 1947

10 ....160.00
11 ....125.00
12-14 ....100.00
15-17 ....90.00

Captain Electron
BCSI

1 ....2.00

Captain Eo 3-D
Eclipse, 1987

1 ....5.00

Captain Fearless Comics
Holyoke, 1941

1 ....475.00
2 ....300.00

Captain Flight Comics
Four Star, 1944

1 ....2,000.00
2 ....1,650.00
3 ....1,400.00
4 ....1,250.00
5 ....1,500.00
6 ....1,100.00
7-10 ....1,500.00
11 ....1,800.00

Captain Fortune
Rip Off

1-4 ....3.00

Captain Gallant
Charlton, 1955

1 ....11.00
1/A-3 ....8.00
4 ....5.00

Captain Glory
Topps, 1993

0-1 ....3.00

Captain Gravity
Penny-Farthing, 1998

1 ....3.00
2-4 ....3.00

Captain Gravity and the Power of the Vril
Penny-Farthing, 2004

1-6 ....3.00

Captain Gravity: One True Hero
Penny-Farthing, 1999

1 ....3.00

Captain Harlock
Eternity, 1989

1-13 ....3.00
Holiday 1 ....3.00

Captain Harlock: Deathshadow Rising
Eternity

1-6 ....2.00

Captain Harlock: The Fall of the Empire
Eternity, 1992

1-4 ....3.00

Captain Harlock: The Machine People
Eternity

1-4 ....3.00

Capt. Holo and His Adventures in the Holographic Dimension in 3-D
Blackthorne

1 ... 3.00

Captain Jet
Farrell, 1952

1 ... 125.00
2 ... 85.00
3 ... 60.00
4-5 ... 40.00

Captain Johner & the Aliens
Valiant, 1995

1-2 ... 6.00

Captain Justice
Marvel, 1988

1-2 ... 1.00

Captain Kidd
Fox, 1949

24-25 ... 100.00

Captain Marvel
M.F., 1966

1 ... 40.00
2-4 ... 25.00

Captain Marvel
Marvel, 1968

1 ... 60.00
2-3 ... 18.00
4 ... 24.00
5 ... 15.00
6 ... 30.00
7-8 ... 15.00
9 ... 25.00
10-15 ... 15.00
16 ... 25.00
17-24 ... 22.00
☛Thanos War starts
25-27 ... 25.00
28 ... 30.00
29 ... 16.00
30 ... 12.00
31 ... 16.00
32-33 ... 12.00
34 ... 6.00
35-37 ... 3.00
38 ... 5.00
39-44 ... 3.00
44/30¢ ... 20.00
45 ... 3.00
45/30¢ ... 20.00
46-47 ... 3.00
48 ... 9.00
49 ... 3.00
50 ... 10.00
51-52 ... 4.00
52/35¢ ... 15.00
53-54 ... 3.00
55 ... 5.00
56 ... 3.00
57 ... 6.00
58-62 ... 3.00

Captain Marvel
Marvel, 1989

1 ... 2.00

Captain Marvel
Marvel, 1994

1-2 ... 2.00

Captain Marvel
Marvel, 1995

1 ... 3.00
2-6 ... 2.00

Captain Marvel
Marvel, 1999

0-1 ... 3.00
1/A ... 4.00
2-35 ... 3.00

Captain Marvel
Marvel, 2002

1-4 ... 2.00
5-25 ... 3.00

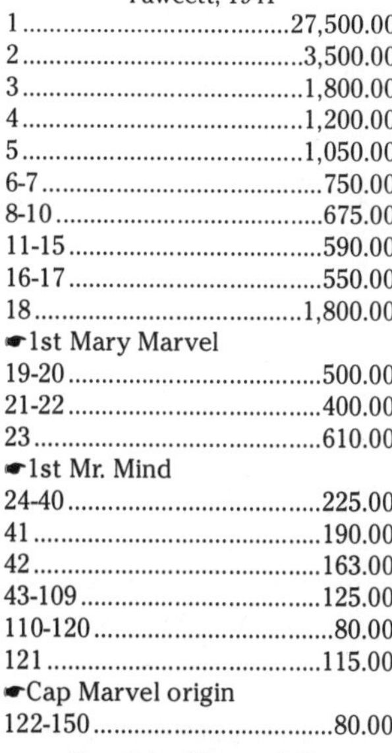

Captain Marvel Adventures
Fawcett, 1941

1 ... 27,500.00
2 ... 3,500.00
3 ... 1,800.00
4 ... 1,200.00
5 ... 1,050.00
6-7 ... 750.00
8-10 ... 675.00
11-15 ... 590.00
16-17 ... 550.00
18 ... 1,800.00
☛1st Mary Marvel
19-20 ... 500.00
21-22 ... 400.00
23 ... 610.00
☛1st Mr. Mind
24-40 ... 225.00
41 ... 190.00
42 ... 163.00
43-109 ... 125.00
110-120 ... 80.00
121 ... 115.00
☛Cap Marvel origin
122-150 ... 80.00

Captain Marvel Jr.
Fawcett, 1942

1 ... 4,000.00
2 ... 1,500.00
3 ... 865.00
4 ... 915.00
5 ... 735.00
6-8 ... 545.00
9-10 ... 500.00
11-15 ... 390.00

Captain Jet

Captain Justice

Captain Marvel Adventures

Captain Marvel Storybook

Captain Midnight

Captain Nice

Captain Paragon

Captain Planet and the Planeteers

16-20 .... 340.00
21-25 .... 275.00
26-30 .... 235.00
31-40 .... 205.00
41-50 .... 180.00
51-70 .... 155.00
71-80 .... 135.00
81-119 .... 120.00

Captain Marvel Presents The Terrible Five

M.F., 1967

1 .... 18.00

Captain Marvel Storybook

Fawcett, 1947

1 .... 450.00
2 .... 310.00
3-4 .... 300.00

Captain Marvel Thrill Book

Fawcett

1 .... 5,000.00

Captain Midnight

Fawcett, 1942

1 .... 2,400.00
2 .... 1,050.00
3-5 .... 750.00
6-10 .... 585.00
11-15 .... 400.00
16-20 .... 375.00
21-30 .... 285.00
31-40 .... 225.00
41-50 .... 200.00
51-60 .... 175.00
61-67 .... 160.00

Captain Nauticus & the Ocean Force

Express, 1994

1-2 .... 3.00

Captain Nice

Gold Key, 1967

1 .... 35.00

Captain N: the Game Master

Valiant, 1990

1-6 .... 2.00

Captain Oblivion

Harrier, 1987

1 .... 2.00

Captain Paragon

AC, 1983

1-4 .... 2.00

Captain Paragon and the Sentinels of Justice

AC

1-6 .... 2.00

Captain Phil

Steeldragon

1 .... 2.00

Captain Planet and the Planeteers

Marvel, 1991

1-12 .... 1.00

Captain Power and the Soldiers of the Future

Continuity, 1988

1-2 .... 2.00

Captain Rocket

P.L., 1951

1 .... 300.00

Captain Salvation

Streetlight

1 .... 2.00

Captain Satan

Millennium

1-2 .... 3.00

Capt. Savage and His Leatherneck Raiders

Marvel, 1968

1 .... 35.00
2 .... 25.00
3-11 .... 15.00
12-19 .... 10.00

Captain Science

Youthful, 1950

1 .... 800.00
2 .... 450.00
3-4 .... 350.00
5-6 .... 300.00
7 .... 275.00

Captain's Jolting Tales

One Shot, 1991

1 .... 3.00
2-4 .... 4.00

Captain Sternn: Running Out of Time

Kitchen Sink, 1993

1 .... 6.00
2-5 .... 5.00

Captain Steve Savage

Avon, 1951

1 .... 120.00
2 .... 85.00
3-13 .... 55.00

Capt. Storm

DC, 1964

1 .... 28.00
2-5 .... 18.00
6 .... 14.00
7-15 .... 12.00
16-18 .... 9.00

Captain Tax Time
Paul Haynes Comics

1 .... 4.00

Captain 3-D
Harvey, 1953

1 .... 75.00

Captain Thunder and Blue Bolt
Hero, 0

1-10 .... 2.00

Captain Thunder and Blue Bolt
Hero, 1992

1-2 .... 4.00

Captain Universe/ Daredevil
Marvel, 2006

1 .... 3.00

Captain Universe/ Invisible Woman
Marvel, 2006

1 .... 3.00

Captain Universe/ Silver Surfer
Marvel, 2006

1 .... 3.00

Captain Universe/ The Incredible Hulk
Marvel, 2006

1 .... 3.00

Captain Universe/X-23
Marvel, 2006

1 .... 3.00

Captain Venture and the Land Beneath the Sea
Gold Key, 1968

1 .... 26.00
2 .... 18.00

Captain Victory and the Galactic Rangers
Pacific, 1981

1-12 .... 1.00
13-Special 1 .... 2.00

Captain Victory and the Galactic Rangers
Jack Kirby, 2000

1-3 .... 3.00

Captain Video
Fawcett, 1951

1 .... 425.00
2 .... 350.00
3-6 .... 225.00

Captain Wings Compact Comics
AC

1-2 .... 4.00

Captain Zephyr and the Tiger Woman
Millennium

1 .... 3.00

Caravan Kidd
Dark Horse, 1992

1-10 .... 3.00

Caravan Kidd Part 2
Dark Horse, 1993

1-10 .... 3.00

Caravan Kidd Part 3
Dark Horse, 1994

1-8 .... 3.00

Carbon Knight
Lunar, 1997

1-4 .... 3.00

Cardcaptor Sakura Comic
Mixx, 2000

1-34 .... 3.00

Cardcaptor Sakura: Master of the Clow
Tokyopop, 2002

1-6 .... 10.00

Care Bears
Marvel, 1985

1-20 .... 1.00

Career Girl Romances
Charlton, 1964

24-31 .... 4.00
32 .... 40.00
33-78 .... 3.00

Car 54 Where Are You?
Dell, 1962

2 .... 75.00
3 .... 45.00
4-5 .... 40.00
6-7 .... 35.00

Carl and Larry Christmas Special
Comics Interview

1 .... 2.00

Carmen
NBM

1 .... 11.00

Carmilla
Aircel, 1991

1-6 .... 3.00

Carnage
Eternity

1 .... 2.00

Captain Science

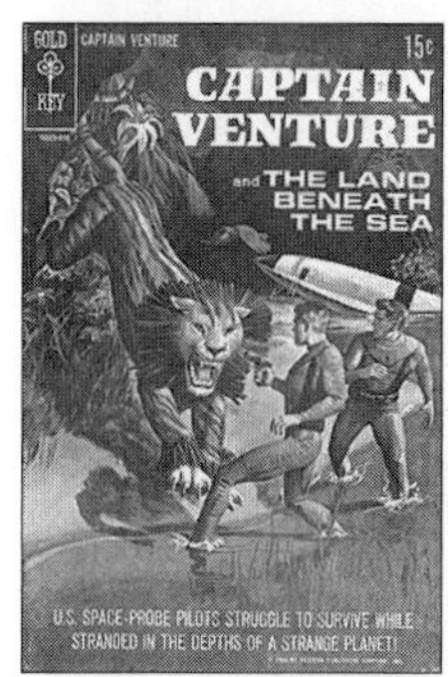

Captain Venture and the Land Beneath the Sea

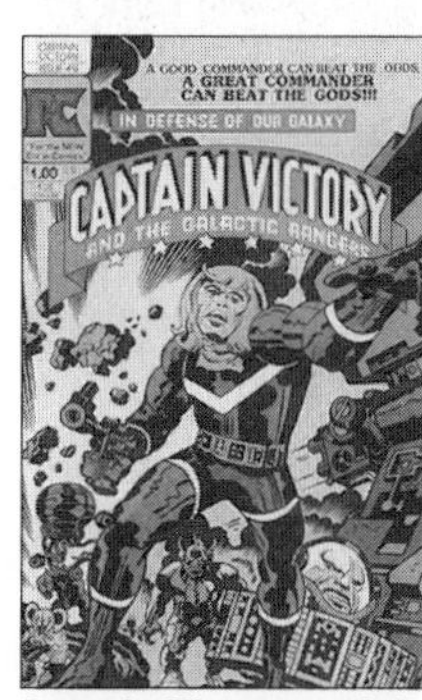

Captain Victory and the Galactic Rangers

Captain Video

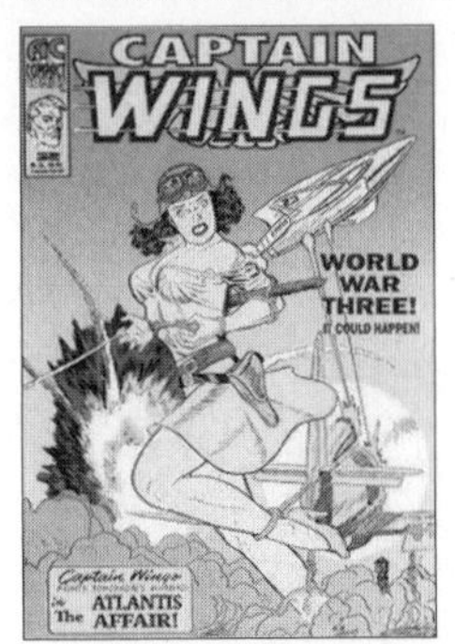

Captain Wings Compact Comics

Caravan Kidd

Care Bears

Carnosaur Carnage

Carnage: It's a Wonderful Life

Marvel, 1996

1 ....2.00

Carnage: Mindbomb

Marvel, 1996

1 ....3.00

Carnal Comics: Anna Malle

Re-Visionary, 1996

1 ....3.00

Carnal Comics: Brittany O'Connell

Re-Visionary, 1996

1 ....3.00

Carnal Comics: Bunny Bleu

Revisionary, 1996

1 ....3.00

Carnal Comics: Christi Lake

Re-Visionary, 1998

1/A 0.00
1 ....4.00

Carnal Comics: Jeanna Fine

Re-Visionary, 1995

1 ....3.00

Carnal Comics: Jenna Jameson

Re-Visionary, 1995

1 ....3.00

Carnal Comics: Jill Kelly

Re-Visionary, 1997

1 ....4.00

Carnal Comics: Julia Ann

Re-Visionary, 1995

1 ....3.00

Carnal Comics: Legends of Porn

Re-Visionary, 1998

1 ....4.00

Carnal Comics: Lisa Ann

Re-Visionary, 1996

1 ....3.00

Carnal Comics: Nici Sterling

Re-Visionary, 1996

1 ....3.00

Carnal Comics: Porsche Lynn

Re-Visionary, 1996

1 ....3.00

Carnal Comics Presents Deja Sin: Fallen Angel

Revolutionary, 1999

1-1/B 4.00

Carnal Comics Presents Demi's Wild Kingdom Adventure

Revisionary, 1999

1 ....4.00

Carnal Comics Presents Ginger Lynn is Torn

Revisionary, 1999

1-1/A 4.00

Carnal Comics Presents Marilyn Chambers Is Still Insatiable

Revisionary, 1999

1-1/A 4.00

Carnal Comics Presents Porn Star Fantasies

Re-Visionary, 1995

1-10 ....3.00

Carnal Comics Presents Wicked Weapon: Official Film Adaptation

Revisionary

1-1/Ashcan 4.00

Carnal Comics: Rebecca Bardoux

Re-Visionary, 1994

1 ....3.00

Carnal Comics: Rebecca Lord

Re-Visionary, 1998

1-1/Nude 4.00

Carnal Comics: Sarah-Jane Hamilton

Revolutionary, 1994

1-3 ....3.00

Carnal Comics: Summer Cummings & Skye Blue

Re-Visionary, 1998

1 ....4.00

Carnal Comics: Taylor Wane

Re-Visionary, 1995

1 ....3.00

Carnal Comics: Zo'

Revisionary, 1998

1-1/Nude 4.00

Carneys

Archie, 1994

1 ....2.00

Carnosaur Carnage
Atomeka
1 .... 5.00

Cartoon Cartoons
DC, 2001
1-33 .... 2.00

Cartoon History of the Universe
Rip Off, 1990
1 .... 5.00
2-5 .... 4.00
6-9 .... 3.00

Cartoonist
Sirius, 1997
1 .... 3.00

Cartoon Network
DC
1 .... 1.00

Cartoon Network Action Pack
DC, 2006
1-45 .... 2.00

Cartoon Network Block Party
DC, 2004
1-2 .... 2.00
3 .... 3.00
4-55 .... 2.00

Cartoon Network Christmas Spectacular
Archie
1 .... 2.00

Cartoon Network Presents
DC, 1997
1-24 .... 2.00

Cartoon Network Presents Space Ghost
Archie, 1997
1 .... 2.00

Cartoon Network Starring
DC, 1999
1-2 .... 3.00
3-18 .... 2.00

Cartoon Quarterly
Gladstone
1 .... 5.00

Cartoon Tales
Disney, 1992
1-4 .... 3.00

Cartune Land
Magic Carpet, 1987
1-4 .... 2.00

Carvers
Image, 1998
1-3 .... 3.00

Car Warriors
Marvel, 1991
1-4 .... 2.00

Casa Howhard
NBM
1-4 .... 11.00

Casanova
Aircel, 1991
1-10 .... 3.00

Casanova
Image, 1991
1-3 .... 3.00
4 .... 2.00
5-6 .... 3.00

Casefiles: Sam & Twitch
Image, 2003
1-25 .... 3.00

Case Morgan, Gumshoe Private Eye
Forbidden Fruit, 1991
1-10 .... 3.00
11 .... 4.00

Case of Blind Fear, A
Eternity, 1989
1-4 .... 2.00

Case of the Wasted Water
Rheem, 1972
1 .... 5.00

Cases of Sherlock Holmes
Renegade, 1986
1-24 .... 2.00

Casey, Crime Photographer
Marvel, 1949
1-4 .... 125.00

Casey Jones & Raphael
Mirage, 1994
1 .... 3.00

Casey Jones: North By Downeast
Mirage, 1994
1-2 .... 3.00

Casper Adventure Digest
Harvey, 1992
1-8 .... 2.00

Casper and Friends
Harvey, 1991
1-5 .... 2.00

Casper and Friends Magazine
Marvel, 1997
1-3 .... 4.00

Casper and Nightmare
Harvey, 1964
6 .... 35.00

Cartoon Cartoons

Cartoon Network Presents

Cases of Sherlock Holmes

Casper and Friends

Casper and Friends Magazine

Casper and the Ghostly Trio

Casper in 3-D

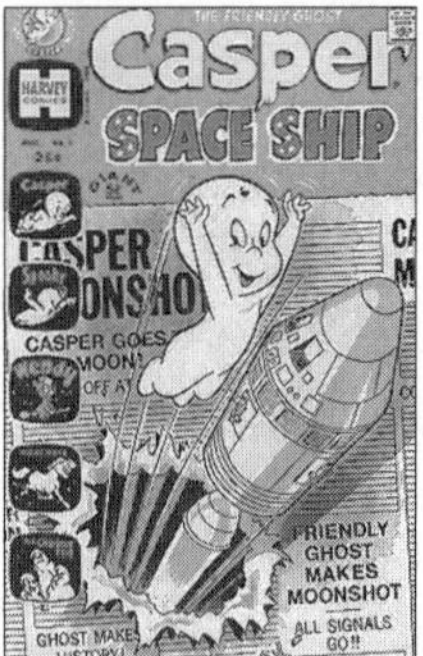

Casper Space Ship

7-10 .... 24.00
11-20 .... 16.00
21-35 .... 14.00
36-46 .... 10.00

Casper and Spooky
Harvey, 1972

1 .... 5.00
2-7 .... 3.00

Casper and the Ghostly Trio
Harvey, 1972

1 .... 20.00
2-4 .... 15.00
5-7 .... 12.00
8-10 .... 2.00

Casper & Wendy
Harvey, 1972

1 .... 9.00
2 .... 5.00
3-5 .... 4.00
6-8 .... 3.00

Casper Digest Magazine
Harvey, 1986

1 .... 3.00
2-13 .... 2.00

Casper Digest Magazine
Harvey, 1991

1-14 .... 2.00

Casper Enchanted Tales Digest
Harvey, 1992

1-10 .... 2.00

Casper Ghostland
Harvey, 1992

1 .... 2.00

Casper Giant Size
Harvey

1-4 .... 2.00

Casper in 3-D
Blackthorne, 1988

1 .... 3.00

Casper's Ghostland
Harvey, 1958

1 .... 175.00
2 .... 75.00
3-5 .... 50.00
6-10 .... 40.00
11-20 .... 25.00
21-30 .... 20.00
31-40 .... 15.00
41-60 .... 10.00
61-81 .... 5.00
82-98 .... 4.00

Casper Space Ship
Harvey, 1972

1 .... 16.00
2-3 .... 13.00
4-5 .... 10.00

Casper, The Friendly Ghost
St. John, 1949

1 .... 2,100.00
2 .... 675.00
3 .... 455.00
4 .... 350.00
5 .... 275.00

Casper, The Friendly Ghost
Harvey, 1952

7 .... 300.00
8 .... 200.00
9-19 .... 100.00
20 .... 500.00
21-39 .... 100.00
40-51 .... 75.00
52-63 .... 60.00
64-70 .... 55.00

Casper, The Friendly Ghost
Harvey, 1949

1 .... 2,100.00
2 .... 675.00
3 .... 455.00
4 .... 350.00
5 .... 275.00
7 .... 225.00
8-10 .... 125.00
11 .... 90.00
12-13 .... 90.00
14-15 .... 90.00
16-17 .... 90.00
18-19 .... 90.00
20 .... 150.00
21 .... 80.00
22-23 .... 80.00
24-25 .... 80.00
26-27 .... 80.00
28-30 .... 80.00
31-40 .... 55.00
41-50 .... 40.00
51-70 .... 30.00

Casper, The Friendly Ghost
Harvey, 1990

254-260 .... 2.00

Casper, The Friendly Ghost
Harvey, 1991

1-GS 4 .... 2.00

Casper, The Friendly Ghost Big Book
Harvey, 1992

1-3 .... 2.00

Cast
Nautilus Comics, 2005

1-2 .... 3.00

Castlevania: The Belmont Legacy
Idea & Design Works, 2005

1-5 .... 4.00

Castle Waiting

Olio, 1997

1 ... 5.00
1/2nd-1/3rd ... 4.00
2-16 ... 3.00
Ashcan 1 ... 10.00

Castle Waiting

Cartoon Books, 2000

1-4 ... 3.00

Casual Heroes

Image, 1996

1-5 ... 2.00

Cat

Marvel, 1972

1 ... 35.00
2 ... 15.00
3 ... 12.00
4 ... 10.00

Cat

Aircel, 1991

1-2 ... 3.00

Catalyst: Agents of Change

Dark Horse, 1994

1-7 ... 2.00

Cat & Mouse

EF Graphics, 1989

1-1/2nd ... 2.00

Cat & Mouse

Aircel, 1990

1-18 ... 2.00

Cat Claw

Eternity, 1990

1-9 ... 3.00

Catfight

Insomnia, 1995

1-1/Gold ... 3.00

Catfight: Dream into Action

Lightning, 1996

1 ... 3.00

Catfight: Dream Warrior

Lightning, 1995

1 ... 3.00

Catfight: Escape from Limbo

Lightning, 1996

1 ... 3.00

Catfight: Sweet Revenge

Lightning, 1997

1 ... 3.00

Catharsis

Being, 1994

1 ... 3.00

Cathexis

NBM

1 ... 14.00

Catholic Comics

Catholic, 1946

1 ... 40.00
2-10 ... 36.00

Catholic Pictorial

Catholic Guild, 1947

1 ... 35.00

Catman

AC, 1995

1-2 ... 6.00

Catman Comics

Continental, 1941

1 ... 3,500.00
2 ... 1,650.00
3 ... 1,400.00
4 ... 1,200.00
5-6 ... 875.00
7-9 ... 800.00
10-14 ... 700.00
15-17 ... 650.00
18-20 ... 590.00
21-22 ... 540.00
23-25 ... 485.00
25/2nd ... 500.00
25/A ... 550.00
26-29 ... 440.00
30-32 ... 375.00

Catnip

Side Show

1 ... 3.00

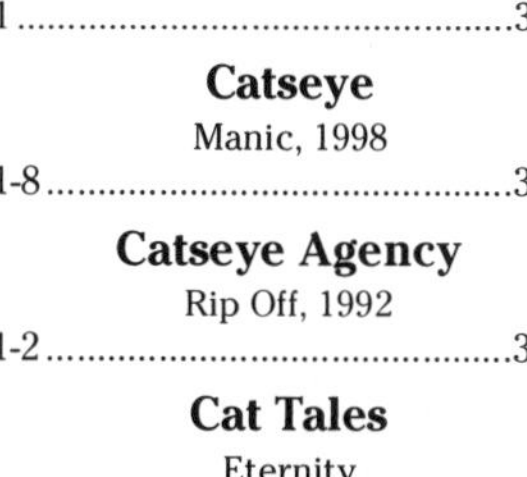

Catseye

Manic, 1998

1-8 ... 3.00

Catseye Agency

Rip Off, 1992

1-2 ... 3.00

Cat Tales

Eternity

1 ... 3.00

Cat, T.H.E.

Dell, 1967

1 ... 18.00
2-4 ... 12.00

Cattle Brain

Itchy Eyeball

1-3 ... 3.00

Catwoman

DC, 1989

1-2 ... 3.00
3-4 ... 2.00

Catwoman

DC, 1993

0 ... 2.00
1-10 ... 3.00

Casper The Friendly Ghost Big Book

Castle Waiting

Catman Comics

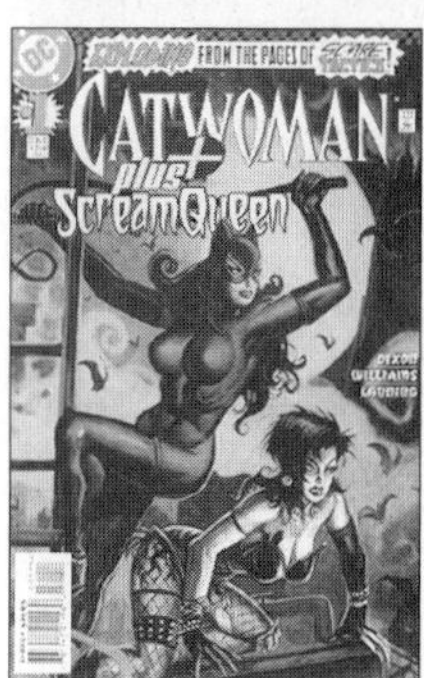

Catwoman Plus

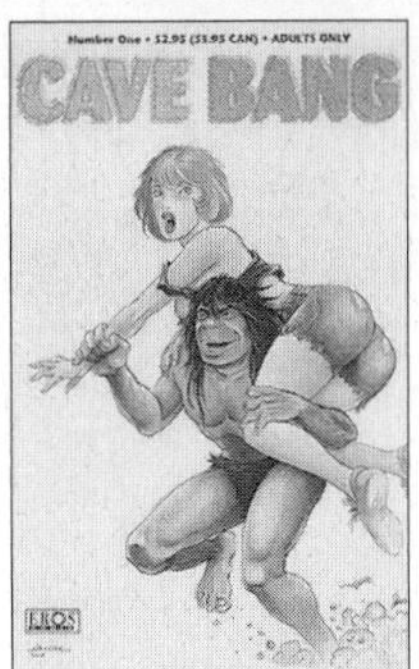
Cave Bang

Cave Girl

Cave Kids

Cavewoman

11-50 .... 2.00
50/A-50/B 3.00
51-94 .... 2.00
1000000 .... 3.00
Ann 1-2 .... 4.00
Ann 3 .... 3.00
Ann 4 .... 4.00

Catwoman
DC, 2002
1 .... 4.00
2-62 .... 3.00

Catwoman: Crooked Little Town
DC, 2003
1 .... 15.00

Catwoman: Guardian of Gotham
DC, 1999
1-2 .... 6.00

Catwoman Plus
DC, 1997
1 .... 3.00

Catwoman Secret Files and Origins
DC, 2002
1 .... 5.00

Catwoman The Movie
DC, 2004
1 .... 5.00

Catwoman/Vampirella: The Furies
DC, 1997
1 .... 5.00

Catwoman: When in Rome
DC, 2004
1-6 .... 4.00

Catwoman/Wildcat
DC, 1998
1-4 .... 3.00

Cave Bang
Fantagraphics, 1996
1-4 .... 3.00

Cave Girl
AC
1 .... 3.00

Cave Girl
Magazine Enterprises, 1954
1 .... 3.00
12-14 .... 185.00

Cave Kids
Gold Key, 1963
1 .... 35.00
2 .... 18.00
3-5 .... 15.00
6-12 .... 12.00
13-16 .... 9.00

Caveman
Caveman, 1998
1-4 .... 4.00
GN 1 .... 10.00

Cavewoman
Basement, 1994
1 .... 26.00
2 .... 20.00
3 .... 15.00
4 .... 12.00
5-6 .... 10.00

Cavewoman Color Special
Avatar, 1999
1 .... 4.00

Cavewoman: Missing Link
Basement, 1997
1-2 .... 3.00

Cavewoman: Odyssey
Caliber
1-5 .... 3.00

Cavewoman One-Shot
Basement, 2001
1 .... 4.00

Cavewoman: Pangaean Sea
Avatar, 1999
0-SE 4.00
Ashcan 1 .... 5.00

Cavewoman: Rain
Basement, 1996
1-1/3rd 3.00
2 .... 4.00
2/2nd-2/3rd 3.00
3 .... 4.00
3/2nd-8 .... 3.00

Cavewoman: Raptor
Basement, 2002
1 .... 3.00

Cecil Kunkle
Darkline
1-2 .... 4.00
3 .... 2.00

Cecil Kunkle
Renegade, 1986
1 .... 2.00

Celebrity
Horizontal
1 .... 3.00

Celestial Mechanics: The Adventures of Widget Wilhelmina Jones
Innovation, 1990
1-3 .... 2.00

Celestine
Image, 1996
1-2 .... 3.00

Cell
Antarctic, 1996
1-3 .... 3.00

Cement Shooz
Horse Feathers, 1991
1-2 .... 3.00

Cenotaph
Northstar
1 .... 4.00

Centerfield
Alternative, 2005
1 .... 4.00

Centrifugal Bumble-Puppy
Fantagraphics
1-7 .... 2.00
8 .... 3.00

Centurions
DC, 1987
1-4 .... 1.00

Century: Distant Sons
Marvel, 1996
1 .... 3.00

Cereal Killings
Fantagraphics, 1992
1-8 .... 3.00

Cerebus Bi-Weekly
Aardvark-Vanaheim, 1988
1-16 .... 2.00
17 .... 4.00
18-19 .... 2.00
20 .... 6.00
21-26 .... 2.00

Cerebus: Church & State
Aardvark-Vanaheim, 1991
1-30 .... 2.00

Cerebus Companion
Win-Mill, 1993
1-2 .... 4.00

Cerebus Guide to Self Publishing
Aardvark-Vanaheim, 1997
1 .... 4.00

Cerebus: Guys Party Pack
Aardvark-Vanaheim
1 .... 4.00

Cerebus High Society
Aardvark-Vanaheim, 1990
1-25 .... 2.00

Cerebus Jam
Aardvark-Vanaheim, 1985
1 .... 3.00

Cerebus the Aardvark
Aardvark-Vanaheim, 1977
0 .... 4.00
0/Gold 6.00
1 .... 700.00
1/Counterfeit 60.00
2 .... 150.00
3 .... 90.00
4 .... 75.00
5 .... 50.00
6 .... 35.00
7 .... 20.00
8-10 .... 15.00
11 .... 12.00
12-22 .... 10.00
23-31 .... 6.00
32-40 .... 5.00
41-50 .... 4.00
51 .... 6.00
52-57 .... 4.00
58-60 .... 3.00
61-62 .... 4.00
63-100 .... 3.00
101-299 .... 2.00
300 .... 4.00

Cerebus World Tour Book
Aardvark-Vanaheim
1 .... 3.00

Ceres Celestial Legend Part 1
Viz, 2001
1-6 .... 3.00

Ceres Celestial Legend Part 2
Viz, 2001
1-5 .... 3.00
6 .... 4.00

Ceres Celestial Legend Part 3
Viz, 2002
1 .... 3.00
2-4 .... 4.00

Ceres Celestial Legend Part 4
Viz, 2002
1-4 .... 4.00

Ceres Celestial Legend Part 5
Viz, 2003
1 .... 4.00

Chadz Frendz
Smiling Face, 1998
1 .... 2.00

Chaingang
Northstar
1-2 .... 3.00

Chain Gang War
DC, 1993
1-1/Silver 3.00
2-4 .... 2.00
5 .... 3.00
6-12 .... 2.00

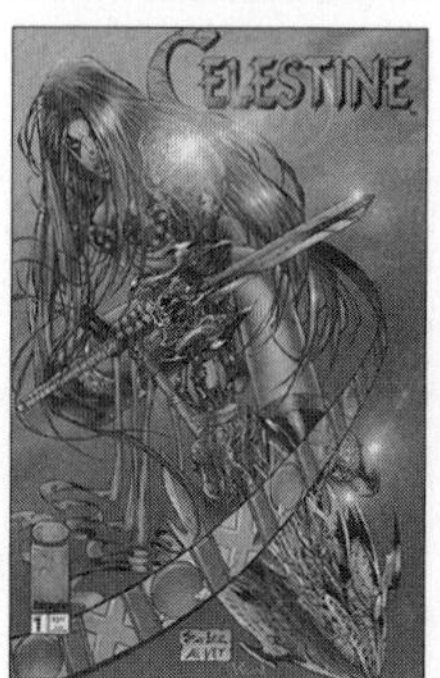

Celestine

Centurions

Cereal Killings

Cerebus the Aardvark

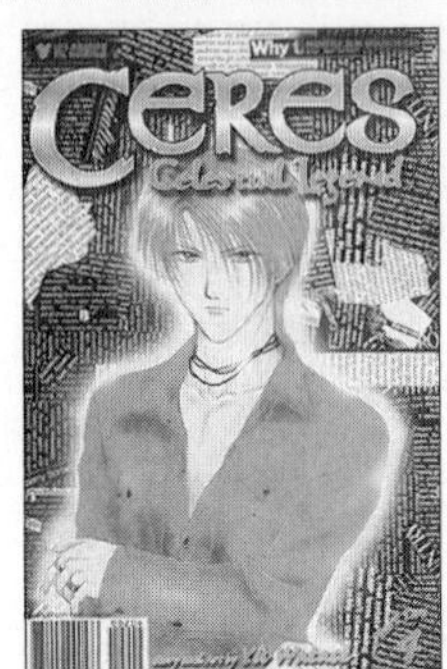
Ceres Celestial Legend Part 2

Chain Gang War

Challenge of the Unknown

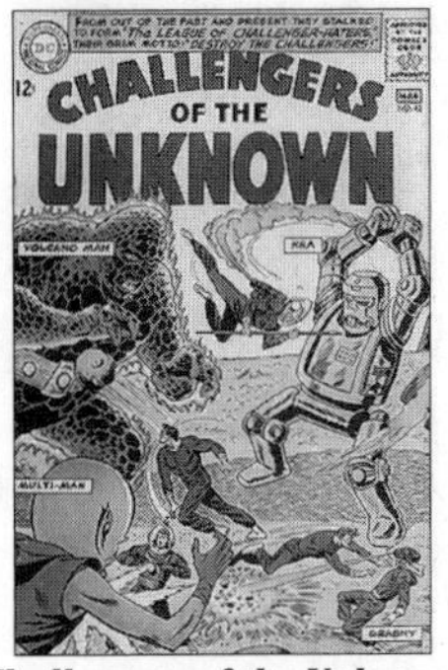
Challengers of the Unknown

Chainsaw Vigilante
NEC
1 ....4.00
1/A 5.00
1/B-1/C 6.00
2-3 ....3.00

Chains of Chaos
Harris, 1994
1-3 ....3.00

Chakan
Rak, 1994
1 ....5.00

Challenge of the Unknown
Ace, 1950
6 ....225.00

Challengers of the Fantastic
Marvel, 1997
1 ....2.00

Challengers of the Unknown
DC, 1958
1 ....1,450.00
2 ....375.00
3-8 ....220.00
9-10 ....140.00
11-15 ....90.00
16-23 ....52.00
24-31 ....25.00
32-49 ....20.00
50-56 ....15.00
57-69 ....11.00
70-73 ....7.00
74 ....14.00
☛Adams art; Deadman
75-80 ....7.00
81 ....6.00
82-87 ....5.00

Challengers of the Unknown
DC, 1997
1-17 ....2.00
18 ....3.00

Challengers of the Unknown
DC, 1991
1-8 ....2.00

Challengers of the Unknown
DC, 2004
1-6 ....3.00

Chamber
Marvel, 2002
1-4 ....3.00

Chamber of Chills
Harvey, 1951
1 ....350.00
2-4 ....275.00
5-9 ....250.00
10-19 ....225.00
20-25 ....200.00
26 ....175.00

Chamber of Chills
Marvel, 1972
1 ....25.00
2-10 ....15.00
11-22 ....12.00
22/30¢ 20.00
23 ....12.00
23/30¢ 20.00
24-25 ....12.00

Chamber of Clues
Harvey, 1955
27 ....30.00
28 ....25.00

Chamber of Darkness
Marvel, 1968
1 ....60.00
2 ....35.00
3 ....30.00
4 ....60.00
☛BWS Conan tryout
5-7 ....30.00
8-1/Special 20.00

Chamber of Evil
Comax
1 ....3.00

Champ Comics
Harvey, 1940
11 ....850.00
12-13 ....750.00
14-15 ....700.00
16-18 ....650.00
19-21 ....600.00
22-25 ....550.00

Champion
Special Studio
1 ....3.00

Champion Comics
Harvey, 1939
2 ....950.00
3-4 ....700.00
5-7 ....600.00
8-10 ....475.00

Champion of Katara
Mu, 1992
1-2 ....3.00

Champion of Katara: Dum-Dums & Dragons
Mu, 1995
1-3 ....3.00

Champions
Marvel, 1975
1 .... 15.00
2-3 .... 6.00
4-5 .... 5.00
5/30¢ 20.00
6 .... 4.00
6/30¢ 20.00
7 .... 4.00
7/30¢ 20.00
8-14 .... 4.00
14/35¢ 15.00
15 .... 4.00
15/35¢ 15.00
16-17 .... 4.00

Champions
Eclipse, 1986
1-6 .... 1.00

Champions
Hero, 1987
1-14 .... 2.00
15 .... 4.00
Ann 1 .... 3.00
Ann 2 .... 4.00

Champions Classics
Hero, 1993
1 .... 1.00
13-15 .... 4.00

Champions Classics/Flare Adventures
Hero, 1993
2-3 .... 3.00
4-7 .... 4.00

Champion Sports
DC, 1973
1 .... 5.00
2-3 .... 4.00

Change Commander Goku
Antarctic, 1993
1-5 .... 3.00

Change Commander Goku 2
Antarctic, 1996
1-4 .... 3.00

Changes
Tundra
1 .... 8.00

Channel Zero
Image, 1998
1-6 .... 3.00

Channel Zero: Dupe
Image, 1999
1 .... 3.00

Chaos! Bible
Chaos, 1995
1 .... 4.00

Chaos! Chronicles
Chaos, 2000
1 .... 4.00

Chaos Effect: Alpha
Valiant, 1994
1 .... 3.00
1/Red foil 90.00

Chaos Effect: Epilogue
Valiant, 1994
1-2 .... 2.00

Chaos Effect: Omega
Valiant, 1994
1 .... 2.00
1/Gold 20.00

Chaos Effect: Beta
Valiant
1 .... 2.00

Chaos! Gallery
Chaos!, 1997
1 .... 3.00

Chaos! Presents Jade
Chaos, 2001
1-4 .... 3.00

Chaos! Quarterly
Chaos, 1995
1-2 .... 5.00
3 .... 4.00

Chapel
Image, 1995
1-2 .... 3.00
2/Variant 4.00

Chapel
Image, 1995
1-2 .... 3.00

Chapel
Image, 1995
1-7 .... 3.00

Chapel
Awesome, 1997
1 .... 3.00

Charlemagne
Defiant, 1994
0 .... 1.00
1-8 .... 3.00

Charles Burns' Modern Horror Sketchbook
Kitchen Sink
1 .... 7.00

Charlie Chan
Crestwood, 1948
1 .... 550.00
2 .... 340.00
3 .... 250.00
4-5 .... 175.00
6-9 .... 140.00

Chamber of Darkness

Champion Comics

Champion Sports

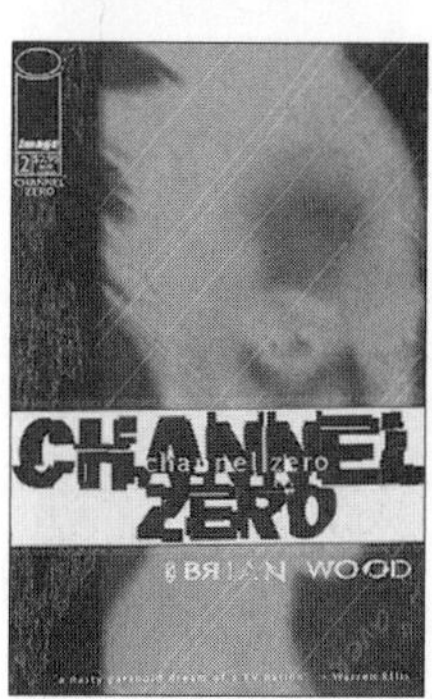

Channel Zero

Chapel

Charlemagne

Charlton Classics

Chase

Charlie Chan
Dell, 1965

1 ....35.00
2 ....25.00

Charlie Chan
Eternity, 1989

1-6 ....2.00

Charlie McCarthy
Dell, 1949

1 ....125.00
2 ....75.00
3-5 ....50.00
6-9 ....45.00

Charlie the Caveman
Fantasy General

1 ....2.00

Charlton Action Featuring Static
Charlton, 1985

11-12 ....2.00

Charlton Bullseye
Charlton, 1981

1 ....7.00
2-10 ....2.00

Charlton Classics
Charlton, 1980

1 ....3.00
2-9 ....2.00

Charlton Premiere
Charlton, 1967

19 ....20.00

Charlton Premiere
Charlton, 1967

1 ....6.00
2-4 ....4.00

Charlton Sport Library: Professional Football
Charlton, 1969

1 ....35.00

Charm School
Slave Labor, 2000

1-3 ....3.00

Chase
DC, 1998

1-9 ....3.00
1000000 ....2.00

Chase
APComics, 2004

1 ....4.00
1/Sketch 5.00
2-4 ....4.00

Chaser Platoon
Aircel, 1991

1-6 ....2.00

Chasing Dogma
Image

1 ....15.00

Chassis
Millennium, 1996

1-3 ....3.00

Chassis
Hurricane, 1998

0-3 ....3.00

Chassis
Image, 1999

0-5 ....3.00

Chastity
Chaos!, 2001

½-3 ....3.00

Chastity: Lust for Life
Chaos!, 1999

1 ....4.00
1/Dynamic 5.00
1/Ltd. 20.00
2-3 ....3.00

Chastity: Reign of Terror
Chaos!, 2000

1 ....3.00

Chastity: Rocked
Chaos!, 1998

1-4 ....3.00

Chastity: Theatre of Pain
Chaos!, 1997

1 ....3.00
1/Variant 4.00
2-3 ....3.00
3/Variant 4.00

Cheapskin
Fantagraphics

1 ....3.00

Checkmate
DC, 2006

1-30 ....3.00

Checkmate
Gold Key, 1962

1 ....30.00
2 ....20.00

Checkmate
DC, 1988

1 ....3.00
2-12 ....1.00
13-33 ....2.00

Check-Up
Fantagraphics

1 ....3.00

Cheech Wizard
Last Gasp

1 ....3.00

Cheeky Angel

Viz, 2004

1-8 .... 10.00

Cheerleaders from Hell

Caliber, 1988

1 .... 3.00

Cheese Heads

Tragedy Strikes

1-5 .... 3.00

Cheese Weasel

Side Show

1-7 .... 3.00

Cheese Weasel: Innocent Until Proven Guilty

Side Show

1 .... 10.00

Cheeta Pop

Fantagraphics, 1996

1-3 .... 3.00

Cheeta Pop Scream Queen

Antarctic, 1994

1-5 .... 3.00

Chemical Warfare

Checker Comics, 1998

1-3 .... 3.00

Chen -n- Solly

Thwack! Pow!, 1997

1-2 .... 1.00

Cheque, Mate

Fantagraphics

1 .... 4.00

Cherry

Last Gasp, 1982

1 .... 8.00

1/2nd-11/2nd 4.00

12-20 .... 3.00

Cherry Deluxe

Cherry, 1998

1 .... 4.00

Cherry's Jubilee

Tundra, 1994

1-4 .... 3.00

Cheryl Blossom

Archie, 1995

1 .... 3.00

2-3 .... 2.00

Cheryl Blossom

Archie, 1996

1-3 .... 2.00

Cheryl Blossom

Archie, 1997

1-37 .... 2.00

Cheryl Blossom Goes Hollywood

Archie, 1996

1-3 .... 2.00

Cheryl Blossom Special

Archie

1-4 .... 2.00

Chesty Sanchez

Antarctic, 1995

1-3 .... 3.00

Special 1 .... 6.00

Cheval Noir

Dark Horse, 1989

1-19 .... 4.00

20 .... 5.00

21 .... 4.00

22 .... 5.00

23-26 .... 4.00

27-50 .... 3.00

Cheyenne

Dell, 1957

4-5 .... 35.00

6-10 .... 25.00

11-25 .... 20.00

Cheyenne Kid

Charlton, 1957

8 .... 30.00

9 .... 20.00

10 .... 35.00

11 .... 30.00

12-15 .... 20.00

16-20 .... 16.00

21-30 .... 14.00

31-40 .... 10.00

41-50 .... 8.00

51-70 .... 6.00

71-87 .... 4.00

87/2nd 2.00

88-89 .... 4.00

89/2nd 2.00

90 .... 4.00

91-99 .... 3.00

Chiaroscuro

DC, 1995

1-10 .... 3.00

Chicanos

Idea & Design Works, 2005

1-8 .... 4.00

Chi Chian

Sirius, 1997

1-6 .... 3.00

Chick Magnet

Voluptuous

1 .... 3.00

Chaser Platoon

Cheerleaders from Hell

Cheese Weasel

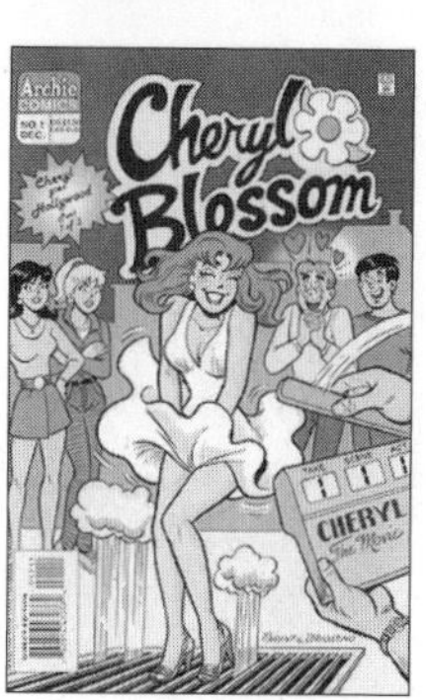

Cheryl Blossom Goes Hollywood

Cheyenne Kid

Children of Fire

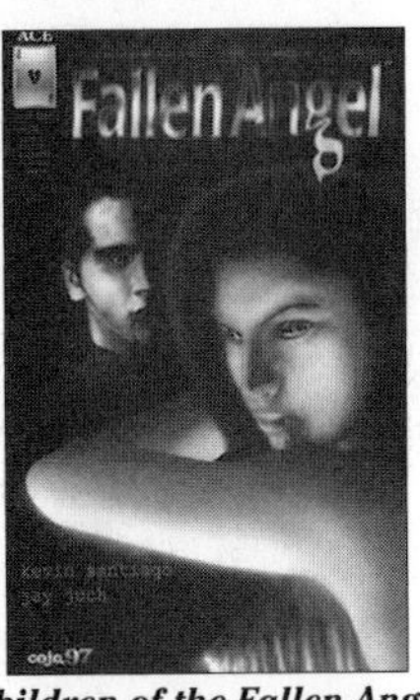
Children of the Fallen Angel

Children of the Night

Chief Victorio's Apache Massacre
Avon, 1951

1 .... 275.00

Childhood's End
Image, 1997

1-5 .... 3.00

Children of Fire
Fantagor

1-3 .... 2.00

Children of the Fallen Angel
Ace, 1997

1 .... 3.00

Children of the Night
Nightwynd

1-4 .... 3.00

Children of the Voyager
Marvel, 1993

1 .... 3.00
2-4 .... 2.00

Children's Crusade
DC, 1993

1 .... 5.00
2 .... 4.00

Child's Play 2: The Official Movie Adaptation
Innovation

1-3 .... 3.00

Child's Play 3
Innovation, 1992

1-4 .... 3.00

Child's Play: The Series
Innovation

1-5 .... 3.00

Chili
Marvel, 1969

1 .... 22.00
2 .... 14.00
3-5 .... 10.00
6-10 .... 8.00
11-26 .... 6.00
Special 1 .... 14.00

Chiller
Marvel, 1993

1-2 .... 3.00

Chilling Adventures in Sorcery
Archie, 1972

1 .... 42.00
2 .... 25.00
3-5 .... 15.00
☛Becomes Red Circle Sorcery

Chilling Tales
Youthful, 1952

13 .... 450.00
14-15 .... 300.00
16-17 .... 250.00

Chilling Tales of Horror
Stanley, 1969

1 .... 12.00
2-7 .... 10.00

Chilling Tales of Horror
Stanley, 1971

1 .... 9.00
2/A-2/B 8.00
3-5 .... 6.00

Chillins
Moonstone

0 .... 3.00

Chimera
CrossGen, 2003

1-4 .... 3.00

Chinago and Other Stories
Tome

1 .... 3.00

China Sea
Nightwynd

1-4 .... 3.00

Chipmunks & Squirrels
Original Syndicate, 1994

1 .... 6.00

Chip 'n' Dale
Dell, 1955

4-5 .... 35.00
6-10 .... 30.00
11-14 .... 24.00
14/A 30.00
15-20 .... 24.00
21-30 .... 20.00

Chip 'n' Dale
Gold Key, 1967

1 .... 20.00
2 .... 12.00
3-5 .... 8.00
6-20 .... 5.00
21-64 .... 3.00
65-66 .... 5.00
67 .... 20.00
68-69 .... 17.00
70-77 .... 3.00
78-83 .... 10.00

Chip 'n' Dale
Disney

1 .... 4.00

Chip 'n' Dale Rescue Rangers
Disney, 1990

1-19 .... 2.00

Chips and Vanilla
Kitchen Sink, 1988

1 .... 2.00

Chirality
CPM, 1997

1-18 .... 3.00

Chirn
Hammac

1-3 .... 2.00

Chisuji
Antarctic, 2004

1-4 .... 3.00

Chitty Chitty Bang Bang
Gold Key, 1969

1 .... 35.00

C.H.I.X.
Image, 1998

1-1/Variant 3.00

C.H.I.X. that Time Forgot
Image, 1998

1 .... 3.00

Chobits
Tokyopop, 2002

1-8 .... 10.00

Choice Comics
Great Comics, 1941

1 .... 950.00
2 .... 650.00
3 .... 485.00

Choices
Angry Isis

1 .... 4.00

Choke
Anubis, 1993

1-Ann 1 .... 3.00

Cholly & Flytrap
Image, 2004

1-4 .... 5.00

Choo-Choo Charlie
Gold Key, 1969

1 .... 60.00

Chopper: Earth, Wind & Fire
Fleetway-Quality

1-2 .... 3.00

Chopper: Song of the Surfer
Fleetway-Quality

1 .... 10.00

Chosen
Martinez, 1995

1 .... 3.00

Chosen
Dark Horse, 2004

1-3 .... 3.00

Christian Comics & Games Magazine
Aida-Zee

0-1 .... 4.00

Christina Winters: Agent of Death
Fantagraphics, 1995

1-3 .... 3.00

Christmas Classics (Walt Kelly's...)
Eclipse, 1987

1 .... 2.00

Christmas Treasury, A
Dell, 1954

1 .... 50.00

Christmas with Superswine
Fantagraphics

1 .... 2.00

Christmas with the Super-Heroes
DC, 1988

1-2 .... 3.00

Chroma-Tick
New England, 1992

1-9 .... 4.00

Chrome
Hot Comics, 1986

1-3 .... 2.00

Chromium Man
Triumphant, 1994

0-15 .... 3.00

Chromium Man: Violent Past
Triumphant

1-2 .... 3.00

Chronic Apathy
Illiterature, 1995

1-4 .... 3.00

Chronic Idiocy
Caliber

1-3 .... 3.00

Chronicles of Corum
First, 1987

1-12 .... 2.00

Chronicles of Crime and Mystery: Sherlock Holmes
Northstar

1 .... 2.00

Chronicles of Panda Khan
Abacus, 1987

1-4 .... 2.00

Children of the Voyager

Chili

Chilling Adventures in Sorcery

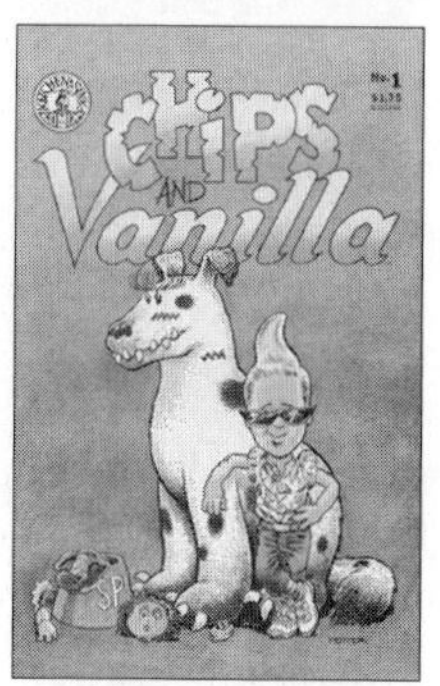

Chips and Vanilla

Choo-Choo Charlie

Christmas with the Super-Heroes

Chrome

Chronos

Chronicles of the Cursed Sword
Tokyopop, 2003

1-20 .... 10.00

Chrono Code
Tokyopop, 2005

1-2 .... 10.00

Chrono Crusade
ADV Manga, 2004

1-6 .... 10.00

Chronos
DC, 1998

1-11 .... 3.00
1000000 .... 4.00

Chronowar
Dark Horse, 1996

1-9 .... 3.00

Chuck Norris
Marvel, 1987

1 .... 2.00
2-5 .... 1.00

Chuk the Barbaric
Avatar

1-3 .... 1.00

Chyna
Chaos!, 2000

1-1/Variant 3.00

Cinderalla
Viz, 2002

1 .... 16.00

Cinder and Ashe
DC, 1988

1-4 .... 2.00

Cinderella
Gold Key, 1965

1 .... 24.00

Cinderella Love
Ziff-Davis, 1950

1 .... 85.00
2 .... 48.00
3 .... 40.00
4-10 .... 35.00
11-29 .... 28.00

Cindy
Timely, 1947

27 .... 75.00
28-40 .... 50.00

Cinnamon El Ciclo
DC, 2003

1-5 .... 3.00

Circle Unleashed
Epoch, 1995

1 .... 3.00

Circle Weave: Apprentice to a God
Abalone

1-4 .... 2.00

Circus the Comic Riot
Globe, 1938

1-3 .... 6,500.00

Circus World
Hammac

1-3 .... 3.00

Cisco Kid
Dell, 1951

2 .... 100.00
3 .... 85.00
4-5 .... 80.00
6-10 .... 75.00
11-20 .... 55.00
21-30 .... 45.00
31-36 .... 30.00
37-41 .... 60.00

Citizen V and the V-Battalion
Marvel, 2001

1-3 .... 3.00

Citizen V and the V-Battalion: The Everlasting
Marvel, 2002

1-4 .... 3.00

Citizen V Battlebook
Marvel, 1998

1 .... 4.00

City of Heroes
Blue King Studios, 2004

1-12 .... 3.00

City of Heroes
Image, 2005

1 .... 3.00
1/Keown 5.00
1/Perez 4.00
2-17 .... 3.00

City of Silence
Image, 2000

1-3 .... 3.00

City of the Living Dead
Avon, 1952

1 .... 300.00

City of Tomorrow
DC, 2005

1 .... 5.00
2-6 .... 3.00

City People Notebook
DC, 2000

1 .... 10.00

City Surgeon
Gold Key, 1963

1 .... 18.00

Civil War
Marvel, 2006

1 .... 5.00
2 .... 7.00
2/Variant 8.00
3 .... 5.00
3/2nd 3.00
4 .... 5.00
4/Variant 3.00
5 .... 4.00
5/Variant 3.00
6 .... 4.00

Civil War: Choosing Sides
Marvel, 2007

1 .... 4.00

Civil War Files
Marvel, 2006

1 .... 4.00

Civil War: Front Line
Marvel, 2006

1-10 .... 3.00

Civil War: The Confession
Marvel, 2007

1 .... 8.00

Civil War: The Initiative
Marvel, 2007

1 .... 6.00

Civil War: War Crimes One-Shot
Marvel, 2007

1 .... 4.00

Civil War: X-Men
Marvel, 2006

1-4 .... 3.00

Civil War: Young Avengers & Runaways
Marvel, 2006

1-4 .... 3.00

Claire Voyant
Leader, 1946

1 .... 375.00
2 .... 225.00
3-4 .... 165.00

Clair Voyant
Lightning, 1996

1 .... 4.00

Clan Apis
Active Synapse, 1998

1-4 .... 3.00
5 .... 4.00

Clandestine
Marvel, 1994

1-12 .... 3.00
Ashcan 1 .... 2.00

Claritin Syrup Presents Looney Tunes
DC, 1998

1 .... 3.00

Clash
DC, 1991

1-3 .... 5.00

Classic Adventure Strips
Dragon Lady, 1985

1-12 .... 4.00

Classic Alex Toth Zorro
Image, 1998

1-2 .... 16.00

Classic Girls
Eternity, 1991

1-4 .... 3.00

Classic Jonny Quest: Skull & Double Crossbones
Illustrated Productions, 1996

1 .... 1.00

Classic Jonny Quest: The Quetong Missile Mystery
Illustrated Productions, 1996

1 .... 1.00

Classic Judge Dredd
Fleetway-Quality

1-15 .... 3.00

Classic Punisher
Marvel, 1989

1 .... 5.00

Classics Desecrated
NBM

1 .... 9.00

Classics Illustrated
Gilberton, 1941

1 .... 4,400.00
1/2nd 325.00
1/3rd 135.00
1/4th 100.00
1/5th 90.00
1/6th 75.00
1/7th 35.00
1/8th 24.00
1/9th 20.00
1/10th-1/11th 18.00
1/12th-1/15th 15.00
1/16th-1/23rd 10.00
2 .... 1,750.00
2/2nd 250.00
2/3rd 130.00
2/4th 100.00
2/5th 90.00
2/6th 75.00
2/7th 35.00
2/8th 24.00
2/9th 20.00

Cinder and Ashe

Cinderella Love

Citizen V and the V-Battalion

Classic Girls

Classics Illustrated

Classics Illustrated Junior

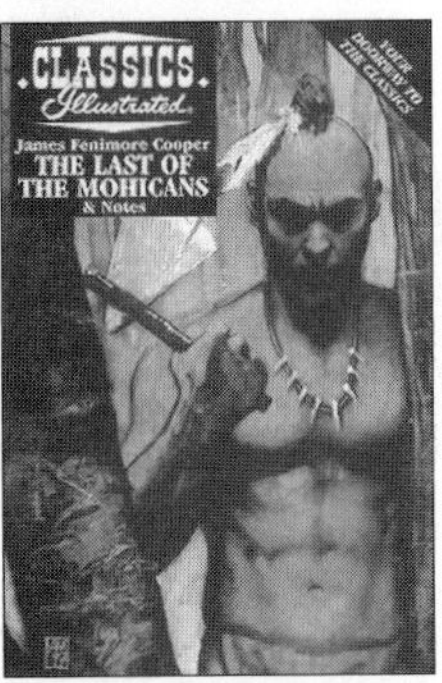

Classics Illustrated Study Guide

Classic X-Men

2/10th....................18.00
2/11th....................16.00
2/12th-2/14th....................15.00
2/15th-2/A/22nd....................10.00
2/B/22nd....................35.00
2/23rd-2/25th....................10.00
3....................1,250.00
3/2nd....................240.00
3/3rd....................125.00
3/4th....................100.00
3/5th....................90.00
3/6th....................85.00
3/7th....................75.00
3/8th....................40.00
3/9th....................24.00
3/10th....................20.00
3/11th....................18.00
3/12th....................16.00
3/13th-3/15th....................15.00
3/16th-3/23rd....................10.00
4....................1,050.00
4/2nd....................240.00
4/3rd....................125.00
4/4th....................100.00
4/5th....................90.00
4/6th....................75.00
4/7th....................40.00
4/8th....................24.00
4/9th....................20.00
4/10th....................18.00
4/11th....................16.00
4/12th-4/13th....................15.00
4/14th-4/15th....................12.00
4/16th-4/22nd....................10.00
5....................1,150.00
5/A....................1,900.00
5/2nd....................235.00
5/3rd....................175.00
5/4th....................160.00
5/5th....................125.00
5/6th....................100.00
5/7th....................90.00
5/8th....................45.00
5/9th....................30.00
5/10th-5/11th....................24.00
5/12th-5/14th....................15.00
5/15th-5/24th....................10.00
6....................1,050.00
6/2nd....................240.00
6/3rd....................185.00
6/4th....................135.00
6/5th....................80.00
6/6th....................45.00
6/7th....................30.00
6/8th....................25.00
6/9th-6/11th....................15.00
6/12th-6/22nd....................10.00
7....................800.00
7/2nd....................225.00
7/3rd....................165.00
7/4th....................130.00
7/5th....................100.00
7/6th....................90.00
7/7th....................45.00
7/8th....................28.00
7/9th-7/10th....................25.00
7/11th-7/12th....................18.00
7/13th-7/14th....................15.00
7/15th-7/23rd....................10.00
8....................1,550.00
8/2nd....................525.00
8/3rd....................425.00
8/A/4th-8/B/4th....................350.00
8/5th....................185.00
8/6th....................135.00
8/7th....................120.00
8/8th....................110.00
9....................750.00
9/A....................800.00
9/2nd....................185.00
9/3rd....................165.00
9/4th....................135.00
9/5th....................100.00
9/6th....................45.00
9/7th-9/8th....................28.00
9/9th....................25.00
9/10th-9/11th....................15.00
9/12th....................10.00
10/A....................675.00
10/B....................700.00
10/A/2nd....................235.00
10/B/2nd....................200.00
10/3rd....................125.00
10/4th....................110.00
10/5th....................85.00
10/6th....................45.00
10/7th....................28.00
10/8th....................24.00
10/9th....................18.00
10/10th-10/12th....................15.00
10/13th-10/21st....................10.00
11....................750.00
11/2nd....................225.00
11/3rd....................135.00
11/4th....................100.00
11/5th....................25.00
11/6th....................15.00
11/7th-11/10th....................10.00
12....................750.00
12/2nd....................225.00
12/3rd....................135.00
12/4th....................110.00
12/5th....................90.00
12/6th....................45.00
12/7th....................25.00
12/8th-12/9th....................18.00
12/10th-12/12th....................15.00
12/13th-12/19th....................10.00
13....................985.00
13/2nd....................240.00
13/3rd....................185.00
13/4th....................125.00
13/5th....................45.00
13/6th....................28.00

Issue	Price
13/7th-13/9th	20.00
13/10th-13/16th	10.00
14	1,600.00
14/2nd	525.00
14/3rd	400.00
14/4th	325.00
14/5th	260.00
15	575.00
15/2nd	215.00
15/3rd	135.00
15/4th	85.00
15/5th	40.00
15/6th	28.00
15/7th	24.00
15/8th	18.00
15/9th	15.00
15/10th-15/19th	10.00
16	575.00
16/2nd	185.00
16/3rd	135.00
16/4th	80.00
16/5th	35.00
16/6th	24.00
16/7th	20.00
16/8th-16/9th	15.00
16/10th-16/14th	10.00
17	575.00
17/A/2nd	185.00
17/B/2nd	135.00
17/3rd	80.00
17/4th	28.00
17/5th	24.00
17/6th-17/7th	20.00
17/8th-17/10th	15.00
17/11th-17/12th	12.00
18/A-18/B	675.00
18/2nd	225.00
18/3rd	135.00
18/4th	110.00
18/5th	40.00
18/6th	28.00
18/7th	24.00
18/A/8th-18/12th	18.00
18/13th-18/18th	10.00
19/A-19/B	450.00
19/2nd	200.00
19/3rd	135.00
19/4th	85.00
19/5th	35.00
19/6th	28.00
19/7th-19/8th	18.00
19/9th-19/10th	15.00
19/11th-19/21st	10.00
20/A-20/D	425.00
20/2nd	165.00
20/3rd	140.00
20/4th	85.00
20/A/5th-20/B/5th	65.00
20/6th	55.00
20/7th	40.00
21/A-21/C	825.00
21/2nd	265.00
21/3rd	200.00
21/4th	150.00
21/5th	130.00
21/6th-21/7th	110.00
22/A	365.00
22/B-22/C	335.00
22/2nd	28.00
22/3rd	24.00
22/4th	20.00
22/5th	16.00
22/6th-22/11th	15.00
23	340.00
23/A/2nd	140.00
23/B/2nd	100.00
23/3rd	35.00
23/4th	28.00
23/5th	24.00
23/6th	18.00
23/7th-23/9th	15.00
23/10th	12.00
23/11th-23/17th	10.00
24	325.00
24/2nd	85.00
24/3rd	28.00
24/4th	26.00
24/5th-24/8th	18.00
24/9th	14.00
24/10th-24/15th	10.00
25	325.00
25/2nd	95.00
25/3rd	35.00
25/4th	28.00
25/5th-25/6th	18.00
25/7th	16.00
25/8th	15.00
25/9th-25/12th	10.00
26	800.00
26/A/2nd-26/B/2nd	265.00
26/3rd-26/4th	65.00
26/5th	35.00
26/A/6th	30.00
26/B/6th	35.00
26/7th-26/8th	24.00
26/9th	30.00
26/10th-26/19th	10.00
27	325.00
27/2nd	100.00
27/3rd	28.00
27/4th	20.00
27/5th-27/6th	15.00
27/7th-27/10th	10.00
28	325.00
28/2nd	95.00
28/3rd	20.00
28/4th-28/5th	15.00
28/6th-28/7th	12.00
29	465.00
29/2nd	28.00
29/3rd	24.00
29/4th-29/5th	20.00
29/6th-29/7th	15.00
29/8th-29/15th	10.00

Claw the Unconquered

Cleopatra

Climax

Cloak and Dagger in Predator and Prey

Clonezone Special

Clowns

Clue Comics

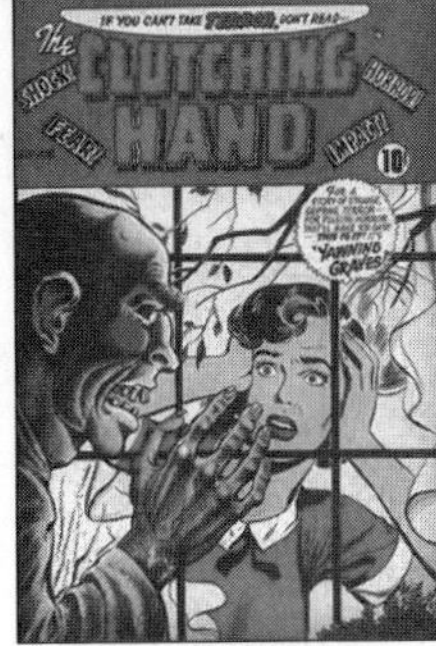

Clutching Hand

30 .... 300.00
30/2nd 36.00
30/3rd-30/4th 32.00
30/5th 20.00
30/6th-30/8th 10.00
31 .... 265.00
31/2nd 35.00
31/3rd 20.00
31/4th 16.00
31/5th-31/7th 15.00
31/8th-31/14th 10.00
32 .... 300.00
32/2nd 45.00
32/3rd 28.00
32/4th-32/5th 20.00
32/6th-32/10th 10.00
33 .... 1,025.00
33/2nd 385.00
33/3rd 295.00
33/A/4th-33/B/4th 240.00
34 .... 285.00
34/2nd 32.00
34/3rd 28.00
34/4th-34/5th 24.00
34/6th 18.00
34/7th-34/8th 15.00
34/9th-34/13th 10.00
35 .... 325.00
35/2nd 32.00
35/3rd-35/5th 12.00
36 .... 215.00
36/2nd 40.00
36/3rd 20.00
36/4th 14.00
36/5th-36/6th 10.00
37 .... 165.00
37/A/2nd 28.00
37/B/2nd 55.00
37/3rd 20.00
37/4th-37/5th 15.00
37/6th-37/8th 12.00
37/9th-37/11th 10.00
38 .... 185.00
38/2nd-38/3rd 24.00
38/4th-38/5th 18.00
39 .... 215.00
39/2nd 28.00
39/3rd-39/5th 24.00
39/6th-39/10th 18.00
39/11th-39/13th 15.00
40 .... 585.00
40/2nd 250.00
40/3rd 175.00
40/4th 130.00
41 .... 365.00
41/2nd 28.00
41/3rd 22.00
41/4th-41/7th 10.00
42 .... 175.00
42/A/2nd 38.00
42/B/2nd 45.00
42/3rd 24.00
42/4th-42/5th 18.00
42/6th-42/9th 15.00
42/10th-42/16th 10.00
43 .... 675.00
43/2nd 450.00
44/A-44/B 550.00
44/A/2nd-44/B/2nd 225.00
44/3rd 135.00
45 .... 95.00
45/2nd 35.00
45/3rd 16.00
45/4th-45/6th 10.00
46 .... 110.00
46/A/2nd 35.00
46/B/2nd 60.00
46/3rd 20.00
46/4th 18.00
46/5th-46/6th 15.00
46/7th-46/17th 10.00
47 .... 100.00
47/2nd 35.00
47/3rd 18.00
47/4th 16.00
47/5th-47/7th 15.00
47/8th-47/16th 10.00
48 .... 90.00
48/2nd 35.00
48/3rd 18.00
48/4th 15.00
48/5th 12.00
48/6th-48/15th 10.00
49 .... 185.00
49/2nd 45.00
49/A/3rd-49/B/3rd 35.00
49/4th 28.00
49/5th-49/6th 24.00
49/7th-49/B/8th 15.00
50/A-50/C 110.00
50/2nd 24.00
50/3rd 18.00
50/4th-50/9th 15.00
50/10th-50/15th 10.00
51/A-51/C 85.00
51/D 100.00
51/2nd 26.00
51/3rd 20.00
51/4th 16.00
51/5th 15.00
51/6th 12.00
51/7th-51/B/8th 10.00
52 .... 80.00
52/2nd 24.00
52/3rd-52/4th 18.00
52/5th-52/10th 10.00
53 .... 125.00
54 .... 110.00
54/2nd 40.00
54/A/3rd-54/B/3rd 32.00
54/4th 20.00
54/5th-54/B/9th 12.00
55 .... 80.00
55/2nd 28.00

Issue	Price
55/3rd-55/4th	15.00
55/5th-55/B/12th	10.00
56	135.00
56/2nd	28.00
56/3rd	24.00
56/4th	20.00
57	85.00
57/2nd	28.00
57/3rd-57/4th	20.00
57/5th-57/7th	15.00
57/8th-57/11th	10.00
58	85.00
58/A/2nd-58/B/2nd	38.00
58/3rd	18.00
58/4th-58/7th	15.00
58/8th-58/11th	10.00
59	110.00
59/2nd	38.00
59/3rd	15.00
59/4th-59/6th	10.00
60	95.00
60/2nd	35.00
60/3rd	24.00
60/4th-60/5th	15.00
60/6th-60/7th	12.00
61/A-61/B	90.00
61/2nd	20.00
61/3rd-61/4th	18.00
62	80.00
62/2nd	28.00
62/3rd	20.00
62/4th	15.00
62/5th-62/9th	10.00
63	90.00
63/2nd	28.00
63/3rd	20.00
63/4th	14.00
63/5th-63/7th	10.00
64	90.00
64/A/2nd-64/B/2nd	30.00
64/3rd	18.00
64/4th	15.00
64/5th-64/14th	10.00
65	85.00
65/2nd	30.00
65/3rd	20.00
65/4th-65/6th	10.00
66	185.00
67	75.00
67/2nd	28.00
67/3rd	18.00
67/4th	15.00
67/5th-67/7th	10.00
68	75.00
68/2nd	28.00
68/3rd-68/4th	20.00
68/5th	16.00
68/6th-68/9th	10.00
69	85.00
69/2nd	28.00
69/3rd	24.00
69/4th	15.00

Issue	Price
69/5th-69/12th	10.00
70	65.00
70/2nd	25.00
70/3rd	18.00
70/4th	16.00
70/5th	15.00
70/6th	10.00
71	110.00
71/2nd	60.00
71/3rd	45.00
72	65.00
72/2nd	30.00
72/3rd	24.00
72/4th	15.00
72/5th-72/11th	10.00
73-74	215.00
75	65.00
75/2nd	32.00
75/3rd	20.00
75/4th	15.00
75/5th-75/9th	10.00
76	65.00
76/2nd	28.00
76/3rd	20.00
76/4th	15.00
76/5th-76/9th	10.00
77	65.00
77/2nd	30.00
77/3rd	20.00
77/4th	15.00
77/5th-77/10th	10.00
78	85.00
78/2nd	30.00
78/3rd	20.00
78/4th	15.00
78/5th-78/12th	10.00
79	65.00
79/2nd	30.00
79/3rd	20.00
79/4th	15.00
79/5th-79/6th	10.00
80	65.00
80/2nd	30.00
80/3rd	20.00
80/4th	15.00
80/5th-80/11th	10.00
81	50.00
81/2nd-81/4th	15.00
82	38.00
82/2nd-82/3rd	15.00
83	40.00
83/2nd	14.00
83/3rd-83/12th	10.00
84	80.00
84/2nd	38.00
85	28.00
85/2nd-85/8th	10.00
86	30.00
86/2nd-86/7th	10.00
87	30.00
87/2nd-87/5th	10.00
88	40.00

Coda

Code Name Ninja

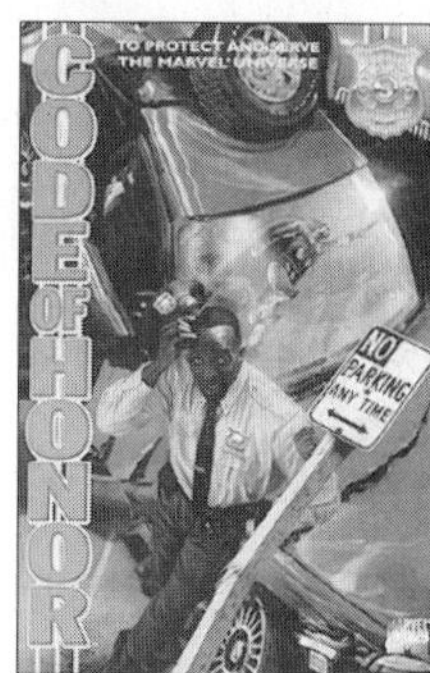

Code of Honor

Cody Starbuck

Coffee World

Cold Blooded

Cold-Blooded Chameleon Commandos

Collection

Issue	Price
88/2nd	12.00
88/3rd-88/4th	10.00
89	35.00
89/2nd-89/5th	10.00
90	25.00
90/2nd-90/6th	10.00
91	28.00
91/2nd	15.00
91/3rd-91/11th	10.00
92/A-92/B	24.00
92/2nd-92/5th	10.00
93	25.00
93/2nd	14.00
93/3rd-93/4th	10.00
94	25.00
94/2nd-94/3rd	10.00
95/A-95/B	55.00
95/2nd	18.00
95/3rd	12.00
96	25.00
96/2nd-96/10th	10.00
97	25.00
97/2nd-97/8th	10.00
98	30.00
98/2nd	12.00
98/3rd-98/10th	10.00
99	30.00
99/2nd-99/8th	10.00
100	25.00
100/2nd-100/9th	10.00
101	25.00
101/2nd-101/8th	10.00
102	45.00
102/2nd	20.00
102/3rd	18.00
103	24.00
103/2nd-103/6th	10.00
104	25.00
104/2nd-104/8th	10.00
105	28.00
105/2nd-105/12th	10.00
106	25.00
106/2nd-106/8th	10.00
107	24.00
107/2nd-107/6th	10.00
108/A	30.00
108/B	35.00
108/2nd-108/7th	10.00
109	24.00
109/2nd	12.00
109/3rd-109/4th	10.00
110	90.00
110/2nd	65.00
111	35.00
111/2nd	12.00
111/3rd-111/4th	10.00
112	30.00
112/2nd-112/9th	10.00
113	60.00
113/2nd	35.00
114	55.00
114/2nd	35.00
115	55.00
115/2nd	28.00
116	60.00
116/2nd	28.00
117	55.00
117/2nd	25.00
117/3rd	20.00
118	55.00
118/2nd	28.00
119	55.00
119/2nd	20.00
119/3rd	15.00
120	50.00
120/2nd	25.00
121	26.00
121/2nd-121/8th	10.00
122	25.00
122/2nd-122/7th	10.00
123	25.00
123/2nd-123/6th	10.00
124	45.00
124/2nd	16.00
124/3rd-124/4th	12.00
124/5th-124/11th	10.00
125	24.00
125/2nd-125/8th	10.00
126	25.00
126/2nd-126/3rd	10.00
127	24.00
127/2nd-127/3rd	10.00
128	28.00
128/2nd-128/8th	10.00
129	65.00
129/2nd	40.00
130	30.00
130/2nd-130/7th	10.00
131	24.00
131/2nd-131/8th	10.00
132	28.00
132/2nd-132/4th	10.00
133	40.00
133/2nd	16.00
133/3rd-133/5th	12.00
133/6th-133/9th	10.00
134	32.00
134/2nd-134/6th	10.00
135	24.00
135/2nd-135/5th	10.00
136	24.00
136/2nd-136/5th	10.00
137	24.00
137/2nd-137/7th	10.00
138	40.00
138/2nd-138/8th	10.00
139	24.00
139/2nd-139/5th	10.00
140	24.00
140/2nd-140/5th	10.00
141	30.00
141/2nd-141/4th	10.00
142	30.00
142/2nd	14.00

142/3rd-142/7th.................... 10.00
143.. 24.00
143/2nd-143/5th.................... 10.00
144.. 35.00
144/2nd.................................. 12.00
144/3rd-144/7th.................... 10.00
145.. 26.00
145/2nd-145/5th.................... 10.00
146.. 26.00
146/2nd-146/4th.................... 10.00
147.. 26.00
147/2nd-147/B/8th................ 10.00
148.. 26.00
148/2nd-148/5th.................... 10.00
149.. 26.00
149/2nd-149/7th.................... 10.00
150.. 45.00
150/2nd-150/3rd.................... 15.00
150/4th.................................. 12.00
151.. 45.00
151/2nd-151/3rd.................... 15.00
151/4th.................................. 12.00
152.. 40.00
152/A/2nd-152/C/2nd.......... 15.00
152/3rd-152/5th.................... 10.00
153.. 45.00
153/A/2nd.............................. 15.00
153/B/2nd.............................. 12.00
153/3rd-154............................ 10.00
154/2nd-154/3rd.................... 15.00
154/4th.................................. 12.00
155.. 28.00
155/2nd-155/3rd.................... 10.00
156.. 28.00
156/2nd-156/4th.................... 10.00
157.. 38.00
157/2nd-157/3rd.................... 15.00
158.. 38.00
158/2nd-158/3rd.................... 18.00
159.. 38.00
159/2nd-159/3rd.................... 15.00
160/A-160/B.......................... 40.00
160/2nd-160/3rd.................... 15.00
161.. 40.00
161/2nd-161/3rd.................... 15.00
162.. 40.00
162/2nd-162/3rd.................... 16.00
163.. 40.00
163/2nd-163/3rd.................... 15.00
164.. 40.00
164/2nd-164/3rd.................... 15.00
165.. 40.00
165/2nd-165/3rd.................... 15.00
166.. 65.00
166/2nd.................................. 20.00
166/3rd.................................. 16.00
167.. 75.00
167/2nd.................................. 35.00
167/3rd.................................. 25.00
168.. 80.00
169.. 75.00
169/2nd.................................. 30.00

Classics Illustrated

First, 1990

1-27..4.00

Classics Illustrated Junior

Famous Authors, 1953

501..75.00
501/2nd..................................12.00
501/3rd-501/9th.....................10.00
502..44.00
502/2nd..................................12.00
502/3rd-502/9th.....................10.00
503..28.00
503/2nd..................................12.00
503/3rd-503/11th...................10.00
504..20.00
504/2nd-504/9th.....................10.00
505..20.00
505/2nd-505/9th.....................10.00
506..18.00
506/2nd-506/8th.....................10.00
507..18.00
507/2nd-507/8th.....................10.00
508..18.00
508/2nd-508/7th.....................10.00
509..18.00
509/2nd-509/8th.....................10.00
510..18.00
510/2nd-510/7th.....................10.00
511-511/2nd...........................18.00
511/3rd-511/7th.....................10.00
512-512/3rd...........................18.00
512/4th..................................15.00
512/5th-512/7th.....................12.00
513..28.00
513/2nd..................................12.00
513/3rd-513/9th.....................10.00
514..24.00
514/2nd-514/5th.....................10.00
515..18.00
515/2nd-515/7th.....................10.00
516..28.00
516/2nd-516/7th.....................10.00
517..18.00
517/2nd-517/6th.....................10.00
518..18.00
518/2nd-518/5th.....................10.00
519..24.00
519/2nd-519/11th...................10.00
520..24.00
520/2nd-520/7th.....................10.00
521..15.00
521/2nd-521/6th.....................10.00
522..18.00
522/2nd-522/5th.....................10.00
523..15.00
523/2nd-523/5th.....................10.00
524..15.00
524/2nd-524/6th.....................10.00
525..22.00
525/2nd-525/6th.....................10.00
526..15.00
526/2nd-526/6th.....................10.00

Colonia

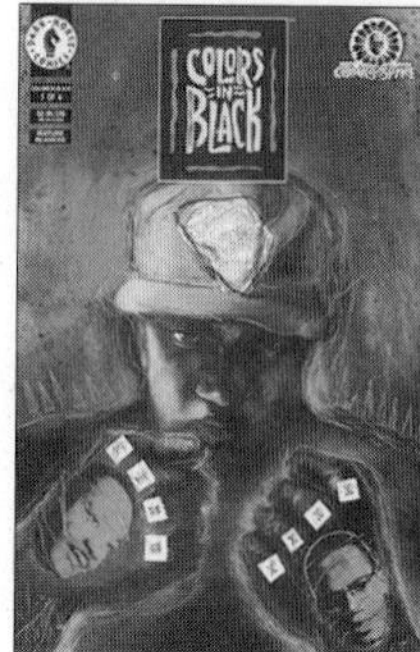

Colors in Black

Colossus

Colossus Comics

Colt

Columbus

Combat Casey

Comedy Comics

527 .... 15.00
527/2nd-527/6th 10.00
528 .... 15.00
528/2nd-528/6th 10.00
529 .... 15.00
529/2nd-529/4th 10.00
530 .... 15.00
530/2nd-530/5th 10.00
531 .... 15.00
531/2nd-531/6th 10.00
532 .... 18.00
532/2nd-532/7th 10.00
533 .... 15.00
533/2nd-533/5th 10.00
534 .... 15.00
534/2nd-534/5th 10.00
535 .... 30.00
535/2nd 15.00
535/3rd-535/7th 10.00
536 .... 15.00
536/2nd-536/6th 10.00
537 .... 15.00
537/2nd-537/5th 10.00
538 .... 15.00
538/2nd-538/5th 10.00
539 .... 15.00
539/2nd-539/6th 10.00
540 .... 15.00
540/2nd-540/6th 10.00
541 .... 20.00
541/2nd-541/5th 10.00
542 .... 16.00
542/2nd-542/5th 10.00
543 .... 15.00
543/2nd-543/5th 10.00
544 .... 26.00
544/2nd 15.00
544/3rd-544/6th 12.00
545 .... 15.00
545/2nd-545/5th 10.00
546 .... 15.00
546/2nd-546/5th 10.00
547 .... 15.00
547/2nd-547/5th 10.00
548 .... 15.00
548/2nd-548/6th 10.00
549 .... 15.00
549/2nd-549/6th 10.00
550 .... 15.00
550/2nd-550/5th 10.00
551 .... 15.00
551/2nd-551/5th 10.00
552 .... 15.00
552/2nd-552/5th 10.00
553 .... 15.00
553/2nd-553/6th 10.00
554 .... 15.00
554/2nd-554/6th 10.00
555 .... 15.00
555/2nd-555/4th 10.00
556 .... 15.00
556/2nd-556/5th 10.00
557 .... 15.00
557/2nd-557/5th 10.00
558 .... 15.00
558/2nd-558/4th 10.00
559 .... 15.00
559/2nd-559/4th 10.00
560 .... 15.00
560/2nd-560/4th 10.00
561 .... 15.00
561/2nd-561/4th 10.00
562 .... 15.00
562/2nd-562/4th 10.00
563 .... 15.00
563/2nd-563/4th 10.00
564 .... 15.00
564/2nd-564/4th 10.00
565 .... 15.00
565/2nd-565/4th 10.00
566 .... 15.00
566/2nd-566/4th 10.00
567 .... 15.00
567/2nd-567/5th 10.00
568 .... 15.00
568/2nd-568/4th 10.00
569 .... 15.00
569/2nd-569/4th 10.00
570 .... 15.00
570/2nd-570/4th 10.00
571 .... 15.00
571/2nd-571/4th 10.00
572 .... 15.00
572/2nd-572/3rd 10.00
573 .... 15.00
573/2nd-573/3rd 10.00
574 .... 15.00
574/2nd-574/3rd 10.00
575 .... 15.00
575/2nd-575/3rd 10.00
576 .... 15.00
576/2nd-576/3rd 10.00
577 .... 18.00

Classics Illustrated Special Issue

Gilberton, 1955

129 .... 50.00
132 .... 45.00
135-138 .... 35.00
138/2nd 25.00
138/3rd 35.00
141-159 .... 40.00
162 .... 75.00
165 .... 45.00
166-167 .... 50.00

Classics Illustrated Study Guide

Acclaim, 1997

1-38 .... 5.00

Classic Star Wars

Dark Horse, 1992

1-3 .... 4.00

4-19 .... 3.00
20 .... 4.00

Classic Star Wars: A Long Time Ago
Dark Horse, 1999
1-6 .... 13.00
Book 1-Book 7 .... 30.00

Classic Star Wars: A New Hope
Dark Horse, 1994
1-2 .... 4.00

Classic Star Wars: Devilworlds
Dark Horse, 1996
1-2 .... 3.00

Classic Star Wars: Han Solo at Stars' End
Dark Horse, 1997
1-3 .... 3.00

Classic Star Wars: Return of the Jedi
Dark Horse, 1994
1-2 .... 4.00

Classic Star Wars: The Early Adventures
Dark Horse, 1994
1-9 .... 3.00

Classic Star Wars: The Empire Strikes Back
Dark Horse, 1994
1-2 .... 4.00

Classic Star Wars: The Vandelhelm Mission
Dark Horse, 1995
1 .... 3.00

Classic Terry & the Pirates
Avalon
1-5 .... 3.00

Classic 2000 A.D.
Fleetway-Quality
1 .... 4.00
2-12 .... 3.00

Classic X-Men
Marvel, 1986
1 .... 6.00
2 .... 4.00
3-29 .... 3.00
30-45 .... 2.00

Claus
Draco, 1997
1-2 .... 3.00

Claws
Marvel, 2006
1-3 .... 4.00

Claw the Unconquered
DC, 1975
1 .... 7.00
2 .... 4.00
3 .... 3.00
4-6 .... 2.00
7 .... 4.00
8-12 .... 2.00

Claw the Unconquered
DC, 2006
1-6 .... 3.00

Clay Cody, Gunslinger
Pines, 1957
1 .... 25.00

Clem: Mall Security
Spit Take, 1997
0 .... 2.00

Cleopatra
Rip Off, 1992
1 .... 3.00

Clerks: The Comic Book
Oni, 1998
1 .... 5.00
1/2nd-2 .... 3.00
Holiday 1 .... 4.00

Cletus and Floyd Show
Asylum, 2002
1 .... 3.00

CLF: Cybernetic Liberation Front
Anubis
1 .... 3.00

Click!
NBM
1 .... 11.00
2-3 .... 13.00
4 .... 11.00

Cliffhanger!
Image, 1997
1 .... 3.00

Cliffhanger Comics
AC, 1989
1-2 .... 3.00

Cliffhanger Comics
AC, 1990
1/A-2/A 3.00

Climax
Gillmor, 1955
1 .... 85.00
2 .... 65.00

Climaxxx
Aircel, 1991
1-4 .... 4.00

Clint
Trigon, 1986
1-2 .... 2.00

Comic Book Confidential

Comic Book Heaven

Comic Cavalcade

Comics and Stories

Comics Magazine

Comics on Parade

Coming of Aphrodite

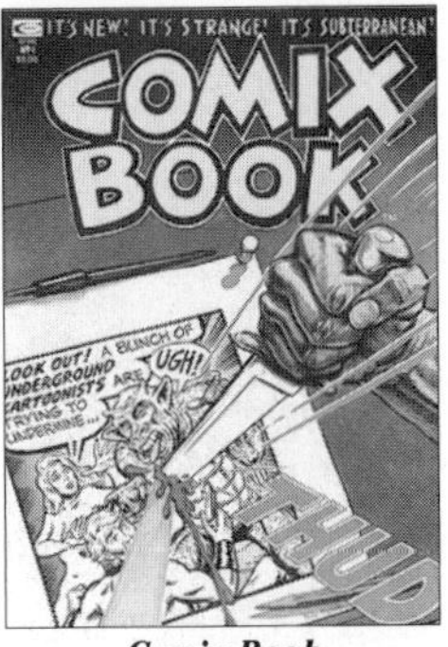

Comix Book

Clint: The Hamster Triumphant
Eclipse
1-2 ....2.00

Clive Barker's The Great and Secret Show
Idea & Design Works, 2006
1-8 ....4.00

Cloak and Dagger
Ziff-Davis, 1952
1 ....100.00

Cloak & Dagger
Marvel, 1983
1-2 ....3.00
3-4 ....2.00
5-10 ....1.00
11 ....2.00

Cloak and Dagger in Predator and Prey
Marvel
1 ....7.00

Clock!
Top Shelf
3 ....3.00

Clockmaker
Image, 2003
1-4 ....3.00

Clockmaker Act 2
Image, 2003
1-2 ....5.00

Clockwork Angels
Image
1 ....11.00

Clonezone Special
Dark Horse, 1989
1 ....2.00

Close Shaves of Pauline Peril
Gold Key, 1970
1 ....20.00
2-4 ....14.00

Cloudfall
Image, 2003
1 ....5.00

Clown Figure
Image, 1994
1 ....1.00

Clown: Nobody's Laughing Now
Fleetway-Quality
1 ....5.00

Clowns
Dark Horse, 1998
1 ....3.00

Clowns
Yahoo Pro
1 ....3.00

Clue Comics
Hillman, 1943
1 ....530.00
2-3 ....360.00
4-6 ....225.00
7-9 ....260.00
10-12 ....155.00

Clue Comic
Hillman, 1947
1 ....530.00
2-3 ....360.00

Clutching Hand
ACG, 1954
1 ....200.00

Clyde Crashcup
Dell, 1963
1 ....90.00
2 ....65.00
3-5 ....48.00

C-M-O Comics
Chicago Mail Order, 1942
1-2 ....1,000.00

Cobalt 60
Tundra
1-2 ....5.00

Cobalt Blue
Power, 1978
1 ....2.00

Cobalt Blue
Innovation, 1989
1-2 ....2.00
GN 1 ....6.00

Cobalt Warrior Angel
Mindchyld Comics, 2005
0 ....4.00

Cobbler's Monster
Image, 2006
1 ....15.00

Cobb: Off the Leash
Idea & Design Works, 2006
1-3 ....4.00

Cobra
Viz, 1990
1-12 ....3.00

Cocomalt Big Book of Comics
Harry A. Chesler, 1938
1 ....1,000.00

Cocopiazo
Slave Labor, 2004
1-4 ....3.00

Coda
Coda
1-4 .... 2.00

Code Blue
Image, 1998
1 .... 3.00

Codename: Danger
Lodestone, 1985
1-4 .... 2.00

Codename: Firearm
Malibu, 1995
0-5 .... 3.00

Codename: Genetix
Marvel, 1993
1-4 .... 2.00

Codename: Knockout
DC, 2001
0-23 .... 3.00

Code Name Ninja
Solson
1 .... 2.00

Codename: Scorpio
Antarctic, 1996
1-4 .... 3.00

Codename: Spitfire
Marvel, 1987
10-13 .... 1.00

Codename: Strikeforce
Spectrum, 1984
1 .... 2.00

Codename: Stryke Force
Image, 1994
0-1/Variant 3.00
2-14 .... 2.00

Code of Honor
Marvel, 1997
1-4 .... 6.00

Code XIII
Comcat, 1989
1-5 .... 7.00

Cody of the Pony Express
Charlton, 1955
8-10 .... 35.00

Cody Starbuck
Star*Reach, 1978
1 .... 2.00

Co-Ed Sexxtasy
Fantagraphics, 1999
1-11 .... 4.00

Coexisting
Alternative, 2005
1 .... 3.00

Coffee World
World
1 .... 2.00

Coffin
Oni, 2000
1 .... 6.00
2-4 .... 4.00

Coffin Blood
Monster
1 .... 4.00

Cold Blooded
Northstar, 1993
1-2 .... 3.00
3 .... 5.00

Cold-Blooded Chameleon Commandos
Blackthorne, 1986
1-5 .... 2.00

Cold Blooded: The Burning Kiss
Northstar, 1993
1 .... 5.00

Cold Eden
Legacy, 1995
4 .... 2.00

Cole Black
Rocky Hartberg
1-6 .... 2.00

Cole Black
Hartberg, 2007
1-5 .... 2.00

Collection
Eternity
1 .... 3.00

Collector's Dracula
Millennium
1-2 .... 4.00

Collectors Guide to the Ultraverse
Malibu, 1994
1 .... 1.00

Collier's
Fantagraphics
1-2 .... 3.00

Colonia
Colonia, 1998
1-10 .... 3.00
11 .... 4.00

Colors in Black
Dark Horse, 1995
1-4 .... 3.00

Colossal Show
Gold Key, 1969
1 .... 25.00

Colossus
Marvel, 1997
1 .... 3.00

Commander Battle and the Atomic Sub

Commies From Mars

Complete Comics

Complete Mystery

Complex City

Conan

Conan Saga

Conan the Adventurer

Colossus Battlebook
Marvel

1 .... 4.00

Colossus Comics
Sun, 1940

1 .... 2,700.00

Colossus: God's Country
Marvel

1 .... 7.00

Colour of Magic (Terry Pratchett's...)
Innovation

1-4 .... 3.00

Colt
Kz Comics, 1986

1-4 .... 1.00

Colt .45
Dell, 1960

4-5 .... 35.00
6 .... 30.00
7-9 .... 20.00

Colt Special
AC, 1985

1 .... 2.00

Columbus
Dark Horse

1 .... 3.00

Colville
King Ink, 1997

1 .... 3.00

Combat
Atlas, 1952

1 .... 135.00
2 .... 80.00
3 .... 75.00
4-5 .... 65.00
6-11 .... 55.00

Combat Casey
Sports Action, 1953

6 .... 40.00
7 .... 34.00
8-10 .... 26.00
11-34 .... 20.00

Combat
Dell, 1961

1 .... 10.00
2 .... 20.00
3 .... 18.00
4 .... 25.00
☛JFK story
5 .... 16.00
6-9 .... 12.00
10-20 .... 9.00
21-27 .... 8.00
28-40 .... 6.00

Combat
Image, 1996

1-2 .... 3.00

Combat Kelly
Marvel, 1951

1 .... 175.00
2 .... 85.00
3-11 .... 70.00
12-28 .... 65.00
29-38 .... 45.00
39-44 .... 30.00

Combat Kelly
Marvel, 1972

1 .... 10.00
2-3 .... 6.00
4-9 .... 4.00

Combat Zone
Avalon

1 .... 3.00

Come Again
Fantagraphics, 1997

1-2 .... 3.00

Comedy Comics
Timely, 1942

9 .... 2,200.00
10 .... 1,600.00
11-13 .... 525.00
14-16 .... 400.00
17-20 .... 300.00
21-24 .... 200.00
25-27 .... 150.00
28-31 .... 100.00
32-34 .... 75.00

Comet
Archie, 1983

1-2 .... 1.00

Comet
DC, 1991

1-18 .... 1.00
Ann 1 .... 2.00

Comet Man
Marvel, 1987

1-6 .... 1.00

Comet Tales
Rocket, 1983

1-3 .... 1.00

Comic Album
Dell, 1958

1 .... 100.00
2 .... 50.00
3 .... 75.00
4-6 .... 30.00
7 .... 40.00
8-10 .... 30.00
11 .... 40.00
12-14 .... 30.00
15 .... 40.00
16 .... 80.00

17 .... 40.00
18 .... 80.00

Comicana
-Ism, 2005

1-3 .... 4.00

Comic Book
Marvel, 1996

1-2 .... 7.00

Comic Book Confidential
Sphinx, 1988

1 .... 2.00

Comic Book Heaven
Slave Labor, 2000

1-9 .... 2.00

Comic Book Talent Search
Silverwolf, 1987

1 .... 2.00

Comic Capers
Timely, 1944

1 .... 120.00
2 .... 85.00
3-4 .... 65.00
5-6 .... 50.00

Comic Cavalcade
DC, 1942

1 .... 7,000.00
2 .... 2,400.00
3 .... 1,650.00
4-5 .... 100.00
6-10 .... 875.00
11-12 .... 750.00
13 .... 950.00
☛Sol. Grundy app.
14-20 .... 750.00
21-29 .... 650.00
30 .... 275.00
31-40 .... 150.00
41-50 .... 100.00
51-62 .... 90.00
63 .... 150.00

Comic Clock (Oscar and Friday's...)
Fawcett

1 .... 15.00

Comic Comics
Fawcett, 1946

1 .... 100.00
2-10 .... 75.00

Comic Land
Fact and Fiction, 1946

1 .... 80.00

Comico Black Book
Comico, 1987

1 .... 2.00

Comico Christmas Special
Comico, 1988

1 .... 3.00

Comico Collection
Comico

1 .... 10.00

Comic Party
Tokyopop, 2004

1-5 .... 10.00

Comics
Dell, 1937

1 .... 1,500.00
2 .... 750.00
3 .... 600.00
4-5 .... 575.00
6-8 .... 500.00
9-11 .... 425.00

Comics and Stories
Dark Horse, 1996

1-4 .... 3.00

Comics Are Dead
Slap Happy, 1999

1 .... 5.00

Comics Artist Showcase
Showcase

1 .... 1.00

Comics for Stoners
Jason Neuman

1 .... 1.00

Comics' Greatest World
Dark Horse, 1993

1 .... 1.00

Comics' Greatest World: Arcadia
Dark Horse, 1993

1 .... 2.00
1/Ltd. 3.00
2 .... 1.00
3 .... 3.00
4 .... 1.00

Comics' Greatest World: Cinnabar Flats
Dark Horse, 1993

1 .... 1.00
1/A-1/Ltd. 3.00
2-4 .... 1.00

Comics' Greatest World: Golden City
Dark Horse, 1993

1 .... 1.00
1/Ltd. 3.00
2-4 .... 1.00

Comics' Greatest World: Out of the Vortex
Dark Horse, 1993

1-4 .... 2.00

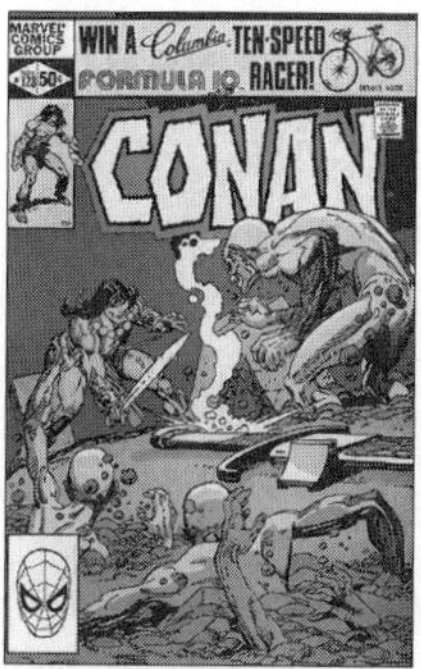

Conan the Barbarian

Conan the Destroyer

Conan the King

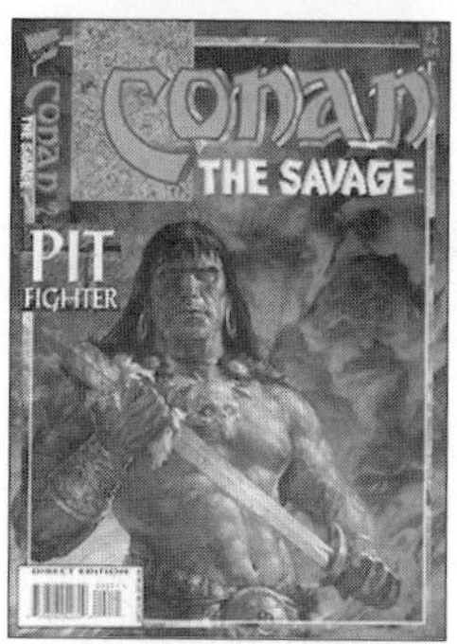

Conan the Savage

Concrete

Concrete Celebrates Earth Day

Concrete Color Special

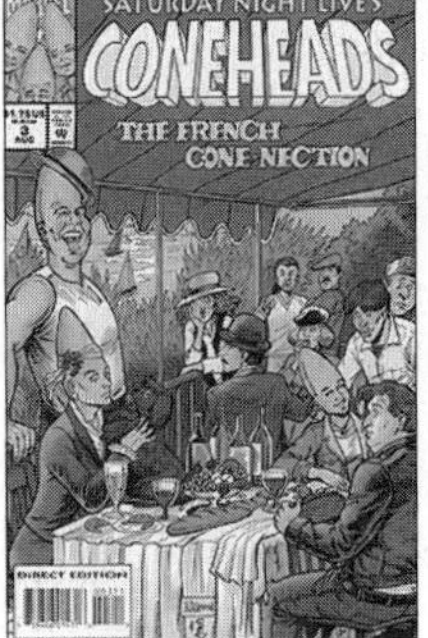

Coneheads

Comics' Greatest World Sourcebook

Dark Horse, 1993

1 .... 1.00

Comics' Greatest World: Steel Harbor

Dark Horse, 1993

1 .... 3.00
2-4 .... 1.00

Comics Magazine

Comics Magazine, 1936

1 .... 8,200.00
2 .... 2,650.00
3 .... 1,500.00
4 .... 1,200.00
5 .... 1,100.00

Comics 101 Presents

Cheap Thrills, 1994

1 .... 2.00

Comics on Parade

United Features, 1938

1 .... 2,800.00
2 .... 1,050.00
3 .... 775.00
4-5 .... 600.00
6-8 .... 420.00
9-10 .... 325.00
11-15 .... 285.00
16-20 .... 260.00
21-25 .... 230.00
26-30 .... 210.00
31-35 .... 135.00
36-40 .... 100.00
41-50 .... 75.00
51-60 .... 60.00
61-80 .... 50.00
81-Special 1 .... 36.00

Comics Reading Libraries

King, 1973

1 .... 10.00
2-5 .... 8.00
6 .... 12.00
7 .... 8.00
8 .... 12.00
9-16 .... 8.00

ComicsTrips (Peter Kuper's...)

Tundra

1 .... 7.00

Coming of Aphrodite

Hero

1 .... 4.00

Comix Book

Marvel, 1974

1 .... 10.00
2-3 .... 8.00
4-5 .... 5.00

Comix International

Warren, 1974

1 .... 125.00
☛Scarce
2 .... 90.00
☛Dracula story
3-5 .... 75.00
☛Spirit story

Commander Battle and the Atomic Sub

ACG, 1954

1 .... 225.00
2 .... 125.00
3-4 .... 100.00
5-7 .... 70.00

Command Review

Thoughts & Images, 1986

1-2 .... 4.00
3-4 .... 5.00

Commies From Mars

Last Gasp

1-5 .... 2.00
6 .... 3.00

Common Foe

Image, 2005

1-4 .... 4.00

Common Grounds

Image, 2004

1-6 .... 3.00

Communion

Fantagraphics, 1991

1 .... 3.00

Complete Cheech Wizard

Rip Off, 1986

1-2 .... 2.00
3-4 .... 3.00

Complete Comics

Timely, 1944

2 .... 1,500.00

Completely Bad Boys

Fantagraphics

1 .... 3.00

Complete Mystery

Marvel, 1948

1 .... 300.00
2 .... 240.00
3-4 .... 200.00

Complete Rog 2000

Pacific, 1982

1 .... 3.00

Complex City

Better, 2000

1-4 .... 3.00

Compost Comics

Gasparotti

1 .... 3.00

Compu-M.E.C.H.

Monolith, 1999

1-2 .... 3.00
3-10 .... 8.00

Comrades of War

Dead Air

1-2 .... 2.00

Conan

Marvel, 1995

1-12 .... 3.00

Conan

Dark Horse, 2004

0 .... 4.00
1 .... 10.00
1/2nd 3.00
2 .... 5.00
2/2nd-50 .... 3.00

Conan Classic

Marvel, 1994

1-11 .... 2.00

Conan and the Daughters of Midora

Dark Horse, 2004

1 .... 5.00

Conan and the Demons of Khitai

Dark Horse, 2005

1-4 .... 3.00

Conan and the Songs of the Dead

Dark Horse, 2006

1-5 .... 3.00

Conan: Book of Thoth

Dark Horse, 2006

1-4 .... 5.00

Conan and the Jewels of Gwahlur

Dark Horse, 2005

1-3 .... 3.00

Conan: Death Covered In Gold

Marvel, 1999

1-3 .... 3.00

Conan: Flame and the Fiend

Marvel, 2000

1-3 .... 3.00

Conan of the Isles

Marvel

1 .... 9.00

Conan: Return of Styrm

Marvel, 1998

1-3 .... 3.00

Conan: River of Blood

Marvel, 1998

1-3 .... 3.00

Conan Saga

Marvel, 1987

1-74 .... 3.00
75 .... 4.00
76-97 .... 2.00

Conan: Scarlet Sword

Marvel, 1998

1-3 .... 3.00

Conan the Adventurer

Marvel, 1994

1-14 .... 2.00

Conan the Barbarian

Marvel, 1970

1 .... 160.00
☛1st comics Conan
2 .... 55.00
3 .... 72.00
4 .... 26.00
5 .... 30.00
6-7 .... 26.00
8 .... 30.00
9 .... 20.00
☛Giant-size
10-11 .... 35.00
☛Giant-size
12 .... 15.00
13-14 .... 20.00
15 .... 17.00
16 .... 20.00
17 .... 17.00
18 .... 20.00
19 .... 17.00
20 .... 27.00
☛1st Red Sonja
21-24 .... 20.00
25 .... 10.00
26-30 .... 8.00
31-35 .... 7.00
36-38 .... 9.00
39-47 .... 7.00
48-50 .... 6.00
51-61 .... 5.00
61/30¢ 20.00
62 .... 5.00
62/30¢ 20.00
63 .... 5.00
63/30¢ 20.00
64 .... 5.00
64/30¢ 20.00
65 .... 5.00
65/30¢ 20.00
66-75/Whitman 5.00
75/35¢ 15.00
76-76/Whitman 5.00
76/35¢ 15.00
77-77/Whitman 5.00
77/35¢ 15.00

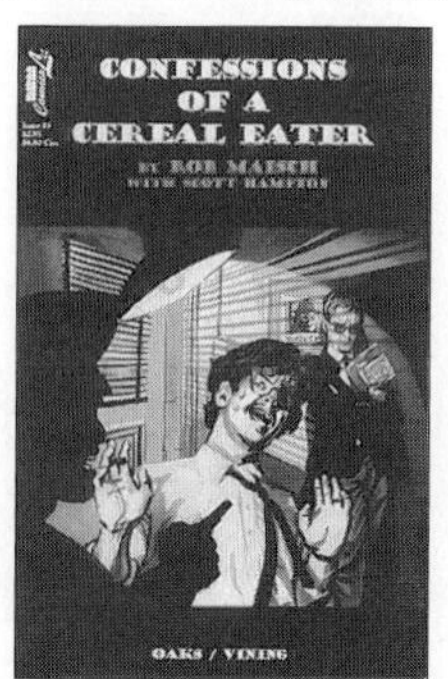

Confessions of a Cereal Eater

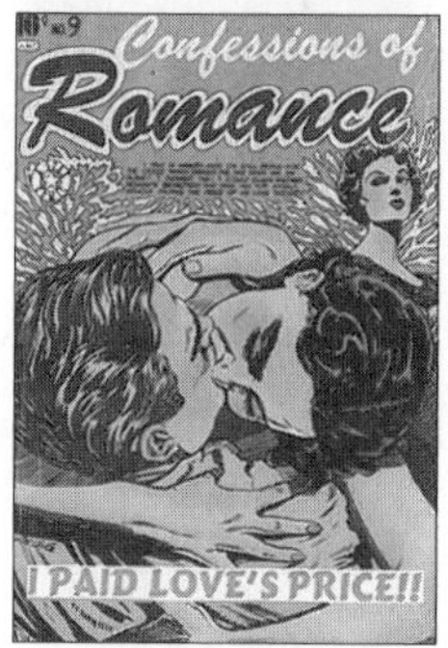

Confessions of Romance

Congorilla

Conjurors

Conqueror

Conqueror Universe

Conservation Corps

Conspiracy

78-78/Whitman.........................5.00
78/35¢-79...............................15.00
79/Whitman.............................5.00
79/35¢...................................15.00
80-93/Whitman.........................5.00
94-99.......................................4.00
100..6.00
101-274....................................2.00
275..3.00
Ann 1......................................10.00
Ann 2-3.....................................6.00
Ann 4-12...................................2.00
Special 1..................................3.00

Conan the Barbarian
Marvel, 1997

1-3...3.00

Conan the Barbarian Movie Special
Marvel, 1982

1-2...1.00

Conan the Barbarian: The Usurper
Marvel, 1997

1-3...3.00

Conan the Destroyer
Marvel, 1985

1-2...1.00

Conan: The Horn of Azoth
Marvel

1..9.00

Conan the King
Marvel, 1984

20-55.......................................2.00

Conan: The Lord of the Spiders
Marvel, 1998

1-3...3.00

Conan: The Ravagers Out of Time
Marvel, 1995

1..10.00

Conan the Reaver
Marvel

1..7.00

Conan the Rogue
Marvel

1..10.00

Conan the Savage
Marvel, 1995

1-12...3.00

Conan: The Skull of Set
Marvel

1..9.00

Conan vs. Rune
Marvel, 1995

1..3.00

Concrete
Dark Horse, 1985

1..3.00
1/2nd-10..................................2.00
Hero ed. 1................................1.00

Concrete: A New Life
Dark Horse, 1989

1..3.00

Concrete Celebrates Earth Day
Dark Horse, 1990

1..4.00

Concrete Color Special
Dark Horse, 1989

1..3.00

Concrete: Eclectica
Dark Horse, 1993

1-2...3.00

Concrete: Fragile Creature
Dark Horse, 1991

1-4...3.00

Concrete Jungle: The Legend of the Black Lion
Acclaim, 1998

1..3.00

Concrete: Killer Smile
Dark Horse, 1994

1-4...3.00

Concrete: Land & Sea
Dark Horse, 1989

1..3.00

Concrete: Odd Jobs
Dark Horse, 1990

1..4.00

Concrete: Strange Armor
Dark Horse, 1997

1-5...3.00

Concrete: The Human Dilemma
Dark Horse, 2005

1-6...4.00

Concrete: Think Like a Mountain
Dark Horse, 1996

1-6...3.00
Ashcan 1..................................1.00

Condom-Man
Aaaahh!!

1..4.00

Condorman
Whitman, 1981

1-3 .... 2.00

Coneheads
Marvel, 1994

1-4 .... 2.00

Confessions of a Cereal Eater
NBM, 2000

1-4 .... 3.00

Confessions of a Teenage Vampire: The Turning
Scholastic, 1997

1 .... 5.00

Confessions of a Teenage Vampire: Zombie Saturday Night
Scholastic, 1997

1 .... 5.00

Confessions of Romance
Star, 1953

7 .... 60.00
8 .... 45.00
9-11 .... 40.00

Confessions of the Lovelorn
ACG, 1954

52-114 .... 20.00

Confessor (Demonicus Ex Deo)
Dark Matter

1 .... 3.00

Confidential Confessions
Tokyopop, 2003

1-6 .... 10.00

Confrontation
Sacred Origin, 1997

1-4 .... 3.00
Special 1 .... 5.00

Congo Bill
DC, 1954

1 .... 1,100.00
2 .... 650.00
3 .... 500.00
4-6 .... 325.00
7 .... 450.00

Congo Bill
DC, 1999

1-4 .... 3.00

Congorilla
DC, 1992

1-4 .... 2.00

Conjurors
DC, 1999

1-3 .... 3.00

Connor Hawke: Dragon's Blood
DC, 2007

1-2 .... 3.00

Conqueror
Harrier, 1984

1-Special 1 .... 2.00

Conqueror of the Barren Earth
DC, 1983

1-4 .... 1.00

Conqueror Universe
Harrier

1 .... 3.00

Conservation Corps
Archie, 1993

1-3 .... 1.00

Conspiracy
Marvel, 1998

1-2 .... 3.00

Conspiracy Comics
Revolutionary, 1991

1-3 .... 3.00

Constantine Movie Adaptation
DC, 2005

0 .... 7.00

Constellation Graphics
Stages

1-2 .... 2.00

Construct
Caliber

1-6 .... 3.00

Contact Comics
Aviation, 1944

1 .... 550.00
2 .... 425.00
3 .... 400.00
4-6 .... 350.00
7-8 .... 300.00
9 .... 275.00
10-11 .... 350.00
12 .... 1,100.00

Containment (Eric Red's)
Idea & Design Works, 2004

1-4 .... 4.00

Contaminated Zone
Brave New Words, 1991

1-3 .... 3.00

Contemporary Bio-Graphics
Revolutionary, 1991

1-8 .... 3.00

Construct

Contact Comics

Contemporary Bio-Graphics

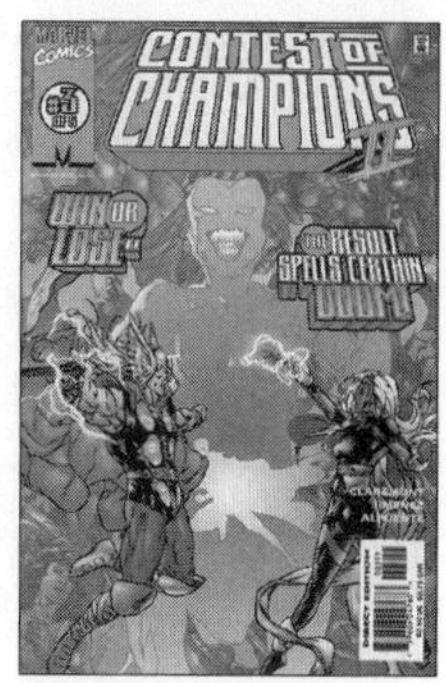

Contest of Champions II

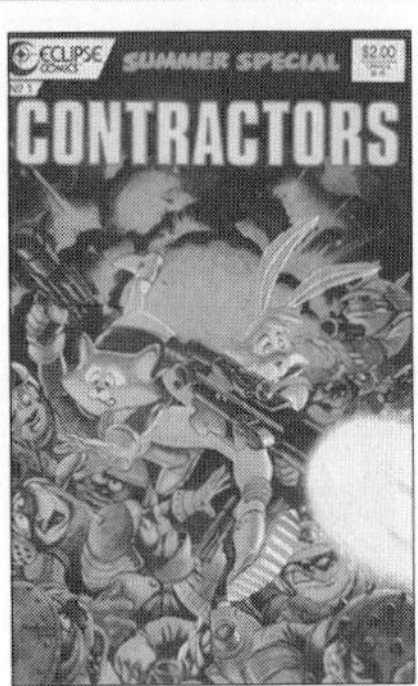

Contractors

Coo Coo Comics

Cool World

COPS

Contender Comics Special
Contender

1 ..... 1.00

Contest of Champions II
Marvel, 1999

1-5 ..... 3.00

Continuum
Continuity, 1988

1 ..... 3.00

Continuum Presents
Continuum, 1988

1-2 ..... 2.00

Contractors
Eclipse, 1987

1 ..... 2.00

Contract With God, A
DC, 2000

1 ..... 13.00

Convent of Hell
NBM

1 ..... 13.00

Convocations: A Magic: The Gathering Gallery
Acclaim, 1995

1 ..... 3.00

Coochy Cooty Men's Comics
Print Mint

1 ..... 3.00

Coo Coo Comics
Animated, 1942

1 ..... 175.00
2 ..... 80.00
3-5 ..... 45.00
6-10 ..... 38.00
11-20 ..... 32.00
21-30 ..... 28.00
31-33 ..... 24.00
34-40 ..... 35.00
41 ..... 85.00
42 ..... 75.00
43-46 ..... 40.00
47 ..... 75.00
48 ..... 40.00
49 ..... 60.00
50-51 ..... 50.00
52-62 ..... 20.00

Cookie
ACG, 1946

1 ..... 90.00
2 ..... 55.00
3-5 ..... 38.00
6-10 ..... 28.00
11-20 ..... 24.00
21-40 ..... 20.00
41-55 ..... 18.00

Cool World
DC, 1992

1-4 ..... 2.00

Cool World Movie Adaptation
DC

1 ..... 4.00

Cop Called Tracy, A
Avalon

1-22 ..... 3.00

COPS
DC, 1988

1-15 ..... 1.00

Cops: The Job
Marvel, 1992

1-4 ..... 1.00

Copybook Tales
Slave Labor, 1996

1-6 ..... 3.00

Corban the Barbearian
Me Comix

1-2 ..... 2.00

Corben Special, A
Pacific, 1984

1 ..... 2.00

Corbo
Sword in Stone

1 ..... 2.00

Cormac Mac Art
Dark Horse, 1989

1-4 ..... 2.00

Corny's Fetish
Dark Horse, 1998

1 ..... 5.00

Corporate Crime Comics
Kitchen Sink, 1977

1-2 ..... 3.00

Corporate Ninja
Slave Labor, 2005

1 ..... 3.00

Cortez and the Fall of the Aztecs
Tome

1-2 ..... 3.00

Corto Maltese: Ballad of the Salt Sea
NBM

1-4 ..... 3.00

Corum: The Bull and the Spear
First

1-4 ..... 2.00

Corvus Rex: A Legacy of Shadows
Crow, 1996
1 .... 2.00

Cosmic Book
Ace
1 .... 2.00

Cosmic Boy
DC, 1986
1-4 .... 1.00

Cosmic Guard
Devil's Due, 2004
1 .... 5.00
2 .... 4.00
3-6 .... 3.00

Cosmic Heroes
Eternity
1-8 .... 2.00
9 .... 3.00
10-11 .... 4.00

Cosmic Kliti
Fantagraphics, 1991
1 .... 2.00

Cosmic Odyssey
DC, 1988
1 .... 4.00
2-4 .... 4.00

Cosmic Powers
Marvel, 1994
1-6 .... 3.00

Cosmic Powers Unlimited
Marvel, 1995
1-5 .... 4.00

Cosmic Ray
Image, 1999
1/A-3 .... 3.00

Cosmic Steller Rebellers
Hammac
1-2 .... 2.00

Cosmic Waves
AmF, 1994
1-3 .... 3.00

Cosmo Cat
Fox, 1946
1 .... 110.00
2-5 .... 85.00

Cosmos
Micmac
1 .... 2.00

Cosmo the Merry Martian
Archie, 1958
1 .... 75.00
2-6 .... 50.00

Cougar
Atlas-Seaboard, 1975
1 .... 5.00
2 .... 3.00

Countdown
DC, 2000
1-8 .... 3.00

Count Duckula
Marvel, 1989
1-15 .... 1.00

Counter Ops
Antarctic, 2003
1-4 .... 4.00

Counterparts
Tundra, 1993
1-3 .... 3.00

Coup D'Etat: Afterword
DC, 2004
1 .... 3.00

Coup D'Etat: The Authority
DC, 2004
1 .... 4.00

Coup D'Etat: Sleeper
DC, 2004
1 .... 6.00
1/Variant 10.00

Coup D'Etat: Stormwatch
DC, 2004
1 .... 5.00
1/Variant 7.00

Coup D'Etat: Wildcats Version 3.0
DC, 2004
1 .... 5.00
1/Variant 6.00

Couple of Winos, A
Fantagraphics, 1991
1 .... 2.00

Courage Comics
J. Edward, 1945
1-3 .... 75.00

Courageous Man Adventures
Moordam, 1998
1-3 .... 3.00

Courageous Princess
Antarctic, 2000
1 .... 12.00

Courtney Crumrin & The Night Things
Oni, 2002
1-4 .... 3.00

Courtney Crumrin Tales
Oni, 2005
1 .... 6.00

Cormac Mac Art

Corporate Crime Comics

Cosmic Boy

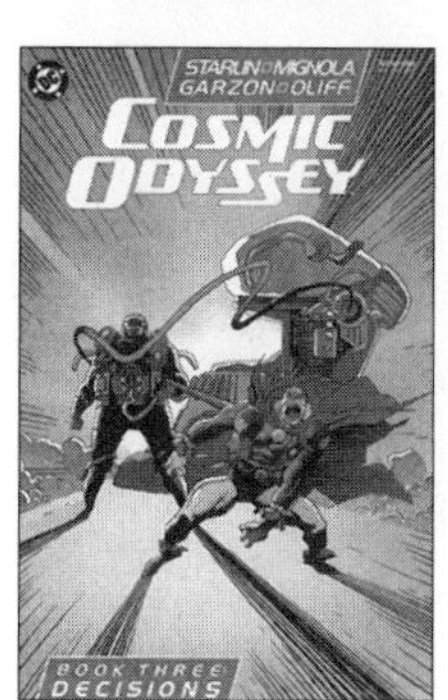

Cosmic Odyssey

Cosmic Powers

Cosmo Cat

Countdown

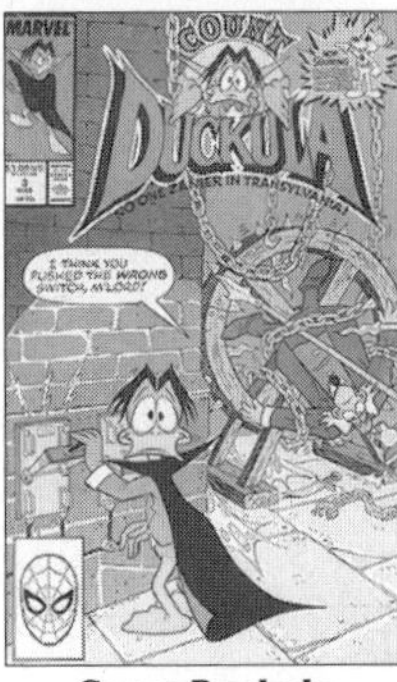

Count Duckula

Courtship of Eddie's Father
Dell, 1970

1 .... 30.00
2 .... 24.00

Courtyard
Avatar, 2003

1-2/A 4.00

Coutoo
Dark Horse

1 .... 4.00

Coven
Awesome, 1997

1/A 5.00
1/B 3.00
1/C 4.00
1/D-6 .... 3.00

Coven
Awesome, 1999

1-4 .... 3.00

Coven Black and White
Awesome, 1998

1 .... 3.00

Coven: Dark Origins
Awesome, 1999

1 .... 3.00

Coven: Fantom
Awesome, 1998

1-1/Gold 3.00

Coven of Angels
Jitterbug, 1995

1-2 .... 4.00
Ashcan 1 .... 8.00

Coven 13
No Mercy, 1997

1 .... 3.00

Coven: Tooth and Nail
Avatar, 2002

1 .... 3.00
1/Ltd. 30.00

Coventry
Fantagraphics, 1996

1-3 .... 4.00

Covert Vampiric Operations
Idea & Design Works, 2003

1 .... 6.00

Covert Vampiric Operations: Artifact
Idea & Design Works, 2003

1-3 .... 4.00

Cow
MonsterPants

1-3 .... 2.00

Cow-Boy
Ogre, 1997

1 .... 4.00

Cowboy Action
Atlas, 1955

5 .... 120.00
6-11 .... 100.00

Cowboy in Africa
Gold Key, 1968

1 .... 40.00

Cowboy Love
Fawcett, 1949

1 .... 100.00
2 .... 75.00
3-11 .... 60.00

Cowboy Love
Avalon

1 .... 3.00

Cowboy Romances
Atlas, 1949

1-2 .... 140.00
3 .... 100.00

Cowboy Western
Charlton, 1948

17 .... 125.00
18-21 .... 100.00
22-25 .... 90.00
26-30 .... 85.00
31-35 .... 80.00
36-39 .... 68.00
46-49 .... 55.00
50-57 .... 42.00
58 .... 68.00
59-60 .... 42.00
61-66 .... 36.00
67 .... 68.00

Cowgirl Romances
Fiction House, 1950

1 .... 225.00
2 .... 150.00
3 .... 125.00
4-6 .... 100.00
7-9 .... 75.00
10-12 .... 50.00

Cowgirl Romances
Marvel, 1950

28 .... 250.00

Cow Puncher
Avon, 1947

1 .... 185.00
2 .... 140.00
2/2nd 50.00
3 .... 90.00
4-5 .... 80.00
6 .... 110.00
7 .... 70.00

Cow Special

Image, 2001

1 ... 3.00

Coyote

Marvel, 1983

1 ... 3.00
2-10 ... 2.00
11 ... 3.00
12-16 ... 2.00

Crabbs

Cat-Head

1 ... 4.00

Crackajack Funnies

Dell, 1938

1 ... 1,800.00
2 ... 900.00
3 ... 650.00
4-5 ... 500.00
6-9 ... 450.00
10-19 ... 350.00
20-25 ... 250.00
26-29 ... 200.00
30-39 ... 175.00
40-43 ... 150.00

CrackBrained Comix

Crackbrained

1-3 ... 2.00

Crack Busters

Showcase, 1986

1-2 ... 2.00

Crack Comics

Quality, 1940

1 ... 3,850.00
2 ... 1,785.00
3 ... 1,200.00
4 ... 1,000.00
5-10 ... 850.00
11-20 ... 650.00
21-24 ... 475.00
25-26 ... 425.00
27 ... 600.00
28-30 ... 350.00
31-40 ... 200.00
41-51 ... 165.00
52-62 ... 145.00

Cracked

Globe, 1958

1 ... 125.00
2 ... 60.00
3-5 ... 35.00
6-10 ... 20.00
11-20 ... 12.00
21-30 ... 10.00
31-50 ... 8.00
51-100 ... 5.00
101-145 ... 4.00
146 ... 8.00
147-149 ... 5.00
150 ... 4.00
151-156 ... 3.00
157 ... 6.00
158-163 ... 3.00
164 ... 4.00
165-168 ... 3.00
169 ... 4.00
170-181 ... 3.00
182 ... 4.00
183-250 ... 3.00
251-350 ... 2.00
351-354 ... 3.00
Ann 1 ... 7.00
Ann 2-3 ... 5.00
Ann 4-19 ... 4.00

Cracked Collectors' Edition

Globe, 1973

4 ... 10.00
5 ... 8.00
6-10 ... 6.00
11-nn (30) ... 5.00
nn (31)-nn (50) ... 4.00
nn (51)-125 ... 3.00

Cracked Guide to the Movies

NBM

1 ... 9.00

Crack Western Comics

Quality, 1949

63 ... 120.00
64-65 ... 85.00
66 ... 75.00
67 ... 85.00
68-70 ... 75.00
71 ... 85.00
72 ... 75.00
73 ... 45.00
74-76 ... 60.00
77 ... 45.00
78-79 ... 60.00
80 ... 45.00
81 ... 60.00
82 ... 45.00
83 ... 60.00
84 ... 65.00

Crap

Fantagraphics, 1993

1-7 ... 3.00

Crash Comics

Tem, 1940

1 ... 2,100.00
2 ... 1,000.00
3 ... 800.00
4 ... 1,650.00
5 ... 750.00

Crash Dummies

Harvey, 1994

1-3 ... 2.00

Cow-Boy

Cow Puncher

Crack Comics

Cracked

Crack Western Comics

Crash Comics

Crash Ryan

Crazyman

Crash Metro & the Star Squad

Oni, 1999

1 ....3.00

Crash Ryan

Marvel, 1984

1-4 ....2.00

Crash Test Dummies

Harvey

1-3 ....2.00

Cray Baby Adventures Special

Electric Milk

1 ....3.00

Cray-Baby Adventures: Wrath of the Pedidlers

Destination Entertainment, 1998

1-3 ....3.00

Crazy

Atlas, 1953

1 ....225.00
2 ....165.00
3 ....125.00
4-7 ....95.00

Crazy

Marvel, 1973

1 ....16.00
2-3 ....10.00

Crazy (Magazine)

Marvel, 1973

1 ....16.00
2-3 ....10.00
4-5 ....5.00
6-15 ....3.00
16-94 ....2.00

Crazy Bob

Blackbird

1 ....3.00
2 ....2.00

Crazyfish Preview

Crazyfish

1-2 ....1.00

Crazy Love Story

Tokyopop, 2004

1-5 ....10.00

Crazyman

Continuity, 1992

1 ....4.00
2-3 ....3.00

Crazyman

Continuity, 1993

1 ....4.00
2-4 ....3.00

Crazy, Man, Crazy

Charlton, 1956

1 ....60.00
2 ....45.00

Creature

Antarctic, 1997

1-2 ....3.00

Creature Commandos

DC, 2000

1-8 ....3.00

Creature Features

Mojo

1 ....5.00

Creature Features (Art Adams'...)

Dark Horse, 1996

1 ....14.00

Creatures of the Id

Caliber, 1990

1 ....11.00

Creatures on the Loose

Marvel, 1971

10 ....50.00
☛1st Kull; Wrightson
11-15 ....15.00
16-22 ....10.00
23-26 ....6.00
27-29 ....5.00
30 ....25.00
☛Man-Wolf

31 ....12.00
32-36 ....8.00
37 ....12.00
King Size 1 ....10.00

Creech

Image, 1997

1-1/A 2.00
2-3 ....3.00

Creech: Out for Blood

Image, 2001

1-2 ....5.00

CreeD

Hall of Heroes, 1994

1 ....4.00
2 ....3.00

CreeD

Lightning, 1995

1-2 ....3.00
2/Platinum 4.00
3-3/Platinum 3.00

CreeD: Apple Tree

Gearbox, 2000

1 ....3.00

CreeD: Cranial Disorder
Lightning, 1996
1-3 .... 3.00

CreeD: Mechanical Evolution
Gearbox, 2000
1-2 .... 3.00

CreeD/Teenage Mutant Ninja Turtles
Lightning, 1996
1 .... 3.00

CreeD: The Good Ship and the New Journey Home
Lightning, 1997
1 .... 3.00

CreeD Use Your Delusion
Avatar, 1998
1-2 .... 3.00

CreeD: Utopiate
Image, 2002
1-4 .... 3.00

Creeper
DC, 1997
1-11 .... 3.00
1,000,000 .... 2.00

Creeper
DC, 2006
1-5 .... 3.00

Creeps
Image, 2001
1-4 .... 3.00

Creepsville
Go-Go
1-5 .... 3.00

Creepy
Warren, 1964
1 .... 160.00
2 .... 50.00
3 .... 25.00
4 .... 35.00
5 .... 18.00
6 .... 15.00
7-8 .... 24.00
9 .... 45.00
10 .... 20.00
11-13 .... 15.00
14 .... 22.00
15 .... 25.00
16-17 .... 30.00
18 .... 25.00
19-20 .... 15.00
21-22 .... 12.00
23-25 .... 11.00
26-31 .... 10.00
32 .... 35.00
33-35 .... 10.00
36 .... 15.00

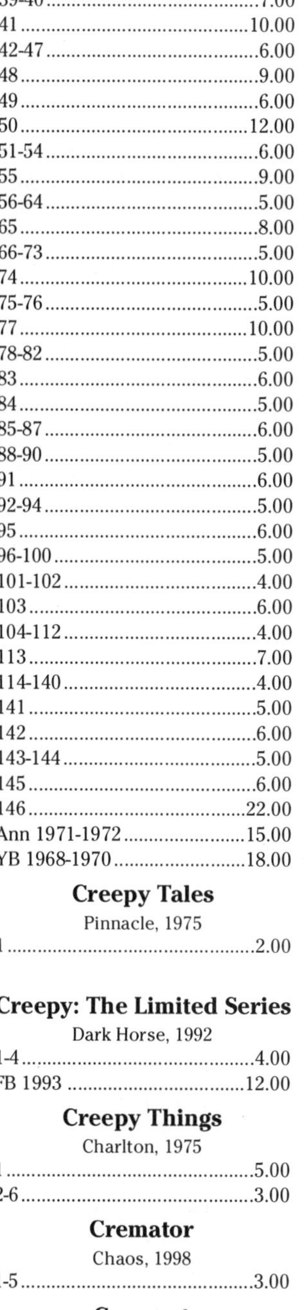

37-38 .... 10.00
39-40 .... 7.00
41 .... 10.00
42-47 .... 6.00
48 .... 9.00
49 .... 6.00
50 .... 12.00
51-54 .... 6.00
55 .... 9.00
56-64 .... 5.00
65 .... 8.00
66-73 .... 5.00
74 .... 10.00
75-76 .... 5.00
77 .... 10.00
78-82 .... 5.00
83 .... 6.00
84 .... 5.00
85-87 .... 6.00
88-90 .... 5.00
91 .... 6.00
92-94 .... 5.00
95 .... 6.00
96-100 .... 5.00
101-102 .... 4.00
103 .... 6.00
104-112 .... 4.00
113 .... 7.00
114-140 .... 4.00
141 .... 5.00
142 .... 6.00
143-144 .... 5.00
145 .... 6.00
146 .... 22.00
Ann 1971-1972 .... 15.00
YB 1968-1970 .... 18.00

Creepy Tales
Pinnacle, 1975
1 .... 2.00

Creepy: The Limited Series
Dark Horse, 1992
1-4 .... 4.00
FB 1993 .... 12.00

Creepy Things
Charlton, 1975
1 .... 5.00
2-6 .... 3.00

Cremator
Chaos, 1998
1-5 .... 3.00

Crescent
B-Line, 1996
0 .... 1.00

Crescent Moon
Tokyopop, 2004
1-6 .... 10.00

Creature Commandos

Creatures on the Loose

CreeD Use Your Delusion

Creeps

Creepy Things

Crime and Punishment

Crimebuster

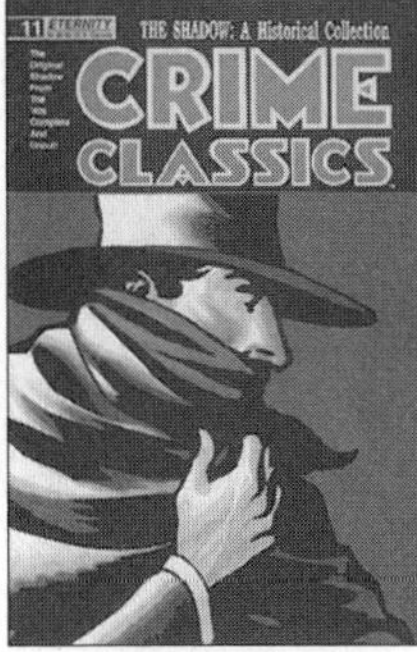

Crime Classics

Crew
Marvel, 2003

1-7 .... 3.00

Crime & Justice
Charlton, 1951

1 .... 240.00
2 .... 125.00
3-5 .... 100.00
6-10 .... 80.00
11-19 .... 65.00
20-23 .... 50.00

Crime & Justice
Avalon, 1998

1 .... 3.00

Crime and Punishment
Lev Gleason, 1948

1 .... 185.00
2 .... 100.00
3-5 .... 60.00
6-10 .... 55.00
11-20 .... 42.00
21-30 .... 38.00
31-38 .... 32.00
39 .... 55.00
40-58 .... 30.00
59 .... 85.00
60-65 .... 28.00
66 .... 175.00
67-68 .... 135.00
69 .... 55.00
70-74 .... 28.00

Crime and Punishment Marshal Law Takes Manhattan
Marvel, 1989

1 .... 5.00

Crimebuster
AC

0 .... 3.00

Crimebuster
Avalon

1 .... 3.00

Crimebuster Classics
AC

1 .... 4.00

Crime Can't Win
Marvel, 1950

1 .... 115.00
2 .... 85.00
3 .... 75.00
4-10 .... 55.00
11-12 .... 48.00

Crime Classics
Eternity, 1988

1-13 .... 2.00

Crime Clinic
Ziff-Davis, 1951

1 .... 225.00
2 .... 165.00
3-5 .... 150.00

Crime Clinic
Slave Labor, 1995

1-2 .... 3.00

Crime Detective Comics (Vol. 1)
Hillman, 1948

1 .... 155.00
2 .... 75.00
3-4 .... 55.00
5 .... 60.00
6-8 .... 55.00
9 .... 125.00
10-12 .... 48.00

Crime Detective Comics (Vol. 2)
Hillman, 1950

1 .... 50.00
2-3 .... 36.00
4 .... 40.00
5-6 .... 30.00
7 .... 45.00
8-12 .... 30.00

Crime Detective Comics (Vol. 3)
Hillman, 1952

1-8 .... 30.00

Crime Detector
Timor, 1954

1 .... 150.00
2 .... 75.00
3 .... 50.00
4 .... 30.00
5 .... 150.00

Crime Does Not Pay
Lev Gleason, 1942

22 .... 800.00
23 .... 525.00
24 .... 375.00
25-30 .... 225.00
31-41 .... 115.00
42 .... 110.00
43-50 .... 90.00
51-60 .... 65.00
61-70 .... 60.00
71-80 .... 50.00
81-90 .... 42.00
91-100 .... 35.00
101-110 .... 32.00
111-130 .... 30.00
131-146 .... 26.00
Ann 1944 .... 700.00
Ann 1945 .... 600.00
Ann 1946-1949 .... 500.00
Ann 1950-1953 .... 400.00

Crime Exposed
Marvel, 1950

1 .... 165.00
2 .... 100.00
3 .... 80.00
4-9 .... 70.00
10-14 .... 60.00

Crimefighters
Marvel, 1948

1 .... 120.00
2-10 .... 80.00

Crime Files
Standard, 1952

5 .... 175.00
6 .... 100.00

Crime Must Lose
Timely, 1950

4 .... 185.00
5-6 .... 150.00
7-10 .... 120.00
11-12 .... 100.00

Crime Must Pay the Penalty
Current, 1948

1 .... 165.00
2 .... 100.00
3-4 .... 85.00
5-7 .... 55.00
8 .... 70.00
9-10 .... 55.00
11-20 .... 45.00
21-30 .... 40.00
31-40 .... 32.00
41 .... 55.00
42-46 .... 32.00

Crime Mysteries
Ribage, 1952

1 .... 450.00
2-3 .... 300.00
4 .... 400.00
5-10 .... 200.00
11-15 .... 175.00

Crime on the Waterfront
Realistic Comics, 1952

4 .... 210.00

Crime Patrol
E.C., 1948

7 .... 600.00
8-9 .... 575.00
10 .... 550.00
11-14 .... 500.00
15 .... 2,200.00
☛1st Cryptkeeper
16 .... 1,500.00

Crime Patrol
Gemstone, 2000

1-5 .... 3.00
Ann 1 .... 14.00

Crime Pays
Boneyard, 1996

1-2 .... 3.00

Crime Reporter
St. John, 1948

1 .... 225.00
2 .... 345.00
3-4 .... 165.00

Crimes by Women
Fox, 1948

1 .... 1,100.00
2 .... 550.00
3 .... 450.00
4-5 .... 375.00
6-10 .... 325.00
11-15 .... 265.00
54 .... 165.00

Crime Smasher
Fawcett, 1949

1 .... 275.00

Crime-Smasher
Blue Comet, 1987

Special 1 .... 2.00

Crime Smashers
Ribage, 1950

1 .... 275.00
2 .... 145.00
3-4 .... 125.00
5 .... 165.00
6-10 .... 90.00
11-12 .... 85.00
13 .... 110.00
14-15 .... 85.00

Crime SuspenStories
E.C., 1950

1 .... 800.00
1/A 1,000.00
☛#1 marked out
2 .... 475.00
3-5 .... 315.00
6-10 .... 235.00
11-12 .... 185.00
13 .... 210.00
14-15 .... 185.00
16 .... 190.00
17 .... 235.00
☛Frazetta art
18-19 .... 170.00
20 .... 215.00
21 .... 115.00
22-23 .... 145.00
24-27 .... 115.00

Crime SuspenStories
Gemstone, 1992

1-15 .... 2.00
16-27 .... 3.00
Ann 1 .... 9.00
Ann 2-3 .... 10.00
Ann 4-6 .... 11.00

Crime Does Not Pay

Crime Must Pay the Penalty

Crime Mysteries

Crime Smashers

Criminals on the Run

Crimson

Crimson Dynamo

Crimson Sourcebook

Criminal
Marvel, 2006

1-3 .... 3.00

Criminal Macabre
Dark Horse, 2003

1-5 .... 3.00

Criminal Macabre: Feat of Clay
Dark Horse, 2006

1 .... 3.00

Criminal Macabre: Two Red Eyes
Dark Horse, 2007

1 .... 3.00

Criminals on the Run
Premium, 1948

1 .... 285.00
2 .... 220.00
3-4 .... 200.00
5-7 .... 165.00
8 .... 175.00
9-10 .... 165.00

Crimson
Image, 1998

1-1/A 4.00
1/B-1/C 6.00
2 .... 3.00
2/A-2/B 6.00
3 .... 3.00
3/A 4.00
4-7 .... 3.00
7/A 15.00
7/B-24 .... 3.00
Special 1 .... 7.00
Special 1/A 8.00

Crimson Avenger
DC, 1988

1-4 .... 2.00

Crimson Dreams
Crimson, 1985

1-11 .... 2.00

Crimson Dynamo
Marvel, 2003

1-6 .... 3.00

Crimson Letters
Adventure, 1990

1 .... 2.00

Crimson Nun
Antarctic, 1997

1-4 .... 3.00

Crimson Plague
Event, 1997

1 .... 3.00
1/Ltd 5.00

Crimson Plague (George Pèrez's...)
Image, 2000

1-2 .... 3.00

Crimson: Scarlet X Blood on the Moon
DC, 1999

1 .... 4.00

Crimson Sourcebook
WildStorm, 1999

1 .... 3.00

Crisis
Fleetway-Quality, 1988

1 .... 4.00
2-10 .... 3.00
11-49 .... 2.00
50-63 .... 3.00

Crisis Aftermath: The Spectre
DC, 2006

1-3 .... 3.00

Crisis on Infinite Earths
DC, 1985

1 .... 5.00
2-3 .... 4.00
4 .... 3.00
5 .... 5.00
6 .... 3.00
7-8 .... 5.00
9-12 .... 3.00

Crisp
Crisp Biscuit, 1997

1-2 .... 3.00

Crisp Biscuit
Crisp Biscuit, 1991

1 .... 2.00

Criss Cross (Doug Mier's ...)
Arcana, 2005

1 .... 4.00

Cristian Dark
Darque, 1993

1-3 .... 3.00

Critical Error
Dark Horse, 1992

1 .... 3.00

Critical Mass
Marvel, 1989

1-7 .... 5.00

Critters
Fantagraphics, 1986

1 .... 10.00
2 .... 3.00
3 .... 8.00
4-5 .... 3.00
6-7 .... 5.00

8-9 .... 3.00
10 .... 4.00
11-22 .... 3.00
23 .... 4.00
24-40 .... 3.00
41-49 .... 2.00
50 .... 5.00
Special 1 .... 2.00

Critturs
Mu, 1992

0 .... 3.00

Cromartie High School
ADV Manga, 2005

5 .... 0.00
1 .... 10.00
2-4 .... 11.00

Cromwell Stone
Dark Horse

1 .... 4.00

Cross
Dark Horse, 1995

0-1 .... 3.00
2 .... 10.00
3 .... 3.00
4-5 .... 10.00
6 .... 3.00

Cross
Tokyopop, 2004

1-5 .... 10.00

Cross and the Switchblade
Spire, 1972

1 .... 3.00
1/2nd 2.00
1/Barbour 1.00

Cross Bronx
Image, 2006

1-4 .... 3.00

Crossed Swords
K-Z, 1986

1 .... 1.00

Crossfire
Eclipse, 1984

1 .... 5.00
2-26 .... 2.00

Crossfire and Rainbow
Eclipse, 1986

1-4 .... 1.00

CrossGen Chronicles
CrossGen, 2000

1-7 .... 4.00

Crossgenesis
CrossGen, 2000

1 .... 5.00

CrossGen Sampler
CrossGen, 2000

1 .... 1.00

Crossing Midnight
DC, 2007

1-2 .... 3.00

Crossovers
CrossGen, 2003

1-9 .... 3.00

Crossroads
First, 1988

1-5 .... 4.00

Crow
Caliber, 1989

1 .... 22.00
☛Crow origin
1/2nd 4.00
1/3rd 3.00
2 .... 12.00
2/2nd 4.00
2/3rd 3.00
3 .... 10.00
3/2nd 4.00
4 .... 10.00

Crow
Tundra, 1992

1-4 .... 5.00

Crow
Image, 1999

1-10 .... 3.00

Crow: City of Angels
Kitchen Sink, 1996

1-3 .... 3.00

Crow: Dead Time
Kitchen Sink, 1996

1-3 .... 3.00

Crow: Flesh & Blood
Kitchen Sink, 1996

1-3 .... 3.00

Crown Comics
Golfing, 1944

1 .... 450.00
2 .... 300.00
3-5 .... 265.00
6 .... 200.00
7-8 .... 175.00
9-10 .... 150.00
11-14 .... 125.00
15-19 .... 100.00

Crow of the Bearclan
Blackthorne, 1986

1-6 .... 2.00

Crow: Waking Nightmares
Kitchen Sink, 1997

1-4 .... 3.00

Crow: Wild Justice
Kitchen Sink, 1996

1-3 .... 3.00

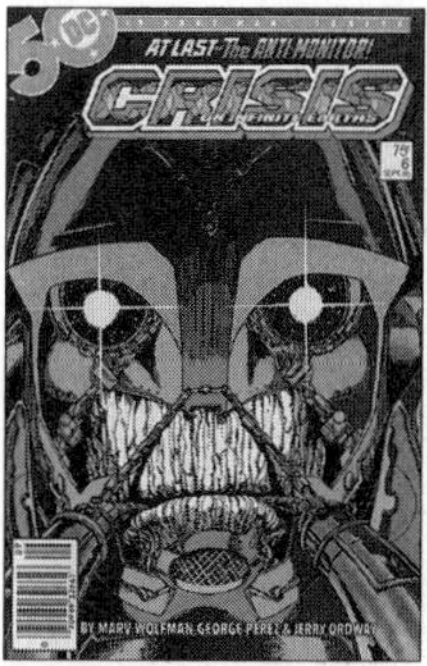

Crisis on Infinite Earths

Critical Error

Critters

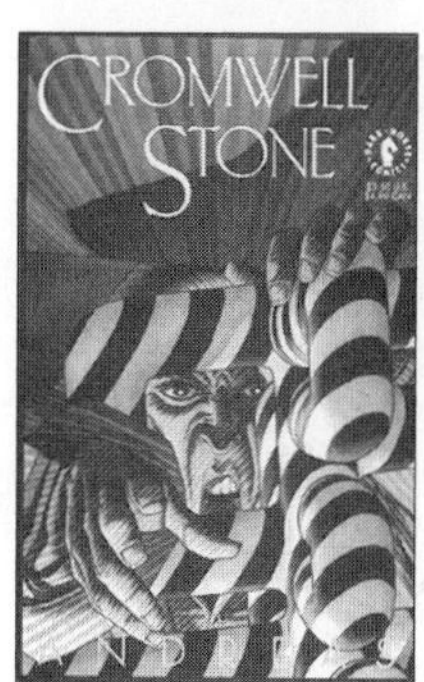

Cromwell Stone

Crossfire

CrossGen Sampler

Crossovers

Crossroads

Crozonia
Image
1 .... 3.00

Crucial Fiction
Fantagraphics, 1992
1 .... 3.00
2-3 .... 2.00

Crucible
DC, 1993
1 .... 2.00
2-6 .... 1.00

Cruel and Unusual
DC, 1999
1-4 .... 3.00

Cruel & Unusual Punishment
Starhead, 1993
1-2 .... 3.00

Cruel World
Fantagraphics
1 .... 4.00

Crusader from Mars
Ziff-Davis, 1952
1 .... 550.00
2 .... 325.00

Crusaders
Guild
1 .... 1.00

Crusaders
Chick, 1974
1-16 .... 2.00

Crusaders
DC, 1992
1-8 .... 1.00

Crusades
DC, 2001
1-20 .... 3.00

Crusades: Urban Decree
DC, 2001
1 .... 4.00

Crush
Aeon, 1995
1-4 .... 3.00

Crush
Dark Horse, 2003
1-4 .... 3.00

Crush
Image, 1996
1-5 .... 2.00

Crusher Joe
Ironcat, 1999
1-3 .... 2.00

Crust
Top Shelf
1 .... 3.00

Crux
CrossGen, 2001
1-33 .... 3.00

Cry for Dawn
Cry for Dawn, 1989
1 .... 45.00
1/A 15.00
1/Counterfeit 2.00
1/2nd 20.00
1/3rd 18.00
2 .... 30.00
2/2nd 15.00
3 .... 25.00
4 .... 15.00
5 .... 15.00
5/2nd 8.00
6 .... 15.00
7 .... 15.00
8 .... 10.00
9 .... 10.00

Crying Freeman Part 1
Viz, 1989
1-8 .... 4.00

Crying Freeman Part 2
Viz, 1990
1-9 .... 4.00

Crying Freeman Part 3
Viz, 1991
1 .... 6.00
2-10 .... 5.00

Crying Freeman Part 4
Viz, 1994
1-3 .... 5.00
4-8 .... 3.00

Crying Freeman Part 5
Viz
1-11 .... 3.00

Crypt
Aaaargh!
1 .... 2.00

Crypt
Image, 1995
1-2 .... 3.00

Cryptics
Image, 2006
1 .... 4.00

Cryptic Tales
Showcase
1 .... 2.00

Cryptic Writings of Megadeth
Chaos!, 1997
1-4 .... 3.00

Crypt of C*m
Fantagraphics, 1999
1 .... 3.00

Crypt of Dawn

Sirius, 1996

1 .... 4.00
1/Ltd. 6.00
2-6 .... 3.00

Crypt of Shadows

Marvel, 1973

1 .... 35.00
2 .... 16.00
3 .... 15.00
4-5 .... 12.00
6-14 .... 10.00
15-21 .... 8.00

Crypt of Terror

E.C., 1950

17 .... 1,000.00
18 .... 800.00
19 .... 750.00

Cryptozoo Crew

NBM, 2005

1-2 .... 3.00

Crystal Balls

Fantagraphics, 1995

1-3 .... 3.00

Crystal Breeze Unleashed

High Impact, 1996

1-3 .... 3.00

Crystal Skull Files

Ink & Feathers

1 .... 12.00

Crystal War

Atlantis

1 .... 4.00

CSI: Bad Rap

Idea & Design Works, 2003

1 .... 6.00
2-5 .... 4.00

CSI: Crime Scene Investigation

Idea & Design Works, 2003

1-5 .... 3.00

CSI: Demon House

Idea & Design Works, 2004

1 .... 5.00
2-5 .... 4.00

CSI: Dying in the Gutters

Idea & Design Works, 2006

1-5 .... 4.00

CSI Miami: Smoking Gun

Idea & Design Works, 2003

1 .... 7.00

CSI Miami: Thou Shalt Not

Idea & Design Works, 2004

1 .... 7.00

CSI: New York Bloody Murder

Idea & Design Works, 2005

1-5 .... 4.00

CSI: Secret Identity

Idea & Design Works, 2005

1-5 .... 4.00

CSI: Serial

Idea & Design Works, 2003

1 .... 20.00

CSI: Thicker Than Blood

Idea & Design Works, 2003

1 .... 7.00

Cthulhu (H.P. Lovecraft's...)

Millennium

1 .... 3.00
1/CS 4.00
2-3 .... 3.00

Cthulhu: The Whisper In Darkness (H.P. Lovecraft's...)

Millennium

1 .... 7.00

Cuckoo

Green Door, 1996

1-5 .... 3.00

Cud

Fantagraphics, 1993

1-8 .... 3.00

Cuda

Avatar, 1998

1-1/A 4.00
1/B 6.00
1/C 4.00

Cuda B.C.

Rebel

1 .... 2.00

Cud Comics

Dark Horse, 1995

1-8 .... 3.00
Ashcan 1 .... 1.00

Cuirass

Harrier

1 .... 2.00

Cult Television

Zone, 1992

1 .... 3.00

Cultural Jet Lag

Fantagraphics, 1991

1 .... 3.00

Culture Vultures

Iconografix

1 .... 3.00

Crown Comics

Crow of the Bearclan

Crucible

Cruel and Unusual

Crusader from Mars

Crying Freeman Part 1

Crypt

Cud

Cupid's Revenge
Fantagraphics
1-2 ....3.00

Curio Shoppe
Phoenix, 1995
1 ....3.00

Cursed
Image, 2003
1-4 ....3.00

Cursed Worlds Source Book
Blue Comet
1 ....3.00

Curse of Dracula
Dark Horse, 1998
1-3 ....3.00

Curse of Dreadwolf
Lightning, 1994
1 ....3.00

Curse of Rune
Malibu, 1995
1/A 0.00
1-4 ....3.00

Curse of the Molemen
Kitchen Sink
1 ....5.00

Curse of the She-Cat
AC, 1989
1 ....3.00

Curse of the Spawn
Image, 1996
1 ....3.00
1/A 4.00
2-15 ....3.00
16-29 ....2.00

Curse of the Weird
Marvel, 1993
1-4 ....2.00

Curse of the Zombie
Marvel
4 ....1.00

CuteGirl
Not Available
1-2 ....1.00

Cutie Pie
Junior Readers' Guild, 1955
1 ....24.00
2-5 ....14.00

Cutting Class
B Comics, 1995
1 ....2.00

Cutting Edge
Marvel, 1995
1 ....3.00

CVO: African Blood
Idea & Design Works, 2006
1 ....4.00

CVO: Covert Vampiric Operations Rogue State
Idea & Design Works, 2004
1-5 ....4.00

Cyber 7
Eclipse, 1989
1-7 ....2.00

Cyber 7 Book Two
Eclipse, 1989
1-10 ....2.00

Cyber City: Part 1
CPM, 1995
1-2 ....3.00

Cyber City: Part 2
CPM, 1995
1-2 ....3.00

Cyber City: Part 3
CPM, 1995
1-2 ....3.00

Cybercom, Heart of the Blue Mesa
Matrix, 1987
1 ....2.00

Cyber Crush: Robots in Revolt
Fleetway-Quality, 1991
1-14 ....2.00

Cyberella
DC, 1996
1-6 ....2.00
7-12 ....3.00

Cyberfarce
Parody
1 ....3.00

Cyber Femmes
Spoof, 1992
1 ....3.00

Cyberforce
Image, 1992
1-2 ....3.00
3-4 ....2.00

Cyberforce
Image, 1993
0-1/Gold 3.00
1/2nd 1.00
2-5 ....3.00
6-7 ....2.00
8-10/Variant 3.00
11-12 ....2.00
13-16 ....3.00
17 ....2.00
18-24 ....3.00
25 ....4.00

26-35 .... 3.00
Ann 1 .... 4.00
Ann 2 .... 3.00

Cyberforce
Image, 2006
0-6 .... 3.00

Cyberforce Origins
Image, 1995
1-1/Gold 3.00
1/2nd 1.00
2-3 .... 3.00

Cyberforce, Stryke Force: Opposing Forces
Image, 1995
1-2 .... 3.00

Cyberforce Universe Sourcebook
Image, 1994
1-2 .... 3.00

Cyberforce/X-Men
Image, 2007
1-1/Variant 4.00

CyberFrog
Harris, 1996
0-4 .... 3.00

Cyberfrog: Reservoir Frog
Harris, 1996
1-2/A 3.00

CyberFrog: 3rd Anniversary Special
Harris, 1997
1-2 .... 3.00

Cyberfrog vs. CreeD
Harris, 1997
1 .... 3.00

Cybergen
CFD, 1996
1 .... 3.00

Cyberhawks
Pyramid, 1987
1-2 .... 2.00

Cyberlust
Aircel, 1991
1-3 .... 3.00

Cybernary
Image, 1995
1-5 .... 3.00

Cybernary 2.0
DC, 2001
1-6 .... 3.00

Cyberpunk (Book 1)
Innovation
1-2 .... 2.00

Cyberpunk (Book 2)
Innovation
1-2 .... 2.00

Cyberpunk Graphic Novel
Innovation
1 .... 7.00

Cyberpunk: The Seraphim Files
Innovation
1-2 .... 3.00
Book 1 .... 7.00

Cyberpunx
Image, 1996
1/A-1/D 3.00

CyberRad
Continuity, 1991
1-7 .... 2.00

Cyberrad
Continuity, 1992
1 .... 3.00
1/A 2.00

CyberRad Deathwatch 2000
Continuity, 1993
1-2 .... 3.00

Cyber Reality Comix
Wonder Comix, 1994
1-2 .... 4.00

Cybersexation
Antarctic, 1997
1 .... 3.00

Cyberspace 3000
Marvel, 1993
1 .... 3.00
2-8 .... 2.00

Cybersuit Arkadyne
Ianus, 1992
1-6 .... 3.00

Cybertrash and the Dog
Silverline, 1998
1 .... 3.00

Cyberzone
Jet-Black Grafiks, 1994
1-8 .... 3.00

Cyblade/Ghost Rider
Marvel, 1997
1 .... 3.00

Cyblade/Shi: The Battle for Independents
Image, 1995
1-1/B 6.00
1/CS 10.00
Ashcan 1 .... 3.00

Curse of the Molemen

Curse of the Spawn

Curse of the Weird

Cutting Edge

Cyber 7

Cybernary

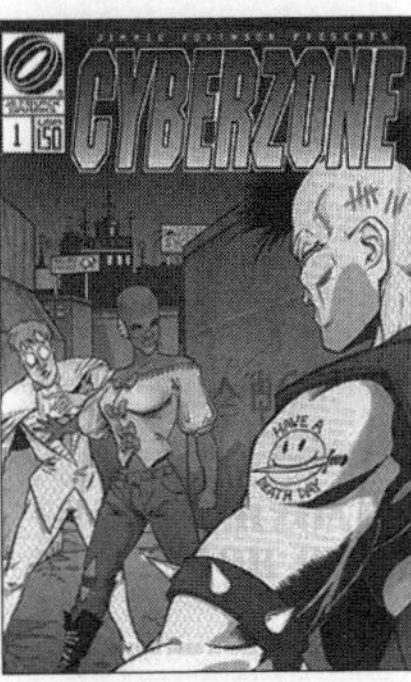

Cyberzone

Cyclops

Cyboars
Vintage, 1996

1-1/A 2.00

Cyborg, the Comic Book
Cannon, 1989

1 ....1.00

Cybrid
Maximum, 1995

1 ....3.00

Cyclone Comics
Bilbara, 1940

1 ....1,300.00
2-3 ....1,000.00
4-5 ....800.00

Cyclops
Marvel, 2000

1-4 ....3.00

Cycops
Comics Interview, 1988

1-3 ....2.00

Cygnus X-1
Twisted Pearl Press, 1994

1-2 ....3.00

Cy-Gor
Image, 1999

1-5 ....3.00

Cylinderhead
Slave Labor, 1989

1 ....2.00

Cynder
Immortelle, 1996

1-Ann 1 ....3.00

Cynder/Hellina Special
Immortelle, 1996

1 ....3.00

Cynosure
Cynosure, 1994

1 ....2.00

Cyntherita
Side Show

1 ....3.00

Czar Chasm
C&T

1-2 ....2.00

Dadaville
Caliber

1 ....3.00

Daemonifuge: The Screaming Cage
Black Library, 2002

1-3 ....3.00

Daemon Mask
Amazing

1 ....2.00

Daemonstorm
Caliber, 1997

1 ....4.00
Ashcan 1 ....1.00

Daffy Duck
Dell, 1956

4-10 ....18.00
11-20 ....10.00
21-40 ....7.00
41-60 ....5.00
61-80 ....4.00
81-100 ....3.00
101-128 ....2.00
129 ....18.00
130 ....25.00
131-134 ....15.00
135-137 ....5.00
138 ....2.00
139-141 ....5.00
142-144 ....15.00
145 ....7.00

Daffy Qaddafi
Comics Unlimited, 1986

1 ....2.00

Dagar, Desert Hawk
Fox, 1948

14 ....475.00
15 ....400.00
16-23 ....300.00

Dagar the Invincible (Tales of Sword and Sorcery...)
Gold Key, 1972

1 ....16.00
2 ....11.00
3-11 ....7.00
12-14 ....5.00
15-18 ....3.00
19 ....2.00

Dagwood Comics
Harvey, 1950

1 ....80.00
2 ....42.00
3-5 ....32.00
6-10 ....26.00
11-20 ....22.00
21-30 ....18.00
31-50 ....15.00
51-70 ....13.00
71-80 ....10.00
81-100 ....8.00
101-120 ....7.00
121-140 ....6.00

Dahmer's Zombie Squad
Boneyard, 1993

1 ....4.00

Dai Kamikaze!

Now, 1987

1-12 .... 2.00

Daikazu

Ground Zero, 1988

1-8 .... 2.00

Daily Bugle

Marvel, 1996

1-3 .... 3.00

Daily Bugle: Civil War Special Edition

Marvel, 2006

1 .... 1.00

Daily Planet Invasion! Extra

DC

1 .... 2.00

Daimons

Cry for Dawn

1 .... 3.00

Daisy and Donald

Gold Key, 1973

1 .... 25.00
2-4 .... 15.00
5-7 .... 10.00
8-10 .... 4.00
11-44 .... 3.00
45-46 .... 25.00
47 .... 60.00
49-54 .... 10.00
55-59 .... 15.00

Daisy and Her Pups Comics

Harvey, 1951

21 (1) 15.00
22 (2)-10 .... 10.00
11-18 .... 7.00

Daisy Kutter: The Last Train

Viper, 2004

1 .... 5.00
1/Conv 6.00
2-4 .... 4.00

Dakkon Blackblade

Acclaim

1 .... 6.00

Dakota North

Marvel, 1986

1-5 .... 2.00

Daktari

Dell, 1967

1 .... 35.00
2-4 .... 30.00

Dale Evans Comics

DC, 1948

1 .... 825.00
2 .... 600.00
3 .... 485.00
4-5 .... 285.00
6-10 .... 250.00
11-20 .... 135.00
21-24 .... 100.00

Dale Kuper's Sketchbook

Green Bay

1 .... 2.00

Dalgoda

Fantagraphics, 1984

1-8 .... 2.00

Dalkiel: The Prophecy

Verotik, 1998

1 .... 4.00

Dalton Boys

Avon, 1951

1 .... 80.00

Dam

Dam

1 .... 3.00

Damage

DC, 1994

0-20 .... 2.00

Damage Control (Vol. 1)

Marvel, 1989

1 .... 2.00
2-4 .... 1.00

Damage Control (Vol. 2)

Marvel, 1989

1 .... 2.00
2-4 .... 1.00

Damage Control (Vol. 3)

Marvel, 1991

1 .... 2.00
2-4 .... 1.00

Dame Patrol

Spoof

1 .... 3.00

Damlog

Pyramid

1 .... 2.00

Damnation

Fantagraphics, 1994

1 .... 3.00

Damned

Image, 1997

1-4 .... 3.00

Damn Nation

Dark Horse, 2005

1-3 .... 3.00

Daemonstorm

Daffy Qaddafi

Daimons

Daisy and Donald

Dale Evans Comics

Damage

Damned

Damonstreik

Damonstreik
Imperial

1-2 .... 2.00

Dampyr
Idea & Design Works, 2005

1-8 .... 8.00

Damselvis, Daughter of Helvis Supermag
Fantagraphics

1 .... 4.00

Dance of Death
Tome

1 .... 3.00

Dance of Lifey Death
Dark Horse, 1994

1 .... 4.00

Dance Party DOA
Slave Labor, 1993

1 .... 4.00

Dances with Demons
Marvel, 1993

1 .... 3.00
2-4 .... 2.00

Dandy Comics
E.C., 1947

1 .... 225.00
2 .... 200.00
3-7 .... 130.00

Danger
Charlton, 1954

1 .... 70.00
2-5 .... 40.00
6-10 .... 30.00
11-14 .... 24.00

Danger
Super, 1964

12-16 .... 14.00

Danger Comics
Danger Comics, 2004

1-2 .... 2.00

Danger Funnies
Cry for Dawn

1 .... 3.00

Danger Girl
Image, 1988

1 .... 5.00
1/Chromium 8.00
1/Mag sized 20.00
1/Tour ed 8.00
1/Go-go cover 31.00
2 .... 3.00
2/Chrome 8.00
2/Gold 6.00
3 .... 3.00
3/A 5.00
3/B-4 .... 3.00
4/A 7.00
5 .... 3.00
6 .... 3.00
6/Gold 5.00
7 .... 6.00
Ashcan 1 .... 5.00
Ashcan 1/Gold 6.00
SP 1 .... 4.00
Deluxe 1 .... 20.00

Danger Girl 3-D
DC, 2003

1 .... 5.00

Danger Girl: Back in Black
DC, 2006

1-4 .... 3.00

Danger Girl: Hawaiian Punch
DC, 2003

1 .... 5.00

Danger Girl Kamikaze
DC, 2001

1-2 .... 3.00

Danger Girls
Animagic

1 .... 3.00

Danger Girl Sketchbook
DC

1 .... 7.00

Danger Girl: Viva Las Danger
DC, 2004

1 .... 5.00

Danger is our Business
Toby, 1953

1 .... 165.00
2 .... 100.00
3-5 .... 75.00
6-10 .... 65.00

Dangerman
Patchwork

1 .... 3.00

Dangerous Times
Evolution

1-6/2nd 2.00

Danger Ranger
Checker, 1998

1-2 .... 2.00

Danger Trail
DC, 1950

1 .... 875.00
2 .... 600.00
3 .... 1,250.00
☛Scarce
4-5 .... 385.00

Danger Trail

DC, 1993

1-4 .... 2.00

Danger Unlimited

Dark Horse, 1994

1-4 .... 3.00

Dangle

Cat-Head

1 .... 3.00

Daniel Boone

Gold Key, 1965

1 .... 45.00
2 .... 28.00
3-5 .... 24.00
6-15 .... 18.00

Dan'l Boone

Magazine Enterprises, 1955

1 .... 70.00
2-8 .... 45.00

Danny Blaze

Charlton, 1955

1 .... 35.00
2 .... 18.00

Dan Panic Funnies

Panic

1 .... 2.00

Danse

Blackthorne, 1987

1 .... 2.00

Dante's Inferno

Tome

1-2 .... 4.00

Dan Turner: Ace in the Hole

Eternity

1 .... 3.00

Dan Turner: Dark Star of Death

Eternity

1 .... 3.00

Dan Turner: Homicide Hunch

Eternity, 1991

1 .... 3.00

Dan Turner: Star Chamber

Eternity, 1991

1 .... 3.00

Dapiek Absaroka: The Killer of Crows

Tome

1 .... 3.00

Darby O'Gill and the Little People

Gold Key, 1970

1 .... 20.00

D'arc Tangent

Ffantasy Ffactory, 1982

1 .... 2.00

Dare

Monster, 1991

1-4 .... 3.00

Daredevil

Lev Gleason, 1941

1 .... 11,000.00
2 .... 2,600.00
3 .... 1,500.00
4 .... 1,200.00
5 .... 975.00
6 .... 825.00
7 .... 725.00
8-10 .... 700.00
11 .... 800.00
12 .... 1,050.00
13 .... 925.00
14 .... 475.00
15 .... 575.00
16-17 .... 425.00
18 .... 950.00
19-20 .... 350.00
21 .... 600.00
22-30 .... 275.00
31 .... 650.00
32-37 .... 200.00
38 .... 350.00
39-41 .... 200.00
42 .... 175.00
43-50 .... 150.00
51-60 .... 115.00
61-69 .... 90.00
70-78 .... 60.00
79-80 .... 70.00
81-99 .... 55.00
100 .... 60.00
101-120 .... 45.00
121-134 .... 36.00

Daredevil

Marvel, 1964

-1 .... 2.00
1 .... 3,000.00
☛1st Daredevil
2 .... 750.00
3 .... 550.00
4 .... 400.00
5 .... 300.00
6 .... 225.00
7 .... 675.00
☛1st red costume
8-10 .... 135.00
11-15 .... 85.00
☛Spider-Man app.
16-17 .... 120.00
☛Spider-Man app.
18 .... 70.00
☛1st Gladiator
19 .... 60.00
20 .... 55.00

Danger Girl

Danger Trail

Daniel Boone

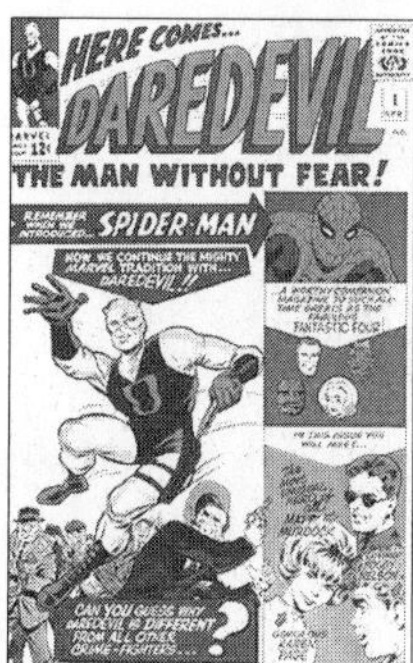

Daredevil

Dare the Impossible

Daring Escapes

Daring Love

Daring Love Stories

21-27 .... 50.00
28-30 .... 45.00
31-42 .... 40.00
43 .... 45.00
44-49 .... 30.00
50-52 .... 33.00
53-71 .... 20.00
72-80 .... 17.00
81 .... 25.00
☛Giant-size
82-83 .... 17.00
84-99 .... 14.00
100 .... 30.00
☛Origin recap
101-130 .... 8.00
131 .... 75.00
☛1st Bullseye
132 .... 15.00
132/30¢ 20.00
133 .... 6.00
133/30¢ 20.00
134 .... 6.00
134/30¢ 20.00
135 .... 6.00
135/30¢ 20.00
136 .... 6.00
136/30¢ 20.00
137-146/Whitman 6.00
146/35¢ 15.00
147 .... 6.00
147/35¢ 15.00
148 .... 6.00
148/35¢ 15.00
149-157 .... 6.00
158 .... 50.00
☛Frank Miller starts
159 .... 22.00
160-161 .... 17.00
162 .... 9.00
163 .... 18.00
164-167 .... 11.00
168 .... 75.00
☛1st Elektra
169 .... 16.00
170 .... 10.00
171 .... 12.00
172-177 .... 7.00
178-180 .... 6.00
181 .... 15.00
☛Elektra dies
182-183 .... 7.00
184 .... 6.00
185 .... 5.00
186 .... 6.00
187-190 .... 5.00
191 .... 6.00
192-195 .... 3.00
196 .... 6.00
197-204 .... 3.00
205 .... 4.00
206-226 .... 3.00
227 .... 4.00
☛Born Again
228-247 .... 3.00
248-249 .... 4.00
250 .... 3.00
251 .... 5.00
252 .... 4.00
253 .... 3.00
254 .... 6.00
☛1st Typhoid Mary
255-257 .... 3.00
258 .... 4.00
259-295 .... 3.00
296-299 .... 2.00
300 .... 3.00
301-303 .... 2.00
304 .... 3.00
305-311 .... 2.00
312 .... 3.00
313-318 .... 2.00
319 .... 5.00
319/2nd-321 .... 2.00
321/Variant 3.00
322-324 .... 2.00
325 .... 3.00
326-349 .... 2.00
350 .... 3.00
350/Variant 4.00
351-374 .... 2.00
375 .... 3.00
376-379 .... 2.00
380 .... 3.00
Ann 1 .... 50.00
Ann 2-3 .... 9.00
Ann 4 .... 8.00
Ann 5 .... 4.00
Ann 6-10 .... 3.00
Ann 1997 .... 4.00

Daredevil

Marvel, 1998

½ 5.00
1 .... 7.00
1/Ltd. 50.00
1/Variant 9.00
2/A-2/B 5.00
3-5 .... 4.00
5/A 5.00
6 .... 3.00
7 .... 4.00
8-15 .... 3.00
16 .... 5.00
16/Unlimited 6.00
17 .... 3.00
17/Unlimited 5.00
☛Newsstand variant
18-20 .... 3.00
20/Unlimited 5.00
21 .... 3.00
21/Unlimited 5.00
22 .... 3.00
22/Unlimited 5.00
23 .... 3.00
23/Unlimited 5.00

24-36 .... 3.00
36/No # 5.00
☛Newsstand; no #
37 .... 3.00
37/Unlimited 5.00
☛Newsstand variant
37/No # 4.00
☛Newsstand; no #
38-56 .... 3.00
57 .... 4.00
58-64 .... 3.00
65 .... 4.00
66-89 .... 3.00
89/Sketch 6.00
90-116 .... 3.00

Daredevil/Batman
Marvel, 1997
1 .... 6.00

Daredevil/Black Widow: Abattoir
Marvel
1 .... 15.00

Daredevil Chronicles
Fantaco, 1982
1 .... 2.00

Daredevil: Father
Marvel, 2004
1 .... 5.00
1/DirCut 4.00
2-5 .... 3.00

Daredevil: Ninja
Marvel, 2000
1-3 .... 3.00

Daredevil/Punisher: Child's Play
Marvel
nn 5.00

Daredevil: Redemption
Marvel, 2005

Daredevil/Shi
Marvel, 1997
1 .... 3.00

Daredevil/Spider-Man
Marvel, 2000
1-4 .... 3.00

Daredevil The Man without Fear
Marvel, 1993
1-3 .... 4.00
4-5 .... 3.00

Daredevil: The Target
Marvel, 2003
1 .... 4.00

Daredevil vs. Vapora
Marvel, 1996
nn 1.00

Daredevil vs. Punisher
Marvel, 2005
1-6 .... 3.00

Daredevil: Yellow
Marvel, 2001
1-6 .... 4.00

Darerat/Tadpole
Mighty Pumpkin, 1987
1 .... 2.00

Dare the Impossible
Fleetway-Quality, 1990
1-15 .... 2.00

Daria Jontak
JMJ, 2001
1 .... 5.00

Daring Adventures
St. John
1 .... 200.00

Daring Adventures
I.W., 1963
9-11 .... 20.00
12 .... 40.00
13-18 .... 20.00

Daring Adventures
B Comics, 1993
1-3 .... 2.00

Daring Comics
Marvel, 1944
9 .... 1,100.00
10 .... 950.00
11-12 .... 875.00

Daring Confessions
Youthful, 1952
4 .... 120.00
5-8 .... 100.00

Daring Escapes
Image, 1998
1-4 .... 3.00

Daring Hero
King-Ganteaume
1 .... 16.00
2-3 .... 10.00

Daring Love
Gilmore, 1953
1 .... 800.00

Daring Love Stories
Fox, 1950
1 .... 250.00

Daring Mystery Comics
Timely, 1940
1 .... 14,500.00
2 .... 3,500.00
3 .... 2,550.00
4 .... 2,200.00
5-9 .... 2,000.00
10 .... 7,000.00

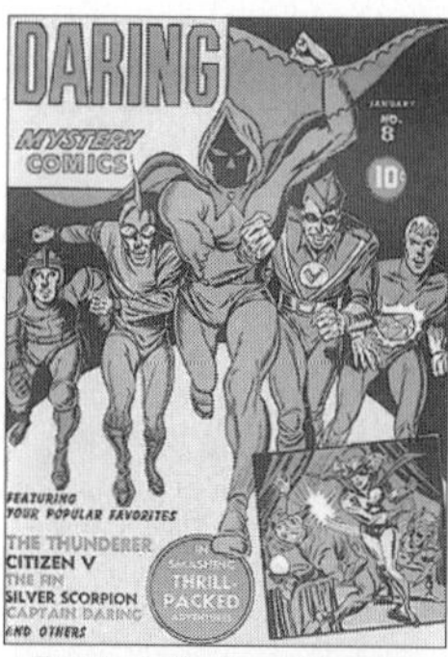

Daring Mystery Comics

Dark Ages

Dark Assassin

Dark Claw Adventures

Dark Comics

Dark Crossings

Darkdevil

Darker Image

11 ....4,500.00
12 ....2,400.00

Daring New Adventures of Supergirl
DC, 1982
1 ....3.00
2-13 ....2.00

Dark
Continuüm, 1993
1-7/2nd 2.00

Dark
Continuüm, 1995
1 ....2.00
1/A 3.00
2 ....2.00
3-4 ....3.00

Dark
August House, 1995
1-2 ....3.00

Dark Adventures
Darkline
1 ....1.00
2-3 ....2.00
4 ....1.00

Dark Ages
Alternate Concepts
1 ....4.00

Dark Angel
Boneyard, 1991
1-3 ....2.00

Dark Angel
Marvel, 1992
6-17 ....2.00

Dark Angel
Boneyard, 1997
1 ....5.00
2-3 ....2.00

Dark Angel
CPM Manga, 1999
1-29 ....3.00

Dark Angel: Death Dreams
Boneyard
1 ....3.00

Dark Angel: Phoenix Resurrection
Image, 2000
1-4 ....3.00

Dark Assassin
Silverwolf, 1987
1 ....2.00

Dark Assassin
Greater Mercury, 1989
1-9 ....2.00

Darkchylde
Maximum, 1996
1-3 ....3.00

Darkchylde Battlebook
WildStorm
1/A-1/B 4.00

Darkchylde
Image, 1996
0/A-½/Variant 3.00
1-1/AmEnt 5.00
1/B 3.00
1/Conv-3 ....5.00
3/A-5/C 3.00
Ashcan 1 ....2.00
Ashcan 1/Gold 3.00
Ashcan 1/Ltd. 5.00

Darkchylde/Painkiller Jane
WildStorm
Ashcan 1 ....3.00

Darkchylde Remastered
Image, 1997
0-3 ....3.00

Darkchylde Sketchbook
Image, 1998
1 ....3.00

Darkchylde Summer Swimsuit Spectacular
DC, 1999
1 ....4.00

Darkchylde Swimsuit Illustrated
Image, 1998
1 ....4.00
1/Gold 5.00

Darkchylde the Diary
Image, 1997
1/A-1/D 3.00

Darkchylde: The Legacy
Image, 1998
1 ....3.00
1/A-1/Variant 4.00
2-3 ....3.00

Dark City Chronicles
Culture
1 ....4.00

Dark Claw Adventures
DC, 1997
1 ....2.00

Dark Comics
Imperial
1 ....2.00

Dark Convention Book
Continuüm, 1993
2 ....0.00
1 ....2.00

Dark Crossings: Dark Cloud Rising

Image, 2003

1 .... 6.00

Dark Crossings

Image, 2000

1-2 .... 6.00

Dark Crossings: Dark Clouds Overhead

Image, 2000

1 .... 6.00

Dark Crystal

Marvel, 1983

1-2 .... 1.00

Dark Destiny

Alpha, 1994

1 .... 4.00

Darkdevil

Marvel, 2000

1-3 .... 3.00

Dark Dominion

Defiant, 1993

1-13 .... 3.00

Darker Image

Image, 1993

1 .... 3.00
1/Gold-1/Ltd. 4.00

Darker Side of Sex

Fantagraphics

1-3 .... 3.00

Darkewood

Aircel

1-5 .... 2.00

Dark Fantasies

Dark Fantasy

1-3 .... 3.00

Dark Fantasy

Apple, 1992

1 .... 3.00

Darkforce

Omega 7

1 .... 3.00
2 .... 4.00

Dark Fringe

Brainstorm, 1996

2 .... 3.00

Dark Fringe: Spirits of the Dead

Brainstorm

1-2 .... 3.00

Dark Gauntlet

Tarescent

1-4 .... 2.00

Dark Guard

Marvel, 1993

1 .... 3.00
2-5 .... 2.00

Darkhawk

Marvel, 1991

1-14 .... 2.00
15-24 .... 1.00
25 .... 3.00
26-38 .... 1.00
39-49 .... 2.00
50-Ann 3 .... 3.00

Darkhold

Marvel, 1992

1/CS 3.00
2-16 .... 2.00

Dark Horse Classics

Dark Horse

1-2 .... 4.00

Dark Horse Classics: Aliens Versus Predator

Dark Horse, 1997

1-6 .... 3.00

Dark Horse Classics: Godzilla

Dark Horse, 1998

1 .... 3.00

Dark Horse Classics: Godzilla: King of the Monsters

Dark Horse, 1998

1-6 .... 3.00

Dark Horse Classics: Star Wars: Dark Empire

Dark Horse, 1997

1-6 .... 3.00

Dark Horse Classics: Terror of Godzilla

Dark Horse, 1998

1-6 .... 3.00

Dark Horse Comics

Dark Horse, 1992

1 .... 4.00
2-6 .... 3.00
7-8 .... 5.00
9 .... 4.00
10-25 .... 3.00

Dark Horse Down Under

Dark Horse, 1994

1-3 .... 3.00

Dark Horse Futures

Dark Horse

1 .... 1.00

Dark Fantasies

Darkhawk

Dark Horse Classics

Dark Horse Comics

Dark Horse Down Under

Dark Horse Monsters

Dark Horse Presents

Darklon the Mystic

Dark Horse Maverick: Happy Endings
Dark Horse, 2002

1 .... 10.00

Dark Horse Maverick 2000
Dark Horse, 2000

0 .... 4.00

Dark Horse Maverick 2001
Dark Horse, 2001

1 .... 5.00

Dark Horse Monsters
Dark Horse, 1997

1 .... 3.00

Dark Horse Presents
Dark Horse, 1986

1 .... 4.00
1/2nd Green-1/2nd Silver 2.00
2-4 .... 3.00
5-9 .... 2.00
10-16 .... 3.00
17 .... 2.00
18 .... 3.00
19-23 .... 2.00
24 .... 6.00
☛1st comics Aliens
25-27 .... 2.00
28 .... 3.00
29-31 .... 2.00
32 .... 4.00
☛Concrete app.
33-35 .... 3.00
36 .... 4.00
36/A 3.00
37-39 .... 2.00
40 .... 3.00
41-49 .... 2.00
50 .... 3.00
51 .... 4.00
☛2nd Sin City
52-53 .... 3.00
54 .... 4.00
55 .... 2.00
56-57 .... 4.00
58 .... 2.00
59-61 .... 3.00
62 .... 4.00
☛All Sin City
63-66 .... 3.00
67 .... 4.00
68-134 .... 3.00
135 .... 4.00
136-149 .... 3.00
150 .... 5.00
151-157 .... 3.00
Ann 1997-2000 .... 5.00

Dark Horse Presents: Aliens
Dark Horse, 1992

1-1/A 5.00

Dark Horse Twenty Years
Dark Horse, 2006

1 .... 1.00

Dark Island
Davdez, 1998

1-3 .... 3.00

Dark Knight Strikes Again
DC, 2001

1 .... 3.00
1/A 5.00
2 .... 3.00
2/A 4.00
3 .... 3.00
3/A 4.00

Darklight: Prelude
Sirius, 1994

1-3 .... 3.00

Darklon the Mystic
Pacific, 1983

1 .... 2.00

Darkman
Marvel, 1990

1-3 .... 2.00

Darkman
Marvel, 1993

1 .... 4.00
2-6 .... 3.00

Darkman (Magazine)
Marvel, 1990

1 .... 2.00

Dark Mansion of Forbidden Love
DC, 1971

1 .... 125.00
2-4 .... 50.00

Darkminds
Image, 1998

½ 3.00
1-1/Variant 4.00
1/2nd-8 .... 3.00

Darkminds
Image, 2000

0-10 .... 3.00

Darkminds: Macropolis
Image, 2002

1/A-2/B 3.00

Darkminds: Macropolis
Dreamwave, 2003

1-4 .... 3.00

Darkminds/Witchblade
Image, 2000

1 .... 6.00

Dark Mists
APComics, 2005
1-2 .... 4.00

Dark Moon Prophesy
Dark Moon Productions, 1995
1 .... 1.00

Dark Mysteries
Master, 1951
1 .... 525.00
2 .... 340.00
3 .... 210.00
4-5 .... 170.00
6-10 .... 140.00
11-20 .... 125.00
21-24 .... 100.00

Dark Nemesis (Villains)
DC, 1998
1 .... 2.00

Darkness
Top Cow, 1996
0-1/Gold 3.00
1/Platinum 8.00
2-10/B 3.00
11/A 8.00
11/B-24 .... 3.00
25 .... 4.00
25/A 20.00
26-28 .... 3.00
28/Graham 5.00
29-Ashcan 1/A 3.00
Deluxe 1 .... 15.00

Darkness
Image, 2002
1 .... 4.00
1/A-24 .... 3.00

Darkness & Tomb Raider
Top Cow, 2005
1 .... 3.00

Darkness/Batman
Image, 1999
1 .... 6.00

Darkness: Black Sails
Image, 2005
0 .... 3.00

Darkness Collected Edition
Image, 2003
1 .... 5.00

Darkness Falls: The Tragic Life of Matilda Dixon
Dark Horse, 2002
1 .... 3.00

Darkness/Hulk
Image, 2004
1 .... 5.00

Darkness Infinity
Image, 1999
1 .... 4.00

Darkness: Level 1
Image, 2007
1-1/2nd variant 3.00

Darkness: Level 0
Image, 2007
1 .... 3.00

Darkness/Painkiller Jane
Image
Ashcan 1-Ashcan 1/A 3.00

Darkness Prelude
Image, 2003
0 .... 4.00
0/A 4.00

Darkness: Spear of Destiny
Image, 2000
1 .... 13.00

Darkness/Superman
Image, 2005
1-2 .... 3.00

Darkness: Wanted Dead One Shot
Image, 2003
1 .... 3.00

Darkness/Witchblade Special
Image, 1999
1 .... 4.00

Darkness/Wolverine
Image, 2006
1 .... 3.00

Dark Oz
Arrow, 1997
1-5 .... 3.00

Dark Peril
Quantum
1-4 .... 3.00

Dark Rat
Maverick Pulp Comix, 1997
1 .... 3.00

Dark Realm
Image, 2000
1-4 .... 3.00

Dark Regions
White Wolf, 1987
1-3 .... 2.00

Darkseed and Other Defamations
Boneyard
1 .... 4.00

Darkminds

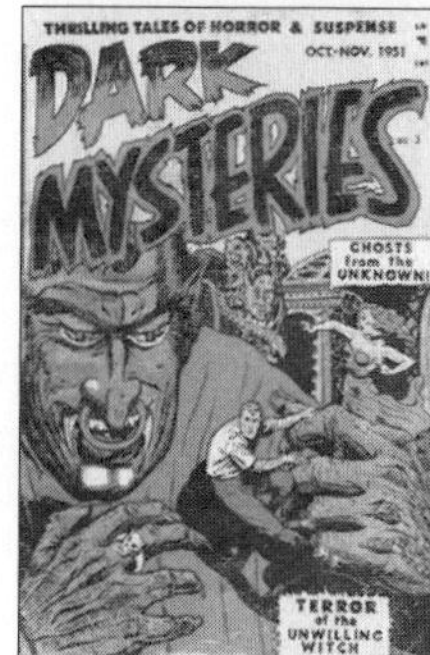

Dark Mysteries

Darkness Infinity

Dark Peril

Dark Realm

Darkside

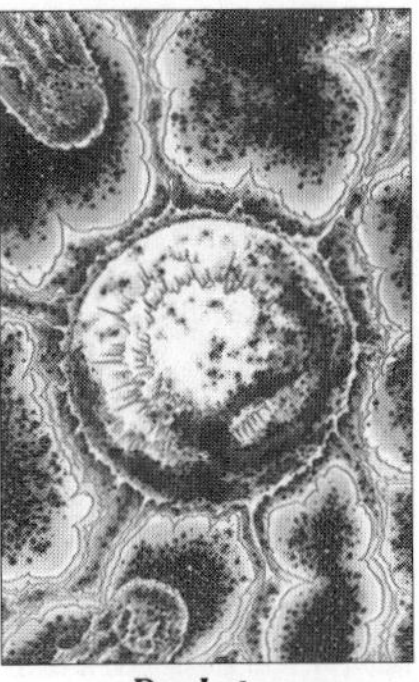
Darkstar

Dark Visions

Darkseid vs. Galactus: The Hunger
DC, 1995
1 ....5.00

Darkseid (Villains)
DC, 1998
1 ....2.00

Dark Shadows
Steinway, 1957
1 ....70.00
2 ....40.00
3 ....36.00

Dark Shadows
Gold Key, 1969
1 ....175.00
1/A 25.00
2-3 ....48.00
4-7 ....25.00
8-16 ....20.00
17-20 ....12.00
21-35 ....10.00

Dark Shadows
Innovation, 1992
1-9 ....3.00

Dark Shrine
Antarctic, 1999
1-2 ....3.00

Dark Shrine Gallery
Basement
1 ....3.00

Darkside
Maximum, 1996
1 ....3.00

Darkside Blues
ADV Manga, 2004
1 ....15.00

Darkstalkers
Devil's Due, 2004
1 ....3.00
1/Variant 4.00
2 ....3.00
2/Variant 4.00
3 ....3.00
3/Variant 4.00
4 ....3.00
4/Variant 4.00
4/Foil 3.00
5 ....4.00
5/Variant 3.00
5/Foil 4.00

Darkstar
Rebel, 1991
1-4 ....2.00

Darkstars
DC, 1992
0-38 ....2.00

Dark Tales of Daily Horror
Antarctic, 1994
1 ....3.00

Dark Tower: The Gunslinger Born
Marvel, 2007
1 ....5.00
2-3 ....4.00

Dark Visions
Pyramid, 1986
1-2 ....2.00

Darkwing Duck Limited Series (Disney's...)
Disney, 1991
1-4 ....2.00

Dark Wolf
Eternity, 1988
1-Ann 1 ....2.00

Dark Wolf
Malibu, 1987
1-4 ....2.00

Dark World
Millennium
1 ....3.00

Darling Love
Close-Up, 1949
1 ....100.00
2-5 ....80.00

Darling Romance
Close-Up, 1949
1 ....350.00
2-7 ....100.00

Darque Passages
Valiant, 1994
1 ....2.00

Darque Passages
Acclaim, 1998
1-4 ....3.00

Darque Razor
London Night, 1997
1 ....3.00

Dart
Image, 1996
1-3 ....3.00

Dartman
Northeastern
1 ....2.00

Data 6
Artist's Unlimited
1 ....2.00

Date with Debbi
DC, 1969
1 ....16.00
2 ....12.00
3-12 ....10.00

13-17 .... 12.00
18 .... 10.00

Date With Judy
DC, 1947

1 .... 120.00
2 .... 95.00
3-5 .... 48.00
6-10 .... 34.00
11-20 .... 22.00
21-40 .... 18.00
41-60 .... 15.00
61-79 .... 10.00

Date with Millie
Atlas, 1956

1 .... 100.00
2 .... 75.00
3-7 .... 60.00

Date with Millie
Atlas, 1959

1 .... 75.00
2 .... 50.00
3-7 .... 45.00

Date with Patsy
Atlas, 1957

1 .... 60.00

Daughters of the Dragon
Marvel, 2006

1-6 .... 3.00

Daughters of the Dragon: Deadly Hands
Marvel, 2006

1 .... 4.00

Daughters of Time 3-D
3-D Zone

1 .... 4.00

David & Goliath
Image, 2003

1-3 .... 3.00

David Cassidy
Charlton, 1972

1 .... 25.00
2-5 .... 16.00
6-9 .... 14.00
10-14 .... 12.00

David Chelsea in Love
Eclipse

1-4 .... 4.00

David Shepherd's Song
Alias, 2005

1-2 .... 3.00

David's Mighty Men
Alias, 2005

1 .... 5.00

Davy Crockett
Gold Key, 1963

1 .... 115.00
2 .... 30.00

Dawn
Sirius Entertainment, 1995

½ 3.00
½/Variant 5.00
1 .... 3.00
1/Black 8.00
1/Sharp 6.00
1/Kids 5.00
2 .... 3.00
2/Mystery 6.00
3-6 .... 3.00

Dawn 15th anniversary Poster Book
Image, 2004

1 .... 5.00

Dawn 2004 Con Sketchbook One-Shot
Image, 2004

1 .... 3.00

Dawn: Convention Sketchbook
Image, 2002

1 .... 3.00

Dawn Convention Sketch Book
Image, 2003

1 .... 3.00

Dawn Hunter
AC

0 .... 3.00

Dawn of the Age of Apocalypse
Marvel

1 .... 9.00

Dawn of the Dead (George Romero's)
Idea & Design Works, 2004

1-3 .... 4.00

Dawn Tenth Anniversary Special
Sirius Entertainment, 1999

1 .... 3.00

Dawn: The Return of the Goddess
Sirius Entertainment, 1999

1 .... 3.00
1/Ltd. 8.00
2-4 .... 3.00

Dawn: Three Tiers
Image, 2003

1-6 .... 3.00

Day Brothers Present
Caliber

1-4 .... 3.00

Dark Wolf

Dark World

Date with Debbi

David Cassidy

Davy Crockett

Day Brothers Present

Dazzler

DC Challenge

Daydreamers
Marvel, 1997

1-3 .... 3.00

Day of Judgment
DC, 1999

1-5 .... 3.00

Day of Judgment Secret Files
DC, 1999

1 .... 5.00

Day of the Defenders
Marvel, 2001

1 .... 4.00

Day of Vengeance
DC, 2005

1 .... 10.00
1/Variant 5.00
☛2nd printing
1/3rd variant 6.00
2 .... 5.00
2/2nd variant 4.00
3-6 .... 3.00

Day of Vengeance: Infinite Crisis Special
DC, 206

1 .... 4.00

Days of Darkness
Apple, 1992

1-5 .... 3.00

Days of Wrath
Apple, 1993

1-4 .... 3.00

Daytona 500 Story
Vortex

1 .... 2.00

Dazzle
Tokyopop, 2006

1 .... 10.00

Dazzler
Marvel, 1981

1 .... 5.00
2 .... 2.00
3-42 .... 1.00

DC 100-Page Super Spectacular: World's Greatest Super-Heroes
DC, 2004

1 .... 7.00

DC Challenge
DC, 1985

1-12 .... 2.00

DC Comics Presents
DC, 1978

1 .... 9.00
1/Whitman 14.00
2 .... 7.00
2/Whitman 12.00
3 .... 4.00
3/Whitman 8.00
4 .... 2.00
4/Whitman 4.00
5 .... 2.00
6 .... 6.00
7-9 .... 2.00
9/Whitman 6.00
10 .... 2.00
10/Whitman 4.00
11 .... 2.00
11/Whitman 4.00
12 .... 2.00
12/Whitman 4.00
13-14 .... 2.00
14/Whitman 3.00
15 .... 2.00
15/Whitman 3.00
16 .... 2.00
16/Whitman 3.00
17-19 .... 2.00
19/Whitman 3.00
20 .... 2.00
20/Whitman 3.00
21 .... 2.00
21/Whitman 3.00
22 .... 2.00
22/Whitman 3.00
23-25 .... 2.00
26 .... 14.00
☛1st New Teen Titans
27 .... 3.00
28-41 .... 2.00
42-43 .... 1.00
44 .... 2.00
45-46 .... 1.00
47 .... 17.00
☛1st Masters Universe
48-50 .... 1.00
51 .... 6.00
52 .... 3.00
53-71 .... 1.00
72 .... 2.00
73-76 .... 1.00
77-78 .... 3.00
79-84 .... 1.00
85 .... 6.00
☛Moore Swamp Thing
86 .... 4.00
87-92 .... 1.00
93 .... 2.00
94-97 .... 1.00
Ann 1-4 .... 3.00

DC Comics Presents: Batman
DC, 2004

1 .... 3.00

DC Comics Presents: Green Lantern
DC, 2004
1 .... 3.00

DC Comics Presents: Hawkman
DC, 2004
1 .... 3.00

DC Comics Presents: JLA
DC, 2004
1 .... 3.00

DC Comics Presents: Mystery in Space
DC, 2004
1 .... 3.00

DC Comics Presents: Superman
DC, 2004
1 .... 3.00

DC Comics Presents: The Atom
DC, 2004
1 .... 3.00

DC Comics Presents: The Flash
DC, 2004
1 .... 3.00

DC Countdown
DC, 2005
1 .... 6.00
1/2nd 3.00

DC First: Batgirl/Joker
DC, 2002
1 .... 4.00

DC First: Flash/Superman
DC, 2002
1 .... 4.00

DC First: Green Lantern/ Green Lantern
DC, 2002
1 .... 4.00

DC First: Superman/Lobo
DC, 2002
1 .... 4.00

DC Graphic Novel
DC, 1985
1-5 .... 6.00
6 .... 7.00
7 .... 6.00

DC/Marvel: All Access
DC, 1996
1-4 .... 3.00

DC 100 Page Super Spectacular
DC, 1971
4 .... 175.00
5 .... 350.00
☛Scarce
5/2nd 7.00
6 .... 150.00
7 .... 60.00
8-9 .... 75.00
10-13 .... 60.00
14-17 .... 45.00
18 .... 30.00
19 .... 24.00
20 .... 35.00
21-22 .... 22.00

DC One Million
DC, 1998
1 .... 3.00
1/Variant 15.00
2-4 .... 2.00
GS 1 .... 5.00

DC Sampler
DC, 1983
1 .... 2.00
2-3 .... 1.00

DC Science Fiction Graphic Novel
DC
1-7 .... 6.00

DC Silver Age Classics Action Comics
DC
252 .... 1.00

DC Silver Age Classics Adventure Comics
DC
247 .... 1.00

DC Silver Age Classics Detective Comics
DC
225-327 .... 1.00

DC Silver Age Classics Green Lantern
DC
76 .... 1.00

DC Silver Age Classics House of Secrets
DC
92 .... 1.00

DC Silver Age Classics Showcase
DC
4-22 .... 1.00

DC Comics Presents

DC One Million

DC Sampler

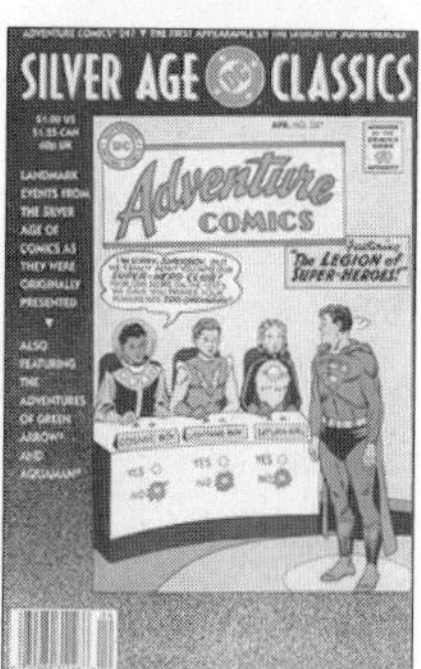

DC Silver Age Classics Adventure Comics

DC Special

DC Super-Stars

DCU Heroes Secret Files

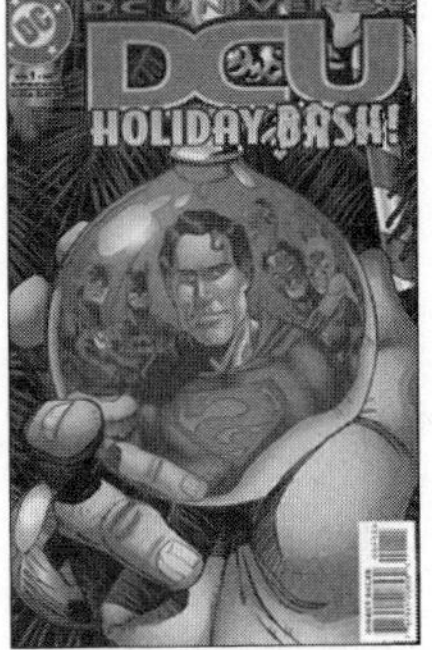

DC Universe Holiday Bash

DC Silver Age Classics Sugar & Spike

DC

99 ....2.00

DC Silver Age Classics The Brave and the Bold

DC

28 ....1.00

DC Sneak Preview

DC

1 ....1.00

DC Special

DC, 1968

1 ....60.00
2 ....50.00
3 ....35.00
4 ....25.00
5-14 ....20.00
15 ....16.00
16-28 ....10.00
29 ....12.00

DC Special Blue Ribbon Digest

DC, 1980

1 ....5.00
2-5 ....4.00
6-17 ....3.00
18 ....4.00
19 ....3.00
20 ....7.00
21-23 ....3.00

DC Special Series

DC, 1977

1 ....10.00
2-5 ....7.00
6-8 ....6.00
9 ....16.00
10-14 ....6.00
15 ....8.00
16 ....20.00
☛Jonah Hex dies
17-18 ....5.00
19-20 ....6.00
21 ....12.00
☛1st Miller Batman
22-26 ....6.00
27 ....18.00

DC Special: The Return of Donna Troy

DC, 2005

1 ....8.00
☛Inf. Crisis tie
2 ....5.00
3-4 ....3.00

DC Spotlight

DC, 1985

1 ....1.00

DC Super-Stars

DC, 1976

1 ....10.00
2-3 ....5.00
4 ....2.00
5 ....10.00
6-7 ....2.00
8 ....4.00
9 ....2.00
10 ....5.00
11 ....7.00
12-13 ....2.00
14-15 ....4.00
16 ....3.00
17 ....16.00
☛1st new Huntress
18 ....2.00

DC: The New Frontier

DC, 2004

1-6 ....7.00

DC 2000

DC, 2000

1-2 ....7.00

DCU: Brave New World

DC, 2006

1 ....1.00

DCU Heroes Secret Files

DC, 1999

1 ....5.00

DCU Infinite Christmas Special

DC, 2007

1 ....5.00

DC Universe Christmas, A

DC, 2000

1 ....20.00

DC Universe Holiday Bash

DC, 1997

1 ....4.00
2-3 ....5.00

DC Universe: Trinity

DC, 1993

1-2 ....3.00

DCU Villains Secret Files

DC, 1999

1 ....5.00

D-Day

Avalon

1 ....3.00

DDP Quarterly

Devil's Due, 2006

1 ....1.00

Dead

Arrow, 1993

1-3 ....3.00

Dead

Arrow

1 .... 3.00

Dead Air

Slave Labor

1 .... 6.00

Dead@17

Viper, 2003

0 .... 27.00
1 .... 35.00
2 .... 22.00
3 .... 10.00
4 .... 7.00

Dead@17: Blood of Saints

Viper, 2004

1-4 .... 3.00

Dead@17: Protectorate

Viper, 2005

1-3 .... 3.00

Dead@17: Revolution

Viper, 2004

1 .... 4.00
2-4 .... 3.00

Dead@17: Rough Cut

Viper, 2004

1-3 .... 3.00

Deadbeats

Claypool, 1992

1 .... 4.00
2-82 .... 3.00

Deadbolt

Hall of Heroes, 1993

1 .... 3.00

Dead Boys

London Night, 1996

1 .... 4.00

Dead Clown

Malibu, 1993

1-3 .... 3.00

Dead Corps(E)

DC, 1998

1-4 .... 3.00

Dead End Crime Stories

Kirby Publications, 1949

1 .... 180.00

Deadenders

DC, 2000

1-16 .... 3.00

Dead Eyes Open

Slave Labor, 2005

1-2 .... 3.00

Dead-Eye Western Comics

Hillman, 1948

1 .... 85.00
2 .... 60.00
3-4 .... 40.00
5-12 .... 30.00

Dead-Eye Western Comics (Vol. 2)

Hillman, 1951

1 .... 85.00
2 .... 60.00
3-4 .... 40.00
5-12 .... 30.00

Dead-Eye Western Comics (Vol. 3)

Hillman, 1953

1 .... 30.00

Deadface

Harrier, 1987

1 .... 5.00
2 .... 4.00
3-8 .... 3.00

Deadface: Doing the Islands with Bacchus

Dark Horse, 1991

1-3 .... 3.00

Deadface: Earth, Water, Air, and Fire

Dark Horse, 1992

1-4 .... 3.00

Deadfish Bedeviled

All American, 1990

1 .... 2.00

Dead Folks (Lansdales & Truman's)

Avatar, 2003

1-3 .... 4.00

Deadforce

Studio Noir, 1996

1 .... 3.00

Deadforce

Antarctic, 1999

1-2 .... 3.00
Ashcan 1 .... 1.00

Dead Grrrl: Dead at 21

Boneyard, 1998

1 .... 3.00

Dead Heat

All American

1 .... 2.00

Dead in the West

Dark Horse, 1993

1-2 .... 4.00

Dead Kid Adventures

Knight, 1998

1 .... 3.00

Dead Killer

Caliber

1 .... 3.00

Deadbeats

Dead Boys

Dead Clown

Deadenders

All comics prices listed are for NEAR MINT condition.

Dead in the West

Deadline USA

Deadly Foes of Spider-Man

Dead Man Walking

Dead King: Burnt
Chaos, 1989
1-4 .... 3.00

Deadliest Creature on Earth...Man
Nicotat, 1989
1 .... 2.00

Deadliest Heroes of Kung Fu
Marvel
1 .... 5.00

Deadline
Deadline, 1988
1-5 .... 6.00
6-58 .... 5.00

Deadline
Marvel, 2002
1-4 .... 3.00

Deadline USA
Dark Horse, 1991
1-8 .... 4.00

Deadly Duo
Image, 1994
1-3 .... 3.00

Deadly Duo
Image, 1995
1-4 .... 3.00

Deadly Foes of Spider-Man
Marvel, 1991
1-4 .... 2.00

Deadly Hands of Kung Fu
Marvel, 1974
1 .... 30.00
2 .... 8.00
3-5 .... 6.00
6-10 .... 5.00
11-19 .... 4.00
20 .... 7.00
21-30 .... 3.00
31 .... 6.00
32-33 .... 3.00
Special 1 .... 4.00

Deadman
DC, 1985
1-7 .... 3.00

Deadman
DC, 1986
1-4 .... 2.00

Deadman
DC, 2002
1-9 .... 3.00

Deadman
DC, 2006
1-5 .... 3.00

Deadman: Dead Again
DC, 2001
1-5 .... 3.00

Deadman: Exorcism
DC
1-2 .... 5.00

Deadman: Love After Death
DC, 1989
1-2 .... 4.00

Dead Man Walking
Boneyard
1 .... 3.00

Dead Meat
Fleetway-Quality
1-3 .... 3.00

Dead Men Tell No Tales
Arcana, 2005
1-3 .... 4.00

Dead Muse
Fantagraphics
1 .... 4.00

Dead of Night
Marvel, 1973
1 .... 35.00
2 .... 12.00
3-10 .... 8.00
11 .... 16.00

Dead or Alive: A Cyberpunk Western
Dark Horse, 1998
1-4 .... 3.00

Deadpan
Ichor, 1995

Deadpan
Slave Labor, 2006
1 .... 6.00

Deadpool
Marvel, 1994
1-4 .... 3.00

Deadpool
Marvel, 1988
-1-0 .... 2.00
1 .... 4.00
2-4 .... 3.00
5-10 .... 2.00
11 .... 4.00
12-22 .... 2.00
23 .... 3.00
24 .... 2.00
25 .... 3.00
26-69 .... 2.00
Ann 1998 .... 3.00

Deadpool Team-Up
Marvel, 1998
1 .... 3.00

Deadpool: The Circle Chase
Marvel, 1993

1 .... 3.00
2-4 .... 2.00

Deadshot
DC, 1988

1-4 .... 2.00

Deadshot
DC, 2005

1-5 .... 3.00

Deadtime Stories
New Comics, 1987

1 .... 2.00

Deadwalkers
Aircel, 1991

1/A-4 .... 3.00

Dead Who Walk
Realistic Comics, 1952

1 .... 180.00

Deadworld
Arrow, 1986

1 .... 6.00
2-26 .... 3.00

Deadworld
Caliber, 1993

1 .... 4.00
2-15 .... 3.00

Deadworld
Image, 2005

1-6 .... 4.00

Deadworld Archives
Caliber

1-3 .... 3.00

Deadworld: Bits and Pieces
Caliber

1 .... 3.00

Deadworld Chronicles: Plague
Caliber

1 .... 3.00

Deadworld: Daemonstorm
Caliber

1 .... 4.00

Deadworld: Necropolis
Caliber

1 .... 4.00

Deadworld: To Kill a King
Caliber

1 .... 3.00
1/Ltd. 6.00
2-3 .... 3.00

Deal with the Devil
Alias, 2005

1-5 .... 3.00

Dear Beatrice Fairfax
Standard, 1950

5-9 .... 100.00

Dear Julia
Black Eye, 1997

1-4 .... 4.00

Dear Lonely Heart
Artful, 1951

1 .... 70.00
2-5 .... 40.00
6-8 .... 36.00

Dear Lonely Hearts
Comic Media, 1953

1 .... 40.00
2-8 .... 25.00

Dearly Beloved
Ziff-Davis, 1952

1 .... 75.00

DearS
Tokyopop, 2005

1-6 .... 10.00

Death3
Marvel, 1993

1 .... 3.00
2-4 .... 2.00

Death & Candy
Fantagraphics, 1999

1-3 .... 4.00
4 .... 5.00

Death & Taxes: The Real Costs of Living
Parody

1 .... 3.00

Deathangel
Lightning, 1997

1/A-1/D 3.00

Death: At Death's Door
DC, 2003

1 .... 10.00

Deathblow
Image, 1993

0-3 .... 3.00
4-9 .... 2.00
10-15 .... 3.00
16 .... 2.00
16/Variant 4.00
17 .... 3.00
17/A 4.00
18-28 .... 3.00
28/Variant 4.00
29 .... 3.00

Dead of Night

Deadpool Team-Up

Deadshot

Deadtime Stories

Deadwalkers

Dear Lonely Heart

Deathblow

Death Dealer

Deathblow
DC, 2007
1-2/Variant 3.00

Deathblow: Byblows
WildStorm, 1999
1-3 ....3.00

Deathblow/Wolverine
Image, 1996
1-2 ....3.00

Death By Chocolate
Sleeping Giant, 1996
1 ....3.00

Death By Chocolate: Sir Geoffrey and the Chocolate Car
Sleeping Giant
1 ....3.00

Death By Chocolate: The Metabolators
Sleeping Giant
1 ....3.00

Death Crazed Teenage Superheroes
Arf! Arf!
1-2 ....2.00

Death Dealer
Verotik, 1995
1 ....6.00
2-4 ....7.00

Death Dreams of Dracula
Apple
1-4 ....3.00

Death Gallery, A
DC
1 ....3.00

Death Hawk
Adventure, 1988
1-3 ....2.00

Death Hunt
Eternity
1 ....2.00

Death Jr.
Image, 2005
1-3 ....5.00

Death Jr.
Image, 2006
1-2 ....5.00

Deathlok
Marvel, 1990
1-4 ....4.00

Deathlok
Marvel, 1991
1 ....3.00
2-34 ....2.00
Ann 1-2 ....3.00
Special 1-4 ....2.00

Deathlok
Marvel, 1999
1-5 ....2.00

Deathmark
Lightning, 1994
1 ....3.00

Deathmask
Future, 2003
1-3 ....3.00

Deathmate
Image, 1993
1 ....3.00
1/Gold 4.00
2 ....3.00
2/Gold 6.00
3 ....5.00
3/Gold 6.00
4 ....5.00
4/Gold 6.00
5 ....5.00
5/Gold 6.00
6 ....3.00
6/Gold 4.00
Ashcan 1 ....1.00

Death Metal
Marvel, 1994
1-4 ....2.00

Death Metal vs. Genetix
Marvel, 1993
1-2 ....3.00

Death Note
Viz, 2005
1-2 ....8.00

Death of Angel Girl
Angel
1 ....3.00

Death of Antisocialman
Not Available
1-10 ....1.00

Death of Hari Kari
Blackout, 1997
0 ....3.00

Death of Lady Vamprè
Blackout
1 ....3.00

Death of Stupidman
Parody
1 ....4.00

Death of Superbabe
Spoof, 1993
1 ....4.00

Death of Vampirella
Harris, 1997
1-1/Variant 15.00

Death Race 2020
Cosmic, 1995

1-5 .... 3.00

Death Rattle
Kitchen Sink, 1985

1-18 .... 2.00

Death Rattle
Kitchen Sink, 1995

½-6 .... 3.00

Deathrow
Heroic, 1993

1 .... 3.00

Death's-Head
Crystal, 1987

1 .... 2.00

Death's Head
Marvel, 1988

1-10 .... 2.00

Death's Head II (Vol. 1)
Marvel, 1992

1 .... 3.00
1/2nd-4 .... 2.00

Death's Head II (Vol. 2)
Marvel, 1992

1-13 .... 2.00
14 .... 3.00
15-16 .... 2.00

Death's Head II & the Origin of Die-Cut
Marvel, 1993

1 .... 3.00
2 .... 2.00

Death's Head II Gold
Marvel

1 .... 4.00

Death Shrike
Brainstorm, 1993

1 .... 3.00

Deathsnake
Fantagraphics, 1994

1-2 .... 3.00

Deathstroke the Terminator
DC, 1991

0 .... 2.00
1 .... 3.00
1/2nd-49 .... 2.00
50 .... 4.00
51-60 .... 2.00
Ann 1-4 .... 4.00

Death Talks About Life
DC

1 .... 2.00

Death: The High Cost of Living
DC, 1993

1 .... 3.00
1/Platinum 6.00
2-3 .... 3.00
3/A 4.00

Death: The Time of Your Life
DC, 1996

1 .... 4.00
2-3 .... 3.00

Death Valley
Charlton, 1953

1 .... 40.00
2-14 .... 20.00

Death Warmed Over
Cat-Head

1 .... 3.00

Deathwatch
Harrier, 1987

1 .... 2.00

Deathwind
Artline

1 .... 3.00

Deathwish
Milestone, 1994

1-4 .... 3.00

Deathworld
Adventure, 1990

1-4 .... 3.00

Deathworld Book II
Adventure, 1991

1-4 .... 3.00

Deathworld Book III
Adventure, 1991

1-4 .... 3.00

Death Wreck
Marvel, 1994

1-4 .... 2.00

Debbie Dean, Career Girl
Civil Service, 1945

1 .... 60.00

Debbie Does Comics
Aircel, 1992

1 .... 3.00

Debbie Does Dallas
Aircel, 1991

1 .... 3.00
1/3D 4.00
1/2nd-18 .... 3.00

Debbi's Dates
DC, 1969

1 .... 30.00
2-5 .... 18.00

Death Hawk

Deathmate

Death of Vampirella

Deathstroke the Terminator

Deathwish

Deathworld

Decoy

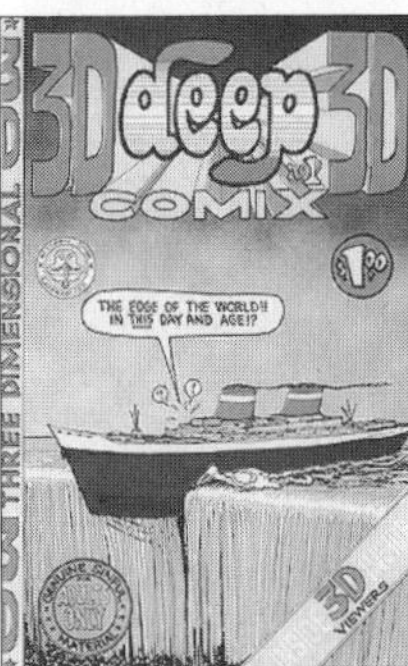

Deep 3D Comix

6 .... 30.00
7-11 .... 18.00

Decade
Dark Horse
1 .... 13.00

Decade of Dark Horse, A
Dark Horse, 1996
1-4 .... 3.00

Decapitator (Randy Bowen's...)
Dark Horse, 1998
1-4 .... 3.00

Deception
Image, 1999
1-3 .... 3.00

Decimation: House of M - The Day After
Marvel, 2006
1 .... 4.00

Decorator
Fantagraphics
1 .... 3.00

Decoy
Penny-Farthing, 1999
1-4 .... 3.00

Decoy: Storm of the Century
Penny-Farthing, 2002
1-4 .... 3.00

Dee Dee
Fantagraphics, 1996
1 .... 3.00

Deep
Marvel, 1977
1 .... 2.00

Deep 3D Comix
Kitchen Sink
1 .... 3.00

Deep Black
Chaos!, 1997
1/A-1/B 2.00

Deep Dimension Horror
AC
1 .... 3.00

Deepest Dimension
Revolutionary, 1993
1-2 .... 3.00

Deep Girl
Ariel Bordeaux
1-2 .... 3.00
3 .... 2.00
4-5 .... 3.00

Deep Sleeper
Oni, 2004
1-2 .... 4.00

Deep Sleeper
Image, 2004
3-4 .... 3.00

Deep Terror
Avalon
1 .... 3.00

Dee Vee
Dee Vee, 1997
1-7 .... 3.00

DefCon 4
Image, 1996
1/A-5 .... 3.00

Defenders
Dell, 1962
1 .... 26.00
2 .... 16.00

Defenders
Marvel, 1972
1 .... 90.00
2 .... 35.00
3 .... 30.00
4-5 .... 26.00
6-7 .... 16.00
8 .... 25.00
9 .... 16.00
10 .... 55.00
☛Avengers War
11 .... 15.00
12-13 .... 9.00
14-16 .... 10.00
17-20 .... 7.00
21-24 .... 6.00
25-29 .... 7.00
30-33 .... 4.00
34 .... 5.00
34/30¢ 20.00
35 .... 5.00
35/30¢ 20.00
36 .... 5.00
36/30¢ 20.00
37 .... 5.00
37/30¢ 20.00
38-38/30¢ 5.00
39-47/Whitman 4.00
48 .... 15.00
48/Whitman 5.00
48/35¢-49 .... 4.00
49/35¢ 15.00
50-50/Whitman 4.00
50/35¢ 15.00
51-51/Whitman 4.00
51/35¢ 15.00
52-52/Whitman 4.00
52/35¢ 15.00
53-62/Whitman 4.00
63-63/Whitman 5.00

64-92 .... 4.00
93-100 .... 3.00
101-152 .... 2.00
Ann 1 .... 12.00

Defenders
Marvel, 2001

1 .... 3.00
2-11 .... 2.00
12 .... 4.00

Defenders
Marvel, 2005

1 .... 5.00
2-5 .... 3.00

Defenders of Dynatron City
Marvel, 1992

1-6 .... 1.00

Defenders of the Earth
Marvel, 1987

1-4 .... 1.00

Defenseless Dead
Adventure, 1991

1-3 .... 3.00

Defex
Devil's Due, 2004

1 .... 5.00
1/Variant 1.00
2-6 .... 3.00

Defiance
Image, 2001

1 .... 4.00
2-8 .... 3.00

Defiant Genesis
Defiant, 1993

1 .... 1.00

Definition
Slave Labor, 1997

1 .... 13.00

Deicide
DC, 2004

1 .... 15.00

Deity
Image, 1997

0 .... 6.00
0/A-3 .... 3.00
3/A 4.00
4-6/A 3.00

Deity
Image, 1998

1-Ashcan 1 .... 3.00

Deity: Requiem
Image, 2005

1 .... 7.00

Deity: Revelations
Image, 1999

1-4 .... 3.00

Deja Vu
Fantaco, 2000

1 .... 3.00

Deja Vu
Radio, 2000

1 .... 3.00

Delia Charm
Red Menace

1-2 .... 3.00

Delirium
Metro

1 .... 2.00

Deliverer
Zion, 1994

1 .... 3.00

Della Vision
Atlas, 1955

1 .... 50.00
2-3 .... 40.00

Dell Giants
Dell, 1959

21 .... 105.00
22 .... 80.00
23 .... 90.00
24-25 .... 75.00
26 .... 140.00
☛Carl Barks art
27-28 .... 75.00
29 .... 90.00
30 .... 75.00
31 .... 90.00
32 .... 65.00
33 .... 85.00
34 .... 65.00
35 .... 95.00
36-37 .... 80.00
38-39 .... 85.00
40 .... 60.00
41 .... 85.00
42 .... 70.00
43 .... 115.00
44 .... 85.00
45-46 .... 55.00
47 .... 60.00
48 .... 125.00
☛1st Flintstones
49 .... 75.00
50 .... 65.00
51-54 .... 40.00
55 .... 60.00

Dell Junior Treasury
Dell, 1955

1 .... 50.00
2-3 .... 40.00
4 .... 35.00
5 .... 40.00
6-10 .... 35.00

Deep Girl

DefCon 4

Delia Charm

Delta Tenn

Demolition Man

Demon Beast Invasion

Demon Dreams

Demon Gun

Delta Squadron
Anderpol
1 .... 2.00

Delta Tenn
Entertainment, 1987
1-10 .... 2.00

Delta, the Ultimate Difference
Apex One, 1997
1 .... 2.00
2 .... 3.00

Delta-Wave
Miller, 1992
1 .... 3.00

Demented Pervert
Print Mint
1-2 .... 3.00

Demented: Scorpion Child
DMF, 2000
1-5 .... 3.00

Demi's Wild Kingdom Adventure
Opus, 2000
1 .... 10.00

Demi the Demoness
Rip Off, 1993
1-5 .... 3.00
6-Special 1 .... 6.00

Demolition Man
DC, 1993
1-4 .... 2.00

Demon
DC, 1972
1 .... 30.00
2 .... 12.00
3-4 .... 10.00
5-9 .... 9.00
10-11 .... 7.00
12-13 .... 10.00
14-16 .... 7.00

Demon
DC, 1987
1-4 .... 2.00

Demon
DC, 1990
0 .... 2.00
1 .... 4.00
2-3 .... 3.00
4-10 .... 2.00
11 .... 3.00
12-18 .... 2.00
19 .... 3.00
20-42 .... 2.00
43 .... 4.00
44-45 .... 3.00
46-49 .... 2.00
50 .... 3.00
51 .... 2.00
52-54 .... 3.00
55-58 .... 2.00
Ann 1 .... 3.00
Ann 2 .... 12.00
☛1st Hitman

Demon Beast Invasion
CPM, 1996
1 .... 3.00

Demon Beast Invasion: The Fallen
CPM, 1998
1-2 .... 3.00

Demonblade
New Comics
1 .... 2.00

Demon Dreams
Pacific, 1984
1-2 .... 2.00

Demon Dreams of Dr. Drew
AC
1 .... 3.00

Demon Driven Out
DC, 2003
1-6 .... 3.00

Demongate
Sirius, 1996
1-9 .... 3.00

Demon Gun
Crusade, 1996
1-3 .... 3.00

Demon-Hunter
Atlas-Seaboard, 1975
1 .... 2.00

Demon Hunter
Atlas-Seaboard, 1975
1 .... 5.00

Demon Hunter
Aircel, 1989
1-4 .... 2.00

Demon Hunter
Davdez, 1998
1 .... 3.00

Demonic Toys
Eternity, 1992
1-4 .... 3.00

Demonique
London Night, 1994
1-4 .... 3.00

Demonique: Angel of Night
London Night, 1997
1 .... 3.00

Demon Ororon
Tokyopop, 2004
1 .... 10.00

Demon Realm
Medeia
0 .... 3.00

Demons & Dark Elves
Weirdworx
1 .... 3.00

Demon's Blood
Odyssey
1 .... 2.00

Demonslayer
Image, 1999
1-3 .... 3.00

Demonslayer
Next
0 .... 3.00

Demonslayer
Image, 2000
1-3 .... 3.00

Demon's Tails
Adventure, 1993
1-4 .... 3.00

Demon Warrior
Eastern, 1987
1-6 .... 2.00

DemonWars: Eye for an Eye (RA Salvatore's)
CrossGen, 2003
1-5 .... 3.00

DemonWars: Trial by Fire (R.A. Salvatore's...)
CrossGen, 2003
1-5 .... 3.00

Demonwish
Pocket Change, 1995
1 .... 3.00

Den
Fantagor
1-10 .... 3.00

Denizens of Deep City
Kitchen Sink, 1988
1-9 .... 2.00

Dennis the Menace
Fawcett, 1953
1 .... 350.00
2 .... 125.00
3 .... 85.00
4-5 .... 70.00
6-10 .... 60.00
11-20 .... 45.00
21-30 .... 35.00
31-40 .... 25.00
41-50 .... 18.00
51-70 .... 14.00
71-90 .... 10.00
91-100 .... 6.00
101-120 .... 4.00
121-140 .... 3.00
141-166 .... 2.00

Dennis the Menace (Giants)
Fawcett, 1955
2-6/A 60.00
7-12 .... 50.00
13-20 .... 35.00
21-29 .... 22.00
30-40 .... 18.00
41-50 .... 15.00
51-60 .... 12.00
61-75 .... 10.00
Special 1 .... 95.00
Special 2 .... 80.00

Dennis the Menace
Marvel, 1981
1-13 .... 2.00

Dennis the Menace and His Dog Ruff
Fawcett, 1961
1 .... 22.00

Dennis the Menace and his Friends
Fawcett, 1969
1-4 .... 12.00
5 .... 8.00
6-10 .... 5.00
11-20 .... 4.00
21-46 .... 3.00

Dennis the Menace and his Pal Joey
Fawcett, 1961
1 .... 42.00

Dennis the Menace Big Bonus Series
Fawcett, 1980
10-11 .... 3.00

Dennis the Menace Bonus Magazine Series
Fawcett, 1970
76-90 .... 8.00
91-120 .... 7.00
121-150 .... 6.00
151-170 .... 4.00
171-194 .... 3.00

Dennis the Menace Comics Digest
Marvel
1 .... 20.00
2-3 .... 1.00

Demon Hunter

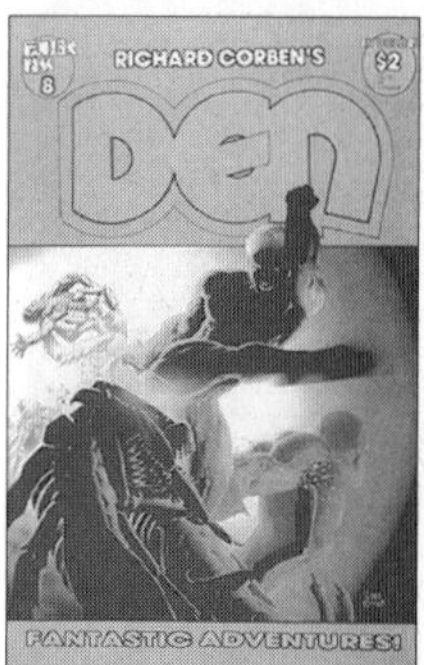

Den

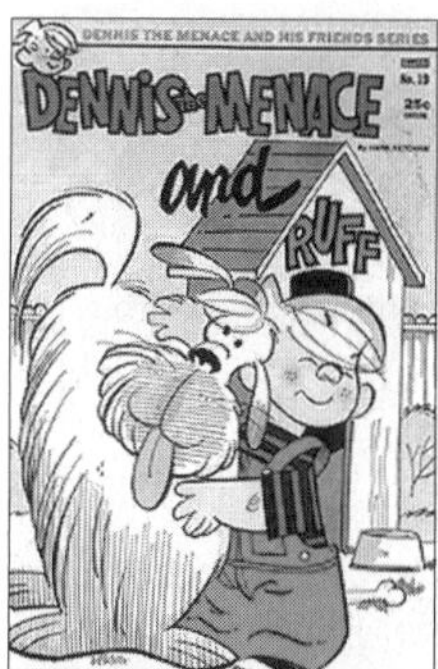

Dennis the Menace and his Friends

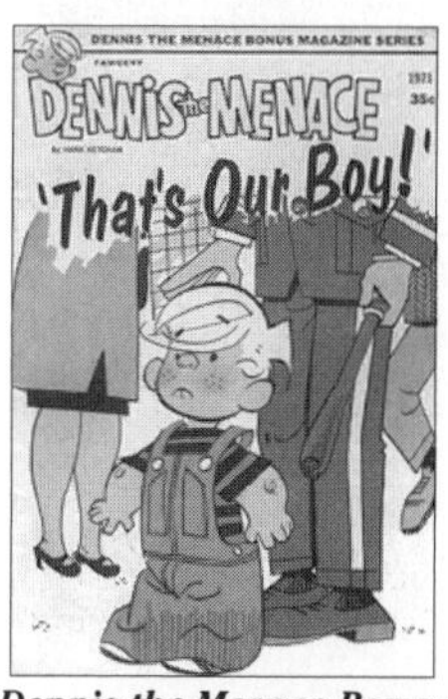

Dennis the Menace Bonus Magazine Series

Dental Hygiene Funnies

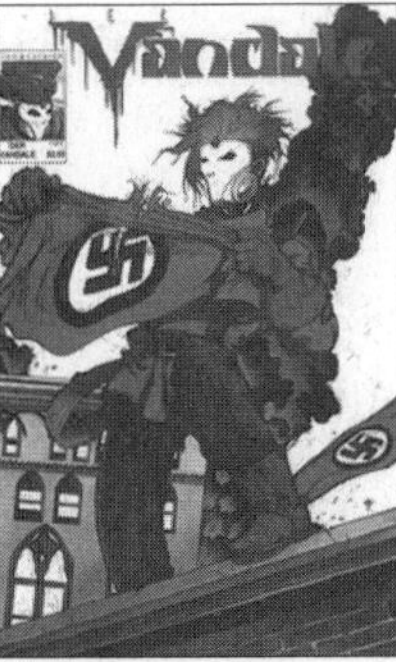
Der Vandale

Descending Angels

Desert Storm Journal

Dennis the Menace Pocket Full of Fun
Fawcett, 1969

1 .... 25.00
2-10 .... 20.00
11-16 .... 15.00
17-50 .... 10.00

Dental Hygiene Funnies
Slave Labor

1 .... 1.00

Depressor
Being

1 .... 3.00

Deputy Dawg
Gold Key, 1965

1 .... 55.00

Deputy Dawg Presents Dinky Duck and Hashimoto-San
Gold Key, 1965

1 .... 30.00

Der Countess
Avalon Communications, 1996

1 .... 3.00

Der Vandale
Innervision

1-3 .... 3.00

Descendants of Toshin
Arrow, 1999

1 .... 3.00

Descending Angels
Millennium

1 .... 3.00

Desert Dawn
E.C., 1935

1 .... 500.00

Desert Peach
Thoughts & Images, 1988

1 .... 10.00
2 .... 6.00
3-6 .... 4.00
7-16 .... 3.00
17 .... 4.00
18 .... 3.00
19-22 .... 5.00
23-30 .... 3.00

Desert Storm Journal
Apple, 1991

1-8 .... 3.00

Desert Storm: Send Hussein to Hell!
Innovation, 1991

1 .... 3.00

Desert Streams
DC

1 .... 6.00

Desolation Jones
DC, 2005

1-8 .... 3.00

Despair
Print Mint, 1969

1 .... 10.00

Desperado
Lev Gleason, 1948

1 .... 85.00
2 .... 45.00
3-8 .... 34.00

Desperadoes
Image, 1997

1-5 .... 3.00

Desperadoes: Banners of Gold
Idea & Design Works, 2004

1-5 .... 4.00

Desperadoes: Epidemic!
DC, 1999

1 .... 6.00

Desperadoes: Quiet of the Grave
DC, 2001

1-5 .... 3.00

Desperate Times
Aaargh, 2000

1-3 .... 3.00
4 .... 2.00

Desperate Times
Image, 1998

0 .... 4.00
1-4 .... 3.00

Desperate Times
Image, 2004

1 .... 3.00

Desso-Lette
Follis Brothers, 1997

1 .... 3.00

Destination Moon
Export, 1950

1 .... 240.00

Destiny: A Chronicle of Deaths Foretold
DC, 1997

1-3 .... 6.00

Destiny Angel
Dark Fantasy

1 .... 4.00

Destroy!!
Eclipse, 1986

1 .... 5.00
1/3D 3.00

Destroy All Comics
Slave Labor, 1994

1-5 ... 4.00

Destroyer Duck
Eclipse, 1982

1 ... 4.00
2-7 ... 2.00

Destroyer (Magazine)
Marvel, 1989

1-8 ... 3.00

Destroyer
Marvel, 1991

1 ... 2.00

Destroyer
Marvel, 1991

1-4 ... 2.00

Destroyer
Valiant, 1995

0 ... 4.00
0/$2.50 ... 10.00

Destructor
Atlas-Seaboard, 1975

1 ... 10.00
2 ... 7.00
3-4 ... 5.00

Detective
Sunset Strips

1-12 ... 3.00

Detective: Chronicles of Max Faccioni
Caliber

1 ... 3.00

Detective Comics
DC, 206

0 ... 3.00
1 ... 80,000.00
2 ... 18,250.00
3 ... 10,800.00
4-5 ... 6,850.00
6-7 ... 4,450.00
8 ... 6,500.00
9-17 ... 4,350.00
18 ... 5,000.00
19 ... 4,150.00
20 ... 6,300.00
21 ... 3,250.00
22 ... 3,950.00
23-26 ... 3,250.00
27 ... 225,000.00
☛1st Batman
27/2nd ... 9.00
28 ... 25,000.00
☛2nd Batman
29 ... 35,000.00
☛3rd Batman
30 ... 7,500.00
31 ... 27,500.00
☛Batman vs. the Monk
32 ... 6,000.00
33 ... 50,000.00
☛Batman origin
34 ... 7,500.00
35 ... 10,000.00
36-37 ... 6,500.00
38 ... 57,500.00
☛1st Robin
39 ... 6,000.00
40 ... 6,500.00
41 ... 4,000.00
42-45 ... 3,000.00
46-50 ... 2,000.00
51-57 ... 1,750.00
58 ... 4,750.00
☛1st Penguin
59 ... 2,000.00
60 ... 1,750.00
61 ... 1,500.00
62 ... 2,250.00
63 ... 1,750.00
64 ... 5,000.00
☛1st Boy Commandos
65 ... 2,250.00
66 ... 4,000.00
☛1st Two-Face
67 ... 2,000.00
68-69 ... 1,750.00
70-71 ... 1,500.00
72-75 ... 1,250.00
76 ... 1,500.00
77-79 ... 1,000.00
80 ... 1,250.00
81-83 ... 1,000.00
84 ... 900.00
85 ... 1,250.00
86-90 ... 900.00
91 ... 1,000.00
92-98 ... 800.00
99 ... 950.00
100 ... 1,000.00
101 ... 700.00
102 ... 950.00
103-108 ... 625.00
109 ... 850.00
110-113 ... 625.00
114 ... 800.00
115-117 ... 625.00
118 ... 825.00
119 ... 600.00
120 ... 800.00
☛Penguin app.
121 ... 600.00
122 ... 1,225.00
123 ... 600.00
124 ... 800.00
125-127 ... 600.00
128 ... 800.00
129-130 ... 600.00
131-136 ... 525.00
137 ... 675.00

Desperadoes

Destination Moon

Destroyer Duck

Detective Comics

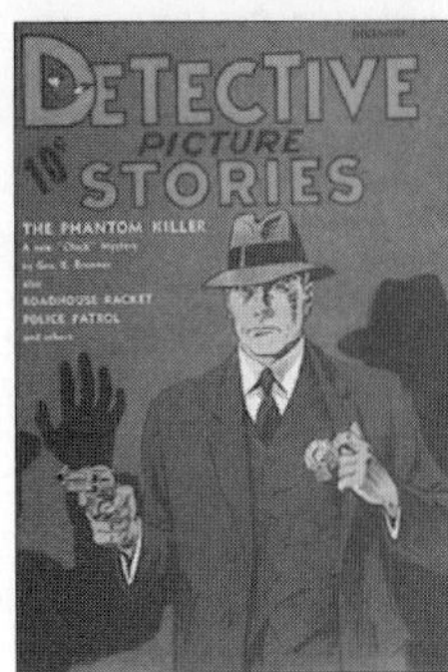

Detective Picture Stories

Detention Comics

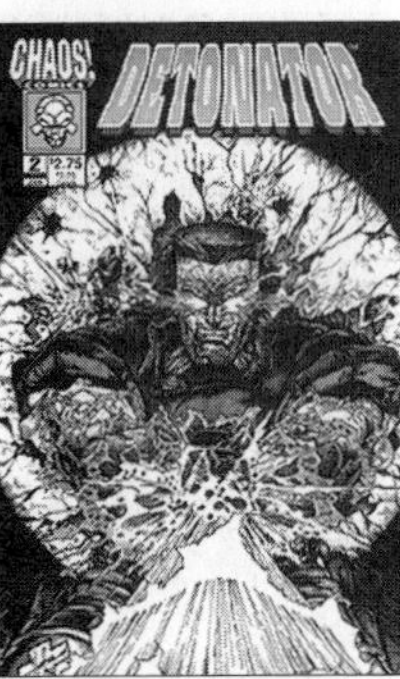

Detonator

Devastator

138 .... 925.00
☛Robotman origin
139 .... 500.00
140 .... 4,000.00
☛1st Riddler
141 .... 575.00
142 .... 1,250.00
☛2nd Riddler
143-148 .... 575.00
149 .... 675.00
150 .... 550.00
151 .... 600.00
152-155 .... 525.00
156 .... 625.00
157-160 .... 500.00
161-167 .... 525.00
168 .... 3,750.00
☛Joker origin
169-170 .... 500.00
171 .... 700.00
172-176 .... 500.00
177-179 .... 400.00
180 .... 450.00
181-186 .... 400.00
187 .... 425.00
188-189 .... 400.00
190 .... 600.00
191-192 .... 400.00
193 .... 450.00
194-199 .... 400.00
200 .... 575.00
201-202 .... 400.00
203 .... 450.00
204 .... 400.00
205 .... 575.00
206-210 .... 400.00
211 .... 450.00
212 .... 400.00
213 .... 525.00
214-224 .... 375.00
225 .... 4,500.00
☛1st Manhunter
226 .... 1,500.00
227-229 .... 500.00
230 .... 550.00
231 .... 400.00
232 .... 300.00
233 .... 1,250.00
☛1st Batwoman
234 .... 325.00
235 .... 600.00
236 .... 350.00
237-240 .... 300.00
241-260 .... 250.00
261-264 .... 200.00
265 .... 325.00
266 .... 200.00
267 .... 250.00
268-271 .... 200.00
272 .... 175.00
273 .... 200.00
274-280 .... 150.00
281-297 .... 125.00
298 .... 200.00
299-310 .... 100.00
311 .... 200.00
☛1st Catman
312-326 .... 100.00
327 .... 225.00
☛New Bat symbol
328 .... 175.00
☛Alfred dies
329-330 .... 75.00
331 .... 65.00
332 .... 115.00
☛Joker
333-340 .... 60.00
341 .... 75.00
342-352 .... 60.00
353-358 .... 75.00
359 .... 350.00
☛1st Batgirl
360-362 .... 65.00
363 .... 100.00
☛2nd Batgirl
364 .... 60.00
365 .... 90.00
366-368 .... 60.00
369 .... 75.00
370 .... 45.00
371 .... 80.00
☛Batmobile
372-376 .... 50.00
377 .... 65.00
378-380 .... 50.00
381-386 .... 40.00
387 .... 75.00
388 .... 50.00
389-390 .... 35.00
391-393 .... 25.00
394 .... 35.00
395 .... 125.00
☛N. Adams art
396-397 .... 35.00
398-399 .... 30.00
400 .... 175.00
☛1st Man-Bat
401 .... 30.00
402 .... 55.00
403-404 .... 35.00
405-407 .... 30.00
408-410 .... 40.00
411 .... 30.00
☛1st Talia
412-424 .... 25.00
425-427 .... 20.00
428-436 .... 15.00
437 .... 20.00
☛100-page issue
438-445 .... 28.00
☛100-page issues
446 .... 12.00
447-450 .... 8.00
451-455 .... 6.00

456-457 .... 9.00
458-462 .... 6.00
463 .... 45.00
☛1st Calculator
464 .... 6.00
465-468 .... 9.00
469-470 .... 5.00
471-473 .... 8.00
☛1st new Deadshot
474-476 .... 15.00
477-479 .... 8.00
480 .... 5.00
481 .... 7.00
482 .... 5.00
483 .... 8.00
484 .... 5.00
485-499 .... 4.00
500 .... 5.00
501-503 .... 4.00
504 .... 6.00
505-523 .... 4.00
524 .... 5.00
525-534 .... 4.00
535 .... 5.00
536-564 .... 4.00
565-568 .... 3.00
569-570 .... 4.00
571 .... 3.00
572 .... 4.00
573-574 .... 3.00
575 .... 4.00
576-577 .... 3.00
578-585 .... 4.00
586-587 .... 3.00
588-590 .... 4.00
591-675 .... 3.00
675/Platinum 5.00
675/Variant 4.00
676 .... 3.00
677-682 .... 2.00
682/Variant 3.00
683-699 .... 2.00
700 .... 4.00
700/Variant 5.00
701-718 .... 2.00
719 .... 3.00
720 .... 4.00
721-722 .... 3.00
723-740 .... 2.00
741 .... 3.00
742-746 .... 2.00
747-749 .... 3.00
750 .... 5.00
751 .... 12.00
☛1st Sasha
752-774 .... 3.00
775 .... 4.00
776-799 .... 3.00
800 .... 4.00
801-816 .... 3.00
817 .... 12.00
818-839 .... 3.00

1000000 .... 4.00
1000000/Variant 15.00
Ann 1 .... 5.00
Ann 2 .... 4.00
Ann 3-7 .... 3.00
Ann 8 .... 4.00
Ann 9 .... 3.00
Ann 10 .... 4.00

Detective Eye
Centaur, 1940
1 .... 1,350.00
2 .... 800.00

Detective Picture Stories
Comics Magazine, 1936
1 .... 3,400.00
2 .... 1,650.00
3-5 .... 850.00

Detectives
Alpha Productions, 1993
1 .... 5.00

Detectives, Inc.: A Terror of Dying Dreams
Eclipse, 1987
1-3 .... 2.00

Detectives Inc. (Micro-Series)
Eclipse, 1980
1-2 .... 2.00

Detention Comics
DC, 1996
1 .... 4.00

Detonator
Image, 2005
1-3 .... 3.00

Detour
Alternative, 1997
1 .... 3.00

Detroit! Murder City Comix
Kent Myers, 1993
1-7 .... 3.00

Devastator
Image, 1998
1-3 .... 3.00

Deviant
Antarctic, 1999
1 .... 3.00

Devil Chef
Dark Horse, 1994
1 .... 3.00

Devil Dinosaur
Marvel, 1978
1 .... 5.00
2-3 .... 4.00
4 .... 5.00
5 .... 4.00
6-9 .... 3.00

Devil Chef

Devil Dinosaur

Devil Kids

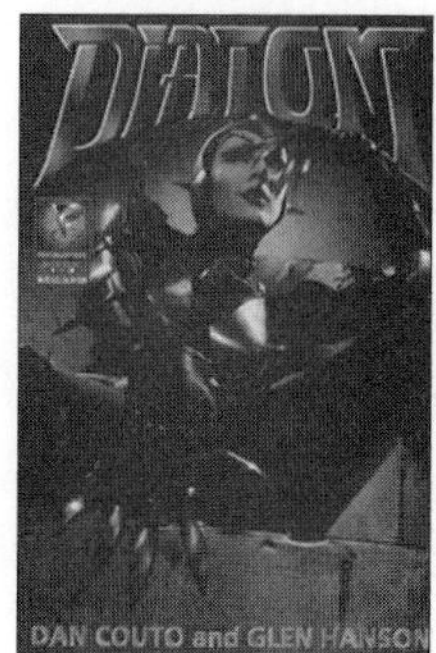

Diatom

Dick Cole

Dickie Dare

Dick Tracy 3-D

Dick Tracy Comics Monthly

Devil Dinosaur Spring Fling
Marvel, 1997

1 ....3.00

Devil-Dog Dugan
Atlas, 1956

1 ....60.00
2 ....40.00
3 ....30.00

Devil Dogs
Street & Smith, 1942

1 ....200.00

Devilina
Atlas-Seaboard, 1975

1 ....9.00
2 ....12.00

Devil Jack
Doom Theater, 1995

1-2 ....3.00

Devil Kids
Harvey, 1962

1 ....150.00
2 ....75.00
3 ....50.00
4-5 ....25.00
6-10 ....20.00
11-17 ....15.00
18-20 ....10.00
21-30 ....8.00
31-40 ....5.00
41-60 ....4.00
61-79 ....3.00
80-107 ....2.00

Devilman
Verotik, 1995

1 ....4.00
2-5 ....3.00
6 ....4.00

Devil May Cry
Dreamwave, 2004

1-3 ....4.00

Devil May Cry 3
Tokyopop, 2005

1 ....10.00

Devil's Angel
Fantagraphics

1 ....3.00

Devil's Bite
Boneyard

1-2 ....3.00

Devil's Brigade
Avalon

1 ....3.00

Devil's Due Studios Previews 2003
Image, 2003

1 ....1.00

Devil's Footprints
Dark Horse, 2003

1-4 ....3.00

Devil's Keeper
Alias, 2005

1 ....1.00
2 ....3.00

Devil's Reign
Image, 1996

½-½/Platinum 3.00

Devil's Rejects
Idea & Design Works, 2005

0/Baby 5.00
0/Otis 6.00
0/Spaulding 5.00
1 ....4.00

Devlin
Maximum, 1996

1 ....3.00

Devlin Demon: Not for Normal Children
Dublin

1 ....3.00

Dewey DeSade
Item

1-2 ....4.00
Ashcan 1 ....1.00

Dexter Comics
Dearfield, 1948

1 ....45.00
2 ....35.00
3-5 ....30.00

Dexter's Laboratory
DC, 1999

1 ....3.00
2-24 ....2.00
25 ....1.00
26-34 ....2.00

Dhampire: Stillborn
DC, 1996

1 ....6.00

Diablo: Tales of Sanctuary
Dark Horse, 2001

1 ....6.00

Dia de los Muertos (Sergio Aragonès')
Dark Horse, 1998

nn 3.00

Diary Loves
Quality, 1949

2 ....60.00
3-15 ....40.00
16-31 ....30.00

Diary of a Dominatrix
Fantagraphics, 1995
1-3 .... 3.00

Diary of Emily K.
Fantagraphics
1 .... 3.00

Diary of Horror
Avon, 1952
1 .... 320.00

Diary Secrets
St. John, 1952
10-30 .... 100.00

Diatom
Photographics, 1995
1-3 .... 5.00

Dick Cole
Curtis Publishing, 1948
1 .... 240.00
2 .... 150.00
3-5 .... 125.00
6-10 .... 100.00

Dick Danger
Olsen, 1998
1-5 .... 3.00

Dick Hercules of St. Markham's
Sports Cartoons
1 .... 30.00
2 .... 15.00
3-7 .... 8.00

Dickie Dare
Eastern, 1942
1 .... 450.00
2 .... 325.00
3-4 .... 275.00

Dicks
Caliber, 1997
1-4 .... 3.00

Dick Tracy
Blackthorne, 1986
1-2 .... 6.00
3-24 .... 7.00

Dick Tracy
Disney, 1990
1 .... 3.00
1/Direct 5.00
2 .... 3.00
2/Direct 6.00
3 .... 3.00
3/Direct 6.00

Dick Tracy 3-D
Blackthorne, 1986
1 .... 3.00

Dick Tracy Adventures
Gladstone, 1991
1 .... 5.00

Dick Tracy Adventures
Hamilton
1 .... 4.00

Dick Tracy Comics Monthly
Harvey, 1950
25 .... 110.00
26-41 .... 85.00
42-50 .... 70.00
51-60 .... 60.00
61-70 .... 52.00
71-80 .... 45.00
81-90 .... 40.00
91-100 .... 32.00
101-110 .... 28.00
111-120 .... 26.00
121-130 .... 24.00
131-140 .... 22.00
141-145 .... 28.00
Giveaway 1 .... 15.00

Dick Tracy Crimebuster
Avalon
1-4 .... 3.00

Dick Tracy Detective
Avalon
1-4 .... 3.00

Dick Tracy Monthly
Dell, 1948
1 .... 365.00
2 .... 250.00
3-5 .... 220.00
6-10 .... 200.00
11-24 .... 140.00

Dick Tracy Monthly
Blackthorne, 1986
1 .... 3.00
2-25 .... 2.00

Dick Tracy Special
Blackthorne, 1988
1-3 .... 3.00

Dick Tracy: The Early Years
Blackthorne, 1987
1-3 .... 7.00
4 .... 3.00

Dick Tracy "Unprinted Stories"
Blackthorne, 1987
1-4 .... 3.00

Dick Tracy Weekly
Blackthorne, 1988
26-99 .... 2.00

Dick Wad
Slave Labor, 1993
1 .... 3.00

Dick Tracy Detective

Dick Tracy Special

Dick Tracy Weekly

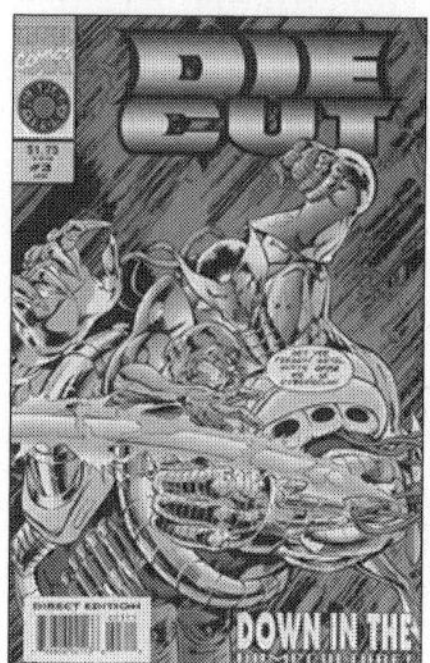

Die-Cut

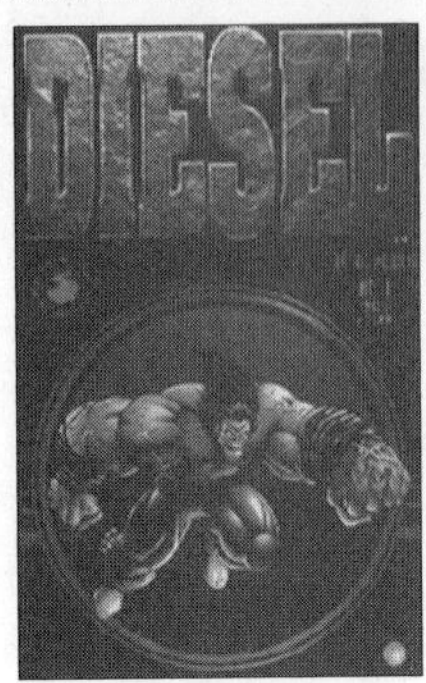
Diesel

Digimon Digital Monsters

Digitek

Dilly

Dick Wingate of the United States Navy
Toby, 1953
1 ....50.00

Dictators of the Twentieth Century: Hitler
Antarctic, 2004
1-4 ....3.00

Dictators of the Twentieth Century: Saddam Hussein
Antarctic, 2004
1-2 ....4.00

Didymous: The Night and Day Worlds
Ironhorse, 1999
1-2 ....3.00

Diebold
Silent Partners, 1996
1-2 ....3.00

Die-Cut
Marvel, 1993
1 ....3.00
2-4 ....2.00

Die-Cut vs. G-Force
Marvel, 1993
1-2 ....3.00

Diesel
Antarctic, 1997
1 ....3.00

Different Beat Comics
Fantagraphics
1 ....4.00

Diggers
C&T
1 ....2.00

Digimon Digital Monsters
Dark Horse, 2000
1-12 ....3.00

Digimon Tamers
Tokyopop, 2004
1 ....10.00

Digital Dragon
Peregrine Entertainment, 1999
1-2 ....3.00

Digital Webbing Presents
Digital Webbing, 2001
1-18 ....3.00
19-20 ....4.00

Digitek
Marvel, 1992
1-4 ....2.00

Dik Skycap
Rip Off, 1991
1-2 ....3.00

Dildo
Fantagraphics, 2003
1 ....6.00
2-10 ....4.00

Dilemma Presents
Dilemma, 1994
1-4 ....3.00

Dilly
Lev Gleason, 1953
1 ....20.00
2-3 ....15.00

Dilton's Strange Science
Archie, 1989
1-5 ....2.00

Dime Comics
Newsbook, 1945
1 ....375.00

Dimension 5
Edge, 1995
1 ....4.00

Dimension X
Karl Art
1 ....4.00

Dimension Z
Pyramid
1-2 ....2.00

Dimm Comics Presents
Dimm, 1996
Ashcan 0-Ashcan 1 ....1.00

Dim-Witted Darryl
Slave Labor, 1998
1-3 ....3.00

Ding Dong
Compix, 1946
1 ....150.00
2 ....75.00
3-5 ....55.00

Dingledorfs
Skylight
1 ....3.00

Dinky Duck
St. John, 1951
1 ....70.00
2 ....55.00
3-5 ....40.00
6-8 ....24.00
9-12 ....18.00
13-15 ....15.00
16-19 ....10.00

Dinky on the Road
Blind Bat, 1994
1 ....2.00

Dino Island
Mirage, 1993
1-2 ....3.00

Dino-Riders
Marvel, 1989
1-3 .... 2.00

Dinosaur Bop
Monster
1-2 .... 3.00

Dinosaur Island
Monster
1 .... 3.00

Dinosaur Mansion
Edge
1 .... 3.00

Dinosaur Rex
Upshot
1-3 .... 2.00

Dinosaurs
Hollywood, 1991
1-2 .... 3.00

Dinosaurs: An Illustrated Guide
Caliber, 1991
1 .... 3.00

Dinosaurs Attack!
Eclipse
1-3 .... 4.00

Dinosaurs, A Celebration
Marvel, 1992
1-4 .... 5.00

Dinosaurs For Hire
Eternity, 1988
1 .... 2.00
1/3D 3.00
1/2nd-9 .... 2.00

Dinosaurs For Hire
Malibu, 1993
1-4 .... 2.00
5-12 .... 3.00

Dinosaurs for Hire: Dinosaurs Rule!
Eternity
1 .... 6.00

Dinosaurs For Hire Fall Classic
Eternity, 1988
1 .... 2.00

Dinosaurs for Hire: Guns 'n' Lizards
Eternity
1 .... 6.00

Dioramas: Love Story
Image, 2004
1 .... 13.00

Dippy Duck
Atlas, 1957
1 .... 30.00

Directory to a Nonexistent Universe
Eclipse, 1987
1 .... 2.00

Dire Wolves: A Chronicle of the Deadworld
Caliber
1 .... 4.00

Dirtbag
Twist N Shout, 1993
1-7 .... 3.00

Dirty Dozen
Dell, 1967
1 .... 25.00

Dirty Pair
Eclipse, 1988
1 .... 4.00
2-4 .... 3.00

Dirty Pair II
Eclipse, 1989
1-5 .... 3.00

Dirty Pair III
Eclipse, 1990
1-5 .... 2.00

Dirty Pair (4th Series)
Viz, 1993
1-5 .... 5.00

Dirty Pair: Dangerous Acquaintances
Dark Horse, 1997
1-5 .... 3.00

Dirty Pair: Fatal but Not Serious
Dark Horse, 1995
1-5 .... 3.00

Dirty Pair: Run from the Future
Dark Horse, 2000
1-4 .... 3.00

Dirty Pair: Sim Hell
Dark Horse, 1993
1-5 .... 3.00

Dirty Pair: Sim Hell Remastered
Dark Horse, 1996
1-4 .... 3.00

Dirty Pair: Start The Violence
Dark Horse, 1999
1/A-1/B 3.00

Dirty Pictures
Aircel, 1991
1-3 .... 3.00

Dime Comics

Dim-Witted Darryl

Ding Dong

Dino Island

Dinosaur Island

Dirty Pair

Disavowed

Dishman

Dirty Plotte
Drawn and Quarterly, 1996
1-9 .... 3.00
10 .... 4.00

Disasters of War
Caliber
1 .... 4.00

Disavowed
DC, 2000
1-6 .... 3.00

Disciples
Image, 2001
1-2 .... 3.00

Dishman
Eclipse, 1988
1 .... 3.00

Disney Afternoon
Marvel, 1994
1-10 .... 2.00

Disney and Me
Fleetway-Quality, 1998
1 .... 4.00
2-165 .... 2.00

Disney Comic Hits
Marvel, 1995
1-16 .... 2.00

Disneyland Birthday Party
Dell, 1958
1 .... 440.00

Disneyland Birthday Party
Gladstone, 1985
1-1/A 10.00

Disney Movie Book
Disney
1 .... 8.00

Disney's Action Club
Acclaim, 1997
1-7 .... 5.00

Disney's Colossal Comics
Disney
1 .... 2.00

Disney's Colossal Comics Collection
Disney
1-10 .... 2.00

Disney's Comics in 3-D
Disney
1 .... 3.00

Disney's Enchanting Stories
Acclaim
1-4 .... 5.00

Disobedient Daisy
Fantagraphics, 1995
1-2 .... 3.00

Distant Soil, A
Warp, 1983
1 .... 8.00
2 .... 5.00
3-5 .... 4.00
6-9 .... 3.00

Distant Soil, A
Aria, 1991
1 .... 5.00
1/2nd 3.00
1/3rd-1/4th 2.00
2 .... 3.00
2/2nd 2.00
3 .... 3.00
3/2nd-8 .... 2.00
9-24 .... 3.00
25 .... 4.00
25/Ltd 8.00
26-27 .... 3.00
28-31 .... 4.00
38 .... 5.00
32-33 .... 4.00
34 .... 5.00
35 .... 4.00
36 .... 5.00

District X
Marvel, 2004
1 .... 4.00
2-13 .... 3.00

Ditko Package
Ditko, 2000
1 .... 9.00

Diva Grafix & Stories
Starhead, 1993
1-2 .... 4.00

Divas
Caliber
1-4 .... 3.00

Divine Intervention/Gen13
DC, 1999
1 .... 3.00

Divine Intervention/ Wildcats
DC, 1999
1 .... 3.00

Divine Right
Image, 1997
1-Ashcan 1/A 3.00

Division 13
Dark Horse, 1994
1-4 .... 3.00

Dixie Dugan
Columbia, 1942
1 .... 90.00

2 ... 60.00
3-6 ... 45.00
7-10 ... 40.00
11-13 ... 35.00

Dixie Road
NBM
1-2 ... 11.00

Dizzy Dames
ACG, 1952
1 ... 90.00
2 ... 65.00
3-6 ... 40.00

Dizzy Dames Special Edition
Avalon
1 ... 3.00

Dizzy Don Comics
F.E. Howard, 1942
1 ... 75.00
2 ... 40.00
4-19 ... 30.00
20-22 ... 20.00

Dizzy Don Comics
F.E. Howard, 1947
3 ... 40.00

Dizzy Duck
Standard, 1950
32-39 ... 40.00

Django and Angel
Caliber
1-5 ... 3.00

DMZ
DC, 2006
1-14 ... 3.00

DNAgents
Eclipse, 1983
1 ... 3.00
2-24 ... 2.00
3D 1 ... 3.00

DNAgents Super Special
Antarctic, 1994
1 ... 4.00

D-N-Angel
Tokyopop, 2004
1-10 ... 10.00

D.O.A.
Saving Grace
1 ... 1.00

Doc Carter VD Comics
Health, 1949
1 ... 125.00

Doc Chaos: The Strange Attractor
Vortex, 1990
1-3 ... 3.00

Doc Frankenstein
Burlyman, 2004
1 ... 7.00
1/Darrow ... 10.00
2 ... 4.00
2/Sketch ... 5.00
3 ... 4.00
3/Variant ... 5.00

Doc Samson
Marvel, 1996
1-4 ... 2.00

Doc Samson
Marvel, 2006
1-5 ... 3.00

Doc Savage
Gold Key, 1966
1 ... 38.00

Doc Savage
Marvel, 1972
1 ... 20.00
2 ... 5.00
3-8 ... 3.00

Doc Savage (Magazine)
Marvel, 1975
1 ... 9.00
2-5 ... 4.00
6-8 ... 3.00

Doc Savage
DC, 1987
1-4 ... 2.00

Doc Savage
DC, 1988
1-24 ... 2.00
Ann 1 ... 4.00

Doc Savage Comics (Vol. 1)
Street & Smith, 1940
1 ... 3,600.00
2 ... 950.00
3 ... 700.00
4-5 ... 465.00
6-7 ... 340.00
8-11 ... 250.00
12 ... 190.00

Doc Savage Comics (Vol. 2)
Street & Smith, 1943
1-2 ... 190.00
3-8 ... 145.00

Doc Savage: Curse of the Fire God
Dark Horse, 1995
1-4 ... 3.00

Disney Comic Hits

District X

Divine Right

Dixie Dugan

Dizzy Dames

DNAgents

Doc Savage

Doc Samson

Doc Savage: Devil's Thoughts

Millennium

1-3 ....3.00

Doc Savage: Doom Dynasty

Millennium

1-2 ....2.00

Doc Savage: Manual of Bronze

Millennium, 1992

1 ....3.00

Doc Savage: Repel

Millennium

1 ....3.00

Doc Savage: The Man of Bronze

Millennium, 1991

1-4 ....3.00

Dr. Andy

Alliance, 1994

1 ....3.00

Dr. Anthony King, Hollywood Love Doctor

Minoan, 1952

1 ....60.00
2-4 ....35.00

Dr. Atomic

Last Gasp

1 ....5.00
2-3 ....4.00
4-6 ....3.00

Doctor Bang

Rip Off, 1992

1 ....3.00

Doctor Boogie

Media Arts

1 ....2.00

Doctor Chaos

Triumphant, 1993

1-12 ....3.00

Doctor Cyborg

Attention!

1 ....3.00
1/Ashcan 1.00
2-3 ....3.00

Doctor Doom's Revenge

Marvel, 1989

1 ....1.00

Doctor Fate

DC, 1987

1-4 ....2.00

Doctor Fate

DC, 2003

1-5 ....3.00

Doctor Fate

DC, 1988

1 ....2.00
2-5 ....1.00
6-41 ....2.00
Ann 1 ....3.00

Doctor Faustus

Anarchy, 1994

1-2 ....3.00
Ashcan 1 ....2.00

Doctor Frankenstein's House of 3-D

3-D Zone, 1992

1 ....4.00

Dr. Fu Manchu

I.W., 1964

1 ....45.00

Dr. Giggles

Dark Horse, 1992

1-2 ....3.00

Doctor Gorpon

Eternity, 1991

1-3 ....3.00

Dr. Goyle Special

Arrow

1 ....3.00

Doctor! I'm Too Big!

NBM

1 ....11.00

Dr. Jekyll and Mr. Hyde

NBM

1 ....16.00

Dr. Kildare

Dell, 1962

2 ....50.00
3-9 ....40.00

Doctor Mid-Nite

DC, 1999

1-3 ....6.00

Dr. Radium and the Gizmos of Boola-Boola

Slave Labor, 1992

1 ....5.00

Dr. Radium, Man of Science

Slave Labor, 1992

1-5 ....3.00

Dr. Robot Special

Dark Horse, 2000

1 ....3.00

Dr. Slump

Viz, 2005

1-4 ....8.00

Doctor Solar, Man of the Atom
Gold Key, 1962

1 .... 150.00
2 .... 80.00
3 .... 50.00
4 .... 60.00
5 .... 30.00
6-10 .... 25.00
11-14 .... 16.00
15 .... 20.00
16-20 .... 16.00
21-27 .... 12.00
28-31 .... 4.00

Dr. Speck
Bug Books

1-4 .... 3.00

Doctor Spectrum
Marvel, 2004

1-6 .... 3.00

Doctor Strange
Marvel, 1968

169 .... 75.00
170-171 .... 30.00
172-173 .... 27.00
174 .... 20.00
175 .... 35.00
176-183 .... 27.00

Doctor Strange
Marvel, 1974

1 .... 25.00
2 .... 18.00
3-4 .... 10.00
5-6 .... 8.00
7 .... 7.00
8-9 .... 4.00
10 .... 7.00
11 .... 6.00
12-13 .... 4.00
13/30¢ 20.00
14 .... 3.00
14/30¢ 20.00
15 .... 3.00
15/30¢ 20.00
16 .... 3.00
16/30¢ 20.00
17 .... 3.00
17/30¢ 20.00
18-23 .... 3.00
23/35¢ 15.00
24 .... 3.00
24/35¢ 15.00
25 .... 3.00
25/35¢ 15.00
26-81 .... 2.00
Ann 1 .... 6.00
Special 1 .... 3.00

Doctor Strange
Marvel, 1999

1-4 .... 3.00

Doctor Strange and Doctor Doom: Triumph and Torment
Marvel, 1989

1 .... 10.00
1/HC 18.00

Doctor Strange Classics
Marvel, 1984

1-4 .... 2.00

Doctor Strange/Ghost Rider Special
Marvel, 1991

1 .... 2.00

Dr. Strange: Oath
Marvel, 2006

1-3 .... 3.00

Doctor Strange: Shamballa
Marvel, 1986

1 .... 7.00

Doctor Strange: Sorcerer Supreme
Marvel, 1988

1 .... 3.00
2-14 .... 2.00
15 .... 3.00
16-49 .... 2.00
50 .... 3.00
51-74 .... 2.00
75 .... 3.00
75/Holo-grafix 4.00
76-90 .... 2.00
Ann 1 .... 3.00
Ann 2 .... 2.00
Ann 3-4 .... 3.00
Ashcan 1 .... 1.00

Dr. Strange vs. Dracula
Marvel, 1994

1 .... 2.00

Doctor Strange: What is it That Disturbs You Stephen?
Marvel, 1997

1 .... 6.00

Doctor Strangefate
DC, 1996

1 .... 2.00

Doctor Tom Brent, Young Intern
Charlton, 1963

1 .... 15.00
2-5 .... 10.00

Dr. Tomorrow
Acclaim, 1997

1-12 .... 3.00

Doctor Chaos

Doctor Strange

Doctor Strange Classics

Doctor Weird

Doctor Who

Doctor Zero

Dodekain

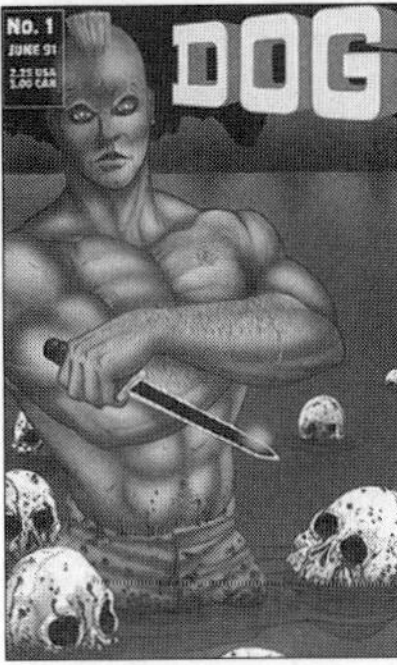

Dog

Doctor Weird
Caliber, 1994

1-2 .... 3.00
Special 1 .... 4.00

Dr. Weird
October, 1997

1-2 .... 3.00

Doctor Who
Marvel, 1984

1 .... 3.00
2-23 .... 2.00

Dr. Who and the Daleks
Dell

1 .... 50.00

Dr. Wirtham's Comix & Stories
Clifford Neal, 1987

1-2 .... 2.00
3 .... 5.00
4-6 .... 2.00
7-8 .... 3.00

Dr. Wonder
Old Town, 1996

1-5 .... 3.00

Doctor Zero
Marvel, 1988

1-8 .... 2.00

Dr. Zomb's House of Freaks
Starhead

1 .... 3.00

Doc Weird's Thrill Book
Pure Imagination

1-3 .... 2.00

Dodekain
Antarctic, 1994

1-8 .... 3.00

Dodges Bullets
Image, 2004

1 .... 10.00

Do-Do
Nationwide, 1950

1 .... 65.00
2-5 .... 45.00
6-7 .... 38.00

Do-Do Man
Edge

1 .... 3.00

Dog
Rebel, 1991

1-2 .... 2.00

Dog Boy
Fantagraphics, 1987

1-9 .... 2.00

Dog Moon
DC

1 .... 7.00

Dogpatch Comics (Al Capp's...)
Toby, 1949

1 .... 90.00
2 .... 70.00
3-4 .... 50.00

Dogs of War
Defiant, 1994

1-8 .... 3.00

Dog Soup
Dog Soup

1 .... 3.00

Dogs-O-War
Crusade, 1996

1-3 .... 3.00

Dog T.A.G.S.: Trained Animal Gun Squadron
Bugged Out, 1993

1 .... 2.00

Dogwitch
Sirius, 2003

1 .... 6.00
2-6 .... 4.00
7-17 .... 3.00

Doin' Time with OJ
Boneyard, 1994

1 .... 4.00

Dojinshi
Antarctic, 1992

1-4 .... 3.00

Doll
Rip Off, 1989

1-8 .... 3.00

Doll and Creature
Image, 2006

1 .... 13.00
2-4 .... 3.00

Doll Man
Quality, 1941

17-19 .... 200.00
20-25 .... 150.00
26-30 .... 130.00
31-36 .... 120.00
37 .... 130.00
38-43 .... 120.00
44-47 .... 100.00

Dollman
Eternity, 1991

1-4 .... 3.00

Doll Man Quarterly
Quality, 1941

1 .... 1,600.00

2 .... 1,000.00
3 .... 680.00
4-5 .... 400.00
6-7 .... 365.00
8 .... 1,000.00
9 .... 365.00
10-16 .... 240.00

Doll Parts
Sirius, 2000
1 .... 3.00

Dolls
Sirius, 1996
1 .... 3.00

Doll
Tokyopop, 2004
1-6 .... 10.00

Dolly
Approved, 1951
1 .... 25.00

Dolly Dill
Marvel, 1945
1 .... 55.00

Dollz
Image, 2001
1/A-2 .... 3.00

Dome: Ground Zero
DC
1 .... 8.00

Domination Factor: Avengers
Marvel, 1999
1-2 .... 3.00

Domination Factor: Fantastic Four
Marvel, 1999
1-2 .... 3.00

Dominion
Eclipse, 1990
1-3 .... 3.00
4-6 .... 2.00

Dominion
Image, 2003
1-2 .... 3.00

Dominion: Conflict 1
Dark Horse, 1996
1-6 .... 3.00

Dominion: Phantom of the Audience
Dark Horse, 1994
1 .... 3.00

Dominique: Family Matters
Caliber
1 .... 3.00

Dominique: Killzone
Caliber, 1995
1 .... 3.00

Dominique: Protect and Serve
Caliber, 1995
1 .... 3.00

Dominique: White Knuckle Drive
Caliber
1 .... 3.00

Domino
Marvel, 1997
1-3 .... 2.00

Domino
Marvel, 2003
1-4 .... 3.00

Domino Chance
Chance, 1982
1 .... 3.00
1/2nd-9 .... 2.00

Domino Chance: Roach Extraordinaire
Amazing
1 .... 2.00

Domino Lady
Fantagraphics, 1990
1-3 .... 2.00

Domino Lady's Jungle Adventure
Fantagraphics, 1992
1-3 .... 3.00

Domu: A Child's Dream
Dark Horse, 1995
1-3 .... 6.00

Donald and Mickey
Gladstone, 1993
19 .... 2.00
20 .... 3.00
21-24 .... 2.00
25 .... 3.00
26-30 .... 2.00

Donald and Mickey in Disneyland
Dell, 1958
1 .... 105.00

Donald and Scrooge
Disney, 1992
1-3 .... 2.00

Donald Duck
Dell, 1952
26 .... 350.00
27-29 .... 100.00
30-44 .... 65.00
45 .... 125.00

Dogs of War

Doll Man Quarterly

Doll Parts

Dolls

Donald Duck Adventures

Donald and Mickey

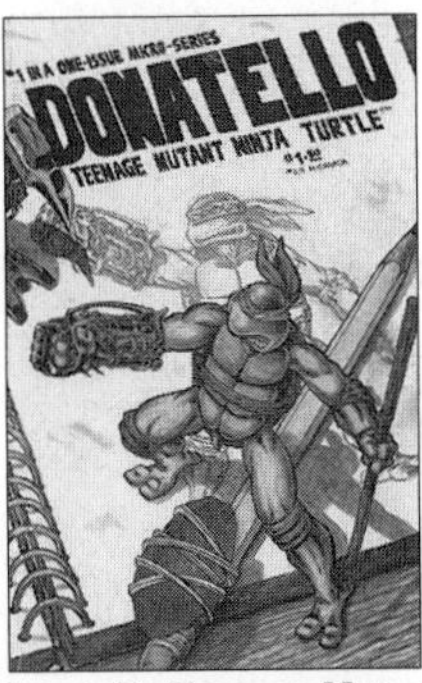

Donatello Teenage Mutant Ninja Turtle

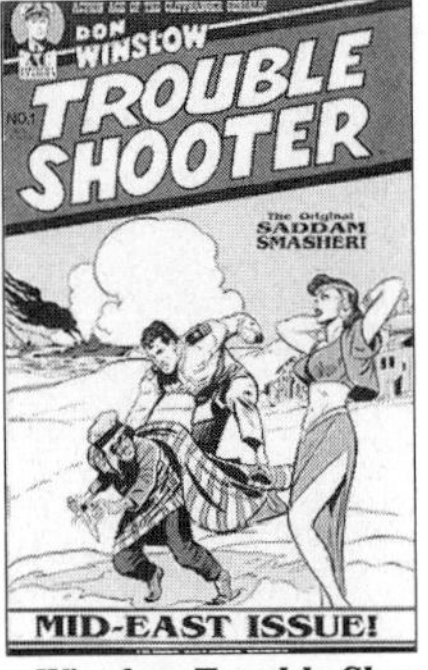

Don Winslow Trouble Shooter

☛Barks art
46 .... 175.00
☛Barks "Secret"
47-51 .... 65.00
52 .... 150.00
☛Barks "Lost"
53 .... 65.00
54 .... 125.00
☛Barks Forbid. Valley
55-58 .... 50.00
59-60 .... 125.00
☛Barks "Ants"
61-67 .... 40.00
68 .... 100.00
☛Barks art
69-70 .... 40.00
71-84 .... 30.00
85-120 .... 25.00
121-135 .... 20.00
136-150 .... 15.00
151-190 .... 10.00
191-210 .... 5.00
211-216 .... 3.00
217 .... 5.00
218-219 .... 10.00
220-228 .... 15.00
229-240 .... 8.00
241-245 .... 15.00
246 .... 17.00
247-249 .... 5.00
250 .... 8.00
251-260 .... 4.00
261-279 .... 3.00
280-285 .... 2.00
286 .... 3.00
287-307 .... 2.00

Donald Duck and Friends

Gemstone, 2003

308-335 .... 3.00

Donald Duck Adventures

Gemstone, 2003

1-14 .... 8.00

Donald Duck Adventures

Disney, 1990

1 .... 3.00
2-38 .... 2.00

Donald Duck Adventures

Gladstone, 1987

1 .... 3.00
2-25 .... 2.00
26 .... 3.00
27-29 .... 2.00
30 .... 3.00
31-48 .... 2.00

Donald Duck Album

Gold Key, 1963

1 .... 50.00
2 .... 40.00

Donald Duck & Mickey Mouse

Gladstone, 1995

1-7 .... 2.00

Donald Duck Beach Party

Gold Key, 1965

1 .... 40.00

Donald Duck Beach Party

Dell, 1954

1 .... 100.00
2 .... 65.00
3-6 .... 55.00

Donald Duck Digest

Gladstone, 1986

1 .... 4.00
2-5 .... 3.00

Donald Duck Fun Book

Dell, 1953

1 .... 320.00
2 .... 240.00

Donald Duck in Disneyland

Dell, 1955

1 .... 110.00

Donald Duck (Whitman Storybook)

Whitman, 1935

978 .... 2,000.00
☛First Whitman

Donatello Teenage Mutant Ninja Turtle

Mirage, 1986

1 .... 2.00

Don Fortune Magazine

Don Fortune, 1946

1 .... 120.00
2 .... 100.00
3-6 .... 80.00

Donielle: Enslaved at Sea

Raging Rhino, 1993

1-9 .... 3.00

Don Martin Magazine

Welsh

1-3 .... 3.00

Donna Matrix

Reactor, 1993

1 .... 4.00

Donna Mia

Avatar, 1996

1-3 .... 3.00

Donna's Day

Slab-O-Concrete

1 .... 1.00

Don Newcombe
Fawcett, 1950
1 .... 145.00

Don Winslow of the Navy
Merwil, 1937
1 .... 1,850.00

Don Winslow of the Navy
Fawcett, 1943
1 .... 750.00
2 .... 360.00
3 .... 225.00
4-6 .... 185.00
7-10 .... 140.00
11-20 .... 100.00
21-30 .... 75.00
31-40 .... 60.00
41-60 .... 46.00
61-73 .... 38.00

Don Winslow Trouble Shooter
AC
1 .... 3.00

Doofer
Fantagraphics
1 .... 3.00

Doofus
Fantagraphics, 1994
1-2 .... 3.00

Doom
Marvel, 2000
1-3 .... 3.00

Doom Force Special
DC, 1992
1 .... 3.00

Doom Patrol
DC, 1964
86 .... 135.00
87 .... 70.00
88-90 .... 50.00
91-98 .... 40.00
99 .... 60.00
100 .... 75.00
101-120 .... 25.00
121 .... 45.00
☛Doom Patrol dies
122-124 .... 2.00

Doom Patrol
DC, 1987
1 .... 3.00
2-18 .... 2.00
19 .... 3.00
20-49 .... 2.00
50 .... 3.00
51-56 .... 2.00
57 .... 3.00
58-87 .... 2.00
Ann 1 .... 1.00
Ann 2 .... 4.00

Doom Patrol
DC, 2001
1-22 .... 3.00

Doom Patrol
DC, 2004
1-18 .... 3.00

Doom Patrol and Suicide Squad Special
DC, 1988
1 .... 2.00

Doomsday + 1
Charlton, 1975
1 .... 8.00
2 .... 5.00
3-6 .... 4.00
7-12 .... 3.00

Doomsday + 1
Avalon
1-2 .... 3.00

Doomsday Annual
DC, 1995
1 .... 4.00

Doomsday Squad
Fantagraphics, 1986
1-2 .... 2.00
3 .... 3.00
4-7 .... 2.00

Doom's IV
Image, 1994
½-4 .... 3.00

Doom: The Emperor Returns
Marvel, 2002
1-3 .... 3.00

Doom 2099
Marvel, 1993
1 .... 3.00
2-10 .... 2.00
11-17 .... 1.00
18-25 .... 2.00
25/Variant 3.00
26-29 .... 2.00
29/Variant 4.00
30-39 .... 2.00
39/Variant 4.00
40-44 .... 2.00

Doorman
Caliber
1 .... 3.00

DoorMan (Cult)
Cult, 1993
1-4 .... 3.00
Ashcan 1 .... 1.00

Doofus

Doom

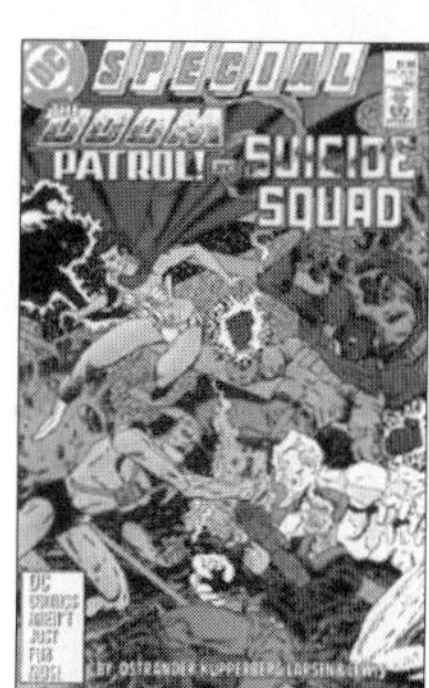

Doom Patrol and Suicide Squad Special

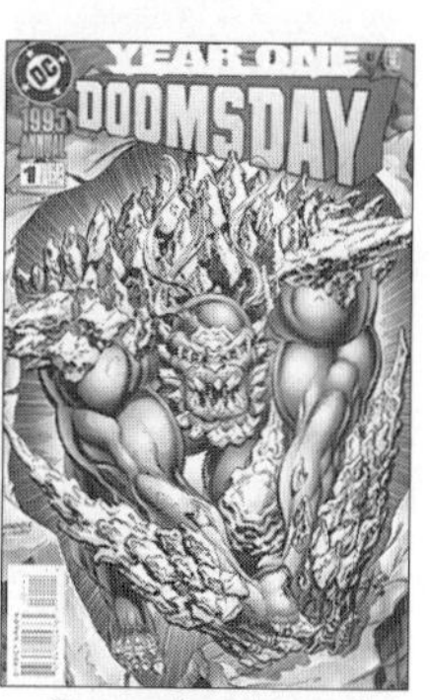

Doomsday Annual

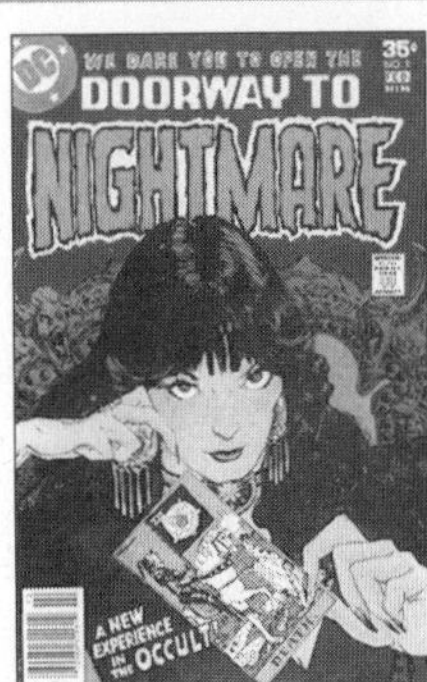

Doorway to Nightmare

Dork

Dorkier Images

Dork Tower

Doorman: Family Secrets
Caliber

1 .... 3.00

Doorway to Nightmare
DC, 1978

1 .... 7.00
2-5 .... 3.00

Dope Comix
Kitchen Sink

1 .... 5.00
2-5 .... 3.00

Dopey Duck
Timely, 1945

1 .... 68.00
2 .... 55.00

Dopin' Dan
Last Gasp, 1972

1 .... 5.00
2-3 .... 3.00

Doris Nelson: Atomic Housewife
Jake Comics, 1995

1 .... 3.00

Dork
Slave Labor, 1993

1-7 .... 3.00
8 .... 4.00
9 .... 3.00

Dork House Comics
Parody

1 .... 3.00

Dorkier Images
Parody, 1993

1-1/Variant 3.00

Dork Tower
Dork Storm, 1998

1 .... 4.00
2-31 .... 3.00

Dothenridge: Tales of the Vampire Monarchy
Dothenridge

½ 2.00

Dotty Dripple Comics
Harvey, 1946

1 .... 22.00
2 .... 14.00
3-5 .... 9.00
6-10 .... 8.00
11-24 .... 6.00

Double Action Comics
DC, 1940

2 .... 10,000.00

Double Comics
Elliott

1 .... 925.00
2 .... 700.00
3 .... 500.00

Double-Dare Adventures
Harvey, 1966

1 .... 20.00
2 .... 16.00

Double Dragon
Marvel, 1991

1-6 .... 1.00

Double Edge: Alpha
Marvel, 1995

1 .... 5.00

Double Edge: Omega
Marvel, 1995

1 .... 5.00

Double Image
Image, 2001

1-5 .... 3.00

Double Impact
High Impact, 1995

1-1/Ltd 4.00
2-5 .... 3.00

Double Impact
High Impact, 1996

0 .... 3.00
1 .... 4.00
2-7 .... 3.00

Double Impact: Art Attack
ABC

1 .... 3.00
1/A-1/B 4.00

Double Impact: Assassins for Hire
High Impact, 1997

1 .... 3.00

Double Impact Bikini Special
High Impact, 1998

1 .... 3.00

Double Impact: From the Ashes
High Impact

1 .... 3.00
2 .... 6.00

Double Impact/Hellina
ABC, 1996

1 .... 3.00
1/Gold 5.00
1/Nude-1/Variant 3.00

Double Impact: One Step Beyond
High Impact, 1998

1 .... 3.00
1/Variant 20.00

Double Impact: Raising Hell
ABC, 1997

1 .... 3.00
1/Nude 4.00

Double Impact: Raw
ABC, 1997

1 .... 3.00
1/A-1/2nd 4.00
2-3 .... 3.00

Double Impact: Raw
ABC, 1998

1/Nude 3.00

Double Impact: Suicide Run
High Impact, 1997

1 .... 3.00
1/A-1/Nude 4.00

Double Impact: Trigger Happy
High Impact, 1997

1-1/B 3.00
1/Ltd. 4.00

Double Life of Private Strong
Archie, 1959

1 .... 340.00
2 .... 160.00

Double Talk
Feature, 1962

1 .... 85.00

Double Trouble
St. John, 1957

1 .... 20.00

Double Up
Eliot, 1941

1 .... 450.00

Dover the Bird
Famous Funnies, 1955

1 .... 30.00

Down
Image, 2006

1-4 .... 3.00

Down with Crime
Fawcett, 1951

1 .... 180.00
2 .... 95.00
3-7 .... 80.00

Do You Believe In Nightmares
St. John, 1957

1 .... 290.00
2 .... 170.00

D.P.7
Marvel, 1986

1-32 .... 1.00
Ann. 1 .... 2.00

Dracula
Dell, 1962

2 .... 20.00
3-4 .... 12.00
6-8 .... 7.00

Dracula
Eternity

1-4 .... 3.00

Dracula (Bram Stoker's...)
Topps, 1992

1 .... 3.00
1/Variant 4.00
2-4 .... 3.00

Dracula 3-D
3-D Zone

1 .... 4.00

Dracula Chronicles
Topps

1-3 .... 3.00

Dracula in Hell
Apple, 1992

1-2 .... 3.00

Dracula Lives! (Magazine)
Marvel, 1973

1 .... 5.00
2 .... 4.00
3-13 .... 3.00
Ann 1 .... 25.00

Dracula: Lord of the Undead
Marvel, 1998

1-3 .... 3.00

Dracula: Return of the Impaler
Slave Labor, 1993

1-4 .... 3.00

Dracula's Daughter
Fantagraphics, 1991

1 .... 3.00

Dracula's Revenge
Idea & Design Works, 2004

1-2 .... 4.00

Dracula: The Lady in the Tomb
Eternity

1 .... 3.00

Dracula: The Suicide Club
Adventure, 1992

1-4 .... 3.00

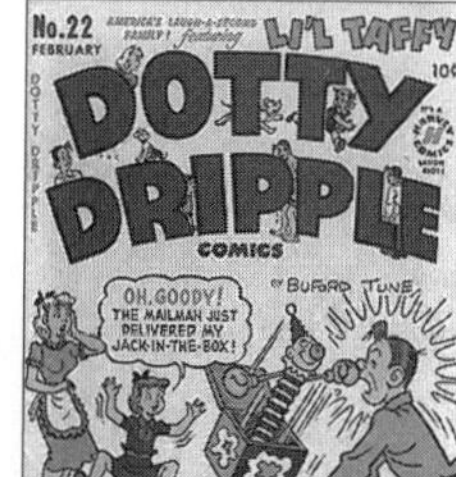

Dotty Dripple Comics

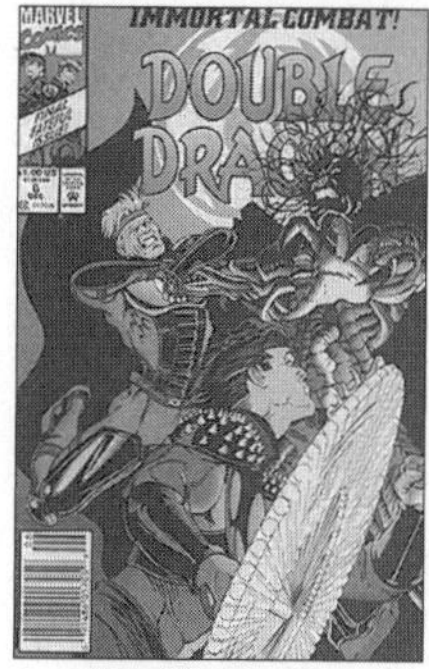

Double Dragon

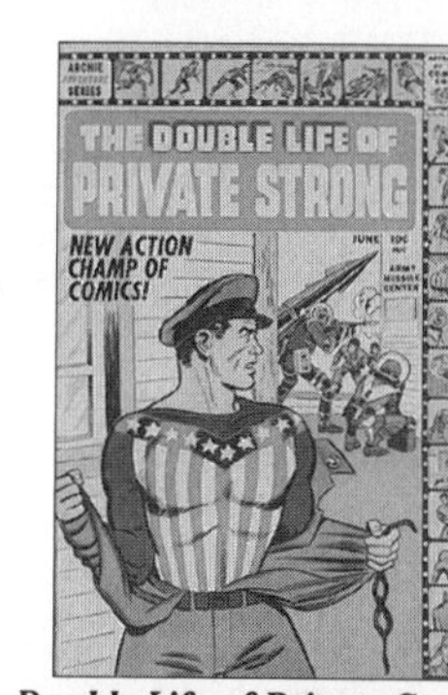

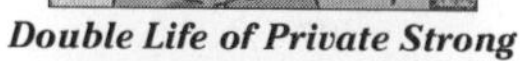

Double Life of Private Strong

Do You Believe In Nightmares

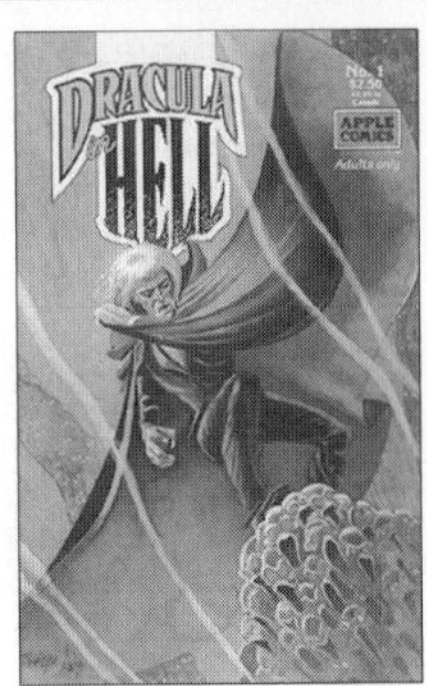
Dracula in Hell

Dragonball

Dragonball Z

Dragon Chiang

Dracula vs. Zorro
Topps, 1993
1-2 .... 4.00

Dracula vs. Zorro (Vol. 2)
Topps, 1994
1 .... 6.00

Dracula vs. Zorro (Vol. 3)
Image, 1998
1-2 .... 3.00

Dracula: Vlad the Impaler
Topps, 1993
1-3 .... 3.00

Draculina
Draculina
1 .... 3.00

Draculina's Cozy Coffin
Draculina, 1994
1-2 .... 3.00

Draft
Marvel, 1988
1 .... 2.00

Drag Comics (Pete Millar's...)
Sham
1 .... 6.00
2 .... 5.00
3-4 .... 4.00

Drag 'n' Wheels
Charlton, 1968
30-35 .... 12.00
36-59 .... 10.00

Dragon
Comics Interview, 1987
1-4 .... 2.00

Dragon
Image, 1996
1-5 .... 2.00

Dragon Arms
Antarctic, 2002
1-6 .... 4.00

Dragon Arms: Chaos Blade
Antarctic, 2004
1-6 .... 3.00

Dragon Arms Stand Alone
Antarctic, 2005
1 .... 3.00

Dragonball
Viz, 1998
1-7 .... 4.00
8-12 .... 3.00

Dragonball Part 2
Viz, 1999
1 .... 4.00
2-15 .... 3.00

Dragonball Part 3
Viz, 2000
1-14 .... 3.00

Dragonball Part 4
Viz, 2001
1-10 .... 3.00

Dragonball Part 5
Viz, 2002
1-7 .... 3.00

Dragonball Part 6
Viz, 2003
1-2 .... 4.00

Dragonball Z
Viz, 1998
1-5 .... 4.00
6-10 .... 3.00

Dragonball Z Part 2
Viz, 1998
1 .... 4.00
2-14 .... 3.00

Dragonball Z Part 3
Viz, 2000
1-10 .... 3.00

Dragonball Z Part 4
Viz, 2000
1-13 .... 3.00

Dragonball Z Part 5
Viz, 2002
1-12 .... 3.00

Dragon: Blood & Guts
Image, 1995
1-3 .... 3.00

Dragon Chiang
Eclipse, 1991
1 .... 4.00

Dragonfire
Nightwynd
1-4 .... 3.00

Dragonfire
Nightwynd, 1992
1-4 .... 3.00

Dragonfire: The Classified Files
Nightwynd
1-4 .... 3.00

Dragonfire: The Early Years
Night Wynd
1-8 .... 3.00

Dragonfire: UFO Wars
Nightwynd
1-3 .... 3.00

Dragonflight
Eclipse, 1991
1-3 .... 5.00

Dragon Flux
Antarctic, 1996
2-3 .... 3.00

Dragonfly
AC, 1985
1-8 .... 2.00

Dragonforce
Aircel, 1988
1-13 .... 2.00

Dragonforce Chronicles
Aircel, 1989
1-5 .... 3.00

Dragon Head
Tokyopop, 2006
1 .... 10.00

Dragonheart
Topps, 1996
1 .... 3.00
2 .... 5.00

Dragon Hunter
Tokyopop, 2003
1-13 .... 10.00

Dragon Knights
Slave Labor, 1998
1-3 .... 2.00

Dragon Knights
Tokyopop, 2002
1-21 .... 10.00

Dragon Lady
Dragon Lady, 1985
1-2 .... 7.00
3-8 .... 6.00

Dragonlance
DC, 1988
1-2 .... 2.00
3-5 .... 1.00
6-34 .... 2.00

Dragonlance Chronicles: Dragons of Autumn Twilight
Devil's Due, 2005
1-2 .... 3.00
2/Special 6.00
3 .... 3.00
3/Special 6.00
4 .... 3.00
4/Special 6.00
5 .... 3.00
5/Special 6.00
6 .... 3.00
6/Special 6.00
7 .... 3.00
7/Special 6.00
8 .... 3.00
8/Variant 6.00

Dragonlance Chronicles: Dragons of Winter Night
Devil's Due, 2006
1 .... 5.00
1/Special 9.00
2 .... 5.00
2/Special 9.00
3 .... 5.00
3/Special 9.00

Dragonlance Comic Book
TSR
1 .... 1.00

Dragonlance Saga
TSR, 1987
1-5 .... 10.00

Dragon Lines
Marvel, 1993
1 .... 3.00
2-4 .... 2.00

Dragon Lines: Way of the Warrior
Marvel, 1993
1-2 .... 2.00

Dragon of the Valkyr
Rak, 1989
1-3 .... 2.00

Dragon Quest
Silverwolf, 1986
1-2 .... 2.00

Dragonring
Aircel, 1986
1-6 .... 2.00

Dragonring
Aircel, 1986
1-15 .... 2.00

Dragonrok Saga
Hanthercraft
1-10 .... 3.00

Dragon's Bane
Hall of Heroes
1 .... 3.00
Ashcan 1 .... 5.00

Dragon's Claws
Marvel, 1988
1-10 .... 2.00

Dragonflight

Dragonfly

Dragonforce Chronicles

Dragonheart

Dragonlance

Dragonslayer

Dragon Strike

Drakuun

Dragons in the Moon
Aircel, 1990
1-4 .... 3.00

Dragon's Lair: Singe's Revenge
CrossGen, 2003
1-3 .... 3.00

Dragonslayer
Marvel, 1981
1-2 .... 2.00

Dragon's Star
Matrix, 1986
1-3 .... 2.00

Dragon's Star 2
Caliber, 1994
1-3 .... 3.00

Dragon's Teeth
Dragon's Teeth
1 .... 3.00

Dragon Strike
Marvel, 1994
1 .... 2.00

Dragonstrike Prime
Illusion, 1996
2 .... 2.00

Dragon Voice
Tokyopop, 2004
1-6 .... 10.00

Dragon Wars
Ironcat, 1998
1-7 .... 3.00

Drag-Strip Hotrodders
Charlton, 1963
1 .... 40.00
2-16 .... 25.00

Drain
Image, 2006
1-1/Variant 3.00

Drake: Demon Box
Image, 2003
1 .... 3.00

Drakkon Wars
Realm, 1997
0 .... 3.00

Drakuun
Dark Horse, 1997
1-24 .... 3.00

Drama
Sirius Entertainment, 1994
1 .... 4.00
1/Ltd. 12.00

Dramacon
Tokyopop, 2005
1 .... 10.00

Drawing on your Nightmares: Halloween 2003 Special
Dark Horse, 2003
1 .... 3.00

Drawn & Quarterly
Drawn & Quarterly, 1990
1-2 .... 3.00
3-8 .... 4.00

Drax the Destroyer
Marvel, 2005
1-4 .... 3.00

Dr. Blink, Super-Hero Shrink
Dork Storm, 2005
1-2 .... 3.00

Dreadlands
Marvel, 1992
1-4 .... 4.00

Dread of Night
Hamilton, 1991
1-2 .... 4.00

Dreadstar
Marvel, 1982
1 .... 3.00
2-49 .... 2.00
50 .... 3.00
51-64 .... 2.00
Ann 1 .... 3.00

Dreadstar
Malibu, 1994
½ 2.00
1/Gold-6 .... 3.00

Dreadstar & Co.
Marvel, 1985
1-6 .... 1.00

Dream Angel
Angel Entertainment, 1996
0 .... 3.00

Dream Angel and Angel Girl
Angel
1 .... 3.00

Dream Angel: The Quantum Dreamer
Angel
0-2 .... 3.00

Dream Book of Love
Magazine Enterprises, 1954
1-2 .... 50.00
3 .... 40.00

Dream Corridor (Harlan Ellison's...)
Dark Horse, 1995
1 .... 4.00

2-5 .... 3.00
Book 1 .... 19.00
Special 1 .... 5.00

Dream Corridor Quarterly (Harlan Ellison's...)

Dark Horse, 1996

1 .... 6.00

Dreamer

DC, 2000

1 .... 8.00

Dreamery

Eclipse, 1986

1-14 .... 2.00

Dreaming

DC, 1996

1-60 .... 3.00
Special 1 .... 6.00

Dreaming

Tokyopop, 2005

1 .... 10.00

Dreamland Chronicles

Astonish, 2004

1/Kunkel-1/Yeagle 4.00
2-3 .... 5.00

Dream Police

Marvel, 2005

1 .... 4.00
☛Straczynski series

Dream-Quest of Unknown Kadath (H.P. Lovecraft's...)

Mock Man, 1998

1-5 .... 3.00

Dreams Cannot Die!

Mark's Giant Economy Size, 1996

1 .... 18.00

Dreams 'n' Schemes of Col. Kilgore

Special Studio, 1991

1-2 .... 3.00

Dreams of a Dog

Rip Off, 1990

1 .... 2.00
2 .... 3.00

Dreams of Everyman

Rip Off, 1992

1 .... 3.00

Dreams of the Darkchylde

Darkchylde, 2000

1-1/A 4.00
1/B 10.00
1/C 6.00
1/D 10.00
1/E 15.00
1/F 5.00
2-6 .... 3.00

Dream Team

Malibu, 1995

1 .... 5.00

Dreamtime

Blind Bat, 1995

3 .... 0.00
1-2 .... 3.00

Dreamwalker

Dreamwalker, 1996

1-5 .... 3.00

Dreamwalker

Caliber, 1996

1-6 .... 3.00

Dreamwalker

Avatar, 1998

0 .... 3.00

Dreamwalker

Marvel

1 .... 7.00

Dreamwalker: Autumn Leaves

Avatar, 1999

1-2 .... 3.00

Dreamwalker: Carousel

Avatar, 1999

1-2 .... 3.00

Dreamwalker: Summer Rain

Avatar, 1999

1 .... 3.00

Dream Weaver

Robert Lankford, 1987

1 .... 2.00

Dream Weavers

Golden Realm Unlimited

1-2 .... 2.00

Dream Wolves

Dramenon, 1994

1-4 .... 3.00

Dream Wolves Swimsuit Bizarre

Gothic, 1995

0 .... 3.00

Dredd By Bisley

Fleetway-Quality

1 .... 6.00

Dredd Rules!

Fleetway-Quality

1 .... 4.00
2-20 .... 3.00

Drifter

Brainstorm

1 .... 3.00

Dreadlands

Dreadstar

Dreaming

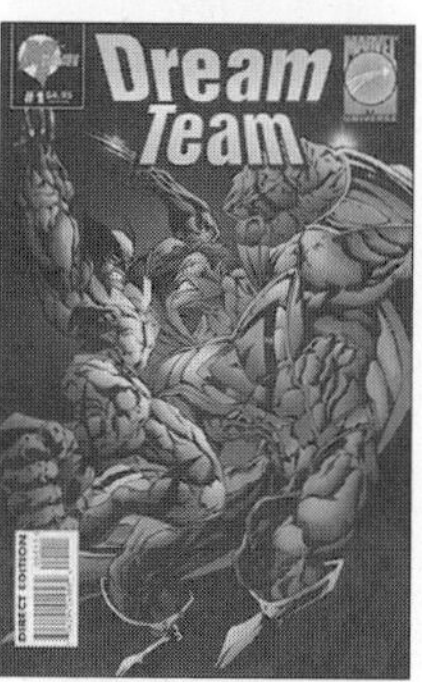

Dream Team

Drifters

Droids

Droopy

Duckman

Drifters
Cornerstone
1 .... 2.00

Drifters
Infinity, 1986
1 .... 2.00

Drive-In (Joe Lansdale's)
Avatar, 2003
1-4 .... 4.00

Droids
Marvel, 1986
1 .... 3.00
2-8 .... 2.00

Drool Magazine
Co. & Sons
1 .... 3.00

Droopy
Dark Horse, 1995
1-3 .... 3.00

Dropsie Avenue: The Neighborhood
Kitchen Sink, 1995
1 .... 16.00

Drug Wars
Pioneer
1 .... 2.00

Druid
Marvel, 1995
1 .... 3.00
2-4 .... 2.00

Drunken Fist
Jademan, 1988
1-54 .... 2.00

Dry Rot
Zolton
1 .... 3.00

Duck and Cover
Cat-Head
1-2 .... 2.00

Duckbots
Blackthorne, 1987
1-2 .... 2.00

Duckman
Dark Horse, 1990
1-Special 1 .... 2.00

Duckman
Topps, 1994
1-6 .... 3.00

Duckman: The Mob Frog Saga
Topps, 1994
1-3 .... 3.00

DuckTales
Gladstone, 1988
1-13 .... 2.00

DuckTales (Disney's...)
Disney, 1990
1-18 .... 2.00

Ducktales: The Movie
Disney
1 .... 6.00

Dudley
Prize, 1949
1 .... 70.00
2-3 .... 60.00

Dudley Do-Right
Charlton, 1970
1 .... 45.00
2 .... 18.00
3 .... 12.00
4-7 .... 10.00

Duel
Antarctic, 2005
0-1 .... 3.00

Duel Masters
Dreamwave, 2003
1 .... 3.00
1/Dynamic 6.00
1/A 3.00
1/B 6.00
2-4 .... 3.00
5 .... 4.00
6-8 .... 3.00

Dumb-Ass Express
McMann & Tate
1 .... 3.00

Dumm $2099
Parody
1 .... 3.00

Dunc and Loo
Dell, 1961
1 .... 50.00
2 .... 40.00
3-5 .... 35.00
6-8 .... 25.00

Dune
Marvel, 1985
1-3 .... 2.00

Dung Boys
Kitchen Sink, 1996
1-3 .... 3.00

Dungeon
NBM, 2002
1 .... 3.00

Dungeoneers
Silverwolf, 1986
1-4 .... 2.00

Dungeons and Dragons: In the Shadow of Dragons
Kenzer and Company, 2001
1-8 .... 3.00

Dungeons & Dragons: Where Shadows Fall
Kenzer and Company, 2003
1-5 .... 4.00

Duplex Planet Illustrated
Fantagraphics, 1993
1-14 .... 3.00
15 .... 5.00

Durango Kid
Magazine Enterprises, 1949
1 .... 300.00
2 .... 200.00
3 .... 165.00
4-5 .... 100.00
6-10 .... 50.00
11-30 .... 40.00
31-41 .... 35.00

Durango Kid
AC
1-2 .... 3.00
3 .... 5.00

Dusk
Deadwood
1 .... 3.00

Dusty Star
Image, 1997
0-1 .... 3.00
2 .... 4.00

Dutch Decker and the Voodoo Queen
Caliber
1 .... 3.00

DV8
DC, 1996
0-14/B 3.00
14/C 5.00
15-Ann 1 .... 3.00
Ann 1999 .... 4.00

DV8 Rave
Image, 1996
1 .... 2.00

DV8 vs. Black Ops
Image, 1997
1-3 .... 3.00

Dyke's Delight
Fanny
1-2 .... 3.00

Dylan Dog
Dark Horse, 1999
1-6 .... 5.00

Dynamic Classics
DC, 1978
1 .... 4.00

Dynamic Comics
Harry A. Chesler, 1941
11 .... 875.00
12 .... 450.00
13 .... 400.00
14-15 .... 300.00
16-17 .... 275.00
18-24 .... 200.00

Dynamite
Comic Media, 1953
1 .... 48.00
2 .... 40.00
3-5 .... 36.00
6-9 .... 30.00

Dynamo
Tower, 1966
1 .... 35.00
2-3 .... 25.00
4 .... 40.00

Dynamo Joe
First, 1986
1 .... 2.00
2-11 .... 1.00
12-15 .... 2.00
Special 1 .... 1.00

Dynomutt
Marvel, 1977
1 .... 10.00
2 .... 5.00
3-6 .... 3.00

Dystopik Snomen
Slave Labor, 1994
1 .... 5.00

Dystopik Snomen
Slave Labor, 1995
1-2 .... 2.00

Eagle
Fox, 1941
1 .... 1,600.00
2 .... 650.00
3-4 .... 450.00

Eagle
Rural Home, 1945
1 .... 325.00
2 .... 165.00

Eagle
Crystal, 1986
1-23 .... 2.00

Eagle
Comic Zone, 1992
1-3 .... 3.00

Eagles Dare
Aager, 1994
1-2 .... 2.00

Dudley Do-Right

Dusty Star

DV8

Dynamic Comics

Dynamo

Eagles Dare

Earthlore

Earthworm Jim

Eagle: The Dark Mirror Saga

Comic Zone, 1992

1-3 .... 3.00

Early Days of the Southern Knights

Comics Interview, 1986

1-4 .... 5.00
5 .... 6.00
6-8 .... 7.00

Earth C.O.R.E.

Independent

1 .... 2.00

Earth 4 (Vol. 2)

Continuity, 1993

1-4 .... 3.00

Earth 4 Deathwatch 2000

Continuity, 1993

0-3 .... 3.00

Earthlore

Eternity

1-2 .... 2.00

Earth Man on Venus, An

Avon, 1951

1 .... 875.00

Earthworm Jim

Marvel, 1995

1-4 .... 2.00

Earth X

Marvel, 1999

0 .... 4.00
0/A 5.00
0/B 4.00
0/C 5.00
1 .... 3.00
1/A 5.00
1/B 30.00
1/C 70.00
2-12 .... 3.00
13 .... 4.00

Earth X Sketchbook

Marvel, 1999

1 .... 5.00

East Meets West

Innovation, 1990

1 .... 3.00

Easy Way

Idea & Design Works, 2005

1-4 .... 4.00

Eating Raoul

Kim Deitch, 1982

1 .... 2.00

Eat-Man

Viz, 1997

1-6 .... 3.00

Eat-Man Second Course

Viz, 1998

1 .... 3.00
2-3 .... 4.00
4-5 .... 3.00

Eberron: Eye of the Wolf

Devil's Due, 2006

1 .... 5.00
1/Special 9.00

Eb'nn

Now, 1986

3-6 .... 2.00

Eb'nn the Raven

Crowquill

1-2 .... 3.00

Ebony Warrior

Africa Rising, 1993

1 .... 2.00

E.C. Classic Reprints

East Coast Comix, 1973

1 .... 4.00
2-12 .... 3.00

EC Classics

Cochran

1-6 .... 5.00

Echo

Image, 2000

0-5 .... 3.00

Echo of Futurepast

Continuity, 1984

1-9 .... 3.00

Eclipse Graphic Album Series

Eclipse, 1978

1 .... 7.00
1/2nd-1/3rd 6.00
2 .... 5.00
3 .... 7.00
4 .... 6.00
5 .... 7.00
6 .... 6.00
7 .... 8.00
7/HC 20.00
7/2nd 8.00
7/3rd 9.00
8 .... 6.00
9-10 .... 14.00
10/HC-11 .... 25.00
12 .... 8.00
12/HC 15.00
12/Ltd 25.00
13 .... 9.00
14 .... 5.00
15 .... 4.00
16 .... 5.00
17 .... 7.00
18 .... 5.00
19 .... 15.00

20 .... 5.00
21 .... 4.00
22-24 .... 5.00
25-26 .... 9.00
27 .... 6.00
28 .... 9.00
29 .... 15.00
30 .... 9.00
30/HC 30.00
31 .... 7.00
31/Ltd. 30.00
32-33 .... 10.00
34 .... 4.00
35 .... 8.00
36 .... 5.00
37 .... 4.00
38 .... 9.00
39-41 .... 5.00
42 .... 9.00
43 .... 8.00
44 .... 6.00
45 .... 11.00
46 .... 8.00
47 .... 15.00
48 .... 10.00
49 .... 7.00
50 .... 13.00
51 .... 8.00
52 .... 5.00

Eclipse Magazine
Eclipse, 1981
1-8 .... 3.00

Eclipse Monthly
Eclipse, 1983
1-10 .... 2.00

Eclipso
DC, 1992
1-5 .... 2.00
6-14 .... 1.00
15-18 .... 2.00
Ann 1 .... 3.00

Eclipso: The Darkness Within
DC, 1992
1-2 .... 3.00

Ectokid
Marvel, 1993
1 .... 3.00
2-9 .... 2.00

Ectokid Unleashed!
Marvel, 1994
1 .... 3.00

Ed
3CG Comics, 1997
1 .... 3.00

Eddie Stanky Baseball Hero
Fawcett, 1951
1 .... 200.00

Eddy Current
Mad Dog, 1987
1-12 .... 3.00

Eden Descendants
Quester Entertainment
1 .... 4.00

Eden Matrix
Adhesive
1/A-1/B 3.00

Eden's Trail
Marvel, 2003
1-5 .... 3.00

Edgar Allan Poe
Eternity, 1988
1-5 .... 2.00

Edge
Silverwolf, 1987
1-2 .... 2.00

Edge
Greater Mercury, 1989
1-11 .... 2.00

Edge
Malibu, 1994
1-3 .... 3.00

Edge of Chaos
Pacific, 1983
1-3 .... 1.00

Ed the Happy Clown
Drawn & Quarterly, 2005
1-3 .... 3.00

Eek! the Cat
Hamilton, 1994
1-3 .... 2.00

Eerie
Avon, 1947
1 .... 850.00
1/2nd 400.00
2 .... 500.00
3 .... 400.00
4-6 .... 350.00
7-8 .... 285.00
9-10 .... 240.00
11-13 .... 200.00
14-17 .... 165.00

Eerie
Warren, 1965
1 .... 175.00
1/2nd 35.00
2 .... 100.00
3 .... 40.00
4-6 .... 30.00
7-10 .... 28.00

Earth X

E.C. Classic Reprints

Echo of Futurepast

Eclipse Magazine

Eclipse Monthly

Eddy Current

Eerie

Eerie Tales

11-16 ....18.00
17 ....60.00
☛Scarce
18-39 ....18.00
40 ....6.00
41-60 ....12.00
61-70 ....10.00
71-80 ....9.00
81 ....70.00
☛Frazetta cover
82-100 ....9.00
101-139 ....8.00
YB 1970 ....36.00
YB 1971 ....25.00
YB 1972 ....18.00

Eerie

I.W.

1 ....24.00
2 ....17.00

Eerie Adventures

Ziff-Davis, 1951

1 ....150.00

Eerie Queerie!

Tokyopop, 2004

1-4 ....10.00

Eerie Tales

Super

12 ....15.00

Egon

Dark Horse, 1998

1-2 ....3.00

Egypt

DC, 1995

1-7 ....3.00

Eh!

Charlton, 1953

1 ....150.00
2 ....90.00
3-4 ....75.00
5 ....60.00
6-7 ....50.00

Ehlissa

Highland Graphics, 1992

1-33 ....2.00

Eightball

Fantagraphics, 1993

1 ....10.00
1/2nd 5.00
1/3rd 4.00
1/4th 3.00
2 ....6.00
3-4 ....5.00
5-8 ....4.00
9-15 ....3.00
16 ....4.00
17-18 ....3.00
19 ....4.00
20-21 ....5.00
22-23 ....3.00

Eighth Wonder

Dark Horse, 1997

1 ....3.00

Eight Legged Freaks

WildStorm, 2002

1 ....7.00

80 Page Giant Magazine

DC, 1964

1 ....295.00
2 ....150.00
3-6 ....125.00
7 ....150.00
8 ....265.00
☛Secret Origins
9-11 ....125.00
12-15 ....80.00

86 Voltz: Dead Girl One-Shot

Image, 2005

1 ....6.00

Ekos Preview

Aspen, 2003

1 ....8.00

El Arsenal Unknown Enemy

Arcana, 2005

1-2 ....3.00

El Cazador

CrossGen, 2003

1-6 ....3.00

El Cazador: Blackjack Tom

CrossGen, 2004

1 ....3.00

El Condün Asesino (Ralf König's...)

Vibora

1-2 ....2.00

El Diablo

DC, 1989

1 ....3.00
2-16 ....2.00

El Diablo

DC, 2001

1-4 ....3.00

Electric Fear

Sparks, 1984

1-2 ....2.00

Electric Girl

Mighty Gremlin, 1998

1 ....4.00
2-3 ....3.00

Electric Warrior

DC, 1986

1-18 ....2.00

Electropolis
Image, 2001

1-3 .... 3.00

Elektra (1st Series)
Marvel, 1995

1 .... 4.00
2-4 .... 3.00

Elektra (2nd Series)
Marvel, 1996

-1 .... 2.00
1 .... 4.00
1/A-3 .... 3.00
4-19 .... 2.00

Elektra (3rd Series)
Marvel, 2001

1 .... 4.00
2-2/A 3.00
3-3/Nude 10.00
4-35 .... 3.00

Elektra & Wolverine: The Redeemer
Marvel, 2002

1-3 .... 6.00

Elektra: Assassin
Marvel, 1986

1-8 .... 3.00

Elektra Battlebook
Marvel, 1998

1 .... 4.00

Elektra/Cyblade
Image, 1997

1-1/A 3.00

Elektra: Glimpse & Echo
Marvel, 2002

1-4 .... 3.00

Elektra Lives Again
Marvel, 1991

1 .... 25.00

Elektra Megazine
Marvel, 1996

1-2 .... 4.00

Elektra Saga
Marvel, 1984

1-4 .... 4.00

Elektra: The Hand
Marvel, 2004

1-5 .... 3.00

Elektra: The Movie
Marvel, 2005

1 .... 6.00

Elementals
Comico, 1984

1 .... 3.00
2-29 .... 2.00
Special 1 .... 3.00
Special 2 .... 2.00

Elementals
Comico, 1989

1 .... 3.00
2-3 .... 2.00
4-41 .... 3.00

Elementals
Comico, 1995

1-3 .... 3.00

Elementals: Ghost of a Chance
Comico, 1995

1 .... 6.00

Elementals: How the War Was Won
Comico, 1996

1-2 .... 3.00

Elementals Lingerie
Comico, 1996

1 .... 3.00

Elementals Sex Special
Comico, 1991

1/Gold 5.00
1-4 .... 3.00

Elementals Sex Special
Comico, 1997

1 .... 3.00

Elemental's Sexy Lingerie Special
Comico, 1993

1/A 3.00
1/B 6.00

Elementals Swimsuit Spectacular 1996
Comico, 1996

1/Gold 4.00
1 .... 3.00

Elementals: The Vampires' Revenge
Comico, 1996

1-2 .... 3.00

Elephantmen
Image, 2006

0-5 .... 3.00

Eleven or One
Sirius Entertainment, 1995

1 .... 4.00
1/2nd 3.00

All comics prices listed are for NEAR MINT condition.

Egon

Eightball

El Diablo

Electric Girl

Electric Warrior

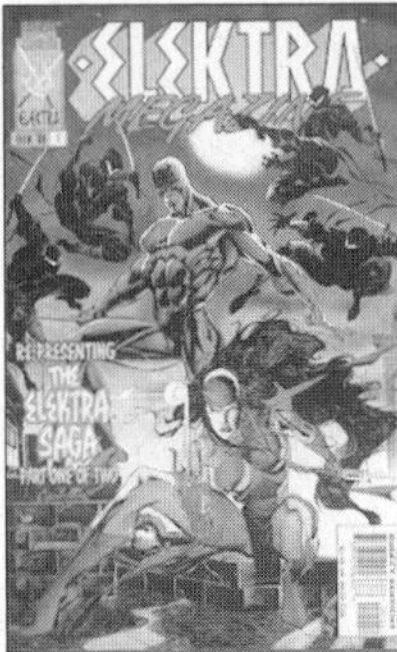

Elektra Megazine

Elfheim

Elfin Romance

Elfheim
Nightwynd, 1991

1-4 .... 3.00

Elfheim (Vol. 2)
Nightwynd

1-4 .... 3.00

Elfheim (Vol. 3)
Nightwynd

1-4 .... 3.00

Elfheim (Vol. 4)
Nightwynd

3-4 .... 0.00
1-2 .... 3.00

Elfheim: Dragon Dream
Night Wynd, 1993

1-4 .... 3.00

Elfin Romance
Mt. Wilson, 1994

1-6 .... 2.00
7 .... 3.00

Elflord
Aircel, 1986

1-8 .... 2.00

Elflord (2nd Series)
Aircel, 1986

1-20 .... 2.00
21 .... 5.00
22-31 .... 2.00

Elflord (3rd Series)
Night Wynd

1-4 .... 3.00

Elflord (4th Series)
Warp, 1997

1-4 .... 3.00

Elflord (5th Series)
Warp, 1997

1-7 .... 3.00

Elflord Chronicles
Aircel, 1990

1-12 .... 3.00

Elflord: Dragon's Eye
Night Wynd, 1993

1-3 .... 3.00

Elflord the Return
Mad Monkey, 1996

1 .... 7.00

Elflord: The Return of the King
Night Wynd

1-4 .... 3.00

Elflore
Nightwynd

1-4 .... 3.00

Elflore (Vol. 2)
Nightwynd

1-4 .... 3.00

Elflore (Vol. 3)
Nightwynd

1-4 .... 3.00

Elflore: High Seas
Night Wynd, 1993

1-3 .... 3.00

Elfquest
Warp, 1978

1 .... 32.00
1/2nd 12.00
1/3rd 8.00
1/4th 5.00
2 .... 18.00
2/2nd 6.00
2/3rd 4.00
2/4th 3.00
3 .... 18.00
3/2nd-3/4th 3.00
4 .... 16.00
4/2nd 5.00
4/3rd 4.00
4/4th 3.00
5 .... 16.00
5/2nd-5/3rd 3.00
6 .... 13.00
6/2nd 4.00
6/3rd 3.00
7 .... 10.00
7/2nd 4.00
7/3rd 3.00
8 .... 10.00
8/2nd 4.00
8/3rd 3.00
9 .... 10.00
9/2nd 4.00
9/3rd 3.00
10-15 .... 8.00
16 .... 10.00
17-21 .... 7.00

Elfquest
Marvel, 1985

1 .... 4.00
2-5 .... 3.00
6-32 .... 2.00

Elfquest

Warp, 1996

1 .... 6.00
2-31 .... 5.00
32-33 .... 3.00

Elfquest (Warp Reprints)

Warp, 1989

1-4 .... 2.00

Elfquest 25th Anniversary Edition

DC, 2003

1 .... 3.00

Elfquest: Blood of Ten Chiefs

Warp, 1993

1-20 .... 3.00

Elfquest: Hidden Years

Warp, 1992

1-29 .... 3.00

Elfquest: Jink

Warp, 1994

1-12 .... 3.00

Elfquest: Kahvi

Warp, 1995

1-6 .... 2.00

Elfquest: Kings Cross

Warp, 1997

1-2 .... 3.00

Elfquest: Kings of the Broken Wheel

Warp, 1990

1 .... 3.00
2-9 .... 2.00

Elfquest: Metamorphosis

Warp, 1996

1 .... 3.00

Elfquest: New Blood

Warp, 1992

1 .... 5.00
2-10 .... 3.00
11-26 .... 2.00
27-33 .... 3.00
34-35 .... 2.00
Special 1 .... 4.00

Elfquest: Recognition Summer 2001 Special

Warp, 2001

2 .... 3.00

Elfquest: Shards

Warp, 1994

1-5 .... 3.00
6-8 .... 2.00
9-12 .... 3.00
13-16 .... 2.00
Ashcan 1 .... 1.00

Elfquest: Siege at Blue Mountain

Warp, 1987

1-2 .... 3.00
2/2nd 2.00
2/3rd-3 .... 3.00
3/2nd 2.00
4-8 .... 3.00

Elfquest: The Discovery

DC, 2006

1-4 .... 4.00

Elfquest: The Grand Quest

DC, 2004

1-4 .... 10.00

Elfquest: The Rebels

Warp, 1994

1 .... 3.00
2-12 .... 2.00

Elfquest: Two-Spear

Warp, 1995

1-5 .... 2.00

Elfquest: Wavedancers

Warp, 1993

1-8 .... 2.00
Special 1 .... 3.00

Elfquest: Wolfrider

DC, 2003

1-8 .... 10.00

Elfquest: Wolfshadow Summer 2001 Special

Warp, 2001

1 .... 4.00

Elfquest: Worldpool

Warp, 1997

1 .... 3.00

Elf-Thing

Eclipse, 1987

1 .... 2.00

Elftrek

Dimension, 1986

1-2 .... 2.00

Elf Warrior

Adventure, 1987

1-4 .... 2.00

El Gato Negro

Azteca, 1993

1-3 .... 2.00
4 .... 3.00

El Gaucho

NBM

1 .... 21.00

El-Hazard

Viz, 1997

1 .... 3.00

Elfquest

Elf-Thing

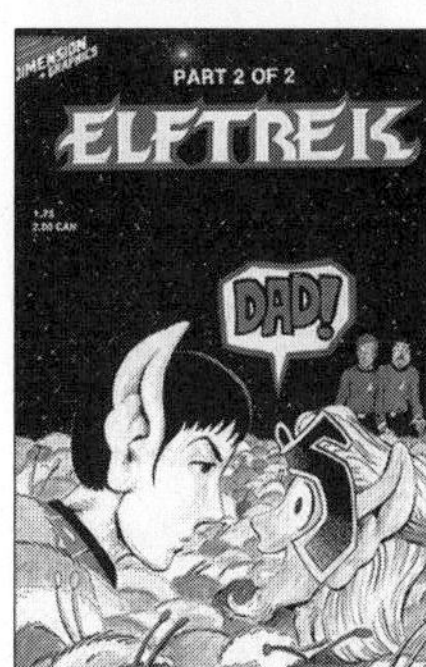

Elftrek

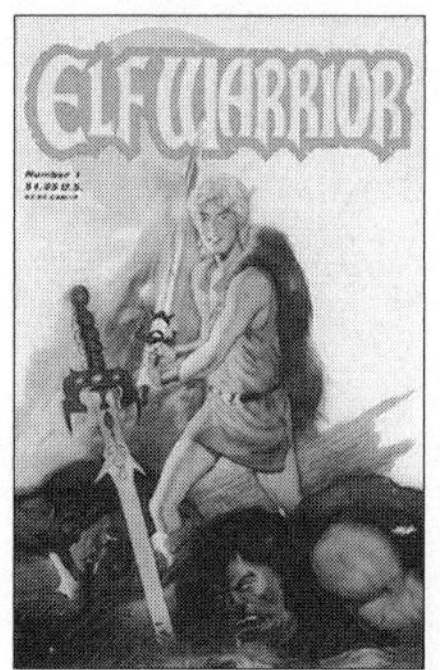

Elf Warrior

El-Hazard

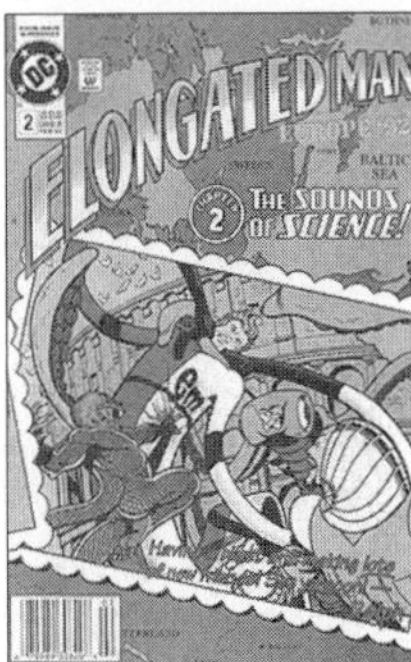
Elongated Man

Elric

Elven

El Hazard: The Magnificent World Part 1
Viz, 2000
1-5 .... 3.00

El Hazard: The Magnificent World Part 2
Viz, 2001
1-5 .... 3.00

El Hazard: The Magnificent World Part 3
Viz, 2001
1-6 .... 3.00

Eliminator
Malibu, 1995
0-1 .... 3.00
1/Variant 4.00
2-3 .... 3.00

Eliminator
Eternity, 1991
1-3 .... 3.00

Eliminator Full Color Special
Eternity, 1991
1 .... 3.00

Elk's Run
Hoarse and Buggy, 2005
1-3 .... 3.00

Ellery Queen Comics
Superior, 1949
1 .... 440.00
2 .... 260.00
3-4 .... 185.00

Ellery Queen
Ziff-Davis, 1952
1 .... 325.00
2 .... 200.00

Elmo Comics
St. John, 1948
1 .... 50.00

Elongated Man
DC, 1992
1-4 .... 1.00

El Perfecto Comics
Print Mint
1 .... 4.00

Elric
Pacific, 1983
1-6 .... 2.00

Elric
Topps, 1996
0 .... 4.00
1-4 .... 3.00

Elric: Sailor on the Seas of Fate
First, 1985
1-7 .... 2.00

Elric: Stormbringer
Dark Horse, 1997
1-7 .... 3.00

Elric: The Bane of the Black Sword
First, 1988
1-6 .... 2.00

Elric: The Making of a Sorcerer
DC, 2004
1-4 .... 6.00

Elric: The Vanishing Tower
First, 1987
1-6 .... 2.00

Elric: Weird of the White Wolf
First, 1986
1-5 .... 2.00

El Salvador: A House Divided
Eclipse
1 .... 3.00

Elsewhere Prince
Marvel, 1990
1-6 .... 2.00

Elseworlds 80-Page Giant
DC, 1999
1 .... 110.00

Elseworld's Finest
DC, 1997
1-2 .... 5.00

Elseworld's Finest: Supergirl & Batgirl
DC, 1998
1 .... 6.00
1/Ltd. 19.00

Elsinore
Alias, 2005
1-7 .... 3.00

Elsinore
Devil's Due, 2005
4-5 .... 3.00

Elven
Malibu, 1994
0 .... 3.00
1 .... 2.00
1/Ltd. 3.00
2-4 .... 2.00

Elvira, Mistress of the Dark
Marvel, 1988
1 .... 4.00

Elvira, Mistress of the Dark
Claypool, 1993
1 .... 4.00
2-166 .... 3.00

Elvira's House of Mystery
DC, 1986
1 .... 3.00
2-10 .... 2.00
11 .... 3.00
Special 1 .... 2.00

Elvis Mandible
DC, 1990
1 .... 4.00

Elvis Presley Experience
Revolutionary, 1992
1-7 .... 3.00

Elvis Shrugged
Revolutionary, 1992
1-2 .... 3.00
3 .... 4.00

El Zombo
Dark Horse, 2004
1-3 .... 3.00

E-Man
Charlton, 1973
1 .... 4.00
2-10 .... 3.00

E-Man
First, 1983
1-5 .... 2.00
6-25 .... 1.00

E-Man
Comico, 1989
1 .... 3.00

E-Man
Comico, 1990
1-3 .... 3.00

E-Man
Alpha, 1993
1 .... 3.00

E-Man Returns
Alpha Productions, 1994
1 .... 3.00

Emblem
Antarctic, 1994
1 .... 4.00
2-8 .... 3.00

Embrace
London Night, 1997
1 .... 5.00
1/Ltd. 10.00

Emeraldas
Eternity, 1990
1-4 .... 2.00

Emergency!
Charlton, 1976
1 .... 20.00
2 .... 16.00
3 .... 14.00
4 .... 16.00

Emergency
Charlton, 1976
1 .... 30.00
2 .... 25.00
3-4 .... 22.00

Emil and the Detectives
Gold Key, 1964
1 .... 25.00

Emily the Strange
Dark Horse, 2005
1-3 .... 8.00

Emissary
Strateia, 1998
1 .... 4.00

Emma Davenport
Lohman Hills, 1995
1-8 .... 3.00

Emma Frost
Marvel, 2003
1 .... 4.00
2-18 .... 3.00

Emo Boy
Slave Labor, 2005
1-4 .... 3.00

Empire
Eternity, 1988
1-4 .... 2.00

Empire
Image, 2000
1-2 .... 3.00

Empire
DC, 2003
0 .... 5.00
1-6 .... 3.00

Empire Lanes
Northern Lights, 1986
1-4 .... 2.00

Empire Lanes
Keyline
1 .... 2.00

Empire Lanes
Keyline, 1989
1 .... 3.00

Empires of Night
Rebel, 1993
1-4 .... 2.00

Emblem

Emeraldas

Emissary

Emma Davenport

Emma Frost

Empire

Empty Zone

Enchanted

Empty Love Stories
Slave Labor, 1994
1-2 .... 3.00

Empty Love Stories
Funny Valentine, 1998
1-Special 1 .... 3.00

Empty Love Stories: 1999
Funny Valentine, 1999
1 .... 3.00

Empty Skull Comics
Fantagraphics, 1996
1 .... 5.00

Empty Zone
Sirius
1-4 .... 3.00

Empty Zone
Sirius, 1998
1-8 .... 3.00

Empty Zone: Trancemissions
Sirius
1 .... 3.00

Enchanted
Sirius, 1997
1-3 .... 3.00

Enchanted (Vol. 2)
Sirius
1-3 .... 3.00

Enchanted Valley
Blackthorne, 1987
1-2 .... 2.00

Enchanted Worlds
Blackmore
1 .... 3.00

Enchanter
Eclipse, 1985
1-8 .... 2.00

Enchanter: Apocalypse Moon
Express
1 .... 3.00

Enchanter: Prelude to Apocalypse
Express
1-3 .... 3.00

Enchanters
Hidden Poet, 1996
1 .... 3.00

Enchanting Love
Kirby Publications, 1949
1-3 .... 75.00

Encyclopêdia Deadpoolica
Marvel, 1998
1 .... 3.00

End: In the Beginning
AFC, 2000
1 .... 3.00

Endless Gallery
DC
1 .... 4.00

Enemy
Dark Horse, 1994
1-5 .... 3.00

Enemy Ace Special
DC, 1990
1 .... 3.00

Enemy Ace: War in Heaven
DC, 2001
1-2 .... 6.00

EnForce
Reoccurring Images
1 .... 3.00

Enginehead
DC, 2004
1-6 .... 3.00

Enigma
DC, 1993
1-8 .... 3.00

Enigma!
Hector Tellez
1 .... 3.00

Eno & Plum
Oni, 1998
1 .... 3.00

Ensign O'Toole
Dell, 1963
1 .... 30.00

Entropy Tales
Entropy
1-4 .... 2.00

Ents
Manic
1-3 .... 3.00

Eo
Rebel
1-4 .... 3.00

Epic
Marvel, 1992
1-4 .... 5.00

Epic Anthology
Marvel, 2004
1 .... 6.00

Epic Graphic Novel: Someplace Strange
Marvel

1 .... 7.00

Epic Graphic Novel: The Death of Groo
Marvel

1-1/3rd 10.00

Epic Illustrated
Marvel, 1980

1 .... 6.00
2-4 .... 4.00
5-34 .... 3.00

Epic Lite
Marvel, 1991

1 .... 5.00

Epicurus the Sage
DC, 1991

1-2 .... 10.00

Epileptic Engine
Epileptic Engine

1-2 .... 3.00

Episode Guides
Celebrity

1 .... 6.00

Epsilon Wave
Independent, 1985

1-8 .... 2.00

Equine the Uncivilized
Graphxpress, 1990

1-6 .... 2.00

Equinox Chronicles
Innovation

1-2 .... 2.00

Eradicator
DC, 1996

1-3 .... 2.00

Eradicators
Silverwolf, 1986

1-4 .... 2.00

Eradicators
Silverwolf, 1989

1-2 .... 2.00

Eric Basaldua Sketchbook
Image, 2006

1 .... 3.00

Eric Preston Is the Flame
B-Movie

1 .... 1.00

Erika Telekinetika
Fantagraphics, 2004

1-3 .... 4.00

Ernie
Kitchen Sink

1 .... 2.00

Ernie Comics
Current, 1948

22-23 .... 30.00
24-25 .... 22.00

Eros Forum
Fantagraphics, 1993

1-3 .... 3.00

Eros Graphic Album
Fantagraphics, 1994

1 .... 10.00
2 .... 13.00
3-4 .... 11.00
5 .... 15.00
6 .... 17.00
7-8 .... 13.00
9 .... 10.00
10 .... 13.00
11 .... 12.00
12-13 .... 13.00
14-16 .... 15.00
17 .... 16.00
18 .... 13.00
19 .... 15.00
20 .... 13.00
21-22 .... 15.00
23-24 .... 13.00
25 .... 17.00
26 .... 14.00
27 .... 12.00
28-29 .... 17.00
30 .... 14.00
31 .... 20.00
32-33 .... 17.00
34-35 .... 15.00
36-42 .... 20.00
43-44 .... 17.00

Eros Hawk
Fantagraphics

1-4 .... 3.00

Eros Hawk III
Fantagraphics, 1994

1 .... 3.00

Erotic Fables & Faerie Tales
Fantagraphics

1-2 .... 3.00

Eroticom
Caliber

1 .... 3.00

Eroticom II
Caliber, 1994

1 .... 3.00

Erotic Orbits
Comax

1 .... 3.00

Erotic Tales
Aircel, 1991

1-3 .... 3.00

Enemy Ace Special

EnForce

Enigma

Epic Illustrated

Eradicator

Esc

Escape to the Stars

Escape Velocity

Erotic Worlds of Frank Thorne
Fantagraphics, 1990
1-6 ....3.00

Erotique
Aircel, 1991
1 ....3.00

Ersatz Peach
Aeon, 1995
1 ....8.00

Ert!
Caliber
1 ....13.00

Esc
Comico, 1996
1-4 ....3.00

Escapade in Florence
Gold Key, 1963
1 ....40.00

Escape from Fear
Planned Parenthood, 1962
1 ....50.00

Escape to the Stars
Solson
1 ....2.00

Escape Velocity
Escape Velocity
1-2 ....2.00

Escapists
Dark Horse, 2006
1 ....1.00
2-6 ....3.00

Espers
Eclipse, 1986
1 ....3.00
2-5 ....2.00

Espers
Halloween, 1996
1-6 ....3.00

Espers
Image, 1997
1 ....4.00
2-9 ....3.00

Espionage
Dell
1 ....18.00
2 ....15.00

Essential Elfquest
Warp, 1995
1 ....2.00

Essential Vertigo: Swamp Thing
DC, 1996
1-5 ....3.00
6-24 ....2.00

Essential Vertigo: The Sandman
DC, 1996
1-5 ....3.00
6-31 ....2.00
32 ....5.00

Essential X-Men
Marvel
1 ....5.00
2-5 ....4.00
6-32 ....3.00

Establishment
DC, 2001
1-13 ....3.00

Etc
DC
1-5 ....5.00

Et Cetera
Tokyopop, 2004
1-6 ....10.00

Eternal
Marvel, 2003
1-6 ....3.00

Eternal Romance
Best Destiny, 1997
1-4 ....3.00

Eternal Romance Labor of Love Sketchbook
Best Destiny
1 ....3.00

Eternals
Marvel, 1976
1 ....10.00
1/30¢ 25.00
2 ....5.00
2/30¢ 15.00
3-5 ....3.00
6-12/Whitman 2.00
12/35¢ 15.00
13-13/Whitman 2.00
13/35¢ 15.00
14-14/Whitman 2.00
14/35¢ 15.00
15-15/Whitman 2.00
15/35¢ 15.00
16-16/Whitman 2.00
16/35¢ 15.00
17-19 ....2.00
Ann 1 ....7.00

Eternals
Marvel, 1985
1 ....2.00
2-12 ....1.00

Eternals
Marvel, 2006
1 ....4.00
1/Variant-1/2nd variant 5.00
2-5/Variant 4.00

Eternals Sketchbook

Marvel, 2006

1 .... 2.00

Eternals: The Herod Factor

Marvel, 1991

1 .... 3.00

Eternal Thirst

Alpha Productions

3-5 .... 2.00

Eternal Warrior

Valiant, 1992

1 .... 4.00
1/GoldEmboss 25.00
1/Gold 10.00
2 .... 3.00
3 .... 2.00
4 .... 5.00
5-7 .... 2.00
8 .... 3.00
9-21 .... 1.00
22 .... 2.00
23-25 .... 1.00
26 .... 4.00
27 .... 1.00
27/VVSS 125.00
28-29 .... 1.00
30-40 .... 2.00
41-45 .... 3.00
46-49 .... 4.00
50 .... 7.00
Special 1 .... 4.00
YB 1-2 .... 5.00

Eternal Warrior: Fist and Steel

Acclaim, 1996

1 .... 5.00
2 .... 6.00

Eternal Warriors

Acclaim, 1997

1-1/Variant 4.00
Ashcan 1 .... 1.00

Eternal Warriors: Archer & Armstrong

Acclaim, 1997

1 .... 4.00

Eternal Warriors Blackworks

Acclaim, 1998

1 .... 4.00

Eternal Warriors: Digital Alchemy

Acclaim, 1997

1 .... 4.00

Eternal Warriors: Mog

Acclaim, 1998

1 .... 4.00

Eternal Warrior Special

Acclaim, 1996

1 .... 3.00

Eternal Warriors: The Immortal Enemy

Acclaim, 1998

1 .... 4.00

Eternal Warriors: Time and Treachery

Acclaim, 1997

1 .... 4.00

Eternity Smith

Renegade, 1986

1-5 .... 2.00

Eternity Smith

Hero, 1987

1-9 .... 2.00

Eternity Triple Action

Eternity

1-4 .... 3.00

Eudaemon

Dark Horse, 1993

1-3 .... 3.00

Eugenus

Eugenus

1-2 .... 4.00
3 .... 3.00

Eureka

Radio, 2000

1-3 .... 3.00

Europa and the Pirate Twins

Powder Monkey, 1996

1-1/A 3.00
Ashcan 1 .... 1.00

Evangeline Special

Lodestone, 1986

1 .... 2.00

Evangeline

Comico, 1984

1 .... 3.00
2 .... 2.00

Evangeline

First, 1987

1 .... 3.00
2-12 .... 2.00

Evel Knievel

Marvel

1 .... 10.00

Evenfall

Slave Labor, 2003

1-7 .... 3.00

Espionage

Essential X-Men

Etc

Eternal Warrior

Evel Knievel

Evil Eye

Ewoks

Excalibur

Even More Secret Origins 80-Page Giant
DC, 2003

1 .... 7.00

E.V.E. Protomecha
Image, 2000

1-6 .... 3.00

Everquest: The Ruins of Kunark
DC, 2002

1 .... 6.00

Everquest: Transformation
DC, 2002

1 .... 6.00

Everwinds
Slave Labor, 1997

1-4 .... 3.00

Every Dog Has His Day
Shiga

1 .... 2.00

Everyman
Marvel, 1991

1 .... 5.00

Everything's Archie
Archie, 1969

1 .... 48.00
2 .... 26.00
3-5 .... 20.00
6-10 .... 12.00
11-20 .... 7.00
21-40 .... 4.00
41-60 .... 3.00
61-157 .... 2.00

Evil Ernie
Eternity, 1991

1 .... 35.00
1/Ltd. 6.00
2 .... 5.00
3-5 .... 4.00

Evil Ernie (Chaos!)
Chaos!, 1997

0 .... 3.00
0/Platinum 5.00
1-10 .... 3.00

Evil Ernie: Baddest Battles
Chaos, 1997

1-1/Variant 2.00

Evil Ernie: Depraved
Chaos!, 1999

1-3 .... 3.00

Evil Ernie: Destroyer
Chaos!, 1997

1-Ashcan 1 .... 3.00

Evil Ernie in Santa Fe
Devil's Due, 2005

1-4 .... 3.00

Evil Ernie: New Year's Evil
Chaos!, 1993

1 .... 5.00

Evil Ernie: Pieces of Me
Chaos!, 2000

1-1/Variant 3.00

Evil Ernie: Revenge
Chaos!, 1993

0-1 .... 3.00
1/Deluxe-1/Ltd. 4.00
2-4 .... 3.00

Evil Ernie: Straight to Hell
Chaos!, 1995

1 .... 3.00
1/A 4.00
2-5 .... 3.00

Evil Ernie: The Lost Sketches
Chaos, 2001

Ashcan 1 .... 1.00

Evil Ernie: The Resurrection
Chaos!, 1993

1 .... 4.00
1/Gold 5.00
2-3 .... 4.00
4 .... 3.00
Ashcan 1 .... 5.00

Evil Ernie vs. the Movie Monsters
Chaos!, 1997

1-1/A 3.00

Evil Ernie vs. the Super Heroes
Chaos!, 1995

1-2 .... 3.00

Evil Ernie: War Of The Dead
Chaos!, 1999

1-3 .... 3.00

Evil Ernie: Youth Gone Wild
Chaos!, 1996

1-5 .... 2.00
Special 1 .... 5.00

Evil Eye
Fantagraphics, 1998

1-3 .... 3.00

Evilman Saves the World
Moonstone, 1996

1 .... 3.00

Evil's Return
Tokyopop, 2004
1-4 .... 10.00

Evo
Image, 2003
1 .... 3.00

Ewoks
Marvel, 1985
1 .... 3.00
2-8 .... 2.00
9 .... 4.00
10-14 .... 2.00

Excalibur
Marvel, 1988
-1 .... 2.00
1 .... 3.00
2-49 .... 2.00
50 .... 3.00
51-70 .... 2.00
71 .... 4.00
☛Hologram cover
72-75 .... 2.00
75/Variant 4.00
76-81 .... 2.00
82 .... 3.00
82/Variant 4.00
83-99 .... 2.00
100 .... 3.00
101-124 .... 2.00
125 .... 3.00
Ann 1 .... 4.00
Ann 2 .... 3.00

Excalibur
Marvel, 2001
1-4 .... 3.00

Excalibur
Marvel, 2004
1-13 .... 3.00

Excalibur: Air Apparent
Marvel, 1991
1 .... 5.00

Excalibur: Mojo Mayhem
Marvel, 1989
1 .... 5.00

Excalibur: Sword of Power
Marvel, 2002
1-4 .... 3.00

Excalibur: The Possession
Marvel, 1991
1 .... 3.00

Excalibur: The Sword Is Drawn
Marvel, 1987
1-1/3rd 4.00

Excalibur: Weird War III
Marvel, 1990
1 .... 10.00

Excalibur: XX Crossing
Marvel, 1992
1 .... 3.00

Exciting Comics
Nedor, 1940
1 .... 2,400.00
2 .... 1,450.00
3 .... 1,000.00
4-6 .... 650.00
7-10 .... 600.00
11-20 .... 465.00
21-30 .... 340.00
31-40 .... 300.00
41-51 .... 240.00
52-60 .... 210.00
61-66 .... 165.00
67-69 .... 100.00

Exciting Romances
Fawcett, 1949
1 .... 50.00
2-12 .... 25.00

Exciting War
Standard, 1952
5 .... 44.00
6-9 .... 32.00

Exciting X-Patrol
Marvel, 1997
1 .... 2.00

Exec
Comics Conspiracy, 2001
1 .... 4.00

Executioner: Death Squad (Don Pendleton's...)
Vivid, 1996
1 .... 13.00

Exhibitionist
Fantagraphics, 1994
1-2 .... 3.00

Exile
Eyeball Soup Designs, 1996
1-2 .... 3.00

Exiled
Exiled, 1998
1-3 .... 3.00

Exile Earth
River City, 1994
1-2 .... 2.00

Exiles
Malibu, 1993
1 .... 2.00
1/Variant 5.00
2 .... 2.00
3 .... 3.00
4 .... 2.00

Exiles
Marvel, 2001
1 .... 4.00

Exciting Comics

Exciting War

Exile Earth

Exit 6

Ex Machina

Exotic Romances

Exposed

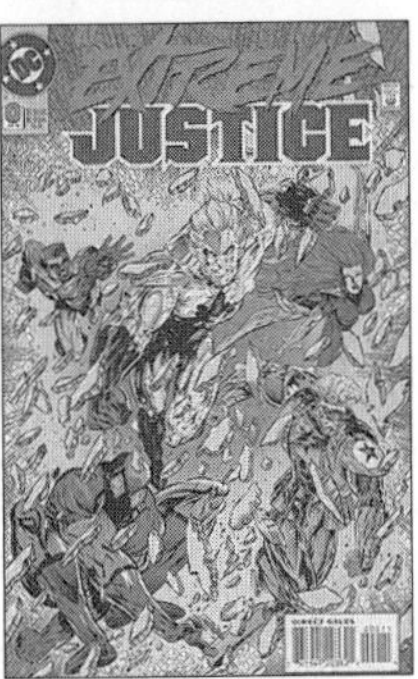

Extreme Justice

2-24 .... 2.00
25-59 .... 3.00
60 .... 5.00
☛Age of Apoc.
61 .... 4.00
☛Age of Apoc.
62-89 .... 3.00
Ann 1 .... 4.00

Exiles
Alpha Productions
1 .... 2.00

Existing Earth
Windwolf Graphics, 1987
1 .... 2.00

Exit
Caliber
1-5 .... 3.00

Exit 6
Plastic Spoon, 1998
1-3/Ashcan 3.00

Exit from Shadow
Bronze Man
4 .... 3.00

Ex-Libris Eroticis
NBM
1 .... 10.00

Ex Machina
DC, 2004
1 .... 8.00
2 .... 4.00
3-25 .... 3.00

Ex Machina Special
DC, 2006
1-2 .... 3.00

Ex-Mutants
Pied Piper, 1987
1-Special 1 .... 2.00

Ex-Mutants
Eternity, 1986
WS 1 .... 0.00
1-Ann 1 .... 2.00

Ex-Mutants
Malibu, 1992
1 .... 2.00
1/Variant 3.00
2-16 .... 2.00
17-18 .... 3.00

Ex-Mutants Microseries: Erin (Lawrence & Lim's...)
Pied Piper
1 .... 2.00

Ex-Mutants Pin-Up Book
Eternity, 1988
1 .... 2.00

Ex-Mutants Special Consumer Electronics Show Edition
Malibu, 1992
1 .... 3.00

Exodus Revelation
Exodus, 1994
1 .... 1.00

Exosquad
Topps, 1994
0 .... 1.00

Exotica
Cry for Dawn, 1993
1 .... 4.00
2 .... 3.00

Exotic Fantasy
Fantagraphics, 1992
1-3 .... 5.00

Exotic Romances
Comic Magazines, 1955
22-29 .... 26.00
30-31 .... 22.00

Expatriate
Image, 2005
1-4 .... 3.00

Experience
Aircel
1 .... 3.00

Exploits of Daniel Boone
Quality, 1955
1 .... 185.00
2 .... 115.00
3-6 .... 80.00

Explorers
Explorer, 1996
1-3 .... 3.00

Explorers
Caliber, 1996
1-3 .... 3.00

Explorers of the Unknown
Archie, 1990
1-6 .... 1.00

Expose
Cracked Pepper, 1993
1 .... 3.00

Exposed
D.S., 1948
1 .... 110.00
2 .... 100.00
3 .... 85.00
4-5 .... 65.00
6 .... 125.00
7 .... 95.00
8-9 .... 55.00

Exposure
Image, 1999
1-4 .... 3.00
5-6 .... 4.00

Exquisite Corpse
Dark Horse
1-3 .... 3.00

Exterminators
DC, 2006
1-13 .... 3.00

Extinct!
New England
1-2 .... 4.00

Extinctioners
Shanda Fantasy Arts, 1999
1-2 .... 3.00

Extinction Event
DC, 2003
1-5 .... 3.00

Extra!
E.C., 1955
1 .... 150.00
2-5 .... 100.00

Extra!
Gemstone, 2000
1-5 .... 3.00
Ann 1 .... 14.00

Extra Terrestrial Trio
Smiling Face, 1995
1 .... 3.00

Extreme
Image, 1993
0-0/Gold 3.00
Holiday 1 .... 1.00

Extreme
Curtis
1 .... 3.00

Extreme Destroyer Epilogue
Image, 1996
1 .... 3.00

Extreme Destroyer Prologue
Image, 1996
1 .... 3.00

Extreme Hero
Image, 1994
1 .... 1.00

Extreme Justice
DC, 1995
0-18 .... 2.00

Extremely Silly
Antarctic
1 .... 3.00

Extremely Silly (Vol. 2)
Antarctic, 1996
1 .... 1.00

Extremely Youngblood
Image, 1996
1 .... 4.00

Extreme Prejudice
Image, 1994
0 .... 3.00

Extreme Previews
Image, 1996
1 .... 1.00

Extreme Previews 1997
Image
1 .... 1.00

Extreme Sacrifice
Image, 1995
1-2 .... 3.00

Extremes of Violet
Blackout, 1995
0-2 .... 3.00

Extreme Super Christmas Special
Image, 1994
1 .... 3.00

Extreme Super Tour Book
Image
1 .... 1.00
1/Gold 2.00

Extreme Tour Book
Image
1-1/Gold 3.00

Extremist
DC, 1993
1 .... 3.00
1/Platinum 4.00
2-4 .... 3.00

Eye
Hamster, 1999
Special 1 .... 3.00

Eyeball Kid
Dark Horse
1-3 .... 3.00

Eyebeam
Adhesive, 1994
1-5 .... 3.00

Eye of Mongombo
Fantagraphics, 1991
1-7 .... 2.00

Eye of the Beholder
NBM
1 .... 11.00

Extremely Youngblood

Extreme Sacrifice

Extreme Super Christmas Special

Eye of Mongombo

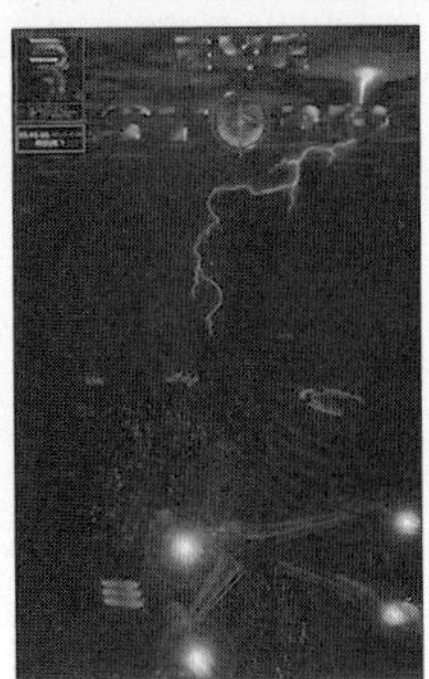
Eye of the Storm

Faans

Fables

Factor-X

Eye of the Storm
Rival, 1994

1 .... 3.00

Eye of the Storm Annual
DC, 2003

1 .... 5.00

Eyeshield 21
Viz, 2005

1-4 .... 8.00

Eyes of Asia
Digital Webbing, 2004

1-2 .... 4.00

Faans
Six Handed

1 .... 3.00

Fables
DC, 2002

1 .... 4.00
2-5 .... 3.00
6-6/Retailer ed. 15.00
7-49 .... 3.00
50 .... 4.00
51-55 .... 3.00
56-80 .... 4.00

Fables By the Brothers Dimm
Dimm, 1995

1 .... 2.00

Fables: Last Castle
DC, 2003

1 .... 5.00

Fabulous Furry Freak Brothers
Rip Off, 1975

0 .... 6.00
1 .... 55.00
1/2nd 30.00
1/3rd 28.00
2 .... 35.00
2/2nd 25.00
3 .... 15.00
4 .... 13.00
5 .... 10.00
6 .... 7.00
7-9 .... 5.00
10 .... 2.00
11-12 .... 4.00
13 .... 3.00

Face
Columbia, 1941

1 .... 400.00
2 .... 250.00
3-4 .... 185.00

Face
DC, 1995

1 .... 5.00

Faction Paradox
Image, 2003

1 .... 3.00
2 .... 4.00

Factor
About Comics, 1998

0 .... 2.00
1-3 .... 3.00

Factor-X
Marvel, 1995

1-4 .... 2.00

Facts o' Life Funnies
Rip Off

1 .... 4.00

Factual Illusions
Blackmore

1 .... 3.00

Faculty Funnies
Archie, 1989

1 .... 4.00
2-5 .... 3.00

Fade from Grace
Beckett, 2004

1-3 .... 2.00

Faerie Codex
Raven, 1997

1-3 .... 3.00

Faeries' Landing
Tokyopop, 2004

1-11 .... 10.00

Fafhrd and the Gray Mouser
Marvel, 1990

1-4 .... 5.00

Failed Universe
Blackthorne, 1986

1 .... 2.00

Fairy Tale Parade
Dell, 1942

1 .... 625.00
2 .... 365.00
3 .... 225.00
4-5 .... 160.00
6-9 .... 125.00

Fairy Tales of the Brothers Grimm
NBM

1 .... 16.00

Fairy Tales
Ziff-Davis, 1951

10-11 .... 165.00

Faith
Lightning, 1997

1/A 3.00

Faith
DC, 1999
1-5 .... 3.00

Faith: A Fable
Carbon-Based Books, 2000
1 .... 9.00

Faithful
Marvel, 1949
1 .... 55.00
2 .... 42.00

Faith of the Foe
Fandom House
1 .... 5.00

Fake
Tokyopop, 2003
1 .... 10.00

Falcon
Marvel, 1983
1-4 .... 2.00

Fall
Big Bad World
1 .... 3.00

Fall
Caliber
1 .... 3.00

Fallen
NBM
1 .... 9.00

Fallen Angel
DC, 2003
1-20 .... 3.00

Fallen Angel
Idea & Design Works, 2006
1-11 .... 4.00

Fallen Angel on the World of Magic: The Gathering
Acclaim, 1996
1 .... 6.00

Fallen Angels
Marvel, 1987
1-8 .... 2.00

Fallen Empires on the World of Magic: The Gathering
Acclaim, 1995
1-2 .... 3.00

Falling in Love
DC, 1955
1 .... 275.00
2 .... 145.00
3 .... 95.00
4-5 .... 65.00
6-10 .... 60.00
11-20 .... 40.00
21-40 .... 28.00
41-59 .... 20.00
60-80 .... 16.00
81-100 .... 14.00
101-120 .... 12.00
121-143 .... 9.00

Falling Man
Image, 1998
1 .... 3.00

Fall of the Roman Empire
Gold Key, 1964
1 .... 25.00

Fallout 3000 (Mike Deodato's...)
Caliber, 1996
1 .... 3.00

Falls The Gotham Rain
Comico
1 .... 5.00

Family Affair
Gold Key, 1970
1 .... 24.00
2 .... 20.00
3-4 .... 14.00

Family Funnies
Harvey, 1950
1 .... 40.00
2 .... 30.00
3-5 .... 25.00
6-8 .... 22.00

Family Guy
Devil's Due, 2006
1-2 .... 7.00

Family Man
DC
1-3 .... 5.00

Famous Comics
King, 1934
1 .... 150.00
2-3 .... 120.00

Famous Crimes
Fox, 1948
1 .... 210.00
2 .... 185.00
3 .... 225.00
4-5 .... 130.00
6 .... 110.00
7 .... 165.00
8-10 .... 110.00
11-15 .... 75.00
16-20 .... 60.00
51-52 .... 38.00

Famous Fairy Tales
K.K., 1942
1 .... 250.00
2-3 .... 165.00

Faculty Funnies

Faerie Codex

Fafhrd and the Gray Mouser

Fairy Tale Parade

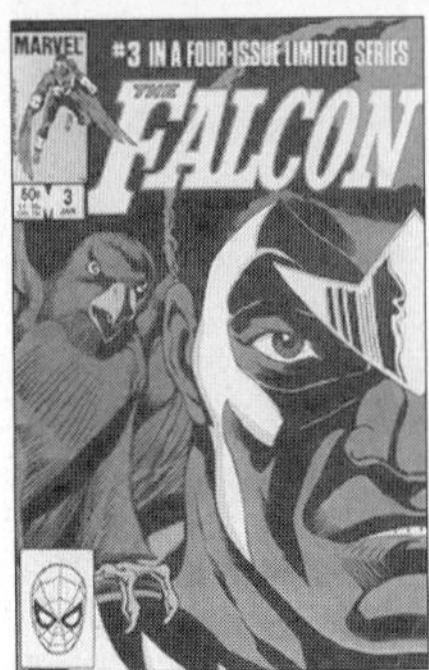

Falcon

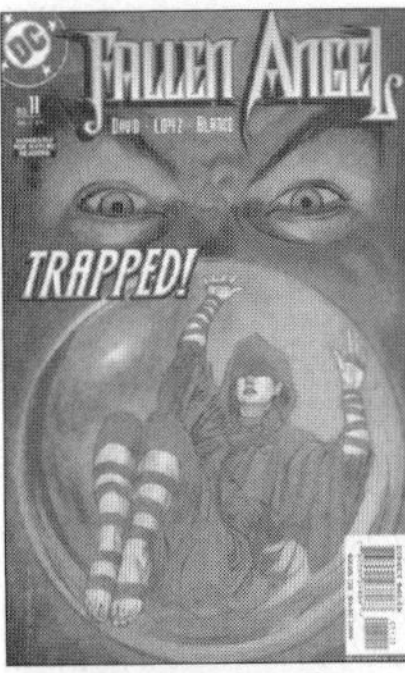

Fallen Angel

Family Affair

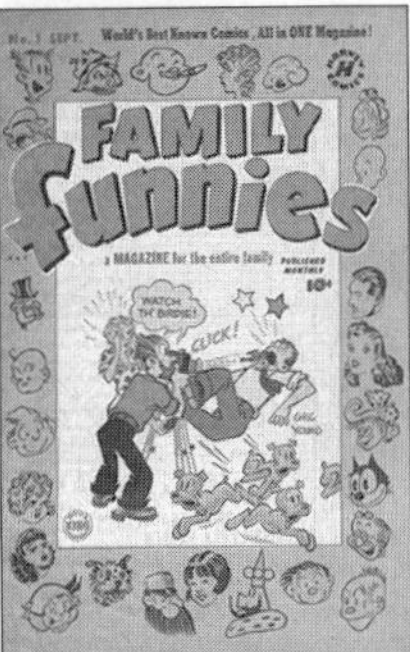

Family Funnies

Famous Features (Jerry Iger's...)

Pacific, 1984

1 ....3.00

Famous Feature Stories

Dell, 1938

1 ....450.00

Famous First Edition

DC, 1974

F-4 ....15.00
☛Whiz #2
F-5 ....13.00
☛Batman #1
F-6 ....10.00
☛W. Woman #1
F-7 ....12.00
☛All-Star #3
F-8 ....9.00
☛Flash #1
C-26....................10.00
☛Action #1
C-28....................9.00
☛Detective #27
C-30....................10.00
☛Sensation #1
C-61....................9.00
☛Superman #1
C-61/Whitman 18.00

Famous Funnies

Famous Funnies, 1934

1 ....16,400.00
2 ....3,850.00
3 ....4,200.00
4 ....1,450.00
5 ....1,100.00
6-10 ....825.00
11-12 ....665.00
13-17 ....415.00
18 ....625.00
19-20 ....415.00
21-22 ....365.00
23-30 ....350.00
31-38 ....235.00
39-40 ....215.00
41-50 ....180.00
51-60 ....165.00
61-70 ....145.00
71-80 ....100.00
81 ....85.00
82 ....105.00
83-90 ....85.00
91-99 ....70.00
100 ....75.00
101-110 ....60.00
111-130 ....50.00
131-150 ....38.00
151-190 ....28.00
191-208 ....25.00
☛Frazetta art
209-216 ....550.00
☛Frazetta art
217-218....................25.00

Famous Funnies: A Carnival of Comics

Eastern Color, 1933

1 ....10,800.00

Famous Gangsters

Avon, 1951

1 ....250.00
2-3....................190.00

Famous Stars

Ziff-Davis, 1950

1 ....165.00
2-3....................90.00
4....................100.00
5-6....................75.00

Famous Stories

Dell

1 ....165.00
2 ....150.00

Famous Western Badmen

Youthful

13....................75.00
14-15 ....50.00

Fana

Comax

1 ....3.00

Fana the Jungle Girl

Comax

1 ....3.00

Fanboy

DC, 1999

1-6....................3.00

Fandom Confidential

Kitchen Sink

1 ....3.00

Fang

Sirius Entertainment, 1995

1-3....................3.00

Fang

Conquest

1 ....3.00

Fang

Tangram

1 ....3.00

Fang: Testament

Sirius Entertainment

1-4....................3.00

Fangraphix

Fangraphix

1-3....................2.00

Fangs of the Cobra

Mythic, 1996

1 ....3.00

Fanny
Fanny
1-2 .... 3.00
3 .... 4.00

Fanny Hill
Shunga
1 .... 3.00

Fantaco's Chronicles Series
Fantaco, 1982
1 .... 2.00

Fantaescape
Zinzinnati, 1988
1 .... 2.00

Fantagor
Last Gasp, 1972
1-3 .... 3.00

FantaSci
Apple, 1988
1-9 .... 2.00

Fantastic
Youthful, 1952
8 .... 165.00
9 .... 120.00

Fantastic Adventures
Super, 1963
10 .... 25.00
11-18 .... 20.00

Fantastic Adventures
Ace, 1987
1-3 .... 2.00

Fantastic Comics
Fox, 1939
1 .... 3,100.00
2 .... 2,000.00
3 .... 6,600.00
4-5 .... 1,600.00
6-9 .... 1,000.00
10-15 .... 800.00
16-23 .... 650.00

Fantastic Comics
Farrell, 1954
10 .... 135.00
11 .... 110.00

Fantastic Fables (Basil Wolverton's...)
Dark Horse, 1993
1-2 .... 3.00

Fantastic Fanzine
Arrow
1-3 .... 2.00

Fantastic Fears
Farrell, 1953
1 .... 265.00
2 .... 185.00
3-5 .... 140.00
6 .... 400.00
7 .... 140.00
8-9 .... 100.00

Fantastic Five
Marvel, 1999
1-3 .... 2.00

Fantastic Force
Marvel, 1994
1 .... 3.00
2-18 .... 2.00

Fantastic Four (Vol. 1)
Marvel, 1961
1 .... 20,000.00
☛1st Fantastic Four
1/Golden 70.00
2 .... 4,500.00
☛1st Skrulls
3 .... 3,000.00
4 .... 3,500.00
5 .... 5,000.00
☛1st Dr. Doom
6 .... 2,000.00
7 .... 1,250.00
8 .... 1,200.00
9-10 .... 1,150.00
11 .... 1,000.00
12 .... 2,700.00
☛Thing vs. Hulk
13 .... 600.00
14 .... 500.00
15 .... 700.00
16-19 .... 500.00
20 .... 600.00
21 .... 450.00
22-23 .... 250.00
24 .... 240.00
25 .... 550.00
☛Avengers app.
26 .... 600.00
☛Avengers app.
27 .... 300.00
28 .... 500.00
☛X-Men app.
29-31 .... 260.00
32-34 .... 250.00
35-40 .... 165.00
41-43 .... 110.00
44 .... 85.00
45 .... 325.00
☛1st Inhumans
46 .... 150.00
47 .... 100.00
48 .... 460.00
☛1st Silver Surfer
49 .... 350.00
50 .... 400.00
51 .... 150.00
52 .... 300.00
☛1st Black Panther
53 .... 140.00
54 .... 105.00

Famous Crimes

Famous Funnies

Fanboy

Fantagor

Fantastic Fears

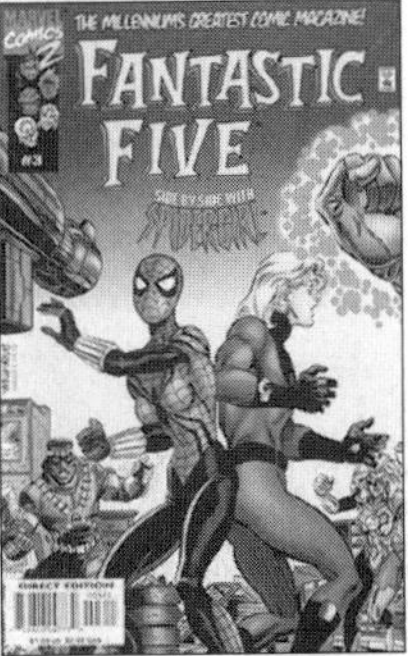

Fantastic Five

Fantastic Four

Fantastic Four Roast

55 ... 210.00
☛Thing vs. Surfer
56 ... 100.00
57 ... 115.00
58 ... 90.00
59 ... 60.00
60 ... 65.00
61 ... 70.00
62-63 ... 60.00
64 ... 50.00
65 ... 55.00
66 ... 115.00
☛1st Warlock
66/2nd ... 2.00
67 ... 105.00
67/2nd ... 2.00
68-69 ... 60.00
70 ... 55.00
71 ... 45.00
72 ... 100.00
☛Silver Surfer app.
73 ... 80.00
74 ... 85.00
75 ... 55.00
76 ... 45.00
77 ... 50.00
78 ... 35.00
79 ... 50.00
80-85 ... 40.00
86 ... 50.00
87 ... 40.00
88-89 ... 35.00
90-93 ... 30.00
94 ... 40.00
95-96 ... 30.00
97-98 ... 25.00
99 ... 30.00
100 ... 70.00
101-105 ... 30.00
106 ... 22.00
107 ... 30.00
108 ... 22.00
109-111 ... 20.00
112 ... 175.00
☛Thing vs. Hulk
113 ... 25.00
114 ... 27.00
115 ... 25.00
116 ... 65.00
☛52 pages
117-120 ... 15.00
121 ... 30.00
☛Galactus app.
122 ... 45.00
123 ... 27.00
124-125 ... 20.00
126 ... 30.00
127 ... 35.00
128 ... 30.00
129 ... 25.00
130-132 ... 15.00
133-145 ... 12.00
146 ... 10.00
147 ... 15.00
148-154 ... 10.00
155 ... 15.00
156-158 ... 12.00
159-163 ... 10.00
164 ... 9.00
165 ... 7.00
166 ... 10.00
167 ... 15.00
168-169 ... 10.00
169/30¢ ... 20.00
170 ... 10.00
170/30¢ ... 20.00
171 ... 6.00
171/30¢ ... 20.00
172 ... 6.00
172/30¢ ... 20.00
173 ... 6.00
173/30¢ ... 20.00
174-183/Whitman ... 6.00
183/35¢ ... 15.00
184-184/Whitman ... 6.00
184/35¢ ... 15.00
185-185/Whitman ... 5.00
185/35¢ ... 15.00
186-186/Whitman ... 5.00
186/35¢ ... 15.00
187-187/Whitman ... 5.00
187/35¢ ... 15.00
188-200 ... 5.00
☛Byrne script/art begins
201-239 ... 4.00
240-248 ... 3.00
249 ... 4.00
250 ... 5.00
251 ... 4.00
252-255 ... 3.00
256 ... 4.00
257-259 ... 3.00
260 ... 5.00
261 ... 4.00
262-268 ... 3.00
269 ... 4.00
270 ... 3.00
271 ... 4.00
272 ... 5.00
273-286 ... 3.00
287-295 ... 2.00
296 ... 3.00
297-299 ... 2.00
300 ... 3.00
301-318 ... 2.00
319 ... 3.00
320-346 ... 2.00
347 ... 3.00
347/2nd ... 2.00
348 ... 3.00
348/2nd ... 2.00
349-350 ... 3.00
351-357 ... 2.00
358 ... 3.00

359-370 .... 2.00
371-371/2nd 3.00
372-374 .... 1.00
375 .... 3.00
376-378 .... 1.00
379-380 .... 2.00
381 .... 3.00
382 .... 2.00
383-387 .... 1.00
387/Variant 3.00
388-394 .... 2.00
394/CS 3.00
395-398 .... 2.00
398/Variant 3.00
399 .... 2.00
399/Variant 3.00
400 .... 4.00
401-415 .... 2.00
416 .... 4.00
500 .... 45.00
500-500/CS 4.00
501 .... 2.00
501 .... 100.00
502-503 .... 2.00
503 .... 85.00
504 .... 55.00
504-505 .... 2.00
505 .... 45.00
506 .... 2.00
507 .... 35.00
507-508 .... 2.00
508 .... 50.00
509 .... 2.00
509 .... 40.00
510 .... 2.00
510 .... 40.00
511 .... 2.00
512-513 .... 3.00
514-516 .... 2.00
517-526 .... 3.00
527 .... 7.00
☛Straczynski starts
527/Variant 4.00
527/DirCut 5.00
527/Conv 7.00
528-535 .... 3.00
536 .... 10.00
537 .... 7.00
537/2nd-565 .... 3.00
Ann 1 .... 900.00
Ann 2 .... 500.00
Ann 3 .... 175.00
Ann 4 .... 90.00
Ann 5 .... 60.00
Ann 6 .... 40.00
Ann 7-8 .... 18.00
Ann 9 .... 10.00
Ann 10-11 .... 8.00
Ann 12-14 .... 5.00
Ann 15-27 .... 3.00
Special 1 .... 2.00
Ashcan 1 .... 1.00

Fantastic Four

Marvel, 1996

1 (417) 4.00
1/Variant 50.00
1/Gold 4.00
2 (418)-11 (427) 2.00
12 (428) 3.00
13 (429) 2.00

Fantastic Four

Marvel, 1998

1 (430) 3.00
1/A 4.00
2 (431)-5 (434) 3.00
6 (435)-24 (453) 2.00
25 (454) 3.00
26 (455)-34 (463) 2.00
35 (464) 3.00
36 (465)-49 (478) 2.00
50 (479)-51 (480) 4.00
52 (481) 2.00
53 (482) 3.00
54 (483) 4.00
55 (484)-59 (488) 2.00
60 (489) 1.00
61 (490)-70 (499) 2.00
Ann 1998 .... 5.00
Ann 1999 .... 4.00
Ann 2001 .... 3.00

Fantastic Four: A Death in the Family

Marvel, 2006

1 .... 4.00

Fantastic Four: Atlantis Rising

Marvel, 1995

1-2 .... 4.00
Ashcan 1 .... 2.00

Fantastic Four: Fireworks

Marvel, 1999

1-3 .... 3.00

Fantastic Four: First Family

Marvel, 2006

1-6 .... 3.00

Fantastic Four: Foes

Marvel, 2005

1-6 .... 3.00

Fantastic Four: Franklin's Adventures

Marvel, 1998

1 .... 2.00

Fantastic Four: House of M

Marvel, 2005

1 .... 5.00
1/Variant 4.00
☛2nd print
2-3 .... 3.00

Fantastic Four Unlimited

Fantastic Four Unplugged

Fantastic Tales

Fantastic Voyages of Sindbad

Fantasy Features

Fantasy Quarterly

Far West

Fast Forward

Fantastic Four/Iron Man: Big in Japan
Marvel, 2006
1-4 ....4.00

Fantastic Four Legends
Marvel, 2003
1 ....14.00

Fantastic Four: 1 2 3 4
Marvel, 2001
1-4 ....3.00

Fantastic Four Roast
Marvel, 1982
1 ....2.00

Fantastic Four Special
Marvel, 1984
1 ....3.00

Fantastic Four Special
Marvel, 2006
1 ....3.00

Fantastic Four: The End
Marvel, 2007
1 ....3.00
1/RoughCut 4.00
2-4 ....3.00

Fantastic Four: The Legend
Marvel, 1996
1 ....4.00

Fantastic Four: The Movie
Marvel, 2005
1 ....5.00

Fantastic Four: The Wedding Special
Marvel, 2006
1 ....5.00

Fantastic Four: The World's Greatest Comics Magazine
Marvel, 2001
1-12 ....3.00

Fantastic Four 2099
Marvel, 1996
1 ....4.00
2-8 ....2.00

Fantastic Four Unlimited
Marvel, 1993
1 ....5.00
2-12 ....4.00

Fantastic Four Unplugged
Marvel, 1995
1-6 ....1.00

Fantastic Four: Unstable Molecules
Marvel, 2003
1-4 ....3.00

Fantastic Four vs. X-Men
Marvel, 1987
1-4 ....3.00

Fantastic Giants
Charlton, 1966
24 ....35.00

Fantastic Panic
Antarctic, 1993
1-8 ....3.00

Fantastic Panic
Antarctic, 1995
1-8 ....3.00

Fantastic Tales
I.W.
1 ....26.00

Fantastic Voyage (Movie)
Gold Key, 1967
1 ....40.00

Fantastic Voyage (TV)
Gold Key, 1969
1 ....25.00
2 ....16.00

Fantastic Voyages of Sindbad
Gold Key, 1965
1 ....18.00
2 ....12.00

Fantastic Worlds
Standard, 1952
5 ....75.00
6-7 ....60.00

Fantastic Worlds
Flashback Comics, 1995
1 ....3.00

Fantasy Features
AC, 1987
1-2 ....2.00

Fantasy Girls
Comax
1 ....3.00

Fantasy Masterpieces
Marvel, 1966
1 ....75.00
2 ....35.00
3 ....30.00
4-8 ....18.00
9 ....30.00
☛Torch origin
10 ....10.00
11 ....15.00

Fantasy Masterpieces
Marvel, 1979
1 ....6.00
2 ....4.00
3-10 ....3.00
11-14 ....2.00

Fantasy Quarterly
Independent Pub. Synd., 1978
1 .... 55.00

Faraway Looks
Faraway Press, 2002
nn 10.00

Farewell, Moonshadow
DC, 1997
1 .... 8.00

Farewell to Weapons
Marvel
1 .... 2.00

Fargo Kid
Prize
3 .... 75.00
4-5 .... 60.00

Farmer's Daughter
Stanhall, 1954
1 .... 110.00
2 .... 85.00
3-4 .... 70.00

Farscape: War Torn
DC, 2002
1-2 .... 5.00

Far West
Antarctic, 1998
1-4 .... 3.00

Fashion in Action
Eclipse, 1986
Summer 1-WS 1 .... 2.00

Fashion Police
Bryce Alan
1 .... 3.00

Fast Fiction
Seaboard, 1949
1 .... 125.00
2-4 .... 100.00
5 .... 60.00

Fast Forward
DC
1-3 .... 5.00

Fastlane Illustrated
Fastlane, 1994
½ 2.00
1-3 .... 3.00

Fast Willie Jackson
Fitzgerald Periodicals, 1976
1 .... 24.00
2-7 .... 16.00

Fatal Beauty
Illustration, 1996
Ashcan 1/A 4.00

Fat Albert
Gold Key, 1974
1 .... 12.00
2 .... 8.00
3-5 .... 7.00
6-10 .... 6.00
11-29 .... 4.00

Fatale
Broadway, 1995
1-6 .... 3.00
Ashcan 1 .... 1.00

Fat and Slat
E.C., 1947
1 .... 165.00
2 .... 110.00
3-4 .... 85.00

Fat and Slat Joke Book
Wise, 1944
1 .... 160.00

Fat Dog Mendoza
Dark Horse, 1992
1 .... 3.00

Fate
DC, 1994
0-1 .... 3.00
2-22 .... 2.00

Fate of the Blade
Dreamwave, 2002
1-5 .... 3.00

Fate's Five
Innervision
1-4 .... 3.00

Fat Freddy's Comics & Stories
Rip Off, 1983
1-2 .... 3.00

Fat Fury Special
Avalon
1 .... 3.00

Father & Son
Kitchen Sink, 1995
1-4 .... 3.00
Ashcan 1 .... 2.00
Special 1 .... 4.00

Fathom (Michael Turner's ...)
Aspen, 2005
1 .... 5.00
1/A cover 4.00
1/B cover 5.00
2-3 .... 3.00

Fathom
Comico, 1987
1-3 .... 2.00

Fathom
Comico, 1992
1-3 .... 3.00

Fat Albert

Fat Dog Mendoza

Fate

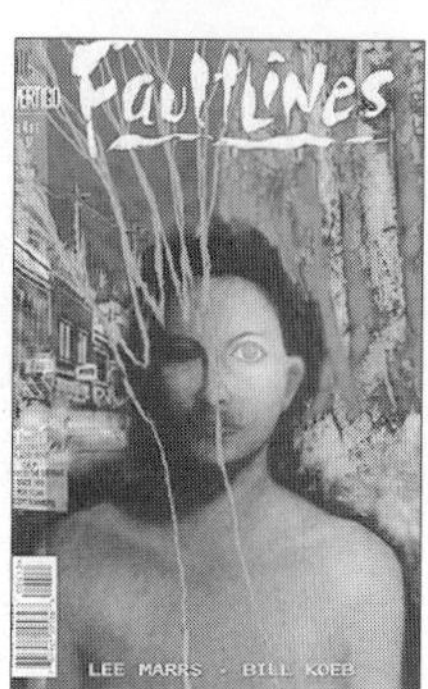

Faultlines

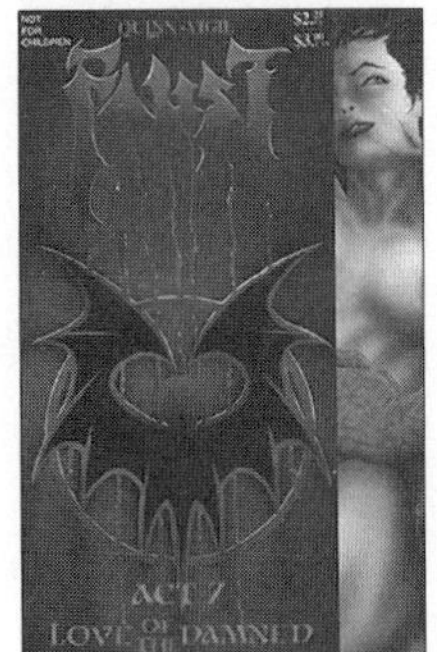

Faust

Fawcett Miniatures

Fawcett Movie Comic

Fax from Sarajevo

Fathom
Image, 1998

0/Dynamic 15.00
0/Conv.................................10.00
0-0/B 5.00
½ 3.00
½/A.......................................4.00
1/A..6.00
1/B-1/C 3.00
1/D....................................115.00
2 ....3.00
2/A....................................100.00
3-8 ....3.00
9 ....5.00
9/A..8.00
9/B 7.00
9/C 5.00
9/D 9.00
10 ....3.00
10/A......................................4.00
10/B 5.00
11 ....3.00
12-12/B 6.00
12/C 5.00
12/D 8.00
13 ....3.00
13/A......................................5.00
13/B-13/C 15.00
14 ....3.00
14/A......................................6.00
Deluxe 1 ....25.00

Fathom: Beginnings
Aspen, 2003

1 ....5.00
1/Conv...................................6.00

Fathom: Cannon Hawke
Aspen, 2004

0 ....6.00
0/Dynamic 15.00
0/Conv.................................10.00

Fathom: Cannon Hawke: Beginnings
Aspen, 2004

1 ....5.00
1/Conv.................................10.00

Fathom: Dawn of War
Aspen, 2004

0 ....5.00
1 ....7.00
1/Jay 10.00
2 ....4.00
2/Conv.................................10.00
3 ....4.00

Fathom: East & West Coast Tour Books
Image, 2004

1 ....3.00

Fathom (Michael Turner's...): Killian's Tide
Image, 2001

1-4/B 3.00

Fathom Preview Special
Image, 1998

1 ....3.00

Fathom Swimsuit Special
Image, 1999

1 ....3.00
2000 ....4.00
2002 ....8.00

Fatman, the Human Flying Saucer
Lightning, 1967

1 ....35.00
2-3 ....25.00

Fat Ninja
Silverwolf, 1986

1-5 ....2.00

Fatt Family
Side Show

1 ....3.00

Faultlines
DC, 1997

1-6 ....3.00

Fauna Rebellion
Fantagraphics, 1990

1-3 ....2.00

Fauntleroy Comics
Archie, 1950

1 ....38.00
2-3 ....24.00

Faust
Northstar, 1988

1 ....8.00
1/2nd 4.00
1/3rd......................................3.00
2 ....6.00
2/2nd 4.00
2/3rd......................................3.00
3 ....5.00
3/2nd 3.00
4 ....4.00
4/2nd 3.00
5 ....4.00
5/2nd 3.00
6 ....4.00
6/2nd 3.00
7 ....4.00
7/2nd 3.00
8 ....4.00
8/2nd-11 ....3.00
Special 1 ....10.00

Faust 777: The Wrath
Avatar, 1998

0-1 ....3.00

1/A 4.00
2-3 3.00

Faust: The Book of M

Avatar, 1999

1 3.00

Fawcett Miniatures

Fawcett

1-3 60.00
4 100.00
5-10 90.00
11 100.00

Fawcett Movie Comic

Fawcett, 1949

0 165.00
1 125.00
2 275.00
3-9 110.00
10-14 80.00
15 750.00
16-20 80.00

Fawcett's Funny Animals

Fawcett, 1942

1 240.00
2 125.00
3 90.00
4-5 65.00
6-10 52.00
11-20 40.00
21-40 32.00
41-60 24.00
61-91 20.00

Fax from Sarajevo

Dark Horse, 1996

1 17.00
1/HC 25.00
Ash 1 5.00

Faze One Fazers

AC

1-4 2.00

Fazers Sketchbook (Vic Bridges'...)

AC

1 2.00

F.B.I.

Dell, 1965

1 60.00

Fear

Marvel, 1970

1 95.00
2 30.00
3-4 15.00
5 20.00
6-9 15.00
10 35.00
☛Man-Thing starts
11 18.00
12 12.00
13-14 9.00
15-17 12.00
18 9.00
19 25.00
☛1st Howard Duck
20 20.00
☛Morbius begins
21 9.00
22 7.00
23 8.00
24 12.00
☛Blade app.
25 8.00
26-29 7.00
30 12.00
31 7.00

Fear Agent

Image, 2005

1-10 3.00

Fear Book

Eclipse, 1986

1 2.00

Fear Effect: Retro Helix

Image, 2002

1-1/Gold 3.00

Fear Effect Special

Image, 2000

1 3.00

Fear Is Hell

C&T

1 2.00

Fearless Fosdick

Kitchen Sink

1 12.00
1/2nd-1/3rd 10.00

Feather

Image, 2003

1-4 3.00
5 6.00

Feature Book

David McKay, 1936

1 1,150.00
2 965.00
3 8,000.00
3/2nd 875.00
4 2,500.00
4/2nd 640.00
5-7 425.00
8 450.00
9 425.00
10-12 310.00
13 250.00
14-15 255.00
16-19 300.00
20-24 260.00
25-26 350.00
27 175.00
28-29 155.00
30 100.00
31 125.00

Faze One Fazers

Fear

Fear Book

Fear Effect Special

Feature Book

Feature Comics

Feature Funnies

Federal Men Comics

32 .... 105.00
33 .... 200.00
34 .... 125.00
35 .... 100.00
36 .... 125.00
37 .... 85.00
38 .... 100.00
39 .... 140.00
40 .... 100.00
41-45 .... 85.00
46 .... 135.00
47 .... 85.00
48-49 .... 185.00
50 .... 165.00
51 .... 150.00
52 .... 125.00
53 .... 120.00
54-57 .... 125.00

Feature Comics

Quality, 1939

21 .... 425.00
22-26 .... 340.00
27 .... 2,750.00
28 .... 1,400.00
29 .... 850.00
30 .... 900.00
31 .... 650.00
32-37 .... 485.00
38-39 .... 350.00
40-50 .... 275.00
51-59 .... 200.00
60-70 .... 140.00
71-80 .... 100.00
81-99 .... 90.00
100 .... 100.00
101-144 .... 60.00

Feature Films

DC, 1950

1 .... 250.00
2 .... 185.00
3-4 .... 150.00

Feature Funnies

Harry A. Chesler, 1937

1 .... 1,500.00
2 .... 800.00
3 .... 550.00
4-5 .... 425.00
6-10 .... 285.00
11-20 .... 200.00

Feature Presentation

Fox, 1950

5 .... 225.00
6 .... 165.00

Federal Men Comics

Gerard, 1945

2 .... 225.00

Feds 'n' Heads

Print Mint

1 .... 8.00

Feeders

Dark Horse, 1999

1 .... 3.00

Feelgood Funnies

Rip Off, 1972

1 .... 3.00

Felicia Hardy: The Black Cat

Marvel, 1994

1-4 .... 2.00

Felix the Cat Silly Stories

Felix, 2005

1 .... 3.00

Felix and His Friends

Toby, 1954

1 .... 250.00
2-3 .... 125.00

Felix's Nephews Inky and Dinky

Harvey, 1957

1 .... 45.00
2-7 .... 24.00

Felix the Cat (Pat Sullivan's...)

Dell, 1948

1 .... 315.00
2 .... 145.00
3 .... 100.00
4-5 .... 85.00
6-10 .... 70.00
11-20 .... 60.00
21-30 .... 85.00
31 .... 45.00
32-33 .... 75.00
34-35 .... 45.00
36 .... 75.00
37 .... 225.00
38-40 .... 75.00
41 .... 60.00
42-51 .... 55.00
52-61 .... 48.00
Ann 1 .... 200.00
Ann 2 .... 165.00

Felix the Cat (1st Series)

Harvey, 1955

62-70 .... 32.00
71-80 .... 26.00
81-90 .... 22.00
91-118 .... 18.00

Felix the Cat (2nd Series)

Dell, 1962

1 .... 35.00
2-12 .... 24.00

Felix the Cat (3rd Series)
Harvey, 1991
1 .... 2.00
2-7 .... 1.00

Felix the Cat and Friends
Felix, 1994
1-5 .... 2.00

Felix the Cat Big Book
Harvey, 1992
1 .... 2.00

Felix the Cat Black & White
Felix
1-8 .... 2.00

Felix the Cat Digest Magazine
Harvey, 1992
1 .... 2.00

Fell
Image, 2005
1 .... 4.00
☛Ellis, Templesmith series
2-4 .... 2.00

Felon
Image, 2001
1-4 .... 3.00

Felt: True Tales of Underground Hip Hop
Image, 2005
1 .... 3.00

Fem 5
Express
1/A-2 .... 3.00

Female Sex Pirates
Friendly
1 .... 3.00

Fem Fantastique
AC, 1988
1 .... 2.00

Femforce
AC, 1984
1-2 .... 4.00
3-86 .... 3.00
87 .... 4.00
88-99 .... 3.00
100 .... 4.00
100/CS 7.00
101-109 .... 5.00
110/A-114 .... 3.00
115-123 .... 6.00
122-133 .... 7.00
Special 1 .... 2.00

Femforce Frightbook
AC
1 .... 3.00

Femforce in the House of Horror
AC, 1989
1 .... 3.00

Femforce: Night of the Demon
AC, 1990
1 .... 3.00

Femforce: Out of the Asylum Special
AC, 1987
1 .... 3.00

Femforce Pin Up Portfolio
AC, 1991
1-3 .... 3.00
4-5 .... 5.00

Femforce: To Die For
AC, 2005
1 .... 16.00

Femforce Uncut
AC
1 .... 10.00

Femforce Up Close
AC, 1992
1-11 .... 3.00

Femforce Victory Reborn
AC, 2005
1 .... 16.00

Femme Macabre
London Night
1 .... 3.00

Femme Noire
Cat-Head
1-2 .... 2.00

Fenry
Raven
1 .... 7.00

Ferret
Malibu, 1992
1 .... 2.00

Ferret
Malibu, 1993
1 .... 2.00
1/Variant-4 .... 3.00
5-10 .... 2.00

Ferro City
Image, 2005
1-4 .... 3.00

Feud
Marvel, 1993
1 .... 3.00
2-4 .... 2.00

Fever
Wonder Comix
1 .... 2.00

Feeders

Feelgood Funnies

Felon

Fem Fantastique

Fifties Terror

Fight Against Crime

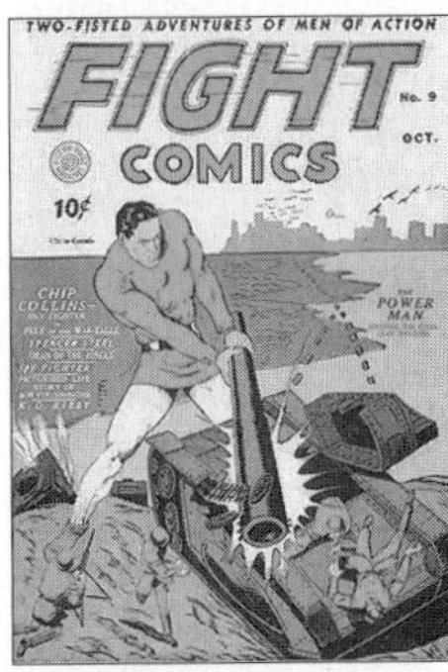
Fight Comics

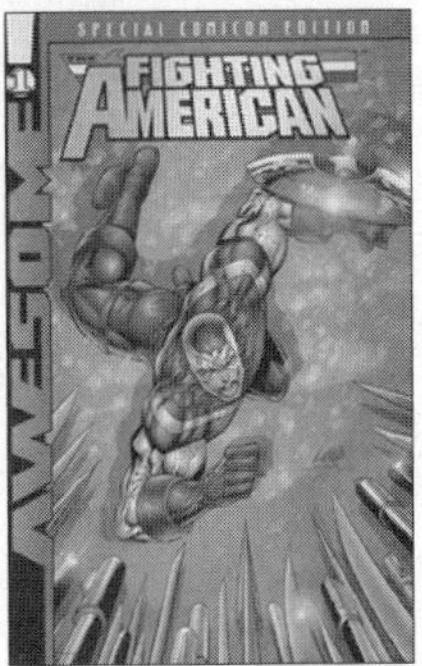
Fighting American Special Comicon Edition

Fever Dreams
Kitchen Sink, 1972
1 .... 3.00

Fever in Urbicand
NBM
1 .... 13.00

F5
Image, 2000
1-Ashcan 1 .... 3.00

F5 Origin
Dark Horse, 2001
1 .... 3.00

Fierce
Dark Horse, 2004
1-4 .... 3.00

15 Minutes
Slave Labor, 2004
1-3 .... 4.00

Fifth Force Featuring Hawk and Animal
Antarctic, 1999
1 .... 2.00
2 .... 3.00

Fifties Terror
Eternity, 1988
1-6 .... 2.00

52
DC, 2006
1 .... 4.00
2-6 .... 3.00
7 .... 4.00
8-36 .... 3.00

Fight Against Crime
Story, 1951
1 .... 240.00
2 .... 185.00
3-5 .... 145.00
6-9 .... 125.00
10-15 .... 175.00
16-21 .... 165.00

Fight Against The Guilty
Story, 1954
22-23 .... 150.00

Fight Comics
Fiction House, 1940
1 .... 3,500.00
2 .... 1,250.00
3 .... 650.00
4 .... 600.00
5 .... 500.00
6-10 .... 450.00
11-14 .... 425.00
15-16 .... 500.00
17-18 .... 425.00
19 .... 450.00
20-30 .... 350.00
31-40 .... 200.00
41-50 .... 175.00
51-60 .... 125.00
61-86 .... 100.00

Fight For Love
United Feature, 1952
1 .... 45.00

Fight for Tomorrow
DC, 2002
1-6 .... 3.00

Fightin' 5
Charlton, 1964
28 .... 20.00
29-30 .... 10.00
31-39 .... 9.00
40 .... 18.00
☛1st Peacemaker
41 .... 10.00
42-49 .... 3.00

Fightin' Air Force
Charlton, 1956
3 .... 32.00
4-5 .... 20.00
6-10 .... 15.00
11-20 .... 12.00
21-53 .... 8.00

Fightin' Army
Charlton, 1956
16 .... 24.00
17-20 .... 18.00
21-30 .... 15.00
31-40 .... 12.00
41-50 .... 10.00
51-75 .... 8.00
76 .... 10.00
☛Willy Schultz
77-100 .... 6.00
101-120 .... 5.00
121-172 .... 4.00

Fighting American
Headline, 1954
1 .... 850.00
2 .... 525.00
3-5 .... 400.00
6-7 .... 285.00

Fighting American
Harvey, 1966
1 .... 20.00

Fighting American
DC, 1994
1-6 .... 2.00

Fighting American
Awesome, 1997
1/A-1/C 3.00
1/D 16.00
2-3 .... 3.00

Fighting American: Dogs of War
Awesome, 1998

1-3 ... 3.00

Fighting American: Rules of the Game
Awesome, 1997

1-3 ... 3.00

Fighting American Special Comicon Edition
Awesome, 1997

1 ... 1.00

Fighting Daniel Boone
Avon, 1953

1 ... 70.00

Fighting Fem Classics
Forbidden Fruit, 1993

1 ... 4.00

Fighting Fems
Forbidden Fruit

1-2 ... 4.00

Fighting Fronts
Harvey, 1952

1 ... 52.00
2-5 ... 40.00

Fighting Indians of the Wild West
Avon, 1952

1 ... 95.00
2 ... 65.00

Fighting Leathernecks
Toby, 1952

1 ... 85.00
2 ... 50.00
3-6 ... 40.00

Fighting Man
Ajax, 1952

1 ... 42.00
2 ... 26.00
3 ... 22.00
4-8 ... 20.00

Fighting Undersea Commandos
Avon, 1952

1 ... 75.00
2 ... 50.00
3 ... 42.00
4-5 ... 38.00

Fighting Yank
Nedor, 1942

1 ... 3,450.00
2 ... 1,400.00
3 ... 800.00
4 ... 725.00
5-10 ... 600.00
11-15 ... 465.00
16-20 ... 385.00
21-26 ... 325.00
27-29 ... 270.00

Fightin' Marines
Charlton, 1951

1 ... 200.00
2 ... 145.00
3 ... 140.00
4-6 ... 110.00
7-9 ... 90.00
10 ... 34.00
11-13 ... 22.00
14 ... 75.00
15 ... 30.00
16 ... 22.00
17 ... 55.00
18-24 ... 16.00
25 ... 36.00
26 ... 40.00
27-29 ... 16.00
30-39 ... 13.00
40-50 ... 10.00
51-70 ... 7.00
71-74 ... 6.00
75-81 ... 4.00
82 ... 6.00
83-100 ... 4.00
101-120 ... 3.00
120/2nd ... 2.00
121-150 ... 3.00
151-176 ... 2.00

Fightin' Navy
Charlton, 1956

74 ... 24.00
75-80 ... 18.00
81-90 ... 15.00
91-100 ... 12.00
101-120 ... 8.00
121-125 ... 5.00
126-133 ... 2.00

Fightin' Texan
St. John, 1952

16-17 ... 55.00

Fight Man
Marvel, 1993

1 ... 2.00

Fight the Enemy
Tower, 1966

1 ... 22.00
2-3 ... 16.00

Figments
Blackthorne

1-2 ... 2.00

Figments Unlimited
Graphik

1-3 ... 1.00

Files of Ms. Tree
Renegade, 1984

1-3 ... 6.00

Fighting Daniel Boone

Fighting Fronts

Fighting Leathernecks

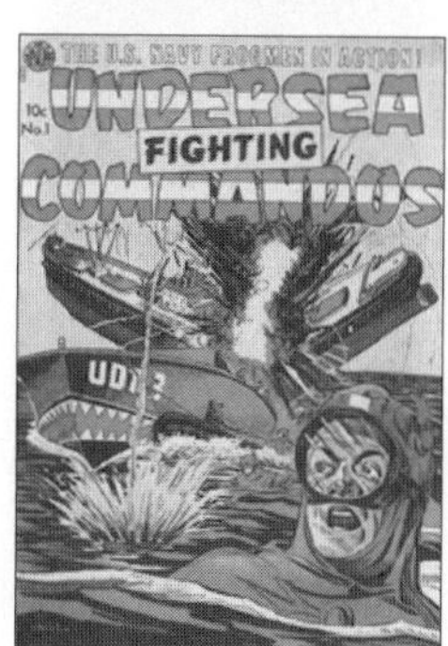

Fighting Undersea Commandos

Fighting Yank

Fight Man

Filthy Habits

Finder

Filibusting Comics
Fantagraphics, 1995

1 .... 3.00

Film Funnies
Marvel, 1949

1 .... 85.00
2 .... 55.00

Film Stars Romances
Star Publications, 1950

1 .... 250.00
2 .... 165.00
3 .... 140.00

Filth
DC, 2002

1-13 .... 3.00

Filthy Animals
Radio, 1997

1-4 .... 3.00

Filthy Habits
Aeon, 1996

1-3 .... 3.00

Final Cycle
Dragon's Teeth, 1987

1-4 .... 2.00

Final Man
C&T

1 .... 2.00

Final Night
DC, 1996

1 .... 6.00
2-4 .... 4.00
Ash 1 .... 1.00

Final Taboo
Aircel, 1991

1-2 .... 3.00

Finals
DC, 1999

1-4 .... 3.00

Finder
Lightspeed, 1996

1-14 .... 4.00
15-35 .... 3.00
Ashcan 1 .... 1.00

Finder Footnotes
Lightspeed

1 .... 6.00

Finieous Treasury
TSR

1 .... 3.00

Fink, Inc.
Fink, Inc.

1 .... 4.00

Finn
Fleetway-Quality

1-4 .... 3.00

Fire
Caliber

1-2 .... 3.00

Firearm
Malibu, 1993

0 .... 15.00
1 .... 2.00
1/Ltd.-2 .... 3.00
3-9 .... 2.00
10 .... 4.00
11-19 .... 2.00

Firebirds One Shot
Image

1 .... 6.00

Firebrand
DC, 1996

1-9 .... 2.00

Firebreather
Image, 2003

1-4 .... 3.00

Firebreather: Iron Saint One-Shot
Image, 2005

1 .... 7.00

Fire from Heaven
Image, 1996

½ 1.00
1-2 .... 3.00

Firehair
Fiction House, 1948

1 .... 400.00
2 .... 200.00
7-9 .... 100.00
10-11 .... 90.00

Fires
Catalan

1 .... 13.00

Fire Sale
Rip Off, 1989

1 .... 3.00

Firestar
Marvel, 1986

1-2 .... 2.00
3-4 .... 1.00

Firestorm
DC, 1978

1 .... 8.00
2 .... 2.00
3 .... 3.00
4-5 .... 2.00

Firestorm
DC, 2004

1 .... 8.00
1-5 .... 3.00
6 .... 5.00
☛Identity Crisis tie
7-29 .... 3.00

Firestorm, the Nuclear Man

DC, 1987

65-93 .... 1.00
30 .... 3.00
94 .... 1.00
31 .... 3.00
95 .... 1.00
32 .... 3.00
96-99 .... 1.00
100 .... 3.00
Ann 5 .... 1.00

Fire Team

Aircel, 1990

1-6 .... 3.00

Firkin

Knockabout

1-6 .... 3.00

First

CrossGen, 2000

1 .... 4.00
2-37 .... 3.00

First Adventures

First, 1985

1-5 .... 1.00

First Deterrent

Devious Drawings, 1996

1 .... 3.00

1st Folio

Pacific, 1984

1 .... 2.00

First Graphic Novel

First, 1984

1-2 .... 6.00
3 .... 12.00
4-5 .... 6.00
6 .... 15.00
7-8 .... 8.00
9-10 .... 10.00
11 .... 15.00
12 .... 8.00
13 .... 12.00
14 .... 8.00
15 .... 10.00
16-17 .... 9.00
18 .... 10.00
19 .... 9.00
20 .... 13.00
21 .... 10.00
22 .... 20.00
23 .... 12.00
24 .... 9.00
25 .... 15.00

1st Issue Special

DC, 1975

1 .... 7.00
2 .... 5.00
3-6 .... 4.00
7 .... 5.00
8 .... 15.00
☛Warlord
9-12 .... 4.00
13 .... 5.00

First King Adventure

ADV Manga, 2005

1-2 .... 10.00

First Kingdom

Bud Plant, 1978

1-5 .... 3.00
6-24 .... 2.00

First Kiss

Charlton, 1957

1 .... 45.00
2 .... 28.00
3 .... 22.00
4-5 .... 18.00
6-10 .... 13.00
11-20 .... 12.00
21-40 .... 8.00

First Love Illustrated

Harvey, 1949

1 .... 100.00
2 .... 65.00
3 .... 45.00
4-10 .... 35.00
11-20 .... 30.00
21-30 .... 28.00
31-40 .... 22.00
41-50 .... 20.00
51-89 .... 16.00

First Man

Image, 1997

1 .... 3.00

First Romance Magazine

Harvey, 1949

1 .... 85.00
2 .... 55.00
3 .... 45.00
4-5 .... 38.00
6-10 .... 32.00
11-20 .... 26.00
21-30 .... 22.00
31-40 .... 18.00
41-52 .... 15.00

First Six Pack

First, 1987

1-2 .... 1.00

First Trip to the Moon

Avalon

1 .... 3.00

First Wave

Andromeda, 2000

1 .... 3.00

Fishmasters

Slave Labor, 1994

1 .... 3.00

Firearm

Firebrand

Firehair

Fire Team

First Kiss

Fish Shticks

Fist of the North Star

Flag Fighters

Fish Police
Fishwrap, 1985

1-3 .... 1.00
4-11 .... 2.00

Fish Police
Comico, 1987

5-16 .... 2.00
17 .... 3.00
18-Special 1 .... 2.00

Fish Police
Marvel, 1992

1-6 .... 1.00

Fish Shticks
Apple, 1991

1-6 .... 2.00

Fission Chicken
Fantagraphics, 1990

1-4 .... 2.00

Fission Chicken: Plan Nine from Vortox
Mu, 1994

1 .... 4.00

Fist of God
Eternity, 1988

1-4 .... 2.00

Fist of the North Star
Viz, 1989

1-8 .... 3.00

Fist of the North Star Part 2
Viz

1-8 .... 3.00

Fist of the North Star Part 3
Viz, 1996

1-5 .... 3.00

Fist of the North Star Part 4
Viz, 1996

1-7 .... 3.00

5-Cent Comics
Fawcett, 1940

1 .... 10,000.00

Five Fists of Science
Image, 2006

1 .... 13.00

Five Little Comics
Scott McCloud

1 .... 4.00

Five Years of Pain
Boneyard, 1997

1 .... 4.00

Flag Fighters
Ironcat, 1997

1-5 .... 3.00

Flame
Fox, 1940

1 .... 1,800.00
2 .... 1,200.00
3 .... 775.00
4 .... 525.00
5 .... 450.00
6-8 .... 340.00

Flamehead
JNCO, 1998

0 .... 1.00

Flame of Recca
Viz, 2003

1-14 .... 10.00

Flame (Ajax)
Ajax

1 .... 285.00
2 .... 165.00
3 .... 150.00

Flame Twisters
Brown Study, 1994

1-2 .... 3.00

Flaming Carrot
Kilian, 1981

1 .... 35.00

Flaming Carrot
Image, 2004

1 .... 3.00
2-4 .... 4.00

Flaming Carrot Comics
Aardvark-Vanaheim, 1984

1 .... 26.00
2 .... 15.00
3 .... 12.00
4 .... 10.00
5-6 .... 8.00
7 .... 7.00
8-9 .... 5.00
10-12 .... 4.00
13-15 .... 3.00
15/A-16 .... 4.00
17-24 .... 3.00
25 .... 4.00
26-30/A 3.00
32 .... 4.00
31 .... 3.00
Ann 1 .... 5.00

Flaming Carrot Stories
Dark Horse

1 .... 5.00

Flaming Love
Quality, 1949

1 .... 225.00
2 .... 125.00

3 .... 85.00
4-6 .... 65.00

Flaming Western Romances

Star Publications, 1950

3 .... 200.00

Flare

Hero, 1988

1-3 .... 3.00

Flare

Hero, 1989

1-16 .... 3.00
Ann 1 .... 5.00

Flare

Heroic

1-29 .... 3.00

Flare Adventures

Heroic, 1992

1 .... 1.00
2-3 .... 3.00
4-14 .... 4.00

Flare First Edition

Hero, 1993

1-3 .... 4.00
4-5 .... 5.00
6-11 .... 4.00

Flash

DC, 1959

105 .... 6,500.00
106 .... 2,000.00
107 .... 1,000.00
108 .... 850.00
109 .... 650.00
110 .... 1,500.00
☛1st Kid Flash
111 .... 450.00
112 .... 600.00
☛1st Elong. Man
113 .... 550.00
114 .... 275.00
115 .... 350.00
116 .... 250.00
117 .... 300.00
118-120 .... 250.00
121-122 .... 200.00
123 .... 1,500.00
☛1st Earth-2
124-128 .... 150.00
129 .... 325.00
☛GA Flash app.
130 .... 150.00
131-136 .... 125.00
137 .... 475.00
☛GA Flash app.
138-140 .... 125.00
141-142 .... 150.00
143 .... 125.00
144-150 .... 100.00
151 .... 80.00
152-153 .... 65.00
154-158 .... 60.00
159 .... 75.00
160 .... 90.00
☛Giant-size
161-164 .... 50.00
165 .... 70.00
166-167 .... 50.00
168 .... 95.00
169 .... 70.00
☛Origin of Flash
170-174 .... 50.00
175 .... 175.00
☛Race w/Superman
176-179 .... 40.00
180 .... 50.00
181-183 .... 35.00
184 .... 50.00
185-186 .... 35.00
187 .... 65.00
188-191 .... 35.00
192-193 .... 25.00
194 .... 40.00
195 .... 25.00
196 .... 40.00
197-200 .... 25.00
201-202 .... 20.00
203 .... 25.00
204 .... 20.00
205 .... 35.00
206 .... 20.00
207-212 .... 17.00
213 .... 25.00
214 .... 40.00
215 .... 35.00
216-219 .... 17.00
220-228 .... 15.00
229 .... 30.00
230-231 .... 15.00
232 .... 30.00
☛100-page issue
233-237 .... 10.00
238-245 .... 7.00
246 .... 12.00
247-262 .... 7.00
263-268 .... 4.00
268/Whitman 12.00
269-273 .... 4.00
273/Whitman 7.00
274 .... 5.00
274/Whitman-275/Whitman ... 7.00
276 .... 4.00
276/Whitman 7.00
277-278 .... 4.00
278/Whitman 7.00
279-283 .... 4.00
283/Whitman 7.00
284-286 .... 4.00
286/Whitman 7.00
287-288 .... 4.00
289 .... 5.00
290-299 .... 3.00

Flame

Flaming Carrot Stories

Flash

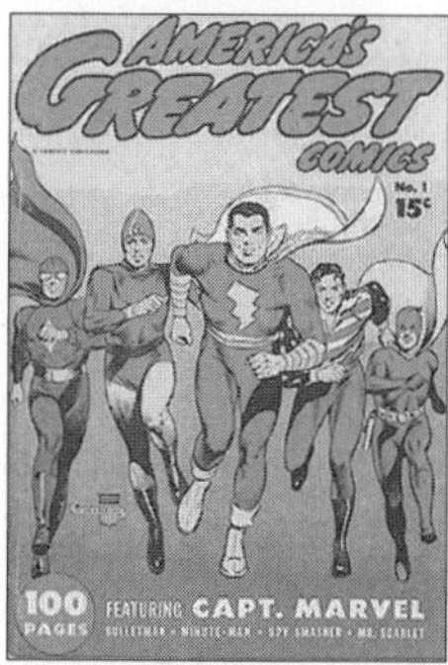

Flashback

Flash Comics

Flash Gordon Comics

Flash Plus

Flesh

300 ....5.00
301-304 ....3.00
305-306 ....4.00
307-349 ....3.00
350 ....7.00
Ann 1 ....400.00
Ann 1/2nd 7.00

Flash

DC, 1987

0 ....4.00
1 ....5.00
2-20 ....3.00
21-49 ....2.00
50 ....3.00
51-78 ....2.00
79 ....3.00
80 ....2.00
80/Variant 3.00
81-90 ....2.00
91 ....4.00
92 ....8.00
☛1st Impulse
93 ....5.00
94-95 ....3.00
96-99 ....2.00
100 ....3.00
100/Variant 4.00
101-149 ....2.00
150 ....3.00
151-187 ....2.00
188 ....3.00
189-199 ....2.00
200 ....4.00
201-205 ....2.00
206 ....6.00
207 ....2.00
208 ....5.00
209 ....4.00
210 ....3.00
210/2nd 2.00
211 ....4.00
212-213 ....2.00
214 ....6.00
☛Identity Crisis tie
215 ....5.00
☛Identity Crisis tie
216 ....6.00
☛Identity Crisis tie
217 ....5.00
☛Identity Crisis tie
218 ....4.00
219 ....9.00
☛Inf. Crisis tie
220 ....6.00
221 ....5.00
222-223 ....4.00
224-1000000 ....3.00
Ann 1 ....5.00
Ann 2-4 ....2.00
Ann 5-7 ....3.00
Ann 8 ....4.00
Ann 9 ....3.00
Ann 10-11 ....4.00
Ann 12 ....3.00
Ann 13 ....4.00
GS 1-2 ....5.00
Special 1 ....4.00
TV 1 ....4.00

Flash & Green Lantern: The Brave and the Bold

DC, 1999

1-6 ....3.00

Flashback

Special, 1974

1-27 ....3.00

Flash Comics

DC, 1940

1 ....70,000.00
☛1st Flash, Hawkman
2 ....8,000.00
3 ....5,500.00
4 ....4,500.00
5 ....3,500.00
6 ....5,000.00
7 ....4,500.00
8 ....3,000.00
9-10 ....3,250.00
11-20 ....2,000.00
21-24 ....1,600.00
25-40 ....1,000.00
41-50 ....800.00
51-61 ....600.00
62 ....1,000.00
☛Kubert Hawkman
63-69 ....600.00
70-85 ....550.00
86 ....2,250.00
☛1st Black Canary
87 ....875.00
88-91 ....900.00
92 ....3,000.00
☛1st solo Black Canary
93 ....700.00
94-99 ....1,000.00
100 ....2,500.00
☛Scarce
101-102 ....2,250.00
☛Scarce
103 ....2,500.00
☛Scarce
104 ....7,000.00
☛Flash origin recap

Flash Gordon

Gold Key, 1965

1 ....26.00

Flash Gordon

King, 1966

1 ....25.00
2-7 ....20.00
8-14 ....10.00
15-19 ....8.00
20-23 ....6.00

24 .... 5.00
25-29 .... 4.00
30 .... 8.00
30/50¢ 4.00
31-37 .... 3.00

Flash Gordon
DC, 1988
1-9 .... 2.00

Flash Gordon
Marvel, 1995
1-2 .... 3.00

Flash Gordon Comics
Harvey, 1950
1 .... 225.00
2 .... 145.00
3-5 .... 110.00

Flash Gordon: The Movie
Golden Press
1 .... 3.00

Flash/Green Lantern: Faster Friends
DC
1 .... 5.00

Flash: Our Worlds at War
DC, 2001
1 .... 3.00

Flash Plus
DC, 1997
1 .... 3.00

Flash Secret Files
DC, 1997
1-3 .... 5.00

Flash: The Fastest Man Alive
DC, 2006
1 .... 6.00
2-7 .... 3.00

Flash: Iron Heights
DC, 2001
1 .... 6.00

Flash: Time Flies
DC, 2002
nn 6.00

Flashmarks
Fantagraphics
1 .... 3.00

Flashpoint
DC, 1999
1-3 .... 3.00

Flatline Comics Presents...
Flatline, 1993
1 .... 3.00

Flat Top
Harvey, 1953
1 .... 28.00

2 .... 16.00
3 .... 12.00
4-7 .... 10.00

Flaxen
Dark Horse
1 .... 3.00

Flaxen: Alter Ego
Caliber, 1995
1 .... 3.00

Fleener
Zongo, 1996
1-3 .... 3.00

Flesh
Fleetway-Quality
1-4 .... 3.00

Flesh & Blood
Brainstorm, 1996
1 .... 3.00
1/Ashcan 1.00

Flesh & Blood: Pre-Existing Conditions
Blindwolf
1 .... 3.00

Flesh and Bones
Upshot
1-4 .... 2.00

Flesh Crawlers
Kitchen Sink, 1994
1-3 .... 3.00

Flesh Gordon
Aircel, 1992
1-4 .... 3.00

Fleshpot
Fantagraphics, 1997
1 .... 3.00

Flex Mentallo
DC, 1996
1 .... 10.00
2-4 .... 8.00

Flickering Flesh
Boneyard, 1993
1 .... 3.00

Flicker's Fleas
Fifth Wheel
1 .... 3.00

Flinch
DC, 1999
1-16 .... 3.00

Flint Armbuster Jr. Special
Alchemy
1 .... 3.00

Flintstone Kids
Marvel, 1987
1-11 .... 2.00

Flesh and Bones

Flesh Crawlers

Flex Mentallo

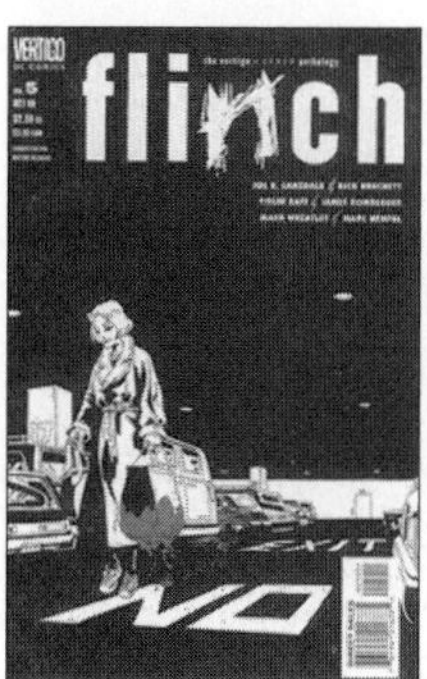

Flinch

Flintstones 3-D

Flintstones Bigger and Boulder

Flintstones Giant Size

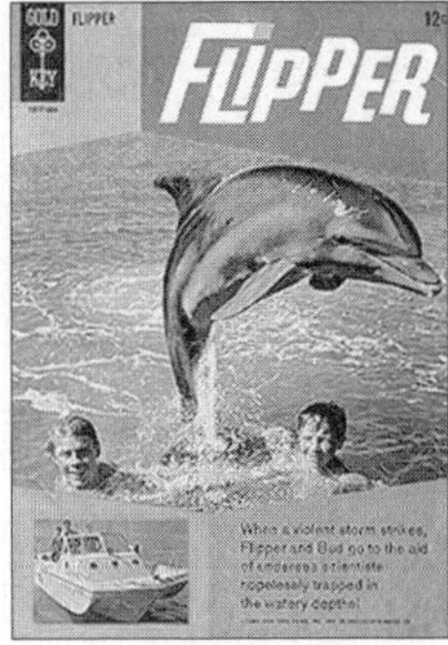
Flipper

Flintstones
Dell, 1961

1 ....55.00
2 ....38.00
3-5 ....30.00
6-7 ....24.00
8-10 ....20.00
11-20 ....18.00
21-30 ....15.00
31-40 ....12.00
41-60 ....9.00

Flintstones
Charlton, 1970

1 ....36.00
2 ....22.00
3-5 ....14.00
6-10 ....9.00
11-20 ....7.00
21-30 ....5.00
31-50 ....4.00

Flintstones 3-D
Blackthorne, 1987

1-4 ....3.00

Flintstones
Marvel, 1977

1 ....5.00
2-9 ....3.00

Flintstones
Harvey, 1992

1 ....3.00
2-13 ....2.00

Flintstones
Archie, 1995

1-22 ....2.00

Flintstones and the Jetsons
DC, 1997

1-21 ....2.00

Flintstones at the New York World's Fair
Dell, 1964

1 ....48.00

Flintstones Big Book
Harvey, 1992

1-2 ....2.00

Flintstones Bigger and Boulder
Gold Key, 1962

1 ....65.00
2 ....45.00

Flintstones Doublevision
Harvey, 1994

1 ....3.00

Flintstones Giant Size
Harvey, 1992

2-3 ....3.00

Flintstones with Pebbles and Bamm-Bamm
Gold Key, 1965

1 ....50.00

Flip
Harvey, 1954

1 ....90.00
2 ....65.00

Flipper
Gold Key, 1966

1 ....25.00
2-3 ....18.00

Flippity and Flop
DC, 1951

1 ....140.00
2 ....85.00
3 ....60.00
4-5 ....45.00
6-10 ....40.00
11-20 ....36.00
21-30 ....30.00
31-40 ....26.00
41-47 ....24.00

Floaters
Dark Horse, 1993

1-5 ....3.00

Flock of Dreamers
Kitchen Sink, 1997

1 ....13.00

Flood Relief
Malibu, 1994

1 ....5.00

Flowers
Drawn and Quarterly

1 ....3.00

Flowers on the Razorwire
Boneyard, 1994

1-10 ....3.00

Fly
Archie, 1983

1 ....3.00
2-9 ....2.00

Fly
DC, 1991

1-17 ....1.00
Ann 1 ....2.00

Fly Man
Archie, 1965

32 ....32.00
33-34 ....20.00
35-39 ....16.00

Flyboy
Ziff-Davis, 1952

1 ....90.00
2-4 ....68.00
5 ....44.00

Flying Aces
Key, 1955

1 .... 35.00
2-5 .... 20.00

Flying A's Range Rider
Dell, 1953

2 .... 60.00
3 .... 45.00
4-5 .... 40.00
6-10 .... 35.00
11-24 .... 28.00

Flying Cadet
Flying Cadet, 1943

1 .... 80.00
2 .... 50.00
3-5 .... 40.00
6-10 .... 35.00
11-17 .... 28.00

Flying Colors 10th Anniversary Special
Flying Colors, 1998

1 .... 3.00

Flying Models
Health, 1954

3 .... 36.00

Flying Nun
Dell, 1968

1 .... 32.00
2-4 .... 20.00

Flying Saucers
Avon, 1950

1 .... 560.00
2 .... 295.00
2/2nd 165.00

Flying Saucers
Dell, 1967

1 .... 26.00
2-5 .... 15.00

Flyin' Jenny
Pentagon, 1946

1 .... 80.00
2 .... 70.00

Focus
DC, 1987

1 .... 1.00

Foes
Ram

1 .... 2.00

Fog City Comics
Stampart

1 .... 1.00

Foodang
Continu¸m, 1994

1 .... 2.00
Ashcan 1 .... 1.00

Foodang
August House, 1995

1-2 .... 3.00

Food First Comics
IFDP

1-1/3rd 3.00

Foodini
Continental, 1950

1 .... 110.00
2 .... 75.00
3 .... 50.00
4 .... 45.00

Foofur
Marvel, 1987

1-6 .... 1.00

Foolkiller
Marvel, 1990

1-10 .... 2.00

FOOM Magazine
Marvel, 1973

1 .... 45.00
2 .... 30.00
3-4 .... 25.00
5-20 .... 20.00
21 .... 25.00
22 .... 40.00

Football Heroes
Personality

1-2 .... 3.00

Football Thrills
Ziff-Davis, 1951

1 .... 165.00
2 .... 110.00

Foot Soldiers
Dark Horse, 1996

1-4 .... 3.00

Foot Soldiers
Image, 1997

1-5 .... 3.00

Foozle
Eclipse, 1985

1-3 .... 2.00

Forbidden 3-D
3-D Zone

1-1/3D 4.00

Forbidden Frankenstein
Fantagraphics, 1991

1 .... 2.00
2 .... 3.00

Forbidden Kingdom
Eastern, 1987

1-8 .... 2.00

Forbidden Knowledge
Last Gasp, 1975

1 .... 4.00

Flippity and Flop

Floaters

Flyboy

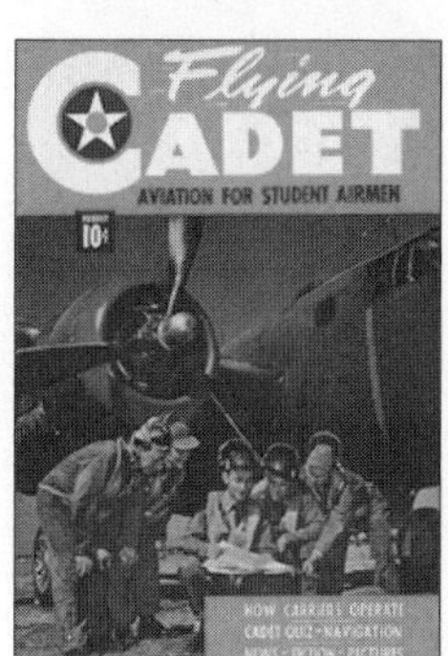

Flying Cadet

Foofur

Foolkiller

Football Heroes

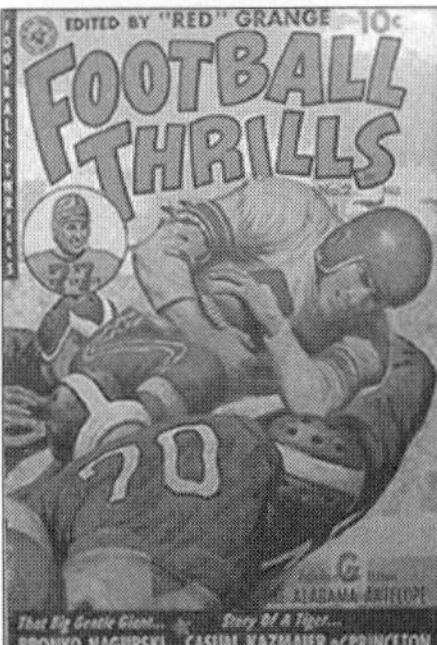

Football Thrills

Forbidden Knowledge: Adventure Beyond the Doorway to Souls with Radical Dreamer

Mark's Giant Economy Size

1 .... 4.00

Forbidden Love

Quality, 1950

1 .... 325.00
2 .... 225.00
3-4 .... 200.00

Forbidden Planet

Innovation, 1992

1-4 .... 3.00

Forbidden Subjects

Angel

0 .... 3.00
0/A-0/B 4.00

Forbidden Subjects: Candy Kisses

Angel

1-1/B 3.00

Forbidden Tales of Dark Mansion

DC, 1972

5 .... 35.00
6-7 .... 17.00
8-9 .... 12.00
10-14 .... 10.00
15 .... 15.00

Forbidden Vampire

Angel

0 .... 3.00

Forbidden Worlds

ACG, 1951

1 .... 875.00
2 .... 500.00
3 .... 465.00
4 .... 270.00
5-6 .... 290.00
7-10 .... 190.00
11-15 .... 135.00
16-20 .... 100.00
21-30 .... 85.00
31-40 .... 75.00
41-50 .... 54.00
51-60 .... 45.00
61-70 .... 40.00
71-72 .... 35.00
73 .... 275.00
☛1st Herbie
74-80 .... 35.00
81-85 .... 24.00
86 .... 30.00
87-90 .... 24.00
91-93 .... 20.00
94 .... 55.00
☛Herbie app.
95-100 .... 20.00
101-109 .... 16.00
110 .... 35.00
☛Herbie app.
111-113 .... 16.00
114 .... 35.00
115 .... 16.00
116 .... 30.00
☛Herbie app.
117-120 .... 16.00
121-124 .... 12.00
125 .... 25.00
☛1st Magicman
126-127 .... 12.00
128 .... 14.00
129 .... 12.00
130 .... 14.00
131-140 .... 12.00
141-145 .... 10.00

Forbidden Worlds (A+)

A-Plus

1 .... 3.00

Forbidden Worlds (Avalon)

Avalon

1 .... 3.00

Forbidden X Angel

Angel, 1997

1 .... 3.00

Forbidden Zone

Galaxy Entertainment

1 .... 6.00

Force 10

Crow

1-1/Ashcan 3.00

Force Majeure: Prairie Bay

Little Rocket, 2002

1 .... 3.00

Force of Buddha's Palm

Jademan, 1988

1-55 .... 2.00

Force Seven

Lone Star, 1999

1-3 .... 3.00

Force Works

Marvel, 1994

1 .... 4.00
2-5 .... 2.00
5/CS 3.00
6-11 .... 2.00
12 .... 3.00
13-22 .... 2.00
Ashcan 1 .... 1.00

Foreplay

NBM

1 .... 19.00

Fore/Punk
Parody
1/A-1/B 3.00

Foreternity
Antarctic, 1997
1-4 .... 3.00

Forever Amber
Image, 1999
1/A-4 .... 3.00

Forever Eve
Shadow Song, 1997
1-4 .... 3.00

Forever Maelstrom
DC, 2003
1-6 .... 3.00

Forever Now
Entertainment
1-2 .... 2.00

Forever People
DC, 1971
1 .... 35.00
2 .... 20.00
3-5 .... 18.00
6-11 .... 14.00

Forever People
DC, 1988
1-6 .... 2.00

Forever Warriors
CFD, 1997
1 .... 3.00

Forge
CrossGen, 2002
1-3 .... 10.00
4-7 .... 12.00
8-13 .... 8.00

Forgotten Realms
DC, 1989
1 .... 2.00
2-25 .... 1.00
Ann 1 .... 2.00

Forgotten Realms: Exile
Devil's Due, 2005
1 .... 5.00
1/Special 9.00
2 .... 5.00
2/Special 9.00
3 .... 5.00
3/Special 9.00

Forgotten Realms: Homeland
Devil's Due, 2005
1 .... 5.00
1/Variant 9.00
1/Conv 10.00
2 .... 5.00
2/Variant 9.00
3 .... 5.00
3/Variant 9.00

Forgotten Realms: Sojourn
Devil's Due, 2006
1 .... 5.00
1/Variant 9.00
2 .... 5.00
2/Special 9.00
3 .... 5.00
3/Special 9.00

Forgotten Realms: The Crystal Shard
Devil's Due, 2006
1 .... 5.00
1/Special 9.00
2 .... 5.00
2/Variant 9.00
3 .... 5.00
3/Silver 9.00

Forgotten Realms: The Grand Tour
TSR
1 .... 1.00

For Lovers Only
Charlton, 1971
60 .... 20.00
61-87 .... 10.00

Formerly Known as the Justice League
DC, 2003
1-6 .... 3.00

Forsaken
Image, 2004
1-3 .... 3.00

Fort: Prophet of the Unexplained
Dark Horse, 2002
1-4 .... 3.00

Fortune and Glory
Oni, 1999
1-3 .... 5.00

Fortune's Fool Story of Jinxer
Cranium, 1999
0 .... 3.00

Fortune's Friends: Hell Week
Aria
1 .... 7.00

Forty Winks
Odd Jobs Limited, 1997
1-4 .... 3.00

Forty Winks Christmas Special
Peregrine Entertainment, 1998
1 .... 3.00

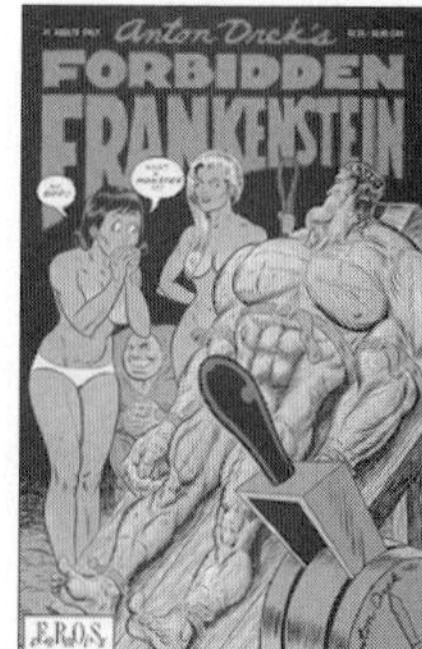

Forbidden Frankenstein

Forbidden Planet

Forbidden Tales of Dark Mansion

Forbidden Worlds

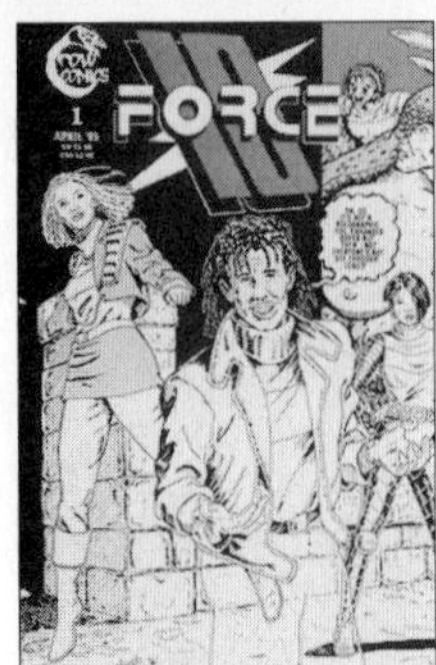

Force 10

Force Seven

Force Works

Forever Amber

Forty Winks Super Special Edition: TV Party Tonite!

Peregrine Entertainment, 1999

1 ....3.00

Foton Effect

Aced, 1986

1-3 ....2.00

Foul!

Traitors Gait

1 ....3.00

4

Marvel, 2000

1 ....4.00

Four Color Comics (1st Series)

Dell, 1939

1 ....7,250.00
2 ....1,500.00
3 ....750.00
4 ....9,000.00
5 ....650.00
6 ....1,500.00
7 ....425.00
8 ....750.00
9 ....630.00
10 ....425.00
11 ....385.00
12 ....550.00
13 ....1,500.00
14-15 ....400.00
16 ....9,800.00
17 ....2,000.00
18-19 ....400.00
20 ....300.00
21 ....675.00
22-23 ....325.00
24 ....400.00
25 ....750.00

Four Color Comics (2nd Series)

Dell, 1942

1 ....550.00
2 ....275.00
3 ....500.00
4-5 ....465.00
6 ....235.00
7 ....325.00
8 ....225.00
9 ....9,000.00
☛1st Donald Duck
10 ....800.00
11 ....310.00
12 ....585.00
13 ....340.00
14 ....350.00
15 ....650.00
16 ....725.00
17 ....525.00
18 ....435.00
19 ....635.00
20 ....235.00
21 ....450.00
22 ....200.00
23 ....380.00
24 ....335.00
25 ....460.00
26 ....475.00
27 ....950.00
☛Became Micky Mouse #1
28 ....220.00
29 ....6,200.00
☛2nd Donald Duck
30 ....575.00
31 ....200.00
32 ....170.00
33 ....775.00
☛Became Bugs Bunny #1
34 ....475.00
35 ....165.00
36 ....210.00
37 ....200.00
38 ....1,440.00
☛Roy Rogers
39 ....350.00
40 ....230.00
41 ....235.00
42 ....190.00
43 ....350.00
44-50 ....450.00
51 ....385.00
52 ....310.00
53 ....170.00
54 ....310.00
55 ....150.00
56 ....365.00
57 ....445.00
58 ....210.00
59 ....220.00
60 ....160.00
61 ....275.00
62 ....2,550.00
☛Donald Duck
63 ....575.00
64-65 ....125.00
66 ....395.00
67 ....190.00
68 ....210.00
69 ....265.00
70 ....300.00
71 ....870.00
☛3 Caballeros
72 ....285.00
73 ....125.00
74 ....1,100.00
☛Little Lulu
75 ....360.00
76 ....285.00
77 ....360.00
78 ....250.00
79 ....1,150.00
☛Mickey Mouse

Issue	Price
80	160.00
81	100.00
82	500.00
83	345.00
84	460.00
85	165.00
86	405.00
87	235.00
88	225.00
89	135.00
90	200.00
91	220.00
92	770.00
93	305.00
94	115.00
95	395.00
96	275.00
97	495.00
98	360.00
99	100.00
100-101	300.00
102	140.00
103	200.00
104	205.00
105	740.00
106	100.00
107	235.00
108	1,650.00
☛Donald Duck	
109	305.00
110	275.00
111	135.00
112	155.00
113	130.00
114	195.00
115	375.00
116	265.00
117	245.00
118	335.00
119	315.00
120	325.00
121	125.00
122	120.00
123	170.00
124	225.00
125	255.00
126	155.00
127	130.00
128	170.00
129	285.00
130	85.00
131	300.00
132	100.00
133	260.00
134	625.00
☛Tarzan	
135	240.00
136	250.00
137	200.00
138	90.00
139	285.00
140	165.00
141	230.00
142	145.00
143	90.00
144/A	165.00
144/B	225.00
145	125.00
146	175.00
147	770.00
☛Donald Duck	
148	640.00
☛Pogo	
149	100.00
150	85.00
151	225.00
152	165.00
153	185.00
154	100.00
155	75.00
156	110.00
157	240.00
158	260.00
159	800.00
☛Donald Duck	
160	190.00
161	475.00
☛Tarzan	
162	200.00
163	190.00
164	140.00
165	245.00
166	175.00
167	195.00
168-169	135.00
170	180.00
171	225.00
172	145.00
173	170.00
174	80.00
175	155.00
176	85.00
177	140.00
178	2,875.00
☛Donald Duck	
179	160.00
180	90.00
181	180.00
182	100.00
183	85.00
184	80.00
185	140.00
186	195.00
187-188	120.00
189	800.00
☛Donald Duck	
190	180.00
191	100.00
192	130.00
193	155.00
194	180.00
195	65.00
196	175.00
197	130.00

Forever Maelstrom

Forever Warriors

For Lovers Only

Four Color Comics (2nd series)

Forty Winks

Four Favorites

Four Horsemen

Four-Star Battle Tales

198 .... 100.00
199 .... 775.00
☛Donald Duck
200 .... 105.00
201 .... 135.00
202 .... 75.00
203 .... 675.00
☛Donald Duck
204 .... 155.00
205 .... 150.00
206 .... 85.00
207 .... 185.00
208 .... 140.00
209 .... 50.00
210 .... 45.00
211 .... 80.00
212 .... 50.00
213 .... 60.00
214 .... 170.00
215 .... 105.00
216 .... 65.00
217 .... 100.00
218 .... 130.00
219 .... 90.00
220 .... 120.00
221 .... 105.00
222 .... 100.00
223 .... 930.00
☛Donald Duck
224-226 .... 80.00
227 .... 160.00
228 .... 260.00
229 .... 50.00
230 .... 85.00
231 .... 150.00
232 .... 65.00
233-234 .... 100.00
235 .... 55.00
236 .... 85.00
237 .... 55.00
238 .... 710.00
☛Donald Duck
239-240 .... 60.00
241 .... 70.00
242 .... 40.00
243 .... 115.00
244 .... 120.00
245-246 .... 55.00
247 .... 130.00
248 .... 165.00
249 .... 60.00
250 .... 110.00
251 .... 45.00
252 .... 120.00
253-254 .... 125.00
255 .... 65.00
256 .... 485.00
☛Donald Duck
257 .... 60.00
258 .... 55.00
259 .... 50.00
260 .... 65.00
261 .... 145.00
262 .... 75.00
263 .... 435.00
264 .... 55.00
265 .... 80.00
266 .... 95.00
267 .... 40.00
268 .... 140.00
269 .... 125.00
270 .... 55.00
271 .... 65.00
272 .... 120.00
273 .... 50.00
274 .... 100.00
275 .... 415.00
☛Donald Duck
276 .... 85.00
277 .... 65.00
278 .... 135.00
279 .... 150.00
280 .... 55.00
281 .... 95.00
282 .... 400.00
☛Donald Duck
283 .... 90.00
284 .... 65.00
285 .... 200.00
286-287 .... 125.00
288 .... 55.00
289 .... 95.00
290 .... 52.00
291 .... 375.00
☛Donald Duck
292 .... 260.00
293 .... 110.00
294 .... 40.00
295 .... 65.00
296 .... 125.00
297 .... 50.00
298 .... 90.00
299 .... 120.00
300 .... 375.00
☛Donald Duck
301 .... 55.00
302 .... 52.00
303 .... 50.00
304 .... 95.00
305 .... 40.00
306 .... 50.00
307 .... 75.00
308 .... 335.00
☛Donald Duck
309 .... 55.00
310 .... 75.00
311 .... 45.00
312 .... 135.00
313 .... 90.00
314 .... 55.00
315 .... 40.00
316 .... 135.00
317 .... 70.00
318 .... 335.00

☛Donald Duck
319 .... 62.00
320 .... 70.00
321 .... 38.00
322-323 .... 40.00
324 .... 75.00
325 .... 90.00
326 .... 35.00
327 .... 65.00
328 .... 335.00
☛Donald Duck
329 .... 100.00
330 .... 40.00
331 .... 155.00
332 .... 40.00
333 .... 48.00
334 .... 90.00
335 .... 85.00
336 .... 32.00
337 .... 40.00
338 .... 65.00
339 .... 85.00
340 .... 70.00
341 .... 150.00
342 .... 35.00
343 .... 80.00
344 .... 135.00
345 .... 32.00
346 .... 52.00
347 .... 65.00
348 .... 140.00
349 .... 65.00
350 .... 32.00
351 .... 35.00
352 .... 70.00
353 .... 85.00
354 .... 45.00
355 .... 65.00
356 .... 135.00
357 .... 45.00
358 .... 32.00
359 .... 85.00
360 .... 35.00
361 .... 52.00
362 .... 75.00
363 .... 60.00
364 .... 28.00
365 .... 40.00
366 .... 65.00
367 .... 330.00
☛Donald Duck
368 .... 250.00
☛Beany & Cecil
369 .... 100.00
370 .... 32.00
371 .... 65.00
372 .... 45.00
373 .... 70.00
374 .... 28.00
375 .... 260.00
☛John Carter of Mars
376 .... 60.00
377 .... 35.00
378 .... 220.00
379 .... 80.00
380 .... 45.00
381 .... 185.00
382 .... 145.00
383 .... 28.00
384 .... 55.00
385 .... 32.00
386 .... 1,050.00
☛Uncle Scrooge
387 .... 65.00
388 .... 40.00
389 .... 35.00
390 .... 28.00
391 .... 50.00
392 .... 65.00
393 .... 60.00
394 .... 155.00
395 .... 42.00
396 .... 110.00
397 .... 65.00
398 .... 35.00
399 .... 32.00
400 .... 165.00
401 .... 50.00
402 .... 80.00
403 .... 65.00
404 .... 100.00
405 .... 28.00
406 .... 65.00
407 .... 55.00
408 .... 350.00
☛Donald Duck
409 .... 28.00
410 .... 32.00
411 .... 50.00
412 .... 35.00
413 .... 135.00
414 .... 175.00
415 .... 130.00
416 .... 28.00
417 .... 30.00
418 .... 48.00
419 .... 70.00
420 .... 50.00
421 .... 145.00
422 .... 335.00
☛Donald Duck
423 .... 40.00
424 .... 120.00
425 .... 175.00
426 .... 32.00
427-428 .... 45.00
429 .... 75.00
430 .... 115.00
431 .... 28.00
432 .... 45.00
433 .... 40.00
434 .... 200.00
435 .... 50.00
436 .... 35.00

Four Women

Fox and the Crow

Fox Comics Legends Series

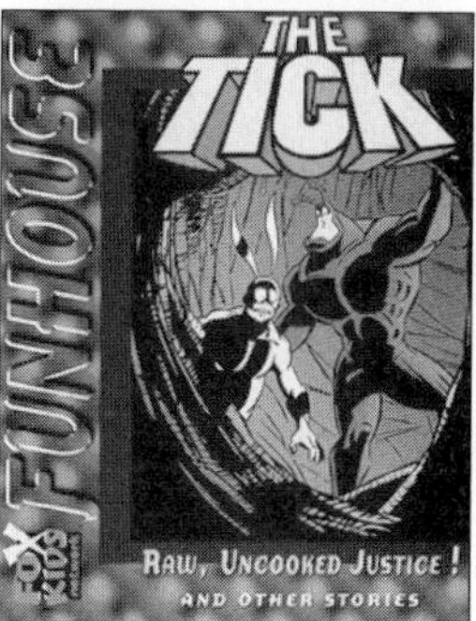

Fox Kids Funhouse

Fractured Fairy Tales

Fragments

Frank Buck

Frankenstein Mobster

437 .... 175.00
438 .... 150.00
439 .... 68.00
440 .... 42.00
441 .... 38.00
442 .... 115.00
443 .... 64.00
444 .... 110.00
445 .... 58.00
446 .... 95.00
447 .... 30.00
448 .... 165.00
449 .... 38.00
450 .... 65.00
451 .... 42.00
452-454 .... 40.00
455 .... 65.00
456 .... 650.00
☛Donald Duck
457 .... 90.00
458 .... 30.00
459 .... 90.00
460 .... 60.00
461 .... 100.00
462 .... 28.00
463 .... 30.00
464 .... 100.00
465 .... 48.00
466 .... 34.00
467 .... 35.00
468 .... 125.00
469 .... 100.00
470 .... 36.00
471 .... 25.00
472 .... 54.00
473 .... 48.00
474 .... 70.00
475 .... 65.00
476 .... 85.00
477 .... 145.00
478 .... 50.00
479 .... 200.00
480 .... 25.00
481 .... 85.00
482-483 .... 30.00
484 .... 32.00
485 .... 65.00
486 .... 40.00
487 .... 65.00
488 .... 165.00
489 .... 35.00
490 .... 75.00
491 .... 80.00
492-493 .... 58.00
494 .... 90.00
495 .... 515.00
☛Donald Duck
496 .... 300.00
☛Green Hornet
497 .... 180.00
498-500 .... 42.00
501 .... 55.00
502 .... 80.00
503 .... 45.00
504 .... 40.00
505 .... 80.00
506 .... 24.00
507 .... 30.00
508 .... 90.00
509 .... 60.00
510 .... 40.00
511 .... 32.00
512 .... 65.00
513 .... 38.00
514 .... 40.00
515-516 .... 25.00
517 .... 70.00
518 .... 30.00
519 .... 80.00
520 .... 45.00
521 .... 48.00
522 .... 30.00
523 .... 80.00
524 .... 30.00
525 .... 44.00
526 .... 26.00
527 .... 45.00
528 .... 110.00
529 .... 30.00
530 .... 145.00
531 .... 48.00
532 .... 32.00
533 .... 35.00
534 .... 55.00
535 .... 470.00
☛I Love Lucy
536 .... 45.00
537 .... 40.00
538 .... 165.00
539 .... 35.00
540 .... 75.00
541 .... 50.00
542 .... 65.00
543 .... 40.00
544 .... 95.00
545 .... 80.00
546-547 .... 48.00
548-549 .... 30.00
550 .... 22.00
551 .... 85.00
552 .... 45.00
553 .... 25.00
554 .... 30.00
555 .... 32.00
556 .... 20.00
557 .... 40.00
558 .... 30.00
559 .... 340.00
☛I Love Lucy
560 .... 48.00
561 .... 125.00
562 .... 70.00
563 .... 36.00
564 .... 40.00

565 .... 48.00
566 .... 35.00
567 .... 125.00
568 .... 45.00
569 .... 28.00
570 .... 145.00
571 .... 45.00
572 .... 42.00
573 .... 32.00
574 .... 165.00
575 .... 85.00
576 .... 30.00
577 .... 25.00
578 .... 55.00
579 .... 40.00
580 .... 36.00
581 .... 50.00
582 .... 45.00
583 .... 32.00
584 .... 50.00
585 .... 36.00
586 .... 45.00
587 .... 22.00
588 .... 110.00
589 .... 45.00
590 .... 65.00
591 .... 60.00
592 .... 50.00
593 .... 30.00
594 .... 85.00
595 .... 40.00
596 .... 375.00
☛Turok
597 .... 55.00
598 .... 40.00
599 .... 35.00
600 .... 65.00
601 .... 35.00
602 .... 135.00
603-604 .... 45.00
605 .... 30.00
606 .... 90.00
607 .... 40.00
608 .... 45.00
609 .... 65.00
610 .... 100.00
611 .... 50.00
612 .... 32.00
613 .... 52.00
614 .... 100.00
615 .... 45.00
616 .... 32.00
617 .... 155.00
618 .... 50.00
619 .... 40.00
620 .... 48.00
621 .... 36.00
622 .... 35.00
623 .... 25.00
624 .... 80.00
625 .... 50.00
626 .... 35.00
627 .... 65.00
628 .... 28.00
629 .... 65.00
630 .... 30.00
631 .... 165.00
632 .... 34.00
633 .... 30.00
634 .... 55.00
635 .... 145.00
636-637 .... 40.00
638 .... 25.00
639 .... 145.00
640 .... 45.00
641 .... 50.00
642 .... 45.00
643 .... 35.00
644 .... 70.00
645 .... 50.00
646 .... 35.00
647 .... 40.00
648 .... 55.00
649 .... 50.00
650 .... 80.00
651 .... 35.00
652 .... 30.00
653 .... 10.00
654 .... 35.00
655 .... 30.00
656 .... 200.00
☛Turok
657 .... 35.00
658 .... 6.00
659 .... 45.00
660 .... 30.00
661 .... 35.00
662 .... 50.00
663 .... 60.00
664 .... 145.00
665 .... 52.00
666 .... 44.00
667 .... 40.00
668 .... 75.00
669 .... 65.00
670 .... 36.00
671 .... 145.00
672 .... 65.00
673 .... 60.00
674 .... 85.00
675 .... 65.00
676 .... 25.00
677 .... 60.00
678 .... 65.00
679 .... 135.00
680 .... 32.00
681 .... 105.00
682 .... 75.00
683 .... 28.00
684 .... 100.00
685-686 .... 50.00
687 .... 60.00
688 .... 75.00
689 .... 30.00

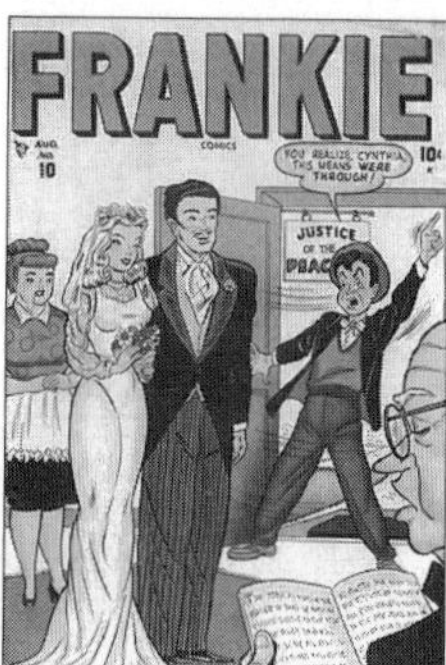

Frankie Comics

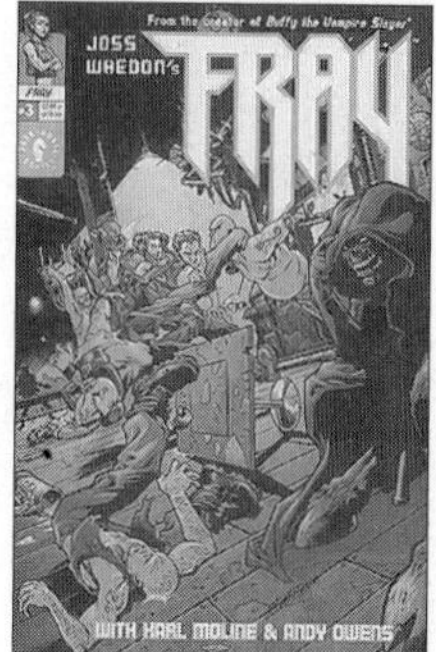

Fray

Freak Out on Infant Earths

Freaks

Fred Hembeck Destroys the Marvel Universe

Fred Hembeck Sells the Marvel Universe

Fred the Possessed Flower

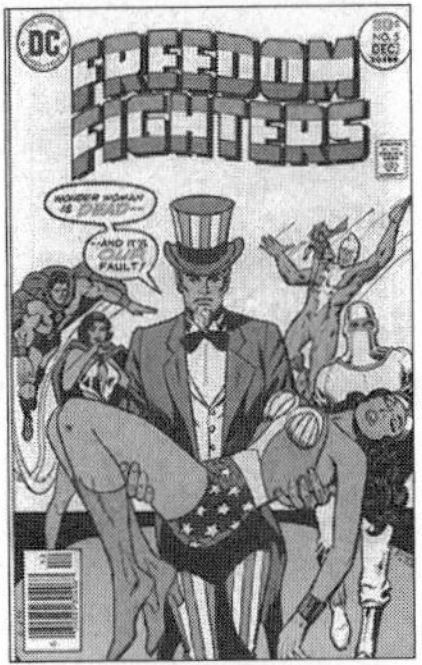

Freedom Fighters

690 .... 140.00
691 .... 25.00
692 .... 30.00
693 .... 85.00
694 .... 55.00
695 .... 30.00
696 .... 35.00
697 .... 25.00
698 .... 32.00
699 .... 68.00
700 .... 55.00
701 .... 90.00
702 .... 75.00
703 .... 85.00
704 .... 30.00
705 .... 55.00
706 .... 45.00
707 .... 70.00
708 .... 65.00
709 .... 225.00
☛The Searchers
710 .... 32.00
711 .... 26.00
712 .... 65.00
713 .... 55.00
714 .... 90.00
715 .... 35.00
716-717 .... 90.00
718 .... 25.00
719 .... 70.00
720 .... 75.00
721 .... 165.00
☛Capt. Kangaroo
722 .... 50.00
723 .... 110.00
724 .... 40.00
725 .... 25.00
726 .... 40.00
727-728 .... 25.00
729 .... 35.00
730 .... 30.00
731 .... 40.00
732 .... 150.00
733 .... 35.00
734 .... 135.00
735 .... 200.00
☛Crusader Rabbit
736 .... 40.00
737 .... 55.00
738 .... 75.00
739 .... 40.00
740 .... 45.00
741 .... 75.00
742-743 .... 40.00
744 .... 30.00
745 .... 32.00
746 .... 25.00
747 .... 60.00
748 .... 35.00
749 .... 60.00
750 .... 65.00
751 .... 80.00
752 .... 115.00
753 .... 30.00
754 .... 55.00
755 .... 40.00
756 .... 34.00
757 .... 90.00
758 .... 70.00
759 .... 100.00
760 .... 135.00
761 .... 115.00
762 .... 90.00
763 .... 60.00
764 .... 26.00
765 .... 25.00
766 .... 40.00
767 .... 75.00
768 .... 50.00
769 .... 75.00
770-771 .... 35.00
772 .... 65.00
773 .... 50.00
774 .... 25.00
775 .... 95.00
776 .... 50.00
777 .... 65.00
778 .... 55.00
779 .... 45.00
780 .... 145.00
781 .... 90.00
782 .... 45.00
783 .... 25.00
784 .... 75.00
785 .... 95.00
786 .... 65.00
787 .... 42.00
788 .... 70.00
789 .... 45.00
790 .... 175.00
☛Wings of Eagles
791 .... 80.00
792 .... 25.00
793 .... 30.00
794 .... 100.00
795 .... 75.00
796 .... 45.00
797 .... 65.00
798 .... 45.00
799 .... 30.00
800 .... 65.00
801 .... 25.00
802 .... 70.00
803-804 .... 55.00
805 .... 140.00
☛Crusader Rabbit
806 .... 60.00
807 .... 35.00
808 .... 80.00
809-810 .... 32.00
811 .... 115.00
812 .... 85.00
813 .... 95.00
814 .... 55.00

815 .... 75.00
816 .... 95.00
817 .... 25.00
818 .... 55.00
819 .... 40.00
820 .... 70.00
821 .... 80.00
822 .... 115.00
823 .... 25.00
824 .... 9.00
825 .... 45.00
826 .... 225.00
☛Spin and Marty
827 .... 30.00
828 .... 35.00
829 .... 55.00
830 .... 95.00
831 .... 65.00
832 .... 40.00
833 .... 60.00
834 .... 45.00
835 .... 40.00
836 .... 75.00
837 .... 60.00
838 .... 50.00
839 .... 75.00
840 .... 45.00
841 .... 25.00
842 .... 64.00
843 .... 75.00
844 .... 65.00
845 .... 125.00
☛Land Unknown
846 .... 115.00
847 .... 45.00
848 .... 40.00
849 .... 65.00
850 .... 35.00
851 .... 75.00
852 .... 25.00
853 .... 45.00
854 .... 135.00
855 .... 45.00
856 .... 40.00
857 .... 65.00
858-859 .... 45.00
860 .... 115.00
861 .... 35.00
862 .... 75.00
863 .... 30.00
864 .... 44.00
865 .... 85.00
866 .... 70.00
867 .... 44.00
868 .... 30.00
869 .... 75.00
870 .... 30.00
871 .... 32.00
872 .... 125.00
☛Capt. Kangaroo
873 .... 45.00
874 .... 75.00
875 .... 30.00
876 .... 95.00
877 .... 100.00
878 .... 225.00
☛Peanuts
879 .... 35.00
880 .... 40.00
881 .... 35.00
882 .... 165.00
883 .... 40.00
884 .... 80.00
885 .... 85.00
886 .... 35.00
887 .... 110.00
888 .... 25.00
889 .... 110.00
890 .... 70.00
891 .... 75.00
892 .... 200.00
☛Maverick
893 .... 55.00
894 .... 25.00
895 .... 105.00
896 .... 85.00
897 .... 65.00
898 .... 40.00
899 .... 45.00
900 .... 65.00
901 .... 45.00
902 .... 26.00
903 .... 25.00
904 .... 34.00
905 .... 200.00
☛Annette
906 .... 30.00
907 .... 125.00
☛Sugarfoot
908 .... 32.00
909 .... 25.00
910 .... 95.00
911 .... 85.00
912 .... 190.00
☛Leave It to Beaver
913 .... 100.00
914 .... 110.00
915 .... 68.00
916 .... 45.00
917 .... 130.00
☛Life of Riley
918-919 .... 75.00
920 .... 160.00
☛Zorro
921 .... 65.00
922 .... 50.00
923 .... 25.00
924 .... 95.00
925 .... 65.00
926 .... 60.00
927 .... 35.00
928 .... 135.00
☛Sea Hunt
929 .... 30.00

Freedom Train

Freejack

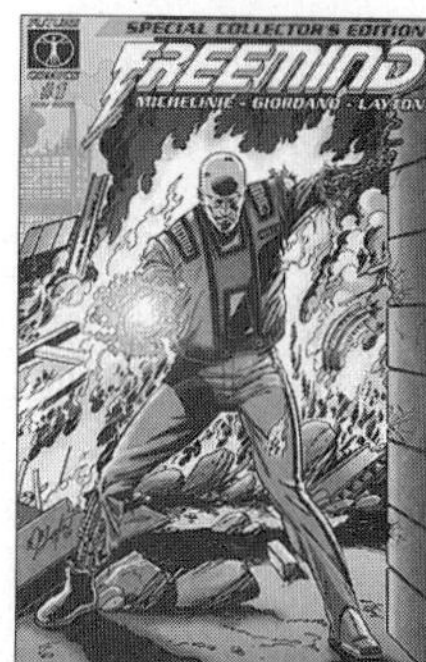

Freemind

Freeway Ninja Hanzo

Freex

Friends

Fright

Fright Night

930 ... 115.00
931 ... 120.00
932 ... 60.00
933 ... 145.00
☛Zorro
934 ... 95.00
935 ... 45.00
936 ... 40.00
937 ... 115.00
938 ... 25.00
939 ... 45.00
940-941 ... 35.00
942 ... 55.00
943 ... 60.00
944 ... 165.00
☛Sinbad
945 ... 95.00
946 ... 75.00
947 ... 48.00
948 ... 45.00
949 ... 58.00
950 ... 40.00
951 ... 110.00
952 ... 40.00
953 ... 36.00
954 ... 80.00
955 ... 25.00
956 ... 180.00
☛Ricky Nelson
957 ... 90.00
958 ... 44.00
959 ... 40.00
960 ... 140.00
☛Zorro
961 ... 55.00
962 ... 95.00
963 ... 45.00
964 ... 105.00
965 ... 50.00
966 ... 70.00
967 ... 36.00
968 ... 80.00
969 ... 165.00
☛Peanuts
970 ... 90.00
971 ... 55.00
972 ... 120.00
973 ... 110.00
974 ... 40.00
975 ... 65.00
976 ... 140.00
977-979 ... 25.00
980 ... 95.00
981-983 ... 70.00
984 ... 100.00
985 ... 65.00
986 ... 70.00
987 ... 45.00
988 ... 40.00
989 ... 60.00
990 ... 90.00
991 ... 30.00
992 ... 90.00
993 ... 55.00
994 ... 110.00
995 ... 45.00
996 ... 32.00
997 ... 70.00
998 ... 175.00
☛Ricky Nelson
999 ... 160.00
1000 ... 85.00
1001 ... 48.00
1002 ... 60.00
1003 ... 145.00
☛Zorro
1004 ... 70.00
1005 ... 90.00
1006 ... 105.00
1007 ... 75.00
1008 ... 60.00
1009 ... 160.00
☛Rifleman
1010 ... 100.00
1011 ... 80.00
1012 ... 70.00
1013 ... 95.00
1014 ... 100.00
1015 ... 150.00
☛Peanuts
1016 ... 45.00
1017 ... 30.00
1018 ... 200.00
☛Rio Bravo
1019 ... 55.00
1020 ... 40.00
1021 ... 55.00
1022 ... 25.00
1023 ... 85.00
1024 ... 90.00
1025 ... 225.00
☛Disneyland
1026 ... 85.00
1027 ... 75.00
1028 ... 225.00
☛Rawhide
1029-1030 ... 50.00
1031 ... 60.00
1032 ... 25.00
1033 ... 45.00
1034 ... 35.00
1035 ... 58.00
1036 ... 55.00
1037 ... 145.00
☛Zorro
1038 ... 60.00
1039 ... 40.00
1040 ... 120.00
1041 ... 110.00
1042 ... 45.00
1043 ... 130.00
☛3 Stooges
1044 ... 75.00
1045 ... 60.00

1046 ... 45.00
1047 ... 185.00
☛Gyro Gearloose
1048 ... 165.00
☛Horse Soldiers
1049 ... 75.00
1050 ... 65.00
☛Donald Duck
1051-1052 ... 120.00
☛Ben-Hur
1053 ... 45.00
1054 ... 65.00
1055 ... 100.00
1056 ... 52.00
1057 ... 45.00
1058 ... 70.00
1059 ... 75.00
1060 ... 140.00
☛Journey/Center
1061 ... 55.00
1062 ... 42.00
1063 ... 44.00
1064 ... 45.00
1065 ... 40.00
1066 ... 125.00
☛77 Sunset Strip
1067 ... 115.00
1068 ... 32.00
1069 ... 115.00
1070 ... 110.00
1071 ... 100.00
1072 ... 48.00
1073 ... 125.00
1074 ... 30.00
1075 ... 75.00
1076 ... 90.00
1077 ... 110.00
1078 ... 90.00
1079 ... 45.00
1080 ... 60.00
1081 ... 25.00
1082 ... 75.00
☛Spin & Marty
1083 ... 70.00
1084 ... 35.00
1085 ... 175.00
☛Time Machine
1086 ... 25.00
1087 ... 120.00
1088 ... 48.00
1089 ... 65.00
1090 ... 26.00
1091 ... 50.00
1092 ... 70.00
1093 ... 65.00
1094 ... 40.00
1095 ... 120.00
1096 ... 65.00
1097 ... 160.00
☛Rawhide
1098 ... 70.00
1099 ... 45.00
1100 ... 220.00
☛Annette's Life
1101 ... 70.00
1102 ... 95.00
1103 ... 160.00
1104 ... 70.00
1105 ... 95.00
1106 ... 100.00
1107-1108 ... 65.00
1109 ... 215.00
☛Life of Donald Duck
1110 ... 295.00
☛Bonanza
1111-1112 ... 55.00
1113 ... 80.00
1114 ... 65.00
1115 ... 160.00
☛Ricky Nelson
1116 ... 55.00
1117 ... 75.00
1118 ... 85.00
1119 ... 45.00
1120 ... 75.00
1121 ... 105.00
1122 ... 30.00
1123-1124 ... 85.00
1125 ... 80.00
1126 ... 65.00
1127 ... 85.00
1128 ... 400.00
☛Rocky & Friends
1129 ... 90.00
1130 ... 85.00
1131 ... 25.00
1132 ... 50.00
1133 ... 60.00
1134 ... 100.00
1135 ... 30.00
1136 ... 60.00
1137 ... 45.00
1138 ... 75.00
1139 ... 165.00
☛Spartacus
1140 ... 45.00
1141-1142 ... 70.00
1143 ... 40.00
1144 ... 85.00
1145 ... 130.00
☛Lost World
1146-1147 ... 65.00
1148 ... 100.00
1149 ... 40.00
1150 ... 100.00
1151 ... 40.00
1152 ... 265.00
☛Rocky & Friends
1153 ... 40.00
1154 ... 440.00
☛Santa Claus Funnies
1155 ... 165.00
1156 ... 95.00
1157 ... 70.00

Fright Night 3-D

Fringe

Frisky Animals

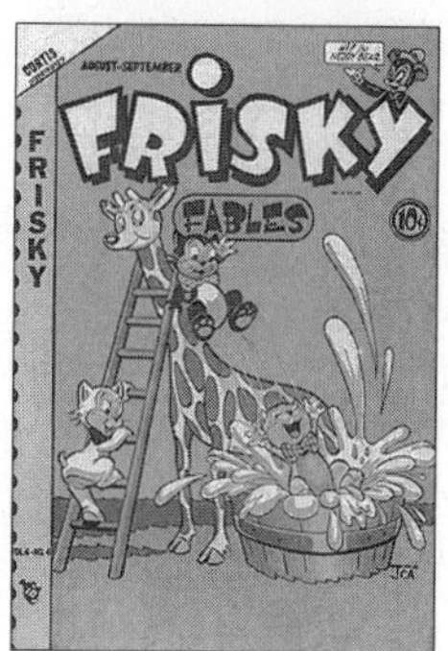

Frisky Fables

Fritzi Ritz

Frogman Comics

From Beyond the Unknown

From Hell

1158 ....85.00
1159 ....90.00
1160 ....165.00
1161 ....95.00
1162 ....75.00
1163 ....70.00
1164 ....75.00
1165 ....120.00
1166 ....235.00
☛Rocky & Friends
1167 ....75.00
1168 ....95.00
1169 ....165.00
☛Sherlock Holmes
1170 ....85.00
1171 ....25.00
1172 ....55.00
1173 ....240.00
☛Twilight Zone
1174 ....35.00
1175 ....26.00
1176 ....45.00
1177 ....30.00
1178 ....60.00
1179 ....75.00
1180 ....140.00
☛Danny Thomas
1181 ....55.00
1182 ....45.00
1183 ....110.00
1184 ....125.00
☛Gyro Gearloose
1185 ....35.00
1186 ....85.00
1187 ....80.00
1188 ....120.00
1189 ....65.00
1190 ....70.00
1191 ....165.00
☛Leave It to Beaver
1192 ....140.00
☛Ricky Nelson
1193 ....85.00
1194 ....40.00
1195 ....70.00
1196 ....45.00
1197 ....65.00
1198 ....75.00
1199 ....80.00
1200 ....65.00
1201 ....40.00
1202 ....150.00
☛Rawhide
1203 ....60.00
1204 ....40.00
1205 ....70.00
1206 ....25.00
1207 ....80.00
1208 ....225.00
☛Rocky & Friends
1209 ....65.00
1210 ....85.00
1211 ....80.00
1212 ....30.00
1213 ....100.00
1214 ....45.00
1215 ....70.00
1216 ....80.00
1218 ....55.00
1219-1220 ....75.00
1221 ....180.00
☛Bonanza
1222 ....25.00
1223 ....55.00
1224 ....40.00
1225 ....85.00
1226 ....55.00
1227 ....85.00
1229 ....115.00
1230 ....120.00
☛Voyage/Bottom Sea
1231 ....130.00
☛Danger Man
1232 ....50.00
1233 ....65.00
1234 ....70.00
1235 ....100.00
1236 ....85.00
1237 ....200.00
☛Untouchables
1238 ....90.00
1239 ....45.00
1240 ....75.00
1241 ....30.00
1242-1243 ....115.00
1244 ....48.00
1245 ....150.00
☛Sherlock Holmes
1246 ....35.00
1247-1248 ....40.00
1249 ....135.00
☛Danny Thomas
1250 ....90.00
1251 ....48.00
1252 ....240.00
☛Andy Griffith
1253 ....85.00
1254 ....60.00
1255 ....80.00
1256 ....65.00
1257 ....80.00
1258 ....75.00
1259 ....70.00
1260 ....100.00
1261 ....140.00
☛Rawhide
1262 ....70.00
1263 ....80.00
1264 ....40.00
1265 ....75.00
1266 ....26.00
1267 ....85.00
1268 ....25.00
1269 ....140.00

☛Rawhide
1270 .... 200.00
☛Bullwinkle
1271 .... 60.00
1272 .... 35.00
1273 .... 65.00
1274 .... 36.00
1275 .... 200.00
☛Rocky & Friends
1276 .... 32.00
1278 .... 110.00
1279 .... 45.00
1280 .... 55.00
1281 .... 28.00
1282 .... 135.00
☛Babes/Toyland
1283 .... 175.00
☛Bonanza
1284 .... 55.00
1285 .... 140.00
☛Leave It to Beaver
1286 .... 170.00
☛Untouchables
1287 .... 60.00
1288 .... 150.00
☛Twilight Zone
1289 .... 100.00
1290 .... 25.00
1291 .... 70.00
1293 .... 25.00
1294 .... 65.00
1295 .... 140.00
☛Mr. Ed
1296 .... 50.00
1297 .... 35.00
1298 .... 48.00
1299 .... 110.00
1300 .... 150.00
☛Comancheros
1301 .... 48.00
1302 .... 38.00
1303 .... 40.00
1304 .... 80.00
1305 .... 100.00
1306 .... 65.00
1307 .... 42.00
1308 .... 125.00
1309 .... 95.00
1310 .... 65.00
1311 .... 200.00
☛Rocky & Friends
1312 .... 55.00
1313-1328 .... 80.00
1330 .... 135.00
☛Brain Boy
1332 .... 80.00
1333 .... 58.00
1335 .... 35.00
1336 .... 48.00
1337 .... 90.00
1341 .... 210.00
☛Andy Griffith
1348 .... 75.00
1349 .... 110.00
1350 .... 55.00
1354 .... 70.00

4-D Monkey

Dr. Leung's, 1988

1-12 .... 2.00

Four Favorites

Ace, 1941

1 .... 1,150.00
2 .... 575.00
3 .... 360.00
4-5 .... 285.00
6-9 .... 250.00
10 .... 300.00
11-12 .... 325.00
13-20 .... 185.00
21-26 .... 125.00
27-32 .... 95.00

Four Horsemen

DC, 2000

1-4 .... 3.00

Four Kunoichi: Bloodlust

Lightning, 1996

1 .... 3.00
1/Nude-1/Platinum 10.00
1/Platinum Nude 4.00

Four Kunoichi: Enter the Sinja

Lightning, 1997

1 .... 3.00

4Most

Premium, 1942

1 .... 700.00
2 .... 325.00
3 .... 275.00
4 .... 240.00
5 .... 90.00
6-7 .... 80.00
8 .... 100.00
9 .... 60.00
10-13 .... 45.00
14-16 .... 32.00
17 .... 35.00
18-24 .... 30.00
25 .... 40.00
26 .... 30.00
27 .... 100.00
28 .... 30.00
29-31 .... 100.00
32 .... 30.00
33-34 .... 110.00
35 .... 30.00
36 .... 110.00
37 .... 30.00
38-40 .... 35.00

411

Marvel, 2003

1-2 .... 4.00

Frontier Fighters

Frontier Western

F-Troop

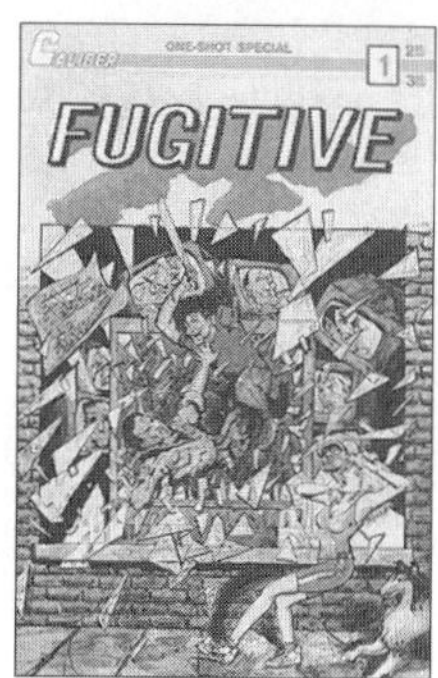

Fugitive

Fugitives from Justice

Fugitoid

Full Metal Fiction

Full Throttle

Four-Star Battle Tales

DC, 1973

1 .... 20.00
2 .... 7.00
3-5 .... 6.00

Four Star Spectacular

DC, 1976

1 .... 12.00
2-6 .... 7.00

Four Teeners

A.A. Wyn, 1948

34 .... 26.00

Fourth World (Jack Kirby's...)

DC, 1997

1 .... 3.00
2-20 .... 2.00

Fourth World Gallery

DC, 1996

1 .... 4.00

Four Women

DC, 2001

1-5 .... 3.00

Fox and the Crow

DC, 1951

1 .... 775.00
2 .... 400.00
3-5 .... 285.00
6-10 .... 195.00
11-15 .... 135.00
16-20 .... 120.00
21-30 .... 90.00
31-40 .... 85.00
41-61 .... 60.00
62-80 .... 42.00
81-94 .... 26.00
☛1st Stanley
95 .... 50.00
96-100 .... 22.00
101-108 .... 18.00

Fox Comics

Fantagraphics

24-Special 1 .... 3.00

Fox Comics Legends Series

Fantagraphics, 1992

1-2 .... 3.00

Foxfire

Malibu, 1996

1-4 .... 2.00

Foxfire

Nightwynd, 1992

1-3 .... 3.00

Foxhole

Mainline, 1954

1 .... 225.00
2 .... 170.00
3-5 .... 125.00
6 .... 100.00
7 .... 125.00

Foxhole (Super)

Super

10-18 .... 14.00

Fox Kids Funhouse

Acclaim

1-2 .... 5.00

Foxy Fagan Comics

Dearfield, 1946

1 .... 60.00
2 .... 40.00
3-5 .... 30.00
6-7 .... 24.00
Ashcan 1-Ashcan 1/2nd 6.00

Fraction

DC, 2004

1-6 .... 3.00

Fractured Fairy Tales

Gold Key, 1962

1 .... 75.00

Fraggle Rock

Marvel, 1985

1 .... 2.00
2-8 .... 1.00

Fraggle Rock

Marvel, 1988

1 .... 2.00
2-5 .... 1.00

Fragile Prophet

Lost in the Dark, 2005

1 .... 3.00

Fragments

Screaming Cat

1 .... 3.00

Francis, Brother of the Universe

Marvel

1 .... 2.00

Frank

Nemesis, 1994

1 .... 2.00
1/Direct 3.00
2 .... 2.00
2/Direct 3.00
3 .... 2.00
3/Direct 3.00
4 .... 2.00
4/Direct 3.00

Frank

Fantagraphics, 1996

1 .... 3.00
2 .... 4.00

Frank Frazetta Fantasy Illustrated

Frank Frazetta Fantasy Illustrated, 1998

1-1/Variant 7.00
2-5 .... 6.00
5/Variant 8.00
6-7/Variant 6.00

Frank in the River

Tundra

1 .... 3.00

Frank Buck

Fox, 1950

70 .... 165.00
71 .... 90.00
3 .... 80.00

Frank Luther's Silly Pilly Comics

Children Comics, 1949

1 .... 35.00

Frank Merriwell at Yale

Charlton, 1955

1 .... 35.00
2 .... 25.00
3-4 .... 16.00

Frank the Unicorn

Fragments West, 1986

1-9 .... 2.00

Frank Zappa: Viva La Bizarre

Revolutionary, 1994

1 .... 3.00

Frankenstein

Prize, 1945

1 .... 1,025.00
2 .... 650.00
3-5 .... 340.00
6-10 .... 275.00
11-20 .... 200.00
21-33 .... 165.00

Frankenstein

Dell, 1963

1 .... 35.00
2 .... 25.00
3-4 .... 15.00

Frankenstein (The Monster of...)

Marvel, 1973

1 .... 40.00
2 .... 15.00
3-5 .... 9.00
6-7 .... 7.00
8 .... 18.00
9 .... 20.00
10 .... 6.00
11-18 .... 5.00

Frankenstein

Eternity, 1989

1 .... 2.00

Frankenstein (Mary Shelley's...)

Topps, 1984

1-4 .... 3.00

Frankenstein/Dracula War

Topps, 1995

1-3 .... 3.00

Frankenstein Jr.

Gold Key, 1967

1 .... 55.00

Frankenstein Mobster

Image, 2003

0-7/B 3.00

Frankenstein: Or the Modern Prometheus

Caliber

1 .... 3.00

Frankie Comics

Margood, 1946

4 .... 35.00
5 .... 25.00
6-10 .... 22.00
11-15 .... 18.00

Frank Ironwine (Warren Ellis')

Avatar

1 .... 4.00
1/Foil 20.00

Franklin Richards: Happy Franksgiving

Marvel, 2007

1 .... 3.00

Franklin Richards, Son of a Genius - Everybody Loves Franklin

Marvel, 2006

1 .... 3.00

Franklin Richards: Son of a Genius Super Summer Spectacular

Marvel, 2006

1 .... 3.00

Fray

Dark Horse, 2001

1-8 .... 3.00

Freak Force

Image, 1993

1-7 .... 2.00
8-18 .... 3.00

Freak Force

Image, 1997

1-3 .... 3.00

Fun and Games Magazine

Fun Comics

Fun-In

Funky Phantom

Funny Films

Funny Folks

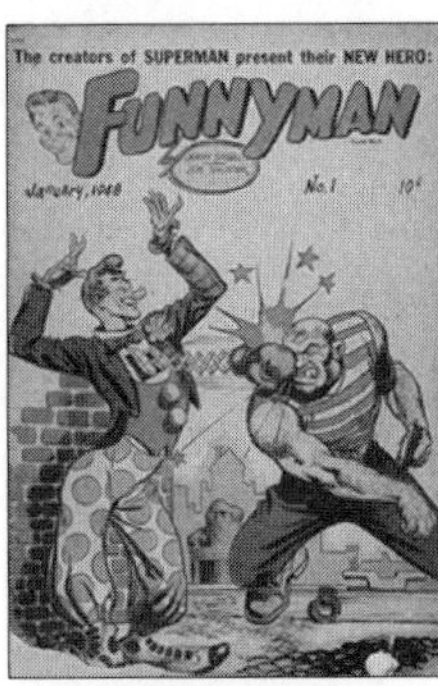

Funnyman

Funny Picture Stories

Freak Out on Infant Earths
Blackthorne, 1987
1-2 .... 2.00

Freaks
Fantagraphics, 1992
1-3 .... 2.00

Freaks' Amour
Dark Horse, 1992
1-3 .... 4.00

Freaks of the Heartland
Dark Horse, 2004
1-6 .... 3.00

Freckles and His Friends
Standard, 1947
1 .... 30.00
2-4 .... 20.00
5-12 .... 20.00

Fred & Bianca Censorship Sucks Special
Comics Interview, 1989
1 .... 2.00

Fred & Bianca Mother's Day Massacre
Comics Interview
1 .... 2.00

Fred & Bianca Valentine's Day Massacre
Comics Interview
1 .... 2.00

Fred the Clown
Hotel Fred, 2001
1-2 .... 3.00

Freddy
Dell, 1964
1 .... 26.00
2-3 .... 18.00

Freddy Krueger's Nightmare on Elm Street
Marvel, 1989
1 .... 5.00
2 .... 4.00

Freddy's Dead: The Final Nightmare
Innovation
1-3/3D 3.00

Freddy vs. Jason vs. Ash
DC, 2007
1 .... 12.00
2 .... 6.00
3-4 .... 4.00

Frederic Remington: The Man Who Painted the West
Tome
1 .... 3.00

Fred Hembeck Destroys the Marvel Universe
Marvel, 1989
1 .... 2.00

Fred Hembeck Sells the Marvel Universe
Marvel, 1990
1 .... 2.00

Fred the Possessed Flower
Happy Predator
1-6 .... 3.00

Free Cerebus
Aardvark-Vanaheim
1 .... 1.00

Free Laughs
Deschaine
1 .... 1.00

Free Speeches
Oni, 1998
1 .... 3.00

Free-View
Acclaim, 1993
1 .... 1.00

Freebooters/Young Gods/ Paradoxman Preview
Dark Horse
1 .... 1.00

Freedom Agent
Gold Key, 1963
1 .... 45.00

Freedom Fighters
DC, 1976
1 .... 12.00
2-3 .... 5.00
4-15 .... 4.00

Freedom Force
Image, 2005
1-6 .... 3.00

Freedom Train
Street & Smith, 1948
1 .... 125.00

Freeflight
Thinkblots, 1994
1 .... 3.00

Freejack
Now, 1992
1 .... 2.00
1/Direct 3.00
2 .... 2.00
2/Direct 3.00
3 .... 2.00
3/Direct 3.00

Freemind
Future, 2002
1-6 .... 4.00
7 .... 3.00

Freeway Ninja Hanzo
SleepyHouse
1 .... 4.00

Freex
Malibu, 1993
1 .... 2.00
1/Hologram 5.00
2-3 .... 2.00
4 .... 3.00
5-14 .... 2.00
15 .... 4.00
16 .... 2.00
17-GS 1 .... 3.00

French Ice
Renegade, 1987
1-13 .... 2.00

French Ticklers
Kitchen Sink, 1989
1-3 .... 2.00

Frenzy
Independent
1-1/A 1.00

Frescazizis
Last Gasp
1 .... 1.00

Fresh Blood Funny Book
Last Gasp
1 .... 1.00

Freshmen
Image, 2005
1/Preview 7.00
☛Seth Green series
1/Linsner 4.00
1/Migliari 3.00
1/Perez 4.00
2-6 .... 3.00

Freshmen II
Image, 2006
1-2 .... 3.00

Freshmen Yearbook One Shot
Image, 2006
1 .... 3.00

Friday Foster
Dell, 1972
1 .... 25.00

Friday the 13th
DC, 2007
1-2 .... 3.00

Friendly Ghost, Casper
Harvey, 1958
1 .... 190.00
2 .... 100.00
3 .... 85.00
4-5 .... 55.00
6-10 .... 46.00
11-20 .... 36.00
21-30 .... 25.00
31-40 .... 18.00
41-50 .... 15.00
51-60 .... 12.00
61-70 .... 10.00
71-80 .... 8.00
81-89 .... 7.00
90-100 .... 6.00
101-120 .... 5.00
121-140 .... 4.00
141-169 .... 3.00
170-253 .... 2.00

Friendly Neighborhood Spider-Man
Marvel, 2005
1 .... 10.00
2-3 .... 6.00
4-16 .... 3.00
17 .... 6.00
18 .... 4.00
19-24 .... 3.00

Friends
Renegade, 1987
1-3 .... 2.00

Friends of Maxx
Image, 1996
1-3 .... 3.00

Fright
Atlas-Seaboard, 1975
1 .... 6.00

Fright
Eternity, 1989
1-12 .... 2.00

Fright Night
Now, 1988
1 .... 3.00
2-22 .... 2.00

Fright Night 1993 Halloween Annual
Now, 1993
1 .... 3.00

Fright Night 3-D
Now, 1992
1-2 .... 3.00

Fright Night 3-D Winter Special
Now, 1993
1 .... 3.00

Fright Night II Graphic Novel
Now
1 .... 4.00

Fringe
Caliber
1-8 .... 3.00

Funny Stuff

Funnytime Features

Funny Tunes

Fury of S.H.I.E.L.D.

Fusion

Future Beat

Future Comics

Futuretech

Frisky Animals
Star Publications, 1951
44-55 ....125.00

Frisky Animals on Parade
Ajax, 1957
1 ....100.00
2 ....36.00
3 ....70.00

Frisky Fables
Premium, 1945
1 ....110.00
2 ....56.00
3 ....38.00
4-5 ....32.00
6-10 ....26.00
11-20 ....24.00
21-30 ....20.00
31-43 ....16.00

Fritzi Ritz
St. John, 1953
3 ....45.00
4-7 ....40.00
27-37 ....25.00
38 ....35.00
39-49 ....25.00
50-59 ....20.00

Frogman Comics
Hillman, 1952
1 ....60.00
2 ....38.00
3-5 ....28.00
6-11 ....24.00

Frogmen
Dell, 1962
2 ....34.00
3 ....26.00
4 ....20.00
5 ....22.00
6 ....20.00
7-11 ....18.00

From Beyonde
Studio Insidio, 1991
1 ....2.00

From Beyond the Unknown
DC, 1969
1 ....45.00
2 ....20.00
3-6 ....15.00
7-10 ....12.00
11-17 ....10.00
18-25 ....8.00

From Dusk Till Dawn
Big
1 ....5.00
1/Deluxe 10.00

From Far Away
Viz, 2004
1-7 ....10.00

From Heaven to Hell
Dead Dog Comics, 2005
1 ....5.00

From Hell
Tundra, 1991
1 ....6.00
☛Alan Moore series
1/2nd-10 ....5.00

From Hell: Dance of the Gull Catchers
Kitchen Sink, 1998
1 ....7.00
☛Alan Moore

From Here to Insanity
Charlton, 1955
8-12 ....45.00
1 ....125.00

From the Darkness
Adventure, 1990
1-4 ....3.00

From the Darkness Book II: Blood Vows
Cry for Dawn
1-3 ....3.00

Front Page Comic Book
Harvey
1 ....250.00

Frontier
Slave Labor, 1994
1 ....3.00

Frontier Fighters
DC, 1955
1 ....220.00
2-3 ....165.00
4-8 ....120.00

Frontier Romances
Avon, 1949
1 ....425.00
2 ....240.00

Frontiers '86 Presents
Frontiers
1-2 ....2.00

Frontier Scout, Dan'l Boone
Charlton, 1956
10 ....60.00
11-13 ....35.00
14 ....22.00

Frontier Western
Atlas, 1956
1 ....125.00
2-3 ....100.00
4-10 ....50.00

Frontline Combat

E.C., 1951

1 ... 535.00
2 ... 340.00
3 ... 250.00
4-5 ... 200.00
6-10 ... 150.00
11-15 ... 120.00

Frontline Combat

Gemstone, 1995

1-4 ... 2.00
5-15 ... 3.00
Ann 1 ... 11.00
Ann 2 ... 13.00

Frost

Caliber

1 ... 2.00

Frostbiter: Wrath of the Wendigo

Caliber

1-3 ... 3.00

Frost: The Dying Breed

Caliber

1-3 ... 3.00

Frozen Embryo

Slave Labor, 1992

1 ... 3.00

Fruits Basket

Tokyopop, 2004

1-12 ... 10.00

F-3 Bandit

Antarctic, 1995

1-10 ... 3.00

F-Troop

Gold Key, 1966

1 ... 50.00
2 ... 40.00
3-5 ... 36.00
6-7 ... 32.00

Fugitive

Caliber, 1989

1 ... 3.00

Fugitives from Justice

St. John, 1952

1 ... 185.00
2 ... 100.00
3 ... 80.00
4-5 ... 60.00

Fugitoid

Mirage, 1985

1 ... 3.00

Full Frontal Nerdity

Dork Storm, 2004

Ann 1 ... 3.00

Full Metal Fiction

London Night, 1997

1 ... 4.00

Full Metal Panic

ADV Manga, 2003

1 ... 10.00
2 ... 10.00

Full Metal Panic!

ADV Manga, 2005

1-2 ... 10.00
3-8 ... 10.00

Full Metal Panic: Overload

ADV Manga, 2005

1-2 ... 10.00

Full Moon

Viz, 2005

1-3 ... 9.00

Full of Fun

Decker, 1957

1 ... 40.00
2 ... 25.00

Full Throttle

Aircel

1-2 ... 3.00

Fun and Games Magazine

Marvel, 1979

1 ... 4.00
2-13 ... 3.00

Fun Boys Spring Special

Tundra

1 ... 2.00

Fun Comics

Star Publications, 1953

9 ... 110.00
10-12 ... 85.00

Fun Comics (Bill Black's...)

AC, 1983

1-4 ... 2.00

Fun House

MN Design

1 ... 7.00

Fun House (J.R. Williams'...)

Starhead, 1993

1 ... 4.00

Fun-In

Gold Key, 1970

1 ... 16.00
2 ... 10.00
3-4 ... 9.00
5-6 ... 8.00
7-10 ... 6.00
11-15 ... 5.00

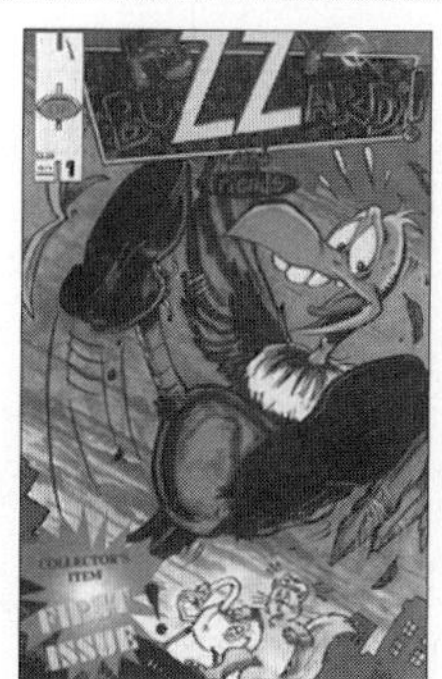

Fuzzy Buzzard and Friends

G-8 and His Battle Aces

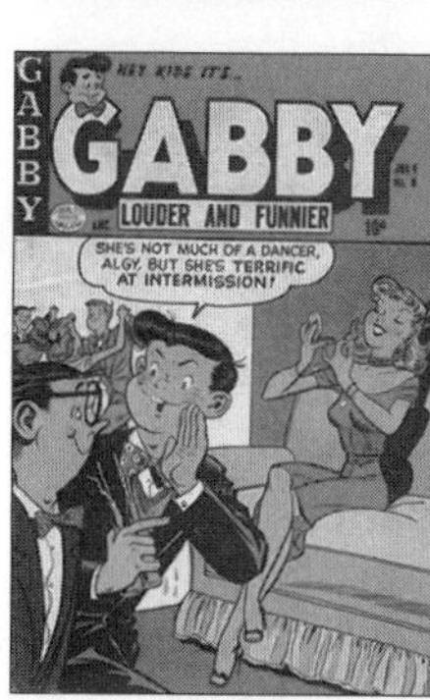

Gabby

Gabby Hayes Western

Galactic Guardians

Galactus the Devourer

Galaxion

Gambit and Associates

Funky Phantom
Gold Key, 1972

1 .... 24.00
2 .... 15.00
3-5 .... 10.00
6-10 .... 8.00
11-13 .... 6.00

Funland
Ziff-Davis, 1949

1 .... 120.00

Funland Comics
Croyden, 1945

1 .... 100.00

Funnies
Dell, 1936

1 .... 1,950.00
2 .... 925.00
3 .... 675.00
4-5 .... 540.00
6-10 .... 425.00
11-20 .... 340.00
21-29 .... 265.00
30 .... 800.00
31 .... 575.00
32-35 .... 500.00
36-44 .... 465.00
45-51 .... 475.00
52-56 .... 460.00
57 .... 3,400.00
58 .... 1,175.00
59-63 .... 575.00
64 .... 600.00

Funnies Annual
Avon, 1959

1 .... 350.00

Funnies on Parade
Eastern Color, 1933

1 .... 14,600.00

Funny Animals
Charlton, 1984

1 .... 450.00
2 .... 250.00

Funnybone
LaSalle, 1943

1 .... 200.00

Funny Book
Parents' Magazine Institute, 1942

1 .... 85.00
2 .... 50.00
3-4 .... 40.00
5-8 .... 35.00

Funny Fables
Decker, 1957

1 .... 28.00
2 .... 20.00

Funny Films
ACG, 1949

1 .... 70.00
2 .... 40.00
3-5 .... 32.00
6-10 .... 26.00
11-20 .... 20.00
21-29 .... 16.00

Funny Folks
DC, 1946

1 .... 225.00
2 .... 90.00
3-5 .... 65.00
6-10 .... 50.00
11-20 .... 38.00
21-26 .... 28.00

Funny Frolics
Marvel, 1945

1 .... 110.00
2 .... 60.00
3-4 .... 45.00
5 .... 35.00

Funny Funnies
Nedor

1 .... 90.00

Funnyman
Magazine Enterprises, 1948

1 .... 185.00
2 .... 140.00
3 .... 125.00
4-6 .... 110.00

Funny Pages
Centaur, 1936

6 .... 1,650.00
7 .... 900.00
8 .... 800.00
9-11 .... 650.00
12-16 .... 540.00
17 .... 600.00
18-20 .... 450.00
21 .... 2,400.00
22 .... 1,450.00
23 .... 885.00
24-29 .... 665.00
30 .... 1,350.00
31-32 .... 665.00
33 .... 1,850.00
34 .... 2,100.00
35 .... 1,350.00
36-38 .... 875.00
39-42 .... 1,000.00

Funny Picture Stories
Comics Magazine, 1936

1 .... 2,650.00
2 .... 1,150.00
3 .... 775.00
4-5 .... 650.00
6-7 .... 485.00

Funny Picture Stories
Centaur, 1937

1 .... 485.00
2-3 .... 365.00

4-5 .... 325.00
6-11 .... 300.00

Funny Picture Stories

Centaur, 1939

1 .... 300.00
2-3 .... 285.00

Funny Stuff

DC, 1944

1 .... 550.00
2 .... 275.00
3-4 .... 150.00
5 .... 140.00
6-10 .... 100.00
11-20 .... 80.00
21 .... 60.00
22 .... 100.00
23-30 .... 60.00
31-40 .... 40.00
41-50 .... 32.00
51-59 .... 26.00
60-70 .... 20.00
71-79 .... 16.00

Funny Stuff Stocking Stuffer

DC, 1985

1 .... 1.00

Funny 3-D

Harvey, 1953

1 .... 75.00

Funnytime Features

Eenieweenie, 1994

1-8 .... 3.00

Funny Tunes

U.S.A., 1944

16 .... 80.00
17 .... 54.00
18-23 .... 38.00

Funny World

Marbak, 1947

1 .... 40.00
2-3 .... 28.00

Funtastic World of Hanna-Barbera

Marvel, 1977

1 .... 13.00
2 .... 9.00
3 .... 6.00

Fun Time

Ace, 1953

1 .... 85.00
2-4 .... 50.00

Furies

Avatar, 1997

0-0/Nude 3.00

Furies

Carbon-Based, 1996

1-8 .... 3.00

Furkindred

Mu, 1991

1 .... 7.00
2 .... 8.00

Furrlough

Antarctic, 1991

1-3 .... 4.00
4-22 .... 3.00
23 .... 4.00
24-34 .... 3.00
35 .... 4.00
36-49 .... 3.00
50 .... 4.00
51-139 .... 3.00
140-144 .... 4.00

Further Adventures of Cyclops and Phoenix

Marvel, 1996

1-4 .... 2.00

Further Adventures of Indiana Jones

Marvel, 1983

1 .... 3.00
2-34 .... 2.00

Further Adventures of Nyoka the Jungle Girl

AC, 2005

1-4 .... 2.00
5 .... 3.00
6-7 .... 7.00

Further Adventures of Young Jeffy Dahmer

Boneyard

1 .... 3.00

Further Fattening Adventures of Pudge, Girl Blimp

Star*Reach

1 .... 4.00
1/A 5.00
2-3 .... 4.00

Fury

Dell, 1962

1 .... 25.00

Fury

Marvel, 1994

1 .... 3.00

Fury

Marvel, 2001

1 .... 4.00
2-6 .... 3.00

Fury/Agent 13

Marvel, 1998

1-2 .... 3.00

Gambit and Bishop

Gambit and Bishop Genesis

Gambit Battlebook

Game Boy

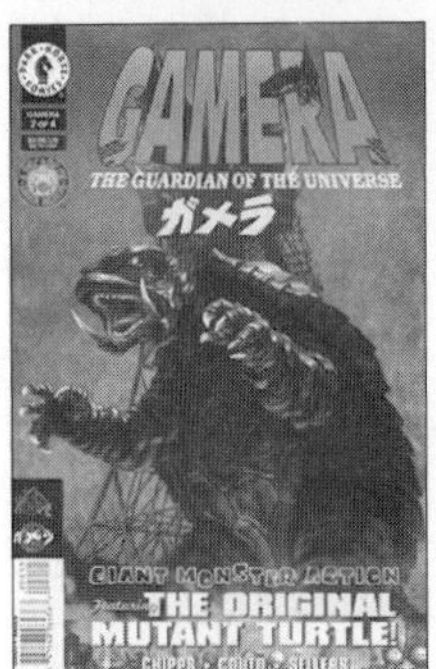

Gamera

Gandy Goose

Gangbusters

Gangsters and Gun Molls

Fury/Black Widow: Death Duty

Marvel, 1995

1 .... 6.00

Fury of Firestorm

DC, 1982

1 .... 6.00
2-10 .... 2.00
11-61 .... 1.00
61/A 10.00
62-64 .... 1.00
Ann 1-4 .... 2.00

Fury of Hellina

Lightning, 1995

1 .... 3.00

Fury of S.H.I.E.L.D.

Marvel, 1995

1 .... 3.00
2-3 .... 2.00
4 .... 3.00

Fused

Image, 2002

1-4 .... 3.00

Fused

Dark Horse, 2004

1-4 .... 3.00

Fushigi Yugi

Viz, 2002

1-16 .... 10.00

Fusion

Eclipse, 1987

1-17 .... 2.00

Futaba-kun Change

Ironcat

1-3 .... 3.00

Futaba-kun Change

Ironcat, 1999

1-4 .... 3.00

Futurama

Slave Labor, 1989

1-3 .... 2.00

Futurama

Bongo, 2000

1 .... 7.00
1/2nd-19 .... 3.00

Futurama/Simpsons Infinitely Secret Crossover Crisis

Bongo, 2002

1-2 .... 3.00

Future Beat

Oasis, 1986

1-2 .... 2.00

Future Comics

David McKay, 1940

1 .... 1,800.00
2 .... 1,100.00
3-4 .... 885.00

Future Cop: L.A.P.D.

DC, 1998

1 .... 5.00
Ashcan 1 .... 1.00

Future Course

Reoccurring Images, 1993

1 .... 3.00

Futuretech

Mushroom, 1995

1 .... 4.00

Future World Comics

George W. Dougherty, 1946

1 .... 200.00
2 .... 160.00

Future World Comix

Warren, 1978

1 .... 4.00

Futurians by Dave Cockrum

Lodestone, 1985

1-3 .... 2.00

Futurians

Aardwolf, 1995

1 .... 3.00

Fuzzy Buzzard and Friends

Hall of Heroes, 1995

1 .... 3.00

G-8 and His Battle Aces

Blazing, 1966

1 .... 2.00

Gabby

Quality, 1953

1 .... 32.00
2 .... 20.00
3 .... 16.00
4-9 .... 12.00

Gabby Hayes Western

Fawcett, 1948

1 .... 315.00
2 .... 160.00
3-5 .... 125.00
6-10 .... 110.00
11-20 .... 80.00
21-30 .... 65.00
31-40 .... 45.00
41-50 .... 36.00
51-59 .... 32.00

Gabriel

Caliber, 1995

1 .... 4.00

!Gag!
Harrier, 1987
1 .... 4.00
2-7 .... 3.00

Gag Reflex (Skip Williamson's...)
Williamson, 1994
1 .... 3.00

Gaijin (Matrix)
Matrix, 1987
1 .... 2.00

Gaijin
Caliber
1 .... 4.00

Gajit Gang
Amazing
1 .... 2.00

Galactic
Dark Horse, 2003
1-3 .... 3.00

Galactica: The New Millennium
Realm, 1999
1 .... 3.00
1/Conv 5.00

Galactic Gladiators
Playdigm, 2001
1-4 .... 3.00

Galactic Guardians
Marvel, 1994
1-4 .... 2.00

Galactic Patrol
Eternity, 1990
1-5 .... 2.00

Galactus the Devourer
Marvel, 1999
1-6 .... 4.00

Galaxina
Aircel, 1991
1-4 .... 3.00

Galaxion
Helikon, 1997
1-11 .... 3.00
Special 1 .... 1.00

Galaxy Girl
Dynamic
1 .... 3.00

Gallegher Boy Reporter
Gold Key, 1965
1 .... 15.00

Gall Force: Eternal Story
CPM, 1995
1-4 .... 3.00

Gambit
Oracle, 1986
1 .... 3.00
2 .... 2.00

Gambit
Eternity, 1988
1 .... 4.00

Gambit
Marvel, 1993
1 .... 3.00
1/Gold 4.00
2-4 .... 3.00

Gambit
Marvel, 1997
1-4 .... 3.00

Gambit
Marvel, 1998
1 .... 3.00
1/A-1/B 4.00
1/C 6.00
1/D 4.00
2-4 .... 3.00
5-24 .... 2.00
25 .... 3.00
Ann 1999-2000 .... 4.00
GS 1 .... 5.00

Gambit
Marvel, 2004
1-12 .... 3.00

Gambit and Associates
Eclectic
1-3 .... 2.00

Gambit and Bishop
Marvel, 2001
1-6 .... 2.00

Gambit and Bishop Alpha
Marvel, 2001
1 .... 2.00

Gambit and Bishop Genesis
Marvel, 2001
1 .... 4.00

Gambit & the X-Ternals
Marvel, 1995
1-4 .... 2.00

Gambit Battlebook
Marvel, 1998
1 .... 4.00

Game Boy
Valiant, 1990
1-4 .... 2.00

Game Guys!
Wonder
1 .... 3.00

Gargoyle

Gargoyles

Gatekeeper

Gates of Eden

Gay Comics

Gazillion

GD Minus 18

Gear

Gamera
Dark Horse, 1996

1-4 .... 3.00

Gammarauders
DC, 1989

1-6 .... 1.00
7-10 .... 2.00

Gamorra Swimsuit Special
Image, 1996

1 .... 3.00

Gandy Goose
St. John, 1953

1 .... 40.00
2 .... 26.00
3 .... 20.00
4 .... 16.00
5-6 .... 14.00

Gangbang Girls: All Wet
Angel

1 .... 3.00

Gangbusters
DC, 1947

1 .... 565.00
2 .... 300.00
3 .... 200.00
4-5 .... 175.00
☛Lady Cop
6-10 .... 140.00
11-13 .... 110.00
14 .... 150.00
15-16 .... 85.00
17 .... 150.00
18-20 .... 85.00
21-30 .... 70.00
31-51 .... 54.00
52-67 .... 44.00

Gangland
DC, 1998

1-4 .... 3.00

Gangsters and Gun Molls
Realistic Comics, 1951

1 .... 240.00
2 .... 185.00
3 .... 155.00
4 .... 135.00

Gangsters Can't Win
D.S., 1948

1 .... 145.00
2 .... 90.00
3 .... 75.00
4-9 .... 58.00

Gantar: The Last Nabu
Target, 1986

1-7 .... 2.00

Gargoyle
Marvel, 1985

1-4 .... 2.00

Gargoyles
Marvel, 1995

1 .... 3.00
2-11 .... 2.00

Garou: The Lone Wolf
Bare Bones, 1999

1 .... 2.00

Garrison's Gorillas
Dell, 1968

1 .... 21.00
2-4 .... 14.00
5 .... 12.00

Gasp!
Quebecor, 1994

1 .... 1.00

Gatecrasher: Ring of Fire
Black Bull, 2000

1-4/A 3.00

Gatekeeper
Gatekeeper

1 .... 3.00

Gate Manga
ADV Manga, 2005

1 .... 10.00

Gates of Eden
Fantaco, 1982

1 .... 4.00

Gates of Pandragon
Ianus

1 .... 2.00

Gatesville Company
Speakeasy Comics, 2005

1 .... 3.00

Gateway to Horror (Basil Wolverton's...)
Dark Horse, 1987

1 .... 2.00

Gathering of Tribes
KC Arts

1 .... 1.00

Gauntlet
Aircel, 1992

1-8 .... 3.00

Gay Comics
U.S.A., 1944

1 .... 375.00
18 .... 220.00
19 .... 185.00
20-25 .... 150.00
26-29 .... 125.00
30-31 .... 65.00
32 .... 45.00
33-34 .... 65.00
35 .... 45.00
36-37 .... 65.00
38-40 .... 45.00

Gay Comics (Bob Ross)

Bob Ross, 1980

1 .... 13.00
2 .... 8.00
3-5 .... 6.00
6-9 .... 5.00
10-16 .... 4.00
17-21 .... 3.00
22-24 .... 5.00
25 .... 4.00
Special 1 .... 3.00

Gazillion

Image, 1998

1-1/Variant 3.00

GD Minus 18

Antarctic, 1998

1 .... 3.00

Gear

Fireman, 1998

1-6 .... 3.00

Gear Station

Image, 2000

1-5 .... 3.00

Geeksville

3 Finger Prints, 1999

1-3 .... 3.00

Geeksville (Vol. 2)

Image, 2000

0-6 .... 3.00

Geisha

Oni, 1998

1-4 .... 3.00

Gem Comics

Spotlight, 1945

1 .... 165.00

Geminar

Image, 2000

Special 1 .... 5.00

Gemini Blood

DC, 1996

1-9 .... 2.00

Gen-Active

WildStorm, 2000

1-6 .... 4.00

Gene Autry and Champion

Dell, 1955

102-121 .... 20.00

Gene Autry Comics

Fawcett, 1942

1 .... 4,500.00
2 .... 1,100.00
3 .... 1,000.00
4-5 .... 875.00
6-10 .... 775.00
11-12 .... 660.00

Gene Autry Comics

Dell, 1946

1 .... 475.00
2 .... 265.00
3 .... 200.00
4-5 .... 145.00
6-10 .... 125.00
11-20 .... 85.00
21-40 .... 60.00
41-60 .... 45.00
61-80 .... 38.00
81-90 .... 30.00
91-100 .... 28.00
101 .... 20.00

Gene Autry's Champion

Dell, 1951

3-19 .... 22.00

Gene Dogs

Marvel, 1993

1 .... 3.00
2-4 .... 2.00

Gene Pool

Idea & Design Works, 2003

1 .... 7.00

Generation Hex

DC, 1997

1 .... 2.00

Generation M

Marvel, 2006

1-5 .... 3.00

Generation Next

Marvel, 1995

1-4 .... 2.00

Generation X

Marvel, 1994

-1 .... 2.00
½-½/Ltd. 3.00
1 .... 4.00
2-24 .... 2.00
25 .... 3.00
26-49 .... 2.00
50-50/Autographed 3.00
51-56 .... 2.00
57 .... 3.00
58-74 .... 2.00
75 .... 3.00
Ann 1995 .... 4.00
Ann 1996-1997 .... 3.00
Ann 1998-1999 .... 4.00
Ashcan 1 .... 2.00
Holiday 1 .... 4.00

Generation X/Gen13

Marvel, 1997

1-1/A 4.00

Generation X Underground

Marvel, 1998

1 .... 3.00

Geeksville

Geisha

Gem Comics

Gemini Blood

Gene Autry and Champion

Gene Dogs

Generation Hex

Generation Next

Generic Comic
Marvel, 1984

1 ....3.00

Generic Comic
Comics Conspiracy, 2001

1-5 ....2.00
5/Variant 6.00
6-9 ....2.00

Genesis
Malibu, 1993

0 ....4.00

Genesis
DC, 1997

1-4 ....2.00

Genesis: The #1 Collection
Image

1 ....10.00

Genetix
Marvel, 1993

1 ....3.00
2-6 ....2.00

Genie
Fc9 Publishing, 2005

1-2 ....3.00

Genocide
Renegade Tribe, 1994

1-1/2nd 3.00

Genocyber
Viz, 1993

1-5 ....3.00

Gen of Hiroshima
Educomics, 1980

1-2 ....2.00

Gensaga
Express

1 ....3.00

Gen12
Image, 1998

1-5 ....3.00

Gen13
Image, 1994

0 ....4.00
½ 2.00
½/A 5.00
1 ....4.00
1/A-1/B 5.00
1/C 4.00
1/2nd-5/A 3.00
Ashcan 1 ....4.00

Gen13
Image, 1994

-1-0 ....3.00
1/3D 5.00
1/A-1/F 3.00
1/G-1/H 4.00
1/I-1/M 3.00
1/N 40.00
1/2nd-10 ....3.00
11-11/A 5.00
12 ....3.00
13/A-13/C 2.00
13/CS-13/D 7.00
14-24 ....3.00
25-25/CS 4.00
26-49 ....3.00
50 ....4.00
51-77 ....3.00
3D 1 ....6.00
3D 1/A 5.00
Ann 1 ....3.00
Ann 1999-2000 ....4.00

Gen13
WildStorm, 2002

0-0/Variant 1.00
1-16 ....3.00

Gen13
DC, 2006

1-4/Variant 3.00

Gen13: A Christmas Caper
WildStorm, 2000

1 ....6.00

Gen13: Backlist
Image, 1996

1 ....3.00

Gen13 Bikini Pin-Up Special
Image

1 ....5.00

Gen13 Bootleg
Image, 1996

1-17 ....3.00
Ann. 1 ....4.00

Gen13: Carny Folk
WildStorm, 2000

1 ....4.00

Gen13/Fantastic Four
WildStorm, 2001

1 ....6.00

Gen13/Generation X
Image, 1997

1/A-1/B 3.00
1/C-1/D 5.00
1/E-1/G 4.00

Gen13: Going West
DC, 1999

1 ....3.00

Gen13: Grunge Saves the World
DC, 1999

1 ....6.00

Gen13 Interactive
Image, 1997
1-3 .... 3.00

Gen13: London, New York, Hell
DC, 2001
1 .... 7.00

Gen13: Magical Drama Queen Roxy
Image, 1998
1-3/A 4.00

Gen13/Maxx
Image, 1995
1 .... 4.00

Gen13: Medicine Song
WildStorm
1 .... 6.00

Gen13/Monkeyman & O'Brien
Image, 1998
1-2/A 3.00

Gen13: Ordinary Heroes
Image, 1996
1-2 .... 3.00

Gen13 Rave
Image, 1995
1 .... 3.00

Gen13: Science Friction
WildStorm, 2001
1 .... 6.00

Gen13: The Unreal World
Image, 1996
1 .... 3.00

Gen13: Wired
DC, 1999
1 .... 3.00

Gen13 Yearbook '97
Image, 1997
1 .... 3.00

Gen13 'Zine
Image, 1996
1 .... 2.00

Gentle Ben
Dell, 1968
1 .... 30.00
2-5 .... 20.00

Genus
Antarctic, 1993
1 .... 4.00
2-57 .... 3.00
58-89 .... 4.00

Genus Greatest Hits
Antarctic, 1996
1-4 .... 5.00

Genus Spotlight
Radio, 1998
1-2 .... 3.00

Geobreeders
CPM Manga, 1999
1-31 .... 3.00

Geomancer
Valiant, 1994
1 .... 2.00
1/VVSS 40.00
2-3 .... 1.00
4-7 .... 2.00
8 .... 4.00

George of the Jungle
Gold Key, 1969
1 .... 35.00
2 .... 24.00

George Romero's Land of the Dead
Idea & Design Works, 2005
1-5 .... 4.00

Georgie Comics
Timely, 1945
1 .... 90.00
2 .... 60.00
3-5 .... 50.00
6-10 .... 40.00
11-20 .... 36.00
21-39 .... 32.00

Gepetto Files
Quick to Fly, 1998
1 .... 3.00

Gerald McBoing Boing and the Nearsighted Mr. Magoo
Dell, 1952
1 .... 85.00
2-6 .... 55.00

Geriatric Gangrene Jujitsu Gerbils
Planet-X
1-2 .... 2.00

Geriatricman
C&T
1 .... 2.00

ge rouge
Verotik, 1997
½-3 .... 3.00

Gertie the Dinosaur Comics
Gertie the Dinosaur, 2000
1 .... 3.00

Gestalt
New England, 1993
1-2 .... 2.00

Generation X

Generation X Underground

Genetix

Genocyber

Gensaga

Genus

Geomancer

Georgie Comics

Gestalt
Caliber
0 ..... 3.00

Get Along Gang
Marvel, 1985
1-6 ..... 1.00

GetBackers
Tokyopop, 2004
1-12 ..... 10.00

Get Bent!
Ben T. Steckler, 1998
1-6 ..... 3.00
7 ..... 2.00
8-9 ..... 3.00

Get Lost
Mikeross, 1954
1 ..... 145.00
2 ..... 90.00

Get Lost
New Comics, 1987
1-3 ..... 2.00

Get Real Comics
Tides Center
1 ..... 2.00

Get Smart
Dell, 1966
1 ..... 45.00
2 ..... 30.00
3-5 ..... 22.00
6-8 ..... 20.00

Ghetto Bitch
Fantagraphics
1 ..... 3.00

Ghetto Blasters
Whiplash, 1997
1 ..... 3.00

Ghost
Dark Horse, 1994
1-24 ..... 3.00
25 ..... 4.00
26-36 ..... 3.00
Special 1-Special 3 ..... 4.00

Ghost
Dark Horse, 1998
1 ..... 4.00
2-22 ..... 3.00

Ghost and the Shadow
Dark Horse, 1995
1 ..... 3.00

Ghost/Batgirl
Dark Horse, 2000
1-4 ..... 3.00

Ghostbusters
First, 1986
1-6 ..... 2.00

Ghostbusters II
Now, 1989
1-3 ..... 2.00

Ghost Comics
Fiction House, 1951
1 ..... 485.00
2 ..... 365.00
3-5 ..... 285.00
6-11 ..... 220.00

Ghostdancing
DC, 1995
1-2 ..... 2.00
3-6 ..... 3.00

Ghost Handbook
Dark Horse, 1999
1 ..... 3.00

Ghost/Hellboy Special
Dark Horse, 1996
1-2 ..... 3.00

Ghost in the Shell
Dark Horse, 1995
1-8 ..... 4.00

Ghost in the Shell 2: Man/Machine Interface
Dark Horse, 2003
1 ..... 4.00
1/Hologram 10.00
2-11 ..... 4.00

Ghost in the Shell 1.5: Human Error Processor
Dark Horse, 2006
1-9 ..... 3.00

Ghostly Haunts
Charlton, 1971
20 ..... 6.00
21-30 ..... 5.00
31-40 ..... 4.00
41-58 ..... 3.00

Ghostly Tales
Charlton, 1966
55 ..... 16.00
56-59 ..... 7.00
60-70 ..... 5.00
71-100 ..... 4.00
101-169 ..... 3.00

Ghostly Weird Stories
Star Publications, 1953
120 ..... 170.00
121-124 ..... 125.00

Ghost Manor
Charlton, 1968
1 ..... 12.00
2-5 ..... 7.00
6-10 ..... 6.00
11-19 ..... 5.00

Ghost Manor
Charlton, 1971

1 ..... 10.00
2-7 ..... 6.00
8 ..... 8.00
9-10 ..... 5.00
11-30 ..... 4.00
31-77 ..... 3.00

Ghost Rider
Magazine Enterprises, 1950

1 ..... 400.00
2-5 ..... 285.00
6-10 ..... 175.00
11 ..... 200.00
12-14 ..... 135.00

Ghost Rider
Marvel, 1967

1 ..... 28.00
2-3 ..... 20.00
4-7 ..... 13.00

Ghost Rider
Marvel, 1973

1 ..... 130.00
2 ..... 37.00
3-4 ..... 25.00
5 ..... 23.00
6-14 ..... 15.00
15-16 ..... 12.00
17 ..... 10.00
17/30¢ 20.00
18 ..... 10.00
18/30¢ 20.00
19 ..... 10.00
19/30¢ 20.00
20 ..... 10.00
21-23 ..... 7.00
24-26/35¢ 15.00
27-30 ..... 7.00
31-49 ..... 6.00
50 ..... 12.00
51-68 ..... 5.00
69-80 ..... 4.00
81 ..... 10.00

Ghost Rider
Marvel, 1990

-1 ..... 2.00
1 ..... 4.00
1/2nd 2.00
2-5/Variant 3.00
5/2nd 2.00
6 ..... 3.00
7-14 ..... 2.00
15 ..... 5.00
15/2nd-27 ..... 2.00
28 ..... 3.00
29-30 ..... 2.00
31 ..... 3.00
32-49 ..... 2.00
50 ..... 3.00
50/Variant 4.00
51-60 ..... 2.00
61 ..... 3.00
62-92 ..... 2.00
93 ..... 3.00
Ann 1 ..... 4.00
Ann 2 ..... 3.00

Ghost Rider
Marvel, 2001

½ 4.00
1-6 ..... 3.00

Ghost Rider
Marvel, 2005

1 ..... 6.00
1/Ribic 18.00
1/DirCut 4.00
1/RRP 45.00
2-6 ..... 3.00

Ghost Rider
Marvel, 2006

1-6 ..... 3.00

Ghost Rider & Cable: Servants of the Dead
Marvel, 1991

1 ..... 4.00

Ghost Rider and the Midnight Sons Magazine
Marvel

1 ..... 4.00

Ghost Rider/Ballistic
Marvel, 1997

1 ..... 3.00

Ghost Rider/Blaze: Spirits of Vengeance
Marvel, 1992

1 ..... 2.00
1/CS 3.00
2-11 ..... 2.00
12 ..... 3.00
13-23 ..... 2.00

Ghost Rider/Captain America: Fear
Marvel, 1992

1 ..... 6.00

Ghost Rider: Crossroads
Marvel, 1995

1 ..... 4.00

Ghost Rider: Highway to Hell
Marvel, 2001

1 ..... 4.00

Ghost Rider Poster Magazine
Marvel, 1992

1 ..... 5.00

Geriatric Gangrene Jujitsu Gerbils

Get Along Gang

Get Lost

Get Real Comics

Get Smart

Ghost and the Shadow

Ghostbusters

Ghostbusters II

Ghost Rider: The Hammer Lane

Marvel, 2001

1-6 .... 3.00

Ghost Rider 2099

Marvel, 1994

1 .... 2.00
1/CS 3.00
2-24 .... 2.00
25 .... 3.00

Ghost Rider; Wolverine; Punisher: The Dark Design

Marvel, 1991

1 .... 6.00

Ghosts

DC, 1971

1 .... 100.00
2 .... 35.00
3-5 .... 17.00
6-10 .... 12.00
11-20 .... 10.00
21-30 .... 6.00
31-39 .... 5.00
40 .... 6.00
41-50 .... 5.00
51-70 .... 4.00
71-112 .... 3.00

Ghost Ship

Slave Labor, 1996

1 .... 4.00
2-3 .... 3.00

Ghosts of Dracula

Eternity, 1991

1-5 .... 3.00

Ghost Spy

Image, 2004

1-5 .... 3.00

Ghost Stories

Dell, 1962

1 .... 36.00
2 .... 20.00
3-5 .... 14.00
6-10 .... 10.00
11-16 .... 7.00
17-20 .... 6.00
21-37 .... 5.00

Ghost Stories

Dark Horse

1 .... 9.00

Ghouls

Eternity

1 .... 2.00

Giant Comics Editions

St. John, 1948

1 .... 575.00
2 .... 340.00
3 .... 425.00
4 .... 1,100.00
5 .... 1,200.00
5/A 500.00
6 .... 675.00
7 .... 525.00
8 .... 485.00
9 .... 650.00
10 .... 525.00
11 .... 650.00
12 .... 1,700.00
13 .... 600.00
14 .... 450.00
15 .... 770.00
16 .... 625.00
17 .... 450.00

Giantkiller

DC, 1999

1-6 .... 3.00

Giantkiller A to Z

DC, 1999

1 .... 3.00

Giant-Size Amazing Spider-Man

Marvel, 1999

1 .... 5.00

Giant-Size Avengers

Marvel, 1974

1 .... 30.00
2 .... 25.00
3-4 .... 20.00
5 .... 15.00

Giant-Size Captain America

Marvel

1 .... 20.00

Giant-Size Captain Marvel

Marvel

1 .... 16.00

Giant-Size Chillers

Marvel, 1974

1 .... 25.00
☛1st Lilith

Giant-Size Chillers

Marvel, 1975

1 .... 20.00
2-3 .... 15.00

Giant-Size Conan

Marvel, 1974

1 .... 16.00
2 .... 10.00
3 .... 7.00
4-5 .... 6.00

Giant-Size Creatures

Marvel, 1974

1 .... 25.00

Giant-Size Daredevil
Marvel, 1975
1 .... 15.00

Giant-Size Defenders
Marvel, 1974
1 .... 20.00
2-3 .... 10.00
4-5 .... 7.00

Giant-Size Doc Savage
Marvel, 1975
1 .... 10.00

Giant-Size Doctor Strange
Marvel, 1975
1 .... 15.00

Giant-Size Dracula
Marvel, 1974
2 .... 22.00
☛was GS Chillers
3-4 .... 15.00
5 .... 20.00
☛1st Marvel Byrne

Giant-Size Fantastic Four
Marvel, 1974
1 .... 20.00
2 .... 12.00
3 .... 10.00
4 .... 12.00
5-6 .... 10.00

Giant-Size Hulk
Marvel, 1975
1 .... 23.00

Giant-Size Hulk
Marvel, 2006
1 .... 8.00

Giant-Size Invaders
Marvel, 1975
2 .... 0.00
1 .... 15.00
☛G.A. Subby origin

Giant-Size Iron Man
Marvel, 1975
1 .... 17.00

Giant-Size Kid Colt
Marvel, 1975
1 .... 27.00
2-3 .... 20.00

Giant-Size Man-Thing
Marvel, 1974
1 .... 15.00
2 .... 9.00
3 .... 12.00
4 .... 10.00
5 .... 12.00

Giant-Size Marvel Triple Action
Marvel, 1975
1 .... 15.00
2 .... 12.00

Giant-Size Master of Kung Fu
Marvel, 1974
1 .... 17.00
2 .... 12.00
3-4 .... 10.00

Giant-Size Mini Comics
Eclipse, 1986
1-4 .... 2.00

Giant-Size Mini-Marvels: Starring Spidey
Marvel, 2002
1 .... 4.00

Giant-Size Ms. Marvel
Marvel, 2006
1 .... 5.00

Giant-Size Official Prince Valiant
Pioneer
1 .... 4.00

Giant-Size Power Man
Marvel, 1975
1 .... 20.00

Giant-Size Spider-Man
Marvel, 1974
1 .... 35.00
2-3 .... 12.00
4 .... 45.00
☛Punisher app.
5 .... 12.00
6 .... 15.00

Giant-Size Spider-Man
Marvel, 1998
1 .... 4.00

Giant-Size Spider-Woman
Marvel, 2005
1 .... 5.00

Giant-Size Super-Heroes
Marvel, 1974
1 .... 25.00

Giant-Size Super-Stars
Marvel, 1974
1 .... 20.00

Giant-Size Super-Villain Team-Up
Marvel, 1975
1 .... 17.00
2 .... 10.00

Giant-Size Thor
Marvel, 1975
1 .... 20.00

Giant-Size Werewolf By Night
Marvel, 1974
2 .... 20.00
3-5 .... 15.00

Ghost Comics

Ghostdancing

Ghost in the Shell

Ghostly Haunts

Ghostly Tales

Ghost Rider and the Midnight Sons Magazine

Ghost Rider Poster Magazine

Ghosts

Giant-Size Wolverine

Marvel, 2006

1 .... 5.00

Giant-Size X-Men

Marvel, 1975

1 .... 800.00
☛1st new X-Men
2 .... 80.00
3-4 .... 5.00

Giant THB Parade

Horse

1 .... 5.00

G.I. Combat

Quality, 1952

1 .... 440.00
2 .... 210.00
3-5 .... 150.00
6-9 .... 125.00
10 .... 135.00
11-20 .... 90.00
21-31 .... 75.00
32 .... 110.00
33-43 .... 75.00

G.I. Combat

DC, 1953

44 .... 500.00
45 .... 300.00
46 .... 250.00
47 .... 225.00
48-50 .... 100.00
51-54 .... 85.00
55 .... 125.00
56-60 .... 85.00
61-66 .... 70.00
67 .... 125.00
☛1st Tank Killer
68 .... 400.00
69-86 .... 70.00
87 .... 300.00
☛1st Haunted Tank
88-100 .... 55.00
101-110 .... 45.00
111-113 .... 38.00
114 .... 75.00
☛Haunted Tank origin
115-120 .... 28.00
121-140 .... 22.00
141-145 .... 8.00
146-150 .... 10.00
151-160 .... 8.00
161-180 .... 7.00
181-200 .... 5.00
201-250 .... 4.00
251-288 .... 3.00

Gideon Hawk

Big Shot, 1994

1-3 .... 2.00

Gidget

Dell, 1966

1 .... 100.00

Gift

Image, 2004

1 .... 3.00
1/DirCut 4.00
2-14 .... 3.00

Gift: A First Publishing Holiday Special

First, 1990

1 .... 6.00

Gifts of the Night

DC, 1999

1-4 .... 3.00

Gigantor

Antarctic, 2000

1 .... 3.00

Giggle Comics

ACG, 1943

1 .... 125.00
2 .... 75.00
3-5 .... 60.00
6-10 .... 45.00
11-20 .... 30.00
21-30 .... 22.00
31-50 .... 20.00
51-70 .... 16.00
71-99 .... 14.00

Gigolo

Fantagraphics, 1995

1-2 .... 3.00

G.I. Government Issued

Paranoid, 1994

1-2 .... 2.00

G.I. in Battle

Four Star, 1952

1 .... 48.00
2 .... 26.00
3-5 .... 20.00
6-9 .... 18.00
Ann 1 .... 38.00
Ann 1/A 115.00
Ann 2-3 .... 24.00
Ann 4-6 .... 20.00

G.I. in Battle

Four Star, 1957

1 .... 55.00
2-6 .... 35.00

G.I. Jackrabbits

Excalibur, 1986

1 .... 2.00

G.I. Jane

Stanhall, 1953

1 .... 75.00
2-6 .... 45.00
7-10 .... 35.00

G.I. Joe
Ziff-Davis, 1950

1 .... 100.00
2-5 .... 60.00
6-10 .... 50.00
11-17 .... 42.00
18 .... 95.00
19-30 .... 36.00
31-40 .... 34.00
41-47 .... 30.00
48 .... 35.00
49-51 .... 30.00

G.I. Joe
Dark Horse, 1995

1-4 .... 2.00

G.I. Joe
Dark Horse, 1996

1-4 .... 3.00

G.I. Joe
Image, 2001

1-3 .... 3.00
4 .... 4.00
5-22 .... 3.00
23-25 .... 3.00

G.I. Joe
Devil's Due, 2004

26-35 .... 3.00
35/Variant 4.00
36-42 .... 3.00

G.I. Joe: America's Elite
Devil's Due, 2005

0 .... 1.00
1 .... 3.00
1/Conv 10.00
2-4 .... 3.00
5-6 .... 5.00
7-13 .... 3.00
13/Special 6.00
14-18 .... 3.00

G.I. Joe: America's Elite Data Desk Handbook
Devil's Due, 2005

1 .... 3.00

G.I. Joe and the Transformers
Marvel, 1987

1-4 .... 1.00

G.I. Joe: Battle Files
Image, 2002

1-3 .... 6.00

G.I. Joe Comics Magazine
Marvel, 1986

1 .... 3.00
2-13 .... 2.00

G.I. Joe: Declassified
Devil's Due, 2006

1 .... 5.00
1/Spaulding 9.00
2 .... 5.00
2/Special 9.00
3 .... 5.00
3/Special 9.00

G.I. Joe: Dreadnoks Declassified
Devil's Due, 2006

1 .... 5.00
1/Special 9.00

G.I. Joe European Missions
Marvel, 1988

1-15 .... 2.00

G.I. Joe: Frontline
Image, 2002

1 .... 3.00
1/Platinum 5.00
2-18 .... 3.00

G.I. Joe in 3-D
Blackthorne, 1987

1-6 .... 3.00

G.I. Joe: Master & Apprentice
Devil's Due, 2004

1-4 .... 3.00

G.I. Joe: Master & Apprentice Vol. II
Devil's Due, 2005

1 .... 3.00
1/Variant 4.00
2 .... 3.00
2/Variant 4.00
3 .... 3.00
3/Variant 4.00

G.I. Joe Order of Battle
Marvel, 1986

1-4 .... 1.00

G.I. Joe, A Real American Hero
Marvel, 1982

1 .... 14.00
2 .... 8.00
2/2nd 2.00
3 .... 4.00
3/2nd 2.00
4 .... 4.00
4/2nd 2.00
5 .... 4.00
5/2nd 2.00
6 .... 4.00
6/2nd 1.00
7 .... 4.00
7/2nd 1.00
8 .... 4.00
8/2nd 1.00
9 .... 4.00
9/2nd 1.00
10 .... 6.00

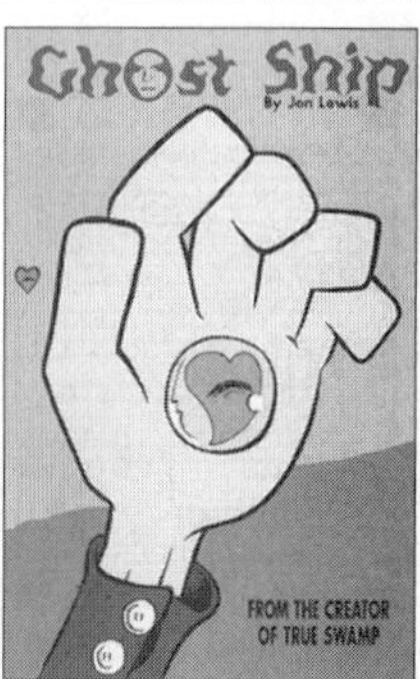

Ghost Ship

Ghost Stories

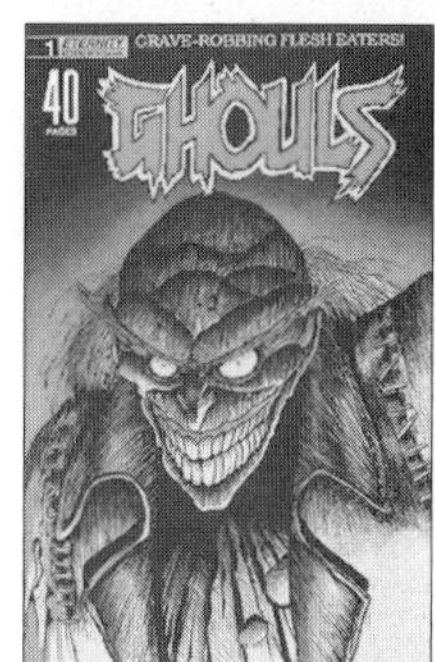

Ghouls

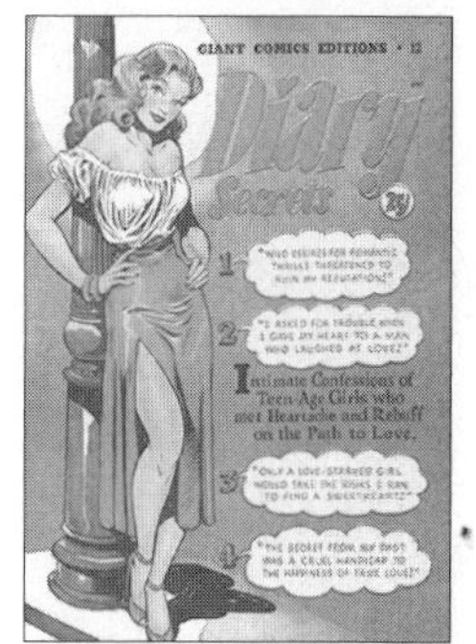

Giant Comics Editions

Giant-Size Amazing Spider-Man

Giant-Size Avengers

Giant-Size Captain Marvel

Giant-Size Conan

10/2nd 1.00
11 ....4.00
11/2nd 1.00
12 ....4.00
12/2nd 1.00
13 ....4.00
13/2nd 1.00
14 ....5.00
14/2nd 1.00
15 ....4.00
15/2nd 1.00
16 ....4.00
16/2nd 1.00
17 ....4.00
17/2nd 1.00
18 ....4.00
18/2nd 1.00
19 ....6.00
19/2nd 1.00
20 ....4.00
20/2nd 1.00
21 ....15.00
☛Silent issue
21/2nd 1.00
22 ....4.00
22/2nd 1.00
23 ....4.00
23/2nd 1.00
24 ....4.00
24/2nd 1.00
25 ....4.00
25/2nd 1.00
26 ....4.00
26/2nd 1.00
27 ....4.00
27/2nd 1.00
28 ....4.00
28/2nd 1.00
29 ....4.00
29/2nd 1.00
30 ....4.00
30/2nd 1.00
31 ....4.00
31/2nd 1.00
32 ....4.00
32/2nd 1.00
33 ....4.00
33/2nd 1.00
34 ....4.00
34/2nd 1.00
35 ....4.00
35/2nd 1.00
36 ....4.00
36/2nd 1.00
37-55 ....4.00
56 ....5.00
57 ....3.00
58 ....4.00
59-151 ....3.00
152-154 ....7.00
155 ....16.00
☛Low circulation

YB 1 ....3.00
YB 2-4 ....2.00
Special 1 ....20.00

G.I. Joe: Reloaded

Devil's Due, 2004

1 ....5.00
2-14 ....3.00

G.I. Joe: Scarlett Declassified

Devil's Due, 2006

1 ....5.00

G.I. Joe: Sigma 6

Devil's Due, 2006

1-6 ....3.00

G.I. Joe: Snake Eyes Declassified

Devil's Due, 2005

1-6 ....3.00

G.I. Joe Special Missions

Marvel, 1986

1 ....2.00
2-28 ....1.00

G.I. Joe Special Missions: Antarctica

Devil's Due, 2006

1 ....5.00

G.I. Joe Special Missions: Manhattan

Devil's Due, 2006

1 ....5.00

G.I. Joe: Special Missions - Manhattan

Devil's Due, 2006

1 ....5.00

G.I. Joe: Special Missions - Tokyo

Devil's Due, 2006

1 ....5.00

G.I. Joe vs. Transformers: The Art of War

Devil's Due, 206

1-4/Variant 3.00

G.I. Joe/Transformers

Image, 2003

1 ....4.00
1/Campbell 3.00
1/Foil 9.00
1/Graham 4.00
1/Graham foil 6.00
1/Miller-2 ....3.00
2/Sketch 12.00
3 ....3.00
3/Conv. 4.00
3/Variant 3.00
4 ....2.00
4/Variant 3.00

5 .... 2.00
5/Variant 3.00
6 .... 2.00

G.I. Joe vs. The Transformers

Devil's Due, 2004

1-1/Variant 4.00
2-4/Variant 3.00

Gilgamesh II

DC, 1989

1-4 .... 4.00

Gimme

Head Imports

1 .... 3.00

Gimoles

Alias, 2005

1 .... 1.00
2-4 .... 3.00

G.I.M.P.: The Monkey Boy and The Short Order Dwarf

Wasteland

1 .... 3.00

G.I. Mutants

Eternity, 1987

1-4 .... 2.00

Ginger

Archie, 1951

1 .... 45.00
2 .... 28.00
3-6 .... 20.00
7-10 .... 30.00

Ginger Fox

Comico, 1988

1-4 .... 2.00

Gin-Ryu

Believe in Yourself, 1995

1-3 .... 3.00
3/Ashcan 1.00
4 .... 3.00

Gipsy

NBM

1-2 .... 11.00

G.I. R.A.M.B.O.T.

Wonder Color, 1987

1 .... 2.00

Girl

Rip Off, 1991

1-4 .... 3.00

Girl

NBM

1 .... 16.00

Girl

DC, 1996

1-3 .... 3.00

Girl Called...Willow!, A

Angel, 1996

1 .... 3.00

Girl Called...Willow! Sketchbook, A

Angel

1 .... 3.00

Girl Comics

Marvel, 1949

1 .... 100.00
2 .... 75.00
3 .... 100.00
4-12 .... 75.00

Girl Confessions

Marvel, 1952

13-35 .... 50.00

Girl Crazy

Dark Horse, 1996

1-3 .... 3.00

Girl Fight Comics

Print Mint

1 .... 3.00

Girl from U.N.C.L.E.

Gold Key, 1967

1 .... 36.00
2 .... 24.00
3 .... 20.00
4-5 .... 15.00

Girl Genius

Studio Foglio, 2000

Ashcan 1 .... 1.00
1-3 .... 3.00
4-12 .... 4.00

Girlhero

High Drive, 1993

1-3 .... 3.00

Girl on Girl College Kink: New Year's Babes

Angel

1 .... 3.00

Girl on Girl: Feedin' Time

Angel

1 .... 3.00

Girl on Girl: Ticklish

Angel

1 .... 3.00

Girls

Image, 2005

1 .... 7.00
1/Variant 5.00
1/Sketch 6.00
2 .... 4.00
2/Variant 5.00
3-20 .... 3.00

Giant-Size Creatures

Giant-Size Daredevil

Giant-Size Defenders

Giant-Size Doc Savage

Giant-Size Doctor Strange

Giant-Size Dracula

Giant-Size Fantastic Four

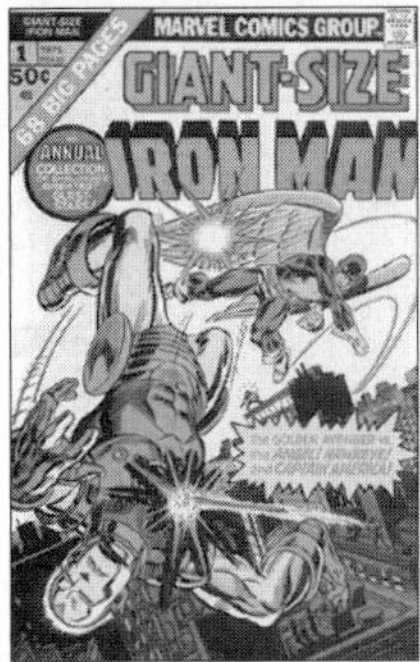

Giant-Size Iron Man

Girls Bravo
Tokyopop, 2005

1-2 .... 10.00

Girls' Love Stories
DC, 1949

1 .... 325.00
2 .... 165.00
3 .... 130.00
4-11 .... 110.00
12-22 .... 75.00
23-32 .... 48.00
33-49 .... 38.00
50-71 .... 30.00
72-94 .... 25.00
95-105 .... 20.00
106-111 .... 17.00
112-123 .... 15.00
124-143 .... 14.00
144-164 .... 9.00
165-180 .... 7.00

Girls of '95: Good, Bad & Deadly
Lost Cause, 1996

1 .... 4.00

Girls of Ninja High School
Antarctic, 1991

1-4 .... 4.00
5 .... 5.00
6-8/B 4.00
9 .... 3.00

Girl Squad X
Fantaco

1 .... 3.00

Girls' Romances
DC, 1950

1 .... 400.00
2 .... 225.00
3-10 .... 115.00
11-20 .... 80.00
21-30 .... 50.00
31-70 .... 40.00
71-90 .... 26.00
91-100 .... 22.00
101-108 .... 18.00
109 .... 65.00
110-120 .... 15.00
121-140 .... 13.00
141-160 .... 8.00

Girl Talk
Fantagraphics, 1996

4 .... 4.00

Girl: The Rule of Darkness
Cry for Dawn

1 .... 3.00

Girl: The Second Coming
NBM

1 .... 11.00

Girl Who Would Be Death
DC, 1998

1-4 .... 3.00

Give It Up! and Other Short Stories
NBM, 1995

1 .... 15.00

Give Me Liberty! (Rip Off)
Rip Off, 1976

1 .... 4.00

Give Me Liberty
Dark Horse, 1990

1-4 .... 5.00

G.I. War Tales
DC, 1973

1 .... 12.00
2 .... 7.00
3-4 .... 6.00

Gizmo
Mirage, 1986

1-6 .... 2.00

Gizmo
Chance

1 .... 3.00

Gizmo and the Fugitoid
Mirage, 1989

1-2 .... 2.00

GLA
Marvel, 2005

1 .... 5.00
2 .... 3.00
3-4 .... 3.00

G.L.A.
Marvel, 2005

2 .... 3.00

Gladiator/Supreme
Marvel, 1997

1 .... 5.00

Glamorous Graphix Presents
Glamorous Graphix, 1996

1 .... 4.00

Glass Jaw
Clay Heeled

1 .... 3.00

Global Force
Silverline

1-2 .... 2.00

Global Frequency
DC, 2002

1-12 .... 3.00

GloomCookie
Slave Labor, 1999

1-2 .... 4.00
3-25 .... 3.00

Gloom
APComics, 2005
1-2 .... 4.00

Glorianna
Press This
1 .... 4.00

Glory
Image, 1995
0-11 .... 3.00
12 .... 4.00
12/A 5.00
13-23 .... 3.00

Glory & Friends Bikini Fest
Image, 1995
1-1/Variant 3.00

Glory & Friends Christmas Special
Image, 1995
1 .... 3.00

Glory & Friends Lingerie Special
Image, 1995
1-1/Variant 3.00

Glory/Angela: Angels in Hell
Image, 1996
1 .... 3.00

Glory/Avengelyne
Image, 1995
1/A-1/B 4.00

Glory/Celestine: Dark Angel
Image, 1996
1-2 .... 3.00

GLX-Mas Special
Marvel, 2006
1 .... 4.00

Glyph
Labor of Love
1-3 .... 5.00

G-Man
Image, 2005
1 .... 6.00

G-Men
Caliber
1 .... 3.00

Gnatrat: The Dark Gnat Returns
Prelude, 1986
1 .... 2.00

Gnatrat: The Movie
Innovation
1 .... 2.00

Gnome-Mobile
Gold Key, 1967
1 .... 25.00

Gnomes, Fairies, and Sex Kittens
Fantagraphics, 2006
1 .... 4.00

G'n'R's Greatest Hits
Revolutionary, 1993
1 .... 3.00

Go-Go
Charlton, 1966
1 .... 40.00
2-9 .... 30.00

Gobbledygook
Mirage
1 .... 110.00
2 .... 70.00

Gobbledygook
Mirage, 1986
1 .... 5.00

Goblin Lord
Goblin, 1996
1-6 .... 3.00

Goblin Magazine
Warren, 1982
1 .... 9.00
2-4 .... 5.00

Goblin Market
Tome
1 .... 3.00

Goblin Studios
Goblin, 1995
1-5 .... 2.00

Go Boy 7 Human Action Machine
Dark Horse, 2003
1-5 .... 3.00

Goddess
DC, 1995
1-8 .... 3.00

Goddess
Twilight Twins
1 .... 2.00

Godhead
Anubis
1-1/Ltd. 4.00
2-3 .... 6.00

Godland
Image, 2005
1-14 .... 3.00

Gods & Tulips
Westhampton
1 .... 3.00

Giant-Size Kid Colt

Giant-Size Master of Kung Fu

Giant Size Official Prince Valiant

Giant-Size Power Man

Giant-Size Spider-Man

Giant-Size Super-Stars

Giant-Size Thor

Giant-Size Werewolf By Night

Godsent
Lock Graphic Publications, 1994

1 .... 2.00

Gods for Hire
Hot, 1986

1-2 .... 2.00

God's Hammer
Caliber, 1990

1-3 .... 3.00

God's Smuggler
Spire

1 .... 6.00

Godwheel
Malibu, 1995

0-3 .... 3.00

Godzilla
Marvel, 1977

1 .... 12.00
1/35¢ 15.00
2 .... 6.00
2/35¢ 15.00
3-3/Whitman 5.00
3/35¢ 15.00
4-5 .... 5.00
6-10 .... 4.00
11-24 .... 3.00

Godzilla
Dark Horse, 1987

1 .... 4.00
2-6 .... 3.00

Godzilla
Dark Horse, 1995

0 .... 4.00
1-16 .... 3.00

Godzilla Color Special
Dark Horse, 1992

1 .... 4.00

Godzilla, King of the Monsters Special
Dark Horse, 1987

1/A-1/B 3.00

Godzilla vs. Barkley
Dark Horse, 1993

1 .... 3.00

Godzilla Versus Hero Zero
Dark Horse, 1995

1 .... 3.00

Go Girl!
Image, 2000

1-5 .... 4.00

Go-Go Boy Ashcan
Mermaid

Ashcan 1 .... 1.00

Gog (Villains)
DC, 1998

1 .... 2.00

Going Home
Aardvark-Vanaheim

1 .... 2.00

Gojin
Antarctic, 1995

1-8 .... 3.00

Gold Digger
Antarctic, 1992

1 .... 35.00
2 .... 20.00
3 .... 15.00
4 .... 13.00
5 .... 3.00
6 .... 3.00
7-22 .... 3.00
23 .... 0.00
24-70 .... 3.00

Gold Digger
Antarctic, 1993

1 .... 5.00
2-50 .... 4.00
50/CS 6.00
Ann 1-5 .... 4.00
Special 1 .... 3.00

Gold Digger
Antarctic, 1999

1 .... 4.00
2-38 .... 3.00
39-44 .... 4.00
45-110 .... 3.00
Ann 4 .... 5.00

Gold Digger Annual 2005
Antarctic, 2005

1 .... 5.00

Gold Digger: Beta
Antarctic, 1998

1 .... 3.00

Gold Digger: Edge Guard
Radio, 2000

1-5 .... 3.00

Gold Digger Halloween Special
Antarctic, 2005

1 .... 3.00

Gold Digger Mangazine
Antarctic, 1994

1-1/2nd 3.00

Gold Digger Perfect Memory
Antarctic, 1996

1 .... 5.00
2-4 .... 7.00

Gold Digger Swimsuit End of Summer Special
Antarctic, 2003

1 .... 5.00

Gold Digger: Swimsuit End of Summer Special 2005

Antarctic, 2005

0 .... 5.00

Gold Digger Swimsuit Special

Antarctic, 2000

1-4 .... 5.00

Golden Age

DC, 1993

1-4 .... 6.00

Golden Age Of Triple-X

Revisionary, 1997

1 .... 4.00

Golden Age of Triple-X: John Holmes Special "Johnny Does Paris"

Re-Visionary

1 .... 3.00

Golden Age Secret Files

DC, 2001

1 .... 5.00

Golden Age Sheena

AC

1 .... 10.00

Golden Arrow

Fawcett, 1942

1 .... 900.00
2 .... 365.00
3-5 .... 250.00
6 .... 235.00

Golden Comics Digest

Gold Key, 1969

1-30 .... 20.00
31-48 .... 15.00

Golden Dragon

Synchronicity, 1987

1 .... 2.00

Golden Features (Jerry Iger's...)

Blackthorne, 1986

1-6 .... 2.00

Golden Lad

Fact and Fiction, 1945

1 .... 650.00
2 .... 375.00
3-4 .... 285.00
5 .... 250.00

Golden Plates

AAA Pop, 2004

1-3 .... 8.00

Golden Warrior

Industrial Design, 1997

1 .... 3.00

Golden Warrior Iczer One

Antarctic, 1994

1-5 .... 3.00

Golden West Rodeo Treasury

Dell, 1957

1 .... 65.00

Goldfish

Image

1 .... 17.00
1/Deluxe 20.00

Gold Key Spotlight

Gold Key, 1976

1 .... 6.00
2-11 .... 4.00

Gold Medal Comics

Cambridge, 1945

1 .... 175.00

Goldyn 3-D

Blackthorne

1 .... 2.00

Golgothika

Caliber, 1996

1-4 .... 3.00

Golgo 13

Lead

1 .... 1.00
2 .... 2.00

Golgo 13

Viz

1-3 .... 5.00

Go-Man!

Caliber, 1989

1-4 .... 3.00

Gomer Pyle

Gold Key, 1966

1 .... 40.00
2-3 .... 25.00

Gon

DC, 1996

1-4 .... 6.00
5 .... 7.00

Gonad the Barbarian

Eternity

1 .... 2.00

Gon Color Spectacular

DC

1 .... 6.00

Gon on Safari

DC, 2000

1 .... 8.00

Gon Underground

DC

1 .... 8.00

Giant-Size X-Men

Gideon Hawk

Gifts of the Night

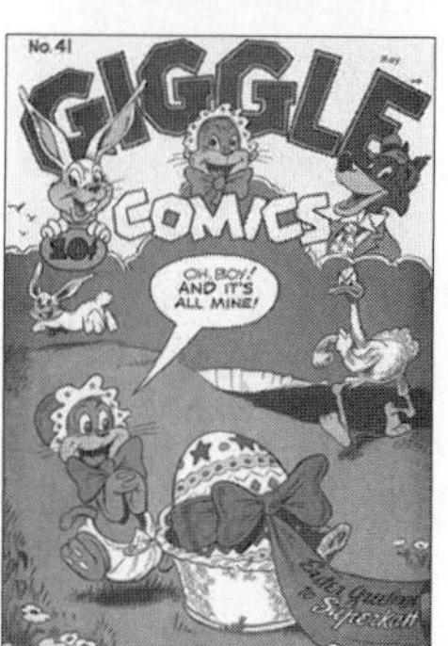

Giggle Comics

All comics prices listed are for NEAR MINT condition.

Gigolo

G.I. Government Issued

G-I in Battle

G.I. Jackrabbits

Good-Bye, Chunky Rice
Top Shelf, 1999

1 ....15.00

Good Girl Art Quarterly
AC, 1990

1-18 ....4.00
19 ....7.00

Good Girls
Fantagraphics, 1987

1-6 ....2.00

Good Guys
Defiant, 1993

1-12 ....3.00

Goody Good Comics
Fantagraphics, 2000

1 ....3.00

Goofy
Dell, 1962

-211 ....40.00

Goofy Adventures
Disney, 1990

1 ....3.00
2-17 ....2.00

Goofy Comics
Nedor, 1943

1 ....125.00
2 ....60.00
3-5 ....45.00
6-10 ....38.00
11-19 ....32.00
20-29 ....45.00
30-35 ....38.00
36-48 ....24.00

Goon
Avatar, 1999

1 ....15.00
2-3 ....10.00

Goon
Albatross Exploding, 2002

1-1/Variant 10.00
2-4 ....5.00

Goon
Dark Horse, 2003

1-30 ....3.00

Goon Noir
Dark Horse, 2006

1-2 ....3.00

Goon Patrol
Pinnacle

1 ....2.00

Gordon Yamamoto and the King of the Geeks
Humble, 1997

1 ....3.00

Gore Shriek
Fantaco, 1986

1-4 ....3.00
5-6 ....4.00
Ann 1 ....5.00

Gore Shriek
Fantaco

1-3 ....3.00

Gore Shriek Delectus
Fantaco

1 ....9.00

Gorgana's Ghoul Gallery
AC

1-2 ....3.00

Gorgo
Charlton, 1961

1 ....200.00
2-3 ....100.00
4 ....75.00
5 ....50.00
6-10 ....40.00
11-16 ....30.00
17-23 ....20.00

Gorgon
Venus, 1996

1-5 ....3.00

Gorilla Gunslinger
Mojo

0 ....1.00

Gotcha!
Rip Off, 1991

1 ....3.00

G.O.T.H.
Verotik, 1996

1-3 ....3.00

Gotham Central
DC, 2003

1-40 ....3.00

Gotham Girls
DC, 2002

1-5 ....2.00

Gotham Nights
DC, 1992

1-4 ....2.00

Gotham Nights II
DC, 1995

1-4 ....2.00

Gothic
5th Panel, 1997

1-2 ....3.00

Gothic Moon
Anarchy Bridgeworks

1 ....6.00

Gothic Nights
Rebel
1-2 .... 2.00

Gothic Red
Boneyard, 1997
1-3 .... 3.00

Gothic Scrolls: Drayven
Davdez, 1997
1-3 .... 3.00
Ashcan 1 .... 2.00

Grackle
Acclaim, 1997
1-4 .... 3.00

Graffiti Kitchen
Tundra
1 .... 3.00

Grafik Muzik
Caliber, 1990
1 .... 15.00
2 .... 10.00
3-4 .... 6.00

Grammar Patrol
Castel
1 .... 2.00

Grand Prix
Charlton, 1967
16 .... 14.00
17-20 .... 8.00
21-31 .... 5.00

Grand Slam Comics
Double A Comics, 1943
51-53 .... 45.00

Graphic
Fantaco
1 .... 4.00

Graphic Heroes in House of Cards
Graphic Staffing
1 .... 1.00

Graphic Story Monthly
Fantagraphics
1-7 .... 4.00

Graphique Musique
Slave Labor, 1989
1-3 .... 8.00

Grasa Del Sol
Estatua, 1998
1 .... 3.00

Grateful Dead Comix
Kitchen Sink, 1992
1 .... 6.00
2-7 .... 5.00

Grateful Dead Comix
Kitchen Sink, 1994
1-2 .... 4.00

Gravediggers
Acclaim, 1996
1-4 .... 3.00

Gravedigger Tales
Avalon
1 .... 3.00

Grave Grrrls: Destroyers of the Dead
Moonstone, 2005
1 .... 4.00

Gravestone
Malibu, 1993
1-7 .... 2.00

Gravestown
Ariel, 1997
1 .... 3.00

Grave Tales
Hamilton, 1991
1-3 .... 4.00

Gravity
Marvel, 2005
1-5 .... 3.00

Gray Area
Image, 2004
1 .... 7.00
1/Incentive 8.00
1/SigSeries 20.00
1/Conv 15.00
2-3 .... 6.00

Grease Monkey
Kitchen Sink, 1995
1-2 .... 4.00

Grease Monkey
Image, 1998
1-2 .... 3.00

Great Action Comics
I.W.
8-9 .... 70.00

Great American Western
AC, 1988
1 .... 2.00
2-3 .... 3.00
4 .... 4.00
5 .... 5.00

Great Big Beef
ERR, 1996
97-99 .... 2.00

Great Comics
Great Comics, 1941
1 .... 500.00
2 .... 285.00
3 .... 660.00
☛Hitler story

Great Comics
Novack, 1945
1 .... 165.00

G.I. Jane

G.I. Joe and the Transformers

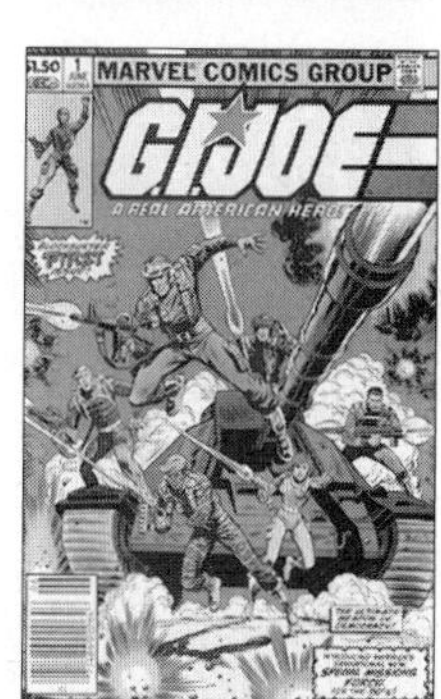

G.I. Joe A Real American Hero

G.I. Joe in 3-D

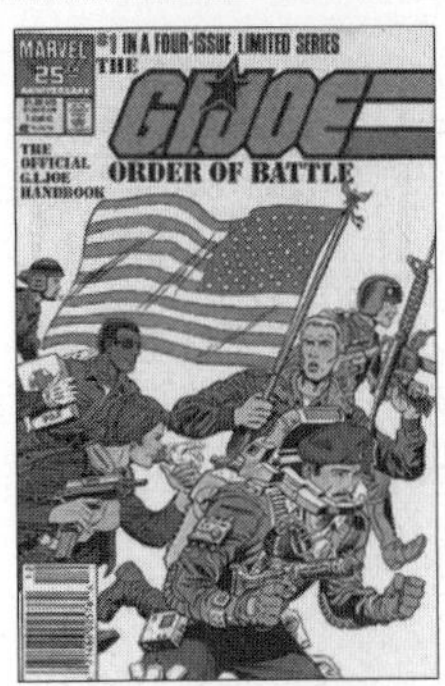

G.I. Joe Order of Battle

G.I. Joe Special Missions

Gilgamesh II

Gimme

1/A....................................200.00
1/B....................................140.00
1/C....................................85.00

Great Detective

Avalon

1-7....................................3.00

Greater Mercury Comics Action

Greater Mercury, 1990

5-9....................................2.00

Greatest American Comic Book

Ocean, 1992

1....................................3.00

Greatest Diggs of All Time!

Rip Off, 1991

1....................................2.00

Greatest Stars of the NBA: Allen Iverson

Tokyopop, 2005

1....................................8.00

Greatest Stars of the NBA: Future Greats

Tokyopop, 2005

1....................................8.00

Great Exploits

Decker, 1957

1....................................25.00

Great Galaxies

Zub

0-5....................................3.00
6/Ashcan....................................1.00

Great Gazoo

Charlton, 1973

1....................................20.00
2....................................12.00
3-20....................................10.00

Great Morons in History

Revolutionary, 1993

1....................................3.00

Great Society Comic Book

Parallax

1....................................16.00
2....................................12.00

Greeenlock

Aircel

1....................................3.00

Green Arrow

DC, 1983

1-2....................................3.00
3-4....................................2.00

Green Arrow

DC, 1988

0....................................3.00
1....................................4.00
2-20....................................2.00
21....................................3.00
22-49....................................2.00
50....................................3.00
51-74....................................2.00
75....................................3.00
76-95....................................2.00
96-99....................................3.00
100....................................7.00
101....................................18.00
☛Death of O. Queen
102-124....................................2.00
125....................................4.00
126-136....................................3.00
137....................................4.00
1000000....................................3.00
Ann 1....................................4.00
Ann 2-5....................................3.00
Ann 6-7....................................4.00

Green Arrow (2nd Series)

DC, 1998

1-2....................................6.00
3-42....................................3.00
43....................................7.00
☛Speedy HIV
44....................................4.00
45-49....................................3.00
50....................................4.00
51-70....................................3.00

Green Arrow: Archer's Quest

DC, 2003

1....................................20.00
1/2nd....................................15.00

Green Arrow by Jack Kirby

DC, 2001

nn....................................6.00

Green Arrow: The Longbow Hunters

DC, 1987

1....................................4.00
1/2nd-3....................................3.00

Green Arrow: The Wonder Year

DC, 1993

1-4....................................2.00

Green Candles

DC, 1995

1-3....................................6.00

Greener Pastures

Kronos, 1994

1-4....................................3.00
4.5....................................2.00
5-7....................................3.00

Green Giant Comics
Pelican, 1940
1 .... 6,000.00

Green Goblin
Marvel, 1995
1 .... 3.00
2-13 .... 2.00

Green-Grey Sponge-Suit Sushi Turtles
Mirage
1 .... 4.00

Greenhaven
Aircel
1-3 .... 2.00

Green Hornet
Gold Key, 1967
1 .... 120.00
2-3 .... 80.00

Green Hornet
Now, 1989
1-1/2nd 4.00
2 .... 3.00
3-14 .... 2.00

Green Hornet
Now, 1991
1-11 .... 2.00
12 .... 3.00
13-21 .... 2.00
22-23 .... 3.00
24-26 .... 2.00
27 .... 3.00
28-37 .... 2.00
38 .... 3.00
39 .... 2.00
40-Ann 1994 .... 3.00

Green Hornet Anniversary Special
Now, 1992
1 .... 3.00
2-3 .... 2.00

Green Hornet Comics
Harvey, 1940
1 .... 4,500.00
2 .... 1,500.00
3 .... 1,250.00
4-6 .... 1,000.00
7 .... 900.00
8 .... 750.00
9 .... 900.00
10 .... 650.00
11-19 .... 600.00
20 .... 700.00
21-31 .... 400.00
32-38 .... 300.00
39 .... 350.00
40-47 .... 250.00

Green Hornet: Dark Tomorrow
Now, 1993
1-3 .... 3.00

Green Hornet: Solitary Sentinel
Now, 1992
1-3 .... 3.00

Green Lama
Spark, 1944
1 .... 750.00
2 .... 475.00
3 .... 340.00
4-5 .... 240.00
6-8 .... 180.00

Green Lantern
DC, 1941
1 .... 37,500.00
☛Green Lantern origin
2 .... 7,500.00
3 .... 5,500.00
4 .... 4,000.00
5 .... 2,750.00
6 .... 2,250.00
7-10 .... 2,000.00
11-20 .... 1,500.00
21-30 .... 1,250.00
31-34 .... 1,000.00
35-38 .... 1,250.00

Green Lantern
DC, 1960
1 .... 4,500.00
☛1st Guardians
2 .... 1,000.00
3 .... 600.00
4-5 .... 450.00
6 .... 400.00
7-10 .... 300.00
11-12 .... 200.00
13 .... 250.00
14-16 .... 175.00
17-20 .... 150.00
21-27 .... 125.00
28-30 .... 100.00
31-39 .... 75.00
40 .... 350.00
☛GA Lantern app.
41-49 .... 75.00
50-51 .... 60.00
52 .... 80.00
53-58 .... 55.00
59 .... 125.00
☛1st Guy Gardner
60-75 .... 50.00
76 .... 375.00
☛Green Arrow starts
77-78 .... 75.00
79-84 .... 60.00
85 .... 50.00
86 .... 60.00

G.I. Mutants

Ginger

Gin-Ryu

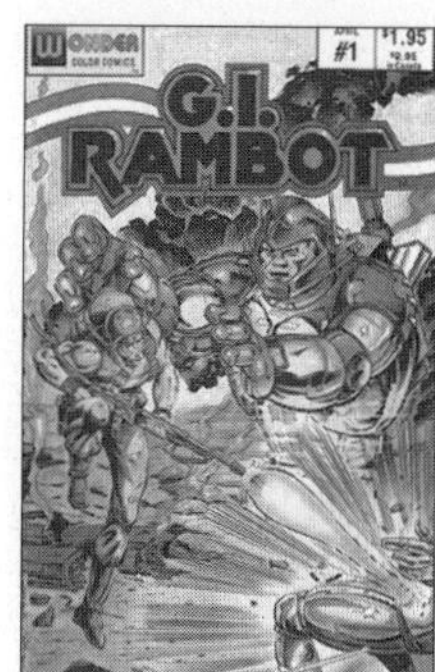

G.I. R.A.M.B.O.T.

Girl Fight Comics

Girl Genius

Girls of Ninja High School

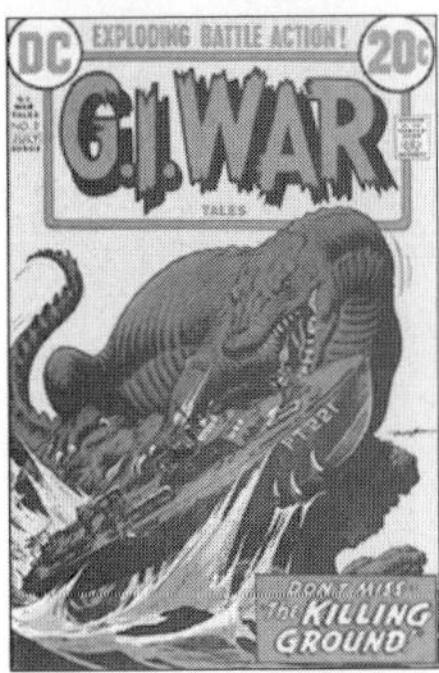

G.I. War Tales

☛Drug issue
87 ....50.00
88 ....30.00
89 ....45.00
90-92 ....10.00
93-99 ....9.00
100 ....10.00
101 ....9.00
102-111 ....4.00
112 ....8.00
113-115 ....3.00
116 ....8.00
116/Whitman 16.00
117 ....3.00
117/Whitman 6.00
118 ....3.00
118/Whitman 6.00
119 ....3.00
119/Whitman 5.00
120 ....3.00
120/Whitman 5.00
121 ....3.00
121/Whitman 5.00
122 ....4.00
123 ....6.00
124-130 ....3.00
131-135 ....2.00
136-139 ....3.00
140 ....2.00
141 ....5.00
☛1st Omega Men
142-144 ....3.00
145-149 ....2.00
150 ....5.00
151-173 ....2.00
174 ....3.00
175-178 ....2.00
179 ....3.00
180-193 ....2.00
194 ....3.00
195 ....4.00
196-205 ....2.00
Special 1-2 ....3.00

Green Lantern
DC, 1990

0 ....4.00
1 ....7.00
2 ....3.00
3-26 ....2.00
27-45 ....1.00
46 ....4.00
47 ....2.00
48-50 ....5.00
51 ....3.00
52-80 ....2.00
81 ....3.00
81/Variant 4.00
82-99 ....2.00
100/A 5.00
100/B 3.00
101-149 ....2.00
150 ....4.00
151-174 ....2.00
175 ....4.00
176 ....8.00
177 ....4.00
178-181 ....2.00
1000000 ....3.00
Ann 1 ....4.00
Ann 2-3 ....3.00
Ann 4 ....4.00
Ann 5 ....3.00
Ann 6 ....4.00
Ann 7-8 ....3.00
Ann 9 ....4.00
Ann 1963 ....6.00
GS 1-2 ....5.00
GS 3 ....6.00
3D 1 ....5.00
3D 1/Ltd. 17.00

Green Lantern
DC, 2005

1 ....6.00
2 ....4.00
3-24 ....3.00
25 ....5.00
26-240 ....3.00

Green Lantern/Adam Strange
DC, 2000

1 ....3.00

Green Lantern/Atom
DC, 2000

1 ....3.00

Green Lantern: Brightest Day, Blackest Night
DC, 2002

1 ....6.00

Green Lantern: Circle of Fire
DC, 2000

1-2 ....5.00

Green Lantern Corps
DC, 1985

206-224 ....2.00
Ann 1 ....3.00
Ann 2-3 ....2.00

Green Lantern Corps Quarterly
DC, 1992

1-8 ....3.00

Green Lantern Corps: Recharge
DC, 2005

1 ....4.00
2-5 ....3.00

Green Lantern Corps
DC, 2006

1-40 ....3.00

Green Lantern: Dragon Lord
DC, 2001
1-3 .... 5.00

Green Lantern: Emerald Allies
DC, 2000
1 .... 15.00

Green Lantern: Emerald Dawn
DC, 1989
1-6 .... 2.00

Green Lantern: Emerald Dawn II
DC, 1991
1 .... 2.00
2-6 .... 1.00

Green Lantern: Emerald Twilight New Dawn
DC, 2003
1 .... 20.00

Green Lantern: Evil's Might
DC, 2002
1-3 .... 6.00

Green Lantern/Firestorm
DC, 2000
1 .... 3.00

Green Lantern/Flash: Faster Friends
DC
1 .... 5.00

Green Lantern Gallery
DC, 1996
1 .... 4.00

Green Lantern: Ganthet's Tale
DC, 1992
1 .... 6.00

Green Lantern/Green Arrow
DC, 1983
1-7 .... 4.00

Green Lantern/Green Lantern
DC, 2000
1 .... 3.00

Green Lantern-Legacy: The Last Will & Testament of Hal Jordan
DC, 2002
1 .... 25.00

Green Lantern: Mosaic
DC, 1992
1-18 .... 1.00

Green Lantern: 1001 Emerald Nights
DC, 2001
1 .... 7.00

Green Lantern: Our Worlds At War
DC, 2001
1 .... 3.00

Green Lantern Plus
DC, 1996
1 .... 3.00

Green Lantern/Power Girl
DC, 2000
1 .... 3.00

Green Lantern: Rebirth
DC, 2004
1 .... 10.00
1/2nd 12.00
1/3rd 5.00
2 .... 6.00
2/2nd 3.00
3 .... 4.00
4-6 .... 3.00

Green Lantern Secret Files
DC, 1998
1-3 .... 5.00

Green Lantern/Sentinel: Heart of Darkness
DC, 1998
1-3 .... 2.00

Green Lantern/Silver Surfer: Unholy Alliances
DC, 1995
1 .... 5.00

Green Lantern Sinestro Corps Special
DC, 2007
1 .... 5.00

Green Lantern/Superman: Legend of the Green Flame
DC, 2000
1 .... 6.00

Green Lantern: The New Corps
DC, 1999
1 .... 5.00
2 .... 5.00

Green Lantern vs. Aliens
DC, 2000
1-4 .... 3.00

Gizmo and the Fugitoid

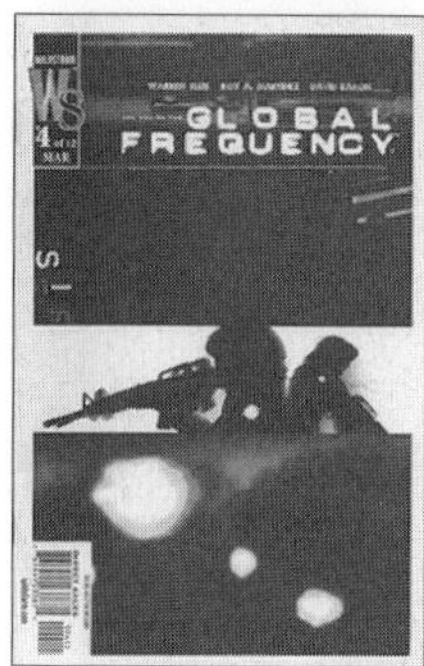

Global Frequency

GloomCookie

Glorianna

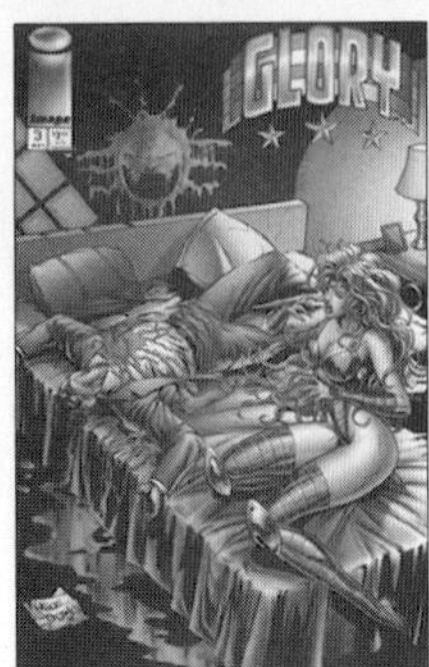
Glory

Goblin Lord

Goddess

Godhead

Green Lantern: Willworld
DC, 2001

1 ....25.00
2 ....18.00

Greenleaf in Exile
Cat's Paw

1-6 ....3.00

Greenlock
Aircel, 1991

1 ....3.00

Green Mask
Fox, 1940

1 ....2,850.00
2 ....1,200.00
3 ....650.00
4-5 ....475.00
6 ....345.00
7-10 ....250.00
11 ....185.00
12-17 ....140.00

Green Planet
Charlton, 1962

1 ....26.00

Green Skull
Known Associates

1 ....3.00

Gregory
DC, 2004

1-1/2nd 8.00
2 ....5.00
3 ....8.00
3/Gold 9.00
4 ....5.00

Gremlin Trouble
Anti-Ballistic, 1960

1 ....4.00
2-29 ....3.00
29-30 ....5.00
Special 1-2 ....3.00

Grendel
Comico, 1983

1 ....45.00
2 ....35.00
3 ....26.00

Grendel
Comico, 1986

1 ....5.00
1/2nd 3.00
2-5 ....4.00
6-15 ....3.00
16 ....4.00
17-32 ....3.00
33 ....4.00
34-39 ....3.00
40 ....4.00

Grendel: Black, White, & Red
Dark Horse, 1998

1-4 ....4.00

Grendel Classics
Dark Horse, 1995

1-2 ....4.00

Grendel Cycle
Dark Horse, 1995

1 ....6.00

Grendel: Devil By the Deed
Comico, 1993

1 ....4.00
1/Ltd 8.00
1/2nd 4.00

Grendel: Devil Child
Dark Horse, 1999

1-2 ....3.00

Grendel: Devil Quest
Dark Horse, 1995

1 ....5.00

Grendel: Devil's Legacy
Comico, 2000

1-12 ....3.00

Grendel: Devil's Reign
Dark Horse, 2004

1-7 ....4.00

Grendel: Devil's Vagary
Comico

1 ....8.00

Grendel: God & the Devil
Dark Horse, 2003

1-9 ....4.00
10 ....5.00

Grendel: Past Prime
Dark Horse, 2000

1 ....15.00

Grendel: Red, White & Black
Dark Horse, 2002

1-4 ....5.00

Grendel Tales: Devils and Deaths
Dark Horse, 1994

1-2 ....3.00

Grendel Tales: Devil's Choices
Dark Horse, 1995

1-4 ....3.00

Grendel Tales: Devil's Hammer
Dark Horse, 1994

1-3 ....3.00

Grendel Tales: Four Devils, One Hell
Dark Horse, 1993
1-6 .... 3.00

Grendel Tales: Homecoming
Dark Horse, 1994
1-3 .... 3.00

Grendel Tales: The Devil in Our Midst
Dark Horse, 1994
1-5 .... 3.00

Grendel Tales: The Devil May Care
Dark Horse, 1995
1-6 .... 3.00

Grendel Tales: The Devil's Apprentice
Dark Horse, 1997
1-3 .... 3.00

Grendel: The Devil Inside
Comico, 2001
1-3 .... 3.00

Grendel: War Child
Dark Horse, 1992
1 .... 4.00
2-9 .... 3.00
10 .... 4.00

Grenuord
Fantagraphics, 2005
1 .... 6.00

Grey
Viz, 1989
1-5 .... 4.00
6-9 .... 3.00

Grey Legacy
Fragile Elite
1 .... 3.00

Greylore
Sirius Comics, 1985
1-5 .... 2.00

Greymatter
Alaffinity, 1993
1-11 .... 3.00

Greyshirt: Indigo Sunset
DC, 2001
1-6 .... 4.00

Griffin (Slave Labor)
Slave Labor, 1988
1-3 .... 2.00

Griffin
DC, 1991
1-6 .... 5.00

Griffin
Slave Labor, 1997
1 .... 3.00

Griffith Observatory
Fantagraphics
1 .... 5.00

Grifter and the Mask
Dark Horse, 1996
1-2 .... 3.00

Grifter/Badrock
Image, 1995
1/A-2/B 3.00

Grifter: One Shot
Image, 1995
1 .... 5.00

Grifter/Shi
Image, 1996
1-2 .... 3.00

Grifter
Image, 1995
1 .... 3.00
1/Direct 4.00
2-10 .... 2.00

Grifter
Image, 1996
1-14 .... 3.00

Grim Ghost
Atlas-Seaboard, 1975
1 .... 10.00
2-3 .... 5.00

Grimjack
First, 1984
1 .... 3.00
2-25 .... 2.00
26 .... 3.00
27-74 .... 2.00
75 .... 4.00
76-81 .... 2.00

Grimjack Casefiles
First, 1990
1-5 .... 2.00

Grimjack: Killer Instinct
Idea & Design Works, 2004
1-6 .... 4.00

Grimlock
Asylum, 1996
1-3 .... 3.00

Grimmax
Defiant, 1994
0 .... 1.00

Grimm's Ghost Stories
Gold Key, 1972
1 .... 14.00
2-5 .... 8.00
6-10 .... 6.00
11-30 .... 4.00

Gods for Hire

Godwheel

Godzilla

Godzilla Color Special

Godzilla Versus Hero Zero

Gojin

Golden Age Secret Files

Golden Arrow

31-42 ....3.00
43-44 ....4.00
45-54 ....3.00
55-60 ....5.00

Grimoire

Speakeasy Comics, 2005

1-5 ....3.00

Gringo

Caliber

1 ....2.00

Grips

Silverwolf, 1986

1 ....3.00
1/Ltd. 10.00
2-4 ....3.00

Grips

Greater Mercury, 1990

1-9 ....2.00
10-12 ....3.00

Grips Adventures

Greater Mercury, 1989

1-8 ....3.00

Grip: The Strange World of Men

DC, 2002

1-5 ....3.00

Grit Bath

Fantagraphics, 1993

1-3 ....3.00

Groo

Image, 1994

1 ....4.00
2-3 ....3.00
4-12 ....2.00

Groo

Dark Horse, 1998

1-4 ....3.00

Groo and Rufferto (Sergio Aragonès')

Dark Horse, 1998

1-4 ....3.00

Groo: Death & Taxes (Sergio Aragonès'...)

Dark Horse, 2001

1-4 ....3.00

Groo: Mightier than the Sword (Sergio Aragonès')

Dark Horse, 2000

1-4 ....3.00

Groo Special

Eclipse, 1984

1 ....3.00

Groo The Wanderer (Sergio Aragonès')

Pacific, 1982

1 ....7.00
2 ....5.00
3-4 ....4.00
5-8 ....3.00

Groo the Wanderer

Marvel, 1985

1 ....5.00
2-3 ....4.00
4-30 ....3.00
31-49 ....2.00
50 ....3.00
51-99 ....2.00
100 ....3.00
101-120 ....2.00

Grootlore

Fantagraphics

1-2 ....2.00

Grootlore

Fantagraphics, 1991

1-3 ....2.00

Groovy

Marvel, 1968

1 ....25.00
2-3 ....16.00

Gross Point

DC, 1997

1-14 ....3.00

Grounded

Image, 2005

1 ....5.00
1/Variant 4.00
☛2nd print
2-5 ....3.00
16 ....4.00

Ground Pound! Comix

Blackthorne, 1987

1 ....2.00

Ground Zero

Eternity, 1991

1-2 ....3.00

Group LaRue (Mike Baron's...)

Innovation, 1989

1-4 ....2.00

Growing Up Enchanted

Too Hip Gotta Go, 2002

1-3 ....3.00

Grrl Scouts (Jim Mahfood's...)

Oni, 1999

1-4 ....3.00

Grrl Scouts: Work Sucks
Image, 2003
1-4 .... 3.00

Grrrl Squad
Amazing Aaron, 1999
1 .... 3.00

Grumpy Old Monsters
Idea & Design Works, 2003
1-3 .... 4.00

Grun
Harrier, 1987
1-4 .... 2.00

Grunts
Mirage, 1987
1 .... 2.00

Guano Comix
Print Mint
4 .... 3.00

Guardian
Spectrum, 1984
1-2 .... 1.00

Guardian Angel
Image, 2002
1-2 .... 3.00

Guardian Knights: Demon's Knight
Limelight
1-2 .... 3.00

Guardians
Marvel, 2004
1-5 .... 3.00

Guardians of Metropolis
DC, 1994
1-4 .... 2.00

Guardians of the Galaxy
Marvel, 1990
1-24 .... 2.00
25-25/Variant 3.00
26-29 .... 2.00
30-35 .... 1.00
35/Variant 3.00
36-38 .... 1.00
39 .... 3.00
40-47 .... 1.00
48-50 .... 2.00
50/Variant 3.00
51-61 .... 2.00
62 .... 3.00
Ann 1 .... 4.00
Ann 2-4 .... 3.00

Guerrilla Groundhog
Eclipse, 1987
1-2 .... 2.00

Guerrilla War
Dell, 1965
12-14 .... 10.00

Guff!
Dark Horse, 1998
1 .... 2.00

Gullivera
NBM, 1996
1 .... 14.00

Gumbo
Deadline Studios, 1994
1-2 .... 3.00

Gumby 3-D
Blackthorne
1-7 .... 3.00

Gumby's Summer Fun Special
Comico, 1987
1 .... 3.00

Gumby's Winter Fun Special
Comico
1 .... 3.00

Gumps
Bridgeport Herald, 1947
1 .... 75.00
2 .... 48.00
3 .... 38.00
4-5 .... 32.00

Guncandy
Image, 2005
1-2 .... 6.00

Gundam Seed Astray R
Tokyopop, 2005
1-4 .... 10.00

Gundam: The Origin
Viz, 2002
1-2 .... 8.00

Gundam Wing: Blind Target
Viz, 2001
1-4 .... 3.00

Gundam Wing: Episode Zero
Viz, 2001
1-8 .... 3.00

Gunfighter
E.C., 1948
5 .... 340.00
6 .... 315.00
7-10 .... 235.00
11-14 .... 190.00

Gunfighters
Charlton, 1966
51-52 .... 6.00
53 .... 4.00
54-85 .... 3.00

Golden Lad

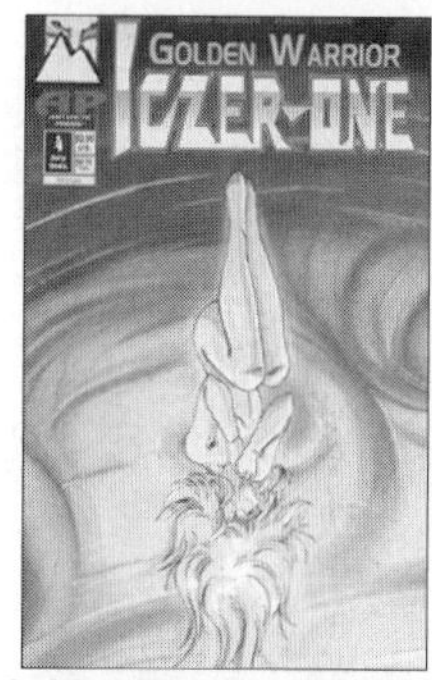

Golden Warrior Iczer One

Goldfish

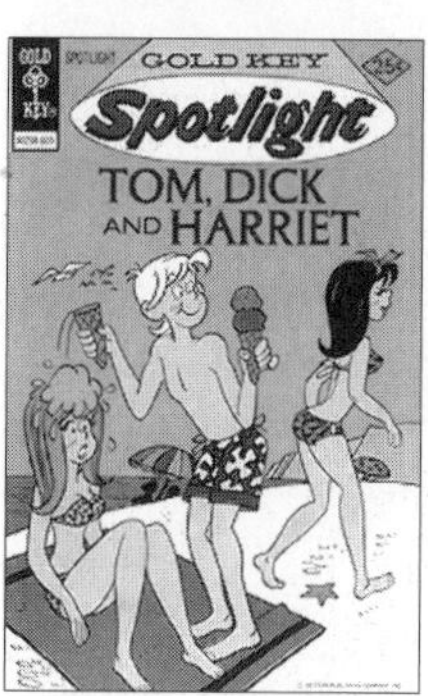

Gold Key Spotlight

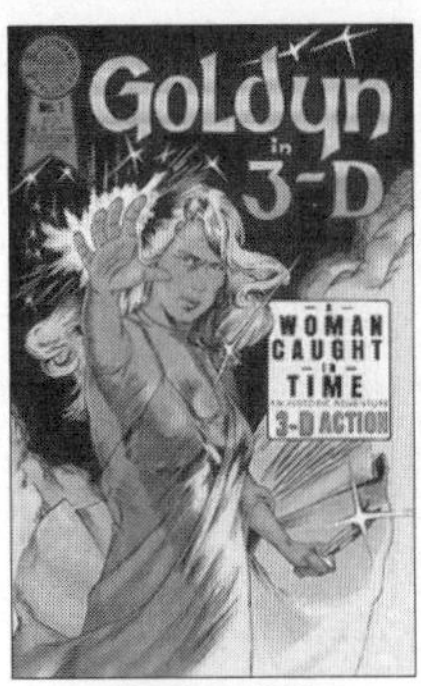

Goldyn 3-D

Golgothika

Gomer Pyle

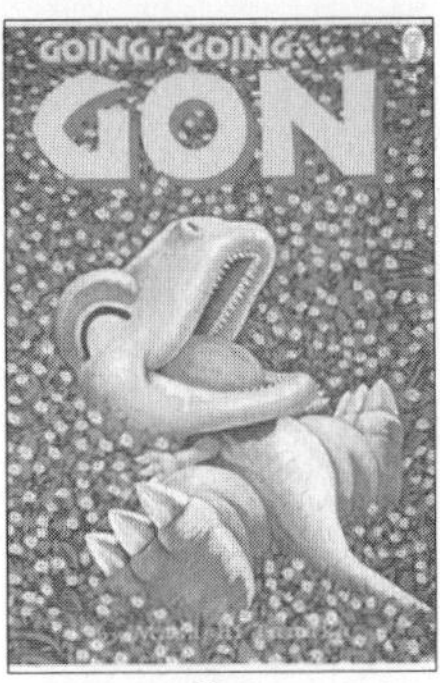

Gon

Gunfighters
Super
15 .... 8.00

Gun Fighters in Hell
Rebel
1-5 .... 2.00

Gunfire
DC, 1994
0-13 .... 2.00

Gun Fury
Aircel, 1989
1-10 .... 2.00

Gun Fury Returns
Aircel, 1990
1-4 .... 2.00

Gun Fu: Showgirls Are Forever
Image, 2006
1 .... 4.00

Gung Ho
Avalon
1 .... 3.00

Gunhawk
Atlas, 1950
12 .... 95.00
13 .... 70.00
14-18 .... 65.00

Gunhawks
Marvel, 1972
1 .... 50.00
2 .... 18.00
3-7 .... 8.00

Gunhed
Viz
1-3 .... 6.00

Gunner
Gun Dog, 1999
1 .... 3.00

Gunparade March
ADV Manga, 2004
1-3 .... 10.00

Gunpowder Girl & The Outlaw Squaw
Active Images, 2005
1 .... 13.00

Gun Runner
Marvel, 1993
1 .... 3.00
2-6 .... 2.00

Guns Against Gangsters
Novelty, 1948
1 .... 365.00
2 .... 225.00
3-7 .... 180.00

Gunslinger Girl
ADV Manga, 2004
1-3 .... 10.00

Gunslingers
Marvel, 2000
1 .... 3.00

Gunsmith Cats
Dark Horse, 1995
1-10 .... 3.00

Gunsmith Cats: Bad Trip
Dark Horse, 1998
1-6 .... 3.00

Gunsmith Cats: Bean Bandit
Dark Horse, 1999
1-9 .... 3.00

Gunsmith Cats: Goldie vs. Misty
Dark Horse, 1997
1-7 .... 3.00

Gunsmith Cats: Kidnapped
Dark Horse, 1999
1-10 .... 3.00

Gunsmith Cats: Mister V
Dark Horse, 2000
1-11 .... 4.00

Gunsmith Cats: Shades of Gray
Dark Horse, 1997
1-5 .... 3.00

Gunsmith Cats Special
Dark Horse, 2001
1 .... 3.00

Gunsmith Cats: The Return of Gray
Dark Horse, 1996
1-7 .... 3.00

Gunsmoke Western
Marvel, 1955
32 .... 90.00
33-35 .... 70.00
36-40 .... 60.00
41-50 .... 52.00
51-60 .... 44.00
61-69 .... 36.00
70 .... 30.00
71 .... 26.00
72 .... 34.00
73-77 .... 26.00

Gunsmoke
Dell, 1957
6-10 .... 35.00
11-20 .... 25.00
21-27 .... 22.00

Gunsmoke
Gold Key, 1969
1 .... 30.00
2-6 .... 20.00

Guns of Shar-Pei
Caliber
1-3 .... 3.00

Guns of the Dragon
DC, 1998
1-4 .... 3.00

Gun That Won the West
Winchester
1 .... 24.00

Gun Theory
Marvel, 2003
1-2 .... 3.00

Gunwitch: Outskirts of Doom
Oni, 2001
1 .... 3.00

Gustav P.I.
NBM
1 .... 10.00

Gutwallow
Numbskull, 1998
1-12 .... 3.00

Gutwallow
Numbskull, 2000
1-3 .... 3.00

Guy Gardner
DC, 1992
1-5 .... 2.00
6-14 .... 1.00
15-16 .... 2.00

Guy Gardner: Collateral Damage
DC, 2007
1-2 .... 6.00

Guy Gardner Reborn
DC, 1992
1-3 .... 5.00

Guy Gardner: Warrior
DC, 1994
0-24 .... 2.00
25 .... 3.00
26-29 .... 2.00
29/Variant 3.00
30-44 .... 2.00
Ann 1 .... 4.00
Ann 2 .... 3.00

Guy Pumpkinhead
Saint Gray
1 .... 3.00

Guzzi Lemans
Antarctic, 1996
1-2 .... 3.00

Gyre
Abaculus, 1997
1 .... 4.00
2-3 .... 3.00
Ashcan 1 .... 1.00
Special 1 .... 5.00

Gyre: Traditions & Interruptions
Abaculus
1 .... 1.00

Gyro Comics
Rip Off, 1988
1-3 .... 2.00

Gyro Gearloose
Dell, 1962
-207 .... 50.00

Hacker Files
DC, 1992
1-12 .... 2.00

Hackmasters of EverKnight
Kenzer and Company, 2000
1 .... 4.00
2-10 .... 3.00

Hack Slash: Land of Lost Toys
Devil's Due, 2005
1-3/Variant 3.00

Hack/Slash: Slice Hard
Devil's Due, 2006
1-1/Variant 5.00

Hack/Slash: Trailers
Devil's Due, 2006
1-1/2nd variant 3.00

Hägar the Horrible
Avalon
0 .... 2.00

Ha Ha Comics
ACG, 1943
1 .... 150.00
2 .... 85.00
3 .... 65.00
4-5 .... 60.00
6-10 .... 45.00
11-20 .... 35.00
21-30 .... 28.00
31-40 .... 24.00
41-50 .... 20.00
51-70 .... 18.00
71-90 .... 16.00
91-98 .... 13.00
99 .... 55.00

Gon Color Spectacular

Gon on Safari

Good Girl Art Quarterly

Goody Good Comics

Goofy Adventures

Goofy Comics

Goon Patrol

Gordon Yamamoto and the King of the Geeks

Hairbat
Screaming Rice

1-4 .... 3.00

Hairbat
Slave Labor, 1995

1 .... 3.00

Hair Bear Bunch
Gold Key, 1972

1 .... 10.00
2 .... 7.00
3-5 .... 6.00
6-9 .... 4.00

Hairbutt the Hippo
Rat Race, 1992

1-3 .... 3.00

Hairbutt the Hippo Crime Files
Rat Race, 1995

1-6 .... 4.00

Hairbutt the Hippo: Private Eye
Ratrace, 1997

1-3 .... 3.00

Halifax Explosion
Halifax, 1997

1 .... 3.00

Hallelujah Trail
Dell, 1966

1 .... 30.00

Hall of Fame
J.C., 1983

1-3 .... 2.00

Hall of Heroes
Hall of Heroes, 1997

1-3 .... 3.00

Hall of Heroes Halloween Special
Hall of Heroes, 1997

1 .... 3.00

Hall of Heroes Presents
Hall of Heroes, 1993

1-3 .... 3.00

Hall of Heroes Presents
Hall of Heroes, 1996

0/A-5 .... 3.00

Hall of Horrors
Hall of Heroes, 1997

1 .... 3.00

Hallowed Knight
Shea, 1997

1-2 .... 3.00

Halloween
Chaos, 2000

1 .... 3.00

Halloween Horror
Eclipse, 1987

1 .... 2.00

Halloween Megazine
Marvel, 1996

1 .... 3.00

Halloween Terror
Eternity

1 .... 3.00

Halls of Horror
Fleetway-Quality

1 .... 4.00
2-26 .... 3.00

Halls of Horror (John Bolton's...)
Eclipse, 1985

1-3 .... 2.00

Halo, an Angel's Story
Sirius, 1996

1-4 .... 3.00

Halo Graphic Novel
Marvel, 2006

1 .... 25.00

Halo: Uprising
Marvel, 2007

1-2 .... 4.00

Hammer
Dark Horse, 1997

1-4 .... 3.00

Hammerlocke
DC, 1992

1-9 .... 2.00

Hammer of God
First, 1990

1-4 .... 2.00

Hammer of God: Butch
Dark Horse, 1994

1-3 .... 3.00

Hammer of God: Pentathlon
Dark Horse

1 .... 3.00

Hammer of God: Sword of Justice
First, 1991

1-2 .... 5.00

Hammer of the Gods
Insight, 2001

1-5 .... 3.00

Hammer of the Gods Color Saga
Insight, 2001

nn 5.00

Hammer of the Gods: Hammer Hits China
Image, 2003
1-3 .... 3.00

Hammer: The Outsider
Dark Horse, 1999
1-3 .... 3.00

Hammer: Uncle Alex
Dark Horse, 1998
1 .... 3.00

Hamster Vice
Blackthorne, 1986
1-9 .... 2.00
3D 1-2 .... 3.00

Hamster Vice
Eternity, 1989
1-2 .... 2.00

Hana-Kimi
Viz, 2004
1-8 .... 10.00

Hand of Fate (Ace)
Ace, 1951
8 .... 200.00
9-10 .... 140.00
11-15 .... 120.00
16-20 .... 100.00
21-23 .... 85.00
24 .... 115.00
25-25/A 85.00

Hand of Fate
Eclipse, 1988
1-3 .... 2.00

Hand Shadows
Doyan, 1986
1-2 .... 2.00

Hands Off!
Tokyopop, 2004
1-5 .... 10.00

Hands Off!
Ward Sutton
1 .... 3.00

Hands of the Dragon
Atlas-Seaboard, 1975
1 .... 6.00

Hangman Comics
M.L.J., 1942
2 .... 1,850.00
3 .... 1,300.00
4-8 .... 950.00

Hanna-Barbera All-Stars
Archie, 1995
1-4 .... 2.00

Hanna-Barbera Bandwagon
Gold Key, 1962
1 .... 70.00
2-3 .... 50.00

Hanna-Barbera Big Book
Harvey, 1993
1 .... 2.00
3 .... 3.00

Hanna-Barbera Giant Size
Harvey, 1992
1-3 .... 0.00
2 .... 2.00

Hanna-Barbera Parade
Charlton, 1971
1 .... 35.00
2 .... 18.00
3 .... 15.00
4 .... 13.00
5 .... 14.00
6-10 .... 12.00

Hanna-Barbera Presents
Archie, 1995
1-8 .... 2.00

Hanna-Barbera Presents All-New Comics
Harvey
1 .... 1.00

Hanna-Barbera Super TV Heroes
Gold Key, 1968
1 .... 58.00
☛Herculoids Birdman
2-3 .... 36.00
4-5 .... 30.00
6-7 .... 35.00

Hansi, the Girl Who Loved the Swastika
Spire, 1973
1 .... 28.00

Hap Hazard
Fandom House
1 .... 2.00

Hap Hazard Comics
Ace, 1944
1 .... 75.00
2-6 .... 50.00
7-24 .... 40.00

Happenstance Jack, III
-Ism, 1998
1 .... 3.00

Happiest Millionaire
Gold Key, 1968
1 .... 25.00

Gorgo

G.O.T.H.

Gotham Central

Gotham Nights

Gothic Nights

Gothic Red

Graffiti Kitchen

Grafik Muzik

Happy
Wonder Comics

1 .... 2.00

Happy Birthday Gnatrat!
Dimension

1 .... 2.00

Happy Birthday Martha Washington
Dark Horse, 1995

1 .... 3.00

Happy Comics
Standard, 1943

1 .... 125.00
2 .... 75.00
3-5 .... 45.00
6-10 .... 35.00
11-20 .... 28.00
21-31 .... 35.00
32 .... 90.00
33 .... 125.00
34-37 .... 35.00
38-40 .... 18.00

Happydale: Devils in the Desert
DC

1-2 .... 7.00

Happy Days
Gold Key, 1979

1 .... 20.00
2-6 .... 10.00

Happy Houlihans
E.C., 1947

1 .... 200.00
2 .... 165.00

Happy Rabbit
Standard, 1951

41-48 .... 40.00

Harbinger
Valiant, 1992

0 .... 6.00
0/Pink 65.00
0/2nd 3.00
1 .... 30.00
2-3 .... 8.00
4 .... 11.00
5 .... 10.00
6 .... 9.00
7 .... 7.00
8-10 .... 4.00
11 .... 2.00
12-28 .... 1.00
29 .... 2.00
30-34 .... 1.00
35 .... 2.00
36-38 .... 1.00
39 .... 3.00
40 .... 4.00
41 .... 5.00

Harbinger: Acts of God
Acclaim, 1998

1 .... 4.00

Harbinger Files
Valiant, 1994

1 .... 2.00
2 .... 4.00

Hardball
Aircel, 1991

1-4 .... 3.00

Hard Boiled
Dark Horse, 1990

1 .... 5.00
2-3 .... 6.00

Hardcase
Malibu, 1993

1 .... 3.00
1/Hologram 5.00
1/Ltd. 3.00
2-15 .... 2.00
16 .... 4.00
17-19 .... 2.00
20-26 .... 3.00

Hardcore Station
DC, 1998

1-6 .... 3.00

H.A.R.D. Corps
Valiant, 1992

1 .... 1.00
1/Gold 12.00
2-5 .... 1.00
6-17 .... 1.00
18 .... 2.00
19-25 .... 1.00
26-28 .... 2.00
29 .... 3.00
30 .... 5.00

Hardkorr
Aircel, 1991

1-4 .... 3.00

Hard Looks
Dark Horse, 1992

1-9 .... 3.00
10 .... 4.00

Hard Rock Comics
Revolutionary, 1992

1 .... 5.00
2 .... 4.00
3 .... 3.00
4 .... 4.00
5 .... 8.00
5/2nd 5.00
6-20 .... 3.00

Hard Time
DC, 2004

1-12 .... 3.00

Hard Time: Season Two
DC, 2006
1-7 .... 3.00

Hardware
DC, 1993
1 .... 2.00
1/CS-1/Platinum 3.00
2-15 .... 2.00
16 .... 3.00
16/Variant 4.00
17-24 .... 2.00
25 .... 3.00
26-28 .... 2.00
29-49 .... 3.00
50 .... 4.00

Hardwired
Bangtro, 1994
1 .... 2.00

Hardy Boys
Gold Key, 1970
1 .... 28.00
2-4 .... 18.00

Har*Har
Fantagraphics
1-2 .... 2.00

Hari Kari
Black Out
0-1 .... 3.00

Hari Kari: Live & Untamed
Blackout
0 .... 3.00
0/Variant 4.00
1 .... 3.00

Hari Kari Private Gallery
Blackout
0-1 .... 3.00

Hari Kari: Rebirth
Black Out
1 .... 3.00

Hari Kari Resurrection
Blackout
1 .... 3.00

Hari Kari: The Beginning
Black Out
1 .... 3.00

Hari Kari: The Diary of Kari Sun
Blackout
½ 3.00

Hari Kari: The Silence of Evil
Black Out
0 .... 3.00

Harlem Globetrotters
Gold Key, 1972
1 .... 13.00
2 .... 9.00
3-5 .... 7.00
6-12 .... 5.00

Harlem Heroes
Fleetway-Quality
1-6 .... 2.00

Harlequin
Caliber, 1993
1 .... 3.00

Harley & Ivy: Love on the Lam
DC, 2001
1 .... 6.00

Harley Quinn
DC, 2000
1 .... 4.00
2-10 .... 3.00
11 .... 2.00
12 .... 3.00
13-22 .... 2.00
23-38 .... 3.00

Harley Quinn: Our Worlds At War
DC, 2001
1 .... 3.00

Harley Rider
Hungness
1 .... 2.00

Harold Hedd
Last Gasp Eco-Funnies
1 .... 8.00
2 .... 4.00

Harold Hedd in "Hitler's Cocaine"
Kitchen Sink, 1984
1-2 .... 40.00

Harpy Pin-Up Special
Peregrine Entertainment, 1998
1 .... 3.00

Harpy Preview
Ground Zero, 1996
1 .... 3.00

Harpy: Prize of the Overlord
Ground Zero, 1996
1-6 .... 3.00

Harrier Preview
Harrier
1 .... 1.00

Harriers
Express
1-3 .... 3.00

Harrowers (Clive Barker's)
Marvel, 1993
1-6 .... 3.00

Grand Prix

Graphique Musique

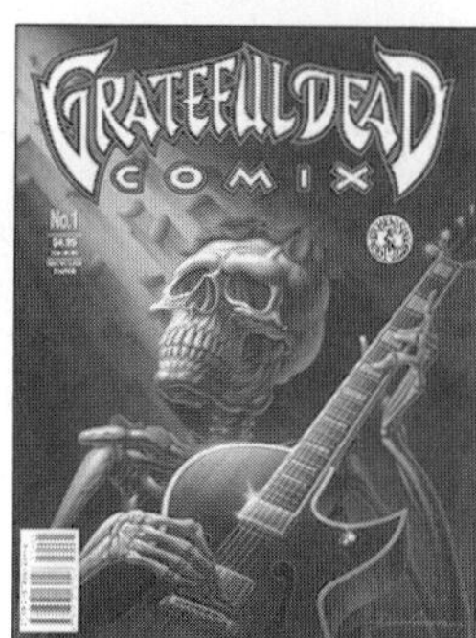

Grateful Dead Comix

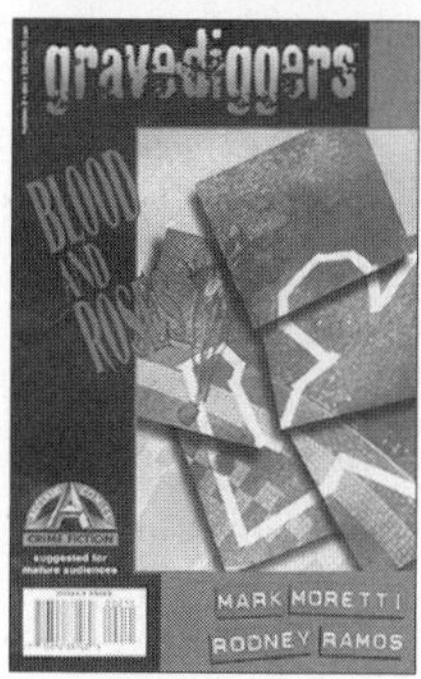

Gravediggers

Gravestone

Grave Tales

Grease Monkey

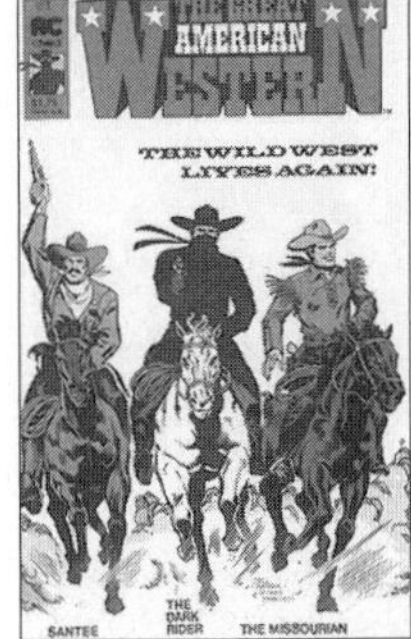

Great American Western

Harry the Cop
Slave Labor, 1992

1-1/2nd	3.00

Harsh Realm
Harris, 1994

1-6	3.00

Harte of Darkness
Eternity

1-4	3.00

Harvey
Marvel, 1970

1	50.00
2	18.00
3	8.00
4-6	6.00

Harvey Collectors Comics
Harvey, 1975

1	7.00
2	4.00
3-16	3.00

Harvey Comics Hits
Harvey, 1951

51	120.00
52	85.00
53	110.00
54	55.00
55	45.00
56	100.00
57	70.00
58	35.00
59	40.00
60	125.00
61	140.00
62	55.00

Harvey Comics Library
Harvey, 1952

1	650.00
2	140.00

Harvey Hits
Harvey, 1957

1	165.00
2	24.00
3	550.00
4	105.00
5	18.00
6	115.00
7	120.00
8	35.00
9	315.00
10	85.00
11	55.00
12	100.00
13	65.00
14	16.00
15	100.00
16	80.00
17	34.00
18	16.00
19	36.00
20	45.00
21	48.00
22	26.00
23	40.00
24	50.00
25	14.00
26	75.00
27	40.00
28	20.00
29	24.00
30	40.00
31	12.00
32	15.00
33	32.00
34	18.00
35	12.00
36	65.00
37	30.00
38	16.00
39	12.00
40-41	10.00
42	12.00
43	9.00
44	52.00
45	22.00
46-47	10.00
48	45.00
49	55.00
50-51	8.00
52	20.00
53	8.00
54	40.00
55	8.00
56	18.00
57	30.00
58	8.00
59	18.00
60	26.00
61	6.00
62	15.00
63	24.00
64	6.00
65	15.00
66	24.00
67	6.00
68	15.00
69	24.00
70	5.00
71	12.00
72	20.00
73-74	6.00
75	12.00
76-77	6.00
78	24.00
79-87	6.00
88	15.00
89-90	6.00
91-122	5.00

Harvey Hits Comics
Harvey, 1986

1	2.00
2	2.00

3 .... 2.00
4 .... 2.00
5-6 .... 2.00

Harvey Spotlite

Harvey, 1987

1 .... 4.00
2-4 .... 3.00

Hate

Fantagraphics, 1990

1 .... 8.00
1/2nd 4.00
1/3rd 2.00
2 .... 5.00
2/2nd-2/3rd 3.00
3 .... 4.00
3/2nd-3/3rd 3.00
4 .... 4.00
4/2nd 2.00
5 .... 4.00
5/2nd 2.00
6 .... 4.00
7-30 .... 3.00

Hateball

Fantagraphics

1 .... 1.00
Annual 1-6 .... 5.00

Hate Jamboree!

Fantagraphics, 1998

1 .... 4.00

Haunted

Charlton, 1971

1 .... 12.00
2-3 .... 6.00
4-6 .... 5.00
7-10 .... 4.00
11-75 .... 3.00

Haunted

Chaos, 2001

1-4 .... 3.00

Haunted Love

Charlton, 1973

1 .... 10.00
2 .... 6.00
3 .... 5.00
4-11 .... 4.00

Haunted Man

Dark Horse, 2000

1-3 .... 3.00

Haunted Mansion

Slave Labor, 2005

1 .... 3.00

Haunted Thrills

Farrell, 1952

1 .... 300.00
2 .... 220.00
3 .... 165.00
4-5 .... 125.00
6-15 .... 100.00
16-18 .... 85.00

Haunt of Fear

E.C., 1950

1 .... 2,750.00
2-3 .... 1,000.00
4 .... 750.00
5 .... 550.00
6 .... 425.00
7-9 .... 400.00
10 .... 375.00
11-13 .... 300.00
14 .... 450.00
15-18 .... 300.00
19 .... 375.00
20 .... 300.00
21-28 .... 250.00

Haunt of Fear

Gladstone, 1991

1-2 .... 3.00

Haunt of Fear

Cochran, 1991

1-5 .... 2.00

Haunt of Fear

Gemstone, 1992

1-15 .... 2.00
16-28 .... 3.00
Ann 1 .... 9.00
Ann 2 .... 10.00
Ann 3-4 .... 11.00
Ann 5 .... 12.00
Ann 6 .... 9.00

Haunt of Horror

Marvel, 1974

1 .... 8.00
2 .... 6.00
3-5 .... 5.00

Haunt of Horror: Edgar Allan Poe

Marvel, 2006

1-3 .... 4.00

Have Gun, Will Travel

Dell, 1960

4-5 .... 38.00
6-10 .... 35.00
11-14 .... 28.00

Haven: The Broken City

DC, 2002

1-9 .... 3.00

Havoc, Inc.

Radio, 1998

1-9 .... 3.00

Havok & Wolverine: Meltdown

Marvel, 1989

1-4 .... 4.00

Hawaiian Dick

Image, 2002

1-3 .... 3.00

Great Galaxies

Greeenlock

Green Arrow

Green Candles

Green Giant Comics

Green Goblin

Greenhaven

Green Hornet Comics

Hawaiian Dick: The Last Resort

Image, 2004

1-2 .... 3.00

Hawk

Ziff-Davis, 1951

1 .... 145.00
2 .... 90.00
3-6 .... 60.00
7-12 .... 55.00
3D 1 .... 250.00

Hawk & the Dove

DC, 1968

1 .... 60.00
2-5 .... 40.00
6 .... 30.00

Hawk and Dove

DC, 1988

1-2 .... 3.00
3-5 .... 2.00

Hawk and Dove

DC, 1989

1 .... 2.00
2-24 .... 1.00
25 .... 2.00
26-27 .... 1.00
28 .... 2.00
Ann 1 .... 3.00
Ann 2 .... 2.00

Hawk and Dove

DC, 1997

1-5 .... 3.00

Hawk & Windblade

Warp, 1997

1-2 .... 3.00

Hawkeye

Marvel, 1983

1 .... 3.00
2-4 .... 2.00

Hawkeye

Marvel, 1994

1-4 .... 2.00

Hawkeye

Marvel, 2003

1-8 .... 3.00

Hawkeye: Earth's Mightiest Marksman

Marvel, 1998

1 .... 3.00

Hawkgirl

DC, 2006

50-59 .... 3.00

Hawkman

DC, 1964

1 .... 475.00
2 .... 200.00
3 .... 75.00
4 .... 200.00
☛1st Zatanna
5-9 .... 65.00
10-12 .... 50.00
13-15 .... 40.00
16-19 .... 36.00
20-27 .... 32.00

Hawkman

DC, 1986

1 .... 3.00
2-17 .... 2.00
Special 1 .... 3.00

Hawkman

DC, 1993

0-1 .... 3.00
2-33 .... 2.00
Ann 1-2 .... 4.00

Hawkman

DC, 2002

1-40 .... 3.00
41 .... 8.00
42 .... 4.00
43-49 .... 3.00

Hawkman Secret Files and Origins

DC, 2002

1 .... 5.00

Hawkmoon: The Jewel in the Skull

First, 1986

1-4 .... 2.00

Hawkmoon: The Mad God's Amulet

First, 1987

1-4 .... 2.00

Hawkmoon: The Runestaff

First, 1988

1-4 .... 2.00

Hawkmoon: The Sword of the Dawn

First, 1987

1-4 .... 2.00

Hawkshaws

Image, 2000

1 .... 3.00

Hawk, Street Avenger

Taurus, 1996

1 .... 3.00

Hawkworld

DC, 1989

1-3 .... 4.00

Hawkworld

DC, 1990

1 .... 3.00
2-32 .... 2.00
Ann 1-3 .... 3.00

Haywire
DC, 1988

1-13 .... 1.00

Hazard
Image, 1996

1-7 .... 2.00

Hazard!
Motion

1 .... 3.00

Hazard!
Reckless Vision

1 .... 3.00

H-Bomb
Antarctic, 1993

1 .... 3.00

Head
Fantagraphics, 2002

1 .... 7.00
2-13 .... 4.00

Headbanger
Parody

1 .... 3.00

Headbuster
Antarctic, 1998

1 .... 3.00

Headhunters
Image, 1997

1-3 .... 3.00

Headless Horseman
Eternity

1-2 .... 2.00

Headline Comics
Headline, 1943

1 .... 325.00
2 .... 275.00
3 .... 140.00
4-5 .... 100.00
6-7 .... 85.00
8 .... 110.00
9-10 .... 85.00
11-15 .... 70.00
16 .... 175.00
17-18 .... 65.00
19 .... 175.00
20-22 .... 60.00
23-24 .... 155.00
25-35 .... 120.00
36 .... 100.00
37 .... 58.00
38-44 .... 38.00
45 .... 45.00
46-50 .... 28.00
51-55 .... 26.00
56 .... 60.00
57-60 .... 26.00
61-70 .... 22.00
71-77 .... 18.00

Headman
Innovation

1 .... 3.00

Health
David Tompkins

1 .... 1.00
2-5 .... 2.00
6 .... 5.00

Heap
Skywald, 1971

1 .... 16.00

Heartbreak Comics
Eclipse

1 .... 4.00

Heartbreakers
Dark Horse, 1996

1-4 .... 3.00

Heartbreakers Superdigest: Year Ten
Image, 1999

1 .... 14.00

Heartland
DC, 1997

1 .... 5.00

Heart of Darkness
Hardline

1 .... 3.00

Heart of Empire
Dark Horse, 1999

1-9 .... 3.00

Heart of the Beast
DC

1 .... 20.00

Hearts of Africa
Slave Labor

1 .... 11.00

Hearts of Darkness
Marvel, 1991

1 .... 5.00

Heart Throbs
DC, 1949

1 .... 240.00
2 .... 135.00
3 .... 65.00
4 .... 85.00
5 .... 50.00
6 .... 80.00
7 .... 48.00
8 .... 80.00
9-10 .... 48.00
11-15 .... 30.00
16-20 .... 26.00
21 .... 45.00
22-23 .... 35.00
24-40 .... 22.00
41-46 .... 18.00
47 .... 125.00

Green Lama

Green Lantern Corps Quarterly

Green Lantern Gallery

Green Lantern Plus

Green Lantern Secret Files

Greenleaf in Exile

Green Mask

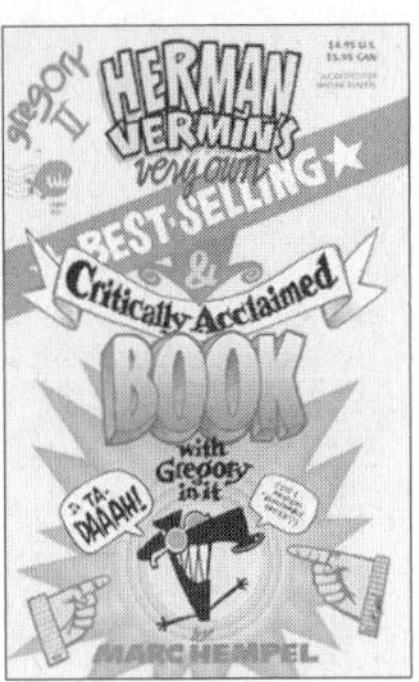
Gregory

48 .....65.00
49-50 .....60.00
51-60 .....48.00
61-70 .....38.00
71-80 .....27.00
81-90 .....20.00
91-100 .....16.00
101 .....60.00
102-110 .....13.00
111-130 .....10.00
131-146 .....9.00

Heartthrobs
DC, 1999
1-4 .....3.00

Heathcliff
Marvel, 1985
1 .....2.00
2-49 .....1.00
50 .....2.00
51-Ann 1 .....1.00

Heathcliff's Funhouse
Marvel, 1987
1-10 .....1.00

Heatseeker
Fantaco
1 .....6.00

Heaven Above Heaven
Tokyopop, 2005
1-3 .....10.00

Heaven LLC
Image, 2004
1 .....13.00

Heaven's Devils
Image, 2003
1 .....3.00
2-4 .....4.00

Heaven Sent
Antarctic, 2004
1-11 .....3.00

Heaven's War
Image, 2003
0 .....13.00

Heavy Armor
Fantasy General
1-3 .....2.00

Heavy Hitters
Marvel, 1993
Ann 1 .....4.00

Heavy Liquid
DC, 1999
1-5 .....6.00

Heavy Metal
Metal Mammoth, 1977
1 .....20.00
2-3 .....10.00
4-11 .....7.00
12-22 .....5.00
23-193 .....4.00
194 .....5.00

Heavy Metal Greatest Hits
HM Communications, 1992
1 .....6.00

Heavy Metal Havoc
HM Communications
1 .....6.00

Heavy Metal Monsters
Revolutionary, 1992
1 .....3.00
2 .....4.00

Heavy Metal War Machine
HM Communications
1 .....6.00

Heck!
Rip Off
1 .....8.00

Heckle and Jeckle
Pines, 1952
1 .....140.00
2 .....75.00
3 .....52.00
4-5 .....45.00
6-10 .....32.00
11-20 .....28.00
21-34 .....20.00

Heckle and Jeckle
Gold Key, 1962
1 .....36.00
2 .....18.00
3-4 .....16.00

Heckle and Jeckle
Dell, 1966
1 .....25.00
2-3 .....13.00

Heckler
DC, 1992
1-6 .....1.00

Hector Plasm
Image, 2006
1 .....6.00

Hector Heathcote
Gold Key, 1964
1 .....30.00

Hedge Knight
Image, 2003
1-2 .....3.00
2/A 6.00
3 .....3.00

Hedy De Vine Comics
Red Circle, 1947
22 .....75.00
23-30 .....60.00
31-40 .....42.00
41-50 .....36.00

Hee Haw

Charlton, 1970

1 .... 13.00
2 .... 8.00
3-7 .... 6.00

Heirs of Eternity

Image, 2003

1-5 .... 3.00

He Is Just a Rat

Exclaim! Brand Comics, 1995

1-5 .... 3.00

Hell

Dark Horse, 2003

1-4 .... 3.00

Hellbender

Eternity

1 .... 2.00

Hellblazer

DC, 1988

1 .... 10.00
2 .... 5.00
3-13 .... 4.00
14-26 .... 3.00
27 .... 9.00
☛Gaiman story
28-39 .... 3.00
40 .... 4.00
41 .... 6.00
☛1st Ennis story
42-46 .... 4.00
47-49 .... 3.00
50 .... 4.00
51-74 .... 3.00
75 .... 4.00
76-199 .... 3.00
200 .... 5.00
201-260 .... 3.00
Ann 1 .... 6.00
Special 1 .... 5.00

Hellblazer Special: Bad Blood

DC, 2000

1-4 .... 3.00

Hellblazer Special: Lady Constantine

DC, 2003

1-4 .... 3.00

Hellblazer/The Books of Magic

DC, 1997

1-2 .... 4.00

Hellboy: Almost Colossus

Dark Horse, 1997

1-2 .... 3.00

Hellboy: Art of the Movie

Dark Horse, 2004

1 .... 25.00

Hellboy: Box Full of Evil

Dark Horse, 1999

1-2 .... 3.00

Hellboy Christmas Special

Dark Horse, 1997

1 .... 4.00

Hellboy: Conqueror Worm

Dark Horse, 2001

1-4 .... 3.00

Hellboy, the Corpse and The Iron Shoes

Dark Horse

1 .... 4.00

Hellboy: Makoma

Dark Horse, 2006

1-2 .... 3.00

Hellboy: Seed of Destruction

Dark Horse, 1994

1 .... 6.00
2-4 .... 4.00

Hellboy: The Island

Dark Horse, 2005

1-2 .... 3.00

Hellboy: The Third Wish

Dark Horse, 2002

1-2 .... 3.00

Hellboy: The Wolves of Saint August

Dark Horse

1 .... 5.00

Hellboy: Wake the Devil

Dark Horse, 1996

1-5 .... 4.00

Hellboy: Weird Tales

Dark Horse, 2003

1-8 .... 3.00

Hellboy Jr.

Dark Horse, 1999

1-2 .... 3.00

Hellboy Jr. Halloween Special

Dark Horse, 1997

1 .... 4.00

Hell Car Comix

Alternating Crimes, 1998

1 .... 3.00

Hellcat

Marvel, 2000

1-3 .... 3.00

Hell City, Hell

Diablo Musica

1 .... 2.00

Gremlin Trouble

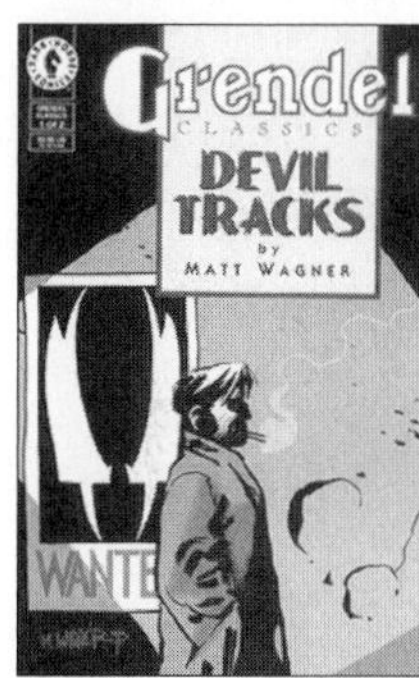

Grendel Classics

Grey

Greylore

Greymatter

Grifter and the Mask

Grimjack

Gringo

Hellcop
Image, 1998

1-4 .... 3.00

Hell Eternal
DC

1 .... 7.00

Hellgate: London
Dark Horse, 2006

0-Bk 1-2 .... 0.00
1-2 .... 3.00

Hellgirl: Demonseed
Knight, 1995

1 .... 3.00

Hellhole
Image, 1999

1-3 .... 3.00

Hellhounds
Image, 2003

1-4 .... 3.00

Hellhounds: Panzer Corps
Dark Horse, 1994

1-6 .... 3.00

Hellhound: The Redemption Quest
Marvel, 1993

1-4 .... 2.00

Hellina
Lightning, 1994

1 .... 3.00

Hellina 1997 Pin-Up Special
Lightning, 1997

1 .... 4.00

Hellina/Catfight
Lightning, 1995

1-1/2nd 3.00

Hellina: Christmas in Hell
Lightning, 1996

1 .... 3.00
1/A-1/C 4.00

Hellina/Cynder
Lightning, 1997

1-1/C 3.00

Hellina/Double Impact
Lightning, 1996

1-1/C 3.00
1/Nude 4.00
1/Platinum 3.00

Hellina: Genesis
Lightning, 1996

1-1/Nude 4.00

Hellina: Heart of Thorns
Lightning, 1996

1-2/Nude 4.00

Hellina: Hellborn
Lightning, 1997

1-2/B 3.00

Hellina: Hell's Angel
Lightning, 1996

1-2/Nude 3.00

Hellina: in the Flesh
Lightning, 1997

1-1/B 3.00

Hellina: Kiss of Death
Lightning, 1995

1-1/Gold 3.00
1/Nude 4.00
1/2nd 3.00

Hellina: Naked Desire
Lightning, 1997

1-1/B 3.00

Hellina/Nira X
Lightning, 1996

1-1/B 3.00

Hellina: Skybolt Toyz Limited Edition
Lightning, 1997

1/A-1/B 2.00

Hellina: Taking Back the Night
Lightning, 1995

1-1/A 5.00

Hellina: Wicked Ways
Lightning, 1995

1/A-1/B 3.00
1/Nude 10.00
1/Silver 3.00

Hell Magician
Fc9 Publishing, 2005

1 .... 3.00

Hell Michigan
Fc9 Publishing, 2005

1-2 .... 3.00
1/Ashcan 4.00

Hello Pal
Harvey, 1943

1-3 .... 400.00

Hellraiser (Clive Barker's)
Marvel, 1989

Summer 1 .... 6.00
Spring 1 .... 7.00

Hellraiser III: Hell on Earth
Marvel

1 .... 5.00

Hellraiser Nightbreed: Jihad
Marvel
1-2 .... 5.00

Hellraiser Posterbook (Clive Barker's)
Marvel
1 .... 5.00

Hellraiser: Spring Slaughter
Marvel
1 .... 7.00

Hellsaint
Black Diamond, 1998
1 .... 3.00

Hell's Angel
Marvel, 1993
1-5 .... 2.00

Hellshock
Image, 1994
1-4/B 2.00
Ashcan 1 .... 1.00

Hellshock
Image, 1997
1-6 .... 3.00
7 .... 4.00

Hellsing
Dark Horse, 2003
1 .... 0.00

Hellspawn
Image, 2000
1-16 .... 3.00

Hellspock
Express
1 .... 3.00

Hellstalker
Rebel Creations, 1989
1-2 .... 2.00

Hellstorm: Prince of Lies
Marvel, 1993
1 .... 3.00
2-21 .... 2.00

Hellstorm: Son of Satan
Marvel, 2006
1-3 .... 4.00

Helm Premiere
Helm, 1995
1 .... 3.00

Help
Jeff Levine
1 .... 0.00

Help
Warren, 1964
1 .... 45.00
2 .... 28.00
3-12 .... 20.00

Help
Warren
1 .... 26.00
2-3 .... 16.00

Helsing
Caliber, 2008
1-2 .... 3.00

Helter Skelter
Antarctic, 1997
0-6 .... 3.00

Helyun: Bones of the Backwoods
Slave Labor, 1991
1 .... 3.00

Helyun Book 1
Slave Labor, 1990
1 .... 7.00

He-Man
Toby, 1954
1 .... 85.00
2 .... 65.00

Hembeck
Fantaco, 1980
1-2 .... 3.00
3-4 .... 2.00
5 .... 3.00
6-7 .... 2.00

Hemp for Victory
Starhead, 1993
1 .... 3.00

Henry (Carl Anderson's...)
Dell, 1948
1 .... 75.00
2 .... 40.00
3 .... 30.00
4-5 .... 25.00
6-10 .... 22.00
11-21 .... 18.00
22-30 .... 15.00
31-40 .... 12.00
41-50 .... 10.00
51-65 .... 8.00

Henry Aldrich
Dell, 1950
1 .... 50.00
2 .... 25.00
3 .... 18.00
4-10 .... 15.00
11-22 .... 12.00

Henry V
Caliber
1 .... 3.00

Hepcats
Double Diamond, 1989
1 .... 5.00
2 .... 4.00

Grit Bath

Groo the Wanderer

Groovy

Gross Point

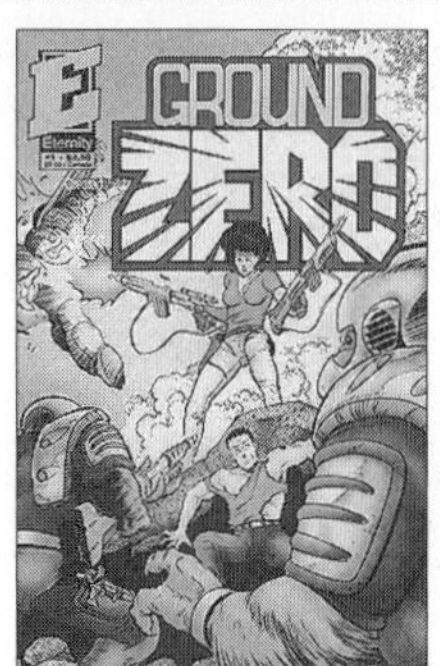

Ground Zero

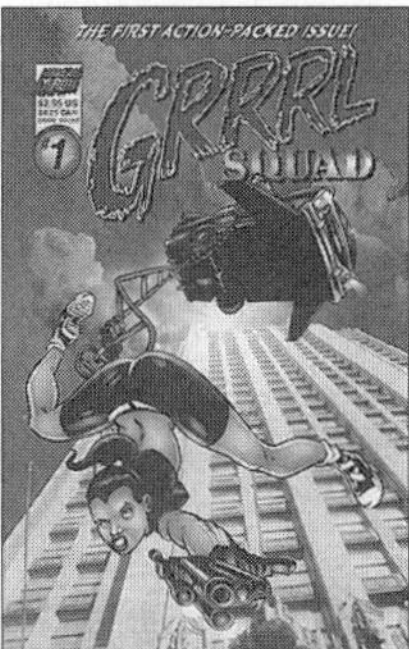

Grrrl Squad

Grun

Grunts

3-14 ... 3.00
Special 1-Special 2 ... 4.00

Hepcats
Antarctic, 1996

0 ... 4.00
0/A ... 6.00
0/Deluxe ... 10.00
1-2 ... 4.00
3-12 ... 3.00

Herbie
Dark Horse, 1992

1-2 ... 3.00

Herbie (A+)
A-Plus

1-6 ... 3.00

Herbie
ACG, 1964

1 ... 95.00
2 ... 60.00
3-5 ... 48.00
6-7 ... 40.00
8 ... 50.00
9-10 ... 38.00
11-23 ... 30.00

Hercules
Charlton, 1967

1 ... 14.00
2 ... 9.00
3-5 ... 6.00
6-8 ... 5.00
8/A ... 10.00
9-13 ... 5.00

Hercules
Marvel, 1982

1-4 ... 2.00

Hercules
Marvel, 1984

1 ... 2.00
2 ... 1.00
3-4 ... 1.00

Hercules
Marvel, 2005

1 ... 3.00
2-3 ... 3.00
4-5 ... 3.00

Hercules
Avalon, 2002

1-2 ... 6.00

Hercules: Heart of Chaos
Marvel, 1997

1-3 ... 3.00

Hercules: Official Comics Movie Adaptation
Acclaim

1 ... 5.00

Hercules Project
Monster, 1991

1-2 ... 2.00

Hercules: The Legendary Journeys
Topps, 1996

1-5 ... 3.00

Hercules Unbound
DC, 1975

1 ... 12.00
2 ... 7.00
3 ... 4.00
4-12 ... 3.00

Here Come the Big People
Event, 1997

1-1/A ... 3.00

Here Come the Lovejoys Again
Fantagraphics, 2005

1-3 ... 4.00

Here Is Greenwood
Viz, 2004

1-9 ... 10.00

Here's Howie
DC, 1952

1 ... 120.00
2 ... 75.00
3-5 ... 60.00
6-10 ... 48.00
11-18 ... 36.00

Heretic
Dark Horse, 1996

1-4 ... 3.00

Heretics
Iguana, 1993

1-3 ... 3.00

Hermes vs. the Eyeball Kid
Dark Horse, 1994

1-3 ... 3.00

Hero
Marvel, 1990

1-6 ... 2.00

Hero Alliance
Wonder Color, 1987

1 ... 2.00

Hero Alliance
Innovation, 1989

1-16 ... 2.00
17-Special 1 ... 3.00

Hero Alliance & Justice Machine: Identity Crisis
Innovation, 1990

1 ... 3.00

Hero Alliance: End of the Golden Age
Innovation, 1989
1-3 .... 2.00

Hero Alliance Quarterly
Innovation, 1991
1-4 .... 3.00

Hero at Large
Speakeasy Comics, 2005
1 .... 3.00

Herobear And The Kid
Astonish, 1999
1-2/2nd 3.00
3-5 .... 4.00

Herobear and the Kid and Decoy
Astonish, 2002
1-2 .... 3.00

Hero Camp
Image, 2005
1-4 .... 3.00

H-E-R-O
DC, 2003
1 .... 3.00
1/2nd 5.00
2-22 .... 3.00

Hero Double Feature
DC, 2003
1 .... 5.00

Heroes
Blackbird, 1985
1 .... 3.00
2-6 .... 2.00

Heroes
DC, 1996
1-6 .... 3.00

Heroes
Marvel, 2001
1 .... 7.00
1/2nd 4.00

Heroes Against Hunger
DC, 1986
1 .... 3.00

Heroes All (Vol. 1)
Heroes All, 1943
1 .... 150.00
2 .... 120.00

Heroes All (Vol. 2)
Heroes All, 1944
1 .... 95.00
2-3 .... 85.00

Heroes All (Vol. 3)
Heroes All, 1945
1-5 .... 80.00
6-10 .... 70.00

Heroes All (Vol. 4)
Heroes All, 1946
1-35 .... 65.00

Heroes All (Vol. 5)
Heroes All, 1947
1-20 .... 60.00

Heroes All (Vol. 6)
Heroes All, 1948
1-10 .... 60.00

Heroes Anonymous
Bongo, 2003
1-6 .... 3.00

Heroes for Hire
Marvel, 1997
1 .... 3.00
2/A-11 .... 2.00
12 .... 3.00
13-19 .... 2.00
Ann 1998 .... 3.00

Heroes for Hire
Marvel, 2006
1 .... 3.00
2 .... 2.00
3-5 .... 3.00

Heroes for Hope
Marvel, 1985
1 .... 5.00

Heroes from Wordsmith
Special Studio
1 .... 3.00

Heroes Incorporated
Double Edge, 1995
1 .... 3.00

Heroes, Inc. Presents Cannon
Armed Services, 1969
1 .... 13.00
2 .... 10.00

Heroes of Faith
Coretoons, 1992
1 .... 3.00

Heroes of Rock 'n Fire
Wonder Comix, 1987
1-2 .... 2.00

Heroes of the Equinox
Fantasy Flight
1 .... 9.00

Guano Comix

Guardian Angel

Guardians

Guardians of the Galaxy

Gumby 3-D

Gunfighter

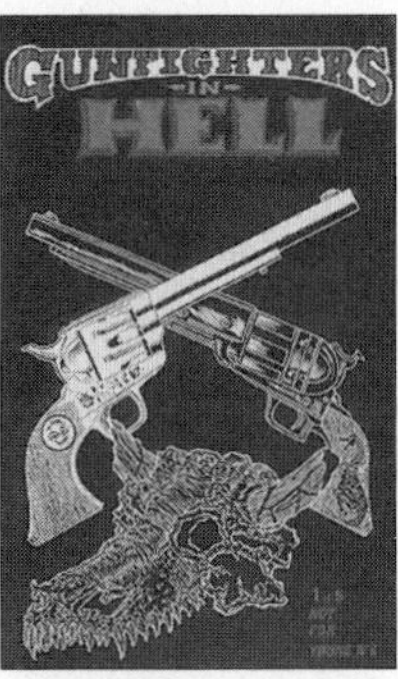

Gun Fighters in Hell

Gunfire

Heroes Reborn
Marvel, 1996

½ ... 3.00

Heroes Reborn: Ashema
Marvel, 2000

1 ... 2.00

Heroes Reborn: Doom
Marvel, 2000

1 ... 2.00

Heroes Reborn: Doomsday
Marvel, 2000

1 ... 2.00

Heroes Reborn: Masters Of Evil
Marvel, 1999

1 ... 2.00

Heroes Reborn Mini Comic
Marvel, 1996

1 ... 1.00

Heroes Reborn: Rebel
Marvel, 2000

1 ... 2.00

Heroes Reborn: Remnants
Marvel, 2000

1 ... 2.00

Heroes Reborn: The Return
Marvel, 1997

1-4/Variant ... 3.00
Ashcan 1 ... 1.00

Heroes Reborn: Young Allies
Marvel, 2000

1 ... 2.00

Hero for Hire
Marvel, 1972

1 ... 125.00
2 ... 30.00
3 ... 14.00
4-6 ... 12.00
7-9 ... 9.00
10 ... 8.00
11-16 ... 9.00

Hero Graphics Super-Spectacular
Hero

1 ... 4.00

Hero Hotline
DC, 1989

1-6 ... 2.00

Heroic
Lightning

1 ... 2.00

Heroic 17
Pennacle, 1993

1 ... 3.00

Heroic Comics
Famous Funnies, 1940

1 ... 850.00
2 ... 475.00
3 ... 375.00
4 ... 340.00
5-6 ... 285.00
7 ... 300.00
8-10 ... 200.00
11-13 ... 185.00
14 ... 200.00
15 ... 210.00
16-20 ... 130.00
21-29 ... 90.00
30 ... 42.00
31-33 ... 44.00
34 ... 32.00
35-42 ... 44.00
43-47 ... 38.00
48 ... 30.00
49-50 ... 38.00
51 ... 42.00
52 ... 38.00
53 ... 32.00
54-55 ... 26.00
56 ... 38.00
57-60 ... 34.00
61-64 ... 24.00
65 ... 60.00
66-67 ... 35.00
68 ... 26.00
69 ... 44.00
70-71 ... 36.00
72 ... 44.00
73 ... 36.00
74 ... 26.00
75 ... 36.00
76-80 ... 18.00
81-82 ... 20.00
83-85 ... 18.00
86-87 ... 25.00
88-97 ... 18.00

Heroic Tales
Lone Star, 1997

1-10 ... 3.00

Heroine
Axess

0/A-0/B ... 3.00

Heroines Inc.
Avatar, 1989

1 ... 2.00

Heroman
Dimension, 1986

1 ... 2.00

Hero on a Stick
Big-Baby

1 .... 3.00

Hero Premiere Edition
Warrior, 1993

1-9 .... 2.00

Heros
OK

1 .... 3.00

Hero Sandwich
Slave Labor, 1987

1-7 .... 2.00

8-9 .... 3.00

Hero Squared
Boom Studios, 2005

1-1/Finger 4.00

Hero Zero
Dark Horse, 1994

0 .... 3.00

Heru, Son of Ausar
Ania, 1993

1 .... 2.00

He Said/She Said Comics
First Amendment

1-6 .... 3.00

Hex
DC, 1985

1 .... 5.00

2-18 .... 2.00

Hexbreaker: A Badger Graphic Novel
First, 1988

1 .... 9.00

Hex Of The Wicked Witch
Asylum, 1999

0/A 2.00

0/B 4.00

Hey, Boss!
Visionary

1 .... 2.00

Hey, Mister
Insomnia, 1997

1-4 .... 3.00

Hey Mister: After School Special
Top Shelf

1 .... 5.00

Hi-Adventure Heroes
Gold Key, 1969

1 .... 12.00

2 .... 7.00

Hickory
Quality, 1949

1 .... 48.00

2 .... 34.00

3-6 .... 24.00

Hideo Li Files
Raging Rhino

1 .... 3.00

Hideo Li Files Comic Novella
Raging Rhino

1 .... 13.00

Hiding Place
DC

1 .... 13.00

Hiding Place
Spire, 1973

1 .... 5.00

Hieroglyph
Dark Horse, 1999

1-4 .... 3.00

High Adventure
Red Top, 1957

1 .... 40.00

Highbrow Entertainment
Image

Ashcan 1 .... 1.00

High Caliber
Caliber

1 .... 10.00

2-4 .... 4.00

High Chaparral
Gold Key, 1968

1 .... 40.00

High Octane Theatre
Infiniti

1 .... 3.00

High Roads
DC, 2002

1-6 .... 3.00

High School Agent
Sun

1-4 .... 3.00

High Shining Brass
Apple, 1990

1-4 .... 3.00

High Stakes Adventures
Antarctic, 1998

1 .... 3.00

1/Deluxe 6.00

Hightop Ninja
Authority, 1997

1-3 .... 3.00

High Voltage
Black Out

0 .... 3.00

Highway 61
Vortex

1 .... 12.00

Gun Fury

Gunhawks

Gunhed

Gun Runner

Gunsmith Cats

Gunsmith Cats Special

Gunsmoke Western

Guns of the Dragon

Hi Hi Puffy Amiyumi
DC, 2006

1-3 .... 2.00

Hi-Jinx
ACG, 1947

1 .... 140.00
2-3 .... 100.00
4-7 .... 120.00

Hikaru No Go
Viz, 2004

1-5 .... 8.00

Hilly Rose
Astro, 1995

1-1/A 3.00
2 .... 4.00
3-9 .... 3.00

Hip Flask
Comicraft, 1998

½ 3.00

Hip Flask: Elephantmen
Active Images, 2003

1/Desert 6.00
1/Street 5.00
1/Sushi 4.00
1/Townhouse 6.00

Hip Flask: Ladronn Sketchbook
Active Images, 2005

1-3 .... 10.00

Hip Flask: Mystery City
Active Images, 2005

0 .... 5.00

Hiroshima: The Atomic Holocaust
Antarctic, 2005

1 .... 4.00

Hi-School Romance
Home, 1949

1 .... 75.00
2 .... 45.00
3-10 .... 32.00
11-20 .... 20.00
21-31 .... 16.00
32 .... 25.00
33-40 .... 13.00
41-75 .... 10.00

His Name Is... Savage
Adventure House

1 .... 24.00

Hi-Spot Comics
Hawley, 1940

2 .... 1,000.00

History of Marvels Comics
Marvel, 2000

1 .... 1.00

History of the DC Universe
DC, 1986

1-2 .... 3.00

History of Violence
DC

1 .... 10.00

Hitchhiker's Guide to the Galaxy
DC, 1993

1-3 .... 5.00

Hit Comics
Quality, 1940

1 .... 4,550.00
2 .... 2,250.00
3 .... 1,700.00
4 .... 1,500.00
5 .... 2,350.00
6-10 .... 1,300.00
11 .... 1,175.00
12-20 .... 825.00
21-23 .... 700.00
24 .... 1,100.00
25 .... 850.00
26 .... 525.00
27-29 .... 700.00
30-35 .... 500.00
36-39 .... 350.00
40-49 .... 200.00
50-55 .... 165.00
56-65 .... 135.00

Hitman
DC, 1996

1-10 .... 3.00
11-29 .... 2.00
30-1000000 .... 3.00
Ann 1 .... 4.00

Hitman/Lobo: That Stupid Bastich
DC, 2000

1 .... 4.00

Hitomi 2
Antarctic, 1993

1-9 .... 3.00
10 .... 4.00

Hitomi and Her Girl Commandos
Antarctic, 1992

1-4 .... 3.00

Hit the Beach
Antarctic, 1993

1 .... 3.00
1/Gold 5.00
2-5 .... 3.00
5/CS 5.00
6 .... 4.00

Hobbit (J.R.R. Tolkien's...)
Eclipse, 1989
1-3 .... 5.00

Hockey Masters
Revolutionary, 1993
1 .... 3.00

Hoe
Thunderball
1 .... 3.00

Hogan's Heroes
Dell, 1966
1 .... 50.00
2 .... 40.00
3-5 .... 32.00
6-9 .... 26.00

Hokum & Hex
Marvel, 1993
1 .... 3.00
2-9 .... 2.00

Holed Up (Rich Johnson's)
Avatar, 2004
1 .... 4.00

Holiday Comics
Star Publications, 1951
1 .... 165.00
2-4 .... 125.00
5-8 .... 90.00

Holiday for Screams
Malibu
1 .... 5.00

Holiday Out
Renegade, 1987
1-3 .... 2.00

Hollow Earth
Vision, 1996
1-3 .... 3.00

Hollow Grounds
DC, 2000
1 .... 20.00

Hollywood Film Stories
Feature Publications, 1950
1 .... 120.00
2-4 .... 80.00

Hollywood Funny Folks
DC, 1950
27 .... 90.00
28-30 .... 70.00
31-37 .... 50.00
38-49 .... 40.00
50-60 .... 30.00

Hollywood Romances
Charlton, 1966
46 .... 35.00
47-49 .... 18.00
50-59 .... 12.00

Hollywood Superstars
Marvel, 1990
1 .... 3.00
2-5 .... 2.00

Holo Brothers
Monster, 1988
1-Special 1 .... 2.00

Holy Avenger
Slave Labor, 1996
1 .... 5.00

Holy Cross
Fantagraphics, 1994
0 .... 5.00
1-2 .... 3.00

Holy Knight
Pocket Change, 1994
1-8 .... 3.00

Holy Terror
Image, 2002
1 .... 3.00

Homage Studios Swimsuit Special
Image, 1993
1 .... 2.00

Home Grown Funnies
Kitchen Sink, 1971
1 .... 55.00
1/2nd 22.00
1/3rd 10.00
1/4th 6.00
1/5th-1/15th 4.00

Homelands on The World of Magic: The Gathering
Acclaim
1 .... 6.00

Homer, The Happy Ghost
Atlas, 1955
1 .... 150.00
2-9 .... 100.00
10-17 .... 80.00
18-22 .... 60.00

Homer, The Happy Ghost
Marvel, 1969
1 .... 40.00
2-4 .... 30.00

Homicide
Dark Horse, 1990
1 .... 2.00

Homicide: Tears of the Dead
Chaos, 1997
1 .... 3.00

Homo Patrol
Helpless Anger
1 .... 4.00

Gun Theory

Gustav P.I.

Gutwallow

Guy Gardner

Guy Gardner Reborn

Guy Pumpkinhead

Guzzi Lemans

Gyre

Honeymoon
Marvel, 1950

41 ....100.00

Honeymooners
Lodestone, 1986

1 ....2.00

Honeymooners
Triad, 1987

1-2 ....2.00
3 ....4.00
4-13 ....2.00

Honey Mustard
Tokyopop, 2005

1-3 ....10.00

Honey West
Gold Key, 1966

1 ....25.00

Hong Kong Phooey
Charlton, 1975

1 ....40.00
2 ....20.00
3-9 ....10.00

Hong on the Range
Image, 1997

1-3 ....3.00

Honk!
Fantagraphics, 1986

1-5 ....2.00

Honko the Clown
C&T

1 ....2.00

Honor Among Thieves
Gateway, 1987

1 ....2.00

Honor of the Damned
-Ism, 2005

1 ....4.00

Hood
South Central

1 ....3.00

Hood
Marvel, 2002

1-6 ....3.00

Hooded Horseman
ACG, 1952

21-24 ....20.00
25 ....25.00
26 ....30.00
27 ....20.00

Hooded Horseman
ACG, 1954

18 ....30.00
19 ....20.00
20 ....25.00
21-22 ....20.00

Hooded Menace
Avon, 1951

1 ....250.00

Hooded Rider Comics
Action

1 ....60.00
2 ....42.00
3 ....32.00
4-5 ....25.00
6-10 ....18.00
11-20 ....15.00
21-44 ....12.00
Special 1 ....20.00

Hood Magazine
Oakland

1-2 ....3.00

Hoodoo
3-D Zone, 1988

1 ....3.00

Hook
Marvel, 1992

1-4 ....1.00

Hook (Magazine)
Marvel

1 ....3.00

Hoon
Eenieweenie, 1995

1-6 ....3.00

Hoon (Vol. 2)
Caliber, 1996

1-2 ....3.00

Hopalong Cassidy
Fawcett, 1943

1 ....4,000.00
2 ....1,000.00
3 ....500.00
4-7 ....400.00
8-11 ....300.00
12-14 ....200.00
15-62 ....100.00
63-74 ....75.00
75-85 ....50.00

Hopalong Cassidy
DC, 1954

86 ....200.00
87-89 ....150.00
90-96 ....100.00
97-105 ....80.00
106-117 ....60.00
118-135 ....50.00

Hopeless Savages
Oni, 2001

1-4 ....3.00

Hopeless Savages: Ground Zero
Oni, 2002

1-4 ....3.00

Hoppy the Marvel Bunny
Fawcett, 1945
1 .... 150.00
2-15 .... 100.00

Hopster's Tracks
Bongo
1-2 .... 3.00

Horde
Swing Shift
1 .... 2.00

Horde
DC, 2004
1 .... 18.00

Horizontal Lieutenant
Dell, 1962
1 .... 30.00

Horny Biker Sluts
Last Gasp, 1991
1-5 .... 3.00
6-13 .... 4.00

Horny Comix & Stories
Rip Off, 1991
1-4 .... 3.00

Horny Tails
NBM
1 .... 13.00

Horny Toads (Wallace Wood's...)
Fantagraphics
1 .... 3.00

Horobi Part 1
Viz, 1990
1-8 .... 4.00

Horobi Part 2
Viz, 1990
1-7 .... 4.00

Horrible Truth About Comics
Alternative, 1999
1 .... 3.00

Horrific
Comic Media, 1952
1 .... 120.00
2-8 .... 100.00
9-13 .... 80.00

Horror House
AC, 1994
1 .... 3.00

Horror Illustrated Book of Fears
Northstar, 1990
1-2 .... 4.00

Horror in the Dark
Fantagor
1-4 .... 2.00

Horrorist
DC, 1995
1-2 .... 6.00

Horror of Collier County
Dark Horse, 1999
1-5 .... 3.00

Horror (Robert E. Howard's...)
Cross Plains, 2000
nn 6.00

Horrors
Star Publications, 1953
11-15 .... 200.00

Horror Show
Caliber, 1991
1 .... 4.00

Horror Show
Dead Dog Comics, 2005
1 .... 5.00

Horrors of the Haunter
AC
1 .... 3.00

Horse
Slave Labor, 1989
1-3 .... 3.00

Horseman
Kevlar, 1996
0-2 .... 3.00

Hosie's Heroines
Slave Labor, 1993
1 .... 3.00

Hostile Takeover
Malibu, 1994
Ashcan 1 .... 1.00

Hot Comics Premiere
Hot Comics, 1994
1-2 .... 3.00

Hot Dog
Magazine Enterprises
1 .... 28.00
2 .... 20.00
3-4 .... 16.00

Hotel Harbour View
Viz
1 .... 10.00

Hothead Paisan: Homicidal Lesbian Terrorist
Giant Ass
1-13 .... 4.00

Hot Line
Fantagraphics, 1992
1 .... 3.00

Gyro Comics

Hackmasters of EverKnight

Ha Ha Comics

Hairbutt the Hippo

Hairbutt the Hippo Crime Files

Hall of Fame

Hall of Heroes

Hall of Heroes Halloween Special

Hot Mexican Love Comics
Hot Mexican Love Comics

1-5 .... 4.00

Hot N' Cold Heroes
A-Plus, 1991

1-2 .... 3.00

Hot Nights in Rangoon
Fantagraphics, 1994

1-3 .... 3.00

Hot Rod and Speedway Comics
Hillman, 1952

1 .... 150.00
2-5 .... 100.00

Hot Rod Comics
Fawcett, 1951

1 .... 125.00
2-6 .... 100.00
7 .... 80.00

Hot Rod Racers
Charlton, 1965

1 .... 30.00
2-15 .... 20.00

Hot Rods and Racing Cars
Charlton, 1951

1 .... 135.00
2 .... 90.00
3 .... 58.00
4-10 .... 50.00
11-20 .... 36.00
21-30 .... 28.00
31-50 .... 24.00
51-60 .... 18.00
61-80 .... 13.00
81-100 .... 10.00
101-120 .... 7.00

Hot Shots
Hot, 1987

1 .... 2.00

Hot Shots: Avengers
Marvel, 1995

1 .... 3.00

Hot Shots: Spider-Man
Marvel, 1996

1 .... 3.00

Hot Shots: X-Men
Marvel, 1996

1 .... 3.00

Hotspur
Eclipse, 1987

1-3 .... 2.00

Hot Stuf'
Sal Quartuccio, 1976

1 .... 4.00
2-8 .... 3.00

Hot Stuff
Harvey, 1991

1 .... 2.00
2-8 .... 1.00
9-12 .... 2.00

Hot Stuff Big Book
Harvey, 1992

1-2 .... 2.00

Hot Stuff Creepy Caves
Harvey, 1974

1 .... 12.00
2-3 .... 8.00
4-5 .... 8.00
6-7 .... 8.00

Hot Stuff Digest
Harvey, 1992

1-5 .... 2.00

Hot Stuff Giant Size
Harvey, 1992

1-3 .... 2.00

Hot Stuff Little Devil
Harvey, 1957

1 .... 450.00
2 .... 200.00
3 .... 150.00
4-5 .... 100.00
6-10 .... 75.00
11-20 .... 60.00
21-30 .... 40.00
31-40 .... 25.00
41-50 .... 20.00
51-70 .... 15.00
71-100 .... 10.00
101-121 .... 7.00
122-145 .... 5.00
146-177 .... 3.00

Hot Stuff Sizzlers
Harvey, 1960

1 .... 90.00
2-5 .... 45.00
6-19 .... 25.00
20-44 .... 12.00
45-52 .... 7.00
53-59 .... 5.00

Hot Stuff Sizzlers
Harvey, 1992

1 .... 1.00

Hot Tails
Fantagraphics, 1996

1 .... 4.00

Hot Wheels
DC, 1970

1 .... 45.00
2 .... 30.00
3-5 .... 24.00
6 .... 30.00

Hourman

DC, 1999

1 .... 3.00
2-25 .... 3.00

House II The Second Story

Marvel, 1987

1 .... 2.00

House of Frightenstein

AC

1 .... 3.00

House of Java

NBM, 2000

1-4 .... 3.00

House of M

Marvel, 2005

1 .... 4.00
1/Quesada 30.00
1/DirCut 4.00
1/Gatefold 5.00
1/Madurera 12.00
2 .... 3.00
2/Dodson 25.00
3 .... 6.00
☛Hawkeye returns
3/Cassaday 20.00
4 .... 3.00
4/Peterson 15.00
5 .... 5.00
5/McKone 15.00
6 .... 3.00
6/Land 15.00
7 .... 4.00
8 .... 3.00

House of Mystery

DC, 1951

1 .... 2,000.00
2 .... 850.00
3 .... 600.00
4-5 .... 450.00
6-10 .... 350.00
11-15 .... 300.00
16-25 .... 220.00
26-35 .... 170.00
36-50 .... 140.00
51-61 .... 95.00
62 .... 70.00
63 .... 85.00
64 .... 70.00
65 .... 85.00
66-69 .... 70.00
70 .... 85.00
71-75 .... 65.00
76 .... 85.00
77-79 .... 65.00
80-83 .... 54.00
84-85 .... 85.00
86-99 .... 54.00
100 .... 65.00
101-116 .... 45.00
117-119 .... 35.00
120 .... 45.00
121-130 .... 28.00
131-142 .... 22.00
143 .... 175.00
☛J'onn J'onzz starts
144 .... 75.00
145-155 .... 50.00
156 .... 75.00
☛1st Robby Reed
157-159 .... 50.00
160 .... 90.00
☛1st S.A. Plastic Man
161 .... 35.00
162-173 .... 32.00
174 .... 50.00
175 .... 45.00
176-177 .... 24.00
178 .... 45.00
☛Neal Adams art
179 .... 60.00
☛1st Bernie Wrightson art
180-181 .... 25.00
182 .... 18.00
183 .... 25.00
184 .... 18.00
185 .... 30.00
186 .... 75.00
☛Wrightson art
187 .... 20.00
188 .... 30.00
189-190 .... 20.00
191 .... 25.00
192 .... 20.00
193 .... 25.00
194 .... 30.00
195 .... 45.00
☛Wrightson swamp man
196-201 .... 20.00
202-203 .... 14.00
204 .... 20.00
205-206 .... 12.00
207 .... 40.00
☛Wrightson art
208 .... 12.00
209-213 .... 10.00
214-220 .... 6.00
221 .... 12.00
222-223 .... 6.00
224 .... 35.00
225-226 .... 18.00
227 .... 27.00
228-229 .... 18.00
230-250 .... 5.00
251-259 .... 4.00
260-321 .... 3.00

House of Secrets

DC, 1956

1 .... 1,500.00
2 .... 550.00
3 .... 450.00
4 .... 350.00
5-7 .... 200.00

Halloween

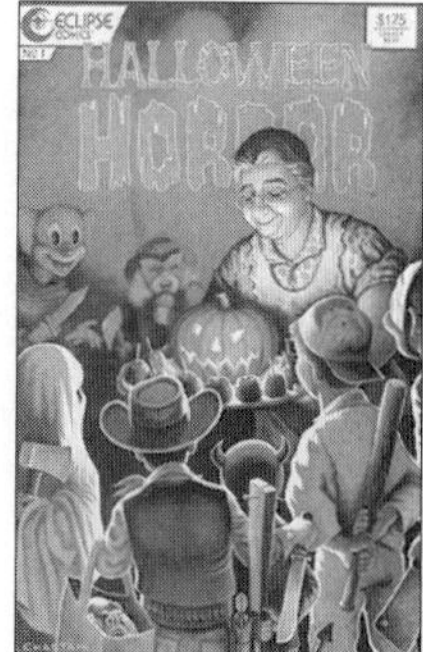

Halloween Horror

Halloween Megazine

Halloween Terror

Halls of Horror

Hammerlocke

Hands of the Dragon

Hangman Comics

8 .... 230.00
9-12 .... 200.00
13-15 .... 125.00
16-20 .... 110.00
21 .... 85.00
22 .... 80.00
23 .... 100.00
☛1st Mark Merlin
24-30 .... 80.00
31-50 .... 65.00
51-60 .... 52.00
61 .... 125.00
☛1st Eclipso
62 .... 60.00
63-65 .... 50.00
66 .... 65.00
☛Eclipso cover
67 .... 40.00
68-79 .... 36.00
80 .... 45.00
81 .... 55.00
☛1st Abel
82-84 .... 20.00
85 .... 32.00
86 .... 20.00
87 .... 45.00
☛Wrightson art
88-91 .... 40.00
92 .... 450.00
☛1st Swamp Thing
93-99 .... 25.00
100 .... 27.00
101-112 .... 18.00
113-141 .... 10.00
142-154 .... 7.00

House of Secrets

DC, 1996

1-25 .... 3.00

House of Secrets: Facade

DC, 2001

1-2 .... 6.00

House of Yang

Charlton, 1975

1 .... 5.00
2 .... 3.00
3 .... 10.00
4 .... 3.00
5 .... 10.00
6 .... 3.00

House of Yang

Modern, 1978

1-2 .... 2.00

Housewives at Play

Fantagraphics, 1999

1-3 .... 3.00

Howard the Duck

Marvel, 1976

1 .... 5.00
2-3 .... 2.00
3/A-3/30¢ 20.00
4 .... 2.00
4/A-4/30¢ 20.00
5-11 .... 2.00
12 .... 6.00
13 .... 4.00
13/A 15.00
13/Whitman 5.00
13/35¢ 15.00
14 .... 2.00
14/A-14/35¢ 15.00
15 .... 2.00
15/A-15/35¢ 15.00
16 .... 2.00
16/A-16/35¢ 15.00
17 .... 2.00
17/A-17/35¢ 15.00
18-33 .... 2.00
Anl 1 .... 5.00

Howard the Duck

Marvel, 2002

1-6 .... 3.00

Howard the Duck (Magazine)

Marvel, 1979

1 .... 4.00
2-3 .... 3.00
4 .... 4.00
5-9 .... 3.00

Howard the Duck Holiday Special

Marvel, 1997

1 .... 3.00

Howard the Duck: The Movie

Marvel, 1986

1-3 .... 1.00

Howdy Doody Comics

Dell, 1950

1 .... 425.00
2 .... 185.00
3 .... 125.00
4-5 .... 100.00
6 .... 125.00
7-10 .... 75.00
11-20 .... 55.00
21-30 .... 40.00
31-38 .... 36.00

Howl

Eternity, 1989

1-2 .... 2.00

Howl's Moving Castle Film Comics

Viz, 2005

1-4 .... 10.00

How The West Was Won

Gold Key, 1963

1 .... 18.00

How To Break Into Comics
Antarctic, 2005
1 .... 3.00

How to Draw Comics Comic
Solson, 1985
1 .... 2.00

How To Draw Felix The Cat And His Friends
Felix, 1992
1 .... 2.00

How to Draw Manga
Antarctic, 2000
1-25 .... 5.00

How to Draw Manga: Next Generation
Antarctic, 2005
1/A-10 .... 5.00

How to Draw Teenage Mutant Ninja Turtles
Solson
1 .... 2.00

How To Pick Up Girls If You're A Comic Book Geek
3 Finger Prints, 1997
1 .... 4.00

How to Publish Comics
Solson
1 .... 2.00

How to Self-Publish Comics ... Not Just Create Them
Devil's Due, 2006
1-4 .... 5.00

H.R. Pufnstuf
Gold Key, 1970
1 .... 55.00
2-3 .... 40.00
4-6 .... 35.00
7-8 .... 25.00

Hsu and Chan
Slave Labor, 2003
1-7 .... 3.00

Huckleberry Hound
Gold Key, 1960
3-5 .... 35.00
6-10 .... 30.00
11-17 .... 20.00
18-19 .... 26.00
20 .... 20.00
21-30 .... 15.00
31-39 .... 9.00
40-43 .... 6.00

Huckleberry Hound & Quick Draw McGraw Giant-Size Flip Book
Harvey, 1993
1 .... 2.00

Huey, Dewey, and Louie Junior Woodchucks
Gold Key, 1966
1 .... 36.00
2 .... 20.00
3 .... 16.00
4-10 .... 12.00
11-20 .... 10.00
21-40 .... 8.00
41-60 .... 6.00
61-81 .... 4.00

Hugga Bunch
Marvel, 1986
1-6 .... 1.00

Hugo
Fantagraphics, 1985
1-3 .... 2.00

Hulk
Marvel, 1978
☛Magazine
10-21 .... 7.00
22-27 .... 5.00

Hulk
Marvel, 1999
1 .... 4.00
1/A 5.00
2-11 .... 3.00

Hulk
Marvel, 2008
1 .... 6.00
1/2nd 3.00
2 .... 4.00
3-18 .... 3.00

Hulk and Thing: Hard Knocks
Marvel, 2004
1-4 .... 4.00

Hulk Comic
Marvel UK, 1979
1 .... 15.00
2 .... 10.00
3 .... 7.00
4-5 .... 6.00
6-10 .... 5.00
11-30 .... 4.00
31-63 .... 3.00

Hulk: Destruction
Marvel, 2005
1-4 .... 3.00

Hulk: Gamma Games
Marvel, 2004
1-3 .... 3.00

Hanna-Barbera Bandwagon

Hanna-Barbera Big Book

Hanna-Barbera Giant Size

Hanna-Barbera Parade

Hanna-Barbera Super TV Heroes

Hap Hazard

Happy Birthday Martha Washington

Happy Comics

Hulk: Gray
Marvel, 2003

1 .... 5.00
2 .... 4.00
3 .... 5.00
4 .... 4.00
5 .... 5.00
6 .... 4.00

Hulk Legends
Marvel, 2003

1 .... 14.00

Hulk Movie
Marvel, 2003

1 .... 13.00

Hulk/Pitt
Marvel, 1996

1 .... 6.00

Hulk: Project H.I.D.E.
Marvel, 1998

1 .... 2.00

Hulk Smash
Marvel, 2001

1-2 .... 3.00

Hulk: The Movie Adaptation
Marvel, 2003

1 .... 4.00

Hulk 2099
Marvel, 1994

1 .... 3.00
2-10 .... 2.00

Hulk: Unchained
Marvel, 2004

1-3 .... 3.00

Hulk Versus Thing
Marvel, 1999

1 .... 4.00

Hulk/Wolverine: 6 Hours
Marvel, 2003

1-4 .... 3.00

Human Defense Corps
DC, 2003

1-6 .... 3.00

Human Fly
Marvel, 1977

1 .... 3.00
1/35¢ 15.00
2-2/Whitman 2.00
2/35¢ 15.00
3-19 .... 2.00

Human Gargoyles
Eternity, 1988

1-4 .... 2.00

Human Head Comix
Iconografix

1 .... 3.00

Humankind
Image, 2004

1 .... 4.00
1/A 2.00
2-5 .... 3.00

Human Powerhouse
Pure Imagination

1 .... 2.00

Human Race
DC, 2005

1-7 .... 3.00

Human Remains
Black Eye

1 .... 4.00

Human Target
DC, 1999

1-4 .... 3.00

Human Target
DC, 2003

1-21 .... 3.00

Human Target Special
DC, 1991

1 .... 2.00

Human Target: Strike Zone
DC, 2004

1 .... 10.00

Human Torch
Marvel, 1940

1 .... 32,000.00
2 .... 7,400.00
3 .... 4,800.00
4 .... 3,400.00
5 .... 4,650.00
6-7 .... 2,100.00
8 .... 3,400.00
9 .... 2,100.00
10 .... 2,750.00
11-15 .... 1,850.00
16-20 .... 1,250.00
21-30 .... 1,025.00
31-38 .... 850.00

Human Torch
Marvel, 1974

1 .... 9.00
2 .... 4.00
3-8 .... 3.00

Human Torch
Marvel, 2003

1-12 .... 3.00

Humants
Legacy

1-2 .... 2.00

Humbug

1 .... 120.00
2-11 .... 100.00

Hummingbird
Slave Labor, 1996

1 .... 5.00

Humongous Man
Alternative, 1997

1-2 .... 2.00

Humor on the Cutting...Edge
Edge

1-4 .... 3.00

Humphrey Comics
Harvey, 1948

1 .... 50.00
2 .... 30.00
3 .... 22.00
4-10 .... 20.00
11-22 .... 16.00

Hunchback of Notre Dame (Disney's...)
Marvel, 1996

1 .... 5.00

Hunger
Speakeasy Comics, 2005

1-4 .... 3.00

Hunter-Killer
Image, 2004

0 .... 1.00
0/Ltd. 5.00
0/Autographed 20.00
0/Conv 6.00
1/Campbell 3.00
1/Hairsine 4.00
1/Silvestri 5.00
2/Silvestri 3.00
2/Linsner 4.00
3-10 .... 3.00

Hunter-Killer Dossier
Image, 2005

0 .... 3.00

Hunter's Heart
DC

1-3 .... 6.00

Hunter: The Age of Magic
DC, 2001

1 .... 4.00
2-25 .... 3.00

Hunter x Hunter
Viz, 2005

1-5 .... 8.00

Hunt for Black Widow
Fleetway-Quality

1 .... 3.00

Hunting
Northstar, 1993

1 .... 4.00

Huntress
DC, 1989

1 .... 3.00
2-5 .... 2.00
6-19 .... 1.00

Huntress
DC, 1994

1-4 .... 2.00

Hup
Last Gasp, 1986

1-4 .... 3.00

Hurricane Girls
Antarctic, 1995

1-7 .... 4.00

Hurricane LeRoux
Inferno

1 .... 3.00

Hustler Comix
L.F.P., 1997

1-4 .... 5.00

Hustler Comix
L.F.P., 1998

1-5 .... 5.00

Hustler Comix XXX
L.F.P., 1999

1 .... 6.00

Hutch Owen's Working Hard
New Hat

1 .... 4.00

Hy-Breed
Division, 1994

1-3 .... 2.00
4-10 .... 3.00

Hybrid: Etherworlds
Dimension 5

1-3 .... 3.00

Hybrids
Continuity, 1993

0 .... 1.00
1-5 .... 3.00

Hybrids
Continuity, 1994

1 .... 3.00

Hybrids: The Origin
Continuity, 1993

2-5 .... 3.00

Hyde-25
Harris, 1995

0 .... 3.00

Hydrogen Bomb Funnies
Rip Off, 1970

1 .... 5.00

Happy Houlihans

Harbinger

Harbinger Files

Hardcase

Hardcore Station

Hard Looks

Hardware

Hardy Boys

Hydrophidian
NBM

1 .... 11.00

Hyena
Tundra

1-4 .... 4.00

Hyperactives
Alias, 2006

0 .... 1.00

Hyper Comix
Kitchen Sink, 1979

1 .... 5.00

Hyper Dolls
Ironcat, 1998

1-2 .... 3.00

Hyper Dolls
Ironcat, 1998

1-6 .... 3.00

Hyperkind
Marvel, 1993

1 .... 3.00
2-9 .... 2.00

Hyperkind Unleashed!
Marvel, 1994

1 .... 3.00

Hyper Mystery Comics
Hyper, 1940

1 .... 1,500.00
2 .... 1,000.00

Hyper Police
Tokyopop, 2005

1-5 .... 10.00

Hyper Rune
Tokyopop, 2004

1-4 .... 10.00

Hypersonic
Dark Horse, 1997

1-4 .... 3.00

Hyper Violents
CFD, 1996

1 .... 3.00

Hypothetical Lizard (Alan Moore's)
Avatar, 2005

1 .... 4.00
1/Wraparound 5.00
1/Platinum 12.00
1/Tarot-2 .... 4.00
2/Wraparound 5.00
3 .... 4.00
3/Foil 6.00
3/Wraparound 5.00

Hysteria: One Man Gang
Image, 2006

1-2 .... 3.00

i 4 N i
Mermaid, 1994

1-2 .... 2.00

I Am Legend
Eclipse

1-4 .... 6.00

I am Legion: Dancing Faun
DC, 2004

1 .... 7.00

I Before E
Fantagraphics, 1994

1-2 .... 4.00

Ibis the Invincible
Fawcett, 1943

1 .... 1,400.00
2 .... 750.00
3 .... 575.00
4-6 .... 400.00

I-Bots (Isaac Asimov's...)
Tekno, 1995

1-7 .... 2.00

I-Bots (Isaac Asimov's...)
Big, 1996

1-9 .... 2.00

iCandy
DC, 2003

1-6 .... 3.00

Icarus
Aircel, 1987

1-5 .... 2.00

Icarus
Kardia, 1992

1 .... 2.00

Ice Age on the World of Magic: The Gathering
Acclaim, 1995

1-4 .... 3.00

Iceman
Marvel, 1984

1 .... 4.00
2-4 .... 3.00

Iceman
Marvel, 2001

1 .... 4.00
2-4 .... 3.00

Icicle
Hero, 1992

1 .... 5.00
2-5 .... 4.00

I Come In Peace
Greater Mercury

1 .... 2.00

Icon
DC, 1993

1 .... 2.00
1/CS 3.00
2-24 .... 2.00
25 .... 3.00
26 .... 2.00
27-30 .... 3.00
31 .... 1.00
32-42 .... 3.00

Icon Devil
Spider

1-2 .... 2.00

Icon Devil
Spider

2 .... 2.00

Iconografix Special
Iconografix

1 .... 3.00

Iczer 3
CPM, 1996

1-2 .... 3.00

Id
Fantagraphics, 1995

1-3/2nd 3.00

ID4: Independence Day
Marvel, 1996

0 .... 3.00
1-2 .... 2.00

Idaho
Dell, 1963

1 .... 28.00
2-8 .... 18.00

Ideal
Timely, 1948

1 .... 250.00
2 .... 225.00
3-4 .... 200.00
5 .... 150.00

Ideal Comics
Timely, 1944

1 .... 150.00
2 .... 100.00
3-4 .... 75.00

Ideal Romance
Key, 1954

3 .... 50.00
4-8 .... 35.00

Id_entity
Tokyopop, 2005

1-4 .... 10.00

Identity Crisis
DC, 2004

1 .... 15.00
1/2nd 6.00
1/3rd 5.00
1/Sketch 225.00
2 .... 8.00
3 .... 7.00
4 .... 8.00
5 .... 7.00
6 .... 8.00
7 .... 7.00

Identity Disc
Marvel, 2004

1-5 .... 3.00

I Die at Midnight
DC, 2000

1 .... 3.00

Idiotland
Fantagraphics, 1993

1-6 .... 3.00

Idle Worship
Visceral

1 .... 3.00

Idol
Marvel

1-3 .... 3.00

I Dream of Jeannie
Dell, 1966

1 .... 60.00
2 .... 40.00

I Dream of Jeannie
Airwave, 2002

1 .... 3.00
Ann 1 .... 4.00

I Feel Sick
Slave Labor, 1999

1 .... 4.00

If the Devil Would Talk
Catholic Guild, 1950

1 .... 850.00

If the Devil Would Talk
Impact, 1958

1 .... 450.00

Igrat
Verotik, 1995

1 .... 3.00

Igrat Illustrations
Verotik, 1997

1 .... 4.00

I Had a Dream
King Ink Empire, 1995

1 .... 3.00

I (Heart) Marvel: Marvel AI
Marvel, 2006

1 .... 3.00

I (Heart) Marvel: Masked Intentions
Marvel, 2006

1 .... 3.00

Hari Kari

Harlem Globetrotters

Harlem Heroes

Harlequin

Harley Quinn

Harley Rider

Harpy Preview

Harrier Preview

I (Heart) Marvel: My Mutant Heart
Marvel, 2006
1 .... 3.00

I (Heart) Marvel: Outlaw Love
Marvel, 2006
1 .... 3.00

I (Heart) Marvel: Web of Romance
Marvel, 2006
1 .... 3.00

I Hunt Monsters
Antarctic, 2004
1-9 .... 3.00

I Hunt Monsters
Antarctic, 2005
1-9 .... 3.00

Ike and Kitzi
A Capella
1 .... 3.00

Iliad
Slave Labor, 1997
1-2 .... 3.00

Iliad II
Micmac, 1986
1-3 .... 2.00

Illegal Alien
Kitchen Sink
1 .... 10.00

Illegal Aliens
Eclipse, 1999
1 .... 3.00

Illuminations
Monolith, 1995
1-5 .... 3.00

Illuminator
Marvel, 1993
1-2 .... 5.00
3 .... 3.00

Illuminatus
Eye-N-Apple
1-2 .... 2.00

Illuminatus!
Rip Off, 1990
1-3 .... 3.00

Illustrated Classex
Comic Zone, 1991
1 .... 3.00

Illustrated Dore: Book of Genesis
Tome
1 .... 3.00

Illustrated Dore: Book of the Apocrypha
Tome
1 .... 3.00

Illustrated Editions
Thwack! Pow!, 1995
1 .... 2.00

Illustrated Kama Sutra
NBM
1 .... 13.00

Illustrated Life of Seymour
Sofa Comics
1-4 .... 3.00

Illustrated Stories of the Operas
Bailey, 1943
1-4 .... 400.00

Illustrated Tales (Jaxon's...)
FTR
1 .... 2.00

I Loved
Fox, 1949
29-32 .... 75.00

I Love Lucy
Eternity, 1990
1-6 .... 3.00

I Love Lucy Book Two
Eternity, 1990
1-6 .... 3.00

I Love Lucy Comics
Dell, 1954
3 .... 110.00
4 .... 85.00
5 .... 70.00
6-10 .... 55.00
11-20 .... 45.00
21-35 .... 36.00

I Love Lucy in 3-D
Eternity
1 .... 4.00

I Love Lucy in Full Color
Eternity
1 .... 6.00

I Love New York
Linsner.com, 2002
1 .... 10.00

I Love You
Charlton, 1955
7 .... 55.00
8-10 .... 16.00
11-16 .... 14.00
17 .... 18.00
18-20 .... 14.00
21-30 .... 12.00
31-50 .... 10.00

51-59 .... 8.00
60 .... 60.00
61-69 .... 4.00
70-121 .... 3.00
122-130 .... 2.00

I Love You
Avalon
1 .... 3.00

I Love You Special
Avalon
1 .... 3.00

I, Lusiphur
Mulehide
1 .... 20.00
2 .... 12.00
3 .... 15.00
4 .... 12.00
5 .... 10.00
6-7 .... 8.00

I Luv Halloween
Tokyopop, 2005
1 .... 10.00

Image
Image, 1993
0 .... 4.00

Image Comics Holiday Special 2005
Image, 2006
1 .... 10.00

Image Introduces... Believer
Image, 2001
1 .... 3.00

Image Introduces... Cryptopia
Image, 2002
1 .... 3.00

Image Introduces... Dog Soldiers
Image, 2002
1 .... 3.00

Image Introduces... Legend of Isis
Image, 2002
1 .... 3.00

Image Introduces... Primate
Image, 2001
1/A-1/B 3.00

Image of the Beast
Last Gasp, 1979
1 .... 3.00

Image Plus
Image, 1993
1 .... 2.00

Images of a Distant Soil
Image, 1997
1 .... 3.00

Images of Omaha
Kitchen Sink, 1992
1-2 .... 4.00

Images of Shadowhawk
Image, 1993
1-3 .... 2.00

Image Two-In-One
Image, 2001
1 .... 3.00

Imagi-Mation
Imagi-Mation
1-2 .... 2.00

Imaginaries
Image, 2005
1-4 .... 3.00

Imagine
Star*Reach, 1978
1 .... 20.00
1/2nd-2 .... 10.00
3 .... 15.00
4 .... 10.00
5-6 .... 6.00

I'm Dickens... He's Fenster
Dell, 1963
1 .... 25.00
2 .... 20.00

Immortal Combat
Express, 1995
1 .... 3.00

Immortal Doctor Fate
DC, 1985
1-3 .... 2.00

Immortal II
Image, 1997
1-5 .... 3.00

Immortal Iron Fist
Marvel, 2007
1 .... 8.00
2 .... 6.00

Immortals
Comics By Day
1 .... 1.00

Imp
Slave Labor, 1994
1 .... 3.00

Impact
E.C., 1955
1 .... 225.00
2 .... 125.00
3-4 .... 90.00
5 .... 80.00

Harriers

Harry the Cop

Harsh Realm

Harvey

Harvey Collectors Comics

Harvey Comics Library

Harvey Hits

Hate

Impact

RCP, 1999

1-5 .... 3.00
Ann 1 .... 14.00

Impact Christmas Special

DC, 1991

1 .... 3.00

Impact Comics Who's Who

DC, 1991

1-3 .... 5.00

Impaler

Image, 2006

1-2 .... 3.00

Imperial Dragons

Alias, 2005

1 .... 1.00

Imperial Guard

Marvel, 1997

1-3 .... 2.00

Impossible Man Summer Vacation Spectacular

Marvel, 1990

1-2 .... 2.00

Impulse

DC, 1995

1-2 .... 4.00
3-5 .... 3.00
6-64 .... 2.00
65-89 .... 3.00
1000000 .... 4.00
Ann 1 .... 5.00
Ann 2 .... 4.00

Impulse/Atom Double-Shot

DC, 1998

1 .... 2.00

Impulse: Bart Saves the Universe

DC

1 .... 6.00

Impulse Plus

DC, 1997

1 .... 3.00

Imp-Unity

Spoof

1 .... 3.00

Incomplete Death's Head

Marvel, 1993

1 .... 3.00
2-12 .... 2.00

In-Country Nam

Survival Arts

1-2 .... 2.00

Incredible Drinkin' Buddies

Luxurious

1 .... 3.00

Incredible Hulk

Marvel, 1962

-1 .... 2.00
1 .... 13,000.00
☛1st Hulk
2 .... 3,500.00
3 .... 2,000.00
4-5 .... 1,750.00
6 .... 2,250.00
102 .... 150.00
103 .... 100.00
104 .... 75.00
105 .... 70.00
106-112 .... 50.00
113-115 .... 40.00
116-121 .... 35.00
122 .... 55.00
☛Thing vs. Hulk
123-125 .... 30.00
126-130 .... 25.00
131 .... 30.00
132 .... 25.00
133 .... 20.00
134-136 .... 16.00
137-140 .... 20.00
☛Harlan Ellison
140/2nd 3.00
☛1st Doc Samson
141-151 .... 20.00
152 .... 25.00
153-160 .... 20.00
161 .... 30.00
162 .... 55.00
☛1st Wendigo
163-171 .... 15.00
172 .... 25.00
☛X-Men app.
173-176 .... 15.00
177-178 .... 17.00
179 .... 16.00
180 .... 180.00
☛Wolverine cameo
181 .... 750.00
☛1st Wolverine story
181/Ace 5.00
182 .... 100.00
☛2nd Wolverine
183 .... 12.00
184-190 .... 10.00
191-198 .... 8.00
198/30¢ 20.00
199 .... 8.00
199/30¢ 20.00
200 .... 11.00
200/30¢ 30.00
201 .... 7.00
201/30¢ 20.00

202 .... 7.00
202/30¢ 20.00
203-212/Whitman 7.00
212/35¢ 15.00
213-213/Whitman 7.00
213/35¢ 15.00
214-214/Whitman 7.00
214/35¢ 15.00
215-215/Whitman 7.00
215/35¢ 15.00
216-216/Whitman 7.00
216/35¢ 15.00
217-218/Whitman 7.00
219-240 .... 5.00
241-249 .... 4.00
250 .... 7.00
251-285 .... 3.00
286 .... 4.00
287-295 .... 3.00
296 .... 5.00
297 .... 4.00
298-299 .... 3.00
300 .... 4.00
301-319 .... 3.00
320-323 .... 2.00
324 .... 5.00
325 .... 3.00
326 .... 4.00
327-328 .... 3.00
329 .... 2.00
☛1st McFarlane
330-334 .... 5.00
335 .... 2.00
336-339 .... 3.00
340 .... 14.00
☛vs. Wolverine
341 .... 4.00
342-349 .... 2.00
350 .... 5.00
☛1st Dale Keown
351-371 .... 2.00
372 .... 3.00
373-376 .... 2.00
377 .... 3.00
377/2nd-377/3rd 2.00
378 .... 3.00
379-384 .... 2.00
385 .... 4.00
386 .... 3.00
387-391 .... 2.00
392 .... 3.00
393 .... 4.00
393/2nd-394 .... 3.00
395-399 .... 2.00
400-400/2nd 3.00
401-418 .... 2.00
418/Variant 3.00
419-425 .... 2.00
425/Variant 4.00
426-448 .... 2.00
449 .... 8.00
450 .... 5.00
451-474 .... 2.00
Ann 1 .... 115.00
Ann 2 .... 40.00
Ann 3-4 .... 25.00
Ann 5 .... 9.00
Ann 6 .... 7.00
Ann 7 .... 9.00
Ann 8 .... 5.00
Ann 9 .... 3.00
Ann 10 .... 4.00
Ann 11-19 .... 3.00
Ann 20 .... 4.00
Ann 1997-1998 .... 3.00
Ashcan 1 .... 1.00

Incredible Hulk

Marvel, 1999

☛Cont'd from Hulk
12-20 .... 3.00
21-24 .... 2.00
25 .... 3.00
26-33 .... 2.00
34 .... 13.00
☛Bruce Jones starts
35 .... 6.00
36-38 .... 5.00
39-41 .... 4.00
42-46 .... 3.00
47-49 .... 2.00
50 .... 5.00
51 .... 4.00
52-54 .... 3.00
55-63 .... 2.00
64 .... 3.00
65-66 .... 2.00
67-72 .... 3.00
73-74 .... 2.00
75-76 .... 4.00
77-82 .... 3.00
83 .... 5.00
83/Variant 4.00
☛2nd print
84 .... 3.00
84/Variant 4.00
☛2nd print
85-91 .... 3.00
92 .... 25.00
92/2nd 6.00
93-99 .... 3.00
100-100/Variant 4.00
101-115 .... 3.00
Ann 1999 .... 5.00
Ann 2000 .... 4.00
Ann 2001 .... 3.00

Incredible Hulk and the Thing: The Big Chance

Marvel

1 .... 6.00

Haunted

Haunted Love

Haunted Thrills

Haunt of Horror

Hawkshaws

Haywire

H-Bomb

Headbanger

Incredible Hulk and Wolverine

Marvel, 1986

1 .... 7.00
1/2nd 4.00

Incredible Hulk: Future Imperfect

Marvel, 1993

1-2 .... 6.00

Incredible Hulk: Hercules Unleashed

Marvel, 1996

1 .... 3.00

Incredible Hulk Megazine

Marvel, 1996

1 .... 4.00

Incredible Hulk: Nightmerica

Marvel, 2003

1-6 .... 3.00

Incredible Hulk Poster Magazine

Marvel

1/A 4.00
1/B 2.00

Incredible Hulk: The End

Marvel, 2002

1 .... 6.00

Incredible Hulk Versus Quasimodo

Marvel, 1983

1 .... 2.00

Incredible Hulk vs. Superman

Marvel, 1999

1 .... 6.00

Incredible Hulk vs. Venom

Marvel, 1994

1 .... 3.00

Incredible Mr. Limpet

Dell, 1964

1 .... 25.00

Incredible Science Fiction

E.C., 1955

30-33 .... 250.00

Incredibles

Dark Horse, 2004

1-4 .... 3.00

Incubus

Palliard

1-2 .... 3.00

Independent Publisher's Group Spotlight

Hero, 1993

0 .... 4.00

Independent Voices

Peregrine Entertainment, 1998

1 .... 2.00
2-3 .... 3.00

Indiana Jones and the Arms of Gold

Dark Horse, 1994

1-6 .... 3.00

Indiana Jones and the Fate of Atlantis

Dark Horse, 1991

1-4 .... 3.00

Indiana Jones and the Golden Fleece

Dark Horse, 1994

1-2 .... 3.00

Indiana Jones and the Iron Phoenix

Dark Horse, 1994

1-4 .... 3.00

Indiana Jones and the Last Crusade

Marvel, 1989

1-4 .... 1.00

Indiana Jones and the Last Crusade (Magazine)

Marvel, 1989

1 .... 3.00

Indiana Jones and the Sargasso Pirates

Dark Horse, 1995

1-4 .... 3.00

Indiana Jones and the Shrine of the Sea Devil

Dark Horse, 1994

1 .... 3.00

Indiana Jones and the Spear of Destiny

Dark Horse, 1995

1-4 .... 3.00

Indiana Jones and the Temple of Doom

Marvel, 1984

1-3 .... 2.00

Indiana Jones: Thunder in the Orient

Dark Horse, 1993

1-6 .... 3.00

Indian Chief
Dell, 1951
3 .... 40.00
4-12 .... 30.00
13-29 .... 25.00
30-33 .... 22.00

Indian Fighter
Dell, 1950
1 .... 75.00
2 .... 50.00
3-11 .... 35.00

Indians
Fiction House, 1950
1 .... 200.00
2 .... 135.00
3-5 .... 100.00
6-10 .... 70.00
11-17 .... 48.00

Indians on the Warpath
St. John, 1949
1 .... 200.00

Indian Summer
NBM
1 .... 22.00

Indian Warriors
Star Publications, 1951
7 .... 100.00
8 .... 80.00

Indigo Vertigo One Shot
Image
1 .... 5.00

In Dream World
Tokyopop, 2005
1-3 .... 10.00

Industrial Gothic
DC, 1995
1-5 .... 3.00

Industrial Strength Preview
Silver Skull
1 .... 2.00

Industry of War One-Shot
Image, 2006
1 .... 8.00

Indy Buzz
Blindwolf, 1999
1 .... 3.00

Inedible Adventures of Clint the Carrot
Hot Leg, 1994
1 .... 3.00

Infantry
Devil's Due, 2004
1 .... 3.00
1/Alternative 4.00
2-3 .... 3.00

Infectious
Fantaco
1 .... 4.00

Inferior Five
DC, 1967
1 .... 24.00
2 .... 16.00
3-10 .... 14.00
11-12 .... 10.00

Inferno
Aircel, 1990
1-4 .... 3.00

Inferno
Caliber, 1995
1 .... 3.00

Inferno
DC, 1997
1-4 .... 3.00

Inferno: Hellbound
Image, 2002
0-3 .... 3.00

Infinite Crisis
DC, 2005
1/Perez-1/Lee 6.00
1/2nd 4.00
1/RRP 450.00
2/Perez-4/Lee 6.00
5/Perez-7 .... 4.00

Infinite Crisis Secret Files 2006
DC, 2006
1 .... 12.00

Infinite Kung Fu
Kagan McLeod, 2000
1-1/2nd 5.00

Infinity Abyss
Marvel, 2002
1-5 .... 3.00
6 .... 4.00

Infinity Charade
Parody
1/A-1/B 3.00
1/Gold 4.00

Infinity Crusade
Marvel, 1993
1 .... 4.00
2-6 .... 3.00

Infinity Gauntlet
Marvel, 1991
1-6 .... 3.00

Infinity Graphics Presents
Infinity, 1987
1 .... 2.00

Infinity, Inc.
DC, 1984
1 .... 3.00

Headbuster

Headhunters

Headless Horseman

Headline Comics

Heap

Heartbreak Comics

Heartbreakers

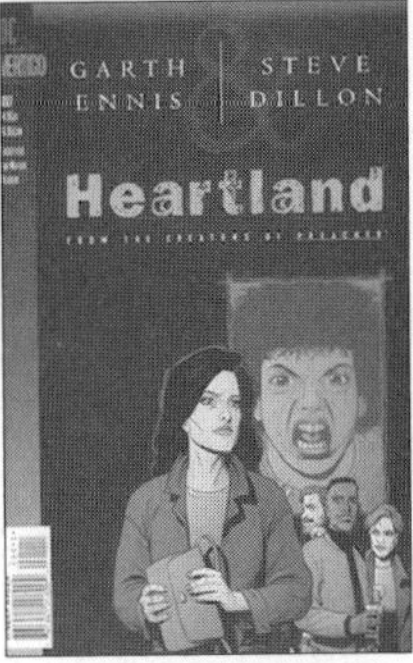

Heartland

2-10 .... 2.00
11-13 .... 1.00
14 .... 4.00
☛McFarlane starts
15-37 .... 3.00
38-45 .... 1.00
46 .... 2.00
47-49 .... 1.00
50 .... 3.00
51-52 .... 1.00
53 .... 2.00
Ann 1-2 .... 3.00
Special 1 .... 2.00

Infinity of Warriors
Ominous, 1994
1 .... 2.00

Infinity War
Marvel, 1992
1-6 .... 3.00

Infochameleon: Company Cult
Mediawarp, 1997
1 .... 5.00

Informer
Feature, 1954
1 .... 48.00
2 .... 34.00
3-5 .... 28.00

In His Steps
Marvel
1 .... 10.00

Inhumanoids
Marvel, 1987
1-4 .... 1.00

Inhumans
Marvel, 1975
1 .... 8.00
2-4 .... 4.00
4/30¢ 7.00
5 .... 4.00
6 .... 3.00
6/30¢ 20.00
7-11 .... 3.00
11/35¢ 15.00
12 .... 3.00
12/35¢ 15.00
Special 1 .... 4.00

Inhumans
Marvel, 1998
1-1/Variant 4.00
2/A-12 .... 3.00

Inhumans
Marvel, 2000
1-4 .... 3.00

Inhumans
Marvel, 2003
1-12 .... 3.00

Inhumans: The Great Refuge
Marvel, 1995
1 .... 3.00

Inhumans: The Untold Saga
Marvel, 1977
1 .... 4.00

Initial D
Tokyopop, 2002
1-20 .... 10.00

Inkpunks Quarterly
Funk-O-Tron
1-3 .... 3.00

In Love
Mainline, 1954
1 .... 130.00
2 .... 85.00
3-4 .... 70.00
5-6 .... 35.00

Inmates Prisoners Of Society
Delta, 1997
1-4 .... 3.00

Innercircle
Mushroom, 1995
0.1-0.3 .... 3.00

Inner-City Products
Hype
1 .... 2.00

Inner City Romance
Last Gasp, 1972
1 .... 5.00
2-5 .... 3.00

Innocent Bystander
Ollie Ollie! Oxen Free, 1997
1-6 .... 3.00

Innocent Ones
Fantagraphics, 2005
1 .... 8.00

Innocents
Image, 2006
1 .... 3.00

Innovation Preview Special
Innovation, 1989
1 .... 1.00

Innovation Spectacular
Innovation, 1990
1-2 .... 3.00

Innovation Summer Fun Special
Innovation
1 .... 4.00

Inovators
Dark Moon, 1995

1 .... 3.00

In Rage
CFD, 1994

1 .... 3.00

Insane
Dark Horse, 1988

1-2 .... 2.00

Insane Clown Posse
Chaos!, 1999

1 .... 3.00
1/A 4.00
2 .... 3.00
2/CS 4.00
3 .... 3.00
3/A 4.00
4 .... 3.00
4/CS 4.00
5 .... 3.00
5/CS 4.00
6 .... 3.00
6/CS 4.00
7 .... 3.00
7/CS 4.00
8 .... 3.00
8/CS 4.00
9-11 .... 3.00
11/CS 4.00
12-12/CS 3.00

In Search of Shirley
NBM

1 .... 10.00

In Search of the Castaways
Gold Key, 1963

1 .... 20.00

Insect Man's 25th Anniversary Special
Entertainment, 1991

1 .... 2.00

Inside Crime
Fox, 1950

1 .... 150.00
2-3 .... 140.00

Inside Out King
Free Fall

1-1/2nd 3.00

Insomnia
Fantagraphics, 2005

1 .... 8.00

Insomnia
Fantagraphics, 2005

1 .... 8.00

Inspector
Gold Key, 1974

1 .... 20.00
2 .... 10.00
3-19 .... 5.00

Inspector Gill of the Fish Police
Apple, 1991

0 .... 3.00

Instant Piano
Dark Horse, 1994

1-4 .... 4.00

Intense!
Pure Imagination

1-3 .... 3.00

Interactive Comics
Adventure

1-2 .... 5.00

Interface
Marvel, 1989

1 .... 3.00
2-8 .... 2.00

Internal Fury
Fierce Comics, 2005

1 .... 2.00
2 .... 2.00
3-4 .... 4.00

International Comics
E.C., 1947

1 .... 425.00
2 .... 275.00
3-5 .... 240.00

International Cowgirl Magazine
Iconografix

1-2 .... 3.00

International Crime Patrol
E.C., 1948

6 .... 375.00

International Fallout Shelter Zone
KHB

1-4 .... 1.00

Interplanetary Lizards of the Texas Plains
Leadbelly, 1991

0 .... 3.00
1-7 .... 2.00
8 .... 3.00

Interstellar Overdrive
Leonine, 1990

1-2 .... 1.00

Interview With the Vampire (Anne Rice's...)
Innovation, 1991

1-12 .... 3.00

In the Days of the Ace Rock 'n' Roll Club
Fantagraphics

1 .... 5.00

Heart of Darkness

Heart of Empire

Hearts of Darkness

Heathcliff

Heavy Armor

Heavy Liquid

Heavy Metal

Heavy Metal Havoc

In The Days of the Mob
DC, 1971

1 .... 50.00

In the Presence of Mine Enemies
Spire

1 .... 7.00

In Thin Air
Tome

1/A-1/B 3.00

Intimate Confessions
I.W., 1964

9-10 .... 12.00

Intimate Confessions
Realistic Comics, 1951

1 .... 375.00
2 .... 150.00
3-7 .... 115.00

Intimate Love
Standard, 1950

5-10 .... 24.00
11-20 .... 14.00
21-28 .... 10.00

Intimates
DC, 2005

1-12 .... 3.00

Intimate Secrets of Romance
Star Publications, 1953

1 .... 95.00
2 .... 65.00

Intimidators
Image, 2006

1-4 .... 4.00

Intrazone
Brainstorm, 1993

1 .... 3.00
1/Ltd. 6.00
2 .... 3.00
2/Ltd. 6.00

Intrigue
Quality, 1955

1 .... 150.00

Intrigue
Image, 1999

1/A-3 .... 3.00

Intruder Comics Module
TSR

1-9 .... 3.00

Inu-Yasha
Viz, 1997

1-15 .... 3.00

Inu-Yasha Part 2
Viz, 1998

1-9 .... 3.00

Inu-Yasha Part 3
Viz, 1999

1-7 .... 3.00

Inu-Yasha Part 4
Viz, 1999

1-7 .... 3.00

Inu-Yasha Part 5
Viz, 2000

1-11 .... 3.00

Inu-Yasha Part 6
Viz, 2001

1-15 .... 3.00

Inu-Yasha Part 7
Viz, 2002

1-7 .... 3.00

Invaders
Gold Key, 1967

1 .... 40.00
2-4 .... 28.00

Invaders
Marvel, 1975

1 .... 18.00
2 .... 10.00
3-4 .... 6.00
5-6 .... 5.00
6/30¢ 20.00
7 .... 5.00
7/30¢ 20.00
8-9 .... 5.00
10-17/Whitman 4.00
17/35¢ 7.00
18-18/Whitman 4.00
18/35¢ 7.00
19-19/Whitman 4.00
19/35¢ 7.00
20-20/Whitman 5.00
20/35¢ 10.00
21-21/Whitman 3.00
21/35¢ 6.00
22-30 .... 4.00
31-32 .... 3.00
33 .... 4.00
34-40 .... 3.00
41 .... 4.00
Ann 1 .... 12.00

Invaders
Marvel, 1993

1-4 .... 2.00

Invaders
Marvel, 2004
0-9 .... 3.00

Invaders from Home
DC
1-6 .... 3.00

Invaders from Mars
Eternity, 1990
1-3 .... 3.00

Invaders from Mars (Book II)
Eternity, 1990
1-3 .... 3.00

Invasion!
DC, 1989
1-3 .... 3.00

Invasion
Avalon
1 .... 3.00

Invasion '55
Apple, 1990
1-3 .... 2.00

Invasion of the Mind Sappers
Fantagraphics, 1996
1 .... 9.00

Invasion of the Space Amazons from the Purple Planet
Grizmart, 1997
1-3 .... 2.00

Invert
Caliber
1 .... 3.00

Invincible
Image, 2003
0 .... 1.00
1 .... 25.00
2-4 .... 12.00
5-11 .... 7.00
12-15 .... 5.00
16-24 .... 3.00
25 .... 5.00
26-37 .... 3.00

Invincible Ed
Summertime, 2002
1-2 .... 4.00

Invincible Ed
Dark Horse, 2003
1-4 .... 3.00

Invincible Four of Kung Fu & Ninja
Dr. Leung's
1-5 .... 2.00

Invincible Man
Junko, 1998
1 .... 5.00
1/Ltd. 8.00

Invincibles
CFD, 1997
1 .... 3.00

Invincible Script Book
Image, 2006
1 .... 4.00

Invisible 9
Flypaper, 1998
1 .... 3.00

Invisible Dirty Old Man
Red Giant
1 .... 4.00

Invisible Frontier
NBM
1 .... 16.00

Invisible People
Kitchen Sink
1-3 .... 3.00

Invisible Scarlet O'Neil
Harvey, 1950
1 .... 165.00
2 .... 90.00
3 .... 75.00

Invisibles
DC, 1994
1 .... 4.00
2-3 .... 3.00
4-8 .... 2.00
9-24 .... 3.00
25 .... 4.00

Invisibles
DC, 1997
1-22 .... 3.00

Invisibles
DC, 1999
12-1 .... 3.00

Invisoworld
Eternity
1 .... 2.00

I.N.V.U.
Tokyopop, 2003
1-2 .... 10.00

Io
Invictus, 1994
1-3 .... 2.00

Ion
DC, 2006
1-9 .... 3.00

Hectic Planet

Hedy De Vine Comics

Hee Haw

He Is Just a Rat

Hellbender

Hellblazer

Hellboy Christmas Special

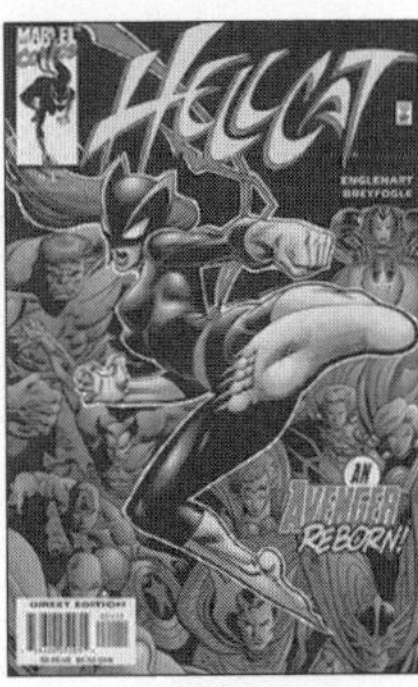

Hellcat

I, Paparazzi

DC

1 .... 30.00

Ironcat

Ironcat, 1999

1-2 .... 3.00

Iron Corporal

Charlton, 1985

23-25 .... 2.00

Iron Corporal

Avalon

1 .... 3.00

Iron Devil

Fantagraphics, 1994

1-3 .... 3.00

Iron Fist

Marvel, 1975

1 .... 35.00
2 .... 12.00
3 .... 10.00
4 .... 8.00
4/30¢ 20.00
5 .... 8.00
5/30¢ 20.00
6 .... 8.00
6/30¢ 20.00
7-13 .... 8.00
13/35¢ 10.00
14 .... 80.00
☛1st Sabretooth
14/35¢ 150.00
15 .... 27.00
☛X-Men app.
15/35¢ 75.00

Iron Fist

Marvel, 1996

1-2 .... 2.00

Iron Fist

Marvel, 1998

1-3 .... 3.00

Iron Fist

Marvel, 2004

1-6 .... 3.00

Iron Fist: Wolverine

Marvel, 2000

1-4 .... 3.00

Iron Ghost

Image, 2005

1-6 .... 3.00

Ironhand of Almuric

Dark Horse

1-4 .... 2.00

Ironjaw

Atlas-Seaboard, 1975

1 .... 9.00
2-3 .... 6.00
4 .... 8.00

Iron Lantern

Marvel, 1997

1 .... 2.00

Iron Man

Marvel, 1968

1 .... 275.00
2-4 .... 60.00
5 .... 55.00
6-7 .... 50.00
8 .... 40.00
9 .... 90.00
10 .... 42.00
11-12 .... 35.00
13-17 .... 27.00
18-20 .... 25.00
21-30 .... 20.00
31-40 .... 15.00
41-42 .... 12.00
43 .... 35.00
☛1st Guardsman
44 .... 12.00
45-46 .... 15.00
47 .... 35.00
☛Barry Smith art
48-50 .... 12.00
51 .... 17.00
52-53 .... 10.00
54 .... 16.00
55 .... 110.00
☛1st Thanos
56-67 .... 15.00
68-85 .... 10.00
85/30¢ 20.00
86 .... 10.00
86/30¢ 20.00
87 .... 10.00
87/30¢ 20.00
88 .... 10.00
88/30¢ 20.00
89 .... 10.00
89/30¢ 20.00
90-95 .... 10.00
95/Whitman 18.00
96 .... 10.00
96/Whitman 18.00
97 .... 10.00
98 .... 8.00
98/Whitman 18.00
99 .... 8.00
99/Whitman 18.00
99/35¢ 15.00
100 .... 12.00
100/Whitman 20.00
100/35¢ 18.00
101 .... 7.00
101/Whitman 14.00
101/35¢ 12.00
102 .... 7.00
102/Whitman 14.00
102/35¢ 12.00
103 .... 7.00
103/Whitman 14.00

103/35¢ 12.00
104 .... 7.00
104/Whitman 14.00
105-113 .... 7.00
113/Whitman 14.00
114 .... 7.00
114/Whitman 14.00
115 .... 7.00
115/Whitman 14.00
116 .... 7.00
116/Whitman 14.00
117 .... 7.00
117/Whitman 14.00
118 .... 7.00
118/Whitman 14.00
119 .... 7.00
119/Whitman 14.00
120-122 .... 7.00
122/Whitman 14.00
☛Alcoholism issue
123-129 .... 7.00
130-149 .... 5.00
150 .... 7.00
151-153 .... 5.00
154 .... 7.00
155-159 .... 5.00
160 .... 7.00
161-170 .... 5.00
171-181 .... 3.00
182 .... 4.00
183-185 .... 3.00
186 .... 4.00
187-191 .... 3.00
192 .... 4.00
193-200 .... 3.00
201-224 .... 2.00
225-232/A 3.00
233-243 .... 2.00
244 .... 3.00
245-250 .... 2.00
251-257 .... 1.00
258-280 .... 2.00
281-282 .... 3.00
283-284 .... 2.00
285-287 .... 1.00
288 .... 3.00
289 .... 1.00
290 .... 4.00
291-299 .... 1.00
300 .... 3.00
300/Variant 4.00
301-304 .... 1.00
305-310 .... 2.00
310/CS 3.00
311-316 .... 2.00
317 .... 3.00
318-324 .... 2.00
325 .... 3.00
326-332 .... 2.00
Ann 1 .... 27.00
Ann 2 .... 20.00
Ann 3 .... 10.00
Ann 4 .... 4.00
Ann 5-10 .... 3.00
Ann 11-13 .... 2.00
Ann 14-15 .... 3.00
Ashcan 1 .... 2.00

Iron Man
Marvel, 1996

1-1/A 3.00
2-11 .... 2.00
12 .... 4.00
13 .... 3.00

Iron Man
Marvel, 1998

1-1/A 4.00
2 .... 2.00
2/Variant 3.00
3-12 .... 2.00
13 .... 3.00
14-45 .... 2.00
46 .... 4.00
47-49 .... 2.00
50 .... 3.00
51-66 .... 2.00
67-83 .... 3.00
84 .... 8.00
☛Avengers Disassemble
85 .... 5.00
86-89 .... 3.00
Ann 1998-2000 .... 4.00
Ann 2001 .... 3.00

Iron Man
Marvel, 2004

1 .... 4.00
2-16 .... 3.00
16/Variant 14.00
17-30 .... 3.00

Iron Man & Sub-Mariner
Marvel, 1968

1 .... 100.00

Iron Man: Bad Blood
Marvel, 2000

1-4 .... 3.00

Iron Man Battlebook
Marvel, 1998

1 .... 4.00

Iron Man/Captain America: Casualties of War
Marvel, 2007

1 .... 4.00

Iron Man: House of M
Marvel, 2005

1 .... 5.00
1/Variant 4.00
☛2nd print
2-3 .... 3.00

Iron Man: Hypervelocity
Marvel, 2007

1 .... 3.00

Hellcop

Hellhole

Hellsaint

Hellsing

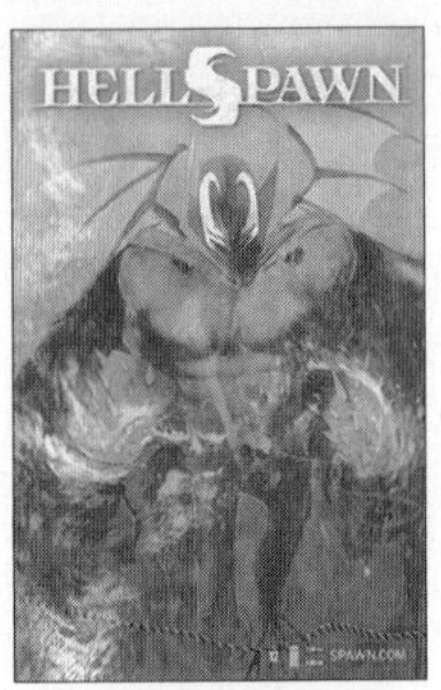

Hellspawn

Hellstalker

Helter Skelter

He-Man

Iron Man: The Inevitable
Marvel, 2006

1-6 ....3.00

Iron Man: The Iron Age
Marvel, 1998

1-2 ....6.00

Iron Man: The Legend
Marvel, 1996

1 ....4.00

Iron Man 2020
Marvel, 1994

1 ....6.00

Iron Manual
Marvel, 1993

1 ....2.00

Iron Man/X-O Manowar: Heavy Metal
Marvel, 1996

1 ....3.00

Iron Marshal
Jademan, 1990

1-32 ....2.00

Iron Saga's Anthology
Iron Saga, 1987

1 ....2.00

Iron West
Image, 2006

1 ....15.00

Iron Wings
Action, 1999

1 ....3.00

Iron Wings
Image, 2000

1 ....3.00

Ironwolf
DC, 1986

1 ....2.00

Ironwood
Fantagraphics, 1991

1-6 ....2.00
7-10 ....3.00

Irredeemable Ant-Man
Marvel, 2006

1-4 ....3.00

I Saw It
Educomics

1 ....2.00

Isis
DC, 1976

1 ....6.00
2-8 ....4.00

Island of Dr. Moreau
Marvel, 1977

1 ....3.00

Ismet
Canis, 1981

1-5 ....1.00

I Spy
Gold Key, 1966

1 ....55.00
2 ....40.00
3-6 ....33.00

Is This Tomorrow?
Catechetical Guild, 1947

1-1/B 125.00

Itchy & Scratchy Comics
Bongo, 1993

1 ....3.00
2-Holiday 1 ....2.00

Itchy Planet
Fantagraphics, 1988

1-3 ....2.00

It Really Happened
Visual Editions, 1945

1 ....85.00
2 ....60.00
3-5 ....45.00
6-7 ....38.00
8 ....70.00
9 ....38.00
10 ....50.00
11 ....38.00

It's a Bird
DC, 2004

1 ....25.00

It's About Time
Gold Key, 1967

1 ....25.00

It's a Duck's Life
Atlas, 1950

1 ....55.00
2 ....40.00
3-5 ....35.00
6-11 ....26.00

It's Fun to Stay Alive
National Automobile Dealers Association, 1947

1 ....60.00

It's Game Time
DC, 1955

1 ....285.00
2-3 ....190.00
4 ....165.00

Itsi Kitsi
Funny Book Institute, 2000

1 ....3.00

It's Love, Love, Love
St. John, 1957

1 ....30.00
2 ....26.00

It's Only a Matter of Life and Death
Fantagraphics
1 .... 4.00

It's Science With Dr. Radium
Slave Labor, 1986
1-7 .... 2.00
Special 1 .... 3.00

It! The Terror from Beyond Space
Millennium, 1993
1-4 .... 3.00

I Want to Be Your Dog
Fantagraphics, 1990
1-5 .... 2.00

J2
Marvel, 1998
1-12 .... 2.00

Jab
Adhesive, 1993
1-5 .... 3.00

Jab
Cummings Design Group, 1994
3 .... 3.00

Jab
Funny Papers, 1993
1-2 .... 3.00

Jace Pearson of the Texas Rangers
Dell, 1951
1 .... 0.00
2-9 .... 45.00

Jace Pearson's Tales of the Texas Rangers
Dell, 1956
11 .... 35.00
12-20 .... 42.00

Jack
Med Systems Company, 1995
1 .... 3.00

Jack Armstrong
Parents' Magazine Institute, 1947
1 .... 225.00
2 .... 95.00
3-5 .... 58.00
6-11 .... 52.00
12 .... 85.00
13 .... 52.00

Jackaroo
Eternity, 1990
1-3 .... 2.00

Jack Cross
DC, 2005
1-4 .... 3.00

Jack Frost
Amazing
1-2 .... 2.00

Jack Hunter
Blackthorne, 1988
1 .... 1.00

Jackie Gleason
St. John, 1955
1 .... 385.00
2 .... 225.00
3-4 .... 185.00

Jackie Gleason and the Honeymooners
DC, 1956
1 .... 440.00
2 .... 300.00
3-4 .... 220.00
5-6 .... 165.00
7-9 .... 135.00
10-11 .... 125.00
12 .... 250.00

Jackie Jokers
Harvey, 1973
1 .... 12.00
2-4 .... 10.00

Jackie Robinson
Fawcett, 1950
1 .... 400.00
2 .... 225.00
3-5 .... 200.00
6 .... 165.00

Jack in the Box Comics
Charlton, 1946
11 .... 85.00
12 .... 45.00
13 .... 60.00
14-16 .... 45.00

Jack Kirby's Galactic Bounty Hunters
Marvel, 2006
1 .... 4.00
2-3 .... 3.00

Jack of Fables
DC, 2006
1-35 .... 3.00

Jack of Hearts
Marvel, 1984
1-4 .... 2.00

Jackpot Comics
Archie, 1941
1 .... 3,000.00
2 .... 1,250.00
3 .... 1,000.00
4 .... 3,850.00
☛Archie starts
5 .... 1,600.00
6 .... 800.00
7-9 .... 450.00

Hembeck

Hemp for Victory

Hepcats

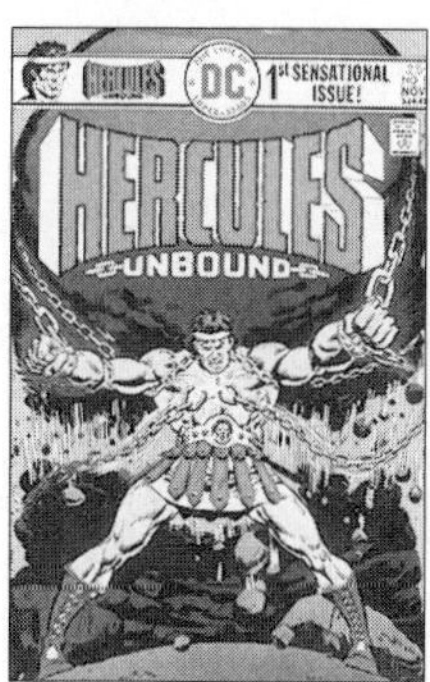

Hercules Unbound

Here Come the Big People

Heretics

Hero

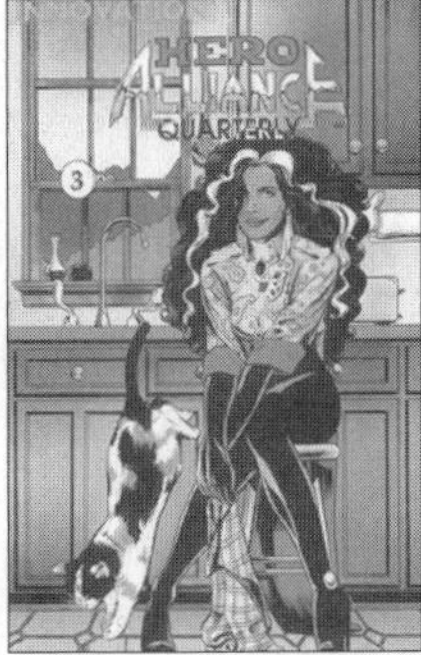
Hero Alliance Quarterly

Jack's Luck Runs Out
Beekeeper Cartoon Amusements
1 ....4.00

Jack Staff
Image, 2003
1-4 ....3.00
5-12 ....4.00

Jack the Giant Killer
Dell, 1963
1 ....32.00

Jack the Ripper
Caliber, 1998
1 ....3.00

Jack the Ripper
Eternity
1-3 ....2.00

Jacquelyn the Ripper
Fantagraphics, 1994
1-2 ....3.00

Jacque's Voice of Doom
Doomed Comics
1 ....2.00

Jademan Collection
Jademan, 1990
1-3 ....3.00

Jademan Kung Fu Special
Jademan
1 ....2.00

Jade Warriors
Image, 2000
1-2 ....3.00

J.A.G.
ThwackPow
1-3 ....2.00

Jaguar
DC, 1991
1-14 ....1.00
Ann 1 ....3.00

Jaguar God
Verotik, 1995
0-5 ....4.00
6-8 ....3.00

Jaguar God Illustrations
Verotik, 2000
nn 4.00

Jaguar God: Return to Xibalba
Verotik, 2003
1 ....5.00

Jailbait
Fantagraphics, 1998
1 ....3.00

Jake Thrash
Aircel
1-2 ....2.00

Jam
Slave Labor, 1989
1 ....3.00
2-3 ....2.00
4-13 ....3.00

Jamar Chronicles
Sweat Shop
1 ....2.00

Jamboree Comics
Round, 1946
1 ....70.00
2-3 ....35.00

James Bond 007: A Silent Armageddon
Dark Horse, 1993
1-2 ....3.00

James Bond 007/ Goldeneye
Topps, 1995
1-3 ....3.00

James Bond 007: Serpent's Tooth
Dark Horse, 1992
1-3 ....5.00

James Bond 007: Shattered Helix
Dark Horse, 1994
1-2 ....3.00

James Bond 007: The Quasimodo Gambit
Dark Horse, 1995
1-3 ....4.00

James Bond for Your Eyes Only
Marvel, 1981
1-2 ....2.00

James Bond Jr.
Marvel, 1992
1-12 ....1.00

James Bond: Permission to Die
Eclipse, 1989
1-2 ....4.00
3 ....5.00

Jam Quacky
JQ
1 ....2.00

Jam Special
Matrix
1 ....3.00

Jam Super Cool Color-Injected Turbo Adventure from Hell

Comico, 1988

1 .... 3.00

Jam Urban Adventure

Tundra, 1992

1-3 .... 3.00

Jane Arden

St. John, 1948

1 .... 70.00
2 .... 50.00

Jane Bondage

Fantagraphics, 1992

1-2 .... 3.00

Jane Bond: Thunderballs

Fantagraphics, 1992

1 .... 3.00

Jane Doe

Raging Rhino

1-3 .... 3.00

Jane's World

Girl Twirl, 2003

1-8 .... 3.00
9-16 .... 6.00

Jann of the Jungle

Atlas, 1955

8 .... 125.00
9-10 .... 100.00
11-15 .... 85.00
16-17 .... 90.00

Janx

Es Graphics

1-2 .... 1.00

J.A.P.A.N.

Outerealm

1 .... 2.00

Jaq Hammer

Anubis, 1994

0 .... 1.00
1 .... 3.00

Jar of Fools Part One

Penny Dreadful, 1994

1 .... 6.00

Jason and the Argonauts

Tome

1-5 .... 3.00

Jason Goes to Hell: The Final Friday

Topps, 1993

1-3 .... 3.00

Jason Monarch

Oracle, 1979

1 .... 2.00

Jason vs. Leatherface

Topps, 1995

1-3 .... 3.00

Java Town

Slave Labor, 1992

1-6 .... 3.00

Javerts

Firstlight, 1997

1 .... 3.00

Jax and the Hell Hound

Blackthorne, 1986

1-4 .... 2.00

Jay Anacleto Sketchbook

Image, 1999

1-1/A 2.00

Jay & Silent Bob

Oni, 1998

1 .... 4.00
1/Variant 5.00
1/2nd-4 .... 3.00

Jazz

High Impact, 1996

1-2 .... 3.00

Jazz Age Chronicles

EF Graphics, 1989

1-3 .... 2.00

Jazz Age Chronicles

Caliber, 1990

1-5 .... 3.00

Jazzbo Comics That Swing

Slave Labor, 1994

1-2 .... 3.00

Jazz: Solitaire

High Impact, 1998

1 .... 3.00
1/A-1/Gold 4.00
2 .... 3.00
2/A-2/B 5.00
3 .... 3.00
3/A-3/B 5.00

JCP Features

J.C., 1981

1 .... 3.00

Jeanie

Timely, 1947

13 .... 145.00
14-17 .... 100.00
18-23 .... 85.00
24-27 .... 65.00

Jeep Comics

R.B. Leffingwell, 1944

1 .... 265.00
2 .... 165.00
3 .... 200.00

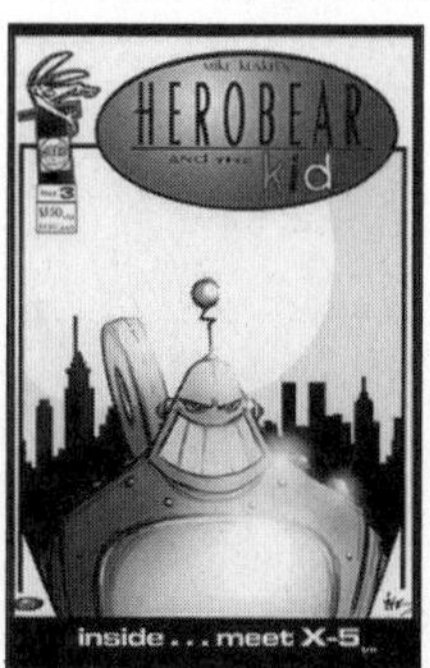

Herobear And The Kid

Hero Double Feature

Heroes Against Hunger

Heroes for Hire

Heroes for Hope

Heroes from Wordsmith

Heroes of Faith

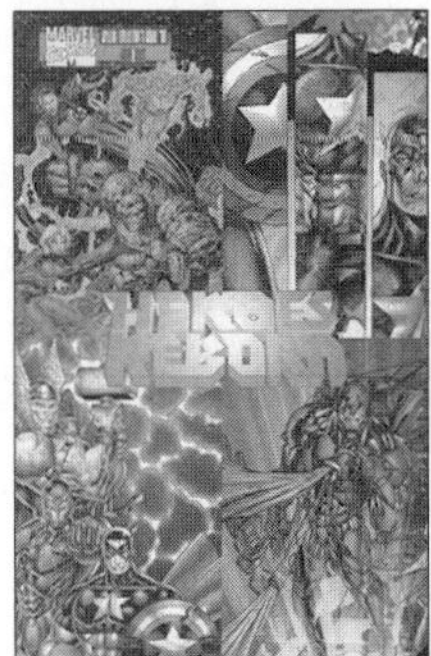
Heroes Reborn Mini Comic

Jeff Jordan, U.S. Agent
D.S., 1947

1 .... 90.00

Jeffrey Dahmer: An Unauthorized Biography of a Serial Killer
Boneyard, 1992

1 .... 4.00
1/2nd 3.00

Jeffrey Dahmer vs. Jesus Christ
Boneyard, 1993

1 .... 4.00

Jemm, Son of Saturn
DC, 1984

1 .... 2.00
2-12 .... 1.00

Jennifer Daydreamer: Oliver
Top Shelf, 2003

1 .... 5.00

Jenny Finn
Oni, 1999

1-4 .... 3.00

Jenny Finn: Messiah
Oni

1 .... 7.00

Jenny Sparks: The Secret History of the Authority
DC, 2000

1-5 .... 3.00

Jeremiah: A Fistful of Sand
Adventure, 1991

1-2 .... 3.00

Jeremiah: Birds of Prey
Adventure, 1991

1-2 .... 3.00

Jeremiah: The Heirs
Adventure

1-2 .... 3.00

Jeremy Brood
Fantagor, 1982

1 .... 6.00
1/2nd 12.00

Jerkbox & Punk'nhead
Jerkbox Studios, 1999

1 .... 3.00

Jerry Drummer
Charlton

10-12 .... 18.00

Jersey Devil
South Jersey Rebellion, 1992

1 .... 2.00
2 .... 3.00
3-7 .... 2.00

Jesse James
Avon, 1950

1 .... 60.00
2 .... 30.00
3-5 .... 40.00
6-9 .... 35.00
15-19 .... 30.00
20-21 .... 28.00
22-29 .... 24.00

Jesse James
AC

1 .... 4.00

Jest
Harry A. Chesler, 1944

10-11 .... 85.00

Jester's Moon
One Shot, 1996

1 .... 1.00

Jesus Comics (Foolbert Sturgeon's...)
Rip Off, 1972

1 .... 5.00
2-3 .... 4.00

Jet
Authority, 1996

1 .... 3.00

Jet
DC, 2000

1-4 .... 3.00

Jet Aces
Fiction House, 1952

1 .... 90.00
2-4 .... 55.00

Jet Black
Monolith, 1997

1 .... 3.00

Jet Comics
Slave Labor, 1997

1-3 .... 3.00

Jet Dream
Gold Key, 1968

1 .... 18.00

Jet Fighters
Standard, 1953

5 .... 80.00
6 .... 50.00
7 .... 80.00

Jet Fury
Herald Gravure

1 .... 20.00
2-24 .... 14.00

Jet Powers
Magazine Enterprises, 1950

1 .... 140.00
2 .... 110.00
3-4 .... 100.00

Jetsons
Gold Key, 1963
1 .... 90.00
2 .... 65.00
3-5 .... 48.00
6-10 .... 40.00
11-20 .... 24.00
21-30 .... 16.00
31-36 .... 14.00

Jetsons
Charlton, 1970
1 .... 35.00
2 .... 22.00
3-5 .... 14.00
6-10 .... 10.00
11-20 .... 7.00

Jetsons
Harvey, 1992
1-5 .... 2.00

Jetsons
Archie, 1995
1-12 .... 2.00

Jetsons Big Book
Harvey, 1992
1-3 .... 2.00

Jetsons GS
Harvey, 1992
1-3 .... 3.00

Jetta of the 21st Century
Standard, 1952
5 .... 110.00
6-7 .... 75.00

Jew in Communist Prague, A
NBM
1-2 .... 12.00

Jezebel Jade
Comico, 1988
1-3 .... 2.00

Jezebelle
WildStorm, 2001
1/A-6 .... 3.00

JFK Assassination
Zone
1 .... 4.00

Jhereg
Marvel
1 .... 9.00

Jigaboo Devil
Millennium
0 .... 3.00

Jiggs & Maggie
Harvey, 1953
11-12 .... 20.00
13-14 .... 20.00
15-16 .... 20.00
17-18 .... 20.00
19-20 .... 20.00
21-22 .... 20.00
23-24 .... 20.00
25-26 .... 20.00
27 .... 20.00

Jiggs is Back
Celtic
1 .... 13.00

Jigsaw
Harvey, 1966
1 .... 16.00
2 .... 10.00

Jill: Part-Time Lover
NBM
1 .... 12.00

Jim (Vol. 1)
Fantagraphics
1 .... 8.00
2 .... 6.00
3-4 .... 5.00

Jim (Vol. 2)
Fantagraphics, 1993
1 .... 5.00
2-3 .... 4.00
4-6 .... 3.00
Special 1 .... 4.00

Jimbo
Bongo, 1995
1-7 .... 3.00

Jim Dandy
Lev Gleason, 1956
1 .... 40.00
2-3 .... 25.00

Jim Hardy
United Feature, 1944
1 .... 300.00

Jim Hardy
United Feature, 1947
1 .... 100.00
2 .... 60.00

Jim Lee Sketchbook
WildStorm
1 .... 40.00

Jimmy Durante
Magazine Enterprises, 1948
1 .... 365.00
2 .... 275.00

Jimmy Wakely
DC, 1949
1 .... 850.00
2 .... 525.00
3-4 .... 465.00
5 .... 325.00
6-7 .... 425.00
8-10 .... 275.00
11-18 .... 225.00

Hero for Hire

Hero Hotline

Heroic 17

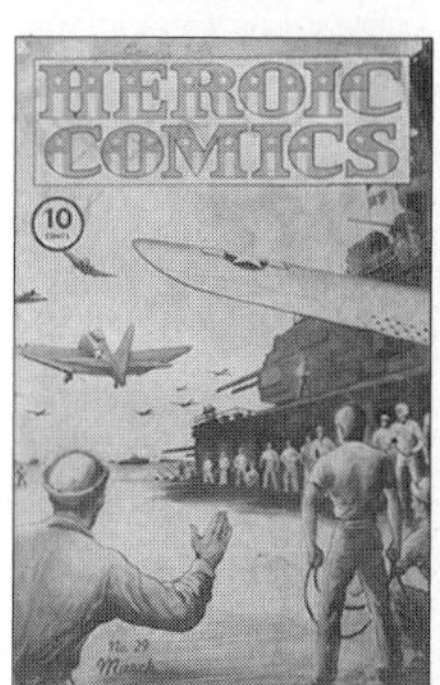

Heroic Comics

Heroines Inc.

Hero on a Stick

Hero Sandwich

Hero Zero

Jim Ray's Aviation Sketchbook
Vital, 1946

1..........200.00
2..........180.00

Jing: King of Bandits
Tokyopop, 2003

1-7..........10.00

Jing: King of Bandits - Twilight Tales
Tokyopop, 2004

1-6..........10.00

Jingle Belle
Oni, 1999

1-2..........3.00

Jingle Belle (Paul Dini's...): The Mighty Elves
Oni, 2001

1..........3.00

Jingle Belle
Dark Horse, 2004

1-4..........3.00

Jingle Belle Jubilee
Oni, 2001

nn..........3.00

Jingle Belle's All-Star Holiday Hullabaloo
Oni, 2000

1..........5.00

Jingle Belle: The Fight Before Christmas
Dark Horse, 2006

1..........3.00

Jingle Belle Winter Wingding
Oni, 2002

nn..........3.00

Jingle Jangle Comics
Eastern Color, 1943

1..........225.00
2..........200.00
3..........175.00
4..........150.00
5-6..........125.00
7-9..........100.00
10-12..........80.00
13-15..........75.00
16-18..........60.00
19-25..........50.00
26-29..........45.00
30-35..........40.00
36-39..........35.00
40-42..........30.00

Jing Pals
Victory, 1946

1..........80.00
2..........40.00
3-4..........30.00

Jinn
Image, 2000

1-3..........3.00

Jinx
Caliber, 1996

1..........4.00
2-7..........3.00
8-9..........5.00
10-11..........3.00
12-17..........4.00
18-19..........3.00
20-21..........4.00
Book 1/Deluxe..........18.00
Book 2..........11.00
Special 1..........5.00

Jinx Pop Culture Hoo-Hah
Image

1..........4.00

Jizz
Fantagraphics

1-7..........2.00
8-10..........3.00

JLA
DC, 1997

1..........6.00
2-6..........4.00
7-15..........3.00
16-40..........2.00
41..........3.00
42-49..........2.00
50..........4.00
51-74..........2.00
75..........4.00
76-99..........2.00
100..........4.00
101-106..........2.00
☛Post ID Crisis
107-108..........5.00
☛Post ID Crisis
109-114..........2.00
115..........12.00
☛ID Crisis follow-up
116..........5.00
117-125..........3.00
1000000..........2.00
Ann 1..........6.00
Ann 2..........5.00
Ann 3..........4.00
GS 1-2..........5.00
GS 3..........6.00

JLA: Act of God
DC, 2001

1-3..........5.00

JLA: Age of Wonder
DC, 2003

1-2..........6.00

JLA/Avengers
Marvel, 2003

1 .... 7.00
3 .... 6.00
3/2nd 7.00

JLA: Black Baptism
DC, 2001

1-4 .... 3.00

JLA: Classified
DC, 2005

1 .... 6.00
2 .... 4.00
3-31 .... 3.00

JLA Classified: Cold Steel
DC, 2006

1-2 .... 6.00

JLA: Created Equal
DC, 2000

1-2 .... 6.00

JLA/Cyberforce
DC, 2005

0 .... 6.00

JLA: Destiny
DC, 2002

1-4 .... 6.00

JLA: Foreign Bodies
DC, 1999

1 .... 6.00

JLA Gallery
DC, 1997

1 .... 3.00

JLA: Gatekeeper
DC, 2001

1-3 .... 5.00

JLA: Gods and Monsters
DC, 2001

1 .... 7.00

JLA/Haven: Anathema
DC, 2002

1 .... 6.00

JLA/Haven: Arrival
DC, 2002

1 .... 6.00

JLA: Heaven's Ladder
DC, 2000

1 .... 10.00

JLA: Incarnations
DC, 2001

1-7 .... 4.00

JLA in Crisis Secret Files
DC, 1998

1 .... 5.00

JLA/JSA: Virtue & Vice
DC, 2003

1 .... 18.00

JLA: Liberty & Justice
DC, 2004

1 .... 10.00

JLA: Obsidian Age
DC, 2003

1-2 .... 13.00

JLA: One Million
DC, 2004

1 .... 20.00

JLA: Our Worlds At War
DC, 2001

1 .... 3.00

JLA: Paradise Lost
DC, 1998

1-3 .... 2.00

JLA: Primeval
DC, 1999

1 .... 6.00

JLA: Scary Monsters
DC, 2003

1-6 .... 3.00

JLA Secret Files
DC, 1997

1 .... 5.00
2 .... 4.00
3 .... 5.00

JLA Secret Files 2004
DC, 2004

1 .... 5.00

JLA: Secret Society of Super-Heroes
DC, 2000

1-2 .... 6.00

JLA: Seven Caskets
DC

1 .... 6.00

JLA: Shogun of Steel
DC, 2002

1 .... 7.00

JLA Showcase
DC, 2000

GS 1 .... 5.00

JLA/Spectre: Soul War
DC, 2003

1-2 .... 6.00

JLA: Superpower
DC, 1999

1 .... 6.00

JLA: The Island of Dr. Moreau
DC, 2002

1 .... 7.00

JLA: The Nail
DC, 1998

1 .... 6.00
2-3 .... 5.00

Hex

Hi-Adventure Heroes

Hieroglyph

High Caliber

High Octane Theatre

High Roads

High Shining Brass

High Stakes Adventures

JLA/Titans
DC, 1998
1....3.00
1/Ltd....5.00
2-3....3.00

JLA: Tomorrow Woman
DC, 1998
1....2.00

JLA: Tower of Babel
DC
1....13.00

JLA Versus Predator
DC, 2000
1....6.00

JLA: Welcome to Working Week
DC, 2003
1....7.00

JLA/WildC.A.T.s
DC, 1997
1....6.00

JLA/Witchblade
DC, 2000
1....6.00

JLA: World without Grown-Ups
DC, 1998
1....6.00
2....5.00

JLA: Year One
DC, 1998
1....4.00
2-5....3.00
6-11....2.00
12....3.00

JLA-Z
DC, 2003
1-3....3.00

JLA: Zatanna's Search
DC, 2003
1....13.00

JLX
DC, 1996
1....2.00

JLX Unleashed
DC, 1997
1....2.00

Joan of Arc
Magazine Enterprises, 1949
1....300.00

Joe 90
Fleetway-Quality
1....4.00
2-7....3.00

Joe College
Hillman, 1949
1....50.00
2....38.00

Joe Dimaggio
Celebrity
1....7.00

Joe Louis
Fawcett, 1950
1....385.00
2....225.00

Joe Palooka
Columbia, 1942
1....525.00
2....265.00
3....200.00
4....175.00

Joe Palooka
Harvey, 1945
1....240.00
2....160.00
3-4....90.00
5....135.00
☛Simon/Kirby issue
6-7....95.00
8-10....75.00
11-14....55.00
15....75.00
☛Humphrey origin
16-20....55.00
21-30....44.00
31-44....38.00
45-51....32.00
52-60....28.00
61....26.00
62....42.00
63-80....26.00
81-115....24.00
116-118....34.00

Joe Palooka Fights His Way Back
Harvey, 1945
1....100.00

Joe Palooka Hi There
American Red Cross, 1949
1....75.00

Joe Psycho & Moo Frog
Goblin, 1996
1....4.00
2-5....3.00
Ashcan 1....2.00

Joe Psycho Full Color Extravagarbonzo
Goblin, 1998
1....3.00

Joe Sinn
Caliber
1-2....3.00

Joe Yank

Standard, 1952

5 .... 50.00
6 .... 55.00
7 .... 25.00
8 .... 35.00
9-16 .... 18.00

Johan & Peewit: The Black Arrow

Fantasy Flight

1 .... 9.00

John Carter of Mars (Edgar Rice Burroughs'...)

Gold Key, 1964

1 .... 30.00
2-3 .... 16.00

John Carter, Warlord of Mars

Marvel, 1977

1 .... 8.00
1/35¢ 15.00
2 .... 4.00
2/35¢ 8.00
2/Whitman 4.00
3-5/35¢ 8.00
6-28 .... 3.00
Ann 1-3 .... 2.00

John Constantine Hellblazer: Papa Midnite

DC, 2005

1-5 .... 3.00

John F. Kennedy

Dell, 1964

1 .... 45.00
1/2nd 30.00
1/3rd 22.00

John Hix Scrapbook

Eastern Color, 1937

1 .... 200.00
2 .... 145.00

John Law Detective

Eclipse, 1983

1 .... 2.00

Johnny Atomic

Eternity

1-3 .... 3.00

Johnny Comet

Avalon, 1999

1-5 .... 3.00

Johnny Cosmic

Thorby

1 .... 3.00

Johnny Danger

Toby, 1954

1 .... 90.00

Johnny Dynamite

Dark Horse, 1994

1-4 .... 3.00

Johnny Gambit

Hot, 1987

1 .... 2.00

Johnny Hazard

Best, 1948

5 .... 90.00
6-7 .... 70.00
8 .... 55.00

Johnny Hazard

Pioneer, 1988

1 .... 2.00

Johnny Hazard Quarterly

Dragon Lady

1-4 .... 6.00

Johnny Jason, Teen Reporter

Dell, 1962

2 .... 20.00

Johnny Law, Sky Ranger

Good, 1955

1 .... 50.00
2-4 .... 35.00

Johnny Mack Brown Comics

Dell, 1950

2 .... 110.00
3 .... 85.00
4-5 .... 75.00
6-8 .... 60.00
9 .... 75.00
10 .... 60.00

Johnny Nemo Magazine

Eclipse, 1985

1-6 .... 3.00

Johnny the Homicidal Maniac

Slave Labor, 1995

1 .... 13.00
1/2nd 4.00
1/3rd-1/4th 3.00
2 .... 9.00
2/2nd 3.00
3 .... 7.00
3/2nd 3.00
4 .... 6.00
4/2nd 3.00
5 .... 5.00
5/2nd 3.00
6-7 .... 4.00
Special 1 .... 20.00

Johnny Thunder

DC, 1973

1 .... 12.00
2-3 .... 8.00

Hightop Ninja

High Voltage

Hilly Rose

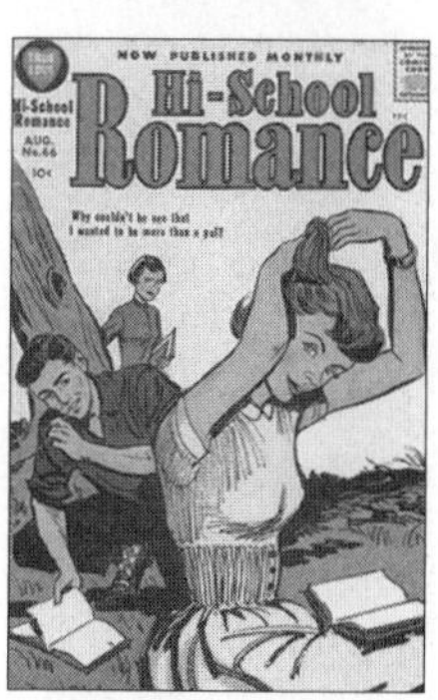

Hi-School Romance

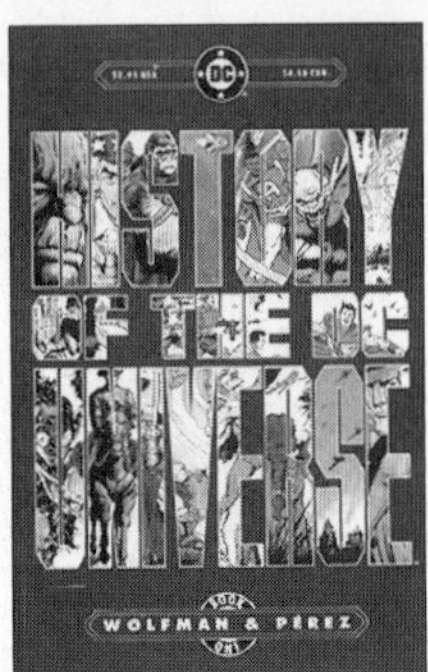

History of the DC Universe

Hit Comics

Hitman

Hitomi 2

John Steele, Secret Agent

Gold Key, 1964

1 ... 18.00

John Wayne Adventure Comics

Toby, 1949

1 ... 1,285.00
2 ... 640.00
3 ... 550.00
4 ... 525.00
5-9 ... 485.00
10-12 ... 425.00
13-16 ... 275.00
17 ... 325.00
18-20 ... 275.00
21-24 ... 240.00
25-31 ... 300.00

Jo-Jo Comics

Fox, 1946

1 ... 125.00
2-3 ... 75.00
4-6 ... 60.00
7 ... 825.00
8 ... 500.00
9-10 ... 375.00
11-20 ... 300.00
21-29 ... 240.00

Joker

DC, 1975

1 ... 16.00
2 ... 12.00
3-5 ... 8.00
6-9 ... 7.00

Joker Comics

Timely, 1942

1 ... 2,000.00
2 ... 775.00
3 ... 400.00
4-5 ... 325.00
6-10 ... 260.00
11-20 ... 205.00
21-27 ... 155.00
28 ... 60.00
29-30 ... 155.00
31 ... 125.00
32 ... 80.00
33 ... 40.00
34-35 ... 80.00
36-42 ... 48.00

Joker: Last Laugh

DC, 2001

1-6 ... 3.00

Joker: Last Laugh Secret Files

DC, 2001

1 ... 6.00

Joker/Mask

Dark Horse, 2000

1-4 ... 3.00

Jolly Jack Starjumper Summer of '92 One-Shot

Conquest

1 ... 3.00

Jolly Jingles

Archie, 1943

10 ... 160.00
11 ... 85.00
12 ... 60.00
13-16 ... 35.00

Jonah Hex

DC, 1977

1 ... 28.00
2 ... 10.00
3-5 ... 7.00
6 ... 6.00
7-8 ... 7.00
9-10 ... 5.00
11-20 ... 4.00
21-92 ... 3.00

Jonah Hex

DC, 2006

1 ... 8.00
2-20 ... 2.00
21-50 ... 3.00

Jonah Hex and Other Western Tales

DC, 1979

1-3 ... 7.00

Jonah Hex: Riders of the Worm and Such

DC, 1995

1-5 ... 3.00

Jonah Hex: Shadows West

DC, 1999

1-3 ... 3.00

Jonah Hex: Two-Gun Mojo

DC, 1993

1 ... 4.00
☛Lansdale, Truman series
1/Silver ... 6.00
2-5 ... 3.00

Jonas! (Mike Deodato's...)

Caliber

1 ... 3.00

Jonathan Fox

Mariah Graphics

1 ... 2.00

Jones Touch

Fantagraphics, 1993

1 ... 3.00

Jonesy

Quality, 1953

1 .... 40.00
2-4 .... 25.00
5-8 .... 20.00

Jon Juan

Toby, 1950

1 .... 425.00

Jonni Thunder

DC, 1985

1-4 .... 1.00

Jonny Demon

Dark Horse, 1994

1-3 .... 3.00

Jonny Double

DC, 1998

1-4 .... 3.00

Jonny Quest

Gold Key, 1964

1 .... 85.00

Jonny Quest

Comico, 1986

1-5 .... 3.00
6-Special 2 .... 2.00

Jonny Quest Classics

Comico, 1987

1-3 .... 2.00

Jon Sable, Freelance

First, 1983

1 .... 3.00
2-56 .... 2.00

Jon Sable, Freelance: Bloodline

Idea & Design Works, 2005

1-6 .... 4.00

Jontar Returns

Miller

1-4 .... 2.00

Josie

Archie, 1965

17-20 .... 16.00
21-30 .... 10.00
31-44 .... 8.00

Josie & the Pussycats

Archie, 1969

45 .... 12.00
46-60 .... 6.00
61-70 .... 5.00
71-90 .... 4.00
91-106 .... 3.00

Josie & the Pussycats

Archie, 1993

1-2 .... 2.00

Journey

Aardvark-Vanaheim, 1983

1 .... 4.00
2-10 .... 3.00
11-27 .... 2.00

Journey Into Fear

Superior, 1951

1 .... 400.00
2 .... 240.00
3-5 .... 210.00
6-10 .... 165.00
11-21 .... 125.00

Journey into Mystery

Marvel, 1952

-1 .... 2.00
1 .... 3,100.00
2 .... 950.00
3-4 .... 700.00
5 .... 800.00
6-11 .... 450.00
12-22 .... 350.00
23-32 .... 225.00
33 .... 250.00
34-40 .... 225.00
41-49 .... 200.00
50 .... 160.00
51-61 .... 155.00
62 .... 250.00
63-71 .... 145.00
72 .... 140.00
73 .... 200.00
74-81 .... 140.00
82 .... 160.00
83 .... 4,500.00
☛1st Thor
83/Golden Record 60.00
84 .... 725.00
85 .... 450.00
86 .... 400.00
87 .... 600.00
88 .... 250.00
89 .... 300.00
90 .... 150.00
91-92 .... 130.00
93 .... 160.00
94-96 .... 130.00
97 .... 325.00
98 .... 120.00
99 .... 105.00
100 .... 115.00
101 .... 150.00
102-108 .... 75.00
109 .... 90.00
110-111 .... 75.00
112 .... 210.00
☛Thor vs. Hulk
113-114 .... 75.00
115 .... 90.00
116 .... 75.00
117-125 .... 70.00
503-521 .... 2.00
Ann 1 .... 150.00

Holiday Comics

Holiday Out

Hollywood Funny Folks

Hollywood Romances

Hollywood Superstars

Holy Cross

Homicide

Hong on the Range

Journey into Mystery

Marvel, 1972

1 .... 17.00
2-3 .... 7.00
4-5 .... 6.00
6-19 .... 5.00

Journey Into Unknown Worlds

Atlas, 1950

1 .... 1,535.00
2 .... 700.00
3 .... 540.00
4-6 .... 400.00
7 .... 560.00
8-10 .... 400.00
11-13 .... 260.00
14-15 .... 445.00
16-20 .... 225.00
21-30 .... 160.00
31-40 .... 110.00
41-54 .... 85.00
55-59 .... 100.00

Journeyman

Image, 1999

1-3 .... 3.00

Journeyman/Dark Ages

Lucid, 1997

1 .... 3.00

Journey: Wardrums

Fantagraphics, 1987

1-2 .... 2.00

Jr. Carrot Patrol

Dark Horse, 1989

1-2 .... 2.00

JSA

DC, 1999

1 .... 5.00
2-36 .... 3.00
37 .... 4.00
38-49 .... 3.00
50 .... 4.00
51-57 .... 3.00
58 .... 4.00
59-66 .... 3.00
67 .... 7.00
☛Identity Crisis tie
68 .... 5.00
69-70 .... 4.00
71 .... 3.00
72 .... 4.00
73 .... 5.00
☛Infinite Crisis tie
74 .... 4.00
☛Infinite Crisis tie
75-87 .... 3.00
Ann 1 .... 5.00

JSA: All Stars

DC, 2003

1-6 .... 3.00
7 .... 4.00
8 .... 3.00

JSA: Classified

DC, 2005

1/Conner 16.00
1/Hughes 24.00
1/Sketch 7.00
☛Hughes, 2nd print
2 .... 9.00
2/Sketch 4.00
3-4 .... 5.00
5-20 .... 3.00

JSA: Our Worlds At War

DC, 2001

1 .... 3.00

JSA Secret Files

DC, 1999

1-2 .... 5.00

JSA: Strange Adventures

DC, 2004

1-6 .... 4.00

JSA: The Liberty File

DC, 2000

1-2 .... 7.00

JSA: Unholy Three

DC, 2003

1-2 .... 7.00

Jubilee

Marvel, 2004

1-6 .... 3.00

Judge Dredd Versus Aliens: Incubus

Dark Horse, 2003

1-4 .... 3.00

Jude, the Forgotten Saint

Catechetical Guild

1 .... 14.00

Judge Child

Eagle

1-5 .... 2.00

Judge Colt

Gold Key, 1969

1 .... 15.00
2-4 .... 10.00

Judge Dredd

Eagle, 1983

1 .... 4.00
2-10 .... 3.00
11-35 .... 2.00

Judge Dredd

Fleetway-Quality, 1986

1-2 .... 3.00
3-61 .... 2.00
Special 1 .... 3.00

Judge Dredd
DC, 1994

1-3 .... 3.00
4-18 .... 2.00

Judge Dredd: America
Fleetway-Quality

1-2 .... 3.00

Judge Dredd Classics
Fleetway-Quality

62-77 .... 2.00

Judge Dredd: Emerald Isle
Fleetway-Quality, 1991

1 .... 5.00

Judge Dredd-Lawman of the Future
Fleetway-Quality

1-3 .... 2.00

Judge Dredd: Legends of the Law
DC, 1994

1 .... 3.00
2-13 .... 2.00

Judge Dredd Megazine
Fleetway-Quality

1 .... 8.00
2-5 .... 6.00
6-15 .... 5.00
16-20 .... 4.00
Ann 1986 .... 9.00
Ann 1989 .... 8.00

Judge Dredd Megazine
Fleetway-Quality

1 .... 6.00
2-83 .... 3.00
MS 1988-1994 .... 4.00
YB 1993-1994 .... 8.00

Judge Dredd Megazine
Fleetway-Quality, 2000

1 .... 4.00
2-42 .... 3.00
43-45 .... 4.00
46 .... 7.00
47-80 .... 4.00

Judge Dredd: Raptaur
Fleetway-Quality

1-2 .... 3.00

Judge Dredd's Crime File
Eagle, 1985

1-6 .... 3.00

Judge Dredd's Crime File
Fleetway-Quality

1-4 .... 4.00

Judge Dredd the Early Cases
Eagle, 1986

1-6 .... 3.00

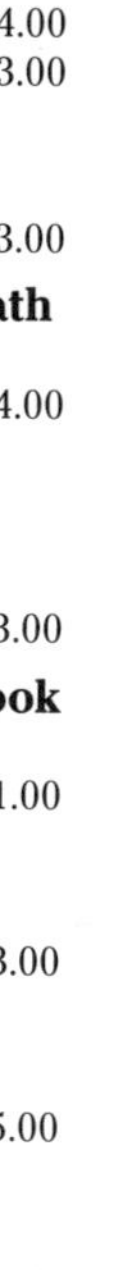

Judge Dredd the Megazine
Fleetway-Quality

1-3 ....5.00

Judge Dredd: The Official Movie Adaptation
DC

1 ....6.00

Judge Parker
Argo, 1956

1 ....35.00
2 ....25.00

J.U.D.G.E.: Secret Rage
Image, 2000

1 ....3.00

Judgment Day
Lightning, 1993

1/A-1/Platinum 4.00
2-8 ....3.00

Judgment Day
Awesome, 1997

1-3/A 3.00

Judgment Day: Aftermath
Awesome, 1998

1-1/A 4.00

Judgment Day: Final Judgment
Awesome, 1997

3 ....3.00

Judgment Day Sourcebook
Awesome

1 ....1.00

Judgment Pawns
Antarctic, 1997

1-3 ....3.00

Judgments
NBM

1 ....15.00

Judo Girl
Alias, 2005

0/Conv......................................8.00
1/Balan......................................3.00
1/Taylor 4.00
2/Balan......................................3.00
2/Taylor 4.00
3/Balan......................................3.00
3/Taylor 4.00
4/Balan......................................3.00
4/Miller 4.00

Judo Joe
Jay-Jay Corp., 1953

1 ....30.00
2-3 ....24.00

Judomaster
Charlton, 1966

89 ....12.00
90-98 ....9.00

Honor Among Thieves

Hooded Rider Comics

Hood Magazine

Hook

Hopalong Cassidy

Horny Biker Sluts

Horobi Part 1

Horror House

Judomaster
Modern, 1977

93-98 .... 2.00

Judy Canova
Fox, 1950

1 .... 110.00
2-3 .... 80.00

Juggernaut
Marvel, 1997

1 .... 3.00

Juggernaut
Marvel, 1999

1 .... 3.00

Jughead's Folly
Archie, 1957

1 .... 120.00

Jughead
Archie, 1965

127-130 .... 12.00
131-140 .... 9.00
141-150 .... 8.00
151-171 .... 7.00
172-200 .... 5.00
201-220 .... 4.00
221-240 .... 3.00
241-352 .... 2.00

Jughead
Archie, 1987

1 .... 3.00
2-176 .... 2.00

Jughead and His Friends Digest
Archie, 2005

1-16 .... 2.00

Jughead as Captain Hero
Archie, 1966

1 .... 28.00
2 .... 15.00
3 .... 10.00
4-7 .... 7.00

Jughead Jones Digest Magazine
Archie, 1977

1 .... 16.00
2 .... 12.00
3-6 .... 6.00
7 .... 8.00
8-10 .... 6.00
11-20 .... 5.00
21-30 .... 4.00
31-50 .... 3.00
51-100 .... 2.00

Jughead's Baby Tales
Archie, 1994

1-2 .... 2.00

Jughead's Diner
Archie, 1990

1-7 .... 2.00

Jughead's Double Digest
Archie, 1989

1 .... 6.00
2-5 .... 4.00
6-79 .... 3.00
80-127 .... 4.00

Jughead's Fantasy
Archie, 1960

1 .... 80.00
2-3 .... 55.00

Jughead's Jokes
Archie, 1967

1 .... 60.00
2 .... 35.00
3 .... 25.00
4-5 .... 18.00
6-10 .... 15.00
11-15 .... 12.00
16-20 .... 10.00
21-30 .... 7.00
31-40 .... 5.00
41-60 .... 4.00
61-78 .... 3.00

Jughead's Pal Hot Dog
Archie, 1990

1-5 .... 1.00

Jughead's Time Police
Archie, 1990

1-6 .... 1.00

Jughead with Archie Digest Magazine
Archie, 1974

1 .... 12.00
2-10 .... 7.00
11-20 .... 4.00
21-50 .... 3.00
51-199 .... 2.00

Jugular
Black Out

0 .... 3.00

Juke Box Comics
Famous Funnies, 1948

1 .... 185.00
2 .... 125.00
3-6 .... 110.00

Jumbo Comics
Fiction House, 1938

1 .... 18,500.00
2 .... 6,000.00
3-4 .... 4,200.00
5 .... 3,300.00
6-7 .... 2,900.00
8 .... 2,975.00
9 .... 2,550.00
10 .... 1,500.00

11-12 .... 1,200.00
13-14 .... 1,100.00
15-20 .... 750.00
21-30 .... 575.00
31-40 .... 475.00
41-50 .... 350.00
51-60 .... 295.00
61-70 .... 220.00
71-80 .... 180.00
81-90 .... 155.00
91-110 .... 135.00
111-120 .... 100.00
121-167 .... 90.00

Jumper
Zav

1-2 .... 3.00

Jun
Disney

1 .... 2.00

Junction 17
Antarctic, 2003

1 .... 4.00
2-4 .... 3.00

Jungle Action
Atlas, 1954

1 .... 240.00
2-6 .... 200.00

Jungle Tales
Atlas, 1954

1 .... 250.00
2 .... 175.00
3-4 .... 145.00
5-7 .... 130.00

Jungle Action
Marvel, 1972

1 .... 15.00
2-4 .... 7.00
5 .... 35.00
☛Black Panther begins
6 .... 12.00
7 .... 8.00
8 .... 15.00
9 .... 7.00
10-16 .... 6.00
17-21 .... 5.00
21/30¢ 20.00
22 .... 5.00
22/30¢ 20.00
23-24 .... 5.00

Jungle Adventures
Super, 1963

10-18 .... 28.00

Jungle Adventures
Skywald, 1971

1 .... 10.00
2-3 .... 7.00

Jungle Book
Gold Key, 1968

1 .... 25.00

Jungle Book
Disney, 1990

1/A 3.00
1/B 6.00

Jungle Book
NBM

1 .... 17.00

Jungle Comics
Fiction House, 1940

1 .... 4,000.00
2 .... 1,500.00
3-4 .... 1,250.00
5 .... 1,500.00
6 .... 650.00
7 .... 600.00
8-10 .... 545.00
11-15 .... 475.00
16-20 .... 425.00
21-25 .... 370.00
26-30 .... 340.00
31-35 .... 290.00
36-40 .... 250.00
41-50 .... 215.00
51-60 .... 200.00
61-70 .... 180.00
71-80 .... 165.00
81-90 .... 150.00
91-97 .... 140.00
98 .... 210.00
99-100 .... 140.00
101-110 .... 130.00
111-130 .... 125.00
131-150 .... 115.00
151-163 .... 100.00

Jungle Comics
A-List, 1997

1-5 .... 3.00

Jungle Fantasy
Avatar, 2002

1-3 .... 4.00

Jungle Girl
Fawcett, 1942

1 .... 975.00

Jungle Girls
AC, 1988

1-2 .... 2.00
3-16 .... 3.00

Jungle Girls!
Eternity

8 .... 3.00

Jungle Jim
Standard, 1949

11 .... 60.00
12-15 .... 40.00
16-20 .... 35.00

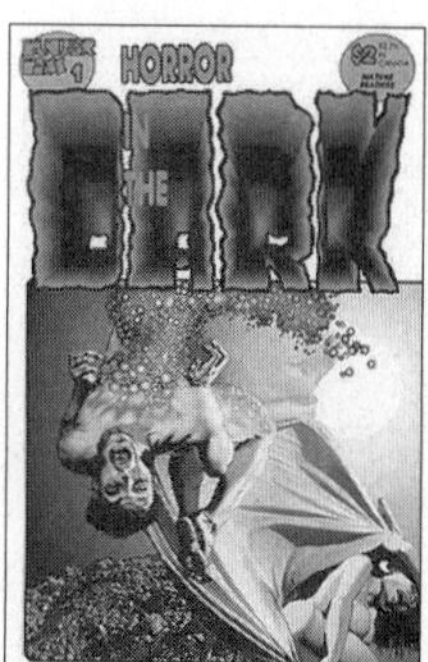

Horror in the Dark

Horse

Hot Dog

Hot Rod Racers

Hot Rods and Racing Cars

Hot Shots

Hot Stuff Big Book

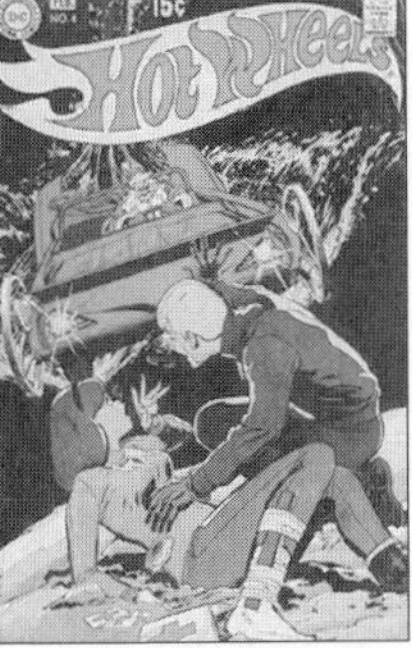

Hot Wheels

Jungle Jim
Dell, 1954

3 .... 30.00
4-9 .... 25.00
10-19 .... 20.00

Jungle Jim
King, 1967

5 .... 9.00

Jungle Jim
Charlton, 1969

22 .... 24.00
23-24 .... 18.00
25-28 .... 16.00

Jungle Jim
Avalon

1 .... 3.00

Jungle Jo
Fox, 1950

0 .... 300.00
1 .... 375.00
2 .... 285.00
3 .... 240.00

Jungle Lil
Fox, 1950

1 .... 325.00

Jungle Love
Aircel

1-3 .... 3.00

Jungle Tales of Cavewoman
Basement

1 .... 3.00

Jungle Tales of Tarzan
Charlton, 1965

1 .... 45.00
2-4 .... 35.00

Jungle Twins
Gold Key, 1972

1 .... 10.00
2 .... 7.00
3-5 .... 4.00
6-17 .... 3.00
18 .... 2.00

Jungle War Stories
Dell, 1962

1 .... 24.00
2-5 .... 16.00
6-11 .... 14.00

Junie Prom
Dearfield, 1947

1 .... 50.00
2 .... 36.00
3-7 .... 30.00

Junior Carrot Patrol
Dark Horse, 1989

1-2 .... 2.00

Junior Comics
Fox, 1947

9 .... 220.00
10 .... 165.00
11-16 .... 125.00

Junior Hopp Comics
Stanmor, 1952

1 .... 40.00
2-3 .... 30.00

Junior Jackalope
Nevada City, 1982

1-2 .... 2.00

Junior Miss
Timely, 1947

24-26 .... 75.00
27-29 .... 65.00
30-33 .... 60.00
34-36 .... 55.00
37-39 .... 50.00

Junior Woodchucks
Disney, 1991

1-4 .... 2.00

Junk Culture
DC, 1997

1-2 .... 3.00

Junker
Fleetway-Quality

1-4 .... 3.00

Junkfood Noir
Oktober Black, 1996

1 .... 2.00

Junk Force
ComicsOne, 2004

1 .... 10.00

Junkwaffel
Print Mint, 1972

1 .... 5.00
2-3 .... 3.00

Junkyard Enforcer
Boxcar, 1998

1 .... 3.00

Jupiter
Sandberg, 1999

1-3 .... 3.00

Jurassic Lark Deluxe Edition
Parody

1 .... 3.00

Jurassic Park
Topps, 1993

0-4/Direct. 3.00

Jurassic Park (Magazine)
Dark Horse

1 .... 4.00
2-15 .... 3.00

Jurassic Park Adventures
Topps, 1994

1-10 .... 2.00

Jurassic Park: Raptor
Topps, 1993

1-2 .... 3.00

Jurassic Park: Raptors Attack
Topps, 1994

1-4 .... 3.00

Jurassic Park: Raptors Hijack
Topps, 1994

1-4 .... 3.00

Just a Pilgrim
Black Bull, 2000

1 .... 4.00
2-5 .... 3.00

Justice
Atlas, 1947

7 (1) 130.00
8 (2) 90.00
9 (3) 75.00
4-5 .... 65.00
6-9 .... 55.00
10-15 .... 65.00
16-20 .... 55.00
21-30 .... 48.00
31-40 .... 42.00
41-52 .... 34.00

Justice
Marvel, 1986

1-25 .... 1.00
26-32 .... 2.00

Justice
Antarctic, 1994

1 .... 4.00

Justice Brigade
TCB Comics

1-8 .... 2.00

Justice
DC, 2005

1/Heroes 5.00
1/Villains-12 .... 4.00

Justice: Four Balance
Marvel, 1994

1-4 .... 2.00

Justice, Inc.
DC, 1975

1 .... 3.00
2-4 .... 2.00

Justice, Inc.
DC, 1989

1-2 .... 4.00

Justice League
DC, 1987

1 .... 6.00
2-3 .... 3.00
3/Ltd. 10.00
4 .... 3.00
5-6 .... 2.00
Ann 1 .... 3.00

Justice League Adventures
DC, 2002

1 .... 3.00
2-34 .... 2.00

Justice League America
DC, 1989

0-50 .... 2.00
51-68 .... 1.00
69 .... 3.00
69/2nd-99 .... 2.00
100 .... 3.00
100/Variant 4.00
101-113 .... 2.00
Ann 4-8 .... 3.00
Ann 9 .... 4.00
Ann 10 .... 3.00
Special 1 .... 2.00
Special 2 .... 3.00

Justice League: A Midsummer's Nightmare
DC, 1996

1-3 .... 3.00

Justice League Elite
DC, 2004

1-11 .... 3.00

Justice League Europe
DC, 1989

1-20 .... 2.00
21-49 .... 1.00
50 .... 3.00
Ann 1-2 .... 2.00
Ann 3 .... 3.00

Justice League International
DC, 1987

7-10 .... 2.00
11-23 .... 1.00
24 .... 2.00
25-58 .... 1.00
59-68 .... 2.00
Ann 2-5 .... 3.00
Special 1 .... 2.00
Special 2 .... 3.00

Justice League of America
DC, 1960

1 .... 5,000.00
2 .... 1,250.00
3 .... 1,000.00
4 .... 700.00
5 .... 600.00
6-8 .... 400.00

Hourman

House of Frightenstein

House of Java

House of Mystery

Howard the Duck Holiday Special

Howdy Doody Comics

How The West Was Won

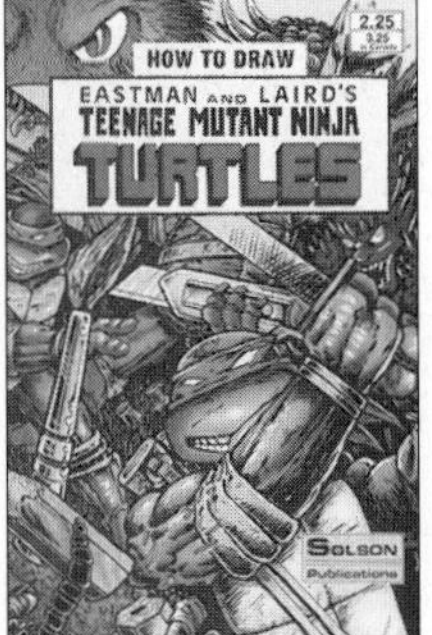

How to Draw Teenage Mutant Ninja Turtles

9 .... 1,000.00
☛JLA origin
10 .... 400.00
11-15 .... 250.00
16-20 .... 225.00
21 .... 350.00
☛Earth-2 visit
22 .... 325.00
23-30 .... 150.00
31 .... 100.00
32-33 .... 90.00
34-36 .... 75.00
☛Supes vs. Cap. Mrv.
37-39 .... 125.00
40-41 .... 75.00
42-45 .... 60.00
☛1st SA Sandman
46 .... 110.00
☛JSA app.
47 .... 95.00
48 .... 140.00
☛Giant issue
49-52 .... 60.00
53-54 .... 55.00
55 .... 115.00
☛JSA team-up
56 .... 100.00
☛JSA team-up
57-62 .... 55.00
63-66 .... 45.00
67 .... 60.00
☛Giant
68 .... 50.00
69-72 .... 45.00
☛Giant
73-81 .... 35.00
82 .... 45.00
☛G.A. Batman app.
83-84 .... 30.00
85 .... 40.00
☛Giant
86-90 .... 25.00
91 .... 35.00
92 .... 32.00
93 .... 25.00
☛Giant
94 .... 60.00
☛Sandman origin
95-99 .... 20.00
100 .... 65.00
101-106 .... 20.00
107-108 .... 25.00
109 .... 20.00
110-116 .... 25.00
117-125 .... 15.00
126-136 .... 10.00
137 .... 20.00
138-150 .... 7.00
151-158 .... 5.00
158/Whitman 10.00
159-160 .... 5.00
160/Whitman 10.00
161 .... 5.00
161/Whitman 10.00
162 .... 5.00
162/Whitman 10.00
163-165 .... 5.00
166 .... 12.00
166/Whitman 25.00
167 .... 12.00
167/Whitman-168 .... 25.00
☛Mindwipe story
168/Whitman 35.00
169 .... 5.00
169/Whitman 10.00
170-171 .... 5.00
171/Whitman 10.00
172 .... 5.00
172/Whitman 10.00
173 .... 5.00
173/Whitman 10.00
174-176 .... 5.00
176/Whitman 10.00
177 .... 5.00
177/Whitman 10.00
178 .... 5.00
178/Whitman 10.00
179 .... 5.00
179/Whitman 10.00
180-181 .... 5.00
181/Whitman 10.00
182-199 .... 5.00
200 .... 7.00
201-217 .... 3.00
218 .... 4.00
219 .... 3.00
220 .... 4.00
221-226 .... 3.00
227 .... 4.00
228-260 .... 3.00
261 .... 4.00
Ann 1 .... 5.00
Ann 2-3 .... 4.00

Justice League of America

DC, 2006

0-1/Variant 6.00
2-2/Variant 4.00
3-38 .... 3.00

Justice League of America: Another Nail

DC, 2004

1-3 .... 6.00

Justice League of America Index

Eclipse, 1986

1-8 .... 2.00

Justice League of America Super Spectacular

DC, 1999

1 .... 6.00

Justice League Quarterly
DC, 1990

1-17 .... 3.00

Justice Leagues: JL?
DC, 2001

1 .... 3.00

Justice Leagues: JLA
DC, 2001

1 .... 3.00

Justice Leagues: Justice League of Aliens
DC, 2001

1 .... 3.00

Justice Leagues: Justice League of Amazons
DC, 2001

1 .... 3.00

Justice Leagues: Justice League of Arkham
DC, 2001

1 .... 3.00

Justice Leagues: Justice League of Atlantis
DC, 2001

1 .... 3.00

Justice League Task Force
DC, 1993

0-5 .... 2.00
6 .... 1.00
7-37 .... 2.00

Justice League Unlimited
DC, 2004

1-29 .... 2.00

Justice Machine (Noble)
Noble, 1981

1-5 .... 3.00
Ann 1 .... 5.00

Justice Machine
Comico, 1987

1 .... 3.00
2-29 .... 2.00
Ann 1 .... 3.00

Justice Machine
Innovation, 1990

1-7 .... 2.00

Justice Machine
Millennium, 1992

1-2 .... 3.00

Justice Machine Featuring the Elementals
Comico, 1986

1-4 .... 2.00

Justice Machine Summer Spectacular
Innovation

1 .... 3.00

Justice Riders
DC, 1997

1 .... 6.00

Justice Society of America
DC, 1991

1-8 .... 2.00

Justice Society of America
DC, 1992

1-5 .... 2.00
6-10 .... 1.00

Justice Society of America
DC, 2007

1-1/Variant 6.00
2 .... 4.00
3-30 .... 3.00

Justice Society of America 100-Page Super Spectacular
DC

1 .... 7.00

Justice Traps the Guilty
Headline, 1947

1 .... 350.00
2 .... 210.00
3 .... 175.00
4-6 .... 160.00
7-10 .... 135.00
11-12 .... 85.00
13 .... 90.00
14-20 .... 58.00
21-30 .... 42.00
31-40 .... 28.00
41-50 .... 24.00
51-70 .... 20.00
71-92 .... 18.00

Just Imagine Comics and Stories
Just Imagine, 1982

1-Special 1 .... 2.00

Just Imagine's Special
Just Imagine, 1986

1 .... 2.00

Just Imagine Stan Lee... Secret Files and Origins
DC, 2002

1 .... 5.00

Just Imagine Stan Lee With Chris Bachalo Creating Catwoman
DC, 2002

1 .... 6.00

How to Publish Comics

H.R. Pufnstuf

Hugga Bunch

Hugo

Hulk Smash

Hulk Versus Thing

Human Defense Corps

Human Target

Just Imagine Stan Lee With Dave Gibbons Creating Green Lantern

DC, 2001

1 .... 6.00

Just Imagine Stan Lee With Gary Frank Creating Shazam!

DC, 2002

1 .... 6.00

Just Imagine Stan Lee With Jerry Ordway Creating JLA

DC, 2002

1 .... 6.00

Just Imagine Stan Lee With Jim Lee Creating Wonder Woman

DC, 2001

1 .... 6.00

Just Imagine Stan Lee With Joe Kubert Creating Batman

DC, 2001

1 .... 6.00

Just Imagine Stan Lee With John Buscema Creating Superman

DC, 2001

1 .... 6.00

Just Imagine Stan Lee With John Byrne Creating Robin

DC, 2002

1 .... 6.00

Just Imagine Stan Lee With John Cassaday Creating Crisis

DC, 2002

1 .... 6.00

Just Imagine Stan Lee With Kevin Maguire Creating The Flash

DC, 2002

1 .... 6.00

Just Imagine Stan Lee With Scott McDaniel Creating Aquaman

DC, 2002

1 .... 6.00

Just Imagine Stan Lee with Walter Simonson Creating Sandman

DC, 2002

1 .... 6.00

Just Married

Charlton, 1958

1 .... 40.00
2 .... 24.00
3-5 .... 15.00
6-10 .... 10.00
11-20 .... 9.00
21-30 .... 6.00
31-60 .... 5.00
61-80 .... 4.00
81-114 .... 3.00

Just Twisted

Necromics

1 .... 2.00

Justy

Viz, 1988

1-9 .... 2.00

Ka'a'nga Comics

Fiction House, 1949

1 .... 500.00
2 .... 270.00
3 .... 185.00
4-5 .... 150.00
6-10 .... 125.00
11-20 .... 100.00

Kaboom

Awesome, 1997

1-Ashcan-1/Gold 3.00

Kabuki

Image, 1997

½ 3.00
½/A 4.00
1-1/A 5.00
2-4 .... 4.00
5-9 .... 3.00

Kabuki Agents

Image, 1999

1-8 .... 3.00

Kabuki: Circle of Blood

Caliber, 1995

1 .... 4.00
1/Ltd 5.00
1/2nd-3 .... 4.00
4-6 .... 3.00
6/Ltd 15.00

Kabuki Classics

Image, 1999

1-2 .... 3.00
3 .... 5.00
4-12 .... 3.00

Kabuki Color Special
Caliber, 1996
1 .... 4.00

Kabuki Compilation
Caliber, 1995
1 .... 8.00

Kabuki: Dance of Death
London Night, 1995
1 .... 4.00

Kabuki Dreams
Image, 1998
nn 5.00

Kabuki: Dreams of the Dead
Caliber, 1996
1 .... 3.00

Kabuki: Fear the Reaper
Caliber, 1994
1 .... 4.00

Kabuki Gallery
Caliber, 1995
1 .... 3.00
1/A 15.00

Kabuki: The Ghost Play
Image, 2002
1 .... 3.00

Kabuki-Images
Image, 1998
1-2 .... 5.00

Kabuki
Marvel, 2004
1 .... 4.00
1/Variant 5.00
2-4 .... 3.00
4/Hughes 4.00
5-7 .... 3.00

Kabuki: Masks of the Noh
Image, 1996
1-4 .... 3.00

Kabuki Reflections
Image, 1998
1-4 .... 5.00

Kabuki: Reflections
Marvel, 2007
1 .... 6.00

Kabuki: Skin Deep
Caliber, 1996
1 .... 4.00
2-2/A 3.00
2/Ltd 8.00
3 .... 3.00

Kafka
Renegade, 1987
1-6 .... 3.00

Kafka: The Execution
Fantagraphics
1 .... 3.00

Kaktus
Fantagraphics
1 .... 3.00

Kalamazoo Comix
Discount Hobby, 1996
1-3 .... 2.00
4-5 .... 3.00

Kalgan the Golden
Harrier, 1988
1 .... 2.00

Kamandi: At Earth's End
DC, 1993
1-6 .... 2.00

Kamandi, the Last Boy on Earth
DC, 1972
1 .... 20.00
2 .... 15.00
3 .... 10.00
4-10 .... 8.00
11-19 .... 7.00
20-38 .... 6.00
39-40 .... 5.00
41-54 .... 4.00
55-58 .... 3.00
59 .... 4.00

Kama Sutra (Manara's...)
NBM
1 .... 13.00

Kama Sutra (Girl's...)
Black Lace
1 .... 3.00

Kamichama Karin
Tokyopop, 2005
1-2 .... 10.00

Kamikaze
DC, 2003
1-6 .... 3.00

Kamikaze Cat
Pied Piper, 1987
1 .... 2.00

Kane
Dancing Elephant, 1998
1-22 .... 4.00
23-26 .... 3.00
27 .... 5.00
28-32 .... 3.00

Kanpai!
Tokyopop, 2005
1-2 .... 10.00

Human Target Special

Humbug

Humongous Man

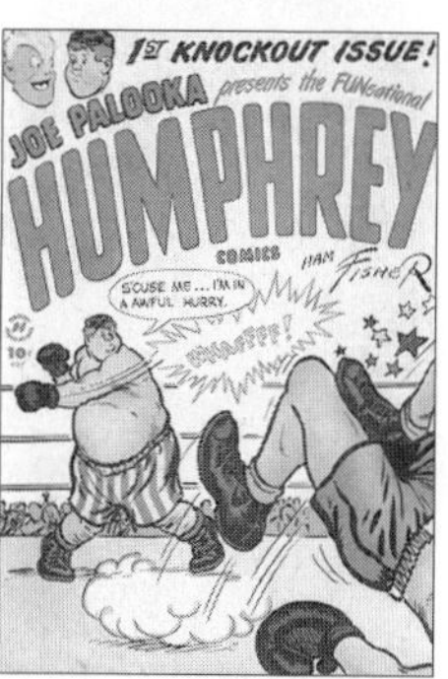

Humphrey Comics

Hup

Hurricane LeRoux

Hyde-25

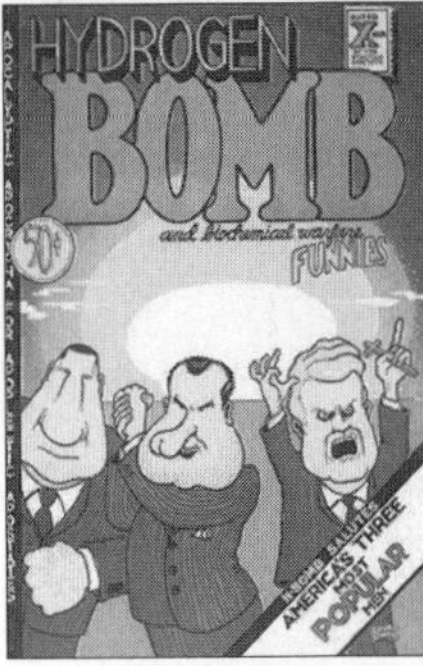

Hydrogen Bomb Funnies

Kansas Thunder
Red Menace
1 .... 3.00

Kaos
Tommy Regalado, 1994
1 .... 2.00

Kaos Moon
Caliber, 1996
1-4 .... 3.00

Kaptain Keen & Kompany
Vortex, 1986
1-6 .... 2.00

Karas
Dark Horse, 2005
1 .... 3.00

Karate Girl
Fantagraphics, 1993
1-2 .... 3.00

Karate Girl Tengu Wars
Fantagraphics, 1995
1-3 .... 3.00

Karate Kid
DC, 1976
1 .... 12.00
2-3 .... 7.00
4-15 .... 5.00

Karate Kreatures
Ma, 1989
1-2 .... 2.00

Kare Kano
Tokyopop, 2003
1-18 .... 10.00

Karma Incorporated
Viper, 2005
1-2 .... 3.00

Karney
Idea & Design Works, 2005
1-4 .... 4.00

Karza
Image, 2003
1-4 .... 3.00

Kasco Comics
Kasko Grainfeed, 1949
1 .... 55.00
2 .... 48.00

Kathy (Standard)
Standard, 1949
1 .... 70.00
2 .... 48.00
3-4 .... 42.00
5-7 .... 36.00
8-17 .... 32.00

Kathy
Atlas, 1959
1 .... 48.00
2-5 .... 35.00
6-9 .... 30.00
10-27 .... 26.00

Katmandu
Antarctic, 1993
1-7 .... 3.00
8-12 .... 2.00
13-25 .... 3.00
26-Ann 4 .... 5.00

Kato of the Green Hornet
Now, 1991
1-4 .... 3.00

Kato of the Green Hornet II
Now, 1992
1-2 .... 3.00

Katy Keene
Archie, 1949
1 .... 650.00
2 .... 375.00
3-5 .... 240.00
6-10 .... 170.00
11-20 .... 125.00
21-30 .... 90.00
31-50 .... 70.00
51-62 .... 55.00
Ann 1 .... 285.00
Ann 2 .... 165.00
3D 1 .... 325.00

Katy Keene
Archie, 1985
8-20 .... 2.00
21-33 .... 1.00

Katy Keene Fashion Book Magazine
Archie, 1955
1 .... 325.00
2 .... 180.00
13-14 .... 140.00
15-16 .... 110.00
17-19 .... 95.00
20-21 .... 85.00
22-23 .... 80.00

Katy Keene Pin Up Parade
Archie, 1955
1 .... 300.00
2 .... 175.00
3 .... 165.00
4-5 .... 145.00
6-8 .... 125.00
9-10 .... 110.00
11-15 .... 80.00

Katy Keene Special
Archie, 1983
1 .... 3.00
2-7 .... 2.00

Katzenjammer Kids

David McKay, 1947

1 ... 110.00
2 ... 80.00
3 ... 65.00
4-5 ... 50.00
6-9 ... 42.00
10-16 ... 36.00
17-22 ... 30.00
23-27 ... 24.00

Ka-Zar

Marvel, 1970

1 ... 35.00
2-3 ... 15.00

Ka-Zar

Marvel, 1974

1 ... 17.00
2 ... 7.00
3-7 ... 5.00
8-15 ... 3.00
15/30¢ ... 20.00
16 ... 3.00
16/30¢ ... 20.00
17 ... 3.00
17/30¢ ... 20.00
18-20 ... 3.00

Ka-Zar

Marvel, 1997

-1 ... 2.00
1 ... 3.00
2-20 ... 2.00
Ann 1997 ... 3.00

Kazar of the Savage Land

Marvel, 1997

1 ... 3.00

Ka-Zar the Savage

Marvel, 1981

1 ... 5.00
2-12 ... 2.00
12/2nd ... 1.00
13-34 ... 2.00

K Chronicles

Keith Knight, 1998

1-9 ... 2.00

Keen Detective Funnies (Vol. 1)

Centaur, 1938

8 ... 1,400.00
9 ... 650.00
10-11 ... 550.00

Keen Detective Funnies (Vol. 2)

Centaur, 1939

1 ... 550.00
2 ... 500.00
3-6 ... 440.00
7 ... 1,650.00
8 ... 585.00
9-11 ... 525.00
12 ... 610.00

Keen Detective Funnies (Vol. 3)

Centaur, 1940

17 ... 475.00
18-19 ... 500.00
20 ... 640.00
21-22 ... 475.00
23-24 ... 625.00

Keen Komics

Centaur, 1939

1 ... 575.00
2 ... 285.00
3 ... 265.00

Keenspot Spotlight

Keenspot, 2002

2002-2003 ... 1.00

Keen Teens

Life's Romances, 1945

1 ... 145.00
2 ... 165.00
3 ... 58.00
4 ... 50.00
5 ... 55.00
6 ... 50.00

Keep

Idea & Design Works, 2005

1-5 ... 4.00

Keif Llama

Oni, 1999

1 ... 3.00

Keif Llama Xeno-Tech

Fantagraphics, 1987

1-6 ... 2.00

Keif Llama: Xenotech

Aeon, 2005

1-2 ... 3.00

Kekkaishi

Viz, 2005

1-3 ... 10.00

Kelly Belle Police Detective

Newcomers

1-3 ... 3.00

Kelly Green

Dargaud

1-2 ... 15.00

Kelvin Mace

Vortex, 1988

1 ... 3.00
2 ... 2.00

Kendra: Legacy of the Blood

Perrydog, 1987

1-2 ... 2.00

Hyper Dolls

Hyperkind

Hypersonic

I Am Legend

I Before E

Ibis the Invincible

Icicle

I Come In Peace

Ken Maynard Western

Fawcett, 1950

1 .... 375.00
2 .... 265.00
3 .... 185.00
4-5 .... 165.00
6-8 .... 150.00

Ken Shannon

Quality, 1951

1 .... 175.00
2 .... 120.00
3-5 .... 90.00
6-10 .... 75.00

Ken Stuart

Publication Enterprises, 1949

1 .... 38.00

Kent Blake of the Secret Service

Atlas, 1951

1 .... 150.00
2 .... 90.00
3-5 .... 65.00
6-14 .... 45.00

Kents

DC, 1997

1-12 .... 3.00

Kerry Drake

Blackthorne, 1986

1-5 .... 7.00

Kerry Drake Detective Cases

Life's Romances, 1944

1 .... 150.00
2 .... 115.00
3 .... 95.00
4-5 .... 85.00
6-8 .... 65.00
9-10 .... 80.00
11-15 .... 50.00
16-20 .... 42.00
21-30 .... 38.00
31-33 .... 32.00

Kewpies

Will Eisner, 1949

1 .... 125.00

Key Comics

Consolidated, 1944

1 .... 215.00
2 .... 170.00
3-5 .... 150.00

Keyhole

Millennium, 1996

1-5 .... 3.00

Key Ring Comics

Dell, 1941

1-5 .... 45.00

Khan

Moonstone, 2005

1 .... 3.00

Kick Ass

Marvel, 2008

1 .... 8.00
2 .... 4.00

Kickers, Inc.

Marvel, 1986

1-12 .... 1.00

Kid's Joker

ADV Manga, 2005

1 .... 10.00

Kid Anarchy

Fantagraphics, 1990

1-3 .... 3.00

Kid Blastoff

Slave Labor, 1996

1 .... 3.00

Kid Cannibal

Eternity, 1991

1-4 .... 3.00

Kid Carrots

St. John, 1953

1 .... 35.00

Kid Colt Outlaw

Marvel, 1948

1 .... 665.00
2 .... 335.00
3-5 .... 250.00
6-10 .... 175.00
11 .... 225.00
12-20 .... 150.00
21-30 .... 105.00
31-40 .... 90.00
41-50 .... 80.00
51-60 .... 65.00
61-70 .... 48.00
71-100 .... 40.00
101-110 .... 28.00
111-120 .... 18.00
121-130 .... 14.00
131-139 .... 10.00
140-170 .... 5.00
171-200 .... 4.00
201-205 .... 3.00
205/30¢ 20.00
206-219 .... 3.00
219/35¢ 15.00
220 .... 3.00
220/35¢ 15.00
221-229 .... 3.00

Kid Cowboy

Ziff-Davis, 1950

1 .... 75.00
2 .... 70.00
3 .... 60.00
4 .... 50.00

5-6 .... 45.00
7-9 .... 40.00
10-11 .... 35.00
12-14 .... 30.00

Kid Death & Fluffy: Halloween Special
Event, 1997
1 .... 3.00

Kid Death & Fluffy Spring Break Special
Event, 1996
1 .... 3.00

Kiddie Kapers
Kiddie Kapers
1 .... 40.00
2 .... 30.00

Kiddie Karnival
Ziff-Davis, 1952
1 .... 165.00

Kid Eternity
Quality, 1946
1 .... 560.00
2 .... 290.00
3 .... 250.00
4-5 .... 175.00
6-10 .... 135.00
11-18 .... 105.00

Kid Eternity
DC, 1991
1-3 .... 5.00

Kid Eternity
DC, 1993
1-16 .... 2.00

Kid from Dodge City
Atlas, 1957
1 .... 60.00
2 .... 40.00

Kid from Texas
Atlas, 1957
1 .... 60.00
2 .... 40.00

Kid Komics
Timely, 1943
1 .... 2,800.00
2 .... 1,150.00
3-4 .... 1,000.00
5-7 .... 650.00
8-10 .... 515.00

Kid Montana
Charlton, 1957
9 .... 28.00
10 .... 18.00
11-12 .... 14.00
13 .... 18.00
14-20 .... 14.00
21-30 .... 9.00
31-40 .... 6.00
41-50 .... 4.00

Kid 'n Play
Marvel, 1992
1-9 .... 1.00

Kid Slade, Gunfighter
Atlas, 1957
5 .... 45.00
6-7 .... 40.00

Kid Supreme
Image, 1996
1-3/A 3.00

Kid's WB Jam Packed Action
DC, 2004
1 .... 8.00

Kid Terrific
Image, 1998
1 .... 3.00

Kidz of the King
King, 1994
1-3 .... 3.00

Kid Zoo Comics
Street & Smith, 1948
1 .... 130.00

Ki-Gorr the Killer
AC
1 .... 4.00

Kiku San
Aircel, 1988
1-6 .... 2.00

Kilgore
Renegade, 1987
1-4 .... 2.00

Kill Barny
Express, 1992
1 .... 3.00

Kill Barny 3
Express, 1992
1 .... 3.00

Killbox
Antarctic, 2002
1-3 .... 5.00

Killer Fly
Slave Labor, 1995
1-3 .... 3.00

Killer Instinct
Acclaim, 1996
1-6 .... 3.00

Killer Instinct Nintendo Power Exclusive Edition
Acclaim
1 .... 1.00

Killer Instinct Tour Book
Image
1/A-1/Gold 3.00

Icon

Iczer 3

Id

Idaho

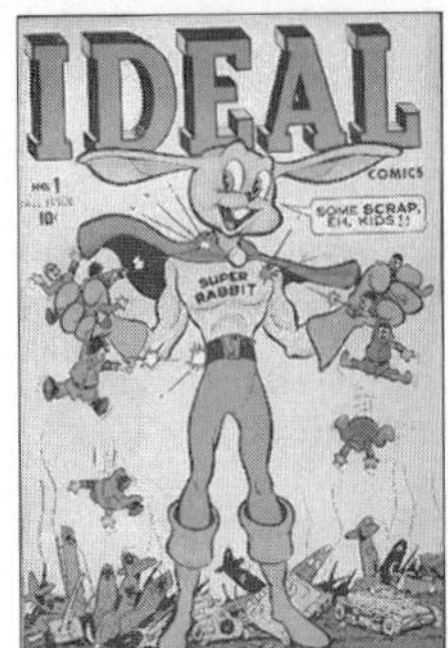

Ideal Comics

Ideal Romance

Identity Crisis

Identity Disc

Killers
Magazine Enterprises, 1947

1 ..... 650.00
2 ..... 575.00

Killer 7
Devil's Due, 2006

1-3 ..... 3.00
3/Special 6.00
4 ..... 3.00
4/Special 6.00

Killer Stunts, Inc.
Alias, 2005

1-4 ..... 3.00

Killer...Tales by Timothy Truman
Eclipse, 1985

1 ..... 2.00

Kill Image
Boneyard

1 ..... 4.00

Killing Stroke
Eternity

1-4 ..... 3.00

Kill Marvel
Boneyard

1/Ltd 5.00

Killpower: The Early Years
Marvel, 1993

1-4 ..... 2.00

Killraven
Marvel, 2001

1 ..... 3.00

Killraven
Marvel, 2002

1-6 ..... 3.00

Kill Razor Special
Image, 1995

1 ..... 3.00

Kill Your Boyfriend
DC, 1995

1 ..... 5.00
1/2nd 6.00

Kilroy: Daemonstorm
Caliber, 1997

..... 3.00

Kilroy
Caliber, 1998

1-1/A 3.00

Kilroy Is Here
Caliber, 1994

0-10 ..... 3.00

Kilroy: Revelations
Caliber, 1994

1 ..... 3.00

Kilroys
ACG, 1947

1 ..... 90.00
2 ..... 55.00
3-5 ..... 38.00
6-10 ..... 30.00
11-20 ..... 20.00
21-30 ..... 16.00
31-40 ..... 14.00
41-47 ..... 12.00
48-49 ..... 40.00
50-54 ..... 12.00

Kilroys
Avalon, 2002

1 ..... 3.00

Kilroy: The Short Stories
Caliber, 1995

1 ..... 3.00

Kimber, Prince of the Feylons
Antarctic, 1992

1-2 ..... 3.00

Kimera
ADV Manga, 2005

1 ..... 10.00

Kimura
Nightwynd, 1991

1-4 ..... 3.00

Kin
Image, 1999

1-5 ..... 3.00
6 ..... 4.00

Kindred
Image, 1994

1 ..... 3.00
2-3/A 2.00
4 ..... 3.00

Kindred II
DC, 2002

1-4 ..... 3.00

Kinetic
DC, 2004

1-8 ..... 3.00

King Arthur and the Knights of Justice
Marvel, 1993

1-3 ..... 1.00

King Comics
David McKay, 1936

1 ..... 8,000.00
2 ..... 2,650.00
3 ..... 1,350.00
4 ..... 1,100.00
5 ..... 850.00
6-10 ..... 625.00
11-15 ..... 450.00
16-20 ..... 390.00

21-30 .... 275.00
31-40 .... 220.00
41-50 .... 175.00
51-60 .... 135.00
61-70 .... 110.00
71-80 .... 95.00
81-90 .... 75.00
91-100 .... 65.00
101-120 .... 50.00
121-140 .... 35.00
141-159 .... 25.00

King Comics Presents
King Comics
1 .... 2.00

King Conan
Marvel, 1980
1 .... 5.00
2-10 .... 2.00
11-19 .... 1.00

King David
DC, 2002
1 .... 20.00

Kingdom
DC, 1999
1 .... 3.00
2 .... 3.00

Kingdom Come
DC, 1996
1-4 .... 5.00

Kingdom Hearts
Tokyopop, 2005
1-4 .... 6.00

Kingdom: Kid Flash
DC, 1999
1 .... 2.00

Kingdom: Nightstar
DC, 1999
1 .... 2.00

Kingdom: Offspring
DC, 1999
1 .... 2.00

Kingdom of the Dwarfs
Comico
1 .... 5.00

Kingdom of the Wicked
Caliber, 1996
1-4 .... 3.00

Kingdom: Planet Krypton
DC, 1999
1 .... 2.00

Kingdom: Son of the Bat
DC, 1999
1 .... 2.00

King Kong
Gold Key, 1968
1 .... 12.00

King Kong
Monster, 1991
1-6 .... 3.00

King Leonardo and His Short Subjects
Gold Key, 1962
1 .... 35.00
2-4 .... 25.00

King Louie and Mowgli
Gold Key, 1968
1 .... 20.00

King of Diamonds
Dell, 1962
1 .... 30.00

King of Hell
Tokyopop, 2003
1-11 .... 10.00

King of the Dead
Fantaco, 1988
0-3 .... 2.00
4 .... 3.00

King of the Royal Mounted
Dell, 1952
8 .... 35.00
9-10 .... 32.00
11-28 .... 28.00

Kingpin
Marvel, 1997
1 .... 6.00

Kingpin
Marvel, 2003
1-7 .... 3.00

Kings in Disguise
Kitchen Sink, 1988
1-6 .... 2.00

Kings of the Night
Dark Horse, 1990
1-2 .... 2.00

King Tiger & Motorhead
Dark Horse, 1996
1-2 .... 3.00

Kinki Klitt Komics
Rip Off, 1992
1-2 .... 3.00

Kinky Hook
Fantagraphics
1 .... 3.00

Kip
Hammer & Anvil
1 .... 3.00

Kirby King of the Serials
Blackthorne, 1989
1 .... 2.00

Idiotland

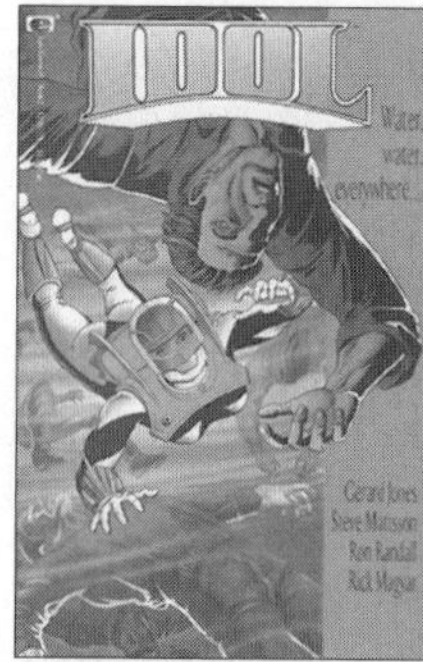

Idol

I Feel Sick

I Had a Dream

Iliad

Illegal Aliens

Illuminator

Illustrated Editions

Kiss
Personality
1 ....4.00
2-3 ....3.00

Kiss
Dark Horse, 2002
1-13/Photo 3.00

Kiss & Tell
Patricia Breen, 1995
1 ....3.00

Kiss & Tell
Sirius, 1996
1 ....3.00

Kiss Classics
Marvel
1 ....10.00

Kisses
Spoof, 1996
1 ....3.00

Kissing Canvas
MN Design
1 ....6.00

Kiss Kiss Bang Bang
CrossGen, 2004
1 ....4.00
1/2nd-5 ....3.00

Kissnation
Marvel
1 ....11.00

Kiss of Death
Acme, 1987
1 ....2.00

Kiss of the Vampire
Brainstorm, 1996
1 ....3.00

Kiss Pre-History
Revolutionary, 1993
1-3 ....3.00

Kiss: Psycho Circus
Image, 1997
1-28 ....2.00
29-31 ....3.00
Special 1 ....2.00

Kiss: Satan's Music?
Celebrity
1 ....4.00

Kissyfur
DC, 1989
1 ....2.00

Kiss: You Wanted the Best, You Got the Best
Wizard, 1998
1 ....1.00

Kit Carson and the Blackfeet Warriors
Realistic Comics, 1953
1 ....40.00

Kitchen Sink Classics
Kitchen Sink, 1994
1 ....5.00
2-3 ....3.00

Kitty
St. John, 1948
1 ....34.00

Kitty Pryde & Wolverine
Marvel, 1984
1-6 ....3.00

Kitty Pryde, Agent of Shield
Marvel, 1997
1-3 ....3.00

Kitz 'n' Katz Komiks
Phantasy, 1986
1-6 ....2.00

Kiwanni: Daughter of the Dawn
C&T, 1988
1 ....2.00

Klor
Sirius, 1998
1-3 ....3.00

Klownshock
Northstar, 1992
1 ....3.00

Knewts of the Round Table
Pan, 1998
1-5 ....3.00

Knight
Bear Claw, 1993
0 ....3.00

Knightfool: The Fall of the Splatman
Parody
1 ....3.00

Knighthawk
Acclaim, 1995
1-6 ....3.00

Knightmare (Antarctic)
Antarctic, 1994
1-6 ....3.00

Knightmare
Image, 1995
0 ....4.00
1-8 ....3.00

Knightshift
London Night, 1996
1-2 .... 3.00

Knights' Kingdom
Lego
1 .... 5.00

Knights of Pendragon
Marvel, 1990
1 .... 3.00
2-18 .... 2.00

Knights of Pendragon
Marvel, 1992
1-15 .... 2.00

Knights of the Dinner Table
Kenzer, 1994
1 .... 150.00
2 .... 45.00
3 .... 25.00
4 .... 30.00
4/2nd-5 .... 25.00
6-10 .... 18.00
11-15 .... 14.00
16-21 .... 10.00
22-30 .... 6.00
31-32 .... 4.00
33-49 .... 3.00
50 .... 5.00
51-69 .... 3.00
70-99 .... 4.00
100 .... 8.00
101-108 .... 4.00
109-155 .... 5.00

Knights of the Dinner Table: Black Hands Gaming Society Special
Kenzer and Company, 2003
1-2 .... 3.00

Knights of the Dinner Table: Everknights
Kenzer and Company, 2002
Special 1 .... 3.00

Knights of the Dinner Table/Faans Crossover Special
Six Handed, 1999
1 .... 3.00

Knights of the Dinner Table Illustrated
Kenzer, 2000
1-41 .... 3.00

Knights of the Jaguar Super Limited One Shot
Image, 2004
1 .... 3.00

Knights of the Zodiac
Viz, 8
1-12 .... 8.00

Knights on Broadway
Broadway, 1996
1-3 .... 3.00

Knight's Round Table
Knight, 1996
1-1/A 3.00

Knightstrike
Image, 1995
1 .... 3.00

Knight Watchman
Image, 1998
1-4 .... 3.00

Knight Watchman: Graveyard Shift
Caliber, 1994
1-2 .... 3.00

Knight Wolf
Five Star
1-3 .... 3.00

Knockout Adventures
Fiction House, 1954
1 .... 75.00

Knuckles
Archie, 1997
1 .... 4.00
2-3 .... 3.00
4-29 .... 2.00

Knuckles' Chaotix
Archie, 1996
1 .... 3.00

Knuckles the Malevolent Nun
Fantagraphics, 1991
1-2 .... 2.00

Kobalt
DC, 1994
1-12 .... 2.00
13-16 .... 3.00

Kobier and Oso
Gebhart
1 .... 2.00

Kobra
DC, 1976
1 .... 9.00
2-7 .... 3.00

Kodocha: Sana's Stage
Tokyopop, 2002
1-3 .... 10.00

Kogaratsu: The Lotus of Blood
Acme
1 .... 6.00

I Love Lucy

I Love Lucy Comics

I Love Lucy in Full Color

Image

Image Introduces... Believer

Image Introduces... Cryptopia

Image Introduces... Legend of Isis

Image Plus

Kokey Koala
Toby, 1952

1 .... 25.00

Koko and Kola
Magazine Enterprises, 1947

1 .... 45.00
2 .... 35.00
3-6 .... 25.00

K.O. Komics
Gerona, 1945

1 .... 425.00

Kolchak Tales: Black & White & Red All Over
Moonstone, 2005

1/A cover-1/B cover 5.00

Kolchak: Tales of the Night Stalker
Moonstone, 2004

1/A-6/B 4.00

Kolchak: The Night Stalker: Get of Belial
Moonstone, 2002

1 .... 7.00

Kolchak: The Night Stalker
Moonstone, 2002

1 .... 7.00

Kolynos Presents the White Guard
Whitehall Pharmacal, 1949

1 .... 20.00

Komic Kartoons
Timely, 1945

1 .... 70.00
2 .... 65.00

Komik Pages
Harry A. Chesler, 1945

10 .... 125.00

Komodo and the Defiants
Victory, 1987

1-2 .... 2.00

Kona
Dell, 1962

2 .... 18.00
3-5 .... 15.00
6-14 .... 12.00
15-21 .... 10.00

Konga
Charlton, 1960

1 .... 75.00
2 .... 50.00
3-4 .... 35.00
5-10 .... 25.00
11-20 .... 16.00
21-23 .... 14.00

Konga's Revenge
Charlton, 1963

1 .... 10.00
2-3 .... 7.00

Kong, 8th Wonder of the World - Movie Adaptation
Dark Horse, 2006

1 .... 4.00

Kong the Untamed
DC, 1975

1 .... 9.00
2-5 .... 3.00

Konny and Czu
Antarctic, 1994

1-4 .... 3.00

Koolau the Leper (Jack London's...)
Tome

1 .... 3.00

Koosh Kins
Archie, 1991

1-4 .... 1.00

K.O. Punch
E.C., 1948

1 .... 650.00

Korak, Son of Tarzan
Gold Key, 1964

1 .... 65.00
2-5 .... 45.00
6-11 .... 30.00
12-18 .... 25.00
19-37 .... 20.00
38-46 .... 17.00
47-51 .... 15.00
52-59 .... 10.00

Kore
Image, 2003

1-5 .... 3.00

Korg: 70,000 B.C.
Charlton, 1975

1 .... 8.00
2-9 .... 5.00

Korvus
Arrow, 1998

0-3 .... 3.00

Korvus
Arrow, 1998

1-2 .... 3.00

Kosmic Kat
Image, 1999

1 .... 3.00

Kosmic Kat Activity Book
Image, 1999

1 .... 3.00

Krazy Kat
Dell, 1951

1	40.00
2-5	25.00

Krazy Kat
Gold Key, 1964

1	15.00

Krazy Komics
Timely, 1942

1	300.00
2	165.00
3	120.00
4-5	95.00
6-9	80.00
10-11	70.00
12	100.00
13-15	65.00
16-19	45.00
20-22	30.00
23-26	25.00

Krazy Krow
Marvel, 1945

1	100.00
2	65.00
3	55.00

Krazy Life
Fox, 1945

1	60.00

Kree-Skrull War Starring The Avengers
Marvel, 1983

1-2	3.00

Kremen
Grey Productions

1-3	3.00

Krey
Gauntlet, 1992

1-3	3.00
Special 1	4.00

Krofft Supershow
Gold Key, 1978

1	6.00
2-6	4.00

Krull
Marvel, 1983

1-2	1.00

Krusty Comics
Bongo, 1995

1-3	3.00

Krypton Chronicles
DC, 1981

1-3	2.00

Krypto the Super Dog
DC, 2006

1	2.00
2	3.00
3-4	2.00

Kull and the Barbarians
Marvel, 1975

1	16.00
2	4.00
3	5.00

Kull in 3-D
Blackthorne

1-2	3.00

Kull the Conqueror
Marvel, 1971

1	20.00
2	12.00
3-4	8.00
5	7.00
6-10	5.00

Kull the Conqueror
Marvel, 1982

1	5.00
2	3.00

Kull the Conqueror
Marvel, 1983

1-5	2.00
6-10	1.00

Kull the Destroyer
Marvel, 1973

11-16	2.00
16/30¢	20.00
17-21	2.00
21/35¢	15.00
22	2.00
22/35¢	15.00
23-23/Whitman	2.00
23/35¢	15.00
24-29	2.00

Kunoichi
Lightning, 1996

1	3.00

Kwaiden
Dark Horse, 2004

1	15.00

Kyra
Elsewhere, 1985

1-6	2.00

Kyrie
ADV Manga, 2005

1	10.00

K-Z Comics Presents
K-Z, 1985

1	2.00

Lab
Astonish, 2001

1	4.00
2	3.00

La Blue Girl
CPM, 1996

1-12	3.00

Images of Omaha

Images of Shadowhawk

Imagi-Mation

Immortal Combat

Immortal II

Imp

Impact

Impact Christmas Special

Labman
Image, 1996

1-1/C 4.00
2-3 ....3.00

Labman Sourcebook
Image, 1996

1 ....1.00

Labor Force
Blackthorne, 1986

1-8 ....2.00

Labor is a Partner
Catechetical Guild, 1949

1 ....120.00

Labours of Hercules
Malan Classical Enterprises

1 ....3.00

Lab Rats
DC, 2002

1-7 ....3.00

Labyrinth of Madness
TSR

1 ....1.00

Labyrinth: The Movie
Marvel, 1986

1-3 ....2.00

Lackluster World
Gen: Eric Publishing, 2004

L.A. Comics
Los Angeles, 1971

1-2 ....3.00

La Cosa Nostroid
Fireman, 1996

1-9 ....3.00

Lad, A Dog
Dell, 1962

2 ....30.00

Lady and the Tramp
Dell, 1955

1 ....25.00

Lady and the Tramp
Gold Key, 1963

1 ....25.00
1 (1973) 14.00

Lady and the Vampire
NBM

1 ....11.00

Lady Arcane
Hero Graphics, 1992

1 ....5.00
2-3 ....4.00
4 ....3.00

Lady Crime
AC, 1992

1 ....3.00

Lady Death 10th Anniversary Edition
Avatar, 2004

1 ....4.00
1/Leather 30.00
1/Painted 4.00
1/Platinum-1/Premium 10.00

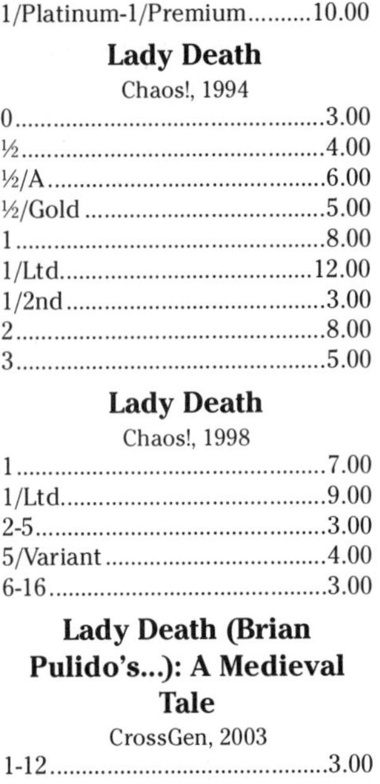

Lady Death
Chaos!, 1994

0 ....3.00
½ 4.00
½/A 6.00
½/Gold 5.00
1 ....8.00
1/Ltd 12.00
1/2nd 3.00
2 ....8.00
3 ....5.00

Lady Death
Chaos!, 1998

1 ....7.00
1/Ltd 9.00
2-5 ....3.00
5/Variant 4.00
6-16 ....3.00

Lady Death (Brian Pulido's...): A Medieval Tale
CrossGen, 2003

1-12 ....3.00

Lady Death: Alive
Chaos, 2001

1-4 ....3.00

Lady Death and the Women of Chaos! Gallery
Chaos, 1996

1 ....2.00

Lady Death/Bad Kitty
Chaos, 2001

1 ....3.00

Lady Death (Brian Pulido's...): Wild Hunt
CrossGen, 2004

1-2 ....3.00

Lady Death: Dark Millennium
Chaos, 2000

1-2 ....3.00

Lady Death: Dragon Wars
Chaos, 1998

1 ....3.00

Lady Death IV: The Crucible
Chaos!, 1996

½ 5.00
½/A 8.00

1 .... 3.00
1/A 13.00
1/B 16.00
1/Silver 4.00
2-5 .... 3.00
5/Variant 5.00
6 .... 3.00

Lady Death: Heartbreaker
Chaos, 2002

1-4 .... 3.00
Ashcan 1 .... 1.00

Lady Death in Lingerie
Chaos!, 1995

1 .... 3.00
1/Ltd. 10.00

Lady Death: Judgement War
Chaos!, 1999

1-3 .... 3.00

Lady Death: Judgement War Prelude
Chaos!, 1999

1 .... 3.00

Lady Death: Retribution
Chaos!, 1998

1 .... 3.00
1/A-1/Ltd. 4.00

Lady Death Swimsuit 2005
Avatar

0 .... 4.00
0/Battle 6.00
0/Gold 10.00
0/Leather 25.00
0/Platinum 15.00
0/Wraparound 4.00

Lady Death Swimsuit Special
Chaos!, 1994

1 .... 3.00
1/Variant 8.00

Lady Death: The Gauntlet
Chaos, 2002

1-2 .... 3.00

Lady Death: The Rapture
Chaos!, 1999

1-4 .... 3.00

Lady Death III: The Odyssey
Chaos!, 1996

-1 .... 2.00
1 .... 4.00
1/Variant 5.00
2-4 .... 3.00
4/A 8.00

Lady Death: Tribulation
Chaos!, 2000

1-2 .... 3.00

Lady Death II: Between Heaven & Hell
Chaos!, 1995

1-1/A 4.00
1/B-1/Ltd. 5.00
1/2nd-4 .... 3.00
4/Variant 5.00

Lady Death/Vampirella: Dark Hearts
Chaos!, 1999

1 .... 4.00
1/A 8.00

Lady Death vs. Purgatori
Chaos!, 1999

1 .... 3.00
1/A 5.00

Lady Death vs. Vampirella
Chaos, 2000

Ashcan 1 .... 1.00

Lady Death: Wicked Ways
Chaos!, 1998

1 .... 3.00
1/Variant 5.00

Lady Dracula
Fantaco

1-2 .... 5.00

Lady Justice (Vol. 1) (Neil Gaiman's...)
Tekno, 1995

1-11 .... 2.00

Lady Justice (Vol. 2) (Neil Gaiman's...)
Big, 1996

1-9 .... 2.00

Lady Luck
Quality, 1949

86 .... 550.00
87-88 .... 375.00
89-90 .... 325.00

Lady Pendragon
Maximum, 1996

1-1/A 3.00
1/Autographed 6.00
1/2nd 3.00
Ashcan 1 .... 4.00
Ashcan 1/Autogr 6.00

Lady Pendragon
Image, 1998

0 .... 3.00
0/A 4.00
1-1/2nd 3.00
2 .... 4.00
2/A-3/A 3.00
Ashcan 1 .... 2.00

Imperial Guard

Impulse

Impulse Plus

Incredible Hulk and Wolverine

Incredible Science Fiction

Indiana Jones and the Fate of Atlantis

Indiana Jones and the Last Crusade

Indiana Jones and the Sargasso Pirates

Lady Pendragon
Image, 1999
1-1/A....3.00
1/B....4.00
2-6....3.00
7....4.00
8-10....3.00

Lady Pendragon Gallery Edition
Image, 1999
1-1/A....3.00

Lady Pendragon: Merlin
Image, 2000
1....3.00

Lady Pendragon/ More Than Mortal
Image, 1999
1....3.00
1/A....4.00
1/B....5.00
Ashcan 1....2.00

Lady Rawhide
Topps, 1995
1-5....3.00

Lady Rawhide
Topps, 1996
½....5.00
1-5....3.00

Lady Rawhide Mini Comic
Topps, 1995
1....1.00

Lady Rawhide: Other People's Blood
Image, 1999
1-5....3.00

Lady Rawhide Special Edition
Topps, 1995
1....4.00

Lady Spectra & Sparky Special
J. Kevin Carrier, 1995
1....3.00

Lady Supreme
Image, 1996
1-2....3.00

Lady Vamprè
Black Out
0-1....3.00

Lady Vamprè: Pleasures of the Flesh
Black Out
1....3.00

Lady Vamprè vs. Black Lace
Black Out, 1996
1....3.00

Laff-a-Lympics
Marvel, 1978
1....18.00
2....10.00
3-5....8.00
6-13....6.00

Laffin' Gas
Blackthorne, 1986
1-12....2.00

Laffy-Daffy Comics
Rural Home, 1945
1-2....40.00

Lagoon Engine Einsatz
ADV Manga, 2005
1....11.00

Lament of the Lamb
Tokyopop, 2004
1....10.00

Lana
Timely, 1948
1....100.00
2....65.00
3-7....40.00

Lance Barnes: Post Nuke Dick
Marvel, 1993
1-4....3.00

Lancelot Link, Secret Chimp
Gold Key, 1971
1....30.00
2....17.00
3-8....10.00

Lancelot Strong, the Shield
Archie, 1983
1....2.00

Lance O'Casey
Fawcett, 1946
1....250.00
2....150.00
3-4....100.00

Lancer
Gold Key, 1969
1....25.00
2-3....20.00

Land of Nod
Dark Horse, 1997
1-4....3.00

Land of Oz
Arrow, 1998
1-9....3.00

Land of the Giants
Gold Key, 1968

1 .... 30.00
2 .... 18.00
3-5 .... 15.00

Land of the Lost Comics
E.C., 1946

1 .... 200.00
2 .... 135.00
3 .... 100.00
4-9 .... 85.00

Landra Special
Alchemy

1 .... 2.00

Lands of Prester John
Noble

1 .... 15.00

Lann
Fantagraphics, 1991

1 .... 3.00

La Pacifica
DC

1-3 .... 5.00

L.A. Phoenix
David G. Brown, 1994

1-3 .... 2.00

L.A. Raptor
Morbid, 1995

1 .... 3.00

Large Feature Comics
Dell, 1939

1 .... 1,250.00
2 .... 1,100.00
3 .... 1,000.00
4 .... 650.00
5-7 .... 750.00
8-15 .... 600.00
16-19 .... 500.00
20-23 .... 400.00
24-30 .... 350.00

Large Feature Comics
Dell, 1942

1-3 .... 400.00
4 .... 365.00
5 .... 325.00
6 .... 340.00
7 .... 350.00
8 .... 600.00
9 .... 385.00
10 .... 350.00
11 .... 325.00
12 .... 300.00
13 .... 350.00

Larry Doby, Baseball Hero
Fawcett, 1950

1 .... 400.00

Lars of Mars
Ziff-Davis, 1951

10 .... 500.00
11 .... 400.00

Lars of Mars 3-D
Eclipse, 1987

1 .... 3.00

Laser Eraser & Pressbutton
Eclipse, 1985

1-6 .... 2.00
3D 1 .... 3.00

Laser Quest Comics
Laser Quest

1 .... 3.00

Lash LaRue Western
Fawcett, 1949

1 .... 625.00
2 .... 385.00
3 .... 310.00
4-5 .... 270.00
6-10 .... 215.00
11-20 .... 172.00
21-30 .... 130.00
31-40 .... 100.00
41-50 .... 75.00
51-60 .... 65.00
61-70 .... 58.00
71-80 .... 50.00
81-84 .... 42.00

Lash Larue Western
AC

1 .... 4.00
Ann 1 .... 3.00

Lassie
Dell, 1950

1 .... 90.00
2 .... 54.00
3-5 .... 38.00
6-10 .... 26.00
11-20 .... 20.00
21-23 .... 18.00
24-50 .... 16.00
51-59 .... 15.00
60-70 .... 13.00

Lassie
Golden Press, 1978

1 .... 22.00

Last American
Marvel, 1990

1-4 .... 2.00

Last Avengers
Marvel, 1995

1-2 .... 6.00

Last Christmas
Image, 2006

1-5 .... 3.00

Indiana Jones and the Shrine of the Sea Devil

Indiana Jones and the Spear of Destiny

Indians

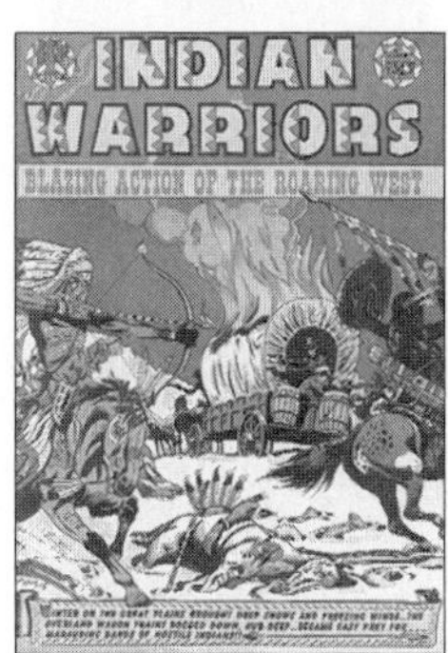

Indian Warriors

Industrial Gothic

Infinite Kung Fu

Infinity Abyss

Infinity Gauntlet

Last Dangerous Christmas
Aeon
1 ....6.00

Last Days of Hollywood, U.S.A.
Morgan
1-5 ....3.00

Last Days of the Justice Society Special
DC, 1986
1 ....3.00

Last Daze of the Bat-Guy
Mythic
1 ....3.00

Last Defender of Camelot
Zim
1 ....2.00

Last Ditch
Edge
1 ....3.00

Last Gasp Comics and Stories
Last Gasp Eco-Funnies, 1994
1-4 ....4.00

Last Generation
Black Tie, 1987
1-5 ....2.00

Last Hero Standing
Marvel, 2005
1-5 ....3.00

Last Kiss
Eclipse, 1990
1 ....4.00

Last Kiss
Shanda, 2001
1-3 ....5.00

Last Knight
NBM
1 ....16.00

Last Minute
-Ism, 2004
1-6 ....3.00

Last of the Dragons
Marvel
1 ....7.00

Last of the Viking Heroes
Genesis West, 1987
1-10 ....2.00
Summer 1-3....................3.00

Last One
DC, 1993
1-6 ....3.00

Last Planet
MBS
1 ....3.00

Last Planet Standing
Marvel, 206
1-5 ....3.00

Last Shot
Image, 2001
1-4 ....3.00

Last Shot: First Draw
Image, 2001
1 ....3.00

Last Starfighter
Marvel, 1984
1-3 ....2.00

Last Temptation
Marvel Music, 1994
1-3 ....5.00

Last Train to Deadsville: A Cal McDonald Mystery
Dark Horse, 2004
1-4 ....3.00

Latest Comics
Spotlight, 1945
1 ....80.00
2 ....50.00

Latigo Kid Western
AC
1 ....2.00

Laugh
Archie, 1987
1 ....3.00
2-5 ....2.00
6-29 ....1.00

Laugh Comics
Archie, 1946
20 ....200.00
21-25 ....160.00
26-30 ....130.00
31-40 ....94.00
41-50 ....62.00
51-60 ....46.00
61-70 ....30.00
71-80 ....25.00
81-90 ....20.00
91-100 ....18.00
101-130 ....15.00
131-170 ....12.00
171-189 ....9.00
190-200 ....8.00
201-250 ....6.00
251-300 ....4.00
301-350 ....3.00
351-400 ....2.00

Laugh Comix
M.L.J., 1944
46 ....115.00
47-48 ....80.00

Laugh Digest Magazine
Archie, 1974
1 .... 10.00
2-5 .... 8.00
6-10 .... 4.00
11-20 .... 3.00
21-200 .... 2.00

Launch!
Elsewhere
1 .... 2.00

Laundryland
Fantagraphics, 1991
1 .... 2.00
2-4 .... 3.00

Laurel and Hardy
Dell, 1962
-210 .... 30.00
2-4 .... 20.00

Laurel and Hardy
Gold Key, 1967
1 .... 24.00
2 .... 18.00

Laurel and Hardy
DC, 1972
1 .... 40.00

Laurel & Hardy in 3-D
Blackthorne, 1987
1-2 .... 3.00

Lava
Crossbreed
1 .... 3.00

Law
Asylum Graphics
1 .... 2.00

Law Against Crime
Essenkay, 1948
1 .... 625.00
2 .... 350.00
3 .... 550.00

Law and Order
Maximum, 1995
1-3 .... 3.00

Lawbreakers Always Lose!
Atlas, 1948
1 .... 235.00
2 .... 160.00
3-5 .... 95.00
6 .... 75.00
7 .... 80.00
8-10 .... 75.00

Lawbreakers Suspense Stories
Charlton, 1953
10 .... 235.00
11 .... 325.00
12-14 .... 145.00
15 .... 275.00

Lawdog
Marvel, 1993
1 .... 3.00
2-10 .... 2.00

Lawdog and Grimrod: Terror at the Crossroads
Marvel, 1993
1 .... 4.00

L.A.W. (Living Assault Weapons)
DC, 1999
1-6 .... 3.00

Lawman
Dell, 1960
3-4 .... 30.00
5-11 .... 26.00

Law of Dredd
Fleetway-Quality
1-33 .... 2.00

Lawrence
Dell, 1963
1 .... 14.00

Lazarus Churchyard
Tundra, 2001
1-3 .... 5.00

Lazarus Five
DC, 2000
1-5 .... 3.00

Lazarus Pits
Boneyard, 1993
1 .... 4.00

Leading Comics
DC, 1941
1 .... 3,500.00
2 .... 1,100.00
3 .... 850.00
4-5 .... 675.00
6-10 .... 580.00
11-15 .... 440.00
16-22 .... 70.00
23 .... 110.00
24-30 .... 55.00
31-41 .... 40.00

Leading Screen Comics
DC, 1950
42 .... 40.00
43-60 .... 30.00
61-77 .... 24.00

Leaf
Nab
1 .... 2.00
1/Deluxe 5.00
2 .... 2.00

League of Champions
Hero, 1990
1-3 .... 3.00

In His Steps

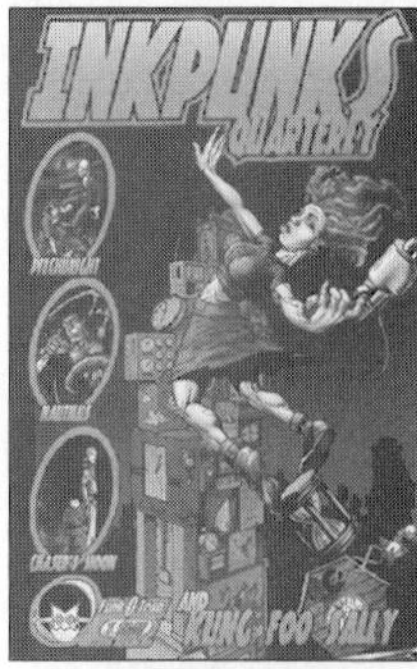

Inkpunks Quarterly

Innocent Bystander

Innovation Preview Special

Innovation Spectacular

Inovators

Insane

Insane Clown Posse

4-11 .... 4.00
12 .... 3.00

League of Extraordinary Gentlemen
DC, 1999

1 .... 8.00
1/A-2 .... 5.00
3-5 .... 4.00
5/A 65.00
☛Recalled edition
6 .... 4.00

League of Extraordinary Gentlemen (Vol. 2)
America's Best, 2002

1-6 .... 4.00

League of Justice
DC, 1996

1-2 .... 6.00

League of Rats
Caliber

1 .... 3.00

League of Super Groovy Crimefighters
Ancient, 2000

1-5 .... 3.00

Leather & Lace
Aircel, 1989

1/A 3.00
1/B 2.00
2/A 3.00
2/B 2.00
3/A 3.00
3/B 2.00
4/A 3.00
4/B 2.00
5/A 3.00
5/B 2.00
6/A 3.00
6/B 2.00
7/A 3.00
7/B 2.00
8/A 3.00
8/B 2.00
9-25 .... 3.00

Leather & Lace: Blood, Sex, & Tears
Aircel, 1991

1-4 .... 3.00

Leather & Lace Summer Special
Aircel, 1990

1 .... 3.00

Leatherboy
Fantagraphics, 1994

1-3 .... 3.00

Leatherface
Arpad, 1991

1 .... 3.00

Leather Underwear
Fantagraphics

1 .... 3.00

Leave it to Beaver
Dell, 1962

-207 .... 100.00

Leave It To Binky
DC, 1948

1 .... 200.00
2 .... 175.00
3 .... 110.00
4 .... 80.00
5-6 .... 55.00
7-10 .... 48.00
11-20 .... 35.00
21-30 .... 28.00
31-40 .... 24.00
41-50 .... 18.00
51-60 .... 12.00
61-71 .... 5.00

Leave It to Chance
Image, 1996

1-12 .... 3.00
13 .... 5.00

Led Zeppelin
Personality

1-4 .... 3.00

Led Zeppelin Experience
Revolutionary, 1992

1-5 .... 3.00

Left-Field Funnies
Apex Novelties

1 .... 4.00

Legacy
Majestic, 1993

0-2 .... 2.00

Legacy (Fred Perry's...)
Antarctic, 1999

1 .... 3.00

Legacy
Image, 2003

1-4 .... 3.00

Legacy of Kain: Defiance One Shot
Image, 2004

1 .... 3.00

Legacy of Kain: Soul Reaver
Top Cow, 1999

1 .... 2.00

Legend
DC, 2005

1-3 .... 6.00

Legend Lore
Arrow

1-2 .... 2.00

Legendlore
Caliber

1-4 .... 3.00

LegendLore: Wrath of the Dragon
Caliber

1-2 .... 3.00

Legend of Isis
Alias, 2005

1 .... 4.00
1/B cover 3.00
1/C cover 4.00
2 .... 3.00
2/B cover 4.00
3 .... 3.00
3/B cover 4.00
4-7 .... 3.00

Legend of Jedit Ojanen on the World of Magic: The Gathering
Acclaim, 1996

1-2 .... 3.00

Legend of Jesse James
Gold Key, 1966

1 .... 24.00

Legend of Kamui
Eclipse, 1987

1 .... 3.00
1/2nd-37 .... 2.00

Legend of Lemnear
CPM, 1998

1-14 .... 3.00

Legend of Lilith
Image

0 .... 5.00

Legend of Mother Sarah
Dark Horse, 1995

1 .... 4.00
2-8 .... 3.00

Legend of Mother Sarah: City of the Angels
Dark Horse, 1997

1-9 .... 4.00

Legend of Mother Sarah, The: City of the Children
Dark Horse, 1996

1-7 .... 4.00

Legend of Sleepy Hollow
Tundra

1 .... 7.00

Legend of Supreme
Image, 1994

1-3 .... 3.00

Legend of the Elflord
Davdez, 1998

1-3 .... 3.00

Legend of the Hawkman
DC, 2000

1-3 .... 5.00

Legend of the Shield
DC, 1991

1 .... 2.00
2-16 .... 1.00
Ann 1 .... 3.00

Legend of Wonder Woman
DC, 1986

1-4 .... 2.00

Legend of Young Dick Turpin
Gold Key, 1966

1 .... 16.00

Legend of Zelda
Valiant, 1990

1-5 .... 2.00

Legend of Zelda
Valiant, 1990

1-5 .... 2.00

Legends
DC, 1986

1-5 .... 2.00
6 .... 3.00

Legends and Folklore
Zone, 1992

1 .... 4.00
2 .... 3.00

Legends from Darkwood
Antarctic, 2003

1-3 .... 4.00

Legends from Darkwood: Summer Fun Special
Antarctic, 2005

0 .... 3.00

Legends of Daniel Boone
DC, 1955

1 .... 300.00
2 .... 135.00
3 .... 110.00
4-8 .... 75.00

Legends of Elfinwild
Wehner

1 .... 2.00

Legends of Kid Death & Fluffy
Event, 1997

1 .... 3.00

Inside Crime

Instant Piano

Interactive Comics

Interface

International Comics

International Fallout Shelter Zone

Interplanetary Lizards of the Texas Plains

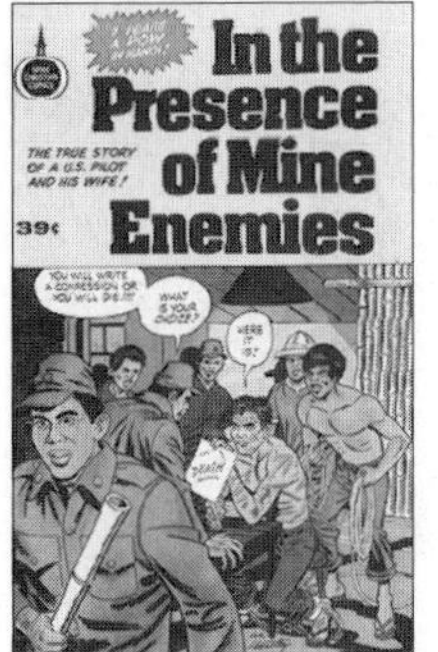

In the Presence of Mine Enemies

Legends of Luxura
Brainstorm, 1996

1 ....3.00
1/Ltd. 4.00

Legends of NASCAR
Vortex

1 ....4.00
1/2nd 2.00
1/3rd 3.00
2 ....2.00
2/Variant 3.00
3-16 ....2.00

Legends of the Dark Claw
DC, 1996

1 ....2.00

Legends of the DCU: Crisis on Infinite Earths
DC, 1999

1 ....5.00

Legends of the DC Universe
DC, 1998

1-5 ....3.00
6-30 ....2.00
31-41 ....3.00
GS 1-2 ....5.00

Legends of the DC Universe 3-D Gallery
DC, 1998

1 ....3.00

Legends of the Legion
DC, 1998

1-4 ....2.00

Legends of the Living Dead
Fantaco

1 ....4.00

Legends of the Stargrazers
Innovation, 1989

1-6 ....2.00

Legends of the World's Finest
DC, 1994

1 ....6.00
2-3 ....5.00

Legendz
Viz, 2005

1-3 ....8.00

L.E.G.I.O.N.
DC, 1989

1 ....3.00
2-22 ....2.00
23 ....3.00
24-49 ....2.00
50 ....4.00
51-69 ....2.00
70 ....3.00
Ann 1 ....4.00
Ann 2-3 ....3.00
Ann 4-5 ....4.00

Legion
DC, 2001

1-24 ....3.00
25 ....4.00
26-38 ....3.00

Legion Anthology
Limelight

1-2 ....3.00

Legion Lost
DC, 2000

1-12 ....3.00

Legion Manga Anthology
Limelight

1-4 ....3.00

Legionnaires
DC, 1993

0 ....2.00
1 ....3.00
2-49 ....2.00
50 ....4.00
51-64 ....2.00
65-80 ....3.00
1000000 ....4.00
Ann 1 ....5.00
Ann 2 ....4.00
Ann 3 ....3.00

Legionnaires Three
DC, 1986

1-4 ....1.00

Legion of Monsters
Marvel

1 ....35.00

Legion of Night
Marvel, 1991

1-2 ....5.00

Legion of Stupid Heroes
Alternate Concepts, 1997

1-4 ....3.00

Legion of Stupid Knights
Alternate Concepts, 1998

Special 1 ....3.00

Legion of Substitute Heroes Special
DC, 1985

1 ....2.00

Legion of Super-Heroes
DC, 1973

1 ....15.00
2 ....8.00
3-4 ....7.00

Legion of Super-Heroes
DC, 1980

259 ....4.00

260-261 .... 3.00
261/Whitman 5.00
262 .... 3.00
262/Whitman 5.00
263 .... 3.00
263/Whitman 5.00
264 .... 3.00
264/Whitman 5.00
265 .... 3.00
265/Whitman 5.00
266 .... 3.00
266/Whitman 5.00
267-270 .... 3.00
271-284 .... 2.00
285 .... 3.00
286-296 .... 2.00
297 .... 3.00
298-309 .... 2.00
310 .... 3.00
311-313 .... 2.00
Ann 1 .... 3.00
Ann 2-3 .... 2.00

Legion of Super-Heroes

DC, 1984

1 .... 5.00
2-5 .... 4.00
6-36 .... 2.00
37-38 .... 5.00
39-44 .... 2.00
45 .... 3.00
46-63 .... 2.00
Ann 1 .... 3.00
Ann 2-3 .... 2.00
Ann 4 .... 3.00

Legion of Super-Heroes

DC, 1989

0 .... 2.00
1 .... 3.00
2-37 .... 2.00
38 .... 3.00
39-49 .... 2.00
50 .... 4.00
51-53 .... 2.00
54 .... 3.00
55-99 .... 2.00
100 .... 6.00
101-108 .... 2.00
109-123 .... 3.00
1000000 .... 4.00
Ann 1 .... 5.00
Ann 2-Ann 6 .... 4.00
Ann 7 .... 3.00
Book 1 .... 18.00

Legion of Super-Heroes

DC, 2005

1 .... 4.00
2-50 .... 3.00

Legion of Super-Heroes Index

Eclipse, 1987

1-5 .... 2.00

Legion of Super-Heroes Secret Files

DC, 1998

1-2 .... 5.00

Legion of the Stupid-Heroes

Blackthorne

1 .... 2.00

Legion: Science Police

DC, 1998

1-4 .... 2.00

Legion Secret Files 3003

DC, 2004

1 .... 5.00

Legions of Ludicrous Heroes

C&T

1 .... 2.00

Legion Worlds

DC, 2001

1-6 .... 4.00

Legion X-1

Silverwolf, 1987

1-2 .... 2.00

Legion X-1

Greater Mercury, 1989

1-3 .... 2.00

Legion X-2

Greater Mercury, 1989

1-7 .... 2.00

Lejentia

Opus, 1987

1-2 .... 2.00

Lemonade Kid

AC

1 .... 3.00

Lena's Bambinas

Fantagraphics

1 .... 4.00

Lenore

Slave Labor, 1998

1-7 .... 3.00

Lensman

Eternity, 1990

1 .... 2.00
1/Variant 4.00
2-6 .... 2.00

Intimate Love

Intruder Comics Module

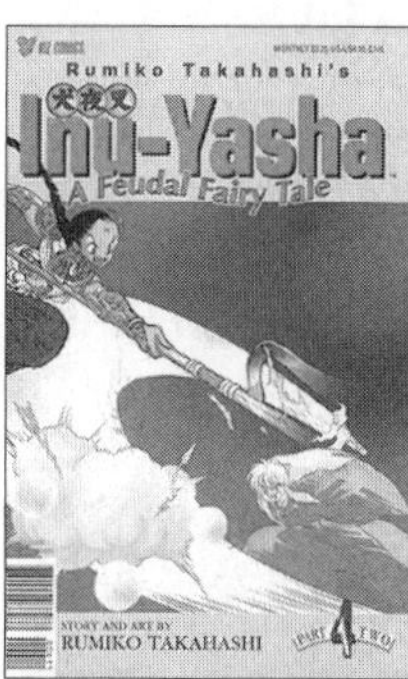

Inu-Yasha Part 2

Invaders from Home

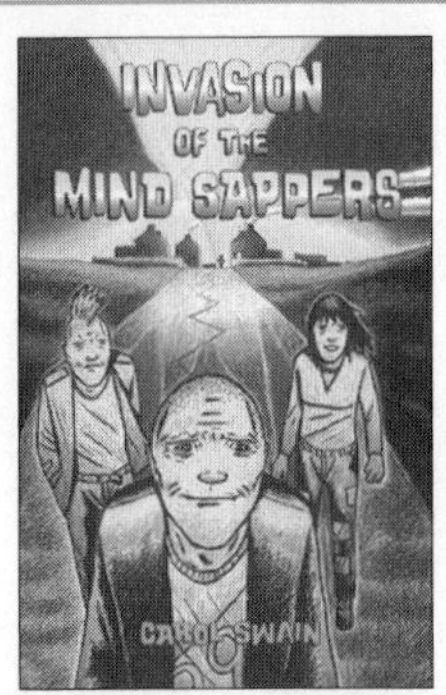

Invasion of the Mind Sappers

Invert

Invincible

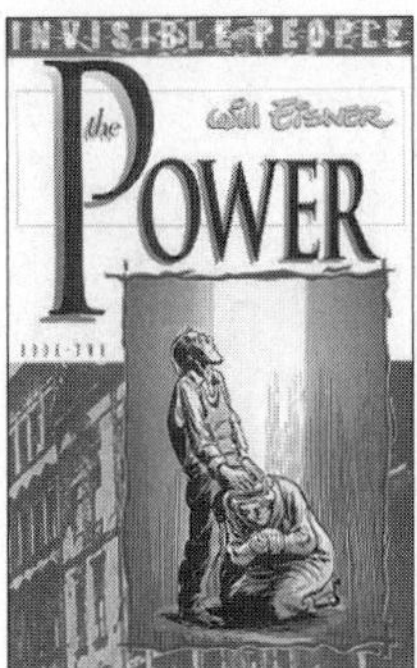

Invisible People

Lensman: War of the Galaxies
Eternity, 1990
1-7 .... 2.00

Leonard Nimoy
Celebrity
1 .... 6.00

Leonardo Teenage Mutant Ninja Turtle
Mirage, 1986
1 .... 4.00

Leopold and Brink
Faultline, 1997
1-3 .... 3.00

Leroy
Standard, 1949
1 .... 30.00
2 .... 25.00
3-6 .... 18.00

Lester Girls: The Lizard's Trail
Eternity
1-3 .... 3.00

Lethal
Image, 1996
1 .... 3.00

Lethal Enforcer
Alias, 2005
1 .... 1.00

Lethal Foes of Spider-Man
Marvel, 1993
1-4 .... 2.00

Lethal Instinct
Alias, 2005
1-5 .... 3.00

Lethal Orgasm
NBM
1 .... 10.00

Lethal Strike
London Night, 1995
0 .... 6.00
½-Ann 1 .... 3.00

Lethal Strike/Double Impact: Lethal Impact
London Night, 1996
1 .... 3.00

Lethargic Comics
Alpha, 1994
1 .... 4.00
2-14 .... 3.00

Lethargic Comics, Weakly
Lethargic, 1991
1 .... 4.00
2-12 .... 3.00

Lethargic Lad
Crusade, 1996
1-3 .... 3.00

Lethargic Lad
Crusade, 1997
1-9 .... 3.00

Let's Pretend
D.S., 1950
1 .... 95.00
2-3 .... 65.00

Let's Take a Trip
Pines, 1958
1 .... 24.00

Level X
Caliber
1-2 .... 4.00

Levi's World
Moordam, 1998
1-4 .... 3.00

Lewd Moana
Fantagraphics
1 .... 3.00

The Lexian Chronicles: Full Circle
APComics, 2005
1/Preview 5.00
1 .... 4.00

Lex Luthor: Man of Steel
DC, 2005
1-5 .... 3.00

Lex Luthor: The Unauthorized Biography
DC, 1989
1 .... 4.00

Lex Talionis: Jungle Tale One Shot
Image, 2004
1 .... 6.00

Liaisons Delicieuses
Fantagraphics, 1990
1-6 .... 2.00

Libby Ellis
Eternity, 1988
1-4 .... 2.00

Libby Ellis
Malibu
1-4 .... 2.00

Liberality For All
-Ism, 2005
1 .... 3.00

Liberator
Malibu, 1987
1-6 .... 2.00

Liberator
Images & Realities
1 .... 2.00

Libertine
Fantagraphics
1 .... 2.00
2 .... 3.00

Liberty Comics
Green, 1945
5-9 .... 125.00
10-15 .... 90.00

Liberty Guards
Chicago Mail Order, 1942
1 .... 250.00

Liberty Meadows
Insight, 1999
1 .... 18.00
1/2nd 3.00
2 .... 10.00
3-4 .... 6.00
5 .... 5.00
6-10 .... 4.00
11-37 .... 3.00

Liberty Meadows Source Book
Image, 2005
1 .... 5.00

Liberty Meadows Wedding Album
Insight, 2001
nn 3.00

Liberty Project
Eclipse, 1987
1-8 .... 2.00

Liberty Scouts
Centaur, 1941
2 .... 775.00
3 .... 550.00

Libra
Eternity, 1987
1 .... 2.00

Librarian
Fantagraphics
1 .... 3.00

Licensable Bear
About, 2003
1-2 .... 3.00

License to Kill
Eclipse
1 .... 8.00

Lidsville
Gold Key, 1972
1 .... 20.00
2 .... 14.00
3-5 .... 12.00

Lieutenant Blueberry: General Golden Mane
Marvel
1 .... 15.00

Lt. Robin Crusoe, U.S.N.
Gold Key, 1966
1 .... 20.00

Life and Adventures of Santa Clause
Tundra, 1992
nn 25.00

L.I.F.E. Brigade
Blue Comet
1-3 .... 2.00

Life Eaters
DC, 2003
1 .... 30.00

Life Force, A
Kitchen Sink
1-1/2nd 13.00

Life of Captain Marvel
Marvel, 1985
1-5 .... 3.00

Life of Christ
Marvel, 1993
1 .... 3.00

Life of Christ: The Easter Story
Marvel
1 .... 3.00

Life of Pope John Paul II
Marvel, 1983
1 .... 3.00

Life on Another Planet
DC, 2000
1 .... 13.00

Lifequest
Caliber, 1997
1-5 .... 3.00

Life Story
Fawcett, 1949
1 .... 60.00
2 .... 45.00
3-9 .... 30.00
10-29 .... 25.00
30-47 .... 20.00

Life Under Sanctions
Fantagraphics, 1994
1 .... 3.00

Life, the Universe and Everything
DC
1-3 .... 7.00

I.N.V.U.

Iron Fist

Ironhand of Almuric

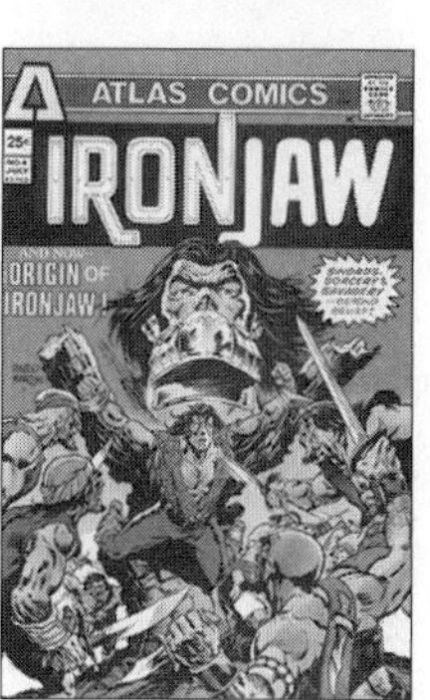

Ironjaw

Iron Manual

Iron Marshal

Iron Wings

Ironwolf

Life with Archie

Archie, 1958

1 .... 225.00
2 .... 110.00
3-5 .... 85.00
6-10 .... 55.00
11-20 .... 32.00
21-31 .... 25.00
32-40 .... 16.00
41-50 .... 12.00
51-60 .... 8.00
61-70 .... 5.00
71-80 .... 4.00
81-120 .... 3.00
121-250 .... 2.00
251-285 .... 1.00

Life with Millie

Atlas, 1960

8 .... 35.00
9-10 .... 28.00
11-20 .... 26.00

Life with Snarky Parker

Fox, 1950

1 .... 145.00

Light and Darkness War

Marvel, 1988

1-6 .... 2.00

Light Brigade

DC, 2004

1-4 .... 6.00

Light Fantastic (Terry Pratchett's...)

Innovation, 1992

0-4 .... 3.00

Lightning Comics

Feature, 1940

4 .... 700.00
5 .... 450.00
6 .... 400.00
7-13 .... 325.00

Lightning Comics Presents

Lightning, 1994

1 .... 4.00

Lights Out

Tokyopop, 2005

1 .... 10.00

Li'l Abner

Harvey, 1947

61 .... 175.00
62 .... 125.00
63 .... 105.00
64-67 .... 85.00
68-71 .... 60.00
72-73 .... 40.00
74-77 .... 35.00
78-82 .... 32.00
83-87 .... 28.00
88-95 .... 25.00
96-97 .... 20.00

Li'l Genius

Charlton, 1955

1-4 .... 0.00
5-30 .... 10.00
31-54 .... 8.00
55 .... 2.00

Lili

Image, 1999

0 .... 5.00

Liling-Po

Tokyopop, 2005

1-3 .... 10.00

Li'l Jinx

Archie, 1956

11 .... 50.00
12-16 .... 32.00

Li'l Keiki

Kiddieland Books, 2005

1 .... 4.00

Li'l Kids

Marvel, 1970

1 .... 35.00
2-5 .... 22.00
6-12 .... 16.00

Lillith: Demon Princess

Antarctic, 1996

0 .... 2.00
0/Variant-3 .... 5.00

Li'l Menace

Fago, 1958

1 .... 30.00
2 .... 18.00
3 .... 16.00

Li'l Pals

Marvel, 1972

1 .... 25.00
2-5 .... 20.00

Li'l Pan

Fox, 1946

6 .... 40.00
7-8 .... 30.00

Li'l Rascal Twins

Charlton, 1957

6 .... 20.00
7-10 .... 12.00
11-18 .... 8.00

Li'l Santa

NBM

1 .... 15.00

Li'l Tomboy

Charlton, 1956

92-100 .... 18.00
101-107 .... 15.00

Limited Collectors' Edition

DC, 1973

C-20 .... 32.00

☛Rudolph
C-21 .... 16.00
C-22 .... 14.00
C-23 .... 16.00
C-24 .... 26.00
☛Rudolph
C-25 .... 28.00
☛Batman
C-27 .... 16.00
C-29 .... 10.00
C-31 .... 15.00
C-32 .... 10.00
C-33 .... 16.00
C-34 .... 12.00
C-35 .... 10.00
C-36 .... 16.00
C-37 .... 20.00
☛Batman
C-38-C-39 .... 10.00
C-40 .... 12.00
C-41-C-43 .... 10.00
C-44 .... 12.00
C-45-C-47 .... 10.00
C-48 .... 12.00
C-49-C-50 .... 10.00
C-51 .... 12.00
C-52 .... 10.00
C-57-C-59 .... 14.00

Lincoln-16

Skarwood, 1997
1-2 .... 3.00

Linda

Ajax, 1954
1 .... 60.00
2 .... 42.00
3-4 .... 36.00

Linda Carter, Student Nurse

Atlas, 1961
1 .... 60.00
2-5 .... 40.00
6-9 .... 30.00

Linda Lark

Dell, 1961
1 .... 15.00
2-8 .... 10.00

Line the Dustbin Funnies

East Willis, 1997
1 .... 3.00

Lionheart

Awesome, 1999
1/A 4.00
1/B-Ashcan 1 .... 3.00

Lion King (Disney's...)

Marvel, 1994
1 .... 3.00

Lions, Tigers & Bears

Image, 2005
1-3 .... 3.00

Lions, Tigers & Bears

Image, 2006
1-3 .... 3.00

Lippy the Lion and Hardy Har Har

Gold Key, 1963
1 .... 60.00

Lipstick

Rip Off, 1992
1 .... 3.00

Lisa Comics

Bongo
1 .... 2.00

Lita Ford: The Queen of Heavy Metal

Rock-It Comics
1 .... 5.00

Little Scrowlie

Slave Labor, 2004
1-12 .... 3.00

Little Al of the FBI

Ziff-Davis, 1950
10 .... 95.00
11 .... 70.00

Little Al of the Secret Service

Ziff-Davis, 1951
1 .... 95.00
2-3 .... 70.00

Little Ambrose

Archie, 1958
1 .... 60.00

Little Angel

Pines, 1954
5 .... 24.00
6-9 .... 20.00
10-16 .... 16.00

Little Annie Rooney

David McKay, 1948
1 .... 48.00
2-3 .... 35.00

Little Archie

Archie, 1956
1 .... 525.00
2 .... 210.00
3 .... 150.00
4-5 .... 115.00
6-10 .... 80.00
11-20 .... 52.00
21-40 .... 32.00
41-60 .... 22.00
☛Giant-size
61-80 .... 16.00

I Saw It

Isis

I Spy

Itchy Planet

It Really Happened

J2

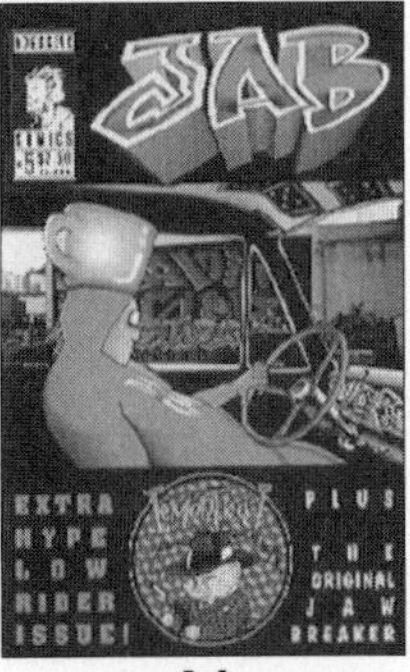

Jab

Jack Armstrong

81-100 .... 11.00
101-120 .... 6.00
121-140 .... 4.00
141-180 .... 3.00

Little Archie Digest Magazine
Archie, 1991

1 .... 3.00
2-25 .... 2.00

Little Archie Mystery
Archie, 1963

1 .... 60.00
2 .... 42.00

Little Aspirin
Marvel, 1949

1 .... 60.00
2 .... 45.00
3 .... 24.00

Little Audrey
St. John, 1948

2 .... 100.00
3-5 .... 65.00
6-10 .... 48.00
11-21 .... 38.00
22-24 .... 30.00

Little Audrey
Harvey, 1945

25 .... 125.00
26-29 .... 75.00
30-40 .... 50.00
41-53 .... 40.00

Little Audrey
Harvey, 1992

1 .... 2.00
2-9 .... 1.00

Little Audrey and Melvin
Harvey, 1962

1 .... 45.00
2 .... 25.00
3-5 .... 18.00
6-10 .... 14.00
11-20 .... 12.00
21-30 .... 9.00
31-40 .... 6.00
41-61 .... 4.00

Little Audrey TV Funtime
Harvey, 1962

1 .... 45.00
2 .... 28.00
3 .... 24.00
4-5 .... 20.00
6-10 .... 16.00
11-20 .... 12.00
21-33 .... 9.00

Little Beaver
Dell, 1951

3 .... 24.00
4-8 .... 20.00

Little Bit
St. John, 1949

1-2 .... 25.00

Little Dot
Harvey, 1953

1 .... 1,250.00
2 .... 500.00
3 .... 400.00
4-5 .... 325.00
6 .... 400.00
7 .... 200.00
8-10 .... 125.00
11-20 .... 100.00
21-30 .... 60.00
31-40 .... 45.00
41-50 .... 25.00
51-60 .... 20.00
61-80 .... 15.00
81-100 .... 10.00
101-141 .... 7.00
142-145 .... 10.00
146-164 .... 5.00

Little Dot
Harvey, 1992

1-7 .... 2.00

Little Dot Dotland
Harvey, 1962

1 .... 75.00
2-3 .... 40.00
4-5 .... 35.00
6-10 .... 24.00
11-20 .... 20.00
21-29 .... 16.00
30-39 .... 12.00
40-54 .... 10.00
55-61 .... 8.00
62-63 .... 10.00

Little Dot in 3-D
Blackthorne

1 .... 3.00

Little Dot's Uncles and Aunts
Harvey, 1961

1 .... 70.00
2-3 .... 42.00
4-5 .... 36.00
6-10 .... 28.00
11-35 .... 22.00
36-52 .... 14.00

Little Dracula
Harvey, 1992

1-3 .... 2.00

Little Ego
NBM

1 .... 11.00

Little Endless Storybook
DC, 2001

1 .... 6.00

Little Eva 3-D
St. John, 1953
1 .... 80.00
2 .... 70.00

Little Fir Tree
W.T. Grant, 1943
1 .... 40.00

Little Ghost
St. John, 1959
1 .... 38.00
2-3 .... 25.00

Little Giant Comics
Centaur, 1938
1 .... 425.00
2 .... 335.00
3-4 .... 260.00

Little Giant Detective Funnies
Centaur, 1938
1 .... 500.00
2 .... 375.00
3-4 .... 330.00

Little Giant Movie Funnies
Centaur, 1938
1 .... 360.00
2 .... 310.00

Little Gloomy
Slave Labor, 1999
1 .... 3.00

Little Gloomy's Super Scary Monster Show
Slave Labor, 2005
1-2 .... 3.00

Little Greta Garbage
Rip Off, 1990
1-2 .... 3.00

Little Grey Man
Image
1 .... 7.00

Little Groucho
Reston, 1955
1 .... 35.00
2 .... 25.00

Little Ike
St. John, 1953
1 .... 40.00
2 .... 26.00
3-4 .... 24.00

Little Iodine
Dell, 1950
1 .... 45.00
2-5 .... 30.00
6-10 .... 25.00
11-19 .... 20.00
20-29 .... 16.00
30-39 .... 13.00
40-56 .... 9.00

Little Italy
Fantagraphics
1 .... 4.00

Little Jack Frost
Avon, 1952
1 .... 38.00

Little Jim-Bob Big Foot
Jump Back, 1998
1-2 .... 3.00

Little Joe
St. John, 1953
1 .... 24.00

Little Lana
Marvel, 1949
8 .... 36.00
9 .... 30.00

Little Lenny
Marvel, 1949
1 .... 50.00
2-3 .... 30.00

Little Lizzie
Marvel, 1949
1 .... 50.00
2-5 .... 28.00

Little Lizzie
Marvel, 1953
1 .... 40.00
2-3 .... 28.00

Little Lotta
Harvey, 1955
1 .... 225.00
2 .... 90.00
3 .... 75.00
4-5 .... 55.00
6-10 .... 40.00
11-20 .... 28.00
21-30 .... 22.00
31-40 .... 18.00
41-50 .... 15.00
51-70 .... 12.00
71-90 .... 8.00
91-98 .... 5.00
99-102 .... 6.00
103-120 .... 3.00

Little Lotta
Harvey, 1992
1-4 .... 2.00

Little Lotta Foodland
Harvey, 1963
1 .... 45.00
2-3 .... 35.00
4-5 .... 30.00
6-10 .... 24.00
11-15 .... 16.00
16-20 .... 12.00
21-29 .... 8.00

Jack Frost

Jack Hunter

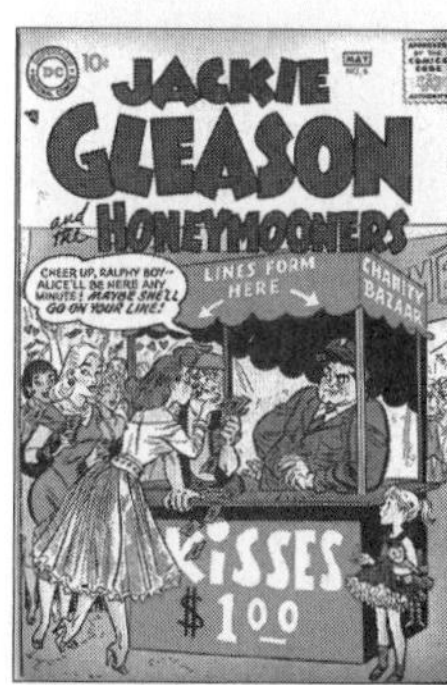

Jackie Gleason and the Honeymooners

Jackie Robinson

Jack of Hearts

Jademan Collection

Jade Warriors

Jaguar God

Little Lulu

Dell, 1948

1 .... 600.00
2 .... 300.00
3 .... 225.00
4-5 .... 200.00
6-10 .... 165.00
11-20 .... 125.00
21-30 .... 105.00
31-38 .... 90.00
39 .... 125.00
40 .... 90.00
41-50 .... 70.00
51-60 .... 60.00
61-70 .... 55.00
71-80 .... 45.00
81-90 .... 40.00
91-99 .... 35.00
100 .... 50.00
101-120 .... 30.00
121-140 .... 28.00
141-160 .... 25.00
161-164 .... 20.00
☛...in Paris
165-166 .... 70.00
☛Christmas Diary
167-180 .... 20.00
181-200 .... 15.00
201-220 .... 9.00
221-240 .... 6.00
241-250 .... 4.00
251-257 .... 3.00
258-259 .... 12.00
260 .... 325.00
☛Sold only in packs
261 .... 45.00
☛Sold only in packs
262-265 .... 12.00
☛Sold only in packs
266-268 .... 15.00
☛Sold only in packs
Ann 1 .... 225.00
Ann 2 .... 175.00

Little Lulu and Her Special Friends

Dell, 1955

3-4 .... 125.00

Little Lulu and Tubby at Summer Camp

Dell, 1957

1 .... 35.00
2 .... 30.00

Little Lulu and Tubby Halloween Fun

Dell, 1957

1 .... 35.00
2 .... 30.00

Little Lulu and Tubby in Alaska

Dell, 1959

1 .... 35.00

Little Max Comics

Harvey, 1949

1 .... 85.00
2 .... 60.00
3 .... 50.00
4-5 .... 40.00
6-9 .... 35.00
10-19 .... 30.00
20-39 .... 25.00
40-59 .... 20.00
60-73 .... 15.00

Little Mermaid (Disney's...)

Marvel, 1994

1 .... 3.00
2-12 .... 2.00

Little Mermaid Limited Series (Disney's...)

Disney, 1992

1-4 .... 2.00

Little Mermaid

W.D.

1 .... 4.00

Little Mermaid: Underwater Engagements (Disney's...)

Acclaim

1 .... 5.00

Little Mermaid

Disney

1 .... 3.00
1/Direct. 6.00

Little Miss Muffet

Best, 1948

11 .... 40.00
12-13 .... 28.00

Little Miss Strange

Millennium

1 .... 3.00

Little Miss Sunbeam

Magazine Enterprises, 1950

1 .... 65.00
2-4 .... 40.00

Little Mister Man

Slave Labor, 1995

1-3 .... 3.00

Little Monsters

Gold Key, 1964

1 .... 20.00
2 .... 12.00
3-5 .... 8.00
6-9 .... 6.00

10-20 .... 5.00
21-44 .... 4.00

Little Monsters
Now, 1990
1-6 .... 2.00

Little Nemo in Slumberland 3-D
Blackthorne, 1987
1 .... 3.00

Little Orphan Annie
David McKay, 1948
1 .... 125.00
2-3 .... 80.00

Little Oz Squad
Patchwork, 1995
1 .... 3.00

Little Red Hot: Bound
Image, 2001
1-3 .... 3.00

Little Red Hot: Chane of Fools
Image, 1999
1-3 .... 3.00

Little Ronzo in Slumberland
Slave Labor, 1987
1 .... 2.00

Little Roquefort
St. John, 1952
1 .... 40.00
2 .... 30.00
3-10 .... 24.00

Little Sad Sack
Harvey, 1964
1 .... 7.00
2-5 .... 4.00
6-19 .... 3.00

Little Scouts
Dell, 1951
2-6 .... 15.00

Little Shop of Horrors
DC, 1987
1 .... 2.00

Little Snow Fairy Sugar Manga
ADV Manga, 2006
1-3 .... 10.00

Little Star
Oni, 2005
1-5 .... 3.00

Little Stooges
Gold Key, 1972
1 .... 16.00
2-3 .... 12.00
4-7 .... 9.00

Little White Mouse
Caliber, 1997
1-4 .... 3.00

Little White Mouse
Caliber, 1998
1-4 .... 3.00

Little White Mouse: Entropy Dreaming
Caliber, 2000
1 .... 3.00

Little White Mouse: Open Space
Blue Line, 2002
1-3 .... 3.00

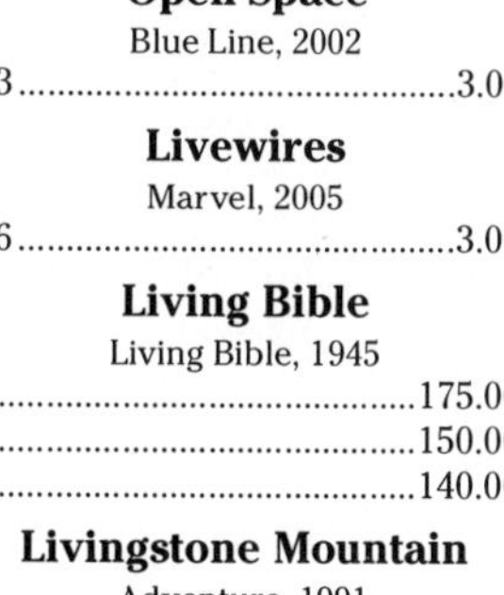

Livewires
Marvel, 2005
1-6 .... 3.00

Living Bible
Living Bible, 1945
1 .... 175.00
2 .... 150.00
3 .... 140.00

Livingstone Mountain
Adventure, 1991
1-4 .... 3.00

Living with Zombies
Frightworld Studios, 2005
1-3 .... 3.00

Liz and Beth
Fantagraphics, 1991
1-4 .... 3.00

Liz and Beth
Fantagraphics, 1992
1-4 .... 3.00

Liz and Beth
Fantagraphics, 1993
1-7 .... 3.00

Lizard Lady
Aircel, 1991
1-4 .... 3.00

Lizards Summer Fun Special
Caliber
1 .... 4.00

Lizzie McGuire Cine-Manga
Tokyopop, 2003
1 .... 8.00

Llisica
NBM
1 .... 10.00

Lloyd Llewellyn
Fantagraphics, 1986
1-6 .... 2.00
Special 1-Special 1/2nd 3.00

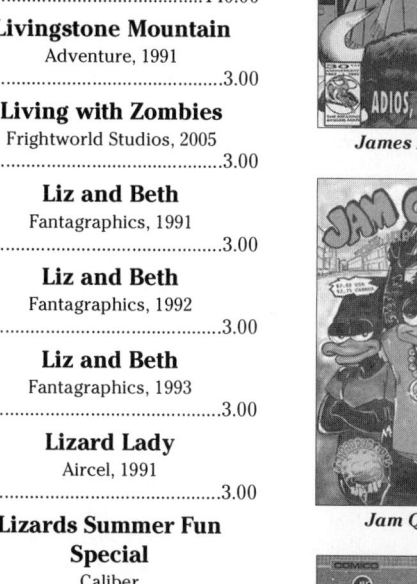

Jamboree Comics

James Bond Jr.

Jam Quacky

Jam Super Cool Color-Injected Turbo Adventure from Hell

J.A.P.A.N.

Jason and the Argonauts

Jason Monarch

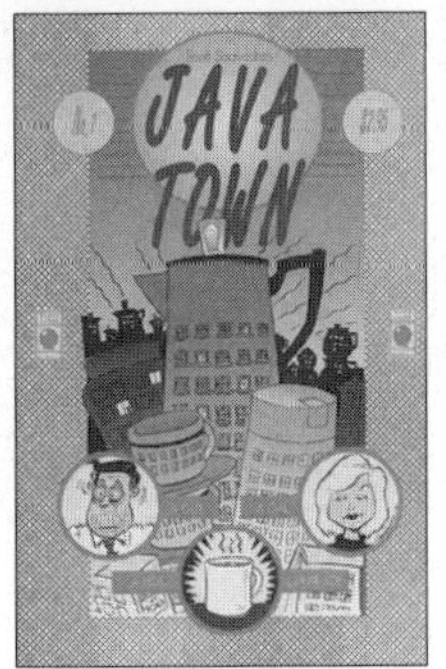

Java Town

Loaded
Interplay
1 .... 1.00

Lobo
DC, 1990
1 .... 3.00
1/2nd-4 .... 2.00

Lobo
DC, 1993
0 .... 3.00
1 .... 4.00
2-10 .... 3.00
11-55 .... 2.00
56-64 .... 3.00
1000000 .... 4.00
Ann 1 .... 5.00
Ann 2-3 .... 4.00

Lobo: A Contract on Gawd
DC, 1994
1-4 .... 2.00

Lobo: Blazing Chain of Love
DC, 1992
1 .... 2.00

Lobo: Bounty Hunting for Fun and Profit
DC
1 .... 5.00

Lobo: Chained
DC, 1997
1 .... 3.00

Lobo Convention Special
DC, 1993
1 .... 2.00

Lobo/Deadman: The Brave and the Bald
DC, 1995
1 .... 4.00

Lobo: Death and Taxes
DC, 1996
1-4 .... 2.00

Lobo/Demon: Helloween
DC, 1996
1 .... 2.00

Lobo: Fragtastic Voyage
DC, 1998
1 .... 6.00

Lobo Gallery: Portraits of a Bastich
DC, 1995
1 .... 4.00

Lobo Goes to Hollywood
DC, 1996
1 .... 2.00

Lobo: Infanticide
DC, 1992
1-4 .... 2.00

Lobo: in the Chair
DC, 1994
1 .... 2.00

Lobo: I Quit
DC, 1995
1 .... 3.00

Lobo/Judge Dredd: Psycho-Bikers Vs. The Mutants from Hell
DC
1 .... 5.00

Lobo/Mask
DC, 1997
1-2 .... 6.00

Lobo Paramilitary Christmas Special
DC, 1991
1 .... 3.00

Lobo: Portrait of a Victim
DC, 1993
1 .... 2.00

Lobo's Back
DC, 1992
1-4 .... 2.00

Lobo's Big Babe Spring Break Special
DC, 1995
1 .... 2.00

Lobo the Duck
DC, 1997
1 .... 2.00

Lobo: Un-American Gladiators
DC, 1993
1-4 .... 2.00

Lobo Unbound
DC, 2003
1-6 .... 3.00

Lobocop
DC, 1994
1 .... 2.00

Local
Oni, 2005
1-2 .... 3.00

Loco vs. Pulverine
Eclipse, 1992
1 .... 3.00

Logan: Path of the Warlord
Marvel, 1996
1 .... 6.00

Logan: Shadow Society
Marvel, 1996

1 .... 6.00

Logan's Run
Marvel, 1977

1 .... 5.00
2-5 .... 2.00
☛Thanos back-up
6-7 .... 15.00
7/35¢ 5.00

Logan's Run
Adventure, 1990

1-6 .... 3.00

Logan's World
Adventure, 1991

1-6 .... 3.00

Lois Lane
DC, 1986

1-2 .... 2.00

Loki
Marvel, 2004

1 .... 12.00
2 .... 6.00
3-4 .... 4.00

Lolita
NBM

1-2 .... 11.00
3-4 .... 10.00

London's Dark
Titan

1 .... 9.00

Lone
Dark Horse, 2003

1-6 .... 3.00

Lone Gunmen
Dark Horse, 2001

Special 1 .... 3.00

Lonely Heart
Ajax, 1955

9 .... 40.00
10-14 .... 35.00

Lonely Nights Comics
Last Gasp

1 .... 2.00

Lonely Tombstone One Shot
Image, 2005

1 .... 6.00

Lonely War of Willy Schultz
Avalon

1-4 .... 3.00

Loner
Fleetway-Quality

1-7 .... 2.00

Lone Ranger
Dell, 1948

1 .... 660.00
2 .... 360.00
3 .... 265.00
4-5 .... 230.00
6-7 .... 195.00
8 .... 275.00
☛Lone Ranger origin
9-10 .... 195.00
11-20 .... 138.00
21-30 .... 100.00
31-40 .... 75.00
41-50 .... 58.00
51-60 .... 50.00
61-70 .... 48.00
71-80 .... 38.00
81-100 .... 34.00
101-111 .... 30.00
112 .... 55.00
113-117 .... 45.00
118 .... 50.00
119-145 .... 45.00

Lone Ranger
Gold Key, 1964

1 .... 35.00
2 .... 18.00
3 .... 14.00
4-6 .... 12.00
7-10 .... 10.00
11-20 .... 9.00
21-28 .... 5.00

Lone Ranger
Pure Imagination, 1996

1 .... 3.00

Lone Ranger and Tonto
Topps, 1994

1 .... 3.00
1/Variant 4.00
2 .... 3.00
2/Variant 4.00
3-4/Variant 3.00

Lone Ranger Comics
Lone Ranger Inc., 1939

1 .... 2,450.00

Lone Ranger Golden West
Gold Key, 1966

1 .... 45.00

Lone Ranger in Milk for Big Mike
Dell, 1955

1 .... 90.00

Lone Ranger Movie Story
Dell, 1956

1 .... 285.00

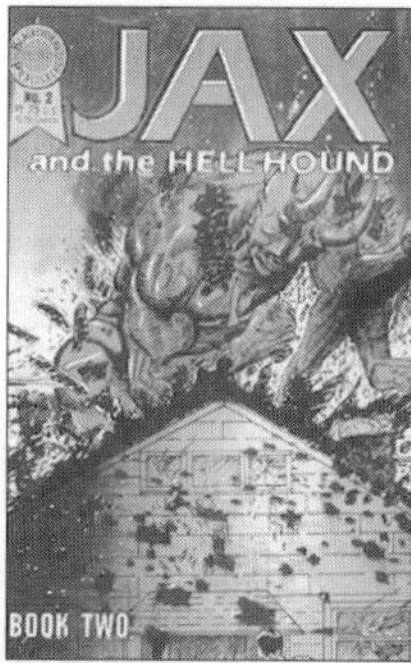

Jax and the Hell Hound

Jazz

Jazzbo Comics That Swing

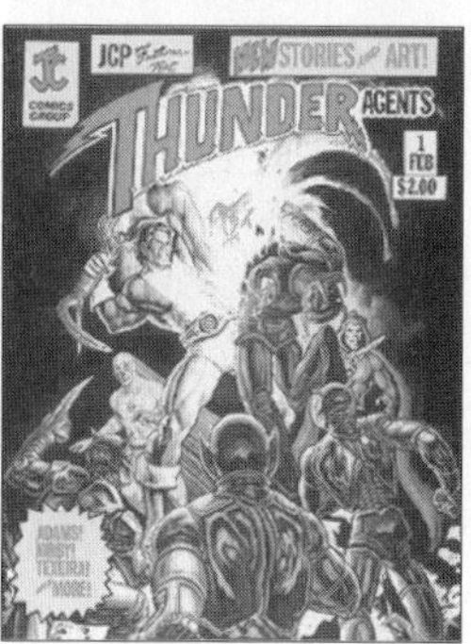

JCP Features

Jeanie

Jeep Comics

Jenny Finn

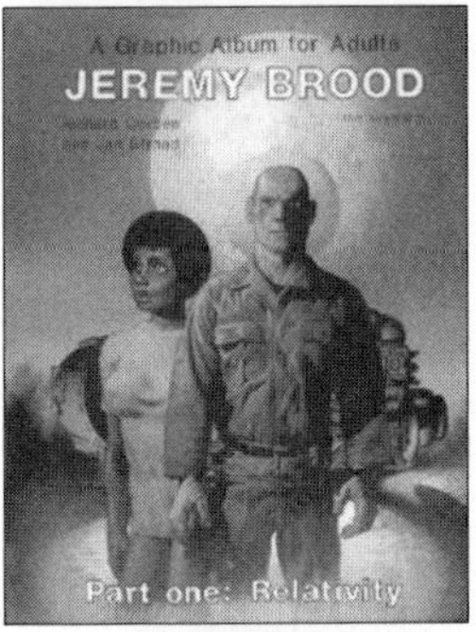

Jeremy Brood

Lone Ranger's Companion Tonto

Dell, 1951

2 .... 50.00
3-5 .... 32.00
6-10 .... 25.00
11-20 .... 22.00
21-33 .... 18.00

Lone Ranger's Famous Horse Hi-Yo Silver

Dell, 1952

3 .... 45.00
4-5 .... 32.00
6-10 .... 25.00
11-20 .... 21.00
21-36 .... 18.00

Lone Ranger's Golden West

Dell, 1955

3 .... 50.00

Lone Ranger's Western Treasury

Dell, 1953

1 .... 125.00
2 .... 100.00

Lone Rider

Superior, 1951

1 .... 95.00
2 .... 60.00
3-5 .... 45.00
6-10 .... 36.00
11-20 .... 32.00
21-26 .... 28.00

Lone Wolf 2100: Red Files

Dark Horse, 2003

1 .... 3.00

Lone Wolf and Cub

First, 1987

1 .... 6.00
1/2nd-1/3rd 3.00
2 .... 4.00
2/2nd 3.00
3 .... 4.00
3/2nd-38 .... 3.00
39 .... 6.00
☛Giant-size
40 .... 3.00
41-49 .... 4.00

Lone Wolf and Cub

Dark Horse, 2000

1-28 .... 10.00

Lone Wolf 2100

Dark Horse, 2002

1-11 .... 3.00

Long Bow

Fiction House, 1951

1 .... 85.00
2 .... 60.00
3 .... 50.00
4-9 .... 40.00

Long, Hot Summer

DC, 1995

1-3 .... 3.00

Longshot

Marvel, 1985

1 .... 4.00
2-4 .... 3.00
5 .... 2.00
6 .... 3.00

Longshot

Marvel, 1998

1 .... 4.00

Longshot Comics

Slave Labor, 1995

1-2 .... 3.00

Lookers

Avatar, 1997

1-2 .... 3.00

Lookers: Slaves of Anubis

Avatar, 1998

1 .... 4.00

Looking Glass Wars: Hatter M

Image, 2006

1-4 .... 4.00

Looney Tunes: Back in Action The Movie

DC, 2003

1 .... 4.00

Looney Tunes

Gold Key, 1975

1 .... 12.00
2 .... 7.00
3-5 .... 5.00
6-10 .... 4.00
11-20 .... 3.00
21-32 .... 2.00
33 .... 25.00
34 .... 40.00
35 .... 30.00
36-42 .... 2.00
43-44 .... 15.00
45-47 .... 20.00

Looney Tunes

DC, 1994

1-190 .... 2.00

Looney Tunes and Merrie Melodies Comics

Dell, 1941

1 .... 9,500.00
2 .... 1,750.00
3 .... 1,100.00
4-5 .... 850.00
6-10 .... 575.00

11-15 .... 425.00
16-20 .... 350.00
21-29 .... 265.00
30-40 .... 200.00
41-50 .... 140.00
51-60 .... 110.00
61-70 .... 85.00
71-80 .... 60.00
81-90 .... 45.00
91-99 .... 32.00
100 .... 38.00
101-110 .... 22.00
111-120 .... 20.00
121-130 .... 18.00
131-140 .... 15.00
141-150 .... 12.00
151-170 .... 10.00
171-200 .... 8.00
201-221 .... 6.00
222-246 .... 4.00

Looney Tunes Magazine

DC, 1994

1 .... 3.00
2-20 .... 2.00

Loose Cannon

DC, 1995

1-4 .... 2.00

Loose Teeth

Fantagraphics

1-3 .... 3.00

Lord Farris: Slavemaster

Fantagraphics, 1996

1-2 .... 3.00

Lord Jim

Gold Key, 1965

1 .... 18.00

Lord of the Dead

Conquest

1 .... 3.00

Lord Pumpkin

Malibu, 1994

0-0/A 3.00

Lord Pumpkin/ NecroMantra

Malibu, 1995

1-4 .... 3.00

Lords

Legend (Not Dark Horse Imprint)

1 .... 2.00

Lords of Misrule

Dark Horse, 1997

1-6 .... 3.00

Lords of Misrule

Atomeka

1 .... 7.00

Lords of the Ultra-Realm

DC, 1986

1-Special 1 .... 2.00

Lore

Idea & Design Works, 2003

1 .... 6.00
2-3 .... 4.00
4 .... 6.00

Lorelei

Starwarp, 1994

1 .... 3.00

Lorelei of the Red Mist

Conquest

1-2 .... 3.00

Lori Lovecraft: My Favorite Redhead

Caliber, 1997

1 .... 4.00

Lori Lovecraft: Repression

A V, 2002

1 .... 3.00

Lori Lovecraft: The Big Comeback

Caliber

1 .... 3.00

Lori Lovecraft: The Dark Lady

Caliber

1 .... 3.00

Lorna the Jungle Girl

Atlas, 1953

1 .... 265.00
2 .... 185.00
3 .... 165.00
4-5 .... 140.00
6-10 .... 110.00
11-14 .... 75.00
15-19 .... 60.00
20-26 .... 50.00

Lortnoc

Radio, 1998

1 .... 3.00

Losers

DC, 2003

1-32 .... 3.00

Losers Special

DC, 1985

1 .... 3.00

Lost and Found Season of the Most PopeJoey

Abanne, 2001

1 .... 3.00

Jersey Devil

Jet Aces

Jet Comics

Jet Fury

Jet Powers

Jezebel Jade

Jezebelle

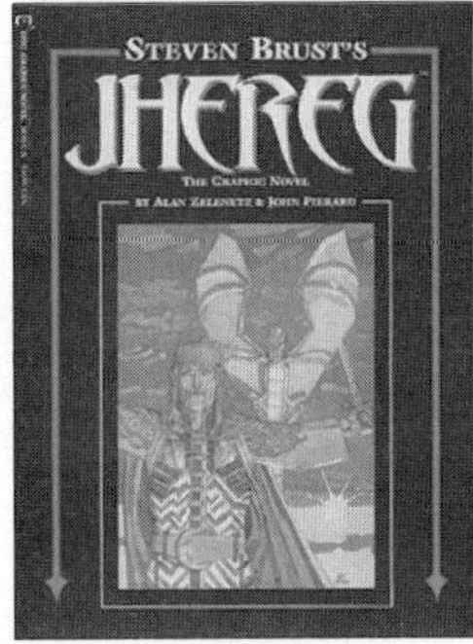

Jhereg

Lost Angel
Caliber
1 .... 3.00

Lost
Caliber, 1996
1-2 .... 3.00

Lost
Chaos, 1997
1-3 .... 3.00

Lost Continent
Eclipse, 1990
1-6 .... 4.00

Lost Girl
NBM
1 .... 10.00

Lost Girls
Kitchen Sink, 1995
1-2 .... 6.00

Lost Heroes
Davdez, 1998
0-4 .... 3.00

Lost in Space
Innovation, 1991
1-12 .... 3.00
13 .... 4.00
13/Gold 5.00
14-Ann 2 .... 3.00
Special 1 .... 4.00
Special 2 .... 3.00

Lost in Space
Dark Horse, 1998
1-3 .... 3.00

Lost in Space: Project Robinson
Innovation, 1993
1 .... 3.00

Lost in the Alps
NBM
1 .... 14.00

Lost Laughter
Bad Habit, 1994
1-4 .... 3.00

Lost Ones
Image, 2000
1 .... 3.00

Lost Ones: For Your Eyes Only
Image, 2000
1 .... 1.00

Lost Planet
Eclipse, 1987
1-6 .... 2.00

Lost Squad
Devil's Due, 2005
1-5 .... 3.00

Lost Universe (Gene Roddenberry's...)
Tekno, 1995
0-7 .... 2.00

Lost World
Millennium, 1996
1-2 .... 3.00

Lost World: Jurassic Park
Topps, 1997
1-3 .... 3.00

Lost Worlds
Standard, 1952
5 .... 150.00
6 .... 120.00

Lothar
Powerhouse Graphics, 1995
1 .... 3.00

Loud Cannoli
Crazyfish
1 .... 3.00

Louder than Words (Sergio Aragonès')
Dark Horse, 1997
1-6 .... 3.00

Louie the Rune Soldier
ADV Manga, 2004
1-4 .... 10.00

Louis Riel
Drawn & Quarterly, 2000
1-5 .... 3.00

Louis vs. Ali
Revolutionary, 1993
1 .... 3.00

Love Adventures
Marvel, 1949
1 .... 90.00
2 .... 70.00
3 .... 60.00
4-5 .... 50.00
6-12 .... 40.00

Love and Marriage
Superior, 1952
1 .... 60.00
2 .... 35.00
3-5 .... 24.00
6-10 .... 20.00
11-16 .... 16.00

Love & Rockets
Fantagraphics, 1982
1 .... 25.00
1/2nd-1/3rd 4.00
1/4th-1/5th 5.00
2 .... 12.00
2/2nd 4.00
2/3rd 5.00
3 .... 9.00

3/2nd.. 4.00
4... 8.00
4/2nd-4/3rd.............................. 4.00
5... 7.00
5/2nd.. 3.00
6... 5.00
6/2nd.. 3.00
7... 5.00
7/2nd.. 3.00
8... 5.00
8/2nd.. 3.00
9... 5.00
9/2nd.. 3.00
10... 5.00
10/2nd...................................... 3.00
11... 4.00
11/2nd...................................... 3.00
12... 4.00
12/2nd...................................... 3.00
13... 4.00
13/2nd...................................... 3.00
14... 4.00
14/2nd...................................... 3.00
15... 4.00
15/2nd-20................................. 3.00
21-27.. 2.00
28-29.. 3.00
29/2nd...................................... 2.00
30-39.. 3.00
40... 4.00
41-49.. 3.00
50... 5.00

Love & Rockets
Fantagraphics, 2001
1... 6.00
2-9.. 4.00
10... 6.00
11-15.. 5.00

Love & Rockets Bonanza
Fantagraphics, 1989
1-1/2nd.................................... 3.00

Love and Romance
Charlton, 1971
1... 24.00
2... 16.00
3-5.. 12.00
6-10.. 8.00
11-20.. 6.00
21-24.. 4.00

Love as a Foreign Language
Oni, 2005
1-4.. 7.00

Love at First Sight
Ace, 1949
1... 85.00
2... 50.00
3-9.. 30.00
10-20.. 25.00
21-35.. 20.00
36-43.. 15.00

Love Bites
Fantagraphics, 1991
1-2..2.00

Love Bites
Radio, 2000
1...3.00

Love Bomb
Abaculus
1-2..3.00

Love Bug
Gold Key, 1969
1...15.00

Lovebunny & Mr. Hell: Day in the Love Life
Image, 2003
1...3.00

Lovebunny & Mr. Hell: Savage Love
Image, 2003
1...3.00

Love Classics
Marvel, 1949
1...75.00
2...65.00

Love Confessions
Quality, 1949
1...150.00
2...125.00
3-5..50.00
6-9..35.00
10...50.00
11-20..40.00
21-30..30.00
31-39..25.00
40-54..20.00

Lovecraft
DC, 2004
1...25.00

Lovecraft
Adventure, 1992
1-4..3.00

Love Diary
Our Publishing, 1949
1...90.00
2...60.00
3...50.00
4-5..30.00
6-10..25.00
11-20..22.00
21-30..16.00
31-40..13.00
41-48..10.00

Love Diary
Quality, 1949
1...165.00

Jiggs is Back

Jigsaw

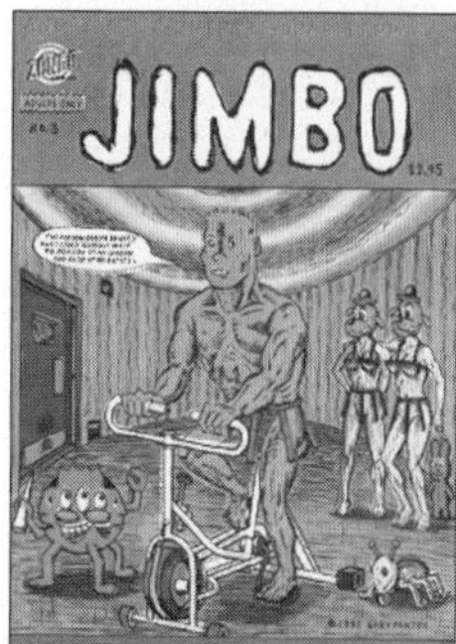

Jimbo

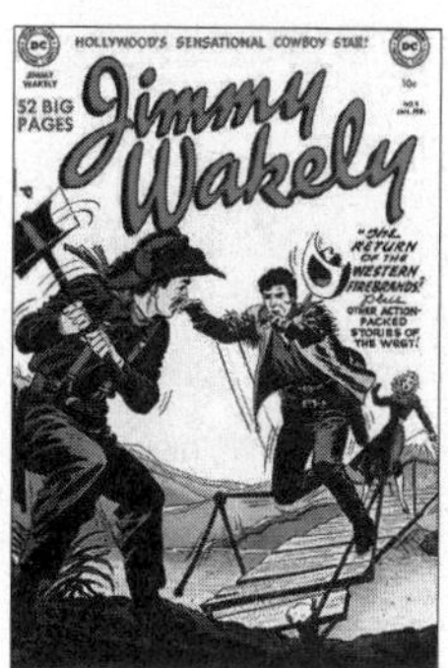

Jimmy Wakely

Jingle Belle

Jingle Jangle Comics

Jing Pals

Jinn

Love Diary
Charlton, 1958

1 ... 45.00
2 ... 24.00
3-4 ... 16.00
5 ... 14.00
6 ... 20.00
7-10 ... 14.00
11-15 ... 12.00
16-20 ... 10.00
21-30 ... 7.00
31-40 ... 5.00
41-60 ... 4.00
61-102 ... 3.00

Love Dramas
Marvel, 1949

1 ... 90.00
2 ... 70.00

Love Eternal: A Tortured Soul
Vlad Ent.

1 ... 2.00

Love Experiences
Ace, 1949

1 ... 60.00
2 ... 30.00
3-5 ... 22.00
6-10 ... 16.00
11-20 ... 13.00
21-30 ... 11.00
31-38 ... 10.00

Love Fantasy
Renegade

1 ... 2.00

Love Hina
Tokyopop, 2002

1-5 ... 3.00

Love in Tights
Slave Labor, 1998

1 ... 3.00

Love Journal
Our, 1951

10 ... 50.00
11-20 ... 25.00
21-25 ... 20.00

Loveland
Marvel, 1949

1 ... 45.00
2 ... 40.00

Loveless
DC, 2005

1-14 ... 3.00

Love Lessons
Harvey, 1949

1 ... 75.00
2 ... 40.00
3-5 ... 30.00

Love Letters
Quality, 1949

1 ... 110.00
2 ... 85.00
3 ... 60.00
4 ... 80.00
5-11 ... 20.00
12-20 ... 16.00
21-48 ... 12.00
49-50 ... 35.00
51 ... 24.00

Love Letters in the Hand
Fantagraphics, 1991

1-2 ... 2.00
3 ... 3.00

Lovelorn
ACG, 1949

1 ... 65.00
2-3 ... 40.00
4-5 ... 35.00
6-10 ... 30.00
11-20 ... 24.00
21-30 ... 22.00
31-39 ... 18.00
40-51 ... 15.00

Lovely as a Lie
Illustration, 1994

1 ... 3.00

Lovely Ladies
Caliber

1 ... 4.00

Lovely Prudence
All the Rage, 1995

1-3 ... 3.00

Love Memories
Fawcett, 1949

1 ... 70.00
2-4 ... 40.00

Love Me Tenderloin
Dark Horse, 2004

1 ... 3.00

Love Mystery
Fawcett, 1950

1 ... 100.00
2 ... 75.00
3 ... 65.00

Love or Money
Tokyopop, 2004

1-4 ... 10.00

Love Problems
Fox

1 ... 125.00

Love Romances
Timely, 1949

6 ... 100.00
7-10 ... 75.00
11-50 ... 65.00

51-59 .... 60.00
60-70 .... 48.00
71-80 .... 42.00
81-100 .... 36.00
101-106 .... 32.00

Lovers
Marvel, 1949

23 .... 70.00
24-25 .... 40.00
26-40 .... 30.00
41-60 .... 24.00
61-70 .... 20.00
71-86 .... 18.00

Lovers' Lane
Lev Gleason, 1949

1 .... 50.00
2 .... 30.00
3-5 .... 22.00
6-10 .... 16.00
11-20 .... 12.00
21-30 .... 10.00
31-41 .... 8.00

Love Scandals
Quality, 1950

1 .... 175.00
2-5 .... 100.00

Love Secrets
Marvel, 1949

1 .... 75.00
2 .... 50.00

Love Secrets
Quality, 1953

32-56 .... 12.00

Love Stories
DC, 1972

147-152 .... 8.00

Love Stories of Mary Worth
Harvey, 1949

1 .... 40.00
2-5 .... 25.00

Love Sucks
Ace

1 .... 3.00

Love Tales
Marvel, 1949

36 .... 75.00
37 .... 50.00
38-40 .... 40.00
41-50 .... 36.00
51-60 .... 32.00
61-70 .... 28.00
71-75 .... 25.00

Love Trails
Marvel, 1949

1 .... 75.00
2 .... 65.00

Lowlife
Caliber, 1994

1-4 .... 3.00

L.T. Caper
Spotlight

1 .... 2.00

Luba
Fantagraphics, 1998

1-3 .... 3.00
4-9 .... 4.00

Lucifer
DC, 2000

1 .... 4.00
2-49 .... 3.00
50 .... 4.00
51-74 .... 3.00
75 .... 4.00

Lucifer
Trident, 1990

1-3 .... 2.00

Lucifer: Nirvana
DC, 2002

1 .... 6.00

Lucifer's Hammer
Innovation, 1993

1-6 .... 3.00

Luck of the Draw
Radio, 2000

1 .... 4.00

Lucky
Howard, 1945

1 .... 300.00

Lucky 7
Howard, 1944

1 .... 225.00

Lucky 7
Runaway Graphics, 1993

1 .... 2.00

Lucky Comics
Holyoke, 1944

1 .... 150.00
2 .... 125.00
3-5 .... 75.00

Lucky Duck
Standard, 1953

5 .... 50.00
6-8 .... 35.00

Lucky Fights It Through
E.C., 1949

1 .... 750.00

Lucky Luke: Jesse James
Fantasy Flight

1 .... 9.00

Jinx

JLA

JLX

Joe Dimaggio

Joe Louis

Joe Sinn

Joe Yank

John F. Kennedy

Lucky Luke: The Stage Coach

Fantasy Flight

1 .... 9.00

Lucky Star

Nationwide, 1950

1 .... 60.00
2 .... 45.00
3-5 .... 36.00
6-14 .... 28.00

Lucy Show

Gold Key, 1963

1 .... 65.00
2 .... 40.00
3-5 .... 32.00

Ludwig Von Drake

Dell, 1961

1 .... 16.00
2 .... 10.00
3-4 .... 8.00

Luftwaffe: 1946 Technical Manual

Antarctic, 1998

3-6 .... 0.00
1-2 .... 4.00

Luftwaffe: 1946

Antarctic, 1996

1 .... 5.00
2-Ann 1 .... 4.00

Luftwaffe: 1946

Antarctic, 1997

1-4 .... 4.00
5 .... 3.00
Special 1-Special 2 .... 4.00

Luftwaffe: 1946

Antarctic, 2002

1-17 .... 6.00

Luftwaffe 1946

Antarctic, 2005

1-3 .... 6.00

Luger

Eclipse, 1986

1-3 .... 2.00

Lugh, Lord of Light

Flagship, 1987

1-4 .... 2.00

Lugo

Lost Boys

½ 1.00

Lullaby

Alias, 2005

1 .... 3.00

Lullaby: Wisdom Seeker

Image, 2005

1 .... 3.00
1/B cover 4.00
2 .... 3.00
2/B cover 4.00
3-4 .... 3.00

Lumenagerie

NBM

1 .... 12.00

Lum Urusei*Yatsura

Viz

1 .... 5.00
2-8 .... 4.00

Lunar Donut

Lunar Donut, 1997

0-6 .... 3.00

Lunatic Binge

Eternity

1-2 .... 4.00

Lunatic Fringe

Innovation, 1989

1-2 .... 2.00

Lunatik

Marvel, 1995

1-3 .... 2.00

Lurid

Idea & Design Works, 2003

1-3 .... 3.00

Lurid Tales

Fantagraphics

1 .... 3.00

Lust

Fantagraphics, 1997

1-6 .... 3.00

Lust for Life

Slave Labor, 1997

1-4 .... 3.00

Lust of the Nazi Weasel Women

Fantagraphics, 1991

1-4 .... 2.00

Lux & Alby Sign on and Save the Universe

Dark Horse, 1993

1-9 .... 3.00

Luxura & Vampfire

Brainstorm

1 .... 3.00

Luxura Collection (Kirk Lindo's...)

Brainstorm

1 .... 5.00

Luxura Leather Special

Brainstorm, 1996

1 .... 3.00

Lycanthrope Leo
Viz
1-7 .... 3.00

Lyceum
Hunter, 1996
1-2 .... 3.00

Lycra-Woman and Spandex-Girl
Comic Zone, 1992
1 .... 3.00

Lycra Woman and Spandex Girl Christmas '77 Special
Comic Zone
1 .... 3.00

Lycra Woman and Spandex Girl Halloween Special
Lost Cause
1 .... 3.00

Lycra Woman and Spandex Girl Jurassic Dinosaur Special
Comic Zone
1 .... 3.00

Lycra Woman and Spandex Girl Summer Vacation Special
Comic Zone
1 .... 3.00

Lycra Woman and Spandex Girl Time Travel Special
Comic Zone
1 .... 3.00

Lycra Woman and Spandex Girl Valentine Special
Comic Zone
1 .... 3.00

Lynch
Image, 1997
1 .... 3.00

Lynch Mob
Chaos, 1994
1-4 .... 3.00

Lynx: An Elflord Tale
Peregrine Entertainment, 1999
1 .... 3.00

M
Eclipse, 1990
1-3 .... 5.00
4 .... 6.00

Maburaho
ADV Manga, 2005
1 .... 10.00

Macabre
Lighthouse, 1989
1-6 .... 3.00

Macabre (Vol. 2)
Lighthouse, 1989
1-2 .... 3.00

Macbeth (William Shakespeare's ...)
Black Dog & Leventhal, 2006
1 .... 13.00

Mace: Bounty Hunter
Image, 2003
1 .... 3.00

M.A.C.H. 1
Fleetway-Quality
1-9 .... 2.00

Machine
Dark Horse, 1994
1-4 .... 3.00

Machine Man
Marvel, 1978
1 .... 3.00
2-18 .... 2.00
☛Alpha Flight app.
19 .... 13.00
☛1st Jack O'Lantern

Machine Man
Marvel, 1984
1-4 .... 2.00

Machine Man/Bastion '98
Marvel, 1998
1 .... 3.00

Machine Man 2020
Marvel, 1994
1-2 .... 2.00

Machine Teen
Marvel, 2005
1-5 .... 3.00

Mack Bolan: The Executioner (Don Pendleton's...)
Innovation, 1993
1 .... 3.00
1/A-1/B 4.00
2-4 .... 3.00

Mackenzie Queen
Matrix
1-5 .... 2.00

Mack the Knife: Monochrome Memories
Caliber
1 .... 3.00

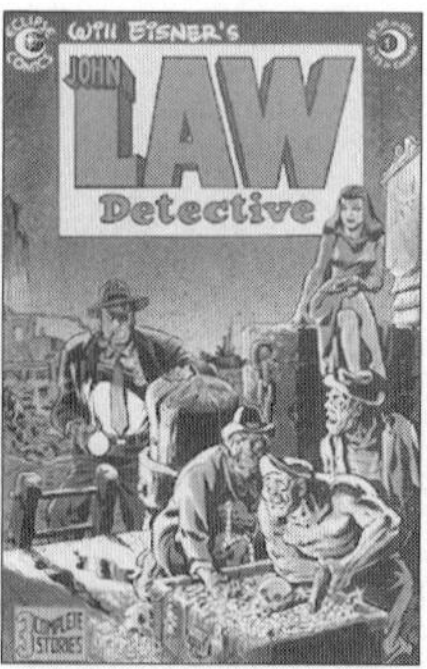

John Law Detective

Johnny Atomic

Johnny Dynamite

Johnny Gambit

Johnny the Homicidal Maniac

John Wayne Adventure Comics

Joker Comics

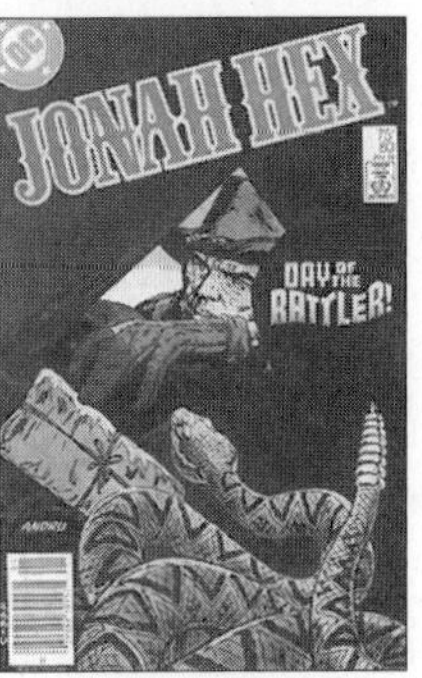

Jonah Hex

Macross II
Viz, 1992

1-10 .... 3.00

Macross II: The Micron Conspiracy
Viz, 1995

1-5 .... 3.00

Mad
E.C., 1952

1 .... 5,000.00
2 .... 1,250.00
3 .... 725.00
4 .... 700.00
5 .... 1,200.00
☛Low distribution
6-11 .... 525.00
12-19 .... 425.00
20-23 .... 300.00
24 .... 785.00
☛1st magazine issue
25 .... 300.00
26-27 .... 250.00
28-29 .... 225.00
30 .... 350.00
31 .... 200.00
32 .... 175.00
33 .... 165.00
34-35 .... 140.00
36-40 .... 110.00
41-50 .... 80.00
51-60 .... 60.00
61-70 .... 48.00
71-80 .... 36.00
81-100 .... 32.00
101-120 .... 18.00
121 .... 22.00
122 .... 18.00
123-140 .... 15.00
141-150 .... 12.00
151-160 .... 9.00
161-170 .... 8.00
171-189 .... 7.00
190-200 .... 5.00
201-220 .... 4.00
221-260 .... 3.00
261-342 .... 2.00
343-417 .... 3.00
418-501 .... 4.00

Mad 2992
Graphic Image

Ashcan 2 .... 1.00

Mad About Millie
Marvel, 1969

1 .... 50.00
2 .... 35.00
3 .... 30.00
4-5 .... 18.00
6-9 .... 15.00
10-17 .... 14.00
Ann 1 .... 20.00

Madagascar
Tokyopop, 2005

1 .... 8.00

Madame Xanadu
DC, 1981

1 .... 3.00

Madballs
Marvel, 1986

1-10 .... 1.00

Mad Classics
DC, 2005

1-12 .... 5.00

Mad-Dog
Marvel, 1993

1-6 .... 1.00

Mad Dog Magazine
Blackthorne, 1986

1-3 .... 2.00

Mad Dogs
Eclipse, 1992

1-3 .... 3.00

Mad Follies
E.C., 1963

1 .... 250.00
2 .... 200.00
3 .... 150.00
4-7 .... 100.00

Mad Hatter
O.W., 1946

1 .... 550.00
2 .... 245.00

Mad House
Red Circle, 1974

95-96 .... 4.00
97-130 .... 3.00

Madhouse
Ajax, 1954

1 .... 95.00
2-4 .... 55.00

Madhouse Glads
Archie, 1970

73-77 .... 3.00
78-92 .... 5.00
93-94 .... 3.00

Madhouse Ma-ad Freakout
Archie, 1969

71-72 .... 3.00

Madhouse Ma-ad Jokes
Archie, 1969

66-70 .... 4.00

Mad Kids
DC, 2005

1-5 .... 5.00

Madman
Tundra, 1992

1 .... 8.00
1/4th-1/2nd 5.00
1/3rd 4.00
2-3 .... 6.00

Madman Adventures
Tundra, 1992

1 .... 5.00
2-3 .... 4.00

Madman Comics
Dark Horse, 1994

1-3 .... 4.00
4-20 .... 3.00
YB 1995 .... 18.00

Madman Picture Exhibition
AAA Pop, 2002

1-4 .... 4.00

Madman/The Jam
Dark Horse, 1998

1-2 .... 3.00

Mad Monster Party
Dell, 1967

1 .... 40.00

Mad Monster Party Adaptation
Black Bear

1-4 .... 3.00

Madonna
Personality

1 .... 3.00
2 .... 3.00

Madonna Sex Goddess
Friendly, 1990

1-3 .... 3.00

Madonna Special
Revolutionary, 1993

1 .... 3.00

Madonna vs. Marilyn
Celebrity

1 .... 3.00

Mad Raccoons
Mu, 1991

1-6 .... 3.00

Madraven Halloween Special
Hamilton, 1995

1 .... 3.00

Madrox
Marvel, 2004

1-5 .... 3.00

Mad Super Special
E.C., 1970

1 .... 90.00
2 .... 54.00
3-5 .... 44.00
6-10 .... 38.00
11-15 .... 26.00
16-20 .... 20.00
21-25 .... 16.00
26-30 .... 12.00
31-40 .... 10.00
41-50 .... 6.00
51-60 .... 5.00
61-135 .... 4.00

Mad TV
E.C., 2000

1 .... 4.00

Mad XL
E.C., 2000

1-33 .... 5.00

Mael's Rage
Ominous, 1994

2-2/Variant 3.00

Maelstrom
Aircel, 1987

1-10 .... 2.00

Magdalena
Image, 2000

1-3/A 3.00

Magdalena
Image, 2003

1 .... 3.00
1/A 5.00
2-4 .... 3.00

Magdalena/Angelus
Image, 2001

0-½ 3.00

Magdalena/Vampirella
Image, 2003

1 .... 3.00

Mage
Comico, 1984

1 .... 5.00
2 .... 4.00
3-5 .... 3.00
6 .... 15.00
☛1st Grendel
7 .... 8.00
8 .... 4.00
9-12 .... 3.00
13 .... 4.00
14 .... 3.00
15 .... 6.00

Mage
Image, 1997

0 .... 3.00
1 .... 4.00
1/3D 5.00
2-3 .... 4.00
4-15 .... 3.00
15/Variant 6.00

Jonathan Fox

Jon Juan

Jonni Thunder

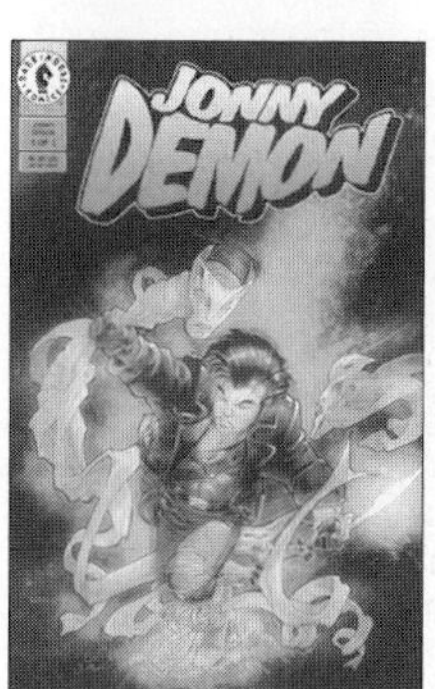

Jonny Demon

Jonny Double

Jonny Quest Classics

Jontar Returns

Josie

Magebook
Comico, 1985
1 .... 9.00
2 .... 8.00

Mage Knight: Stolen Destiny
Idea & Design Works, 2002
1-5 .... 4.00

Mage: The Hero Discovered
Image, 1998
1-8 .... 5.00

Maggie and Hopey Color Special
Fantagraphics, 1997
1 .... 4.00

Maggie the Cat
Image, 1996
1-4 .... 3.00

Maggots
Hamilton, 1991
1-3 .... 4.00

Magical Mates
Antarctic, 1996
1-9 .... 3.00

Magical Nymphini
Rip Off, 1991
1-5/2nd 3.00

Magical Twilight
Graphic Visions
1 .... 3.00

Magic Boy and Girlfriend
Top Shelf, 1998
1 .... 9.00

Magic Boy & the Robot Elf
Slave Labor, 1996
1 .... 10.00

Magic Carpet
Shanda Fantasy Arts, 1999
1 .... 5.00

Magic Comics
David McKay, 1939
1 .... 2,800.00
2 .... 1,150.00
3 .... 685.00
4 .... 415.00
5 .... 330.00
6-11 .... 275.00
12-20 .... 210.00
21-30 .... 130.00
31-40 .... 95.00
41-50 .... 75.00
51-60 .... 58.00
61-80 .... 46.00
81-100 .... 40.00
101-123 .... 34.00

Magic Flute
Eclipse, 1990
1-3 .... 5.00

Magicians' Village
Mad Monkey, 1995
1 .... 2.00

Magic Inkwell Comic Strip Theatre
Moordam, 1998
1 .... 3.00

Magic Knight Rayearth
Mixx, 2001
1-6 .... 0.00

Magicman
A-Plus
1 .... 3.00

Magic Pickle
Oni, 2001
1-4 .... 3.00

Magic Priest
Antarctic, 1998
1 .... 3.00

Magic: The Gathering: Antiquities War
Acclaim, 1995
1-4 .... 3.00

Magic: The Gathering: Elder Dragons
Acclaim, 1996
1-2 .... 3.00

Magic: The Gathering: Gerard's Quest
Dark Horse, 1998
1-4 .... 3.00

Magic: The Gathering: Nightmare
Acclaim, 1995
1 .... 3.00

Magic: The Gathering: Shandalar
Acclaim, 1996
1-2 .... 3.00

Magic: The Gathering: The Shadow Mage
Acclaim, 1995
1-4 .... 3.00

Magic: The Gathering: Wayfarer
Acclaim, 1995
1-5 .... 3.00

Magic Whistle
Alternative, 1998
1-2 .... 3.00

Magic Words (Alan Moore's...)

Avatar, 2002

1 .... 7.00

Magik

Marvel, 1983

1-4 .... 2.00

Magik

Marvel, 2000

1-4 .... 3.00

Magilla Gorilla

Gold Key, 1964

1 .... 30.00
2 .... 15.00
3-5 .... 12.00
6-10 .... 10.00

Magna-Man: The Last Superhero

Comics Interview, 1988

1-3 .... 2.00

Magnesium Arc

Iconografix

1 .... 4.00

Magnetic Men Featuring Magneto

Marvel, 1997

1 .... 2.00

Magneto

Marvel, 1993

0 .... 3.00

Magneto

Marvel, 1996

1-4 .... 2.00

Magneto and the Magnetic Men

Marvel, 1996

1 .... 2.00

Magneto Ascendant

Marvel, 1999

1 .... 4.00

Magneto: Dark Seduction

Marvel, 2000

1-4 .... 3.00

Magneto Rex

Marvel, 1999

1-3 .... 3.00

Magnets: Robot Dismantler

Parody

1 .... 3.00

Magnus, Robot Fighter

Gold Key, 1963

1 .... 200.00
2-3 .... 125.00
4-10 .... 60.00
11-20 .... 35.00
21-28 .... 20.00
29-45 .... 10.00
45/Whitman 18.00
46 .... 10.00

Magnus Robot Fighter

Valiant, 1991

0/card 40.00
0/no card 30.00
1 .... 10.00
2 .... 8.00
3-4 .... 5.00
☛Flip-book with Rai #1
5-6 .... 6.00
7-8 .... 4.00
9-10 .... 3.00
11 .... 6.00
12 .... 20.00
☛1st Valiant Turok
13-16 .... 3.00
17-21 .... 2.00
21/Gold 20.00
22-25 .... 2.00
25/VVSS 15.00
26-35 .... 1.00
36 .... 2.00
37-43 .... 1.00
44 .... 3.00
45-54 .... 2.00
55-57 .... 3.00
57/error 10.00
58-60 .... 3.00
61-62 .... 4.00
63 .... 5.00
64 .... 12.00
YB 1 .... 5.00

Magnus Robot Fighter

Acclaim, 1997

1-18 .... 3.00
Ashcan 1 .... 1.00

Magnus Robot Fighter/ Nexus

Valiant, 1993

0/Preview 10.00
1-2 .... 3.00

Magus

Caliber

1-2 .... 3.00

Mahoromatic: Automatic Maiden

Tokyopop, 2004

1-7 .... 10.00

Maine Zombie Lobstermen

Maine Stream Comics

1-2 .... 3.00
3 .... 4.00

Mai, the Psychic Girl

Eclipse, 1987

1 .... 4.00
1/2nd 2.00

Journey

Journey Into Unknown Worlds

Journeyman

Journey Saga

Jr. Carrot Patrol

JSA

JSA Secret Files

Jubilee

2 ....3.00
2/2nd 2.00
3 ....3.00
4-28 ....2.00

Maison Ikkoku Part 1
Viz, 1992
1-7 ....4.00

Maison Ikkoku Part 2
Viz, 1993
1 ....4.00
2-6 ....3.00

Maison Ikkoku Part 3
Viz, 1993
1-6 ....3.00

Maison Ikkoku Part 4
Viz, 1994
1-10 ....3.00

Maison Ikkoku Part 5
Viz, 1995
1-2 ....3.00
3-5 ....4.00
6 ....3.00
7-8 ....4.00
9 ....3.00

Maison Ikkoku Part 6
Viz, 1996
1 ....4.00
2 ....3.00
3-4 ....4.00
5 ....3.00
6 ....4.00
7-10 ....3.00
11 ....4.00

Maison Ikkoku Part 7
Viz, 1997
1-2 ....4.00
3-13 ....3.00

Maison Ikkoku Part 8
Viz, 1998
1 ....3.00
2 ....4.00
3 ....3.00
4-7 ....4.00
8 ....3.00

Maison Ikkoku Part 9
Viz, 1999
1-10 ....3.00

Majcans
P.S.
1 ....1.00

Majestic
DC, 2004
1-5 ....3.00

Majestic
DC, 2005
1-16 ....3.00

Major Bummer
DC, 1997
1-15 ....3.00

Major Damage
Invictus, 1994
1-2 ....2.00

Major Inapak the Space Ace
Magazine Enterprises, 1952
1 ....8.00

Major Power And Spunky
Fantagraphics, 1994
1 ....4.00

Major Victory Comics
Harry A. Chesler, 1944
1 ....400.00
2 ....255.00
3 ....220.00

Makebelieve
Liar
1 ....3.00

Malcolm-10
Onli
1 ....2.00

Malcolm X
Millennium, 1993
1 ....4.00

Malcolm X Angriest Man in America
London Publishing
1 ....7.00

Malibu Ashcan: UltraForce
Malibu, 1994
1 ....1.00

Malibu Signature Series
Malibu
1993-1994 ....1.00

Malice in Wonderland
Fantagraphics, 1993
1 ....3.00

Malinky Robot Bicycle
Slave Labor, 2005
1 ....3.00

Mallimalou
Chance
1 ....2.00

Malu in the Land of Adventure
I.W., 1964
1 ....50.00

Mammoth Comics
K.K., 1939
1 ....1,250.00

Man Against Time
Image, 1996

1-6 .... 2.00

Man-Bat
DC, 1975

1 .... 10.00
2 .... 4.00

Man-Bat
DC, 1984

1 .... 3.00

Man-Bat
DC, 1996

1-3 .... 3.00

Man-Bat
DC, 2006

1-5 .... 3.00

Man Called A-X
Malibu, 1994

0-5 .... 3.00

Man Called A-X
DC, 1997

1-8 .... 3.00

Man Called Loco, A
Avalon

1 .... 3.00

Man Comics
Marvel, 1949

1 .... 100.00
2 .... 65.00
3-5 .... 45.00
6-10 .... 38.00
11-20 .... 32.00
21-28 .... 28.00

Mandrake the Magician
King, 1966

1 .... 32.00
2 .... 20.00
3 .... 14.00
4-5 .... 13.00
6-7 .... 10.00
8 .... 16.00
9 .... 9.00
10 .... 24.00

Mandrake the Magician
Marvel, 1995

1-2 .... 3.00

Man-Eating Cow
NEC, 1992

1 .... 5.00
2-4 .... 4.00
5-10 .... 3.00

Man-Frog
Mad Dog, 1987

1-2 .... 2.00

Man from Atlantis
Marvel, 1978

1 .... 3.00
2-7 .... 2.00

Man from U.N.C.L.E.
Gold Key, 1965

1 .... 150.00
2 .... 75.00
3-5 .... 50.00
6-20 .... 35.00
21-22 .... 25.00

Man from U.N.C.L.E.
Entertainment, 1987

1-11 .... 2.00

Man From U.N.C.L.E.: The Birds of Prey Affair
Millennium, 1993

1-2 .... 3.00

Manga Caliente
Fantagraphics, 2003

1-3 .... 4.00

Manga Darkchylde
Dark Horse, 2005

1-2 .... 3.00

Manga Horror
Avalon

1 .... 3.00

Mangaphile
Radio, 1999

1-7 .... 3.00

Manga Shi
Crusade, 1996

1 .... 3.00

Manga Shi: Shiseji
Crusade

1 .... 3.00

Manga Shi 2000
Crusade, 1997

1-3 .... 3.00

Manga Surprise!
Morning & Afternoon, Kodansha Ltd., 1996

1 .... 2.00

Manga Vizion
Viz, 1995

1-10 .... 5.00

Manga Vizion (Vol. 2)
Viz, 1996

1-12 .... 5.00

Manga Vizion (Vol. 3)
Viz, 1997

1-8 .... 5.00

Judge Child

Judge Colt

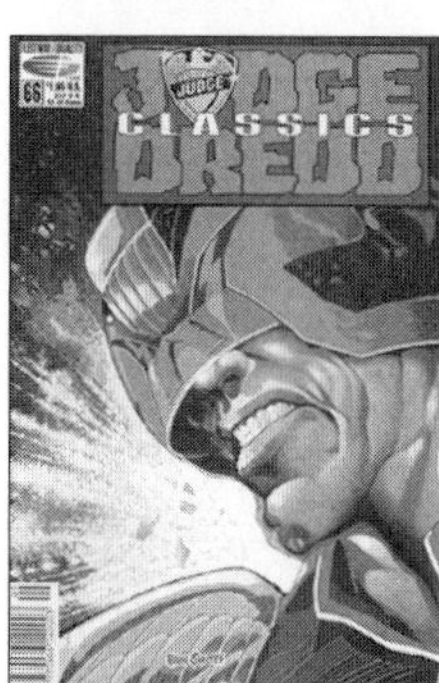

Judge Dredd Classics

Judge Dredd-Lawman of the Future

Judge Dredd the Early Cases

Judge Dredd the Megazine

Judgment Pawns

Judomaster

Manga Vizion (Vol. 4)

Viz

1-8 .... 5.00

Manga Zen

Zen Comics

1 .... 3.00

Mangazine

Antarctic, 1985

1 .... 4.00
1/2nd 2.00
2 .... 4.00
3 .... 2.00
4-5 .... 4.00

Mangazine (Vol. 2)

Antarctic, 1989

1 .... 4.00
2 .... 3.00
3-5 .... 2.00
6-44 .... 3.00

Mangazine (Vol. 3)

Antarctic, 1999

1-53 .... 9.00
54-71 .... 10.00

Mangle Tangle Tales

Innovation

1 .... 3.00

Manhunt

Print Mint, 1973

1 .... 4.00
2 .... 3.00

Manhunter

DC, 1984

1 .... 3.00

Manhunter

DC, 1988

1 .... 2.00
2-24 .... 1.00

Manhunter

DC, 1994

0-12 .... 2.00

Manhunter

DC, 2004

1-4 .... 3.00
5 .... 4.00
☛Identity Crisis tie
6 .... 8.00
7-27 .... 3.00

Manhunter: The Special Edition

DC, 1999

1 .... 10.00

Manhunt!

Magazine Enterprises, 1947

1 .... 285.00
2 .... 240.00
3 .... 200.00
4-11 .... 165.00

Maniac Chainsaw Weilding Duckbilled Platypus

Duncwadd Comics, 1995

1 .... 1.00

Manic One-Shot

Image, 2004

1 .... 4.00

Manifest Eternity

DC, 2006

1-6 .... 3.00

Manik

Millennium, 1995

1-3 .... 3.00

Manimal

Renegade, 1986

1 .... 2.00

Man in Black

Harvey, 1957

1 .... 110.00
2 .... 75.00
3-4 .... 60.00

Man in Black

Recollections, 1991

1-2 .... 2.00

Mankind

Chaos, 1999

1 .... 3.00

Mann and Superman

DC, 2000

1 .... 6.00

Man of Many Faces

Tokyopop, 2003

1 .... 10.00

Man of Rust

Blackthorne, 1986

1/A-1/B 2.00

Man of Steel

DC, 1986

1-6/Silver 3.00

Man of the Atom

Acclaim, 1997

1 .... 4.00

Man of War

Centaur, 1941

1 .... 1,050.00
2 .... 775.00

Man of War

Eclipse, 1987

1-5 .... 2.00

Man of War
Malibu, 1993

1 .... 2.00
1/Direct-5 .... 3.00
6-8 .... 2.00

Man O' Mars
Fiction House, 1953

1 .... 275.00
1/2nd 100.00

Manosaurs
Express

1-2 .... 3.00

Mantech Robot Warriors
Archie, 1984

1-4 .... 1.00

Man-Thing
Marvel, 1974

1 .... 30.00
2 .... 14.00
3 .... 10.00
4 .... 8.00
5 .... 10.00
6-10 .... 5.00
11-22 .... 3.00

Man-Thing
Marvel, 1979

1 .... 3.00
2-11 .... 2.00

Man-Thing
Marvel, 1997

1-8 .... 3.00

Man-Thing
Marvel, 2004

1-3 .... 3.00

Mantra
Malibu, 1993

1-1/Ltd. 3.00
1/Hologram 6.00
2-3 .... 2.00
4 .... 3.00
5-9 .... 2.00
10 .... 4.00
11-17 .... 2.00
18 .... 3.00
19-20 .... 2.00
21-24 .... 3.00
GS 1 .... 4.00

Mantra
Malibu, 1995

0-7 .... 2.00

Mantra: Spear of Destiny
Malibu, 1995

1-2 .... 3.00

Mantus Files
Eternity

1-4 .... 3.00

Man Who Would Be King
Tome

1 .... 3.00

Man with the Screaming Brain
Dark Horse, 2005

1/A-4/B 3.00

Many Ghosts of Dr. Graves
Charlton, 1967

1 .... 30.00
2 .... 18.00
3 .... 12.00
4-10 .... 10.00
11-20 .... 8.00
21-45 .... 6.00
46-53 .... 4.00
54 .... 6.00
☛Byrne cover
55-71 .... 4.00
72 .... 5.00

Many Loves of Dobie Gillis
DC, 1960

1 .... 85.00
2 .... 65.00
3 .... 50.00
4-5 .... 45.00
6-10 .... 35.00
11-20 .... 26.00
21-26 .... 24.00

Many Reincarnations of Lazarus
Fisher, 1998

1 .... 3.00
Ashcan 1 .... 1.00

Many Worlds of Tesla Strong
DC, 2003

1 .... 3.00

Mara
Aircel, 1991

1-4 .... 3.00

Mara Celtic Shamaness
Fantagraphics, 1995

1-6 .... 3.00

Mara of the Celts Book 1
Rip Off, 1993

Special 1 .... 3.00

Mara of the Celts Book 2
Fantagraphics, 1995

1 .... 3.00

Marauder
Silverline, 1998

1-4 .... 3.00

Judy Canova

Jughead as Captain Hero

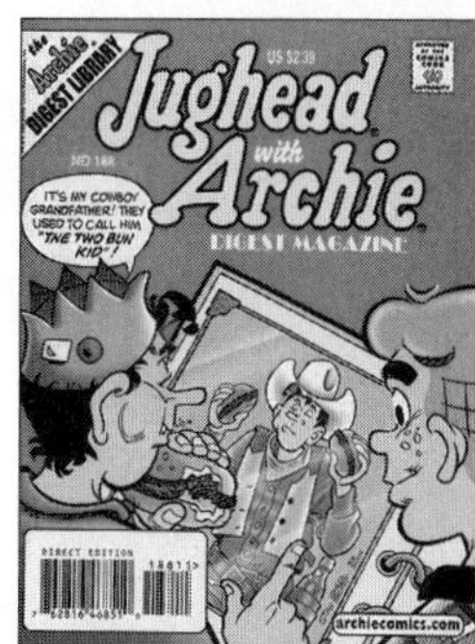

Jughead with Archie Digest Magazine

Jumbo Comics

Jungle Comics

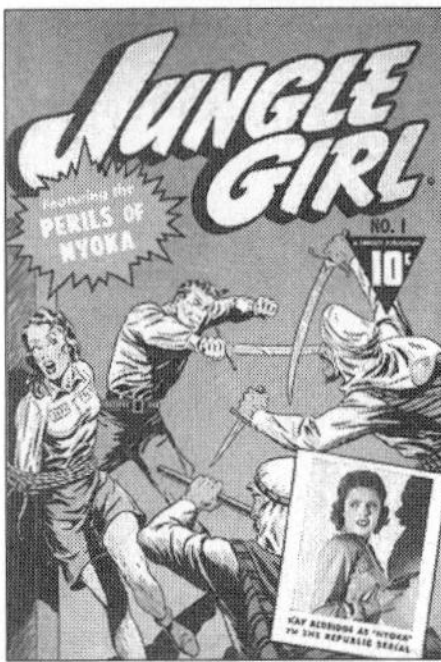

Jungle Girl

Jungle Girls

Jungle Lil

March Hare

Lodestone

Issue	Price
1	2.00

March of Comics (Boys' and Girls'...)

K.K., 1946

Issue	Price
1	340.00
2	250.00
3	295.00
4	5,150.00
5	175.00
6	160.00
7	125.00
8	400.00
9-10	75.00
11	60.00
12-14	55.00
15	45.00
16	85.00
17	175.00
18	100.00
19	85.00
20	3,225.00
21	80.00
22	85.00
23	100.00
24	185.00
25	195.00
26	200.00
27	250.00
28	185.00
29-33	40.00
34	70.00
35	165.00
36	140.00
37	110.00
38	45.00
39	165.00
40	60.00
41	2,775.00
42	60.00
43	45.00
44	70.00
45	210.00
46	65.00
47	150.00
48-50	40.00
51	115.00
52	90.00
53	40.00
54	165.00
55	55.00
56	260.00
57	55.00
58	40.00
59	70.00
60	190.00
61	55.00
62	145.00
63-65	35.00
66	80.00
67	30.00
68	115.00
69	190.00
70	45.00
71	50.00
72	60.00
73	110.00
74	175.00
75	45.00
76	50.00
77	110.00
78	90.00
79	30.00
80	65.00
81	25.00
82	90.00
83	40.00
84	35.00
85	30.00
86	120.00
87	55.00
88	45.00
89	30.00
90	120.00
91	115.00
92	28.00
93	20.00
94	55.00
95	25.00
96	50.00
97	35.00
98	85.00
99	25.00
100	80.00
101	20.00
102	110.00
103	25.00
104	80.00
105	65.00
106-108	30.00
109	20.00
110	40.00
111	25.00
112-113	20.00
114	75.00
115	25.00
116	65.00
117	50.00
118	75.00
119	20.00
120-121	70.00
122-123	26.00
124	18.00
125	75.00
126	20.00
127	35.00
128-130	20.00
131	65.00
132	20.00
133	70.00
134	40.00
135-136	60.00

Issue	Price
137-138	20.00
139	18.00
140	30.00
141	18.00
142	70.00
143	18.00
144	80.00
145	18.00
146	55.00
147	18.00
148	40.00
149	18.00
150-151	60.00
152-153	20.00
154	18.00
155	75.00
156	18.00
157	35.00
158	18.00
159	30.00
160	18.00
161	50.00
162	18.00
163	50.00
164	18.00
165	60.00
166	20.00
167	55.00
168	20.00
169-170	30.00
171	18.00
172	70.00
173	18.00
174	55.00
175	18.00
176	50.00
177-179	18.00
180	45.00
181-182	15.00
183	18.00
184	15.00
185	65.00
186	15.00
187	30.00
188-190	15.00
191	45.00
192	15.00
193	55.00
194	30.00
195	40.00
197-198	18.00
199	40.00
200	25.00
201	15.00
202	50.00
203	15.00
204	60.00
205	35.00
206	45.00
207	15.00
208	55.00
209	15.00
210	35.00
212-213	15.00
214	30.00
215	40.00
216	50.00
217	30.00
218	10.00
219	25.00
220	10.00
221	35.00
222	10.00
223	55.00
224	10.00
225	45.00
226-228	15.00
229	50.00
230	30.00
231	10.00
232	55.00
233	50.00
234-235	25.00
236-237	30.00
238	40.00
239	10.00
240	50.00
241-242	15.00
243	40.00
244	35.00
245	10.00
246-247	25.00
248	50.00
249	10.00
250	30.00
251	85.00
252	45.00
253	40.00
254	30.00
255-256	15.00
257	25.00
258	40.00
259	10.00
260	20.00
261	10.00
262	40.00
263	45.00
264	20.00
265	30.00
266	25.00
267	70.00
268	45.00
269-270	15.00
271-272	40.00
273	10.00
274	20.00
275	60.00
276	75.00
277	10.00
278	20.00
279	25.00
280	45.00
281	10.00
282	20.00

Jungle Tales of Tarzan

Jungle War Stories

Junie Prom

Junior Comics

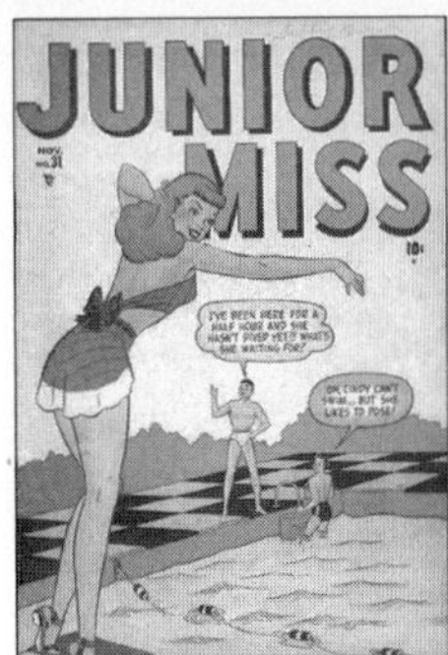

Junior Miss

Junk Culture

Junker

Junk Force

Issue	Price
283-284	15.00
285	150.00
286	35.00
287-288	10.00
289	35.00
290	15.00
291	20.00
292	40.00
293	35.00
294	20.00
295	10.00
296-298	15.00
299-300	30.00
301	10.00
302	25.00
303	10.00
304	40.00
305	10.00
306-307	30.00
308	15.00
309	20.00
310	40.00
311-312	15.00
313	10.00
314	25.00
315	10.00
316	35.00
317-318	30.00
319	20.00
320	65.00
321	10.00
322	35.00
323	20.00
324-326	15.00
327	30.00
328	60.00
329	10.00
330	50.00
331	8.00
332	25.00
333	8.00
334	15.00
335	20.00
336	30.00
337	20.00
338	35.00
340	15.00
341-342	25.00
343	8.00
344	15.00
345	8.00
346	15.00
347	8.00
348	40.00
349	20.00
350	30.00
351	10.00
352	50.00
353	8.00
354-355	20.00
356	35.00
357	8.00
358	15.00
359	10.00
360	40.00
361	8.00
362	15.00
363	8.00
364	25.00
365	6.00
366	20.00
367	8.00
368	25.00
369-370	15.00
371	6.00
372	15.00
373	25.00
374-375	6.00
376	10.00
377	6.00
378	50.00
379-380	6.00
381	10.00
382	15.00
383	10.00
384	6.00
385	15.00
386-388	6.00
389	15.00
390	6.00
391	15.00
392-393	5.00
394	10.00
395	8.00
396-398	5.00
399	40.00
400	5.00
401-403	4.00
404	35.00
405	5.00
406	10.00
407	8.00
408	30.00
409-410	4.00
411	10.00
412-413	4.00
414	30.00
415-416	4.00
417	10.00
418-425	4.00
426	15.00
427	6.00
428-437	4.00
438	12.00
439	5.00
440-446	4.00
447	5.00
448-456	4.00
457-458	3.00
459	4.00
460	3.00
461-466	4.00
467	8.00
468-478	4.00

479 .... 6.00
480-488 .... 4.00

March of Crime
Fox, 1950

1 .... 245.00
2 .... 225.00
3 .... 115.00

Marco Polo
Charlton, 1962

1 .... 68.00

Marc Silvestri Sketchbook
Image, 2004

1 .... 3.00

Marc Silvestri Sketchbook
Image, 2006

1 .... 3.00

Marc Spector: Moon Knight
Marvel, 1989

1 .... 3.00
2-7 .... 2.00
8-9 .... 3.00
10-18 .... 2.00
19-25 .... 3.00
26-31 .... 2.00
32-33 .... 3.00
34-49 .... 2.00
50 .... 3.00
51-54 .... 2.00
55-57 .... 3.00
58-60 .... 2.00
Special 1 .... 3.00

Margie
Dell, 1962

2 .... 25.00

Margie Comics
Marvel, 1946

35 .... 100.00
36-38 .... 50.00
39-41 .... 75.00
42 .... 50.00
43-44 .... 75.00
45 .... 50.00
46 .... 75.00
47-49 .... 50.00

Marginal Prophets
Marginal Prophets

1 .... 1.00

Marie-Gabrielle
NBM

1 .... 16.00

Marilyn Monroe: Suicide or Murder?
Revolutionary, 1993

1 .... 3.00

Marines Attack
Charlton, 1964

1 .... 16.00
2 .... 12.00
3-5 .... 9.00
6-9 .... 6.00

Marines in Action
Atlas, 1955

1 .... 65.00
2-10 .... 42.00
11-14 .... 36.00

Marines in Battle
Marvel, 1954

1 .... 110.00
2 .... 60.00
3-19 .... 45.00
20-25 .... 36.00

Marine War Heroes
Charlton, 1964

1 .... 15.00
2-3 .... 12.00
4-5 .... 9.00
6-10 .... 7.00
11-18 .... 5.00

Marionette
Alpha Productions

1-3 .... 3.00

Marionette
Raven, 1987

1-3 .... 1.00

Mark
Dark Horse, 1987

1-6 .... 2.00

Mark
Dark Horse, 1993

1-4 .... 3.00

Markam
Gauntlet

1 .... 3.00

Mark Hazzard: Merc
Marvel, 1986

1-Ann 1 .... 1.00

Mark of Charon
CrossGen, 2003

1-5 .... 3.00

Mark of the Succubus
Tokyopop, 2005

1 .... 10.00

Marksman
Hero, 1988

1-5 .... 2.00
Ann 1 .... 3.00

Mark Trail
Standard, 1955

1 .... 35.00
5 .... 18.00

Marmaduke Mouse
Quality, 1946

1 .... 70.00

Junkyard Enforcer

Jurassic Park Adventures

Just a Pilgrim

Justice Brigade

Justice League

Justice League Adventures

Justice League America

Justice League Europe

2 .... 40.00
3-5 .... 28.00
6-10 .... 20.00
11-20 .... 16.00
21-40 .... 12.00
41-65 .... 9.00

Marmalade Boy
Tokyopop, 2001
1-3 .... 3.00

Marooned!
Fantagraphics, 1990
1 .... 2.00

Marquis: Danse Macabre
Oni, 2000
1-3 .... 3.00

Marquis: Les Preludes
Caliber, 1997
1 .... 3.00

Marriage of Hercules and Xena
Topps, 1998
1 .... 3.00

Married...With Children
Now, 1990
1 .... 3.00
1/2nd-7 .... 2.00

Married...With Children
Now, 1991
1 .... 3.00
2-7 .... 2.00
Ann 1994 .... 3.00
Special 1 .... 2.00

Married...With Children: Buck's Tale
Now, 1994
1 .... 2.00

Married...With Children: Bud Bundy, Fanboy in Paradise
Now
1 .... 3.00

Married...With Children: Flashback Special
Now, 1993
1-3 .... 2.00

Married...With Children: Kelly Bundy
Now, 1992
1-3 .... 2.00

Married...With Children: Kelly Goes to Kollege
Now
1-3 .... 3.00

Married...With Children: Off Broadway
Now, 1993
1 .... 2.00

Married...With Children: Quantum Quartet
Now, 1993
1-2 .... 2.00
3 .... 3.00

Married...With Children 3-D Special
Now, 1993
1 .... 3.00

Married...With Children: 2099
Now, 1993
1-3 .... 2.00

Mars
First, 1984
1 .... 2.00
2-12 .... 1.00

Mars
Tokyopop, 2002
1-3 .... 10.00

Mars Attacks
Topps, 1994
1-1/Ltd 4.00
2-5 .... 3.00

Mars Attacks
Topps, 1995
1 .... 4.00
2-8 .... 3.00

Mars Attacks Baseball Special
Topps, 1996
1 .... 3.00

Mars Attacks High School
Topps, 1997
1-2 .... 3.00

Mars Attacks Image
Image, 1996
1-4 .... 3.00

Mars Attacks the Savage Dragon
Topps, 1996
1-4 .... 3.00

Marshal Law
Marvel, 1987
1 .... 4.00
2-6 .... 3.00

Marshal Law: Kingdom of the Blind
Apocalypse
1 .... 4.00
1/Direct 6.00

Marshal Law: Secret Tribunal

Dark Horse, 1993

1-2 .... 3.00

Marshal Law: Super Babylon

Dark Horse, 1992

1 .... 5.00

Marshal Law: The Hateful Dead

Apocalypse

1 .... 6.00

M.A.R.S. Patrol Total War

Gold Key, 1966

3 .... 50.00

☛Was Total War

4-5 .... 35.00

6-10 .... 25.00

Martha Splatterhead's Weirdest Stories Ever Told

Monster

1 .... 4.00

Martha Washington Goes to War

Dark Horse, 1994

1-5 .... 3.00

Martha Washington Saves the World

Dark Horse, 1997

1-3 .... 4.00

Martha Washington: Stranded in Space

Dark Horse, 1995

1 .... 3.00

☛Reprint from DHP; Miller, Gibbons

Martian Manhunter

DC, 1988

1-4 .... 2.00

Martian Manhunter

DC, 1998

0-1 .... 3.00

2-21 .... 2.00

22-36 .... 3.00

1000000 .... 4.00

Ann 1-2 .... 3.00

Martian Manhunter: American Secrets

DC, 1992

1-3 .... 5.00

Martian Manhunter

DC, 2006

1-5 .... 3.00

Martian Manhunter Special

DC, 1996

1 .... 4.00

Martin Kane

Fox, 1949

1 .... 210.00

2 .... 135.00

Martin Mystery

Dark Horse, 1999

1-6 .... 5.00

Martin the Satanic Racoon

Gabe Martinez

1 .... 1.00

2 .... 2.00

Marvel Westerns: Western Legends

Marvel, 2006

1 .... 4.00

Marvel Action Hour, Featuring Iron Man

Marvel, 1994

1 .... 2.00

1/CS 3.00

2-8 .... 2.00

Marvel Action Hour, Featuring the Fantastic Four

Marvel, 1994

1 .... 2.00

1/CS 3.00

2-8 .... 2.00

Marvel Action Universe

Marvel, 1989

1 .... 1.00

Marvel Adventure

Marvel, 1975

1 .... 8.00

2-3 .... 5.00

3/30¢ 20.00

4 .... 5.00

4/30¢ 20.00

5 .... 4.00

5/30¢ 20.00

6 .... 4.00

Marvel Adventures

Marvel, 1997

1-18 .... 2.00

Marvel Adventures: Avengers

Marvel, 2006

1-8 .... 3.00

Marvel Adventures: Fantastic Four

Marvel, 2005

0-19 .... 3.00

Justice League of America

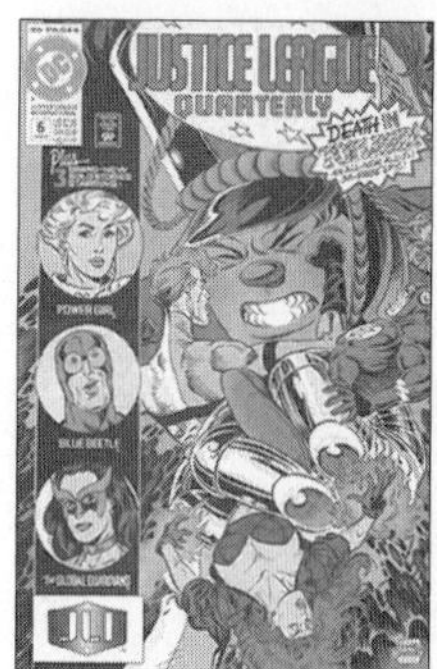

Justice League Quarterly

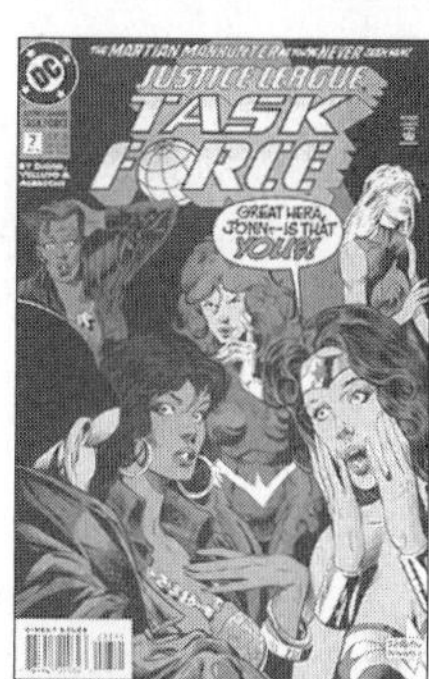

Justice League Task Force

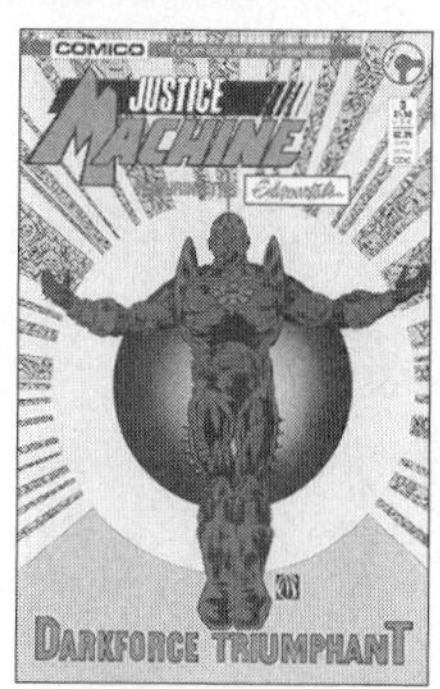

Justice Machine Featuring the Elementals

Justice Riders

Justice Traps the Guilty

Just Imagine Stan Lee With Jim Lee Creating Wonder Woman

Just Imagine Stan Lee With John Byrne Creating Robin

Marvel Adventures Flip Magazine

Marvel, 2005

1-11 .... 4.00
13-20 .... 5.00

Marvel Adventures: Spider-Man

Marvel, 2005

1-23 .... 3.00

Marvel Adventures: Spider-Man Vol. 1: The Sinister Six Digest

Marvel, 2005

1 .... 7.00

Marvel Adventures: The Thing

Marvel, 2005

1 .... 2.00
2-3 .... 3.00

Marvel Age

Marvel, 1983

1 .... 2.00
2-133 .... 1.00
134 .... 2.00
135-136 .... 1.00
137-138 .... 2.00
139-Ann 4 .... 1.00

Marvel Age: Fantastic Four

Marvel, 2004

1 .... 3.00
2-12 .... 2.00

Marvel Age: Fantastic Four Tales - The Thing

Marvel, 2005

1 .... 2.00

Marvel Age Hulk

Marvel, 2004

1-4 .... 2.00

Marvel Age Preview

Marvel, 1990

1-2 .... 2.00

Marvel Age: Runaways

Marvel, 2004

1 .... 8.00

Marvel Age: Sentinel

Marvel, 2004

1 .... 8.00

Marvel Age: Spider-Girl

Marvel, 2004

1 .... 8.00

Marvel Age: Spider-Man

Marvel, 2004

1 .... 3.00
1/FCBD 2.00
2-4 .... 3.00
5-20 .... 2.00

Marvel Age Spider-Man Team Up

Marvel, 2004

1-5 .... 2.00

Marvel and DC Present

Marvel, 1982

1 .... 12.00

Marvel Boy

Marvel, 1950

1 .... 875.00
2 .... 610.00

Marvel Boy

Marvel, 2000

1 .... 3.00
1/A 5.00
2-6 .... 3.00

Marvel Chillers

Marvel, 1975

1 .... 12.00
2 .... 7.00
3 .... 10.00
4 .... 7.00
4/30¢ 20.00
5 .... 7.00
5/30¢ 20.00
6 .... 5.00
6/30¢ 20.00
7 .... 5.00

Marvel Chillers: Shades of Green Monsters

Marvel, 1997

1 .... 3.00

Marvel Chillers: The Thing in the Glass Case

Marvel, 1997

1 .... 3.00

Marvel Classics Comics

Marvel, 1976

1 .... 7.00
2-5 .... 5.00
6-27 .... 4.00
28 .... 8.00
☛1st Mike Golden art
29-36 .... 4.00

Marvel Collectible Classics: Amazing Spider-Man

Marvel, 1988

300 .... 14.00

Marvel Collectible Classics: Avengers (Vol. 3)

Marvel, 1998

1 .... 14.00

Marvel Collectible Classics: X-Men

Marvel, 1998

1-GS 1 .... 14.00

Marvel Collectible Classics: X-Men (Vol. 2)

Marvel, 1998

1 .... 14.00

Marvel Collector's Edition

Marvel, 1992

1 .... 3.00

Marvel Collectors' Item Classics

Marvel, 1966

1 .... 125.00
2 .... 70.00
3-4 .... 45.00
5-6 .... 30.00
7-10 .... 15.00
11-20 .... 12.00
21 .... 15.00
22 .... 17.00
23 .... 20.00

Marvel Comics

Marvel, 1939

1 .... 165,000.00
1/A 350,000.00
1/HC 30.00
1/HC/2nd 20.00

Marvel Comics Presents

Marvel, 1988

1 .... 4.00
2-5 .... 3.00
6-53 .... 2.00
54-62 .... 3.00
63-71 .... 2.00
72 .... 4.00
73-86 .... 3.00
87-175 .... 2.00

Marvel Comics Presents Spider-Man

Marvel

1 .... 2.00

Marvel Comics Presents the X-Men

Marvel

1 .... 2.00

Marvel Comics: 2001

Marvel, 2001

1 .... 1.00

Marvel Double Feature

Marvel, 1973

1 .... 40.00
2 .... 20.00
3 .... 15.00
4-8 .... 10.00
9-15 .... 8.00
15/30¢ 20.00
16 .... 8.00
16/30¢-17/30¢ 20.00
18 .... 8.00
19-21 .... 6.00

Marvel Double Shot

Marvel, 2003

1-4 .... 3.00

Marvel Encyclopedia

Marvel, 2003

1-2 .... 30.00
3 .... 20.00
4 .... 25.00
5-6 .... 30.00

Marvel Encyclopedia (Magazine)

Marvel, 2004

1 .... 6.00

Marvel Family

Fawcett, 1945

1 .... 1,100.00
2 .... 525.00
3 .... 425.00
4-5 .... 315.00
6-10 .... 265.00
11-20 .... 200.00
21-30 .... 165.00
31-40 .... 135.00
41-70 .... 100.00
71-81 .... 85.00
82-89 .... 75.00

Marvel Fanfare

Marvel, 1982

1 .... 5.00
2-5 .... 3.00
6-50 .... 2.00
51 .... 3.00
52-60 .... 2.00

Marvel Fanfare

Marvel, 1996

1 .... 2.00
2-6 .... 1.00

Marvel Feature

Marvel, 1971

1 .... 125.00
2 .... 60.00
3 .... 30.00
4 .... 25.00
5-10 .... 10.00
11 .... 55.00
☛Thing vs. Hulk
12 .... 35.00

Just Married

Justy

Kaboom

Kabuki

Kabuki Reflections

Kafka

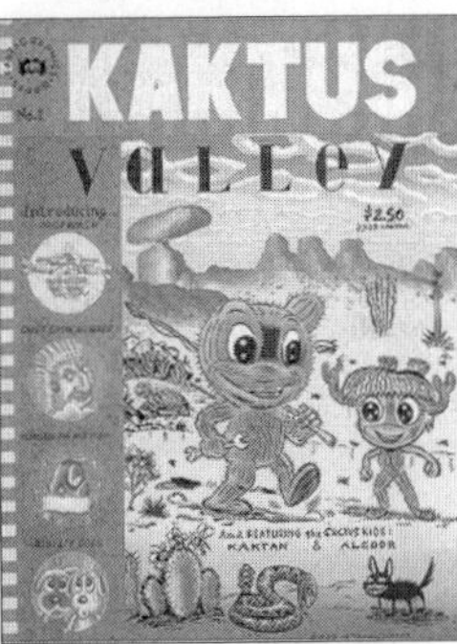

Kaktus

Kalamazoo Comix

Marvel Feature

Marvel, 1975

1 ....10.00
2-4 ....3.00
4/30¢ 35.00
5 ....3.00
5/30¢ 20.00
6-7 ....3.00

Marvel Frontier Comics Unlimited

Marvel, 1994

1 ....3.00

Marvel Fumetti Book

Marvel, 1984

1 ....2.00

Marvel Graphic Novel

Marvel, 1982

1 ....13.00
1/2nd-1/3rd 6.00
2 ....7.00
3 ....8.00
4 ....12.00
4/2nd 6.00
4/3rd 5.00
5 ....20.00
5/2nd 7.00
5/3rd-8 ....6.00
9 ....7.00
10-11 ....6.00
12-13 ....7.00
14-17 ....6.00
18-21 ....7.00
22 ....9.00
23 ....7.00
24 ....8.00
25-28 ....7.00
29 ....8.00
30 ....6.00
31 ....7.00
32 ....10.00
33-34 ....7.00
35 ....13.00
36-37 ....7.00
38 ....16.00

Marvel Graphic Novel: Arena

Marvel

1 ....6.00

Marvel Graphic Novel: Cloak and Dagger and Power Pack: Shelter From the Storm

Marvel

1 ....8.00

Marvel Graphic Novel: Emperor Doom: Starring the Mighty Avengers

Marvel

1 ....6.00

Marvel Graphic Novel: Ka-Zar: Guns of the Savage Land

Marvel

1 ....9.00

Marvel Graphic Novel: Rick Mason, the Agent

Marvel, 1989

1 ....10.00

Marvel Graphic Novel: Roger Rabbit in the Resurrection of Doom

Marvel

1 ....9.00

Marvel Graphic Novel: The Shadow

Marvel

1 ....11.00

Marvel Graphic Novel: Who Framed Roger Rabbit?

Marvel

1 ....7.00

Marvel Guide to Collecting Comics

Marvel, 1982

1 ....3.00

Marvel Halloween Ashcan 2006

Marvel, 2006

1 ....1.00

Marvel Halloween: Supernaturals Tour Book

Marvel, 1998

1 ....3.00

Marvel: Heroes & Legends

Marvel, 1996

1-2 ....3.00

Marvel Heroes Flip Magazine

Marvel, 2005

1-11 ....4.00
13-20 ....5.00

Marvel Holiday Special

Marvel, 1993

1-1996 ....3.00

Marvel Holiday Special 2004

Marvel, 2004

1 .... 16.00

Marvel Holiday Special 2005

Marvel, 2006

1 .... 4.00

Marvel Holiday Special 2006

Marvel, 2007

1 .... 4.00

Marvel Illustrated: Swimsuit Issue

Marvel, 1991

1 .... 4.00

Marvel Kids

Marvel

1-4 .... 4.00

Marvel Knights

Marvel, 2000

1 .... 4.00
1/A 5.00
2/Barreto 4.00
2/Quesada 5.00
3-15 .... 3.00

Marvel Knights

Marvel, 2002

1-6 .... 3.00

Marvel Knights 4

Marvel, 2004

1 .... 4.00
2-29 .... 3.00

Marvel Knights Double-Shot

Marvel, 2002

1-4 .... 3.00

Marvel Knights Magazine

Marvel, 2001

1-6 .... 4.00

Marvel Knights/Marvel Boy Genesis Edition

Marvel, 2000

1 .... 1.00

Marvel Knights: Millennial Visions

Marvel, 2002

1 .... 4.00

Marvel Knights Sketchbook

Marvel

1 .... 1.00

Marvel Knights Spider-Man

Marvel, 2004

1 .... 5.00
2 .... 4.00
3-4 .... 3.00
5 .... 2.00
6-22 .... 3.00

Marvel Knights Tour Book

Marvel, 1998

1 .... 3.00

Marvel Knights 2099: Black Panther

Marvel, 2004

1 .... 4.00

Marvel Knights 2099: Daredevil

Marvel, 2004

1 .... 4.00

Marvel Knights 2099: Inhumans

Marvel, 2004

1 .... 4.00

Marvel Knights 2099: Mutant

Marvel, 2004

1 .... 4.00

Marvel Knights 2099: Punisher

Marvel, 2004

1 .... 4.00

Marvel Knights Wave 2 Sketchbook

Marvel

1 .... 1.00

Marvel Legacy: The 1960s Handbook

Marvel, 2006

1 .... 5.00

Marvel Legends: Thor

Marvel, 2004

1 .... 25.00

Marvel Legends: Wolverine

Marvel, 2003

2 .... 20.00
3 .... 13.00
4-5 .... 14.00
6 .... 20.00

Marvel Legends: X-Men

Marvel, 2003

3 .... 25.00
4 .... 20.00

Kalgan the Golden

Kamikaze Cat

Kane

Kansas Thunder

Kaos Moon

Karate Girl Tengu Wars

Karate Kid

Kare Kano

Marvel Magazine
Marvel, 1998

1-6 ....1.00

Marvel Mangaverse
Marvel, 2002

1-6 ....2.00

Marvel Mangaverse: Avengers Assemble!
Marvel, 2002

1 ....2.00

Marvel Mangaverse: Eternity Twilight
Marvel, 2002

1 ....2.00
1/A 4.00

Marvel Mangaverse: Fantastic Four
Marvel, 2002

1 ....2.00

Marvel Mangaverse: Ghost Riders
Marvel, 2002

1 ....2.00

Marvel Mangaverse: New Dawn
Marvel, 2002

1 ....4.00

Marvel Mangaverse: Punisher
Marvel, 2002

1 ....2.00

Marvel Mangaverse: Spider-Man
Marvel, 2002

1 ....2.00

Marvel Mangaverse: X-Men
Marvel, 2002

1 ....2.00

Marvelman Special
Fleetway-Quality

1 ....5.00

Marvel Masterpieces 2 Collection
Marvel, 1994

1-3 ....3.00

Marvel Masterpieces Collection
Marvel, 1993

1-4 ....3.00

Marvel Milestone Edition: Amazing Fantasy
Marvel, 1992

15 ....3.00

Marvel Milestone Edition: Amazing Spider-Man
Marvel, 1993

1 ....3.00
149 ....3.00

Marvel Milestone Edition: Avengers
Marvel, 1993

1 ....3.00
16 ....3.00

Marvel Milestone Edition: Captain America
Marvel, 1995

1 ....4.00

Marvel Milestone Edition: Fantastic Four
Marvel, 1991

1 ....3.00
5 ....3.00

Marvel Milestone Edition: Giant-Size X-Men
Marvel, 1991

1 ....4.00

Marvel Milestone Edition: Incredible Hulk
Marvel, 1991

1 ....3.00
181 ....3.00

Marvel Milestone Edition: Iron Fist
Marvel

14 ....3.00

Marvel Milestone Edition: Iron Man
Marvel, 1992

55 ....3.00

Marvel Milestone Edition: Iron Man, Ant-Man & Captain America
Marvel, 2005

1 ....4.00

Marvel Milestone Edition: Tales of Suspense
Marvel, 1994

39 ....3.00

Marvel Milestone Edition: X-Men
Marvel, 1991

1 ....3.00

Marvel Milestones: Beast & Kitty
Marvel, 2006

1 ....4.00

Marvel Milestones: Black Panther, Storm, and Ka-Zar
Marvel, 2006
1 .... 4.00

Marvel Milestones: Blade, Man-Thing & Satana
Marvel
1 .... 4.00

Marvel Milestones: Captain Britain, Psylocke, and Golden Age Sub-Mariner
Marvel, 2005
1 .... 4.00

Marvel Milestones: Dragon Lord, Speedball, and Man in the Sky
Marvel, 2006
1 .... 4.00

Marvel Milestones: Dr. Doom, Sub-Mariner, & Red Skull
Marvel, 2005
0 .... 4.00

Marvel Milestones: Dr. Strange, Silver Surfer, Sub-Mariner, Hulk
Marvel, 2005
1 .... 4.00

Marvel Milestones: Ghost Rider, Black Widow & Iceman
Marvel, 2005
1 .... 4.00

Marvel Milestones: Jim Lee and Chris Claremont X-Men and The Starjammers Part #17
Marvel, 2006
1 .... 4.00

Marvel Milestones: Legion of Monsters, Spider-Man, and Brother Voodoo
Marvel, 2006
1 .... 4.00

Marvel Milestones: Millie the Model & Patsy Walker
Marvel, 2006
1 .... 4.00

Marvel Milestones: Onslaught
Marvel, 2007
1 .... 4.00

Marvel Milestones: Rawhide Kid and Two-Gun Kid
Marvel, 2006
1 .... 4.00

Marvel Milestones: Star Brand and Quasar
Marvel, 2006
1 .... 4.00

Marvel Milestones: Ultimate Spider-Man, Ultimate X-Men, Microman & Mantor
Marvel, 2006
1 .... 4.00

Marvel Milestones: Venom and Hercules
Marvel, 2005
1 .... 4.00

Marvel Milestones: Wolverine, X-Men, & Tuk: Cave Boy
Marvel, 2005
1 .... 4.00

Marvel Milestones: X-Men & The Starjammers Part 2
Marvel, 2006
1 .... 4.00

Marvel Monsters: Devil Dinosaur
Marvel, 2005
1 .... 4.00

Marvel Monsters Fin Fang Four
Marvel, 2005
1 .... 4.00

Marvel Monsters: From the Files of Ulysses Bloodstone
Marvel, 2006
1 .... 4.00

Marvel Monsters: Monsters On the Prowl
Marvel, 2005
1 .... 4.00

Marvel Monsters: Where Monsters Dwell
Marvel, 2005
1 .... 4.00

Katy Keene Pin Up Parade

Katy Keene Special

Katzenjammer Kids

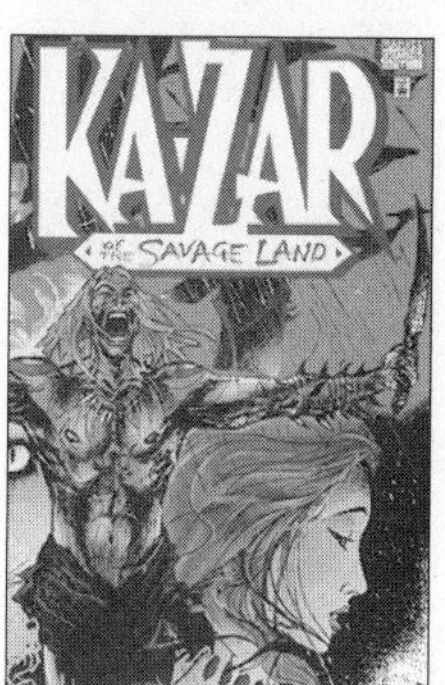

Kazar of the Savage Land

Ka-Zar the Savage

Keen Teens

Kelly Belle Police Detective

Kelvin Mace

Marvel Movie Premiere
Marvel

1 .... 3.00

Marvel Movie Showcase
Marvel, 1982

1-2 .... 1.00

Marvel Movie Spotlight
Marvel, 1982

1 .... 4.00

Marvel Must Haves
Marvel, 2001

1-2 .... 4.00

Marvel Must Haves: Amazing Spider-Man #30-32
Marvel, 2003

1 .... 4.00

Marvel Must Haves: Avengers #500-502
Marvel, 2004

1 .... 4.00

Marvel Must Haves: Incredible Hulk #50-52
Marvel, 2003

1 .... 4.00

Marvel Must Haves: Incredible Hulk #34-36
Marvel, 2003

1 .... 4.00

Marvel Must Haves: New Avengers #1-3
Marvel, 2005

1 .... 4.00

Marvel Must Haves: New X-Men #114-116
Marvel, 2003

1 .... 4.00

Marvel Must Haves: NYX #4-5
Marvel, 2005

1 .... 4.00

Marvel Must Haves: Sentinel #1 & #2 and Runaways #1 & #2
Marvel, 2003

1 .... 4.00

Marvel Must Haves: Spider-Man & Black Cat #1-#3
Marvel, 2006

1 .... 5.00

Marvel Must Haves: The Ultimates #1-3
Marvel, 2003

1 .... 4.00

Marvel Must Haves: Truth: Red, White and Black
Marvel, 2003

1 .... 4.00

Marvel Must Haves: Ultimates 2 #1-3
Marvel, 2005

1 .... 5.00

Marvel Must Haves: Ultimate Spider-Man #1-3
Marvel, 2003

1 .... 4.00

Marvel Must Haves: Ultimate Venom
Marvel, 2003

1 .... 4.00

Marvel Must Haves: Ultimate War
Marvel, 2003

1 .... 4.00

Marvel Must Haves: Ultimate X-Men #1-3
Marvel, 2003

1 .... 4.00

Marvel Must Haves: Ultimate X-Men #34 & #35
Marvel, 2003

1 .... 3.00

Marvel Must Haves: Wolverine #1-3
Marvel, 2003

1 .... 4.00

Marvel Mystery Comics
Marvel, 1939

2 .... 30,000.00
3 .... 15,000.00
4 .... 12,500.00
5 .... 22,500.00
6-7 .... 7,500.00
8 .... 10,000.00
9 .... 25,000.00
10 .... 8,000.00
11 .... 3,800.00
12 .... 4,000.00
13 .... 5,000.00
14-17 .... 2,500.00
18 .... 2,250.00
19-20 .... 2,500.00
21 .... 2,000.00
22-25 .... 1,700.00
26-30 .... 1,475.00
31-41 .... 1,325.00

42-48 .... 1,125.00
49 .... 1,450.00
50 .... 1,125.00
51-67 .... 1,000.00
68-78 .... 860.00
79 .... 810.00
80 .... 1,275.00
81 .... 975.00
82 .... 2,250.00
83 .... 810.00
84 .... 1,250.00
85 .... 810.00
86 .... 890.00
87 .... 785.00
88-91 .... 950.00
92 .... 2,500.00

Marvel Mystery Comics
Marvel, 1999
1 .... 4.00

Marvel Nemesis: The Imperfects
Marvel, 2005
1 .... 4.00
2-6 .... 3.00

Marvel No-Prize Book
Marvel, 1983
1 .... 3.00

Marvelous Adventures of Gus Beezer and Spider-Man
Marvel, 2004
1 .... 3.00

Marvelous Adventures of Gus Beezer: Hulk
Marvel, 2003
1 .... 3.00

Marvelous Adventures of Gus Beezer: Spider-Man
Marvel, 2003
1 .... 3.00

Marvelous Adventures of Gus Beezer: X-Men
Marvel, 2003
1 .... 3.00

Marvelous Dragon Clan
Lunar, 1994
1-2 .... 3.00

Marvelous Wizard of Oz (MGM's...)
Marvel
1 .... 16.00

Marvel: Portraits of a Universe
Marvel, 1995
1-4 .... 3.00

Marvel Poster Book
Marvel, 1991
1 .... 3.00

Marvel Poster Magazine
Marvel, 2001
2 .... 4.00

Marvel Premiere
Marvel, 1972
1 .... 35.00
2 .... 12.00
3 .... 30.00
☛Dr. Strange
4 .... 10.00
5-6 .... 8.00
7 .... 15.00
8 .... 10.00
9 .... 6.00
10 .... 9.00
11-12 .... 5.00
13 .... 8.00
14 .... 12.00
15 .... 80.00
☛1st Iron Fist
16 .... 20.00
☛2nd Iron Fist
17-18 .... 12.00
19-24 .... 10.00
25 .... 15.00
26 .... 4.00
27 .... 10.00
28 .... 13.00
29 .... 3.00
29/30¢ 20.00
30 .... 3.00
30/30¢ 20.00
31 .... 3.00
31/30¢ 20.00
32-36 .... 3.00
36/35¢ 15.00
37-37/Whitman 3.00
37/35¢ 15.00
38-38/Whitman 3.00
38/35¢ 15.00
39-49 .... 3.00
50 .... 13.00
☛1st Alice Cooper
51-56 .... 3.00
57 .... 5.00
58-61 .... 3.00

Marvel Presents
Marvel, 1975
1 .... 11.00
2 .... 5.00
3 .... 10.00
4 .... 4.00
4/30¢ 20.00
5 .... 4.00
5/30¢ 20.00
6 .... 4.00
6/30¢ 20.00
7-10 .... 4.00

Ken Maynard Western

Ken Shannon

Kerry Drake Detective Cases

Key Comics

Keyhole

Kid Blastoff

Kid Cannibal

Kid Carrots

11 ....15.00
11/35¢-12 ....4.00
12/35¢ 15.00

Marvel Preview
Marvel, 1975

1 ....15.00
2 ....50.00
☛Punisher origin
3 ....10.00
☛Blade app.
4 ....7.00
☛Blade app.
5-24 ....5.00

Marvel Preview '93
Marvel, 1993

1 ....4.00

Marvel Riot
Marvel, 1995

1 ....2.00

Marvel Romance Redux: But He Said He Loved Me
Marvel, 20006

1 ....3.00

Marvel Romance Redux: Guys & Dolls
Marvel, 2006

1 ....3.00

Marvel Romance Redux: I Should Have Been a Blonde
Marvel, 2006

1 ....3.00

Marvel Romance Redux: Love Is a Four Letter Word
Marvel, 2006

1 ....3.00

Marvel Romance Redux: Restraining Orders Are for Other Girls
Marvel, 2006

1 ....3.00

Marvels
Marvel, 1994

0 ....4.00
1 ....6.00
1/2nd 3.00
2 ....6.00
2/2nd 3.00
3-4 ....6.00
4/2nd 3.00

Marvel Saga
Marvel, 1985

1 ....3.00
2-25 ....2.00

Marvels Comics: Captain America
Marvel, 2000

1 ....2.00

Marvels Comics: Daredevil
Marvel, 2000

1 ....2.00

Marvels Comics: Fantastic Four
Marvel, 2000

1 ....2.00

Marvels Comics: Spider-Man
Marvel, 2000

1 ....2.00

Marvels Comics: Thor
Marvel, 2000

1 ....2.00

Marvels Comics: X-Men
Marvel, 2000

1 ....2.00

Marvel Select Flip Magazine
Marvel, 2005

1-11 ....4.00
12-20 ....5.00

Marvel Selects: Fantastic Four
Marvel, 2000

1 ....3.00

Marvel Selects: Spider-Man
Marvel, 2000

1-3 ....3.00

Marvel's Greatest Comics
Marvel, 1969

☛Was Marvel Collector's Item Classics
23-34 ....15.00
35-37 ....10.00
38-50 ....4.00
51-63 ....3.00
63/30¢ 20.00
64 ....3.00
64/30¢ 20.00
65-70/Whitman 3.00
71 ....2.00
71/35¢ 15.00
71/Whitman-72/Whitman 2.00
72/35¢ 15.00
73-73/Whitman 2.00
73/35¢ 15.00
74-96 ....2.00

Marvel's Greatest Comics: Fantastic Four #52

Marvel, 2006

1 .... 3.00

Marvel: Shadows & Light

Marvel, 1997

1 .... 3.00

Marvel 1602

Marvel, 2003

1 .... 6.00
2 .... 5.00
3 .... 6.00
4 .... 5.00
5 .... 6.00
6 .... 5.00
7 .... 4.00
8 .... 5.00

Marvel 1602: New World

Marvel, 2005

1-5 .... 4.00

Marvel 1602: Fantastik Four

Marvel, 2006

1-4 .... 4.00

Marvel 65th Anniversary Special

Marvel, 2004

1 .... 5.00

Marvels of Science

Charlton, 1946

1 .... 100.00
2 .... 55.00
3-4 .... 48.00

Marvel Special Edition Featuring Close Encounters of the Third Kind

Marvel, 1978

3 .... 9.00

Marvel Special Edition Featuring Spectacular Spider-Man

Marvel, 1975

1 .... 12.00

Marvel Special Edition Featuring Star Wars

Marvel, 1977

1 .... 14.00
2 .... 12.00
3 .... 14.00

Marvel Spectacular

Marvel, 1973

1 .... 5.00
2-19 .... 3.00

Marvel Spotlight: Brian Michael Bendis/Mark Bagley

Marvel, 2007

1 .... 3.00

Marvel Spotlight: Daniel Way/Oliver Coipel

Marvel, 2006

1 .... 3.00

Marvel Spotlight: David Finch/Roberto Aguirre-Sacasa

Marvel, 2006

1 .... 3.00

Marvel Spotlight: Ed Brubaker/Billy Tan

Marvel, 2006

1 .... 3.00

Marvel Spotlight: Heroes Reborn/Onslaught Reborn

Marvel, 2007

1 .... 3.00

Marvel Spotlight: John Cassaday/Sean McKeever

Marvel, 2006

1 .... 3.00

Marvel Spotlight: Joss Whedon/Michael Lark

Marvel, 2006

1 .... 3.00

Marvel Spotlight: Mark Millar/Steve McNiven

Marvel, 2006

1 .... 3.00

Marvel Spotlight: Neil Gaiman/Salvador Larroca

Marvel, 2006

1 .... 3.00

Marvel Spotlight: Robert Kirkman/Greg Land

Marvel, 2006

1 .... 3.00

Marvel Spotlight: Stan Lee/ Jack Kirby

Marvel, 2006

1 .... 3.00

Marvel Spotlight

Marvel, 1971

1 .... 25.00
2 .... 130.00
☛1st Werewolf
3-4 .... 30.00
5 .... 275.00
☛1st Ghost Rider

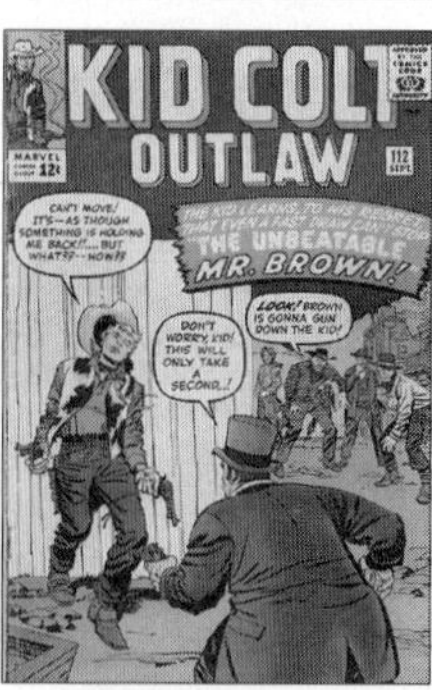

Kid Colt Outlaw

Kiddie Kapers

Kid from Dodge City

Kid Komics

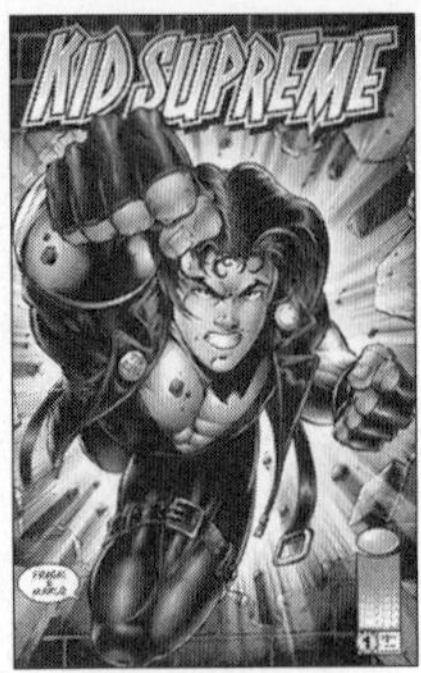
Kid Supreme

Kid Terrific

Kidz of the King

Ki-Gorr the Killer

6 .... 45.00
7 .... 35.00
8 .... 25.00
9 .... 30.00
10 .... 35.00
11-12 .... 22.00
13 .... 12.00
14-15 .... 10.00
16-19 .... 7.00
20-21 .... 5.00
22 .... 6.00
23-24 .... 5.00
25-27 .... 3.00
27/30¢ 20.00
28 .... 10.00
28/30¢ 18.00
29 .... 9.00
29/30¢ 15.00
30-31 .... 3.00
32 .... 50.00
☛1st Spider-Woman
33 .... 3.00

Marvel Spotlight
Marvel, 1979

1 .... 3.00
2-11 .... 2.00

Marvel Spotlight: Warren Ellis/Jim Cheung
Marvel, 2006

1 .... 3.00

Marvel Spring Special
Marvel, 1988

1 .... 3.00

Marvel Super Action
Marvel, 1977

1-1/Whitman 8.00
2 .... 3.00
2/35¢ 15.00
3-3/Whitman 3.00
3/35¢ 15.00
4-4/Whitman 3.00
5-37 .... 2.00

Marvel Super Action (Magazine)
Marvel, 1976

1 .... 35.00

Marvel Super Hero Contest of Champions
Marvel, 1982

1-3 .... 4.00

Marvel Super-Heroes
Marvel, 1966

12 .... 95.00
☛1st Captain Mar-vell; was Fanton Masterpieces
13 .... 50.00
14 .... 75.00
☛Reprints 1st Kirby
15 .... 42.00
16 .... 25.00
17 .... 30.00
18 .... 40.00
☛1st Guardians
19 .... 20.00
20 .... 35.00
21-27 .... 12.00
28-30 .... 10.00
31 .... 20.00
32 .... 6.00
33-38 .... 5.00
39-45 .... 4.00
46-57 .... 3.00
57/30¢ 20.00
58 .... 3.00
58/30¢ 20.00
59-65/Whitman 3.00
65/35¢ 15.00
66-66/Whitman 3.00
66/35¢ 15.00
67-80/Whitman 3.00
81-105 .... 2.00
Special 1 .... 40.00
☛1966 one-shot

Marvel Super-Heroes
Marvel, 1990

1 .... 4.00
2-15 .... 3.00

Marvel Super-Heroes Megazine
Marvel, 1994

1-6 .... 3.00

Marvel Super Heroes Secret Wars
Marvel, 1984

1 .... 4.00
2 .... 2.00
3 .... 3.00
4 .... 4.00
5 .... 3.00
6 .... 4.00
7 .... 3.00
8 .... 15.00
☛1st black costume
9-10 .... 2.00
11 .... 3.00
12 .... 2.00

Marvel Super Hero Island Adventures
Marvel, 1999

1 .... 5.00

Marvel Super Special
Marvel, 1977

1 .... 85.00
☛Kiss
2-3 .... 8.00
4 .... 30.00
☛Beatles

5 ... 55.00
☛Kiss
6 ... 7.00
8 ... 8.00
9 ... 7.00
10 ... 6.00
11-15 ... 5.00
16 ... 7.00
17-41 ... 4.00

Marvel Swimsuit Special

Marvel, 1992

1 ... 4.00
2-4 ... 5.00

Marvel Tails

Marvel, 1983

1 ... 2.00

Marvel Tales

Marvel, 1949

93 ... 1,200.00
94 ... 800.00
95 ... 650.00
96 ... 550.00
97 ... 625.00
98-101 ... 550.00
102 ... 660.00
103 ... 500.00
104 ... 575.00
105 ... 445.00
106-108 ... 390.00
109-120 ... 275.00
121-130 ... 225.00
131 ... 200.00
132-133 ... 155.00
134 ... 175.00
135-145 ... 155.00
146-159 ... 125.00

Marvel Tales

Marvel, 1964

1 ... 175.00
2 ... 85.00
3 ... 45.00
4-5 ... 30.00
6-9 ... 25.00
10 ... 30.00
11-16 ... 25.00
17-21 ... 20.00
22-32 ... 15.00
33-44 ... 12.00
45-65 ... 10.00
66-66/30¢ ... 20.00
67 ... 10.00
67/30¢ ... 20.00
68 ... 10.00
68/30¢ ... 20.00
69 ... 10.00
69/30¢ ... 20.00
70 ... 10.00
70/30¢ ... 20.00
71 ... 10.00
72-79 ... 7.00
79/Whitman ... 10.00
80 ... 7.00
80/Whitman ... 10.00
80/35¢ ... 18.00
81 ... 7.00
81/Whitman ... 14.00
81/35¢ ... 15.00
82 ... 7.00
82/Whitman ... 14.00
82/35¢ ... 15.00
83 ... 7.00
83/Whitman ... 10.00
83/35¢ ... 15.00
84-84/Whitman ... 7.00
84/35¢ ... 15.00
85-85/Whitman ... 7.00
86-122 ... 5.00
123-136 ... 4.00
137 ... 7.00
138-144 ... 5.00
145-183 ... 4.00
184-191 ... 2.00
192 ... 3.00
193-286 ... 2.00
286/CS-286/2nd ... 3.00
287-291 ... 2.00

Marvel Tales Flip Magazine

Marvel, 2005

1-10 ... 4.00
11-19 ... 5.00

Marvel Team-Up

Marvel, 1972

1 ... 185.00
2 ... 30.00
3 ... 25.00
4 ... 45.00
☛X-Men app.
5 ... 18.00
6-10 ... 16.00
11 ... 13.00
12 ... 18.00
☛Werewolf app.
13-20 ... 13.00
21-31 ... 8.00
32-44 ... 5.00
44/30¢ ... 20.00
45 ... 5.00
45/30¢ ... 20.00
46 ... 5.00
46/30¢ ... 20.00
47 ... 4.00
47/30¢ ... 20.00
48 ... 4.00
48/30¢ ... 20.00
49-52 ... 4.00
53 ... 15.00
☛X-Men app.
54-58/Whitman ... 4.00
58/35¢ ... 15.00
59-59/Whitman ... 4.00

Kiku San

Kilgore

Killer Fly

Killer Instinct

Kill Image

Kill Razor Special

Kill Your Boyfriend

Kilroy Is Here

59/35¢ 15.00
60-60/Whitman 4.00
60/35¢ 15.00
61-61/Whitman 4.00
61/35¢ 15.00
62-62/Whitman 4.00
62/35¢ 15.00
63-65 .... 4.00
66 .... 7.00
☛Captain Britain app.
67-94 .... 4.00
95-99 .... 3.00
100 .... 6.00
101-136 .... 3.00
137 .... 4.00
138-143 .... 3.00
144 .... 4.00
145-150 .... 3.00
Ann 1 .... 30.00
Ann 2 .... 6.00
Ann 3 .... 4.00
Ann 4-6 .... 3.00
Ann 7 .... 2.00

Marvel Team-Up

Marvel, 1997

1-11 .... 2.00

Marvel Team-Up

Marvel, 2004

1-8 .... 2.00
9-25 .... 3.00

Marvel: The Lost Generation

Marvel, 2000

12-1 .... 3.00

Marvel Treasury Edition

Marvel, 1974

1 .... 15.00
2-25 .... 10.00
26 .... 12.00
27 .... 10.00
28 .... 25.00

Marvel Treasury of Oz

Marvel, 1975

1 .... 15.00

Marvel Treasury Special Featuring Captain America's Bicentennial Battles

Marvel, 1976

1 .... 16.00

Marvel Treasury Special, Giant Superhero Holiday Grab-Bag

Marvel, 1974

1 .... 10.00

Marvel Triple Action

Marvel, 1972

1 .... 20.00
2-5 .... 12.00
6-29 .... 8.00
29/30¢ 20.00
30 .... 5.00
30/30¢ 20.00
31-36 .... 5.00
36/35¢ 15.00
37 .... 5.00
37/35¢ 15.00
38-47 .... 5.00
GS 1-2 .... 10.00

Marvel Two-In-One

Marvel, 1974

1 .... 55.00
2 .... 15.00
3 .... 10.00
4 .... 7.00
5-6 .... 8.00
7-10 .... 5.00
11-15 .... 3.00
15/30¢ 30.00
16 .... 3.00
16/30¢ 30.00
17 .... 3.00
17/30¢ 30.00
18 .... 3.00
18/30¢ 30.00
19-25/Whitman 3.00
26-28/Whitman 2.00
28/35¢ 20.00
29-29/Whitman 2.00
29/35¢ 20.00
30-30/Whitman 2.00
30/35¢ 20.00
31-31/Whitman 2.00
31/35¢ 20.00
32-50 .... 2.00
51-51/Whitman 3.00
52-53 .... 2.00
54 .... 4.00
55-99 .... 2.00
100 .... 3.00
Ann 1 .... 4.00
Ann 2 .... 15.00
☛Warlock dies
Ann 3-4 .... 2.00
Ann 5 .... 3.00
Ann 6-7 .... 2.00

Marvel Universe

Marvel, 1998

1 .... 3.00
2-7 .... 2.00

Marvel Universe: Millennial Visions

Marvel, 2002

1 .... 4.00

Marvel Universe: The End
Marvel, 2003

1-6 .... 4.00

Marvel Valentine Special
Marvel, 1997

1 .... 2.00

Marvel Versus DC/DC Versus Marvel
DC, 1996

1-4 .... 4.00
Ashcan 1 .... 1.00

Marvel Westerns: Outlaw Files
Marvel, 2006

1 .... 4.00

Marvel Westerns: Strange Westerns Starring Black Rider
Marvel, 2006

1 .... 4.00

Marvel Westerns: Two-Gun Kid
Marvel, 2006

1 .... 4.00

Marvel X-Men Collection
Marvel, 1994

1-3 .... 3.00

Marvel Year in Review
Marvel, 1989

1-5 .... 4.00
6 .... 3.00

Marvel Zombies
Marvel, 2006

1 .... 55.00
1/2nd 35.00
1/3rd 12.00
2 .... 16.00
3 .... 6.00
3/2nd 4.00
4-5 .... 3.00

Marvel Zombies vs. Army of Darkness
Marvel, 2007

1 .... 5.00
1/2nd-5 .... 3.00

Marville
Marvel, 2002

1-7 .... 2.00

Marvin Mouse
Atlas, 1957

1 .... 75.00

Mary Jane
Marvel, 2004

1-4 .... 2.00

Mary Jane: Homecoming
Marvel, 2005

1-3 .... 3.00

Mary Marvel
Fawcett, 1945

1 .... 1,450.00
2 .... 650.00
3 .... 450.00
4 .... 400.00
5 .... 275.00
6-10 .... 250.00
11-20 .... 160.00
21-28 .... 135.00

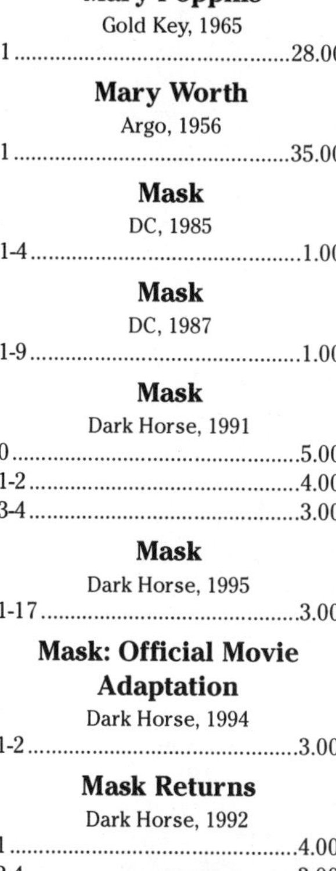

Mary Poppins
Gold Key, 1965

1 .... 28.00

Mary Worth
Argo, 1956

1 .... 35.00

Mask
DC, 1985

1-4 .... 1.00

Mask
DC, 1987

1-9 .... 1.00

Mask
Dark Horse, 1991

0 .... 5.00
1-2 .... 4.00
3-4 .... 3.00

Mask
Dark Horse, 1995

1-17 .... 3.00

Mask: Official Movie Adaptation
Dark Horse, 1994

1-2 .... 3.00

Mask Returns
Dark Horse, 1992

1 .... 4.00
2-4 .... 3.00

Mask: Toys in the Attic
Dark Horse, 1998

1-4 .... 3.00

Mask: Virtual Surreality
Dark Horse, 1997

1 .... 3.00

Mask Comics
Rural Home, 1945

1 .... 2,100.00
2 .... 1,250.00

Mask Conspiracy
Ink & Feathers

1 .... 7.00

Kimura

Kin

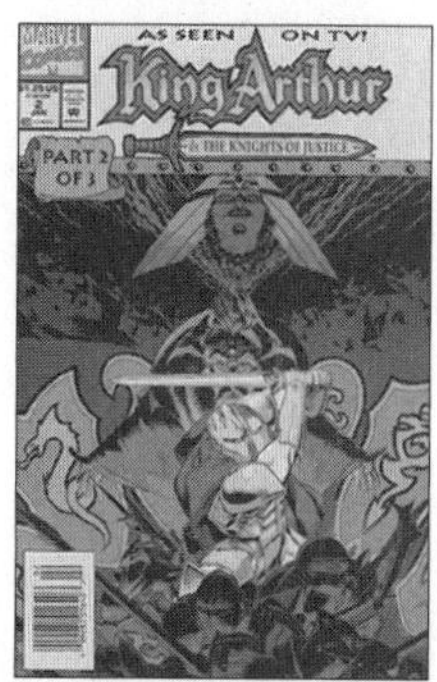

King Arthur and the Knights of Justice

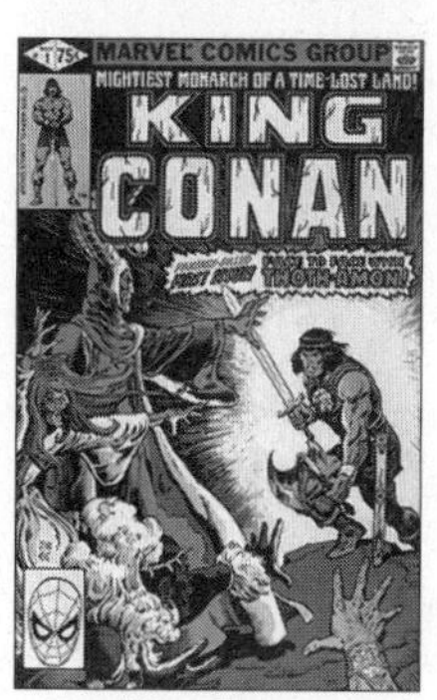

King Conan

Kingdom Come

Kingdom of the Dwarfs

Kingdom of the Wicked

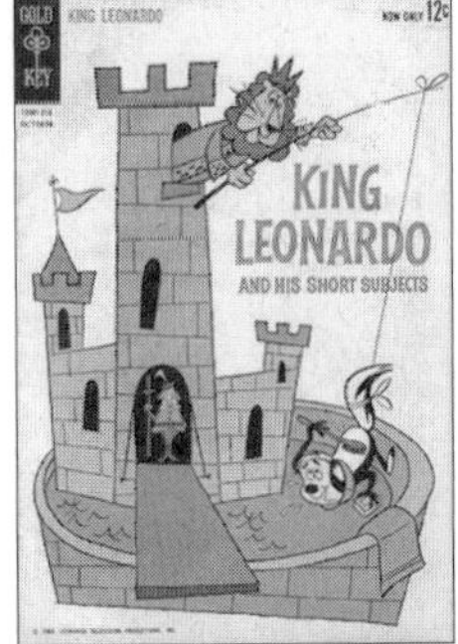

King Leonardo and His Short Subjects

Masked Man
Eclipse, 1984

1-12 .... 2.00

Masked Marvel
Centaur, 1940

1 .... 1,325.00
2 .... 900.00
3 .... 800.00

Masked Ranger
Premier, 1954

1 .... 175.00
2-3 .... 75.00
4-9 .... 65.00

Masked Rider
Marvel, 1996

1 .... 3.00

Masked Warrior X
Antarctic, 1996

1 .... 4.00
2 .... 3.00
3 .... 4.00
4 .... 3.00

Mask/Marshal Law
Dark Horse, 1998

1-2 .... 3.00

Mask of Dr. Fu Manchu
Avon, 1951

1 .... 385.00

Mask of Zorro
Image, 1998

1-4/Variant 3.00

Masks: Too Hot for TV
DC, 2003

1 .... 5.00

Masque of the Red Death
Dell, 1964

1 .... 20.00

Masquerade
Mad Monkey

1-2 .... 4.00
Ashcan 1 .... 2.00

Masques (J.N. Williamson's...)
Innovation, 1992

1-2 .... 5.00

Master
New Comics

1-2 .... 2.00

Master Comics
Fawcett, 1940

1 .... 8,100.00
2 .... 2,275.00
3 .... 1,550.00
4-5 .... 1,275.00
6 .... 1,200.00
7 .... 2,150.00
8 .... 1,325.00
9-10 .... 1,050.00
11 .... 2,300.00
12 .... 1,150.00
13 .... 1,800.00
14-15 .... 1,000.00
16-20 .... 925.00
21 .... 4,550.00
22 .... 3,925.00
23 .... 2,400.00
24-30 .... 860.00
31-40 .... 625.00
41 .... 525.00
42-47 .... 400.00
48 .... 450.00
49 .... 400.00
50 .... 475.00
51-55 .... 280.00
56-65 .... 230.00
66-80 .... 175.00
81-90 .... 145.00
91-100 .... 125.00
101-132 .... 120.00
133 .... 135.00

Master Darque
Acclaim, 1997

1 .... 6.00
Ash 1 .... 4.00

Masterman Comic
United Anglo-American

1 .... 45.00
2 .... 24.00
3-5 .... 18.00
6-12 .... 11.00

Master of Kung Fu
Marvel, 1974

17 .... 15.00
18 .... 7.00
19-20 .... 6.00
21-31 .... 5.00
32-39 .... 4.00
39/30¢ 20.00
40 .... 3.00
40/30¢ 20.00
41 .... 3.00
41/30¢ 20.00
42 .... 3.00
42/30¢ 20.00
43 .... 3.00
43/30¢ 20.00
44-53 .... 3.00
53/35¢ 15.00
54 .... 3.00
54/35¢ 15.00
55 .... 3.00
55/35¢-57/35¢ 15.00
58-99 .... 3.00
100 .... 4.00
101-124 .... 2.00
125 .... 3.00
Ann 1 .... 20.00

Master of Kung Fu: Bleeding Black
Marvel, 1991
1 .... 3.00

Master of Mystics: The Demoncraft
Chakra
1-2 .... 2.00

Master of Rampling Gate (Anne Rice's...)
Innovation, 1991
1 .... 7.00

Masters of the Universe: Icons of Evil: Beast Man
Image, 2003
1 .... 5.00

Master of the Void
Iron Hammer, 1993
1 .... 3.00

Masters of Horror
Idea & Design Works, 2005
1 .... 4.00
3-4 .... 4.00

Masters of the Universe
DC, 1982
1 .... 3.00
2-3 .... 2.00

Masters of the Universe
Marvel, 1986
1 .... 4.00
2-13 .... 3.00

Masters of the Universe
Image, 2002
1-1/B 3.00
1/Gold 6.00
2-4/B 3.00

Masters of the Universe
Image, 2003
1 .... 6.00
1/A-4 .... 3.00
4/A-4/C 6.00
5-8 .... 3.00

Master's Series
Avalon
1 .... 3.00

Masterworks Series of Great Comic Book Artists
DC, 1983
1-3 .... 3.00

Matador
DC, 2005
1-5 .... 3.00

Matt Champion
Metro
1 .... 2.00

Matterbaby
Antarctic, 1997
1-Ann 1 .... 3.00

Matt Slade, Gunflighter
Atlas, 1956
1 .... 90.00
2 .... 60.00
3-4 .... 45.00

Maverick
Dell, 1959
7-10 .... 50.00
11-15 .... 40.00
16-19 .... 30.00

Maverick
Marvel, 1997
1 .... 3.00

Maverick
Marvel, 1997
1 .... 3.00
2-11 .... 2.00
12 .... 3.00

Maverick Marshal
Charlton, 1957
1 .... 30.00
2 .... 20.00
3-7 .... 16.00

Mavericks
Dagger, 1994
1-5 .... 3.00

Mavericks: The New Wave
Dagger
1-3 .... 3.00

Max Brewster: The Universal Soldier
Fleetway-Quality
1-3 .... 3.00

Max Burger PI
Graphic Image
1 .... 2.00
2 .... 3.00

Max Damage: Panic!
Head, 1995
1 .... 3.00

Maximage
Image, 1995
1-10 .... 3.00

Maximo One-Shot
Dreamwave, 2004
1 .... 4.00

Maximortal
Tundra, 1992
1-4 .... 4.00
5-7 .... 3.00

Maximum Security
Marvel, 2000
1-3 .... 3.00

King of the Dead

King of the Royal Mounted

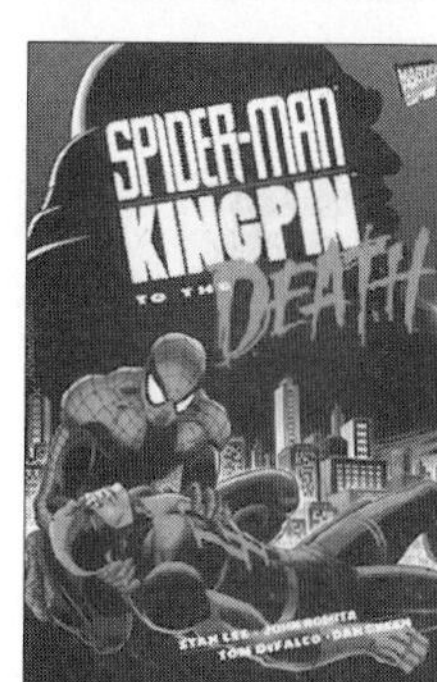

Kingpin

Kings in Disguise

Kings of the Night

Kip

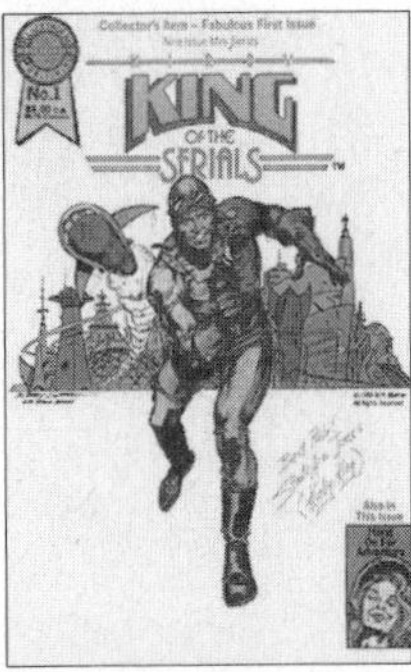

Kirby King of the Serials

Kiss Classics

Maximum Security Dangerous Planet
Marvel, 2000

1 .... 3.00

Maximum Security: Thor vs. Ego
Marvel, 2000

1 .... 3.00

Maximum Volume
Kitchen Sink, 1994

1 .... 15.00

Maxion
CPM Manga, 1999

1-20 .... 3.00

Max of the Regulators
Atlantic

1-4 .... 2.00

Max Rep in the Age of the Astrotitans
Dumbbell, 1997

1-2 .... 3.00

Max the Magnificent
Slave Labor, 1987

1-3 .... 2.00

Maxwell Mouse Follies
Renegade, 1986

1-6 .... 2.00

Maxwell the Magic Cat
Acme

1-3 .... 5.00
4 .... 6.00

Maxx
Image, 1993

½ 5.00
½/Gold 16.00
1 .... 3.00
1/3D 5.00
1/Variant 6.00
2-10 .... 3.00
11-35 .... 2.00

Maxx
DC, 2003

1-3 .... 18.00

M.A.X. Yearbook
Marvel, 1993

1 .... 0.00

Mayhem
Kelva, 1977

1 .... 1.00

Mayhem
Dark Horse, 1989

1-4 .... 4.00

Maze
Metaphrog, 1997

1 .... 4.00

Maze Agency
Idea & Design Works, 2006

1-3 .... 4.00

Maze Agency
Comico, 1988

1-3 .... 3.00
4-6 .... 2.00
7 .... 3.00
8-15 .... 2.00
16-Ann 1 .... 3.00
Special 1-Xmas 1 .... 3.00

Maze Agency
Caliber, 1997

1-3 .... 3.00

Mazie
Nationwide, 1950

1 .... 85.00
2-3 .... 45.00

Mazie and her Boyfriends
Harvey, 1950

1 .... 26.00
2 .... 13.00
3-10 .... 9.00
11-28 .... 7.00

'Mazing Man
DC, 1986

1-12 .... 1.00
Special 1-Special 3 .... 2.00

McHale's Navy
Dell, 1963

1 .... 40.00
2 .... 32.00
3 .... 26.00

McKeever and The Colonel
Dell, 1963

1 .... 28.00
2-3 .... 20.00

M.D.
E.C., 1955

1 .... 80.00
2-5 .... 65.00

M.D.
Gemstone, 1999

1-5 .... 3.00

M.D. Geist
CPM, 1995

1-3 .... 3.00

M.D. Geist: Ground Zero
CPM, 1996

1-3 .... 3.00

Mea Culpa
Four Walls Eight Windows, 1990

1 .... 13.00

Me-A Day With Elvis
Invincible

1 .... 1.00

Meadowlark
Parody
1 .... 3.00

Me and Her
Fantagraphics, 1991
1-3 .... 2.00
Special 1 .... 3.00

Mean, Green Bondo Machine
Mu, 1992
1 .... 3.00

Mean Machine
Fleetway-Quality
1 .... 5.00

Meanwhile...
Crow
1-2 .... 3.00

Measles
Fantagraphics, 1998
1-8 .... 3.00

Meat Cake
Fantagraphics, 1995
1-10 .... 3.00
11 .... 4.00

Meat Cake
Iconografix
1 .... 3.00

Meatface the Amazing Flesh
Monster
1 .... 3.00

Mecha
Dark Horse, 1987
1-6 .... 2.00

Mechanic
Image, 1998
1 .... 6.00

Mechanical Man Blues
Radio, 1998
1 .... 3.00

Mechanics
Fantagraphics, 1985
1-3 .... 2.00

Mechanimals
Novelle
1 .... 4.00
2 .... 3.00

Mechanimoids Special X Anniversary
Mu
1 .... 4.00

Mechanoids
Caliber
1-3 .... 3.00

Mech Destroyer
Image, 2001
1-4 .... 3.00

Mechoverse
Airbrush
1-3 .... 2.00

Mechthings
Renegade, 1987
1-4 .... 2.00

Medabots Part 1
Viz, 2002
1-4 .... 3.00

Medabots Part 2
Viz, 2002
1-4 .... 3.00

Medabots Part 3
Viz, 2002
1-4 .... 3.00

Medabots Part 4
Viz, 2002
1-4 .... 3.00

Medal of Honor
Dark Horse, 1994
1-Special 1 .... 3.00

Media*Starr
Innovation, 1989
1-3 .... 2.00

Medieval Spawn
Image
1-3 .... 2.00

Medieval Spawn/ Witchblade
Image, 1996
1 .... 3.00
1/Gold 6.00
1/Platinum 15.00
2 .... 4.00
3 .... 3.00

Medieval Witchblade
Image
1-3 .... 6.00

Medora
Lobster, 1999
1 .... 3.00

Medusa Comics
Triangle
1 .... 2.00

Meef Comix
Print Mint, 1973
1-2 .... 4.00

Kissing Canvas

Kiss of Death

Kiss Pre-History

Kissyfur

Kitchen Sink Classics

Klor

Knewts of the Round Table

Knighthawk

Meet Corliss Archer
Fox, 1948
1 .... 475.00
2 .... 350.00
3 .... 270.00

Meet Merton
Toby, 1953
1 .... 40.00
2 .... 22.00
3 .... 20.00

Meet Miss Bliss
Atlas, 1955
1 .... 80.00
2 .... 50.00
3-4 .... 44.00

Meet Miss Pepper
St. John, 1954
5 .... 80.00
6 .... 65.00

Meet the Bank
Custom, 1995
1 .... 1.00

Megacity 909
Devil's Due, 2005
1 .... 6.00
1/Variant 5.00
2-8/Variant 3.00

Mega Dragon & Tiger
Image, 1999
1-5 .... 3.00

Megahurtz
Image, 1997
1-3 .... 3.00

Megalith
Continuity, 1989
1-4 .... 2.00
5-9 .... 3.00

Megalith
Continuity, 1993
0-0/A 1.00
1-7 .... 3.00

Megalomaniacal Spider-Man
Marvel, 2002
1 .... 3.00

Megaman
Dreamwave, 2003
1 .... 3.00
2-4 .... 3.00

Mega Morphs
Marvel, 2005
1-4 .... 3.00

Megaton
Megaton, 1983
1-2 .... 3.00
3 .... 5.00
4-7 .... 2.00
8 .... 3.00
Holiday 1 .... 4.00

Megaton Man
Kitchen Sink, 1984
1 .... 3.00
1/2nd 2.00
2-10 .... 3.00

Megaton Man: Bombshell
Image, 1999
1 .... 3.00

Megaton Man: Hardcopy
Image, 1999
1-2 .... 3.00

Megaton Man Meets the Uncategorizable X+Thems
Kitchen Sink, 1989
1 .... 2.00

Megaton Man vs. Forbidden Frankenstein
Fiasco, 1996
1 .... 3.00

Megazzar Dude
Slave Labor, 1991
Special 1 .... 3.00

Mekanix
Marvel, 2002
1-6 .... 3.00

Mel Allen Sports Comics
Standard, 1949
1 .... 85.00
2 .... 58.00

Melissa Moore: Bodyguard
Draculina
1 .... 3.00

Melody
Kitchen Sink, 1988
1 .... 3.00
2-8 .... 2.00

Melonpool Chronicles
Para-Troop
1 .... 3.00

Meltdown
Image, 2006
1 .... 6.00

Melting Pot
Kitchen Sink, 1993
1 .... 4.00
2-3 .... 3.00
4 .... 4.00

Melty Feeling
Antarctic, 1996
1-4 .... 4.00

Melvin Monster
Dell, 1965

1 .... 60.00
2 .... 45.00
3 .... 40.00
4-5 .... 32.00
6-10 .... 26.00

Melvin the Monster
Atlas, 1956

1 .... 55.00
2 .... 40.00
3-5 .... 35.00

Melvis
Chameleon, 1994

1-4 .... 2.00

Memento Mori
Memento Mori, 1995

1-2 .... 2.00

Memories
Marvel, 1992

1 .... 3.00

Memory
NBM

1 .... 25.00

Memoryman
David Markoff

1/Ashcan 1.00

Memory Man (Emergency Stop)
Esp

1 .... 3.00
2-4 .... 2.00
5-Ashcan 1 .... 3.00

Menace
Atlas, 1953

1 .... 400.00
2 .... 300.00
3 .... 250.00
4 .... 215.00
5-6 .... 170.00
7-11 .... 140.00

Men Against Crime
Ace Magazines, 1951

3 .... 70.00
4-7 .... 50.00

Menagerie
Chrome Tiger, 1987

1-2 .... 2.00

Mendy and the Golem
Mendy, 1981

1 .... 3.00
2-19 .... 2.00

Men from Earth
Future-Fun

1 .... 2.00

Men in Action
Marvel, 1952

1 .... 50.00
2 .... 36.00
3-6 .... 28.00
7 .... 32.00
8-9 .... 28.00

Men in Action
Ajax, 1957

1 .... 50.00
2 .... 30.00
3-6 .... 25.00

Men in Black
Aircel, 1990

1 .... 15.00
2 .... 10.00
3 .... 8.00

Men in Black
Aircel, 1991

1 .... 14.00
2 .... 10.00
3 .... 8.00

Men in Black: Far Cry
Marvel, 1997

1 .... 4.00

Men in Black: Retribution
Marvel, 1997

1 .... 4.00

Men in Black: The Movie
Marvel, 1997

1 .... 4.00

Men of Mystery
AC, 2005

1-56 .... 7.00

Men of War
DC, 1977

1 .... 15.00
2-12 .... 6.00
13-26 .... 4.00

Men's Adventure Comix
Penthouse International, 1995

1 .... 6.00
2-7 .... 5.00

Men's Adventures
Atlas, 1950

4 .... 175.00
5 .... 120.00
6-8 .... 100.00
9-20 .... 75.00
21-26 .... 125.00
27-28 .... 675.00

Menthu
Black Inc!, 1998

1-4 .... 3.00

Menz Insana
DC

1 .... 8.00

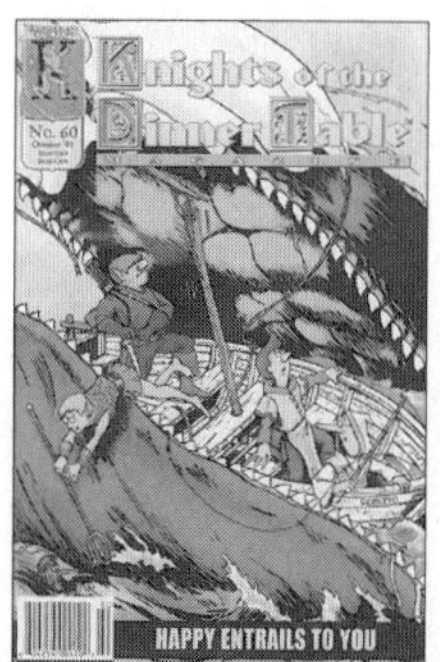

Knights of the Dinner Table

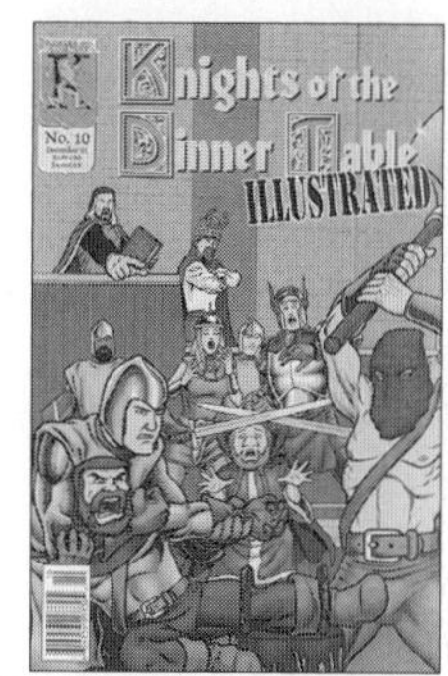

Knights of the Dinner Table Illustrated

Knights on Broadway

Knightstrike

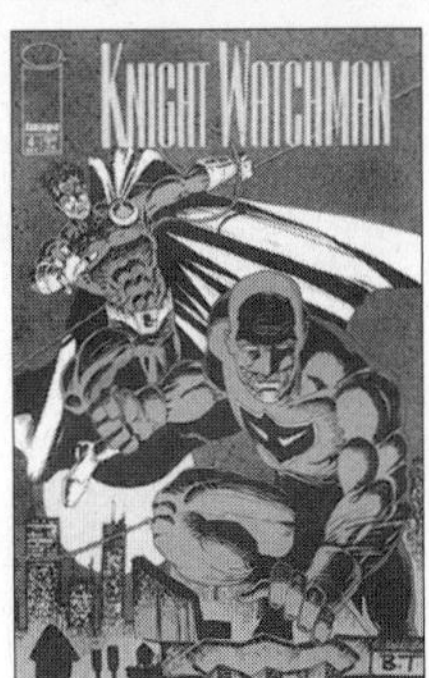

Knight Watchman

Knuckles

Knuckles the Malevolent Nun

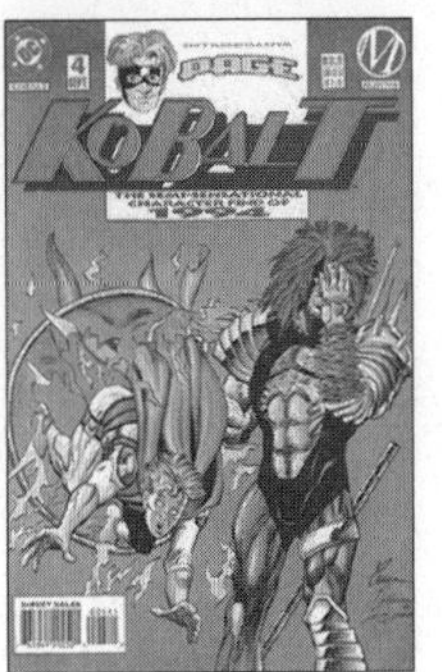

Kobalt

Mephisto Vs.
Marvel, 1987
1 .... 3.00
2-4 .... 2.00

Mercedes
Angus, 1995
1-12 .... 3.00

Merchants of Death
Eclipse, 1988
1-4 .... 4.00

Merchants of Venus
DC
1 .... 6.00

Mercy
DC
1 .... 6.00

Meridian
CrossGen, 2000
1 .... 4.00
2-44 .... 3.00

Merlin
Adventure, 1990
1-6 .... 3.00

Merlin: Idylls of the King
Adventure, 1992
1-2 .... 3.00

Merlin Jones As The Monkey's Uncle
Gold Key, 1965
1 .... 10.00

Merlinrealm 3-D
Blackthorne, 1985
1 .... 2.00

Mermaid
Alternative, 1998
1 .... 3.00

Mermaid Forest
Viz, 1993
1-4 .... 3.00

Mermaid's Dream
Viz, 1985
1-3 .... 3.00

Mermaid's Gaze
Viz
1-4 .... 3.00

Mermaid's Mask
Viz
1-4 .... 3.00

Mermaid's Promise
Viz
1-4 .... 3.00

Mermaid's Scar
Viz, 1994
1-4 .... 3.00

Merry Comics
Charlton, 1945
1 .... 95.00

Merry Mouse
Avon, 1953
1 .... 42.00
2 .... 30.00
3-4 .... 24.00

Merton of the Movement
Last Gasp, 1971
1 .... 4.00

Meru Puri
Viz, 2005
1-2 .... 9.00

Merv Pumpkinhead, Agent of D.R.E.A.M.
DC, 2000
nn 6.00

Messenger
Image, 2000
1 .... 6.00

Messenger 29
September, 1989
1 .... 2.00

Messiah
Pinnacle
1 .... 2.00

Messozoic
Kitchen Sink, 1993
1 .... 3.00

Meta-4
First, 1991
1 .... 4.00
2-3 .... 2.00

Metabarons
DC, 2004
1 .... 15.00

Metabarons
Humanoids, 2000
1-3 .... 4.00
4-14 .... 3.00

Metacops
Fantagraphics, 1991
1-3 .... 2.00

Metadocs: The Super E.R.
Antarctic, 2005
1 .... 5.00

Metal Bikini
Eternity, 1990
1-6 .... 2.00

Metal Gear Solid
Idea & Design Works, 2004
1 .... 4.00
1/Silver 7.00
1/2nd 4.00

1/Incentive 35.00
2-12 .... 4.00
Ashcan 0 .... 1.00

Metal Gear Solid: Sons of Liberty

Idea & Design Works, 2005

0-8 .... 4.00

Metal Guardian Faust

Viz, 1997

1-8 .... 3.00

Metal Hurlant

DC, 2002

1-3 .... 8.00
4-6 .... 7.00
7-8 .... 5.00
9-14 .... 4.00

Metallica

Celebrity

1/A 3.00
1/B 7.00

Metallica

Forbidden Fruit, 1992

1-2 .... 3.00

Metallica

Rock-It Comics

1 .... 5.00

Metallica's Greatest Hits

Revolutionary, 1993

1 .... 3.00

Metallix

Future, 2002

0-5 .... 4.00
6 .... 3.00

Metal Men

DC, 1963

1 .... 500.00
2 .... 225.00
3-5 .... 150.00
6-10 .... 80.00
11-20 .... 55.00
21-26 .... 45.00
27 .... 80.00
☛Metal Men
28-30 .... 42.00
31-41 .... 24.00
42-44 .... 12.00
45-56 .... 6.00

Metal Men

DC, 1993

1 .... 3.00
2-4 .... 2.00

Metal Men of Mars & Other Improbable Tales

Slave Labor, 1989

1 .... 2.00

Metal Militia

Express, 1995

1/Ashcan 1.00
1 .... 3.00
1/A 7.00
2-3 .... 3.00

Metamorpho

DC, 1965

1 .... 75.00
2 .... 45.00
3 .... 40.00
4-9 .... 30.00
10-17 .... 25.00

Metamorpho

DC, 1993

1-4 .... 2.00

Metaphysique

Malibu, 1995

1-6 .... 3.00
Ashcan 1 .... 1.00

Metaphysique

Eclipse, 1992

1 .... 3.00

Meteor Comics

Baird, 1945

1 .... 265.00

Meteor Man

Marvel, 1993

1-6 .... 1.00

Meteor Man: The Movie

Marvel, 1993

1 .... 2.00

Metropol (Ted McKeever's...)

Marvel, 1991

1-12 .... 3.00

Metropol A.D.

Marvel, 1992

1-3 .... 4.00

Metropolis S.C.U.

DC, 1994

1-4 .... 2.00

Mez

C.A.P., 1997

1-2 .... 2.00

Mezz: Galactic Tour 2494

Dark Horse, 1994

1 .... 3.00

M Falling

Vagabond

1 .... 4.00

MFI: The Ghosts of Christmas

Image, 1999

1 .... 4.00

Kobra

Kokey Koala

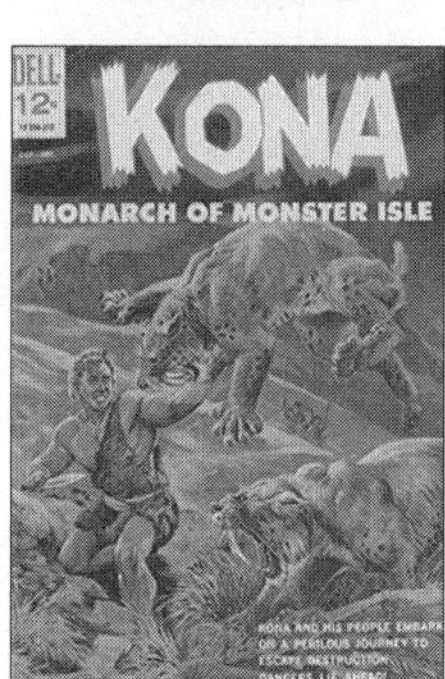

Kona

Konga

Kong the Untamed

Konny and Czu

Koosh Kins

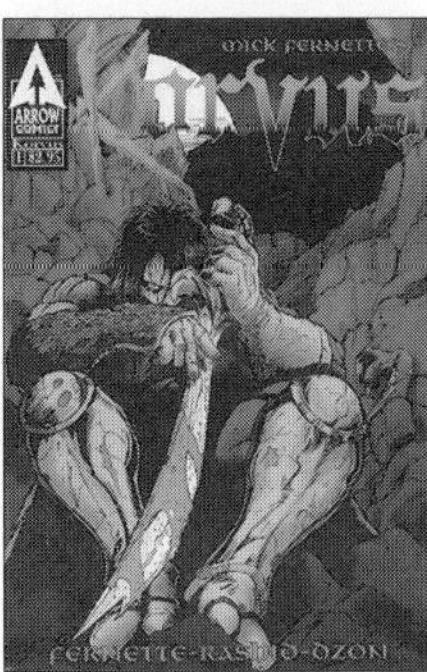
Korvus

Miami Mice
Rip Off, 1986
1-3 ....2.00
3/A 5.00
4 ....2.00

Michaelangelo Christmas Special
Mirage, 1990
1 ....2.00

Michaelangelo Teenage Mutant Ninja Turtle
Mirage, 1985
1 ....3.00

Michael Jordan Tribute
Revolutionary
1 ....3.00

Mickey and Donald
Gladstone, 1988
1-18 ....2.00

Mickey and Friends
Fleetway-Quality, 1996
1-10 ....2.00

Mickey and Goofy Explore Energy
Dell, 1976
1 ....2.00

Mickey & Minnie
W.D.
1 ....4.00

Mickey Finn
Eastern, 1942
1 ....85.00
2 ....45.00
3 ....32.00
4-5 ....24.00
6-15 ....20.00

Mickey Mantle
Magnum, 1991
1-2 ....2.00

Mickey Mouse
Dell, 1952
28-30 ....40.00
31-35 ....30.00
36-40 ....25.00
41-50 ....20.00
51-60 ....16.00
61-70 ....15.00
71-80 ....14.00
81-100 ....12.00
101-120 ....11.00
121-140 ....10.00
141-160 ....8.00
161-180 ....7.00
181-200 ....6.00
201-203 ....5.00
204 ....8.00
205-206 ....5.00
207 ....20.00
208 ....50.00
209 ....20.00
210-214 ....7.00
215-218 ....10.00
219 ....12.00
220 ....4.00
221-240 ....3.00
241-256 ....2.00

Mickey Mouse and Friends
Gemstone, 2003
257-295 ....3.00

Mickey Mouse
Disney
1 ....4.00

Mickey Mouse Adventures
Disney, 1990
1 ....3.00
2-18 ....2.00

Mickey Mouse Album
Gold Key, 1962
-210 ....25.00
1 ....20.00

Mickey Mouse and Goofy Explore Energy Conservation
Disney, 1978
1 ....2.00

Mickey and Goofy Explore the Universe of Energy
Disney, 1985
1 ....3.00

Mickey Mouse Birthday Party
Dell, 1953
1 ....365.00

Mickey Mouse Club
Gold Key, 1964
1 ....25.00

Mickey Mouse Club Parade
Dell, 1955
1 ....150.00

Mickey Mouse Digest
Gladstone, 1986
1 ....5.00
2 ....4.00
3-5 ....3.00

Mickey Mouse in Fantasyland
Dell, 1957
1 ....135.00

Mickey Mouse in Frontierland
Dell, 1956
1 ....125.00

Mickey Mouse Summer Fun
Dell, 1958
1 .... 110.00

Mickey Mouse Surprise Party
Gold Key, 1969
1 .... 18.00

Mickey Rat
Los Angeles Comic Book Co., 1972
1 .... 25.00
2 .... 20.00
3-4 .... 15.00

Micra: Mind Controlled Remote Automaton
Comics Interview, 1986
1-7 .... 2.00

Microbots
Gold Key, 1971
1 .... 10.00

Micronauts
Marvel, 1979
1-1/Whitman 4.00
1/2nd 2.00
2-5/Whitman 3.00
6-58 .... 2.00
59 .... 3.00
Ann 1 .... 4.00
Ann 2 .... 3.00
Special 1-Special 5 .... 2.00

Micronauts (Vol. 2)
Marvel, 1984
1 .... 3.00
2-20 .... 2.00

Micronauts
Image, 2002
1-11 .... 3.00

Middle Class Fantasies
Cartoonists Co-Op
1-2 .... 3.00

Middleman
Viper, 2005
1-4 .... 3.00

Midget Comics
St. John, 1950
1 .... 80.00
2 .... 55.00

Midnight
Ajax, 1957
1 .... 54.00
2 .... 38.00
3-6 .... 26.00

Midnight Days (Neil Gaiman's...)
DC, 2000
1 .... 18.00

Midnighter
DC, 2007
1-15 .... 3.00

Midnight Eye Goku
Viz
1-6 .... 5.00

Midnight Kiss
APComics, 2005
1 .... 4.00

Midnight Mass
DC, 2002
1-2 .... 3.00
3-4 .... 3.00
5-6 .... 3.00
7-8 .... 3.00

Midnight Mass
DC, 2004
1 .... 3.00
2-3 .... 3.00
4-5 .... 3.00
6 .... 3.00

Midnight Men
Marvel, 1993
1 .... 3.00
2-4 .... 2.00

Midnight Mystery
ACG, 1961
1 .... 60.00
2 .... 40.00
3 .... 32.00
4-7 .... 30.00

Midnight Nation
Image, 2000
½ 5.00
½/Gold 9.00
1/A 4.00
1/B 5.00
1/C 8.00
1/D 5.00
2-12 .... 3.00

Midnight Panther
CPM, 1997
1-12 .... 3.00

Midnight Panther: Feudal Fantasy
CPM, 1998
1-2 .... 3.00

Midnight Panther: School Daze
CPM, 1998
1-5 .... 3.00

Kosmic Kat Activity Book

Krazy Komics

Krey

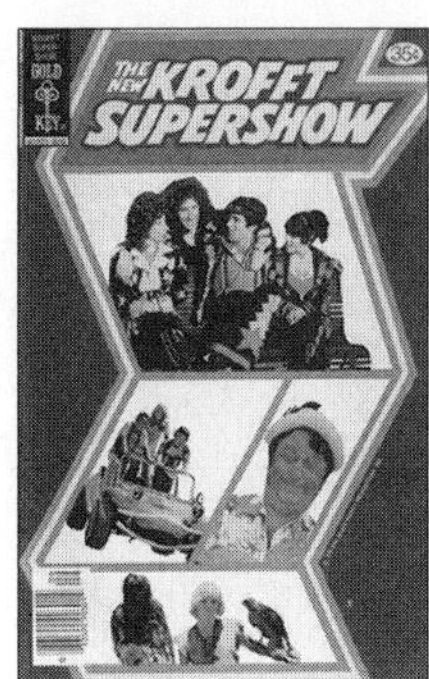

Krofft Supershow

Krull

Krusty Comics

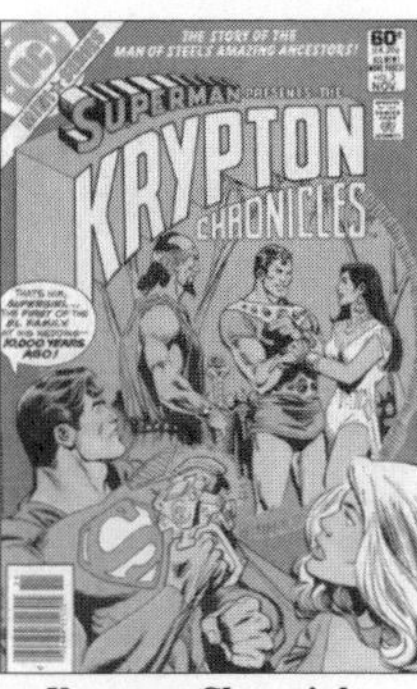

Krypton Chronicles

Kull and the Barbarians

Midnight Screams
Mystery Graphix, 1992

1-2 ....3.00

Midnight Sons Unlimited
Marvel, 1993

1-9 ....4.00
Ashcan 1 ....1.00

Midnight Tales
Charlton, 1972

1 ....18.00
2 ....10.00
3-5 ....8.00
6-17 ....6.00
18 ....8.00

Midnite
Blackthorne, 1986

1-3 ....2.00

Midnite Skulker
Target, 1986

1-7 ....2.00

Midnite's Quickies
One Shot, 1997

1 ....4.00
2-Special 1/B 3.00

Midori Days
Viz, 2005

1-2 ....10.00

Midvale
Mu, 1990

1-2 ....3.00

Mightily Murdered Power Ringers
Express

1 ....3.00

Mighty Midget Comics: Minute Man
Lowe, 1942

12 ....100.00

Mighty Ace
Omega 7

1-2 ....2.00

Mighty Atom
Magazine Enterprises, 1949

6 ....35.00

Mighty Atom
Magazine Enterprises, 1957

1 ....22.00
2-6 ....18.00

Mighty Bomb
Antarctic, 1997

1 ....3.00

Mighty Bombshells
Antarctic, 1993

1-2 ....3.00

Mighty Cartoon Heroes
Karl Art

0 ....3.00

Mighty Comics
Archie, 1966

40-50 ....15.00

Mighty Crusaders
Archie, 1965

1 ....24.00
2 ....15.00
3 ....12.00
4-7 ....10.00

Mighty Crusaders
Archie, 1983

4-13 ....1.00

Mightyguy
C&T, 1987

1-5 ....2.00

Mighty Hercules
Gold Key, 1963

1-2 ....40.00

Mighty Heroes
Dell, 1967

1 ....125.00
2-4 ....60.00

Mighty Heroes
Marvel, 1998

1 ....3.00

Mighty I
Image, 1995

1-2 ....1.00

Mighty Love
DC, 2004

1 ....18.00

Mighty Magnor
Malibu, 1993

1 ....2.00
1/Variant 4.00
2-6 ....2.00

Mighty Man
Image, 2005

1 ....8.00

Mighty Marvel Western
Marvel, 1968

1 ....45.00
2 ....30.00
3-5 ....25.00
6-15 ....20.00
16-21 ....15.00
22-45 ....10.00
45/30¢ 20.00
46 ....10.00

Mighty Midget Comics: Captain Marvel Jr.
Lowe, 1942

11 ....100.00

Mighty Mites
Eternity, 1986
1-3 .... 2.00

Mighty Mites
Eternity, 1987
1-2 .... 2.00

Mighty Morphin Power Rangers (Saban's...)
Marvel, 1995
1 .... 3.00
2-9 .... 2.00

Mighty Morphin Power Rangers: Ninja Rangers/VR Troopers (Saban's...)
Marvel, 1995
1 .... 3.00
2-8 .... 2.00

Mighty Morphin Power Rangers Saga (Saban's...)
Hamilton, 1994
1-3 .... 3.00

Mighty Morphin Power Rangers: The Movie
Marvel, 1995
1 .... 3.00
1/Variant 4.00

Mighty Mouse
Timely, 1946
1 .... 750.00
2 .... 365.00
3-4 .... 200.00

Mighty Mouse
Gold Key, 1964
166-172 .... 0.00
161-169 .... 15.00

Mighty Mouse
Spotlight, 1987
1-2 .... 2.00

Mighty Mouse
Marvel, 1990
1-10 .... 2.00

Mighty Mouse Adventure Magazine
Spotlight
1 .... 2.00

Mighty Mouse Adventures
St. John, 1951
1 .... 185.00

Mighty Mouse and Friends Holiday Special
Spotlight
1 .... 2.00

Mighty Mouse Comics
St. John, 1947
5 .... 225.00
6-8 .... 145.00
9-10 .... 115.00
11-20 .... 75.00
21-30 .... 50.00
31-36 .... 38.00
37 .... 35.00
38-45 .... 60.00
46-49 .... 28.00
50-70 .... 20.00
71-83 .... 16.00

Mighty Mutanimals
Archie, 1991
1 .... 2.00
2-3 .... 1.00

Mighty Mutanimals
Archie, 1992
1-8 .... 1.00

Mighty Samson
Gold Key, 1964
1 .... 75.00
2-4 .... 45.00
5-10 .... 30.00
11-20 .... 20.00
21-31 .... 15.00
32 .... 10.00
Marvel, 2001
1-3 .... 4.00

Mighty Tiny
Antarctic, 1989
1-4 .... 2.00
5 .... 3.00

Mighty Tiny: The Mouse Marines
Antarctic
1 .... 3.00

Mike Barnett, Man Against Crime
Fawcett, 1951
1 .... 125.00
2 .... 85.00
3-6 .... 65.00

Mike Danger (Vol. 1) (Mickey Spillane's...)
Tekno, 1995
1-11 .... 2.00

Mike Danger (Vol. 2) (Mickey Spillane's...)
Big, 1996
1-10 .... 2.00

Kull the Destroyer

Kyra

K-Z Comics Presents

Labman Sourcebook

Labor Force

Lab Rats

L.A. Comics

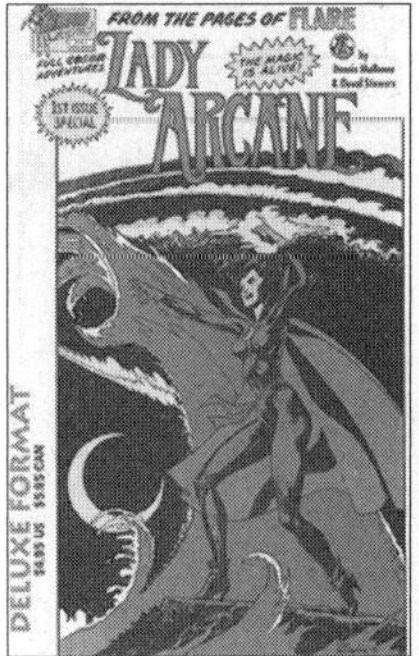

Lady Arcane

Mike Donovan Detective Comic
Arnold

50 .... 9.00

Mike Mauser Files
Avalon, 1999

1 .... 3.00

Mike Mignola's BPRD Collection
Dark Horse, 2004

1 .... 18.00

Mike Mist Minute Mist-Eries
Eclipse, 1981

1 .... 2.00

Mike Regan
Hardboiled

1 .... 3.00

Mike Shayne Private Eye
Dell, 1962

1 .... 16.00
2-3 .... 10.00

Milikardo Knights
Mad Badger, 1997

1-2 .... 3.00

Military Comics
Comic Magazines, 1941

1 .... 9,000.00
2 .... 2,700.00
3 .... 2,150.00
4 .... 1,600.00
5 .... 1,375.00
6-7 .... 1,110.00
8-10 .... 1,000.00
11-12 .... 875.00
13-15 .... 760.00
16-20 .... 650.00
21-22 .... 560.00
23-43 .... 465.00

Milk
Radio, 1997

1-40 .... 3.00
41-43 .... 4.00

Milk & Cheese
Slave Labor, 1991

1 .... 65.00
1/2nd 6.00
1/3rd 5.00
1/4th-1/7th 3.00
2 .... 35.00
2/2nd 5.00
2/3rd 4.00
2/4th-2/5th 3.00
3 .... 28.00
3/2nd 4.00
3/3rd-3/5th 3.00
4 .... 16.00
4/2nd-4/3rd 3.00
5 .... 15.00
5/2nd-5/4th 3.00
6 .... 8.00
6/2nd-7 .... 3.00

Milkman Murders
Dark Horse, 2004

1-4 .... 3.00

Millennium
DC, 1988

1-8 .... 2.00

Millennium 2.5 A.D.
Avalon

1 .... 3.00

Millennium Edition: Action Comics
DC, 2000

1 .... 4.00
252 .... 3.00

Millennium Edition: Adventure Comics
DC, 2000

61 .... 4.00
247 .... 3.00

Millennium Edition: All Star Comics
DC, 2000

3 .... 4.00
3/Variant 10.00
8 .... 4.00

Millennium Edition: All-Star Western
DC, 2000

10 .... 3.00

Millennium Edition: Batman
DC, 2001

1 .... 4.00
1/Chrome 5.00

Millennium Edition: Batman: The Dark Knight Returns
DC, 2000

1 .... 6.00

Millennium Edition: Crisis on Infinite Earths
DC, 2000

1 .... 3.00
1/Chrome 5.00

Millennium Edition: Detective Comics
DC, 2000

1 .... 4.00
38 .... 4.00
225 .... 3.00

327 .... 4.00
359 .... 4.00

Millennium Edition: Flash Comics
DC, 2000
1 .... 4.00

Millennium Edition: Gen13
WildStorm, 2000
1 .... 3.00

Millennium Edition: Green Lantern
DC, 2000
76 .... 3.00

Millennium Edition: Hellblazer
DC, 2000
1 .... 3.00

Millennium Edition: House of Mystery
DC, 2000
1 .... 3.00

Millennium Edition: House of Secrets
DC, 2000
92 .... 3.00

Millennium Edition: JLA
DC, 2000
1 .... 3.00

Millennium Edition: Justice League
DC, 2000
1 .... 3.00
1/Chrome 5.00

Millennium Edition: Kingdom Come
DC, 2000
1 .... 6.00

Millennium Edition: Mad
DC, 2000
1 .... 2.00
1/Recalled 25.00

Millennium Edition: Military Comics
DC, 2000
1 .... 4.00

Millennium Edition: More Fun Comics
DC, 2000
73 .... 4.00
101 .... 3.00

Millennium Edition: Mysterious Suspense
DC, 2000
1 .... 3.00

Millennium Edition: New Gods
DC, 2000
1 .... 3.00

Millennium Edition: Our Army at War
DC, 2000
81 .... 3.00

Millennium Edition: Plop!
DC, 2000
1 .... 3.00

Millennium Edition: Police Comics
DC, 2000
1 .... 4.00

Millennium Edition: Preacher
DC, 2000
1 .... 3.00

Millennium Edition: Sensation Comics
DC, 2000
1 .... 4.00

Millennium Edition: Showcase
DC, 2000
4 .... 3.00
22 .... 3.00

Millennium Edition: Superboy
DC, 2001
1 .... 3.00

Millennium Edition: Superman
DC, 2000
75 .... 3.00

Millennium Edition: Superman (1st Series)
DC, 2000
233 .... 3.00

Millennium Edition: Superman's Pal Jimmy Olsen
DC, 2000
1 .... 3.00

Millennium Edition: Tales Calculated to Drive You Mad
DC, 2000
1 .... 3.00

Millennium Edition: The Brave and the Bold
DC, 2000
85 .... 3.00

Lady Rawhide

Lady Supreme

Laff-a-Lympics

Lament of the Lamb

Land of the Giants

Land of the Lost Comics

La Pacifica

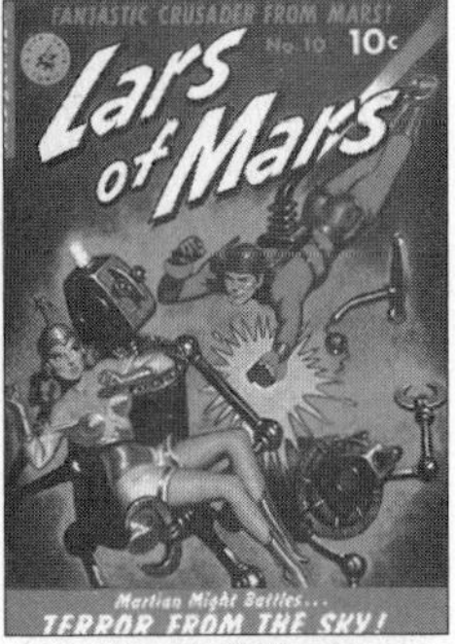

Lars of Mars

Millennium Edition: The Flash
DC, 2000

123 .... 3.00

Millennium Edition: The Man of Steel
DC, 2000

1 .... 3.00

Millennium Edition: The New Teen Titans
DC, 2000

1 .... 3.00

Millennium Edition: The Saga of the Swamp Thing
DC, 2000

21 .... 3.00

Millennium Edition: The Sandman
DC, 2000

1 .... 3.00

Millennium Edition: The Shadow
DC, 2001

1 .... 3.00

Millennium Edition: The Spirit
DC, 2000

1 .... 3.00

Millennium Edition: Watchmen
DC, 2000

1 .... 3.00

Millennium Edition: Whiz Comics
DC, 2000

2 .... 4.00

Millennium Edition: WildC.A.T.S
DC, 2000

1 .... 3.00

Millennium Edition: Wonder Woman (1st Series)
DC, 2000

1 .... 4.00

Millennium Edition: Wonder Woman (2nd Series)
DC, 2000

1 .... 3.00

Millennium Edition: World's Finest
DC, 2000

71 .... 3.00

Millennium Edition: Young Romance Comics
DC, 2000

1 .... 3.00

Millennium Fever
DC, 1995

1-4 .... 3.00
Ashcan 1 .... 1.00

Millennium Index
Eclipse, 1988

1-2 .... 2.00

Millie the Lovable Monster
Dell, 1962

1 .... 22.00
2-3 .... 18.00
4-6 .... 13.00

Millie the Model Comics
Marvel, 1945

1 .... 500.00
2 .... 300.00
3-8 .... 190.00
9 .... 175.00
10 .... 140.00
11 .... 100.00
12 .... 85.00
13-14 .... 110.00
15 .... 85.00
16 .... 110.00
17-20 .... 85.00
21-30 .... 60.00
31-40 .... 38.00
41-60 .... 35.00
61-70 .... 28.00
71-99 .... 25.00
100 .... 32.00
101-130 .... 15.00
131-154 .... 12.00
155-180 .... 10.00
181-207 .... 9.00
Ann 1 .... 140.00
Ann 2 .... 95.00
Ann 3-4 .... 70.00
Ann 5 .... 65.00
Ann 6-10 .... 45.00
Ann 11-12 .... 25.00

Milton the Monster and Fearless Fly
Gold Key, 1966

1 .... 60.00

Mindbenders
MBS

1 .... 3.00

Mindgame Gallery
Mindgame
1 .... 2.00

Mind Probe
Rip Off
1 .... 3.00

Minds' Play
Davan
1 .... 3.00

Minerva
NBM
1 .... 10.00

Mineshaft
Fantagraphics, 2005
1-16 .... 5.00

Minimum Wage
Fantagraphics, 1995
1-10 .... 3.00

Ministry of Space
Image, 2001
1-3 .... 3.00

Mink
Tokyopop, 2004
1 .... 10.00

Minkenstein
Mu, 2005
0 .... 3.00

Minor Miracles
DC, 2000
1 .... 13.00

Minotaur
Labyrinth, 1996
1-4 .... 3.00

Minute Man
Fawcett, 1941
1 .... 1,500.00
2 .... 750.00
3 .... 665.00

Minx
DC, 1998
1-8 .... 3.00

Miracle Comics
St. John, 1940
1 .... 1,150.00
2 .... 675.00
3-4 .... 485.00

Miracle Girls
Tokyopop, 2000
1-19 .... 3.00

Miracleman
Eclipse, 1985
1 .... 10.00
2-4 .... 8.00
4/Gold 15.00
5 .... 8.00
5/Platinum 15.00
6-8 .... 8.00
8/Gold 15.00
9-10 .... 10.00
11-12 .... 14.00
13 .... 18.00
14 .... 24.00
15 .... 35.00
16 .... 16.00
17 .... 25.00
17/Gold 40.00
18 .... 20.00
19-22 .... 15.00
23 .... 16.00
24 .... 25.00
3D 1 .... 10.00
3D 1/Gold 18.00

Miracleman: Apocrypha
Eclipse, 1991
1-3 .... 3.00

Miracleman Family
Eclipse, 1988
1-2 .... 3.00

Miracle Squad
Upshot
1-4 .... 2.00

Miracle Squad: Blood and Dust
Apple, 1989
1-4 .... 2.00

Mirage Mini Comics
Mirage
1 .... 12.00

Mirror Man Comic
Donald F. Peters
21 .... 3.00

Mirrorwalker
Now, 1990
1-2 .... 3.00

Mirrorworld: Rain
Netco, 1997
0-1 .... 3.00

Misadventures Of Breadman And Doughboy
Hemlock Park, 1999
1-2 .... 3.00

Miseroth: Amok Hell
Northstar
1-3 .... 5.00

Misery
Image, 1995
1 .... 3.00

Misplaced
Image, 2003
1-2 .... 3.00

Last Avengers

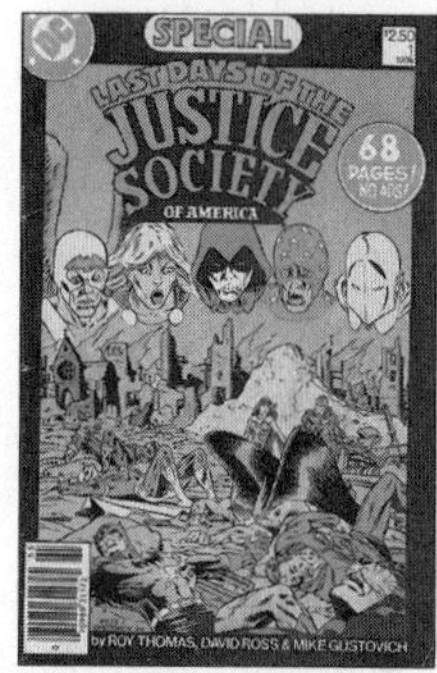

Last Days of the Justice Society Special

Last Gasp Comics and Stories

Last Kiss

Latigo Kid Western

Laugh Comics

Laugh Digest Magazine

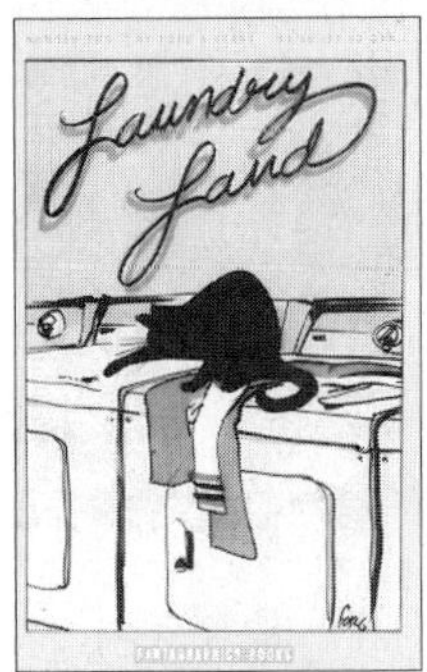

Laundryland

Miss America (Vol. 1)

Timely, 1944

1 ....885.00
2 ....720.00
3-5 ....300.00
6 ....70.00

Miss America (Vol. 2)

Timely, 1945

1-6 ....35.00

Miss America (Vol. 3)

Timely, 1945

1-6 ....35.00

Miss America (Vol. 4)

Timely, 1946

1-2 ....35.00
3 ....55.00
4-6 ....28.00

Miss America (Vol. 5)

Timely, 1946

1-6 ....28.00

Miss America (Vol. 6)

Timely, 1947

1-3 ....24.00

Miss America (Vol. 7)

Atlas, 1947

1-9 ....24.00
10-24 ....20.00
25-93 ....16.00

Miss Beverly Hills of Hollywood

DC, 1949

1 ....325.00
2 ....200.00
3-5 ....165.00
6-9 ....140.00

Miss Cairo Jones

Croyden, 1945

1 ....195.00

Miss Fury

Timely, 1942

1 ....3,000.00
2 ....1,500.00
3 ....1,250.00
4 ....1,000.00
5-6 ....750.00
7-8 ....700.00

Miss Fury

Adventure, 1991

1 ....3.00
1/Ltd 5.00
2-4 ....3.00

Miss Fury

Avalon

1-2 ....3.00

Missing Beings Special

Comics Interview

1 ....2.00

Mission: Impossible

Dell, 1967

1 ....24.00
2-4 ....18.00
5 ....12.00

Mission Impossible

Marvel, 1996

1 ....3.00

Missions in Tibet

Dimension, 1995

1 ....3.00

Miss Melody Lane of Broadway

DC, 1950

1 ....400.00
2 ....225.00
3 ....185.00

Miss Peach

Dell, 1963

1 ....60.00

Misspent Youths

Brave New Words, 1991

1-3 ....3.00

Miss Victory Golden Anniversary Special

AC, 1991

1 ....5.00

Mister America

Endeavor, 1994

1-2 ....3.00

Mr. and Mrs. J. Evil Scientist

Gold Key, 1963

1 ....50.00
2 ....30.00
3-4 ....20.00

Mr. Average

B.S.

1-3 ....2.00

Mr. Beat Adventures

Moordam, 1997

1 ....3.00

Mr. Beat/Craybaby/Weirdsville Post Halloween Leftover

Monster Thanksgiving Special
Blindwolf, 1998
1 .... 3.00

Mr. Beat – Existential Cool
Moordam, 1998
0 .... 3.00

Mr. Beat's Babes and Bongos Annual
Moordam, 1998
1/Blue-1/Red 3.00

Mr. Beat's House of Burning Jazz Love
Moordam, 1997
1 .... 3.00

Mr. Beat's Two-Fisted Atomic Action Super Special
Moordam, 1997
1 .... 3.00

Mr. Beat Superstar
Moordam, 1998
1 .... 3.00

Mister Blank
Slave Labor, 1997
0-5 .... 3.00

Mr. Cream Puff
Blackthorne, 1987
1 .... 2.00

Mr. Day & Mr. Night
Slave Labor, 1993
1 .... 4.00

Mr. District Attorney
DC, 1948
1 .... 600.00
2 .... 265.00
3-5 .... 200.00
6-10 .... 155.00
11-20 .... 110.00
21-30 .... 85.00
31-40 .... 75.00
41-50 .... 60.00
51-67 .... 50.00

Mr. Doom
Pied Piper, 1987
1 .... 2.00

Mister E
DC, 1991
1-4 .... 2.00

Mister Ed, the Talking Horse
Dell, 1962
1 .... 70.00
2 .... 45.00
3-4 .... 40.00
5-6 .... 30.00

Mr. Fixitt
Apple, 1989
1-2 .... 2.00

Mr. Fixitt
Heroic
1 .... 3.00

Mr. Hero-The Newmatic Man (1st Series) (Neil Gaiman's...)
Tekno, 1995
1-17 .... 2.00

Mr. Hero-The Newmatic Man (2nd Series) (Neil Gaiman's...)
Big, 1996
1-4 .... 2.00

Mr. Jigsaw Special
Ocean, 1988
1 .... 2.00

Mr. Lizard 3-D
Now, 1993
1 .... 4.00

Mr. Lizard Annual
Now, 1993
1 .... 3.00

Mr. Majestic
DC, 1999
1-9 .... 3.00

Mister Miracle (1st Series)
DC, 1971
1 .... 50.00
2 .... 25.00
3 .... 20.00
4 .... 25.00
5 .... 30.00
6 .... 22.00
7-8 .... 20.00
9-14 .... 15.00
15-16 .... 12.00
17-18 .... 10.00
19-25 .... 7.00
Special 1 .... 4.00

Mister Miracle (2nd Series)
DC, 1989
1 .... 3.00
2-5 .... 2.00
6-28 .... 1.00

Mister Miracle (3rd Series)
DC, 1996
1-7 .... 2.00

Mr. Monster
Dark Horse, 1988
1-7 .... 2.00
8 .... 5.00

Law Against Crime

Law and Order

Lawbreakers Suspense Stories

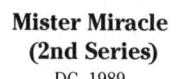

Lawdog

Lazarus Five

Leading Comics

League of Justice

League of Super Groovy Crimefighters

Mr. Monster Attacks!
Tundra, 1992

1-3 .... 4.00

Mr. Monster (Doc Stearn...)
Eclipse, 1985

1 .... 3.00
2-10 .... 2.00

Mr. Monster Presents (Crack-A-Boom!)
Caliber, 1997

1-3 .... 3.00

Mr. Monster's Gal Friday... Kelly!
Image, 2000

1-3 .... 4.00

Mr. Monster's High-Octane Horror
Eclipse, 1986

1 .... 2.00
3D 1 .... 3.00

Mr. Monster's Hi-Shock Schlock
Eclipse, 1987

1-2 .... 2.00

Mr. Monster's Hi-Voltage Super Science
Eclipse, 1987

1 .... 2.00

Mr. Monster's Triple Threat 3-D
3-D Zone, 1993

1 .... 4.00

Mr. Monster's True Crime
Eclipse, 1986

1-2 .... 2.00

Mr. Monster's Weird Tales of the Future
Eclipse, 1987

1 .... 2.00

Mr. Monster vs. Gorzilla
Image, 1998

1 .... 3.00

Mr. Mxyzptlk (Villains)
DC, 1998

1 .... 2.00

Mister Mystery
Aragon, 1951

1 .... 650.00
2 .... 450.00
3 .... 400.00
4-5 .... 340.00
6 .... 300.00
7 .... 525.00
8-10 .... 300.00
11 .... 385.00
12 .... 550.00
13-18 .... 240.00
19 .... 275.00

Mr. Natural
Kitchen Sink, 1970

1 .... 90.00
1/2nd 75.00
1/3rd 50.00
1/4th 35.00
2 .... 50.00
3 .... 45.00
3/2nd 22.00
3/3rd 10.00
3/4th 5.00
3/5th-3/10th 4.00

Mr. Night
Slave Labor, 2005

1 .... 3.00

Mr. Nightmare's Winter Special
Moonstone, 1995

1 .... 4.00

Mr. Nightmare's Wonderful World
Moonstone, 1995

1-5 .... 3.00

Mister Planet
Mr. Planet

1-2 .... 3.00

Mr. Risk
Humor

1 .... 45.00
2 .... 32.00

Mister Sixx
Imagine Nation

1 .... 2.00

Mr. T and the T-Force
Now, 1993

1 .... 3.00
1/Gold 4.00
2-10 .... 2.00

Mister X (Vol. 1)
Vortex, 1984

1 .... 4.00
2-14 .... 3.00

Mister X (Vol. 2)
Vortex

1-5 .... 3.00
6-11 .... 2.00
12 .... 3.00

Mister X (Vol. 3)
Caliber, 1996
1-4 .... 3.00

Mistress of Bondage
Fantagraphics
1-3 .... 3.00

Misty
Marvel, 1985
1-6 .... 1.00

Misty Girl Extreme
Fantagraphics, 1997
1-2 .... 3.00

Mites
Continuüm
1-2 .... 2.00

Mitzi Comics
Timely, 1948
1 .... 150.00

MixxZine
Mixx, 1997
1-6 .... 5.00

Mnemovore
DC, 2005
1-6 .... 3.00

Mobfire
DC, 1994
1-6 .... 3.00
Ashcan 1 .... 1.00

Mobile Police Patlabor Part 1
Viz, 1997
1-6 .... 3.00

Mobile Police Patlabor Part 2
Viz, 1998
1-6 .... 3.00

Mobile Suit Gundam 0079
Viz, 1999
1-8 .... 3.00

Mobile Suit Gundam 0083
Viz, 1999
1-13 .... 5.00

Mobile Suit Gundam Seed Astray
Tokyopop, 2004
1 .... 10.00

Mobile Suit Gundam Wing: Ground Zero
Viz, 2000
1-4 .... 3.00

Mobsters and Monsters Magazine
Original Syndicate, 1995
1 .... 3.00

Moby Dick
NBM
1 .... 16.00

Moby Duck
Gold Key, 1967
1 .... 12.00
2 .... 6.00
3-5 .... 5.00
6-10 .... 4.00
11-30 .... 3.00

Mod
Kitchen Sink, 1981
1 .... 5.00

Model
Tokyopop, 2004
1 .... 10.00

Model
NBM, 2002
1 .... 25.00

Model By Day
Rip Off, 1990
1-2 .... 3.00

Modeling with Millie
Marvel, 1963
21 .... 65.00
22-30 .... 48.00
31-40 .... 36.00
41-54 .... 30.00

Modern Comics
Quality, 1945
44 .... 450.00
45-53 .... 360.00
54-57 .... 250.00
58-80 .... 200.00
81-99 .... 170.00
100 .... 195.00
101 .... 170.00
102 .... 200.00

Modern Grimm
Symptom, 1996
1 .... 3.00

Modern Love
E.C., 1949
1 .... 510.00
2-3 .... 325.00
4-6 .... 450.00
7-8 .... 325.00

Modern Pulp
Special Studio
1 .... 3.00

Modern Romans
Fantagraphics
1-3 .... 2.00

Leatherboy

Leave It To Binky

Leave It to Chance

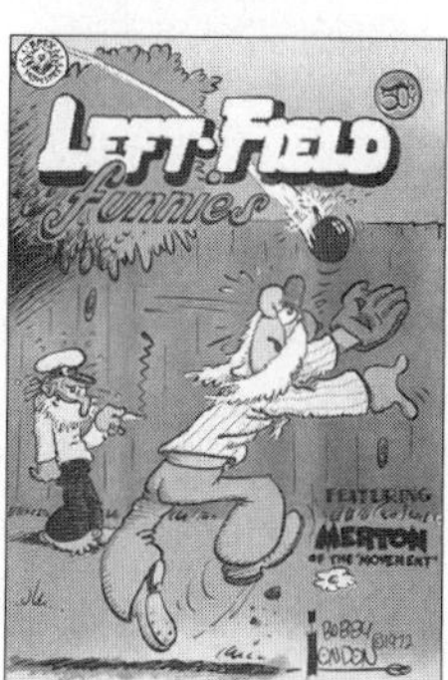

Left-Field Funnies

Legacy

Legend of Jesse James

Legend of Lemnear

Legend of Mother Sarah

Modest Proposal, A
Tome

1-2 .... 3.00

Modesty Blaise
DC

1 .... 20.00

Modniks
Gold Key, 1967

1 .... 8.00
2 .... 4.00

Mod Squad
Dell, 1969

1 .... 20.00
2-5 .... 12.00
6-8 .... 9.00

Mod Wheels
Gold Key, 1971

1 .... 30.00
2-9 .... 20.00
10-16 .... 15.00
17-19 .... 10.00

Moe & Shmoe Comics
O.S., 1948

1 .... 35.00
2 .... 25.00

Moebius Comics
Caliber, 1996

1-6 .... 3.00

Moebius: Exotics
Dark Horse

1 .... 7.00

Moebius: H.P.'s Rock City
Dark Horse, 1996

1 .... 8.00

Moebius: Madwoman of the Sacred Heart
Dark Horse, 1996

1 .... 13.00

Moebius: The Man from the Ciguri
Dark Horse, 1996

1 .... 8.00

Mogobi Desert Rats
Studio 91, 1991

1 .... 2.00

Mojo Action Companion Unit
Exclaim, 1997

1 .... 3.00

Mojo Mechanics
Syndicate

1-2 .... 3.00

Molly Manton's Romances
Marvel, 1949

1 .... 70.00

Molly O' Day
Avon, 1945

1 .... 225.00

Moment of Silence, A
Marvel, 2002

1 .... 4.00

Moment of Freedom, A
Caliber, 1997

nn 5.00

Mona
Kitchen Sink

1 .... 5.00

Monarchy
DC, 2001

1-12 .... 3.00

Mondo 3-D
3-D Zone

1 .... 4.00

Mondo Bondo
LCD

1 .... 3.00

Money Talks
Slave Labor, 1996

1 .... 4.00
2-5 .... 3.00

Mongrel
Northstar, 1994

1/A-3 .... 4.00

Monica's Story
Alternative, 1999

1 .... 4.00

Monkees
Gold Key, 1967

1 .... 45.00
2 .... 30.00
3 .... 24.00
4-5 .... 20.00
6-10 .... 18.00
11-17 .... 12.00

Monkey & The Bear
Avon, 1953

1 .... 45.00
2-3 .... 28.00

Monkey Business
Parody

1-2 .... 3.00

Monkey In A Wagon vs. Lemur On A Big Wheel
Alias, 2005

1 .... 3.00

Monkeyman and O'Brien
Dark Horse, 1996

1 .... 4.00
2-3 .... 3.00
Special 1 .... 3.00

Monkeyshines
Ace, 1944
1 .... 60.00
2 .... 40.00
3-10 .... 30.00
11-15 .... 25.00
16 .... 20.00
17-23 .... 25.00

Monnga
Daikaiju, 1995
1 .... 4.00

Monolith
Comico, 1991
1-4 .... 3.00

Monolith
DC, 2004
1 .... 4.00
2-12 .... 3.00

Monolith
Last Gasp, 1972
1 .... 3.00

Monroe
Conquest
1 .... 5.00

Monster
Fiction House, 1953
1 .... 340.00
2 .... 275.00

Monster (Butler & Hogg's...)
Slave Labor
1 .... 3.00

Monster
Ring
1 .... 2.00

Monster Boy
Monster, 1991
1 .... 3.00

Monster Boy Comics
Slave Labor, 1997
1-3 .... 3.00

Monster Club
APComics, 2002
1 .... 6.00
2 .... 5.00
3-9 .... 4.00

Monster Club
APComics, 2004
0 .... 3.00
1-5 .... 4.00

Monster Crime Comics
Hillman, 1952
1 .... 625.00

Monster Fighters Inc.
Image, 1999
1 .... 4.00

Monster Fighters Inc.: The Black Book
Image, 2000
1 .... 4.00

Monster Fighters Inc.: The Ghosts of Christmas
Image, 1999
1 .... 4.00

Monster Frat House
Eternity, 1989
1 .... 2.00

Monster House
Idea & Design Works, 2006
1 .... 8.00

Monster Hunters
Charlton, 1975
1 .... 6.00
1/2nd 3.00
2 .... 4.00
3-18 .... 3.00

Monster in My Pocket
Harvey, 1991
1-4 .... 2.00

Monster Island
Compass, 1998
1 .... 4.00

Monster Love
Kitchen Sink
1 .... 3.00

Monsterman
Image, 1997
1 .... 3.00

Monster Massacre
Atomeka
1 .... 8.00

Monster Massacre Special
Blackball
1 .... 3.00

Monster Matinee
Chaos!, 1997
1-3 .... 3.00

Monster Menace
Marvel, 1993
1-4 .... 2.00

MonsterMen (Gary Gianni's...)
Dark Horse, 1999
1 .... 3.00

Monster Posse
Adventure, 1992
1-3 .... 3.00

Monsters Attack!
Globe, 1989
1-5 .... 3.00

Legend of Supreme

Legend of the Hawkman

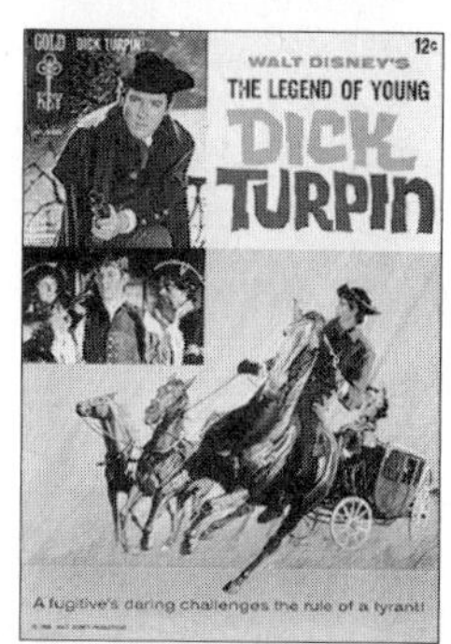

Legend of Young Dick Turpin

Legends

Legends of Daniel Boone

Legends of Luxura

Legends of the Dark Claw

Legends of the DC Universe

Monsters from Outer Space
Adventure, 1992
1-3 .... 3.00

Monsters on the Prowl
Marvel, 1971
9 .... 25.00
☛Was Chamber of Darkness
10-15 .... 15.00
16 .... 18.00
17-30 .... 12.00

Monsters to Laugh With
Marvel, 1964
1 .... 40.00
2-3 .... 30.00

Monsters Unleashed
Marvel, 1973
1 .... 40.00
2 .... 18.00
3-5 .... 15.00
6-8 .... 10.00
9-11 .... 7.00
Ann 1 .... 12.00

Monster War: Magdalena vs. Dracula
Image, 2005
1 .... 3.00

Monster War: Tomb Raider vs. Wolf Men
Image, 2005
2 .... 3.00

Monster War: Witchblade vs. Frankenstein
Image, 2005
3/A-3/B 3.00

Monster War: Darkness vs. Mr. Hyde
Image, 2005
4/A-4/B 3.00

Monster World
DC, 2001
1-4 .... 3.00

Monstrosity
Slap Happy, 1998
1 .... 5.00

Monte Hale Western
Fawcett, 1948
29 .... 200.00
30 .... 100.00
31-36 .... 75.00
37-45 .... 50.00
46-55 .... 45.00
56-70 .... 35.00
71-88 .... 30.00

Monty Hall of the U.S. Marines
Toby, 1951
1 .... 55.00
2 .... 32.00
3-11 .... 24.00

Moon, a Girl ... Romance
E.C., 1949
9 .... 600.00
10-11 .... 500.00
12 .... 600.00

Moon Beast
Avalon
1 .... 3.00

Moonchild
Forbidden Fruit, 1992
1-2 .... 3.00

Moon Child (Vol. 2)
Forbidden Fruit
1-3 .... 4.00

Moondog
Print Mint, 1973
1 .... 4.00
2 .... 3.00

Moonfighting
Harrier, 1988
1 .... 2.00

Moon Girl
E.C., 1947
1 .... 765.00
2 .... 400.00
3 .... 325.00
4 .... 300.00
5 .... 665.00
6-8 .... 325.00
9 .... 450.00
10-11 .... 365.00
12 .... 460.00

Moon Knight
Marvel, 1980
1 .... 10.00
2 .... 7.00
3-4 .... 5.00
5-20 .... 3.00
21-24 .... 2.00
25 .... 3.00
26-34 .... 2.00
35 .... 3.00
36-38 .... 2.00

Moon Knight
Marvel, 1985
1 .... 3.00
2-6 .... 2.00

Moon Knight
Marvel, 1998
1-4 .... 3.00

Moon Knight
Marvel, 1999
1-4 .... 3.00

Moon Knight
Marvel, 2006
1-6 .... 3.00

Moon Knight: Divided We Fall
Marvel, 1992
1 .... 5.00

Moon Knight Special
Marvel, 1992
1 .... 3.00

Moon Knight Special Edition
Marvel, 1983
1-3 .... 3.00

Moon Mullins
ACG, 1947
1 .... 80.00
2 .... 50.00
3-6 .... 45.00

Moon Mullins
St. John, 1948
7-8 .... 35.00

Moonshadow
Marvel, 1985
1 .... 4.00
2-3 .... 3.00
4-12 .... 2.00

Moonshadow
DC, 1994
1-5 .... 3.00
6-11 .... 2.00
12 .... 3.00

Moon Shot, the Flight of Apollo 12
Pepper Pike Graphix, 1994
1 .... 3.00

Moonstone Monsters: Zombies
Moonstone, 2005
1 .... 3.00

Moonstruck
White Wolf, 1987
1 .... 2.00

Moontrap
Caliber
1 .... 2.00

Moonwalker 3-D
Blackthorne
1 .... 3.00

Moordam Christmas Comics
Moordam, 1999
1 .... 3.00

Mopsy
St. John, 1948
1 .... 85.00
2 .... 55.00
3-5 .... 48.00
6-10 .... 40.00
11-15 .... 30.00
16-18 .... 26.00

Mora
Image, 2005
1-4 .... 3.00

Morbid Angel
London Night, 1996
½-1 .... 3.00

Morbid Angel: Penance
London Night, 1996
1 .... 4.00

Morbius Revisited
Marvel, 1993
1-5 .... 2.00

Morbius: The Living Vampire
Marvel, 1992
1 .... 2.00
1/CS 3.00
2-24 .... 2.00
25 .... 3.00
26-32 .... 2.00

More Fetish
Boneyard, 1993
1 .... 3.00

More Fun Comics
DC, 1936
☛Was New Fun Comics
7-8 .... 5,600.00
9 .... 6,500.00
10 .... 3,250.00
11 .... 2,850.00
12-13 .... 2,450.00
14 .... 12,500.00
☛1st Dr. Occult
15-16 .... 5,000.00
17 .... 4,500.00
18-20 .... 2,150.00
21-25 .... 1,950.00
26-29 .... 1,775.00
30-40 .... 1,625.00
41-45 .... 1,325.00
46-50 .... 1,200.00
51 .... 5,000.00
☛Spectre cameo
52 .... 54,000.00
☛1st Spectre story
53 .... 35,000.00

Legends of the Legion

Legends of the Stargrazers

L.E.G.I.O.N.

Legion Anthology

Legion Lost

Legionnaires

Legion of Stupid Heroes

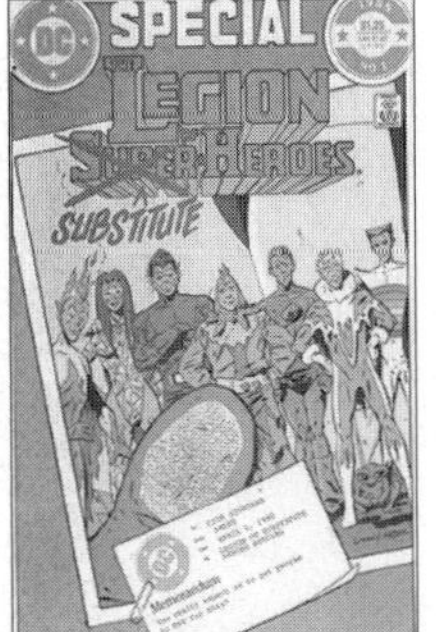
Legion of Substitute Heroes Special

54 ....9,700.00
55 ....12,400.00
☛1st Dr. Fate
56 ....4,400.00
57-59 ....3,100.00
59/15¢ 4,500.00
60 ....3,100.00
61-64 ....2,500.00
65-66 ....2,660.00
67 ....6,850.00
68-70 ....2,100.00
71 ....5,750.00
72 ....1,725.00
73 ....12,200.00
☛1st Aquaman, Green Arrow
74 ....2,450.00
75-80 ....1,725.00
81-88 ....1,150.00
89 ....1,325.00
90-99 ....940.00
100 ....1,060.00
101 ....7,850.00
☛1st Superboy
102 ....1,375.00
103 ....1,025.00
104-105 ....760.00
106-107 ....650.00
108-110 ....165.00
111-120 ....140.00
121-124 ....115.00
125 ....575.00
☛Superman cover
126 ....115.00
127 ....225.00

More Secret Origins Replica Edition
DC, 1999
1 ....5.00

More Starlight To Your Heart
ADV Manga, 2004
1-2 ....10.00

More Tales from Gimbley
Harrier, 1988
1 ....2.00

More Tales From Sleaze Castle
Gratuitous Bunny, 1990
1 ....4.00
2-6 ....3.00

More Than Mortal
Liar, 1997
1-6 ....3.00
Deluxe 1 ....15.00

More Than Mortal/ Lady Pendragon
Image, 1999
1-1/A 3.00

More Than Mortal: Otherworlds
Image, 1999
1-4 ....3.00

More Than Mortal: Sagas
Liar, 1998
1-3 ....3.00

More Than Mortal: Truths & Legends
Liar, 1998
1-1/A 3.00
1/Ltd. 4.00
2-5 ....3.00

More Trash from Mad
E.C., 1958
1 ....60.00
2 ....35.00
3 ....20.00
4-5 ....14.00
6-10 ....10.00
11-12 ....8.00

Morgana X
Fanatic Press
1 ....10.00

Morgana X
Sky Comics, 1993
1-SE 1 ....3.00

Morlocks
Marvel, 2002
1-4 ....3.00

Morlock 2001
Atlas-Seaboard, 1975
1 ....9.00
2 ....6.00
3 ....8.00

Morning Glory
Radio, 1998
1-5 ....3.00

Morningstar Special
Comico, 1990
1 ....3.00

Morphing Period
Shanda, 2000
1 ....5.00

Morphos the Shapechanger
Dark Horse, 1996
1 ....5.00

Morphs
Graphxpress, 1987
1-4 ....2.00

Morrigan
Dimension X, 1993
1 ....3.00

Morrigan
Sirius, 1997
1 .... 3.00

Mortal Coil Ashcan
Mermaid
Ashcan 1 .... 1.00

Mortal Coils: Bloodlines
Red Eye, 2002
1 .... 3.00

Mortal Kombat
Malibu, 1994
0-6 .... 3.00

Mortal Kombat: Baraka
Malibu, 1995
1 .... 3.00

Mortal Kombat: Battlewave
Malibu, 1995
1-6 .... 3.00

Mortal Kombat: Goro, Prince of Pain
Malibu, 1994
1-3 .... 3.00

Mortal Kombat: Kitana & Mileena
Malibu, 1995
1 .... 3.00

Mortal Kombat: Kung Lao
Malibu, 1995
1 .... 3.00

Mortal Kombat: Rayden & Kano
Malibu, 1995
1-3 .... 3.00

Mortal Kombat Special Edition
Malibu, 1994
1-2 .... 3.00

Mortal Kombat: Tournament Edition
Malibu, 1994
1-2 .... 4.00

Mortal Kombat U.S. Special Forces
Malibu, 1995
1-2 .... 4.00

Mortal Souls
Avatar, 2002
1/A 4.00

Mortar Man
Marshall Comics, 1993
1-3 .... 2.00

Mort Grim
Adhouse Books, 2005
0 .... 5.00

Mortie
Magazine Publications, 1952
1 .... 38.00
2-4 .... 24.00

Mortigan Goth: Immortalis
Marvel, 1993
1 .... 2.00
1/Variant 3.00
2-4 .... 2.00

Mort the Dead Teenager
Marvel, 1992
1-4 .... 2.00

Morty the Dog
Mu, 1991
1-2 .... 4.00

Morty the Dog
Starhead
1 .... 2.00

Mosaic
Sirius, 1999
1/A-5 .... 3.00

Mosaic: Hell City Ripper
Sirius, 1999
1-5 .... 3.00

Moses and the Ten Commandments
Dell, 1957
1 .... 80.00

Mostly Wanted
WildStorm, 2000
1-4 .... 3.00

Moth (Steve Rude's)
Dark Horse, 2004
1-4 .... 3.00

Moth (Steve Rude's) Double-Sized Special
Dark Horse, 2004
1 .... 5.00

Motherless Child
Kitchen Sink
1 .... 3.00

Mother's Oats Comix
Rip Off, 1969
1 .... 5.00
2 .... 3.00

Mother Superion
Antarctic, 1997
1 .... 3.00

Mother Teresa of Calcutta
Marvel, 1984
1 .... 2.00

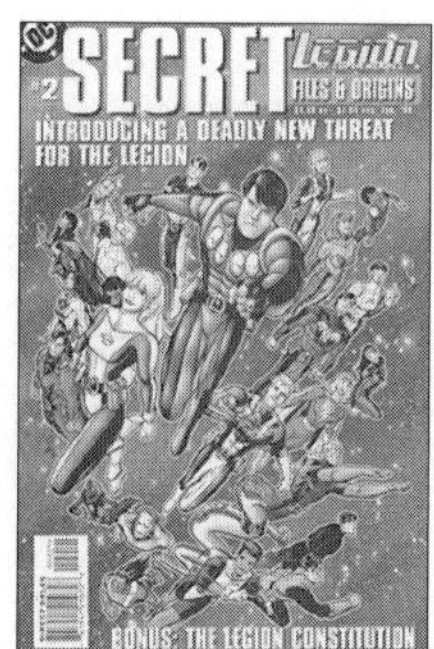

Legion of Super-Heroes Secret Files

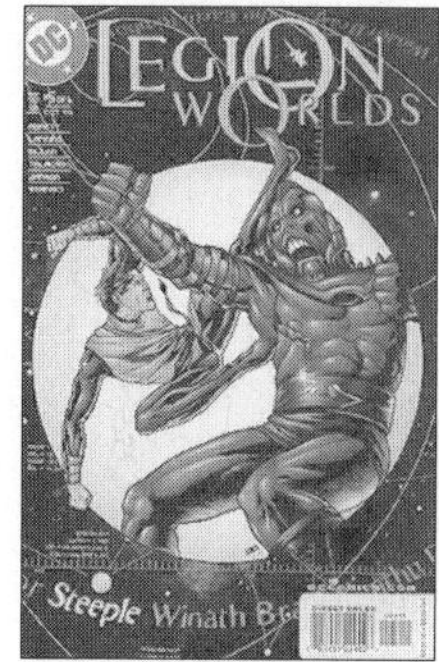

Legion Worlds

Lemonade Kid

Lenore

Leonardo Teenage Mutant Ninja Turtle

Leopold and Brink

Lethal Foes of Spider-Man

Lethal Strike

Motion Picture Comics
Fawcett, 1950

101 .... 115.00
102-104 .... 80.00
105 .... 90.00
106-107 .... 75.00
108-109 .... 60.00
110 .... 215.00
111 .... 90.00
112 .... 50.00
113-114 .... 40.00

Motley Stories
Division

1 .... 3.00

Motorbike Puppies
Dark Zulu Lies, 1992

1-2 .... 3.00

Motorhead
Dark Horse, 1994

1-6 .... 3.00
Special 1 .... 4.00

Motormouth
Marvel, 1992

1-12 .... 2.00

Mountain
Underground

1 .... 3.00

Mountain World
Icicle Ridge

1 .... 2.00

Mouse Guard
Archaia Studios Press, 2006

1 .... 90.00
1/2nd 18.00
2 .... 25.00

Mouse Musketeers (M.G.M.'s...)
Dell, 1957

8 .... 35.00
9-21 .... 30.00

Mouse on the Moon
Dell, 1963

1 .... 15.00

Movie Love
Famous Funnies, 1950

1 .... 60.00
2 .... 50.00
3 .... 45.00
4-9 .... 40.00
10 .... 50.00
11-15 .... 35.00
16-22 .... 30.00

Movie Comics
DC, 1939

1 .... 2,450.00
2 .... 1,700.00
3 .... 1,100.00
4-6 .... 950.00

Movie Comics
Fiction House, 1946

1 .... 400.00
2-3 .... 350.00
4 .... 300.00

Movie Star News
Pure Imagination

1 .... 6.00

Movie Thrillers
Magazine Enterprises, 1949

1 .... 160.00

Moxi
Lightning, 1996

1/A-Ash 1/D 0.00
1 .... 3.00

Moxi's Friends: Bobby Joe & Nitro
Lightning, 1996

1 .... 3.00

Moxi: Strange Daze
Lightning, 1996

1 .... 3.00

M. Rex
Image, 1999

1-2 .... 3.00
Ashcan 1/A-1/B 5.00

Mr. T
APComics, 2005

1-2 .... 4.00

Ms. Anti-Social
Helpless Anger

1 .... 2.00

Ms. Cyanide & Ice
Black Out

0-1 .... 3.00

Ms. Fantastic
Conquest

1-4 .... 3.00

Ms. Fantastic Classics
Conquest

1 .... 3.00

Ms. Fortune
Image, 1998

1 .... 3.00

Ms. Marvel
Marvel, 1977

1 .... 8.00
2-6 .... 3.00
6/35¢ 15.00
7 .... 3.00
7/35¢ 15.00
8 .... 3.00
8/35¢ 15.00
9 .... 3.00
☛1st Mystique
9/35¢ 15.00

10 .... 3.00
10/35¢ 15.00
11-15 .... 2.00
16 .... 15.00
☛Mystique cameo
17 .... 8.00
18 .... 40.00
☛1st Mystique
19 .... 3.00
20-23 .... 2.00

Ms. Marvel
Marvel, 2006
1-45 .... 3.00

Ms. Mystic
Pacific, 1982
1 .... 4.00
2 .... 3.00

Ms. Mystic
Continuity, 1988
1-9 .... 2.00

Ms. Mystic
Continuity, 1993
1-4 .... 3.00

Ms. Mystic Deathwatch 2000
Continuity, 1993
1-3 .... 3.00

Ms. PMS
Aaaahh!!, 1992
0-1 .... 3.00

Ms. PMS
Aaaahh!!, 2005
1 .... 4.00

Ms. Quoted Tales
Chance, 1983
1 .... 2.00

Ms. Tree
Eclipse, 1983
1 .... 4.00
2-5 .... 3.00
6-49 .... 2.00
50-3D 2 .... 3.00
Summer 1 .... 2.00

Ms. Tree Quarterly
DC, 1990
1-10 .... 4.00

Ms. Victory Special
AC
1 .... 2.00

Mu
Devil's Due, 2004
1 .... 3.00
1/Ropie 4.00
2 .... 3.00
2/Suh 4.00
3 .... 3.00
3/MLim 4.00
4 .... 3.00
4/Hyung 4.00

Mucha Lucha
DC, 2003
1-3 .... 2.00

Muggsy Mouse
Magazine Enterprises, 1951
1 .... 40.00
2 .... 30.00
3-5 .... 24.00

Muggy-Doo Boy Cat
Stanhall, 1953
1 .... 36.00
2-4 .... 25.00

Muktuk Wolfsbreath: Hard-Boiled Shaman
DC, 1998
1-3 .... 3.00

Mullkon Empire (John Jakes'...)
Tekno, 1995
1-6 .... 2.00

Multiverse (Michael Moorcock's...)
DC, 1997
1-12 .... 3.00

Mummy
Monster, 1991
1-4 .... 2.00

Mummy
Dell
1 .... 25.00

Mummy Archives
Millennium, 1992
1 .... 3.00

Mummy or Ramses the Damned (Anne Rice's...)
Millennium, 1990
1-12 .... 3.00

Mummy's Curse
Aircel, 1990
1-4 .... 3.00

Mummy: Valley of the Gods
Chaos, 2001
1-3 .... 3.00

Munden's Bar
First, 1988
Ann 1 .... 3.00
Ann 2 .... 6.00

Munsters
Gold Key, 1965
1 .... 120.00
2 .... 75.00

Lethargic Comics

Liberator

Liberty Meadows

Libra

License to Kill

Life on Another Planet

Life Story

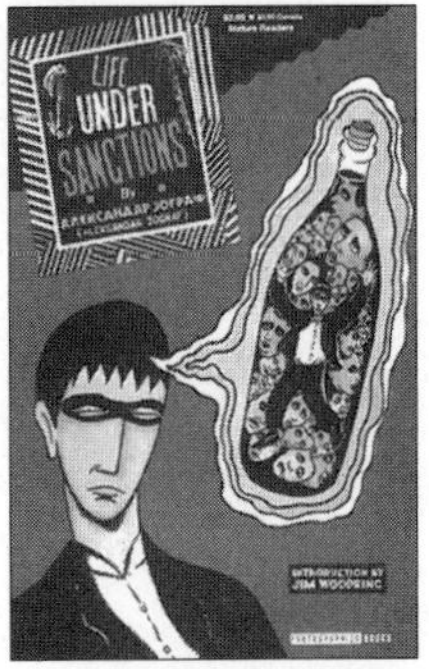

Life Under Sanctions

3-5 .... 48.00
6-10 .... 34.00
11-16 .... 30.00

Munsters
TV Comics, 1997
1-Special 1 .... 3.00

Muppet Babies
Marvel, 1985
1 .... 2.00
2-26 .... 1.00

Muppet Babies
Harvey, 1993
1-6 .... 2.00

Muppet Babies Adventures
Harvey, 1992
1 .... 1.00

Muppet Babies Big Book
Harvey, 1992
1 .... 2.00

Muppets Take Manhattan
Marvel, 1984
1-3 .... 2.00

Murcièlaga She-Bat
Heroic, 1993
1 .... 2.00
2-3 .... 3.00

Murder
Renegade, 1986
1-2 .... 2.00

Murder Can Be Fun
Slave Labor, 1996
1-4 .... 4.00
5-12 .... 3.00

Murder City
Eternity
1 .... 4.00

Murder Incorporated
Fox, 1948
1 .... 400.00
2 .... 300.00
3-6 .... 175.00
7-15 .... 150.00

Murder Me Dead
El Capitan, 2000
1-7 .... 3.00

Murderous Gangsters
Avon, 1951
1 .... 300.00
2 .... 200.00
3-4 .... 150.00

Music Comics
Personality
2-4 .... 3.00

Music Comics on Tour
Personality
1 .... 3.00

Mutant Aliens
NBM
1 .... 11.00

Mutant Book of the Dead
Starhead
1 .... 3.00

Mutant Chronicles
Acclaim, 1996
1-4 .... 3.00

Mutant Chronicles Sourcebook
Acclaim, 1996
1 .... 3.00

Mutant Earth
Image, 2002
1/A-4/B 3.00

Mutant Misadventures of Cloak & Dagger
Marvel, 1988
1-8 .... 2.00
9 .... 3.00
10-18 .... 2.00
19 .... 3.00

Mutants and Misfits
Silverline, 1987
1 .... 2.00

Mutants vs. Ultras: First Encounters
Malibu, 1995
1 .... 7.00

Mutant, Texas: Tales of Sheriff Ida Red
Oni, 2002
1-4 .... 3.00

Mutant X
Marvel, 1998
1 .... 3.00
1/A 4.00
2-5 .... 3.00
6-11 .... 2.00
12 .... 3.00
13-24 .... 2.00
25 .... 3.00
26-32 .... 2.00
Anl 1999-Anl 2000 .... 3.00
Ann 2001 .... 4.00

Mutant X
Marvel, 2001
1 .... 3.00

Mutant X: Dangerous Decisions
Marvel, 2002
1 .... 4.00

Mutant X: Origin
Marvel, 2002
1 .... 4.00

Mutant Zone
Aircel, 1991
1-3 .... 3.00

Mutation
Speakeasy Comics, 2005
1-2 .... 3.00

Mutatis
Marvel, 1992
1-3 .... 3.00

Mutator
Checker, 1998
1-2 .... 2.00

Muties
Marvel, 2002
1-6 .... 3.00

Mutiny
Aragon, 1954
1 .... 65.00
2-3 .... 45.00

Mutopia X
Marvel, 2005
1 .... 4.00
☛House of M
1/Variant-5 .... 3.00

Mutt & Jeff
DC, 1939
1 .... 725.00
2 .... 375.00
3 .... 290.00
4 .... 200.00
5 .... 140.00
6-10 .... 125.00
11-15 .... 90.00
16-20 .... 75.00
21-30 .... 60.00
31-50 .... 40.00
51-70 .... 30.00
71-90 .... 24.00
91-100 .... 18.00
101-120 .... 15.00
121-148 .... 12.00

Muzzle
Dead Fish
1-6 .... 1.00

MX–The Superhero Series
Radical Comix, 1994
1-2 .... 3.00

My Diary
Marvel, 1949
1 .... 85.00
2 .... 65.00

My Date
Hillman, 1947
1 .... 200.00
2-4 .... 145.00

My Experience
Fox, 1949
19 .... 200.00
20 .... 75.00
21 .... 200.00
22 .... 150.00

My Faith in Frankie
DC, 2004
1-4 .... 3.00

My Favorite Martian
Gold Key, 1964
1 .... 55.00
2 .... 35.00
3-4 .... 30.00
5-9 .... 24.00

My First ABC Magazine
Burghley
1-3 .... 2.00

My Flesh is Cool (Steven Grant's)
Avatar, 2004
1 .... 4.00

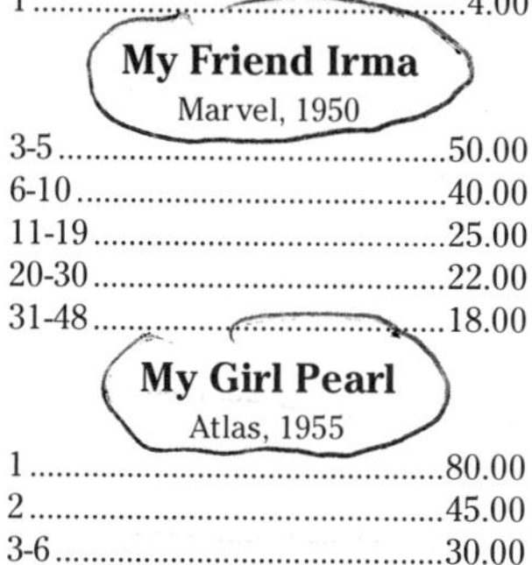

My Friend Irma
Marvel, 1950
3-5 .... 50.00
6-10 .... 40.00
11-19 .... 25.00
20-30 .... 22.00
31-48 .... 18.00

My Girl Pearl
Atlas, 1955
1 .... 80.00
2 .... 45.00
3-6 .... 30.00
7-11 .... 25.00

My Greatest Adventure
DC, 1955
1 .... 1,250.00
2 .... 600.00
3-4 .... 425.00
5-10 .... 325.00
11-14 .... 200.00
15-17 .... 250.00
18 .... 300.00
19 .... 200.00
20-21 .... 225.00
22-27 .... 175.00
28 .... 200.00
29-30 .... 150.00
31-40 .... 125.00
41-61 .... 100.00
62-79 .... 75.00
80 .... 425.00
☛1st Doom Patrol
81-85 .... 150.00

My Great Love
Fox, 1949
1 .... 80.00

Life with Archie

Lightning Comics Presents

Lili

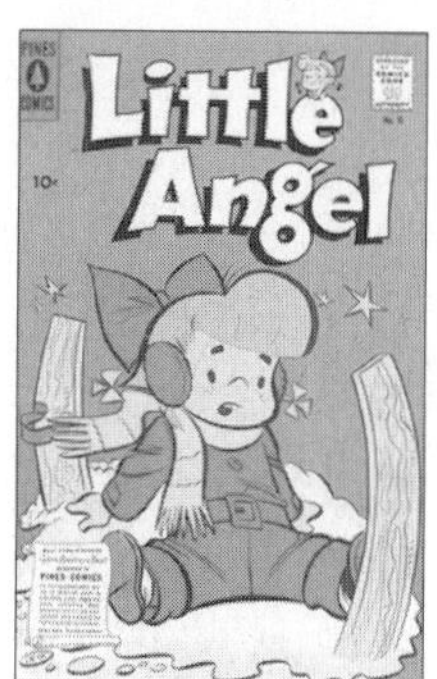

Little Angel

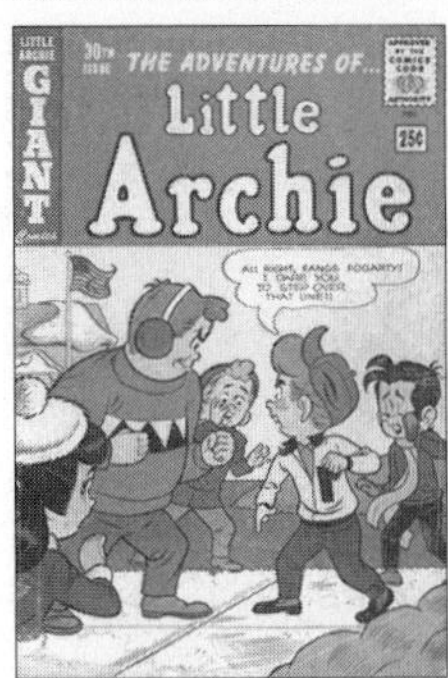

Little Archie

Little Audrey and Melvin

Little Dot in 3-D

Little Gloomy

2	50.00
3-4	40.00

My Intimate Affair
Fox, 1950

1	100.00
2	55.00

My Life
Fox, 1948

4	155.00
5	80.00
6-7	85.00
8-9	40.00
10	90.00
11-15	40.00

My Life With Eddie Vedder
Chemical Brain Comics, 1998

1-3	4.00

My Little Margie
Charlton, 1954

1	110.00
2	60.00
3-5	35.00
6-10	32.00
11-19	26.00
20	45.00
21-30	20.00
31-39	16.00
40-50	12.00
51-53	9.00
54	40.00

My Little Margie's Boyfriends
Charlton, 1955

1	70.00
2	45.00
3-5	40.00
6-11	30.00

My Love
Marvel, 1949

1	80.00
2	60.00
3-4	40.00

My Love
Marvel, 1969

1	20.00
2	12.00
3	10.00
4-9	8.00
10-20	6.00
21-39	4.00
Special 1	15.00

My Love Affair
Fox, 1949

1	90.00
2	50.00
3-6	60.00

My Love Secret
Fox, 1949

24-30	0.00
25	50.00
53	25.00

My Love Story
Fox, 1949

1	90.00
2	50.00
3-4	45.00

My Love Story
Atlas, 1956

1	75.00
2-5	40.00
6-9	35.00

My Monkey's Name is Jennifer
Slave Labor, 2002

1	3.00

My Name Is Chaos
DC, 1992

1-4	5.00

My Name Is Holocaust
DC, 1995

1-5	3.00

My Name is Mud
Incognito, 1994

1	3.00

My Only Love
Charlton, 1975

1	10.00
2	4.00
3-9	3.00

My Own Romance
Marvel, 1949

4	100.00
5	60.00
6-18	50.00
19-55	35.00
56-74	20.00
75	25.00
76	20.00

My Personal Problem
Ajax, 1955

1	50.00
2-4	35.00

My Private Life
Fox, 1950

16-17	60.00

My Real Love
Standard, 1952

5	100.00

Myriad
Approbation, 2005

1-6	3.00

Myrmidon
Red Hills, 1998

1 .... 3.00

My Romance
Marvel, 1948

1 .... 95.00
2 .... 60.00
3 .... 50.00

My Romantic Adventures
ACG, 1956

68 .... 35.00
69-70 .... 28.00
71-80 .... 24.00
81-89 .... 20.00
90-99 .... 16.00
100-110 .... 12.00
111-120 .... 10.00
121-138 .... 8.00

My Romantic Adventures?
Avalon

1 .... 3.00

Myron Moose Funnies
Fantagraphics, 1973

1-3 .... 2.00

My Secret
Superior, 1949

1 .... 75.00
2-3 .... 35.00

My Secret Affair
Fox, 1949

1 .... 125.00
2-3 .... 65.00

My Secret Life
Fox, 1949

22-24 .... 75.00
25-26 .... 60.00

My Secret Life
Charlton, 1957

19 .... 12.00
20-30 .... 6.00
31-47 .... 4.00

My Secret Marriage
Superior, 1953

1 .... 75.00
2 .... 40.00
3-15 .... 30.00
16-24 .... 25.00

My Secret Romance
Fox, 1950

1 .... 100.00
2 .... 85.00

Mysfits
Bon-a-Gram, 1994

1 .... 3.00

Mys-Tech Wars
Marvel, 1993

1-4 .... 2.00

Mysteries
Superior, 1953

1 .... 275.00
2 .... 150.00
3-5 .... 110.00
6-11 .... 85.00

Mysteries of Scotland Yard
Magazine Enterprises, 1954

1 .... 50.00

Mysteries of Unexplored Worlds
Charlton, 1956

1 .... 200.00
2 .... 65.00
3-4 .... 100.00
5-7 .... 135.00
8 .... 100.00
9-10 .... 135.00
11 .... 110.00
12 .... 75.00
13-18 .... 28.00
19 .... 60.00
20 .... 28.00
21-24 .... 60.00
25 .... 20.00
26 .... 55.00
27-30 .... 20.00
31-40 .... 14.00
41-45 .... 10.00
46 .... 22.00
47-48 .... 16.00

Mysterious Adventures
Story, 1951

1 .... 325.00
2 .... 225.00
3-10 .... 175.00
11 .... 200.00
12-13 .... 175.00
14 .... 150.00
15 .... 200.00
16-24 .... 150.00

Mysterious Stories
Premier, 1954

2 .... 300.00
3 .... 200.00
4-7 .... 165.00

Mysterious Suspense
Charlton, 1968

1 .... 35.00

Mysterious Traveler Comics
TransWorld, 1948

1 .... 450.00

Mystery Comics
Wise, 1944

1 .... 725.00
2 .... 585.00
3-4 .... 500.00

Little Iodine

Little Jim-Bob Big Foot

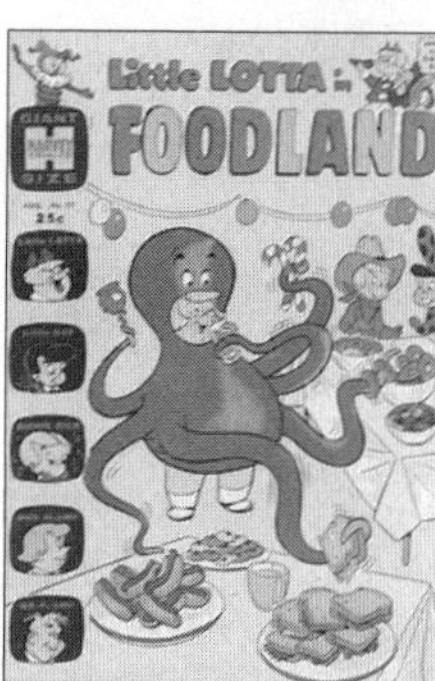

Little Lotta Foodland

Little Max Comics

Little Mister Man

Little Nemo in Slumberland 3-D

Little Orphan Annie

Little Ronzo in Slumberland

Mystery Date
Lightspeed, 1999

1..........3.00

Mystery in Space
DC, 1951

1..........3,000.00
2..........1,250.00
3..........900.00
4-5..........700.00
6-10..........600.00
11-15..........400.00
16-25..........320.00
26-40..........235.00
41-52..........195.00
53..........1,500.00
☛Adam Strange starts
54..........425.00
55..........250.00
56-60..........175.00
61-71..........125.00
72-74..........100.00
75..........225.00
☛JLA app.
76-80..........100.00
81-86..........75.00
87..........175.00
☛Hawkman app.
88-90..........90.00
☛Hawkman app.
91-93..........50.00
94-103..........40.00
104-110..........30.00
111-117..........5.00

Mystery in Space
DC, 2006

1-4..........4.00

Mystery Man
Slave Labor, 1988

1-2..........2.00

Mystery Men Comics
Fox, 1939

1..........10,250.00
2..........9,000.00
3..........3,250.00
4-5..........2,200.00
6..........1,700.00
7..........1,825.00
8..........1,700.00
9..........900.00
10-12..........850.00
13..........550.00
14-19..........500.00
20-31..........425.00

Mystery Men Movie Adaptation
Dark Horse, 1999

1-2..........3.00

Mysterymen Stories
Bob Burden, 1996

1..........5.00

Mystery of Woolverine Woo-Bait
Fantagraphics, 2004

1..........5.00

Mystery Tales
Marvel, 1952

1..........400.00
2..........250.00
3-5..........200.00
6-10..........185.00
11-20..........150.00
21-30..........120.00
31-40..........90.00
41-54..........65.00

Mystic
Marvel, 1951

1..........485.00
2..........335.00
3..........235.00
4..........400.00
5..........175.00
6..........400.00
7..........175.00
8-20..........135.00
21-30..........105.00
31-36..........85.00
37-56..........70.00
57..........100.00
58-61..........70.00

Mystic
CrossGen, 2000

1-43..........3.00

Mystic Comics
Timely, 1940

1..........11,750.00
2..........3,600.00
3-5..........2,850.00
6-7..........2,650.00
8..........1,950.00
9-10..........1,700.00

Mystic Comics
Timely, 1944

1..........2,000.00
2..........1,000.00
3-4..........775.00

Mystic Edge
Antarctic, 1998

1..........3.00

Mystic Trigger
Maelstrom

1..........3.00

Mystical Tales
Atlas, 1956

1..........300.00
2..........185.00

3-5 .... 140.00
6-7 .... 125.00

Mystique
Marvel, 2003
1 .... 3.00
2-24 .... 3.00

Mystique & Sabretooth
Marvel, 1996
1-4 .... 2.00

My Story
Fox, 1949
5 .... 100.00
6-12 .... 80.00

Myst: The Book of the Black Ships
Dark Horse, 1997
0 .... 2.00
1-4 .... 3.00

My Terrible Romance
NEC, 1994
1-2 .... 3.00

Myth
Fygmok, 1996
1-2 .... 3.00

Mythadventures
Warp, 1984
1-12 .... 2.00

Myth Conceptions
Apple, 1987
1-8 .... 2.00

Mythical Detective Loki
ADV Manga, 2004
1-2 .... 10.00

Mythic Heroes
Chapterhouse, 1996
1 .... 3.00

Myth Maker (Robert E. Howard's...)
Cross Plains, 1999
1 .... 7.00

Mythography
Bardic, 1996
1-8 .... 4.00

Mythos
Wonder Comix, 1987
1-3 .... 2.00

Mythos: Hulk
Marvel, 2006
1 .... 4.00

Mythos: The Final Tour
DC, 1996
1-3 .... 6.00

Mythos: X-Men
Marvel, 2006
1 .... 4.00

Mythstalkers
Image, 2003
1-8 .... 3.00

My True Love
Fox, 1949
66 .... 60.00
67-69 .... 50.00

My Uncle Jeff
Origin Comics, 2003
1 .... 4.00

My War With Brian
NBM
1 .... 17.00

Nadesico
CPM Manga, 1999
1-26 .... 3.00

Nagasaki: The Forgotten Bomb
Antarctic, 2004
1-2 .... 4.00

Nail
Dark Horse, 2004
1-4 .... 3.00

Naive Inter-Dimensional Commando Koalas
Eclipse, 1986
1 .... 2.00

Naked Angels
Fantagraphics, 1996
1-2 .... 3.00

Naked Eye (S.A. King's...)
Antarctic, 1994
1-3 .... 3.00

Naked Fangs
Acid Rain, 1994
1-2 .... 3.00

'Nam
Marvel, 1986
1 .... 2.00
1/2nd-25 .... 1.00
26-84 .... 2.00

Nameless
Image, 1997
1-5 .... 3.00

Names of Magic
DC, 2001
1-5 .... 3.00

'Nam Magazine
Marvel, 1988
1-10 .... 3.00

Namor
Marvel, 2003
1 .... 3.00
2-4 .... 2.00
5-12 .... 3.00

Little Roquefort

Little Sad Sack

Little Shop of Horrors

Little Stooges

Little White Mouse

Living Bible

Livingstone Mountain

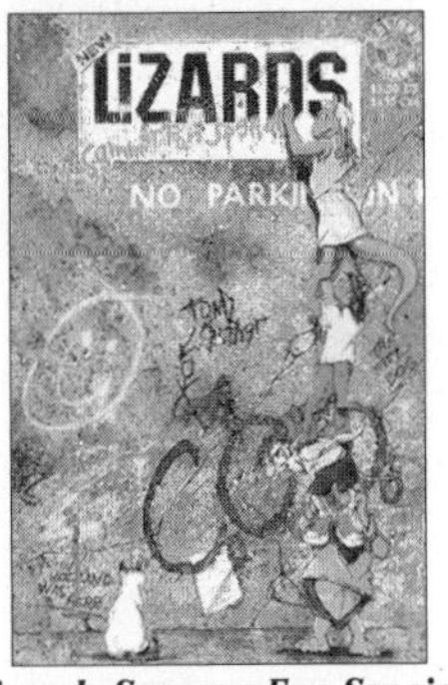

Lizards Summer Fun Special

Namora
Timely, 1948

1 .... 2,000.00
2-3 .... 1,200.00

Namor Sub-Mariner
Marvel, 1990

1-5 .... 2.00
6-36 .... 1.00
37 .... 2.00
38-49 .... 1.00
50 .... 2.00
50/Variant 3.00
51-62 .... 2.00
Ann 1 .... 3.00
Ann 2 .... 2.00
Ann 3-4 .... 3.00

Nancy and Sluggo
St. John, 1955

121 .... 25.00
122-130 .... 15.00
131-145 .... 12.00

Nancy and Sluggo
Dell, 1957

146 .... 25.00
147-187 .... 10.00

Nancy and Sluggo
Gold Key, 1962

188-192 .... 10.00

Nancy and Sluggo Travel Time
Dell, 1958

1 .... 80.00

Nanny and the Professor
Dell, 1970

1 .... 16.00
2 .... 10.00

Nanosoup
Millennium, 1996

1 .... 3.00

Napoleon & Uncle Elby
Eastern, 1942

1 .... 200.00

Narcolepsy Dreams
Slave Labor, 1995

1-2 .... 3.00
4 .... 1.00

Nard n' Pat
Cartoonists Co-Op, 1974

1 .... 3.00

Narrative Illustration
E.C., 1942

1 .... 1,000.00

Nascar Adventures
Vortex, 1992

1-7 .... 3.00

NASCUB Adventures
Vortex, 1991

1 .... 2.00

Nash
Image, 1999

1-Ashcan 1/Varian 3.00

Nasti: Monster Hunter
Schism

1-3 .... 3.00
Ashcan 1/Ltd. 1.00

Nathaniel Dusk
DC, 1984

1-4 .... 2.00

Nathaniel Dusk II
DC, 1985

1-4 .... 2.00

Nathan Never
Dark Horse, 1999

1-6 .... 5.00

National Comics
Quality, 1940

1 .... 4,800.00
2 .... 1,800.00
3 .... 1,300.00
4 .... 975.00
5 .... 1,160.00
6-11 .... 1,000.00
12 .... 675.00
13-16 .... 720.00
17 .... 545.00
18 .... 790.00
19-23 .... 545.00
24-30 .... 376.00
31-34 .... 330.00
35-38 .... 250.00
39 .... 275.00
40-50 .... 170.00
51 .... 230.00
52-60 .... 120.00
61-70 .... 100.00
71-75 .... 80.00

National Comics
DC, 1999

1 .... 2.00

National Lampoon Presents: French Comics (The Kind Men Like)
National Lampoon

1 .... 5.00

National Velvet
Dell, 1962

1-2 .... 30.00

National Velvet
Dell, 1962

1 .... 12.00
2 .... 9.00

Nation of Snitches
DC
1 .... 5.00

Nat Turner
Kyle Baker Publishing, 2005
1-2 .... 3.00

Natural Inquirer
Fantagraphics, 1989
1 .... 2.00

Natural Selection
Atom, 1998
1-2 .... 3.00

Nature Boy
Charlton, 1956
3 .... 55.00
4-5 .... 50.00

Nature of the Beast
Caliber
1-2 .... 3.00

Naughty Bits
Fantagraphics, 1991
1 .... 7.00
1/2nd 3.00
2 .... 5.00
3-5 .... 4.00
6-38 .... 3.00

Näu Headhunter
Neotek Iconography, 1993
1 .... 3.00

Nausicaä of the Valley of Wind Part 1
Viz, 2004
1-7 .... 3.00

Nausicaä of the Valley of Wind Part 2
Viz
1-4 .... 3.00

Nausicaä of the Valley of Wind Part 3
Viz
1-3 .... 4.00

Nausicaä of the Valley of Wind Part 4
Viz, 1995
1-6 .... 3.00

Nausicaä of the Valley of Wind Part 5
Viz, 1995
1-8 .... 3.00

Nautilus
Shanda Fantasy Arts, 1999
1 .... 3.00

Navy Action
Atlas, 1954
1 .... 85.00
2-4 .... 58.00
5-11 .... 45.00
15-18 .... 38.00

Navy Combat
Atlas, 1955
1 .... 140.00
2 .... 85.00
3-7 .... 70.00
8-12 .... 62.00
13-20 .... 48.00

Navy Heroes
Almanac, 1955
1 .... 75.00

Navy Patrol
Key, 1955
1 .... 28.00

Navy Tales
Atlas, 1957
1 .... 85.00
2 .... 75.00
3-4 .... 60.00

Navy Task Force
Stanmor, 1954
1 .... 45.00
2 .... 25.00
3-8 .... 20.00

Navy War Heroes
Charlton, 1964
1 .... 12.00
2 .... 8.00
3-7 .... 6.00

Naza
Dell, 1964
1 .... 15.00
2-5 .... 8.00
6-9 .... 6.00

Nazrat
Imperial, 1986
1-6 .... 2.00

Nazz
DC, 1990
1-4 .... 5.00

NBC Saturday Morning Comics
Harvey, 1991
1 .... 2.00

Near Myths
Rip Off, 1978
1 .... 3.00

Near to Now
Fandom House
1-2 .... 2.00

Lizzie McGuire Cine-Manga

Loaded

Lobo Convention Special

Lobo Goes to Hollywood

Lobo Paramilitary Christmas Special

Lobo the Duck

Lois Lane

Loki

Neat Stuff
Fantagraphics, 1985
1 ... 5.00
1/2nd ... 3.00
2 ... 4.00
2/2nd ... 3.00
3 ... 4.00
3/2nd-15 ... 3.00

Nebbs
Dell, 1945
1 ... 75.00

Neck and Neck
Tokyopop, 2004
1-4 ... 10.00

Necromancer
Anarchy
1 ... 3.00
1/Deluxe ... 4.00
2 ... 3.00
2/Deluxe ... 4.00
3 ... 3.00
3/Deluxe ... 4.00
4 ... 3.00
4/Deluxe ... 4.00

Necromancer
Anarchy
1-4 ... 3.00

Necromancer
Image, 2005
1/Manapul ... 3.00
1/Horn ... 4.00
1/Bachalo-6 ... 3.00

Necropolis
Fleetway-Quality
1-9 ... 3.00

Necroscope
Malibu, 1992
1-5 ... 3.00

Necroscope Book II: Wamphyri
Malibu, 1994
1-5 ... 3.00

Necrowar
Dreamwave, 2003
1-3 ... 3.00

Nefarismo
Fantagraphics, 1994
1-8 ... 3.00

Negation
CrossGen, 2002
1-27 ... 3.00

Negation War
CrossGen, 2004
1-2 ... 3.00

Negation Prequel
CrossGen, 2001
1 ... 3.00

Negative Burn
Caliber, 1993
1-3 ... 6.00
4 ... 4.00
5-6 ... 6.00
7-12 ... 4.00
13 ... 7.00
14-47 ... 4.00
48-49 ... 5.00
50 ... 7.00

Negative Burn
Image, 2006
1-7 ... 6.00

Negative Burn: Summer Special 2005
Image, 2005
1 ... 10.00

Negative One
Eirich Olson, 1999
1 ... 3.00

Negro Heroes
Parents' Magazine Institute, 1947
1 ... 525.00
2 ... 570.00

Negro Romance
Charlton, 1950
1 ... 700.00
2-3 ... 525.00

Neil & Buzz in Space and Time
Fantagraphics, 1989
1 ... 2.00

Neil the Horse Comics and Stories
Aardvark-Vanaheim, 1983
1 ... 3.00
2-13 ... 2.00
14-15 ... 3.00

Nellie the Nurse
Atlas, 1945
1 ... 225.00
2 ... 105.00
3-4 ... 80.00
5 ... 90.00
6-10 ... 75.00
11 ... 80.00
12 ... 75.00
13 ... 55.00
14-16 ... 80.00
17 ... 55.00
18 ... 80.00
19-20 ... 55.00
21-30 ... 50.00
31-36 ... 42.00

Nemesis Comics Special
Nemesis
Ashcan 1 .... 1.00

Nemesister
Cheeky, 1997
1-3 .... 3.00
3/Ashcan 1.00
4-9 .... 3.00

Nemesis the Warlock
Eagle, 1984
1-8 .... 2.00

Nemesis the Warlock
Fleetway-Quality, 1989
1-19 .... 2.00

Neo
Excalibur
1 .... 2.00

Neomen
Slave Labor, 1987
1-2 .... 2.00

Neon City
Innovation
1 .... 2.00

Neon City: After the Fall
Innovation
1 .... 3.00

Neon Cyber
Image, 1999
1 .... 3.00
1/Variant 5.00
2-8 .... 3.00

Neon Genesis Evangelion Book 1
Viz, 1997
1/A-6/B 3.00

Neon Genesis Evangelion Book 2
Viz, 1998
1/A-1/B 4.00
2/A-5/B 3.00

Neon Genesis Evangelion Book 3
Viz, 1998
1/A-6/B 3.00

Neon Genesis Evangelion Book 4
Viz, 1999
1/A-7/B 3.00

Neon Genesis Evangelion Book 5
Viz, 2000
1-7/B 3.00

Neon Genesis Evangelion Book 6
Viz, 2001
1-4/B 4.00

Neon Genesis Evangelion Book 7
Viz, 2002
1-5/B 3.00
6-6/B 4.00

Neotopia
Antarctic, 2003
1-5 .... 4.00

Neotopia (Vol. 2)
Antarctic, 2003
1-5 .... 3.00

Neotopia (Vol. 3)
Antarctic, 2004
1-4 .... 3.00

Neotopia (Vol. 4)
Antarctic, 2004
1-5 .... 3.00

Nerve
Nerve, 1987
1-7 .... 2.00
8 .... 4.00

Nervous Rex
Blackthorne, 1985
1-10 .... 2.00

Nestrobber
Blue Sky Blue, 1992
1-2 .... 2.00

Netherworld
Ambition
1 .... 2.00

Netherworlds
Adventure, 1988
1 .... 2.00

Net Prophet: Trouble on Garamond
Penn & Inc.
Ashcan 1 .... 1.00

Neuro Jack
Big, 1996
1 .... 2.00

Neuromancer: The Graphic Novel
Marvel
1 .... 9.00

Neutro
Dell, 1967
1 .... 35.00

Lonely Nights Comics

Loner

Lone Rider

Long Bow

Longshot

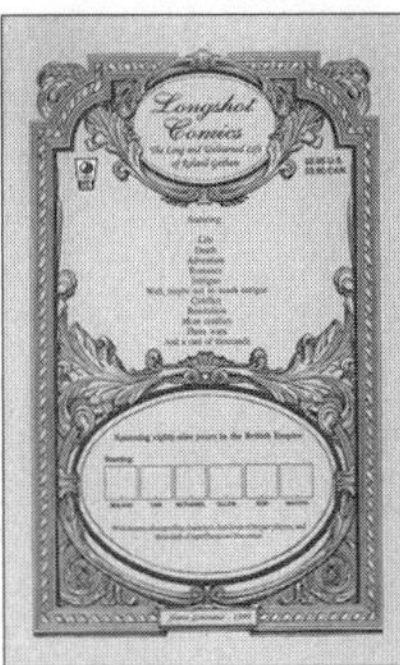
Longshot Comics

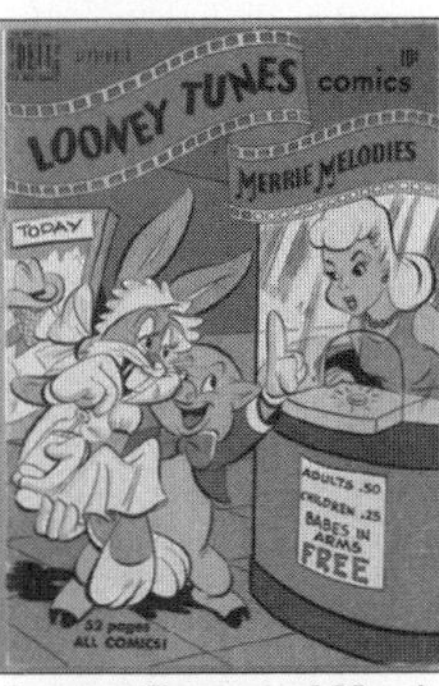

Looney Tunes and Merrie Melodies Comics

Loose Cannon

Nevada
DC, 1998

1-6 .... 3.00

Nevermen
Dark Horse, 2000

1-3 .... 3.00

Nevermen: Streets of Blood
Dark Horse, 2003

1-3 .... 3.00

Neverwhere (Neil Gaiman's)
DC, 2005

1-9 .... 3.00

New Adventure Comics
DC, 1937

12 .... 3,400.00
13 .... 3,200.00
14 .... 2,800.00
15-20 .... 1,975.00
21-22 .... 1,750.00
23-31 .... 1,475.00

New Adventures of Abraham Lincoln
Image

1 .... 20.00

New Adventures of Beauty and the Beast (Disney's...)
Disney, 1992

1-2 .... 2.00

New Adventures of Charlie Chan
DC, 1958

1 .... 425.00
2 .... 275.00
3-6 .... 230.00

New Adventures of Cholly and Flytrap: Till Death Do Us Part
Marvel, 1990

1-3 .... 5.00

New Adventures of Felix the Cat
Felix, 1992

1-7 .... 2.00

New Adventures of Huck Finn
Gold Key, 1968

1 .... 10.00

New Adventures of Jesus
Rip Off

1 .... 5.00

New Adventures of Judo Joe
Ace, 1987

1 .... 2.00

New Adventures of Pinocchio
Dell, 1962

1 .... 65.00
2-3 .... 50.00

New Adventures of Rick O'Shay and Hipshot
Cottonwood

1-2 .... 5.00

New Adventures of Shaloman
Mark 1

1 .... 2.00
2-Special 1 .... 3.00

New Adventures of Speed Racer
Now, 1993

0 .... 4.00
1-3 .... 2.00

New Adventures of Superboy
DC, 1980

1 .... 4.00
1/Whitman 8.00
2 .... 2.00
2/Whitman 3.00
3-4 .... 2.00
4/Whitman 3.00
5 .... 2.00
5/Whitman 3.00
6 .... 2.00
6/Whitman 3.00
7-8 .... 2.00
8/Whitman 3.00
9-20 .... 2.00
21-54 .... 1.00

New Adventures of Terry & the Pirates
Avalon, 1998

1-6 .... 3.00

New Adventures of the Phantom Blot
Gold Key, 1964

1 .... 18.00
2 .... 16.00
3 .... 12.00
4-7 .... 8.00

New Age Comics
Fantagraphics, 1985

1 .... 2.00

New America
Eclipse, 1987

1-4 .... 2.00

New Archies
Archie, 1987

1 .... 3.00
2-5 .... 2.00
6-22 .... 1.00

New Avengers
Marvel, 2005

0/Military 10.00
☛Promo for U.S. troops
1 .... 7.00
1/Retailer ed. 70.00
☛Spider-Man cover
1/DirCut 5.00
1/Quesada 12.00
1/Finch 9.00
1/2nd 3.00
2 .... 2.00
2/Hairsine 45.00
3 .... 2.00
3/Wolverine 45.00
4 .... 3.00
4/Cheung 15.00
4/DF 20.00
5 .... 2.00
5/Granov 15.00
6 .... 2.00
6/Hitch 15.00
7 .... 8.00
7/Adams 25.00
8 .... 3.00
8/Romita 20.00
9 .... 3.00
9/Trimpe 15.00
10-43 .... 3.00
Ann 1 .... 4.00

New Avengers: Illuminati
Marvel, 2007

1 .... 5.00

New Avengers/Illuminati Special
Marvel, 2006

1 .... 14.00

New Avengers: Most Wanted Files
Marvel, 2006

1 .... 4.00

New Beginning
Unicorn

1-3 .... 2.00

New Bondage Fairies
Fantagraphics, 1996

1-12 .... 3.00

New Book of Comics
DC, 1937

1 .... 13,000.00
2 .... 6,500.00

Newcomers Illustrated
Newcomers

1-6 .... 3.00

Newcomers Showcase
Newcomers

1 .... 3.00

New Comics
DC, 1935

1 .... 16,000.00
2 .... 10,000.00
3-7 .... 3,000.00
8-11 .... 2,750.00

New Crew
Personality, 1991

1-10 .... 3.00

New Crime Files of Michael Mauser, Private Eye
Apple, 1992

1 .... 3.00

New DNAgents
Eclipse, 1985

1 .... 2.00
2-17 .... 1.00

New England Gothic
Visigoth, 1986

1-2 .... 2.00

New Eternals
Marvel, 1999

1 .... 4.00

New Excalibur
Marvel, 2006

1-14 .... 3.00

Newforce
Image, 1996

1-4 .... 3.00

New Frontier
Dark Horse, 1992

1-3 .... 3.00

New Frontiers
Evolution, 1989

1-2 .... 2.00

New Fun Comics
DC, 1935

1 .... 46,000.00
☛Becomes More Fun Comics
2 .... 21,000.00
3 .... 12,000.00
4-5 .... 9,000.00
6 .... 24,000.00
☛Becomes More Fun

New Funnies (Walter Lantz...)
Dell, 1942

65 .... 475.00
66-70 .... 255.00
71-75 .... 175.00

Lord Pumpkin

Lords of the Ultra-Realm

Lorelei of the Red Mist

Lorna the Jungle Girl

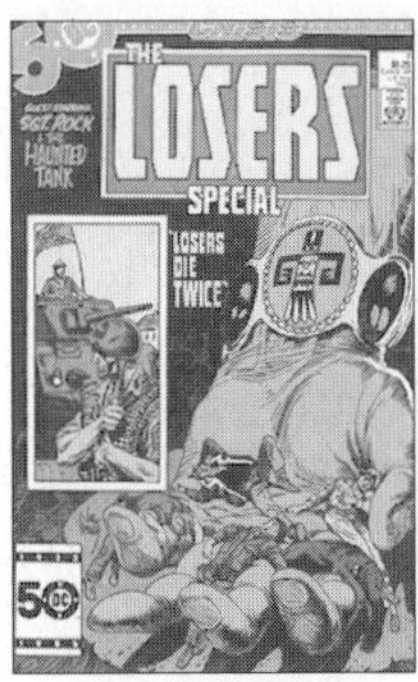

Losers Special

Lost Angel

Lost Continent

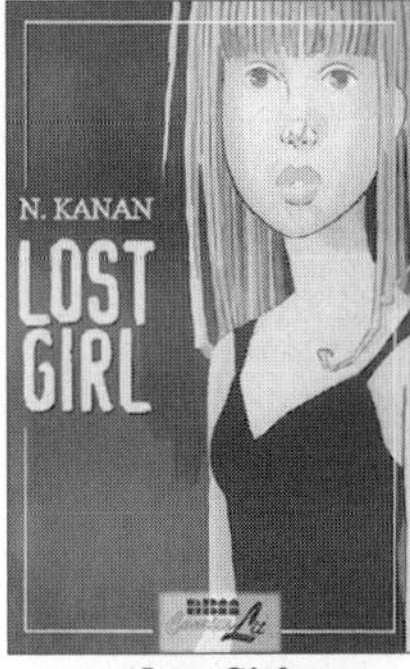

Lost Girl

76 .... 550.00
77-80 .... 145.00
81-90 .... 115.00
91-100 .... 75.00
101-110 .... 54.00
111-120 .... 42.00
121-130 .... 34.00
131-150 .... 26.00
151-170 .... 18.00
171-190 .... 15.00
191-220 .... 12.00
221-240 .... 10.00
241-260 .... 8.00
272-288 .... 6.00

New Gods

DC, 1971

1 .... 35.00
2 .... 18.00
3-11 .... 12.00
12-19 .... 6.00

New Gods

DC, 1984

1-6 .... 2.00

New Gods

DC, 1989

1-28 .... 2.00

New Gods

DC, 1995

1-11 .... 2.00
12 .... 1.00
13-15 .... 2.00

New Gods Secret Files

DC, 1998

1 .... 5.00

New Guardians

DC, 1988

1 .... 2.00
2-12 .... 1.00

New Hat

Black Eye

1 .... 1.00

New Hero Comics

Red Spade

1 .... 1.00

New Horizons

Shanda Fantasy Arts, 1999

1-5 .... 5.00

New Humans

Pied Piper, 1987

1-3 .... 2.00

New Humans

Eternity, 1987

1-17 .... 2.00
Ann 1 .... 3.00

New Justice Machine

Innovation, 1989

1-3 .... 2.00

New Kids on the Block: Backstage Pass

Harvey, 1991

1 .... 1.00

New Kids on the Block: Chillin'

Harvey, 1990

1 .... 2.00
2-7 .... 1.00

New Kids on the Block Comic Tour '90

Harvey, 1991

1 .... 1.00

New Kids on the Block Magic Summer Tour

Harvey, 1991

1 .... 1.00
1/Ltd 4.00

New Kids on the Block: NKOTB

Harvey, 1990

1-5 .... 1.00
6 .... 2.00

New Kids on the Block Step By Step

Harvey, 1991

1 .... 1.00

New Kids on the Block: Valentine Girl

Harvey, 1991

1 .... 1.00

New Love

Fantagraphics, 1996

1-6 .... 3.00

Newman

Image, 1996

1-4 .... 3.00

New Mangaverse

Marvel, 2006

1-4 .... 3.00

Newmen

Image, 1994

1 .... 3.00
2-4 .... 2.00
5-25 .... 3.00

New Mutants

Marvel, 1983

1 .... 6.00
2-24 .... 2.00
25-26 .... 3.00
27-85 .... 2.00
86 .... 3.00
☛Cable cameo
87 .... 6.00
☛1st Cable story
87/2nd 2.00

88 ... 3.00
89-97 ... 2.00
98 ... 5.00
99 ... 3.00
100-100/3rd ... 2.00
Ann 1 ... 3.00
Ann 2 ... 4.00
Ann 3-5 ... 2.00
Ann 6 ... 3.00
Ann 7 ... 2.00
Special 1 ... 3.00
Summer 1 ... 2.00

New Mutants

Marvel, 2003

1 ... 4.00
2-13 ... 3.00

New Mutants: Truth or Death

Marvel, 1997

1-3 ... 3.00

New Night of the Living Dead

Fantaco

0 ... 2.00
1-3 ... 4.00

New Order

Creative Force, 1994

1 ... 3.00

New Paltz Comix

Moods, 1974

1-3 ... 2.00

New Partners in Peril

Blue Comet

1 ... 2.00

New Partners in Peril

Tami

1 ... 2.00

New People

Dell, 1970

1 ... 10.00
2 ... 8.00

New Power Stars

Blue Comet

1 ... 2.00

New Romances

Standard, 1951

5 ... 75.00
6-9 ... 45.00
10 ... 50.00
11 ... 110.00
12-13 ... 40.00
14 ... 50.00
15 ... 40.00
16-17 ... 50.00
18-21 ... 40.00

New Shadowhawk

Image, 1995

1-7 ... 3.00

New Statesmen

Fleetway-Quality

1-5 ... 4.00

Newstime

DC, 1993

1 ... 3.00

Newstralia

Innovation, 1989

1-5 ... 2.00

New Talent Showcase

DC, 1984

1-10 ... 2.00
11-19 ... 1.00

New Teen Titans

DC, 1980

1 ... 8.00
2 ... 10.00
☛1st Deathstroke
3-10 ... 3.00
11-38 ... 2.00
39 ... 3.00
40 ... 2.00
Ann 1 ... 3.00
Ann 2-3 ... 2.00

New Teen Titans

DC, 1984

1-5 ... 3.00
6-49 ... 2.00
Ann 1-4 ... 3.00

New Teen Titans (Giveaways and Promos)

DC

1-5 ... 1.00

New Teen Titans: Terror of Trigon

DC, 2003

1 ... 18.00

New Terrytoons

Dell, 1960

1 ... 45.00
2 ... 22.00
3-8 ... 18.00

New Terrytoons

Gold Key, 1962

1 ... 35.00
2 ... 22.00
3 ... 12.00
4-5 ... 8.00
6-10 ... 6.00
11-20 ... 5.00
21-30 ... 4.00
31-40 ... 3.00
41-54 ... 2.00

Lost Girls

Lost Heroes

Lost Laughter

Lost Planet

Lost Worlds

Louie the Rune Soldier

Love Adventures

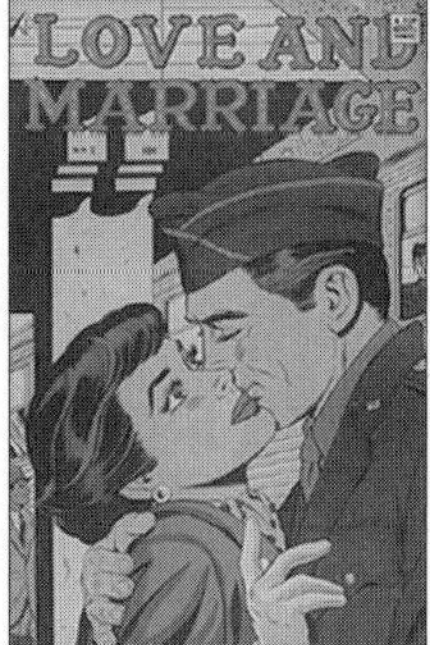

Love and Marriage

New Thunderbolts
Marvel, 2004

1-18 .... 3.00

New Titans
DC, 1988

0-59 .... 2.00
60-61 .... 3.00
62-99 .... 2.00
100 .... 3.00
101-124 .... 2.00
125 .... 4.00
126-130 .... 2.00
Ann 5-7 .... 4.00
Ann 8-10 .... 3.00
Ann 11 .... 4.00

New Triumph Featuring Northguard
Matrix, 1985

1-5 .... 2.00

New Two-Fisted Tales
E.C.

1 .... 6.00

New Two-Fisted Tales
Dark Horse, 1993

1 .... 5.00

newuniversal
Marvel, 2006

1 .... 8.00
2 .... 6.00
3 .... 4.00

New Vampire Miyu (Vol. 1)
Ironcat, 1997

1-6 .... 3.00

New Vampire Miyu (Vol. 2)
Ironcat, 1998

1-6 .... 3.00

New Vampire Miyu (Vol. 3)
Ironcat, 1998

1-7 .... 3.00

New Vampire Miyu (Vol. 4)
Ironcat, 1999

1-6 .... 3.00

New Warriors
Marvel, 1990

1 .... 2.00
1/2nd-24 .... 1.00
25 .... 3.00
26-40 .... 1.00
40/Variant 2.00
41-47 .... 1.00
48-50 .... 2.00
50/Variant 3.00
51-59 .... 2.00
60 .... 3.00
61-75 .... 2.00
Ann 1 .... 3.00
Ann 2 .... 2.00
Ann 3-4 .... 3.00
Ashcan 1 .... 1.00

New Warriors
Marvel, 1999

1-10 .... 3.00

New Warrior
Marvel, 2005

1 .... 4.00
2-6 .... 3.00

New Wave
Eclipse, 1986

1-3 .... 2.00
4-8 .... 1.00
9-13 .... 2.00

New Wave Versus The Volunteers
Eclipse, 1987

1-2 .... 3.00

New World Order
Blazer, 1992

1-8 .... 3.00

New World Order
Pig's Eye

1 .... 1.00

New Worlds Anthology
Caliber, 1996

1 .... 3.00
2-6 .... 4.00

New X-Men (Academy X)
Marvel, 2004

1 .... 4.00
2-16 .... 3.00
☛House of M
16/Variant 4.00
17-43 .... 3.00
44-45 .... 6.00
46 .... 3.00

New X-Men: Academy X Yearbook Special
Marvel, 2005

1 .... 4.00

New X-Men: Hellions
Marvel, 2005

1 .... 4.00
2-4 .... 3.00

New York, the Big City
Kitchen Sink

1 .... 14.00

New York, the Big City
DC, 2000
1 .... 13.00

New York City Outlaws
Outlaw, 1984
1-4 .... 2.00

New York World's Fair Comics
DC, 1939
1939 .... 25,500.00
1940 .... 15,500.00

New York: Year Zero
Eclipse, 1988
1-4 .... 2.00

Next
DC, 2006
1-6 .... 3.00

Next Exit
Slave Labor, 2004
1-6 .... 3.00

Next Man
Comico, 1985
1-5 .... 2.00

Next Men (John Byrne's...)
Dark Horse, 1992
0-20 .... 3.00
21 .... 30.00
☛Hellboy appears
22-30 .... 3.00

Next Nexus
First, 1989
1-4 .... 2.00

Nextwave
Marvel, 2006
1-11 .... 3.00

Next Wave
Overstreet
1 .... 2.00

Nextworld
Dark Horse, 2003
1-2 .... 0.00

Nexus: Alien Justice
Dark Horse, 1992
1-3 .... 4.00

Nexus Legends
First, 1989
1 .... 3.00
2-23 .... 2.00

Nexus Meets Madman
Dark Horse, 1996
1 .... 3.00

Nexus the Liberator
Dark Horse, 1992
1-4 .... 3.00

Nexus: The Origin
Dark Horse, 1995
1 .... 4.00

Nexus: The Wages of Sin
Dark Horse, 1995
1-4 .... 3.00

Nexus
Capital, 1981
1 .... 15.00
2 .... 10.00
3 .... 15.00

Nexus
First, 1983
1 .... 5.00
2 .... 4.00
3-5 .... 3.00
6-49 .... 2.00
50 .... 4.00
51-80 .... 2.00
81-84 .... 4.00
85-98 .... 3.00

NFL Superpro
Marvel, 1991
1-12 .... 1.00
Special 1 .... 2.00
Special 1/Prest 4.00

Nickel Comics
Dell, 1938
1 .... 400.00

Nickel Comics
Fawcett, 1940
1/Ash 0.00
1 .... 2,500.00
2 .... 1,000.00
3 .... 850.00
4 .... 625.00
5-7 .... 600.00
8 .... 700.00

Nick Fury, Agent of SHIELD
Marvel, 1968
1 .... 75.00
2-5 .... 40.00
6-8 .... 30.00
9-13 .... 25.00
14 .... 20.00
15 .... 50.00
☛1st Bullseye
16-18 .... 20.00

Nick Fury, Agent of SHIELD
Marvel, 1983
1-2 .... 3.00

Nick Fury, Agent of S.H.I.E.L.D.
Marvel, 1989
1-47 .... 2.00

Love and Romance

Love at First Sight

Love Bites

Love Bomb

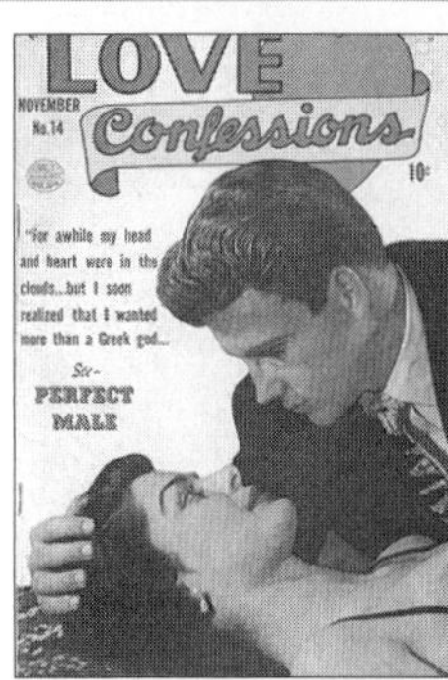

Love Confessions

Love Experiences

Love Fantasy

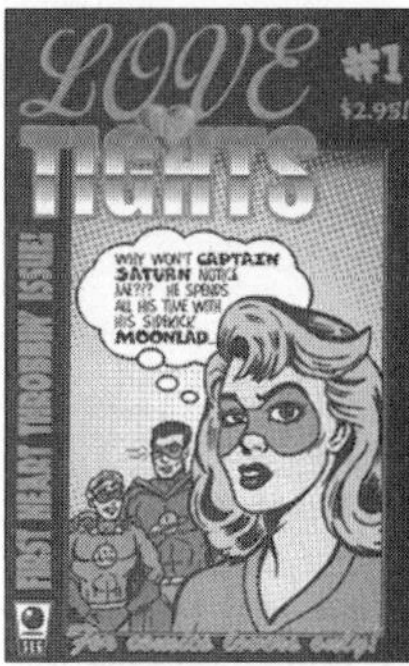

Love in Tights

Nick Fury's Howling Commandos

Marvel, 2005

1 .... 3.00
1/DirCut 4.00
2-6 .... 3.00

Nick Fury vs. S.H.I.E.L.D.

Marvel, 1988

1-6 .... 4.00

Nick Halliday

Argo, 1955

1 .... 40.00

Nick Hazard

Harrier, 1988

1 .... 2.00

Nicki Shadow

Relentless, 1997

0 .... 1.00
1 .... 3.00

Nick Noyz and the Nuisance Tour Book

Red Bullet

1 .... 3.00

Nick Ryan the Skull

Antarctic, 1994

1-3 .... 3.00

Night

Jester Press, 2005

1 .... 3.00

Night

Slave Labor, 1995

0 .... 2.00

Nightbird

Harrier, 1988

1-2 .... 2.00

Night Breed (Clive Barker's)

Marvel, 1990

1-10 .... 3.00
11-19 .... 2.00
20-25 .... 3.00

Night Brigade

Wonder Comix, 1987

1 .... 2.00

Nightcat

Marvel, 1991

1 .... 4.00

Night City

Thorby

1 .... 3.00

Night Club

Image, 2005

1-4 .... 3.00

Nightcrawler (Vol. 1)

Marvel, 1985

1-4 .... 2.00

Nightcrawler (Vol. 2)

Marvel, 2002

1-4 .... 3.00

Nightcrawler (Vol. 3)

Marvel, 2004

1-12 .... 3.00

Nightcry

CFD, 1995

1-6 .... 3.00

NightfalL: The Black Chronicles

Homage, 1999

1-3 .... 3.00

Night Fisher

Fantagraphics, 2005

1 .... 13.00

Night Force

DC, 1982

1 .... 3.00
2-14 .... 2.00

Night Force

DC, 1996

1 .... 3.00
2-11 .... 2.00
12 .... 3.00

Night Glider

Topps, 1993

1 .... 3.00

Nighthawk

Marvel, 1998

1-3 .... 3.00

Night in a Moorish Harem, A

NBM

1 .... 12.00
2 .... 11.00

Nightjar (Alan Moore's)

Avatar, 2004

1 .... 3.00
☛Alan Moore series
1/Platinum 10.00
1/Wraparound 3.00
1/Tarot 4.00
2 .... 3.00
2/Platinum 10.00
2/Wraparound 4.00
3 .... 3.00
3/Platinum 10.00
3/Wraparound-4 .... 4.00
4/Tarot 5.00

Nightjar: Hollow Bones
Avatar, 2004

1 .... 4.00
1/Platinum 10.00
1/Wraparound 4.00

Night Life
Strawberry Jam, 1987

1-7 .... 2.00
8 .... 3.00

Nightlinger
Gauntlet

1-2 .... 3.00

Nightly News
Image, 2006

1-2 .... 3.00

Night Man
Malibu, 1993

1 .... 3.00
1/Ltd. 25.00
2-15 .... 2.00
16 .... 4.00
17-23 .... 3.00
Ann 1 .... 4.00

Night Man
Malibu, 1995

0-4 .... 2.00

Night Man/Gambit
Malibu, 1996

1-3 .... 2.00

Night Man vs. Wolverine
Malibu, 1995

0 .... 5.00

Nightmare
St. John, 1953

10 .... 330.00
11 .... 230.00
12 .... 210.00
13 .... 155.00

Nightmare (Magazine)
Skywald, 1971

1 .... 65.00
2 .... 40.00
3-5 .... 35.00
6 .... 40.00
7 .... 20.00
8-9 .... 35.00
10 .... 40.00
11-19 .... 15.00
20 .... 40.00
21-Ann 1 .... 15.00

Nightmare (Alex Niño's...)
Innovation, 1989

1 .... 2.00

Nightmare
Marvel, 1994

1-4 .... 2.00

Nightmare!
Portman

1 .... 5.00
2 .... 4.00

Nightmare & Casper
Harvey, 1963

1 .... 60.00
2-5 .... 35.00

Nightmare on Elm Street
DC, 2006

1-4 .... 3.00

Nightmare on Elm Street, A (Freddy Krueger's...)
Marvel

1 .... 3.00

Nightmare on Elm Street: The Beginning
Innovation

1-2 .... 3.00

Nightmares
Eclipse, 1985

1-2 .... 2.00

Nightmares & Fairy Tales
Slave Labor, 2002

1 .... 8.00
2 .... 6.00
3-6 .... 5.00
7-14 .... 3.00

Nightmares on Elm Street
Innovation, 1991

1-6 .... 3.00

Nightmare Theater
Chaos!, 1997

1-4 .... 3.00

Nightmare Walker
Boneyard, 1996

1 .... 3.00

Nightmark
Alpha Productions

1 .... 2.00

Nightmark: Blood & Honor
Alpha, 1994

1-3 .... 3.00

Nightmark Mystery Special
Alpha

1 .... 3.00

Night Mary
Idea & Design Works, 2005

1-5 .... 4.00

Nightmask
Marvel, 1986

1-12 .... 1.00

Love Journal

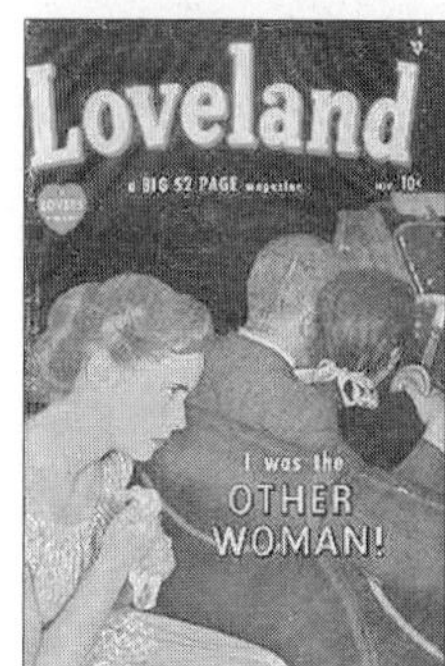

Loveland

Love Lessons

Love Letters

Lovelorn

Lovely Prudence

Love Problems

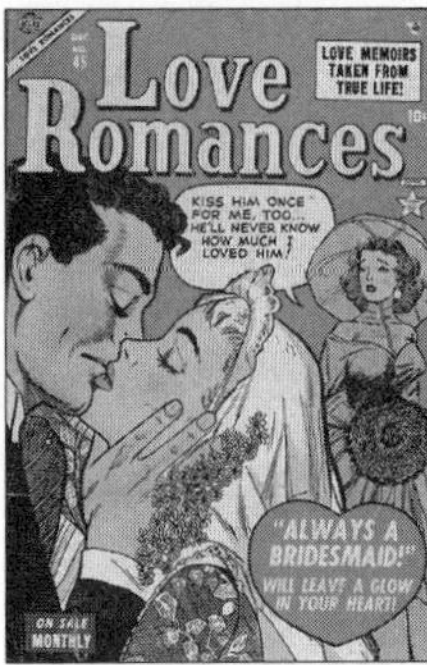

Love Romances

Night Masters
Custom Pic, 1986

1-6 .... 2.00

Night Music
Eclipse, 1984

1-7 .... 2.00
8 .... 4.00
9-11 .... 5.00

Night Nurse
Marvel, 1972

1 .... 110.00
2-4 .... 50.00

Night of Mystery
Avon, 1953

1 .... 275.00

Night of the Living Dead
Fantaco, 1991

0 .... 2.00
1-2 .... 5.00
3-4 .... 6.00

Night of the Living Deadline USA
Dark Horse, 1992

1 .... 3.00

Night of the Living Dead: Aftermath
Fantaco

1 .... 2.00

Night of the Living Dead: London
Fantaco

1-2 .... 6.00

Night of the Living Dead: Prelude
Fantaco, 1991

1 .... 2.00

Night Raven: House of Cards
Marvel, 1991

1 .... 6.00

Night Rider
Marvel, 1974

1 .... 25.00
2-6 .... 10.00

Night's Children
Fantaco

1-4 .... 4.00

Night's Children: Double Indemnity
Fantaco

1 .... 8.00

Night's Children Erotic Fantasies
Fantaco

1 .... 5.00

Night's Children: Foreplay
Fantaco

1 .... 5.00

Night's Children: The Vampire
Millennium

1-2 .... 3.00

Night's Children: Vampyr!
Fantaco

1-3 .... 4.00

Nightshade
No Mercy, 1997

1 .... 3.00

Nightshades
London Night

1 .... 3.00

Nightside
Marvel, 2001

1-4 .... 3.00

Nights into Dreams
Archie, 1998

1-6 .... 2.00

Nightstalkers
Marvel, 1992

1 .... 1.00
1/CS 3.00
2-18 .... 2.00

Nightstreets
Arrow, 1986

1 .... 3.00
2-5 .... 2.00

Night Terrors
Chanting Monks, 2000

1 .... 3.00

Night Thrasher
Marvel, 1993

1 .... 3.00
2-21 .... 2.00

Night Thrasher: Four Control
Marvel, 1992

1-4 .... 2.00

Night Tribes
DC, 1999

1 .... 5.00

Night Trippers
Image, 2006

1 .... 17.00

Nightveil
AC, 1984

1-Special 1 .... 2.00

Nightveil's Cauldron of Horror
AC, 1991

1-3 .... 3.00

Nightvenger
Axis, 1994
Ashcan 1 .... 2.00

Nightvision
Rebel, 1996
1-4 .... 3.00

Nightvision: All About Eve
London Night, 1996
1 .... 3.00

Nightvision (Atomeka)
Atomeka
1 .... 3.00

Night Vixen
ABC
0/A 3.00
0/B-0/C 4.00

Night Walker
Fleetway-Quality
1-3 .... 3.00

Night Warriors: Darkstalkers' Revenge the Comic Series
Viz, 1998
1-6 .... 3.00

Nightwatch
Marvel, 1994
1 .... 2.00
1/Variant 3.00
2-12 .... 2.00

Nightwing
DC, 1995
1 .... 4.00
2-4 .... 3.00

Nightwing
DC, 1996
½ 4.00
½/Platinum 7.00
1 .... 11.00
2 .... 6.00
3-5 .... 4.00
6-15 .... 3.00
16-49 .... 2.00
50 .... 4.00
51-98 .... 2.00
99 .... 3.00
100 .... 4.00
101 .... 6.00
102 .... 5.00
103-104 .... 6.00
105 .... 5.00
106 .... 6.00
107-108 .... 2.00
109-128 .... 3.00
1000000 .... 2.00
Ann 1 .... 5.00
GS 1 .... 6.00

Nightwing: Alfred's Return
DC, 1995
1 .... 4.00

Nightwing and Huntress
DC, 1998
1-4 .... 2.00

Nightwing: Our Worlds at War
DC, 2001
1 .... 3.00

Nightwing Secret Files
DC, 1999
1 .... 5.00

Nightwing: The Target
DC, 2001
1 .... 6.00

Nightwing: Ties that Bind
DC
1 .... 13.00

Nightwolf
Devil's Due, 2006
0 .... 1.00
2-3 .... 3.00

Nightwolf
Entropy
1-2 .... 2.00

Night Zero
Fleetway-Quality
1-4 .... 2.00

Nikki Blade Summer Fun
ABC
1/A-1/B 3.00

Nimrod
Fantagraphics, 1998
1-2 .... 3.00

Nina's All-Time Greatest Collectors' Item Classic Comics
Dark Horse, 1992
1 .... 3.00

Nina's New & Improved All-Time Greatest Collectors' Item Classic Comics
Dark Horse, 1994
1 .... 3.00

9-11: Emergency Relief
Alternative, 2002
1 .... 15.00

Nine Lives of Felix the Cat
Harvey, 1991
1-5 .... 2.00

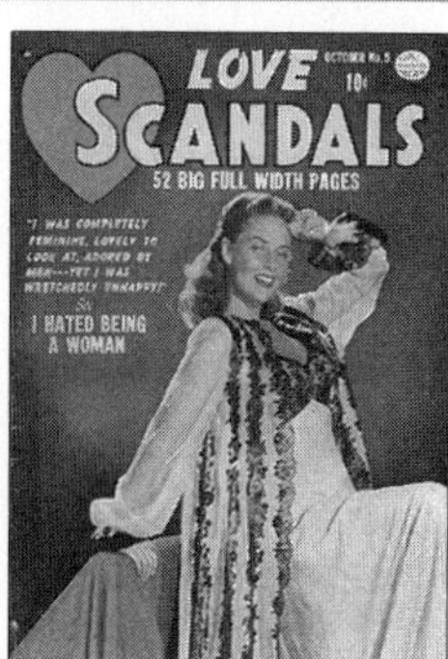

Love Scandals

Love Sucks

Love Tales

L.T. Caper

Luba

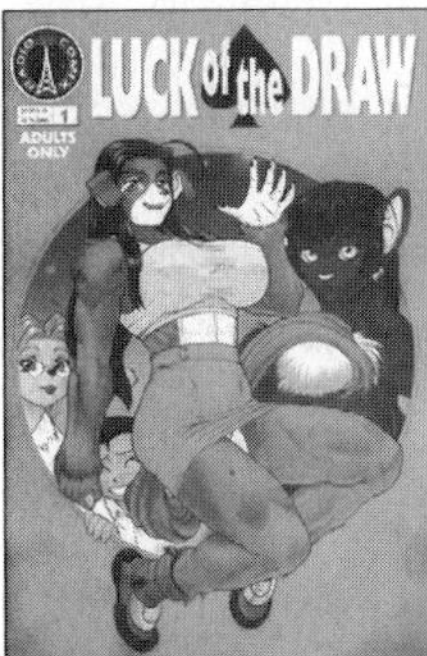

Luck of the Draw

Lucky Comics

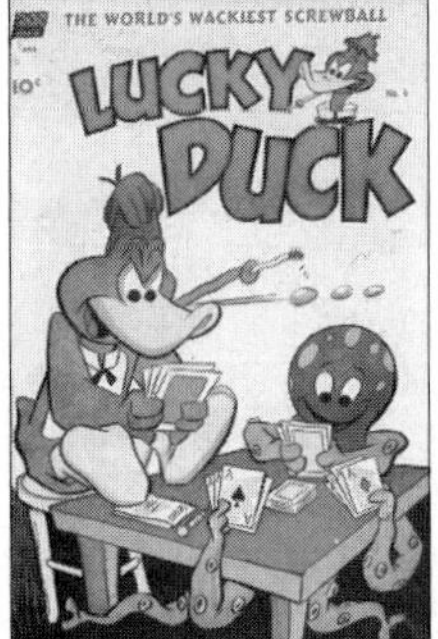

Lucky Duck

Nine Lives of Leather Cat

Forbidden Fruit, 1993

1-6 .... 4.00

Nine Rings of Wu-Tang

Image, 1999

0 .... 2.00
1/A 4.00
1/B 5.00
2-5 .... 3.00

1984 Magazine

Warren, 1978

1 .... 6.00
2-10 .... 4.00

1994 Magazine

Warren, 1980

11-29 .... 3.00

1963

Image, 1993

1 .... 2.00
1/BR 3.00
1/Gold 5.00
1/Silver 3.00
2-6 .... 2.00

Ninety-Nine Girls

Fantagraphics, 1991

1 .... 2.00

Nine Volt

Image, 1997

1-4 .... 3.00

Ninja

Eternity, 1986

1-Special 1 .... 2.00

Ninja-Bots Super Special

Pied Piper

1 .... 2.00

Ninja Boy

DC, 2001

1 .... 4.00
2-6 .... 3.00
Ashcan 1 .... 1.00

Ninja Elite

Adventure, 1987

1-8 .... 2.00

Ninja Funnies

Eternity, 1987

1-5 .... 2.00

Ninja High School

Antarctic, 1987

0 .... 3.00
0/Ltd. 4.00
1 .... 7.00
1/2nd 3.00
2 .... 5.00
2/2nd 2.00
3 .... 4.00
3/2nd 2.00
4 .... 4.00
4/2nd 2.00
5-6 .... 4.00
6/2nd 2.00
7-10 .... 4.00
11-22 .... 3.00
23-31 .... 2.00
32-49 .... 3.00
50 .... 4.00
51-99 .... 3.00
100 .... 5.00
101-115 .... 4.00
116-160 .... 3.00
YB 1 .... 6.00
YB 2-4 .... 5.00
YB 5- 9/B 4.00
YB 10/A-Summer 1 .... 3.00
3D 1 .... 5.00

Ninja High School in Color

Eternity, 1992

1-3 .... 3.00
4-13 .... 2.00

Ninja High School Perfect Memory

Antarctic, 1993

1 .... 5.00
1/2nd-2 .... 6.00
2/Platinum 5.00

Ninja High School Spotlight

Antarctic, 1996

1 .... 4.00
2 .... 3.00
3 .... 4.00
4 .... 3.00

Ninja High School Swimsuit Special

Antarctic, 1992

1-1996 .... 4.00

Ninja High School Talks About Comic Book Printing

Antarctic

1 .... 1.00

Ninja High School Talks About Sexually Transmitted Diseases

Antarctic

1 .... 2.00

Ninja High School: The Prom Formula

Antarctic, 2004

1 .... 6.00

Ninja High School: The Prom Formula

Eternity, 1989

1-2 .... 3.00

Ninja High School: The Special Edition
Eternity
1-4 .... 3.00

Ninja High School Version 2
Antarctic, 1999
1-2 .... 3.00

Ninjak
Valiant, 1994
0 .... 3.00
0/A 4.00
1 .... 2.00
1/Gold 20.00
2-3 .... 1.00
4 .... 2.00
5-11 .... 1.00
12-13 .... 2.00
14 .... 1.00
15-24 .... 2.00
25 .... 3.00
26 .... 5.00
YB 1 .... 3.00

Ninjak
Acclaim, 1996
1-12 .... 3.00
Ashcan 1 .... 1.00

Ninja Scroll
DC, 2006
1-4 .... 3.00

Ninjutsu, Art of the Ninja
Solson
1 .... 2.00

Nintendo Comics System
Valiant, 1990
1-2 .... 5.00

Nintendo Comics System
Valiant, 1991
1-9 .... 2.00

N.I.O.
Acclaim, 1998
1 .... 3.00

Nira X: Anime
Entity, 1997
0 .... 3.00

Nira X: Annual
Express, 1996
1/A 3.00
1/B 10.00

Nira X: Cyberangel
Express, 1994
1-4 .... 3.00
Ashcan 1 .... 1.00

Nira X: Cyberangel
Express, 1994
1 .... 3.00
1/Ltd. 4.00
2-4 .... 3.00

Nira X: Cyberangel
Express
1 .... 3.00

Nira X: Cyberangel - Cynder: Endangered Species
Express
1 .... 3.00
1/Ltd. 13.00

Nira X: Exodus
Avatar, 1997
1 .... 3.00

Nira X: Heatwave
Express, 1995
1 .... 4.00
2-3 .... 3.00

Nira X: Soul Skurge
Express, 1996
1 .... 3.00

Noah's Ark
Barbour
1 .... 2.00

Noble Armour Halberder (John and Jason Waltrip's...)
Academy, 1997
1 .... 3.00

Noble Causes: Extended Family One Shot
Image, 2003
1 .... 7.00

Noble Causes
Image, 2002
1/A-1/B 5.00
2/A-4/B 3.00
5 .... 4.00

Noble Causes: Distant Relatives
Image, 2003
1-4 .... 3.00

Noble Causes: Family Secrets
Image, 2002
1-4/B 3.00

Noble Causes: First Impressions
Image, 2001
1 .... 3.00

Noble Causes
Image, 2004
1/A-24 .... 4.00

Lucky Star

Lucy Show

Luger

Lunatic Binge

Lunatik

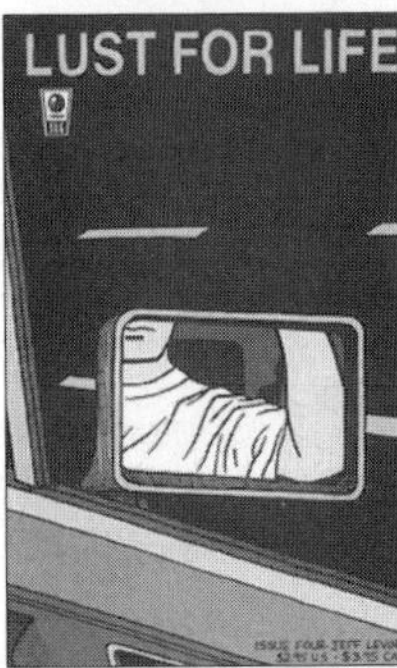

Lust for Life

Lycanthrope Leo

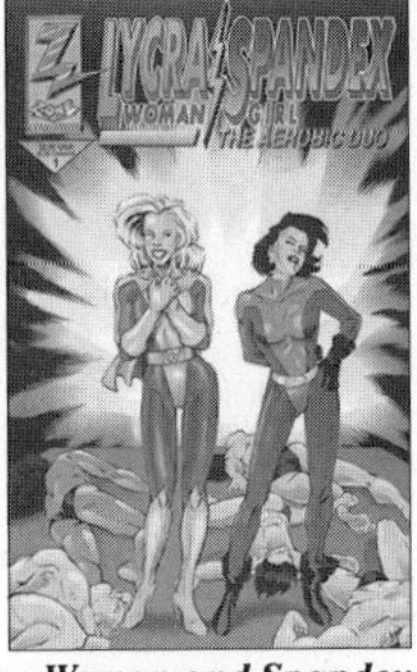

Lycra-Woman and Spandex-Girl

Nobody
Oni, 1998

1-4 ....3.00

No Business Like Show Business
3-D Zone

1 ....3.00

Nocturnal Emissions
Vortex

1 ....3.00

Nocturnals
Malibu, 1995

1 ....4.00
2-6 ....3.00

Nocturnals: Troll Bridge
Oni, 2000

1 ....5.00

Nocturnals: Witching Hour
Dark Horse, 1998

1 ....5.00

Nocturne
Aircel, 1991

1-3 ....3.00

Nocturne
Marvel, 1995

1-4 ....2.00

Nodwick
Henchman, 2000

1-30 ....3.00

No Escape
Marvel, 1994

1-3 ....2.00

Nog the Protector of the Pyramides
Onli

1 ....2.00

No Guts or Glory
Fantaco, 1991

1 ....3.00

No Honor
Image, 2000

0-4 ....3.00

No Hope
Slave Labor, 1993

1-9 ....3.00

Noid in 3-D
Blackthorne

1-2 ....3.00

No Illusions
Comics Defence Fund

1 ....1.00

Noir
Alpha, 1994

1 ....4.00

Noir
Creative Force, 1995

1 ....5.00

No Justice, No Piece!
Head, 1997

1-2 ....3.00

Nolan Ryan
Celebrity

1 ....3.00

Nolan Ryan's 7 No-Hitters
Revolutionary, 1993

1 ....3.00

Nomad
Marvel, 1990

1-4 ....2.00

Nomad
Marvel, 1992

1 ....3.00
2-25 ....2.00

Noman
Tower, 1966

1 ....40.00
2 ....28.00

No Man's Land
Tundra

1 ....15.00

Non
Red Ink

1-3 ....3.00

No Need for Tenchi! Part 1
Viz

1-7 ....3.00

No Need for Tenchi! Part 2
Viz

1-7 ....3.00

No Need for Tenchi! Part 3
Viz, 1996

1-6 ....3.00

No Need for Tenchi! Part 4
Viz, 1997

1-6 ....3.00

No Need for Tenchi! Part 5
Viz, 1998

1-5 ....3.00

No Need for Tenchi! Part 6
Viz, 1998

1-5 ....3.00

No Need for Tenchi! Part 7

Viz, 1999

1-6 .... 3.00

No Need for Tenchi! Part 8

Viz, 1999

1-5 .... 3.00

No Need For Tenchi! Part 9

Viz, 1998

1-6 .... 3.00

No Need for Tenchi! Part 10

Viz, 2001

1-7 .... 3.00

No Need For Tenchi! Part 11

Viz, 2001

1-4 .... 4.00

No Need For Tenchi! Part 12

Viz, 2001

1-6 .... 3.00

No Ninja Man

Custom Pic

1-1/2nd 2.00

No No UFO

Antarctic, 1996

1-4 .... 3.00

Noodle Fighter Miki

ADV Manga, 2005

1 .... 10.00

No Pasaran!

NBM

1 .... 14.00
2 .... 12.00

No Profit for the Wise

CFD, 1996

1 .... 3.00

Norb

Mu, 1992

1 .... 9.00

Normalman

Aardvark-Vanaheim, 1984

1 .... 3.00
2-12 .... 2.00
3D 1 .... 3.00

Normalman 3-D

Renegade, 1986

1 .... 2.00

Normalman-Megaton Man Special

Image, 1994

1 .... 3.00

Northern's Hemisphere

Northern's Hemisphere

5-7 .... 2.00

Northern's Hemisphere Undisguised

Northern's Hemisphere

1 .... 3.00

Northguard: The Mandes Conclusion

Caliber, 1989

1-3 .... 2.00

Northstar

Marvel, 1994

1-4 .... 2.00

Northstar Presents

Northstar, 1994

1-2 .... 3.00

Northwest Cartoon Cookery

Starhead, 1995

1 .... 3.00

Northwest Mounties

St. John, 1948

1 .... 285.00
2 .... 220.00
3-4 .... 230.00

Northwest Passage

NBM, 2005

1 .... 6.00

Nosferatu

Dark Horse, 1991

1 .... 4.00

Nosferatu

Tome, 1991

1-2 .... 3.00

Nosferatu, Plague of Terror

Millennium

1-4 .... 3.00

Nosferatu: The Death Mass

Antarctic, 1997

1-4 .... 3.00

Nostalgic Mad

E.C.

1 .... 5.00
2 .... 4.00

Nostradamus Chronicles: 1559-1821

Tome

1 .... 3.00

Lycra Woman and Spandex Girl Jurassic Dinosaur Special

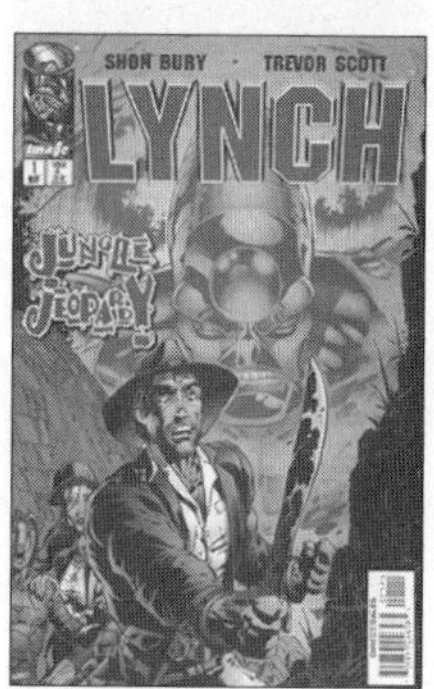

Lynch

Lynch Mob

M

Macabre

M.A.C.H. 1

Machine Man

Macross II

Not Approved Crime
Avalon
1 ....3.00

Not Brand Echh
Marvel, 1967
1 ....45.00
2 ....18.00
3-5 ....15.00
6-8 ....10.00
☛Giant issues start
9-13 ....25.00

Notenki Memoirs
ADV Manga, 2005
1 ....10.00

No Time for Sergeants
Dell, 1965
1-2 ....40.00
3 ....30.00

(Not Only) The Best of Wonder Wart-Hog
Print Mint, 1973
1 ....15.00
2-3 ....12.00

Not Quite Dead
Rip Off, 1993
1-4 ....3.00

Nova
Marvel, 1976
1 ....8.00
2 ....4.00
3-10 ....3.00
10/35¢ 15.00
11 ....3.00
11/35¢ 15.00
12 ....3.00
12/35¢ 15.00
13 ....3.00
13/35¢ 15.00
14 ....3.00
14/35¢ 15.00
15-25 ....3.00

Nova
Marvel, 1994
1 ....2.00
1/Variant 3.00
2-18 ....2.00

Nova
Marvel, 1999
1 ....3.00
2-7 ....2.00

Nova Hunter
Ryal
1 ....3.00

Novavolo
Jungle Boy, 2000
1-Ann 2001 ....4.00

Now Comics Preview
Now
1 ....1.00

Nowheresville
Caliber, 1995
1 ....4.00

Nowheresville: Death By Starlight
Caliber
1-4 ....3.00

Nowheresville: The History of Cool
Caliber
1 ....3.00

Now, on a More Serious Note...
Dawn, 1994
1 ....2.00

Now We Are Sick
Dreamhaven
1 ....12.00

Now What?!
Now
1 ....3.00
2-11 ....2.00

Nth Man, the Ultimate Ninja
Marvel, 1989
1-16 ....1.00

Nuance
Magnetic Ink
1-3 ....3.00

Nuclear War!
NEC, 2000
1-2 ....4.00

Nukla
Dell, 1965
1 ....12.00
2 ....8.00
3 ....6.00
4 ....10.00

Null Patrol
Escape Velocity
1-2 ....2.00

Numidian Force
Kamite, 1991
4 ....2.00

Nurse Betsy Crane
Charlton, 1961
12 ....15.00
13-20 ....12.00
21-27 ....10.00

Nursery Rhymes
Ziff-Davis, 1951
10 ....75.00

Nurses

Gold Key, 1963

1 .... 50.00
2 .... 40.00
3 .... 30.00

Nurture the Devil

Fantagraphics, 1994

2-3 .... 3.00

Nut Runners

Rip Off, 1991

1-2 .... 3.00

Nuts!

Premiere, 1954

1 .... 175.00
2-5 .... 120.00

Nuts & Bots

Excel Graphics, 1998

1 .... 4.00

Nutty Comics

Harvey, 1946

1 .... 0.00
4 .... 50.00
5-8 .... 40.00

Nutty Comics

Fawcett, 1946

1 .... 80.00

Nutty Life

Fox, 1946

2 .... 60.00

NYC Mech

Image, 2004

1-6 .... 3.00

NYC Mech: Beta Love

Image, 2005

1-2 .... 4.00
3-5 .... 3.00

Nyght School

Brainstorm, 1997

2 .... 3.00

Nyoka the Jungle Girl

Fawcett, 1945

2 .... 500.00
3 .... 275.00
4-5 .... 200.00
6-10 .... 160.00
11-20 .... 124.00
21-22 .... 92.00
23 .... 9.00
24-25 .... 29.00
26-30 .... 92.00
31-40 .... 72.00
41-50 .... 56.00
51-60 .... 46.00
61-77 .... 40.00

Nyoka the Jungle Girl

Charlton, 1955

14-22 .... 32.00

NYX

Marvel, 2003

1 .... 9.00
1/Variant 8.00
2 .... 7.00
2/Variant 5.00
3 .... 45.00
☛Wolvie's clone
4 .... 9.00
5 .... 4.00
6-7 .... 3.00

Oak

Fat Cat

1-3 .... 3.00

Oaky Doaks

Eastern Color, 1942

1 .... 210.00

Obergeist: Ragnarok Highway

Image, 2001

1-6 .... 3.00

Obergeist: The Empty Locket

Dark Horse, 2002

1 .... 3.00

Obie

Store, 1953

1 .... 20.00

Objective Five

Image, 2000

1-6 .... 3.00

Oblivion

Comico, 1995

1-3 .... 3.00

Oblivion City

Slave Labor, 1991

1-8 .... 3.00
9 .... 4.00

Obnoxio the Clown

Marvel, 1983

1 .... 2.00

Occult Crimes Taskforce

Image, 2006

1-2 .... 3.00

Occult Files of Dr. Spektor

Gold Key, 1973

1 .... 32.00
2-5 .... 14.00
6-10 .... 8.00
11-13 .... 5.00
14 .... 9.00
☛Solar app.
15-17 .... 5.00
18 .... 7.00
☛Solar app.
19-20 .... 5.00
21-22 .... 3.00

Mad

Mad About Millie

Madame Xanadu

Mad-Dog

Mad Dogs

Mad Hatter

Mad House

Madhouse Glads

23 .... 7.00
☛Solar app.
24 .... 3.00
25 .... 10.00
☛Whitman only

Occult Laff-Parade
Print Mint, 1973
1 .... 3.00

Ocean
DC, 2004
1-6 .... 3.00

Ocean Comics
Ocean
1 .... 2.00

Ocelot
Fantagraphics
1-3 .... 3.00

Octavia
-Ism, 2004
1-3 .... 3.00

Octavia Trilogy
-Ism, 2005
1 .... 6.00

October Yen
Antarctic, 1996
1 .... 4.00
2-3 .... 3.00

Octobriana
Revolution
1 .... 4.00
2-5 .... 3.00

Octobriana: Filling in the Blanks
Artful Salamander, 1998
1 .... 3.00

Odd Adventure-Zine
Zamboni, 1997
1-4 .... 3.00

Oddballs
NBM, 2002
1-7 .... 3.00

Oddballz
NBM, 2002
1-4 .... 3.00

Oddjob
Slave Labor, 1999
1 .... 3.00

Oddly Normal
Viper, 2005
1-4 .... 3.00

Odd Tales
-Ism, 2004
1-4 .... 4.00

Oeming Sketchbook
Michael Avon Oeming
1 .... 5.00

Of Bitter Souls
Speakeasy Comics, 2005
1-2 .... 3.00

Offcastes
Marvel, 1993
1 .... 3.00
2-3 .... 2.00

Offerings
Cry for Dawn, 1993
1-2 .... 3.00

Official, Authorized Zen Intergalactic Ninja Sourcebook
Express
1-1/2nd 4.00

Official Buz Sawyer
Pioneer, 1988
1-5 .... 2.00

Official Crisis on Infinite Earths Index
Eclipse, 1986
1 .... 2.00

Official Handbook of the Conan Universe
Marvel, 1986
1 .... 2.00
2 .... 1.00

Official Handbook of the Invincible Universe
Image, 2007
1 .... 5.00

Official Handbook of the Marvel Universe
Marvel, 1983
1-15 .... 2.00

Official Handbook of the Marvel Universe
Marvel, 1985
1-20 .... 2.00

Official Handbook of the Marvel Universe
Marvel, 1989
1-8 .... 2.00

Official Handbook of the Marvel Universe Master Edition
Marvel, 1990
1-5 .... 5.00
6-12 .... 4.00
13-36 .... 5.00

Official Handbook of the Marvel Universe: Alternate Universes 2005

Marvel, 2005

1 .... 4.00

Official Handbook of the Marvel Universe: Avengers 2005

Marvel, 2005

1 .... 4.00

Official Handbook of the Marvel Universe: Book of the Dead 2004

Marvel, 2004

1 .... 4.00

Official Handbook of the Marvel Universe Daredevil Elektra 2004

Marvel, 2004

1 .... 4.00

Official Handbook of the Marvel Universe: Fantastic Four 2005

Marvel, 2005

1 .... 4.00

Official Handbook of the Marvel Universe: Golden Age Marvel 2004

Marvel, 2004

1 .... 4.00

Official Handbook of the Marvel Universe: Horror 2005

Marvel, 2005

1 .... 4.00

Official Handbook of the Marvel Universe: Hulk

Marvel, 2004

1 .... 4.00

Official Handbook of the Marvel Universe: Marvel Knights 2005

Marvel, 2005

1 .... 4.00

Official Handbook of the Marvel Universe: Spider-Man 2004

Marvel, 2004

1 .... 4.00

Official Handbook of the Marvel Universe: Spider-Man 2005

Marvel, 2005

1 .... 4.00

Official Handbook of the Marvel Universe: The Avengers

Marvel, 2004

1 .... 4.00

Official Handbook of the Marvel Universe: Wolverine 2004

Marvel, 2004

1 .... 4.00

Official Handbook of the Marvel Universe: Women of Marvel 2005

Marvel, 2005

1 .... 4.00

Official Handbook of the Marvel Universe: X-Men 2004

Marvel, 2004

1 .... 4.00

Official Handbook of the Marvel Universe: X-Men - Age of Apocalypse 2005

Marvel, 2005

1 .... 4.00

Official Handbook of the Marvel Universe: X-Men 2005

Marvel, 2006

1 .... 4.00

Official Handbook: Ultimate Marvel Universe 2005

Marvel, 2005

1 .... 4.00

Official Handbook: Ultimate Marvel Universe - Ultimates & X-Men 2005

Marvel, 2006

1 .... 4.00

Official Hawkman Index

Eclipse, 1986

1-2 .... 2.00

Official How to Draw G.I. Joe

Blackthorne, 1987

1-3 .... 2.00

Madhouse Ma-ad Jokes

Madman

Madman Comics

Mad Monster Party Adaptation

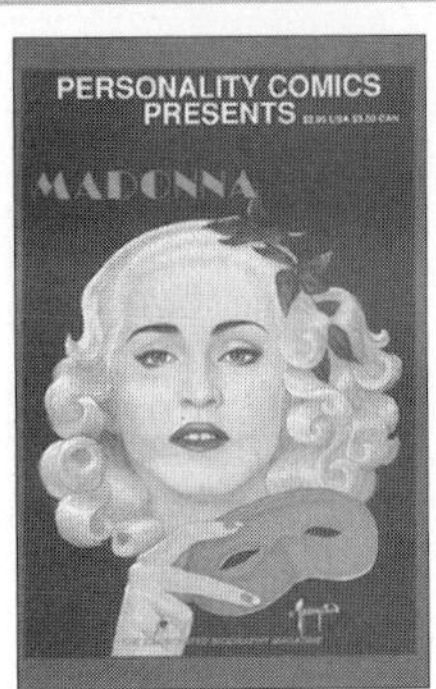

Madonna

Mad Raccoons

Maelstrom

Mage

Official How to Draw Robotech

Blackthorne, 1987

1-14 .... 2.00

Official How to Draw Transformers

Blackthorne, 1987

1-4 .... 2.00

Official Johnny Hazard

Pioneer, 1988

1 .... 2.00

Official Jungle Jim

Pioneer, 1988

1-9 .... 2.00
10-16 .... 3.00
Ann 1 .... 4.00

Official Justice League of America Index

ICG

1-8 .... 2.00

Official Mandrake

Pioneer, 1988

1-9 .... 2.00
10-15 .... 3.00

Official Marvel Index to Marvel Team-Up

Marvel, 1986

1-6 .... 1.00

Official Marvel Index to the Amazing Spider-Man

Marvel, 1985

1-9 .... 1.00

Official Marvel Index to the Avengers

Marvel, 1987

1-7 .... 3.00

Official Marvel Index to The Avengers

Marvel, 1994

1-6 .... 2.00

Official Marvel Index to the Fantastic Four

Marvel, 1985

1-12 .... 1.00

Official Marvel Index to the X-Men

Marvel, 1987

1-7 .... 3.00

Official Marvel Index to the X-Men

Marvel, 1994

1-5 .... 2.00

Official Modesty Blaise

Pioneer, 1988

1-8 .... 2.00
Ann 1 .... 5.00

Official Prince Valiant

Pioneer, 1988

1-9 .... 2.00
10-18 .... 3.00
Ann 1-King Size 1 .... 4.00

Official Prince Valiant Monthly

Pioneer, 1989

1-2 .... 4.00
3-4 .... 5.00
5-8 .... 7.00

Official Rip Kirby

Pioneer, 1988

1-6 .... 2.00

Official Secret Agent

Pioneer, 1988

1-7 .... 2.00

Official Teen Titans Index

Independent, 1985

1-5 .... 2.00

Offworld

Graphic Image

1 .... 4.00

Of Mind and Soul

Rage

1 .... 2.00

Of Myths and Men

Blackthorne, 1987

1-2 .... 2.00

Ogenki Clinic

Akita, 1997

1-2 .... 4.00
3-6 .... 5.00

Ogenki Clinic (Vol. 2)

Akita, 1998

1-6 .... 4.00

Ogenki Clinic (Vol. 3)

Sexy Fruit, 1998

1-7 .... 4.00

Ogenki Clinic (Vol. 4)

Sexy Fruit, 1999

1-6 .... 3.00

Ogenki Clinic (Vol. 5)

Sexy Fruit, 1999

1-7 .... 3.00

Ogenki Clinic (Vol. 6)
Sexy Fruit, 2000
1-7 ..... 3.00

Ogenki Clinic (Vol. 7)
Ironcat, 2000
1-7 ..... 3.00

Ogenki Clinic (Vol. 8)
Ironcat, 2001
1-8 ..... 3.00

Ogenki Clinic (Vol. 9)
Ironcat, 2002
1-8 ..... 3.00

Ogre
Black Diamond, 1994
1-4 ..... 3.00

O.G. Whiz
Gold Key, 1971
1 ..... 25.00
2 ..... 15.00
3-6 ..... 10.00
7-11 ..... 3.00

Oh.
B Publications, 1995
1-22 ..... 3.00

Oh Brother!
Stanhall, 1953
1 ..... 40.00
2-5 ..... 25.00

Ohm's Law
Imperial
1-3 ..... 2.00

Oh My Goddess!
Dark Horse, 1994
1 ..... 5.00
2-6 ..... 3.00
88-95 ..... 4.00
96-105 ..... 3.00
106 ..... 4.00
107-109 ..... 3.00
110-112 ..... 4.00

Oh My Goddess! Part II
Dark Horse, 1995
1-8 ..... 3.00

Oh My Goddess! Part III
Dark Horse, 1995
1-11 ..... 3.00

Oh My Goddess! Part IV
Dark Horse, 1996
1-8 ..... 3.00

Oh My Goddess! Part V
Dark Horse, 1997
1-2 ..... 3.00
3-4 ..... 4.00
5 ..... 3.00
6-7 ..... 4.00
8 ..... 3.00
9-12 ..... 4.00

Oh My Goddess! Part VI
Dark Horse, 1998
1 ..... 4.00
2-6 ..... 3.00

Oh My Goddess! Part VII
Dark Horse, 1999
1-8 ..... 3.00

Oh My Goddess! Part VIII
Dark Horse, 2000
1-6 ..... 4.00

Oh My Goddess! Part IX
Dark Horse, 2000
1-7 ..... 4.00

Oh My Goddess! Part X
Dark Horse, 2001
1-5 ..... 4.00

Oh My Goddess! Part XI
Dark Horse, 2001
1-2 ..... 4.00
3-6 ..... 3.00

Oh My Goddess!: Adventures of the Mini-Goddesses
Dark Horse, 2000
1 ..... 10.00

Oh My Goth
Sirius, 1998
1-4 ..... 3.00

Oh My Goth: Humans Suck!
Sirius, 2000
1-2 ..... 3.00

Oink: Blood and Circus
Kitchen Sink, 1998
1-4 ..... 5.00

Oink: Heaven's Butcher
Kitchen Sink, 1995
1-3 ..... 5.00

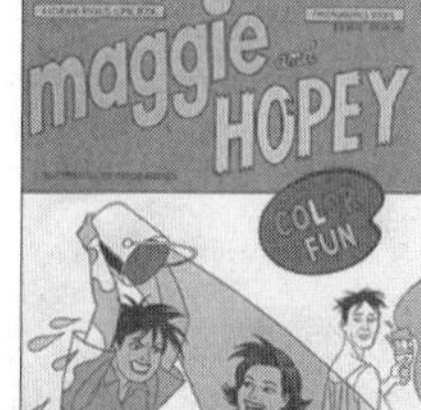

Maggie and Hopey Color Special

Maggie the Cat

Maggots

Magical Mates

Magical Twilight

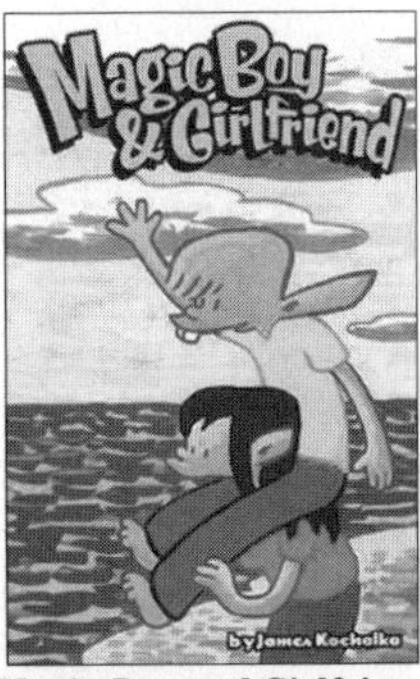

Magic Boy and Girlfriend

Magic Carpet

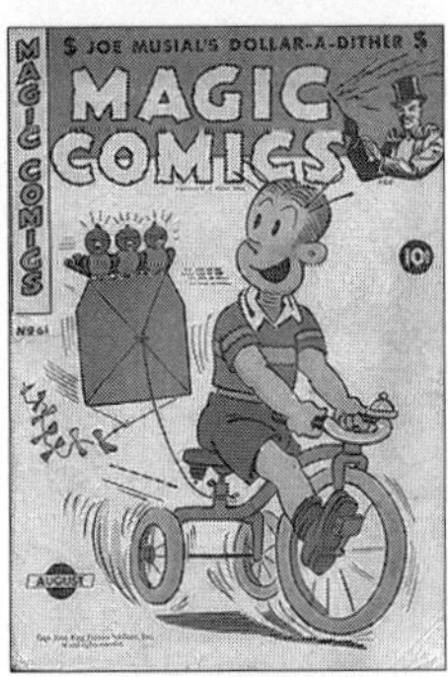

Magic Comics

Ojo
Oni, 2004

1-5 ....3.00

OJ's Big Bust Out
Boneyard, 1995

1 ....4.00

Okay Comics
United Feature, 1940

1 ....250.00

Oklahoma Kid
Ajax, 1957

1 ....75.00
2-4 ....40.00

Oktane
Dark Horse, 1995

1-4 ....3.00

Oldblood
Parody

1-1/2nd 3.00

Olympians
Marvel, 1991

1-2 ....4.00

Olympus Heights
Idea & Design Works, 2004

1-3 ....4.00

OMAC
DC, 1974

1 ....40.00
2 ....15.00
3 ....12.00
4 ....10.00
5-8 ....7.00

OMAC
DC, 2006

1-6 ....3.00

OMAC: One Man Army Corps
DC, 1991

1-4 ....4.00

OMAC Project
DC, 2005

1 ....22.00
1/2nd 7.00
1/3rd 3.00
2 ....6.00
2/2nd 3.00
3 ....4.00
4-6 ....3.00

OMAC Project: Infinite Crisis Special
DC, 2006

1 ....5.00

Omaha: Cat Dancer
Steeldragon, 1984

1 ....12.00
1/Ashcan 3.00
1/2nd 4.00
2 ....8.00

Omaha The Cat Dancer
Kitchen Sink, 1986

0 ....4.00
1 ....10.00
1/2nd 4.00
1/3rd 3.00
2 ....5.00
3-5 ....4.00
6-20 ....3.00

Omaha The Cat Dancer
Fantagraphics, 1994

1-4 ....3.00

O'Malley and the Alley Cats
Gold Key, 1971

1 ....8.00
2-3 ....6.00
4-9 ....4.00

Omar Lennyx
Magnecom

1 ....3.00

Omega Elite
Blackthorne

1 ....4.00

Omega Flight
Marvel, 2007

1 ....7.00
2 ....5.00
3 ....4.00

Omega Force
South Star, 1992

1 ....2.00

Omega Force
Entity, 1995

1 ....3.00

Omega Force II
Entity, 1996

1-3 ....3.00

Omega Knights
Underground, 1992

1-6 ....2.00

Omega Man
Omega 7

0 ....3.00
1 ....4.00
Ashcan 1 ....1.00

Omega Men
DC, 1983

1 ....4.00
2 ....3.00
3-10 ....2.00
11-19 ....1.00
20 ....2.00
21-38 ....1.00
Ann 1-2 ....2.00

Omega Men

DC, 2006

1-3 .... 3.00

Omega the Unknown

Marvel, 1976

1 .... 9.00
2 .... 6.00
2/30¢ 20.00
3 .... 3.00
3/30¢ 20.00
4-8 .... 2.00
9 .... 3.00
9/35¢ 15.00
10 .... 2.00
10/35¢ 15.00

Omen

Chaos!, 1998

1-5 .... 3.00

Omen

Northstar, 1989

1-2 .... 2.00

Omen: Save the Chosen Preview

Chaos!, 1997

1 .... 3.00

Omen: Vexed

Chaos!, 1998

1 .... 3.00

Omicron: Astonishing Adventures on Other Worlds

Pyramid, 1987

1-2 .... 2.00

Omnibus: Modern Perversity

Blackbird, 1992

1 .... 3.00

Omni Comix

Omni, 1995

1-2 .... 4.00
3 .... 5.00

Omni Men

Blackthorne, 1989

1 .... 4.00

On a Pale Horse

Innovation, 1991

1-5 .... 5.00

Once Upon a Time in the Future

Platinum

1 .... 10.00

One

Tokyopop, 2004

1-8 .... 10.00

One

Pacific, 1977

1 .... 3.00

One

Marvel, 1985

1-6 .... 2.00

One-Arm Swordsman

Dr. Leung's

1-7 .... 2.00

One-Fisted Tales

Slave Labor, 1990

1-4/3rd 3.00
5 .... 4.00
5/2nd-11 .... 3.00

One Hundred and One Dalmatians

Disney, 1991

1 .... 3.00

100 Bullets

DC, 1999

1 .... 10.00
2 .... 7.00
3-5 .... 5.00
6-10 .... 4.00
11-49 .... 3.00
50 .... 4.00
51-100 .... 3.00

100 Degrees in the Shade

Fantagraphics, 1992

1-4 .... 3.00

100 Girls

Arcana, 2004

1-1/Variant 5.00
2-6 .... 3.00

100 Greatest Marvels of All Time

Marvel, 2001

1-5 .... 8.00
6-10 .... 4.00

101 Other Uses for a Condom

Apple, 1991

1 .... 5.00

101 Ways to End the Clone Saga

Marvel, 1997

1 .... 3.00

100 Pages of Comics

Dell, 1937

1 .... 1,200.00

100%

DC, 2002

1-5 .... 6.00

Magicman

Magic Pickle

Magic Whistle

Magik

Magnesium Arc

Magnetic Men Featuring Magneto

Magneto

Magneto and the Magnetic Men

100% True?
DC, 1996

1-2 .... 4.00

One Mile Up
Eclipse, 1991

1-2 .... 3.00

One Millennium
Hunter, 1997

1-5 .... 3.00

One Million Years Ago
St. John, 1953

1 .... 100.00

One Piece
Viz, 2004

1-8 .... 8.00

One-Pound Gospel
Viz

1-2 .... 4.00
3-4 .... 3.00

One-Pound Gospel Round 2
Viz, 1997

1-6 .... 3.00

One-Shot Parody
Milky Way, 1986

1 .... 2.00

One-Shot Western
Caliber

1 .... 3.00

1001 Nights of Sheherazade
NBM, 2002

1 .... 13.00

1111
Crusade, 1996

1 .... 3.00

1,001 Nights of Bacchus
Dark Horse, 1993

1 .... 5.00

...One to Go
ƒardwolf

1 .... 3.00

Oni
Dark Horse, 2001

1-3 .... 3.00

Oni Double Feature
Oni, 1998

1 .... 6.00
1/2nd 3.00
2-6 .... 4.00
7-12 .... 3.00

Onigami
Antarctic, 1998

1-3 .... 3.00

Oni Press Color Special
Oni, 2001

2001-2002 .... 6.00

Oni Press Summer Vacation Supercolor Fun Special
Oni, 2000

1 .... 6.00

Only the End of the World Again
Oni, 2000

1 .... 7.00

On Our Butts
Aeon, 1995

1 .... 3.00

On Raven's Wings
Boneyard, 1994

1-2 .... 3.00

Onslaught: Epilogue
Marvel, 1997

1 .... 3.00

Onslaught: Marvel
Marvel, 1996

1 .... 6.00
1/Gold 12.00

Onslaught Reborn
Marvel, 2006

1 .... 6.00
2 .... 4.00

Onslaught: X-Men
Marvel, 1996

1 .... 5.00
1/Gold 10.00
1/Variant 8.00

On The Air
National Broadcasting Company, 1947

1 .... 175.00

On the Bus
Slave Labor, 1994

1 .... 3.00

On the Road to Perdition
DC, 2003

1-3 .... 8.00

On The Spot
Fawcett, 1948

1 .... 250.00

Onyx Overlord
Marvel, 1992

1-4 .... 3.00

Oombah, Jungle Moon Man
Strawberry Jam, 1992

1 .... 3.00

Open Season
Renegade, 1987
1-7 .... 2.00

Open Sore Funnies
Home-Made Euthanasia
1 .... 1.00

Open Space
Marvel, 1989
1-4 .... 5.00

Operation: Kansas City
Motion, 1993
1 .... 3.00

Operation: Knightstrike
Image, 1995
1-3 .... 3.00

Operation Peril
ACG, 1950
1 .... 185.00
2 .... 90.00
3-5 .... 80.00
6-10 .... 75.00
11-12 .... 50.00
13-16 .... 40.00

Operation: Stormbreaker
Acclaim, 1997
1 .... 4.00

Operative: Scorpio
Blackthorne, 1989
1 .... 4.00

Opposite Forces
Funnypages, 2002
1-4 .... 3.00

Opposite Forces
Alias, 2005
1 .... 1.00
2-3 .... 3.00

Optic Nerve
Drawn & Quarterly, 1997
1 .... 5.00
2-7 .... 3.00

Optimism of Youth
Fantagraphics, 1991
1 .... 13.00

Ora
Son of a Treebob, 1999
1 .... 3.00

Oracle
Oracle, 1986
1 .... 3.00

Oracle - A Trespassers Mystery
Amazing Montage
1 .... 5.00

Oracle Presents
Oracle, 1986
1-2 .... 3.00

Oral Roberts' True Stories
Telepix, 1956
101 .... 110.00
102 .... 65.00
103-107 .... 50.00
108-113 .... 45.00
114-119 .... 40.00

Orbit
Eclipse
1-3 .... 5.00

Orb Magazine
Orb, 1974
1-3 .... 1.00

Order
Marvel, 2002
1-6 .... 2.00

Or Else
Drawn and Quarterly, 2005
1 .... 6.00
2-3 .... 4.00

Oriental Heroes
Jademan, 1988
1-55 .... 2.00

Orient Gateway
NBM
1 .... 14.00

Original Adventures of Cholly and Flytrap
Image, 2006
1-2 .... 6.00

Original Astro Boy
Now, 1987
1-20 .... 2.00

Original Black Cat
Recollections, 1988
1-8 .... 2.00
9 .... 3.00
10 .... 1.00

Original Boy: Day of Atonement
Omega 7
1 .... 2.00

Original Crew
Personality, 1991
1-10 .... 3.00

Original Dick Tracy
Gladstone, 1990
1-5 .... 2.00

Original Doctor Solar, Man of the Atom
Valiant, 1995
1 .... 5.00

Magneto Ascendant

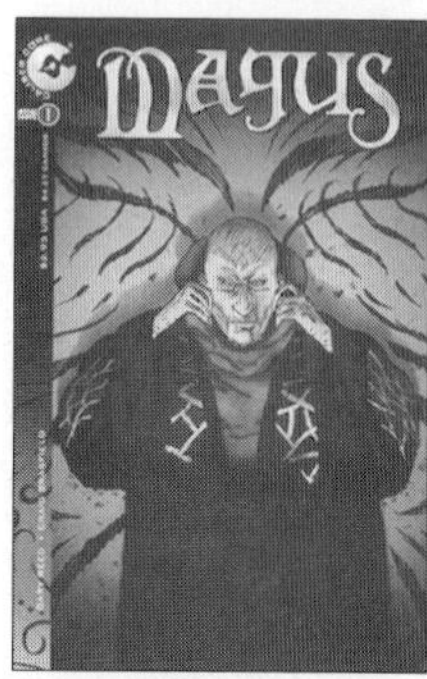

Magus

Maison Ikkoku Part 2

Major Bummer

Major Inapak the Space Ace

Makebelieve

Malcolm-10

Mammoth Comics

Original E-Man
First, 1985

1-7 .... 2.00

Original Ghost Rider
Marvel, 1992

1-20 .... 2.00

Original Ghost Rider Rides Again
Marvel, 1991

1-7 .... 2.00

Original Magnus Robot Fighter
Valiant, 1992

1 .... 4.00

Original Man
Omega 7

1 .... 4.00

Original Man: The Most Powerful Man In the Universe
Omega 7

1 .... 2.00

Original Mysterymen Presents (Bob Burden's...)
Dark Horse, 1999

1-4 .... 3.00

Original Sad Sack
Recollections

1 .... 2.00

Original Shield
Archie, 1984

1-4 .... 1.00

Original Sin
Thwack! Pow!

1-3 .... 1.00

Original Sins
Avalon

1 .... 3.00

Original Street Fighter
Alpha

1 .... 3.00

Original Tom Corbett
Eternity, 1990

1-5 .... 3.00

Original Turok, Son of Stone
Valiant, 1995

1 .... 4.00
2 .... 7.00

Original Tzu: Spirits of Death
Murim, 1997

1 .... 3.00

Origin of Galactus
Marvel, 1996

1 .... 3.00

Origin of the Defiant Universe
Defiant, 1994

1 .... 2.00

Orion
Dark Horse, 1993

1 .... 4.00
2-5 .... 3.00
6 .... 4.00

Orion
DC, 2000

1-25 .... 3.00

Orlak Redux
Caliber, 1991

1 .... 4.00

Ororo: Before the Storm
Marvel, 2005

1-4 .... 3.00

Orphen
ADV Manga, 2005

1-3 .... 10.00

Osborn Journals
Marvel, 1997

1 .... 3.00

Oscar Comics
Marvel, 1947

1 .... 60.00
2 .... 75.00
3-9 .... 35.00
10 .... 40.00

Othello
Tome

1 .... 4.00

Other Big Thing (Colin Upton's...)
Fantagraphics, 1991

1 .... 3.00
2-3 .... 2.00
4 .... 3.00

Others
Image, 1995

0 .... 1.00
1-4 .... 3.00

Others (Cormac)
Cormac

1 .... 2.00

Other Side
DC, 2006

1-4 .... 3.00

Otherworld

DC, 2005

1-7 .... 3.00

Otis Goes Hollywood

Dark Horse, 1997

1-2 .... 3.00

Otto Space!

Manifest Destiny

1-2 .... 2.00

Ouran High School Host Club

Viz, 2005

1-3 .... 9.00

Our Army at War

DC, 1952

1 .... 1,500.00
2 .... 750.00
3-4 .... 600.00
5-7 .... 500.00
8-11 .... 400.00
12 .... 325.00
13 .... 400.00
14 .... 325.00
15-19 .... 300.00
20 .... 275.00
21-31 .... 200.00
32-40 .... 175.00
41-50 .... 125.00
51-70 .... 100.00
71-80 .... 75.00
81 .... 2,500.00
☛1st Sgt. Rock
82 .... 650.00
83 .... 1,800.00
☛1st Kubert Rock
84 .... 300.00
85 .... 350.00
86-87 .... 300.00
88 .... 325.00
89-90 .... 300.00
91 .... 700.00
☛1st all-Rock issue
92-100 .... 175.00
101-112 .... 125.00
113-118 .... 150.00
119 .... 125.00
120-121 .... 80.00
122-125 .... 75.00
126 .... 100.00
127 .... 75.00
128 .... 275.00
☛Sgt. Rock Origin
129-133 .... 75.00
134-137 .... 60.00
138-150 .... 50.00
151 .... 350.00
☛1st Enemy Ace
152 .... 50.00
153 .... 140.00
☛2nd Enemy Ace
154 .... 40.00
155 .... 75.00
☛3rd Enemy Ace
156-157 .... 40.00
158 .... 60.00
☛1st Iron Major
159-163 .... 40.00
164 .... 80.00
☛Giant-sized
165-167 .... 40.00
168 .... 90.00
☛1st Unknown Soldier
169-176 .... 30.00
177 .... 50.00
178-181 .... 30.00
182-183 .... 40.00
184-185 .... 30.00
186 .... 40.00
187-189 .... 30.00
190 .... 40.00
191-198 .... 25.00
199-202 .... 20.00
203 .... 35.00
☛Giant
204-215 .... 20.00
216 .... 55.00
☛Giant-sized
217-228 .... 15.00
229 .... 35.00
☛Giant-sized
230-234 .... 15.00
235-240 .... 25.00
241 .... 15.00
242 .... 20.00
☛100-page issue
243-253 .... 15.00
254 .... 18.00
255 .... 15.00
256 .... 18.00
257 .... 15.00
258-271 .... 10.00
272 .... 15.00
273-301 .... 10.00

Our Cancer Year

Four Walls Eight Windows, 1994

1 .... 18.00

Our Fighting Forces

DC, 1954

1 .... 725.00
2 .... 340.00
3 .... 310.00
4-5 .... 250.00
6-9 .... 190.00
10 .... 205.00
11-15 .... 135.00
16-20 .... 115.00
21-30 .... 90.00
31-40 .... 75.00
41 .... 90.00
42-44 .... 70.00
45 .... 235.00

Man Against Time

Man Comics

Man-Frog

Man from Atlantis

Manga Horror

Manga Shi

Manga Vizion

Mangazine

☛1st Gunner & Sarge
46 ....95.00
47 ....80.00
48-50 ....60.00
51-60 ....35.00
61-64 ....28.00
65-70 ....18.00
71-80 ....15.00
81-90 ....10.00
91-99 ....7.00
100-120 ....6.00
121-150 ....5.00
151-181 ....4.00

Our Flag Comics
Ace, 1941
1 ....1,700.00
2 ....925.00
3-5 ....750.00

Our Gang with Tom & Jerry
Dell, 1942
1 ....600.00
2 ....335.00
3-5 ....190.00
6 ....195.00
7 ....130.00
8 ....175.00
9-10 ....158.00
11 ....146.00
12-20 ....130.00
21-30 ....115.00
31-36 ....90.00
37-40 ....48.00
41-50 ....32.00
51-59 ....26.00

Our Love
Marvel, 1949
1 ....75.00
2 ....50.00

Our Love Story
Marvel, 1969
1 ....55.00
2-4 ....25.00
5 ....75.00
☛Steranko art
6-8 ....25.00
9 ....35.00
10-11 ....25.00
12 ....35.00
13 ....20.00
14-20 ....12.00
21-37 ....8.00
38 ....15.00

Our Secret
Superior, 1949
4 ....100.00
5-8 ....55.00

Outbreed 999
Blackout, 1994
1-5 ....3.00

Outcast
Acclaim, 1995
1 ....5.00

Outcasts
DC, 1987
1-12 ....2.00

Outer Edge
Innovation
1 ....3.00

Outer Limits
Dell, 1964
1 ....125.00
2-5 ....65.00
6-10 ....50.00
11-18 ....35.00

Outer Orbit
Dark Horse, 2007
1 ....3.00

Outer Space
Charlton, 1958
17 ....60.00
☛Was This Magazine Is Haunted
18-20 ....75.00
21-25 ....55.00

Outer Space
Charlton, 1968
1 ....20.00

Outer Space Babes
Silhouette
1 ....3.00

Out For Blood
Dark Horse, 1999
1-4 ....3.00

Outlander
Malibu, 1987
1-7 ....2.00

Outlanders
Dark Horse, 1988
0-1 ....3.00
2-21 ....2.00
22-33 ....3.00
Special 1 ....3.00

Outlanders Epilogue
Dark Horse, 1994
1 ....3.00

Outlaw 7
Dark Horse, 2001
1-3 ....3.00

Outlaw Fighters
Atlas, 1954
1 ....85.00
2-5 ....60.00

Outlaw Kid (1st Series)

Marvel, 1954

1 .... 165.00
2 .... 80.00
3-10 .... 65.00
11-17 .... 54.00
18 .... 58.00
19 .... 54.00

Outlaw Kid (2nd Series)

Marvel, 1970

1 .... 25.00
2-7 .... 10.00
8 .... 15.00
9 .... 8.00
10 .... 20.00
11-20 .... 8.00
21-30 .... 5.00

Outlaw Nation

DC, 2000

1-19 .... 3.00

Outlaw Nation

Boneyard, 1994

1-1/Platinum 5.00

Outlaw Overdrive

Blue Comet

1 .... 3.00

Outlaws

D.S., 1948

1 .... 200.00
2 .... 175.00
3 .... 110.00
4-5 .... 85.00
6 .... 65.00
7-8 .... 90.00
9 .... 200.00

Outlaws

Star, 1952

10 .... 120.00
11-14 .... 90.00

Outlaws

DC, 1991

1-8 .... 2.00

Outlaws of the West

Charlton, 1957

11 .... 20.00
12-20 .... 12.00
21-30 .... 8.00
31-50 .... 5.00
51-60 .... 4.00
61-70 .... 3.00
71-88 .... 2.00

Out of the Night

ACG, 1952

1 .... 400.00
2 .... 285.00
3 .... 150.00
4 .... 230.00
5-10 .... 150.00
11-17 .... 115.00

Out of the Shadows

Standard, 1952

5 .... 350.00
6 .... 225.00
7 .... 160.00
8 .... 285.00
9 .... 160.00
10 .... 145.00
11 .... 160.00
12 .... 215.00
13 .... 190.00
14 .... 160.00

Out of the Vortex (Comics' Greatest World...)

Dark Horse, 1994

5-12 .... 2.00

Out of this World

Charlton, 1956

1 .... 85.00
2 .... 45.00
3-6 .... 60.00
7 .... 65.00
8-10 .... 60.00
11-12 .... 55.00
13-15 .... 20.00
16 .... 55.00

Out of This World

Eternity

1 .... 4.00

Outposts

Blackthorne, 1997

1 .... 2.00

Outsiders

DC, 1984

1-3 .... 2.00
4-28 .... 1.00
Ann 1 .... 3.00
Special 1 .... 2.00

Outsiders

DC, 1993

0 .... 3.00
1/A 4.00
1/B 3.00
2-12 .... 2.00
13 .... 3.00
14-24 .... 2.00

Outsiders

DC, 2003

1-20 .... 3.00
21-23 .... 4.00
24-43 .... 3.00

Outsiders Double Feature

DC, 2003

1 .... 5.00

Mangle Tangle Tales

Manik

Manimal

Mankind

Mann and Superman

Man of Many Faces

Manosaurs

Mantech Robot Warriors

Out There
DC, 2001
1 ....3.00
1/Variant 4.00
2-18 ....3.00
Ashcan 1 ....1.00

Overkill: Witchblade/Aliens/Darkness/Predator
Image, 2000
1-2 ....6.00

Overload Magazine
Eclipse, 1987
1 ....2.00

Overmen
Excel, 1998
1 ....3.00

Over the Edge
Marvel, 1995
1-10 ....1.00

Overture
Innovation, 1990
1-2 ....2.00

Owl
Gold Key, 1967
1 ....50.00
2 ....40.00

Owlhoots
Kitchen Sink
1-2 ....3.00

Ox Cow O' War
Spoof
1 ....3.00

Oz
Caliber, 1995
0 ....4.00
1 ....6.00
2-10 ....4.00
11-20 ....3.00

Oz Collection (Bill Bryan's...)
Arrow
1 ....3.00

Oz: Daemonstorm
Caliber, 1997
1 ....4.00

Ozf5 Gale Force
Alias, 2005
1 ....5.00

Oz: Romance in Rags
Caliber, 1996
1-3 ....3.00

Oz Special: Freedom Fighters
Caliber
1 ....3.00

Oz Special: Lion
Caliber
1 ....3.00

Oz Special: Scarecrow
Caliber
1 ....3.00

Oz Special: Tin Man
Caliber
1 ....3.00

Oz Squad
Brave New Words, 1991
1-4 ....3.00

Oz Squad
Patchwork, 1994
1-10 ....3.00

Oz: Straw & Sorcery
Caliber, 1997
1-3 ....3.00

Oz: The Manga
Antarctic, 2005
1-6 ....3.00

Oz-Wonderland Wars
DC, 1986
1-3 ....3.00

Ozark Ike
Standard, 1948
11-15 ....55.00
16-20 ....44.00
21-25 ....38.00

Ozzie & Babs
Fawcett, 1947
1 ....54.00
2 ....28.00
3-5 ....24.00
6-13 ....18.00

Ozzy Osbourne
Rock-It Comics, 1993
1 ....6.00

Pacific Presents
Pacific, 1982
1 ....4.00
2 ....3.00
3-4 ....2.00

Pac (Preter-Human Assault Corps)
Artifacts, 1993
1 ....2.00

Pact
Image, 1994
1-3 ....2.00

Pact
Image, 2005
1-4 ....3.00

Pageant of Comics
St. John, 1947

1-2 .... 50.00

Pagers Comics Anthology
No Talent, 1997

1-6 .... 3.00

Painkiller Jane
Event, 1997

0 .... 4.00
0/Ltd. 40.00
1 .... 3.00
1/A 4.00
1/Red foil 25.00
2 .... 3.00
2/A 4.00
3 .... 3.00
3/A 4.00
4 .... 3.00
4/A 4.00
5 .... 3.00
5/A 4.00

Painkiller Jane/ Darkchylde
Event, 1998

0 .... 4.00
1 .... 3.00
1/A 30.00
1/B 4.00
1/C 40.00
Ashcan 1 .... 5.00

Painkiller Jane/Hellboy
Event, 1998

1 .... 3.00
1/Ltd. 30.00
1/A 3.00

Painkiller Jane vs. The Darkness: Stripper
Event, 1997

1-1/C 3.00
1/Ltd. 20.00

Paintball Universe 2000
Splattoons

1 .... 3.00

Pajama Chronicles
Blackthorne, 1987

1 .... 2.00

Pakkins' Land
Caliber, 1996

0 .... 2.00
1-6 .... 3.00

Pakkins' Land
Alias, 2005

1-5 .... 3.00

Pakkins' Land: Forgotten Dreams
Caliber, 1998

1-4 .... 3.00

Pakkins' Land: Quest for Kings
Caliber, 1997

1-6 .... 3.00

Palatine
Gryphon Rampant, 1994

1-5 .... 3.00

Palestine
Fantagraphics, 1994

1-9 .... 3.00

Pal-Yat-Chee
Adhesive, 1993

1 .... 3.00

Pamela Anderson Uncovered
Pop

1 .... 3.00

Pancho Villa
L. Miller & Son

1 .... 10.00
2-29 .... 6.00
30-63 .... 4.00

Panda Khan Special
Abacus, 1990

1 .... 3.00

Pandemonium
Chaos!, 1998

1 .... 3.00

Pandora Pill
Acid Rain

1 .... 3.00

Panic
E.C., 1954

1 .... 210.00
2 .... 125.00
3-11 .... 80.00
12 .... 160.00

Panic
Gemstone, 1997

1-12 .... 3.00
Ann 1-2 .... 11.00

Panorama
St.Eve Productions, 1991

1-2 .... 3.00

Pantera
Malibu, 1994

1 .... 4.00

Pantha: Haunted Passion
Harris, 1997

1 .... 3.00

Pantheon
Archer Books & Games, 1995

1-2 .... 3.00

Mantra

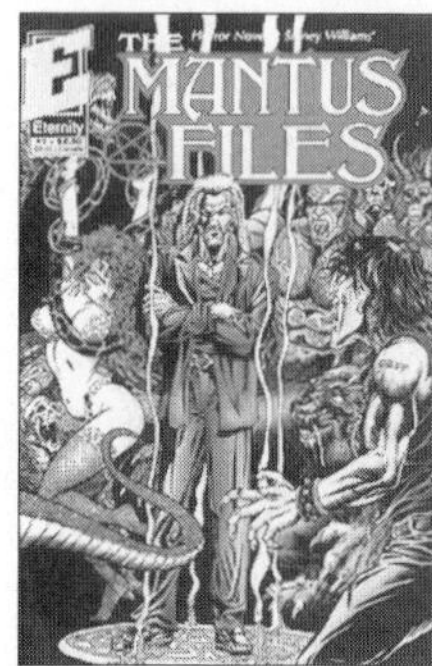

Mantus Files

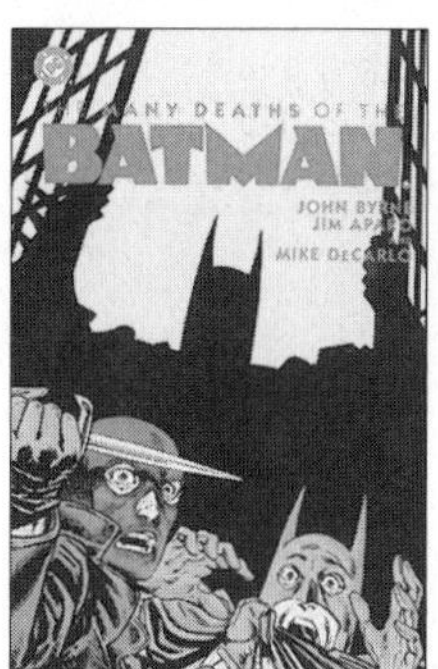

Many Deaths of the Batman

Many Loves of Dobie Gillis

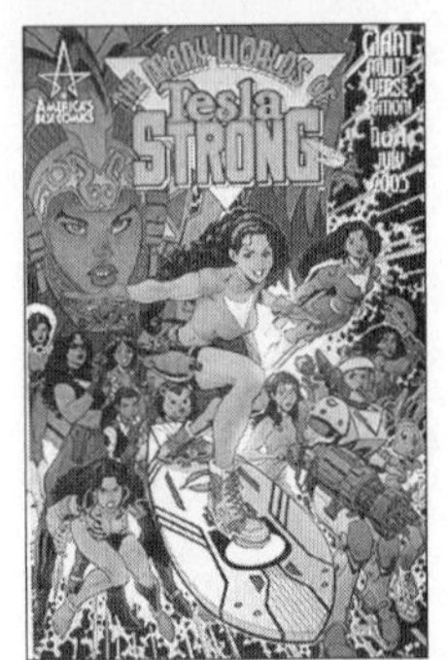
Many Worlds of Tesla Strong

Mara Celtic Shamaness

Marada the She-Wolf

Marauder

Pantheon
Lone Star, 1998
1-6 .... 3.00

Pantheon: Ancient History
Lone Star, 1999
1 .... 4.00

Panzer 1946
Antarctic, 2004
1-5 .... 6.00

Paper Cinema: The Box
Grey Blossom Sequentials, 1998
3 .... 4.00

Paper Cinema: Waves In Space
Grey Blossom Sequentials, 1998
2 .... 4.00

Paper Dolls from the California Girls
Eclipse
1 .... 6.00

Paper Museum
Jungle Boy, 2002
1 .... 3.00

Paper Tales
CLG Comics, 1993
1-2 .... 3.00

Para-Cops
Excel, 1998
1 .... 3.00

Paradax
Vortex, 1987
1-2 .... 2.00

Paradigm
Image, 2002
1-4 .... 4.00
5-8 .... 3.00
9-12 .... 4.00

Paradigm
Gauntlet
1 .... 3.00

Paradise Kiss
Tokyopop, 2002
1 .... 10.00

Paradise Too
Abstract, 2000
nn-14 .... 3.00

Paradise X
Marvel, 2002
0 .... 5.00
1-12 .... 3.00

Paradise X: Devils
Marvel, 2002
1 .... 5.00

Paradise X: Heralds
Marvel, 2001
1-3 .... 4.00

Paradise X: A
Marvel, 2003
1 .... 3.00

Paradise X: X
Marvel, 2003
1 .... 3.00

Paradise X: Ragnarok
Marvel, 2003
1-2 .... 3.00

Paradise X: Xen
Marvel, 2002
1 .... 5.00

Paradox Project: Genesis
Paradox Project, 1998
1 .... 3.00

Paragon: Dark Apocalypse
AC
1-4 .... 3.00

Parallax: Emerald Night
DC, 1996
1 .... 15.00

Paramount Animated Comics
Harvey, 1953
3 .... 125.00
4-6 .... 55.00
7 .... 100.00
8-10 .... 55.00
11-22 .... 45.00

Paranoia
Adventure, 1991
1-6 .... 3.00

Paranoia
Co. & Sons
1 .... 4.00

Paraphernalia
Graphitti
1 .... 2.00

Parasyte
Mixx, 1999
1-2 .... 12.00

Para Troop
Comics Conspiracy, 1998
0 .... 4.00
1-Ashcan 1 .... 3.00

Pardners
Cottonwood Graphics, 1990
1-2 .... 8.00

Paris
Slave Labor, 2005
1-2 .... 3.00

Paris the Man of Plaster
Harrier, 1987
1-6 .... 2.00

Parliament of Justice
Image, 2003
1 .... 6.00

Paro-Dee
Parody
1 .... 3.00

Parody Press Annual Swimsuit Special '93
Parody, 1993
1 .... 3.00

Parole Breakers
Avon, 1951
1 .... 260.00
2 .... 175.00
3 .... 160.00

Particle Dreams
Fantagraphics, 1986
1-6 .... 2.00

Partners in Pandemonium
Caliber
1-3 .... 3.00

Partridge Family
Charlton, 1971
1 .... 30.00
2 .... 16.00
3-4 .... 14.00
5 .... 20.00
☛Giant-sized
6-14 .... 12.00
15-21 .... 10.00

Parts of a Hole
Caliber
1 .... 3.00

Parts Unknown
Eclipse, 1995
1-4 .... 3.00

Parts Unknown Convention Sketchbook
-Ism, 2005
1 .... 10.00

Parts Unknown: Dark Intentions
Knight, 1995
0-4 .... 3.00

Parts Unknown: Hostile Takeover
Image, 2000
1 .... 3.00
1/Ashcan 5.00
2 .... 3.00
2/Ashcan 5.00
3 .... 3.00
3/Ashcan 5.00
4 .... 3.00
4/Ashcan 5.00

Parts Unknown II: The Next Invasion
Eclipse, 1993
1 .... 3.00

Passover
Maximum, 1996
1 .... 3.00

Pat Boone
DC, 1959
1 .... 200.00
2-5 .... 150.00

Patches
Rural Home, 1945
1 .... 300.00
2 .... 125.00
3-7 .... 100.00
8-11 .... 75.00

Pater Contrarius
Robot
1 .... 2.00

Path
CrossGen, 2002
1-23 .... 3.00

Path Prequel
CrossGen, 2002
1 .... 3.00

Pathways to Fantasy
Pacific, 1984
1 .... 2.00

Patient Zero
Image, 2004
1-4 .... 3.00

Patrick Rabbit
Fragments West, 1988
1-7 .... 2.00

Patrick Stewart
Celebrity
1 .... 3.00

Patrick Stewart vs. William Shatner
Celebrity, 1992
1 .... 6.00

Patriots
WildStorm, 2000
1-10 .... 3.00

Pat Savage: The Woman of Bronze
Millennium, 1992
1 .... 3.00

Patsy and Hedy
Marvel, 1952
1 .... 135.00
2 .... 70.00

March of Crime

Marines Attack

Marines in Action

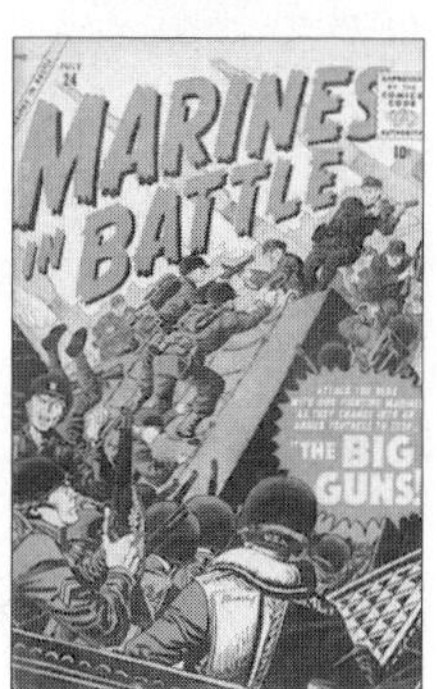

Marines in Battle

Marine War Heroes

Markam

Mark of Charon

Marmaduke Mouse

3-10 .... 48.00
11-20 .... 32.00
21-30 .... 25.00
31-50 .... 23.00
51-60 .... 15.00
61-90 .... 12.00
91-110 .... 10.00
Ann 1 .... 55.00

Patsy & Her Pals
Atlas, 1953

1 .... 125.00
2-4 .... 75.00
5-9 .... 60.00
10-15 .... 55.00
16-19 .... 50.00
20-25 .... 45.00
26-29 .... 40.00

Patsy Walker
Marvel, 1945

1 .... 400.00
2 .... 175.00
3-10 .... 125.00
11-12 .... 70.00
13-14 .... 80.00
15-16 .... 70.00
17 .... 80.00
18 .... 70.00
19-22 .... 80.00
23-24 .... 55.00
25 .... 80.00
26-29 .... 55.00
30 .... 70.00
31-41 .... 30.00
42-50 .... 25.00
51-60 .... 22.00
61-80 .... 16.00
81-100 .... 13.00
101-124 .... 10.00
Special 1 .... 45.00

Pat the Brat
Archie, 1955

1 .... 35.00
2 .... 24.00
3-4 .... 20.00
15-33 .... 14.00

Patty Cake
Permanent Press, 1995

1-9 .... 3.00

Patty Cake
Caliber, 1996

1-Holiday 1 .... 3.00

Patty Cake & Friends
Slave Labor, 1997

1-15 .... 3.00
Special 1 .... 4.00

Patty Cake & Friends
Slave Labor, 2000

1-15 .... 5.00

Patty Powers
Atlas, 1955

4 .... 50.00
5-7 .... 30.00

Paul Terry's Comics
St. John, 1951

85 .... 40.00
86-90 .... 35.00
91-96 .... 25.00
97-105 .... 20.00
106-120 .... 15.00
121-125 .... 10.00

Paul the Samurai
New England, 1992

1 .... 4.00
2 .... 3.00
3 .... 6.00
4 .... 4.00
5-10 .... 3.00

Paul the Samurai
NEC, 1990

1 .... 4.00
2-3 .... 3.00

Pawnee Bill
Story, 1951

1 .... 65.00
2-3 .... 45.00

Payne
Dream Catcher, 1995

1 .... 3.00

Pay-off
D.S., 1948

1 .... 150.00
2 .... 90.00
3-5 .... 75.00

P. City Parade
Horse, 1996

1 .... 5.00

Peacemaker
Charlton, 1967

1 .... 10.00
2-3 .... 6.00
4 .... 8.00
5 .... 6.00

Peacemaker
Modern, 1978

1-2 .... 3.00

Peacemaker
DC, 1988

1-4 .... 2.00

Peacemaker Kurogane
ADV Manga, 2004

1-3 .... 10.00

Peacemakers
Kinetic

1 .... 3.00

Peace Party
Blue Corn
1 .... 3.00

Peace Posse
Mellon Bank
1 .... 3.00

Peanut Butter and Jeremy
Alternative, 2000
1-3 .... 3.00
4/FCBD 2.00

Peanuts
Dell, 1954
1 .... 125.00
4 .... 75.00
5-13 .... 55.00

Peanuts
Gold Key, 1963
1 .... 125.00
2-4 .... 75.00

Peasant and the Devil
Fantagraphics
1 .... 3.00

Pebbles and Bamm-Bamm
Charlton, 1972
1 .... 18.00
2 .... 12.00
3-5 .... 9.00
6-10 .... 7.00
11-20 .... 5.00
21-30 .... 4.00
31-36 .... 3.00

Pebbles & Bamm-Bamm
Harvey, 1993
1-Summer 1 .... 2.00

Pebbles Flintstone
Gold Key, 1963
1 .... 75.00

Pedestrian Vulgarity
Fantagraphics
1 .... 3.00

Pedro
Fox, 1950
1 .... 150.00
2 .... 100.00

Peek-A-Boo 3-D
3-D Zone
1 .... 4.00

Peepshow
Drawn & Quarterly, 1992
1-9 .... 3.00

Pellestar
Eternity, 1987
1-2 .... 2.00

Pendragon
Aircel, 1991
1-2 .... 3.00

Pendulum
Adventure, 1992
1-4 .... 3.00

Pendulum's Illustrated Stories
Pendulum
1-6 .... 5.00

Peng One Shot
Oni, 2005
1 .... 6.00

Penguin & Pencilguin
Fragments West, 1987
1-6 .... 2.00

Penguin Bros.
Labyrinth, 1998
1-2 .... 3.00

Penny
Avon, 1947
1 .... 55.00
2-5 .... 30.00
6 .... 35.00

Penny & Aggie
Alias, 2005
1-4 .... 3.00

Penny Century
Fantagraphics, 1997
1-7 .... 3.00

Pentacle: The Sign of the Five
Eternity, 1991
1-4 .... 2.00

Penthouse Comix
Penthouse International, 1994
1 .... 6.00
1/2nd-33 .... 5.00

Penthouse Max
Penthouse International, 1996
1-3 .... 5.00

Penthouse Men's Adventure Comix
Penthouse, 1995
1-7 .... 5.00

People are Phony
Siegel and Simon, 1976
1 .... 4.00

People's Comics
Golden Gate, 1972
1 .... 4.00

Pep
Archie, 1940
1 .... 6,850.00
2 .... 1,850.00
3 .... 1,375.00
4-5 .... 1,050.00
6 .... 825.00

Marmalade Boy

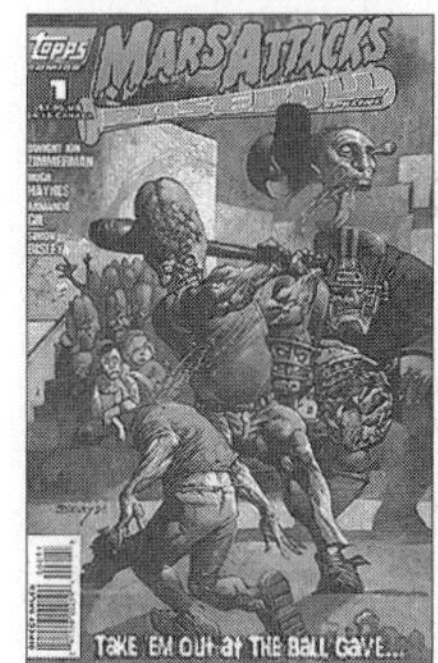

Mars Attacks Baseball Special

Mars Attacks Image

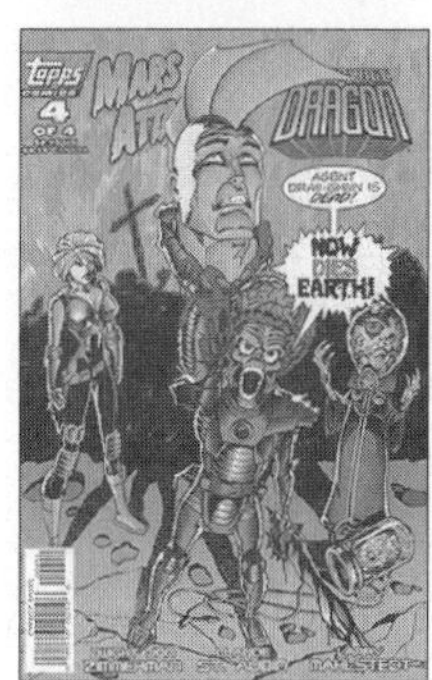

Mars Attacks the Savage Dragon

Marshal Law

M.A.R.S. Patrol Total War

Martha Washington Goes to War

Martha Washington Saves the World

7-11..800.00
12..925.00
13-15.......................................675.00
16..1,000.00
17..2,700.00
☛1st Hangman
18-21.......................................560.00
22.......................................12,000.00
23..1,150.00
24-25.......................................935.00
26..1,475.00
27-30.......................................750.00
31-35.......................................585.00
36..1,050.00
37-40.......................................410.00
41-47.......................................230.00
48..280.00
49-50.......................................230.00
51-55.......................................185.00
56-60.......................................180.00
61-65.......................................140.00
66-70.......................................100.00
71-80..82.00
81-99..62.00
100..90.00
101-110......................................40.00
111-120......................................28.00
121-130......................................23.00
131-140......................................19.00
141-160......................................15.00
161-177.......................................7.00
178-200.......................................6.00
201-220.......................................5.00
221-250.......................................4.00
251-300.......................................2.00
301-411.......................................1.00

Perazim
Antarctic, 1996
1-3...3.00

Percevan: The Three Stars of Ingaar
Fantasy Flight
1...9.00

Peregrine
Alliance, 1994
1-2...3.00

Perfect Love
Ziff-Davis, 1951
1...115.00
2..80.00
3-10...65.00

Perfect Crime
Cross, 1949
1...210.00
2...120.00
3-9...100.00
10-14..85.00
15...90.00
16-25..65.00
26..110.00
27-30..65.00
31-33..60.00

Perg
Lightning, 1993
1-1/Gold......................................4.00
1/Platinum....................................3.00
1/Variant.....................................4.00
2-8...3.00

Perhapanauts
Dark Horse, 2005
1-4...3.00

Perhapanauts: Second Chances
Dark Horse, 2006
1-3...3.00

Periphery
Arch-Type
1...3.00

Perramus: Escape from the Past
Fantagraphics, 1991
1-4...4.00

Perry
Lightning, 1997
1...3.00

Perry Mason
Dell, 1964
1-2..40.00

Personality Classics
Personality, 1992
1-4...3.00

Personality Comics Presents
Personality, 1991
1-18..3.00

Personal Love
Famous Funnies, 1950
1...100.00
2..55.00
3-7..45.00
8-9..50.00
10...45.00
11...55.00
12...45.00
13-15..40.00
16-17..45.00
18-30..40.00
31...55.00
32-33..40.00

Pest
Pest Comics
1-7...2.00

Pet
Fantagraphics, 1997
1...3.00

Pete Mangan
L. Miller & Son

51 .... 8.00
52-55 .... 6.00

Peter and the Wolf
NBM

1 .... 16.00

Peter Cannon-Thunderbolt
DC, 1992

1-3 .... 2.00
4-12 .... 1.00

Martian Manhunter Special

Peter Cottontail
Key, 1954

1 .... 50.00
2 .... 35.00

Peter Kock
Fantagraphics, 1994

1 .... 4.00
2-6 .... 3.00

Peter Pan
Gold Key, 1969

1 .... 20.00
2 .... 12.00

Peter Pan
Tundra

1-2 .... 15.00

Martin Kane

Peter Pan
Disney

1 .... 6.00

Peter Pan and the Warlords of Oz
Hand of Doom, 1998

1 .... 3.00

Peter Pan & the Warlords of Oz: Dead Head Water
Hand of Doom, 1999

1 .... 3.00

Peter Pan: Return to Never-Never Land
Adventure, 1991

1-2 .... 3.00

Peter Panda
DC, 1953

1 .... 245.00
2 .... 120.00
3-8 .... 100.00
9 .... 110.00
10 .... 100.00
11-31 .... 60.00

Peter Pan Treasure Chest
Dell, 1953

1 .... 1,500.00

Peter Parker: Spider-Man
Marvel, 1998

1 .... 5.00
1/Sunburst 6.00
1/Dynamic 14.00
2/A-2/B 2.00
3-21 .... 4.00
25/Variant 6.00
22-29 .... 4.00
30-49 .... 3.00
50 .... 4.00
51-57 .... 3.00
Ann 1998-1999 .... 4.00

Peter Porkchops
DC, 1949

1 .... 165.00
2 .... 85.00
3-5 .... 60.00
6-10 .... 50.00
11-20 .... 45.00
21-30 .... 40.00
31-40 .... 32.00
41-50 .... 25.00
51-60 .... 20.00
61-62 .... 18.00

Peter Porker, the Spectacular Spider-Ham
Marvel, 1985

1-17 .... 1.00

Peter Rabbit
Avon, 1947

1 .... 150.00
2 .... 90.00
3-6 .... 70.00
7-10 .... 20.00
11-20 .... 14.00
21-34 .... 10.00

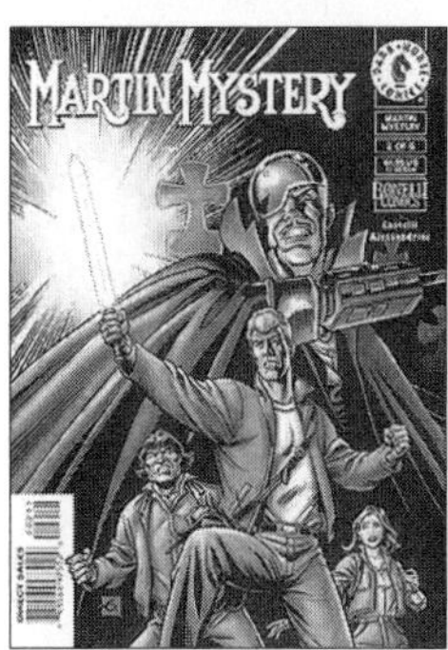

Martin Mystery

Peter Rabbit 3-D
Eternity

1 .... 3.00

Peter the Little Pest
Marvel, 1969

1 .... 75.00
2-4 .... 50.00

Pete the P.O.'d Postal Worker
Sharkbait, 1997

1 .... 4.00
2-10 .... 3.00

Petticoat Junction
Dell, 1964

1 .... 40.00
2-3 .... 30.00
4 .... 25.00
5 .... 30.00

Petworks vs. WildK.A.T.S.
Parody

1 .... 3.00

Phaedra
Express, 1994

1 .... 3.00

Marvel Action Universe

Marvel Adventure

Marvel Adventures

Marvel Age

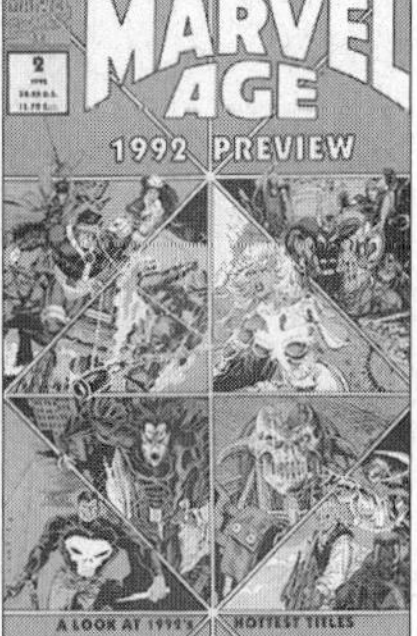

Marvel Age Preview

Phage: ShadowDeath (Neil Gaiman's...)
Big, 1996

1-6 .... 2.00

Phantacea: Phase One
Mcpherson, 1987

1 .... 5.00

Phantasmagoria
Tome

1 .... 3.00

Phantasy Against Hunger
Tiger, 1987

1 .... 2.00

Phantom
Gold Key, 1962

1 .... 90.00
2 .... 55.00
3-10 .... 36.00
11-17 .... 28.00
18 .... 32.00
19-28 .... 24.00
30-40 .... 15.00
41-59 .... 12.00
60-70 .... 9.00
71-74 .... 7.00

Phantom
DC, 1988

1-4 .... 2.00

Phantom
DC, 1989

1-13 .... 2.00

Phantom
Wolf, 1992

0/Ltd. 4.00
1 .... 3.00
2-8 .... 2.00

Phantom Force
Image, 1993

0-Ashcan 1 .... 3.00

Phantom
Moonstone, 2003

1-8 .... 4.00

Phantom Force
Genesis West

0 .... 3.00

Phantom Guard
Image, 1997

1-6 .... 3.00

Phantom Jack
Image, 2004

1-4 .... 3.00
4/Error 4.00
5 .... 3.00

Phantom Lady
Fox, 1947

13 .... 2,400.00
14-16 .... 1,500.00
17 .... 3,300.00
18-19 .... 1,050.00
20-22 .... 825.00
23 .... 925.00

Phantom Lady
Ajax, 1954

5 .... 1,000.00
2-4 .... 800.00

Phantom Lady
Verotik, 1994

1 .... 10.00

Phantom of Fear City
Claypool, 1993

1-12 .... 3.00

Phantom of the Opera
Eternity

1 .... 2.00

Phantom of the Opera
Innovation, 1991

1 .... 7.00

Phantom Quest Corp.
Pioneer, 1997

1 .... 3.00

Phantom Stranger (1st Series)
DC, 1952

1 .... 1,500.00
2 .... 1,000.00
3-6 .... 750.00

Phantom Stranger (2nd Series)
DC, 1969

1 .... 125.00
2-3 .... 60.00
4 .... 70.00
5-7 .... 50.00
8-13 .... 40.00
14-17 .... 35.00
18-21 .... 25.00
22-41 .... 15.00

Phantom Stranger
DC, 1987

1-4 .... 3.00

Phantom: The Ghost Killer
Moonstone, 2002

nn 6.00

Phantom: The Hunt
Moonstone, 2003

nn 7.00

Phantom: The Singh Web
Moonstone, 2002

nn 7.00

Phantom: The Ghost Who Walks (Lee Falk's...)
Marvel, 1995
1-3 .... 3.00

Phantom: The Treasure of Bangalla
Moonstone, 2002
nn 7.00

Phantom 2040
Marvel, 1995
1-4 .... 2.00

Phantom Witch Doctor
Avon, 1952
1 .... 300.00

Phantom Zone
DC, 1982
1 .... 2.00
2-4 .... 1.00

Phase One
Victory, 1986
1-5 .... 2.00

Phathom
Blatant, 1999
1 .... 3.00

Phatwars
Bon
1 .... 2.00

Phaze
Eclipse, 1988
1-2 .... 2.00

PhD: Phantasy Degree
Tokyopop, 2005
1-4 .... 10.00

Phenomerama
Caliber
1 .... 3.00

Phigments
Amazing
1-2 .... 2.00

Philbert Desanex' Dreams
Rip Off, 1993
1 .... 3.00

Philistine
One Shot, 1993
1-6 .... 3.00

Phil Rizzuto, Baseball Hero
Fawcett, 1951
1 .... 500.00

Phineus: Magician for Hire
Piffle, 1994
1 .... 3.00

Phobos
Flashpoint, 1994
1 .... 3.00

Phoebe & the Pigeon People
Kitchen Sink
1 .... 3.00

Phoebe: Angel in Black
Angel
1 .... 3.00

Phoebe Chronicles
NBM
1-2 .... 10.00

Phoenix
Atlas-Seaboard, 1975
1 .... 7.00
2 .... 5.00
3-4 .... 3.00

Phoenix Restaurant
Fandom House
1 .... 4.00

Phoenix Resurrection: Aftermath
Malibu, 1996
1 .... 4.00

Phoenix Resurrection: Genesis
Malibu, 1995
1-2 .... 4.00

Phoenix Resurrection: Red Shift
Malibu, 1995
0-0/Ltd. 3.00

Phoenix Resurrection: Revelations
Malibu, 1995
1 .... 4.00

Phoenix Square
Slave Labor, 1997
1-2 .... 3.00

Phoenix: The Untold Story
Marvel, 1984
1 .... 8.00

Phonogram
Image, 2006
1-3 .... 4.00

Phony Pages (Terry Beatty's...)
Renegade, 1986
1-2 .... 2.00

Picnic Party
Dell, 1955
6-7 .... 150.00
8 .... 225.00

Marvel and DC Present

Marvel Chillers

Marvel Classics Comics

Marvel Comics

Marvel Comics Presents

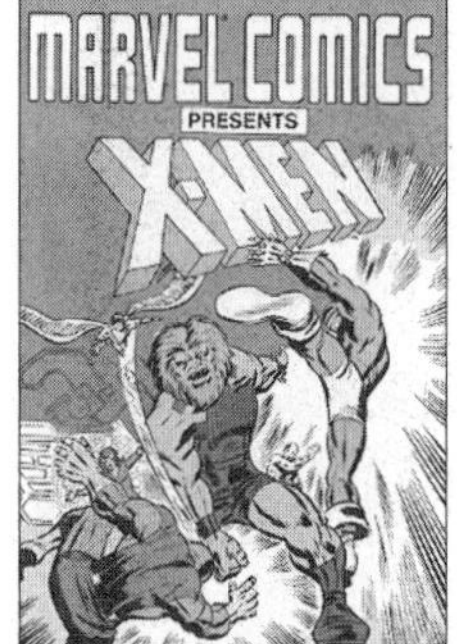

Marvel Comics Presents the X-Men

Marvel Double Feature

Marvel Double Shot

Pictorial Confessions
St. John, 1949
1 .... 200.00
2 .... 125.00
3 .... 100.00

Pictorial Love Stories
Charlton, 1949
22-26 .... 110.00

Pictorial Romances
St. John, 1950
4 .... 160.00
5 .... 120.00
6-9 .... 90.00
10 .... 120.00
11 .... 100.00
12-13 .... 90.00
14 .... 80.00
15-16 .... 90.00
17-20 .... 165.00
21-24 .... 80.00

Picture News
News in Color and Action, 1946
1 .... 120.00
2 .... 100.00
3 .... 80.00
4 .... 95.00
5-10 .... 60.00

Picture Parade
Gilberton, 1953
1 .... 110.00
2-4 .... 60.00

Picture Progress
Gilberton, 1954
5-9 .... 38.00

Picture Progress
Gilberton, 1954
1-9 .... 38.00

Picture Stories From American History
E.C., 1946
1 .... 140.00
2-4 .... 110.00

Picture Stories from Science
E.C., 1947
1 .... 75.00
2 .... 50.00

Picture Stories from the Bible (New Testament)
E.C., 1944
1 .... 50.00
2-3 .... 38.00

Picture Stories from the Bible (Old Testament)
E.C., 1943
1 .... 100.00
2-4 .... 75.00

Picture Stories from World History
E.C., 1947
1 .... 210.00
2 .... 160.00

Picture Taker
Slave Labor, 1998
1 .... 3.00

Pie
Wow Cool
1 .... 3.00

Piece of Steak
Tome
1 .... 3.00

Pieces
5th Panel, 1997
1-3 .... 3.00

Pied Piper Graphic Album
Pied Piper
1-3 .... 7.00

Pied Piper of Hamelin
Tome
1 .... 3.00

Pigeonman
Above & Beyond, 1997
1 .... 3.00

Pigeon-Man, the Bird-Brain
Ferry Tail, 1993
1 .... 3.00

Pighead
Williamson
1 .... 3.00

Pigtale
Image, 2005
1-4 .... 3.00

Pilgrim's Progress
Marvel, 1992
1 .... 10.00

Pineapple Army
Viz, 1988
1-10 .... 2.00

Pinhead
Marvel, 1993
1-6 .... 3.00

Pinhead & Foodini
Fawcett, 1951
1 .... 180.00
2-3 .... 90.00
4 .... 75.00

Pinhead vs. Marshal Law: Law in Hell
Marvel, 1993
1-2 .... 3.00

Pink Dust
Kitchen Sink, 1998
1 .... 4.00

Pink Floyd
Personality
1-2 .... 3.00

Pink Floyd Experience
Revolutionary, 1991
1-5 .... 3.00

Pink Panther
Gold Key, 1971
1 .... 40.00
2 .... 17.00
3-5 .... 15.00
6-10 .... 8.00
11-20 .... 6.00
21-40 .... 4.00
41-74 .... 3.00
75-76 .... 15.00
77 .... 17.00
78-83 .... 8.00
84-87 .... 15.00

Pink Panther
Harvey, 1993
1-SS 1 .... 2.00

Pinky and the Brain
DC, 1996
1 .... 3.00
2-27 .... 2.00
Holiday 1 .... 3.00

Pinocchia
NBM
1 .... 12.00

Pinocchio and the Emperor of the Night
Marvel, 1988
1 .... 1.00

Pinocchio Special
Gladstone, 1990
1 .... 2.00

Pint-Sized X-Babies
Marvel, 1998
1 .... 3.00

Pioneer Picture Stories
Street & Smith, 1941
1 .... 165.00
2 .... 85.00
3-9 .... 75.00

Pipsqueak Papers (Wallace Wood's...)
Fantagraphics
1 .... 3.00

Piracy
E.C., 1954
1 .... 160.00
2 .... 115.00
3-7 .... 85.00

Piracy
Gemstone, 1998
1-7 .... 3.00

Piranha Is Loose!
Special Studio
1-2 .... 3.00

Pirate Club
Slave Labor, 2004
1-8 .... 3.00

Pirate Corps
Eternity, 1987
1-4 .... 3.00

Pirate Corp$!
Slave Labor, 1989
1-5/2nd 3.00
Special 1 .... 2.00
Special 1/2nd 3.00

Pirate Queen
Comax
1 .... 3.00

Pirates Comics
Hillman, 1950
1 .... 135.00
2 .... 100.00
3-4 .... 90.00

Pirates of Coney Island
Image, 2006
1-2 .... 3.00
3-3/Variant 4.00

Pirates of Dark Water
Marvel, 1991
1-9 .... 1.00

P.I.'s: Michael Mauser and Ms. Tree
First, 1985
1-3 .... 2.00

Pistolero
Eternity
1 .... 4.00

Pita Ten Official Fan Club Book
Tokyopop, 2005
1 .... 10.00

Pi: The Book of Ants
Artisan Entertainment
1 .... 3.00

Pitt
Image, 1993
½ 2.00
1 .... 3.00
1/Gold 4.00
2-13 .... 2.00
14-20 .... 3.00

Marvel Fanfare

Marvel Frontier Comics Unlimited

Marvel Graphic Novel

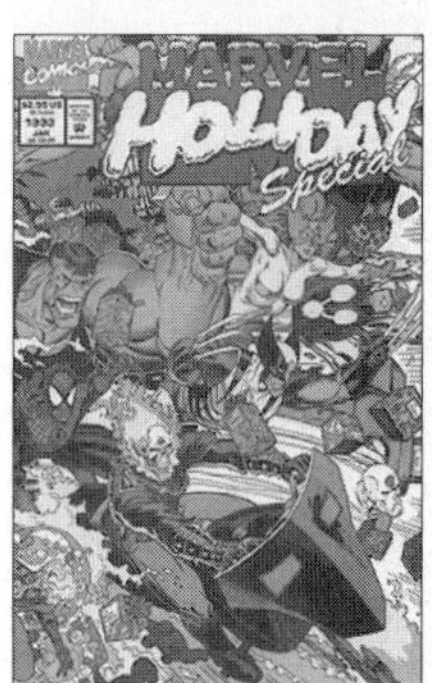

Marvel Holiday Special

Marvel Knights

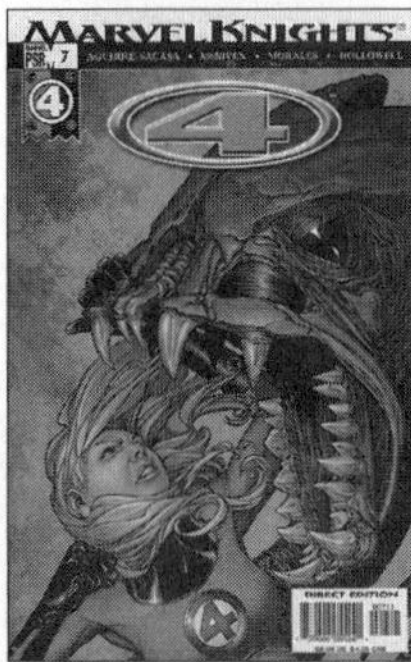
Marvel Knights 4

Marvel Knights Magazine

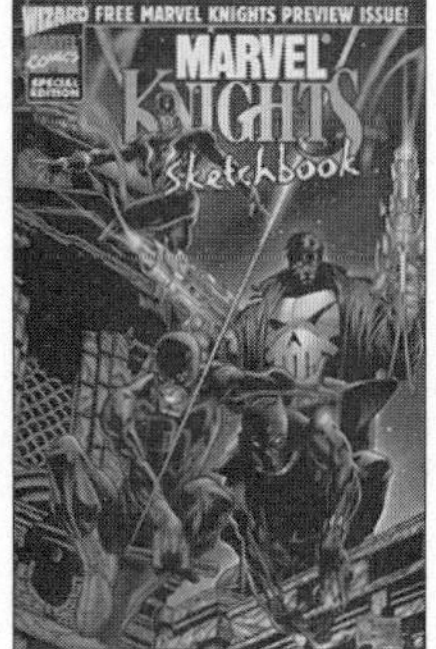
Marvel Knights Sketchbook

Pitt
Marvel
1 .... 3.00

Pitt Crew
Full Bleed, 1998
1 .... 3.00

Pitt: In the Blood
Full Bleed, 1996
1 .... 3.00

Pixie and Dixie and Mr. Jinks
Gold Key, 1963
1 .... 60.00

Pixies
Magazine Enterprises, 1946
1 .... 50.00
2-5 .... 30.00

Pixy Junket
Viz
1-6 .... 3.00

P.J. Warlock
Eclipse, 1986
1-3 .... 2.00

Places That Are Gone
Aeon, 1994
1-2 .... 3.00

Plague
Tome
1 .... 3.00

Plan 9 from Outer Space
Eternity, 1990
1-1/2nd 5.00

Plan 9 from Outer Space: Thirty Years Later
Eternity, 1991
1-3 .... 3.00

Planet 29
Caliber
1-2 .... 3.00

Planetary
DC, 1999
1 .... 8.00
☛Warren Ellis series
2-26 .... 3.00

Planetary/Batman: Night on Earth
DC, 2003
1 .... 6.00

Planetary: Crossing Worlds
DC, 2004
1 .... 15.00

Planetary/JLA: Terra Occulta
WildStorm, 2002
1 .... 6.00

Planetary/The Authority: Ruling the World
DC, 2000
nn 6.00

Planet Blood
Tokyopop, 2005
1-3 .... 10.00

Planet Comics
Fiction House, 1940
1 .... 12,500.00
2 .... 5,000.00
3 .... 3,250.00
4-7 .... 2,500.00
8-12 .... 2,000.00
13-14 .... 1,500.00
15 .... 2,700.00
☛Scarce
16-18 .... 1,350.00
19-24 .... 1,225.00
25-30 .... 1,000.00
31-40 .... 850.00
41-50 .... 600.00
51-60 .... 500.00
61-70 .... 400.00
71-73 .... 300.00

Planet Comics
Blackthorne, 1988
1-3 .... 2.00

Planet Comics
A-List, 1997
1-3 .... 3.00

Planet Comics
Avalon
1 .... 6.00

Planet Hulk: Gladiator Guidebook
Marvel, 2006
1 .... 4.00

Planet Ladder
Tokyopop, 2002
1-2 .... 10.00

Planet of Geeks
Starhead
1 .... 3.00

Planet of Terror (Basil Wolverton's...)
Dark Horse, 1987
1 .... 2.00

Planet of the Apes
Marvel, 1974
1 .... 20.00
1/2nd 5.00

2 ... 10.00
3 ... 9.00
4-5 ... 8.00
6 ... 6.00
7-29 ... 5.00
Ann 1 ... 4.00

Planet of the Apes
Adventure, 1990
1-1/Ltd. ... 4.00
1/2nd-24 ... 3.00
Ann 1 ... 4.00

Planet of the Apes
Dark Horse, 2001
1-3/Variant ... 3.00

Planet of the Apes
Dark Horse, 2001
1-6/Variant ... 3.00

Planet of the Apes: Blood of the Apes
Adventure, 1991
1-4 ... 3.00

Planet of the Apes: Forbidden Zone
Adventure, 1992
1-4 ... 3.00

Planet of the Apes: Sins of the Father
Adventure, 1992
1 ... 3.00

Planet of the Apes: Urchak's Folly
Adventure, 1991
1-4 ... 3.00

Planet of Vampires
Atlas-Seaboard, 1975
1 ... 12.00
2-3 ... 8.00

Planet Patrol
Edge
1 ... 3.00

Planet Terry
Marvel, 1985
1-12 ... 1.00

Planet-X
Eternity
1 ... 3.00

Planet X Reprint Comic
Planet X, 1987
1 ... 2.00

Plaque X
Aholattafun, 2004
1 ... 3.00

Plasm
Defiant, 1993
0 ... 1.00

Plasma Baby
Caliber
1-3 ... 3.00

Plasmer
Marvel, 1993
1 ... 3.00
2-4 ... 2.00

Plastic Forks
Marvel, 1990
1-5 ... 5.00

Plastic Little
CPM, 1997
1-5 ... 3.00

Plastic Man
Comic Magazines, 1943
1 ... 3,200.00
2 ... 1,300.00
3 ... 800.00
4 ... 700.00
5 ... 565.00
6-10 ... 450.00
11-20 ... 375.00
21-30 ... 310.00
31-40 ... 240.00
41-50 ... 200.00
51-64 ... 165.00

Plastic Man
DC, 1966
1 ... 150.00
2 ... 50.00
3 ... 30.00
4-5 ... 20.00
6-10 ... 15.00
11-20 ... 8.00

Plastic Man
DC, 2004
1-20 ... 3.00

Plastic Man
DC, 1988
1-4 ... 1.00

Plastic Man Lost Annual
DC, 2004
1 ... 7.00

Plastic Man Special
DC, 1999
1 ... 4.00

Plastron Cafè
Mirage, 1992
1-4 ... 2.00

Platinum
Komodo
1 ... 4.00

Platinum.44
Comax
1 ... 3.00

Marvel Knights Spider-Man

Marvel Knights Wave 2 Sketchbook

Marvel Magazine

Marvel Mangaverse

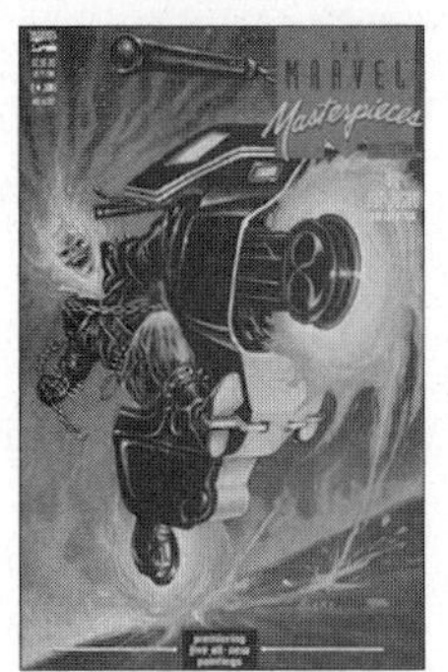
Marvel Masterpieces Collection

Marvel Movie Premiere

Marvel Must Haves

Marvel Mystery Comics

Platinum Grit
Dead Numbat, 1994
1-6 .... 4.00

Playbear
Fantagraphics, 1995
1-3 .... 3.00

Playful Little Audrey
Harvey, 1957
1 .... 90.00
2 .... 50.00
3-5 .... 35.00
6-10 .... 24.00
11-21 .... 15.00
22-40 .... 12.00
41-50 .... 10.00
51-60 .... 8.00
61-80 .... 5.00
81-99 .... 3.00
100-103 .... 4.00
104-121 .... 3.00

Playground
Caliber
1 .... 3.00

Playgrounds
Fantagraphics
1 .... 2.00

Pleasure & Passion (Alazar's...)
Brainstorm, 1997
1 .... 3.00

Pleasure Bound
Fantagraphics, 1996
1 .... 3.00

Plop!
DC, 1973
1 .... 18.00
2-3 .... 8.00
4-5 .... 7.00
6-10 .... 6.00
11-23 .... 5.00
24 .... 8.00

PMS Book
Ivory Tower
1-1/7th 4.00

Pocahontas (Disney's...)
Marvel, 1995
1 .... 5.00

Pocket Comics
Harvey, 1941
1 .... 1,100.00
2 .... 775.00
3-4 .... 525.00

Poe
Cheese, 1996
1-11 .... 3.00

Poe
Sirius, 1997
1-Special 1 .... 3.00

Poets Prosper: Rhyme & Revelry
Tome
1 .... 4.00

Pogo Parade
Dell, 1953
1 .... 275.00

Pogo Possum
Dell, 1949
1 .... 500.00
2 .... 400.00
3-5 .... 300.00
6-8 .... 250.00
9-13 .... 200.00
14-16 .... 150.00

Point Blank
WildStorm, 2002
1-5 .... 3.00

Point-Blank
Eclipse
1-2 .... 3.00

Point Pleasant
Ape Entertainment, 2004
1 .... 4.00

Poison Elves: Hyena
Sirius Entertainment, 2004
1-4 .... 3.00

Poison Elves
Mulehide, 1993
8 .... 15.00
9-10 .... 12.00
11-15 .... 10.00
15/2nd 3.00
16-17 .... 8.00
17/2nd 3.00
18-20 .... 5.00
Deluxe 1 .... 35.00

Poison Elves
Sirius, 1995
1 .... 6.00
1/2nd 3.00
2-3 .... 4.00
4-70 .... 3.00
Special 1 .... 4.00

Poison Elves: Ventures
Sirius, 2005
1 .... 4.00

Poizon
London Night, 1995
0 .... 3.00
0/Nude 4.00
½-1 .... 3.00
1/A 15.00
1/Nude 5.00
2-3 .... 3.00

Pokèmon: The Electric Tale of Pikachu

Viz, 1998

1 .... 4.00
1/2nd-4 .... 3.00

Pokèmon Part 2

Viz, 1999

1-4 .... 3.00

Pokèmon Part 3

Viz, 1999

1-4 .... 4.00

Pokèmon Adventures

Viz, 1999

1-5 .... 6.00

Pokèmon Adventures Part 2

Viz, 2000

1-6 .... 3.00

Pokèmon Adventures Part 3

Viz, 2000

1-7 .... 3.00

Pokèmon Adventures Part 4

Viz, 2001

1-2 .... 3.00
3-4 .... 5.00

Pokèmon Adventures Part 5

Viz, 2001

1-5 .... 5.00

Pokèmon Adventures Part 6

Viz, 2001

1-4 .... 5.00

Pokèmon Adventures Part 7

Viz, 2002

1-5 .... 5.00

Pokèthulhu Adventure Game

Dork Storm

1 .... 6.00

Police Academy

Marvel, 1989

1-6 .... 1.00

Police Action

Marvel, 1954

1 .... 140.00
2 .... 85.00
3-7 .... 55.00

Police Action

Atlas-Seaboard, 1975

1 .... 11.00
2-3 .... 5.00

Police Against Crime

Premiere, 1954

1 .... 150.00
2 .... 75.00
3-9 .... 50.00

Police Badge #479

Atlas, 1955

5 .... 75.00

Police Comics

Comic Magazines, 1941

1 .... 6,000.00
2 .... 2,250.00
3 .... 1,700.00
4-5 .... 1,450.00
6-7 .... 1,350.00
8 .... 1,500.00
9-10 .... 1,100.00
11 .... 1,750.00
12-13 .... 985.00
14-20 .... 725.00
21-22 .... 575.00
23-30 .... 500.00
31-40 .... 375.00
41-43 .... 315.00
44-50 .... 260.00
51-60 .... 195.00
61-70 .... 175.00
71-80 .... 160.00
81-93 .... 145.00
94-102 .... 225.00
103 .... 140.00
104-127 .... 110.00

Police Line-Up

Avon, 1951

1 .... 225.00
2 .... 150.00
3-4 .... 115.00

Police Trap

Mainline, 1954

1 .... 165.00
2-4 .... 100.00
5-6 .... 130.00

Polis

Brave New Words

1-2 .... 3.00

Political Action Comics

Comicfix, 2004

1 .... 5.00

Polly and Her Pals

Eternity, 1990

1-5 .... 3.00

Polly and the Pirates

Oni, 2005

1-2 .... 3.00

Polly Pigtails

Parents' Magazine Institute, 1946

1 .... 75.00
2 .... 35.00

Marvel Poster Book

Marvel Premiere

Marvel Preview

Marvel Riot

Marvels

Marvel Saga

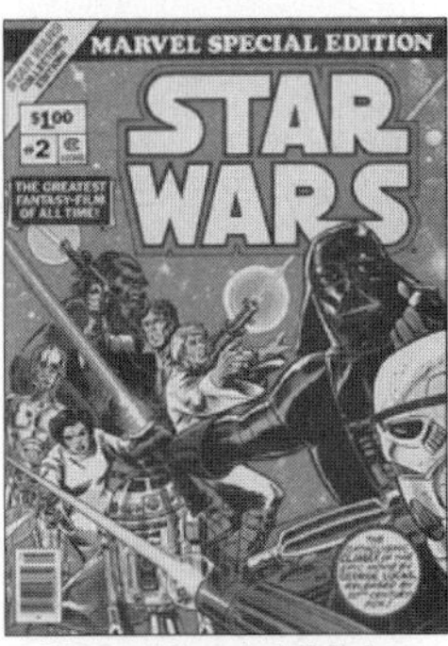

Marvel Special Edition Featuring Star Wars

Marvel Spring Special

3-5 .... 30.00
6-20 .... 25.00
21-30 .... 20.00
31-43 .... 15.00

Ponytail
Dell, 1962

-209 .... 12.00
2-12 .... 8.00

Ponytail
Charlton, 1969

13 .... 6.00
14-20 .... 4.00

Poot
Fantagraphics, 1997

1-3 .... 3.00
4 .... 4.00

Popbot
Idea & Design Works, 2002

1-4 .... 8.00
5-7 .... 10.00

Popcorn!
Discovery

1 .... 4.00

Popcorn Pimps
Fantagraphics, 1996

1 .... 9.00

Popeye
Dell, 1948

1 .... 250.00
2 .... 150.00
3-5 .... 125.00
6-10 .... 100.00
11-20 .... 75.00
21-30 .... 60.00
31-50 .... 50.00
51-69 .... 40.00
70-80 .... 30.00
81-92 .... 25.00
93-100 .... 20.00
101-120 .... 15.00
121-138 .... 10.00
139-149 .... 7.00
150-155 .... 5.00
156-157 .... 10.00
158 .... 35.00
159 .... 30.00
162-167 .... 10.00
168-171 .... 18.00
Special 1 .... 2.00

Popeye (Educational Series)
King, 1972

E 1-E 15 .... 4.00

Popeye
Harvey, 1993

1-Summer 1 .... 2.00

Popeye Special
Ocean, 1987

1-2 .... 2.00

Pop Life
Fantagraphics, 1998

1-2 .... 4.00

Popples
Marvel, 1986

1-4 .... 1.00

Poppo of the Popcorn Theatre
Fuller, 1955

1 .... 25.00
2 .... 15.00
3-5 .... 12.00
6-13 .... 10.00

Popular Comics
Dell, 1936

1 .... 3,650.00
2 .... 1,285.00
3 .... 1,025.00
4 .... 815.00
5 .... 750.00
6-7 .... 600.00
8-10 .... 565.00
11-15 .... 455.00
16-20 .... 400.00
21-30 .... 345.00
31-40 .... 300.00
41-45 .... 240.00
46 .... 310.00
☛1st Marvel Man
47-50 .... 240.00
51-60 .... 205.00
61-71 .... 160.00
72-75 .... 140.00
76-78 .... 200.00
79-80 .... 140.00
81-90 .... 130.00
91-100 .... 110.00
101-110 .... 85.00
111 .... 50.00
112-130 .... 80.00
131-145 .... 65.00

Popular Romance
Better, 1949

5 .... 60.00
6-10 .... 40.00
11-21 .... 35.00
22-27 .... 45.00
28-29 .... 35.00

Popular Teenagers
Star, 1950

5 .... 185.00
6-8 .... 170.00
9 .... 110.00
10 .... 105.00
11 .... 85.00
12-13 .... 95.00

14 .... 120.00
15 .... 100.00
16 .... 85.00
17 .... 95.00
18-19 .... 85.00
20-21 .... 95.00
22-23 .... 85.00

Pork Knight: This Little Piggy

Silver Snail, 1986

1 .... 2.00

Porky Pig

Dell, 1952

25-30 .... 12.00
31-50 .... 9.00
51-70 .... 7.00
71-81 .... 6.00

Porky Pig

Gold Key, 1965

1 .... 30.00
2 .... 14.00
3-5 .... 12.00
6-10 .... 8.00
11-20 .... 5.00
21-30 .... 4.00
31-50 .... 3.00
51-109 .... 2.00

Pornotopia

Radio, 1999

1 .... 3.00

Port

Silverwolf, 1987

1-2 .... 2.00

Portable Lowlife

Aeon, 1993

1 .... 5.00

Portals of Elondar

Storybook, 1996

1 .... 3.00

Portent

Image, 2006

1-4 .... 3.00

Portfolios

Delta, 1994

1-3 .... 3.00

Portfolios Preview

Delta

Ashcan 1 .... 1.00

Portia Prinz of the Glamazons

Eclipse, 1986

1-6 .... 2.00

Portrait of a Young Man as a Cartoonist

Hammer & Anvil, 1996

1-8 .... 3.00

Possessed

DC, 2003

1-6 .... 3.00

Possibleman

Blackthorne, 1987

1-2 .... 2.00

Post Apocalypse

Slave Labor, 1994

1 .... 3.00

(Post-Atomic) Cyborg Gerbils

Trigon, 1986

1-2 .... 3.00

Post Brothers

Rip Off, 1991

19-38 .... 3.00

Potential

Slave Labor, 1998

1-2 .... 4.00
3 .... 5.00
4 .... 4.00

Pound

Radio, 2000

1 .... 3.00

Pounded

Oni, 2002

1-3 .... 3.00

Powder Burn

Antarctic, 1999

1-1/A 3.00
1/CS 6.00

Power

Aircel, 1991

1-4 .... 2.00

Power & Glory

Malibu, 1994

1/A-4 .... 3.00
WS 1 .... 3.00

Power Brigade

Moving Target

1 .... 2.00

Power Comics

Holyoke, 1944

1 .... 1,500.00
2-4 .... 1,250.00

Power Comics

Power, 1977

1-5 .... 2.00

Power Comics

Eclipse, 1988

1-4 .... 2.00

Power Company

DC, 2002

1-18 .... 3.00

Marvel Super Action

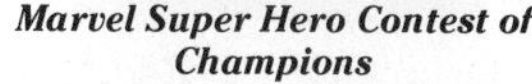

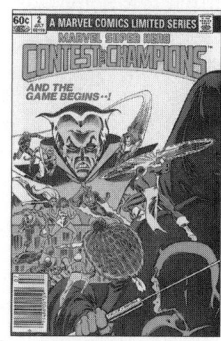

Marvel Super Hero Contest of Champions

Marvel Super-Heroes Megazine

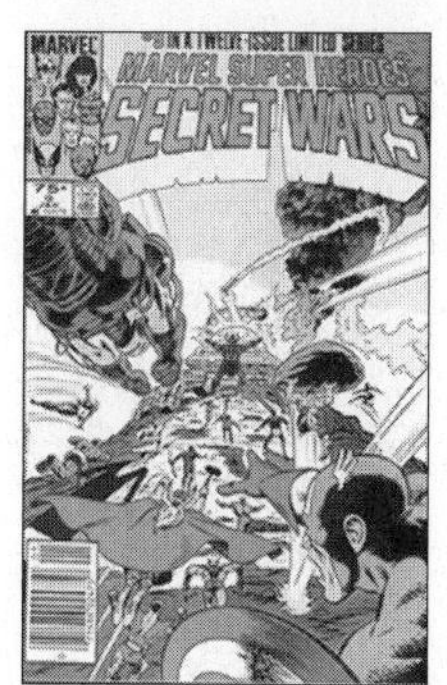

Marvel Super Heroes Secret Wars

Marvel Super Special

Marvel Team-Up

Marvel Treasury Edition

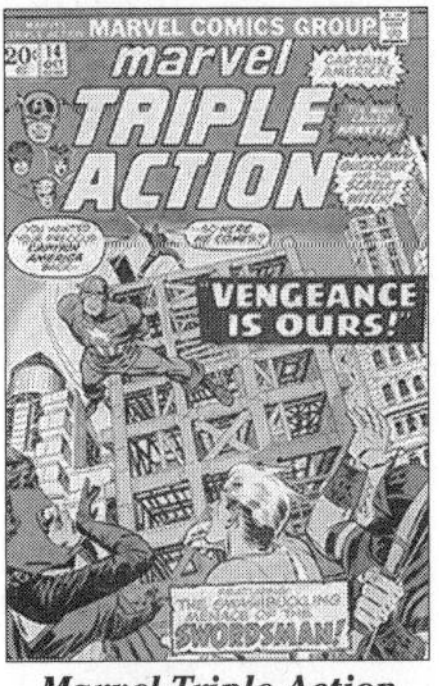

Marvel Triple Action

Power Company: Bork
DC, 2002

1 ....3.00

Power Company: Josiah Power
DC, 2002

1 ....3.00

Power Company: Manhunter
DC, 2002

1 ....3.00

Power Company: Sapphire
DC, 2002

1 ....3.00

Power Company: Skyrocket
DC, 2002

1 ....3.00

Power Company: Striker Z
DC, 2002

1 ....3.00

Power Company: Witchfire
DC, 2002

1 ....3.00

Power Defense
Miller

1 ....3.00

Power Factor
Wonder, 1986

1-2 ....2.00

Power Factor
Innovation, 1990

1-3 ....2.00
Special 1 ....3.00

Power Girl
DC, 1988

1-4 ....1.00

Powerhouse Pepper Comics
Timely, 1943

1 ....1,025.00
2 ....525.00
3-4 ....485.00
5 ....570.00

Powerless
Marvel, 2004

1-6 ....3.00

Power Line
Marvel, 1988

1-8 ....2.00

Power Lords
DC, 1983

1-3 ....1.00

Power Man & Iron Fist
Marvel, 1974

17 ....8.00
18-20 ....5.00
21-30 ....4.00
30/30¢ 20.00
31 ....4.00
31/30¢ 20.00
32 ....3.00
32/30¢ 20.00
33 ....3.00
33/30¢ 20.00
34 ....3.00
34/30¢ 20.00
35-44 ....3.00
44/35¢ 15.00
45 ....3.00
45/35¢ 15.00
46 ....3.00
46/35¢ 15.00
47-47/Whitman 3.00
47/35¢ 15.00
48 ....10.00
49-50 ....6.00
51-52 ....3.00
53-55 ....4.00
56 ....3.00
57 ....12.00
58-65 ....3.00
66 ....20.00
☛2nd Sabretooth
67-77 ....2.00
78 ....5.00
79-83 ....2.00
84 ....6.00
☛Sabretooth app.
85-125 ....2.00
Ann 1 ....4.00

Power of Prime
Malibu, 1995

1-4 ....3.00

Power of Shazam
DC, 1994

1 ....3.00
2-42 ....2.00
43-47 ....3.00
1000000 ....4.00
Ann 1 ....3.00

Power of Strong Man
AC

1 ....3.00

Power of the Atom
DC, 1988

1-18 ....1.00

Power Pachyderms
Marvel, 1989

1 ....1.00

Power Pack

Marvel, 1984

1-2 .... 2.00
3-9 .... 1.00
10 .... 2.00
11-18 .... 1.00
19 .... 2.00
20-26 .... 1.00
27 .... 4.00
28-43 .... 1.00
44-62 .... 2.00
Holiday 1 .... 3.00

Power Pack

Marvel, 2000

1-4 .... 3.00

Power Pack

Marvel, 2005

1-4 .... 3.00

Power Plays

Millennium, 1995

1 .... 3.00

Power Plays

AC, 1985

1-2 .... 2.00

Power Plays

Extrava-Gandt

1-3 .... 2.00

Powerpuff Girls

DC, 2000

1 .... 5.00
2-3 .... 3.00
4-70 .... 2.00

Powerpuff Girls Double Whammy

DC, 2000

1 .... 5.00

Power Rangers Turbo: Into the Fire

Acclaim

1 .... 5.00

Power Rangers Zeo

Image, 1996

1-2 .... 3.00

Powers

Image, 2000

1 .... 7.00
2 .... 6.00
3 .... 5.00
4-10 .... 4.00
11-37 .... 3.00
Ann 1 .... 4.00

Powers Coloring/Activity Book

Image, 2001

1 .... 2.00

Powers

Marvel, 2004

1-11 .... 3.00
12/Bendis 4.00
12/Oeming-21 .... 3.00

Powers That Be

Broadway, 1995

1 .... 2.00
2 .... 3.00
2/Ashcan 1.00
3 .... 3.00
3/Ashcan 1.00
4-9 .... 3.00

Prairie Moon and Other Stories

Dark Horse

1 .... 2.00

Preacher

DC, 1995

1 .... 13.00
2 .... 6.00
3-5 .... 5.00
6-10 .... 4.00
11-49 .... 3.00
50-66 .... 4.00

Preacher Special: Cassidy: Blood & Whiskey

DC, 1998

1 .... 6.00

Preacher Special: One Man's War

DC, 1998

1 .... 5.00

Preacher Special: Saint of Killers

DC, 1996

1-4 .... 3.00

Preacher Special: Tall in the Saddle

DC, 2000

1 .... 5.00

Preacher Special: The Good Old Boys

DC, 1997

1 .... 5.00

Preacher Special: The Story of You-Know-Who

DC, 1996

1 .... 5.00

Precious Metal

Arts Industria, 1990

1 .... 3.00

Predator

Dark Horse, 1989

1 .... 5.00
1/2nd 3.00

Marvel Two-In-One

Marvel Valentine Special

Marville

Mary Jane

Mary Marvel

Mary Worth

Masked Ranger

Masked Rider

2 .... 4.00
3-4 .... 3.00

Predator 2

Dark Horse, 1991

1-2 .... 3.00

Predator: Bad Blood

Dark Horse, 1993

1-4 .... 3.00

Predator: Big Game

Dark Horse, 1991

1-4 .... 3.00

Predator: Captive

Dark Horse, 1998

1 .... 3.00

Predator: Cold War

Dark Horse, 1991

1-4 .... 3.00

Predator: Dark River

Dark Horse, 1996

1-4 .... 3.00

Predator: Hell & Hot Water

Dark Horse, 1997

1-3 .... 3.00

Predator: Hell Come a Walkin'

Dark Horse, 1998

1-2 .... 3.00

Predator: Homeworld

Dark Horse, 1999

1-4 .... 3.00

Predator: Invaders from the Fourth Dimension

Dark Horse, 1994

1 .... 4.00

Predator: Jungle Tales

Dark Horse, 1995

1 .... 3.00

Predator: Kindred

Dark Horse, 1996

1-4 .... 3.00

Predator: Nemesis

Dark Horse, 1997

1-2 .... 3.00

Predator: Primal

Dark Horse, 1997

1-2 .... 3.00

Predator: Race War

Dark Horse, 1993

0-4 .... 3.00

Predator: Strange Roux

Dark Horse, 1996

1 .... 3.00

Predator: The Bloody Sands of Time

Dark Horse, 1992

1-2 .... 3.00

Predator versus Judge Dredd

Dark Horse, 1997

1-3 .... 3.00

Predator vs. Magnus Robot Fighter

Dark Horse, 1992

1 .... 3.00
1/Platinum 10.00
2 .... 3.00

Predator: Xenogenesis

Dark Horse, 1999

1-4 .... 3.00

Prelude to Blue Dog

Ground Zero, 1996

1 .... 4.00

Premiere

Diversity

1 .... 3.00
1/Gold 4.00
1/Ltd.-2 .... 3.00

Preservation of Obscurity

Lump of Squid

1-2 .... 3.00

President Dad

Tokyopop, 2004

1-4 .... 10.00

Pressed Tongue (Dave Cooper's...)

Fantagraphics, 1994

1-3 .... 3.00

Presto Kid

AC

1 .... 3.00

Pretear

ADV Manga, 2004

1-4 .... 10.00

Pre-Teen Dirty-Gene Kung-Fu Kangaroos

Blackthorne, 1986

1-3 .... 2.00

Prey

Monster

1-3 .... 2.00

Prey for Us Sinners

Fantaco

1 .... 5.00

Prez
DC, 1973

1 .... 12.00
2 .... 6.00
3-4 .... 5.00

Pride & Joy
DC, 1997

1-4 .... 3.00

Pride of the Yankees
Magazine Enterprises, 1949

1 .... 450.00

Priest
Maximum, 1996

1-3 .... 3.00

Primal
Dark Horse, 1992

1-2 .... 3.00

Primal Force
DC, 1994

0-14 .... 2.00

Primal Rage
Sirius, 1996

1-4 .... 3.00

Prime
Malibu, 1993

½-1 .... 3.00
1/Hologram 5.00
1/Ltd. 3.00
2-11 .... 2.00
12 .... 4.00
13-26 .... 2.00
Ann 1 .... 4.00
Ashcan 1 .... 1.00

Prime
Malibu, 1995

0-15 .... 2.00

Prime 8 Creation
Two Morrows, 2001

1 .... 4.00

Prime/Captain America
Malibu, 1996

1 .... 4.00

Prime Cuts
Fantagraphics, 1987

1-10 .... 4.00

Prime Cuts (Mike Deodato's...)
Caliber

1 .... 3.00

Primer
Comico, 1982

1 .... 5.00
2 .... 55.00
☛1st Grendel
3-4 .... 4.00
5 .... 50.00
☛1st Sam Kieth art
6 .... 5.00

Primer
Comico, 1996

1 .... 3.00

Prime Slime Tales
Mirage, 1986

1-4 .... 2.00

Prime vs. the Incredible Hulk
Malibu, 1995

0 .... 5.00

Primitives
Sparetime, 1995

1-3 .... 3.00

Primortals (Vol. 1) (Leonard Nimoy's...)
Tekno, 1995

1-16 .... 2.00

Primortals (Vol. 2) (Leonard Nimoy's...)
Big, 1996

0-8 .... 2.00

Primortals Origins (Leonard Nimoy's...)
Tekno, 1995

1-2 .... 2.00

Primus
Charlton, 1972

1 .... 7.00
2-4 .... 4.00
5-7 .... 3.00

Prince: Alter Ego
Piranha Music, 1991

1 .... 2.00

Prince and the New Power Generation: Three Chains of Gold
DC

1 .... 4.00

Prince and the Pauper
Dell, 1962

1 .... 15.00

Prince and the Pauper (Disney's...)
Disney

1 .... 6.00

Prince Namor, the Sub-Mariner
Marvel, 1984

1-4 .... 2.00

Masked Warrior X

Master Comics

Masterman Comic

Master of Kung Fu

Master of the Void

Matt Champion

Matterbaby

Max Burger PI

Prince Nightmare
Aaaargh!

1 ....3.00

Princess and the Frog
NBM

1 ....16.00

Princess Karanam and the Djinn of the Green Jug
Mu

1 ....3.00

Princess Natasha
DC, 2006

1-3 ....2.00

Princess Prince
CPM Manga, 2000

1-10 ....3.00

Princess Sally
Archie, 1995

1-3 ....2.00

Princess Tutu
ADV Manga, 2005

1-2 ....10.00

Prince Valiant
Marvel, 1994

1-4 ....4.00

Prince Valiant Monthly
Pioneer

1-4 ....5.00

Prince Vandal
Triumphant, 1993

1-6 ....3.00

Priority: White Heat
AC, 1987

1-2 ....2.00

Prison Break
Realistic Comics, 1951

1 ....250.00
2 ....175.00
3 ....145.00
4-5 ....125.00

Prisoner
DC, 1988

1-4 ....4.00

Prisoner of Chillon
Tome

1 ....3.00

Prisonopolis
Mediawarp, 1997

1-4 ....3.00

Prison Riot
Avon, 1952

1 ....200.00

Private Beach: Fun and Perils in the Trudyverse
Antarctic, 1995

1-3 ....3.00

Private Commissions (Gray Morrow's...)
Forbidden Fruit, 1992

1-2 ....3.00

Privateers
Vanguard, 1987

1-2 ....2.00

Private Eye
Atlas, 1951

1 ....150.00
2-3 ....90.00
4-8 ....70.00

Private Eyes
Eternity, 1988

1-3 ....2.00
4 ....3.00
5-6 ....4.00

Prize Comics
Feature, 1940

1 ....1,700.00
2 ....825.00
3-5 ....625.00
6 ....545.00
7 ....1,200.00
8-9 ....600.00
10-12 ....510.00
13 ....550.00
14-20 ....445.00
21-24 ....345.00
25-30 ....280.00
31-35 ....215.00
36-40 ....160.00
41-45 ....130.00
46-50 ....105.00
51-60 ....78.00
61-68 ....62.00

Prize Comics Western
Feature, 1948

69 ....100.00
70-90 ....90.00
91-112 ....80.00
113 ....125.00
114-119 ....80.00

Prize Mystery
Key, 1955

1 ....75.00
2-3 ....50.00

Pro
Image, 2002

1 ....6.00

Pro Action Magazine
Marvel, 1994

1-3 ....3.00

Probe

Imperial

1-3 .... 2.00

Prof. Coffin

Charlton, 1985

19-21 .... 2.00

Professional: Golgo 13

Viz

1-3 .... 5.00

Professor Om

Innovation, 1990

1 .... 3.00

Professor Xavier and the X-Men

Marvel, 1995

1-3 .... 2.00

4-18 .... 1.00

Profolio

Alchemy, 1989

1 .... 2.00

2-3 .... 3.00

Profolio

Alchemy

1 .... 6.00

Progeny

Caliber

1 .... 5.00

Program Error: Battlebot

Phantasy

1 .... 2.00

Project

DC, 1997

1-2 .... 6.00

Project A-Ko

Malibu, 1994

1-4 .... 3.00

Project A-Ko 2

CPM, 1995

1-3 .... 3.00

Project A-Ko versus

CPM, 1995

1-5 .... 3.00

Project Arms

Viz, 2002

1-5 .... 3.00

Project: Dark Matter

Dimm Comics, 1996

1-4 .... 3.00

Project: Generation

Truth, 2000

1-2 .... 1.00

Project: Hero

Vanguard, 1987

1-2 .... 2.00

Project Sex

Fantagraphics, 1991

1 .... 3.00

Project: Superior

Adhouse Books, 2005

1 .... 20.00

Project X

Kitchen Sink

1 .... 3.00

Promethea

DC, 1999

1 .... 6.00

☛Alan Moore series

1/Variant 7.00

2 .... 4.00

3-22 .... 3.00

23 .... 4.00

24-31 .... 3.00

32 .... 4.00

32/Ltd 125.00

Prometheus' Gift

Cat-Head

1 .... 2.00

Prometheus (Villains)

DC, 1998

1 .... 2.00

Promise

Viz

1 .... 6.00

Propellerman

Dark Horse, 1993

1-8 .... 3.00

Prophecy of the Soul Sorcerer

Arcane, 1998

1-3 .... 3.00

Ashcan 1 .... 2.00

Prophecy of the Soul Sorcerer Preview Issue

Arcane

1 .... 2.00

Prophecy of the Soul Sorcerer

Arcane, 2000

1-3 .... 3.00

Prophet

Image, 1993

0-10 .... 3.00

Prophet

Image, 1995

1 .... 4.00

1/Chromium 5.00

1/Holochrome 6.00

2 .... 3.00

2/Platt 4.00

Maximum Security

Max the Magnificent

Maxwell Mouse Follies

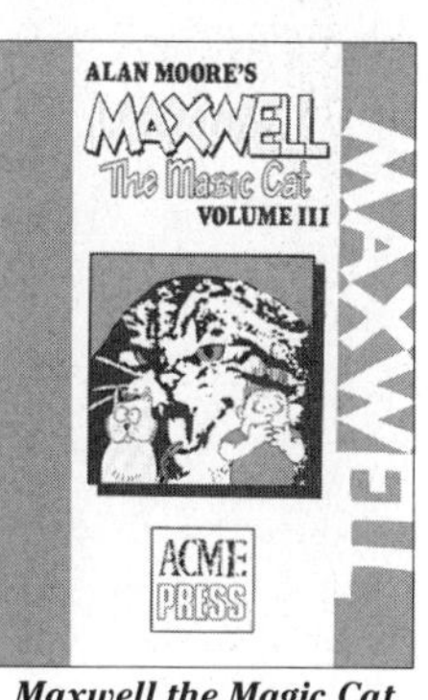

Maxwell the Magic Cat

Maxx

Mayhem

Mazie and her Boyfriends

M.D. Geist

3-8 ....3.00
Ann 1/A-1/B 4.00

Prophet
Awesome, 2000

1-1/A 3.00

Prophet Babewatch
Image, 1995

1 ....3.00

Prophet/Cable
Maximum, 1997

1-2 ....4.00

Prophet/Chapel: Super Soldiers
Image, 1996

1/A-2 ....3.00

Proposition Player
DC, 1999

1-6 ....3.00

Protectors Handbook
Malibu, 1992

1 ....3.00

Protectors
Malibu, 1992

1 ....2.00
1/CS-12 ....3.00
13-16 ....2.00
17 ....3.00
18 ....2.00
19-20 ....3.00

Protectors
New York

1-2 ....2.00

Protheus (Mike Deodato's...)
Caliber, 1996

1-2 ....3.00

Protista Chronicles
Xulu

1 ....2.00

Prototykes Holiday Special/Hero Illustrated Holiday Special
Dark Horse, 1994

1-2 ....1.00

Prototype
Malibu, 1993

0 ....2.00
1 ....3.00
1/Hologram 5.00
2 ....2.00
3 ....3.00
4-12 ....2.00
13 ....4.00
14-17 ....2.00
18-GS 1 ....3.00

Prowler
Eclipse, 1987

1-4 ....2.00

Prowler
Marvel, 1994

1-4 ....2.00

Prowler in "White Zombie"
Eclipse, 1988

1 ....2.00

Pro Wrestling's True Facts
Dan Pettiglio, 1994

1 ....3.00

Proximity Effect
Image, 2004

1 ....10.00

Prudence & Caution
Defiant, 1994

1-6 ....3.00

Pryde & Wisdom
Marvel, 1996

1-3 ....2.00

Pscythe
Image, 2004

1-2 ....4.00

Psi-Force
Marvel, 1986

1-Ann 1 ....1.00

Psi-Judge Anderson
Fleetway-Quality

1-15 ....2.00

Psi-Judge Anderson: Engrams
Fleetway-Quality

1-2 ....2.00

Psi-Judge Anderson: Psifiles
Fleetway-Quality

1 ....3.00

Psi-Lords
Valiant, 1994

1 ....4.00
1/VVSS 70.00
1/Gold 20.00
2-4 ....1.00
5-8 ....2.00
9 ....3.00
10 ....5.00

PS238
Dork Storm, 2002

0-9 ....3.00

Psyba-Rats
DC, 1995

1-3 ....3.00

Psychic Academy
Tokyopop, 2004
1-10 .... 10.00

Psycho
DC, 1991
1-3 .... 5.00

Psycho (Alfred Hitchcock's...)
Innovation
1-3 .... 3.00

Psychoanalysis
E.C., 1955
1 .... 100.00
2-4 .... 85.00

Psychoanalysis
Gemstone, 1999
1-4 .... 3.00
Ann 1 .... 11.00

Psychoblast
First, 1987
1-9 .... 2.00

Psycho Killers
Comic Zone, 1992
1 .... 4.00
1/2nd 3.00
2 .... 4.00
2/2nd 3.00
3 .... 4.00
3/2nd-10 .... 3.00
11 .... 4.00
12-15 .... 3.00

Psycho Killers PMS Special
Zone, 1993
1 .... 3.00

Psycho (Magazine)
Skywald, 1971
1 .... 20.00
2 .... 12.00
3 .... 10.00
4-10 .... 8.00
11-20 .... 6.00
21-24 .... 5.00
Anl 1972-Anl 1974 .... 5.00

Psychoman
Revolutionary, 1992
1 .... 3.00

Psychonaut
Fantagraphics, 1996
1-3 .... 4.00

Psychonauts
Marvel, 1993
1-4 .... 5.00

Psycho-Path
Venusian, 1990
1-2 .... 2.00

Psycho-Path The Ultimate Vigilante
Greater Mercury, 1990
1 .... 2.00

Psychotic Adventures Illustrated
Last Gasp, 1972
1-3 .... 3.00

Psy-Comm
Tokyopop, 2005
1 .... 10.00

Psyence Fiction
Abaculus, 1998
½ 1.00
1 .... 3.00

Psylocke & Archangel: Crimson Dawn
Marvel, 1997
1-4 .... 3.00

PT 109
K.K., 1964
1 .... 12.00

Pteranoman
Kitchen Sink, 1990
1 .... 2.00

Public Enemies
D.S., 1948
1 .... 115.00
2 .... 100.00
3-5 .... 65.00
6-7 .... 55.00

Public Enemies
Eternity
1-2 .... 4.00

Pubo
Dark Horse, 2002
1-3 .... 4.00

Pudgy Pig
Charlton, 1958
1-2 .... 20.00

Puffed
Image, 2003
1-3 .... 3.00

Puke & Explode
Northstar, 1990
1-2 .... 3.00

Pulp (Vol. 1)
Viz, 1997
1 .... 6.00

Pulp (Vol. 2)
Viz, 1998
1-12 .... 6.00

Mea Culpa

Me-A Day With Elvis

Mean Machine

Meanwhile...

Measles

Meatface the Amazing Flesh

Mecha

Mechanical Man Blues

Pulp (Vol. 3)

Viz, 1999

1-12 .... 6.00

Pulp (Vol. 4)

Viz, 2000

1-6 .... 6.00

Pulp (Vol. 5)

Viz, 2001

1-12 .... 6.00

Pulp (Vol. 6)

Viz

1-8 .... 6.00

Pulp Action

Avalon

1-8 .... 3.00

Pulp Dreams

Fantagraphics, 1991

1 .... 3.00

Pulp Fantastic

DC, 2000

1-3 .... 3.00

Pulp Fiction

A List, 1997

1-6 .... 3.00

Pulp Western

Avalon

1 .... 3.00

Pulse

Blackjack, 1997

1 .... 2.00

Pulse

Marvel, 2004

1 .... 5.00
2-4 .... 3.00
5 .... 2.00
6-9 .... 3.00
10 .... 6.00
☛House of M
10/Variant 4.00
☛2nd print
11-14 .... 3.00

Pulse: House of M Special Edition

Marvel, 2005

1 .... 1.00

Puma Blues

Aardvark One, 1986

1-23 .... 2.00

Pummeler

Parody, 1992

1 .... 3.00

Pummeler $2099

Parody

1 .... 3.00

Pumpkinhead: The Rites of Exorcism

Dark Horse, 1992

1-4 .... 3.00

Punch & Judy (Vol. 1)

Hillman, 1944

1 .... 125.00
2 .... 70.00
3-12 .... 60.00

Punch & Judy (Vol. 2)

Hillman, 1949

1 .... 40.00
2 .... 125.00
3-9 .... 40.00
10-12 .... 125.00

Punch & Judy (Vol. 3)

Hillman, 1951

1 .... 125.00
2 .... 115.00
3-9 .... 40.00

Punch Comics

Harry A. Chesler, 1941

1 .... 800.00
2 .... 525.00
9 .... 500.00
10 .... 380.00
11 .... 340.00
12 .... 400.00
13 .... 380.00
14-15 .... 330.00
16-17 .... 310.00
18 .... 400.00
19 .... 330.00
20 .... 600.00
21 .... 330.00
22-23 .... 150.00

Punisher

Marvel, 1986

1 .... 13.00
2-3 .... 7.00
4-5 .... 6.00

Punisher

Marvel, 1987

1 .... 7.00
2-3 .... 4.00
4-9 .... 3.00
10 .... 4.00
11-62 .... 2.00
63-74 .... 1.00
75 .... 3.00
76-80 .... 2.00
81-85 .... 1.00

86 .... 3.00
87-90 .... 1.00
91-99 .... 2.00
100 .... 3.00
100/Variant-101 .... 4.00
102-104 .... 2.00
Ann 1 .... 4.00
Ann 2-3 .... 3.00
Ann 4-5 .... 2.00
Ann 6-7 .... 3.00

Punisher
Marvel, 1995
1 .... 3.00
2-18 .... 2.00

Punisher
Marvel, 1998
1 .... 3.00
1/Variant 6.00
2-4 .... 3.00

Punisher
Marvel, 2000
1 .... 4.00
1/Variant 9.00
2 .... 4.00
2/Variant 6.00
3 .... 4.00
4-12 .... 3.00

Punisher
Marvel, 2001
1-37 .... 3.00

Punisher
Marvel, 2004
1 .... 5.00
2 .... 4.00
3-60 .... 3.00

Punisher: A Man Named Frank
Marvel, 1994
1 .... 7.00

Punisher Anniversary Magazine
Marvel
1 .... 5.00

Punisher Armory
Marvel, 1990
1-10 .... 2.00

Punisher Back to School Special
Marvel, 1992
1 .... 4.00
2-3 .... 3.00

Punisher/Batman: Deadly Knights
Marvel, 1994
1 .... 5.00

Punisher/Black Widow: Spinning Doomsday's Web
Marvel
1 .... 10.00

Punisher: Bloodlines
Marvel, 1991
1 .... 6.00

Punisher: Blood on the Moors
Marvel
1 .... 17.00

Punisher: Bloody Valentine
Marvel, 2006
1 .... 4.00

Punisher: Die Hard in the Big Easy
Marvel, 1992
1 .... 5.00

Punisher: Empty Quarter
Marvel, 1994
1 .... 7.00

Punisher: G-Force
Marvel, 1992
1 .... 5.00

Punisher Holiday Special
Marvel, 1993
1-3 .... 3.00

Punisher Invades the 'Nam: Final Invasion
Marvel, 1994
1 .... 7.00

Punisher Kills the Marvel Universe
Marvel, 1995
1 .... 20.00
1/2nd 6.00

Punisher: Kingdom Gone
Marvel, 1990
1 .... 17.00

Punisher Magazine
Marvel, 1989
1-16 .... 3.00

Punisher Meets Archie
Marvel, 1994
1 .... 4.00
1/Variant 5.00

Punisher Movie Special
Marvel, 1990
1 .... 6.00

Punisher: No Escape
Marvel, 1990
1 .... 5.00

Mechanics

Mechanoids

Mech Destroyer

Medal of Honor

Meef Comix

Meet Corliss Archer

Megahurtz

Megaton

Punisher: Official Movie Adaptation
Marvel, 2004

1-3 .... 3.00

Punisher: Origin of Micro Chip
Marvel, 1993

1-2 .... 2.00

Punisher/Painkiller Jane
Marvel, 2001

1 .... 4.00

Punisher: P.O.V.
Marvel, 1991

1-4 .... 5.00

Punisher: Red X-Mas
Marvel, 2004

1 .... 4.00

Punisher: Silent Night
Marvel, 2006

1 .... 4.00

Punisher Summer Special
Marvel, 1991

1-4 .... 3.00

Punisher: The Cell
Marvel, 2005

1 .... 5.00

Punisher: The End
Marvel, 2004

1 .... 5.00

Punisher: The Ghosts of Innocents
Marvel, 1993

1-2 .... 6.00

Punisher: The Movie
Marvel, 2004

1-3 .... 3.00

Punisher: The Prize
Marvel, 1990

1 .... 5.00

Punisher: The Tyger
Marvel, 2006

1 .... 5.00

Punisher 2099
Marvel, 1993

1 .... 2.00
2-15 .... 1.00
16-25 .... 2.00
25/Variant 3.00
26-34 .... 2.00

Punisher vss Bullseye
Marvel, 2006

1-5 .... 3.00

Punisher vs. Daredevil
Marvel, 2000

1 .... 4.00

Punisher War Journal
Marvel, 1988

1 .... 5.00
2-7 .... 3.00
8-49 .... 2.00
50 .... 3.00
51-60 .... 2.00
61 .... 3.00
62-64/Variant 2.00
65 .... 3.00
66-74 .... 2.00
75 .... 4.00
76 .... 3.00
77-80 .... 2.00

Punisher War Journal
Marvel, 2006

1-5 .... 3.00
6 .... 6.00
7 .... 3.00

Punisher War Zone
Marvel, 1992

1 .... 3.00
2-22 .... 2.00
23 .... 3.00
24-41 .... 2.00
Ann 1-2 .... 3.00

Punisher/Wolverine African Saga
Marvel, 1988

1 .... 6.00

Punisher X-Mas Special
Marvel, 2007

1 .... 4.00

Punisher: Year One
Marvel, 1994

1-4 .... 3.00

Punx
Acclaim, 1995

1-3 .... 3.00

Punx (Manga) Special
Acclaim, 1996

1 .... 3.00

Puppet Comics
George W. Dougherty, 1946

1-2 .... 75.00

Puppet Master
Eternity

1-4 .... 3.00

Puppet Master: Children of the Puppet Master
Eternity, 1991

1-2 .... 3.00

Puppetoons (George Pal's ...)
Fawcett, 1945

1 .... 300.00

2 .... 150.00
3-19 .... 100.00

Puppy Action!
Northstar

1 .... 3.00

Puppy in My Pocket
Burghley

1-35 .... 3.00

Pure Images
Pure Imagination, 1990

1-4 .... 3.00

Purgatori
Chaos!, 1998

½-Ashcan 1 .... 3.00

Purgatori
Devil's Due, 2000

1-6 .... 3.00

Purgatori: Empire
Chaos, 2000

1-3 .... 3.00

Purgatori: Goddess Rising
Chaos!, 1999

1-4 .... 3.00

Purgatori: The Dracula Gambit
Chaos!, 1997

1-1/Variant 3.00

Purgatori: The Dracula Gambit Sketchbook
Chaos!, 1997

1 .... 3.00

Purgatori: The Vampires Myth
Chaos!, 1996

-1 .... 2.00
1 .... 4.00
1/Ltd. 5.00
1/Variant 8.00
2-6 .... 3.00

Purgatori vs. Vampirella
Chaos, 2000

nn 3.00

Purgatory USA
Slave Labor, 1989

1 .... 2.00

Purge
Ania, 1993

0-1 .... 2.00

Purge
Amara

0 .... 2.00

Purple Claw
Toby, 1953

8 .... 0.00
1 .... 175.00
2-3 .... 125.00

Purple Claw Mysteries
AC

1 .... 3.00

Purple Hood
John Spencer & Co.

1-2 .... 5.00

Purr
Blue Eyed Dog

1 .... 8.00

Pussycat
Marvel, 1968

1 .... 150.00

PvP
Dork Storm, 2001

1 .... 3.00

PvP
Image, 2003

1 .... 5.00
2-19 .... 3.00

PvP
Image, 2005

0 .... 1.00
20-29 .... 3.00

Pyrite
Samson

1 .... 1.00

Q-Loc
Chiasmus, 1994

1 .... 3.00

Quack!
Star*Reach, 1976

1-6 .... 3.00

Quadrant
Quadrant, 1983

1-8 .... 2.00

Quadro Gang
Nonsense Unlimited

1 .... 1.00

Quagmire
Kitchen Sink, 1970

1 .... 3.00

Quagmire U.S.A.
Antarctic, 1994

1-3 .... 3.00

Quagmire U.S.A.
Antarctic, 2004

1-5 .... 3.00

Quality Special
Fleetway-Quality

1-2 .... 2.00

Quantum & Woody
Acclaim, 1997

17 .... 3.00
Ashcan 1 .... 1.00

Megaton Man

Mekanix

Melody

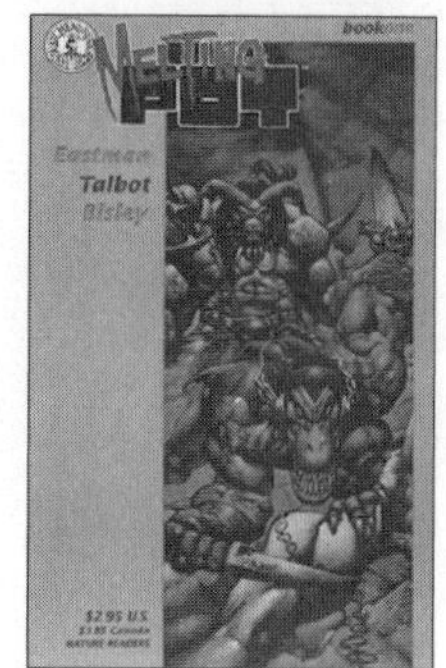

Melting Pot

Melty Feeling

Memories

Menace

Menagerie

Quantum Creep
Parody, 1992

1 .... 3.00

Quantum Leap
Innovation, 1991

1 .... 5.00
2-5 .... 4.00
6-13 .... 3.00
Ann 1 .... 4.00
Special 1 .... 5.00

Quantum: Rock of Ages
Dreamchilde Press, 2003

1-4 .... 3.00

Quasar
Marvel, 1989

1 .... 2.00
2-46 .... 1.00
47 .... 2.00
☛1st Thunderstrike
48-49 .... 1.00
50 .... 3.00
51-60 .... 1.00
Special 1-3 .... 2.00

Queen & Country
Oni, 2001

1 .... 9.00
1/FCBD 1.00
2 .... 7.00
3 .... 6.00
4-15 .... 5.00
16-20 .... 4.00
21-24 .... 3.00
25 .... 6.00
26-28 .... 3.00

Queen & Country: Declassified
Oni, 2002

1-3 .... 3.00

Queen & Country: Declassified
Oni, 2005

1 .... 3.00

Queen & Country: Declassified
Oni, 2005

1-3 .... 3.00

Queen of the Damned (Anne Rice's...)
Innovation, 1991

1-12 .... 3.00

Queen of the West, Dale Evans
Dell, 1954

3 .... 60.00
4-5 .... 55.00
6-10 .... 48.00
11-22 .... 44.00

Queen's Greatest Hits
Revolutionary, 1993

1 .... 3.00

Quest for Camelot
DC, 1998

1 .... 5.00

Quest for Dreams Lost
Literacy Volunteers, 1987

1 .... 2.00

Question
DC, 1987

1-36 .... 2.00
Ann 1 .... 3.00
Ann 2 .... 4.00

Question
DC, 2005

1-6 .... 3.00

Question Quarterly
DC, 1990

1-5 .... 3.00

Question Returns
DC, 1997

1 .... 4.00

Quest of the Tiger Woman
Millennium

1 .... 3.00

Quest Presents
Quest, 1983

1-3 .... 2.00

Questprobe
Marvel, 1984

1-3 .... 2.00

Quick Draw McGraw
Dell, 1960

2 .... 15.00
3-7 .... 10.00
8-12 .... 8.00
13-14 .... 6.00
15 .... 10.00

Quick Draw McGraw
Charlton, 1970

1 .... 10.00
2 .... 7.00
3-5 .... 5.00
6-8 .... 4.00

Quicken Forbidden
Cryptic, 1996

1-13 .... 3.00

Quicksilver
Marvel, 1997

1 .... 3.00
2-13 .... 2.00

Quick-Trigger Western
Atlas, 1956

12-19 .... 100.00

Quincy Looks Into His Future
General Electric
1 .... 2.00

Quit City (Warren Ellis')
Avatar, 2004
1 .... 4.00
1/Foil 15.00

Quit Your Job
Alternative
1 .... 7.00

Quivers
Caliber, 1991
1-2 .... 3.00

Q-Unit
Harris, 1993
1 .... 3.00

Qwan
Tokyopop, 2005
1-3 .... 10.00

Rabbit
Sharkbait, 1999
1 .... 3.00

Rabid
Fantaco
1 .... 6.00

Rabid Animal Komix
Krankin' Komix, 1995
1-2 .... 3.00

Rabid Monkey
D.B.I. Comics, 1997
1 .... 2.00

Rabid Rachel
Miller
1 .... 2.00

Race Against Time
Dark Angel, 1997
1-2 .... 3.00

Race for the Moon
Harvey, 1958
1 .... 100.00
2-3 .... 150.00

Race of Scorpions
Dark Horse, 1990
1-2 .... 5.00

Race of Scorpions
Dark Horse, 1991
1 .... 2.00
2-4 .... 3.00

Racer X
Now, 1988
1-11 .... 2.00

Racer X
Now, 1989
1-10 .... 2.00

Racer X
WildStorm, 2000
1-3 .... 3.00

Racer X Premiere
Now, 1988
1 .... 4.00

Rack & Pain
Dark Horse, 1994
1-4 .... 3.00

Rack & Pain: Killers
Chaos, 1996
1-4 .... 3.00

Racket Squad in Action
Charlton, 1952
1 .... 150.00
2-4 .... 80.00
5 .... 120.00
6 .... 80.00
7-10 .... 75.00
11 .... 165.00
12 .... 300.00
13 .... 55.00
14 .... 75.00
15-28 .... 55.00
29 .... 60.00

Radical Dreamer
Blackball, 1994
0 .... 3.00
1 .... 2.00
2-4 .... 3.00

Radical Dreamer
Mark's Giant Economy Size, 1995
1-5 .... 3.00

Radioactive Man
Bongo, 1993
1-88 .... 5.00
216-1000 .... 3.00

Radioactive Man
Bongo, 2000
1-9 .... 3.00

Radioactive Man 80 Page Colossal
Bongo, 1995
1 .... 5.00

Radio Boy
Eclipse, 1987
1 .... 2.00

Radiskull & Devil Doll: Radiskull Love-Hate One Shot
Image, 2003
1 .... 3.00

Mendy and the Golem

Men of War

Menthu

Menz Insana

Mephisto Vs.

Mercedes

Mercy

Meridian

Radix
Image, 2001

1-2 .... 3.00

Radrex
Bullet, 1990

1 .... 2.00

Ragamuffins
Eclipse, 1985

1 .... 2.00

Rage
Anarchy Bridgeworks

1 .... 3.00

Raggedy Ann and Andy
Dell, 1946

1 .... 180.00
2-4 .... 125.00
5-9 .... 100.00
10-15 .... 75.00
16-19 .... 60.00
20-39 .... 50.00

Raggedy Ann and Andy
Dell, 1964

1 .... 35.00
2-4 .... 20.00

Raggedy Ann and Andy
Gold Key, 1971

1 .... 5.00
2-6 .... 4.00

Raggedyman
Cult, 1993

1-1/Variant 3.00
2-3 .... 2.00
4-6 .... 3.00

Raging Angels
Classic Hippie

1 .... 3.00

Ragman
DC, 1976

1 .... 5.00
2-5 .... 3.00

Ragman
DC, 1991

1-8 .... 2.00

Ragman: Cry of the Dead
DC, 1993

1-6 .... 2.00

Ragmop
Planet Lucy, 1995

1-7 .... 3.00

Ragmop
Image, 1997

1-3 .... 3.00

Ragnarok Guy
Sun

1 .... 3.00

Rags Rabbit
Harvey, 1951

11 .... 25.00
12-18 .... 20.00

Rahrwl
Northstar

1 .... 3.00
1/2nd 2.00

Rai
Valiant, 1992

0 .... 4.00
1 .... 8.00
1/Companion 1.00
2 .... 6.00
3 .... 16.00
4 .... 15.00
5 .... 6.00
6-8 .... 3.00
☛adds ...Future Force
25-28 .... 1.00
29-31 .... 2.00
32 .... 3.00
33 .... 5.00

Rai and the Future Force
Valiant, 1993

9 .... 1.00
☛was Rai
9/Gold 18.00
9/VVSS 10.00
10-20 .... 1.00
21 .... 2.00
21/VVSS 60.00
22-24 .... 1.00
☛becomes Rai again

Rai Companion
Valiant, 1993

1 .... 1.00

Raiders of the Lost Ark
Marvel, 1981

1-3 .... 2.00

Raider 3000
Gauntlet

1-2 .... 3.00

Raijin Comics
Gutsoon, 2002

1-36 .... 5.00
37-41 .... 6.00

Raika
Sun

1-20 .... 3.00

Rain
Tundra

1-6 .... 2.00

Rainbow Brite and the Star Stealer
DC, 1985

1 .... 1.00

Raisin Pie
Fantagraphics, 2002
1-4 .... 4.00

Rak
Rak Graphics
1 .... 5.00

Rakehell
Draculina
1 .... 3.00

Ralfy Roach
Bugged Out, 1993
1 .... 3.00

Ralph Kiner, Home Run King
Fawcett, 1950
1 .... 250.00

Ralph Snart Adventures
Now, 1986
1 .... 3.00
2-3 .... 2.00

Ralph Snart Adventures
Now, 1986
1-9 .... 2.00

Ralph Snart Adventures
Now, 1988
1 .... 2.00
1/3D 3.00
1/CS 4.00
2-23 .... 2.00
24 .... 3.00
25-26 .... 2.00

Ralph Snart Adventures
Now, 1992
1-3 .... 3.00

Ralph Snart Adventures
Now, 1993
1-5 .... 3.00

Ralph Snart: The Lost Issues
Now, 1993
1-3 .... 3.00

Ramar of the Jungle
Charlton, 1954
1 .... 125.00
2-5 .... 75.00

Ramba
Fantagraphics, 1992
1-8 .... 3.00

Ramblin' Dawg
Edge, 1994
1 .... 3.00

Rambo
Blackthorne, 1988
1 .... 2.00

Rambo III
Blackthorne
1 .... 2.00
3D 1 .... 3.00

Ramm
Megaton, 1987
1-2 .... 2.00

Rampage
Slap Happy, 1997
1 .... 10.00

Rampaging Hulk
Marvel, 1998
1-6 .... 2.00

Rampaging Hulk (Magazine)
Marvel, 1977
1 .... 35.00
2 .... 14.00
3-5 .... 5.00
6-9 .... 4.00

Ramthar (Mike Deodato's...)
Caliber, 1996
1 .... 3.00

Rana 7
NGNG
1-4 .... 3.00

Rana 7: Warriors of Vengeance
NGNG, 1995
1-2 .... 3.00

Random Encounter
Viper, 2005
1-4 .... 3.00

Randy O'Donnell is the M@n
Image, 2001
1-3 .... 3.00

Range Busters
Charlton, 1955
8 .... 50.00
9-10 .... 30.00

Rangeland Love
Atlas, 1949
1 .... 100.00
2 .... 85.00

Range Romances
Quality, 1949
1-2 .... 165.00
3 .... 130.00
4-5 .... 110.00

Rangers Comics
Fiction House, 1941
1 .... 2,750.00
2 .... 850.00

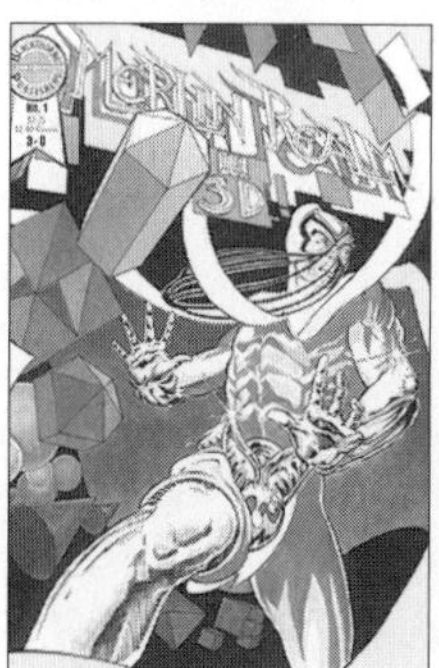

Merlinrealm 3-D

Mermaid

Mermaid Forest

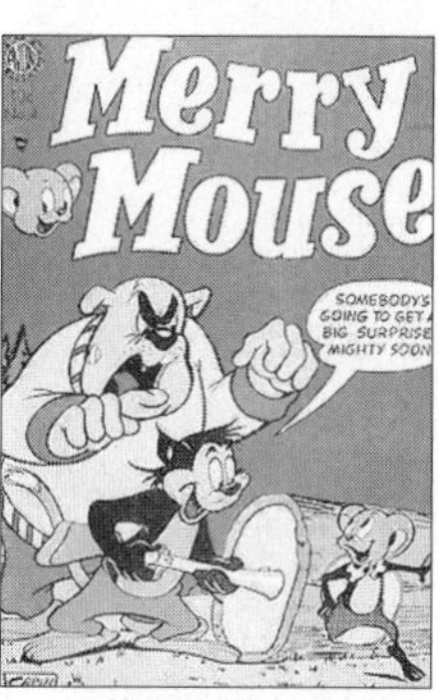

Merry Mouse

Merton of the Movement

Messenger 29

Messiah

Messozoic

3 .... 650.00
4-5 .... 500.00
6-12 .... 425.00
13-19 .... 350.00
20-24 .... 300.00
25-29 .... 250.00
30-39 .... 175.00
40-59 .... 120.00
60-69 .... 90.00

Rango
Dell, 1967

1 .... 25.00

Rank & Stinky
Parody

1-Special 1 .... 3.00

Ranma 1/2
Viz, 1991

1 .... 25.00
2 .... 10.00
3 .... 8.00
4-5 .... 6.00
6-7 .... 5.00

Ranma 1/2 Part 2
Viz, 1992

1 .... 7.00
2 .... 5.00
3-11 .... 4.00

Ranma 1/2 Part 3
Viz, 1992

1-13 .... 3.00

Ranma 1/2 Part 4
Viz, 1994

1-11 .... 3.00

Ranma 1/2 Part 5
Viz, 1994

1-12 .... 3.00

Ranma 1/2 Part 6
Viz, 1996

1-14 .... 3.00

Ranma 1/2 Part 7
Viz, 1998

1-14 .... 3.00

Ranma 1/2 Part 8
Viz, 1999

1-13 .... 3.00

Ranma 1/2 Part 9
Viz, 2000

1-11 .... 3.00

Ranma 1/2 Part 10
Viz, 2001

1-11 .... 3.00

Ranma 1/2 Part 11
Viz, 2002

1-11 .... 3.00

Ranma 1/2 Part 12
Viz, 2003

1 .... 3.00

Rann-Thanagar War
DC, 2005

1 .... 8.00
1/Variant 5.00
☛2nd printing
2 .... 4.00
3-6 .... 3.00

Rann/Thanagar War: Infinite Crisis Special
DC, 2006

1 .... 5.00

Rant
Boneyard, 1994

1-Ashcan 1 .... 3.00

Raphael Teenage Mutant Ninja Turtle
Mirage, 1987

1 .... 3.00
1/2nd 2.00

Rare Breed
Chrysalis, 1995

1-2 .... 3.00

Rascals in Paradise
Dark Horse, 1994

1-3 .... 4.00

Rat Bastard
Crucial, 1997

1-1/Ashcan 3.00
2-6 .... 2.00

Rated X
Aircel, 1991

1-Special 1 .... 3.00

Rat Fink Comics
World of Fandom

1-3 .... 3.00

Rat Fink Comix (Ed "Big Daddy" Roth's...)
Starhead

1 .... 2.00

Ratfoo
Spit Wad, 1997
1 .... 3.00

Rat Patrol
Dell, 1967
1-5 .... 40.00
6 .... 25.00

Rat Preview (Justin Hampton's...)
Aeon, 1997
1 .... 1.00

Rats!
Slave Labor, 1992
1 .... 3.00

Ravage 2099
Marvel, 1992
1 .... 2.00
2-18 .... 1.00
19-25 .... 2.00
25/Variant 3.00
26-33 .... 2.00

Rave Master
Tokyopop, 2003
1-18 .... 10.00

Raven
Malan Classical Enterprises
1 .... 5.00

Raven
Renaissance, 1993
1-4 .... 3.00

Raven Chronicles
Caliber, 1995
1-14 .... 3.00
15 .... 4.00

Ravens and Rainbows
Pacific, 1983
1 .... 2.00

Ravenwind
Pariah, 1996
1 .... 3.00

Raver
Malibu, 1993
1 .... 3.00
2-3 .... 2.00

Raw City
Dramenon
1 .... 3.00

Rawhide
Dell, 1962
1 .... 200.00

Rawhide
Gold Key, 1963
1 .... 175.00
2 .... 150.00

Rawhide Kid
Marvel, 1955
1 .... 800.00
2 .... 350.00
3-5 .... 185.00
6-10 .... 140.00
11-16 .... 110.00
17 .... 400.00
☛Origin, Kirby art
18-21 .... 95.00
22 .... 90.00
23 .... 200.00
☛Origin retold, Kirby
24-30 .... 90.00
31-44 .... 75.00
45 .... 90.00
46 .... 60.00
47-60 .... 35.00
61-70 .... 25.00
71-86 .... 18.00
87-92 .... 15.00
93-99 .... 12.00
100 .... 18.00
101-113 .... 12.00
114-120 .... 10.00
121-133 .... 7.00
133/30¢ 20.00
134 .... 7.00
134/30¢ 20.00
135-139 .... 7.00
140-140/35¢ 15.00
141-151 .... 6.00
Special 1 .... 12.00

Rawhide Kid
Marvel, 1985
1-4 .... 2.00

Rawhide Kid
Marvel, 2003
1 .... 5.00
2 .... 4.00
3-5 .... 3.00

Raw Media Illustrated
ABC, 1998
1-1/Nude 3.00

Raw Media Mags
Rebel, 1994
1-4 .... 5.00

Raw Periphery
Slave Labor
1 .... 3.00

Ray
ADV Manga, 2004
1-3 .... 10.00

Ray
DC, 1992
1 .... 3.00
2-6 .... 2.00

Meta-4

Metacops

Metal Bikini

Metal Guardian Faust

Metallix

Metal Men

Metal Militia

Metamorpho

Ray
DC, 1994

0-1 .... 2.00
1/Variant 3.00
2-24 .... 2.00
25 .... 4.00
26-28 .... 2.00
Ann 1 .... 4.00

Ray Bradbury Comics
Topps, 1993

1-Special 1 .... 4.00

Ray Bradbury Comics: Martian Chronicles
Topps, 1994

1 .... 3.00

Ray Bradbury Comics: Trilogy of Terror
Topps, 1994

1 .... 3.00

Ray Bradbury Special: Tales of Horror
Topps, 1994

1 .... 3.00

Ray-Mond
Deep-Sea

1-2 .... 3.00

Rayne
Sheet Happies, 1995

1-4 .... 3.00

Razor
London Night, 1991

0 .... 3.00
0/A 4.00
0/2nd-½ 3.00
1 .... 4.00
1/2nd-2 .... 3.00
2/Platinum 4.00
2/Variant 5.00
3 .... 3.00
3/CS 4.00
4 .... 3.00
4/Platinum 4.00
5 .... 3.00
5/Platinum 4.00
6-12 .... 3.00
Ann 1 .... 15.00
Ann 1/Gold 20.00
Ann 2 .... 4.00

Razor
London Night, 1996

1-7 .... 3.00

Razor & Shi Special
London Night, 1994

1 .... 3.00
1/Platinum 4.00

Razor Archives
London Night, 1997

1 .... 4.00
2-4 .... 5.00

Razor: Burn
London Night, 1995

1-4 .... 3.00

Razor/Cry No More
London Night, 1995

1 .... 4.00

Razor/Dark Angel: The Final Nail
London Night, 1994

1 .... 3.00

Razorguts
Monster, 1992

1-4 .... 2.00

Razorline: The First Cut
Marvel, 1993

1 .... 1.00

Razor/Morbid Angel
London Night, 1996

1-3 .... 3.00

Razor Nights (Mike Deodato's...)
Caliber, 1996

1 .... 3.00

Razor's Edge
Innovation, 1999

1 .... 3.00

Razor's Edge: Warblade
DC, 2005

1-5 .... 3.00

Razor: The Suffering
London Night

1-3 .... 3.00

Razor: Torture
London Night, 1995

0 .... 4.00
1-6 .... 3.00

Razor: Uncut
London Night, 1995

13-51 .... 3.00

Razor/Warrior Nun Areala: Faith
London Night, 1996

1 .... 4.00

Razorwire
5th Panel, 1996

1-2 .... 2.00

Reaction: The Ultimate Man
Studio Archein

1 .... 3.00

Reacto-Man

B-Movie

1-3 .... 2.00

Reactor Girl

Tragedy Strikes, 1991

1-5 .... 3.00

Reagan's Raiders

Solson, 1986

1-3 .... 2.00

Real Adventure Comics

Gilmore, 1955

1 .... 40.00

Real Adventures of Jonny Quest

Dark Horse, 1996

1-12 .... 3.00

Real Americans Admit: "The Worst Thing I've Ever Done!"

NBM

1 .... 9.00

Real Bout High School

Tokyopop, 2002

1-2 .... 10.00

Real Clue Crime Stories

Hillman, 1943

1 .... 275.00
2-4 .... 200.00
5-9 .... 55.00
10-21 .... 45.00
22-33 .... 40.00
34-45 .... 34.00
46-57 .... 28.00
58-73 .... 20.00

Real Deal Magazine

Real Deal

5 .... 2.00

Real Experiences

Atlas, 1950

25 .... 35.00

Real Fact Comics

DC, 1946

1 .... 370.00
2 .... 220.00
3 .... 200.00
4 .... 220.00
5 .... 850.00
☛Making of Batman
6 .... 700.00
☛1st Harlan Ellison
7 .... 105.00
8 .... 380.00
9 .... 160.00
10 .... 150.00
11-12 .... 85.00
13 .... 300.00
14 .... 80.00
15 .... 105.00
16 .... 270.00
17-18 .... 80.00
19 .... 90.00
20 .... 100.00
21 .... 80.00

Real Funnies

Nedor, 1943

1 .... 180.00
2-3 .... 90.00

Real Ghostbusters Summer Special

Now, 1993

1 .... 3.00

Real Ghostbusters 3-D Summer Special

Now, 1993

1 .... 3.00

Real Ghostbusters

Now, 1988

1-28 .... 2.00
3D 1 .... 3.00

Real Ghostbusters

Now, 1991

1 .... 2.00
1/3D 3.00
2-4 .... 2.00
Ann 1992 .... 1.00
Ann 1993 .... 3.00

Real Girl

Fantagraphics, 1990

1-4 .... 3.00
5-7 .... 4.00

Real Heroes

Parents' Magazine Institute, 1941

1 .... 125.00
2 .... 75.00
3-5 .... 60.00
6 .... 90.00
7-10 .... 45.00
11-16 .... 40.00

Realistic Romances

Realistic Comics, 1951

1 .... 125.00
2-4 .... 50.00
5-17 .... 45.00

Real Life

Fantagraphics, 1990

1 .... 3.00

Real Life Comics

Standard, 1941

1 .... 350.00
2 .... 135.00
3 .... 230.00
4-5 .... 95.00
6-10 .... 85.00
11-20 .... 65.00

Meteor Man

Metropolis S.C.U.

Miami Mice

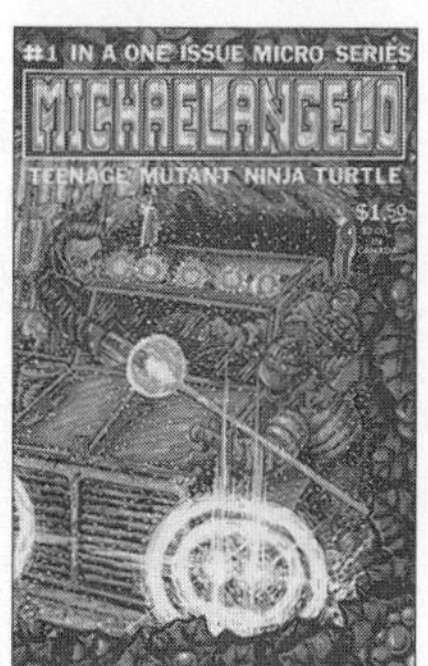

Michaelangelo Teenage Mutant Ninja Turtle

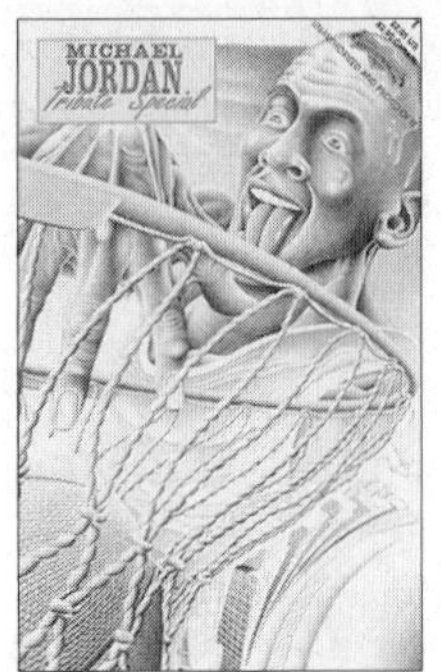

Michael Jordan Tribute

Mickey Finn

Mickey Mouse Surprise Party

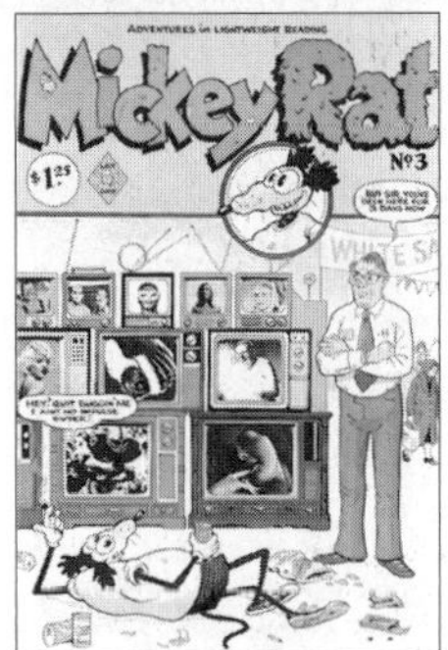

Mickey Rat

21-23 ....50.00
24 ....85.00
25-26 ....50.00
27 ....72.00
28-30 ....50.00
31-40 ....38.00
41-49 ....32.00
50 ....145.00
51 ....28.00
52 ....165.00
53-59 ....28.00

Real Life Secrets
Ace, 1949

1 ....75.00

Real Love
Ace, 1949

25-32 ....35.00
33-46 ....30.00
47-76 ....25.00

Really Fantastic Alien Sex Frenzy (Cynthia Petal's...)
Fantagraphics

1 ....4.00

Realm Handbook
Caliber

1 ....3.00

Realm of the Claw
Image, 2003

0 ....6.00
1/A-2/B 3.00

Realm of the Dead
Caliber

1-3 ....3.00

Realm
Arrow, 1986

1 ....5.00
2-3 ....2.00
4 ....4.00
5-15 ....2.00
16-21 ....3.00

Realm
Caliber

1-13 ....3.00

Real Schmuck
Starhead

1 ....3.00

Real Screen Comics
DC, 1945

1 ....750.00
2 ....325.00
3 ....250.00
4-5 ....175.00
6-10 ....125.00
11-21 ....80.00
22-30 ....55.00
31-39 ....38.00
40-50 ....26.00
51-60 ....18.00
61-70 ....16.00
71-90 ....14.00
91-100 ....10.00
101-128 ....8.00

Real Smut
Fantagraphics, 1993

1-6 ....3.00

Real Sports Comics
Hillman, 1948

1 ....250.00

Real Stuff
Fantagraphics, 1990

1-20 ....3.00

Real War Stories
Eclipse, 1987

1-1/2nd 2.00
2 ....5.00

Real Weird War
Avalon

1 ....3.00

Real Weird West
Avalon

1 ....3.00

Real Western Hero
Fawcett, 1948

70 ....150.00
71 ....75.00
72-73 ....60.00
74-75 ....50.00

Real West Romances
Crestwood, 1949

1 ....75.00
2-4 ....60.00
5-6 ....40.00

Realworlds: Batman
DC

1 ....6.00

Realworlds: Justice League of America
DC, 2000

1 ....6.00

Realworlds: Superman
DC

1 ....6.00

Realworlds: Wonder Woman
DC, 2000

1 ....6.00

Re-Animator
Aircel

1-3 ....3.00

Re-Animator: Dawn of the Re-Animator
Adventure, 1992
1-4 .... 3.00

Re-Animator in Full Color
Adventure, 1991
1-3 .... 3.00

Rear Entry
Fantagraphics, 2004
1-10 .... 4.00

R.E.B.E.L.S.
DC, 1994
0-17 .... 2.00

Rebel Sword
Dark Horse, 1994
1-5 .... 3.00

Rebirth
Tokyopop, 2003
1-16 .... 10.00

Recollections Sampler
Recollections
1 .... 1.00

Record of Lodoss War: Chronicles of the Heroic Knight
CPM Manga, 2000
1-11 .... 3.00

Record of Lodoss War: The Grey Witch
CPM, 1998
1-22 .... 3.00

Record of Lodoss War: The Lady of Pharis
CPM
1-8 .... 3.00

Rectum Errrectum
Boneyard
1 .... 4.00

Red
DC, 2003
1-3 .... 3.00

Red Arrow
P.L., 1951
1 .... 65.00
2-3 .... 50.00

Redblade
Dark Horse, 1993
1-3 .... 3.00

Red Circle
Rural Home, 1945
1 .... 400.00
2 .... 225.00
3-4 .... 125.00

Red Circle Sorcery
Red Circle, 1974
6 .... 10.00
☛Was Chilling Adventures in Sorcery
7-11 .... 5.00

Reddevil
AC
1 .... 3.00

Red Diaries
Caliber, 1997
1-4 .... 4.00

Red Dragon
Comico, 1996
1 .... 3.00

Red Dragon Comics (Vol. 1)
Street & Smith, 1943
5 .... 900.00
6 .... 1,500.00
7 .... 1,000.00
8-9 .... 500.00

Red Dragon Comics (Vol. 2)
Street & Smith, 1947
1 .... 650.00
2 .... 450.00
3 .... 350.00
4-7 .... 250.00

Redeemer
Images & Realities
1 .... 3.00

Redeemers
Antarctic, 1997
1 .... 3.00

Red Flannel Squirrel
Sirius, 1997
1 .... 3.00

Redfox
Harrier, 1986
1 .... 4.00
1/2nd 2.00
2-3 .... 3.00
4-20 .... 2.00

Red Heat
Blackthorne, 1988
1 .... 2.00
1/3D 3.00

Red Iceberg
Impact, 1960
1 .... 300.00

Red Mask
Magazine Enterprises, 1954
54 .... 0.00
42 .... 125.00
43 .... 105.00

Midnight

Midnight Mass

Midnight Men

Midnight Nation

Midnight Sons Unlimited

Midnight Tales

Midvale

Mighty Bomb

44-52 .... 95.00
53 .... 75.00

Redmask of the Rio Grande

AC

1-3 .... 3.00

Red Menace

DC, 2007

1-2/Variant 3.00

Red Moon

Millennium, 1995

1-2 .... 3.00

Red Planet Pioneer

Inesco

1 .... 3.00

Red Rabbit

Dearfield, 1947

1 .... 75.00
2 .... 45.00
3-10 .... 35.00
11-17 .... 30.00
18 .... 42.00
19-22 .... 30.00

Red Raven Comics

Timely, 1940

1 .... 10,000.00

Red Razors: A Dreddworld Adventure

Fleetway-Quality

1-3 .... 3.00

Red Revolution

Caliber

1 .... 3.00

Red Rocket 7

Dark Horse, 1997

1-5 .... 3.00
6-7 .... 4.00

Red Ryder Comics

Dell, 1940

1 .... 2,200.00
3 .... 1,000.00
4-5 .... 550.00
6 .... 400.00
7-10 .... 350.00
11-20 .... 280.00
21-30 .... 185.00
31-40 .... 125.00
41-50 .... 95.00
51-53 .... 68.00
54-73 .... 60.00
74-77 .... 54.00
78-83 .... 50.00
84-89 .... 45.00
90-95 .... 40.00
96-101 .... 35.00
102-107 .... 30.00
108-110 .... 26.00
111-120 .... 24.00
121-130 .... 22.00
131-140 .... 18.00
141-151 .... 16.00

Red Seal Comics

Harry A. Chesler, 1945

14 .... 475.00
15-16 .... 315.00
17-19 .... 285.00
20-22 .... 250.00

Red Shetland

Graphxpress, 1992

1-4 .... 2.00
5-8 .... 3.00
9-11 .... 4.00

Redskin

Youthful, 1950

1 .... 100.00
2-6 .... 50.00
7-12 .... 45.00

Red Sonja

Marvel, 1976

1 .... 8.00
2-4 .... 3.00
4/35¢-5/35¢ 20.00
6 .... 3.00
7-15 .... 2.00

Red Sonja

Marvel, 1983

1-2 .... 1.00

Red Sonja

Marvel, 1983

1-13 .... 2.00

Red Sonja

Dynamite Comics, 2005

0/Black-0/White 3.00
0/Ross 30.00
0/Sketch 150.00
0/Foil 10.00
0/Authentix 20.00
0/DF 25.00
1 .... 20.00
1/Rivera 25.00
1/Adams 35.00
1/Linsner 125.00
1/Ross 40.00
1/Rubi 20.00
1/DF 35.00
5 .... 3.00

Red Sonja: A Death in Scarlet

Cross Plains, 1999

1 .... 3.00

Red Sonja/Claw: Devil's Hands

DC, 2006

1-4 .... 3.00

Red Sonja in 3-D
Blackthorne
1 .... 3.00

Red Sonja: Scavenger Hunt
Marvel, 1995
1 .... 3.00

Red Sonja: The Movie
Marvel, 1985
1-2 .... 1.00

Red Star
Image, 2000
1 .... 4.00
2-9 .... 3.00

Red Star
CrossGen, 2003
1-5 .... 3.00

Red Tornado
DC, 1985
1-4 .... 1.00

Red Warrior
Atlas, 1951
1 .... 100.00
2 .... 50.00
3-6 .... 40.00

Red Wolf
Marvel, 1972
1 .... 35.00
2 .... 18.00
3-5 .... 15.00
6-9 .... 10.00

Reese's Pieces
Eclipse, 1986
1-2 .... 2.00

Reform School Girl
Realistic Comics, 1951
1 .... 1,000.00

Re:Gex
Awesome, 1998
0-1/A 3.00

Reggie and Me
Archie, 1966
19 .... 10.00
20 .... 8.00
21-25 .... 6.00
26-30 .... 5.00
31-50 .... 3.00
51-100 .... 2.00
101-126 .... 1.00

Reggie's Revenge
Archie, 1994
1-3 .... 2.00

Reggie's Wise Guy Jokes
Archie, 1968
1 .... 8.00
2 .... 5.00
3 .... 4.00
4-5 .... 3.00
6-10 .... 2.00
11-60 .... 1.00

Registry of Death
Kitchen Sink, 1996
1 .... 16.00

Regulators
Image, 1995
1-4 .... 3.00

Rehd
Antarctic, 2003
0 .... 3.00

Reid Fleming
Boswell
1 .... 10.00
1/2nd 4.00

Reid Fleming, World's Toughest Milkman
Eclipse, 1986
1 .... 6.00
1/2nd 3.00
1/3rd-1/5th 2.00
1/6th-2 .... 3.00
2/2nd-6 .... 2.00
7-9 .... 3.00

Reign of the Dragonlord
Eternity, 1986
1-2 .... 2.00

Reign of the Zodiac
DC, 2003
1-8 .... 3.00

Reiki Warriors
Revolutionary, 1993
1 .... 3.00

Reinventing Comics
Paradox, 2000
1 .... 23.00

Relative Heroes
DC, 2000
1-6 .... 3.00

Relentless Pursuit
Slave Labor, 1989
1-2 .... 2.00
3 .... 3.00
4 .... 4.00

Reload
DC, 2003
1-3 .... 3.00

Reload/Mek
DC, 2004
1 .... 15.00

Remains
Idea & Design Works, 2004
1-5 .... 4.00

Mighty Cartoon Heroes

Mighty Comics

Mightyguy

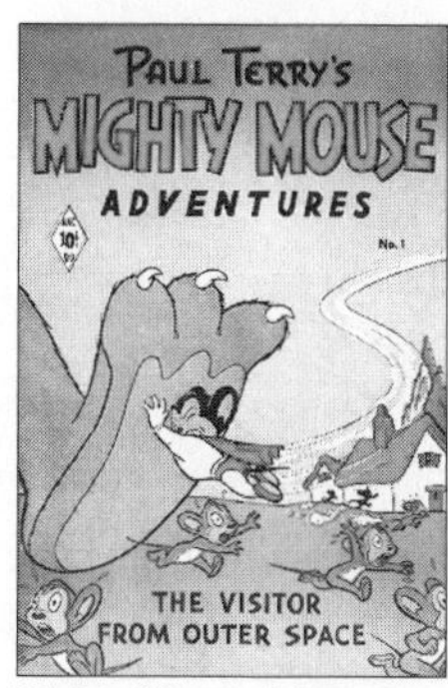

Mighty Mouse Adventures

Mighty Mouse Comics

Mighty Samson

Mighty Tiny

Mike Donovan Detective Comic

Remarkable Worlds of Phineas B. Fuddle
Paradox, 2000

1-4 ....6.00

Remember Pearl Harbor
Street & Smith, 1942

1 ....350.00

Remote
Tokyopop, 2004

1-7 ....10.00

Ren & Stimpy Show
Marvel, 1992

1/A-1/B 3.00
1/2nd-25 ....2.00
25/Variant 3.00
26-44 ....2.00
Special 1-Holiday 1 ....3.00

Ren & Stimpy Show: Radio Daze
Marvel, 1995

1 ....2.00

Ren & Stimpy Show Special: Around the World in a Daze
Marvel, 1996

1 ....3.00

Ren & Stimpy Show Special: Eenteractive
Marvel, 1995

1 ....3.00

Ren & Stimpy Show Special: Four Swerks
Marvel, 1995

1 ....3.00

Ren & Stimpy Show Special: Powdered Toast Man
Marvel, 1994

1 ....3.00

Ren & Stimpy Show Special: Powdered Toastman's Cereal
Marvel, 1995

1 ....3.00

Ren & Stimpy Show Special: Sports
Marvel, 1995

1 ....3.00

Renegade
Rip Off, 1991

1 ....3.00

Renegade!
Magnecom, 1993

1 ....3.00

Renegade Rabbit
Printed Matter

1-5 ....2.00

Renegade Romance
Renegade, 1987

1-2 ....4.00

Renegades
Age of Heroes

1-2 ....1.00

Renegades of Justice
Blue Masque, 1995

1-2 ....3.00

Renfield
Caliber, 1994

1 ....3.00
1/Ltd. 6.00
2-3 ....3.00
Ashcan 1 ....1.00

Rennin Comics (Jim Chadwick's...)
Restless Muse, 1997

1 ....3.00

Reno Browne
Marvel, 1950

50-52 ....150.00

Replacement God
Handicraft, 1998

6 ....7.00

Replacement God
Slave Labor, 1995

1 ....6.00
1/2nd 3.00
2 ....4.00
3-8 ....3.00

Replacement God and Other Stories
Image, 1997

1-5 ....3.00

Reporter
Reporter

1 ....3.00

Reptilicus
Charlton, 1961

1 ....100.00
2 ....50.00

Reptisaurus
Charlton, 1962

3-Special 1 ....25.00

Requiem for Dracula
Marvel, 1992

1 ....2.00

Rescueman
Best

1 ....3.00

Rescuers Down Under (Disney's...)
Disney
1 .... 3.00

Resident Evil
Image, 1998
1 .... 6.00
2-5 .... 5.00

Resident Evil: Code Veronica
DC, 2002
1-3 .... 15.00

Resident Evil: Fire and Ice
WildStorm, 2000
1-4 .... 3.00

Resistance
WildStorm, 2002
1-8 .... 3.00

Restaurant at the End of the Universe
DC, 1994
1-3 .... 7.00

Resurrection Man
DC, 1997
1-27 .... 3.00
1000000 .... 4.00

Retaliator
Eclipse, 1992
1-5 .... 3.00

Retief
Adventure, 1989
1-6 .... 2.00

Retief (Keith Laumer's...)
Mad Dog, 1987
1-6 .... 2.00

Retief and the Warlords
Adventure, 1991
1-4 .... 3.00

Retief: Diplomatic Immunity
Adventure, 1991
1-2 .... 3.00

Retief: Grime and Punishment
Adventure, 1991
1 .... 3.00

Retief of the C.D.T.
Mad Dog
1 .... 2.00

Retief: The Garbage Invasion
Adventure, 1991
1 .... 3.00

Retief: The Giant Killer
Adventure, 1991
1 .... 3.00

Retro 50's Comix
Edge
1-2 .... 3.00
3 .... 4.00

Retro Comics
AC
0-3 .... 6.00

Retro-Dead
Blazer, 1995
1 .... 3.00

Retrograde
Eternity
1-3 .... 2.00

Retro Rocket
Image, 2006
1-3 .... 3.00

Return of Disney's Aladdin
Disney
1-2 .... 2.00

Return of Girl Squad X
Fantaco
1 .... 5.00

Return of Gorgo
Charlton, 1963
2-3 .... 75.00

Return of Happy the Clown
Caliber, 1995
1 .... 4.00
2 .... 3.00

Return of Herbie
Avalon
1 .... 3.00

Return of Konga
Charlton, 1962
1 .... 50.00

Return of Lum Urusei*Yatsura
Viz, 1994
1-8 .... 3.00

Return of Lum Urusei*Yatsura Part 2
Viz, 1995
1-13 .... 3.00

Return of Lum Urusei*Yatsura Part 3
Viz, 1996
1-11 .... 3.00

Mike Mauser Files

Mike Mist Minute Mist-Eries

Military Comics

Millennium

Millennium 2.5 A.D.

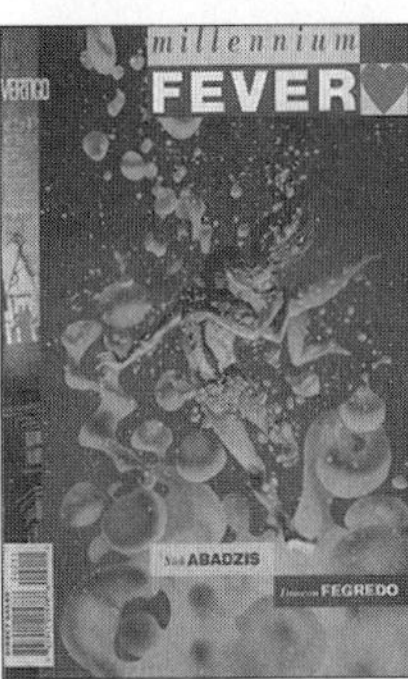

Millennium Fever

Millie the Model Comics

Mindbenders

Return of Lum Urusei*Yatsura Part 4
Viz, 1997

1-11 .... 3.00

Return of Megaton Man
Kitchen Sink, 1988

1-3 .... 3.00

Return of Shadowhawk
Image, 2004

1 .... 3.00

Return of Tarzan (Edgar Rice Burroughs'...)
Dark Horse, 1997

1-3 .... 3.00

Return of the Outlaw
Toby, 1953

1 .... 50.00
2-9 .... 25.00
10-11 .... 20.00

Return of the Skyman
Ace, 1987

1 .... 2.00

Return of Valkyrie
Eclipse

1 .... 10.00

Return to Jurassic Park
Topps, 1995

1-9 .... 3.00

Return to the Eve
Monolith

1 .... 3.00

Reveal
Dark Horse, 2002

1 .... 7.00

Revealing Romances
Ace, 1949

1 .... 50.00
2 .... 30.00
3-6 .... 25.00

Revelations
Dark Horse, 1995

1/Ashcan 1.00

Revelations
Golden Realm Unlimited

1 .... 3.00

Revelations
Dark Horse, 2005

1-6 .... 3.00

Revelations (Clive Barker's)
Eclipse

1 .... 8.00

Revelation: The Comic Book
Draw Near

1-6 .... 4.00

Revelry in Hell
Fantagraphics, 1990

1 .... 3.00

Revenge of the Oil Slick Ducks
Canew Ideas

1 .... 1.00

Revenge of the Prowler
Eclipse, 1988

1 .... 2.00
2 .... 3.00
3-4 .... 2.00

Revengers Featuring Armor and The Silverstreak
Continuity, 1985

1-3 .... 2.00

Revengers Featuring Megalith
Continuity, 1985

1-6 .... 2.00

Revengers: Hybrids Special
Continuity, 1992

1 .... 5.00

Reverend Ablack: Adventures of the Antichrist
Creativeforce Designs, 1996

1-2 .... 3.00

Revisionary
Moonstone, 2005

1 .... 3.00

Revolver
Fleetway-Quality

1-7 .... 3.00

Revolver (Robin Snyder's...)
Renegade, 1985

1-Ann 1 .... 2.00

Revolving Doors
Blackthorne, 1986

1-3 .... 2.00

Revved
Image, 2006

1 .... 10.00

Rex Allen
Dell, 1951

2 .... 60.00
3-9 .... 35.00

10-15 .... 30.00
16-19 .... 25.00
20-31 .... 20.00

Rex Dexter of Mars

Fox, 1940

1 .... 1,500.00

Rex Hart

Marvel, 1949

6-8 .... 100.00

Rex Hellwig

Black Cat

1 .... 3.00

Rex Libris

Slave Labor, 2005

1-2 .... 3.00

Rex Morgan, M.D.

Argo, 1950

1 .... 75.00
2-3 .... 50.00

Rex Mundi

Image, 2003

1-17 .... 3.00

RG Veda

Tokyopop, 2005

1-3 .... 10.00

Rhaj

Mu

1-4 .... 2.00

Rhanes of Terror

Buffalo Nickel, 1999

1-4 .... 3.00

Rhudiprrt, Prince of Fur

Mu, 1990

1-4 .... 2.00
5-8 .... 3.00

Rib

Dilemma, 1996

1 .... 2.00

Rib

Caliber, 1997

1 .... 3.00

Ribit!

Comico, 1989

1-4 .... 2.00

Richard Dragon

DC, 2004

1-12 .... 3.00

Richard Dragon, Kung-Fu Fighter

DC, 1975

1 .... 10.00
2-3 .... 4.00
4-5 .... 3.00
6-18 .... 2.00

Richard Speck

Boneyard, 1993

1 .... 3.00

Richie Rich

Harvey, 1960

1 .... 3,250.00
2 .... 950.00
3 .... 500.00
4-5 .... 375.00
6-9 .... 250.00
10 .... 175.00
11-15 .... 125.00
16-20 .... 90.00
21-30 .... 65.00
31-40 .... 45.00
41-49 .... 35.00
50-60 .... 25.00
61-70 .... 20.00
71-88 .... 15.00
89-102 .... 10.00
103-126 .... 7.00
127-159 .... 5.00
160-200 .... 3.00
201-254 .... 2.00

Richie Rich

Harvey, 1991

1 .... 5.00
2 .... 3.00
3-10 .... 2.00
11-28 .... 1.00

Richie Rich Adventure Digest Magazine

Harvey, 1992

1-6 .... 2.00

Richie Rich and Billy Bellhops

Harvey, 1977

1 .... 5.00

Richie Rich and Cadbury

Harvey, 1977

1 .... 15.00
2-10 .... 10.00
11-12 .... 5.00
13-19 .... 4.00
20-29 .... 3.00

Richie Rich & Casper

Harvey, 1974

1 .... 12.00
2 .... 6.00
3-5 .... 4.00
6-10 .... 3.00
11-45 .... 2.00

Richie Rich and Casper in 3-D

Blackthorne, 1987

1/A-1/B 3.00

Minimum Wage

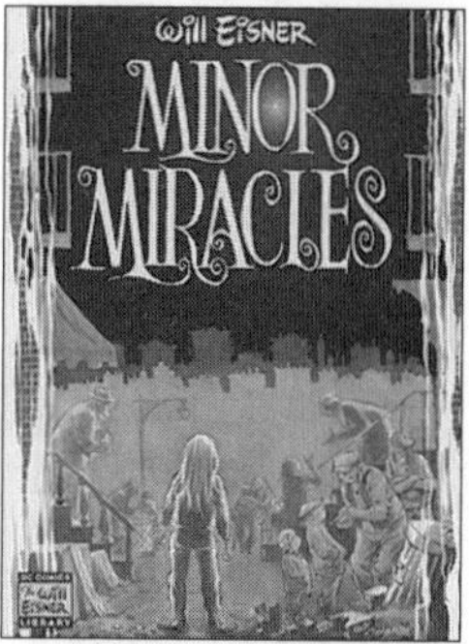

Minor Miracles

Minute Man

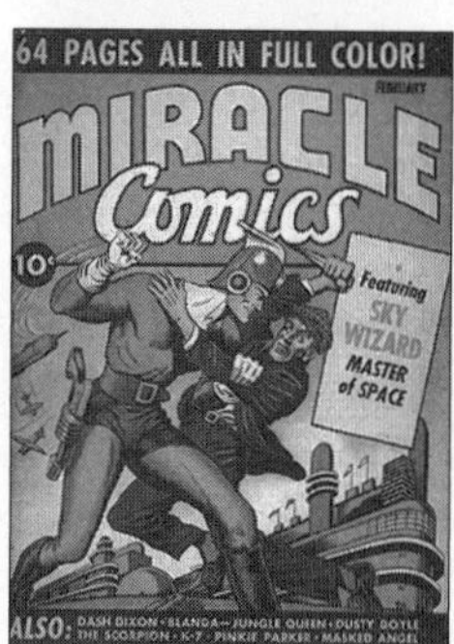

Miracle Comics

Miracle Girls

Miracleman

Miracleman Family

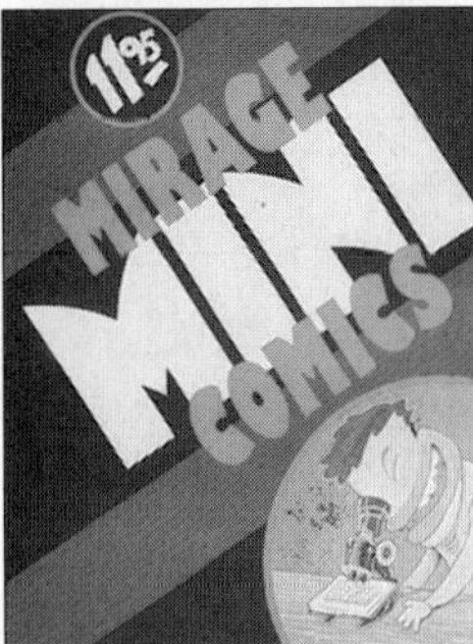

Mirage Mini Comics

Richie Rich & Dollar, the Dog

Harvey, 1977

1 ..... 5.00
2 ..... 3.00
3-24 ..... 2.00

Richie Rich and Dot

Harvey, 1974

1 ..... 20.00

Richie Rich and Gloria

Harvey, 1977

1 ..... 10.00
2-10 ..... 8.00
11-19 ..... 5.00
20-25 ..... 4.00

Richie Rich and His Girlfriends

Harvey, 1979

1 ..... 10.00
2-10 ..... 8.00
11-16 ..... 5.00

Richie Rich and His Mean Cousin Reggie

Harvey, 1979

1 ..... 10.00
2-3 ..... 5.00

Richie Rich & Jackie Jokers

Harvey, 1973

1 ..... 18.00
2 ..... 10.00
3-5 ..... 6.00
6-10 ..... 4.00
11-30 ..... 3.00
31-48 ..... 2.00

Richie Rich and Professor Keenbean

Harvey, 1990

1-2 ..... 1.00

Richie Rich and the New Kids on the Block

Harvey, 1991

1 ..... 2.00

Richie Rich and Timmy Time

Harvey, 1977

1 ..... 8.00

Richie Rich Bank Books

Harvey, 1972

1 ..... 24.00
2 ..... 10.00
3-5 ..... 6.00
6-10 ..... 4.00
11-20 ..... 3.00
21-59 ..... 2.00

Richie Rich Best of the Years

Harvey, 1977

1 ..... 10.00
2-6 ..... 6.00

Richie Rich Big Book (Vol. 2)

Harvey, 1992

1-2 ..... 2.00

Richie Rich Big Bucks

Harvey, 1991

1 ..... 2.00
2-8 ..... 1.00

Richie Rich Billions

Harvey, 1974

1 ..... 12.00
2 ..... 7.00
3 ..... 6.00
4-5 ..... 5.00
6-10 ..... 4.00
11-30 ..... 3.00
31-48 ..... 2.00

Richie Rich Cash

Harvey, 1974

1 ..... 10.00
2 ..... 6.00
3-10 ..... 4.00
11-30 ..... 3.00
31-47 ..... 2.00

Richie Rich Cash Money

Harvey, 1992

1-2 ..... 2.00

Richie Rich, Casper and Wendy

Harvey, 1976

1 ..... 8.00
1/A-2-1/L-2 ..... 5.00

Richie Rich Diamonds

Harvey, 1972

1 ..... 15.00
2 ..... 9.00
3-5 ..... 7.00
6-10 ..... 5.00
11-30 ..... 4.00
31-40 ..... 3.00
41-59 ..... 2.00

Richie Rich Digest Magazine

Harvey, 1986

1 ..... 4.00
2-10 ..... 3.00
11-42 ..... 2.00

Richie Rich Digest Stories

Harvey, 1977

1 ..... 10.00
2-10 ..... 5.00
11-17 ..... 3.00

Richie Rich Digest Winners

Harvey, 1977

1 .... 10.00
2-5 .... 5.00

Richie Rich Dollars & Cents

Harvey, 1963

1 .... 250.00
2 .... 125.00
3-5 .... 85.00
6-10 .... 40.00
11-20 .... 25.00
21-30 .... 15.00
31-40 .... 10.00
41-50 .... 7.00
51-60 .... 5.00
61-70 .... 3.00
71-90 .... 2.00
91-109 .... 1.00

Richie Rich Fortunes

Harvey, 1971

1 .... 25.00
2 .... 10.00
3-5 .... 7.00
6-10 .... 5.00
11-20 .... 4.00
21-40 .... 3.00
41-63 .... 2.00

Richie Rich Gems

Harvey, 1974

1 .... 10.00
2 .... 6.00
3-5 .... 4.00
6-10 .... 3.00
11-43 .... 2.00

Richie Rich Giant Size

Harvey, 1992

1-4 .... 2.00

Richie Rich Gold & Silver

Harvey, 1975

1 .... 10.00
2 .... 6.00
3-5 .... 4.00
6-10 .... 3.00
11-42 .... 2.00

Richie Rich Gold Nuggets Digest Magazine

Harvey, 1990

1 .... 3.00
2-4 .... 2.00

Richie Rich Holiday Digest

Harvey, 1980

1 .... 3.00
2-5 .... 2.00

Richie Rich Inventions

Harvey, 1977

1 .... 10.00
2-10 .... 6.00
11-19 .... 4.00
20-26 .... 3.00

Richie Rich Jackpots

Harvey, 1972

1 .... 30.00
2 .... 12.00
3-5 .... 8.00
6-8 .... 6.00
9-19 .... 4.00
20 .... 6.00
21-40 .... 3.00
41-58 .... 2.00

Richie Rich Million Dollar Digest

Harvey, 1980

1-10 .... 10.00

Richie Rich Million Dollar Digest

Harvey, 1986

1 .... 5.00
2-10 .... 3.00
11-34 .... 2.00

Richie Rich Millions

Harvey, 1961

1 .... 200.00
2-3 .... 100.00
4-10 .... 75.00
11-20 .... 50.00
21-30 .... 40.00
31-37 .... 30.00
38-44 .... 25.00
45-48 .... 20.00
49-56 .... 10.00
57-61 .... 7.00
62-80 .... 5.00
81-90 .... 3.00
91-110 .... 2.00
111-113 .... 1.00

Richie Rich Money World

Harvey, 1972

1 .... 85.00
2 .... 35.00
3 .... 25.00
4-5 .... 20.00
6-10 .... 15.00
11-18 .... 10.00
19-28 .... 7.00
29-38 .... 5.00
39-59 .... 3.00

Richie Rich Money World Digest

Harvey, 1991

1-8 .... 2.00

Richie Rich (Movie Adaptation)

Marvel, 1995

1 .... 3.00

Mirrorwalker

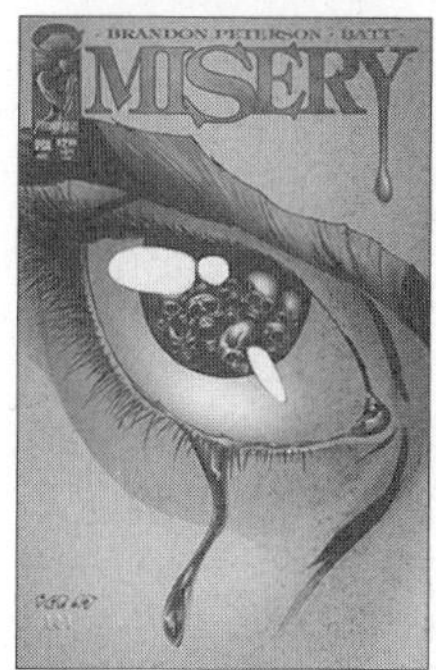

Misery

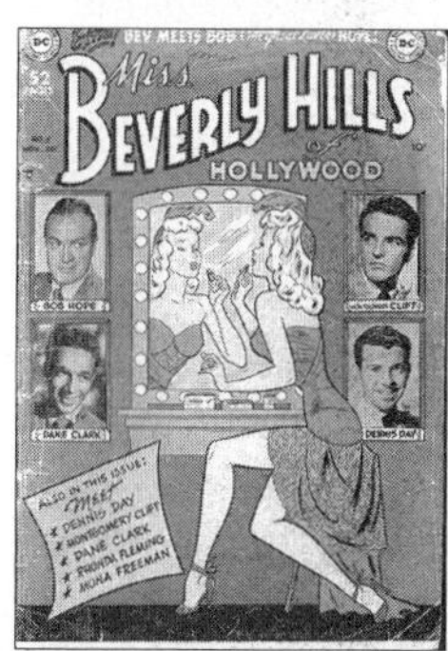

Miss Beverly Hills of Hollywood

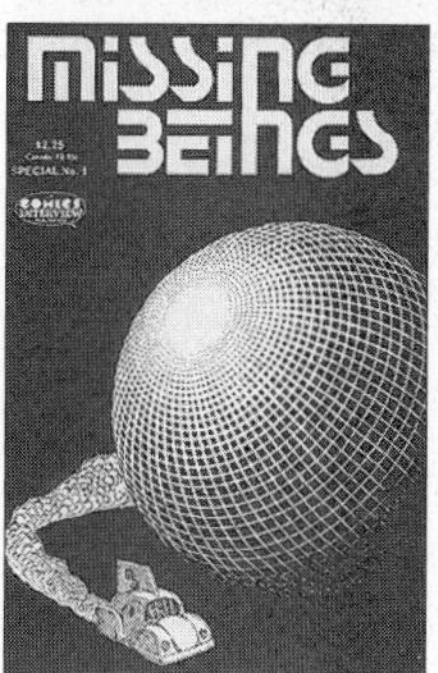

Missing Beings Special

Misspent Youths

Miss Victory Golden Anniversary Special

Mister America

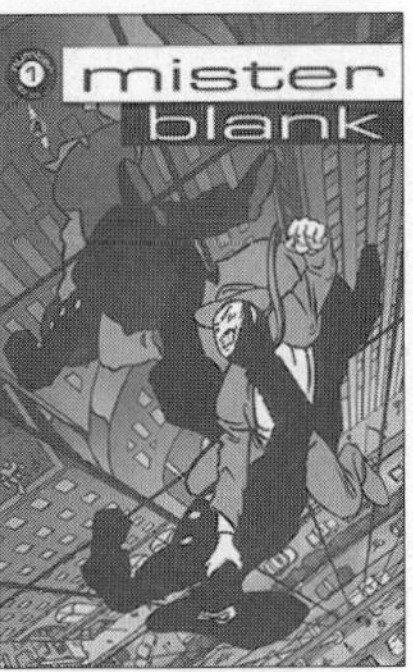
Mister Blank

Richie Rich Profits
Harvey, 1974
1 .... 25.00
2-3 .... 15.00
4-10 .... 10.00
11-19 .... 8.00
20-29 .... 6.00
30-39 .... 5.00
40-47 .... 4.00

Richie Rich Relics
Harvey, 1988
1-4 .... 3.00

Richie Rich Riches
Harvey, 1972
1 .... 28.00
2 .... 13.00
3-5 .... 8.00
6-10 .... 5.00
11-20 .... 4.00
21-30 .... 3.00
31-59 .... 2.00

Richie Rich Success Stories
Harvey, 1964
1 .... 200.00
2 .... 100.00
3-4 .... 75.00
5-10 .... 50.00
11-20 .... 25.00
21-25 .... 20.00
26-30 .... 15.00
31-40 .... 10.00
41-70 .... 7.00
71-89 .... 5.00
90-100 .... 3.00
101-105 .... 2.00

Richie Rich Vacation Digest
Harvey, 1991
1992-1993 .... 2.00

Richie Rich Vacations Digest
Harvey, 1980
1 .... 10.00
2-8 .... 5.00

Richie Rich Vaults of Mystery
Harvey, 1974
1 .... 25.00
2 .... 15.00
3-5 .... 8.00
6-10 .... 5.00
11-20 .... 4.00
21-47 .... 3.00

Richie Rich Zillionz
Harvey, 1976
1 .... 12.00
2-4 .... 6.00
5 .... 4.00
6-10 .... 3.00
11-33 .... 2.00

Ricky
Standard, 1953
5 .... 20.00

Ride
Image, 2004
1-2 .... 3.00

Ride: 2 for the Road One Shot
Image, 2005
1 .... 3.00

Ride: Foreign Parts
Image, 2005
0 .... 3.00

Rider
Ajax, 1957
1 .... 75.00
2-5 .... 40.00

Rifleman
Dell, 1960
2-3 .... 85.00
4-10 .... 70.00
11-20 .... 55.00

Rima, the Jungle Girl
DC, 1974
1 .... 13.00
2-7 .... 7.00

Rime of the Ancient Mariner
Tome
1 .... 4.00

Rimshot
Rip Off, 1990
1-2 .... 2.00
3 .... 3.00

Ring of Bright Water
Dell, 1969
1 .... 7.00

Ring of Roses
Dark Horse, 2005
1-4 .... 3.00

Ring of the Nibelung
DC, 1989
1-4 .... 5.00

Ring of the Nibelung
Dark Horse, 2000
1-4 .... 3.00

Ring of the Nibelung (Vol. 2)
Dark Horse, 2000
1-3 .... 3.00

Ring of the Nibelung (Vol. 3)
Dark Horse, 2000
1-3 .... 3.00

Ring of the Nibelung, The (Vol. 4)
Dark Horse, 2001
1-4 .... 3.00

Ringo Kid
Marvel, 1970
1 .... 20.00
2 .... 8.00
3-10 .... 5.00
11 .... 4.00
12 .... 10.00
13-27 .... 4.00
27/30¢ 20.00
28 .... 4.00
28/30¢ 20.00
29-30 .... 4.00

Ringo Kid Western
Marvel, 1954
1 .... 175.00
2 .... 90.00
3 .... 60.00
4-5 .... 48.00
6-10 .... 42.00
11-21 .... 36.00

Rin Tin Tin
Dell, 1954
4-10 .... 50.00
11-20 .... 40.00
21-38 .... 35.00

Rin Tin Tin & Rusty
Gold Key, 1963
1 .... 50.00

Rio at Bay
Dark Horse, 1992
1-2 .... 3.00

Rio Conchos
Gold Key, 1965
1 .... 22.00

Rio Graphic Novel
Comico, 1987
1 .... 9.00

Rio Kid
Eternity
1-3 .... 3.00

Rion 2990
Rion
1-4 .... 2.00

Riot
Atlas, 1954
1 .... 165.00
2 .... 120.00
3 .... 105.00
4 .... 140.00
5 .... 145.00
6 .... 105.00

Riot, Act 1
Viz, 1995
1-6 .... 3.00

Riot, Act 2
Viz, 1996
1-7 .... 3.00

Riot Gear
Triumphant, 1993
1-Ashcan 1 .... 3.00

Riot Gear: Violent Past
Triumphant, 1994
1-2 .... 3.00

Ripclaw (Vol. 1)
Image, 1995
½ 2.00
½/Gold-4 .... 3.00

Ripclaw (Vol. 2)
Image, 1995
1-Special 1 .... 3.00

R.I.P. Comics Module
TSR
1-8 .... 3.00

R.I.P.D.
Dark Horse, 1999
1-4 .... 3.00

Ripfire
Malibu, 1995
0 .... 3.00

Rip Hunter...Time Master
DC, 1961
1 .... 350.00
2 .... 140.00
3 .... 115.00
4-5 .... 95.00
6-7 .... 85.00
8-15 .... 70.00
16-20 .... 58.00
21-25 .... 48.00
26-29 .... 40.00

Rip in Time
Fantagor
1-5 .... 2.00

Ripley's Believe It or Not!
Gold Key, 1967
4 .... 26.00
5-10 .... 16.00
11-15 .... 12.00
16-20 .... 10.00
21-30 .... 8.00
31-38 .... 5.00
39 .... 6.00
40-50 .... 5.00

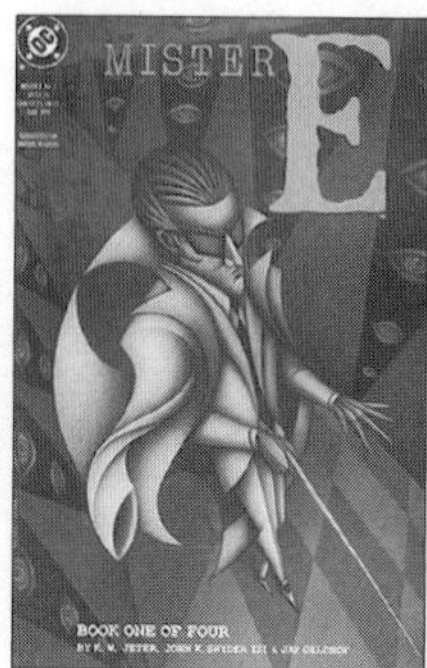

Mister E

Mister Mystery

Mister Sixx

Misty

Misty Girl Extreme

Mobfire

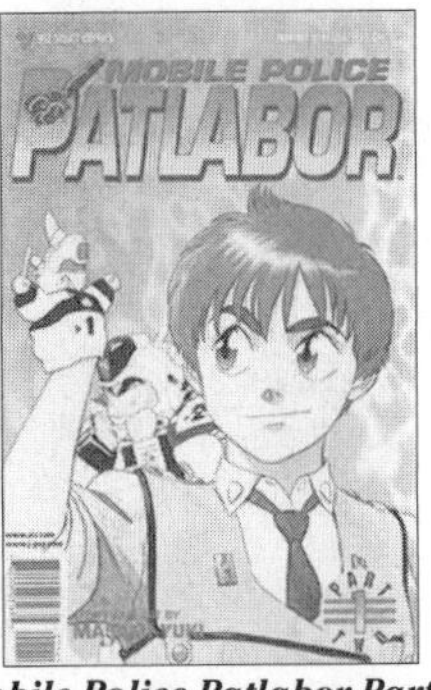

Mobile Police Patlabor Part 2

Mobile Suit Gundam 0079

51-70 .... 4.00
71-94 .... 3.00

Ripley's Believe It or Not!
Dark Horse, 2002

1-4 .... 3.00

Ripley's Believe It or Not!: Beauty & Grooming
Schanes

1 .... 3.00

Ripley's Believe It or Not!: Child Prodigies
Schanes

1 .... 3.00

Ripley's Believe It or Not!: Cruelty
Schanes Products, 1993

1-2 .... 3.00

Ripley's Believe It or Not!: Fairy Tales & Literature
Schanes

1 .... 3.00

Ripley's Believe It or Not!: Feats of Wonder
Schanes

1 .... 3.00

Ripley's Believe It or Not Magazine
Harvey, 1953

1 .... 60.00
2 .... 45.00
3-4 .... 40.00

Ripley's Believe It or Not!: Sports Feats
Schanes Products, 1993

1 .... 3.00

Ripley's Believe It or Not!: Strange Deaths
Schanes Products, 1993

1 .... 3.00

Ripley's Believe It or Not True War Stories
Gold Key, 1966

1 .... 24.00

Rip Off Comix
Rip Off, 1977

1 .... 25.00
2 .... 16.00
3 .... 12.00
4 .... 8.00
5-6 .... 6.00
6/2nd 3.00
7 .... 6.00
8-10 .... 5.00
11-23 .... 4.00
24-26 .... 3.00
27-31 .... 4.00

Ripper
Aircel

1-6 .... 3.00

Ripper Legacy
Caliber

1-3 .... 3.00

Riptide
Image, 1995

1-2 .... 3.00

Rise of Apocalypse
Marvel, 1996

1-4 .... 2.00

Rising Stars
Image, 1999

0 .... 5.00
0/Gold 12.00
½ 3.00
1/Holofoil 8.00
1/Chromium 10.00
1/Kids 7.00
1/Fighting 6.00
1/Funeral 5.00
1/Wizard 4.00
2 .... 3.00
3-24 .... 3.00
Ashcan 1/Conven 6.00
Ashcan 1 .... 3.00

Rising Stars: Bright
Image, 2003

1-3 .... 3.00

Rising Stars: Untouchable
Image, 2006

1 .... 3.00

Rising Stars: Visitations
Image, 2002

1 .... 9.00

Rising Stars: Voices of the Dead
Image, 2005

1-6 .... 3.00

Rite
Knight, 1997

1 .... 3.00

Riverdale High
Archie, 1990

1 .... 2.00
2-5 .... 1.00

Rivets
Argo, 1956

1 .... 30.00
2-3 .... 20.00

Rivets & Ruby
Radio, 1998

1-4 .... 3.00

Rivit
Blackthorne, 1987
1 .... 2.00

Roach Killer
NBM
1 .... 12.00

Roachmill
Blackthorne, 1986
1-6 .... 2.00

Roachmill
Dark Horse, 1988
1-10 .... 2.00

Roadkill
Lighthouse
1-2 .... 2.00

Roadkill: A Chronicle of the Deadworld
Caliber
1 .... 3.00

Road to Hell
Idea & Design Works, 2006
1-3 .... 4.00

Road Trip
Oni, 2000
1 .... 3.00

Roadways
Cult, 1994
1-4 .... 3.00

Roarin' Rick's Rare Bit Fiends
King Hell, 1994
1-21 .... 3.00

Robbin' $3000
Parody
1 .... 3.00

Rob Hanes
WCG, 1991
1 .... 3.00

Rob Hanes Adventures
WCG, 2000
1-10 .... 3.00

Robin
DC, 1991
1 .... 3.00
1/2nd-1/3rd 2.00
2 .... 3.00
2/2nd-5 .... 2.00
Ann 1-2 .... 3.00

Robin
DC, 1993
0 .... 2.00
1-1/Variant 4.00
2-14 .... 2.00
14/Variant 3.00
15-49 .... 2.00
50 .... 3.00
51-74 .... 2.00
75 .... 3.00
76-99 .... 2.00
100 .... 4.00
101-125 .... 2.00
126 .... 5.00
☛Robin quits
127 .... 4.00
☛New Robin
128 .... 3.00
129-138 .... 2.00
139-169 .... 3.00
1000000 .... 4.00
Ann 3 .... 3.00
Ann 4 .... 4.00
Ann 5 .... 3.00
Ann 6 .... 4.00
Ann 7 .... 5.00
GS 1 .... 6.00

Robin Plus
DC, 1996
1-2 .... 3.00

Robin 3000
DC, 1992
1-2 .... 5.00

Robin: Year One
DC, 2000
1-4 .... 5.00

Robin/Argent Double-Shot
DC, 1998
1 .... 2.00

Robin II
DC, 1991
1 .... 1.00
1/A-1/C 2.00
1/CS 10.00
1/D 2.00
2 .... 1.00
2/A-2/C 2.00
2/CS 9.00
3 .... 1.00
3/A-3/B 2.00
3/CS 6.00
4 .... 1.00
4/A 2.00
4/CS 4.00
Deluxe 1 .... 30.00

Robin III: Cry of the Huntress
DC, 1992
1 .... 1.00
1/Variant 3.00
2 .... 1.00
2/Variant 3.00
3 .... 1.00
3/Variant 3.00
4 .... 1.00
4/Variant 3.00

Mobile Suit Gundam 0083

Mobsters and Monsters Magazine

Moby Duck

Modeling with Millie

Modern Love

Modern Pulp

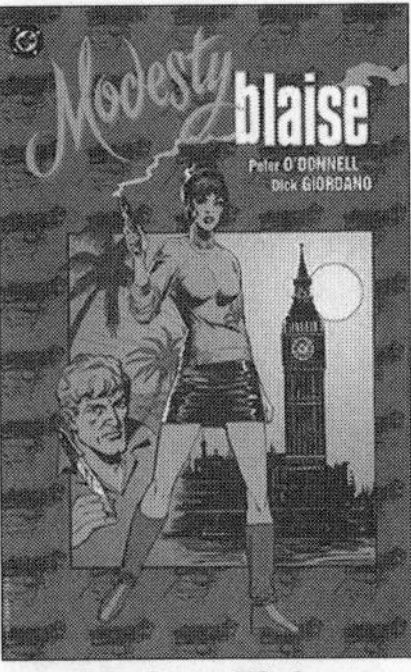

Modesty Blaise

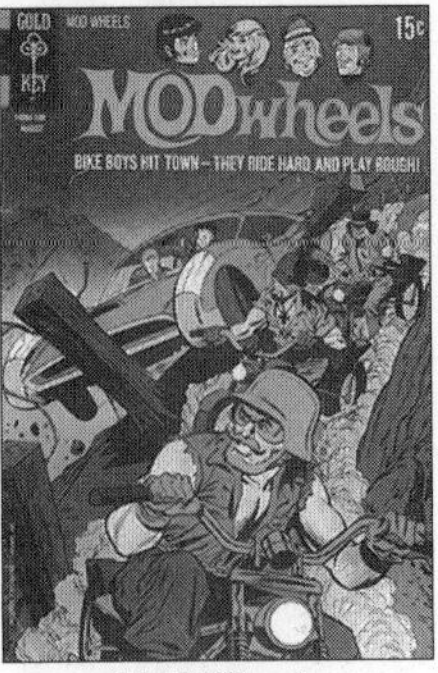

Mod Wheels

5 .... 1.00
5/Variant 3.00
6 .... 1.00
6/Variant 3.00

Robin Hood
Magazine Enterprises, 1955

52 .... 100.00
53-8 .... 90.00

Robin Hood
Charlton, 1956

28 .... 40.00
29-30 .... 35.00
31-37 .... 30.00
38 .... 45.00

Robin Hood
Dell, 1963

1 .... 20.00

Robin Hood
Eternity, 1989

1-4 .... 2.00

Robin Hood
Eclipse, 1991

1-3 .... 3.00

Robin Hood Tales
Quality, 1956

1 .... 190.00
2-6 .... 185.00

Robin Hood Tales
DC, 1957

7 .... 220.00
8-14 .... 185.00

Robin Red and the Lutins
Ace, 1986

1-2 .... 2.00

Robinsonia
NBM

1 .... 12.00

Robocop (Magazine)
Marvel, 1987

1 .... 3.00

Robocop
Marvel, 1990

1 .... 3.00
2-23 .... 2.00

Robocop (Movie Adaptation)
Marvel, 1990

1 .... 5.00

Robocop 2
Marvel, 1990

1-3 .... 2.00

Robocop 2 (Magazine)
Marvel, 1990

1 .... 3.00

Robocop 3
Dark Horse, 1993

1-3 .... 3.00

Robocop (Frank Miller's)
Avatar, 2003

1 .... 5.00
1/Platinum 7.00
1/Wraparound 5.00
2 .... 4.00
2/Platinum 5.00
3 .... 4.00
3/Platinum 6.00
3/Ryp-4 .... 4.00
4/Miller 6.00
4/Platinum 5.00
5 .... 4.00
5/Platinum 5.00
5/Wraparound-6 .... 4.00
6/Miller 6.00
6/Platinum 5.00
7 .... 4.00
7/Miller 6.00
7/Platinum 5.00
7/Wraparound-8 .... 4.00
8/Miller 6.00
8/Platinum 5.00
8/Wraparound 4.00

Robocop: Killing Machine
Avatar, 2004

1 .... 6.00
1/Platinum 15.00
1/Wraparound 6.00

Robocop: Mortal Coils
Dark Horse, 1993

1-4 .... 3.00

Robocop: Prime Suspect
Dark Horse, 1992

1-4 .... 3.00

Robocop: Roulette
Dark Horse, 1993

1-4 .... 3.00

Robocop vs. the Terminator
Dark Horse, 1992

1 .... 3.00
1/Platinum 4.00
2-4 .... 3.00

Robocop: Wild Child
Avatar, 2005

1 .... 3.00
1/Photo 4.00
1/Platinum 12.00
1/Rivalry 5.00
1/Wraparound 6.00

Robocop: Wild Child - Detroit's Finest

Avatar, 2005

1 .... 6.00
1/Detroit 7.00
1/Photo 6.00
1/Platinum 15.00
1/Rivalry 7.00
1/Wraparound 6.00

Robo Dojo

DC, 2002

1-6 .... 3.00

Robo-Hunter

Eagle

1 .... 2.00
2-5 .... 1.00

Robotech

Antarctic, 1997

1-Ann 1 .... 3.00

Robotech (Wildstorm)

DC, 2003

0-6 .... 3.00

Robotech: Amazon World-Escape from Praxis

Academy, 1994

1 .... 3.00

Robotech: Class Reunion

Antarctic, 1998

1 .... 4.00

Robotech: Clone

Academy, 1995

0-5 .... 3.00
Special 1 .... 4.00

Robotech: Covert-Ops

Antarctic, 1998

1-2 .... 3.00

Robotech: Cyber World: Secrets of Haydon IV

Academy, 1994

1 .... 3.00

Robotech Defenders

DC, 1985

1-2 .... 2.00

Robotech: Escape

Antarctic, 1998

1 .... 3.00

Robotech: Final Fire

Antarctic, 1998

1 .... 3.00

Robotech: Firewalkers

Eternity, 1993

1 .... 3.00

Robotech Genesis

Eternity, 1992

1 .... 3.00
1/Ltd. 6.00
2-6 .... 3.00

Robotech in 3-D

Comico, 1985

1 .... 3.00

RoboTech: Invasion

DC, 2004

1-5 .... 3.00

Robotech: Invid War

Eternity, 1992

1-9 .... 3.00
10-13 .... 1.00
14-18 .... 3.00

Robotech: Invid War Aftermath

Eternity, 1993

1-2 .... 3.00

RoboTech: Love & War

DC, 2003

1-6 .... 3.00

RoboTech: Macross Saga

DC, 2003

1-4 .... 15.00

Robotech Masters

Comico, 1985

1-23 .... 2.00

Robotech: Mechangel

Academy

1-3 .... 3.00

Robotech: Megastorm

Antarctic, 1998

1 .... 8.00

Robotech: Prelude to the Shadow Chronicles

DC, 2005

1-5 .... 4.00

Robotech: Return to Macross

Eternity, 1993

1-32 .... 3.00

Robotech: Sentinels - Rubicon

Antarctic, 1998

1-7 .... 3.00

Robotech Special

Comico, 1988

1 .... 3.00

Robotech the Graphic Novel

Comico, 1986

1 .... 6.00

Moebius Comics

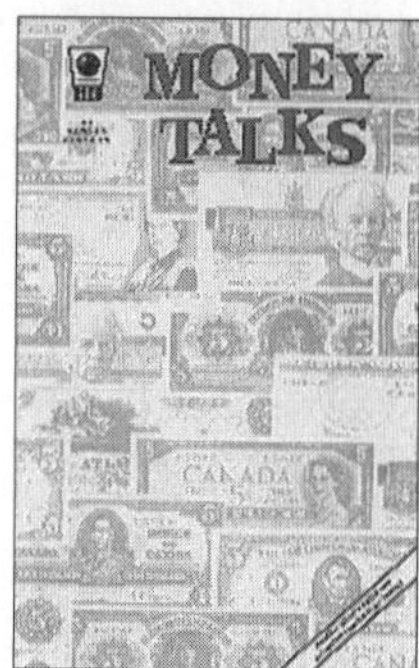

Money Talks

Monkey Business

Monkeyshines

Monnga

Monster Boy

Monster Boy Comics

Monster Crime Comics

Robotech: The Macross Saga

Comico, 1984

1 ....8.00
2 ....4.00
3-5 ....3.00
6-36 ....2.00

Robotech: The New Generation

Comico, 1985

1-25 ....2.00

Robotech II: Invid World, Assault on Optera

Academy, 1994

1 ....3.00

Robotech II: The Sentinels

Eternity, 1988

1 ....4.00
1/2nd 2.00
2-3 ....3.00
3/2nd-16 ....2.00

Robotech II: The Sentinels Book II

Eternity, 1990

1-11 ....2.00
12-20 ....3.00

Robotech II: The Sentinels Book III

Eternity

1-6 ....3.00

Robotech II: The Sentinels Book IV

Academy, 1996

1-6 ....3.00

Robotech II: The Sentinels Cyberpirates

Eternity, 1991

1-4 ....2.00

Robotech II: The Sentinels Special

Eternity, 1989

1-2 ....2.00

Robotech II: The Sentinels Swimsuit Spectacular

Eternity

1 ....3.00

Robotech II: The Sentinels: The Illustrated Handbook

Eternity

1-3 ....3.00

Robotech II: The Sentinels The Malcontent Uprisings

Malibu, 1989

7-12 ....2.00

Robotech II: The Sentinels: The Untold Story

Eternity

1 ....3.00

Robotech II: The Sentinels Wedding Special

Eternity, 1989

1-2 ....2.00

Robotech: Vermilion

Antarctic, 1997

1-4 ....3.00

Robotech Warriors

Academy, 1995

1 ....3.00

Robotech: Wings of Gibraltar

Antarctic, 1998

1-2 ....3.00

Robotix

Marvel, 1986

1 ....1.00

Robotmen of the Lost Planet

Avon, 1952

1 ....1,000.00

Robo Warriors

CFW

1-8 ....2.00

Robyn of Sherwood

Caliber, 1998

1 ....3.00

Rockers

Rip Off, 1988

1-8 ....2.00

Rocket Comics

Hillman, 1940

1 ....1,535.00
2-3 ....775.00

Rocketeer 3-D Comic

Disney, 1991

1 ....5.00

Rocketeer Adventure Magazine

Comico, 1988

1 ....5.00
2 ....4.00
3 ....3.00

Rocketeer Special Edition

Eclipse, 1984

1 ....2.00

Rocketeer: The Official Movie Adaptation
Disney, 1991
1 ... 3.00
1/Direct ... 6.00

Rocket Kelly
Fox, 1944
0 ... 185.00
1 ... 140.00
2-5 ... 120.00

Rocketman
AC
1-Ashcan 2 ... 6.00

Rocketman
Ajax, 1952
1 ... 6.00

Rocketman: King of the Rocket Men
Innovation
1-4 ... 3.00

Rocketo
Speakeasy Comics, 2005
1-5 ... 3.00

Rocketo: Journey to the Hidden Sea
Image, 2006
6-7 ... 3.00
10-12 ... 4.00

Rocket Raccoon
Marvel, 1985
1 ... 2.00
2-4 ... 1.00

Rocket Ranger
Adventure, 1991
1-6 ... 3.00

Rocket Ship X
Fox, 1951
1 ... 525.00

Rocket to the Moon
Avon, 1951
1 ... 815.00

Rock Fantasy
Rock Fantasy, 1990
1-15 ... 3.00
16 ... 5.00
17 ... 3.00

Rockheads
Solson
1 ... 2.00

Rockin' Bones
New England, 1992
1-Holiday 1 ... 3.00

Rockinfreakapotamus Presents the Red Hot Chili Peppers Illustrated Lyrics
Telltale, 1997
1 ... 4.00

Rockin Rollin Miner Ants
Fate, 1991
1 ... 2.00

Rockmeez
Jzink Comics, 1992
1-4 ... 3.00

Rock 'n' Roll Comics
Revolutionary, 1989
1 ... 6.00
1/2nd ... 4.00
1/3rd-1/7th ... 2.00
2 ... 3.00
2/2nd-2/4th ... 2.00
1-2 ... 4.00
2/5th-1-4 ... 2.00
3 ... 10.00
1-5-1-6 ... 2.00
4 ... 50.00
1-7 ... 2.00
4/2nd ... 3.00
5-8 ... 2.00
9 ... 5.00
9/2nd-16 ... 2.00
17 ... 3.00
18 ... 2.00
19-29 ... 3.00
5-2 ... 2.00
30-39 ... 3.00
6-2 ... 2.00
40 ... 3.00
6-3 ... 2.00
41 ... 3.00
6-4 ... 2.00
42-49 ... 3.00
7-2 ... 2.00
50 ... 3.00
7-3 ... 2.00
51-65 ... 3.00

Rock N' Roll Comics Magazine
Revolutionary, 1990
1-5 ... 3.00

Rock 'N' Roll
Image, 2006
1 ... 4.00

Rockola
Mirage
1 ... 2.00

Rocko's Modern Life
Marvel, 1994
1-7 ... 2.00

Monster Fighters Inc.

Monster Frat House

Monster Hunters

Monster Island

Monster Love

Monsterman

Monster Massacre

Monster Massacre Special

Rocky and His Fiendish Friends
Gold Key, 1962

1 .... 100.00
2-3 .... 75.00
4-5 .... 60.00

Rocky Horror Picture Show: The Comic Book
Caliber, 1990

1 .... 7.00
1/2nd 3.00
2-3 .... 4.00

Rocky Lane Western
Fawcett, 1949

1 .... 450.00
2 .... 175.00
3-9 .... 125.00
10-19 .... 75.00
20-35 .... 55.00
36-45 .... 40.00
46-55 .... 35.00

Rocky Lane Western
Charlton, 1954

56 .... 75.00
57-60 .... 45.00
61-70 .... 35.00
71-87 .... 30.00

Rocky Lane Western (AC)
AC

1 .... 3.00
2 .... 6.00
Ann 1 .... 3.00

Rocky Mountain King
L. Miller & Son

1 .... 10.00
2-5 .... 8.00
6-20 .... 6.00
21-50 .... 5.00
51-65 .... 4.00

Rocky: The One and Only
Fantagraphics, 2006

1 .... 13.00

Rod Cameron Western
Fawcett, 1950

1 .... 325.00
2 .... 150.00
3 .... 125.00
4-10 .... 105.00
11-19 .... 85.00
20 .... 90.00

Roel
Sirius, 1997

1 .... 3.00

Rogan Gosh
DC

1 .... 7.00

Roger Dodger
Standard, 1952

5 .... 25.00

Roger Fnord
Rip Off, 1992

1 .... 3.00

Roger Rabbit
Disney, 1990

1-18 .... 2.00
Special 1 .... 4.00

Roger Rabbit in 3-D
Disney

1 .... 3.00

Roger Rabbit's Toontown
Disney, 1991

1-5 .... 2.00

Roger Wilco
Adventure, 1992

1-2 .... 3.00

Rog-2000
Pacific

1 .... 2.00

Rogue
Marvel, 1995

1 .... 4.00
2-4 .... 3.00

Rogue
Marvel, 2001

1-4 .... 3.00

Rogue
Marvel, 2004

1-12 .... 3.00

Rogue
Monster, 1991

1 .... 2.00

Rogue Battlebook
Marvel

1 .... 4.00

Rogue Satellite Comics
Slave Labor, 1996

1-Special 1 .... 3.00

Rogues Gallery
DC

1 .... 4.00

Rogues (Villains)
DC, 1998

1 .... 2.00

Rogue Trooper (1st Series)
Fleetway-Quality

1-49 .... 2.00

Rogue Trooper (2nd Series)

Fleetway-Quality

1-9 .... 3.00

Roja Fusion

Antarctic, 1995

1 .... 3.00

Rokkin

DC, 2006

1-6 .... 3.00

Roland: Days Of Wrath

Terra Major, 1999

1 .... 3.00

Rollercoaster

Fantagraphics, 1996

1 .... 4.00

Rollercoasters Special Edition

Blue Comet

1 .... 2.00

Rolling Stones

Personality

1-3 .... 3.00

Rolling Stones: Voodoo Lounge

Marvel, 1995

1 .... 7.00

Roly Poly Comics

Green, 1945

1 .... 225.00
10 .... 150.00
11-14 .... 100.00

Rom

Marvel, 1979

1 .... 8.00
2-10 .... 2.00
11-16 .... 1.00
17-18 .... 2.00
19-23 .... 1.00
24-25 .... 2.00
26-53 .... 1.00
54 .... 3.00
55 .... 1.00
56 .... 3.00
57-74 .... 1.00
75 .... 2.00
Ann 1-4 .... 1.00

Romance & Confession Stories

St. John, 1949

1 .... 300.00

Romancer

Moonstone, 1996

1 .... 3.00

Romances of Nurse Helen Grant

Atlas, 1957

1 .... 35.00

Romances of the West

Marvel, 1949

1 .... 150.00
2 .... 100.00

Romance Tales

Marvel, 1949

7 .... 75.00
8-9 .... 55.00

Romance Trail

DC, 1949

1 .... 370.00
2 .... 175.00
3 .... 190.00
4 .... 135.00
5-6 .... 120.00

Roman Holidays

Gold Key, 1973

1 .... 20.00
2-3 .... 10.00

Romantic Adventures

ACG, 1949

1 .... 70.00
2 .... 35.00
3-5 .... 24.00
6-10 .... 20.00
11-30 .... 16.00
31-45 .... 14.00
46-48 .... 45.00
49-50 .... 14.00
51-67 .... 12.00

Romantic Confessions (Vol. 1)

Hillman, 1949

1 .... 100.00
2 .... 50.00
3-12 .... 40.00

Romantic Confessions (Vol. 2)

Hillman, 1951

1-2 .... 32.00
3 .... 45.00
4-12 .... 32.00

Romantic Hearts

Story, 1951

1 .... 75.00
2 .... 40.00
3-10 .... 35.00

Romantic Hearts

Story, 1953

1 .... 50.00
2 .... 30.00
3-12 .... 25.00

Monster Matinee

Monster Posse

Monsters from Outer Space

Monsters on the Prowl

Monsters Unleashed

Monster World

Monte Hale Western

Monty Hall of the U.S. Marines

Romantic Love
Avon, 1949

1 .... 130.00
2-5 .... 80.00
6 .... 110.00
7-8 .... 72.00
9-12 .... 80.00
13-23 .... 72.00

Romantic Marriage
Ziff-Davis, 1950

1 .... 125.00
2 .... 70.00
3-9 .... 55.00
10 .... 100.00
11-24 .... 55.00

Romantic Picture Novelettes
Magazine Enterprises, 1946

1 .... 125.00

Romantic Secrets
Fawcett, 1949

1 .... 85.00
2-4 .... 55.00
5-8 .... 40.00
9 .... 55.00
10 .... 40.00
11-23 .... 36.00
24 .... 42.00
25-39 .... 32.00

Romantic Secrets
Charlton, 1955

5 .... 45.00
6-10 .... 22.00
11-20 .... 12.00
21-30 .... 8.00
31-52 .... 6.00

Romantic Story
Charlton, 1949

1 .... 65.00
2 .... 40.00
3 .... 30.00
4-9 .... 20.00
10-22 .... 14.00
23-40 .... 12.00
41-60 .... 10.00
61-80 .... 8.00
81-130 .... 5.00

Romantic Tails
Head, 1998

1 .... 3.00

Romantic Western
Fawcett, 1949

1 .... 90.00
2-3 .... 68.00

Romp One Shot
Image, 2004

1 .... 7.00

Ronald McDonald
Charlton, 1970

1 .... 52.00
2-4 .... 35.00

Ronin
DC, 1983

1 .... 4.00
☛Frank Miller series
2-5 .... 3.00
6 .... 5.00

Rook
Harris, 1995

1-2 .... 3.00

Rook Magazine
Warren, 1979

1 .... 4.00
2-10 .... 3.00
11-14 .... 2.00

Room 222
Dell, 1970

1 .... 30.00
2-4 .... 20.00

Rooter
Custom, 1996

1-6 .... 3.00

Rooter
Custom, 1998

1-2 .... 3.00

Roots of the Oppressor
Northstar

1 .... 3.00

Roots of the Swamp Thing
DC, 1986

1-5 .... 2.00

Roscoe! The Dawg, Ace Detective
Renegade, 1987

1-4 .... 2.00

Rose & Thorn
DC, 2004

1-6 .... 3.00

Rose
Hero, 1992

1 .... 4.00
2 .... 3.00
3-4 .... 4.00
5 .... 3.00

Rose
Cartoon Books, 2000

1-3 .... 6.00

Rose & Gunn
Bishop, 1995

3-5 .... 3.00

Rose & Gunn Creator's Choice
Bishop, 1995

1 .... 3.00

Roswell: Little Green Man
Bongo, 1996

1 .... 4.00
2-6 .... 3.00

Rotogin Junkbotz
Image, 2003

0-3 .... 3.00

Rough Raiders
Blue Comet

1-3 .... 2.00
Ann 1 .... 3.00

Roulette
Caliber

1 .... 3.00

Roundup
D.S., 1948

1 .... 105.00
2-5 .... 75.00

Route 666
CrossGen, 2002

1-22 .... 3.00

Rovers
Malibu, 1987

1-7 .... 2.00

Royal Roy
Marvel, 1985

1-6 .... 1.00

Roy Campanella, Baseball Hero
Fawcett, 1950

1 .... 500.00

Roy Rogers Comics
Dell, 1948

1 .... 600.00
2 .... 275.00
3-5 .... 200.00
6-10 .... 140.00
11-20 .... 105.00
21-30 .... 90.00
31-40 .... 75.00
41-50 .... 55.00
51-60 .... 45.00
61-80 .... 35.00
81-100 .... 30.00
101-145 .... 25.00

Roy Rogers' Trigger
Dell, 1951

2 .... 90.00
3-5 .... 48.00
6-17 .... 35.00

Roy Rogers Western
AC

1 .... 5.00

Roy Rogers Western Classics
AC

1-2 .... 3.00
3-4 .... 4.00
5 .... 3.00

RTA: Personality Crisis
Image, 2005

0 .... 4.00

Rubber Blanket
Rubber Blanket

1 .... 6.00
2-3 .... 8.00

Rubber Duck
Print Mint, 1971

1-2 .... 3.00

Rubes Revue
Fragments West

1 .... 2.00

Ruby Shaft's Tales of the Unexpurgated
Fantagraphics

1 .... 3.00

Ruck Bud Webster and His Screeching Commandos
Pyramid

1 .... 2.00

Rude Awakening
Dennis Mcmillan, 1996

1 .... 13.00

Rudolph the Red-Nosed Reindeer
DC

1 .... 10.00

Rudolph the Red-Nosed Reindeer Annual
DC, 1950

1950 .... 115.00
1951 .... 90.00
1952-1953 .... 75.00
1954-1956 .... 60.00
1957-1961 .... 48.00
1962 .... 75.00

Ruff and Reddy
Dell, 1960

4-8 .... 40.00
9-12 .... 30.00

Rugged Action
Atlas, 1954

1 .... 75.00
2-4 .... 55.00

Moon Beast

Moondog

Moon Girl

Moon Knight Special

Moon Knight Special Edition

Moonshadow

Moonstruck

Moontrap

Rugrats
Marvel UK

1 .... 3.00
2-29 .... 2.00

Rugrats Comic Adventures
Nickelodeon Magazines, 1997

1 .... 4.00
2-10 .... 3.00

Rugrats Comic Adventures
Nickelodeon Magazines, 1998

1 .... 3.00

Ruins
Marvel, 1995

1-2 .... 5.00

Rulah Jungle Goddess
Fox, 1948

17 .... 1,000.00
18 .... 750.00
19-22 .... 600.00
23-27 .... 450.00

Ruler of the Land
ADV Manga, 2004

1-5 .... 10.00

Rumble Girls: Silky Warrior Tansie
Image, 2000

1-6 .... 4.00

Rumic World
Viz, 1993

1 .... 3.00
2 .... 4.00

Rummage $2099
Parody

1 .... 3.00

Runaway
Dell, 1964

1 .... 16.00

Runaway: A Known Associates Mystery
Known Associates

1 .... 3.00

Runaways
Marvel, 2003

1 .... 4.00
2-18 .... 3.00

Runaways
Marvel, 2005

1 .... 6.00
1/Variant 5.00
2-22 .... 3.00

Run, Buddy, Run
Gold Key, 1967

1 .... 15.00

Rune
Malibu, 1994

0 .... 3.00
1-2 .... 2.00
3 .... 4.00
4-9 .... 2.00
GS 1 .... 3.00

Rune
Malibu, 1995

0-7 .... 2.00

Rune: Hearts of Darkness
Malibu, 1996

1-3 .... 2.00

Rune/Silver Surfer
Marvel, 1995

1 .... 3.00
1/Direct 6.00

Runes of Ragnan
Image, 2005

1-3 .... 4.00
4 .... 3.00

Rune vs. Venom
Malibu, 1995

1 .... 4.00

Rune/Wrath
Malibu

1 .... 1.00

Runners: Bad Goods
Serve Man Press, 2003

1-5 .... 3.00

Rurouni Kenshin
Viz, 2003

1-19 .... 8.00

Ruse
CrossGen, 2001

1-26 .... 3.00

Ruse: Archard's Agents: Deadly Dare
CrossGen, 2004

1 .... 3.00

Ruse: Archard's Agents: Pugilistic Pete
CrossGen, 2003

1 .... 3.00

Rush City
DC, 2006

1-3 .... 3.00

Rush Limbaugh Must Die
Boneyard, 1993

1 .... 5.00

Rust
Now, 1987

1-13 .... 2.00

Rust
Now, 1989
1-7 .... 2.00

Rust
Adventure, 1992
1 .... 3.00
1/Ltd. 5.00
2-4 .... 3.00

Rust
Caliber
1-2 .... 3.00

Rusty
Marvel, 1947
12 .... 55.00
13 .... 40.00
14 .... 60.00
15-17 .... 48.00
18-19 .... 30.00
20 .... 55.00
21-22 .... 60.00

Rusty, Boy Detective
Lev Gleason, 1955
1 .... 50.00
2-5 .... 30.00

Ruule: Ganglords of Chinatown
Beckett, 2003
1-5 .... 3.00

Saari
P.L., 1951
1 .... 300.00

Saban Powerhouse
Acclaim, 1997
1-2 .... 5.00

Saban Presents Power Rangers Turbo vs. Beetleborgs Metallix
Acclaim, 1997
1 .... 5.00

Saber Tiger
Viz, 1991
1 .... 13.00

Sabina
Fantagraphics, 1994
1-7 .... 3.00

Sable
First, 1988
1-27 .... 2.00

Sable & Fortune
Marvel, 2006
1-4 .... 3.00

Sable (Mike Grell's...)
First, 1990
1-10 .... 2.00

Sabra Blade
Draculina, 1994
1-1/Variant 3.00

Sabre
Eclipse, 1982
1 .... 3.00
2-14 .... 2.00

Sabre: 20th Anniversary Edition
Image
1 .... 13.00

Sabretooth
Marvel, 1993
1-4 .... 3.00
Special 1 .... 5.00

Sabretooth
Marvel, 1998
1 .... 6.00

Sabretooth
Marvel, 2004
1-4 .... 3.00

Sabretooth Classic
Marvel, 1994
1-15 .... 2.00

Sabretooth: Mary Shelley Overdrive
Marvel, 2002
1-4 .... 3.00

Sabrina
Archie, 1997
1 .... 3.00
2-32 .... 2.00

Sabrina
Archie, 2000
1-105 .... 2.00

Sabrina Online
Vision
2 .... 4.00

Sabrina the Teenage Witch
Archie, 1971
1 .... 45.00
2 .... 20.00
3-5 .... 12.00
6-10 .... 10.00
11-17 .... 8.00
18-20 .... 6.00
21-30 .... 5.00
31-50 .... 4.00
51-60 .... 3.00
61-77 .... 2.00
Holiday 1 .... 3.00
Holiday 2-3 .... 2.00

Sabrina the Teenage Witch
Archie, 1996
1 .... 2.00

Mopsy

Morbid Angel

Morbius Revisited

More Fun Comics

More Tales from Gimbley

More Than Mortal

Morlocks

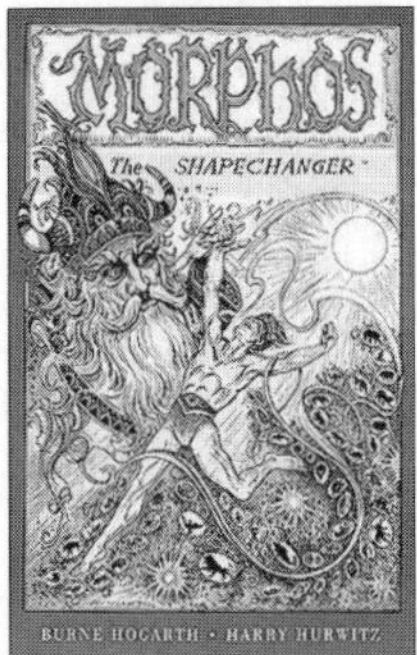

Morphos the Shapechanger

Sachs & Violens
Marvel, 1993

1-1/Platinum 3.00
2-4 ....2.00

Sacred Ruins: The Mystic Wars
Labyrinth, 2000

1 ....3.00

Sacrificed Trees
Mansion, 1995

1 ....3.00

Saddle Justice
E.C., 1948

3 ....300.00
4 ....275.00
5-8 ....250.00

Saddle Romances
E.C., 1949

9-11 ....275.00

Sade/Razor
London Night

1/2nd 3.00

Sad Sack
Harvey, 1949

1 ....500.00
2 ....250.00
3 ....125.00
4-10 ....100.00
11-19 ....70.00
20 ....50.00
21-30 ....35.00
31-40 ....25.00
41-50 ....15.00
51-70 ....10.00
71-90 ....8.00
91-100 ....5.00
101-150 ....3.00
151-287 ....2.00
288-289 ....3.00
290-291 ....2.00
292 ....10.00
293 ....2.00
3D 1 ....125.00

Sad Sack & The Sarge
Harvey, 1957

1 ....80.00
2 ....45.00
3-5 ....30.00
6-10 ....20.00
11-20 ....16.00
21-30 ....12.00
31-40 ....9.00
41-49 ....7.00
50-60 ....6.00
61-80 ....5.00
81-90 ....3.00
91-96 ....4.00
97-100 ....3.00
101-155 ....2.00

Sad Sack Army Life Parade
Harvey, 1963

1 ....35.00
2 ....20.00
3 ....15.00
4-5 ....12.00
6-10 ....10.00
11-20 ....8.00
21-30 ....6.00
31-40 ....5.00
41-50 ....4.00
51-61 ....3.00

Sad Sack at Home for the Holidays
Lorne-Harvey, 1992

1 ....2.00

Sad Sack Comics
Harvey

1 ....15.00
2 ....12.00
3 ....10.00
4 ....10.00
5 ....10.00
6-9 ....8.00
10 ....8.00
11-19 ....6.00
20-29 ....4.00
30-39 ....4.00
40 ....4.00

Sad Sack Fun Around the World
Harvey, 1974

1 ....10.00

Sad Sack in 3-D
Blackthorne, 1988

1 ....2.00

Sad Sack Laugh Special
Harvey, 1958

1 ....90.00
2 ....45.00
3-10 ....25.00
11-20 ....20.00
21-30 ....15.00
31-40 ....12.00
41-60 ....10.00
61-80 ....8.00
81-93 ....6.00

Sad Sack Navy, Gobs 'n' Gals
Harvey, 1972

1 ....12.00
2 ....8.00
3-5 ....6.00
6-8 ....4.00

Sad Sack's Funny Friends
Harvey, 1955

1 ....50.00
2 ....34.00

3 .... 22.00
4-5 .... 20.00
6-10 .... 16.00
11-20 .... 12.00
21-30 .... 10.00
31-40 .... 8.00
41-50 .... 5.00
51-75 .... 3.00

Sad Sack U.S.A.

Harvey, 1972

1 .... 12.00
2-8 .... 6.00

Sad Sack with Sarge & Sadie

Harvey, 1972

1 .... 10.00
2 .... 6.00
3-8 .... 4.00

Sad Sad Sack World

Harvey, 1964

1 .... 45.00
2-10 .... 20.00
11-30 .... 15.00
31-40 .... 12.00
41-46 .... 10.00

Safe Comics

Graphic Graphics, 1998

1-2 .... 3.00

Safest Place in the World

Dark Horse, 1993

1 .... 3.00

Safety-Belt Man

Sirius, 1994

1-6 .... 3.00

Safety-Belt Man: All Hell

Sirius, 1996

1-6 .... 3.00

Saffire

Image, 2000

1-3 .... 3.00

Saga

Odyssey

1 .... 2.00

Saga of Crystar Crystal Warrior

Marvel, 1983

1 .... 2.00
2-11 .... 1.00

Saga of Elf Face

Exter Entrance, 1986

1-3 .... 1.00

Saga of Ra's Al Ghul

DC, 1988

1-4 .... 3.00

Saga of Seven Suns

DC, 2004

1 .... 25.00

Saga of Squadron Supreme

Marvel, 2006

1 .... 4.00

Saga of the Man Elf

Trident, 1989

1-5 .... 2.00

Saga of the Original Human Torch

Marvel, 1990

1-4 .... 2.00

Saga of the Realm

Caliber, 1992

1-3 .... 3.00

Saga of the Sub-Mariner

Marvel, 1988

1-12 .... 2.00

Saga of the Swamp Thing

DC, 1982

1 .... 3.00
2-19 .... 2.00
20 .... 15.00
☛Alan Moore starts
21 .... 12.00
22-25 .... 6.00
26-32 .... 4.00
33 .... 3.00
34 .... 5.00
35-36 .... 3.00
37 .... 55.00
☛1st Hellblazer
38 .... 15.00
39-40 .... 9.00
41-45 .... 4.00
Ann 1 .... 3.00
Ann 2 .... 4.00
Ann 3 .... 3.00

Saigon Chronicles

Avalon

1 .... 3.00

Saikano

Viz, 2004

1-6 .... 10.00

Sailor Moon Comic

Mixxzine, 1998

1 .... 15.00
1/A 12.00
2-4 .... 8.00
5-7 .... 6.00
8 .... 5.00
9 .... 4.00
10-33 .... 3.00

Sailor Moon SuperS

Mixx

1 .... 10.00

Morphs

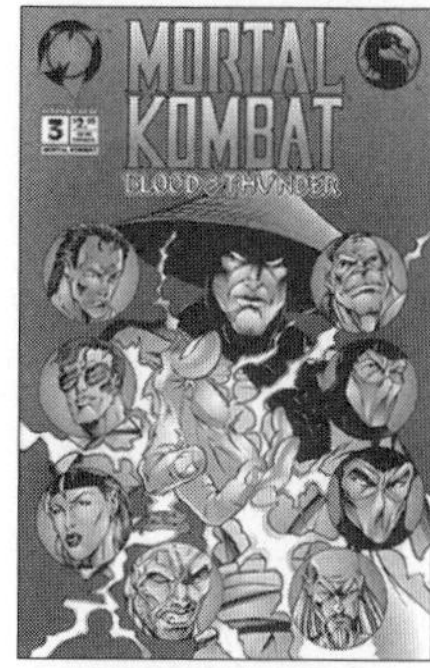

Mortal Kombat

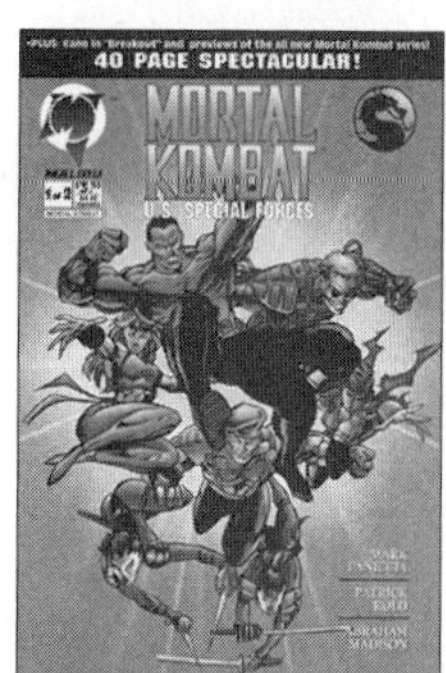

Mortal Kombat U.S. Special Forces

Mortar Man

Mort the Dead Teenager

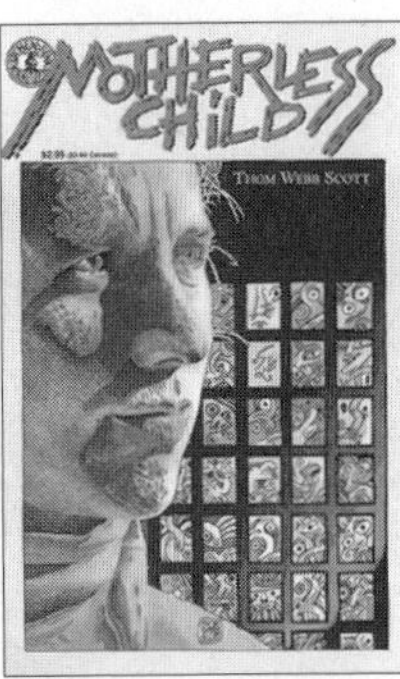
Motherless Child

Mother Superion

Mother Teresa of Calcutta

Sailor's Story, A
Marvel
1 ....6.00

Sailor's Story, A: Winds, Dreams, and Dragons
Marvel
1 ....7.00

Sailor Sweeney
Atlas, 1956
12-14 ....80.00

Saint
Avon, 1947
1 ....475.00
2 ....245.00
3-4 ....200.00
5 ....20.00
6 ....250.00
7 ....160.00
8-10 ....145.00
11 ....100.00
12 ....120.00

Saint Angel
Image, 2000
0 ....3.00
1-4 ....4.00

St. George
Marvel, 1988
1-8 ....2.00

Saint Germaine
Caliber, 1997
1-8 ....3.00

Saint Germaine: Restoration
Caliber, 1997
1 ....4.00

Saints
Saturn, 1995
0-1 ....3.00

Saint Sinner
Marvel, 1993
1 ....3.00
2-8 ....2.00

St. Swithin's Day
Trident, 1990
1-1/2nd 3.00

St. Swithin's Day
Oni, 1998
1 ....3.00

Saiyuki
Tokyopop, 2004
1 ....10.00

Saiyuki Reload
Tokyopop, 2005
1-2 ....10.00

Sakura Taisen
Tokyopop, 2005
1-2 ....10.00

Salamander Dream
Adhouse Books, 2005
1 ....15.00

Salamandroid
Harris
Ashcan 1 ....1.00

Salimba
Blackthorne, 1986
1 ....4.00
3D 1-3D 2 ....3.00

Sally Forth
Fantagraphics, 1993
1-8 ....3.00

Sam & Max, Freelance Police
Marvel
1 ....2.00

Sam & Max Freelance Police Special
Comico, 1989
1 ....3.00

Sam and Max, Freelance Police Special
Fishwrap, 1987
1 ....2.00

Sam & Max Freelance Police Special Color Collection
Marvel
1 ....5.00

Sam and Twitch
Image, 1999
1-26 ....3.00

Sam Bronx and the Robots
Eclipse, 1989
1 ....7.00

Sambu Gassho (A Chorus in Three Parts)
Bodo Genki, 1994
1 ....1.00

Sam Hill, Private Eye
Close-Up, 1950
1 ....175.00
2 ....115.00
3-7 ....80.00

Sammy: Tourist Trap
Image, 2003
1-4 ....3.00

Sammy Very Sammy Day One Shot
Image, 2004
1 .... 6.00

Sam Noir: Samurai Detective
Image, 2006
1-3 .... 3.00

Sam Slade, Robo-Hunter
Fleetway-Quality
1-33 .... 2.00

Samson
Fox, 1940
1 .... 1,400.00
2 .... 550.00
3 .... 425.00
4 .... 375.00
5-6 .... 285.00

Samson
Ajax, 1955
12 .... 175.00
13-14 .... 155.00

Samson
Samson, 1995
½ 3.00

Samson: The Kid Who Never Got a Haircut
Tyndale
1 .... 2.00

Sam Stories: Legs
Image, 1999
1 .... 3.00

Samurai
Aircel, 1986
1 .... 3.00
1/2nd-12 .... 2.00
13-16 .... 3.00
17-23 .... 2.00

Samurai
Aircel, 1987
1-3 .... 2.00

Samurai
Aircel, 1988
1-7 .... 2.00

Samurai
Warp, 1997
1 .... 3.00

Samurai Champloo
Tokyopop, 2005
1 .... 10.00

Samurai 7
Gauntlet
1-3 .... 3.00

Samurai Cat
Marvel, 1991
1-3 .... 2.00

Samurai Compilation Book
Aircel
1-2 .... 5.00

Samurai Deeper Kyo
Tokyopop, 2003
1-16 .... 10.00

Samurai: Demon Sword
Night Wynd
1-4 .... 3.00

Samurai Executioner
Dark Horse, 2004
1-9 .... 10.00

Samurai Funnies
Solson
1-2 .... 2.00

Samurai Guard
Colburn, 1999
1-2 .... 3.00
Ashcan 1 .... 1.00

Samurai: Heaven and Earth
Dark Horse, 2004
1-4 .... 3.00

Samurai: Heaven and Earth
Dark Horse, 2006
1 .... 3.00

Samurai Jack Special
DC, 2002
1-1/2nd 4.00

Samurai Jam
Slave Labor, 1994
1-4 .... 3.00

Samurai: Mystic Cult
Nightwynd, 1992
1-4 .... 3.00

Samurai Penguin
Slave Labor, 1986
1-8 .... 2.00

Samurai Penguin: Food Chain Follies
Slave Labor, 1991
1 .... 6.00

Samurai Squirrel
Spotlight, 1986
1-2 .... 2.00

Samurai: Vampire's Hunt
Nightwynd, 1992
1-4 .... 3.00

Motion Picture Comics

Motorhead

Motormouth

Moxi

M. Rex

Ms. Marvel

Ms. Tree

Mucha Lucha

Samuree
Continuity, 1987

1-9 .... 2.00

Samuree
Continuity, 1993

1-4 .... 3.00

Samuree
Acclaim, 1995

1-2 .... 3.00

Sanctuary Part 1
Viz, 1993

1 .... 6.00
2-9 .... 5.00

Sanctuary Part 2
Viz, 1994

1-9 .... 5.00

Sanctuary Part 3
Viz, 1994

1-8 .... 3.00

Sanctuary Part 4
Viz, 1995

1-5 .... 3.00
6-7 .... 4.00

Sanctuary Part 5
Viz, 1996

1-13 .... 4.00

Sanctum
Blackshoe

1/Ltd. 4.00

San Diego Comic-Con Comics
Dark Horse, 1992

1-4 .... 3.00

Sandmadam
Spoof

1 .... 3.00

Sandman
DC, 1974

1 .... 15.00
2 .... 7.00
3-6 .... 4.00

Sandman
DC, 1989

1 .... 25.00
2-3 .... 12.00
4-7 .... 4.00
8 .... 15.00
☛1st Death
8/Ltd. 35.00
9-14 .... 4.00
15-21 .... 3.00
22 .... 4.00
23-49 .... 3.00
50 .... 5.00
50/Gold 20.00
51-74 .... 3.00
75 .... 4.00
Special 1 .... 5.00

Sandman: A Gallery of Dreams
DC, 1994

1 .... 5.00

Sandman: Endless Nights
DC, 2003

1 .... 3.00
1/2nd 18.00

Sandman Midnight Theatre
DC, 1995

1 .... 7.00

Sandman Mystery Theatre
DC, 1993

1 .... 4.00
2-49 .... 3.00
50 .... 4.00
51-70 .... 3.00
Ann 1 .... 4.00

Sandman Mystery Theatre: Sleep of Reason
DC, 2007

1 .... 3.00

Sandman #1 Special Edition
DC, 2006

1 .... 1.00

Sandman Presents: Bast
DC, 2003

1-3 .... 3.00

Sandman Presents: Love Street
DC, 1999

1-3 .... 3.00

Sandman Presents: Lucifer
DC, 1999

1-3 .... 3.00

Sandman Presents: Petrefax
DC, 2000

1-4 .... 3.00

Sandman Presents: Taller Tales
DC, 2003

1 .... 20.00

Sandman Presents: Deadboy Detectives
DC, 2001
1-4 .... 3.00

Sandman Presents: Everything You Always Wanted to Know About Dreams...But Were Afraid To Ask
DC, 2001
1 .... 4.00

Sandman Presents: The Furies
DC, 2004
1 .... 18.00

Sandman Presents: Thessaly - Witch for Hire
DC, 2004
1-4 .... 3.00

Sandman Presents: The Corinthian
DC, 2001
1-3 .... 3.00

Sandman Presents: The Thessaliad
DC, 2002
1-4 .... 3.00

Sandman: The Dream Hunters
DC, 2008
1-4/A 4.00

Sands
Black Eye, 1997
1-3 .... 3.00

Sandscape
Dreamwave, 2003
1-4 .... 3.00

Sands of the South Pacific
Toby, 1953
1 .... 150.00

San Francisco Comic Book
San Francisco Comic Book Co., 1970
1 .... 6.00
2-7 .... 4.00

Santa Claus Adventures (Walt Kelly's...)
Innovation
1 .... 7.00

Santa Claus Funnies
Dell, 1943
1 .... 300.00
2 .... 225.00

Santa Claws
Eternity
1 .... 3.00

Santa Claws
Thorby
1 .... 3.00

Santana
Malibu, 1994
1 .... 5.00

Santa's Christmas Comics
Standard, 1952
1 .... 100.00

Santa the Barbarian
Maximum, 1996
1 .... 3.00

Sapphire
Aircel, 1990
1-9 .... 3.00

Sapphire
NBM, 2001
1-2 .... 11.00

Sap Tunes
Fantagraphics
1-2 .... 3.00

Sarah-Jane Hamilton Presents Superstars of Erotica
Re-Visionary
1 .... 3.00

Sarge Snorkel
Charlton, 1973
1 .... 8.00
2 .... 5.00
3-5 .... 4.00
6-17 .... 3.00

Sarge Steel
Charlton, 1964
1 .... 15.00
2 .... 10.00
3-5 .... 8.00
6-9 .... 6.00

Satanika
Verotik, 1995
0 .... 4.00
1 .... 5.00
2-3 .... 4.00
4-10 .... 3.00
11 .... 4.00

Satanika Illustrations
Verotik, 1996
1 .... 4.00

Satanika Tales
Verotik, 2005
1-2 .... 4.00

Muggsy Mouse

Muggy-Doo Boy Cat

Murder

Murder Me Dead

Murderous Gangsters

Music Comics

Music Comics on Tour

Mutant Chronicles

Satan Place
Thunderhill
1 .... 4.00

Satan's Planet (A Day in Life On...)
Home-Made Euthanasia
1 .... 1.00
2 .... 2.00

Satan's Six
Topps, 1993
1-4 .... 3.00

Satan's Six: Hellspawn
Topps, 1994
1-3 .... 3.00

Saturday Morning: The Comic
Marvel, 1996
1 .... 2.00

Saturday Nite
Anson Jew, 1999
1-2 .... 3.00

Saucy Little Tart
Fantagraphics, 1995
1 .... 3.00

Saurians: Unnatural Selection
CrossGen, 2002
1-2 .... 3.00

Savage Combat Tales
Atlas-Seaboard, 1975
1 .... 16.00
2-3 .... 10.00

Savage Dragon
Image, 1992
1 .... 3.00

Savage Dragon
Image, 1993
0 .... 2.00
½ 3.00
½/Platinum 4.00
1-3 .... 3.00
4-12 .... 2.00
13-13/A 3.00
14 .... 2.00
15-24 .... 3.00
25-25/A 4.00
26-49 .... 3.00
50 .... 6.00
51/A-74 .... 3.00
75 .... 6.00
76-99 .... 3.00
100 .... 9.00
101-106 .... 3.00
107 .... 4.00
108-123 .... 3.00
125 .... 5.00
126-150 .... 3.00

Savage Dragon Archives
Image, 1998
1-4 .... 3.00

Savage Dragonbert: Full Frontal Nerdity
Image, 2002
1 .... 6.00

Savage Dragon Companion
Image, 2002
1 .... 3.00

Savage Dragon/Destroyer Duck
Image, 1996
1 .... 4.00

Savage Dragon: God War
Image, 2004
1-3 .... 3.00

Savage Dragon/Hellboy
Image, 2002
1 .... 6.00

Savage Dragon/Marshal Law
Image, 1997
1-2 .... 3.00

Savage Dragon: Red Horizon
Image, 1997
1-3 .... 3.00

Savage Dragon: Sex & Violence
Image, 1997
1-2 .... 3.00

Savage Dragon/Teenage Mutant Ninja Turtles Crossover
Mirage, 1993
1 .... 3.00

Savage Dragon vs. The Savage Megaton Man
Image, 1993
1 .... 2.00
1/Gold 3.00

Savage Fists of Kung Fu
Marvel
1 .... 8.00

Savage Funnies
Vision, 1996
1-2 .... 2.00

Savage Henry
Vortex, 1987
1-13 .... 2.00
14-30 .... 3.00

Savage Henry (Iconografix)
Caliber
1-3 .... 3.00

Savage Henry: Headstrong
Caliber, 1995
1-3 .... 3.00

Savage Hulk
Marvel, 1996
1 .... 7.00

Savage Ninja
Cadillac, 1985
1 .... 1.00

Savage Return of Dracula
Marvel, 1992
1 .... 2.00

Savages
Peregrine, 2001
1 .... 3.00

Savages
Comax
1 .... 3.00

Savage She-Hulk
Marvel, 1980
1 .... 8.00
2 .... 5.00
3-5 .... 3.00
6-25 .... 2.00

Savage Sword of Conan
Marvel, 1974
1 .... 60.00
2 .... 28.00
3 .... 16.00
4-10 .... 12.00
11-20 .... 8.00
21-29 .... 6.00
30-50 .... 5.00
51-173 .... 3.00
174-235 .... 2.00
Ann 1 .... 17.00
Special 1 .... 6.00

Savage Sword of Mike
Fandom House
1 .... 2.00

Savage Tales
Marvel, 1971
1 .... 150.00
2 .... 32.00
3-4 .... 20.00
5 .... 12.00
6-11 .... 10.00
12 .... 8.00
Ann 1 .... 25.00

Savage Tales
Marvel, 1985
1 .... 4.00
2-5 .... 3.00
6-9 .... 2.00

Savant Garde
Image, 1997
1-7 .... 3.00
Fan ed. 1/A-3/A 1.00

Saved By the Bell
Harvey, 1992
1-5 .... 1.00

Saviour
Trident, 1989
1 .... 4.00
2 .... 2.00
3-5 .... 3.00

Saw: Rebirth
Idea & Design Works
1 .... 4.00

SB Ninja High School
Antarctic, 1992
1/A 3.00
1/B 5.00
2/A 3.00
2/B 5.00
3/A 3.00
3/B 5.00
4-7 .... 3.00

Scab
Fantaco, 1999
1-2 .... 4.00

Scab
Orphan Underground, 1994
1-2 .... 3.00

Scales of the Dragon
Sundragon, 1997
1 .... 2.00

Scalped
DC, 2007
1-30 .... 3.00

Scamp
Dell, 1958
5 .... 25.00
6-10 .... 10.00
11-16 .... 8.00

Scamp
Gold Key, 1968
1 .... 8.00
2-5 .... 4.00
6-20 .... 3.00
21-45 .... 2.00

Scan
Iconografix
1-2 .... 3.00

Scandals
Thorby
1 .... 3.00

Scandal Sheet
Arriba
1 .... 3.00

Mutant Zone

Mutatis

Muties

My Date

My Favorite Martian

My Friend Irma

My Greatest Adventure

My Intimate Affair

Scarab
DC, 1993

0-8 ....2.00

Scaramouch
Innovation, 1991

1-2 ....2.00

Scarecrow of Romney Marsh
Gold Key, 1964

1 ....30.00
2-3 ....20.00

Scarecrow (Villains)
DC, 1998

1 ....2.00

Scare Tactics
DC, 1996

1-12 ....2.00

Scarface: Scarred for Life
Idea & Design Works, 2006

1 ....4.00
1/Special 20.00

Scarlet Crush
Awesome, 1998

1-2 ....3.00

Scarlet in Gaslight
Eternity, 1988

1-4 ....2.00

Scarlet Kiss: The Vampyre
All American

1 ....3.00

Scarlet Scorpion/ Darkshade
AC, 1995

1-2 ....4.00

Scarlet Spider
Marvel, 1995

1-2 ....2.00

Scarlet Spider Unlimited
Marvel, 1995

1 ....4.00

Scarlett
DC, 1993

1 ....3.00
2-14 ....2.00

Scarlet Thunder
Slave Labor, 1995

1-2 ....2.00
3-4 ....3.00

Scarlett Pilgrim
Last Gasp

1 ....1.00

Scarlet Traces: The Great Game
Dark Horse, 2006

1-4 ....3.00

Scarlet Witch
Marvel, 1994

1-4 ....2.00

Scarlet Zombie
Comax

1 ....3.00

Scars (Warren Ellis')
Avatar, 2003

1-6/A 4.00

Scary Book
Caliber, 1999

1-2 ....3.00
Book 1 ....13.00

Scary Godmother
Sirius, 1997

1-6 ....3.00

Scary Godmother: Bloody Valentine
Sirius, 1998

1 ....4.00

Scary Godmother Holiday Spooktacular
Sirius, 1998

1 ....3.00

Scary Godmother Revenge of Jimmy
Sirius

1 ....20.00

Scary Godmother: Wild About Harry
Sirius, 2000

1-3 ....3.00

Scary Tales
Charlton, 1975

1 ....5.00
2-10 ....3.00
11-46 ....2.00

Scatterbrain
Dark Horse, 1998

1-4 ....3.00

Scattered
Scattered

1-9 ....0.00
24-30 ....3.00

Scavengers
Fleetway-Quality, 1988

1-5 ....1.00
6-14 ....2.00

Scavengers
Triumphant, 1993
0 .... 1.00
0/A-11 .... 3.00

SCC Convention Special
Super Crew
1 .... 2.00

Scenario A
Antarctic, 1998
1-2 .... 3.00

Scene of the Crime
DC, 1999
1-4 .... 3.00

Schizo
Antarctic, 1994
1-3 .... 4.00

School Day Romances
Star, 1949
1 .... 165.00
2-3 .... 120.00
4 .... 185.00

Science Affair, A
Antarctic, 1994
1-2 .... 3.00

Science Comics
Fox, 1940
1 .... 4,000.00
2 .... 1,800.00
3 .... 1,500.00
4 .... 1,350.00
5-8 .... 900.00

Science Comics
Humor, 1946
1 .... 125.00
2-3 .... 75.00
4-5 .... 45.00

Science Fair
Antarctic, 2005
1-3 .... 3.00

Science Fair Story of Electronics – The Discovery That Changed the World!
Radio Shack, 1981
1981-1984 .... 1.00

Science Fiction Classics
Dragon Lady
1 .... 6.00

Sci-Fi
Rough Copy
1 .... 3.00

Scimidar
Eternity, 1988
1-3 .... 3.00
4/A-4/B 2.00

Scimidar Book II
Eternity, 1989
1-4 .... 3.00

Scimidar Book III
Eternity, 1990
1-4 .... 3.00

Scimidar Book IV: "Wild Thing"
Eternity
1-4 .... 3.00

Scimidar Book V: "Living Color"
Eternity, 1991
1-4 .... 3.00

Scimidar
CFD
1-3 .... 3.00

Scimidar Pin-Up Book
Eternity, 1990
1 .... 4.00

Scion
CrossGen, 2000
1-43 .... 3.00

Sci-Spy
DC, 2002
1-6 .... 3.00

Sci-Tech
DC, 1999
1-4 .... 3.00

Scooby-Doo
Marvel, 1977
1-1/35¢ 20.00
2-4 .... 7.00
5-9 .... 4.00

Scooby-Doo
Harvey, 1992
1-Special 2 .... 2.00

Scooby-Doo
Archie, 1995
1-21 .... 2.00

Scooby-Doo
DC, 1997
1 .... 3.00
2-140 .... 2.00
Summer 1 .... 4.00
Special 1 .... 3.00
Special 2 .... 4.00

Scooby-Doo Big Book
Harvey, 1992
1-2 .... 2.00

Scooby-Doo Dollar Comic
DC, 2003
1 .... 1.00

My Life

My Little Margie

My Name Is Chaos

My Name Is Holocaust

My Only Love

My Own Romance

My Romantic Adventures

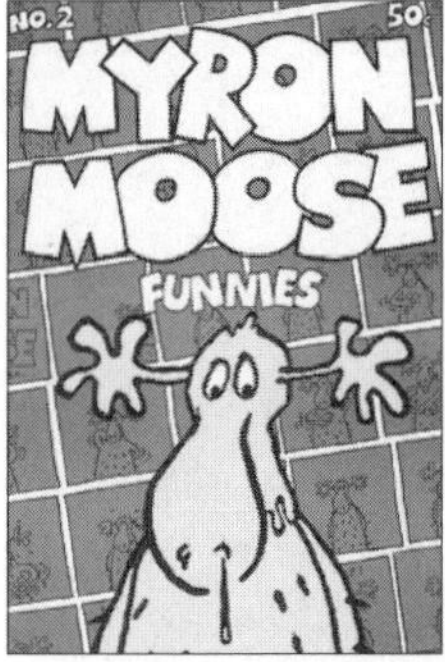

Myron Moose Funnies

Scooby-Doo Super Scarefest
DC, 2002

1 .... 4.00

Scooby Doo, Where Are You?
Gold Key, 1970

1 .... 100.00
2-8 .... 50.00
9-19 .... 25.00
20-30 .... 15.00

Scooby Doo, Where Are You?
Charlton, 1975

1 .... 15.00
2 .... 10.00
3-5 .... 7.00
6-10 .... 6.00
11 .... 5.00

Scoop Comics
Harry A. Chesler, 1941

1 .... 800.00
2 .... 850.00
3 .... 400.00
8 .... 260.00

Scooterman
Wellzee, 1996

1-3 .... 3.00

Scorched Earth
Tundra, 1991

1-3 .... 3.00

Scorchy
Forbidden Fruit

1 .... 4.00

Score
DC, 1989

1-4 .... 5.00

Scorn: Deadly Rebellion
SCC Entertainment, 1996

0 .... 3.00

Scorn: Heatwave
SCC Entertainment, 1997

1 .... 4.00

Scorpia
Miller

1-2 .... 3.00

Scorpion
Annruel

1 .... 3.00

Scorpion
Atlas-Seaboard, 1975

1-2 .... 16.00
3 .... 10.00

Scorpion Corps
Dagger, 1993

1-10 .... 3.00

Scorpion King
Dark Horse, 2002

1-2 .... 3.00

Scorpion Moon
Express, 1994

1 .... 3.00

Scorpio Rising
Marvel, 1994

1 .... 6.00

Scorpio Rose
Eclipse, 1983

1-2 .... 2.00

Scotland Yard
Charlton, 1955

1 .... 85.00
2-4 .... 60.00

Scout
Eclipse, 1985

1-15 .... 2.00
16 .... 4.00
17-18 .... 2.00
19 .... 4.00
20-24 .... 2.00

Scout Handbook
Eclipse, 1987

1 .... 2.00

Scout: War Shaman
Eclipse, 1988

1-16 .... 2.00

Scrap City Pack Rats
Out of the Blue, 1986

1-5 .... 2.00

Scratch
Outside, 1986

1-6 .... 2.00

Scratch
DC, 2004

1-5 .... 3.00

Scream Comics
Humor, 1944

1 .... 100.00
2 .... 55.00
3-10 .... 45.00
11-18 .... 42.00
19 .... 52.00

Screamers
Fantagraphics, 1995

1-3 .... 3.00

Screen Monsters
Zone

1 .... 3.00

Screenplay
Slave Labor, 1989

1 .... 2.00

Screwball Squirrel
Dark Horse, 1995
1-3 .... 3.00

Screw Comics
Fantagraphics, 1994
1 .... 4.00

Scribbly
DC, 1948
1 .... 900.00
2 .... 550.00
3-5 .... 430.00
6-10 .... 325.00
11-15 .... 265.00

Scrubs in Scrubland: The Reflex
Scrubland
1 .... 3.00

Scud: Tales from the Vending Machine
Fireman, 1998
1-4 .... 3.00

Scud: The Disposable Assassin
Fireman, 1994
1 .... 10.00
1/2nd-1/3rd 3.00
2-5 .... 4.00
6-20 .... 3.00

Scum of the Earth
Aircel, 1991
1-2 .... 3.00

Scythe
Caliber, 1996
1 .... 3.00

Sea Devils
DC, 1961
1 .... 500.00
2 .... 300.00
3 .... 200.00
4-5 .... 125.00
6-13 .... 75.00
14-20 .... 50.00
21-35 .... 35.00

Seadragon
Elite, 1986
1-6 .... 2.00

Seaguy
DC, 2004
1-3 .... 3.00

Sea Hound
Avon, 1945
1-2 .... 60.00

Sea Hunt
Dell, 1960
4-6 .... 30.00
7-9 .... 25.00
10-13 .... 20.00

Seals
Studio Aries, 2000
Ashcan 1 .... 1.00

Sea of Red
Image, 2005
1-12 .... 3.00
13 .... 4.00

seaQuest
Nemesis, 1994
1 .... 3.00
2-3 .... 2.00

Searchers
Caliber, 1996
1-4 .... 3.00

Searchers: Apostle of Mercy
Caliber, 1997
1 .... 3.00
2 .... 4.00

Search for Love
ACG, 1950
1 .... 90.00
2 .... 60.00

Season of the Witch
Image, 2005
0 .... 3.00
1-4 .... 4.00

Sebastian O
DC, 1993
1-3 .... 2.00

Sebastivan
Disney, 1991
1-2 .... 2.00

Second City
Harrier, 1986
1-4 .... 2.00

Second Life of Doctor Mirage
Valiant, 1993
1 .... 1.00
1/Gold 15.00
2-6 .... 1.00
7 .... 2.00
8-13 .... 1.00
14-17 .... 2.00
18 .... 4.00

Second Rate Heroes
Foundation
1-2 .... 3.00

Secret Agent
Charlton, 1966
9 .... 8.00
10 .... 6.00

Secret Agent
Gold Key, 1966
1 .... 40.00
2 .... 25.00

Mys-Tech Wars

Mysteries of Scotland Yard

Mysteries of Unexplored Worlds

Mysterious Suspense

Mystery Comics

Mystery in Space

Mystery Men Comics

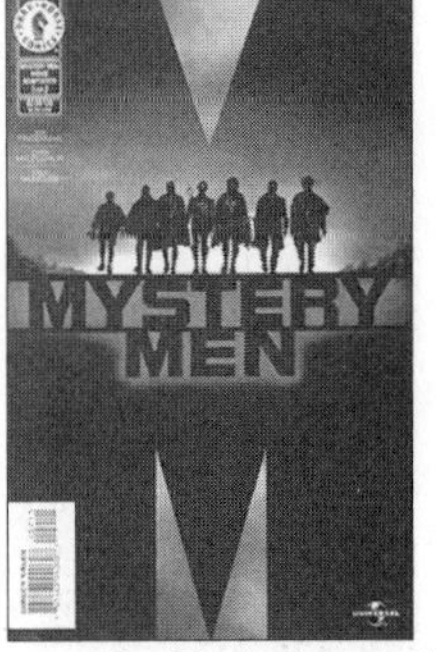

Mystery Men Movie Adaptation

Secret Agents
Personality

1-3 .... 3.00

Secret City Saga (Jack Kirby's...)
Topps, 1993

0-4 .... 3.00

Secret Defenders
Marvel, 1993

1 .... 3.00
2-11 .... 2.00
12 .... 3.00
13-24 .... 2.00
25 .... 3.00

Secret Diary of Eerie Adventures
Avon, 1953

1 .... 1,425.00

Secret Doors
Dimension

1 .... 2.00

Secret Fantasies
Bullseye

1 .... 2.00
2 .... 3.00

Secret Files
Angel, 1996

0 .... 3.00
0/Nude 4.00
1 .... 3.00

Secret Files and Origins Guide to the DC Universe 2000
DC, 2000

1 .... 7.00

Secret Files & Origins Guide to the DC Universe 2001-2002
DC, 2002

1 .... 5.00

Secret Files: Invasion Day
Angel, 1996

1-2/Nude 5.00

Secret Files President Luthor
DC, 2001

1 .... 5.00

Secret Files: The Strange Case
Angel

1 .... 3.00

Secret Hearts
DC, 1949

1 .... 375.00
2 .... 190.00
3 .... 150.00
4-5 .... 155.00
6 .... 150.00
7 .... 260.00
8-10 .... 120.00
11-20 .... 90.00
21-26 .... 78.00
27-40 .... 60.00
41-50 .... 42.00
51-60 .... 35.00
61-75 .... 30.00
76-99 .... 25.00
100 .... 30.00
101-109 .... 25.00
110 .... 30.00
111-119 .... 18.00
120 .... 25.00
121-126 .... 18.00
127 .... 25.00
128-133 .... 14.00
134 .... 25.00
135-142 .... 14.00
143-148 .... 12.00
149 .... 14.00
150-152 .... 12.00
153 .... 14.00

Secret Invasion
Marvel, 2008

1-2 .... 4.00

Secret Killers
Bronze Man, 1997

1-4 .... 3.00

Secret Love
Ajax, 1955

1 .... 50.00
2-3 .... 30.00

Secret Love
Four Star, 1957

1 .... 45.00
2-4 .... 30.00

Secret Loves
Comic Magazines, 1949

1 .... 125.00
2 .... 110.00
3 .... 75.00
4 .... 55.00
5 .... 75.00
6 .... 55.00

Secret Messages
NBM, 2001

1-5 .... 3.00

Secret Missions
St. John, 1950

1 .... 125.00

Secret Mysteries
Ribage, 1954

16 .... 145.00
17-19 .... 100.00

Secret Origins
DC, 1961

Ann 1 .... 400.00

Secret Origins
DC, 1973

1 .... 18.00
2 .... 8.00
3-4 .... 7.00
5-7 .... 6.00

Secret Origins
DC, 1986

1 .... 5.00
2-50 .... 2.00
Ann 1 .... 3.00
Ann 2-3 .... 2.00
GS 1 .... 5.00
Special 1 .... 2.00

Secret Origins of Krankin' Komix
Krankin' Komix, 1996

1 .... 1.00

Secret Origins of Super-Villains
DC, 1999

GS 1 .... 5.00

Secret Origins Replica Edition
DC, 2000

1 .... 5.00

Secret Plot
Fantagraphics, 1997

1-2 .... 3.00

Secret Romance
Charlton, 1968

1 .... 12.00
2 .... 8.00
3-10 .... 7.00
11-30 .... 5.00
31-39 .... 4.00
40-48 .... 3.00

Secret Romances
Superior, 1951

1 .... 45.00
2 .... 25.00
3-5 .... 18.00
6-20 .... 15.00
21-27 .... 12.00

Secret Six
DC, 1968

1 .... 45.00
2 .... 15.00
3-5 .... 12.00
6 .... 15.00
7 .... 20.00

Secret Six
DC, 2006

1 .... 3.00
2-30 .... 3.00

Secret Society of Super-Villains
DC, 1976

1 .... 10.00
2-8 .... 5.00
9-15 .... 3.00

Secrets of Drawing Comics (Rich Buckler's...)
Showcase, 1994

1-4 .... 3.00

Secrets of Haunted House
DC, 1975

1 .... 35.00
2-4 .... 12.00
5 .... 18.00
6-15 .... 10.00
16-20 .... 6.00
21-30 .... 3.00
31 .... 5.00
32-46 .... 3.00

Secrets of Love and Marriage
Charlton, 1956

1 .... 25.00
2 .... 15.00
3-7 .... 10.00
8 .... 20.00
9-25 .... 10.00

Secrets of Sinister House
DC, 1972

5 .... 40.00
☛Was Sinister House of Secret Love
6-9 .... 20.00
10 .... 25.00
11-15 .... 15.00
16-17 .... 12.00
18 .... 15.00

Secrets of the House of M
Marvel, 2005

1 .... 4.00

Secrets of the Legion of Super-Heroes
DC, 1981

1-3 .... 2.00

Secrets of the Valiant Universe
Valiant, 1994

1 .... 5.00
2-3 .... 3.00

Secrets of Young Brides
Charlton, 1957

5 .... 25.00
6-23 .... 20.00
24-34 .... 15.00
35-44 .... 10.00

Mystery Tales

Mystique

Mythadventures

Myth Conceptions

Mythic Heroes

Mythography

Mythos

My War With Brian

Secrets of Young Brides
Charlton, 1975

1 .... 10.00
2-9 .... 7.00

Secret Story Romances
Atlas, 1953

1 .... 100.00
2 .... 75.00
3-21 .... 60.00

Secretum Secretorum
Twilight Twins

0 .... 4.00

Secret Voice
Adhouse Books, 2005

1 .... 5.00

Secret War
Marvel, 2004

1 .... 4.00
1/2nd 5.00
1/3rd 4.00
2 .... 6.00
2/2nd 4.00
3 .... 5.00
4-5 .... 4.00

Secret Wars II
Marvel, 1985

1-4 .... 2.00
5 .... 3.00
6-9 .... 2.00

Secret Weapons
Valiant, 1993

1-11 .... 1.00
11/VVSS 30.00
12-15 .... 1.00
16-19 .... 2.00
20 .... 4.00
21 .... 5.00

Sectaurs
Marvel, 1985

1-8 .... 1.00

Section 12
Mythic

1 .... 3.00

Section Zero
Image, 2000

1-3 .... 3.00

Seduction
Eternity

1 .... 3.00

Seduction of the Innocent
Eclipse, 1985

1 .... 3.00
2-6 .... 2.00
3D 1-3D 2 .... 3.00

Seeker
Caliber, 1994

1-2 .... 3.00

Seekers into the Mystery
DC, 1996

1-15 .... 3.00

Seeker 3000
Marvel, 1998

1-4 .... 3.00

Seeker 3000 Premiere
Marvel, 1998

1 .... 2.00

Seeker: Vengeance
Sky, 1993

1-2 .... 3.00

Select Detective
D.S., 1948

1 .... 150.00
2 .... 100.00
3 .... 85.00

Self-Loathing Comics
Fantagraphics, 1996

1-2 .... 3.00

Semper Fi
Marvel, 1988

1-9 .... 1.00

Sensational Police Cases
Avon, 1954

1 .... 250.00
2-4 .... 100.00

Sensational She-Hulk
Marvel, 1989

1 .... 3.00
2-49 .... 2.00
50 .... 3.00
51-60 .... 2.00

Sensational She-Hulk in Ceremony
Marvel, 1989

1-2 .... 4.00

Sensational Spider-Man
Marvel, 1996

-1 .... 2.00
0 .... 5.00
1 .... 2.00
1/CS 4.00
2-11 .... 2.00
11/CS 7.00
12-24 .... 2.00
25-25/A 3.00
26-33 .... 2.00
Ann 1996 .... 3.00

Sensational Spider-Man
Marvel, 2006

23-34 .... 3.00
35 .... 6.00
36 .... 4.00

Sensation Comics
DC, 1942

1 ... 27,500.00
2 ... 5,200.00
3 ... 2,750.00
4 ... 1,850.00
5 ... 1,550.00
6 ... 1,400.00
7-10 ... 1,140.00
11-20 ... 1,075.00
21-30 ... 840.00
31-34 ... 610.00
35-40 ... 560.00
41-50 ... 495.00
51-60 ... 455.00
61-67 ... 395.00
68 ... 500.00
☛1st Huntress
69-70 ... 395.00
71-80 ... 380.00
81 ... 425.00
82-90 ... 385.00
91-93 ... 190.00
94 ... 350.00
95-99 ... 190.00
100-109 ... 450.00

Sensation Comics
DC, 1999

1 ... 2.00

Sensation Mystery
DC, 1952

110-116 ... 350.00

Sensei
First, 1989

1-4 ... 3.00

Sensual Phrase
Viz, 2004

1-10 ... 10.00

Sentai
Antarctic, 1994

1-7 ... 3.00

Sentinel (Harrier)
Harrier, 1986

1-4 ... 2.00

Sentinel
Marvel, 2003

1-12 ... 3.00

Sentinel
Marvel, 2003

1-5 ... 3.00

Sentinels of Justice
AC

1 ... 4.00
2 ... 6.00
3 ... 4.00

Sentinels of Justice Compact
AC

1-3 ... 4.00

Sentinels Presents... Crystal World: Prisoners of Spheris
Academy, 1996

1 ... 3.00

Sentinel Squad O*N*E
Marvel, 2006

1-5 ... 3.00

Sentry
Marvel, 2000

1 ... 15.00
1/Variant ... 20.00
1/Conv. ... 25.00
2 ... 8.00
3-4 ... 4.00
5 ... 4.00

Sentry
Marvel, 2005

1 ... 3.00
2-3 ... 3.00
4-5 ... 3.00
6-8 ... 3.00

Sentry/Fantastic Four
Marvel, 2001

1 ... 3.00

Sentry/Hulk
Marvel, 2001

1 ... 3.00

Sentry: Rough Cut
Marvel, 2006

1 ... 4.00

Sentry Special
Innovation, 1991

1 ... 3.00

Sentry/Spider-Man
Marvel, 2001

1 ... 3.00

Sentry/The Void
Marvel, 2001

1 ... 5.00

Sentry/X-Men
Marvel, 2001

1 ... 3.00

Sepulcher
Illustration, 2000

1-2 ... 3.00

Sequential
I Don't Get It, 1999

1-3 ... 3.00

Nadesico

Naive Inter-Dimensional Commando Koalas

Names of Magic

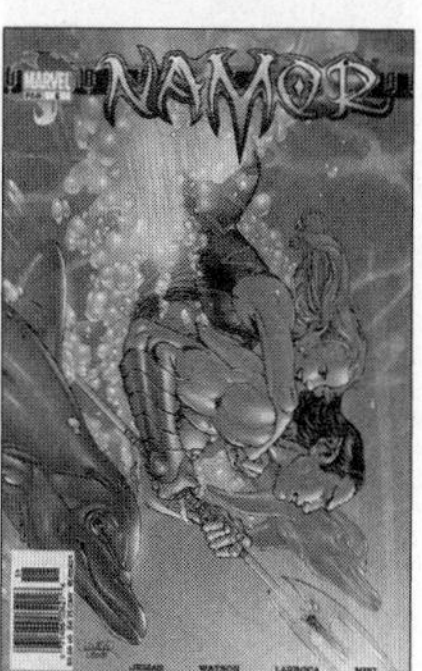

Namor

Nanosoup

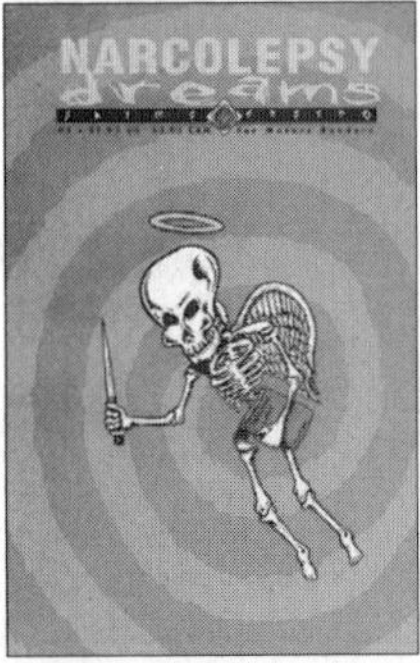

Narcolepsy Dreams

Nascar Adventures

Nash

Seraphim
Innovation, 1990

1-3 ....3.00

Serenity
Dark Horse, 2005

1/Cassaday-1/Jones 12.00
2/Bradstreet-2/DHP 7.00
3/Middleton-3/Yu 5.00

Serenity: Better Days
Dark Horse, 2008

1-2 ....3.00

Sergeant Barney Barker
Atlas, 1956

1 ....105.00
2-3 ....85.00

7 Days to Fame
-Ism, 2005

1 ....4.00

Sgt. Bilko
DC, 1957

1 ....350.00
2 ....150.00
3-5 ....100.00
6-13 ....75.00
14-18 ....60.00

Sgt. Bilko's Pvt. Doberman
DC, 1958

1 ....150.00
2 ....110.00
3 ....90.00
4-5 ....70.00
6-11 ....50.00

Sgt. Frog
Tokyopop, 2004

1-10 ....10.00

Sgt. Fury
Marvel, 1963

1 ....1,500.00
2 ....400.00
3-5 ....225.00
6-10 ....150.00
11-12 ....100.00
13 ....500.00
☛Cap. America app.
13/2nd 2.00
14-15 ....80.00
16-19 ....75.00
20-23 ....50.00
24 ....30.00
25-27 ....50.00
28-31 ....40.00
32-38 ....25.00
39-40 ....20.00
41-63 ....15.00
64-99 ....12.00
100 ....25.00
101 ....12.00
102 ....10.00
103-110 ....8.00
111-121 ....6.00
122-131 ....5.00
132-133 ....4.00
133/30¢ 20.00
134 ....4.00
134/30¢ 20.00
135-140 ....4.00
141-142/35¢ 15.00
143-151 ....4.00
152-167 ....3.00
Ann 1 ....125.00
Ann 2 ....55.00
Ann 3 ....30.00
Ann 4 ....22.00
Ann 5 ....10.00
Ann 6-7 ....9.00

Sgt. Fury: Peacemaker
Marvel, 2006

1-6 ....4.00

Sgt. Preston of the Yukon
Dell, 1952

5 ....45.00
6-12 ....40.00
13 ....50.00
14-17 ....40.00
18 ....45.00
19-29 ....30.00

Sgt. Rock
DC, 1977

302 ....25.00
☛Was Our Army at War
303-307 ....15.00
308-312 ....10.00
313-320 ....8.00
321-329 ....6.00
329/Whitman 15.00
330 ....6.00
331-341 ....5.00
342-350 ....4.00
351-390 ....3.00
391-422 ....2.00
Ann 1-2 ....4.00
Ann 3-4 ....3.00

Sgt. Rock
DC, 1991

14-22 ....2.00
Special 1-Special 2 ....3.00

Sgt. Rock: Between Hell and a Hard Place
DC, 2003

1 ....25.00

Sgt. Rock Special
DC, 1988

1-13 ....3.00

Sgt. Rock's Prize Battle Tales Replica Edition
DC, 2000

1 ....6.00

Sgt. Rock: The Prophecy
DC, 2006
1-6 .... 3.00

Sergio Aragonès Destroys DC
DC, 1996
1 .... 4.00

Sergio Aragonès Massacres Marvel
Marvel, 1996
1 .... 4.00

Sergio Aragonès Stomps Star Wars
Dark Horse, 2000
1 .... 3.00

Serial Repercussions
Chalk Outlines Studios, 1999
1-3 .... 3.00

Serina
Antarctic, 1996
1-3 .... 3.00

Serius Bounty Hunter
Blackthorne, 1987
1-3 .... 2.00

Serpentina
Lightning, 1998
1/A-1/B 3.00

Serpentyne
Nightwynd, 1992
1-3 .... 3.00

Serra Angel on the World of Magic: The Gathering
Acclaim, 1996
1 .... 6.00

Seth Throb Underground Artist
Slave Labor, 1994
1-7 .... 3.00

Settei
Antarctic, 1993
1-2 .... 8.00

Settei Super Special Featuring: Project A-Ko
Antarctic, 1994
1 .... 3.00

Seven Block
Marvel, 1990
1 .... 5.00

Seven Guys of Justice
False Idol, 2000
1-10 .... 2.00

777: Wrath/Faust Fearbook
Rebel
1 .... 14.00

Seven Miles a Second
DC, 1996
1 .... 8.00

Seven Seas Comics
Universal Phoenix, 1946
1 .... 575.00
2 .... 490.00
3-6 .... 450.00

Seven Soldiers
DC, 2005
0 .... 5.00
0/Faces 3.00
1 .... 4.00

Seven Soldiers: Frankenstein
DC, 2006
1-4 .... 3.00

Seven Soldiers: Guardian
DC, 2005
1-4 .... 3.00

Seven Soldiers: Klarion the Witch Boy
DC, 2005
1 .... 4.00
2-4 .... 3.00

Seven Soldiers: Mister Miracle
DC, 2005
1-4 .... 3.00

Seven Soldiers: Shining Knight
DC, 2005
1-4 .... 3.00

Seven Soldiers: The Bulleteer
DC, 2006
1-4 .... 3.00

Seven Soldiers: Zatanna
DC, 2005
1-4 .... 3.00

7th Millennium
Allied
1-4 .... 3.00

Seventh Shrine
Image, 2005
1 .... 6.00

7th System
Sirius, 1998
1-6 .... 3.00

77 Sunset Strip
Dell, 1962
1 .... 150.00

77 Sunset Strip
Gold Key, 1962
1-2 .... 100.00

Nathaniel Dusk

Nathan Never

National Comics

Nation of Snitches

Nature of the Beast

Nautilus

Navy Combat

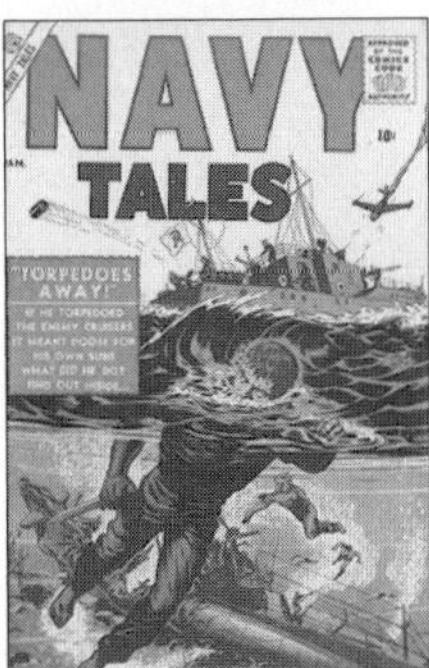
Navy Tales

Sewage Dragoon
Parody
1-1/2nd 3.00

Sex & Death
Acid Rain, 1995
1 ....4.00

Sex and Death
Acid Rain
1 ....3.00

Sexcapades
Fantagraphics, 1996
1-3 ....3.00

Sex Drive
M.A.I.N.
1 ....3.00

Sexecutioner
Fantagraphics, 1991
1-3 ....3.00

Sexhibition
Fantagraphics, 1996
1-4 ....3.00

Sex in the Sinema
Comic Zone, 1991
1-4 ....3.00

Sex, Lies and Mutual Funds of the Yuppies From Hell
Marvel
1 ....3.00

Sex Machine
Fantagraphics, 1997
1-3 ....3.00

Sexploitation Cinema: A Cartoon History
Revisionary, 1998
1 ....4.00

Sex Trek: The Next Infiltration
Friendly
1 ....3.00

Sex Wad
Fantagraphics
1-2 ....3.00

Sex Warrior
Dark Horse
1-2 ....3.00

Sex Warrior Isane XXX
Fantagraphics, 2004
1-8 ....4.00

Sexx Wars
Immortal
1 ....3.00

Sexy Stories from the World Religions
Last Gasp, 1990
1 ....3.00

Sexy Superspy
Forbidden Fruit, 1991
1-7 ....3.00

Sexy Women
Celebrity
1-2 ....3.00

Seymour
Teddy Bear Press, 1994
1 ....2.00

SFA Spotlight
Shanda Fantasy Arts, 1999
1-4 ....3.00
5 ....5.00

Shade
DC, 1997
1-4 ....3.00

Shade Changing Man
DC, 1977
1 ....10.00
2-8 ....4.00

Shade Changing Man
DC, 1990
1 ....3.00
2-49 ....2.00
50 ....3.00
51-70 ....2.00

Shades and Angels
Candle Light
1 ....3.00

Shades of Blue
AMP, 1999
1-2 ....3.00

Shades of Gray
Lady Luck, 1994
1-11 ....3.00

Shades of Gray Comics and Stories
Tapestry, 1996
1-4 ....3.00

Shade Special
AC, 1984
1 ....2.00

Shado: Song of the Dragon
DC, 1992
1-4 ....5.00

Shadow
Archie, 1964
1 ....30.00
2-8 ....18.00

Shadow
DC, 1973

1 .... 12.00
2-3 .... 8.00
4 .... 6.00
5 .... 4.00
6 .... 5.00
7-12 .... 4.00

Shadow
DC, 1986

1 .... 3.00
2-4 .... 2.00

Shadow
DC, 1987

1 .... 3.00
2-19 .... 2.00
Ann 1- 2 .... 3.00

Shadow (Movie Adaptation)
Dark Horse, 1994

1-2 .... 3.00

Shadow Agents
Armageddon, 1991

1 .... 3.00

Shadowalker
Aircel

1 .... 2.00

Shadowalker Chronicles
Ground Zero

1-2 .... 2.00

Shadow and Doc Savage
Dark Horse, 1995

1-2 .... 3.00

Shadow and the Mysterious 3
Dark Horse, 1994

1 .... 3.00

Shadowblade
Hot

1 .... 2.00

Shadow: Blood and Judgment
DC

1 .... 13.00

Shadow Cabinet
DC, 1994

0 .... 3.00
1-12 .... 2.00
13-17 .... 3.00

Shadow Comics (Vol. 1)
Street & Smith, 1940

1 .... 2,800.00
2 .... 1,200.00
3 .... 800.00
4 .... 675.00
5-6 .... 625.00
7 .... 525.00
8-11 .... 400.00
12 .... 325.00

Shadow Comics (Vol. 2)
Street & Smith, 1941

1-2 .... 325.00
3 .... 550.00
4-5 .... 425.00
6-10 .... 375.00
11-12 .... 350.00

Shadow Comics (Vol. 3)
Street & Smith, 1943

1-10 .... 325.00
11-12 .... 300.00

Shadow Comics (Vol. 4)
Street & Smith, 1944

1-12 .... 300.00

Shadow Comics (Vol. 5)
Street & Smith, 1945

1 .... 275.00
2 .... 325.00
3-7 .... 300.00
8-12 .... 275.00

Shadow Comics (Vol. 6)
Street & Smith, 1946

1-12 .... 250.00

Shadow Comics (Vol. 7)
Street & Smith, 1947

1-12 .... 250.00

Shadow Comics (Vol. 8)
Street & Smith, 1948

1 .... 250.00
2-12 .... 225.00

Shadow Comics (Vol. 9)
Street & Smith, 1949

1-5 .... 200.00

Shadow Comix Showcase
Shadow Comix, 1996

1 .... 3.00

Shadow Cross
Darkside, 1995

1 .... 3.00

Shadowdragon
DC, 1995

Ann 1 .... 4.00

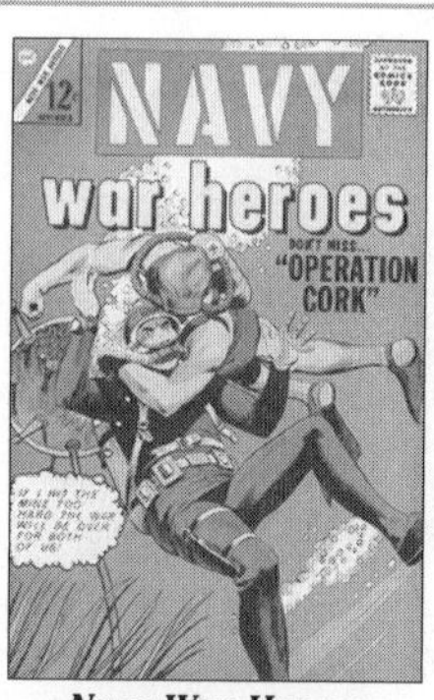

Navy War Heroes

Nazrat

NBC Saturday Morning Comics

Near Myths

Neat Stuff

Necromancer

Necropolis

Nefarismo

Shadow Empires: Faith Conquers
Dark Horse, 1994
1-4 .... 3.00

ShadowGear
Antarctic, 1999
1-3 .... 3.00

ShadowHawk (Vol. 1)
Image, 1992
1 .... 3.00
1/A 2.00
2-3 .... 3.00
4 .... 2.00

ShadowHawk (Vol. 2)
Image, 1993
1 .... 4.00
1/Gold 3.00
2 .... 2.00
2/Gold-3 .... 3.00

ShadowHawk (Vol. 3)
Image, 1993
0-1 .... 3.00
2 .... 2.00
3-4 .... 3.00
12-13 .... 2.00
14-18 .... 3.00
Special 1 .... 4.00

Shadowhawk (Vol. 4)
Image, 2005
1-7 .... 3.00
8-15 .... 4.00

Shadowhawk Gallery
Image, 1994
1 .... 2.00

Shadowhawk One-Shot
Image, 2006
1 .... 2.00

Shadowhawk Saga
Image
1 .... 1.00

Shadowhawks of Legend
Image, 1995
1 .... 5.00

Shadowhawk-Vampirella
Image, 1995
2 .... 5.00

Shadow: Hell's Heat Wave
Dark Horse, 1995
1-3 .... 3.00

Shadow House
Shadow House, 1997
1-5 .... 3.00

Shadowhunt Special
Image, 1996
1/A-1/B 3.00

Shadow: In the Coils of Leviathan
Dark Horse, 1993
1-4 .... 3.00

Shadow Lady (Masakazu Katsura's...)
Dark Horse, 1998
1-24 .... 3.00
Special 1 .... 4.00

Shadowland
Fantagraphics, 1989
1-2 .... 2.00

Shadowline Special
Image
1 .... 1.00

Shadowlord/Triune
Jet City, 1986
1 .... 2.00

Shadowman
Valiant, 1992
0/Non-chromium 5.00
0/VVSS 45.00
0 .... 3.00
0/Gold 20.00
1 .... 8.00
2-3 .... 5.00
4-6 .... 3.00
7 .... 2.00
8 .... 4.00
9 .... 2.00
10-15 .... 1.00
16 .... 2.00
17-18 .... 1.00
19 .... 5.00
20-24 .... 1.00
25 .... 2.00
26-31 .... 1.00
32-39 .... 2.00
40-41 .... 3.00
42 .... 4.00
43 .... 7.00
YB 1 .... 4.00

Shadowman
Acclaim, 1996
1 .... 3.00
1/Variant-5 .... 3.00
5/Ashcan 1.00
6-20 .... 3.00
Ashcan 1 .... 1.00

Shadowman
Acclaim, 1999
1-3 .... 4.00
4-6 .... 3.00

Shadow Master
Psygnosis
0 .... 1.00

Shadowmasters
Marvel, 1989
1-4 .... 4.00

Shadowmen
Trident
1-2 .... 2.00

Shadow of the Batman
DC, 1985
1 .... 3.00
2-5 .... 2.00

Shadow of the Torturer (Gene Wolfe's...)
Innovation, 1991
1-6 .... 3.00

Shadowpact
DC, 2006
1-8 .... 3.00

Shadowplay
Idea & Design Works, 2005
1-4 .... 4.00

Shadow Play
Whitman, 1982
1 .... 3.00

Shadow Raven
Poc-It, 1995
1 .... 3.00

Shadow Reavers
Black Bull, 2001
1-2 .... 3.00

Shadow Reigns
Aix C.C., 1997
0 .... 3.00

Shadow Riders
Marvel, 1992
1 .... 3.00
2-4 .... 2.00

Shadows
Image, 2003
1-4 .... 3.00

Shadows & Light
Marvel, 1998
1-3 .... 3.00

Shadows and Light
NBM
1-4 .... 11.00

Shadow's Edge
Lion
1 .... 4.00

Shadows Fall
DC, 1994
1-6 .... 3.00

Shadows from Beyond
Charlton, 1966
50 .... 20.00

Shadows from the Grave
Renegade, 1988
1-2 .... 2.00

Shadow Slasher
Pocket Change, 1994
0-7 .... 3.00

Shadow Slayer
Eternity
0 .... 2.00

Shadowstar
Shadowstar, 1985
1-3 .... 2.00

Shadow State
Broadway, 1995
1-7 .... 3.00
Ashcan 1 .... 1.00

Shadow Strikes!
DC, 1989
1 .... 3.00
2-31 .... 2.00
Ann 1 .... 4.00

Shadowtown
Iconografix
1 .... 3.00

Shadowtown: Black Fist Rising
Madheart
1 .... 3.00

Shadow War of Hawkman
DC, 1985
1 .... 2.00
2-4 .... 1.00

Shadow Warrior
Gateway
1 .... 2.00

Shaiana
Express, 1995
1 .... 3.00
1/Chromium 10.00
1/Holochrome 15.00
2-3 .... 3.00

Shaloman
Mark 1
1-9 .... 2.00

Shaman
Continuity, 1994
0 .... 2.00

Shaman's Tears
Image, 1993
0-1 .... 3.00
1/Platinum 4.00
2 .... 3.00
3 .... 2.00

Negation

Negation Prequel

Negative Burn

Negative One

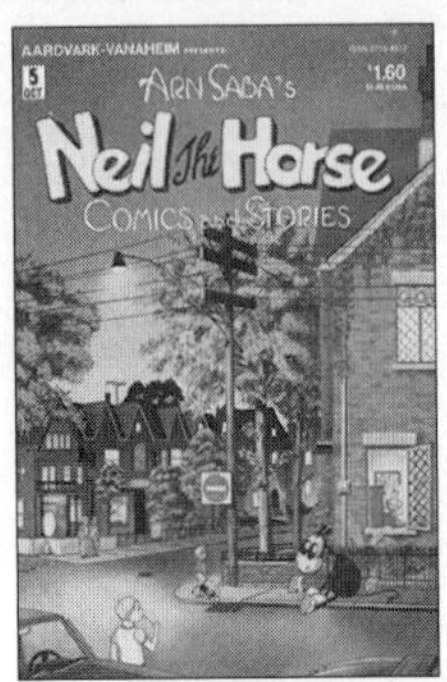

Neil the Horse Comics and Stories

Nemesister

Neo

Neomen

3/Ashcan 3.00
4-12 .... 2.00

Shanda the Panda
Mu, 1992

1 .... 3.00

Shanda the Panda
Antarctic, 1993

1-15 .... 3.00
16-20 .... 2.00
21-24 .... 3.00
25 .... 5.00
26-33 .... 3.00
34-43 .... 5.00
Ann 1-2 .... 4.00
Ann 3-4 .... 5.00

Shang Chi: Master of Kung Fu
Marvel, 2002

1-6 .... 3.00

Shanghai: Big Machine
Brick House Digital, 2000

1 .... 3.00

Shanghaied: The Saga of the Black Kite
Eternity, 1987

1-3 .... 2.00

Shangri La
Image, 2004

1 .... 8.00

Shanna the She-Devil
Marvel, 1972

1 .... 27.00
2 .... 6.00
3-5 .... 4.00

Shanna the She-Devil
Marvel, 2005

1 .... 6.00
2-7 .... 4.00

Shaolin
Black Tiger

1-5 .... 3.00

Shaolin Cowboy
Burlyman, 2004

1 .... 4.00
1/Variant 5.00
2 .... 4.00
2/Mignola 8.00
3 .... 4.00

Shaolin Sisters
Tokyopop, 2003

1-2 .... 10.00

Shaolin Sisters: Reborn
Tokyopop, 2005

1-3 .... 10.00

Shaquille O'Neal vs. Michael Jordan
Personality

1-2 .... 3.00

Shards
Ascension, 1994

1 .... 3.00

Sharky
Image, 1998

1/A-4/A 3.00

Sharp Comics
Blackerby, 1945

1 .... 235.00
2 .... 210.00

Shatter
First, 1985

1 .... 3.00
1/2nd 2.00

Shatter
First, 1985

1 .... 3.00
2-14 .... 2.00

Shattered Earth
Eternity, 1988

1-9 .... 2.00

Shattered Image
Image, 1996

1-4 .... 3.00

Shatterpoint
Eternity, 1990

1-4 .... 2.00

Shaun of the Dead
Idea & Design Works, 2005

1 .... 4.00
2-4 .... 4.00

Shazam!
DC, 1973

1 .... 20.00
2-7 .... 10.00
8 .... 20.00
☛100-page issue
9-17 .... 10.00
18-35 .... 7.00

Shazam! and the Shazam Family
DC, 2002

Ann 1 .... 6.00

Shazam! Power of Hope
DC, 2000

1-1/2nd 10.00

Shazam: The New Beginning
DC, 1987

1-4 .... 2.00

Sheba
Sick Mind, 1996

1-4 .... 3.00

Sheba
Sirius, 1997

1-8 .... 3.00

Sheba Pantheon
Sirius, 1998

1 .... 3.00

She Buccaneer
Monster, 1992

1-2 .... 2.00

She-Cat
AC, 1989

1-4 .... 3.00

Sheedeva
Fantagraphics, 1994

1-2 .... 3.00

Sheena
Marvel, 1984

1-2 .... 2.00

Sheena 3-D Special
Blackthorne, 1985

1 .... 2.00

Sheena, Queen of the Jungle (Fiction House)
Fiction House, 1942

1 .... 1,600.00
2 .... 850.00
3 .... 575.00
4-5 .... 465.00
6 .... 415.00
7-10 .... 365.00
11-14 .... 315.00
15-18 .... 210.00

Sheena-Queen of the Jungle
London Night, 1998

1/A-1/C 5.00
1/D 3.00
1/Ltd. 15.00

Sheena, Queen of the Jungle 3-D
Blackthorne, 1985

1 .... 3.00

She-Hulk
Marvel, 2004

1 .... 12.00
2 .... 7.00
3 .... 4.00
4-12 .... 3.00

She-Hulk
Marvel, 2005

1-2 .... 3.00
3 .... 4.00
4-7 .... 3.00
8 .... 22.00
9-28 .... 3.00

She Hulk 2
Marvel, 2005

1-2 .... 3.00
3 .... 4.00
4-14 .... 3.00

Sheila Trent: Vampire Hunter
Draculina

1-2 .... 3.00

Shell Shock
Mirage, 1989

1 .... 13.00

Sheriff of Tombstone
Charlton, 1958

1 .... 50.00
2 .... 30.00
3-10 .... 20.00
11-17 .... 18.00

Sherlock Holmes
DC, 1975

1 .... 8.00

Sherlock Holmes
Eternity, 1988

1-20 .... 2.00
21-23 .... 3.00

Sherlock Holmes
Avalon, 1997

1 .... 3.00

Sherlock Holmes: Adventures of the Opera Ghost
Caliber

1-2 .... 3.00

Sherlock Holmes Casebook
Eternity

1-2 .... 2.00

Sherlock Holmes: Dr. Jekyll & Mr. Holmes
Caliber, 1998

1 .... 3.00

Sherlock Holmes in the Case of the Missing Martian
Eternity, 1990

1-4 .... 2.00

Sherlock Holmes in the Curious Case of the Vanishing Villain
Atomeka

1 .... 5.00

Sherlock Holmes Mysteries
Moonstone

1 .... 3.00

Neon Cyber

Nervous Rex

Netherworlds

Netman

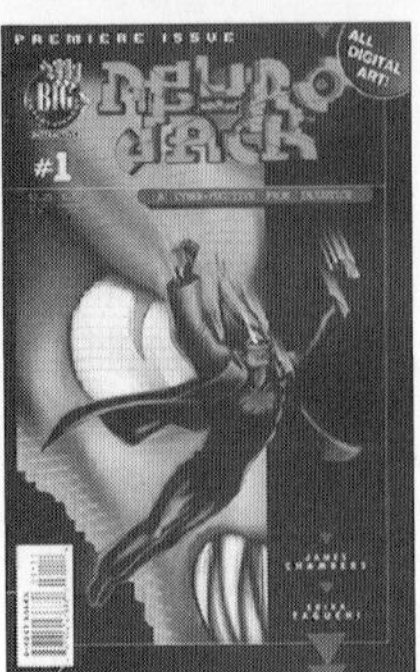
Neuro Jack

Nevada

New Adventure Comics

New Adventures of Charlie Chan

Sherlock Holmes of the '30s
Eternity

1-7 .... 3.00

Sherlock Holmes Reader
Tome, 1998

1-4 .... 4.00

Sherlock Holmes: Return of the Devil
Adventure, 1992

1-2 .... 3.00

Sherlock Jr.
Eternity, 1990

1-3 .... 3.00

Sherman's Room
-Ism, 2005

1 .... 3.00

Sherman's March Through Atlanta to the Sea
Heritage Collection

1 .... 4.00

Sherlock Holmes
Charlton, 1955

1 .... 225.00
2 .... 175.00

Sherry the Showgirl
Atlas, 1956

1 .... 100.00
2 .... 70.00
3-7 .... 55.00

She's Josie
Archie, 1963

1 .... 85.00
2 .... 55.00
3 .... 30.00
4-5 .... 25.00
6-10 .... 20.00
11-16 .... 16.00

Sheva's War
DC, 1998

1-5 .... 3.00

Shi
Crusade, 1996

0-½ 3.00

Shi: Art of War Tour Book
Crusade, 1998

1 .... 5.00

Shi: Black, White, and Red
Crusade, 1998

1-2 .... 3.00

Shi/Cyblade: The Battle for Independents
Crusade, 1995

1 .... 4.00
1/Variant 5.00

Shi/Daredevil: Honor Thy Mother
Crusade, 1997

1 .... 3.00
1/Ltd 6.00

Shidima
Image, 2001

0/A-4 .... 3.00

Shi: East Wind Rain
Crusade, 1997

1-2 .... 4.00
Ashcan 1 .... 1.00

SHIELD
Marvel, 1973

1 .... 15.00
2-5 .... 5.00

Shield
Archie, 1983

2 .... 1.00

Shield: Spotlight
Idea & Design Works, 2004

1-5 .... 4.00

Shield – Steel Sterling
Archie, 1983

3 .... 1.00

Shield Wizard Comics
M.L.J., 1940

1 .... 2,900.00
2 .... 1,350.00
3-4 .... 850.00
5 .... 740.00
6-8 .... 700.00
9-13 .... 525.00

Shi: Heaven & Earth
Crusade, 1997

1-Ashcan 1 .... 3.00

Shi: Ju Nen
Dark Horse, 2004

1-3 .... 3.00

Shi: Kaidan
Crusade, 1996

1-1/A 3.00

Shiloh: The Devil's Own Day
Heritage Collection

1 .... 4.00

Shi: Masquerade
Crusade, 1998

1 .... 4.00

Shimmer
Avatar, 1998

1 .... 4.00

Shi: Nightstalkers
Crusade, 1997

1 .... 4.00

Shion: Blade of the Minstrel
Viz, 1990

1 .... 10.00

Ship Ahoy
Spotlight, 1944

1 .... 135.00

Shi: Pandora's Box
Avatar, 2003

1 .... 4.00

Ship of Fools
Image, 1997

0-3 .... 3.00

Ship of Fools
Caliber

1-6 .... 3.00

Ship of Fools
NBM, 1999

1 .... 11.00

Shipwrecked!
Disney

1 .... 6.00

Shi: Rekishi
Crusade, 1997

1-2 .... 3.00

Shi: Sempo
Avatar, 2003

1-2 .... 4.00

Shi: Senryaku
Crusade, 1995

1 .... 3.00
1/Variant 4.00
2-3 .... 3.00

Shi: The Blood of Saints
Crusade, 1996

1 .... 3.00
Fan ed. 1/A 2.00

Shi: The Series
Crusade, 1997

1-1/A 4.00
2-16 .... 3.00

Shi: The Way of the Warrior
Crusade, 1994

½ 3.00
½/Platinum 4.00
1 .... 6.00
1/A 5.00
1/B-1/C 8.00
2 .... 5.00
2/A 3.00
2/B 6.00
2/Ashcan 5.00
3-4 .... 4.00
4/2nd-5 .... 3.00
5/Variant 5.00
6-6/A 3.00
6/Ashcan 4.00
7 .... 3.00
7/Variant 4.00
8 .... 3.00
8/A 5.00
9-12 .... 3.00
Fan ed. 1/A-Fan ed. 3/A 1.00

Shi/Vampirella
Crusade, 1997

1 .... 3.00

Shi vs. Tomoe
Crusade, 1996

1 .... 4.00
1/Ltd. 5.00

Shi: Year of the Dragon
Crusade, 2000

1 .... 3.00

Shmoo Comics (Al Capp's...)
Toby, 1949

1 .... 250.00
2-5 .... 175.00

Shock & Spank the Monkeyboys Special
Arrow

1 .... 3.00

Shock Detective Cases
Star, 1952

20-21 .... 150.00

Shock Illustrated
E.C., 1955

1-2 .... 200.00
3 .... 800.00

Shocking Mystery Cases
Star, 1952

50 .... 325.00
51 .... 150.00
52-60 .... 135.00

Shockrockets
Image, 2000

1-6 .... 3.00

Shock SuspenStories
E.C., 1952

1 .... 850.00
2 .... 500.00
3 .... 350.00
4 .... 325.00
5 .... 290.00
6-7 .... 350.00
8 .... 260.00
9-11 .... 210.00
12 .... 225.00
13 .... 350.00
☛Frazetta art
14-15 .... 200.00
16-18 .... 170.00

New Age Comics

New America

Newcomers Illustrated

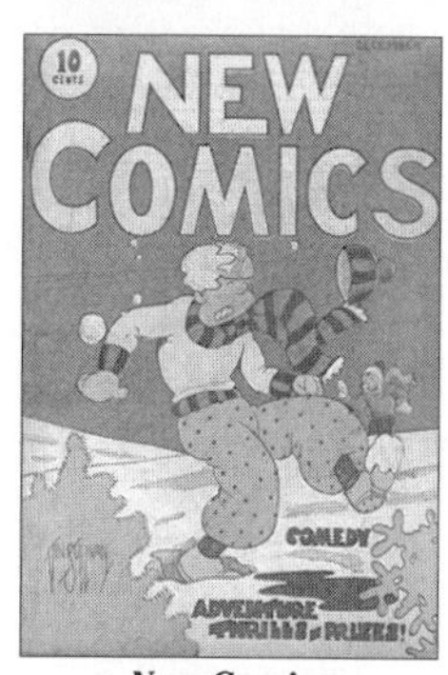

New Comics

New England Gothic

Newforce

New Frontiers

New Gods Secret Files

Shock SuspenStories (RCP)

Gemstone, 1992

1-16 .... 2.00
17-18 .... 3.00
Ann 1 .... 9.00
Ann 2 .... 10.00
Ann 3 .... 9.00
Ann 4 .... 10.00

Shock the Monkey

Millennium

1 .... 3.00
2 .... 4.00

Shock Therapy

Harrier, 1986

1-5 .... 2.00

Shogun Warriors

Marvel, 1979

1-1/Whitman 5.00
2-20 .... 2.00

Shojo Zen

Zen, 1997

1 .... 3.00

Shonen Jump

Viz, 2002

0-36 .... 5.00

Shoney Bear and His Friends

Golden Press, 1986

1 .... 2.00

Shoney's Fun and Adventure Magazine

Paragon, 1983

1-8 .... 1.00

Shooty Beagle

Fantagraphics, 1991

1-3 .... 2.00

Short on Plot!

Mu

1 .... 3.00

Short Order

Head, 1974

1 .... 20.00
2 .... 15.00

Shorts (Pat Kelley's...)

Antarctic, 1997

1-2 .... 3.00

Shortstop Squad

Ultimate Sports Force, 1999

1 .... 4.00

Shotgun Mary

Antarctic, 1995

1 .... 4.00
1/CS 10.00
1/Variant-Ashcan 1 .... 3.00

Shotgun Mary

Antarctic, 1998

1 .... 3.00
1/Variant 4.00
2-3 .... 3.00

Shotgun Mary: Blood Lore

Antarctic, 1997

1-4 .... 3.00

Shotgun Mary: Deviltown

Antarctic, 1996

1 .... 3.00
1/Ltd. 5.00

Shotgun Mary Shooting Gallery

Antarctic, 1996

1 .... 3.00

Shotgun Mary: Son of the Beast

Antarctic, 1997

1 .... 3.00

Shottloose

Absolute

1-2 .... 1.00

Shoujo

Antarctic, 2003

1-3 .... 6.00

Showcase

DC, 1956

1 .... 3,500.00
2-3 .... 1,000.00
4 .... 27,500.00
☛1st Silver Age Flash
5 .... 1,000.00
6 .... 4,000.00
7 .... 2,000.00
8 .... 11,500.00
☛2nd Silver Age Flash
9 .... 7,500.00
10 .... 3,000.00
11-12 .... 1,750.00
13-14 .... 4,500.00
15 .... 2,000.00
16 .... 1,000.00
17 .... 2,750.00
☛1st Adam Strange
18 .... 1,200.00
19 .... 1,500.00
20 .... 1,000.00
21 .... 500.00
22 .... 5,600.00
☛1st Silver Age Green Lantern
23-24 .... 1,750.00
25-26 .... 350.00
27 .... 900.00
28-29 .... 400.00
30 .... 800.00
31-32 .... 400.00
33 .... 375.00

34 .... 1,250.00
35 .... 700.00
36 .... 525.00
37 .... 700.00
38 .... 400.00
39 .... 350.00
40 .... 300.00
41-42 .... 150.00
43 .... 450.00
44 .... 100.00
45 .... 325.00
46-47 .... 100.00
48-52 .... 80.00
53-54 .... 100.00
55 .... 275.00
☛Dr. Fate origin
56 .... 125.00
57 .... 225.00
58 .... 150.00
59 .... 125.00
60 .... 225.00
☛Spectre origin
61 .... 100.00
62 .... 80.00
63 .... 50.00
64 .... 100.00
☛Spectre appearance
65 .... 50.00
66-72 .... 30.00
73 .... 85.00
☛1st Creeper
74 .... 45.00
☛1st Anthro
75 .... 75.00
☛1st Hawk & Dove
76-77 .... 50.00
78 .... 35.00
79-81 .... 45.00
82-84 .... 40.00
85-87 .... 20.00
88-93 .... 15.00
94 .... 20.00
☛New Doom Patrol
95-96 .... 8.00
97-103 .... 6.00
104 .... 5.00
Book 1 .... 20.00

Showcase '93

DC, 1993

1-6 .... 2.00
7-8 .... 3.00
9-12 .... 2.00

Showcase '94

DC, 1994

1-12 .... 2.00

Showcase '95

DC, 1995

1-12 .... 3.00

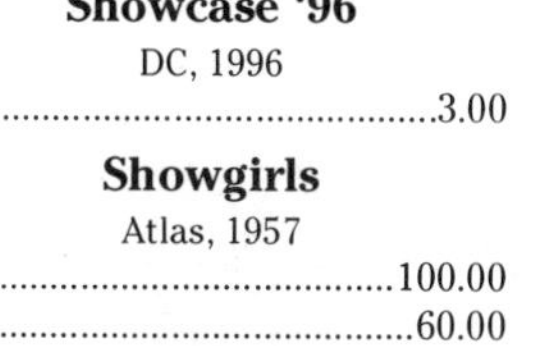

Showcase '96

DC, 1996

1-12 .... 3.00

Showgirls

Atlas, 1957

1 .... 100.00
2 .... 60.00

Shred

CFW, 1989

1-8 .... 2.00

Shrek

Dark Horse, 2003

1-3 .... 3.00

Shriek

Fantaco

1-2 .... 5.00
Special 1-3 .... 4.00

Shriek Show: Mark of Shadow

-Ism, 2005

1-2 .... 3.00

Shrike

Victory, 1987

1-2 .... 2.00

Shroud

Marvel, 1994

1-4 .... 2.00

Shugga

Fantagraphics

1-2 .... 3.00

Shuriken

Victory, 1985

1-8 .... 2.00

Shuriken

Eternity, 1991

1-6 .... 3.00

Shuriken

Blackthorne

1 .... 8.00

Shuriken: Cold Steel

Eternity, 1989

1-6 .... 2.00

Shuriken Team-Up

Eternity, 1989

1 .... 2.00

Shut Up and Die!

Image, 1998

1-5 .... 3.00

Sick Smiles

Aiiie!, 1994

1-8 .... 3.00

Sidekick

Image, 2006

1-4 .... 4.00

New Horizons

New Love

Newman

Newmen

New Paltz Comix

New Statesmen

Newstralia

New Talent Showcase

Sidekicks
Fanboy, 2000
1 .... 3.00

Sidekicks: The Substitute
Oni, 2002
1 .... 3.00

Side Show
Mature Magic, 1987
1 .... 2.00

Sideshow Comics
Pan Graphics
1-5 .... 2.00

Siege
Image, 1997
1-4 .... 3.00

Siegel and Shuster: Dateline 1930s
Eclipse, 1984
1-2 .... 2.00

Siege of the Alamo
Tome, 1991
1 .... 3.00

Sight Unseen
Fantagraphics, 1997
1 .... 3.00

Sigil
CrossGen, 2000
1 .... 4.00
2-42 .... 3.00

Sigma
Image, 1996
1-3 .... 3.00

Signal to Noise
Dark Horse, 1993
1-1/2nd 15.00

Silbuster
Antarctic, 1994
1-19 .... 3.00

Silencers
Caliber, 1991
1-4 .... 3.00

Silencers
Moonstone, 2003
1-2 .... 4.00

Silencers
Image, 2005
1 .... 3.00

Silent Hill: Paint It Black
Idea & Design Works, 2005
0 .... 7.00

Silent City
Kitchen Sink, 1995
1 .... 25.00

Silent Dragon
DC, 2005
1-6 .... 3.00

Silent Hill: Dead/Alive
Idea & Design Works, 2005
1-4 .... 4.00

Silent Hill: Dying Inside
Idea & Design Works, 2004
1-3 .... 4.00
4-5 .... 4.00

Silent Invasion
Renegade, 1986
1-2 .... 2.00
3-12 .... 3.00

Silent Invasion: Abductions
Caliber, 1998
1 .... 3.00

Silent Mobius Part 1
Viz, 1991
1-6 .... 5.00

Silent Mobius Part 2
Viz, 1992
1-5 .... 5.00

Silent Mobius Part 3
Viz, 1992
1-5 .... 3.00

Silent Mobius Part 4
Viz, 1992
1-5 .... 3.00

Silent Mobius Part 5: Into the Labyrinth
Viz, 1999
1-6 .... 3.00

Silent Mobius Part 6: Karma
Viz, 1999
1-7 .... 3.00

Silent Mobius Part 7: Catastrophe
Viz, 2000
1-6 .... 3.00

Silent Mobius Part 8: Love & Chaos
Viz, 2000
1-7 .... 3.00

Silent Mobius Part 9: Advent
Viz, 2001
1-6 .... 3.00

Silent Mobius Part 10: Turnabout
Viz, 2002
1-6 .... 3.00

Silent Mobius Part 11: Blood
Viz, 2002
1-5 .... 3.00

Silent Mobius Part 12: Hell
Viz, 2002
1-2 .... 3.00

Silent Rapture
Avatar, 1997
1-2 .... 3.00

Silent Screamers: Nosferatu
Image, 2000
1 .... 5.00

Silent Winter/ Pineappleman
Limelight
1 .... 3.00

Silke
Dark Horse, 2001
1-4 .... 3.00

Silken Ghost
CrossGen, 2003
1-5 .... 3.00

Silly Symphonies
Dell, 1952
1 .... 200.00
2 .... 175.00
3-4 .... 125.00
5-9 .... 110.00

Silly-Cat
Joe Chiappetta, 1997
1 .... 1.00

Silly Daddy
Joe Chiappetta, 1995
1-18 .... 3.00

Silly Tunes
Timely, 1945
1 .... 150.00
2 .... 85.00
3-7 .... 60.00

Silver
Comicolor, 1996
1 .... 2.00

Silver Age
DC, 2000
1 .... 3.00
GS 1 .... 6.00

Silver Age: Challengers of the Unknown
DC, 2000
1 .... 3.00

Silver Age: Dial H for Hero
DC, 2000
1 .... 3.00

Silver Age: Doom Patrol
DC, 2000
1 .... 3.00

Silver Age: Flash
DC, 2000
1 .... 3.00

Silver Age: Green Lantern
DC, 2000
1 .... 3.00

Silver Age: Justice League of America
DC, 2000
1 .... 3.00

Silver Age Secret Files
DC, 2000
1 .... 5.00

Silver Age: Showcase
DC, 2000
1 .... 3.00

Silver Age: Teen Titans
DC, 2000
1 .... 3.00

Silver Age: The Brave and the Bold
DC, 2000
1 .... 3.00

Silverback
Comico, 1989
1-3 .... 3.00

Silverblade
DC, 1987
1-12 .... 1.00

Silver Cross
Antarctic, 1997
1-3 .... 3.00

Silverfawn
Caliber
1 .... 2.00

Silverhawks
Marvel, 1987
1-7 .... 1.00

Silverheels
Pacific, 1983
1-3 .... 2.00

All comics prices listed are for NEAR MINT condition.

New Triumph Featuring Northguard

New World Order

New Worlds Anthology

Next Man

Nextwave

Nexus Legends

Nexus Meets Madman

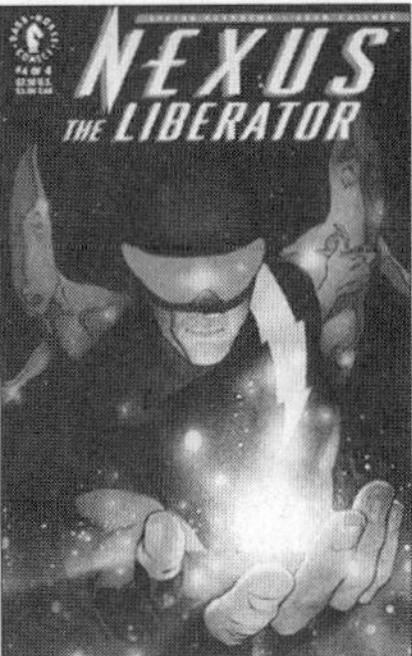

Nexus the Liberator

Silver Kid Western

Key, 1954

1 .... 60.00
2 .... 40.00
3-5 .... 30.00

Silver Sable

Marvel, 1992

1-4 .... 2.00
5-23 .... 1.00
24-35 .... 2.00

Silver Scream

Recollections, 1991

1-3 .... 2.00

Silver Star

Pacific, 1983

1-6 .... 1.00

Silver Star (Jack Kirby's...)

Topps, 1993

1 .... 3.00

Silverstorm

Aircel, 1990

1-4 .... 2.00

Silverstorm

Silverline, 1998

1-4 .... 3.00

Silver Streak Comics

Lev Gleason, 1939

1 .... 11,000.00
2 .... 4,000.00
3 .... 3,500.00
4 .... 1,750.00
5 .... 2,000.00
6 .... 13,500.00
7 .... 8,300.00
8 .... 3,200.00
9 .... 1,900.00
10 .... 1,500.00
11 .... 1,000.00
12-14 .... 850.00
15-19 .... 700.00
20-23 .... 600.00

Silver Surfer

Marvel, 1968

1 .... 400.00
2 .... 160.00
3 .... 135.00
4 .... 265.00
☛Surfer vs. Thor
5-6 .... 75.00
7 .... 90.00
8 .... 95.00
9-10 .... 60.00
11 .... 65.00
12 .... 50.00
13 .... 70.00
14 .... 125.00
☛Spider-Man app.
15-18 .... 55.00

Silver Surfer

Marvel, 1988

1-2 .... 3.00

Silver Surfer

Marvel, 1987

-1-½ 3.00
½/Platinum 6.00
1 .... 7.00
2 .... 6.00
3-10 .... 4.00
11-14 .... 3.00
15 .... 4.00
16-24 .... 3.00
25 .... 4.00
26-31 .... 3.00
32-33 .... 2.00
34 .... 5.00
35 .... 4.00
36-38 .... 3.00
39-45 .... 2.00
46-47 .... 3.00
48-49 .... 2.00
50 .... 5.00
50/2nd-74 .... 2.00
75 .... 4.00
76-85 .... 2.00
85/CS 3.00
86-90 .... 2.00
91 .... 1.00
92-99 .... 2.00
100 .... 3.00
100/Variant 4.00
101-124 .... 2.00
125 .... 3.00
126-146 .... 2.00
Ann 1 .... 4.00
Ann 2-7 .... 3.00
Ann 1997 .... 4.00
Ann 1998 .... 3.00

Silver Surfer

Marvel, 2003

1-6 .... 2.00
7-14 .... 3.00
Book 1 .... 15.00

Silver Surfer

Marvel, 1982

1 .... 12.00

Silver Surfer: Dangerous Artifacts

Marvel, 1996

1 .... 4.00

Silver Surfer: Inner Demons

Marvel, 1998

1 .... 4.00

Silver Surfer: Judgment Day

Marvel, 1988

1 .... 15.00

Silver Surfer: Loftier Than Mortals
Marvel, 1999
1-2 .... 3.00

Silver Surfer: Rebirth of Thanos
Marvel, 2006
1 .... 13.00

Silver Surfer/Superman
Marvel, 1996
1 .... 6.00

Silver Surfer: The Enslavers
Marvel, 1990
1 .... 17.00

Silver Surfer vs. Dracula
Marvel, 1994
1 .... 2.00

Silver Surfer/Warlock: Resurrection
Marvel, 1993
1-4 .... 3.00

Silver Surfer/Weapon Zero
Marvel, 1997
1 .... 3.00

Silver Sweetie
Spoof
1 .... 3.00

Silverwing Special
Now, 1987
1 .... 1.00

Silverwolf Comic Book Trivia Comic Book
Silverwolf, 1987
1-3 .... 2.00

Simon and Kirby Classics
Pure Imagination, 1986
1 .... 2.00

Simon Cat in Taxi
Slab-O-Concrete
1 .... 2.00

Simon Spector (Warren Ellis'...)
Avatar, 2005
1 .... 4.00

Simpsons Comics
Bongo, 1992
1 .... 5.00
2 .... 4.00
3-10 .... 3.00
11-31 .... 2.00
32 .... 3.00
33-39 .... 2.00
40-150 .... 3.00

Simpsons Comics and Stories
Welsh, 1993
1 .... 4.00

Simpsons Comics (Magazine)
Bongo, 1997
1 .... 4.00
2-25 .... 3.00

Simpsons Comics Presents Bart Simpson
Bongo, 2000
1-50 .... 3.00

Simpsons/Futurama Crossover Crisis Part 2
Bongo, 2005
1 .... 3.00

Simpsons Super Spectacular
Bongo, 2005
1 .... 5.00

Simulators
Neatly Chiseled Features
1 .... 3.00

Sin
Tragedy Strikes, 1992
1-3 .... 3.00

Sinbad
Adventure, 1989
1-4 .... 2.00

Sinbad Book II
Adventure, 1991
1-4 .... 3.00

Sin City
Cozmic
1 .... 2.00

Sin City: A Dame to Kill For
Dark Horse, 1993
1 .... 4.00
1/2nd-6 .... 3.00

Sin City Angels
Fantagraphics, 2004
1 .... 4.00

Sin City: Family Values
Dark Horse, 1997
1 .... 15.00
1/A 18.00
1/Ltd 75.00

Sin City: Hell and Back
Dark Horse, 1999
1-9 .... 3.00

NFL Superpro

Nick Hazard

Nicki Shadow

Nick Ryan the Skull

Nightbird

Night Brigade

Nightcat

Night City

Sin City: Just Another Saturday Night
Dark Horse, 1997

½-1 .... 3.00

Sin City: Lost, Lonely, & Lethal
Dark Horse, 1996

1 .... 3.00

Sin City: Sex & Violence
Dark Horse, 1997

1 .... 3.00

Sin City: Silent Night
Dark Horse, 1995

1 .... 3.00

Sin City: That Yellow Bastard
Dark Horse, 1996

1-5 .... 3.00
6 .... 4.00

Sin City: The Babe Wore Red and Other Stories
Dark Horse, 1994

1 .... 3.00

Sin City: The Big Fat Kill
Dark Horse, 1994

1-5 .... 3.00

Sindy
Forbidden Fruit

1-5 .... 3.00

Sinergy
Caliber, 1994

1 .... 3.00
1/Ltd. 6.00
2 .... 3.00
2/Ltd. 6.00
3 .... 3.00
3/Ltd. 6.00
4 .... 3.00
4/Ltd. 6.00
5 .... 3.00
5/Ltd. 6.00

Single Series
United Feature, 1939

1 .... 750.00
2 .... 375.00
3 .... 300.00
4 .... 600.00
5 .... 200.00
6 .... 300.00
7-11 .... 200.00
12-17 .... 190.00
18 .... 500.00
19 .... 300.00
20 .... 600.00
21 .... 265.00
22 .... 200.00
23 .... 265.00
24 .... 375.00
25 .... 300.00
26-28 .... 185.00

Singularity 7
Idea & Design Works, 2004

1-4 .... 4.00

Sinister House of Secret Love
DC, 1971

1 .... 125.00
2-4 .... 75.00

Sinister Romance
Harrier, 1988

1-4 .... 2.00

Sinja: Deadly Sins
Lightning, 1996

1 .... 3.00
1/A 6.00
1/B 10.00

Sinja: Resurrection
Lightning, 1996

1 .... 3.00

Sinnamon
Catfish, 1995

1 .... 3.00

Sinnamon
Catfish, 1996

1-4 .... 3.00
4/Variant 5.00
5 .... 3.00
5/Variant 4.00
6-8 .... 3.00

Sinner
Fantagraphics, 1987

1-5 .... 3.00

Sinners
DC

1 .... 10.00

Sinnin!
Fantagraphics, 1991

1-2 .... 2.00

Sin of the Mummy
Fantagraphics

1 .... 3.00

Sins of Youth: Aquaboy/Lagoon Man
DC, 2000

1 .... 3.00

Sins of Youth: Batboy and Robin
DC, 2000

1 .... 3.00

Sins of Youth: JLA, Jr.
DC, 2000

1 .... 3.00

Sins of Youth: Kid Flash/ Impulse

DC, 2000

1 .... 3.00

Sins of Youth Secret Files

DC, 2000

1 .... 5.00

Sins of Youth: Starwoman and the JSA (Junior Society)

DC, 2000

1 .... 3.00

Sins of Youth: Superman, Jr./Superboy, Sr.

DC, 2000

1 .... 3.00

Sins of Youth: The Secret/ Deadboy

DC, 2000

1 .... 3.00

Sins of Youth: Wonder Girls

DC, 2000

1 .... 3.00

Sinthia

Lightning, 1997

1/A-1/B 3.00
1/Platinum 4.00
2/A-2/B 3.00

Sir Charles Barkley and the Referee Murders

Hamilton, 1993

1 .... 10.00

Siren

0-Special 1 .... 2.00

Sirens

Caliber, 1994

1-2 .... 4.00

Siren: Shapes

Image, 1998

1-3 .... 3.00

Sirens of the Lost World

Comax

1 .... 3.00

Sirius Gallery

Sirius, 1997

1-3 .... 3.00

Sister Armageddon

Draculina

1-4 .... 3.00

Sisterhood of Steel

Marvel, 1984

1-8 .... 2.00

Sister Red

ComicsOne, 2004

1-2 .... 10.00

Sisters of Darkness

Illustration, 1997

1/A-3 .... 3.00

Sisters of Mercy

Maximum, 1995

1-5 .... 3.00

Sisters of Mercy

London Night, 1997

0 .... 2.00

Sisters of Mercy: When Razors Cry Crimson Tears

No Mercy, 1996

1 .... 3.00

Sister Vampire

Angel

1 .... 3.00

Six

Image, 2004

0 .... 6.00

6

Virtual, 1996

1-3 .... 3.00

6: Lethal Origins

Virtual, 1996

1 .... 4.00

Six Degrees

Heretic

1 .... 4.00
2-5 .... 3.00

Six From Sirius

Marvel, 1984

1-4 .... 2.00

Six From Sirius 2

Marvel, 1986

1-4 .... 2.00

Six-Gun Heroes

Fawcett, 1950

1 .... 325.00
2 .... 175.00
3-5 .... 120.00
6-15 .... 90.00
16-22 .... 75.00
23 .... 85.00

Six-Gun Heroes

Charlton, 1954

24 .... 125.00
25-30 .... 65.00
31-40 .... 55.00
41-50 .... 48.00
51-60 .... 32.00
61-70 .... 22.00
71-83 .... 16.00

Nightcry

Night Force

Night Glider

Nighthawk

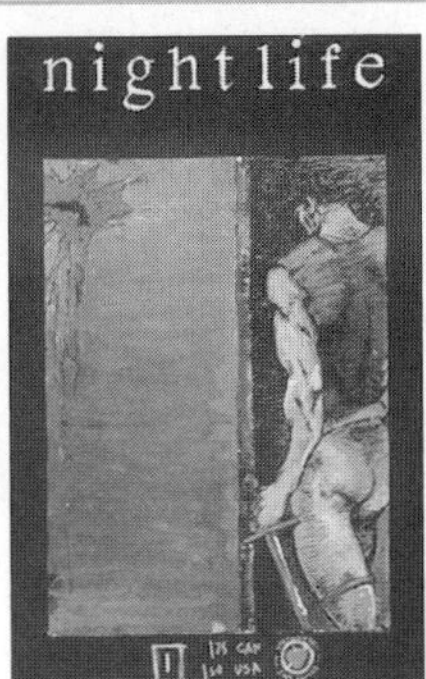

Night Life

Nightlinger

Nightmares

Nightmares on Elm Street

Six-Gun Samurai
Alias, 2005

1 .... 1.00
2 .... 3.00

Six-Gun Western
Atlas, 1957

1 .... 120.00
2-3 .... 85.00
4 .... 60.00

Six Million Dollar Man
Charlton, 1976

1 .... 12.00
2 .... 6.00
3-5 .... 5.00
6-9 .... 4.00

Six Million Dollar Man (Magazine)
Charlton, 1976

1 .... 10.00
2 .... 8.00
3-7 .... 5.00

666: The Mark of the Beast
Fleetway-Quality, 1986

1 .... 3.00
2-18 .... 2.00

Six String Samurai
Awesome, 1998

1 .... 3.00

68
Image, 2007

1 .... 4.00

Sixty Nine
Fantagraphics, 1993

1-4 .... 3.00

67 Seconds
Marvel, 1992

1 .... 16.00

Sixx
Zygotic

1-4 .... 3.00

Sizzle Theatre
Slave Labor, 1991

1 .... 3.00

Sizzlin' Sisters
Fantagraphics, 1997

1-2 .... 3.00

Skateman
Pacific, 1983

1 .... 2.00

Skeleton Girl
Slave Labor, 1995

1-3 .... 3.00

Skeleton Hand
ACG, 1952

1 .... 260.00
2 .... 175.00
3-6 .... 145.00

Skeleton Hand
Avalon

1 .... 3.00

Skeleton Key
Amaze Ink, 1995

1-30 .... 2.00

Skeleton Warriors
Marvel, 1995

1-4 .... 2.00

Sketchbook Series
Tundra

1-9 .... 4.00
10 .... 5.00

Skidmarks
Tundra

0-3 .... 3.00

Skid Roze
London Night, 1998

1 .... 3.00

Skim Lizard
Puppy Toss

1 .... 3.00

Skin
Tundra

1 .... 9.00

Skin Graft
Iconografix

1 .... 4.00

Skin Graft: The Adventures of a Tattooed Man
DC, 1993

1-4 .... 3.00

Skinheads in Love
Fantagraphics, 1992

1 .... 2.00

Skinners
Image

1/A-1/C 3.00

Skin13
Express, 1995

½/A-1/C 3.00

Skizz
Fleetway-Quality

1-3 .... 2.00

Skreemer
DC, 1989

1 .... 2.00
2-6 .... 2.00

Skrog
Comico

1 .... 2.00

Skrog (Yip, Yip, Yay) Special
Crystal
1 .... 3.00

Skrull Kill Krew
Marvel, 1995
1-5 .... 3.00

Skulker
Thorby
1 .... 3.00

Skull & Bones
DC, 1992
1-3 .... 5.00

Skull Comics
Last Gasp, 1970
1 .... 18.00
2 .... 10.00
3-6 .... 6.00

Skull the Slayer
Marvel, 1975
1 .... 12.00
2 .... 5.00
3 .... 2.00
4-5 .... 4.00
5/30¢ 20.00
6 .... 3.00
6/30¢ 20.00
7-8 .... 3.00

Skunk
Express, 1996
1-6 .... 3.00
GN 1 .... 5.00

Skunk
Mu, 1993
1 .... 3.00

Sky Ape (Les Adventures)
Slave Labor, 1997
1-3 .... 3.00
Book 1 .... 13.00

Sky Comics Presents Monthly
Sky Comics, 1992
1 .... 3.00

Skye Blue
Mu, 1992
1-3 .... 3.00

Skye Runner
DC, 2006
1-5 .... 3.00

Sky Gal
AC
1-3 .... 4.00

Skyman
Columbia, 1941
1-2 .... 800.00
3 .... 400.00

Sky Masters
Pure Imagination, 1991
1 .... 8.00

Skynn & Bones
Brainstorm
1 .... 3.00

Skynn & Bones: Deadly Angels
Brainstorm, 1996
1 .... 3.00

Sky Pilot
Ziff-Davis, 1951
10-11 .... 85.00

Skyscrapers of the Midwest
Adhouse Books, 2004
1-2 .... 5.00

Skywolf
Eclipse, 1988
1-3 .... 2.00

Slacker Comics
Slave Labor, 1994
1-18 .... 3.00

Slaine the Berserker
Fleetway-Quality, 1987
1-20 .... 2.00

Slaine the Horned God
Fleetway-Quality, 1990
1 .... 4.00
2-6 .... 3.00

Slaine the King
Fleetway-Quality, 1989
21-28 .... 2.00

Slam Bang Comics
Fawcett, 1940
1 .... 1,375.00
2 .... 575.00
3 .... 850.00
4-7 .... 450.00

Slam Dunk Kings
Personality, 1992
1-4 .... 3.00

Slapstick
Marvel, 1992
1-4 .... 1.00

Slash
Northstar, 1993
1 .... 3.00
1/Special 5.00
2-5 .... 3.00

Slash Maraud
DC, 1987
1-6 .... 2.00

Slaughterman
Comico
1-2 .... 4.00

Nightmark Mystery Special

Nightmask

Night Masters

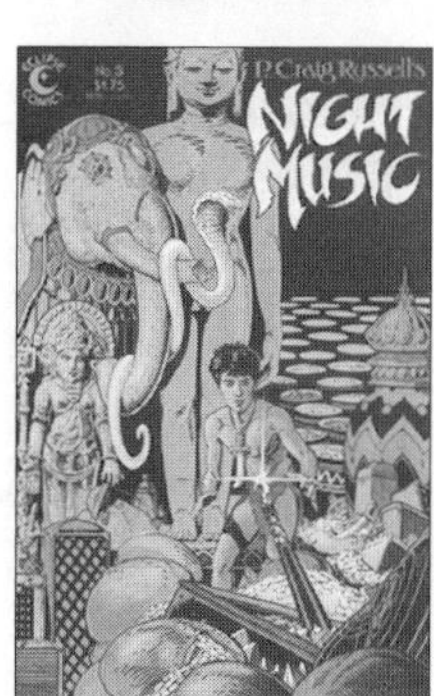

Night Music

Night Nurse

Night of the Living Dead

Night Rider

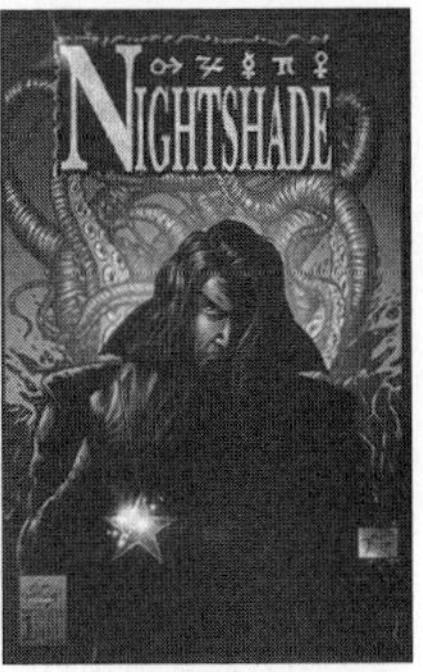

Nightshade

Slave Girl
Eternity, 1989

1 ....2.00

Slave Girl Comics
Avon, 1949

1 ....750.00
2 ....600.00

Slave Labor Stories
Slave Labor, 1992

1-4 ....3.00

Slave Pit Funnies
Slave Pit, 1995

1 ....5.00

Slayers
CPM Manga, 1998

1-5 ....3.00

Slayers
Tokyopop, 2002

1-6 ....3.00

Sleazy Scandals of the Silver Screen
Kitchen Sink, 1993

1 ....3.00

Sledge Hammer
Marvel, 1988

1-2 ....1.00

Sleeper
DC, 2003

1-12 ....3.00

Sleeper: Season 2
DC, 2004

1-11 ....3.00

Sleeping Dragons
Slave Labor, 2000

1-4 ....3.00

Sleepwalker
Marvel, 1991

1 ....2.00
2-18 ....1.00
19 ....2.00
20-24 ....1.00
25 ....3.00
26-33 ....1.00
Holiday 1 ....2.00

Sleepwalking
Hall of Heroes, 1996

1 ....3.00
1/Variant 10.00
2-3 ....3.00

Sleepy Hollow
DC, 2000

1 ....8.00

Sleeze Brothers
Marvel, 1989

1-6 ....2.00

Sleeze Brothers
Marvel, 1991

1 ....4.00

Slice
Express, 1996

1 ....3.00

Slick Chick
Leader, 1946

1 ....90.00
2-3 ....60.00

Sliders
Acclaim, 1996

1-7 ....3.00
Special 1-3 ....4.00

Slightly Bent Comics
Slightly Bent, 1998

1-2 ....3.00

Slimer!
Now, 1989

1-19 ....2.00

Slingers
Marvel, 1998

0 ....1.00
1/A-1/D 3.00
2-12 ....2.00

Sloth Park
Blatant, 1998

1 ....3.00

Slow Burn
Fantagraphics

1 ....3.00

Slow Death
Last Gasp, 1970

1 ....20.00
1/Silver 25.00
2 ....12.00
3-5 ....10.00
6-11 ....6.00

Slowpoke Comix
Alternative, 1998

1 ....3.00

Sludge
Malibu, 1993

1-1/Ltd 3.00
2-11 ....2.00
12 ....4.00
13 ....2.00

Sludge: Red X-Mas
Malibu, 1994

1 ....3.00

Slugger
Lev Gleason, 1956

1 ....30.00

Slug 'n' Ginger
Fantagraphics

1 ....2.00

Slutburger Stories
Rip Off, 1990
1-2 .... 3.00

Small Favors
Fantagraphics, 2000
1-4 .... 4.00

Small Gods
Image, 2004
1 .... 4.00
2-12 .... 3.00

Small Gods Special
Image, 2005
0 .... 3.00

Small Killing, A
VG, 1993
1 .... 15.00
1/2nd 12.00

Small Press Expo
Insight, 1995
1995-1997 .... 3.00

Small Press Swimsuit Spectacular
Allied, 1995
1 .... 3.00

Smallville
DC, 2003
1-11 .... 4.00

Smash Comics
Quality, 1939
1 .... 1,900.00
2 .... 775.00
3 .... 535.00
4-5 .... 475.00
6-10 .... 375.00
11-12 .... 350.00
13 .... 375.00
14 .... 1,700.00
15 .... 825.00
16 .... 800.00
17 .... 900.00
18 .... 1,150.00
19-20 .... 640.00
21-30 .... 585.00
31-40 .... 425.00
41-50 .... 295.00
51-60 .... 200.00
61-70 .... 146.00
71-85 .... 110.00

Smash Comics
DC, 1999
1 .... 2.00

Smax
DC, 2003
1-5 .... 3.00

Smile
Mixx, 1998
1-12 .... 4.00
13-29 .... 5.00

Smile
Kitchen Sink
1 .... 3.00

Smiley
Chaos, 1998
1 .... 3.00

Smiley Anti-Holiday Special
Chaos!, 1999
1 .... 3.00

Smiley Burnett Western
Fawcett, 1950
1 .... 275.00
2-4 .... 200.00

Smiley's Spring Break
Chaos!, 1999
1 .... 3.00

Smiley Wrestling Special
Chaos!, 1999
1 .... 3.00

Smilin' Ed
Fantaco, 1982
1-4 .... 1.00

Smilin' Jack
Dell, 1948
1 .... 65.00
2 .... 35.00
3-8 .... 30.00

Smith Brown Jones
Kiwi, 1997
1 .... 4.00
2-5 .... 3.00

Smith Brown Jones: Alien Accountant
Slave Labor, 1998
1-4 .... 3.00

Smith Brown Jones: Halloween Special
Slave Labor, 1998
1 .... 3.00

Smitty
Dell, 1948
1 .... 55.00
2 .... 35.00
3-5 .... 25.00
6-7 .... 20.00

Smoke
Idea & Design Works, 2005
1 .... 10.00
2-3 .... 7.00

Smoke and Mirrors
Speakeasy Comics, 2005
1 .... 3.00

Nightshades

Nightstalkers

Night Thrasher

Night Tribes

Nightveil

Nightvision

Night Walker

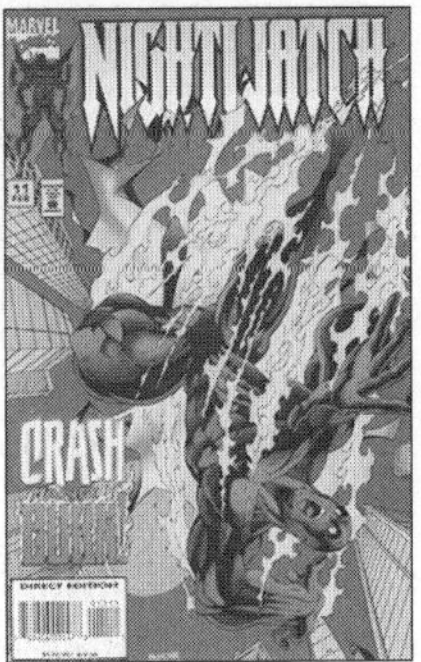

Nightwatch

Smokey Bear
Gold Key, 1970

1 .... 8.00
2 .... 5.00
3 .... 4.00
4-13 .... 3.00

Smoot
Skip Williamson

1 .... 3.00

Smurfs
Marvel, 1982

1 .... 4.00

Smut the Alternative Comic
Wiltshire

1 .... 3.00

Snack Bar
Big Town

1 .... 3.00

Snagglepuss
Gold Key, 1962

1 .... 45.00
2-4 .... 30.00

Snake
Special Studio, 1989

1 .... 4.00

Snake Eyes
Fantagraphics

1-3 .... 8.00

Snake Plissken Chronicles (John Carpenter's...)
CrossGen, 2003

1/A-2 .... 3.00

Snakes on a Plane
DC, 2006

1-2 .... 3.00

Snak Posse
HCOM, 1994

1-2 .... 2.00

Snap
Harry A. Chesler, 1944

9 .... 125.00

Snap Dragons
Dork Storm, 2002

1-3 .... 3.00

Snap the Punk Turtle
Super Crew

½ 2.00

Snarf
Kitchen Sink, 1972

1 .... 10.00
2-4 .... 8.00
5-10 .... 6.00
11-14 .... 4.00
15 .... 5.00

Snarl
Caliber

1-3 .... 3.00

Sniffy the Pup
Standard, 1949

5 .... 60.00
6-10 .... 35.00
11-18 .... 25.00

Snoid Comics
Kitchen Sink, 1979

1 .... 2.00

Snooper and Blabber Detectives
Gold Key, 1962

1 .... 100.00
2-3 .... 75.00

S'Not for Kids
Vortex

1 .... 7.00

Snowbuni
Mu, 1991

1 .... 3.00

Snow Drop
Tokyopop, 2004

1-11 .... 10.00

Snowman
Express, 1996

1 .... 5.00
1/A 6.00
1/2nd 3.00
2 .... 4.00
2/A 5.00
2/2nd-3/A 3.00

Snowman: 1944
Entity, 1996

1 .... 3.00

Snow White
Marvel, 1995

1 .... 2.00

Snow White and the Seven Dwarfs
Gladstone

1 .... 4.00

Snuff
Boneyard, 1997

1 .... 3.00

Soap Opera Love
Charlton, 1983

1 .... 25.00
2-3 .... 15.00

Soap Opera Romances
Charlton, 1982

1 .... 12.00
2-5 .... 8.00

SOB: Special Operations Branch

Promethean, 1994

1 .... 2.00

Socketeer

Kardia

1 .... 2.00

Sock Monkey

Dark Horse, 1998

1-2 .... 3.00

Sock Monkey (Tony Millionaire's...)

Dark Horse, 1999

1-2 .... 3.00

Sock Monkey (Tony Millionaire's...)

Dark Horse, 2000

1-2 .... 3.00

Sock Monkey (Tony Millionaire's)

Dark Horse, 2003

1-2 .... 3.00

Sock Monkey: The Inches Incident

Dark Horse, 2006

1-2 .... 3.00

Socrates in Love

Viz, 2005

1 .... 9.00

So Dark the Rose

CFD, 1995

1 .... 3.00

Sofa Jet City Crisis

Visual Assault

1 .... 7.00

S.O.F.T. Corps

Spoof

1 .... 3.00

Sojourn

Dreamer, 1998

1-5 .... 2.00
6-10 .... 3.00

Sojourn

CrossGen, 2001

1 .... 5.00
2-24 .... 3.00
25 .... 1.00
26-34/2nd 3.00
Special 1 .... 4.00

Sojourn Prequel

CrossGen, 2001

1 .... 5.00

Solar Lord

Image, 1999

1-7 .... 3.00

Solarman

Marvel, 1989

1-2 .... 1.00

Solar, Man of the Atom

Valiant, 1991

1 .... 7.00
2-7 .... 5.00
8-9 .... 6.00
10 .... 16.00
☛1st Eternal Warrior
10/2nd 3.00
11 .... 5.00
12 .... 4.00
13 .... 2.00
14 .... 4.00
15-16 .... 2.00
17-32 .... 1.00
33 .... 2.00
34-41 .... 1.00
42-50 .... 2.00
51-56 .... 3.00
57-58 .... 4.00
59 .... 5.00
60 .... 10.00

Solar, Man of the Atom

Acclaim, 1997

1 .... 4.00

Solar, Man of the Atom: Hell on Earth

Acclaim, 1998

1-4 .... 3.00

Solar, Man of the Atom: Revelations

Acclaim, 1997

1 .... 4.00

Solar Stella

Sirius, 2000

1 .... 3.00

Soldier & Marine Comics

Charlton, 1954

11-12 .... 30.00
13-15 .... 25.00
9 .... 45.00

Soldier Comics

Fawcett, 1952

1 .... 55.00
2-3 .... 30.00
4-5 .... 25.00
6-11 .... 16.00

Soldiers of Fortune

ACG, 1951

1 .... 175.00
2 .... 100.00
3-5 .... 85.00
6-10 .... 75.00
11-13 .... 60.00

Nightwing and Huntress

Nightwing Secret Files

Nightwolf

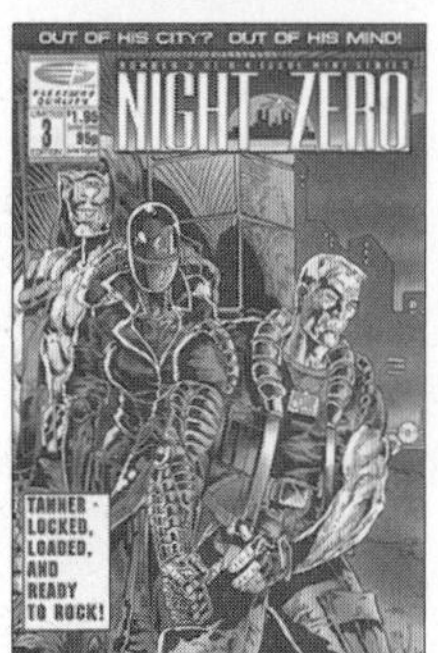

Night Zero

Nine Lives of Felix the Cat

Nine Volt

Ninja

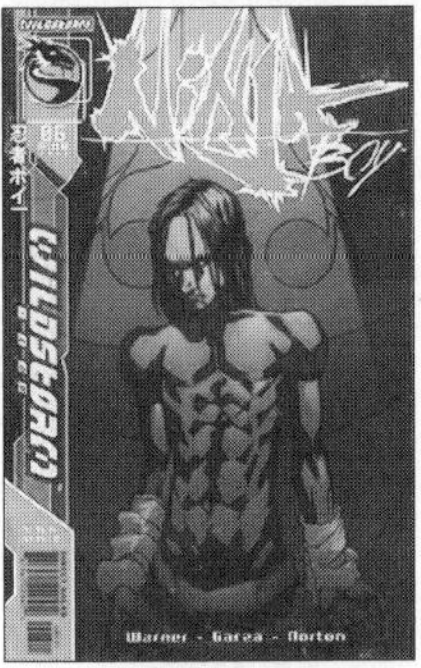
Ninja Boy

Soldiers of Freedom
AC, 1987

1-2 ....2.00

Soldier X
Marvel, 2002

1 ....3.00
2-6 ....2.00
7-12 ....3.00

Sold Out
Fantaco, 1986

1-2 ....2.00

Solitaire
Malibu, 1993

1 ....2.00
1/CS 3.00
2-12 ....2.00

Solo
Marvel, 1994

1-4 ....2.00

Solo
Dark Horse, 1996

1-2 ....3.00

Solo
DC, 2005

1-12 ....5.00

Solo Avengers
Marvel, 1987

1-20 ....1.00

Solo Ex-Mutants
Eternity, 1987

1-6 ....2.00

Solomon Kane
Marvel, 1985

1 ....2.00
2-6 ....1.00

Solomon Kane in 3-D
Blackthorne

1 ....3.00

Solson Christmas Special
Solson, 1986

1 ....3.00

Solson's Comic Talent Starsearch
Solson

1-2 ....2.00

Solus
CrossGen, 2003

1-8 ....3.00

Solution
Malibu, 1993

0 ....3.00
1 ....2.00
1/Ltd.-2 ....3.00
3-15 ....2.00
16 ....4.00
17 ....3.00

Someplace Strange
Marvel

1 ....7.00

Somerset Holmes
Pacific, 1983

1 ....3.00
2-6 ....2.00

Some Tales from Gimbley
Harrier, 1987

1 ....2.00

Something
Strictly Underground

1 ....3.00

Something at the Window is Scratching
Slave Labor

1 ....10.00

Something Different
Wooga Central, 1992

1-3 ....2.00

Something Wicked
Image, 2003

1-3 ....3.00

Some Trouble of a SeRRious Nature
Crusade, 2001

1 ....4.00

Somnambulo: Sleep of the Just
9th Circle, 1996

1 ....3.00

Son of Vulcan
DC, 1965

1-6 ....3.00

Songbook (Alan Moore's...)
Caliber

1 ....6.00

Song of Mykal: Atlantis Fantasyworld 25th Anniversary Comic
Atlantis Fantasyworld, 2001

1 ....3.00

Song of the Cid
Tome

1-2 ....3.00

Song of the Sirens
Millennium

1-2 ....3.00

Songs of Bastards
Conquest

1 ....3.00

Sonic & Knuckles: Mecha Madness Special
Archie, 1995
1 .... 2.00

Sonic & Knuckles Special
Archie, 1995
1 .... 2.00

Sonic Blast Special
Archie, 1996
1 .... 2.00

Sonic Disruptors
DC, 1987
1-7 .... 1.00

Sonic Live Special
Archie
1 .... 2.00

Sonic Quest - The Death Egg Saga
Archie, 1997
2 .... 2.00

Sonic's Friendly Nemesis Knuckles
Archie, 1996
1 .... 3.00
2-3 .... 2.00

Sonic the Hedgehog
Archie, 1993
1 .... 20.00
2-3 .... 10.00

Sonic the Hedgehog
Archie, 1993
0 .... 9.00
1 .... 12.00
2-3 .... 9.00
4-5 .... 7.00
6-10 .... 6.00
11-20 .... 4.00
21-50 .... 3.00
51-185 .... 2.00
Special 1 .... 3.00
Special 2-15 .... 2.00

Sonic the Hedgehog in Your Face Special
Archie
1 .... 2.00

Sonic the Hedgehog Triple Trouble Special
Archie, 1995
1 .... 2.00

Sonic vs. Knuckles Battle Royal Special
Archie, 1997
1 .... 2.00

Sonic X
Archie, 2005
1-15 .... 2.00

Son of Ambush Bug
DC, 1986
1-6 .... 2.00

Son of M
Marvel, 2006
1-6 .... 3.00

Son of Mutant World
Fantagor, 1990
1-2 .... 3.00
3-5 .... 2.00

Son of Rampage
Slap Happy, 1998
2 .... 14.00

Son of Satan
Marvel, 1975
1 .... 20.00
2 .... 15.00
3 .... 10.00
3/30¢ 15.00
4 .... 10.00
4/30¢ 15.00
5 .... 10.00
5/30¢ 15.00
6-8 .... 10.00

Son of Sinbad
St. John, 1950
1 .... 250.00

Son of Yuppies From Hell
Marvel
1 .... 4.00

Sons of Katie Elder
Dell, 1965
1 .... 125.00

Sophistikats Katch-Up Kollection
Silk Purrs, 1995
1 .... 6.00

Sorcerer's Children
Sillwill, 1998
1-4 .... 3.00

Sorority Secrets
Toby, 1954
1 .... 50.00

S.O.S.
Fantagraphics
1 .... 3.00

Soul
Flashpoint, 1994
1-1/Gold 3.00

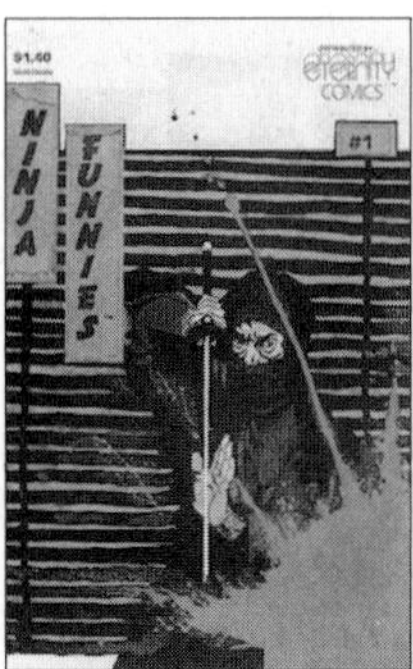

Ninja Funnies

Ninja High School

Ninja High School Spotlight

Ninja High School Swimsuit Special

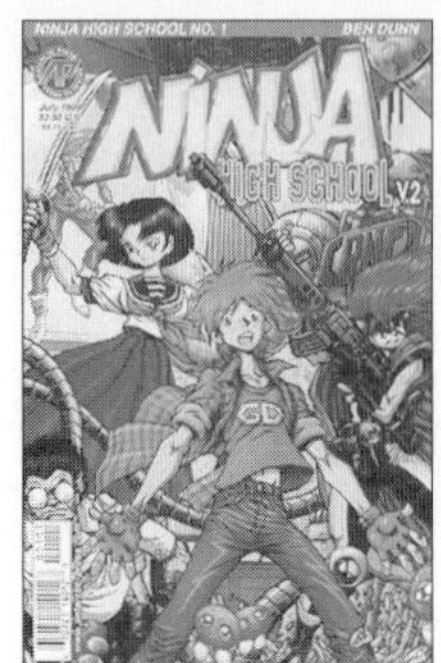

Ninja High School Version 2

Ninjak

N.I.O.

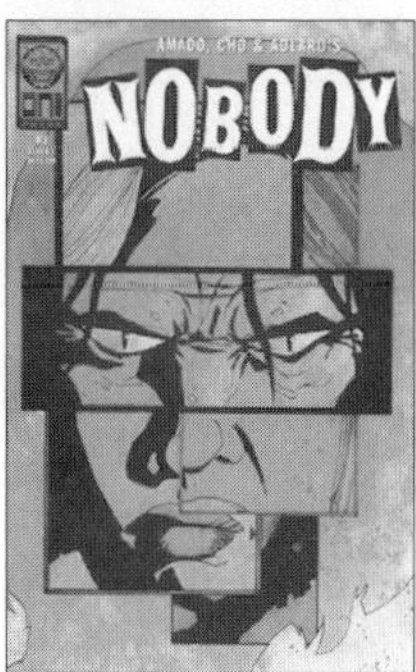

Nobody

Soulfire (Michael Turner's ...)

Aspen, 2004

0 .... 5.00
0/Conv 7.00
1 .... 7.00
1/Virgin 8.00
2 .... 6.00
2/Rupps 10.00
3 .... 5.00
4 .... 3.00
4/Variant 4.00
4/Campbell 3.00
4/Lee 4.00
4/Conv 10.00

Soulfire: Beginnings

Aspen, 2003

1 .... 4.00
1/Conv 10.00

Soulfire: Dying of the Light

Aspen, 2005

0 .... 3.00
0/Conv 15.00
1-2 .... 3.00

Soulfire Preview

Aspen, 2003

1 .... 4.00
1/Conv 8.00

Soul of a Samurai

Image, 2003

1-4 .... 6.00

Soulquest

Innovation, 1989

1 .... 4.00

Soul Saga

Top Cow, 2000

1-5 .... 3.00

Soulsearchers and Company

Claypool, 1993

1 .... 4.00
2-69 .... 3.00

Soul to Seoul

Tokyopop, 2005

1-3 .... 10.00

Soul Trek

Spoof, 1992

1-2 .... 3.00

Soulwind

Image, 1997

1-8 .... 3.00

Soupy Sales Comic Book

Archie, 1965

1 .... 80.00

Southern Blood

Jm Comics, 1992

1-2 .... 3.00

Southern Cumfort

Fantagraphics

1 .... 3.00

Southern-Fried Homicide

Cremo

1 .... 8.00

Southern Knights

Guild, 1983

2-34 .... 2.00
35-36 .... 4.00
Holiday 1-Special 1 .... 2.00

Southern Knights Primer

Comics Interview

1 .... 2.00

Southern Squadron

Aircel, 1990

1-4 .... 2.00

Southern Squadron

Eternity, 1991

1-4 .... 3.00

Southern Squadron: The Freedom of Information Act

Eternity, 1992

1-3 .... 3.00

Sovereign Seven

DC, 1995

1 .... 3.00
1/Variant 4.00
2-36 .... 2.00
Ann 1 .... 4.00
Ann 2 .... 3.00

Sovereign Seven Plus

DC, 1997

1 .... 3.00

Soviet Super Soldiers

Marvel, 1992

1 .... 2.00

Space Action

Ace, 1952

1 .... 525.00
2-3 .... 350.00

Space Squadron

Atlas, 1951

1 .... 400.00
2 .... 340.00
3-5 .... 275.00

Space: 1999

Charlton, 1975

1 .... 10.00
2-4 .... 7.00
5-7 .... 5.00

Space: 34-24-34
MN Design
1 .... 5.00

Space: Above and Beyond
Topps, 1996
1-3 .... 3.00

Space: Above and Beyond: The Gauntlet
Topps, 1996
1-2 .... 3.00

Space Ace
Magazine Enterprises, 1952
5 .... 400.00

Space Adventures
Charlton, 1952
1 .... 240.00
2 .... 125.00
3-5 .... 105.00
6-9 .... 90.00
10-12 .... 225.00
13-19 .... 90.00
20 .... 110.00
21 .... 80.00
23 .... 100.00
24-32 .... 70.00
33 .... 325.00
☛1st Captain Atom
34 .... 150.00
35-40 .... 125.00
41 .... 25.00
42 .... 75.00
43-50 .... 25.00
51-60 .... 18.00
61-72 .... 12.00

Space Ark
AC, 1987
1-5 .... 2.00

Space Bananas
Karl Art
0 .... 2.00

Space Beaver
Ten-Buck, 1986
1-11 .... 2.00

Space Busters
Ziff-Davis, 1952
1 .... 525.00
2 .... 450.00

Space Circus
Dark Horse, 2000
1-4 .... 3.00

Space Comics
Avon, 1954
4-5 .... 40.00

Space Cowboy Annual 2001
Vanguard, 2001
1/Frazetta-1/Williamson 5.00

Spaced
Unbridled Ambition, 1985
1-13 .... 2.00

Spaced
Comics and Comix
1 .... 4.00

Space Detective
Avon, 1951
1 .... 775.00
2 .... 575.00
3-4 .... 300.00

Spaced Out
Forbidden Fruit, 1992
1 .... 3.00

Spaced Out
Print Mint
1 .... 3.00

Space Family Robinson
Gold Key, 1962
1 .... 225.00
2 .... 100.00
3-5 .... 75.00
6-10 .... 50.00
11-15 .... 35.00
16-20 .... 25.00
21-44 .... 20.00
45-54 .... 10.00
55-59 .... 6.00

Space Funnies
Archival, 1990
1 .... 6.00

Spacegal Comics
Thorby
1-2 .... 3.00

Space Ghost
Gold Key, 1967
1 .... 150.00

Space Ghost
Comico, 1987
1 .... 4.00

Space Ghost
DC, 2005
1 .... 22.00
2 .... 10.00
3-6 .... 3.00

Space Giants
Boneyard
1 .... 3.00

Spacegirl Comics
Bill Jones Graphics, 1995
1-2 .... 3.00

Spacehawk
Dark Horse, 1989
1-4 .... 2.00
5 .... 3.00

Nodwick

Nomad

Normalman

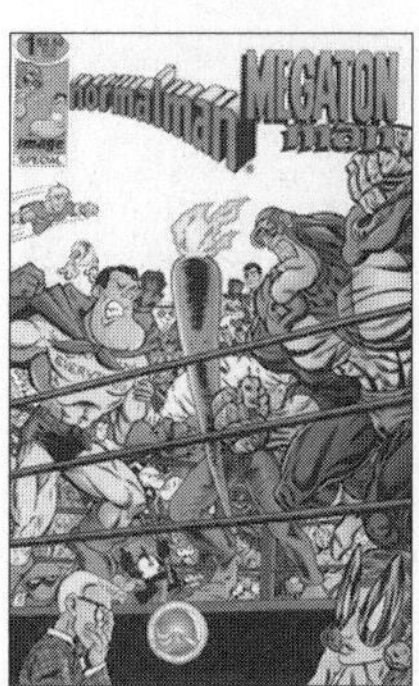

Normalman-Megaton Man Special

Northstar

Northwest Cartoon Cookery

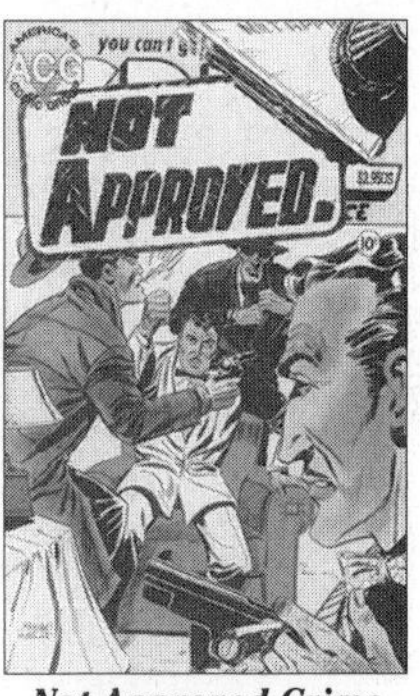

Not Approved Crime

Not Brand Echh

Space Hustlers
Slave Labor, 1997

1 ....3.00

Space Jam
DC, 1996

1 ....6.00

Spaceknights
Marvel, 2000

1-5 ....3.00

Spaceman
Atlas, 1953

1 ....400.00
2 ....260.00
3-6 ....225.00

Spaceman
Dell, 1962

2 ....40.00
3 ....32.00
4-6 ....24.00
7-8 ....22.00
9-10 ....5.00

Spaceman
Oni, 2002

nn 3.00

Space Mouse
Avon, 1953

1 ....65.00
2 ....40.00
3-5 ....30.00

Space: 1999 (Magazine)
Charlton, 1975

1 ....30.00
2-8 ....20.00

Space Patrol
Ziff-Davis, 1952

1 ....550.00
2 ....390.00

Space Patrol
Adventure

1-3 ....3.00

Space Slutz
Comic Zone

1 ....4.00

Space Thrillers
Avon, 1954

1 ....850.00

Space Time Shuffle a Trilogy
Alpha Productions

1-2 ....2.00

Space Trip to the Moon
Avalon, 1999

1 ....3.00

Space Usagi
Mirage, 1992

1-3 ....3.00

Space Usagi
Mirage, 1993

1-3 ....3.00

Space Usagi
Dark Horse, 1996

1-3 ....3.00

Space War
Charlton, 1959

1 ....95.00
2-3 ....55.00
4-6 ....100.00
7 ....30.00
8 ....100.00
9 ....30.00
10 ....100.00
11-15 ....30.00
16-27 ....16.00
28-32 ....4.00

Space War Classics
Avalon

1 ....3.00

Space Western
Charlton, 1952

40 ....180.00
41 ....130.00
42 ....140.00
43-45 ....130.00

Space Wolf
Antarctic, 1992

1-2 ....3.00

Space Worlds
Atlas, 1952

6 ....300.00

Spam
Alpha Productions

1-2 ....2.00

Spandex Tights
Lost Cause, 1994

1 ....3.00
2-5 ....2.00
6 ....3.00

Spandex Tights
Lost Cause, 1997

1-3 ....3.00

Spanish Fly
Fantagraphics, 1996

1-5 ....3.00

Spank
Fantagraphics

2-4 ....2.00

Spank the Monkey
Arrow, 1999

1 ....3.00

Spanner's Galaxy
DC, 1984

1-6 ..... 1.00

Sparkle Comics
United Feature, 1948

1 ..... 85.00
2 ..... 50.00
3-10 ..... 38.00
11-25 ..... 26.00
26-33 ..... 20.00

Sparkler Comics
United Feature, 1940

1 ..... 315.00
2 ..... 240.00

Sparkler Comics
United Feature Syndicate, 1941

1 ..... 1,500.00
2 ..... 650.00
3-4 ..... 425.00
5-10 ..... 375.00
11-20 ..... 300.00
21-29 ..... 235.00
30-40 ..... 165.00
41-50 ..... 150.00
51-60 ..... 100.00
61-70 ..... 75.00
71-90 ..... 55.00
91-100 ..... 42.00
101-120 ..... 30.00

Sparkling Stars
Holyoke, 1944

1 ..... 100.00
2 ..... 65.00
3 ..... 50.00
4-10 ..... 42.00
11-33 ..... 35.00

Sparkplug
Heroic, 1993

1-3 ..... 3.00

Sparky & Tim
Aaron Warner, 1999

1 ..... 6.00

Sparky Watts
Publication Enterprises, 1942

1 ..... 300.00
2 ..... 165.00
3 ..... 110.00
4 ..... 85.00
5-6 ..... 55.00
7 ..... 42.00
8-10 ..... 34.00

Sparrow
Millennium, 1995

1-4 ..... 3.00

Spartan: Warrior Spirit
Image, 1995

1-4 ..... 3.00

Spartan X: Hell-Bent-Hero-For-Hire (Jackie Chan's...)
Image, 1998

1-4 ..... 3.00

Spartan X: The Armour of Heaven (Jackie Chan's...)
Topps, 1997

1 ..... 3.00

Spasm
Parody

1 ..... 10.00

Spasm
Rough Copy

1-5 ..... 3.00

Spawn
Image, 1992

1 ..... 5.00
1/A 3.00
2 ..... 4.00
3-6 ..... 3.00
7-9 ..... 4.00
10-50 ..... 3.00
51-97 ..... 2.00
98-99 ..... 3.00
100/A 6.00
100/B-100/F 5.00
101-149 ..... 3.00
150 ..... 5.00
151-171 ..... 3.00
Ann 1 ..... 5.00
Fan ed. 1/A-3/B 1.00

Spawn-Batman
Image, 1994

1 ..... 4.00

Spawn Bible
Image, 1996

1 ..... 2.00

Spawn Blood and Salvation
Image, 1999

1 ..... 5.00

Spawn Blood Feud
Image, 1995

1-4 ..... 2.00

Spawn: Godslayer
Image, 2006

1 ..... 7.00

Spawn Movie Adaptation
Image, 1997

1 ..... 5.00

Spawn #1 in 3-D
Image, 2006

1 ..... 6.00

Not Quite Dead

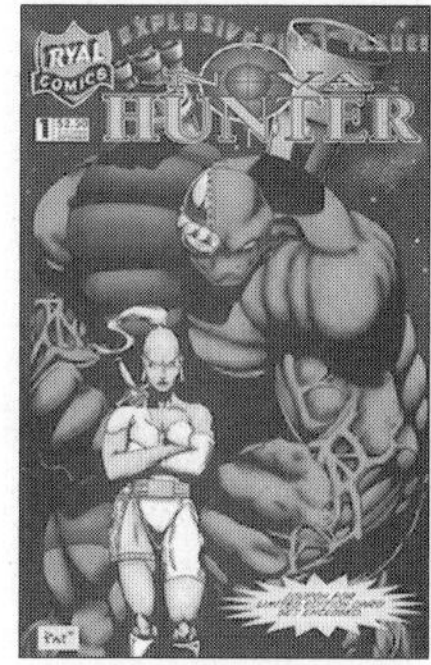

Nova Hunter

Nukla

Null Patrol

Nurse Betsy Crane

Nyoka the Jungle Girl

NYX

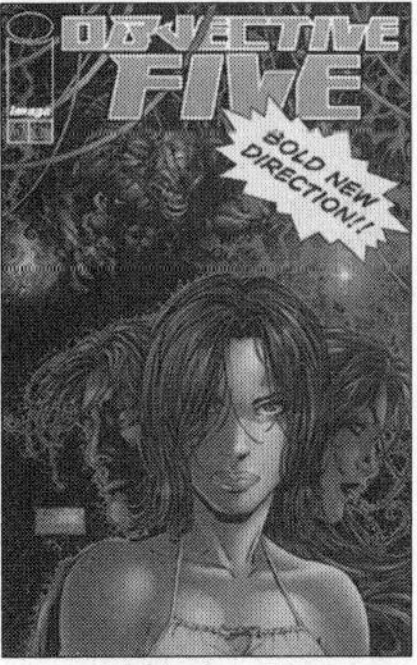

Objective Five

Spawn: Simony One-Shot
Image, 2004

1 .... 8.00

Spawn: The Dark Ages
Image, 1999

1-28 .... 3.00

Spawn the Impaler
Image, 1996

1-3 .... 3.00

Spawn the Undead
Image, 1999

1-9 .... 2.00

Spawn/WildC.A.T.S
Image, 1996

1-4 .... 3.00

Spaztic Colon
-Ism, 2005

1-3 .... 4.00

Special Agent
Parents' Magazine Institute, 1947

1 .... 75.00
2 .... 45.00
3-8 .... 35.00

Special Comics
M.L.J., 1941

1 .... 2,500.00

Special Edition
DC, 1944

1 .... 475.00
2 .... 300.00
3-5 .... 350.00
6 .... 300.00

Special Edition Comics
Fawcett, 1940

1 .... 9,000.00

Special Hugging and Other Childhood Tales
Slave Labor, 1989

1 .... 2.00

Special Marvel Edition
Marvel, 1971

1 .... 20.00
2-4 .... 15.00
5-14 .... 7.00
15 .... 45.00
☛1st Shang-Chi
16 .... 18.00

Special War Series
Charlton, 1965

1 .... 10.00
2-3 .... 8.00
4 .... 16.00

Species
Dark Horse, 1995

1-4 .... 3.00

Species: Human Race
Dark Horse, 1996

1-4 .... 3.00

Spectacles
Alternative, 1997

1-4 .... 3.00

Spectacular Features Magazine
Fox, 1950

11-12 .... 165.00
3 .... 125.00

Spectacular Scarlet Spider
Marvel, 1995

1-2 .... 2.00

Spectacular Spider-Man (Magazine)
Marvel, 1968

1 .... 90.00
2 .... 75.00

Spectacular Spider-Man
Marvel, 1976

-1 .... 2.00
1 .... 25.00
2 .... 15.00
3-3/Whitman 8.00
4-7/Whitman 5.00
7/35¢ 15.00
8-8/Whitman 5.00
8/35¢ 15.00
9-9/Whitman 5.00
9/35¢ 15.00
10-10/Whitman 4.00
10/35¢ 15.00
11-11/Whitman 4.00
11/35¢ 15.00
12-20 .... 4.00
21-26/Whitman 3.00
☛1st Miller Daredevil
27-28 .... 15.00
☛2nd Miller Daredevil
29-55 .... 3.00
56 .... 5.00
57-63 .... 3.00
64 .... 5.00
☛1st Cloak & Dagger
65-82 .... 3.00
83 .... 7.00
☛Punisher app.
84 .... 3.00
85 .... 5.00
86-99 .... 3.00
100 .... 5.00
101 .... 3.00
102-115 .... 2.00
116 .... 3.00
117-129 .... 2.00
130 .... 3.00
131 .... 5.00
132 .... 4.00

133 ... 3.00
134-142 ... 2.00
143 ... 4.00
144-146 ... 2.00
147 ... 8.00
☛New Hobgoblin
148 ... 2.00
149 ... 3.00
150-157 ... 2.00
158 ... 5.00
159 ... 4.00
160-188 ... 2.00
189 ... 4.00
189/2nd ... 3.00
190-195 ... 2.00
195/CS ... 3.00
196-199 ... 2.00
200 ... 4.00
201-213 ... 2.00
213/CS ... 3.00
214-217 ... 2.00
217/Variant ... 3.00
218-219 ... 2.00
220-221 ... 3.00
222 ... 2.00
223-223/Variant ... 3.00
224 ... 2.00
225 ... 5.00
225/Variant ... 4.00
226-228 ... 2.00
229 ... 3.00
229/Variant-230 ... 4.00
231-249 ... 2.00
250 ... 3.00
251-255 ... 2.00
255/Variant ... 5.00
256-263 ... 2.00
Ann 1 ... 5.00
Ann 2 ... 4.00
Ann 3-7 ... 3.00
Ann 8 ... 4.00
Ann 9-1997 ... 3.00
Special 1 ... 4.00

Spectacular Spider-Man

Marvel, 2003

1 ... 4.00
1/CanExpo ... 6.00
2-3 ... 3.00
4 ... 4.00
5-7 ... 3.00
8-13 ... 2.00
14 ... 3.00
15 ... 7.00
☛Avengers Disassmbled
16 ... 5.00
☛Avengers Disassmbled
17-19 ... 2.00
20 ... 3.00
☛Organic webshooters
21-27 ... 2.00

Spectacular Spider-Man Adventures

Marvel UK, 1999

1 ... 4.00
2-46 ... 3.00

Spectacular Spider-Man Super Special

Marvel, 1995

1 ... 4.00

Spectacular Stories Magazine

Fox, 1950

3 ... 250.00
4 ... 175.00

Spectre

DC, 1967

1 ... 150.00
2 ... 60.00
3-5 ... 50.00
6-10 ... 40.00

Spectre

DC, 1987

1-5 ... 3.00
6-31 ... 2.00
Ann 1 ... 3.00

Spectre

DC, 1992

0 ... 3.00
1 ... 6.00
2 ... 5.00
3 ... 4.00
4-7 ... 3.00
8 ... 4.00
9-20 ... 3.00
21-36 ... 2.00
37-62 ... 3.00
Ann 1 ... 4.00

Spectre

DC, 2001

1-27 ... 3.00

Spectrescope

Spectre, 1994

1 ... 1.00

Spectrum

New Horizons, 1987

1 ... 2.00

Spectrum Comics Previews

Spectrum, 1983

1 ... 3.00

Speedball

Marvel, 1988

1-10 ... 1.00

Speed Buggy

Charlton, 1975

1 ... 12.00
2-9 ... 8.00

Oblivion

Obnoxio the Clown

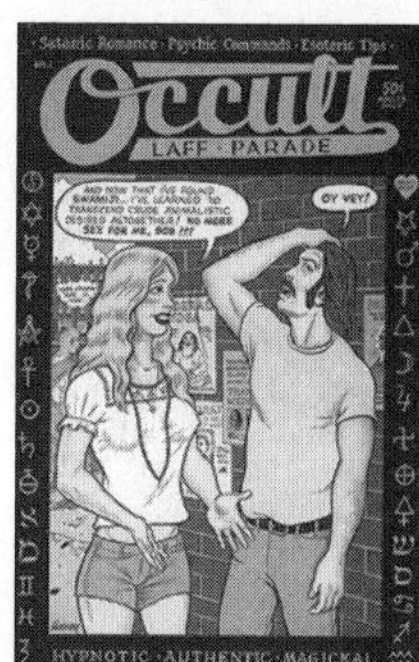

Occult Laff-Parade

October Yen

Oddjob

Official Buz Sawyer

Official Crisis on Infinite Earths Index

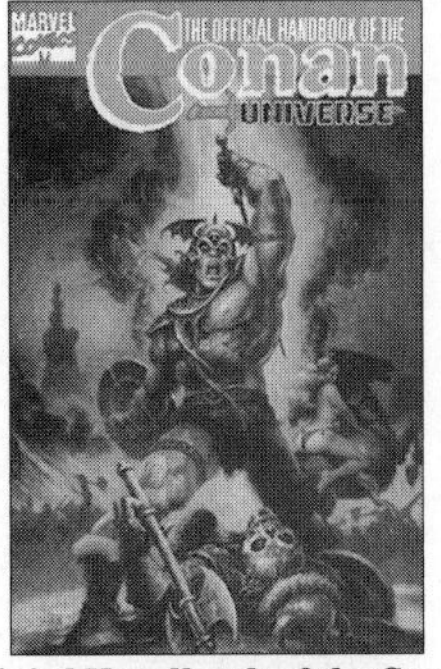

Official Handbook of the Conan Universe

Speed Comics
Harvey, 1939

1 .... 3,000.00
2 .... 1,100.00
3 .... 525.00
4-5 .... 450.00
6-10 .... 400.00
11-13 .... 365.00
14-16 .... 500.00
17 .... 550.00
18-20 .... 365.00
21-30 .... 300.00
31-37 .... 250.00
38 .... 450.00
39-44 .... 250.00

Speed Demon
Marvel, 1996

1 .... 2.00

Speed Force
DC, 1997

1 .... 4.00

Speed Racer
Now, 1987

1 .... 3.00
1/2nd-38 .... 2.00
Special 1 .... 3.00
Special 1/2nd 2.00

Speed Racer
DC, 1999

1-3 .... 3.00

Speed Racer
Now

1-3 .... 3.00

Speed Racer 3-D Special
Now, 1993

1 .... 3.00

Speed Racer Classics
Now, 1988

1-2 .... 4.00

Speed Racer Featuring Ninja High School
Now, 1993

1-2 .... 3.00

Speed Racer: Return of the GRX
Now, 1994

1-2 .... 2.00

Speed Racer: The Original Manga
DC

1 .... 10.00

Speed Smith, the Hot Rod King
Ziff-Davis, 1952

1 .... 100.00

Speed Tribes
Nemicron, 1998

1 .... 3.00

Spellbinders
Fleetway-Quality, 1986

1-12 .... 2.00

Spellbinders
Marvel, 2005

1-6 .... 3.00

Spellbound
Atlas, 1952

1 .... 400.00
2 .... 210.00
3-6 .... 180.00
7-10 .... 155.00
11-20 .... 125.00
21-23 .... 105.00
24-28 .... 95.00
29 .... 105.00
30-33 .... 95.00

Spellbound
Marvel, 1988

1-6 .... 2.00

Spellcaster
Medusa

1-3 .... 3.00

Spelljammer
DC, 1990

1-18 .... 2.00

Spex-7
Shadow Shock, 1994

1 .... 2.00

Sphinx
Print Mint, 1972

1-3 .... 3.00

Spicecapades
Fantagraphics, 1999

1 .... 5.00

Spicy Adult Stories
Aircel, 1991

1-4 .... 3.00

Spicy Tales
Eternity, 1988

1-17 .... 2.00
18-20 .... 3.00
Special 1-2 .... 2.00

Spider
Eclipse, 1991

1-3 .... 5.00

Spiderbaby Comix (S.R. Bissette's...)
Spiderbaby, 1996

1 .... 4.00

Spider-Boy
Marvel, 1996

1 .... 3.00

Spider-Boy Team-Up
Marvel, 1997
1 .... 2.00

Spider-Femme
Spoof
1 .... 3.00

Spider Garden
NBM
1 .... 13.00

Spider-Girl
Marvel, 1998
0 .... 2.00
½ 3.00
1-1/A 4.00
2-5 .... 3.00
6-16 .... 2.00
17 .... 3.00
18-24 .... 2.00
25 .... 3.00
26-58 .... 2.00
59-74 .... 3.00
75 .... 8.00
76-99 .... 3.00
100-Ann 1999 .... 4.00

Spider-Girl Battlebook
Marvel, 1998
1 .... 4.00

Spider-Man
Marvel, 1990
-1 .... 2.00
½ 4.00
½/Platinum 6.00
1-1/CS 5.00
1/Platinum 42.00
1/Silver 5.00
1/2nd 50.00
1/Direct/2n 5.00
2-8 .... 3.00
9 .... 6.00
10 .... 4.00
11-12 .... 3.00
13 .... 5.00
14 .... 3.00
15-25 .... 2.00
26 .... 4.00
27-46 .... 2.00
46/CS 3.00
47-49 .... 2.00
50 .... 3.00
50/Variant 4.00
51-51/Variant 3.00
52-56 .... 2.00
57-57/Variant 3.00
58-74 .... 2.00
75 .... 4.00
76-98/B 2.00
Ann 1997-1998 .... 3.00
GS 1 .... 4.00
Holiday 1995 .... 3.00

Spider-Man Adventures
Marvel, 1994
1 .... 2.00
1/Variant 3.00
2-15 .... 2.00

Spider-Man and Arana Special
Marvel, 2006
1 .... 4.00

Spider-Man and Batman
Marvel, 1995
1 .... 6.00

Spider-Man and Daredevil Special Edition
Marvel, 1984
1 .... 2.00

Spider-Man and Doctor Octopus: Negative Exposure
Marvel, 2003
1-5 .... 3.00

Spider-Man and His Amazing Friends
Marvel, 1981
1 .... 10.00

Spider-Man and Mysterio
Marvel, 2001
1-3 .... 3.00

Spider-Man and Power Pack
Marvel, 2007
1-3 .... 3.00

Spider-Man and the Dallas Cowboys
Marvel, 1983
1 .... 10.00

Spider-Man and the Incredible Hulk
Marvel, 1981
1 .... 10.00

Spider-Man & the New Mutants
Marvel
1 .... 3.00

Spider-Man & Wolverine
Marvel, 2003
1-4 .... 3.00

Spider-Man and X-Factor: Shadowgames
Marvel, 1994
1-3 .... 2.00

Spider-Man/Badrock
Maximum, 1997
1/A-1/B 3.00

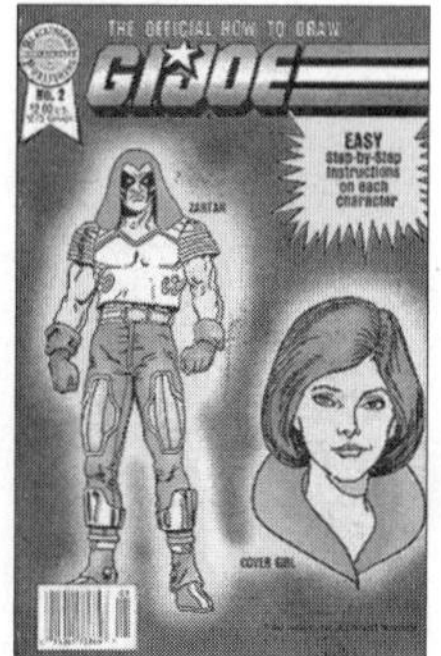

Official How to Draw G.I. Joe

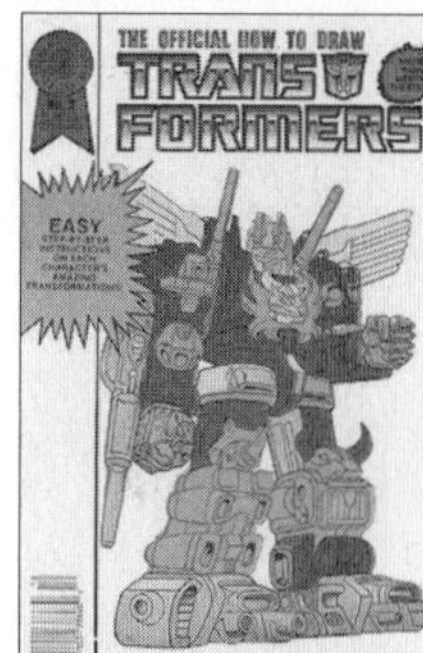

Official How to Draw Transformers

Official Johnny Hazard

Official Jungle Jim

Official Justice League of America Index

Official Marvel Index to Marvel Team-Up

Official Prince Valiant Monthly

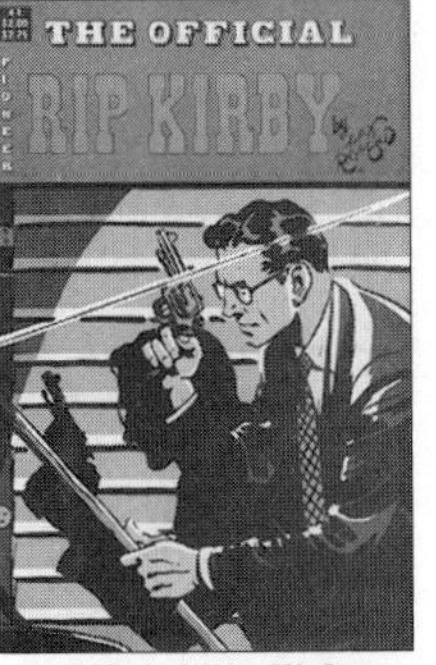

Official Rip Kirby

Spider-Man Battlebook
Marvel, 1998

1 ....4.00

Spider-Man/Black Cat: The Evil That Men Do
Marvel, 2002

1 ....5.00
2-6 ....3.00

Spider-Man: Blue
Marvel, 2002

1 ....6.00
2 ....5.00
3-6 ....4.00

Spider-Man: Breakout
Marvel, 2005

1-5 ....3.00

Spider-Man: Carnage
Marvel

1 ....9.00

Spider-Man: Chapter One
Marvel, 1998

0-1 ....3.00
1/A 4.00
1/B-1/C 14.00
2/A-2/B 3.00
2/C 4.00
3-12 ....3.00
Deluxe 1-Deluxe 1/Ltd. 30.00

Spider-Man: Christmas in Dallas
Marvel, 1983

1 ....10.00

Spider-Man Classics
Marvel, 1993

1-12 ....2.00
13-15 ....1.00
15/CS 3.00
16 ....1.00

Spider-Man Collectors' Preview
Marvel, 1994

1 ....2.00

Spider-Man Comics Magazine
Marvel, 1987

1-13 ....2.00

Spider-Man/Daredevil
Marvel, 2002

1 ....3.00

Spider-Man: Dead Man's Hand
Marvel, 1997

1 ....3.00

Spider-Man: Death and Destiny
Marvel, 2000

1-3 ....3.00

Spider-Man/Doctor Octopus: Out of Reach
Marvel, 2004

1 ....4.00
2-5 ....3.00

Spider-Man/Doctor Octopus: Year One
Marvel, 2004

1-5 ....3.00

Spider-Man/Dr. Strange: The Way to Dusty Death
Marvel, 1992

1 ....7.00

Spider-Man Family
Marvel, 2005

1 ....5.00

Spider-Man Family: Amazing Friends
Marvel, 2006

1 ....5.00

Spider-Man Family Featuring Spider-Clan
Marvel, 2007

1 ....5.00

Spider-Man: Fear Itself
Marvel, 1992

1 ....13.00

Spider-Man, Fire-Star and Iceman
Marvel, 1983

1 ....10.00

Spider-Man: Friends & Enemies
Marvel, 1995

1-4 ....2.00

Spider-Man: Funeral for an Octopus
Marvel, 1995

1-4 ....2.00

Spider-Man/Gen13
Marvel, 1996

1 ....5.00

Spider-Man: Get Kraven
Marvel, 2002

1-6 ....2.00

Spider-Man: Hobgoblin Lives
Marvel, 1997

1-3 ....3.00

Spider-Man: House of M
Marvel, 2005
1 .... 6.00
1/Conv 15.00
2 .... 5.00
2/Variant 4.00
☛2nd print
3-5 .... 3.00

Spider-Man/Human Torch
Marvel, 2005
1-5 .... 3.00

Spider-Man: India
Marvel, 2004
1-4 .... 3.00

Spider-Man: Legacy of Evil
Marvel, 1996
1 .... 4.00

Spider-Man Legends
Marvel, 2003
2 .... 20.00
3 .... 25.00
4 .... 14.00

Spider-Man: Lifeline
Marvel, 2001
1-3 .... 3.00

Spider-Man Loves Mary Jane
Marvel, 2006
1-13 .... 3.00

Spider-Man: Made Men
Marvel, 1999
1 .... 6.00

Spider-Man Magazine
Marvel, 1994
1-10 .... 2.00

Spider-Man Magazine
Marvel, 1995
1 .... 3.00

Spider-Man: Maximum Clonage Alpha
Marvel, 1995
1 .... 10.00

Spider-Man: Maximum Clonage Omega
Marvel, 1995
1 .... 10.00

Spider-Man Megazine
Marvel, 1994
1-6 .... 3.00

Spider-Man 2 Movie Adaptation
Marvel, 2004
1 .... 4.00

Spider-Man Mysteries
Marvel, 1998
1 .... 1.00

Spider-Man: Power of Terror
Marvel, 1995
1-4 .... 2.00

Spider-Man, Power Pack
Marvel, 1984
1 .... 1.00

Spider-Man/Punisher: Family Plot
Marvel, 1996
1-2 .... 3.00

Spider-Man, Punisher, Sabretooth: Designer Genes
Marvel, 1993
1 .... 9.00

Spider-Man: Quality of Life
Marvel, 2002
1-4 .... 3.00

Spider-Man: Redemption
Marvel, 1996
1-4 .... 2.00

Spider-Man: Reign
Marvel, 2006
2 .... 18.00

Spider-Man: Revenge of the Green Goblin
Marvel, 2000
1-3 .... 3.00

Spider-Man Saga
Marvel, 1991
1-4 .... 3.00

Spider-Man: Son of the Goblin
Marvel, 2004
1 .... 16.00

Spider-Man Special Edition
Marvel, 1992
1 .... 7.00

Spider-Man, Storm and Power Man
Marvel, 1982
1 .... 2.00

Spider-Man Super Special
Marvel, 1995
1 .... 4.00

Spider-Man: Sweet Charity
Marvel, 2002
1 .... 5.00

Offworld

Of Mind and Soul

Of Myths and Men

O.G. Whiz

Oh My Goth

Okay Comics

Oktane

Oldblood

Spider-Man Team-Up
Marvel, 1995

1-7 .... 3.00

Spider-Man Team-Up Special
Marvel, 2005

0 .... 3.00

Spider-Man: The Arachnis Project
Marvel, 1994

1-6 .... 2.00

Spider-Man: The Clone Journal
Marvel, 1995

1 .... 3.00

Spider-Man: The Death of Captain Stacy
Marvel, 2000

1 .... 4.00

Spider-Man: The Final Adventure
Marvel, 1995

1-4 .... 3.00

Spider-Man: The Jackal Files
Marvel, 1995

1 .... 2.00

Spider-Man: The Lost Years
Marvel, 1995

0 .... 4.00
1-3 .... 3.00

Spider-Man: The Manga
Marvel, 1997

1 .... 4.00
2-31 .... 3.00

Spider-Man: The Mutant Agenda
Marvel, 1994

0 .... 1.00
1-3 .... 2.00

Spider-Man: The Official Movie Adaptation
Marvel, 2002

1 .... 6.00

Spider-Man: The Other Sketchbook
Marvel, 2005

1 .... 3.00

Spider-Man: The Parker Years
Marvel, 1995

1 .... 3.00

Spider-Man 2099
Marvel, 1992

1 .... 3.00
2-18 .... 1.00
19-25 .... 2.00
25/Variant 3.00
26-46 .... 2.00
Ann 1 .... 3.00
Special 1 .... 4.00

Spider-Man 2099 Meets Spider-Man
Marvel, 1995

1 .... 6.00

Spider-Man Universe
Marvel, 2000

1-5 .... 5.00
6-7 .... 4.00

Spider-Man Unlimited
Marvel, 1993

1-12 .... 4.00
13-22 .... 3.00

Spider-Man Unlimited
Marvel, 1999

1 .... 3.00

Spider-Man Unlimited
Marvel, 2004

1-15 .... 3.00

Spider-Man Unmasked
Marvel, 1996

1 .... 6.00

Spider-Man: Venom Agenda
Marvel, 1998

1 .... 3.00

Spider-Man vs. Dracula
Marvel, 1994

1 .... 2.00

Spider-Man vs. Punisher
Marvel, 2000

1 .... 3.00

Spider-Man vs. the Hulk
Marvel, 1979

1 .... 7.00

Spider-Man vs. Wolverine
Marvel, 1987

1 .... 6.00
1/2nd 5.00

Spider-Man: Web of Doom
Marvel, 1994

1-3 .... 2.00

Spider: Reign of the Vampire King
Eclipse, 1992

1-3 .... 5.00

Spider Sneak Preview

Argosy, 2001

1 .... 5.00

Spider's Web

Blazing

1 .... 2.00

Spider-Woman

Marvel, 1978

1 .... 6.00
2-3 .... 3.00
4-36 .... 2.00
☛1st Siryn
37-38 .... 4.00
☛X-Men app.
39-49 .... 1.00
50 .... 4.00

Spider-Woman

Marvel, 1993

1-4 .... 2.00

Spider-Woman

Marvel, 1999

1-2 .... 3.00
3-18 .... 2.00

Spider-Woman: Origin

Marvel, 2006

1-5 .... 3.00

Spidery-Mon: Maximum Carcass

Parody

1/A-1/C 3.00

Spidey and the Mini-Marvels

Marvel, 2003

1 .... 4.00

Spidey Super Stories

Marvel, 1974

1 .... 20.00
☛Spider-Man origin
2 .... 6.00
3-57 .... 5.00

Spike and Tyke (M.G.M.'s...)

Dell, 1955

4 .... 14.00
5 .... 12.00
6-10 .... 10.00
11-24 .... 8.00

Spike: Asylum

Idea & Design Works, 2006

1-4 .... 4.00

Spike: Lost and Found

Idea & Design Works, 2006

1 .... 7.00

Spike: Old Times

Idea & Design Works, 2005

0 .... 7.00

Spike: Old Wounds

Idea & Design Works, 2006

1 .... 7.00

Spike vs. Dracula

Idea & Design Works, 2006

1-5 .... 4.00

Spin and Marty

Dell, 1958

5 .... 60.00
6-9 .... 45.00

Spineless-Man $2099

Parody

1 .... 3.00

Spine-Tingling Tales (Dr. Spektor Presents...)

Gold Key, 1975

1 .... 20.00
2-4 .... 8.00

Spinworld

Slave Labor, 1997

1-4 .... 3.00

Spiral Path

Eclipse, 1986

1-2 .... 2.00

Spiral Zone

DC, 1988

1-4 .... 1.00

Spirit

Newspaper, 1940

1 .... 700.00
2 .... 325.00
3 .... 175.00
4-5 .... 125.00
6-10 .... 100.00
11-20 .... 75.00
21-52 .... 55.00
53-83 .... 45.00
84-135 .... 35.00
136-187 .... 28.00
188-240 .... 20.00
241-290 .... 16.00
291-396 .... 35.00
397-585 .... 30.00
586-634 .... 15.00
635-641 .... 125.00
642 .... 75.00
643-644 .... 125.00
645 .... 75.00

Spirit

Quality, 1944

1 .... 600.00
2 .... 350.00
3 .... 250.00
4-5 .... 185.00
6-10 .... 150.00
11 .... 125.00
12-17 .... 200.00
18-21 .... 250.00
22 .... 350.00

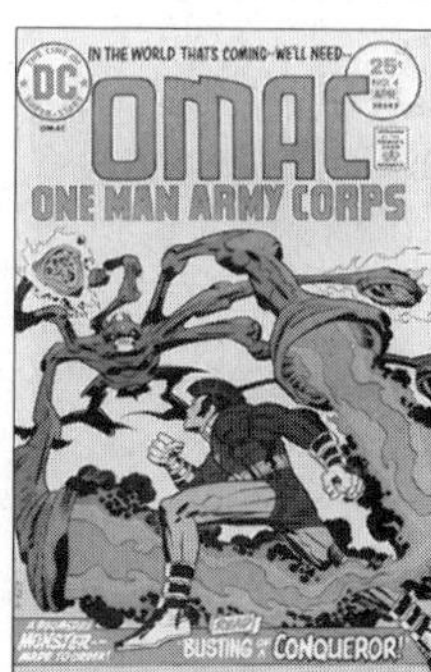

OMAC

Omega Force II

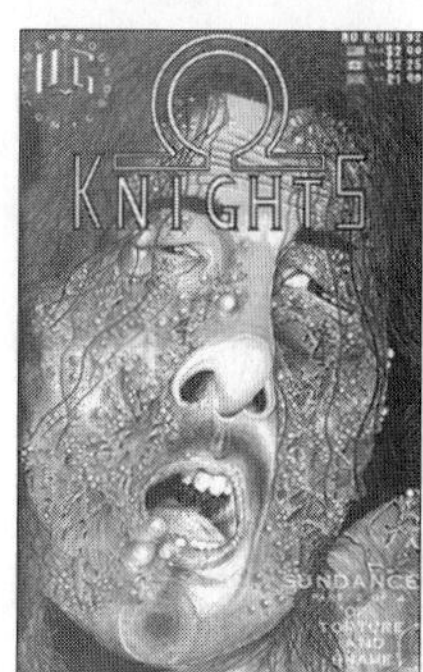

Omega Knights

Omega the Unknown

Omni Comix

On a Pale Horse

One-Fisted Tales

One Mile Up

Spirit
Fiction House, 1952

1 ......250.00
2 ......225.00
3-4 ......175.00
5 ......200.00

Spirit
Super

11-12 ......15.00

Spirit
Harvey, 1966

1 ......50.00
2 ......42.00

Spirit
Kitchen Sink, 1973

1-2 ......14.00

Spirit
Ken Pierce

1-4 ......18.00

Spirit (Magazine)
Warren, 1974

1 ......22.00
2 ......10.00
3 ......7.00
4-12 ......6.00
13-15 ......5.00
16 ......7.00
17-41 ......4.00
Special 1 ......35.00
☛Mail-in only

Spirit
Kitchen Sink, 1983

1 ......5.00
2-9 ......4.00
10-11 ......3.00
12-87 ......2.00

Spirit
DC, 2007

1-30 ......3.00

Spirit Casebook
Kitchen Sink

1 ......13.00

Spirit Collector's Edition Reprints
Will Eisner, 1972

1-40 ......2.00
Deluxe 1-4 ......20.00

Spirit Jam
Kitchen Sink, 1998

1 ......6.00

Spirit of the Tao
Image, 1998

1-13 ......3.00
Ashcan 1 ......5.00

Spirit of the Wind
Chocolate Mouse

1 ......2.00

Spirit of Wonder
Dark Horse, 1996

1-5 ......3.00

Spirits
Mind Walker, 1995

3 ......3.00

Spirits of Venom
Marvel, 1993

1 ......10.00

Spirit: The New Adventures
Kitchen Sink, 1998

1-8 ......4.00

Spirit: The Origin Years
Kitchen Sink, 1992

1-10 ......3.00

Spirit World
DC, 1971

1 ......35.00

Spirou & Fantasio: Z Is for Zorglub
Fantasy Flight

1 ......9.00

Spitfire and the Troubleshooters
Marvel, 1986

1-9 ......1.00

Spitfire Comics
Harvey, 1941

1-2 ......150.00

Spittin' Image
Eclipse

1 ......3.00

Spit Wad Comics
Spit Wad, 1983

1 ......3.00

Splat!
Mad Dog, 1987

1-3 ......2.00

Splatter
Arpad

1 ......3.00

Splatter
Northstar, 1991

1 ......5.00
2-8 ......3.00
Ann 1 ......5.00

Splitting Image
Image, 1993

1-2 ......2.00

Spoof
Marvel, 1970
1 .... 15.00
2 .... 7.00
3 .... 8.00
4-5 .... 7.00

Spoof Comics
Spoof, 1992
0-12 .... 3.00

Spook (1st Series)
Star, 1946
1 .... 200.00

Spook (2nd Series)
Star, 1953
22 .... 225.00
23 .... 150.00
24 .... 160.00
25-30 .... 150.00

Spook City
Mythic, 1997
1 .... 3.00

Spookgirl
Slave Labor, 2000
1 .... 3.00

Spooky
Harvey, 1955
1 .... 200.00
2 .... 110.00
3 .... 65.00
4-5 .... 50.00
6-10 .... 35.00
11-20 .... 24.00
21-29 .... 20.00
30-39 .... 18.00
40-50 .... 15.00
51-70 .... 12.00
71-90 .... 8.00
91-110 .... 6.00
111-130 .... 5.00
131-161 .... 4.00

Spooky
Harvey, 1991
1-4 .... 1.00

Spooky Digest
Harvey, 1992
1-2 .... 2.00

Spooky Haunted House
Harvey, 1972
1 .... 15.00
2-11 .... 10.00

Spooky Mysteries
Your Guide, 1947
1 .... 58.00

Spooky Spooktown
Harvey, 1961
1 .... 85.00
2 .... 45.00
3-5 .... 30.00
6-10 .... 22.00
11-20 .... 15.00
21-29 .... 8.00
30-40 .... 5.00
41-66 .... 3.00

Spooky the Dog Catcher
Paw Prints, 1994
1-3 .... 3.00

Sport Comics
Street & Smith, 1940
1 .... 350.00
2 .... 175.00
3-4 .... 150.00

Sports Action
Atlas, 1950
2 .... 250.00
3 .... 130.00
4-11 .... 115.00
12-13 .... 125.00
14 .... 115.00

Sports Classics
Personality
1 .... 3.00
1/Ltd. 6.00
2-5 .... 3.00

Sports Comics
Personality
1-4 .... 3.00

Sports Hall of Shame in 3-D
Blackthorne
1 .... 3.00

Sports Legends
Revolutionary, 1992
1-9 .... 3.00

Sports Legends Special - Breaking the Color Barrier
Revolutionary, 1993
1 .... 3.00

Sports Personalities
Personality, 1991
1-13 .... 3.00

Sport Stars
Parents' Magazine Institute, 1946
1 .... 225.00
2 .... 145.00
3-4 .... 125.00

Sport Stars
Atlas, 1949
1 .... 250.00

Sports Superstars
Revolutionary, 1992
1-Ann 1 .... 3.00

Spotlight
Marvel, 1978
1 .... 8.00
2-4 .... 6.00

One Million Years Ago

One-Pound Gospel Round 2

Oni

Onigami

Oni Press Summer Vacation Supercolor Fun Special

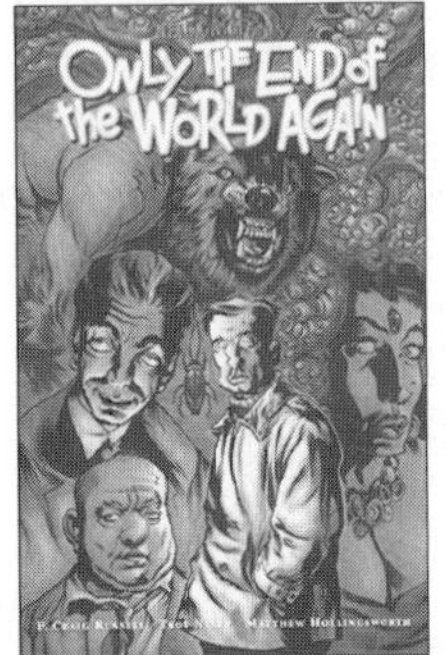

Only the End of the World Again

On the Bus

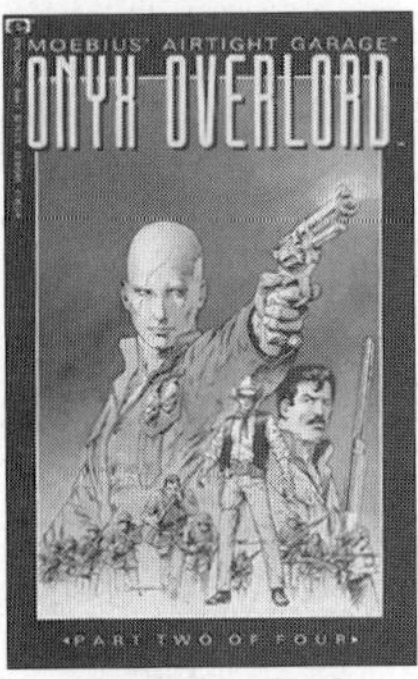

Onyx Overlord

Spotlight Comics
Harry A. Chesler, 1944
1 .... 400.00
2 .... 330.00
3 .... 340.00

Spotlight on the Genius That Is Joe Sacco
Fantagraphics
1 .... 5.00

Spotty the Pup
Avon, 1953
1-3 .... 25.00

Spring Break Comics
AC, 1987
1 .... 2.00

Spring-Heel Jack
Rebel
1-2 .... 2.00

Springtime Tales (Walt Kelly's...)
Eclipse, 1988
1 .... 3.00

Spud
Spud, 1996
1 .... 4.00

Spunky
Standard, 1949
1 .... 75.00
2 .... 50.00
3-7 .... 30.00

Spunky Knight
Fantagraphics, 1996
1-3 .... 3.00

Spunky Knight Extreme
Fantagraphics, 2004
1-4 .... 4.00

Spunky Knight XXX
Fantagraphics, 2005
1-4 .... 4.00

Spunky the Smiling Spook
Ajax, 1957
1 .... 50.00
2-4 .... 30.00

Spunky Todd: The Psychic Boy
Caliber
1 .... 3.00

Spy and Counterspy
ACG, 1949
1 .... 150.00
2 .... 100.00

SpyBoy
Dark Horse, 1999
1-17 .... 3.00
Special 1 .... 5.00

Spyboy 13: Manga Affair
Dark Horse, 2003
1-3 .... 3.00

Spyboy: Final Exam
Dark Horse, 2004
1-4 .... 3.00

Spyboy/Young Justice
Dark Horse, 2002
1-3 .... 3.00

Spy Cases
Atlas, 1950
26 .... 160.00
27-28 .... 105.00
4-7 .... 90.00
8 .... 100.00
9-10 .... 90.00
11-19 .... 75.00

Spy Fighters
Atlas, 1951
1 .... 130.00
2 .... 75.00
3-13 .... 60.00
14-15 .... 65.00

Spy Hunters
ACG, 1949
3 .... 125.00
4-10 .... 75.00
11-15 .... 55.00
16 .... 85.00
17-24 .... 55.00

Spyke
Marvel, 1993
1 .... 3.00
2-4 .... 2.00

Spyman
Harvey, 1966
1 .... 30.00
2-3 .... 24.00

Spy Smasher
Fawcett, 1941
1 .... 2,500.00
2 .... 750.00
3-7 .... 450.00
8-9 .... 350.00
10 .... 375.00
11 .... 350.00

Spy Thrillers
Atlas, 1954
1 .... 125.00
2 .... 85.00
3-4 .... 70.00

Squadron Supreme
Marvel, 1985
1 .... 2.00
2-12 .... 1.00

Squadron Supreme
Marvel, 2006
1-6 .... 3.00

Squadron Supreme: New World Order
Marvel, 1998
1 .... 6.00

Squalor
First, 1989
1-4 .... 3.00

Squee!
Slave Labor, 1997
1 .... 7.00
1/2nd 3.00
2 .... 5.00
3-4 .... 4.00

Squeeks
Lev Gleason, 1953
1 .... 45.00
2 .... 25.00
3-5 .... 15.00

Sri Krishna
Chakra
1 .... 4.00

Stacia Stories
Kitchen Sink, 1995
1 .... 3.00

Stagger Lee
Image, 2006
1 .... 18.00

Stain
Fathom, 1988
1 .... 3.00

Stainless Steel Armadillo
Antarctic, 1995
1-5 .... 3.00

Stainless Steel Rat
Eagle, 1985
1-6 .... 3.00

Stalker
DC, 1975
1 .... 7.00
2-4 .... 4.00

Stalkers
Marvel, 1990
1-12 .... 2.00

Stalking Ralph
Aeon, 1995
1 .... 5.00

Stamps Comics
Youthful, 1951
1 .... 225.00
2 .... 125.00
3-6 .... 100.00
7 .... 125.00

Stand Up Comix (Bob Rumba's...)
Grey
1 .... 3.00

Stan Lee Meets Dr. Doom
Marvel, 2007
1 .... 4.00

Stan Lee Meets Dr. Strange
Marvel, 2006
1 .... 4.00

Stan Lee Meets Silver Surfer
Marvel, 2007
1 .... 4.00

Stan Lee Meets Spider-Man
Marvel, 2006
1 .... 4.00

Stan Lee Meets Thing
Marvel, 2007
1 .... 4.00

Stanley & His Monster
DC, 1968
109 .... 20.00
110-112 .... 15.00

Stanley and His Monster
DC, 1993
1 .... 3.00
2-4 .... 2.00

Stanley the Snake with the Overactive Imagination
Emerald
1-2 .... 2.00

Star
Image, 1995
1-4 .... 3.00

Starbikers
Renegade
1 .... 2.00

Starblast
Marvel, 1994
1-4 .... 2.00

Star Blazers
Comico, 1987
1-4 .... 2.00

Star Blazers
Comico, 1989
1-2 .... 2.00
3-5 .... 3.00

Star Blazers: The Magazine of Space Battleship Yamato
Argo, 1995
0-1 .... 3.00

Open Season

Open Sore Funnies

Open Space

Operation Peril

Optimism of Youth

Oracle - A Trespassers Mystery

Orb Magazine

Oriental Heroes

Star Blecch: Deep Space Diner
Parody
1/A-1/B 3.00

Star Blecch: Generation Gap
Parody, 1995
1 ....4.00

Star Brand
Marvel, 1986
1-Ann 1 ....1.00

Starchild
Taliesen, 1993
0-1 ....4.00
1/2nd 3.00
2 ....4.00
2/2nd-14 ....3.00

Starchild: Crossroads
Coppervale, 1995
1-3 ....3.00

Starchild: Mythopolis
Image, 1997
0-6 ....3.00

Starchy
Excel
1 ....2.00

Star Comics Magazine
Marvel, 1986
1 ....3.00
2-13 ....2.00

S.T.A.R. Corps
DC, 1993
1-6 ....2.00

Star Crossed
DC, 1997
1-3 ....3.00

Stardust (Neil Gaiman and Charles Vess'...)
DC, 1998
1 ....7.00
2-4 ....6.00

Stardusters
Nightwynd, 1991
1-4 ....3.00

Stardust Kid
Image, 2005
1-3 ....4.00

Starfire
DC, 1976
1 ....7.00
2-8 ....3.00

Star Forces
The Other Faculty
1 ....3.00

Starforce Six Special
AC, 1984
1 ....2.00

Stargate
Express, 1996
1 ....3.00
1/Variant 4.00
2 ....3.00
2/Variant 4.00
3 ....3.00
3/Variant 4.00
4 ....3.00
4/Variant 4.00

Stargate Doomsday World
Entity, 1996
1-3 ....3.00

Stargate SG1: Aris Boch
Avatar, 2004
1 ....4.00
1/Platinum 10.00

Stargate SG1 Con Special 2003
Avatar, 2003
1 ....4.00

Stargate SG1 Con Special 2004
Avatar, 2004
1 ....3.00
1/A 4.00

Stargate SG-1: Daniel's Song
Avatar, 2005
1 ....3.00
1/Photo 4.00
1/Wraparound 3.00
1/Glow 20.00
1/Gold Foil 6.00
1/PlatFoil 10.00
1/Adversary 6.00

Stargate SG1: Fall of Rome
Avatar
0/Preview 6.00
1-1/Foil 4.00
1/Platinum 10.00
2 ....4.00
2/Painted 6.00
2/Photo 4.00
2/Platinum 10.00
3 ....4.00
3/Painted 6.00
3/Platinum 10.00
3/Photo 4.00

Stargate SG1: P.O.W.
Avatar, 2004
1-3 ....4.00

Stargate: The New Adventures Collection
Entity, 1997

1 .... 6.00

Stargate Underworld
Entity, 1997

1 .... 3.00

Stargods
Antarctic, 1998

1 .... 3.00
1/CS 6.00
2 .... 3.00
2/CS 6.00

Stargods: Visions
Antarctic, 1998

1 .... 3.00

Star Hawks
Avalon, 1986

1-2 .... 3.00
3-8 .... 3.00

Starhead Presents
Starhead, 1987

1-3 .... 1.00

Star Hunters
DC, 1977

1-7 .... 1.00

Star Jacks
Antarctic, 1994

1 .... 3.00

Star Jam Comics
Revolutionary, 1992

1-10 .... 3.00

Starjammers
Marvel, 1995

1-4 .... 3.00

Starjammers
Marvel, 2004

1-6 .... 3.00

Stark: Future
Aircel, 1986

1-17 .... 2.00

Starkid
Dark Horse, 1998

1 .... 3.00

Stark Raven
Endless Horizons, 2000

1 .... 3.00

Starkweather
Arcana, 2004

1 .... 4.00
1/Ltd. 5.00
2-5 .... 4.00

Starlet O'Hara in Hollywood
Standard, 1948

1 .... 145.00
2 .... 85.00
3-4 .... 70.00

Starlight
Eternity, 1987

1 .... 2.00

Starlight Agency
Antarctic, 1991

1-3 .... 3.00

Starlion: A Pawn's Game
Storm, 1993

1 .... 2.00

Starlord
Marvel, 1996

1-3 .... 3.00

Starlord Megazine
Marvel, 1996

1 .... 3.00

Star-Lord Special Edition
Marvel, 1982

1 .... 2.00

Starlove
Forbidden Fruit

1 .... 3.00
2 .... 4.00

Starman (1st Series)
DC, 1988

1-10 .... 2.00
11-25 .... 1.00
26 .... 2.00
27-45 .... 1.00

Starman (2nd Series)
DC, 1994

0-1 .... 5.00
2-3 .... 4.00
4-40 .... 3.00
41-46 .... 2.00
47-49 .... 3.00
50 .... 4.00
51-80 .... 3.00
1000000 .... 4.00
Ann 1 .... 5.00
Ann 2 .... 4.00
GS 1 .... 5.00

Starman: Secret Files
DC, 1998

1 .... 5.00

Starman: The Mist
DC, 1998

1 .... 2.00

Original Sins

Osborn Journals

Oscar Comics

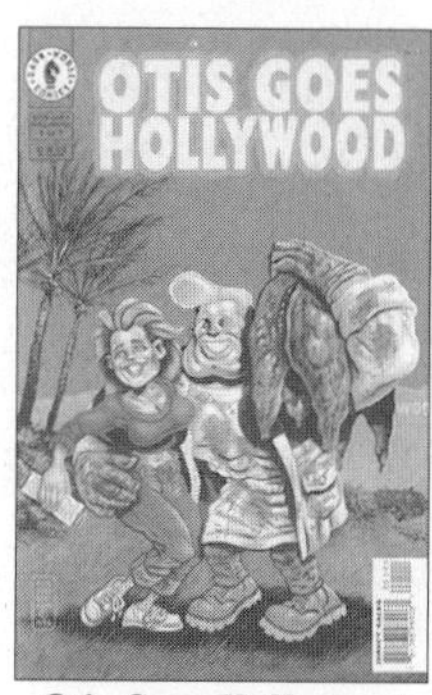

Otis Goes Hollywood

Our Army at War

Our Fighting Forces

Our Love Story

Outbreed 999

Star Masters

Marvel, 1995

1-3 .... 2.00

Starmasters

AC, 1989

1 .... 2.00

Star Ranger

Centaur, 1937

1 .... 1,150.00
2 .... 525.00
3-6 .... 450.00
7-10 .... 360.00
11-12 .... 325.00

Star Ranger Funnies

Centaur, 1939

15 .... 625.00
1 .... 450.00
2-5 .... 375.00

Star Rangers

Adventure, 1987

1-3 .... 2.00

Star*Reach

Star*Reach, 1974

1-18 .... 2.00

Star*Reach Classics

Eclipse, 1984

1-6 .... 2.00

Starriors

Marvel, 1984

1-4 .... 1.00

Star Rovers

Comax

1 .... 3.00

Stars and S.T.R.I.P.E.

DC, 1999

0-14 .... 3.00

Stars and Stripes Comics

Centaur, 1941

2 .... 2,100.00
3 .... 1,100.00
4 .... 1,000.00
5-6 .... 675.00

Star Seed

Broadway, 1996

7-9 .... 3.00

Starship Troopers

Dark Horse, 1997

1-2 .... 3.00

Starship Troopers: Brute Creations

Dark Horse, 1997

1 .... 3.00

Starship Troopers: Dominant Species

Dark Horse, 1998

1-4 .... 3.00

Starship Troopers: Insect Touch

Dark Horse, 1997

1-3 .... 3.00

Star Slammers

Malibu, 1994

1-4 .... 3.00

Star Slammers Special

Dark Horse, 1996

1 .... 3.00

Starslayer

Pacific, 1982

1 .... 2.00
2 .... 4.00
3 .... 2.00
4 .... 1.00
5 .... 2.00
6-9 .... 1.00
10 .... 2.00
11-34 .... 1.00

Starslayer: The Director's Cut

Acclaim, 1995

1-8 .... 3.00

Star Spangled Comics

DC, 1941

1 .... 4,500.00
2 .... 1,800.00
3 .... 1,000.00
4-5 .... 875.00
6 .... 800.00
7 .... 8,000.00
☛1st Newsboy Legion
8-10 .... 1,600.00
11-16 .... 1,175.00
17 .... 1,500.00
18-19 .... 1,000.00
20-30 .... 850.00
31-40 .... 525.00
41-50 .... 425.00
51-60 .... 400.00
61-64 .... 375.00
65 .... 1,050.00
☛Robin stories start
66-68 .... 690.00
69 .... 800.00
☛1st Tomahawk
70 .... 690.00
71-80 .... 575.00
81-83 .... 450.00
84 .... 625.00
85-86 .... 450.00
87 .... 625.00
88-94 .... 500.00
95-99 .... 265.00

100 .... 300.00
101-110 .... 225.00
111-112 .... 200.00
113 .... 375.00
114 .... 325.00
115-131 .... 200.00

Star Spangled Comics

DC, 1999

1 .... 2.00

Star Spangled War Stories

DC, 1952

132 (1) 750.00
133 (2) 550.00
3 .... 475.00
4-6 .... 285.00
7-10 .... 220.00
11-20 .... 185.00
21-30 .... 130.00
31-40 .... 90.00
41-50 .... 70.00
51-70 .... 60.00
71-83 .... 55.00
84 .... 125.00
☛1st Mlle. Marie
85-87 .... 80.00
88-89 .... 65.00
90 .... 325.00
☛1st Dinosaur Island
91 .... 45.00
92 .... 110.00
93 .... 45.00
94-99 .... 110.00
100 .... 145.00
☛1st Sgt. Gorilla
101-133 .... 60.00
134 .... 65.00
135-138 .... 60.00
139 .... 50.00
140-143 .... 24.00
144 .... 27.00
145 .... 35.00
146-150 .... 20.00
151 .... 125.00
☛1st Unknown Soldier
152-153 .... 20.00
154 .... 55.00
☛Unknown Soldier origin
155 .... 16.00
156-161 .... 14.00
162-180 .... 6.00
181-204 .... 5.00

Starstone

Aircel

1-3 .... 2.00

Starstream

Gold Key, 1976

1-4 .... 3.00

Starstruck

Marvel, 1985

1 .... 3.00
2-6 .... 2.00

Starstruck

Dark Horse, 1990

1-4 .... 3.00

Star Studded

Superior, 1945

1 .... 200.00

Startling Comics

Avalon

1 .... 3.00

Startling Comics

Better, 1940

1 .... 1,800.00
2 .... 1,000.00
3 .... 800.00
4 .... 575.00
5-9 .... 450.00
10 .... 3,200.00
11 .... 900.00
12 .... 750.00
13-29 .... 450.00
30-40 .... 400.00
41-43 .... 350.00
44-45 .... 500.00
46-53 .... 400.00

Startling Crime Illustrated

Caliber, 1991

1 .... 3.00

Startling Stories: Banner

Marvel, 2001

1-4 .... 3.00

Startling Stories: The Thing

Marvel, 2003

1 .... 4.00

Startling Stories: The Thing – Night Falls on Yancy Street

Marvel, 2003

1-4 .... 4.00

Startling Terror Tales

Star, 1952

10 .... 480.00
11 .... 750.00
12 .... 155.00
13 .... 170.00
14 .... 155.00

Startling Terror Tales

Star, 1953

4-9 .... 160.00
10 .... 210.00
11 .... 160.00

Star Trek

Gold Key, 1967

1 .... 350.00
2 .... 125.00
3 .... 100.00
4 .... 90.00

Outcasts

Outlaw 7

Outlaw Overdrive

Outlaws of the West

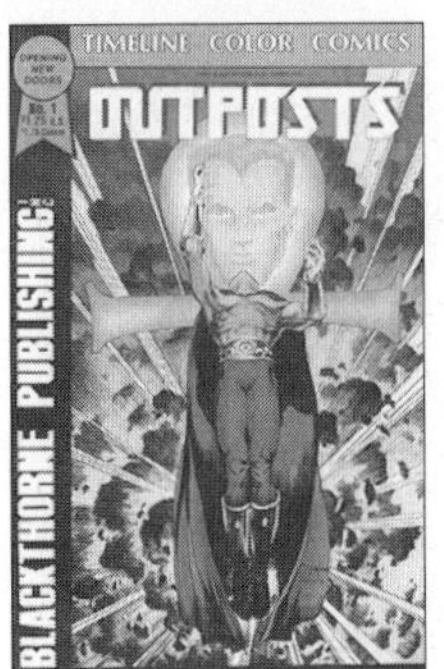

Outposts

Out There

Over the Edge

Oz

5-6 .... 75.00
7 .... 60.00
8-9 .... 50.00
10 .... 40.00
11-19 .... 30.00
20-20/Whitman 45.00
21-22 .... 30.00
23-23/Whitman 45.00
24-25/Whitman 35.00
26 .... 25.00
26/Whitman 35.00
27-27/Whitman 30.00
28 .... 20.00
29-29/Whitman 30.00
30-31 .... 20.00
31/Whitman-36/Whitman 30.00
37-38 .... 20.00
38/Whitman-40/Whitman 30.00
41-41/Whitman 25.00
42-43 .... 15.00
44-48/Whitman 25.00
49-50 .... 15.00
51-51/Whitman 25.00
52 .... 15.00
52/Whitman-55/Whitman 25.00
56 .... 15.00
56/Whitman-59/Whitman 25.00
60-60/Whitman 20.00
61 .... 12.00

Star Trek
Marvel, 1980

1 .... 5.00
2 .... 3.00
3-18 .... 2.00

Star Trek
DC, 1984

1 .... 4.00
2-10 .... 3.00
11-56 .... 2.00
Ann 1-3 .... 3.00

Star Trek
DC, 1989

1 .... 5.00
2 .... 4.00
3-10 .... 3.00
11-23 .... 2.00
24 .... 3.00
25-49 .... 2.00
50 .... 4.00
51-70 .... 2.00
71-74 .... 3.00
75 .... 4.00
76-80 .... 3.00
Ann 1 .... 4.00
Ann 2 .... 3.00
Ann 3-3 .... 4.00

Star Trek: Deep Space Nine
Malibu, 1993

0-1/B 3.00
1/C 4.00
2-24 .... 3.00
25 .... 4.00
26-30 .... 3.00
31-Ann 1 .... 4.00
Ashcan 1 .... 5.00
Special 1 .... 4.00

Star Trek: Deep Space Nine
Marvel, 1996

1-15 .... 2.00

Star Trek: Deep Space Nine, the Celebrity Series: Blood and Honor
Malibu, 1995

1 .... 3.00

Star Trek: Deep Space Nine Hearts and Minds
Malibu, 1994

1-4 .... 3.00

Star Trek: Deep Space Nine: Lightstorm
Malibu, 1994

1 .... 4.00

Star Trek: Deep Space Nine: N-Vector
DC, 2000

1-4 .... 3.00

Star Trek: Deep Space Nine: Rules of Diplomacy
Malibu, 1995

1 .... 3.00

Star Trek: Deep Space Nine/Star Trek: The Next Generation
Malibu, 1994

1-2 .... 3.00
Ashcan 1 .... 1.00

Star Trek: Deep Space Nine: Terok Nor
Malibu, 1995

0 .... 3.00

Star Trek: Deep Space Nine Maquis
Malibu, 1995

1-3 .... 3.00

Star Trek: Deep Space Nine, Ultimate Annual
Malibu, 1995

1 .... 6.00

Star Trek: Deep Space Nine, Worf Special
Malibu, 1995

0 .... 4.00

Star Trek: Divided We Fall
DC, 2001

1-4 .... 3.00

Star Trek: Early Voyages
Marvel, 1997

1 .... 3.00
2-17 .... 2.00

Star Trek: Enter the Wolves
WildStorm, 2001

1 .... 6.00

Star Trek: First Contact
Marvel, 1996

1 .... 6.00

Star Trek Generations
DC, 1994

1 .... 4.00
1/Prestige 6.00

Star Trekker
Antarctic, 1991

1 .... 3.00

Star Trek: Mirror Mirror
Marvel, 1997

1 .... 4.00

Star Trek Movie Special
DC, 1984

3-5 .... 2.00

Star Trek: New Frontier: Double Time
DC, 2000

1 .... 6.00

Star Trek: Operation Assimilation
Marvel, 1997

1 .... 3.00

Star Trek VI: The Undiscovered Country
DC, 1992

1 .... 3.00
1/Direct 6.00

Star Trek Special
WildStorm, 2001

1 .... 7.00

Star Trek: Starfleet Academy
Marvel, 1996

1-19 .... 2.00

Star Trek: Telepathy War
Marvel, 1997

1 .... 3.00

Star Trek: The Modala Imperative
DC, 1991

1 .... 3.00
2-4 .... 2.00

Star Trek: The Next Generation
DC, 1988

1 .... 3.00
2-6 .... 2.00

Star Trek: The Next Generation
DC, 1989

1 .... 5.00
2 .... 4.00
3-20 .... 3.00
21-49 .... 2.00
50 .... 4.00
51-71 .... 2.00
72-74 .... 3.00
75 .... 4.00
76-80 .... 3.00
Ann 1-6 .... 4.00
Special 1-3 .... 5.00

Star Trek: The Next Generation/Deep Space Nine
DC, 1994

1-2 .... 3.00
Ashcan 1 .... 1.00

Star Trek: The Next Generation: Ill Wind
DC, 1995

1-4 .... 3.00

Star Trek: The Next Generation: Perchance to Dream
DC, 2000

1-4 .... 3.00

Star Trek: The Next Generation: Riker
Marvel, 1998

1 .... 4.00

Star Trek:The Next Generation: Shadowheart
DC, 1994

1-4 .... 2.00

Star Trek: The Next Generation: The Killing Shadows
DC, 2000

1-4 .... 3.00

Star Trek: The Next Generation: The Modala Imperative
DC, 1991

1-4 .... 2.00

Oz-Wonderland Wars

Ozzy Osbourne

Painkiller Jane

Panda Khan Special

Panic

Paradise Kiss

Paradise X

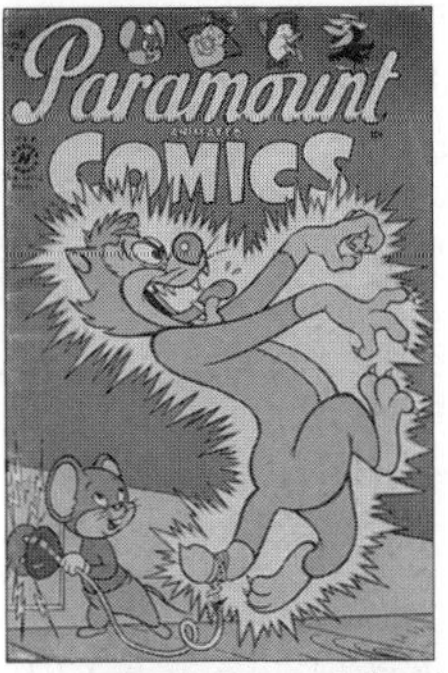

Paramount Animated Comics

Star Trek: The Next Generation: The Series Finale

DC, 1994

1 .... 4.00

Star Trek Unlimited

Marvel, 1996

1-10 .... 3.00

Star Trek: Untold Voyages

Marvel, 1998

1-4 .... 3.00
5 .... 4.00

Star Trek: Voyager

Marvel, 1996

1-15 .... 2.00

Star Trek: Voyager: Avalon Rising

DC, 2000

1 .... 6.00

Star Trek: Voyager: Encounters with the Unknown

DC

1 .... 20.00

Star Trek: Voyager: False Colors

DC, 2000

1 .... 6.00

Star Trek: Voyager: Splashdown

Marvel, 1998

1-4 .... 3.00

Star Trek: Voyager: The Planet Killer

DC, 2001

1-3 .... 3.00

Star Trek/X-Men

Marvel, 1996

1 .... 5.00

Star Trek/X-Men: Second Contact

Marvel, 1998

1-1/Variant 5.00

Star Wars

Marvel, 1977

1 .... 20.00
1/35¢ 800.00
1/2nd-1/Whitman 3rd 4.00
2 .... 10.00
2/35¢ 5.00
2/2nd 4.00
2/Whitman-2/Whitman 3rd 10.00
3 .... 8.00
3/35¢ 5.00
3/2nd 4.00
3/Whitman-3/Whitman 3rd 8.00
4 .... 7.00
4/35¢ 5.00
4/2nd 4.00
4/Whitman-5/2nd 7.00
5/Whitman-5/Whitman 2nd 4.00
6-6/2nd 7.00
6/Whitman-6/Whitman 2nd 4.00
7 .... 7.00
7/Whitman 0.00
8 .... 7.00
8/Whitman 3.00
9 .... 7.00
9/Whitman 3.00
10-19 .... 7.00
20-21 .... 6.00
22-23/Whitman 5.00
24-48 .... 4.00
49 .... 5.00
50-106 .... 4.00
107 .... 25.00
☛Low distribution
Ann 1 .... 8.00
Ann 2-3 .... 5.00

Star Wars (Magazine)

Dark Horse, 1992

1 .... 5.00
2 .... 4.00
3-10 .... 3.00

Star Wars

Dark Horse, 1998

0 .... 10.00
1 .... 4.00
2-49 .... 3.00
50 .... 6.00
☛Title becomes Star Wars Republic
51-83 .... 3.00

Star Wars: A New Hope Manga

Dark Horse, 1998

1-4 .... 10.00

Star Wars: A New Hope: The Special Edition

Dark Horse, 1997

1-4 .... 3.00

Star Wars: Boba Fett

Dark Horse, 1995

½ 3.00
½/Gold 5.00
1-3 .... 4.00

Star Wars: Boba Fett: Agent of Doom

Dark Horse, 2000

1 .... 3.00

Star Wars: Boba Fett: Enemy of the Empire

Dark Horse, 1999

1-4 .... 3.00

Star Wars: Boba Fett One-Shot

Dark Horse, 2006

1 .... 3.00

Star Wars: Boba Fett: Twin Engines of Destruction

Dark Horse, 1997

1 .... 3.00

Star Wars: Chewbacca

Dark Horse, 2000

1-4 .... 3.00

Star Wars: Clone Wars

Dark Horse, 2003

1-9 .... 31.00

Star Wars: Crimson Empire

Dark Horse, 1997

1 .... 6.00
2-6 .... 5.00

Star Wars: Crimson Empire II: Council of Blood

Dark Horse, 1998

1 .... 4.00
2-6 .... 3.00

Star Wars: Dark Empire

Dark Horse, 1993

1 .... 6.00
1/2nd 3.00
1/Gold 5.00
1/Platinum 6.00
2 .... 4.00
2/2nd 3.00
2/Gold 4.00
2/Platinum 5.00
3 .... 4.00
3/2nd 3.00
3/Gold 4.00
3/Platinum 5.00
4-4/Gold 4.00
4/Platinum 5.00
5 .... 3.00
5/Gold 4.00
5/Platinum 5.00
6 .... 3.00
6/Gold 4.00
6/Platinum 5.00
Ashcan 1 .... 1.00

Star Wars: Dark Empire II

Dark Horse, 1994

1 .... 3.00
1/Gold 4.00
2 .... 3.00
2/Gold 4.00
3 .... 3.00
3/Gold 4.00
4 .... 3.00
4/Gold 4.00
5 .... 3.00
5/Gold 4.00
6 .... 3.00
6/Gold 4.00

Star Wars: Dark Force Rising

Dark Horse, 1997

1-6 .... 3.00

Star Wars: Dark Times

Dark Horse, 2006

1 .... 3.00

Star Wars: Darth Maul

Dark Horse, 2000

1-4/Variant 3.00

Star Wars: Droids

Dark Horse, 1994

1-6 .... 3.00
Special 1 .... 3.00

Star Wars: Droids

Dark Horse, 1995

1-8 .... 3.00

Star Wars: Empire

Dark Horse, 2002

1-40 .... 3.00

Star Wars: Empire's End

Dark Horse, 1995

1-2 .... 3.00

Star Wars: Episode I Anakin Skywalker

Dark Horse, 1999

1-1/Variant 3.00

Star Wars: Episode III: Revenge of the Sith

Dark Horse, 2005

1-4 .... 3.00

Star Wars: Episode I Obi-Wan Kenobi

Dark Horse, 1999

1-1/Variant 3.00

Star Wars: Episode I Queen Amidala

Dark Horse, 1999

1-1/Variant 3.00

Star Wars: Episode I Qui-Gon Jinn

Dark Horse, 1999

1-1/Variant 3.00

Star Wars: Episode I The Phantom Menace

Dark Horse, 1999

1-4/Variant 3.00

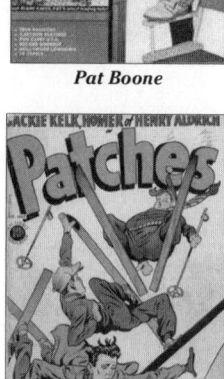

Pat Boone

Patches

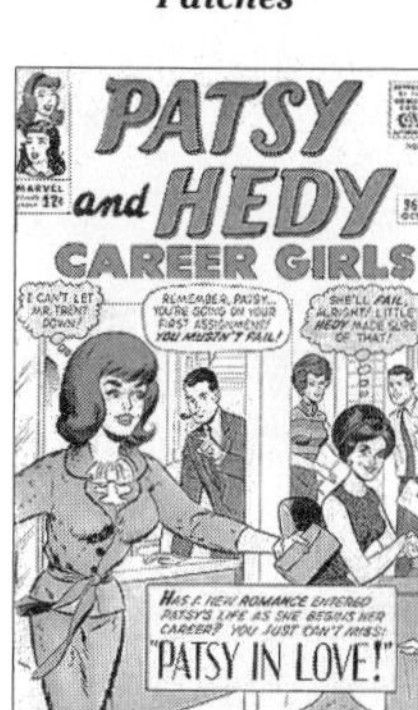

Patsy and Hedy

Patsy Walker

Pat the Brat

Patty Cake

Pebbles and Bamm-Bamm

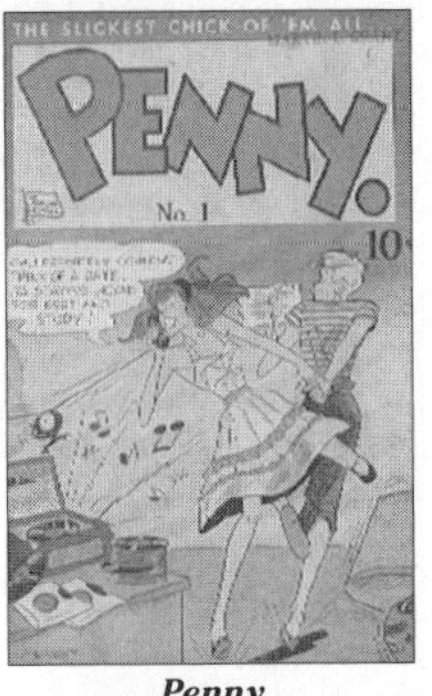

Penny

Star Wars: Episode II: Attack of the Clones
Dark Horse
1-4/Variant....4.00

Star Wars: General Grievous
Dark Horse, 2005
1-4....3.00

Star Wars Handbook
Dark Horse, 1998
1-2....3.00

Star Wars: Heir to the Empire
Dark Horse, 1995
1-6....3.00

Star Wars in 3-D
Blackthorne, 1987
1....3.00

Star Wars: Infinities: A New Hope
Dark Horse, 2001
1-4....3.00

Star Wars: Infinities: Return of the Jedi
Dark Horse, 2003
1-4....3.00

Star Wars: Infinities: The Empire Strikes Back
Dark Horse, 2002
1-4....3.00

Star Wars: Jabba the Hutt
Dark Horse, 1995
1-4....3.00

Star Wars: Jango Fett: Open Seasons
Dark Horse, 2002
1-4....3.00

Star Wars: Jedi - Aayla Secura
Dark Horse, 2003
1....5.00

Star Wars: Jedi Academy: Leviathan
Dark Horse, 1998
1-4....3.00

Star Wars: Jedi Council: Acts of War
Dark Horse, 2000
1-4....3.00

Star Wars: Jedi - Dooku Clone Wars
Dark Horse, 2003
1....5.00

Star Wars: Jedi - Mace Windu
Dark Horse, 2003
1....5.00

Star Wars: Jedi Quest
Dark Horse, 2001
1-4....3.00

Star Wars: Jedi - Shaak Ti
Dark Horse, 2003
1....5.00

Star Wars: Jedi vs. Sith
Dark Horse, 2001
1-6....3.00

Star Wars: Jedi - Yoda
Dark Horse, 2004
1....5.00

Star Wars: Knights of the Old Republic
Dark Horse, 2006
1....12.00
2-4....6.00
5-6....5.00
7-8....4.00
9-40....3.00

Star Wars: Knights of the Old Republic 25¢ Flip Book
Dark Horse, 2006
1....2.00

Star Wars: Legacy
Dark Horse, 2006
0....1.00
1....12.00
2-7....3.00

Star Wars: Mara Jade
Dark Horse, 1998
1-6....3.00

Star Wars: Obsession
Dark Horse, 2004
1....8.00
2....4.00
3-5....3.00

Star Wars: Purge
Dark Horse, 2005
1....25.00

Star Wars: Qui-Gon & Obi-Wan: Last Stand on Ord Mantell
Dark Horse, 2000
1/A-3/B....3.00

Star Wars: Qui-Gon & Obi-Wan: The Aurorient Express
Dark Horse, 2002
1-2....3.00

Star Wars: Rebellion
Dark Horse, 2006
1 .... 8.00
3-5 .... 3.00

Star Wars: Return of the Jedi
Marvel, 1983
1-4 .... 4.00

Star Wars: River of Chaos
Dark Horse, 1995
1-4 .... 3.00

Star Wars: Shadows of Empire: Evolution
Dark Horse, 1998
1-5 .... 3.00

Star Wars: Shadows of the Empire
Dark Horse, 1995
1-6 .... 3.00

Star Wars: Shadow Stalker
Dark Horse, 1997
1 .... 3.00

Star Wars: Splinter of the Mind's Eye
Dark Horse, 1995
1-4 .... 3.00

Star Wars: Starfighter: Crossbones
Dark Horse, 2002
1-3 .... 3.00

Star Wars: Tag & Bink are Dead
Dark Horse, 2001
1-2 .... 3.00

Star Wars: Tag & Bink Episode I - Revenge of the Clone Menace
Dark Horse, 2006
1 .... 3.00

Star Wars Tales
Dark Horse, 1999
1-4 .... 5.00
5-21 .... 6.00
22/Art 7.00
22/Photo 6.00
23/Art 7.00
23/Photo 6.00
24/Art 7.00
24/Photo 6.00

Star Wars Tales-A Jedi's Weapon
Dark Horse
1 .... 1.00

Star Wars: Tales: A Jedi's Weapon
Dark Horse, 2002
1 .... 2.00

Star Wars: Tales from Mos Eisley
Dark Horse, 1996
1 .... 3.00

Star Wars: Tales of the Jedi
Dark Horse, 1993
1 .... 4.00
1/Special 6.00
2 .... 4.00
2/Special 5.00
3 .... 3.00
3/Special 5.00
4 .... 3.00
4/Special 5.00
5 .... 3.00
5/Special 5.00

Star Wars: Tales of the Jedi: Dark Lords of the Sith
Dark Horse, 1994
1-6 .... 3.00

Star Wars: Tales of the Jedi: Fall of the Sith Empire
Dark Horse, 1997
1-5 .... 3.00

Star Wars: Tales of the Jedi: Redemption
Dark Horse, 1998
1-5 .... 3.00

Star Wars: Tales of the Jedi: The Freedon Nadd Uprising
Dark Horse, 1994
1-2 .... 3.00

Star Wars: Tales of the Jedi: The Golden Age of the Sith
Dark Horse, 1996
0 .... 1.00
1-5 .... 3.00

Star Wars: Tales of the Jedi: The Sith War
Dark Horse, 1995
1-6 .... 3.00

Star Wars: The Bounty Hunters: Aurra Sing
Dark Horse, 1999
1 .... 3.00

Pep

Perg

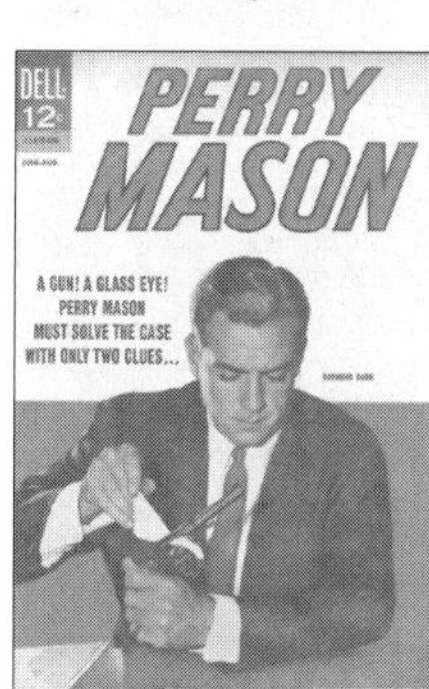

Perry Mason

Personal Love

Peter Cannon-Thunderbolt

Peter Porkchops

Phantom 2040

Phantom Force

Star Wars: The Bounty Hunters: Kenix Kil

Dark Horse, 1999

1 .... 3.00

Star Wars: The Bounty Hunters: Scoundrel's Wages

Dark Horse, 1999

1 .... 3.00

Star Wars: The Empire Strikes Back: Manga

Dark Horse, 1999

1-4 .... 10.00

Star Wars: The Jabba Tape

Dark Horse, 1998

1 .... 3.00

Star Wars: The Last Command

Dark Horse, 1997

1 .... 4.00
2-6 .... 3.00

Star Wars: The Protocol Offensive

Dark Horse, 1997

1 .... 5.00

Star Wars: The Return of Tag & Bink Special Edition

Dark Horse, 2006

1 .... 3.00

Star Wars: Underworld: The Yavin Vassilika

Dark Horse, 2000

1/A-5/B 3.00

Star Wars: Union

Dark Horse, 1999

1 .... 14.00
2 .... 10.00
3 .... 7.00
4 .... 5.00

Star Wars: Vader's Quest

Dark Horse, 1999

1-4 .... 3.00

Star Wars: Valentines Story

Dark Horse, 2003

1 .... 4.00

Star Wars: X-Wing Rogue Leader

Dark Horse, 2005

1-3 .... 3.00

Star Wars: X-Wing Rogue Squadron

Dark Horse, 1995

½ 3.00
½/Platinum 5.00
1-4 .... 4.00
5-24 .... 3.00
25 .... 4.00
26-35 .... 3.00
Special 1 .... 1.00

Star Weevils

Rip Off

1 .... 1.00

Star Western

Avalon

1-5 .... 6.00

S.T.A.T.

Majestic, 1993

1-1/Variant 2.00

Static

DC, 1993

1 .... 2.00
1/CS-1/Silver 3.00
2-13 .... 2.00
14 .... 3.00
15-24 .... 2.00
25 .... 4.00
26-30 .... 3.00
31 .... 1.00
32-47 .... 3.00

Static Shock!: Rebirth of the Cool

DC, 2001

1-4 .... 3.00

Stay Puffed

Image, 2004

1 .... 4.00

Steady Beat

Tokyopop, 2005

1 .... 10.00

Stealth Force

Malibu, 1987

1-8 .... 2.00

Stealth Squad

Petra, 1995

0-4 .... 3.00

Steampunk

DC, 2000

1-4 .... 3.00
5 .... 4.00
6-11 .... 3.00
12 .... 4.00

Steampunk: Catechism

DC, 2000

1 .... 3.00

Stech

Silverwolf, 1986

1 .... 2.00

Steed and Mrs. Peel

Eclipse, 1990

1-3 .... 5.00

Steel
DC, 1994

0-46 .... 2.00
47-52 .... 3.00
Ann 1-2 .... 4.00

Steel Angel
Gauntlet

1 .... 3.00

Steel Claw
Fleetway-Quality, 1986

1-5 .... 2.00

Steeldragon Stories
Steeldragon

1 .... 2.00

Steele Destinies
Nightscapes, 1995

1-3 .... 3.00

Steelgrip Starkey
Marvel, 1986

1-6 .... 2.00

Steel Pulse
True Fiction, 1986

1-3 .... 2.00
4 .... 4.00

Steel Sterling
Archie, 1984

4-7 .... 1.00

Steel, the Indestructible Man
DC, 1978

1 .... 5.00
2-5 .... 2.00

Steel: The Official Comic Adaptation of the Warner Bros. Motion Picture
DC, 1997

1 .... 5.00

Steeltown Rockers
Marvel, 1990

1-6 .... 1.00

Stellar Comics
Stellar

1 .... 3.00

Stellar Losers
Antarctic, 1993

1-3 .... 3.00

Stephen Darklord
Rak, 1987

1-3 .... 2.00

Steps to a Drug Free Life
David G. Brown, 1998

1 .... 1.00

Stern Wheeler
Spotlight

1 .... 2.00

Steve Canyon Comics
Harvey, 1948

1 .... 110.00
2 .... 75.00
3-6 .... 55.00

Steve Canyon Magazine (Milton Caniff's...)
Kitchen Sink, 1983

1-4 .... 3.00
5-7 .... 4.00
8-12 .... 5.00
13 .... 6.00
14 .... 5.00
3D 1 .... 2.00

Steven
Kitchen Sink, 1996

1-4 .... 3.00
5-8 .... 4.00

Steven Presents Dumpy
Fantagraphics, 1999

1 .... 3.00

Steven's Comics
DK Press

1 .... 1.00
3 .... 3.00
2 .... 2.00
4 .... 4.00

Steve Roper
Famous Funnies, 1948

1 .... 65.00
2 .... 45.00
3-5 .... 35.00

Steve Zodiak and the Fireball XL-5
Gold Key, 1964

1 .... 65.00

Stevie
Magazine Publications, 1952

1 .... 45.00
2-6 .... 25.00

Stewart the Rat
About, 2003

1 .... 4.00

Stickboy
Fantagraphics, 1990

1-5 .... 3.00

Stickboy
Revolutionary, 1990

1-4 .... 3.00

Stickboy
Starhead, 1993

1-6 .... 3.00

Stig's Inferno
Vortex, 1989

1-2 .... 2.00
3-4 .... 4.00
5-7 .... 2.00

Phantom Jack

Phantom of Fear City

Pictorial Romances

Picture News

Pieces

Pigeonman

Pinky and the Brain

Pitt

Stimulator
Fantagraphics, 1991

1 .... 3.00

Sting
Artline

1 .... 3.00

Sting of the Green Hornet
Now, 1992

1-4/CS 3.00

Stinktooth
Stinktooth, 1991

1 .... 1.00

Stinz
Fantagraphics, 1989

1 .... 4.00
2-5 .... 3.00

Stinz
Brave New Words, 1990

1-3 .... 3.00

Stinz
Mu, 1994

1-4 .... 3.00
5 .... 5.00
6 .... 6.00
7 .... 5.00

Stoker's Dracula
Marvel, 2004

1-4 .... 4.00

Stone
Image, 1998

1-2 .... 3.00
2/A 6.00
2/B 4.00
3-4 .... 3.00

Stone
Image, 1999

1 .... 3.00
1/Variant 7.00
2-3 .... 3.00

Stone Cold Steve Austin
Chaos, 1999

1-4 .... 3.00

Stone Protcctors
Harvey, 1994

1-3 .... 2.00

Stonewall in the Shenandoah
Heritage Collection

1 .... 4.00

Stoney Burke
Dell, 1963

1 .... 25.00
2 .... 20.00

Stories by Famous Authors Illustrated
Seaboard, 1950

1-13 .... 200.00

Stories from Bosnia
Drawn and Quarterly

1 .... 4.00

Stories of Romance
Atlas, 1956

5 .... 55.00
6-13 .... 35.00

Stories of the Fantastic
NBM

1-2 .... 10.00
3 .... 13.00

Storm
Marvel, 1996

1-4 .... 3.00

Storm Battlebook
Marvel, 1998

1 .... 4.00

Stormbreaker: The Saga of Beta Ray Bill
Marvel, 2005

1-6 .... 3.00

Storm
Marvel, 2006

1-6 .... 3.00

Stormquest
Caliber, 1955

1-6 .... 2.00

Stormwatch
Image, 1993

0-1/Gold 3.00
2-8 .... 2.00
9 .... 3.00
10 .... 2.00
10/A-10/B 3.00
11-16 .... 2.00
17-36 .... 3.00
37 .... 4.00
38-49 .... 3.00
50 .... 5.00
Special 1 .... 4.00
Special 2 .... 3.00

Stormwatch
Image, 1997

1-12 .... 3.00

Stormwatcher
Eclipse, 1989

1-4 .... 2.00

Stormwatch: PHD
DC, 2007

1-2/Variant 3.00

Stormwatch Sourcebook

Image, 1994

1 .... 3.00

StormWatch: Team Achilles

WildStorm, 2002

1-23 .... 3.00

Story of Electronics: The Discovery that Changed the World!

Radio Shack, 1980

1 .... 3.00

Story of Martha Wayne

Argo

1 .... 25.00

Straight Arrow

Magazine Enterprises, 1950

1 .... 260.00
2 .... 150.00
3 .... 175.00
4-5 .... 75.00
6-10 .... 70.00
11-20 .... 62.00
21 .... 55.00
22 .... 110.00
23-30 .... 50.00
31-40 .... 42.00
41-50 .... 30.00
51-55 .... 24.00

Straitjacket Studios Presents

Straitjacket

0 .... 3.00

Strand

Trident, 1990

1-2 .... 3.00

Stranded On Planet X

Radio, 1999

1 .... 3.00

Strange

Marvel, 2004

1-6 .... 4.00

Strange Adventures

DC, 1950

1 .... 2,500.00
2 .... 1,150.00
3 .... 850.00
4 .... 800.00
5-6 .... 650.00
7 .... 625.00
8 .... 550.00
9 .... 1,250.00
☛1st Captain Comet
10 .... 400.00
11 .... 500.00
12 .... 400.00
13 .... 500.00
14 .... 650.00
15 .... 500.00
16 .... 450.00
17 .... 275.00
18-20 .... 450.00
21-23 .... 350.00
24 .... 375.00
25 .... 350.00
26-29 .... 300.00
30 .... 425.00
31-38 .... 275.00
39 .... 400.00
40-41 .... 250.00
42 .... 275.00
43 .... 250.00
44 .... 325.00
45-46 .... 250.00
47 .... 200.00
48 .... 250.00
49 .... 200.00
50 .... 225.00
51 .... 200.00
52-53 .... 225.00
54 .... 150.00
55 .... 200.00
56-60 .... 150.00
61-70 .... 125.00
71-74 .... 100.00
75 .... 75.00
76-78 .... 100.00
79 .... 150.00
80-83 .... 100.00
84 .... 125.00
85-90 .... 100.00
91 .... 90.00
92-93 .... 80.00
94 .... 75.00
95 .... 90.00
96 .... 65.00
97 .... 90.00
98 .... 75.00
99 .... 90.00
100 .... 125.00
101 .... 65.00
102-103 .... 90.00
104-106 .... 65.00
107 .... 75.00
108-109 .... 65.00
110 .... 75.00
111 .... 65.00
112 .... 60.00
113 .... 90.00
114 .... 125.00
☛1st Star Hawkins
115-116 .... 60.00
117 .... 550.00
☛1st Atomic Knights
118 .... 75.00
119 .... 90.00
120 .... 200.00
☛2nd Atomic Knights
121-123 .... 75.00

Pixy Junket

Planetary

Planet Ladder

Planet Terry

Plasmer

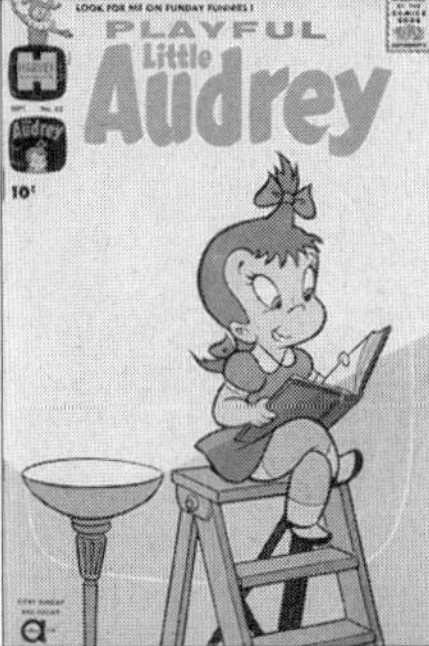

Playful Little Audrey

Pogo Possum

Police Comics

124 .... 90.00
125-126 .... 75.00
127 .... 50.00
128 .... 75.00
129 .... 90.00
130-131 .... 50.00
132 .... 75.00
133-135 .... 65.00
136-137 .... 50.00
138 .... 55.00
139-140 .... 50.00
141 .... 55.00
142-145 .... 50.00
146 .... 40.00
147-148 .... 50.00
149 .... 40.00
150-160 .... 50.00
161-167 .... 35.00
168 .... 30.00
169 .... 35.00
170 .... 50.00
171-172 .... 30.00
173 .... 40.00
174 .... 30.00
175 .... 40.00
176-177 .... 30.00
178 .... 25.00
179 .... 30.00
180 .... 150.00
☛1st Animal Man
181 .... 25.00
182-183 .... 30.00
184 .... 60.00
☛Animal Man app.
185-186 .... 25.00
187 .... 20.00
188 .... 25.00
189 .... 30.00
190 .... 100.00
☛Animal Man app.
191 .... 20.00
192-193 .... 25.00
194 .... 20.00
195 .... 35.00
☛Animal Man app.
196-197 .... 25.00
198 .... 20.00
199 .... 30.00
200 .... 25.00
201 .... 40.00
202-204 .... 20.00
205 .... 125.00
☛Deadman begins
206 .... 60.00
☛Adams Deadman
207 .... 50.00
208-212 .... 60.00
213 .... 40.00
214 .... 60.00
215 .... 45.00
216 .... 40.00
217-219 .... 20.00
220 .... 25.00
221-223 .... 20.00
224-230 .... 15.00
231-244 .... 10.00

Strange Adventures

DC, 1999

1-4 .... 3.00

Strange Attractors

Retrografix, 1993

1 .... 4.00
1/2nd 3.00
2 .... 4.00
2/2nd 3.00
3 .... 4.00
3/2nd-15 .... 3.00

Strange Attractors: Moon Fever

Caliber, 1997

1-3 .... 3.00

Strange Avenging Tales (Steve Ditko's...)

Fantagraphics, 1997

1 .... 3.00

Strange Bedfellows

Hippy, 2002

1-2 .... 6.00

Strange Brew

Aardvark-Vanaheim

1 .... 3.00

Strange Combat Tales

Marvel, 1984

1-4 .... 3.00

Strange Confessions

Ziff-Davis, 1952

1 .... 285.00
2-4 .... 200.00

Strange Day

Alternative, 2005

1 .... 4.00

Strange Days

Eclipse, 1984

1-3 .... 2.00

Strange Detective Tales: Dead Love

Oddgod Press, 2005

1 .... 4.00

Strange Embrace

Atomeka, 1993

1-3 .... 4.00

Strange Fantasy

Farrell, 1952

1 .... 300.00
2 .... 250.00
3 .... 200.00
4-6 .... 125.00
7 .... 150.00

8 .... 125.00
9 .... 150.00
10 .... 125.00
11-14 .... 100.00

Strange Girl
Image, 2005

1-12 .... 3.00

Strangehaven
Abiogenesis, 1995

1 .... 5.00
1/2nd 3.00
2 .... 4.00
2/2nd 3.00
3 .... 4.00
3/2nd-18 .... 3.00

Strange Heroes
Lone Star, 2000

1-2 .... 3.00

Strange Journey
America's Best, 1957

1 .... 105.00
2-4 .... 75.00

Strange Killings: Body Orchard (Warren Ellis')
Avatar, 2002

1-6 .... 4.00

Strange Killings: Necromancer (Warren Eilis')
Avatar, 2004

1-2 .... 4.00

Strange Killings: Strong Medicine (Warren Ellis')
Avatar, 2003

1-3 .... 4.00

Strange Looking Exile
Robert Kirby

1-3 .... 2.00

Strangelove
Express

1-2 .... 3.00

Strange Mysteries
Superior, 1951

1 .... 375.00
2 .... 200.00
3-5 .... 175.00
6-9 .... 145.00
10 .... 130.00
11-18 .... 115.00
19 .... 125.00
20-21 .... 90.00

Strange Planets
Super, 1958

1 .... 60.00
9 .... 35.00
10-12 .... 20.00
13-16 .... 15.00

Stranger in a Strange Land
Rip Off, 1989

1-2 .... 2.00
3 .... 3.00

Strangers
Malibu, 1993

1 .... 2.00
1/Hologram 5.00
1/Ltd. 4.00
2-4 .... 2.00
5 .... 3.00
6-12 .... 2.00
13 .... 4.00
14-24 .... 2.00
Ann 1 .... 4.00

Strangers
Image, 2003

1-6 .... 3.00

Strangers in Paradise
Antarctic, 1993

0 .... 75.00
1 .... 65.00
1/2nd 5.00
1/3rd 3.00
2 .... 24.00
3 .... 18.00

Strangers in Paradise
Abstract, 1994

1 .... 30.00
1/Gold 4.00
1/2nd 3.00
2 .... 15.00
2/Gold 3.00
3 .... 12.00
3/Gold 3.00
4 .... 10.00
4/Gold 3.00
5 .... 10.00
5/Gold 3.00
6 .... 8.00
6/Gold 3.00
7 .... 8.00
7/Gold 3.00
8 .... 8.00
8/Gold 3.00
9 .... 8.00
9/Gold 3.00
10 .... 8.00
10/Gold 3.00
11 .... 5.00
11/Gold 3.00
12 .... 5.00
12/Gold 3.00
13 .... 4.00
13/Gold-14 .... 3.00

Polly Pigtails

Popeye

Popeye Special

Popular Comics

Popular Romance

Popular Teenagers

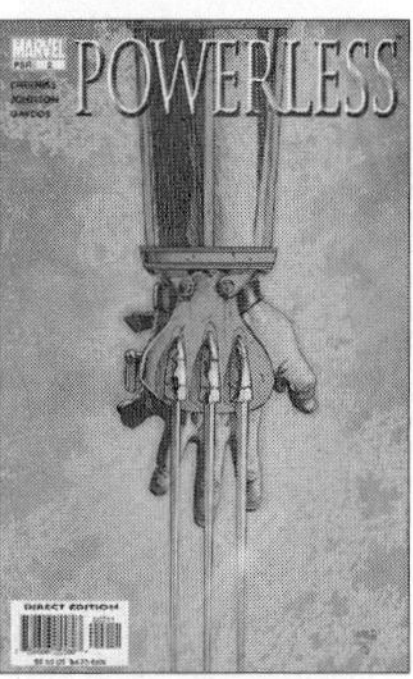

Powerless

Power of Strong Man

Strangers in Paradise

Homage, 1996

1....4.00
2-78....3.00
Special 1....4.00

Strangers in Paradise Sourcebook

Abstract, 2003

1....3.00

Stranger's Tale, A

Vineyard

1....2.00

Stranger than Fiction

Impact, 1998

1-4....2.00

Strange Sports Stories

DC, 1973

1....18.00
2....9.00
3-6....7.00

Strange Sports Stories

Adventure, 1992

1-3....3.00

Strange Stories

Avalon

1....3.00

Strange Stories from Another World

Fawcett, 1952

2....300.00
3-5....220.00

Strange Stories of Suspense

Atlas, 1955

5....220.00
6....130.00
7....135.00
8....140.00
9....130.00
10....135.00
11-13....110.00
14-16....120.00

Strange Suspense Stories

Charlton, 1952

1....450.00
2....325.00
3-5....275.00
16....150.00
17....110.00
18....160.00
19....200.00
20....160.00
21....110.00
22....135.00
27....60.00
28-30....50.00
31-33....100.00
34....200.00
35....100.00
36....145.00
37....100.00
38....45.00
39-41....80.00
42-44....20.00
45....80.00
46....20.00
47-48....80.00
49....20.00
50-51....75.00
52-54....50.00
55-60....20.00
61-74....14.00
75....90.00
76-77....20.00

Strange Suspense Stories

Charlton, 1967

1....20.00
2-9....12.00

Strange Tales

Marvel, 1951

1....2,750.00
2....800.00
3-5....700.00
6-10....550.00
11-20....350.00
21-30....275.00
31-44....225.00
45-58....200.00
59....225.00
60....200.00
61....225.00
62-63....175.00
64....200.00
65-66....175.00
67-78....200.00
79....250.00
80....200.00
81-83....175.00
84....200.00
85-88....175.00
89....400.00
☛Kirby Fin Fang Foom
90-92....175.00
93-96....150.00
97....350.00
☛Aunt May & Uncle Ben
98-100....150.00
101....900.00
☛Human Torch starts
102....425.00
☛Human Torch app.
103-105....300.00
106....225.00
107....250.00
108-109....225.00
110....1,250.00
☛1st Dr. Strange
111....350.00

112-113 .... 150.00
114 .... 350.00
115 .... 450.00
☛Dr. Strange origin
116 .... 125.00
117-118 .... 100.00
119-123 .... 125.00
124-125 .... 75.00
126 .... 90.00
127-129 .... 75.00
130 .... 90.00
131-134 .... 75.00
135 .... 125.00
☛1st S.H.I.E.L.D.
136 .... 75.00
137-147 .... 50.00
148 .... 75.00
☛Ancient One origin
149-150 .... 50.00
151 .... 75.00
152-158 .... 50.00
159 .... 60.00
160-168 .... 50.00
169 .... 15.00
☛Series restarted
170 .... 10.00
171-177 .... 7.00
178 .... 15.00
☛Warlock origin
179-181 .... 10.00
182-185 .... 3.00
185/30¢ 20.00
186 .... 3.00
186/30¢ 20.00
187-188 .... 3.00
Ann 1 .... 325.00
Ann 2 .... 350.00

Strange Tales

Marvel, 1987

1 .... 2.00
2-12 .... 1.00
13-14 .... 2.00
15-16 .... 1.00
17 .... 2.00
18-19 .... 1.00

Strange Tales

Marvel, 1994

1 .... 7.00

Strange Tales

Marvel, 1998

1-4 .... 5.00

Strange Tales: Dark Corners

Marvel, 1998

1 .... 4.00

Strange Tales of the Unusual

Atlas, 1955

1 .... 300.00
2-3 .... 165.00
4 .... 125.00
5 .... 150.00
6 .... 125.00
7 .... 135.00
8 .... 125.00
9 .... 135.00
10-11 .... 125.00

Strange Terrors

St. John, 1952

1 .... 500.00
2 .... 250.00
3 .... 350.00
4 .... 500.00
5 .... 350.00
6 .... 500.00
7 .... 525.00

Strange Weather Lately

Metaphrog, 1997

1-6 .... 4.00
7-9 .... 3.00
10 .... 4.00

Strange Wink (John Bolton's...)

Dark Horse, 1998

1-3 .... 3.00

Strange World of Your Dreams

Prize, 1952

1 .... 400.00
2-3 .... 300.00
4 .... 240.00

Strange Worlds

Avon, 1950

1 .... 1,000.00
2-9 .... 800.00
18-19 .... 175.00
20 .... 55.00
21-22 .... 40.00

Strange Worlds

Atlas, 1958

1 .... 525.00
2 .... 300.00
3 .... 235.00
4 .... 210.00
5 .... 180.00

Strange Worlds

Eternity

1 .... 4.00

Strange Worlds

North Coast

1 .... 4.00

Strangling Desdemona

Ningen Manga

1 .... 3.00

Power of the Atom

Power Pack

Powers

Preacher

Predator

Pre-Teen Dirty-Gene Kung-Fu Kangaroos

Prez

Primal Force

Strapped (Derreck Wayne Jackson's...)

Gothic Images, 1994

1-4 .... 2.00

Strata

Renegade, 1986

1-5 .... 2.00

Stratonaut

Nightwynd, 1991

1-4 .... 3.00

Stratosfear

Caliber

1 .... 3.00

Strawberry Shortcake

Marvel, 1985

1-6 .... 1.00

Straw Men

All American, 1989

1-8 .... 2.00

Stray

DC, 2001

1 .... 6.00

Stray Bullets

El Capitan, 1995

1 .... 4.00
1/2nd-21 .... 3.00
22-35 .... 4.00

Stray Cats

Twilight Twins, 1999

1 .... 3.00

Stray Toasters

Marvel

1-4 .... 5.00

Streak of Chalk

NBM

1 .... 16.00

Street Fighter

Devil's Due, 2004

7 .... 3.00
7/Foil 8.00
8 .... 3.00
8/Foil 13.00
9 .... 3.00
9/Foil 8.00
10 .... 3.00
10/Foil 4.00
11 .... 3.00
11/Variant 4.00
11/Foil 13.00
12 .... 3.00
12/Variant 4.00
13 .... 3.00
13/Variant 4.00
14 .... 3.00
14/Variant 4.00

Streetfighter

Ocean, 1986

1-4 .... 2.00

Street Fighter

Malibu, 1993

1 .... 3.00
1/Gold 5.00
2 .... 3.00
2/Gold 4.00
3 .... 3.00
3/Gold 4.00

Street Fighter

Image, 2003

1 .... 3.00
1/A/2nd 5.00
1.1 .... 2.00
1/A-3 .... 3.00
3/C 5.00
3/A-4 .... 3.00
4/C 5.00
4/A-5 .... 3.00
5/A 5.00
6 .... 3.00
6/Dynamic 5.00

Street Fighter: The Battle for Shadaloo

DC

1 .... 4.00

Street Fighter II (Tokuma Shoten)

Tokuma Shoten, 1994

1 .... 3.00

Street Fighter II

Viz, 1994

1-8 .... 3.00

Street Fighter II: The Animated Movie

Viz

1-5 .... 3.00

Street Heroes 2005

Eternity, 1989

1-3 .... 2.00

Street Music

Fantagraphics

1-6 .... 3.00

Street Poet Ray

Blackthorne, 1989

1-2 .... 2.00

Street Poet Ray

Marvel, 1990

1-4 .... 3.00

Streets

DC, 1993

1-3 .... 5.00

Street Sharks
Archie, 1996
1-3 .... 2.00

Street Sharks
Archie, 1996
1-3 .... 2.00

Street Wolf
Blackthorne, 1986
1-3 .... 2.00

Strictly Independent!
One Shot, 1996
1-2 .... 2.00

Strictly Private
Eastern Color, 1942
1-2 .... 135.00

Strike!
Eclipse, 1987
1-6 .... 2.00

Strikeback!
Malibu, 1994
1-3 .... 3.00

Strikeback!
Image, 1996
1-6 .... 3.00

Strike Force America
Comico, 1992
1 .... 3.00

Strike Force America
Comico
1 .... 3.00

Strike Force Legacy
Comico, 1993
1 .... 4.00

Strikeforce: Morituri
Marvel, 1986
1-4 .... 2.00
5-12 .... 1.00
13 .... 2.00
14-23 .... 1.00
24-31 .... 2.00

Strikeforce: Morituri: Electric Undertow
Marvel, 1989
1-5 .... 4.00

Striker
Viz, 1998
1-4 .... 3.00

Striker: Secret of the Berserker
Viz
1-4 .... 3.00

Strike! Versus Sgt. Strike Special
Eclipse, 1988
1 .... 2.00

Strippers and Sex Queens of the Exotic World
Fantagraphics, 1994
1-4 .... 4.00

Strips
Rip Off, 1989
1-10 .... 3.00
Special 1-2 .... 4.00

Strong Guy Reborn
Marvel, 1997
1 .... 3.00

Stronghold
Devil's Due, 2005
1 .... 5.00

Strontium Bitch
Fleetway-Quality
1-2 .... 3.00

Strontium Dog
Eagle, 1985
1-4 .... 2.00

Strontium Dog
Fleetway-Quality, 1987
1 .... 2.00
2-12 .... 1.00
13-Special 1 .... 2.00

Str¸del War
Rough Copy
1 .... 3.00

Stryfe's Strike File
Marvel, 1993
1-1/2nd 2.00

Stryke
London Night
0 .... 3.00
0/A 4.00
1 .... 3.00

Strykeforce
Image, 2004
1-5 .... 3.00

St. Tail Comic
Mixx, 2000
1-9 .... 3.00

Students of the Unusual
3 Finger Prints, 2005
1-4 .... 3.00
5-6 .... 4.00

Studio Comics Presents
Studio, 1995
1 .... 3.00

Stuff of Dreams
Fantagraphics
1-3 .... 4.00

Stumbo Tinytown
Harvey, 1963
1 .... 85.00

Primer

Prince Nightmare

Prize Comics

Professor Xavier and the X-Men

Project A-Ko

Promethea

Propellerman

Prophet

2 ....50.00
3 ....35.00
4-5 ....25.00
6-13 ....18.00

Stunt Dawgs
Harvey, 1993
1 ....1.00

Stuntman Comics
Harvey, 1946
1 ....685.00
2-3 ....425.00

Stupid
Image, 1993
1 ....2.00

Stupid Comics
Oni, 2000
1 ....3.00

Stupid Comics
Image, 2003
1-3 ....3.00

Stupid Heroes
Mirage, 1994
1-3 ....3.00

Stupidman
Parody
1 ....3.00

Stupidman: Burial for a Buddy
Parody
1/A-1/B 3.00

Stupidman: Rain on the Stupidmen
Parody
1/A-1/B 3.00

Stupid, Stupid Rat Tails
Cartoon Books, 1999
1-3 ....3.00

Stygmata
Express, 1994
0-3 ....3.00

Subhuman
Dark Horse, 1998
1-4 ....3.00

Submarine Attack
Charlton, 1958
11 ....24.00
12-20 ....16.00
21-30 ....12.00
31-40 ....9.00
41-54 ....7.00

Sub-Mariner
Timely, 1941
1 ....25,000.00
2 ....7,000.00
3 ....5,000.00
4 ....4,500.00
5 ....3,500.00
6-11 ....2,500.00
12-15 ....1,500.00
16-20 ....1,200.00
21-31 ....1,000.00
32 ....1,250.00
33-35 ....900.00
36-41 ....700.00
42 ....1,000.00

Sub-Mariner
Marvel, 1968
1 ....125.00
2 ....45.00
3-4 ....35.00
5 ....30.00
6-7 ....25.00
8 ....75.00
☛vs. The Thing
8/2nd 2.00
9 ....30.00
10 ....25.00
11-13 ....20.00
14 ....50.00
☛Toro dies
15-30 ....20.00
31-33 ....15.00
34 ....70.00
☛Hulk, Surfer app.
35 ....35.00
☛Hulk, Surfer app.
36-40 ....15.00
41-Special 1 ....10.00
Special 2 ....15.00

Submissive Suzanne
Fantagraphics, 1998
1-6 ....3.00

Subspecies
Eternity, 1991
1-4 ....3.00

Substance Affect
Crazyfish
1 ....3.00

Substance Quarterly
Substance, 1994
1-3 ....3.00

Subtle Violents
Cry for Dawn, 1991
1 ....15.00
1/A 160.00

Suburban High Life
Slave Labor, 1987
1-3 ....2.00

Suburban High Life
Slave Labor, 1988
1 ....6.00

Suburban Nightmares
Renegade, 1988
1-4 .... 2.00

Suburban She-Devils
Marvel, 1991
1 .... 2.00

Suburban Voodoo
Fantagraphics, 1992
1 .... 3.00

Succubus
Fantagraphics
1 .... 3.00

Sucker the Comic
Troma
1 .... 3.00

Suckle
Fantagraphics, 1996
1 .... 15.00

Sugar & Spike
DC, 1956
1 .... 1,700.00
1/2nd 3.00
2 .... 700.00
3-5 .... 500.00
6-10 .... 350.00
11-20 .... 250.00
21-30 .... 150.00
31-40 .... 125.00
41-50 .... 75.00
51-60 .... 55.00
61-80 .... 50.00
81-98 .... 35.00

Sugar Bowl Comics
Famous Funnies, 1948
1 .... 75.00
2 .... 42.00
3 .... 55.00
4-5 .... 42.00

Sugar Buzz
Slave Labor, 1998
1-4 .... 3.00

Sugar Ray Finhead
Wolf, 1994
1-11 .... 3.00

Sugarvirus
Atomeka
1 .... 4.00

Suicide Squad
DC, 1987
1-22 .... 1.00
23 .... 15.00
☛1st Oracle
24-49 .... 1.00
50 .... 2.00
51-66 .... 1.00
Ann 1 .... 2.00

Suicide Squad
DC, 2001
1-30 .... 3.00

Suikoden III: The Successor of Fate
Tokyopop, 2004
1-8 .... 10.00

Suit
Virtual, 1996
1 .... 3.00
1/A-2/A 4.00

Sullengray
Ape Entertainment, 2005
1 .... 4.00

Sultry Teenage Super Foxes
Solson
1-2 .... 2.00

Summer Fun
Dell, 1959
2 .... 175.00

Summer Love
Charlton, 1965
46 .... 95.00
47 .... 70.00
48 .... 15.00

Sunburn
Alternative, 2000
1 .... 3.00

Sun Devils
DC, 1984
1-12 .... 2.00

Sundiata: A Legend of Africa
NBM
1 .... 16.00

Sundown
Arcana, 2005
1 .... 3.00

Sunfire & Big Hero Six
Marvel, 1998
1-3 .... 3.00

Sun Fun Komiks
Sun, 1939
1 .... 175.00

Sun Girl
Marvel, 1948
1 .... 1,000.00
2-3 .... 675.00

Sunglasses After Dark
Verotik, 1995
1-5 .... 3.00
6 .... 4.00

Prototype

Psi-Force

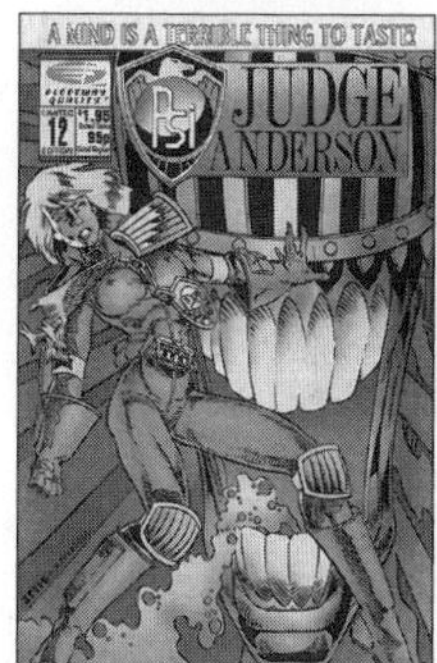

Psi-Judge Anderson

Psi-Lords

Psychic Academy

Psychoanalysis

Psycho Killers

Psyence Fiction

Sunny, America's Sweetheart

Fox, 1947

11 .... 475.00
12-14 .... 375.00

Sunrise

Harrier, 1986

1-2 .... 2.00

Sun-Runners

Pacific, 1984

1-Special 1 .... 2.00

Sunset Carson

Charlton, 1951

1 .... 530.00
2 .... 380.00
3-4 .... 280.00

Super Bad James Dynomite

Idea & Design Works, 2006

1-4 .... 4.00

Superboy

DC, 1949

1 .... 7,000.00
2 .... 2,000.00
3 .... 1,500.00
4-5 .... 1,000.00
6-10 .... 800.00
11-15 .... 600.00
16-20 .... 450.00
21-30 .... 350.00
31-38 .... 275.00
39-50 .... 225.00
51-60 .... 175.00
61-67 .... 125.00
68 .... 500.00
☛1st Bizarro
69-77 .... 100.00
78 .... 175.00
☛Mxyzptlk origin
79 .... 100.00
80 .... 150.00
☛Meets Supergirl
81-85 .... 90.00
86 .... 200.00
☛Legion app.
87-88 .... 90.00
89 .... 275.00
☛1st Mon-El
90-93 .... 90.00
94-97 .... 75.00
98 .... 100.00
99 .... 75.00
100 .... 175.00
☛Phtm. Zone villains
101-120 .... 60.00
121-128 .... 50.00
129 .... 75.00
130-137 .... 40.00
138 .... 55.00
☛Giant-sized
139-140 .... 40.00
141-146 .... 35.00
147 .... 50.00
☛Saturn Girl origin
148-155 .... 25.00
156 .... 65.00
☛Giant-size
157-164 .... 25.00
165 .... 50.00
☛Giant-size
166-168 .... 25.00
169-173 .... 20.00
174 .... 30.00
175-178 .... 20.00
☛Giant-sized
179-181 .... 15.00
182 .... 20.00
183-196 .... 12.00
197 .... 20.00
☛Legion stories start
198-199 .... 12.00
200 .... 15.00
201 .... 12.00
202 .... 30.00
203-204 .... 12.00
205 .... 40.00
206-207 .... 12.00
208 .... 15.00
209 .... 10.00
210 .... 15.00
211-212 .... 10.00
213-221 .... 7.00
222-230 .... 5.00
Ann 1 .... 175.00
SP 1 .... 4.00

Superboy

DC, 1990

1-18 .... 2.00
Special 1 .... 3.00

Superboy

DC, 1994

0 .... 2.00
1 .... 3.00
2-24 .... 2.00
25 .... 3.00
26-99 .... 2.00
100 .... 3.00
1000000 .... 4.00
Ann 1 .... 3.00
Ann 2 .... 4.00
Ann 3 .... 3.00
Ann 4 .... 4.00

Superboy and the Legion of Super-Heroes

DC, 1977

244/A-258/A 0.00
231-241 .... 5.00
241/Whitman 8.00
242 .... 5.00
242/Whitman 8.00

243 .... 5.00
243/Whitman 8.00
244 .... 5.00
244/Whitman 8.00
245 .... 5.00
245/Whitman 8.00
246 .... 5.00
246/Whitman 8.00
247 .... 5.00
247/Whitman 8.00
248 .... 5.00
248/Whitman 8.00
249-250 .... 5.00
251 .... 4.00
251/Whitman 7.00
252 .... 4.00
252/Whitman 7.00
253 .... 4.00
253/Whitman 7.00
254 .... 4.00
254/Whitman 7.00
255 .... 4.00
255/Whitman 7.00
256 .... 4.00
256/Whitman 7.00
257 .... 4.00
257/Whitman 7.00
258 .... 4.00
258/Whitman 7.00

Superboy & the Ravers

DC, 1996

1-19 .... 2.00

Superboy Plus

DC, 1997

1-2 .... 3.00

Superboy/Risk Double-Shot

DC, 1998

1 .... 2.00

Superboy/Robin: World's Finest Three

DC, 1996

1-2 .... 5.00

Superboy's Legion

DC, 2001

1-2 .... 6.00

Super Brat

Toby, 1954

1 .... 40.00
2-4 .... 25.00

Supercar

Gold Key, 1962

1 .... 250.00
2-4 .... 200.00

Super Cat

Star, 1953

56-58 .... 120.00

Super Cat

Ajax, 1957

1 ....55.00
2-4 ....35.00

Super Circus

Cross, 1951

1 ....85.00
2 ....55.00
3-5 ....45.00

Super Comics

Dell, 1938

1 ....1,600.00
2 ....600.00
3 ....510.00
4-5 ....400.00
6-10 ....315.00
11-25 ....260.00
26-29 ....182.00
30 ....265.00
31-40 ....138.00
41-50 ....124.00
51-70 ....78.00
71-90 ....58.00
91-100 ....48.00
101-110 ....34.00
111-121 ....25.00

Supercops

Now, 1990

1 ....3.00
2-4 ....2.00

Super Cops

Red Circle, 1974

1 ....2.00

Super DC Giant

DC, 1970

13 ....75.00
14-16 ....30.00
17 ....125.00
18-19 ....50.00
20 ....40.00
21 ....175.00
22 ....25.00
☛Westerns
23 ....40.00
24 ....30.00
☛Supergirl comics
25-26 ....25.00
27 ....15.00

Super Deluxe Hero Happy Hour: The Lost Episode

Idea & Design Works, 2006

1 ....10.00

Super Duck Comics

Archie, 1944

1 ....350.00
2 ....145.00
3 ....105.00
4-5 ....85.00
6-10 ....68.00

Public Enemies

Pulp Fiction

Punch Comics

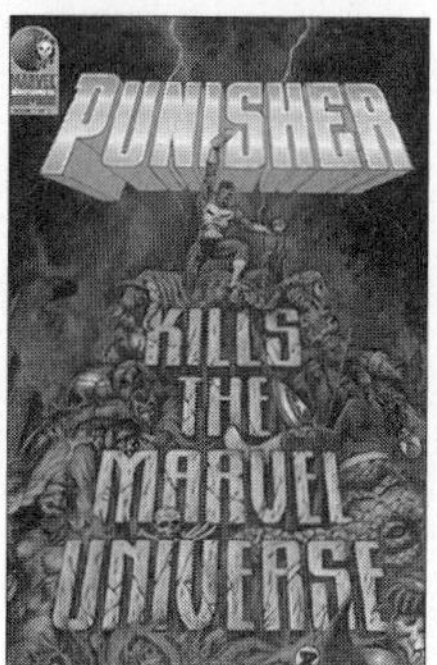

Punisher Kills the Marvel Universe

Purgatori

Purple Claw Mysteries

Quadrant

Quagmire U.S.A.

11-20 ....56.00
21-30 ....45.00
31-50 ....32.00
51-70 ....24.00
71-94 ....20.00

Superfan
Mark 1

1 ....2.00

Superfist Ayumi
Fantagraphics, 1996

1-2 ....3.00

Super Friends
DC, 1976

1 ....20.00
2 ....9.00
3-5 ....7.00
6-10 ....6.00
11-13 ....4.00
13/Whitman 8.00
14 ....6.00
14/Whitman 12.00
15 ....4.00
15/Whitman 12.00
16 ....6.00
16/Whitman 12.00
17-20 ....4.00
20/Whitman 12.00
21 ....6.00
21/Whitman 12.00
22 ....6.00
22/Whitman 12.00
23 ....6.00
23/Whitman 12.00
24-25 ....4.00
25/Whitman 8.00
26-31 ....4.00
32 ....5.00
32/Whitman 10.00
33-47 ....4.00
Special 1 ....5.00

Super Funnies
Superior, 1953

1 ....300.00
2 ....100.00
3-4 ....50.00

Supergirl
DC, 1972

1 ....15.00
2 ....10.00
3-10 ....8.00

Supergirl
DC, 1983

14-23 ....3.00
DOT 1-2 ....4.00

Supergirl
DC, 1996

1 ....10.00
☛Matrix, Linda merge
1/2nd 3.00
2-3 ....4.00
4-7 ....3.00
8-49 ....2.00
50 ....4.00
51-72 ....2.00
73-75 ....3.00
76-80 ....3.00
1000000 ....4.00
Ann 1 ....3.00
Ann 2 ....4.00

Supergirl
DC, 2005

1/A-6/A 0.00
0 ....5.00
1 ....7.00
1/Turner 10.00
1/Sketch 4.00
☛2nd print
2-4 ....3.00
5 ....4.00
6-38 ....3.00

Supergirl and the Legion of Super-Heroes
DC, 2006

17-25 ....3.00

Supergirl/Lex Luthor Special
DC, 1993

1 ....3.00

Supergirl
DC, 1994

1-4 ....3.00

Supergirl Movie Special
DC

1 ....1.00

Supergirl Plus
DC, 1997

1 ....3.00

Supergirl/Prysm Double Shot
DC, 1998

1 ....2.00

Supergirl: Wings
DC, 2001

1 ....6.00

Super Goof
Gold Key, 1965

1 ....24.00
2-3 ....12.00
4-10 ....10.00
11-20 ....7.00
21-30 ....5.00
31-57 ....3.00
58-59 ....4.00
60 ....15.00
61 ....70.00
62 ....15.00

63 .... 3.00
64-66 .... 5.00
67-69 .... 8.00
70-74 .... 15.00

Super Green Beret

Milson, 1967

1 .... 30.00
2 .... 24.00

Superheroes

Dell, 1967

1 .... 20.00
2-4 .... 12.00

Super Heroes Battle Super Gorillas

DC, 1976

1 .... 10.00

Super Heroes Stamp Album

USPS, 2000

1-6 .... 3.00
7-10 .... 4.00

Super Heroes Versus Super Villains

Archie, 1966

1 .... 50.00

Super Hero Happy Hour

GeekPunk, 2002

1-4 .... 3.00

SupeRichie

Harvey, 1975

1 .... 5.00
2-5 .... 3.00
6-18 .... 2.00

Super Information Hijinks: Reality Check

Tavicat, 1995

1-5 .... 3.00

Super Information Hijinks: Reality Check!

Sirius, 1996

1-10 .... 3.00

Superior Seven

Imagine This, 1992

1-5 .... 2.00

Superior Stories

Nesbit, 1955

1 .... 120.00
2-4 .... 50.00

Super Magic

Street & Smith, 1941

1 .... 1,200.00

Super Magician (Vol. 1)

Street & Smith, 1941

2 .... 325.00
3 .... 250.00
4-5 .... 225.00
6-7 .... 200.00
8 .... 225.00
9-10 .... 200.00
11-12 .... 175.00

Super Magician (Vol. 2)

Street & Smith, 1943

1 .... 225.00
2-12 .... 110.00

Super Magician (Vol. 3)

Street & Smith, 1944

1-12 .... 100.00

Super Magician (Vol. 4)

Street & Smith, 1945

1-12 .... 90.00

Super Magician (Vol. 5)

Street & Smith, 1946

1-8 .... 75.00

Superman (1st Series)

DC, 1939

1 .... 160,000.00
2 .... 16,000.00
3 .... 9,200.00
4 .... 6,500.00
5 .... 6,000.00
6-7 .... 3,500.00
8-10 .... 2,850.00
11-13 .... 2,200.00
14 .... 4,500.00
☛U.S. flag cover
15 .... 2,050.00
16-20 .... 1,650.00
21 .... 1,500.00
22-23 .... 1,100.00
24 .... 1,400.00
25 .... 1,050.00
26 .... 1,250.00
27-29 .... 950.00
30 .... 1,350.00
☛1st Mr. Mxyzptlk
31-40 .... 825.00
41-50 .... 650.00
51-52 .... 525.00
53 .... 1,800.00
☛Superman origin
54-60 .... 500.00
61 .... 1,000.00
☛1st Kryptonite
62-70 .... 475.00
71-75 .... 450.00
76 .... 1,100.00
☛Batman team-up
77-80 .... 400.00

Quantum Creep

Quantum Leap

Quasar

Quest for Dreams Lost

Quest Presents

Questprobe

Quicken Forbidden

Quicksilver

Issue	Price
81-90	375.00
91-95	360.00
96-99	325.00
100	1,500.00
101-110	280.00
111-120	240.00
121-130	195.00
131-139	155.00
140	175.00
☛1st Bizarro Jr.	
141-145	115.00
146	160.00
☛Superman origin	
147	135.00
148	115.00
149	125.00
☛Legion app.	
150-161	68.00
162-180	58.00
181-186	55.00
187	60.00
188-192	55.00
193	60.00
194-198	55.00
199	180.00
☛1st race with Flash	
200	60.00
201	24.00
202	30.00
203-211	24.00
212	50.00
☛Superbabies	
213-216	24.00
217	30.00
218-221	20.00
222	30.00
223-226	20.00
227	30.00
228-231	20.00
232	30.00
233	40.00
☛Kryptonite destroyed	
234-238	18.00
239	30.00
☛Giant-sized	
240-244	18.00
245	22.00
246-251	18.00
252	60.00
☛100-page issue	
253	18.00
254	22.00
255-264	9.00
265-271	8.00
272	20.00
☛100-page issue	
273-277	7.00
278	17.00
☛100-page issue	
279-283	5.00
284	7.00
285-286	5.00
287-292	4.00
293-299	3.00
300	11.00
301-321	3.00
321/Whitman	5.00
322	3.00
322/Whitman	5.00
323	3.00
323/Whitman	5.00
324	3.00
324/Whitman	5.00
325	3.00
325/Whitman	5.00
326	3.00
326/Whitman	5.00
327	3.00
327/Whitman	5.00
328	3.00
328/Whitman	5.00
329	3.00
329/Whitman	5.00
330	3.00
330/Whitman	5.00
331	3.00
331/Whitman	5.00
332	3.00
332/Whitman	5.00
333	3.00
333/Whitman	5.00
334	3.00
334/Whitman	5.00
335	3.00
335/Whitman	5.00
336	3.00
336/Whitman	5.00
337	3.00
337/Whitman	5.00
338	3.00
338/Whitman	5.00
339	3.00
339/Whitman	5.00
340	3.00
340/Whitman	5.00
341	3.00
341/Whitman	5.00
342	3.00
342/Whitman	5.00
343	3.00
343/Whitman	5.00
344	3.00
344/Whitman	5.00
345	3.00
345/Whitman	5.00
346	3.00
346/Whitman	5.00
347	3.00
347/Whitman	5.00
348	3.00
348/Whitman	5.00
349	3.00
349/Whitman	5.00
350	3.00

350/Whitman 5.00
351-399 .... 2.00
400 .... 5.00
401-422 .... 2.00
423 .... 5.00
Ann 1 .... 600.00
Ann 1/2nd 5.00
Ann 2 .... 325.00
Ann 3 .... 210.00
Ann 4 .... 180.00
Ann 5 .... 105.00
Ann 6 .... 90.00
Ann 7 .... 62.00
Ann 8 .... 46.00
Ann 9-10 .... 5.00
Ann 11 .... 4.00
Ann 12 .... 3.00
Special 1-3 .... 4.00

Superman

DC, 1987

0 .... 3.00
1-2 .... 4.00
3-5 .... 3.00
6-8 .... 2.00
9 .... 4.00
10-49 .... 2.00
50 .... 4.00
50/2nd-52/2nd 2.00
53 .... 3.00
53/2nd-72 .... 2.00
73 .... 3.00
73/2nd 2.00
74 .... 4.00
74/2nd 2.00
75 .... 5.00
☛Death of Superman
75/CS 12.00
75/Platinum 40.00
75/2nd-75/4th 2.00
76-77 .... 3.00
78 .... 2.00
78/CS 3.00
79-82 .... 2.00
82/Variant 4.00
83-99 .... 2.00
100 .... 3.00
100/Variant 4.00
101-122 .... 2.00
123 .... 3.00
123/Variant 5.00
124-150 .... 2.00
150/Variant 4.00
151-170 .... 2.00
171 .... 4.00
172-174 .... 2.00
175 .... 4.00
176-190 .... 2.00
190/A 4.00
191 .... 2.00
192 .... 3.00
193-199 .... 2.00
200 .... 4.00
201 ....8.00
202 ....2.00
203 ....6.00
☛Lee sketchbook
204 ....4.00
204/Sketch 250.00
204/DF Lee 30.00
204/DF Azzarell 25.00
205/Lee 4.00
205/Turner-205/DF Lee 3.00
205/DF Turner 30.00
206-207 ....3.00
208 ....5.00
209 ....4.00
210-215 ....3.00
216 ....5.00
☛Infinite Crisis tie
217 ....7.00
☛OMAC appearance
218 ....5.00
219 ....6.00
219/Variant-226 ....3.00
650 ....8.00
651-680 ....3.00
1000000 ....4.00
1000000/Ltd. 15.00
Ann 1 ....4.00
Ann 2-3 ....3.00
Ann 3/2nd-3/3rd 2.00
Ann 4-6 ....3.00
Ann 7 ....4.00
Ann 8-11 ....3.00
Ann 12 ....4.00
GS 1-GS 2 ....5.00
GS 3 ....6.00
Special 1 ....4.00
3D 1 ....5.00

Superman 3-D

DC, 1998

1 ....4.00

Superman Adventures

DC, 1996

1-3 ....3.00
4-20 ....2.00
21 ....4.00
22-66 ....2.00
Ann 1 ....4.00
Special 1 ....3.00

Superman/Aliens 2: God War

DC, 2002

1-4 ....3.00

Superman: A Nation Divided

DC

1 ....5.00

Q-Unit

Racket Squad in Action

Radical Dreamer

Radix

Ragman

Rai

Rain

Rampaging Hulk

Superman & Batman: Generations
DC, 1999

1-4 ....5.00

Superman & Batman: Generations II
DC, 2001

1-4 ....6.00

Superman & Batman: Generations III
DC, 2003

1-12 ....3.00

Superman & Batman Magazine
Welsh, 1993

1 ....3.00
2 ....2.00
3 ....3.00
4-8 ....2.00

Superman and Batman: World's Funnest
DC, 2000

1 ....7.00

Superman & Bugs Bunny
DC, 2000

1-4 ....3.00

Superman & Savage Dragon: Chicago
DC, 2002

1 ....6.00

Superman & Savage Dragon: Metropolis
DC, 1999

nn 5.00

Superman: At Earth's End
DC, 1995

1 ....5.00

Superman/Batman Secret Files
DC, 2003

1 ....5.00

Superman/Batman
DC, 2003

1 ....8.00
1/Retailer ed. 125.00
1/2nd-1/3rd 4.00
2 ....6.00
3 ....5.00
3/2nd 3.00
4 ....4.00
5 ....3.00
6 ....4.00
7 ....3.00
8 ....10.00
☛1st new Supergirl
8/2nd 7.00
☛Sketch cover
8/3rd 6.00
☛Wonder Woman cover
8/4th 3.00
9 ....5.00
9/2nd 4.00
9/3rd 3.00
10 ....5.00
10/2nd 4.00
11 ....5.00
12 ....4.00
13 ....5.00
13/Supergirl 7.00
14 ....5.00
15 ....4.00
16 ....5.00
17 ....4.00
18 ....3.00
19 ....4.00
20 ....3.00
21 ....4.00
22-24 ....3.00
26 ....4.00
27-60 ....3.00
Ann 1 ....4.00

Superman: Birthright
DC, 2003

1-12 ....3.00

Superman: Bizarro's World
DC

1 ....10.00

Superman: Blood of My Ancestors
DC, 2003

1 ....7.00

Superman Confidential
DC, 2007

1-10 ....3.00

Superman: Day of Doom
DC, 2003

1 ....10.00

Superman: Distant Fires
DC, 1998

1 ....6.00

Superman/Doomsday: Hunter/Prey
DC, 1994

1-3 ....6.00

Superman: Emperor Joker
DC, 2000

1 ....4.00

Superman: Endgame
DC, 2001

1 ....15.00

Superman Family
DC, 1974

164 ....35.00

165-169 .... 13.00
☛100-page issue
170-177 .... 11.00
178-180 .... 5.00
181-200 .... 4.00
201-222 .... 3.00

Superman/Fantastic Four
DC, 1999
1 .... 10.00

Superman for All Seasons
DC, 1998
1-4 .... 5.00

Superman for Earth
DC, 1991
1 .... 5.00

Superman Forever
DC, 1998
1 .... 6.00
1/Variant 7.00

Super Manga Blast!
Dark Horse, 2000
1-18 .... 5.00
19-59 .... 6.00

Superman Gallery
DC, 1993
1 .... 3.00

Superman/Gen13
WildStorm, 2000
1-3 .... 3.00

Superman (Giveaways)
DC, 1980
1-5 .... 1.00

Superman, Inc.
DC, 2000
1 .... 7.00

Superman IV Movie Special
DC, 1987
1 .... 2.00

Superman: Kal
DC
1 .... 6.00

Superman: Kansas Sighting
DC, 2004
1-2 .... 7.00

Superman: King of the World
DC, 1999
1 .... 4.00
1/Gold 5.00

Superman: Krisis of the Krimson Kryptonite
DC, 1996
1 .... 13.00

Superman: Last Son of Earth
DC, 2000
1-2 .... 6.00

Superman: Last Stand on Krypton
DC, 2003
1 .... 7.00

Superman: Lex 2000
DC, 2001
1 .... 4.00

Superman: Lois Lane
DC, 1998
1 .... 2.00

Superman/Madman Hullabaloo
Dark Horse, 1997
1-3 .... 3.00

Superman Meets the Motorsports Champions
DC, 1999
1 .... 1.00

Superman Meets the Quik Bunny
DC
1 .... 1.00

Superman: Metropolis
DC, 2003
1-12 .... 3.00

Superman Metropolis Secret Files
DC, 2000
1 .... 5.00

Superman Monster
DC
1 .... 6.00

Superman Movie Special
DC, 1983
1 .... 2.00

Superman: No Limits!
DC, 2001
1 .... 15.00

Superman: Our Worlds at War Secret Files
DC, 2001
1 .... 6.00

Superman: Peace on Earth
DC, 1999
1-1/2nd 10.00

Superman Plus
DC, 1997
1 .... 3.00

Rat Bastard

Raver

Razor

Razorwire

Real Bout High School

Real Heroes

Real Life Comics

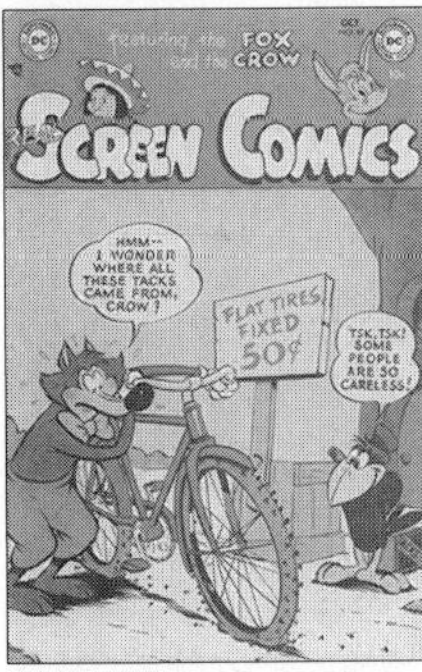

Real Screen Comics

Superman: President Lex
DC, 2003

1 .... 18.00

Superman: Red Son
DC, 2003

1 .... 7.00
2-3 .... 6.00

Superman Red/Superman Blue
DC, 1998

1 .... 4.00
Deluxe 1 .... 5.00

Superman Returns: Krypton to Earth
DC, 2006

1-4 .... 4.00

Superman Returns: The Movie Adaptation
DC, 2006

1 .... 7.00

Superman: Return to Krypton
DC, 2004

1 .... 18.00

Superman: Save the Planet
DC, 1998

1 .... 3.00
1/Variant 4.00

Superman: Secret Files
DC, 1998

1-2 .... 5.00

Superman: Secret Files 2004
DC, 2004

1 .... 5.00

Superman Secret Files and Origins 2004
DC, 2005

0 .... 6.00
☛Infinite Crisis tie

Superman Secret Files 2005
DC, 2006

1 .... 5.00

Superman: Secret Identity
DC, 2004

1-4 .... 6.00

Superman's Girl Friend Lois Lane
DC, 1958

1 .... 2,600.00
2 .... 625.00
3 .... 415.00
4-5 .... 300.00
6-10 .... 220.00
11-18 .... 125.00
19 .... 215.00
20 .... 125.00
21-29 .... 86.00
30-50 .... 48.00
51-67 .... 34.00
68 .... 44.00
69 .... 34.00
70 .... 175.00
☛1st SA Catwoman
71 .... 105.00
☛Catwoman app.
72-73 .... 15.00
74 .... 34.00
75-76 .... 15.00
77 .... 24.00
78 .... 15.00
79-85 .... 10.00
86 .... 16.00
87-94 .... 10.00
95 .... 25.00
☛Giant-sized
96-103 .... 8.00
104 .... 16.00
105-106 .... 14.00
107-110 .... 6.00
111 .... 10.00
112 .... 6.00
113 .... 14.00
114-120 .... 6.00
121 .... 5.00
122-123 .... 8.00
124-137 .... 5.00
Ann 1 .... 75.00
Ann 2 .... 50.00

Superman/Shazam: First Thunder
DC, 2005

1-4 .... 4.00

Superman: Silver Banshee
DC, 1998

1-2 .... 2.00

Superman's Metropolis
DC, 1997

1 .... 6.00

Superman's Nemesis: Lex Luthor
DC, 1999

1-4 .... 3.00

Superman's Pal Jimmy Olsen
DC, 1954

1 .... 4,000.00
2 .... 1,250.00
3 .... 675.00
4-5 .... 475.00
6-10 .... 335.00
11-20 .... 235.00
21-30 .... 150.00

31-40 .... 100.00
41-50 .... 75.00
51-56 .... 50.00
57-70 .... 30.00
71 .... 25.00
72-73 .... 30.00
74-75 .... 25.00
76 .... 30.00
77-88 .... 25.00
89-90 .... 20.00
91-94 .... 16.00
95 .... 25.00
96-99 .... 16.00
100 .... 25.00
101-103 .... 12.00
104 .... 35.00
☛Weird Adventures
105-112 .... 12.00
113 .... 25.00
☛Anti-Superman ish
114-119 .... 12.00
120-126 .... 10.00
127 .... 16.00
128-130 .... 10.00
131-132 .... 8.00
133 .... 10.00
134 .... 25.00
135-140 .... 12.00
141-150 .... 10.00
151 .... 8.00
152-163 .... 7.00

Superman Spectacular

DC

1 .... 3.00

Superman: Speeding Bullets

DC, 1993

1 .... 5.00

Superman: Strength

DC, 2005

1-3 .... 6.00

Superman/Tarzan: Sons of the Jungle

Dark Horse, 2001

1-3 .... 3.00

Superman: The Dark Side

DC, 1998

1-3 .... 5.00

Superman: The Doomsday Wars

DC, 1999

1 .... 5.00
1/Ltd. 25.00
2-3 .... 5.00

Superman: The Earth Stealers

DC, 1988

1 .... 3.00

Superman: The Last God of Krypton

DC, 1999

1 .... 5.00

Superman: The Legacy of Superman

DC, 1993

1 .... 3.00

Superman: The Man of Steel

DC, 1991

0 .... 3.00
1 .... 6.00
2-3 .... 3.00
4-16 .... 2.00
17 .... 3.00
18 .... 4.00
18/2nd-18/3rd 2.00
19-21 .... 3.00
22 .... 2.00
22/Variant 3.00
23-30 .... 2.00
30/Variant 3.00
31-49 .... 2.00
50 .... 3.00
51-99 .... 2.00
100 .... 3.00
100/Variant 4.00
101-134 .... 2.00
1000000-Ann 5 .... 3.00
Ann 6 .... 4.00

Superman: The Man of Steel Gallery

DC, 1995

1 .... 4.00

Superman: The Man of Tomorrow

DC, 1995

1-14 .... 2.00
15 .... 3.00
1000000 .... 2.00

Superman: The Odyssey

DC, 1999

1 .... 5.00

Superman: The Secret Years

DC, 1985

1-4 .... 2.00

Superman: The Trial of Superman

DC

1 .... 15.00

Real Sports Comics

Real Stuff

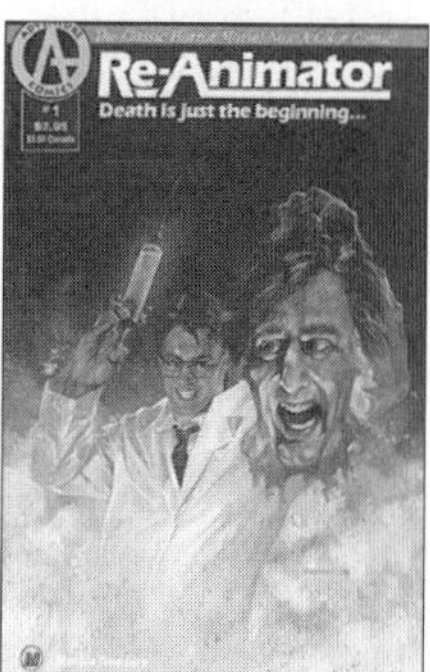

Re-Animator in Full Color

R.E.B.E.L.S.

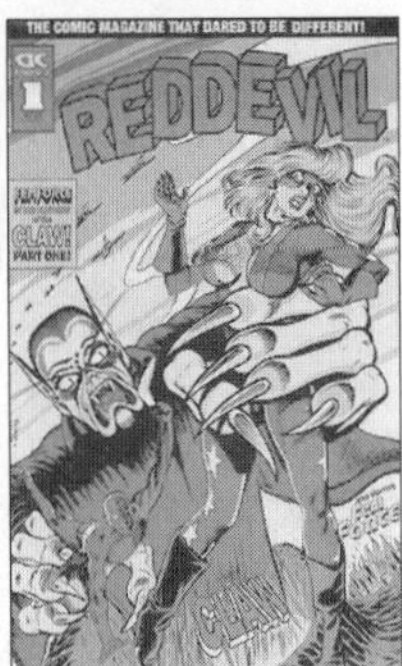

Reddevil

Redfox

Redmask of the Rio Grande

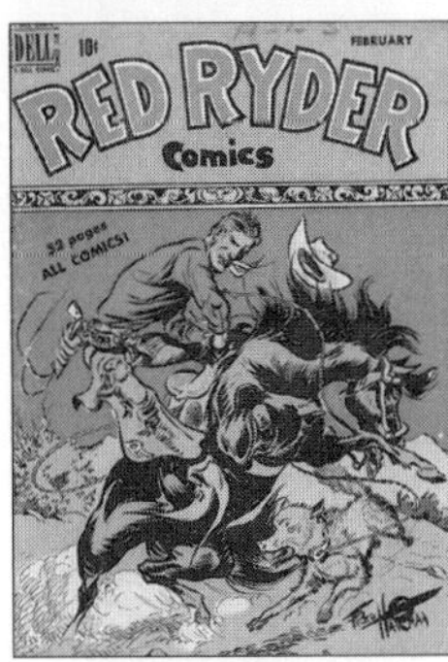

Red Ryder Comics

Superman: The Wedding Album

DC, 1996

1 .... 6.00
1/Direct 5.00
1/Gold 10.00

Superman/Thundercats

1 .... 6.00

Superman/Toyman

DC, 1996

1 .... 2.00

Superman: Under a Yellow Sun

DC, 1994

1 .... 6.00

Superman vs. Aliens

DC, 1995

1-3 .... 5.00

Superman vs. Predator

DC, 2000

1-3 .... 5.00

Superman vs. the Amazing Spider-Man

DC

1 .... 20.00

Superman vs. the Revenge Squad

DC

1 .... 13.00

Superman vs. The Terminator: Death to the Future

Dark Horse, 1999

1-4 .... 3.00

Superman Villains Secret Files

DC, 1998

1 .... 5.00

Superman vs. Darkseid: Apokolips Now

DC, 2003

1 .... 3.00

Superman: War of the Worlds

DC, 1998

1 .... 6.00
1/Ltd. 19.00

Superman: Where is Thy Sting?

DC, 2001

1 .... 7.00

Superman/Wonder Woman: Whom Gods Destroy

DC, 1996

1-4 .... 5.00

Superman Y2K

DC, 2000

nn 5.00

Super Mario Bros.

Valiant, 1990

1-6 .... 2.00
Special 1 .... 3.00

Super Mario Bros.

Valiant, 1991

1-5 .... 2.00

Supermarket

Idea & Design Works, 2006

1-4 .... 4.00

Supermen of America

DC, 1999

1 .... 4.00
1/CS 5.00
2-4 .... 3.00

Supermodels in the Rainforest

Sirius, 1998

1-3 .... 3.00

Supermouse Big Cheese

Pines, 1948

1 .... 200.00
2 .... 125.00
3 .... 85.00
4-6 .... 65.00
7-10 .... 35.00
11-20 .... 25.00
21-40 .... 18.00
41-45 .... 15.00
GS 1 .... 75.00
GS 2 .... 50.00

Super-Mystery Comics (1st Series)

Ace, 1940

1 .... 1,700.00
2 .... 950.00
3 .... 675.00
4 .... 450.00
5 .... 500.00
6 .... 450.00

Super-Mystery Comics (2nd Series)

Ace, 1941

1 .... 2,000.00
2-6 .... 350.00

Super-Mystery Comics (3rd Series)
Ace, 1942

1-6 .... 300.00

Super-Mystery Comics (4th Series)
Ace, 1944

1 .... 300.00
2-6 .... 250.00

Super-Mystery Comics (5th Series)
Ace, 1945

1-6 .... 250.00

Super-Mystery Comics (6th Series)
Ace, 1946

1 .... 225.00
2-4 .... 200.00
5 .... 250.00
6 .... 200.00

Super-Mystery Comics (7th Series)
Ace, 1947

1-6 .... 200.00

Super-Mystery Comics (8th Series)
Ace, 1948

1-6 .... 200.00

Supernatural Freak Machine
Idea & Design Works, 2005

1-2 .... 4.00

Supernatural Law
Exhibit A, 1999

24-38 .... 3.00

Supernaturals
Marvel, 1998

1/A-1/D 4.00
1/E 5.00
1/Ltd. 30.00
2/A-4/E 4.00
Ashcan 1 .... 3.00

Supernaturals Tour Book
Marvel, 1998

1 .... 3.00

Supernatural Thrillers
Marvel, 1972

1 .... 27.00
2-4 .... 10.00
5 .... 27.00
☛1st Living Mummy
6-15 .... 10.00

Superpatriot
Image, 1993

1-4 .... 2.00

SuperPatriot: America's Fighting Force
Image, 2002

1-4 .... 3.00

Superpatriot: Liberty & Justice
Image, 1995

1 .... 3.00
2-4 .... 3.00

Superpatriot: War on Terror
Image, 2004

1 .... 4.00
2 .... 3.00

Super Powers
DC, 1984

1 .... 2.00
2-5 .... 1.00

Super Powers
DC, 1985

1-6 .... 1.00

Super Powers
DC, 1986

1-4 .... 1.00

Super Pup
Avon, 1940

4-5 .... 25.00

Super Rabbit
Timely, 1943

1 .... 500.00
1/2nd 35.00
2 .... 275.00
2/2nd 25.00
3-5 .... 175.00
6 .... 150.00
7-10 .... 100.00
10/2nd 22.00
11-14 .... 90.00

Super Sexxx
Fantagraphics

1 .... 3.00

Super Shark Humanoids
Fish Tales, 1992

1 .... 3.00

Supersnipe Comics
Street & Smith, 1942

6 .... 600.00
7 .... 390.00
8 .... 415.00
9 .... 440.00
10 .... 365.00
11-12 .... 335.00

Supersnipe Comics (Vol. 2)
Street & Smith, 1944

1 .... 250.00

All comics prices listed are for NEAR MINT condition.

Red Tornado

Red Wolf

Regulators

Relative Heroes

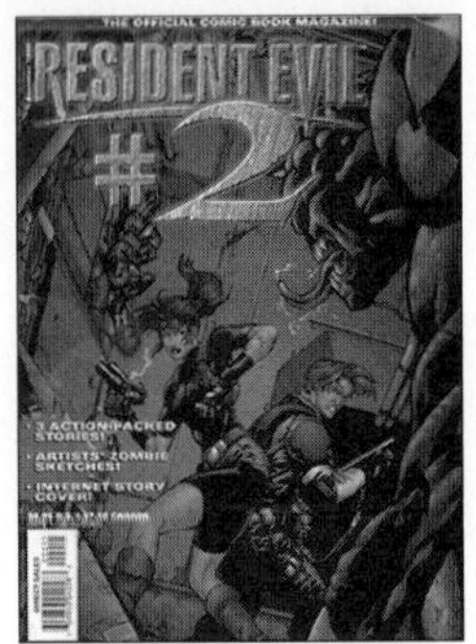

Resident Evil

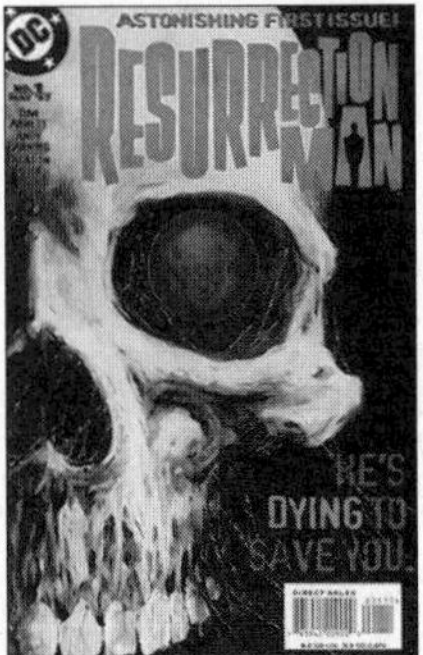

Resurrection Man

Retief and the Warlords

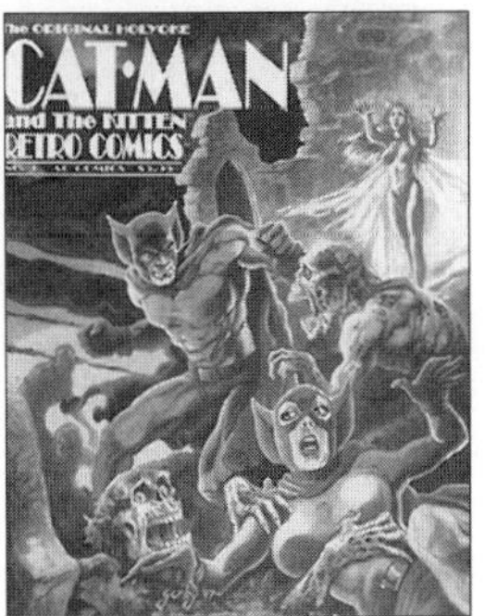

Retro Comics

2-3 ....220.00
4-12 ....210.00

Supersnipe Comics (Vol. 3)

Street & Smith, 1946

1 ....190.00
2-12 ....165.00

Supersnipe Comics (Vol. 4)

Street & Smith, 1947

1-12 ....130.00

Supersnipe Comics (Vol. 5)

Street & Smith, 1949

1 ....105.00

Super Soldier

DC, 1996

1 ....2.00

Super Soldier: Man of War

DC, 1997

1 ....2.00

Super Soldiers

Marvel, 1993

1 ....3.00
2-8 ....2.00

Supersonic Soul Puddin Comics & Stories

Four Cats Funny Books, 1995

1 ....4.00

Super Sonic vs. Hyper Knuckles

Archie

1 ....2.00

Super Spy

Centaur, 1940

1 ....1,000.00
2 ....600.00

Superstar: As Seen on TV

Image, 1999

1 ....6.00

Superswine

Caliber

1-2 ....3.00

Super Taboo

Fantagraphics, 1995

1-2 ....3.00

Super-Team Family

DC, 1975

1 ....12.00
2-4 ....6.00
5-10 ....4.00
11-15 ....3.00

Super-Villain Classics

Marvel, 1983

1 ....3.00

Super-Villain Team-Up

Marvel, 1975

1 ....7.00
2 ....5.00
3-5 ....4.00
5/30¢ 20.00
6 ....3.00
6/30¢ 20.00
7 ....3.00
7/30¢ 20.00
8-12/Whitman 3.00
12/35¢ 15.00
13 ....5.00
13/35¢ 15.00
14-14/Whitman 3.00
14/35¢ 15.00
15-17 ....3.00

Super Western Comics

Youthful, 1950

1 ....70.00

Superworld Comics

Hugo Gernsback, 1940

1 ....4,000.00
2 ....2,350.00
3 ....1,825.00

Suppressed!

Tome

1 ....3.00

Supreme

Image, 1992

0-1/Gold 3.00
2-12 ....2.00
13-40 ....3.00
41 ....4.00
41/Ltd 15.00
41/AmEnt 9.00
41/2nd-56 ....3.00
Ann 1 ....4.00

Supreme: Glory Days

Image, 1994

1-2 ....3.00

Supreme Power

Marvel, 2003

1 ....4.00
1/Special 5.00
2-4 ....3.00
5 ....4.00
6-18 ....3.00

Supreme Power: Hyperion

Marvel, 2005

1-5 ....3.00

Supreme Power: Nighthawk

Marvel, 2005

1-6 ....3.00

Supreme: The Return

Awesome, 1999

1-6 ....3.00

Supremie
Parody

1 .... 3.00

Sure-Fire Comics
Ace, 1940

1 .... 1,025.00
2 .... 485.00
3 .... 375.00
4 .... 500.00

Surfcrazed Comics
Pacifica

1 .... 3.00
3 .... 4.00
4 .... 3.00

Surf 'n' Wheels
Charlton, 1969

1-6 .... 12.00

Surf Sumo
Star Tiger, 1997

1-1/2nd 3.00

Surge
Eclipse, 1984

1-4 .... 2.00

Surreal School Stories
Gratuitous Bunny, 1995

1-5 .... 2.00

Surrogates
Top Shelf Productions, 2005

1 .... 3.00

Surrogate Saviour
Hot Brazen Comics, 1995

1-3 .... 3.00

Survive!
Apple

1 .... 3.00

Survivors
Fantagraphics

1-2 .... 3.00

Survivors
Prelude, 1986

1-2 .... 2.00

Survivors
Burnside, 1987

1 .... 2.00

Sushi
Shunga, 1990

1-8 .... 3.00

Suspense
Atlas, 1949

1 .... 370.00
2 .... 190.00
3 .... 210.00
4 .... 155.00
5-6 .... 165.00
7-10 .... 155.00
11-13 .... 120.00
14 .... 190.00
15-17 .... 120.00
18 .... 130.00
19-20 .... 120.00
21 .... 115.00
22 .... 130.00
23-24 .... 115.00
25 .... 160.00
26-29 .... 115.00

Suspense Comics
Continental, 1943

1 .... 2,500.00
2 .... 1,850.00
3 .... 6,000.00
4-6 .... 1,400.00
7-10 .... 1,050.00
11 .... 1,925.00
12 .... 1,050.00

Suspense Detective
Fawcett, 1952

1 .... 260.00
2 .... 155.00
3-5 .... 125.00

Suspira: The Great Working
Chaos, 1997

1-4 .... 3.00

Sussex Vampire
Caliber

1 .... 3.00

Sustah-Girl: Queen of the Black Age
Onli

1 .... 2.00

Suzie Comics
M.L.J., 1945

49 .... 125.00
50-55 .... 80.00
56 .... 75.00
57-100 .... 55.00

Swamp Fever
Big Muddy

1 .... 3.00

Swamp Thing
DC, 1972

1 .... 60.00
2 .... 30.00
3-4 .... 20.00
5-6 .... 15.00
7 .... 12.00
8-10 .... 10.00
11-24 .... 5.00

Swamp Thing
DC, 1986

46 .... 4.00
47-49 .... 3.00
50 .... 4.00
51 .... 3.00

Revolver

Rex Allen

Richie Rich Cash

Richie Rich Diamonds

Richie Rich Fortunes

Richie Rich Gems

Richie Rich Jackpots

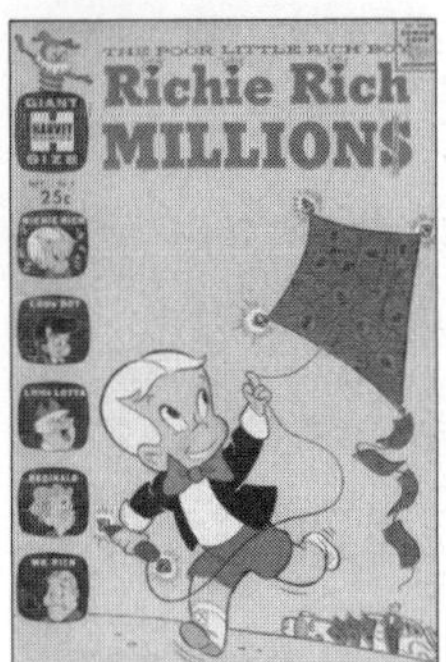

Richie Rich Millions

52 ....4.00
53 ....5.00
☛Batman appearance
54-81 ....3.00
82-83 ....2.00
84 ....5.00
☛Sandman appearance
85-89 ....2.00
90 ....3.00
91-99 ....2.00
100 ....3.00
101-124 ....2.00
125 ....3.00
126-140 ....2.00
140/Platinum 6.00
141-149 ....2.00
150 ....3.00
151-158 ....2.00
159-171 ....3.00
Ann 4-5 ....4.00
Ann 6 ....3.00
Ann 7 ....4.00

Swamp Thing
DC, 2000
1 ....4.00
2-20 ....3.00

Swamp Thing
DC, 2004
1 ....4.00
2-29 ....3.00

Swamp Thing: Roots
DC
1 ....8.00

Swan
Little Idylls, 1995
1-4 ....3.00

Swarm
Mushroom
1 ....3.00

Sweatshop
DC, 2003
1-6 ....3.00

Sweeney
Standard, 1949
4-5 ....45.00

Sweet
Adept
1 ....4.00

Sweetchilde
New Moon
1 ....3.00

Sweet Childe: Lost Confessions
Anarchy Bridgeworks
1 ....3.00

Sweetheart Diary
Fawcett, 1949
1 ....90.00
2 ....50.00
3-4 ....75.00
5-10 ....45.00
11-14 ....32.00

Sweetheart Diary
Charlton, 1955
32 ....35.00
33-41 ....25.00
42-60 ....15.00
61-65 ....12.00

Sweethearts
Fawcett, 1948
68 ....85.00
69-70 ....50.00
71-80 ....40.00
81-99 ....34.00
100 ....40.00
101-115 ....30.00
116-122 ....25.00

Sweethearts
Charlton, 1954
23-30 ....12.00
31-39 ....10.00
40 ....16.00
41 ....9.00
42 ....35.00
43-45 ....9.00
46 ....15.00
47-50 ....9.00
51-60 ....7.00
61-70 ....6.00
71-100 ....4.00
101-137 ....3.00

Sweetie Pie
Ajax, 1955
1 ....45.00
2 ....25.00

Sweet Love
Harvey, 1949
1 ....55.00
2 ....35.00
3-4 ....25.00
5 ....40.00

Sweet Lucy
Brainstorm, 1993
1-2 ....3.00

Sweet Lucy: Blonde Steele
Brainstorm
1 ....3.00

Sweet Lucy Commemorative Edition
Brainstorm, 1994
1 ....4.00

Sweetmeats
Atomeka
1 .... 4.00

Sweet Sixteen
Parents' Magazine Institute, 1946
1 .... 100.00
2 .... 75.00
3-13 .... 50.00

Sweet XVI
Marvel, 1991
1-6 .... 1.00
Special 1 .... 2.00

Swerve
Slave Labor, 1995
1-2 .... 2.00

Swift Arrow
Ajax, 1954
1 .... 85.00
2 .... 50.00
3-5 .... 35.00

Swift Arrow
Ajax, 1957
1 .... 45.00
2-3 .... 35.00

Swift Arrow's Gunfighters
Ajax, 1957
4 .... 35.00

Swiftsure
Harrier, 1985
1-18 .... 2.00

Swiftsure & Conqueror
Harrier, 1985
1-8 .... 2.00
9 .... 3.00
10-18 .... 2.00

Swimsuits & Mermaids
Image Guild
1-1/2nd 4.00

Swing with Scooter
DC, 1966
1 .... 30.00
2 .... 18.00
3 .... 15.00
4-5 .... 12.00
6-10 .... 10.00
11-20 .... 8.00
21-30 .... 6.00
31-36 .... 5.00

Switchblade
Silverline, 1997
1 .... 3.00

Sword in the Stone
Gold Key, 1964
1 .... 30.00

Sword of Damocles
Image, 1996
1-2 .... 3.00

Sword of Dracula
Image, 2003
1-6 .... 3.00

Sword of Sorcery
DC, 1973
1 .... 10.00
2-3 .... 8.00
4-5 .... 6.00

Sword of the Atom
DC, 1983
1-Special 3 .... 2.00

Sword of the Samurai
Avalon, 1996
1 .... 3.00

Sword of Valor
A+
1-4 .... 3.00

Swordsmen and Saurians
Eclipse
1 .... 20.00

Swords of Cerebus
Aardvark-Vanaheim
1-2/2nd 5.00
3-4/2nd 6.00
5-6 .... 5.00

Swords of Cerebus Supplement
Aardvark-Vanaheim
1 .... 1.00

Swords of Shar-Pei
Caliber
1-2 .... 3.00

Swords of Texas
Eclipse, 1987
1-4 .... 2.00

Swords of the Swashbucklers
Marvel, 1985
1-12 .... 2.00

Swords of Valor
A-Plus
1-4 .... 3.00

Sylvia Faust
Image, 2004
1-2 .... 3.00

Symbols of Justice
High Impact, 1995
1 .... 3.00

Syn
Dark Horse, 2003
1-5 .... 3.00

Richie Rich Money World

Richie Rich Profits

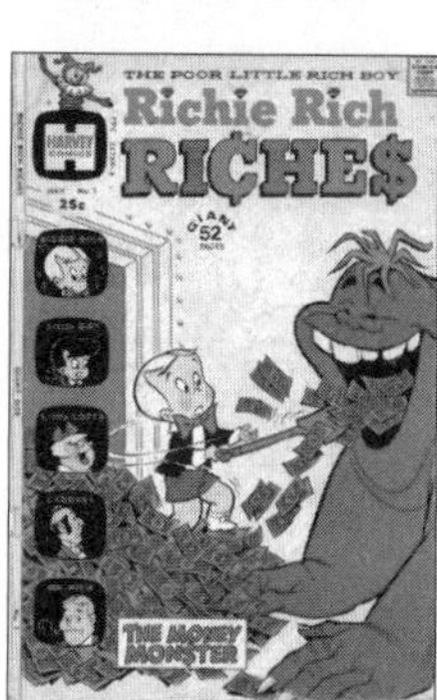

Richie Rich Riches

Richie Rich Vaults of Mystery

Richie Rich Zillionz

Rin Tin Tin

Rio at Bay

Rip Hunter...Time Master

Synn, the Girl from LSD
AC, 1990

1 .... 4.00

Synthetic Assassin
Night Realm

1 .... 2.00

Syphons
Now, 1986

1-7 .... 2.00

Syphons
Now, 1993

0 .... 1.00
1-3 .... 3.00

Syphons: The Sygate Stratagem
Now, 1994

1-3 .... 3.00

System
DC, 1996

1-3 .... 3.00

System Seven
Arrow, 1987

1-3 .... 2.00

Taboo
Spiderbaby, 1995

1-3 .... 10.00
4-9 .... 15.00

Taboux
Antarctic, 1996

1-2 .... 4.00

Tabula Rasa
Image, 2006

1 .... 5.00

Tactics
ADV Manga, 2004

1-2 .... 10.00

Taffy Comics
Rural Home, 1945

1 .... 150.00
2 .... 110.00
3 .... 90.00
4-5 .... 75.00
6-10 .... 50.00
11-12 .... 40.00

Tailgunner Jo
DC, 1988

1-6 .... 1.00

Tails
Archie, 1995

1-3 .... 2.00

Tainted
DC, 1995

1 .... 5.00

Tainted Blood
Weirdling, 1996

1 .... 3.00

Taken Under Compendium
Caliber

1 .... 3.00

Takion
DC, 1996

1-7 .... 2.00

Tale of Halima
Fantagraphics

1-2 .... 3.00

Tale of Mya Rom
Aircel

1 .... 2.00

Tale of One Bad Rat
Dark Horse, 1994

1 .... 4.00
2-4 .... 3.00

Tale of the Body Thief (Anne Rice's...)
Sicilian Dragon, 1999

1-12 .... 3.00

Tales Calculated to Drive You Bats
Archie, 1961

1 .... 75.00
2 .... 50.00
3-7 .... 30.00
Ann 1 .... 50.00

Tales Calculated to Drive You Mad
E.C., 1997

1-8 .... 4.00

Tales Designed to Thrizzle
Fantagraphics, 2005

1 .... 5.00

Tales from Ground Zero
Excel

1 .... 5.00

Tales From Necropolis
Brainstorm

1 .... 3.00

Tales From ... Riverdale Digest Magazine
Archie, 2005

7-17 .... 2.00

Tales from Shock City
Fantagraphics, 2001

nn 4.00

Tales From Sleaze Castle
Gratuitous Bunny

1-3 .... 3.00

Tales From the Age of Apocalypse
Marvel, 1996

1 .... 6.00

Tales from the Age of Apocalypse: Sinister Bloodlines
Marvel, 1997

1 .... 6.00

Tales from the Aniverse
Massive, 1992

1-3 .... 2.00

Tales from the Aniverse
Arrow

1-6 .... 2.00

Tales from the Bog
Aberration, 1995

1-Ashcan 1 .... 3.00

Tales from the Bog (Director's Cut)
Aberration, 1998

1 .... 3.00

Tales from the Bully Pulpit One Shot
Image, 2004

1 .... 7.00

Tales from the Clonezone
Dark Horse

1 .... 2.00

Tales From the Crypt
E.C., 1950

20 .... 775.00
21 .... 900.00
22 .... 700.00
23-25 .... 520.00
26-30 .... 400.00
31 .... 460.00
32 .... 300.00
33 .... 675.00
☛Crypt Keeper origin
34-46 .... 295.00

Tales from the Crypt
Gladstone, 1990

1-6 .... 3.00

Tales from the Crypt
Cochran, 1991

1 .... 4.00

Tales from the Crypt
Cochran, 1991

1-7 .... 2.00

Tales from the Crypt
Gemstone, 1992

1-15 .... 2.00
16-30 .... 3.00
Ann 1 .... 9.00
Ann 2 .... 10.00
Ann 3 .... 11.00
Ann 4 .... 13.00
Ann 5 .... 14.00

Tales from the Edge!
Vanguard, 1993

1 .... 4.00
2 .... 5.00
3-7 .... 3.00
8 .... 4.00
9 .... 5.00
10 .... 4.00
11 .... 5.00
12 .... 4.00
13 .... 3.00
14 .... 5.00
15 .... 6.00
Summer 1 .... 4.00

Tales from the Fridge
Kitchen Sink, 1973

1 .... 3.00

Tales from the Great Book
Famous Funnies, 1955

1 .... 30.00
2-4 .... 24.00

Tales from the Heart
Entropy, 1988

1 .... 4.00
2-11 .... 3.00

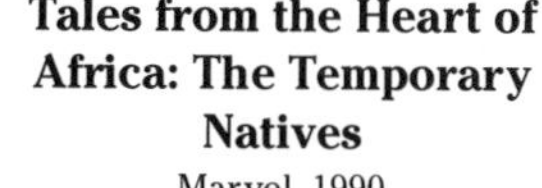

Tales from the Heart of Africa: The Temporary Natives
Marvel, 1990

1 .... 4.00

Tales from the Kids
David G. Brown, 1996

1 .... 2.00

Tales From the Leather Nun
Last Gasp

1 .... 14.00

Tales From the Mahabharata
Amar Chitra Katha

16 .... 4.00

Tales from the Outer Boroughs
Fantagraphics

1-3 .... 2.00
4-5 .... 3.00

Tales from the Plague
Eclipse

1 .... 4.00

Tales from the Ravaged Lands
Magi, 1996

0 .... 2.00
1-6 .... 3.00

Rip Off Comix

Rising Stars

Robin Red and the Lutins

Robotech Masters

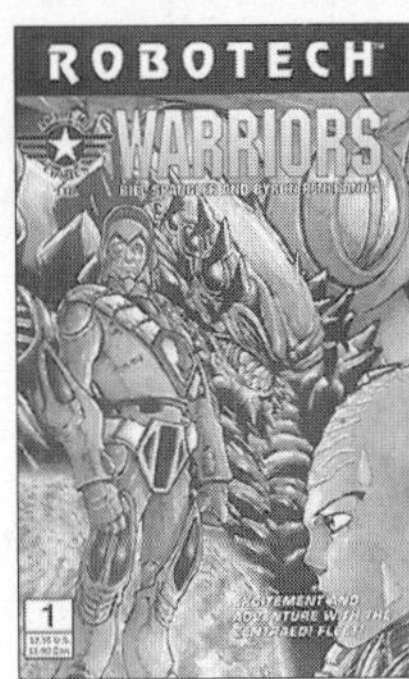

Robotech Warriors

Rocket Ranger

Roger Rabbit

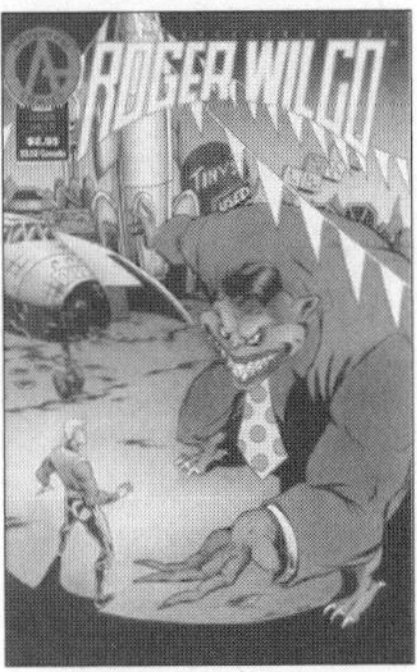

Roger Wilco

Tales from the Stone Troll Cafè

Planet X, 1986

1 .... 2.00

Tales from the Tomb

Dell, 1962

1 .... 125.00

Tales from the Tomb (Magazine, Vol. 1)

Eerie, 1969

6 .... 40.00
7-8 .... 34.00

Tales from the Tomb (Magazine, Vol. 2)

Eerie, 1970

1-6 .... 30.00

Tales from the Tomb (Magazine, Vol. 3)

Eerie, 1971

1-6 .... 25.00

Tales from the Tomb (Magazine, Vol. 4)

Eerie, 1972

1-5 .... 25.00

Tales from the Tomb (Magazine, Vol. 5)

Eerie, 1973

1-6 .... 20.00

Tales from the Tomb (Magazine, Vol. 6)

Eerie, 1974

1-6 .... 20.00

Tales from the Tomb (Magazine, Vol. 7)

Eerie, 1975

1-3 .... 15.00

Tales from the Tube

Print Mint

1 .... 3.00

Tales of a Checkered Man

D.W. Brubaker

1 .... 2.00

Tales of Asgard

Marvel, 1968

1 .... 30.00

Tales of Asgard

Marvel, 1984

1 .... 2.00

Tales of Beatrix Farmer

Mu, 1996

1 .... 3.00

Tales of Blue & Grey

Avalon

1 .... 3.00

Tales of Evil

Atlas-Seaboard, 1975

1 .... 9.00
2-3 .... 7.00

Tales of Ghost Castle

DC, 1975

1 .... 10.00
2-3 .... 9.00

Tales of G.I. Joe

Marvel, 1988

1-15 .... 1.00

Tales of Horror

Toby, 1952

1 .... 250.00
2 .... 175.00
3-13 .... 150.00

Tales of Jerry

Hacienda

1-10 .... 3.00

Tales of Lethargy

Alpha

1-3 .... 3.00

Tales of Ordinary Madness

Dark Horse, 2004

1-4 .... 3.00

Tales of Screaming Horror

Fantaco, 1992

1 .... 4.00

Tales of Sex and Death

Print Mint, 1971

1-2 .... 3.00

Tales of Shaundra

Rip Off

1 .... 13.00

Tales of Suspense

Marvel, 1959

1 .... 1,400.00
2 .... 540.00
3 .... 475.00
4 .... 450.00
5-10 .... 325.00
11-20 .... 240.00
21-32 .... 150.00
33-38 .... 135.00
39 .... 3,500.00
☛1st Iron Man
40 .... 1,100.00
41 .... 650.00
42-45 .... 325.00
☛1st Crimson Dynamo
46-47 .... 210.00
48 .... 265.00
☛1st red/gold armor
49 .... 210.00
50 .... 155.00
51 .... 105.00
52 .... 140.00
53 .... 120.00

☛Watcher origin
54-56 .... 62.00
57 .... 170.00
☛Cap America appearance
58-59 .... 210.00
☛Cap stories start
60 .... 120.00
61-62 .... 82.00
63 .... 180.00
☛Bucky origin
64 .... 72.00
65-66 .... 125.00
☛Red Skull origin
67-70 .... 52.00
71-80 .... 42.00
81-99 .... 32.00

Tales of Suspense
Marvel, 1995
1 .... 7.00

Tales of Suspense: Captain America/Iron Man
Marvel, 2005
1 .... 6.00

Tales of Tellos
Image, 2004
1-3 .... 4.00

Tales of Terror
Eclipse, 1985
1-13 .... 2.00

Tales of Terror Annual
E.C., 1951
1 .... 2,500.00
2 .... 2,000.00
3 .... 1,500.00

Tales of the Armorkins
Co. & Sons
1 .... 3.00

Tales of the Beanworld
Eclipse, 1985
1 .... 4.00
2-10 .... 3.00
11-19 .... 2.00
20-21 .... 3.00

Tales of the Closet
Hetric-Martin, 1987
1-8 .... 3.00

Tales of the Crimson Lion
Gary Lankford, 1987
1 .... 2.00

Tales of the Cyborg Gerbils
Harrier, 1987
1 .... 2.00

Tales of the Darkness
Image, 1998
½ 3.00
½/A 4.00
1-4 .... 3.00

Tales of the Fehnnik
Antarctic, 1995
1 .... 3.00

Tales of the Fehnnik
Radio, 1998
1 .... 3.00

Tales of the Great Unspoken
Top Shelf
1 .... 4.00

Tales of the Green Beret
Dell, 1967
1 .... 25.00
2-5 .... 18.00

Tales of the Green Berets
Avalon
1-7 .... 3.00

Tales of the Green Hornet
Now, 1990
1-2 .... 2.00

Tales of the Green Hornet
Now, 1992
1-4 .... 2.00

Tales of the Green Hornet
Now, 1992
1-3 .... 3.00

Tales of the Green Lantern Corps
DC, 1981
1 .... 2.00
2-3 .... 1.00
Ann 1 .... 2.00

Tales of the Jackalope
Blackthorne, 1986
1-7 .... 2.00

Tales of the Kung Fu Warriors
CFW, 1989
1-14 .... 2.00

Tales of the Legion
DC, 1984
314-324 .... 1.00
325 .... 2.00
326-354 .... 1.00
Ann 4-5 .... 2.00

Tales of the Mans
Skit
Ashcan 1 .... 1.00

Tales of the Marvels: Blockbuster
Marvel, 1995
1 .... 6.00

Rom

Romantic Adventures

Romantic Story

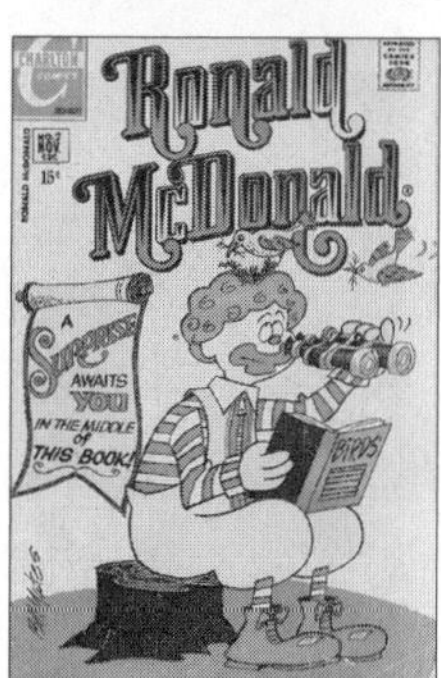

Ronald McDonald

Ronin

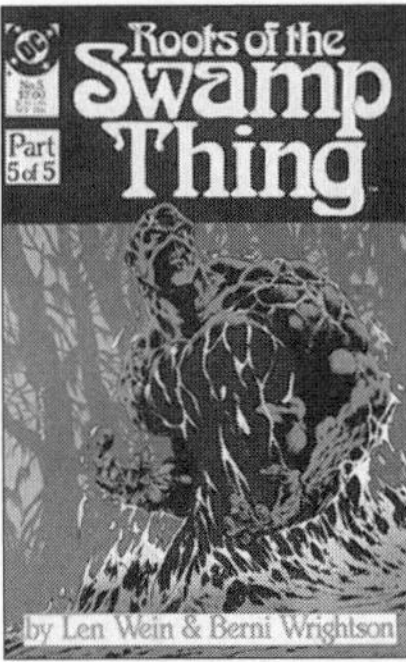

Roots of the Swamp Thing

Roy Rogers Comics

Roy Rogers Western

Tales of the Marvels: Inner Demons

Marvel, 1995

1 .... 6.00

Tales of the Marvels: Wonder Years

Marvel, 1995

1-2 .... 5.00

Tales of the Marvel Universe

Marvel, 1997

1 .... 3.00

Tales of the Mysterious Traveler

Charlton, 1956

1 .... 220.00
2 .... 170.00
3 .... 135.00
4-5 .... 115.00
6-10 .... 92.00
11-13 .... 80.00
14-15 .... 3.00

Tales of the Mysterious Traveler

Eclipse

1 .... 3.00

Tales of the New Teen Titans

DC, 1982

1 .... 2.00
2-4 .... 1.00

Tales of the Ninja Warriors

CFW, 1988

1-16 .... 2.00

Tales of the Sun Runners

Sirius, 1986

1-3 .... 2.00

Tales of the Teenage Mutant Ninja Turtles

Mirage, 1987

1 .... 3.00
2-7 .... 2.00

Tales of the Teenage Mutant Ninja Turtles

Mirage, 2004

1-5 .... 3.00

Tales of the Teen Titans

DC, 1984

41-42 .... 2.00
43 .... 3.00
44 .... 6.00
45-59 .... 2.00
60-91 .... 1.00
Ann 4 .... 2.00

Tales of the Unexpected

DC, 1956

1 .... 750.00
2 .... 385.00
3 .... 275.00
4-5 .... 225.00
6-10 .... 165.00
11-20 .... 125.00
21-30 .... 100.00
31-39 .... 85.00
40 .... 650.00
☛Spacc Rangcr starts
41-42 .... 275.00
43 .... 450.00
☛Space Ranger cover
44-45 .... 200.00
46-50 .... 150.00
51-55 .... 125.00
56-60 .... 100.00
61-70 .... 85.00
71-74 .... 60.00
75-82 .... 50.00
83-90 .... 30.00
91-100 .... 22.00
101-104 .... 20.00
☛Becomes Unexpected

Tales of the Unexpected

DC, 2006

1-3 .... 4.00

Tales of the Vampires

Dark Horse, 2003

1-5 .... 3.00

Tales of the Witchblade

Image, 1996

½ 4.00
½/A 8.00
½/Gold 5.00
1-1/Gold 3.00
1/Platinum 5.00
2-9 .... 3.00
Deluxe 1 .... 15.00

Tales of the Zombie

Marvel, 1973

1 .... 25.00
2 .... 18.00
3-5 .... 15.00
6-10 .... 10.00
Ann 1 .... 15.00

Tales of Toad

Print Mint, 1970

1 .... 20.00
2-3 .... 15.00

Tales of Torment

Mirage, 2004

1 .... 3.00

Tale Spin

Disney, 1991

1-7 .... 2.00

Tale Spin Limited Series

Disney, 1991

1-4 .... 2.00

Talespin

Disney

1 .... 4.00

Tales Sleepy Hollow: The Lost Chronicles of "I Hunt Monsters"

Antarctic, 2005

1 .... 3.00

Tales to Astonish

Marvel, 1959

1 .... 2,000.00
2 .... 635.00
3-5 .... 440.00
6-10 .... 355.00
11-20 .... 265.00
21-26 .... 200.00
27 .... 3,600.00
☛1st Hank Pym
28-34 .... 175.00
35 .... 1,900.00
☛1st Ant-Man
36 .... 625.00
37-40 .... 350.00
41-43 .... 230.00
44 .... 500.00
☛1st Wasp
45-48 .... 150.00
49 .... 250.00
☛1st Giant Man
50-56 .... 95.00
57 .... 125.00
☛Spider-Man appearance
58 .... 95.00
59 .... 150.00
☛Giant-Man vs. Hulk
60 .... 175.00
☛Hulk stories start
61 .... 75.00
62 .... 90.00
☛1st Leader
63-65 .... 75.00
66-69 .... 70.00
70 .... 100.00
☛Namor stories start
71-81 .... 55.00
82 .... 78.00
☛Iron Man appearance
83-90 .... 55.00
91 .... 52.00
☛Silver Surfer appearance
92-93 .... 75.00
☛Silver Surfer appearance
94-99 .... 50.00
100 .... 75.00
101 .... 85.00

Tales to Astonish

Marvel, 1979

1-14 .... 2.00

Tales to Astonish

Marvel, 1994

1 .... 7.00

Tales to Offend

Dark Horse, 1997

1 .... 3.00

Tales Too Terrible to Tell

NEC, 1990

1 .... 3.00
1/2nd-7 .... 4.00

Taleweaver

WildStorm, 2001

1 .... 4.00
2-6 .... 3.00

Talismen: SCSI Voodoo

Blink

1-3 .... 3.00

Talk Dirty

Fantagraphics, 1992

1-3 .... 3.00

Talking Orangutans in Borneo

GT-Labs, 1999

1 .... 4.00

Tall Tails

Golden Realm, 1993

1-2 .... 2.00
3-7 .... 3.00

Tally-Ho Comics

Bailey, 1944

1 .... 350.00

Talonz

Stop Dragon, 1987

1 .... 2.00

Talos of the Wilderness Sea

DC, 1985

1 .... 2.00

Tammas

Pandemonium, 1986

1 .... 2.00

Tangent Comics/Doom Patrol

DC, 1997

1 .... 3.00

Tangent Comics/Green Lantern

DC, 1997

1 .... 3.00

Tangent Comics/JLA

DC, 1998

1 .... 2.00

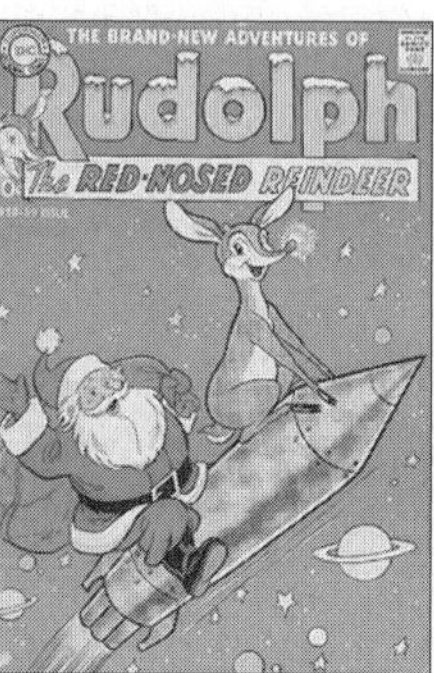

Rudolph the Red-Nosed Reindeer Annual

Runaways

Rune

Ruse

Rusty

Sable

Sabre

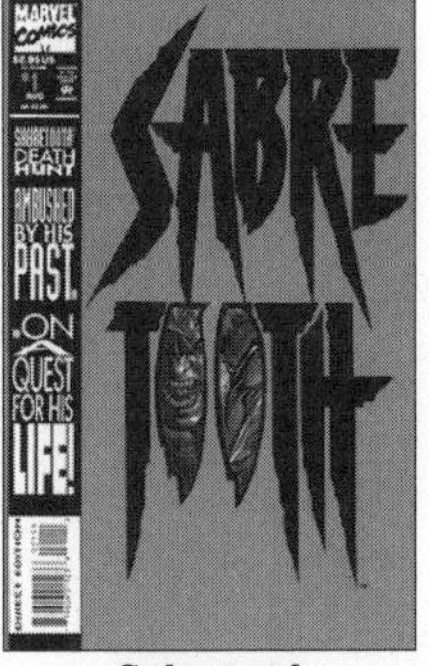

Sabretooth

Tangent Comics/Metal Men
DC, 1997

1 ....3.00

Tangent Comics/Nightwing
DC, 1997

1 ....3.00

Tangent Comics/ Nightwing: Night Force
DC, 1998

1 ....2.00

Tangent Comics/Powergirl
DC, 1998

1 ....2.00

Tangent Comics/Sea Devils
DC, 1997

1 ....3.00

Tangent Comics/Secret Six
DC, 1997

1 ....3.00

Tangent Comics/Tales of the Green Lantern
DC, 1998

1 ....2.00

Tangent Comics/The Atom
DC, 1997

1 ....3.00

Tangent Comics/The Batman
DC, 1998

1 ....2.00

Tangent Comics/The Flash
DC, 1997

1 ....3.00

Tangent Comics/The Joker
DC, 1997

1 ....3.00

Tangent Comics/The Joker's Wild
DC, 1998

1 ....2.00

Tangent Comics/ The Superman
DC, 1998

1 ....2.00

Tangent Comics/ The Trials of the Flash
DC, 1998

1 ....2.00

Tangent Comics/ Wonder Woman
DC, 1998

1 ....2.00

Tangents
NBM

1 ....17.00

Tangled Web
Marvel, 2001

1-22 ....3.00

Tank Girl
Dark Horse, 1991

1 ....4.00
2-4 ....3.00

Tank Girl 2
Dark Horse, 1993

1-4 ....3.00

Tank Girl: Apocalypse
DC, 1995

1-4 ....2.00

Tank Girl Movie Adaptation
DC

1 ....6.00

Tank Girl: The Odyssey
DC, 1995

1-4 ....3.00

Tank Vixens
Antarctic, 1994

1-4 ....3.00

Tantalizing Stories
Tundra, 1992

1-5 ....2.00
6 ....3.00

TaoLand
Sumitek, 1994

1 ....2.00
2-5 ....6.00

TaoLand Adventures
Antarctic, 1999

1-2 ....4.00

Tap
Promethean, 1994

1-3 ....3.00

Tapestry
Superior Junk, 1994

1-5 ....2.00

Tapestry Anthology
Caliber, 1997

1 ....3.00

Tapping the Vein
Eclipse

1 ....8.00
2-3 ....7.00
4-5 ....8.00

Target: Airboy
Eclipse, 1988

1 ....2.00

Target Comics

Novelty, 1940

1 .... 3,500.00
2 .... 1,650.00
3-4 .... 1,100.00
5 .... 3,100.00
6 .... 1,450.00
7 .... 3,300.00
8-9 .... 1,100.00
10 .... 1,375.00
11 .... 1,200.00
12 .... 1,100.00
13 .... 615.00
14 .... 585.00
15-24 .... 500.00
25-34 .... 450.00
35-36 .... 95.00
37-48 .... 68.00
49-56 .... 56.00
57-66 .... 50.00
67-90 .... 45.00
91-102 .... 38.00
103-105 .... 32.00

Target: The Corruptors

Dell, 1962

2-3 .... 25.00

Target Western Romances

Star, 1949

106 .... 200.00
107 .... 175.00

Targitt

Atlas-Seaboard, 1975

1 .... 9.00
2 .... 8.00
3 .... 7.00

Tarot Cafe

Tokyopop, 2005

1-4 .... 10.00

Tarot: Witch of the Black Rose

Broadsword, 2000

1 .... 5.00
2-29 .... 3.00
29/Variant 4.00
30 .... 3.00
30/Variant 20.00
31 .... 3.00
31/Deluxe 20.00
31/Photo 15.00
32 .... 3.00
32/Variant 5.00
33-55 .... 3.00
33/Deluxe 20.00

Tarzan

Dell, 1948

1 .... 900.00
2 .... 525.00
3-5 .... 385.00
6-9 .... 290.00
10 .... 260.00
11 .... 235.00
12-15 .... 220.00
16-20 .... 160.00
21-30 .... 135.00
31-54 .... 80.00
55-70 .... 50.00
71-79 .... 42.00
80-99 .... 30.00
100 .... 40.00
101-110 .... 28.00
111-120 .... 25.00
121-131 .... 20.00

Tarzan

Gold Key, 1962

132-154 .... 14.00
155 .... 18.00
156-162 .... 10.00
163-164 .... 8.00
165 .... 10.00
166-167 .... 8.00
168 .... 10.00
169-170 .... 8.00
171 .... 10.00
172-200 .... 7.00
201-206 .... 6.00

Tarzan

DC, 1972

207 .... 17.00
208 .... 10.00
209-210 .... 6.00
211-229 .... 4.00
230-235 .... 8.00
236-258 .... 3.00

Tarzan

Marvel, 1977

1 .... 3.00
1/35¢ 15.00
2-2/Whitman 2.00
2/35¢ 15.00
3 .... 2.00
3/35¢ 15.00
4 .... 2.00
4/35¢ 15.00
5 .... 2.00
5/35¢ 15.00
6-29 .... 2.00
Ann 1 .... 3.00
Ann 2-3 .... 2.00

Tarzan

Dark Horse, 1996

1-20 .... 3.00

Tarzan (Disney's...)

Dark Horse, 1999

1-2 .... 3.00

Sabrina the Teenage Witch

Saddle Justice

Sad Sack

Sad Sack Army Life Parade

Sad Sack Laugh Special

Safety-Belt Man

Saga of the Original Human Torch

Saga of the Sub-Mariner

Tarzan and the Jewels of Opar (Edgar Rice Burroughs'...)
Dark Horse, 1999
1 ....11.00

Tarzan: A Tale of Mugambi (Edgar Rice Burroughs'...)
Dark Horse, 1995
1 ....3.00

Tarzan/Carson of Venus
Dark Horse, 1998
1-4 ....3.00

Tarzan Digest
DC, 1972
1 ....3.00

Tarzan Family
DC, 1975
60-61 ....5.00
62-66 ....4.00

Tarzan/John Carter: Warlords of Mars
Dark Horse, 1996
1-4 ....3.00

Tarzan, Lord of the Jungle
Gold Key, 1965
1 ....40.00

Tarzan: Love, Lies and the Lost City
Malibu, 1992
1-3 ....4.00

Tarzan of the Apes
Marvel, 1984
1-2 ....3.00

Tarzan of the Apes (Edgar Rice Burroughs'...)
Dark Horse, 1999
1 ....13.00

Tarzan's Jungle Annual
Dell, 1952
1 ....100.00
2 ....75.00
3-7 ....55.00

Tarzan: The Beckoning
Malibu, 1992
1-7 ....3.00

Tarzan: The Lost Adventure (Edgar Rice Burroughs'...)
Dark Horse, 1995
1-4 ....3.00

Tarzan: The Rivers of Blood (Edgar Rice Burroughs'...)
Dark Horse, 1999
1-4 ....3.00

Tarzan: The Savage Heart
Dark Horse, 1999
1-4 ....3.00

Tarzan The Warrior
Malibu, 1992
1-5 ....3.00

Tarzan vs. Predator at the Earth's Core
Dark Horse, 1996
1-4 ....3.00

Tarzan Weekly
Byblos
1 ....5.00

T.A.S.E.R.
Comicreations, 1992
1-2 ....2.00

Task Force One
Image, 2006
1-4 ....4.00

Taskmaster
Marvel, 2002
1-4 ....3.00

Tasmanian Devil and His Tasty Friends
Gold Key, 1962
1 ....75.00

Tastee-Freez Comics
Harvey, 1957
1-6 ....25.00

Tasty Bits
Avalon, 1999
1 ....3.00

Tattered Banners
DC, 1998
1-4 ....3.00

Tattoo
Caliber
1-2 ....3.00

Tattoo Man
Fantagraphics
1 ....3.00

Taxx
Express
½ 2.00
1 ....3.00

T-Bird Chronicles
Me Comix
1-2 ....2.00

Team 7

Image, 1994

1-4 .... 3.00
Ashcan 1 .... 1.00

Team 7: Dead Reckoning

Image, 1996

1-4 .... 3.00

Team 7: Objective: Hell

Image, 1995

1-3 .... 3.00

Team America

Marvel, 1982

1-12 .... 1.00

Team Anarchy

Dagger, 1993

1-7 .... 3.00

Team Nippon

Aircel, 1989

1-7 .... 2.00

Team One: Stormwatch

Image, 1995

1-2 .... 3.00

Team One: WildC.A.T.S

Image, 1995

1-2 .... 3.00

Team Superman

DC, 1999

1 .... 3.00

Team Superman Secret Files

DC, 1998

1 .... 5.00

Team Titans

DC, 1992

1/A 4.00
1/B-1/E 3.00
2-24 .... 2.00
Ann 1 .... 4.00
Ann 2 .... 3.00

Team X

Marvel, 1999

2000 .... 4.00

Team X/Team 7

Marvel, 1997

1 .... 5.00

Team Yankee

First, 1989

1-6 .... 2.00

Team Youngblood

Image, 1993

1-9 .... 2.00
10 .... 3.00
11 .... 2.00
12-22 .... 3.00

Team Zero

DC, 2006

1-6 .... 3.00

Tears

Boneyard, 1992

1-2 .... 3.00

Teaser and the Blacksmith

Fantagraphics

1 .... 4.00

Tech High

Virtually Real Enterprises, 1996

1-3 .... 3.00

Tech Jacket

Image, 2003

1-6 .... 3.00

Techno Maniacs

Independent

1 .... 2.00

Technopolis

Caliber

1-4 .... 3.00

Technopriests

DC, 2004

1 .... 15.00

Teddy Roosevelt and His Rough Riders

Avon, 1950

1 .... 125.00

Teen-Age Brides

Home, 1953

1 .... 40.00
2 .... 25.00
3-7 .... 20.00

Teen-Age Confidential Confessions

Charlton, 1960

1 .... 20.00
2 .... 12.00
3-5 .... 10.00
6-9 .... 8.00
10-22 .... 6.00

Teen-Aged Dope Slaves and Reform School Girls

Eclipse

1 .... 10.00

Teen-Age Diary Secrets

St. John, 1949

4 .... 150.00
5-9 .... 125.00

Teenage Hotrodders

Charlton, 1963

1 .... 35.00
2-10 .... 20.00
11-24 .... 15.00

Sailor Moon Comic

Saint Angel

Saiyuki

Sam and Twitch

Samurai

Samurai Penguin

Sanctuary Part 2

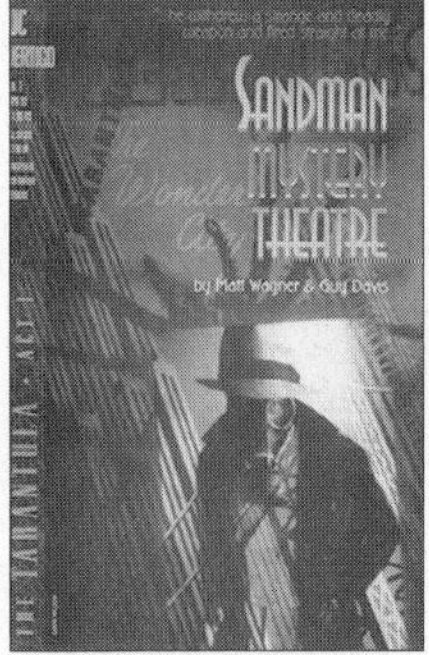
Sandman Mystery Theatre

Teen-Age Love
Charlton, 1958

4 .... 30.00
5 .... 16.00
6-10 .... 14.00
11-20 .... 9.00
21-30 .... 7.00
31-50 .... 5.00
51-70 .... 4.00
71-96 .... 2.00

Teenage Mutant Ninja Turtles
Mirage, 1984

1 .... 300.00
1/Counterfeit 2.00
1/2nd 15.00
1/3rd 8.00
1/4th 4.00
1/5th 3.00
2 .... 28.00
2/Counterfeit 2.00
2/2nd 6.00
2/3rd 3.00
2/4th 4.00
3-3/Misprint 15.00
3/2nd 3.00
4 .... 12.00
4/2nd 2.00
5 .... 4.00
5/2nd 2.00
6 .... 3.00
6/2nd 2.00
7 .... 5.00
7/2nd 2.00
8 .... 4.00
9-10 .... 3.00
11 .... 4.00
12-15 .... 3.00
16-62 .... 2.00

Teenage Mutant Ninja Turtles
Mirage, 1993

1-13 .... 3.00
Special 1 .... 4.00

Teenage Mutant Ninja Turtles
Image, 1996

1 .... 4.00
2-23 .... 3.00

Teenage Mutant Ninja Turtles Adventures
Archie, 1988

1-3 .... 3.00

Teenage Mutant Ninja Turtles Adventures
Archie, 1989

1-3 .... 3.00
4-72 .... 2.00
Special 1-5 .... 3.00
Special 6-11 .... 2.00

Teenage Mutant Ninja Turtles Adventures
Archie, 1996

1-3 .... 2.00

Teenage Mutant Ninja Turtles Animated
Dreamwave, 2003

1-7 .... 3.00

Teenage Mutant Ninja Turtles Authorized Martial Arts Training Manual
Solson, 1986

1-4 .... 3.00

Teenage Mutant Ninja Turtles Classics Digest
Archie, 1993

1-8 .... 2.00

Teenage Mutant Ninja Turtles/Flaming Carrot Crossover
Mirage, 1993

1-4 .... 3.00

Teenage Mutant Ninja Turtles III The Movie: The Turtles are Back...In Time
Archie

1 .... 3.00
1/Prestige 5.00

Teenage Mutant Ninja Turtles II: The Secret of the Ooze
Mirage

1 .... 6.00

Teenage Mutant Ninja Turtles Meet the Conservation Corps
Archie

1 .... 3.00

Teenage Mutant Ninja Turtles Michaelangelo Christmas Special
Mirage, 1990

1 .... 2.00

Teenage Mutant Ninja Turtles Movie II
Archie, 1991

1 .... 3.00

Teenage Mutant Ninja Turtles Mutant Universe Sourcebook
Archie, 1993

1-3 .... 2.00

Teenage Mutant Ninja Turtles Present: April O'Neil

Archie, 1993

1-3 .... 1.00

Teenage Mutant Ninja Turtles Presents: Donatello and Leatherhead

Archie, 1993

1-3 .... 1.00

Teenage Mutant Ninja Turtles Presents Merdude and Michaelangelo

Archie, 1993

1-3 .... 1.00

Teenage Mutant Ninja Turtles-Savage Dragon Crossover

Mirage, 1995

1 .... 3.00

Teenage Mutant Ninja Turtles: The Movie

Archie, 1990

1 .... 3.00
1/Direct 5.00
1/Prestige 6.00

Teenage Mutant Ninja Turtles: The Movie

Mirage, 1990

1 .... 6.00

Teenagents (Jack Kirby's...)

Topps, 1993

1-4 .... 3.00

Teen-Age Romance

Atlas, 1960

77-81 .... 15.00

Teen-Age Romance

Marvel, 1961

82-86 .... 20.00

Teen-Age Romances

St. John, 1949

1 .... 250.00
2-3 .... 160.00
4-8 .... 150.00
9 .... 160.00
10-12 .... 145.00
13-22 .... 160.00
23-30 .... 125.00
31-45 .... 105.00

Teen-Age Temptations

St. John, 1952

1 .... 250.00
2-9 .... 125.00

Teen Comics

Marvel, 1947

22-23 .... 55.00
24 .... 60.00
25 .... 55.00
26 .... 60.00
27 .... 55.00
28 .... 60.00
29 .... 55.00
30 .... 60.00
31-35 .... 55.00

Teen Comics

Personality, 1992

1-6 .... 3.00

Teen Confessions

Charlton, 1959

1 .... 75.00
2 .... 40.00
3-10 .... 30.00
11-30 .... 25.00
31 .... 125.00
32-50 .... 20.00
51-58 .... 15.00
59 .... 20.00
60-97 .... 12.00

Teenie Weenies

Ziff-Davis, 1951

10-11 .... 125.00

Teens at Play

1 .... 5.00

Teen Tales: The Library Comic

David G. Brown, 1997

1 .... 1.00

Teen Titans

DC, 1966

1 .... 260.00
2 .... 100.00
3-5 .... 40.00
6-10 .... 32.00
11-17 .... 28.00
18-22 .... 33.00
23-25 .... 18.00
26-30 .... 12.00
31 .... 20.00
☛Giant-sized
32-38 .... 18.00
39-43 .... 12.00
44-47 .... 7.00
48 .... 12.00
☛1st Harlequin
49 .... 7.00
50 .... 20.00
☛Batgirl returns
51-53 .... 6.00

Teen Titans

DC, 1996

1 .... 4.00
2-10 .... 3.00

Sarge Snorkel

Sarge Steel

Savage Combat Tales

Savage Sword of Conan

Scarab

Scarlet Spider

Scarlett

Scary Godmother

11 ....2.00
12 ....3.00
13-24 ....2.00
42 ....3.00
Ann 1 ....4.00
Ann 1999 ....5.00

Teen Titans
DC, 2003

½ 16.00
1 ....12.00
1/2nd 5.00
1/3rd 4.00
1/4th 8.00
2-15 ....3.00
16 ....5.00
17 ....4.00
18-19 ....3.00
20 ....4.00
☛Identity Crisis tie
21-41 ....3.00
Ann 1 ....12.00

Teen Titans Go!
DC, 2003

1-12 ....2.00
13-14 ....3.00
15-38 ....2.00

Teen Titans/Legion Special
DC, 2004

1 ....4.00

Teen Titans/Outsiders Secret Files
DC, 2003

1 ....6.00

Teen Titans/Outsiders Secret Files 2005
DC, 2005

1 ....5.00

Teen Titans Spotlight
DC, 1986

1-21 ....1.00

Tekken Forever
Image, 2001

1/A-1/B 3.00

Tek Knights
Artline

1 ....3.00

Tekno*Comix Handbook
Tekno, 1996

1 ....4.00

Teknophage (Neil Gaiman's...)
Tekno, 1995

1 ....2.00
1/Variant 3.00
2-10 ....2.00

Teknophage vs. Zeerus
Big, 1996

1 ....3.00

TEKQ
Gauntlet

1-4 ....3.00

Tekworld
Marvel, 1992

1 ....3.00
2-24 ....2.00

Telepathic Wanderers
Tokyopop, 2005

1 ....10.00

Television Comics
Standard, 1950

5 ....45.00
6-8 ....35.00

Television Puppet Show
Avon, 1950

1 ....100.00
2 ....75.00

Tell It to the Marines
Toby, 1952

1 ....135.00
2 ....90.00
3-5 ....68.00
6-7 ....58.00
8-11 ....50.00
12-15 ....40.00

Tellos
Image, 1999

1-4/A 3.00
4/B 4.00
5-10 ....3.00
Ashcan 1 ....2.00

Tellos: Maiden Voyage
Image, 2001

1 ....6.00

Tellos: Sons & Moons
Image, 2002

1 ....6.00

Tellos: The Last Heist
Image, 2001

1 ....6.00

Telltale Heart
Mojo

1 ....5.00

Tell Tale Heart and Other Stories
Fantagraphics

1 ....3.00

Telluria
Zub

1-3 ....3.00

Tempest
DC, 1996

1-4 .... 2.00

Template
Head, 1995

0-Special 1 .... 3.00
Spec 1/Ashcan 1.00
Special 1/Varia 3.00

Temple Snare
Mu

1 .... 2.00

Temptress: The Blood of Eve
Caliber

1 .... 3.00

Tempus Fugitive
DC, 1990

1-4 .... 5.00

Tenchi Muyo!
Pioneer, 1997

1-6 .... 3.00

Tender Love Stories
Skywald, 1971

1 .... 15.00
2-4 .... 10.00

Tender Romance
Key, 1953

1 .... 100.00
2 .... 60.00

Tense Suspense
Fago, 1958

1 .... 55.00
2 .... 40.00

Tenth
Image, 1997

0 .... 3.00
½ 5.00
1 .... 3.00
1/A 4.00
2-4 .... 3.00

Tenth
Image, 1997

0 .... 3.00
0/A 8.00
1 .... 3.00
2-3/A 3.00
3/B 8.00
4-14/A 3.00

Tenth
Image, 1999

1-1/A 3.00
1/B 10.00
2-4 .... 3.00

Tenth
Image, 1999

1 .... 3.00
1/A 6.00
1/B-4 .... 3.00

Tenth Configuration
Image, 1998

1 .... 3.00

10th Muse
Image, 2000

1-9/B 3.00

10th Muse
Alias, 2002

1 .... 4.00
1/B 5.00
1/C 4.00
1/D 5.00
1/Photo foil 6.00
2 .... 3.00
2/B 4.00
2/Photo foil 5.00
3 .... 3.00
3/B 4.00
3/C 3.00
4 .... 4.00
5 .... 3.00
5/Special 20.00
6-8 .... 3.00

Tenth: Resurrected
Dark Horse, 2001

1/A-4 .... 3.00

Ten Years of Love & Rockets
Fantagraphics, 1992

1 .... 2.00

Terminal City
DC, 1996

1 .... 3.00
2-9 .... 3.00

Terminal City: Aerial Graffiti
DC, 1997

1-5 .... 3.00

Terminal Point
Dark Horse, 1993

1-3 .... 3.00

Terminator
Now, 1988

1-17 .... 2.00

Terminator
Dark Horse, 1990

1-4 .... 3.00

Terminator
Dark Horse, 1991

1 .... 3.00

Terminator
Dark Horse, 1998

1-4 .... 3.00

Terminator (Magazine)
Trident

1-4 .... 3.00

Scary Tales

Scattered

Scene of the Crime

Scion

Scorpion

Scorpio Rose

Scout

Screwball Squirrel

Terminator 2: Judgment Day
Marvel, 1991
1-3 .... 2.00

Terminator 2: Judgment Day (Magazine)
Marvel, 1991
1 .... 3.00

Terminator 3
Beckett, 2003
1-6 .... 6.00

Terminator: All My Futures Past
Now, 1990
1-2 .... 3.00

Terminator: Endgame
Dark Horse, 1992
1-3 .... 3.00

Terminator: Hunters and Killers
Dark Horse, 1992
1-3 .... 3.00

Terminator: One Shot
Dark Horse, 1991
1 .... 6.00

Terminator: Secondary Objectives
Dark Horse, 1991
1-4 .... 3.00

Terminator: Tempest
Dark Horse
1-4 .... 3.00

Terminator: The Burning Earth
Now, 1990
1 .... 8.00
2-3 .... 5.00
4-5 .... 6.00

Terminator: The Dark Years
Dark Horse, 1999
1-4 .... 3.00

Terminator: The Enemy Within
Dark Horse, 1991
1-4 .... 3.00

Terraformers
Wonder Color, 1987
1-2 .... 2.00

Terranauts
Fantasy General, 1986
1 .... 2.00

Terra Obscura
DC, 2003
1-5 .... 3.00
6 .... 4.00

Terra Obscura
DC, 2004
1-6 .... 3.00

Terrarists
Marvel, 1993
1-4 .... 3.00

Terrific Comics
Continental, 1944
1 .... 3,500.00
2-3 .... 2,000.00
4 .... 3,600.00
5 .... 4,500.00
6 .... 1,800.00

Terrific Comics
Ajax, 1954
14 .... 200.00
16 .... 150.00

Terrifying Tales
Star, 1953
11 .... 350.00
12 .... 310.00
13 .... 350.00
14-15 .... 275.00

Territory
Dark Horse, 1999
1-4 .... 3.00

Terror
Leadslinger, 1991
1 .... 3.00

Terroress
Helpless Anger, 1990
1 .... 3.00

Terror Illustrated
E.C., 1955
1 .... 100.00
2 .... 75.00

Terror, Inc.
Marvel, 1992
1-13 .... 2.00

Terror on the Planet of the Apes
Adventure, 1991
1-4 .... 3.00

Terrors of the Jungle
Star, 1952
17 .... 525.00
18 .... 385.00
19-21 .... 345.00
4-10 .... 300.00

Terror Tales
Eternity, 1991
1 .... 3.00

Terry and the Pirates
Avalon

1-2 ... 3.00

Terry and the Pirates Comics
Harvey, 1947

3 ... 285.00
4 ... 160.00
5 ... 100.00
6-10 ... 65.00
11-20 ... 55.00
21-25 ... 45.00
26-28 ... 28.00

Terry-Bears Comics
St. John, 1952

1 ... 55.00
2-3 ... 35.00

Terry-Toons Comics
Timely, 1942

1 ... 1,025.00
2 ... 380.00
3-5 ... 255.00
6-10 ... 200.00
11-20 ... 125.00
21-37 ... 85.00
38 ... 700.00
39 ... 250.00
40-50 ... 110.00
51-59 ... 70.00

Terry-Toons Comics
St. John, 1947

60 ... 70.00
61-71 ... 60.00
72-83 ... 55.00
84-86 ... 48.00

Terry-Toons Comics
Pines, 1952

1 ... 110.00
2 ... 55.00
3-9 ... 50.00

Tessie the Typist
Marvel, 1944

1 ... 325.00
2 ... 190.00
3 ... 60.00
4-8 ... 125.00
9-13 ... 138.00
14-23 ... 40.00

Testament
DC, 2006

1-13 ... 3.00

Test Dirt
Fantagraphics

1 ... 3.00

Test Drive
M.A.I.N.

1 ... 3.00

Texan
St. John, 1948

1 ... 100.00
2 ... 75.00
3 ... 65.00
4-10 ... 50.00
11 ... 75.00
12 ... 85.00
13-15 ... 50.00

Texas Chainsaw Massacre
DC, 2007

1-2 ... 3.00

Texas Kid
Leading, 1951

1 ... 95.00
2 ... 60.00
3-5 ... 50.00
6-10 ... 40.00

Texas Rangers in Action
Charlton, 1956

5 ... 30.00
6-7 ... 22.00
8 ... 32.00
9-10 ... 22.00
11 ... 36.00
12 ... 16.00
13 ... 28.00
14-20 ... 16.00
21-30 ... 12.00
31-40 ... 9.00
41-50 ... 7.00
51-60 ... 5.00
61-70 ... 4.00
71-79 ... 2.00

Tex Benson
3-D Zone

1-2 ... 3.00

Tex Benson
Metro

1-4 ... 2.00

Tex Dawson, Gunslinger
Marvel, 1973

1 ... 12.00

Tex Farrell
D.S., 1948

1 ... 75.00

Tex Granger
Parents' Magazine Institute, 1948

18 ... 55.00
19 ... 45.00
20-24 ... 35.00

Tex Morgan
Marvel, 1948

1 ... 150.00
2 ... 105.00
3-6 ... 60.00
7-9 ... 105.00

Scribbly

Sea Devils

Sea Hunt

Secret Defenders

Secret Six

Secret Society of Super-Villains

Secrets of Haunted House

Secrets of the Legion of Super-Heroes

Tex Ritter Western
Charlton, 1950

1 .... 375.00
2 .... 230.00
3 .... 100.00
4-5 .... 72.00
6-10 .... 55.00
11-20 .... 40.00
21 .... 22.00
22 .... 40.00
23-30 .... 22.00
31-46 .... 20.00

Tex Taylor
Marvel, 1948

1 .... 175.00
2 .... 90.00
3 .... 80.00
4-6 .... 95.00
7-9 .... 110.00

Teykwa
Gemstone, 1988

1 .... 2.00

Thacker's Revenge
Explorer

1 .... 3.00

Thane of Bagarth
Avalon

1 .... 3.00

Thanos
Marvel, 2003

1 .... 4.00
2-12 .... 3.00

Thanos Quest
Marvel, 1990

1-2/2nd 5.00
Special 1 .... 4.00

That Chemical Reflex
CFD

1-3 .... 3.00

That Wilkin Boy
Archie, 1969

1 .... 15.00
2 .... 9.00
3-5 .... 6.00
6-10 .... 5.00
11 .... 4.00
12-20 .... 6.00
21-26 .... 5.00
27-30 .... 4.00
31-52 .... 3.00

THB
Horse, 1994

1 .... 12.00
1/2nd 6.00
2 .... 10.00
3-4 .... 8.00
5-6 .... 6.00
69 .... 5.00

T.H.E. Cat
Gold Key, 1967

1 .... 12.00
2-4 .... 10.00

TheComicStore.com Presents
TheComicStore.com

1 .... 1.00

There's a Madman in My Mirror
Bench, 1999

1 .... 4.00

Thespian
Dark Moon, 1995

1 .... 3.00

They Call Me...The Skul
Virtual, 1996

1 .... 3.00
1/A 4.00
2 .... 3.00

They Came from the '50s
Eternity

1 .... 10.00

They Were 11
Viz

1-4 .... 3.00

They Were Chosen to be the Survivors
Spectrum, 1983

1-4 .... 2.00

Thief
Penguin Palace, 1995

1 .... 3.00

Thief of Sherwood
A-Plus

1 .... 2.00

Thieves
Silverwolf, 1986

1 .... 2.00

Thieves & Kings
I Box, 1994

1 .... 4.00
1/2nd-3 .... 3.00
3/2nd 2.00
4-20 .... 3.00
21-24 .... 2.00
25-36 .... 3.00

Thing
Charlton, 1952

1 .... 735.00
2-4 .... 585.00
5-9 .... 540.00
10-14 .... 390.00
15-17 .... 295.00

Thing
Marvel, 1983

1 .... 6.00
2-10 .... 2.00
11-13 .... 1.00
14 .... 2.00
15-36 .... 1.00

Thing
Marvel, 2006

1-8 .... 3.00

Thing: Freakshow
Marvel, 2002

1-4 .... 3.00

Thing from Another World
Dark Horse, 1993

1-4 .... 3.00

Thing From Another World: Climate of Fear
Dark Horse, 1994

1-4 .... 3.00

Thing From Another World: Eternal Vows
Dark Horse, 1993

1-4 .... 3.00

Thing/She-Hulk: The Long Night
Marvel, 2002

1 .... 3.00

3rd Degree
NBM

1 .... 3.00

Third Eye (Dark One's...)
Sirius, 1998

1-2 .... 5.00

Third World War
Fleetway-Quality

1-6 .... 3.00

Thirteen
Dell, 1961

1 .... 35.00
2 .... 24.00
3-4 .... 20.00
5-10 .... 18.00
11-25 .... 14.00
26-29 .... 8.00

13: Assassin Comics Module
TSR

1-8 .... 2.00

13 Days of Christmas: A Tale of the Lost Lunar Bestiary
Sirius

1 .... 3.00

Thirteen O'Clock
Dark Horse

1 .... 3.00

Thirteen Something!
Global

1 .... 2.00

13th Son: Worse Thing Waiting
Dark Horse, 2005

1-4 .... 3.00

30 Days of Night
Idea & Design Works, 2002

1 .... 55.00
1/2nd 7.00
2 .... 25.00
3 .... 10.00
Ann 2004 .... 5.00

30 Days of Night: Bloodsucker Tales
Idea & Design Works, 2004

1 .... 4.00
2-7 .... 4.00
8 .... 3.00

30 Days of Night: Dead Space
Idea & Design Works, 2006

1 .... 4.00
2-3 .... 4.00

30 Days of Night: Return to Barrow
Idea & Design Works, 2004

1 .... 12.00
1/2nd 4.00
2 .... 8.00
3 .... 5.00
4-6 .... 4.00

Dark Days: A 30 Days of Night Sequel
Idea & Design Works, 2003

1 .... 8.00
2 .... 5.00
3-6 .... 4.00

30 Days of Night: Spreading the Disease
Idea & Design Works, 2006

1 .... 4.00

39 Screams
Thunder Baas, 1986

1-6 .... 2.00

32 Pages
Sirius, 2001

1 .... 3.00

This Is Heat
Aeon

1 .... 3.00

Secrets of the Valiant Universe

Secret War

Secret Weapons

Sectaurs

Seekers into the Mystery

Sensation Comics

Sensation Mystery

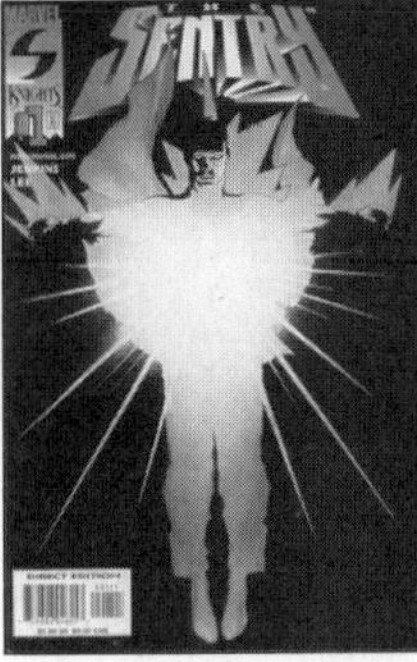
Sentry

This Is Not an Exit

Draculina

1-2 ....3.00

This Is Sick!

Silver Skull

1-2 ....3.00

This Is Suspense

Charlton, 1955

23 ....145.00
24 ....75.00
25-26 ....45.00

This is War

Standard, 1952

5 ....100.00
6 ....75.00
7-9 ....50.00

This Magazine Is Haunted

Fawcett, 1951

1 ....350.00
2 ....265.00
3 ....200.00
4-5 ....175.00
6-8 ....150.00
9 ....125.00
10 ....200.00
11-12 ....125.00
13 ....200.00
14 ....125.00
15 ....100.00
16 ....225.00
17 ....250.00
18 ....225.00
19 ....215.00
20 ....100.00
21 ....200.00

This Magazine is Haunted (2nd Series)

Charlton, 1957

12-14 ....300.00
15-16 ....200.00

Thor

Marvel, 1966

126 ....125.00
127-140 ....45.00
141-160 ....32.00
161-164 ....25.00
165 ....40.00
☛Warlock appearance
166 ....36.00
167 ....24.00
☛Galactus origin
168-169 ....36.00
☛Galactus origin
170-177 ....20.00
178-179 ....18.00
180 ....24.00
☛Thor vs. Mephisto
181 ....23.00
182-192 ....12.00
193 ....55.00
☛Silver Surfer appearance
194-199 ....12.00
200 ....16.00
201-205 ....9.00
206-224 ....7.00
225 ....14.00
☛1st Firelord
226 ....7.00
227-246 ....5.00
246/30¢ 20.00
247 ....5.00
247/30¢ 20.00
248 ....5.00
248/30¢ 20.00
249-260/Whitman 5.00
260/35¢ 15.00
261-261/Whitman 5.00
261/35¢ 15.00
262-262/Whitman 5.00
262/35¢ 15.00
263-263/Whitman 5.00
263/35¢ 15.00
264-264/Whitman 5.00
264/35¢ 15.00
265-299 ....3.00
300 ....8.00
301-336 ....2.00
337 ....7.00
☛1st Beta Ray Bill
338 ....3.00
339 ....5.00
340 ....4.00
341 ....3.00
342 ....4.00
343-348 ....2.00
349 ....3.00
350-373 ....2.00
374 ....3.00
375-400 ....2.00
401-410 ....1.00
411 ....3.00
412 ....2.00
413-431 ....1.00
432-433 ....2.00
434-449 ....1.00
450 ....3.00
451-473 ....1.00
474-475 ....2.00
475/Variant 3.00
476-481 ....2.00
482 ....3.00
483-499 ....2.00
500 ....3.00
501-502 ....2.00
Ann 2 ....65.00
Ann 2/2nd 3.00
Ann 3 ....12.00
Ann 4 ....10.00
Ann 5-6 ....8.00
Ann 7 ....7.00
Ann 8 ....6.00

Ann 9-12 .... 4.00
Ann 13-19 .... 3.00

Thor

Marvel, 1998

1 .... 5.00
1/A 20.00
1/B 5.00
1/C 6.00
1/D 8.00
1/E 5.00
2-2/A 3.00
3-11 .... 2.00
12 .... 3.00
12/DF 15.00
13-25 .... 2.00
25/Gold 5.00
26-31 .... 2.00
32 .... 4.00
33-34 .... 2.00
35 .... 3.00
36-61 .... 2.00
62-79 .... 3.00
80 .... 28.00
☛Avengers Disassembled
81 .... 5.00
82-84 .... 4.00
85 .... 3.00
Ann 1999-2001 .... 4.00

Thor

Marvel, 2007

1 .... 3.00
1/Suydam-1/Zombie 7.00
1/2nd 4.00
1/3rd-2 .... 3.00
2/Dell Otto 5.00
2/2nd-14 .... 3.00

Thor Battlebook

Marvel, 1998

1 .... 4.00

Thor: Blood Oath

Marvel, 2005

1-6 .... 3.00

Thor Corps

Marvel, 1993

1-4 .... 2.00

Thorion of the New Asgods

Marvel, 1997

1 .... 2.00

Thorr-Sverd

Vincent

1-3 .... 1.00

Thor: Son of Asgard

Marvel, 2004

1-12 .... 3.00

Thor: The Legend

Marvel, 1996

1 .... 4.00

Thor: Vikings

Marvel, 2003

1-5 .... 4.00

Those Annoying Post Bros.

Vortex, 1994

1 .... 3.00
2-18 .... 2.00
39-48 .... 3.00
Ann 1 .... 5.00

Those Crazy Peckers

U.S.Comics, 1987

1 .... 2.00

Those Magnificent Men In Their Flying Machines

Gold Key, 1965

1 .... 25.00

Those Unstoppable Rogues

Original Syndicate, 1995

1 .... 4.00

Those Who Hunt Elves

ADV Manga, 2003

1 .... 10.00

Thrax

Event, 1996

1-2 .... 3.00

Threat!

Fantagraphics, 1986

1-10 .... 2.00

Three

Invincible

1-4 .... 2.00

3-D Action

Atlas, 1954

1 .... 250.00

3-D Adventure Comics

Stats Etc., 1986

1 .... 2.00

3-D Alien Terror

Eclipse, 1986

1 .... 3.00

3-D Dolly

Harvey, 1953

1 .... 175.00

3-D-ell

Dell, 1953

1 .... 265.00
2-3 .... 190.00

3-D Exotic Beauties

3-D Zone, 1990

1 .... 4.00

3-D Heroes

Blackthorne

1 .... 3.00

SFA International Presents

SFA Spotlight

Shadow Cabinet

Shadowman

Shadowmasters

Shadow of the Batman

Shadow State

Shanda the Panda

3-D Hollywood
3-D Zone
1.....3.00

Three Dimensional Adventures
DC
1.....900.00
1/2nd.....3.00

Three Dimensional E.C. Classics
E.C., 1954
1.....550.00

Three Dimension Comics
St. John, 1953
1.....100.00
2-3.....80.00

3-D Sheena, Jungle Queen
Real Adventures, 1953
1.....325.00
4-5.....250.00

3-D Space Zombies
3-D Zone
1.....4.00

3-D Substance
3-D Zone
1.....3.00
2.....4.00

3-D Tales of the West
Atlas, 1954
1.....250.00

3-D Three Stooges
Eclipse
1-3.....3.00

3-D True Crime
3-D Zone, 1992
1.....4.00

3-D Zone
3-D Zone, 1986
1-20.....3.00

.357!
Mu, 1990
1.....3.00

3 Geeks
3 Finger Prints, 1997
1-7.....3.00
8.....4.00
9-11.....3.00

300
Dark Horse, 1998
1-2.....4.00
3-4.....3.00
5.....4.00

3 Little Kittens: Purr-Fect Weapons (Jim Balent's...)
Broadsword, 2002
1-3/A.....3.00

Three Mouseketeers
DC, 1956
1.....140.00
2.....58.00
3-10.....50.00
11-26.....40.00

Three Mouseketeers
DC, 1970
1.....35.00
2-4.....18.00
5-7.....22.00

Three Musketeers
Eternity, 1988
1-3.....2.00

Three Musketeers
Marvel, 1993
1-2.....2.00

3 Ninjas Kick Back
Now, 1994
1-3.....2.00

303
Avatar, 2004
0.....1.00
1.....5.00
☛Garth Ennis series
1/Wraparound.....10.00
2.....4.00
2/Platinum.....10.00
2/Wraparound-3.....4.00
3/Wraparound.....5.00
4.....4.00
4/Wraparound.....5.00
5.....4.00
5/Incentive.....7.00
5/Wraparound.....4.00

Three Stooges
Jubilee, 1949
1.....700.00
2.....500.00

Three Stooges
St. John, 1953
1.....400.00
2.....300.00
3.....275.00
4-7.....200.00

Three Stooges
Gold Key, 1961
6.....65.00
7.....48.00
8-10.....40.00
11-20.....28.00
21-30.....22.00
31-40.....18.00
41-55.....15.00

Three Stooges in 3-D
Eternity
1 .... 4.00

Three Stooges in Full Color
Eternity
1 .... 6.00

Three Stooges Meet Hercules
Dell, 1962
1 .... 75.00

3x3 Eyes
Innovation, 1991
1 .... 3.00
2-5 .... 2.00

3x3 Eyes: Curse of the Gesu
Dark Horse, 1995
1-5 .... 3.00

3x3 Eyes: Descent of the Mystic City
Dark Horse, 2004
1 .... 19.00

Threshold
Sleeping Giant, 1996
1-2 .... 3.00

Threshold
Sleeping Giant, 1997
1-3 .... 3.00

Threshold
Avatar, 1998
1-50 .... 5.00

Threshold of Reality
Maintech, 1986
1-3 .... 1.00

Threshold: The Stamp Collector
Sleeping Giant, 1997
1-2 .... 3.00

Thriller
DC, 1983
1-12 .... 2.00

Thrilling Adventure Stories
Atlas-Seaboard, 1975
1 .... 18.00
2 .... 25.00

Thrilling Adventure Strips
Dragon Lady, 1986
5-10 .... 3.00

Thrilling Comics
Better, 1940
1 .... 2,000.00
2 .... 800.00
3 .... 650.00
4-10 .... 500.00
11-18 .... 425.00
19 .... 500.00
☛1st American Crusader
20 .... 425.00
21-30 .... 350.00
31-40 .... 310.00
41 .... 700.00
☛Hitler cover
42-52 .... 270.00
53-70 .... 225.00
71-80 .... 90.00

Thrilling Comics
DC, 1999
1 .... 2.00

Thrilling Crime Cases
Star Publications, 1950
41 .... 140.00
42-45 .... 65.00
46-48 .... 55.00
49 .... 200.00

Thrilling Romances
Standard, 1949
5 .... 60.00
6-8 .... 40.00
9-10 .... 45.00
11-26 .... 40.00

Thrilling Science Fiction
Paragon
1 .... 10.00

Thrilling Science Tales
AC
1-2 .... 4.00

Thrilling True Story of the Baseball Giants
Fawcett, 1952
1 .... 425.00

Thrilling True Story of the Baseball Yankees
Fawcett, 1952
1 .... 400.00

Thrilling Wonder Tales
AC, 1991
1 .... 3.00

Thrill Kill
Caliber
1 .... 3.00

Thrillkiller
DC, 1997
1 .... 3.00
2-3 .... 3.00

Thrillkiller '62
DC, 1998
1 .... 5.00

Thrillogy
Pacific, 1984
1 .... 2.00

Shanna the She-Devil

She-Cat

SHIELD

Shockrockets

Shogun Warriors

Shonen Jump

Shottloose

Showcase

Thrill-O-Rama
Harvey, 1965
1 .... 25.00
2 .... 16.00
3 .... 14.00

Thrills of Tomorrow
Harvey, 1954
17 .... 80.00
18 .... 65.00
19-20 .... 195.00

Through Gates of Splendor
Spire, 1974
1 .... 8.00

Thumb Screw
Caliber
1-3 .... 4.00

Thump'n Guts
Kitchen Sink, 1993
1 .... 3.00

Thun'da Comics
Magazine Enterprises, 1952
1 .... 850.00
2 .... 165.00
3 .... 135.00
4-6 .... 95.00

Thun'Da, King of the Congo
AC
1 .... 3.00

Thun'da Tales (Frank Frazetta's...)
Fantagraphics, 1986
1 .... 2.00

T.H.U.N.D.E.R.
Solson
1 .... 2.00

THUNDER Agents
Tower, 1965
1 .... 140.00
2 .... 75.00
3-5 .... 55.00
6-8 .... 42.00
9-10 .... 35.00
11-15 .... 38.00
16-19 .... 22.00
20 .... 15.00

T.H.U.N.D.E.R. Agents
J.C., 1983
1-2 .... 2.00

Thunder Agents (Wally Wood's)
Deluxe, 1984
1-5 .... 2.00

Thunderbolt
Charlton, 1966
1 .... 16.00
51 .... 10.00
52-60 .... 9.00

Thunderbolt and Jaxon
DC, 2006
1-5 .... 3.00

Thunderbolts
Marvel, 1997
-1 .... 2.00
0 .... 1.00
1 .... 4.00
2-5 .... 3.00
6-11 .... 2.00
12 .... 6.00
13-24 .... 2.00
25 .... 3.00
26-49 .... 2.00
50 .... 3.00
51-76 .... 2.00
77-78 .... 3.00
79-81 .... 2.00
100 .... 4.00
101-102 .... 3.00
103 .... 8.00
104-109 .... 3.00
110-140 .... 5.00
Ann 1997-Ashcan 1 .... 3.00

Thunderbolts: Life Sentences
Marvel, 2001
1 .... 4.00

Thunderbunny
Archie, 1984
1 .... 2.00

Thunderbunny
Warp, 1985
1-12 .... 2.00

Thundercats
Marvel, 1985
1 .... 4.00
2-24 .... 2.00

Thundercats/Battle of the Planets
DC, 2003
1 .... 5.00

Thundercats: Dogs of War
DC, 2003
1 .... 3.00

Thundercats: Enemy's Pride
DC, 2004
1-5 .... 3.00

Thundercats: Hammerhand's Revenge
DC, 2003
1-5 .... 3.00

Thundercats Origins: Heroes & Villains
DC, 2004

1 .... 4.00

Thundercats Origins: Villains & Heroes
DC, 2004

1 .... 4.00

Thundercats: Reclaiming Thundera
DC, 2003

1 .... 13.00

Thundercats: The Return
DC, 2003

1-5 .... 3.00

ThunderCats (DC/WildStorm)
DC, 2002

0-5 .... 3.00

Thunder Girls
Pin & Ink, 1997

1-3 .... 3.00

Thundergod
Crusade, 1996

1-3 .... 3.00

Thundermace
Rak, 1986

1-7 .... 2.00

Thundersaurs: The Bodacious Adventures of Biff Thundersaur
Innovation

1 .... 2.00

Thunderskull! (Sidney Mellon's...)
Slave Labor, 1989

1 .... 2.00

Thunderstrike
Marvel, 1993

1 .... 3.00
2-8 .... 1.00
9-13 .... 2.00
13/A 3.00
14 .... 2.00
14/A 3.00
15 .... 2.00
15/A 3.00
16 .... 2.00
16/A 3.00
17-24 .... 2.00

Tick
NEC, 1988

1 .... 15.00
1/2nd-1/3rd 3.00
1/4th 2.00
1/5th 3.00
2 .... 8.00
2/Variant 15.00
2/2nd 3.00
2/3rd-2/4th 2.00
2/5th 3.00
3 .... 6.00
3/2nd-3/4th 3.00
4 .... 8.00
4/2nd 2.00
4/3rd-4/5th 3.00
5 .... 8.00
5/2nd 3.00
6 .... 5.00
6/2nd-6/3rd 3.00
7 .... 5.00
7/2nd-7/3rd 3.00
8-8/Variant 8.00
8/2nd-12 .... 3.00
12/Ltd. 20.00
13 .... 4.00
Special 1 .... 50.00
Special 2 .... 25.00

Tick & Arthur
NEC, 1999

1 .... 4.00

Tick & Artie
NEC, 2002

1/A-1/B 4.00

Tick Big Blue Destiny
NEC, 1997

1 .... 3.00
1/A 5.00
1/Ashcan 3.00
1/B 19.00
2-2/Variant 3.00
3-5 .... 4.00

Tick Big Red-n-Green Christmas Spectacle
NEC, 2001

1 .... 4.00

Tick Big Summer Annual
NEC, 1999

1 .... 4.00

Tick: Circus Maximus
NEC, 2000

1-4 .... 4.00

Tick: Days of Drama
New England, 2005

1 .... 5.00

Tick: Heroes of the City
NEC, 1999

1 .... 4.00

Tick Incredible Internet Comic
NEC, 2001

1 .... 4.00

Shrek

Sick Smiles

Sigil

Silly Daddy

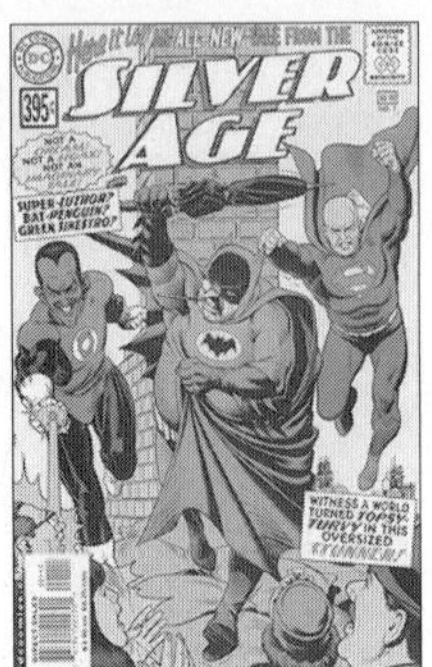
Silver Age

Silverblade

Silver Sable

Silver Streak Comics

Tick: Karma Tornado
NEC, 1993
1 .... 4.00
1/2nd 3.00
2 .... 4.00
2/2nd 3.00
3 .... 5.00
3/2nd 3.00
4 .... 5.00
4/2nd 3.00
5 .... 5.00
5/2nd 3.00
6 .... 4.00
6/2nd 3.00
7 .... 4.00
7/2nd 3.00
8 .... 4.00
8/2nd-9/2nd 3.00

Tick: Luny Bin Trilogy
NEC, 1998
0 .... 2.00
1-3 .... 4.00

Tick's Back
NEC, 1997
0 .... 3.00
0/A 5.00
0/B 8.00
0/C 10.00

Tick's Big Back to School Special
NEC, 1998
1 .... 4.00

Tick's Big Cruise Ship Vacation Special
NEC, 2000
1 .... 4.00

Tick's Big Father's Day Special
NEC, 2000
1 .... 4.00

Tick's Big Halloween Special
NEC, 1999
1 .... 4.00

Tick's Big Mother's Day Special
NEC, 2000
1 .... 4.00

Tick's Big Romantic Adventure
NEC, 1998
1 .... 3.00

Tick's Big Summer Fun Special
NEC, 1998
1 .... 4.00

Tick's Big Tax Time Terror
NEC, 2000
1 .... 4.00

Tick's Big Year 2000 Special
NEC, 2000
1 .... 4.00

Tick's Big Yule Log Special
NEC, 1997
1 .... 4.00
2000/Ltd. 5.00
2001 .... 4.00

Tick's Giant Circus of the Mighty
NEC, 1992
1-2 .... 3.00

Tick's Golden Age Comic
NEC, 2002
1/A-2/B 5.00

Tick's Massive Summer Double Spectacle
NEC, 2000
1-2/B 4.00

Tick-Tock Follies
Slave Labor, 1996
1 .... 3.00

Tick Tock Tales
Magazine Enterprises, 1946
1 .... 75.00
2 .... 40.00
3-10 .... 35.00
11-33 .... 30.00

Tic Toc Tom
Detonator Canada, 1995
1-3 .... 3.00

Tiger
King, 1970
1 .... 10.00
1/2nd 6.00
2 .... 5.00
3-6 .... 4.00

Tiger 2021
Anubis, 1994
Ashcan 1 .... 4.00

Tiger Girl
Gold Key, 1968
1 .... 35.00

Tigerman
Atlas-Seaboard, 1975
1 .... 9.00
2-3 .... 8.00

Tigers of Terra
Mind-Visions, 1990
1-8 .... 3.00
9-12 .... 4.00

Tigers of Terra
Antarctic, 1993
0-23 .... 3.00
24 .... 4.00
25 .... 3.00

Tigers of Terra
Antarctic, 2000
1 .... 3.00

Tigers of Terra: Technical Manual
Antarctic, 1995
1-2 .... 3.00

Tiger Woman
Millennium, 1994
1-2 .... 3.00

Tiger Woman: The Last Place on Earth
Caliber
1 .... 3.00

Tiger-X
Eternity, 1988
1-3 .... 2.00
Special 1-Special 1/2nd 2.00

Tiger-X Book II
Eternity, 1989
1-4 .... 2.00

Tigra
Marvel, 2002
1-4 .... 3.00

Tigress
Hero, 1992
1-5 .... 3.00
6 .... 4.00

Tigress
Basement, 1998
1 .... 3.00

Tijuana Bible
Starhead, 1997
1-9 .... 3.00

Tilazeus Meets the Messiah
Aiiie
1 .... 3.00

Timber Wolf
DC, 1992
1-5 .... 2.00

Time Bandits
Marvel, 1982
1 .... 2.00

Time Breakers
DC, 1997
1-5 .... 2.00

Time City
Rocket, 1992
1 .... 3.00

Timecop
Dark Horse, 1994
1-2 .... 3.00

Timedrifter (Gerard Jones'...)
Innovation, 1990
1-3 .... 2.00

Time for Love
Charlton, 1967
1 .... 7.00
2-5 .... 5.00
6-10 .... 4.00
11-30 .... 3.00
31-47 .... 2.00

Time Gates
Double Edge
1-3 .... 2.00

Timejump War
Apple, 1989
1-3 .... 2.00

Time Killers
Fleetway-Quality
1-7 .... 3.00

Timeless Tales (Bob Powell's...)
Eclipse, 1989
1 .... 2.00

Timely Presents: All-Winners
Marvel, 1999
1 .... 4.00

Timely Presents: Human Torch
Marvel, 1999
1 .... 4.00

Time Machine
Eternity, 1990
1-3 .... 3.00

Time Masters
DC, 1990
1-8 .... 2.00

Time Out of Mind
Graphic Serials
1-3 .... 2.00

Timeslip Collection
Marvel, 1998
1 .... 3.00

Timeslip Special
Marvel, 1998
1 .... 6.00

Timespell
Club 408 Graphics, 1997
0-4 .... 3.00
Ashcan 1 .... 1.00

Simpsons Comics

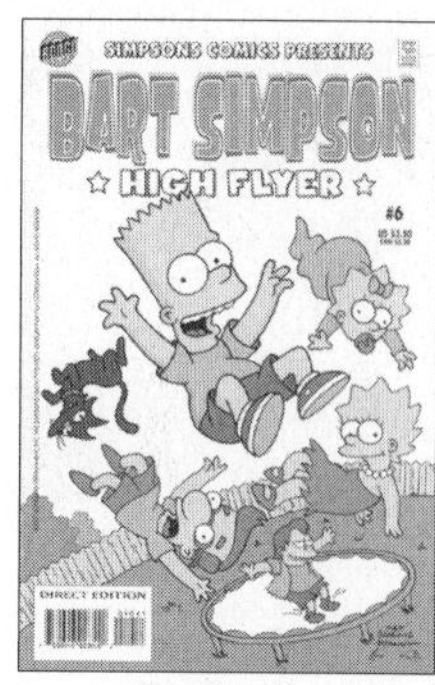

Simpsons Comics Presents Bart Simpson

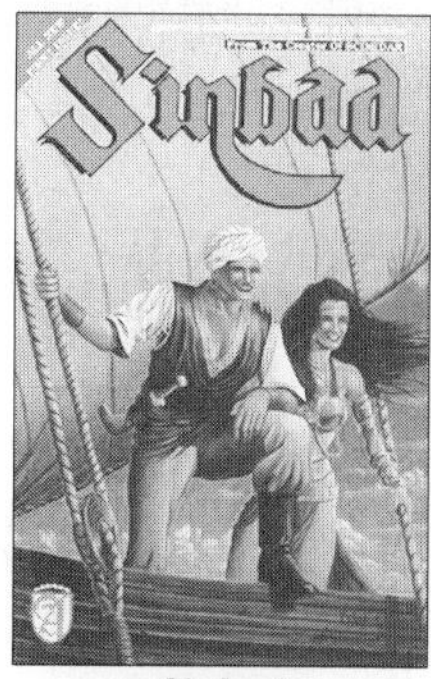

Sinbad

Sisterhood of Steel

Sister Red

Six

Six From Sirius

Six String Samurai

Timespell: The Director's Cut

Club 408 Graphics, 1998

1 .... 3.00

Timespirits

Marvel, 1984

1-8 .... 2.00

Time Traveler Ai

CPM Manga, 1999

1-6 .... 3.00

Time Traveler Herbie

Avalon

1 .... 3.00

Time Tunnel

Gold Key, 1967

1 .... 40.00
2 .... 35.00

Time Twisted Tales

Rip Off

1 .... 2.00

Time Twisters

Fleetway-Quality

1-21 .... 2.00

Timewalker

Acclaim, 1995

0 .... 5.00
1 .... 2.00
1/VVSS 75.00
2-3 .... 1.00
4-15 .... 2.00
YB 1 .... 3.00

Time Wankers

Fantagraphics, 1991

1-5 .... 2.00

Time Warp

DC, 1979

1 .... 4.00
2-5 .... 2.00

Time Warrior

Blazing, 1993

1 .... 3.00

Time Warriors: The Beginning

Fantasy General

1 .... 2.00

Tim Holt

Magazine Enterprises, 1948

1 .... 350.00
2 .... 175.00
3 .... 130.00
4-5 .... 95.00
6 .... 155.00
7-10 .... 90.00
11 .... 220.00
12-19 .... 72.00
20 .... 95.00
21-30 .... 58.00
31-41 .... 48.00

Tim Holt Western Annual

AC

1 .... 3.00

Tim McCoy

Charlton, 1947

16 .... 275.00
17-21 .... 225.00

Timmy the Timid Ghost

Charlton, 1956

3 .... 36.00
4-10 .... 20.00
11-20 .... 18.00
21-45 .... 10.00

Timmy the Timid Ghost

Charlton, 1967

1 .... 10.00
2-10 .... 6.00
11-26 .... 4.00

Tim Tyler

Standard, 1948

11 .... 40.00
12-18 .... 30.00

Tincan Man

Image, 1999

1-Ashcan 1 .... 3.00

Tiny Deaths

YUGP, 1997

1-2 .... 2.00

Tiny Tessie

Marvel, 1949

24 .... 50.00

Tiny Toon Adventures

DC, 1994

1-7 .... 2.00

Tiny Tot Comics

E.C., 1946

1 .... 225.00
2 .... 155.00
3-5 .... 125.00
6-10 .... 100.00

Tipper Gore's Comics and Stories

Revolutionary, 1989

1-5 .... 2.00

Tippy Teen

Tower, 1965

1 .... 25.00
2 .... 14.00
3 .... 8.00
4-5 .... 6.00
6-27 .... 5.00

Tip Top Comics

St. John, 1936

1 .... 7,200.00

2 .... 2,400.00
3 .... 1,600.00
4-5 .... 1,000.00
6-10 .... 760.00
11-20 .... 560.00
21-30 .... 350.00
31-40 .... 250.00
41-50 .... 200.00
51-60 .... 140.00
61-80 .... 110.00
81-100 .... 85.00
101-110 .... 72.00
111-120 .... 60.00
121-130 .... 52.00
131-150 .... 45.00
151-180 .... 40.00
181-200 .... 35.00
201-225 .... 28.00

Tip-Topper Comics

United Features, 1949

1 .... 45.00
2 .... 30.00
3-5 .... 25.00
6-10 .... 15.00
11-28 .... 14.00

Titan A.E.

Dark Horse, 2000

1-3 .... 3.00

Titans

DC, 1999

1 .... 3.00
2-24 .... 3.00
25 .... 4.00
26-50 .... 3.00
Ann 1 .... 4.00

Titans/Legion of Super-Heroes: Universe Ablaze

DC, 2000

1-4 .... 5.00

Titan Special

Dark Horse, 1994

1 .... 4.00

Titans: Scissors, Paper, Stone

DC, 1997

1 .... 5.00

Titans Secret Files

DC, 1999

1-2 .... 5.00

Titans Sell-Out! Special

DC, 1992

1 .... 4.00

Titans/Young Justice: Graduation Day

DC, 2003

1-3 .... 3.00

Tiyu

Express, 1996

1 .... 10.00

T-Man

Quality, 1951

1 .... 210.00
2 .... 110.00
3 .... 100.00
4-5 .... 105.00
6 .... 110.00
7-8 .... 100.00
9-10 .... 85.00
11 .... 65.00
12-13 .... 55.00
14 .... 65.00
15-19 .... 55.00
20 .... 70.00
21-26 .... 55.00
27-38 .... 50.00

T-Minus-1

Renegade, 1988

1 .... 2.00

TMNT Mutant Universe Sourcebook

Archie

1-2 .... 2.00

TMNT: Teenage Mutant Ninja Turtles

Mirage, 2001

1-9 .... 3.00
10 .... 4.00
11-18 .... 3.00

To Be Announced

Strawberry Jam, 1986

1-7 .... 2.00

Today's Brides

Ajax, 1955

1 .... 45.00
2-4 .... 30.00

Today's Romance

Standard, 1952

5 .... 30.00
6 .... 24.00
7-8 .... 15.00

Todd Mcfarlane Presents: Kiss Psycho Circus

Image, 1998

1 .... 7.00
2-5 .... 5.00

Todd Mcfarlane Presents: Ozzy Osbourne

Image, 1999

1 .... 5.00

Todd McFarlane Presents: The Crow Magazine

Image, 2000

1 .... 5.00

Skeleton Key

Skreemer

Skull the Slayer

Sky Gal

Slacker Comics

Slash Maraud

Sleepwalker

Sleeze Brothers

To Die For
Blackthorne

1 ....2.00
1/3D 3.00

Toe Tags Featuring George Romero
DC, 2004

1-6 ....3.00

Toka
Dell, 1964

1 ....25.00
2 ....15.00
3-10 ....10.00

Tokyo Babylon
Tokyopop, 2004

1 ....10.00

Tokyo Boys & Girls
Viz, 2005

1-2 ....9.00

Tokyo Mew Mew
Tokyopop, 2003

1 ....10.00

TokyoPop (Vol. 3)
Mixx, 1999

1-7 ....5.00

TokyoPop (Vol. 4)
Mixx, 2000

1-3 ....5.00

Tokyo Storm Warning
DC, 2003

1-3 ....3.00

Tokyo Tribes
Tokyopop, 2004

1-4 ....10.00

Tomahawk
DC, 1950

1 ....850.00
2 ....400.00
3-5 ....290.00
6-10 ....195.00
11-20 ....125.00
21-27 ....100.00
28 ....110.00
29 ....130.00
☛Frazetta art
30 ....90.00
31-40 ....70.00
41-50 ....56.00
51-56 ....45.00
57 ....85.00
☛Frazetta art
58-60 ....40.00
61-80 ....32.00
81-90 ....25.00
91-100 ....15.00
101-110 ....10.00
111-120 ....8.00
121-132 ....6.00
133-140 ....5.00

Tom & Jerry 50th Anniversary Special
Harvey, 1991

1 ....3.00

Tom & Jerry Adventures
Harvey, 1992

1 ....1.00

Tom & Jerry and Friends
Harvey, 1991

1-4 ....1.00

Tom & Jerry Big Book
Harvey, 1992

1-2 ....2.00

Tom & Jerry Comics
Dell, 1949

60 ....50.00
61-65 ....40.00
66-70 ....36.00
71-80 ....28.00
81-90 ....24.00
91-100 ....18.00
101-110 ....14.00
111-120 ....12.00
121-130 ....9.00
131-150 ....7.00
151-170 ....6.00
171-190 ....5.00
191-200 ....4.00
201-230 ....3.00
231-300 ....2.00
301-327 ....1.00
328-329 ....5.00
330 ....20.00
331-341 ....7.00
342-344 ....15.00

Tom & Jerry
Harvey, 1991

1 ....2.00
2-8 ....1.00
9-Ann 1 ....2.00

Tom & Jerry Digest
Harvey, 1992

1 ....2.00

Tom & Jerry Giant Size
Harvey, 1992

1-2 ....2.00

Tom & Jerry Picnic Time
Dell, 1958

1 ....75.00

Tom & Jerry's Back to School
Dell, 1956

1 ....90.00

Tom & Jerry's Toy Fair
Dell, 1958
1 .... 65.00

Tom & Jerry Summer Fun
Dell, 1954
1 .... 100.00
2-4 .... 50.00

Tom & Jerry Summer Fun
Gold Key, 1967
1 .... 35.00

Tom & Jerry's Winter Fun
Dell, 1954
3 .... 50.00
4-7 .... 40.00

Tom & Jerry Winter Carnival
Dell, 1952
1 .... 150.00
2 .... 125.00

Tomato
Starhead, 1994
1-2 .... 3.00

Tomb of Darkness
Marvel, 1974
9 .... 20.00
☛Cont'd from Beware
10-20 .... 10.00
20/30¢ 20.00
21 .... 10.00
21/30¢ 20.00
22-23 .... 10.00

Tomb of Dracula
Marvel, 1972
1 .... 100.00
2-3 .... 35.00
4 .... 30.00
5-6 .... 18.00
7 .... 15.00
8-9 .... 12.00
10 .... 100.00
☛1st Blade
11 .... 10.00
12 .... 12.00
13 .... 35.00
☛Blade origin
14 .... 12.00
15-16 .... 10.00
17 .... 12.00
18 .... 10.00
19 .... 12.00
20-21 .... 10.00
22-25 .... 8.00
25/2nd 2.00
26-29 .... 8.00
30 .... 10.00
31-32 .... 8.00
33-41 .... 7.00
42-43 .... 6.00
43/30¢ 18.00
44 .... 6.00
44/30¢ 18.00
45 .... 6.00
45/30¢ 18.00
46 .... 6.00
46/30¢ 18.00
47 .... 6.00
47/30¢ 18.00
48-49 .... 6.00
50 .... 10.00
51-56 .... 6.00
57-57/35¢ 12.00
58 .... 6.00
58/35¢ 12.00
59 .... 6.00
59/35¢ 12.00
60 .... 6.00
60/35¢ 12.00
61-69 .... 5.00
70 .... 8.00

Tomb of Dracula
Marvel, 2004
1-4 .... 3.00

Tomb of Dracula (Magazine)
Marvel, 1979
1 .... 15.00
2-6 .... 6.00

Tomb of Dracula
Marvel, 1991
1-4 .... 5.00

Tomb of Ligeia
Dell, 1965
1 .... 12.00

Tomb of Terror
Harvey, 1952
1 .... 500.00
2-3 .... 300.00
4-12 .... 250.00
13-14 .... 340.00
15 .... 550.00
16 .... 300.00

Tomb Raider: Arabian Nights
Image, 2004
1 .... 6.00

Tomb Raider Cover Gallery
Image, 2006
1 .... 3.00

Tomb Raider/Darkness Special
Image, 2001
1 .... 4.00
1/A 6.00

Slick Chick

Sliders

Sludge

Smash Comics

Smith Brown Jones

Smurfs

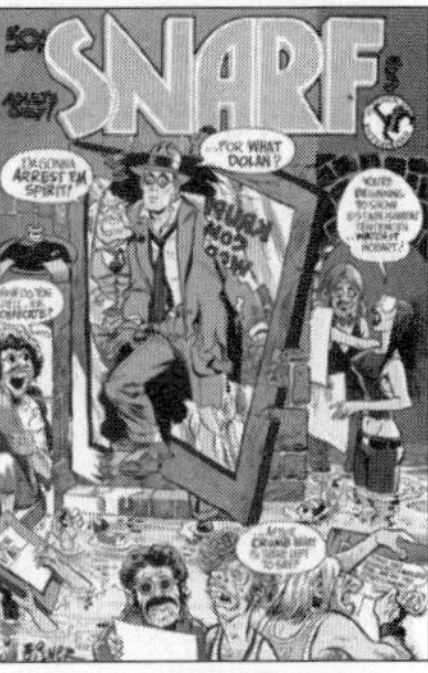

Snarf

Sniffy the Pup

Tomb Raider: Epiphany
Image, 2003

1 .... 5.00

Tomb Raider Gallery
Image, 2000

1 .... 3.00

Tomb Raider: Greatest Treasure of All One Shot
Image

1 .... 7.00

Tomb Raider: Journeys
Image, 2002

1-12 .... 3.00

Tomb Raider Magazine
Image, 2001

1 .... 5.00

Tomb Raider: Takeover One Shot
Image, 2003

1 .... 3.00

Tomb Raider: The Series
Image, 1999

0 .... 3.00
0/Dynamic 5.00
½-1/D 3.00
1/Holofoil 7.00
1/Another Unive 5.00
1/Tower Gold 6.00
1/Tower 5.00
2 .... 3.00
2/Tower 5.00
2/Tower foil 7.00
3 .... 3.00
3/Monster Mart 7.00
3/Gold Mart 125.00
4 .... 3.00
4/Dynamic 4.00
4/Dynamic with 8.00
5 .... 3.00
5/Dynamic 6.00
6-7 .... 3.00
7/Museum 125.00
8-9 .... 3.00
9/White 4.00
9/Dynamic 6.00
9/Dynamic blue 7.00
9/Sketch 10.00
10 .... 3.00
10/Gold foil 12.00
10/Red foil 10.00
11 .... 3.00
11/Graham 7.00
12 .... 3.00
12/Graham 8.00
13-15 .... 3.00
15/Dynamic 10.00
16-46 .... 3.00
47 .... 4.00
47/Variant 3.00
48 .... 4.00
48/Variant-50 .... 3.00
Ashcan 1 .... 5.00

Tomb Raider/Witchblade
Image, 1997

1-1/A 6.00
1/B 20.00
1/2nd 3.00

Tomb Tales
Cryptic, 1997

1-2 .... 3.00

Tom Corbett
Eternity, 1990

1-4 .... 2.00

Tom Corbett Book Two
Eternity, 1990

1-4 .... 2.00

Tom Corbett, Space Cadet
Dell, 1953

4-11 .... 55.00

Tom Corbett, Space Cadet
Prize, 1955

1 .... 200.00
2-3 .... 140.00

Tom Judge: End of Days
Image, 2003

1 .... 4.00

Tom Landry
Spire, 1973

1 .... 3.00

Tommi Gunn
London Night, 1996

1 .... 3.00

Tommi Gunn: Killer's Lust
London Night, 1997

1-1/Nude 3.00

Tom Mix
Ralston-Purina, 1940

1 .... 2,500.00
2 .... 1,250.00
3-9 .... 800.00
10-11 .... 500.00

Tom Mix Western
Fawcett, 1948

1 .... 1,400.00
2 .... 550.00
3-5 .... 375.00
6-10 .... 285.00
11-25 .... 225.00
26-40 .... 115.00
41-61 .... 75.00

Tom Mix Western
AC

1-2 .... 3.00

Tommy and the Monsters
New Comics
1 .... 2.00

Tommy Looks At Farming
B.F. Goodrich, 1955
1 .... 20.00

Tommy of the Big Top
Best, 1948
10 .... 30.00
11-12 .... 24.00

Tomoe
Crusade, 1996
0 .... 3.00
0/Ltd. 4.00
0/Variant-1 .... 3.00
1/Ltd. 4.00
1/2nd-3 .... 3.00

Tomoe: Unforgettable Fire
Crusade, 1997
1 .... 3.00
1/Ltd. 4.00

Tomoe/Witchblade: Fire Sermon
Crusade, 1996
1 .... 4.00
1/A 5.00

Tomorrow Knights
Marvel, 1990
1-6 .... 2.00

Tomorrow Man
Antarctic, 1993
1 .... 3.00

Tomorrow Man & Knight Hunter: Last Rites
Antarctic, 1994
1-6 .... 3.00

Tomorrow Stories
DC, 1999
1 .... 4.00
1/Variant 6.00
2-12 .... 3.00

Tomorrow Stories Special
DC, 2006
1-2 .... 7.00

Tom Strong
DC, 1999
1 .... 4.00
1/Variant 5.00
2-36 .... 3.00

Tom Strong's Terrific Tales
1 .... 4.00
2-12 .... 3.00

Tom Terrific
Pines, 1957
1 .... 135.00
2-6 .... 95.00

Tongue*Lash
Dark Horse, 1996
1-2 .... 3.00

Tongue*Lash II
Dark Horse, 1999
1-2 .... 3.00

Tony Bravado, Trouble-Shooter
Renegade, 1989
1-2 .... 2.00
3-4 .... 3.00

Tool & Die
Flashpoint, 1994
1 .... 3.00

Too Much Coffee Man
Adhesive, 1993
1 .... 12.00
2 .... 8.00
3 .... 6.00
4-5 .... 5.00
6-8 .... 3.00
MC 1 .... 10.00
MC 1/2nd 3.00
MC 2 .... 8.00
MC 2/2nd 3.00
MC 3 .... 8.00
MC 3/2nd 3.00
MC 4 .... 6.00
MC 4/2nd-Special 2 .... 3.00

Too Much Hopeless Savages
Oni, 2003
1-4 .... 3.00

Toon Warz: The Fandom Menace
Sirius, 1999
1/A-1/D 3.00

Tooth and Claw
Image, 1999
1-3 .... 3.00
Ashcan 1 .... 2.00

Top 10
DC, 1999
1 .... 5.00
1/Variant 6.00
2-12 .... 3.00

Top Cat
Dell, 1961
1 .... 60.00
2 .... 35.00
3-5 .... 25.00
6-10 .... 20.00
11-20 .... 15.00
21-31 .... 12.00

Top Cat
Charlton, 1970
1 .... 20.00

Sock Monkey

Soldiers of Freedom

Soldier X

Solitaire

Solo Avengers

Solus

Somerset Holmes

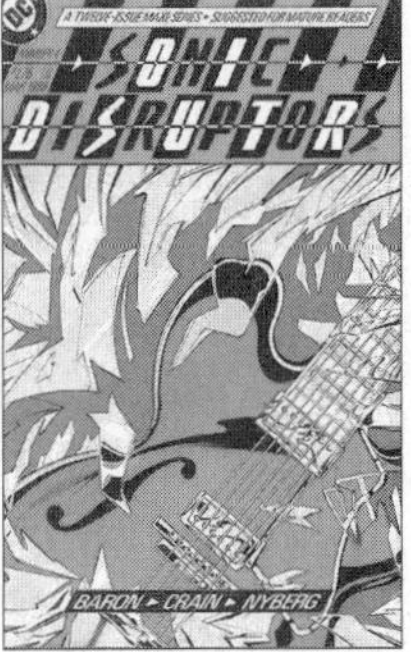

Sonic Disruptors

2....12.00
3-5....8.00
6-10....5.00
11-20....4.00

Top Comics: Flintstones
Gold Key, 1967
1-2....10.00
3-4....15.00

Top Comics: Flipper
Gold Key, 1967
1....10.00

Top Comics: Lassie
Gold Key, 1967
1....10.00

Top Comics: Mickey Mouse
Gold Key, 1967
1-2....10.00
3-4....15.00

Top Comics: Tweety & Sylvester
Gold Key, 1967
1-2....10.00

Top Comics: Yogi Bear
Gold Key, 1967
1....16.00

Top Cow 2003 Compilation Special
Image, 2003
1....3.00

Top Cow 2005 Preview Book
Top Cow, 2005
0....1.00

Top Cow: Book of Revelation 2003
Image, 2003
1....4.00

Top Cow Classics in Black and White: Aphrodite IX
Image, 2000
1....3.00

Top Cow Classics in Black and White: Ascenscion
Image, 2000
1-1/A....3.00

Top Cow Classics in Black and White: Fathom
Image, 2000
1....3.00

Top Cow Classics in Black and White: Magdalena
Image, 2002
1....3.00

Top Cow Classics in Black and White: Midnight Nation
Image, 2001
1....3.00

Top Cow Classics in Black and White: Rising Stars
Image, 2000
1....3.00

Top Cow Classics in Black and White: The Darkness
Image, 2000
1....3.00

Top Cow Classics in Black and White: Tomb Raider
Image, 2000
1....3.00

Top Cow Classics in Black and White: Witchblade
Image, 2000
1....3.00
1/A....5.00
25....3.00

Top Cow Con Sketchbook 2004
Image, 2004
1....3.00

Top Cow Productions Inc./ Ballistic Studios Swimsuit Special
Image, 1995
1....3.00

Top Cow Secrets
Image, 1996
WS 1....3.00

Top Cow Special
Image
1....3.00

Top Dog
Marvel, 1985
1-14....1.00

Top Eliminator
Charlton, 1967
25-29....10.00

Top Flight Comics
St. John, 1952
1....60.00

Topix (Vol. 1)
Catechetical Guild, 1942
1....225.00
2....120.00
3....90.00
4-8....70.00

Topix (Vol. 2)
Catechetical Guild, 1943

1-10 .... 55.00

Topix (Vol. 3)
Catechetical Guild, 1944

1-10 .... 45.00

Topix (Vol. 4)
Catechetical Guild, 1945

1-10 .... 36.00

Topix (Vol. 5)
Catechetical Guild, 1946

1-4 .... 32.00
5 .... 75.00
6-15 .... 32.00

Topix (Vol. 6)
Catechetical Guild, 1948

4-14 .... 30.00

Topix (Vol. 7)
Catechetical Guild, 1948

1-20 .... 26.00

Topix (Vol. 8)
Catechetical Guild, 1949

1-30 .... 26.00

Topix (Vol. 9)
Catechetical Guild, 1950

1-30 .... 22.00

Topix (Vol. 10)
Catechetical Guild, 1951

1-15 .... 20.00

Top Love Stories
Star, 1951

3 .... 185.00
4-9 .... 150.00
10-19 .... 135.00

Top-Notch Comics
M.L.J., 1939

1 .... 3,500.00
2 .... 1,500.00
3 .... 1,000.00
4 .... 825.00
5 .... 900.00
6-8 .... 650.00
9 .... 3,000.00
☛1st Black Hood
10 .... 1,000.00
☛2nd Black Hood
11-15 .... 625.00
16-20 .... 550.00
21-30 .... 425.00
31-45 .... 250.00

Topps Comics Presents
Topps, 1993

0 .... 2.00
1 .... 1.00

Tops
Lev Gleason, 1949

1 .... 1,100.00
2 .... 900.00

Top Secret
Hillman, 1952

1 .... 150.00

Top Secrets
Street & Smith, 1947

1 .... 200.00
2-10 .... 125.00

Top Shelf
Primal Groove, 1995

1 .... 5.00

Top Shelf
Top Shelf, 1996

1-7 .... 7.00

Tops in Adventure
Ziff-Davis, 1952

1 .... 300.00

Top 10: Beyond the Farthest Precinct
DC, 2005

1-5 .... 3.00

Tor
DC, 1975

1 .... 8.00
2-6 .... 4.00

Tor
Marvel, 1993

1-4 .... 6.00

Eclipse, 1986

1-2 .... 3.00

Torch of Liberty Special
Dark Horse, 1995

1 .... 3.00

Torchy
Innovation, 1992

1-9 .... 3.00
Summer 1 .... 3.00

Torchy
Quality, 1949

1 .... 1,000.00
2-3 .... 405.00
4 .... 510.00
5-6 .... 640.00
16 .... 0.00

Son of Ambush Bug

Soulsearchers and Company

Southern Knights

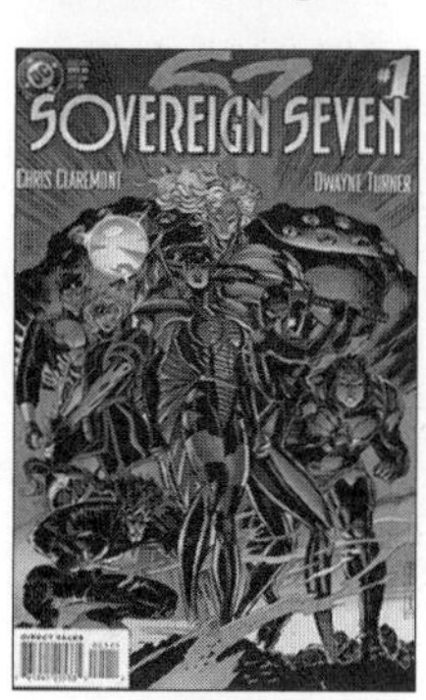

Sovereign Seven

Space Adventures

Space Ark

Space Family Robinson

Spacehawk

Torg
Adventure, 1992

1-4 .... 3.00

Tori Do
Penguin Palace, 1994

1-1/2nd 2.00

To Riverdale and Back Again
Archie, 1990

1 .... 3.00

Tor Johnson: Hollywood Star
Monster

1 .... 3.00

Tor Love Betty
Fantagraphics, 1991

1 .... 3.00

Torment
Aircel

1-3 .... 3.00

Torpedo
Hard Boiled, 1993

1-4 .... 3.00

Torrid Affairs
Eternity, 1988

1-2/B 2.00
3-5 .... 3.00

Torso
Image, 1999

1-2 .... 4.00
3-6 .... 5.00

Tortoise and The Hare
Last Gasp

1 .... 3.00

To See the Stars
NBM

1 .... 14.00

Total Eclipse
Eclipse, 1988

1-5 .... 4.00

Total Eclipse: The Seraphim Objective
Eclipse, 1988

1 .... 2.00

Total Justice
DC, 1996

1-3 .... 2.00

Totally Alien
Trigon

1-5 .... 3.00

Totally Horses!
Painted Pony, 1997

1-5 .... 2.00

Total Recall
DC, 1990

1 .... 3.00

Total War
Gold Key, 1965

1 .... 40.00
2 .... 35.00

Totems
DC, 2000

1 .... 6.00

Totems
Cartoon Frolics

1-3 .... 3.00

Totem: Sign of the Wardog
Alpha Productions, 1991

1-2 .... 2.00

Totem: Sign of the Wardog
Alpha Productions, 1992

1-2 .... 3.00
Ann 1 .... 4.00

Touch
DC, 2004

1-6 .... 3.00

Touch of Silk, a Taste of Leather, A
Boneyard, 1994

1 .... 3.00

Touch of Silver, A
Image, 1997

1-6 .... 3.00

Tough
Viz, 2005

1-4 .... 10.00

Tough Guys and Wild Women
Eternity, 1989

1-2 .... 2.00

Tough Kid Squad
Timely, 1942

1 .... 7,500.00

Tower of Shadows
Marvel, 1969

1 .... 55.00
2-5 .... 25.00
6-8 .... 15.00
9 .... 8.00
Special 1 .... 22.00

Townscapes
DC, 2004

1 .... 18.00

Toxic!
Apocalypse

1-19 .... 3.00

Toxic Avenger
Marvel, 1991
1-11 .... 2.00

Toxic Crusaders
Marvel, 1992
1-8 .... 1.00

Toxic Gumbo
DC, 1998
1 .... 6.00

Toxic Paradise
Slave Labor
1 .... 5.00

Toxin
Marvel, 2005
1-6 .... 3.00

Toxine
Nose, 1991
1 .... 3.00

Toyboy
Continuity, 1986
1-7 .... 2.00

Toyland Comics
Fiction House, 1947
1 .... 200.00
2-3 .... 125.00

Toy Story (Disney's...)
Marvel, 1995
1 .... 5.00

Toytown Comics
Toytown, 1945
1 .... 150.00
2 .... 100.00
3-7 .... 75.00

Traci Lords: The Outlaw Years
Boneyard
1 .... 3.00

Tracker
Blackthorne, 1988
1-2 .... 2.00

Tragg and the Sky Gods
Whitman, 1975
1 .... 5.00
2-9 .... 3.00

Trail Blazers
Street & Smith, 1941
1 .... 170.00
2 .... 130.00
3-4 .... 120.00

Trailer Trash
Tundra, 1996
1 .... 2.00
4-8 .... 3.00

Trakk: Monster Hunter
Image, 2003
1-2 .... 3.00

Tramps Like Us
Tokyopop, 2004
1-7 .... 10.00

Tranceptor
NBM
1 .... 12.00

Trancers
Eternity, 1991
1-2 .... 3.00

Tranquility
Dreamsmith, 1998
1-3 .... 3.00

Tranquilizer
Luxurious
1-2 .... 3.00

Transformers
Marvel, 1984
1 .... 10.00
2-3 .... 5.00
4-20 .... 3.00
21-69 .... 2.00
70-76 .... 5.00
77-79 .... 10.00
80 .... 18.00

Transformers
Idea & Design Works, 2005
0-5 .... 1.00

Transformers Animated Movie Adaptation
Idea & Design Works, 2006
1-3 .... 4.00

Transformers: Armada
Dreamwave, 2002
1-7 .... 3.00
7/A 4.00
8-18 .... 3.00

Transformers Armada: More Than Meets the Eye
Dark Horse, 2004
1-3 .... 5.00

Transformers: Beast Wars
Idea & Design Works, 2006
1-4 .... 3.00

Transformers Comics Magazine
Marvel, 1987
1-10 .... 2.00

Transformers: Energon
Dark Horse, 2004
19-30 .... 3.00

Space War

Space Wolf

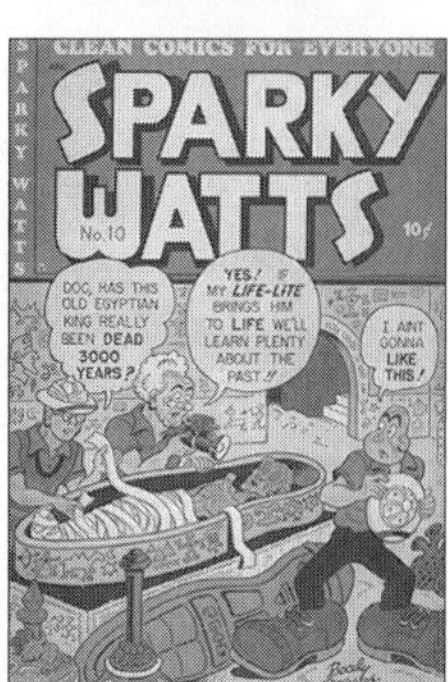

Sparky Watts

Spawn

Special Marvel Edition

Speedball

Speed Comics

Spelljammer

Transformers: Escalation
Idea & Design Works, 2006

1-2 ....4.00

Transformers: Evolutions
Idea & Design Works, 2006

1-4 ....3.00

Transformers/Gen13
Marvel

Ashcan 1 ....1.00

Transformers: Generation 1
Dreamwave, 2002

1/Autobot-1/Decepticon 4.00
1/Chromium 6.00
1/2nd-1/3rd 3.00
2/Autobot-2/Decepticon 4.00
2/2nd-6/Decepticon 3.00

Transformers: Generation 1
Dreamwave, 2003

1 ....3.00
1/Counterfeit 6.00
2-6 ....3.00

Transformers: Generation 1
Dreamwave, 2003

0 ....3.00
1 ....4.00
1/SilvSnail 5.00
2-10 ....3.00

Transformers: Generation 1 Preview
Dreamwave, 2002

1/A-1/B 4.00

Transformers: Generation 2
Marvel, 1993

1 ....2.00
1/Variant 3.00
2-12 ....2.00

Transformers: Generations
Idea & Design Works, 2006

1-9 ....2.00
10 ....3.00

Transformers/G.I.Joe
Dreamwave, 2003

1 ....3.00
2-6 ....3.00

Transformers: Headmasters
Marvel, 1987

1-4 ....1.00

Transformers in 3-D
Blackthorne, 1987

1-3 ....3.00

Transformers: Infiltration
Idea & Design Works, 2006

1-6 ....3.00

Transformers: Infiltration Cover Gallery
Idea & Design Works, 2006

1 ....6.00

Transformers: Micromasters
Dreamwave, 2004

1-3 ....3.00

Transformers: More than Meets the Eye Official Guide
Dreamwave, 2003

1-8 ....5.00

Transformers Movie
Marvel, 1986

1-3 ....1.00

Transformers Spotlight: Hot Rod
Idea & Design Works, 2006

1 ....4.00

Transformers Spotlight: Nightbeat
Idea & Design Works, 2006

1 ....4.00

Transformers Spotlight: Shockwave
Idea & Design Works, 2006

1 ....4.00

Transformers Spotlight: Six Shot
Idea & Design Works, 2006

1 ....4.00

Transformers: Stormbringer
Idea & Design Works, 2006

1-4 ....3.00

Transformers 2004 Summer Special
Dreamwave, 2004

1 ....5.00

Transformers: The War Within
Dreamwave, 2002

1-1/Variant 7.00
2-5 ....3.00
5/A 5.00
6 ....3.00
Ashcan 1 ....3.00

Transformers: The War Within

Dreamwave, 2003

1-6 .... 3.00

Transformers: The War Within

Dreamwave, 2004

1-3 .... 3.00

Transformers Universe

Marvel, 1986

1 .... 20.00
1/DirCut-2 .... 10.00
2/FanClub 25.00
2/Conv 20.00
3 .... 5.00
4 .... 2.00

Transit

Vortex, 1987

1-5 .... 2.00

Transmetropolitan

DC, 1997

1 .... 8.00
2 .... 6.00
3-5 .... 4.00
6-60 .... 3.00

Transmetropolitan: Filth of the City

DC, 2001

1 .... 6.00

Transmetropolitan: I Hate it Here

DC, 2000

1 .... 6.00

Transmutation of Ike Garuda

Marvel, 1992

1-2 .... 4.00

Trans Nubians

Adeola

1 .... 3.00

Trash

Fleetway-Quality

1-2 .... 3.00

Trauma Corps

Anubis, 1994

1 .... 3.00

Travelers

South Jersey Rebellion Productions

1-3 .... 2.00

Traveller's Tale, A

Antarctic, 1992

1-3 .... 3.00

Travels of Jaimie McPheeters

Gold Key, 1963

1 .... 12.00

Treasure Chest of Fun and Fact (Vol. 1)

George A. Pflaum, 1946

1 .... 275.00
2 .... 150.00
3 .... 85.00
4-6 .... 70.00

Treasure Chest of Fun and Fact (Vol. 2)

George A. Pflaum, 1946

1 .... 55.00
2-20 .... 50.00

Treasure Chest of Fun and Fact (Vol. 3)

George A. Pflaum, 1947

1 .... 40.00
2-20 .... 35.00

Treasure Chest of Fun and Fact (Vol. 4)

George A. Pflaum, 1948

1-20 .... 32.00

Treasure Chest of Fun and Fact (Vol. 5)

George A. Pflaum, 1949

1 .... 32.00
2-20 .... 30.00

Treasure Chest of Fun and Fact (Vol. 6)

George A. Pflaum, 1950

1-20 .... 30.00

Treasure Chest of Fun and Fact (Vol. 7)

George A. Pflaum, 1951

1 .... 30.00
2-20 .... 26.00

Treasure Chest of Fun and Fact (Vol. 8)

George A. Pflaum, 1952

1-20 .... 26.00

Spider-Girl

Spider-Man

Spider-Man Classics

Spider-Man Megazine

Spider-Woman

Spidey and the Mini-Marvels

Spidey Super Stories

Splitting Image

Treasure Chest of Fun and Fact (Vol. 9)

George A. Pflaum, 1953

1-20 ....26.00

Treasure Chest of Fun and Fact (Vol. 10)

George A. Pflaum, 1954

1-20 ....24.00

Treasure Chest of Fun and Fact (Vol. 11)

George A. Pflaum, 1955

1-20 ....24.00

Treasure Chest of Fun and Fact (Vol. 12)

George A. Pflaum, 1956

1-20 ....24.00

Treasure Chest of Fun and Fact (Vol. 13)

George A. Pflaum, 1957

1-20 ....24.00

Treasure Chest of Fun and Fact (Vol. 14)

George A. Pflaum, 1958

1-20 ....24.00

Treasure Chest of Fun and Fact (Vol. 15)

George A. Pflaum, 1959

1-20 ....24.00

Treasure Chest of Fun and Fact (Vol. 16)

George A. Pflaum, 1960

1-20 ....20.00

Treasure Chest of Fun and Fact (Vol. 17)

George A. Pflaum, 1961

1 ....20.00
2 ....100.00
3 ....20.00
4 ....65.00
5 ....20.00
6 ....65.00
7 ....20.00
8 ....65.00
9 ....20.00
10 ....65.00
11 ....20.00
12 ....65.00
13 ....20.00
14 ....65.00
15 ....20.00
16 ....65.00
17 ....20.00
18 ....65.00
19 ....20.00
20 ....65.00

Treasure Chest of Fun and Fact (Vol. 18)

George A. Pflaum, 1962

1-20 ....20.00

Treasure Chest of Fun and Fact (Vol. 19)

George A. Pflaum, 1963

1-20 ....20.00

Treasure Chest of Fun and Fact (Vol. 20)

George A. Pflaum, 1964

1-20 ....18.00

Treasure Chest of Fun and Fact (Vol. 21)

George A. Pflaum, 1965

1-20 ....18.00

Treasure Chest of Fun and Fact (Vol. 22)

George A. Pflaum, 1966

1-20 ....18.00

Treasure Chest of Fun and Fact (Vol. 23)

George A. Pflaum, 1967

1-20 ....18.00

Treasure Chest of Fun and Fact (Vol. 24)

George A. Pflaum, 1968

1-18 ....18.00

Treasure Chest of Fun and Fact (Vol. 25)

George A. Pflaum, 1969

1-16 ....15.00

Treasure Chest of Fun and Fact (Vol. 26)

George A. Pflaum, 1970

1-8 ....15.00

Treasure Chest of Fun and Fact (Vol. 27)

George A. Pflaum, 1969

1-8 ....15.00

Treasure Chests
Fantagraphics, 1999
1-5 .... 3.00

Treasure Chest Summer (Vol. 1)
George A. Pflaum, 1966
1-6 .... 5.00

Treasure Comics
Prize, 1945
1 .... 175.00
2-6 .... 100.00
7-8 .... 200.00
9 .... 100.00
10 .... 175.00
11 .... 100.00

Treasury of Dogs, A
Dell, 1956
1 .... 25.00

Treasury of Horses, A
Dell, 1955
1 .... 25.00

Treasury of Victorian Murder, A
NBM
1 .... 9.00

Treehouse of Horror (Bart Simpson's...)
Bongo, 1995
1 .... 4.00
2-4 .... 3.00
5 .... 4.00
6-7 .... 5.00
8 .... 4.00
9-10 .... 5.00

Trekker
Dark Horse, 1987
1-9 .... 2.00
Special 1 .... 3.00

Trekker
Image, 1999
Special 1 .... 3.00

Trek Teens
Parody, 1993
1-1/A 3.00

Trenchcoat Brigade
DC, 1999
1-4 .... 3.00

Trencher
Image, 1993
1-4 .... 2.00

Trencher X-Mas Bites Holiday Blow-Out
Blackball, 1993
1 .... 3.00

Trespassers
Amazing Montage
1-5 .... 3.00

Triad Universe
Triad, 1994
1-2 .... 2.00

Trial Run
Miller
1-7 .... 2.00
14-15 .... 3.00

Trials of Shazam!
DC, 2006
1-4 .... 3.00

Triarch
Caliber
1-2 .... 3.00

Tribe
Image, 1993
1-1/Variant 3.00
2-3 .... 2.00

Tribe
Good, 1996
0 .... 3.00

Trickster King Monkey
Eastern, 1988
1 .... 2.00

Trident
Trident, 1989
1-8 .... 4.00

Trident Sampler
Trident
1-2 .... 1.00

Trigger
DC, 2005
1-8 .... 3.00

Triggerman
Caliber, 1996
1-2 .... 3.00

Trigger Twins
DC, 1973
1 .... 18.00

Trilogy Tour
Cartoon, 1997
1 .... 2.00

Trilogy Tour II
Cartoon, 1998
1 .... 5.00

Trinity Angels
Acclaim, 1997
1-12 .... 3.00
Ashcan 1 .... 1.00

Triple Dare
Alternative, 1998
1 .... 3.00

Spooky Spooktown

Sports Action

Spring Break Comics

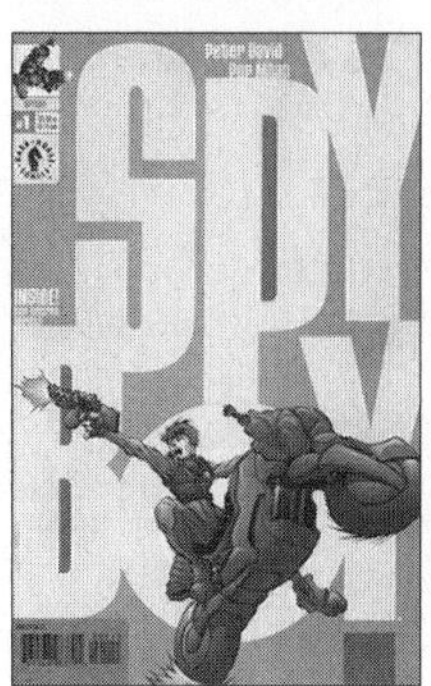

SpyBoy

Spy Smasher

Squadron Supreme

Star

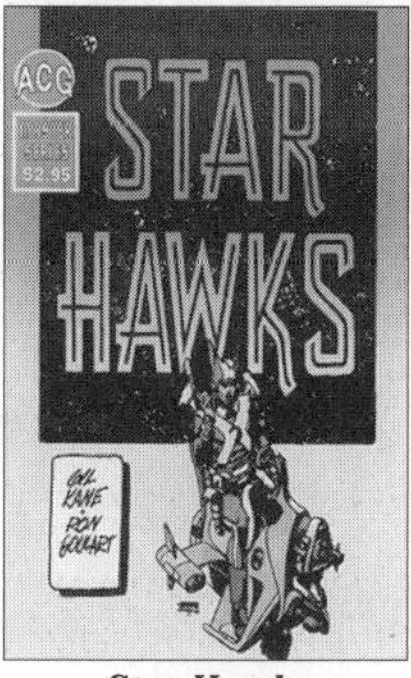

Star Hawks

Triple Threat
Holyoke, 1946

1 ... 150.00

TripleïX
Dark Horse, 1994

1-6 ... 4.00
7 ... 5.00

Triple-X Cinema: A Cartoon History
Re-Visionary, 1997

1-3 ... 4.00

Triumph
DC, 1995

1-4 ... 2.00

Triumphant Unleashed
Triumphant, 1993

0 ... 3.00
0/A ... 1.00
0/Variant ... 4.00
1 ... 3.00

Triumvirate
Catacomb

1 ... 3.00

Troll
Image, 1993

1 ... 3.00

Troll II
Image, 1994

1 ... 4.00

Troll: Halloween Special
Image, 1994

1 ... 3.00

Troll: Once a Hero
Image, 1994

1 ... 3.00

Trollords: Death and Kisses
Apple, 1989

1-5 ... 2.00
6 ... 3.00

Trollords
Tru, 1986

1-15 ... 2.00
Special 1 ... 2.00

Trollords
Comico, 1988

1-3 ... 2.00
4 ... 3.00

Troll Patrol
Harvey, 1993

1 ... 2.00

Trombone
Knockabout

1 ... 3.00

Tropo
Blackbird

1-5 ... 3.00

Trouble
Marvel, 2003

1-5 ... 3.00

Trouble Express
Radio, 1998

1-2 ... 3.00

Trouble Magnet
DC, 2000

1-4 ... 3.00

Troublemakers
Acclaim, 1996

1-19 ... 3.00
Ashcan 1 ... 1.00

Troubleman
Image, 1996

1-3 ... 2.00

Troubleshooters Inc.
Nightwolf, 1995

1-2 ... 3.00

Trouble With Girls
Malibu, 1987

1 ... 3.00
2-14 ... 2.00
Ann 1 ... 3.00
Holiday 1 ... 3.00

Trouble With Girls
Comico, 1989

1 ... 3.00
2-23 ... 2.00

Trouble With Girls: The Night of the Lizard
Marvel, 1993

1 ... 3.00
2-4 ... 2.00

Trouble with Tigers
Antarctic, 1992

1-2 ... 3.00

Trout Fission
Tall Tale, 1998

1-2 ... 2.00

Troy
Tome

1 ... 3.00

TRS-80 Computer Whiz Kids
Archie

1 ... 2.00

Truckin'
Print Mint, 1972

1-2 ... 3.00

True Adventures of Adam and Bryon

American Mule, 1998

1-3 .... 3.00

True Aviation Picture Stories

Parents' Magazine Institute, 1942

1 .... 100.00
2 .... 80.00
3-5 .... 60.00
6-14 .... 50.00

True Comics

Parents' Magazine Institute, 1941

1 .... 210.00
2 .... 105.00
3 .... 150.00
4-5 .... 100.00
6 .... 105.00
7-10 .... 58.00
11-20 .... 56.00
21-30 .... 45.00
31-50 .... 35.00
51-54 .... 30.00
55 .... 50.00
56-60 .... 30.00
61-70 .... 25.00
71 .... 45.00
72-73 .... 35.00
74-77 .... 25.00
78 .... 35.00
79 .... 25.00
80-84 .... 80.00

True Complete Mystery

Superior, 1949

5 .... 145.00
6 .... 110.00

True Confidences

Fawcett, 1949

1 .... 80.00
2-4 .... 60.00

True Confusions

Fantagraphics

1 .... 3.00

True Crime Comics

Magazine Village, 1947

2 .... 900.00
3 .... 825.00
4 .... 750.00
5-6 .... 550.00

True Crime Comics

Magazine Village, 1949

1 .... 850.00

True Crime Comics

Eclipse

1-2 .... 3.00

True Faith

DC

1 .... 13.00

True Gein

Boneyard, 1993

1 .... 3.00

True Glitz

Rip Off

1 .... 3.00

True Life Secrets

Charlton, 1951

1 .... 50.00
2 .... 25.00
3-5 .... 18.00
6-10 .... 15.00
11-20 .... 12.00
21-29 .... 9.00

True Life Tales

Marvel, 1949

8 .... 50.00
2 .... 40.00

True Love

Eclipse, 1986

1-2 .... 2.00

True Love Pictorial

St. John, 1952

1 .... 75.00
2 .... 100.00
3-5 .... 175.00
6-9 .... 100.00
10-11 .... 75.00

True Love Problems & Advice Illustrated

Harvey, 1949

1 .... 75.00
2 .... 50.00
3-10 .... 35.00
11-31 .... 25.00
32-44 .... 20.00

True Movie and Television

Toby, 1950

1 .... 300.00
2 .... 400.00
3-4 .... 150.00

True North

Comic Legends Defense Fund, 1988

1 .... 4.00

True North II

Comic Legends Defense Fund, 1990

1 .... 5.00

True Secrets

Atlas, 1950

3 .... 80.00
4-9 .... 60.00
10-21 .... 50.00
22-40 .... 40.00

True Sin

Boneyard

1 .... 3.00

Starjammers

Star Rangers

Stars and S.T.R.I.P.E.

Starslayer

Star Spangled Comics

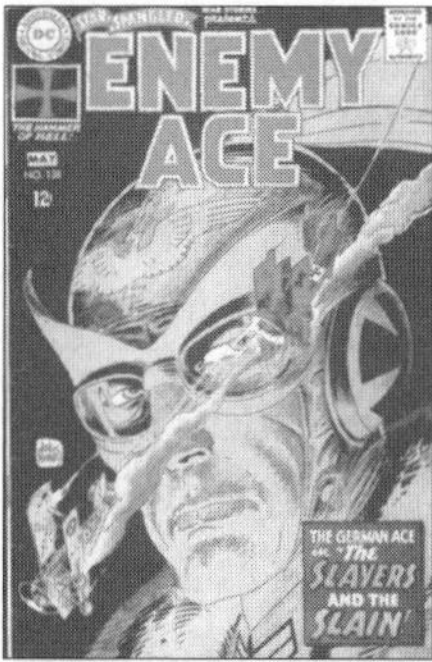

Star Spangled War Stories

Star Trek (3rd series)

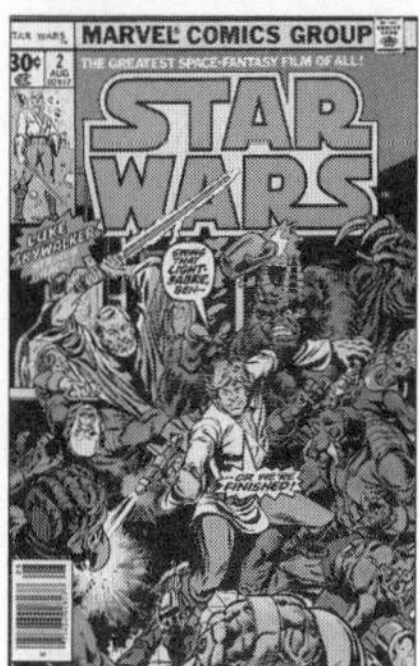

Star Wars

True Sport Picture Stories (Vol. 1)

Street & Smith, 1942

5 .... 185.00
6-12 .... 120.00

True Sport Picture Stories (Vol. 2)

Street & Smith, 1943

1-12 .... 100.00

True Sport Picture Stories (Vol. 3)

Street & Smith, 1945

1-12 .... 85.00

True Sport Picture Stories (Vol. 4)

Street & Smith, 1947

1-12 .... 75.00

True Sport Picture Stories (Vol. 5)

Street & Smith, 1949

1-2 .... 75.00

True Spy Stories

Caliber

1 .... 3.00

True Story, Swear to God

Image, 2006

1-2 .... 3.00

True Swamp

Peristaltic, 1994

1-5 .... 3.00

True Sweetheart Secrets

Fawcett, 1950

1 .... 40.00
2-11 .... 25.00

True 3-D

Harvey, 1953

1-2 .... 30.00

True Travel Tales

-Ism, 2004

1-4 .... 3.00

True War Experiences

Harvey, 1952

1 .... 75.00
2-4 .... 40.00

Trufan Adventures Theatre

Paragraphics, 1986

1-2 .... 2.00

Truly Tasteless and Tacky

Caliber

1 .... 3.00

Trump

Playboy, 1957

1 .... 175.00
2 .... 125.00

Truth

Dark Horse, 1999

0 .... 1.00
1 .... 18.00

Truth, Justin, and the American Way

Image, 2006

1-4 .... 3.00

Truth: Red, White & Black

Marvel, 2003

1 .... 5.00
2-7 .... 4.00

Truth Serum

Slave Labor, 2002

1-3 .... 3.00

Trypto the Acid Dog

Renegade

1 .... 2.00

TSC Jams

TSC

0-1 .... 4.00

TSR Worlds

DC, 1990

Ann 1 .... 2.00

Tsukuyomi - Moon Phase

Tokyopop, 2005

1 .... 10.00

Tsunami Girl

Image, 1999

1-3 .... 3.00

Tsunami, the Irresistlble Force

Epoch

1 .... 2.00

T2: Cybernetic Dawn

Malibu, 1995

0-4 .... 3.00

T2: Nuclear Twilight

Malibu, 1995

0-4 .... 3.00

Tubby

Dell, 1953

5 .... 45.00
6-10 .... 30.00
11-20 .... 26.00
21-40 .... 24.00
41-49 .... 20.00

Tubby and His Clubhouse Pals

Dell, 1956

1 .... 75.00

Tubby and the Little Men From Mars

Gold Key, 1964

1 .... 75.00

Tuesday
Kim-Rehr, 2003
1-3 .... 3.00

Tuff Ghosts, Starring Spooky
Harvey, 1962
1 .... 35.00
2-5 .... 18.00
6-10 .... 12.00
11-30 .... 10.00
31-40 .... 8.00
41-43 .... 6.00

Tuff Sh*t
Print Mint
1 .... 3.00

Tuffy
Standard, 1949
5 .... 24.00
6-9 .... 18.00

Tug & Buster
Art & Soul, 1995
1-7 .... 3.00

Tug & Buster
Image, 1998
1 .... 3.00

Tumbling Boxes
Fantagraphics, 1994
1 .... 3.00

Tundra Sketchbook Series
Tundra
1-9 .... 4.00
10 .... 5.00
11-12 .... 4.00

Turbo Jones: Pathfinder
Fleetway-Quality
1 .... 10.00

Turistas: Other Side of Paradise – Book One
Idea & Design Works, 2006
1 .... 4.00

Turok
Acclaim, 1998
1-4 .... 3.00

Turok Adon's Curse
Acclaim
1 .... 5.00

Turok: Child of Blood
Acclaim, 1998
1 .... 4.00

Turok, Dinosaur Hunter
Acclaim, 1993
0 .... 5.00
1 .... 2.00
1/Gold 14.00
1/VVSS 20.00
2-10 .... 1.00
11 .... 2.00
12-19 .... 1.00
20 .... 2.00
21 .... 1.00
22-38 .... 2.00
39 .... 3.00
40-42 .... 4.00
43-44 .... 3.00
45 .... 6.00
46 .... 9.00
47 .... 18.00
YB 1 .... 4.00

Turok: Evolution
Acclaim, 2002
1 .... 3.00

Turok: Redpath
Acclaim, 1997
1 .... 4.00

Turok: Seeds of Evil
Acclaim
1-1/Direct 5.00

Turok/Shadowman
Acclaim, 1999
1 .... 4.00

Turok: Shadow of Oblivion
Acclaim, 2000
1 .... 5.00

Turok, Son of Stone
Dell, 1956
3 .... 155.00
4-5 .... 125.00
6-7 .... 110.00
7/15¢ 135.00
8-10 .... 110.00
11-20 .... 75.00
21-30 .... 48.00
31-40 .... 38.00
41-50 .... 28.00
51-60 .... 22.00
61-70 .... 15.00
71-90 .... 10.00
91-110 .... 8.00
111-130 .... 6.00
GS 1 .... 100.00

Turok: Spring Break in the Lost Land
Acclaim, 1997
1 .... 4.00

Turok: Tales of the Lost Land
Acclaim, 1998
1 .... 4.00

Turok: The Empty Souls
Acclaim, 1996
1-1/Variant 4.00
Ashcan 1 .... 1.00

Star Wars Tales

Star Western

Static

Stealth Force

Steampunk

Steel

Steelgrip Starkey

Steve Canyon Comics

Turok the Hunted
Acclaim, 1996
1-2 .... 5.00

Turok, Timewalker: Seventh Sabbath
Acclaim, 1997
1-2 .... 3.00

Turtle Soup
Mirage, 1987
1 .... 5.00

Turtle Soup
Mirage, 1991
1-4 .... 3.00

Turtle Soup
Astonish, 2003
1 .... 4.00

Tusk World Tour Book 2001
Tusk, 2001
nn 5.00

Tutenstein
Marvel, 2004
1 .... 1.00

Tuxedo Gin
Viz, 2003
1-14 .... 10.00

TV Casper and Company
Harvey, 1963
1 .... 75.00
2-5 .... 30.00
6-10 .... 20.00
11-20 .... 15.00
21-31 .... 10.00
32-46 .... 8.00

TV Funnies (Walter Lantz...)
Dell, 1958
261-271 .... 4.00

TV Stars
Marvel, 1978
1 .... 15.00
2-4 .... 7.00

TV Western
AC, 2001
1 .... 6.00

Tweety and Sylvester
Dell, 1951
4-11 .... 20.00
12-37 .... 15.00

Tweety and Sylvester
Gold Key, 1964
1 .... 35.00
2-5 .... 20.00
6-10 .... 8.00
11-20 .... 5.00
21-40 .... 4.00
41-100 .... 3.00
101-102 .... 2.00
103-104 .... 5.00
105-106 .... 12.00
107 .... 17.00
108-116 .... 8.00
117-121 .... 10.00

21st Centurions
AC, 2005
1 .... 4.00

24 Hour Comics
About, 2004
1 .... 12.00

24: Midnight Sun
Idea & Design Works, 2005
0 .... 7.00

24: Nightfall
Idea & Design Works, 2006
1 .... 4.00
2 .... 4.00

24 One-shot
Idea & Design Works, 2004
1 .... 7.00

20 Nude Dancers 20 Year Two
Tundra
1 .... 4.00

21
Image, 1996
1-3 .... 3.00

21 Down
DC, 2002
1-12 .... 3.00

22 Brides
Event, 1996
1 .... 3.00
1/Ltd 4.00
2-4 .... 3.00
4/A 4.00
CS 1 .... 35.00

Twice-Told Tales of Unsupervised Existence
Rip Off, 1989
1 .... 2.00

Twilight
DC, 1991
1-3 .... 5.00

Twilight
Avatar, 1997
1-2 .... 3.00

Twilight Avenger
Elite, 1986
1-2 .... 2.00

Twilight Avenger
Eternity, 1988

1-8 .... 2.00

Twilight Experiment
DC, 2005

1-6 .... 3.00

Twilight Girl
Cross Plains, 2000

1-3 .... 3.00

Twilight Man
First, 1989

1-4 .... 3.00

Twilight People
Caliber

1-2 .... 3.00

Twilight X
Pork Chop

1-3 .... 2.00

Twilight X
Antarctic, 1993

1-5 .... 3.00

Twilight-X: Interlude
Antarctic, 1992

1-6 .... 3.00

Twilight-X: Interlude
Antarctic, 1993

1-5 .... 3.00

Twilight X Quarterly
Antarctic, 1994

1-3 .... 3.00

Twilight X: Storm
Antarctic, 2003

1-6 .... 4.00

Twilight: X War
Antarctic, 2005

1 .... 3.00

Twilight Zone
Dell, 1962

-207 .... 250.00
-210 .... 200.00

Twilight Zone
Gold Key, 1962

1 .... 90.00
2 .... 55.00
3 .... 42.00
4-10 .... 35.00
11-20 .... 30.00
21-27 .... 16.00
28-30 .... 10.00
31-40 .... 8.00
41-51 .... 6.00
52-70 .... 5.00
71-92 .... 4.00

Twilight Zone
Now, 1991

1-1/Direct 3.00
2-8 .... 2.00
9 .... 3.00
9/Prestige 5.00
10-16 .... 2.00
SF 1 .... 4.00

Twilight Zone
Now, 1993

1-Ann 1993 .... 3.00

Twilight Zone 3-D Special
Now, 1993

1 .... 3.00

Twilight Zone Premiere
Now, 1991

1-1/Direct 3.00
1/Prestige 5.00
1/2nd-1/Direct/2n 3.00

Twin Earths
R. Susor

1-2 .... 6.00

Twist
Dell, 1962

1 .... 5.00

Twist
Kitchen Sink, 1988

1-3 .... 2.00

Twisted
Alchemy

1 .... 4.00

Twisted 3-D Tales
Blackthorne, 1986

1 .... 3.00

Twisted Sisters
Kitchen Sink, 1994

1-4 .... 4.00

Twisted Tales
Pacific, 1954

1 .... 4.00
2-3D 1 .... 3.00

Twisted Tales of Bruce Jones
Eclipse, 1985

1-4 .... 2.00

Twisted Tantrums of the Purple Snit
Blackthorne

1-2 .... 2.00

Twister
Harris

1 .... 3.00

Twitch (Justin Hampton's...)
Aeon

1 .... 3.00

Steven

Stevie

Stormwatch

Straight Arrow

Strange Adventures

Strange Attractors

Strange Fantasy

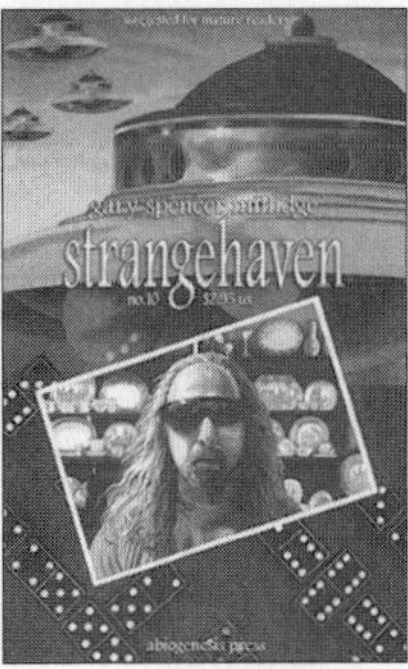

Strangehaven

Two-Bits
Image, 2005

1 .... 1.00

Two Faces of Tomorrow
Dark Horse, 1997

1-13 .... 3.00

Two-Fisted Science
General Tektronics Labs, 2001

1 .... 3.00

Two-Fisted Tales
E.C., 1950

18 .... 700.00
19 .... 500.00
20 .... 325.00
21-22 .... 260.00
23-25 .... 210.00
26-30 .... 160.00
31-35 .... 130.00
36-41 .... 115.00
Ann 1 .... 550.00
Ann 2 .... 400.00

Two-Fisted Tales
Gemstone, 1992

1-15 .... 2.00
16-24 .... 3.00
Ann 1 .... 9.00
Ann 2 .... 10.00
Ann 3 .... 11.00
Ann 4 .... 13.00
Ann 5 .... 14.00

Two Fools
Last Gasp

1 .... 1.00

Two-Gun Kid
Marvel, 1948

1 .... 660.00
2 .... 300.00
3-4 .... 220.00
5 .... 200.00
6-10 .... 165.00
11-12 .... 125.00
13-20 .... 90.00
21-30 .... 80.00
31-44 .... 60.00
45-46 .... 55.00
47 .... 45.00
48 .... 50.00
49-50 .... 40.00
51 .... 50.00
52 .... 40.00
53-54 .... 20.00
55 .... 40.00
56 .... 20.00
57 .... 40.00
58-59 .... 20.00
60 .... 30.00
☛Two-Gun Kid origin
61-80 .... 12.00
81-92 .... 8.00
93-129 .... 4.00
129/30¢ 20.00
130 .... 4.00
130/30¢ 20.00
131 .... 4.00
131/30¢ 20.00
132-136 .... 4.00

Two-Gun Kid: Sunset Riders
Marvel, 1995

1-2 .... 7.00

2-Gun Western
Atlas, 1956

4 .... 100.00

Two Gun Western
Marvel, 1950

5 .... 90.00
6-14 .... 70.00

2-Headed Giant
A Is A, 1995

1 .... 3.00

2 Hot Girls on a Hot Summer Night
Fantagraphics, 1991

1-4 .... 3.00

2 Live Crew Comics
Fantagraphics

1 .... 3.00

Two Over Ten
Second 2 Some Studios, 2001

1-5 .... 3.00

Two Step
DC, 2003

1-3 .... 3.00

2000 A.D. Monthly
Eagle, 1985

1-6 .... 2.00

2000 A.D. Monthly
Eagle, 1986

1-3 .... 2.00

2000 A.D. Presents
Fleetway-Quality, 1986

4-25 .... 2.00

2000 A.D. Showcase
Fleetway-Quality

25-54 .... 2.00

2000 A.D. Showcase
Fleetway-Quality

1-11 .... 3.00

2002 Tokyopop Manga Sampler
Mixx, 2002

1 .... 1.00

Two Thousand Maniacs
Aircel
1-3 .... 3.00

2099 A.D.
Marvel, 1995
1 .... 4.00

2099 A.D. Apocalypse
Marvel, 1995
1 .... 5.00

2099 A.D. Genesis
Marvel, 1996
1 .... 5.00

2099: Manifest Destiny
Marvel, 1998
1 .... 6.00

2099 Special: The World of Doom
Marvel, 1995
1 .... 2.00

2099 Unlimited
Marvel, 1993
1-10 .... 4.00
Ashcan 1 .... 1.00

2099: World of Tomorrow
Marvel, 1996
1-8 .... 3.00

2001 Nights
Viz, 1990
1-10 .... 4.00

2001, A Space Odyssey
Marvel, 1976
1-7 .... 5.00
7/35¢ 20.00
8 .... 12.00
8/35¢ 20.00
9 .... 5.00
9/35¢ 20.00
10 .... 5.00
10/35¢ 20.00
GS 1 .... 12.00

2010
Marvel, 1984
1-2 .... 2.00

2112 (John Byrne's...)
Dark Horse, 1991
1-1/3rd 10.00

2024
NBM
1 .... 17.00

2020 Visions
DC, 1997
1-12 .... 3.00

2 to Chest
Dark Horse, 2004
1 .... 3.00

Two x Justice
Graphic Serials
1 .... 2.00

Tykes
Alternative, 1997
1-Ashcan 1 .... 3.00

Tyler Kirkham Sketchbook
Image, 2006
1 .... 3.00

Typhoid
Marvel, 1995
1-4 .... 4.00

Tyrannosaurus Tex
Monster, 1991
1-3 .... 3.00

Tyrant (S.R. Bissette's...)
Spider Baby, 1994
1-3 .... 3.00
3/Gold 4.00
4-6 .... 3.00

Tzu the Reaper
Murim, 1997
1-3 .... 3.00

Uberdub
Caliber, 1991
1-3 .... 3.00

UFO & Outer Space
Whitman, 1978
14 .... 8.00
15-20 .... 6.00
21-25 .... 5.00

UFO Encounters
Golden Press
1 .... 2.00

UFO Flying Saucers
Gold Key, 1968
1 .... 25.00
2-4 .... 15.00
5-13 .... 10.00

Ultiman Giant Annual
Image, 2001
1 .... 5.00

Ultimate Adventures
Marvel, 2002
1-4 .... 2.00
5-6 .... 3.00

Ultimate Daredevil & Elektra
Marvel, 2003
1 .... 3.00
2-4 .... 2.00

Strangers in Paradise

Strange Sports Stories

Strange Suspense Stories

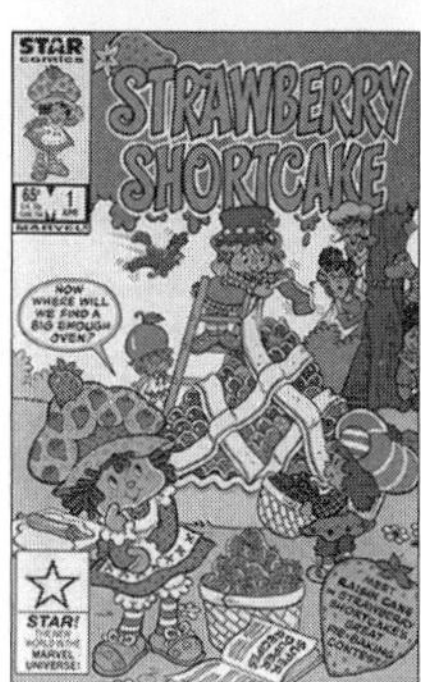

Strawberry Shortcake

All comics prices listed are for NEAR MINT condition.

Stray Bullets

Stray Toasters

Sugar Ray Finhead

Suicide Squad

Ultimate Elektra

Marvel, 2004

1-5 .... 2.00

Ultimate Extinction

Marvel, 2006

1-5 .... 3.00

Ultimate Fantastic Four

Marvel, 2004

1 .... 5.00
2 .... 4.00
3 .... 3.00
4 .... 2.00
5 .... 3.00
6 .... 2.00
7 .... 3.00
8 .... 4.00
9-13 .... 2.00
13/Sketch 6.00
14-18 .... 2.00
19 .... 5.00
20 .... 4.00
21 .... 6.00
21/Variant 8.00
22 .... 16.00
23 .... 7.00
24-55 .... 3.00
Ann 1-2 .... 4.00

Ultimate Fantastic Four/ X-Men Special

Marvel, 2006

1 .... 3.00

Ultimate Iron Man

Marvel, 2005

1/Kubert 5.00
1/Hitch 4.00
1/Sketch 6.00
2-5 .... 3.00

Ultimate Marvel Flip Magazine

Marvel, 2005

1-11 .... 4.00
12-20 .... 5.00

Ultimate Marvel Magazine

Marvel, 2001

1 .... 6.00
2-11 .... 4.00

Ultimate Marvel Team-Up

Marvel, 2001

1-16 .... 3.00

Ultimate Nightmare

Marvel, 2004

1 .... 3.00
2-5 .... 2.00

Ultimate Power

Marvel, 2006

1-3 .... 3.00

Ultimates

Marvel, 2002

1 .... 7.00
2 .... 9.00
3 .... 6.00
4 .... 10.00
5 .... 8.00
6 .... 7.00
7 .... 6.00
8 .... 5.00
9 .... 6.00
10 .... 4.00
11 .... 3.00
12 .... 2.00
13 .... 4.00

Ultimates 2

Marvel, 2005

1-1/2nd 3.00
1/Sketch 35.00
2-11 .... 3.00
12-Ann 2 .... 4.00

Ultimate Secret

Marvel, 2005

1-4 .... 3.00

Ultimate Six

Marvel, 2003

1 .... 4.00
2 .... 3.00
3 .... 2.00
4 .... 3.00
5 .... 2.00
6 .... 3.00
7 .... 2.00

Ultimate Spider-Man

Marvel, 2000

½ 8.00
½/A 18.00
1 .... 65.00
1/White 375.00
1/Kay-Bee 4.00
1/FCBD 3.00
1/Checkers 7.00
1/Payless 6.00
1/Target 175.00
2 .... 30.00
2/Swinging 25.00
3 .... 16.00
4 .... 8.00
5 .... 55.00
6 .... 9.00
6/Niagara 35.00
7 .... 9.00
8 .... 8.00
8/Payless 6.00
9-10 .... 6.00
11 .... 5.00
12 .... 4.00
13 .... 5.00
14 .... 4.00
15 .... 5.00

16-21 .... 3.00
22 .... 4.00
23-26 .... 3.00
27 .... 4.00
28 .... 3.00
29 .... 4.00
30 .... 3.00
31 .... 4.00
32 .... 3.00
33 .... 4.00
34-46 .... 3.00
47 .... 4.00
48-49 .... 3.00
50 .... 4.00
51 .... 2.00
52 .... 5.00
53 .... 3.00
54-55 .... 2.00
56 .... 4.00
57-59 .... 2.00
60 .... 8.00
61 .... 5.00
62 .... 8.00
63 .... 5.00
☛Gwen Stacy returns
64 .... 4.00
65 .... 5.00
66 .... 2.00
67 .... 3.00
68-71 .... 2.00
72 .... 4.00
73-77 .... 2.00
78-99 .... 3.00
100 .... 4.00
101-103 .... 3.00
Ann 1 .... 4.00
Ann 2 .... 3.00
SP 1 .... 4.00

Ultimate Tales Flip Magazine

Marvel, 2005

1-11 .... 4.00
12-20 .... 5.00

Ultimate Vision

Marvel, 2007

0-2 .... 3.00

Ultimate War

Marvel, 2003

1-4 .... 3.00

Ultimate Wolverine vs. Hulk

Marvel, 2006

1-2 .... 3.00

Ultimate X-Men

Marvel, 2000

½ 5.00
1 .... 14.00
1/Sketch 20.00
1/Checkers 30.00
1/NYPost 8.00
1/Universal 60.00
2 .... 7.00
3 .... 6.00
4-5 .... 5.00
6-10 .... 4.00
11-12 .... 3.00
13 .... 4.00
14 .... 3.00
15 .... 4.00
16-17 .... 3.00
18 .... 5.00
19 .... 4.00
20-26 .... 3.00
27-32 .... 2.00
33 .... 5.00
34 .... 4.00
35 .... 3.00
36 .... 4.00
37 .... 3.00
38 .... 2.00
39 .... 3.00
40 .... 2.00
41 .... 5.00
42 .... 4.00
43-49 .... 2.00
50 .... 5.00
50/Conv 15.00
51-59 .... 2.00
60-61 .... 3.00
61/Coipel 5.00
62-74 .... 3.00
75 .... 4.00
76-77 .... 3.00
Ann 1-2 .... 4.00

Ultimate X-Men/Fantastic Four Special

Marvel, 2006

1 .... 3.00

Ultra

Image, 2004

1 .... 4.00
2-8 .... 3.00

UltraForce (Vol. 1)

Malibu, 1994

0 .... 3.00
0/Variant 1.00
1 .... 3.00
1/Hologram 5.00
2-5 .... 2.00
6-10 .... 3.00
Ashcan 1 .... 1.00

UltraForce

Malibu, 1995

0-15 .... 2.00

UltraForce/Avengers

Malibu, 1995

1 .... 4.00

Sun-Runners

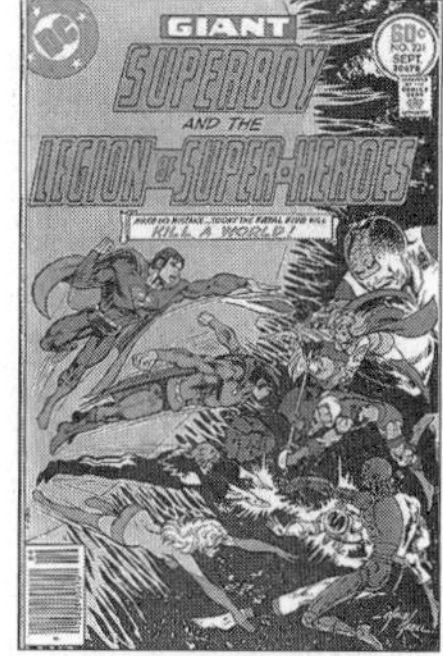

Superboy and the Legion of Super-Heroes

Super Comics

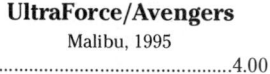

Super DC Giant

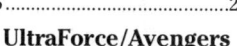

Super Duck Comics

Super Friends

Super Green Beret

Super Heroes Stamp Album

UltraForce/Avengers Prelude

Malibu, 1995

1 .... 3.00

UltraForce/Spider-Man

Malibu, 1996

1-1/Variant 4.00

Ultragirl

Marvel, 1996

1-3 .... 2.00

Ultrahawk

D.M.S.

1 .... 2.00

Ultra Klutz

Onward, 1986

1-31 .... 2.00

Ultra Klutz '81

Onward, 1981

1 .... 2.00

Ultra Klutz Dreams

Bad Habit

1 .... 3.00

Ultraman (Ultracomics)

Harvey, 1993

1 .... 2.00
1/CS 3.00
1/Direct 4.00
2 .... 2.00
2/CS-2/Direct 3.00
3 .... 2.00
3/CS-3/Direct 3.00

Ultraman

Nemesis, 1994

-1-1 .... 3.00
1/A-5 .... 2.00

Ultraman Classic: Battle of the Ultra-Brothers

Viz

1-5 .... 5.00

Ultraman Tiga

Dark Horse, 2003

1-5 .... 4.00
6-7 .... 3.00
8-10 .... 4.00

Ultra Monthly

Malibu, 1993

1-6 .... 1.00

Ultraverse/Avengers Prelude

Malibu, 1995

1 .... 3.00

Ultraverse Double Feature: Prime and Solitaire

Malibu, 1995

1 .... 4.00

Ultraverse: Future Shock

Malibu, 1997

1 .... 3.00

Ultraverse Origins

Malibu, 1994

1 .... 1.00

Ultraverse Prcmiere

Malibu, 1993

0 .... 1.00

Ultraverse Unlimited

Malibu, 1996

1-2 .... 3.00

Ultraverse Year One

Malibu, 1994

1 .... 5.00

Ultraverse Year Two

Malibu, 1995

1 .... 5.00

Ultraverse Year Zero: The Death of The Squad

Malibu, 1995

1-4 .... 3.00

Umbra

Image, 2006

1-3 .... 6.00

Umbrella Academy: Apocalypse Suite

Dark Horse, 2007

1 .... 8.00
1/2nd 4.00
2-6 .... 3.00

Unbound

Image, 1998

1 .... 3.00

Uncanny Origins

Marvel, 1996

1-14 .... 1.00

Uncanny Tales

Marvel, 1952

1 .... 700.00
2 .... 400.00
3-5 .... 325.00
6-10 .... 285.00
11-20 .... 210.00
21-25 .... 165.00
26 .... 225.00
27-28 .... 165.00
29-40 .... 80.00
41-56 .... 65.00

Uncanny Tales

Marvel, 1973

1 .... 20.00
2-12 .... 12.00

Uncanny X-Men

Marvel, 1970

Issue	Price
-1	2.00
142	25.00
☛Future Past	
143	8.00
144	6.00
145	7.00
146-148	6.00
149-157	5.00
158	6.00
☛Rogue appearance	
159-161	5.00
162	6.00
163-166	5.00
167	4.00
☛Rogue joins team	
168-175	5.00
176-177	4.00
178	5.00
179	4.00
180	3.00
181	4.00
182-183	5.00
184-186	4.00
187-188	3.00
189-190	4.00
191	5.00
192	4.00
193	5.00
194-199	3.00
200	6.00
201	5.00
☛Portacio art	
202-209	4.00
210-211	5.00
☛Wolverine vs. Sabretooth	
212-213	8.00
☛Wolverine vs. Sabretooth	
214-215	3.00
216	4.00
217-218	3.00
219-220	4.00
221	7.00
☛1st Mr. Sinister	
222	5.00
☛Wolverine vs. Sabretooth	
223	4.00
224-231	3.00
232	4.00
233-243	3.00
244	5.00
☛1st Jubilee	
245-247	3.00
248	5.00
☛1st Jim Lee X-Men	
248/2nd	2.00
249-258	3.00
259	4.00
260-265	3.00
266	14.00
☛1st Gambit	
267-268	6.00
269	3.00
270	4.00
270/2nd	2.00
271-275	3.00
275/2nd	2.00
276-280	3.00
281-281/2nd	2.00
282	3.00
282/2nd	1.00
283	5.00
284	4.00
285	3.00
286	2.00
287	3.00
288-291	2.00
292	3.00
293	2.00
294/CS	3.00
295/CS	2.00
296/CS	3.00
297-299	2.00
300	3.00
301-302	2.00
303	3.00
304-306	2.00
307	5.00
308-328	2.00
329	4.00
330-352	2.00
353	3.00
354-362	2.00
363	4.00
364	3.00
365-374	2.00
375	3.00
376-378	2.00
379	3.00
380-381	2.00
381/Dynamic	7.00
382	2.00
383	3.00
384-386	2.00
387	3.00
388-399	2.00
400	4.00
401-403	2.00
404	4.00
405-415	2.00
416	3.00
417-421	2.00
422	4.00
423-429	2.00
430-438	3.00
439	2.00
440-441	3.00
442	2.00
443	3.00
444	4.00
445-449	2.00
450	7.00
☛1st X-23	

Superman (1st series)

Superman Adventures

Supernatural Law

Superpatriot

Supersnipe Comics

Super-Team Family

Super-Villain Team-Up

Supreme

451 .... 6.00
☛X-23 appearance
452 .... 3.00
453-454 .... 2.00
455 .... 4.00
456-459 .... 2.00
460-461 .... 3.00
461/Kubert 15.00
☛House of M
462-493 .... 3.00
Ann 1 .... 50.00
Ann 2 .... 45.00
Ann 3 .... 14.00
Ann 4 .... 6.00
Ann 5 .... 5.00
Ann 6 .... 7.00
Ann 7 .... 5.00
Ann 8 .... 4.00
Ann 9 .... 10.00
Ann 10 .... 8.00
Ann 11-12 .... 4.00
Ann 13 .... 3.00
Ann 14 .... 6.00
Ann 15 .... 4.00
Ann 16 .... 2.00
Ann 17-18 .... 3.00
Ann 1995 .... 4.00
Ann 1996-1998 .... 3.00
Ann 2000-2001 .... 4.00

Uncanny X-Men in Days of Future Past

Marvel

1 .... 4.00

Uncensored Mouse

Eternity, 1989

1-2 .... 3.00

Uncle Charlie's Fables

Lev Gleason, 1952

1 .... 50.00
2 .... 30.00
3-5 .... 24.00

Uncle Joe's Commie Book Featuring Cutey Bunny

Rip Off, 1995

1 .... 3.00

Uncle Joe's Funnies

Centaur, 1938

1 .... 250.00

Uncle Milty

Victoria, 1950

1 .... 325.00
2 .... 200.00
3-4 .... 165.00

Uncle Sam

DC, 1997

1-2 .... 5.00

Uncle Sam and the Freedom Fighters

DC, 2006

1-6 .... 3.00

Uncle Sam Quarterly

Quality, 1941

1 .... 1,500.00
2 .... 750.00
3 .... 600.00
4 .... 550.00
5-8 .... 500.00

Uncle Scrooge

Dell, 1953

4 .... 310.00
5 .... 220.00
6-7 .... 185.00
8 .... 140.00
9-10 .... 125.00
11-15 .... 100.00
16-20 .... 80.00
21-30 .... 65.00
31-40 .... 55.00
41-50 .... 45.00
51-70 .... 40.00
71 .... 38.00
72-100 .... 32.00
101-120 .... 20.00
121-140 .... 18.00
141-160 .... 12.00
161-171 .... 10.00
172-176 .... 15.00
177-178 .... 25.00
179 .... 225.00
180 .... 35.00
181-185 .... 15.00
186-197 .... 10.00
198 .... 15.00
199-200 .... 10.00
201-219 .... 6.00
220-240 .... 5.00
241-260 .... 4.00
261-299 .... 3.00
300-308 .... 2.00
309-318 .... 7.00

Uncle Scrooge

Gemstone, 2003

319-349 .... 7.00

Uncle Scrooge Adventures

Gladstone, 1987

1 .... 5.00
2 .... 3.00
3-4 .... 2.00
5 .... 6.00
6-8 .... 2.00
9 .... 5.00
10-13 .... 2.00
14 .... 5.00
15-19 .... 2.00
20-21 .... 5.00
22 .... 2.00

23 .... 3.00
24-25 .... 2.00
26 .... 3.00
27 .... 2.00
28 .... 3.00
29 .... 2.00
30 .... 3.00
31-32 .... 2.00
33 .... 3.00
34-54 .... 2.00

Uncle Scrooge and Donald Duck
Gold Key, 1965
1 .... 50.00

Uncle Scrooge & Donald Duck
Gladstone, 1998
1-2 .... 2.00

Uncle Scrooge and Money
Gold Key, 1967
1 .... 6.00

Uncle Scrooge Classics
Whitman, 1979
1 .... 3.00

Uncle Scrooge Comics Digest
Gladstone, 1986
1 .... 3.00
2-5 .... 2.00

Uncle Scrooge Goes to Disneyland
Gladstone, 1985
1 .... 275.00
1/A-1/A/2nd 5.00
1/2nd 6.00

Uncle Scrooge the Golden Fleecing
Whitman
1 .... 8.00

Uncle Sham
Print Mint
1 .... 4.00

Uncle Slam & Fire Dog
Action Planet, 1997
1-2 .... 3.00

Uncut Comics
Uncut Comics, 1997
1 .... 1.00
1/A-2 .... 2.00

Undercover Genie
DC, 2003
1 .... 15.00

Undercover Girl
Magazine Enterprises, 1952
5 .... 230.00
6-7 .... 220.00

Underdog
Charlton, 1970
1 .... 60.00
2 .... 38.00
3-5 .... 30.00
6-10 .... 25.00

Underdog
Gold Key, 1975
1 .... 35.00
2 .... 20.00
3 .... 12.00
4-5 .... 8.00
6-10 .... 6.00
11-20 .... 5.00
21-23 .... 4.00

Underdog
Spotlight, 1987
1-2 .... 3.00

Underdog
Harvey, 1993
1-Summer 1 .... 2.00

Underdog 3-D
Blackthorne
1 .... 3.00

Underground
Aircel
1 .... 2.00

Underground (Andrew Vachss'...)
Dark Horse, 1993
1-4 .... 4.00

Underground Classics
Rip Off, 1985
1 .... 6.00
2 .... 10.00
2/2nd 2.00
2/3rd 3.00
3 .... 8.00
3/2nd 2.00
4 .... 3.00
5 .... 8.00
6 .... 5.00
7 .... 6.00
8 .... 5.00
9-11 .... 4.00
12 .... 5.00
12/2nd 3.00
13-15 .... 4.00

Underlords
Eidolon Entertainment, 2005
1-4 .... 3.00

Undersea Agent
Tower, 1966
1 .... 32.00
2 .... 22.00
3-6 .... 18.00

Supreme Power

Sweet

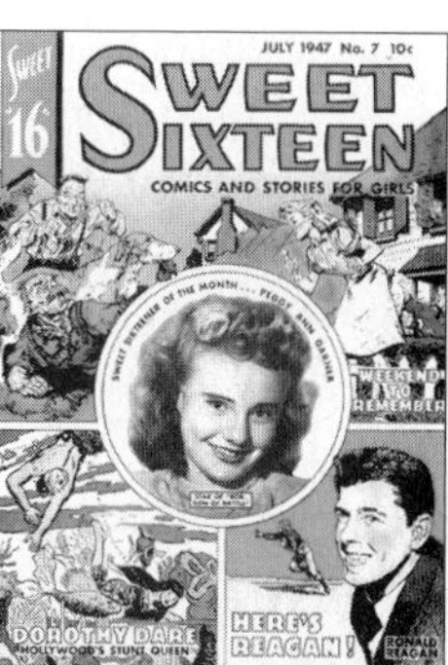

Sweet Sixteen

Sword of Sorcery

Sword of the Atom

Sword of Valor

Swords of the Swashbucklers

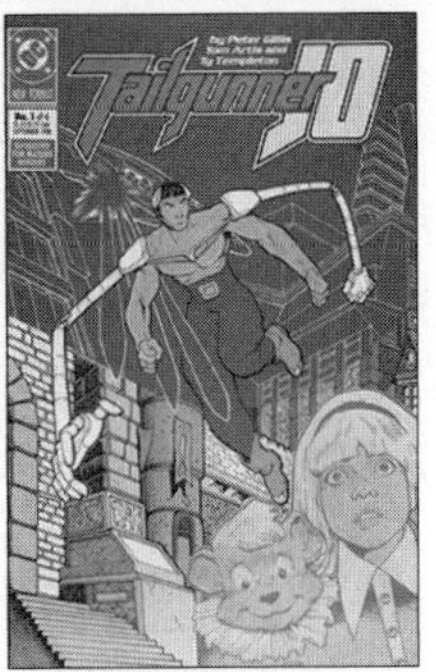
Tailgunner Jo

Underside
Caliber
1 .....3.00

Undertaker
Chaos, 1999
0 .....3.00
½-1 .....4.00
1/A 6.00
1/B 8.00
1/Variant 4.00
2-Holiday 1 .....3.00

Under Terra
Predawn
2-6 .....2.00

Undertow
NBM
1 .....9.00

Underwater
Drawn and Quarterly, 1994
1 .....3.00

Underworld
Marvel, 2006
1-5 .....3.00

Underworld
D.S., 1948
1 .....400.00
2-6 .....250.00
7-9 .....175.00

Underworld
DC, 1987
1-4 .....3.00

Underworld
Death
1 .....2.00

Underworld Crime
Fawcett, 1952
1 .....200.00
2-7 .....100.00

Underworld: Evolution
Idea & Design Works, 2006
1 .....7.00

Underworld Unleashed
DC, 1995
1 .....4.00
2-3 .....3.00

Underworld Unleashed: Abyss: Hell's Sentinel
DC, 1995
1 .....3.00

Underworld Unleashed: Apokolips: Dark Uprising
DC, 1995
1 .....2.00

Underworld Unleashed: Batman: Devil's Asylum
DC, 1995
1 .....3.00

Underworld Unleashed: Patterns of Fear
DC, 1995
1 .....3.00

Undie Dog
Halley's
1 .....2.00

Unearthly Spectaculars
Harvey, 1965
1 .....20.00
2-3 .....16.00

Uneeda Comix
Print Mint
1 .....20.00

Unexpected
DC, 1968
105 .....50.00
☛Was Tales of ...
106-113 .....35.00
114-116 .....30.00
117-127 .....25.00
128 .....45.00
☛Wrightson art
129-139 .....20.00
140-156 .....15.00
157-162 .....30.00
☛100 pages
163-188 .....10.00
189-190 .....7.00
191 .....10.00
192-206 .....7.00
207-222 .....5.00

U.N. Force
Gauntlet, 1995
1-5 .....3.00

Unforgiven
Mythic
1 .....3.00

Unfunnies (Mark Millar's)
Avatar, 2004
1 .....5.00
2 .....4.00

Unfunny X-Cons
Parody, 1992
1-1/2nd 3.00

Unholy (Brian Pulido's ...)
Avatar, 2005
1 .....4.00
1/Foil 5.00
1/Platinum 10.00
1/Haunted 6.00

1/Premium 8.00
1/Wraparound 5.00
2 .... 4.00

Unicorn Isle
Apple, 1986

1-5 .... 2.00

Unicorn King
Kz Comics, 1986

1 .... 2.00

Union
Image, 1993

0-1 .... 3.00
2-4 .... 2.00

Union
Image, 1995

1-9 .... 3.00

Union: Final Vengeance
Image, 1997

1 .... 3.00

Union Jack
Marvel, 1998

1-3 .... 3.00

Union Jack (2nd series)
Marvel, 2006

1-4 .... 3.00

Union Jacks
Anacom

1 .... 2.00

United Comics
United Feature Syndicate, 1940

1 .... 125.00
8-20 .... 25.00
21 .... 18.00
22 .... 25.00
23 .... 18.00
24 .... 25.00
25-26 .... 18.00

United States Marines
Magazine Enterprises, 1943

1 .... 100.00
2 .... 150.00
3 .... 125.00
4 .... 100.00
5-8 .... 40.00

Unity
Valiant, 1992

0 .... 5.00
0/Red 75.00
1 .... 4.00
1/Gold 10.00
1/Platinum 12.00
YB 1 .... 4.00

Unity: The Lost Chapter
Valiant, 1995

1 .... 5.00

Unity 2000
Acclaim, 1999

1 ....3.00
1/A 5.00
2-3 ....3.00

Universal Monsters: Dracula
Dark Horse, 1993

1 ....5.00

Universal Monsters: Frankenstein
Dark Horse, 1993

1 ....4.00

Universal Monsters: The Creature from the Black Lagoon
Dark Horse, 1993

1 ....5.00

Universal Monsters: The Mummy
Dark Horse, 1993

1 ....5.00

Universal Pictures Presents Dracula
Dell, 1963

1 ....160.00

Universal Soldier
Now, 1992

1 ....2.00
1/Direct-1/Variant 3.00
2 ....2.00
2/Direct 3.00
3 ....2.00
3/Direct 3.00

Universe
Image, 2001

1-7 ....3.00
8 ....5.00

Universe X
Marvel, 2000

0-X 4.00

Universe X: Beasts
Marvel, 2001

1 ....4.00

Universe X: Cap
Marvel, 2001

1 ....5.00

Universe X: Iron Men
Marvel, 2001

1 ....4.00

Universe X: Omnibus
Marvel, 2001

1 ....4.00

Tales Calculated to Drive You Bats

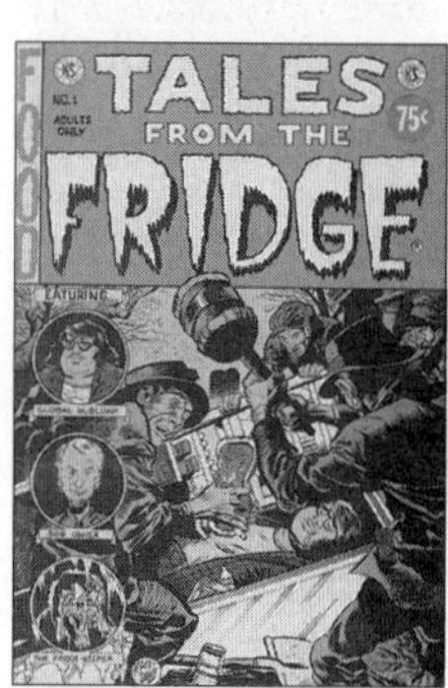

Tales from the Fridge

Tales from the Heart

Tales of G.I. Joe

Tales of Lethargy

Tales of Suspense

Tales of Terror

Tales of the Armorkins

Universe X: Spidey
Marvel, 2001

1 ...10.00
1/A ...6.00
1/B ...10.00
1/C ...90.00

Unknown Soldier
DC, 1977

205-210 ...5.00
211-229 ...4.00
230-247 ...3.00
248-249 ...5.00
250-267 ...3.00
268 ...5.00

Unknown Soldier
DC, 1988

1-12 ...3.00

Unknown Soldier
DC, 1997

1-4 ...3.00

Unknown World
Fawcett, 1952

1 ...250.00

Unknown Worlds
ACG, 1960

1 ...90.00
2 ...60.00
3 ...45.00
4-5 ...40.00
6-8 ...35.00
9 ...50.00
10 ...35.00
11-20 ...28.00
21-30 ...20.00
31-40 ...16.00
41-57 ...12.00

Unknown Worlds of Frank Brunner
Eclipse, 1985

1-2 ...2.00

Unknown Worlds of Science Fiction
Marvel, 1975

1 ...12.00
2-6 ...7.00
Special 1 ...10.00

Unleashed!
Triumphant

1 ...3.00

Unlimited Access
Marvel, 1997

1 ...3.00
2-3 ...2.00
4 ...3.00

Unseen
Standard, 1952

5 ...225.00
6-7 ...180.00
8-11 ...150.00
12-14 ...160.00

Unsupervised Existence
Fantagraphics

1-7/2nd ...2.00

Untamed
Marvel, 1993

1 ...3.00
2-3 ...2.00

Untamed Love
Comic Magazines, 1950

1-2 ...125.00
3-4 ...100.00
5 ...125.00

Untamed Love (Frank Frazetta's...)
Fantagraphics, 1987

1 ...2.00

Untold Legend of Captain Marvel
Marvel, 1997

1-3 ...3.00

Untold Legend of the Batman
DC, 1980

1 ...3.00
1/2nd ...1.00
1/3rd-3 ...2.00

Untold Origin of Femforce
AC, 1989

1 ...5.00

Untold Origin of Ms. Victory
AC, 1989

1 ...3.00

Untold Tales of Chastity
Chaos, 2000

1 ...3.00

Untold Tales of Lady Death
Chaos, 2000

1 ...3.00

Untold Tales of Purgatori
Chaos, 2000

1 ...3.00

Untold Tales of Spider-Man
Marvel, 1995

-1 ...1.00
1 ...2.00
2-25 ...1.00
Ann 1996-1997 ...2.00

Untold Tales of the New Universe: Justice
Marvel, 2006

1 ...3.00

Untold Tales of the New Universe: D.P. 7
Marvel, 2006
1 .... 3.00

Untold Tales of the New Universe: Nightmask
Marvel, 2006
1 .... 3.00

Untold Tales of the New Universe: Psi-Force
Marvel, 2006
1 .... 3.00

Untold Tales of the New Universe: Star Brand
Marvel, 2006
1 .... 3.00

Untouchables
Dell, 1962
3-4 .... 50.00

Untouchables
Caliber, 1997
1-4 .... 3.00

Untouchables
Eastern
1-2 .... 1.00

Unusual Tales
Charlton, 1955
1 .... 125.00
2 .... 75.00
3-5 .... 45.00
6-11 .... 80.00
12 .... 56.00
13 .... 30.00
14-15 .... 56.00
16 .... 30.00
17-21 .... 22.00
22 .... 35.00
23 .... 14.00
24-27 .... 30.00
28-29 .... 14.00
30-40 .... 10.00
41-49 .... 6.00

Up from Bondage
Fantagraphics, 1991
1 .... 3.00

Up From the Deep
Rip Off, 1971
1 .... 3.00

Urban Hipster
Alternative, 1998
1 .... 3.00

Urban Legends
Dark Horse, 1993
1 .... 3.00

Urotsukidoji: Legend of the Overfiend
CPM, 1998
1-3 .... 3.00

Urth 4
Continuity, 1989
1-4 .... 2.00

Urza-Mishra War on the World of Magic: The Gathering
Acclaim, 1996
1-2 .... 6.00

U.S. 1
Marvel, 1983
1-12 .... 1.00

USA Comics
Timely, 1941
1 .... 12,000.00
2 .... 4,400.00
3 .... 3,100.00
4-5 .... 2,500.00
6 .... 3,550.00
7 .... 3,400.00
8-10 .... 2,250.00
11-12 .... 1,500.00
13-17 .... 1,250.00

U.S.Agent
Marvel, 1993
1-4 .... 2.00

USAgent
Marvel, 2001
1-3 .... 3.00

Usagi Yojimbo
Fantagraphics, 1986
1 .... 8.00
1/2nd 3.00
2-3 .... 5.00
4-5 .... 4.00
6-10 .... 3.00
10/2nd 2.00
11-38 .... 3.00
Special 1-3 .... 4.00
Summer 1 .... 5.00

Usagi Yojimbo
Mirage, 1993
1 .... 5.00
2-5 .... 4.00
6-16 .... 3.00

Usagi Yojimbo
Dark Horse, 1996
1 .... 4.00
2-120 .... 3.00
Special 4 .... 4.00

U.S. Air Force
Charlton, 1958
1 .... 45.00
2 .... 25.00

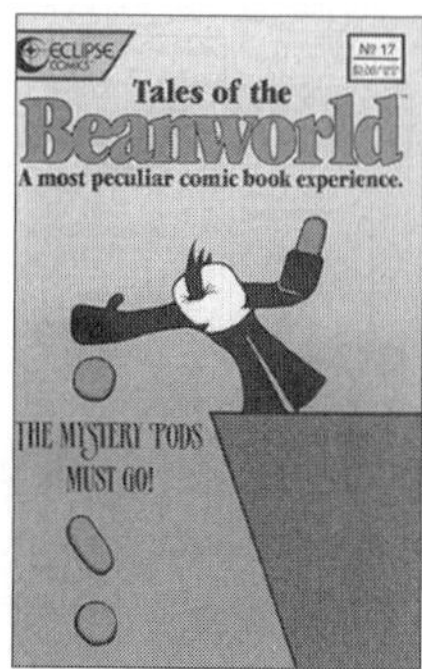

Tales of the Beanworld

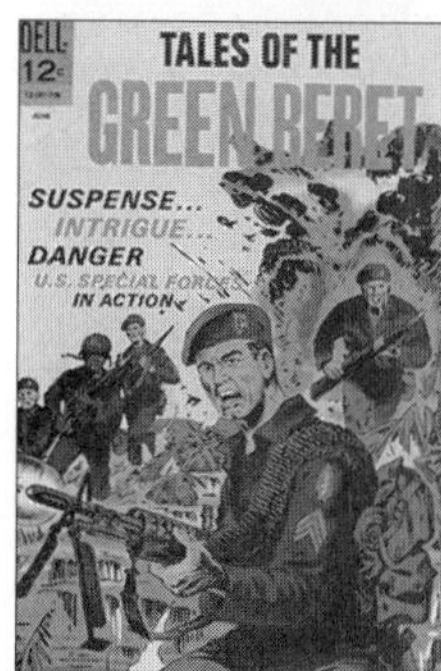

Tales of the Green Beret

Tales of the Green Berets

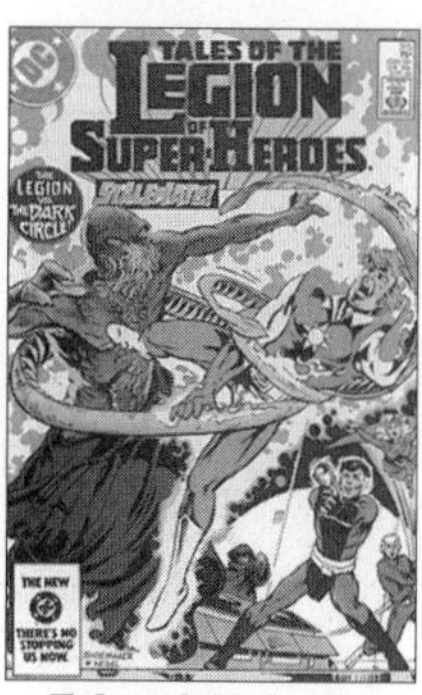

Tales of the Legion

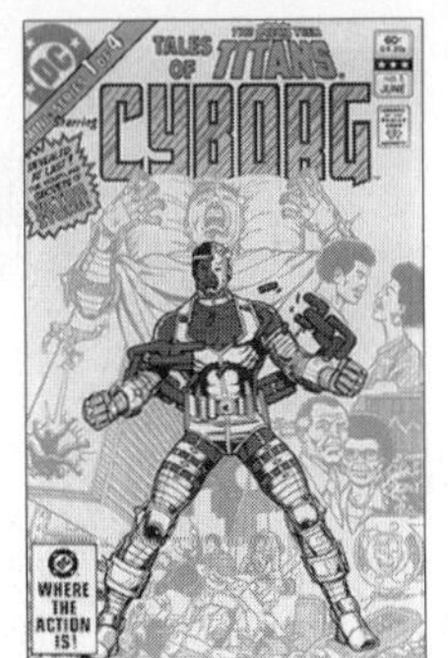
Tales of the New Teen Titans

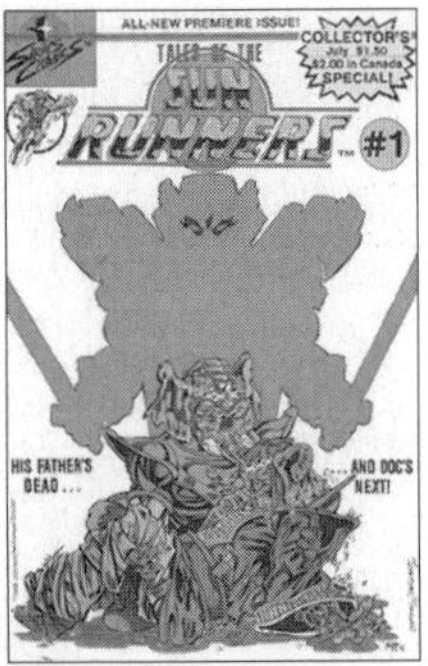
Tales of the Sun Runners

Tales of the Teenage Mutant Ninja Turtles

Tales of the Teen Titans

3-5 ....15.00
6-10 ....12.00
11-20 ....10.00
21-37 ....8.00

User
DC, 2001
1-3 ....6.00

U.S. Fighting Air Force
Superior, 1952
1 ....55.00
2-3 ....38.00
4-5 ....30.00
6-10 ....25.00
11-28 ....20.00

U.S. Fighting Men
Super, 1963
10-11 ....15.00
12-18 ....12.00

V
DC, 1985
1 ....2.00
2-18 ....1.00

Vacation in Disneyland
Dell, 1958
1 ....125.00

Vagabond
Image, 2000
1/A-1/B 3.00

Vagabond (Viz)
Viz, 2001
1-15 ....5.00

Vaistron
Slave Labor, 2005
1-2 ....3.00

Valentine
Redeye, 1997
1 ....3.00

Valentino
Renegade, 1985
1-3 ....2.00

Valerian
Fantasy Flight, 1996
1 ....3.00

Valeria, the She-Bat (Continuity)
Continuity, 1993
1-4 ....3.00
5 ....2.00

Valeria the She-Bat (Windjammer)
Acclaim, 1995
1-2 ....3.00

Valhalla
Antarctic, 1999
1 ....3.00

Valiant Efforts
Valiant Comics, 1991
1 ....2.00

Valiant Reader
Valiant, 1993
1 ....1.00

Valiant Varmints
Shanda Fantasy Arts
1 ....5.00

Valiant Vision Starter Kit
Valiant, 1994
1 ....3.00

Valkyr
Ironcat, 1999
1-5 ....3.00

Valkyrie
Eclipse, 1987
1-3 ....2.00

Valkyrie
Eclipse, 1988
1-3 ....2.00

Valkyrie
Marvel, 1997
1 ....3.00

Valley of the Dinosaurs
Harvey, 1975
1 ....10.00
2-5 ....6.00
6-11 ....4.00

Valor
E.C., 1955
1 ....190.00
2 ....140.00
3-4 ....115.00
5 ....105.00

Valor
DC, 1992
1-12 ....1.00
13-23 ....2.00

Valor
Gemstone, 1998
1-5 ....3.00

Valor Thunderstar and His Fireflies
Now, 1986
1-3 ....2.00

Vamperotica
Brainstorm, 1994
1 ....8.00
1/Gold-1/Platinum 10.00
1/2nd 4.00
1/3rd 3.00
2 ....5.00

3-16 .... 3.00
16/Nude 5.00
17 .... 3.00
17/A 5.00
18 .... 3.00
18/Nude 5.00
19-19/A 3.00
19/Nude 5.00
20 .... 3.00
20/Nude 5.00
21-22 .... 3.00
22/Nude 5.00
23-24 .... 3.00
24/Nude 5.00
25-45 .... 3.00
45/Variant 4.00
46-49 .... 3.00
Ann 1 .... 4.00
Ann 1/Gold 8.00
SS 1 .... 4.00

Vamperotica Magazine

Brainstorm

1 .... 5.00
1/Nude 6.00
1/Variant 10.00
2 .... 5.00
2/Nude-2/Variant 6.00
3 .... 5.00
3/Nude-10/Variant 6.00
11-12/Nude 3.00

Vamperotica Presents Countess Vladimira

Brainstorm, 2001

1 .... 3.00

Vampfire

Brainstorm, 1996

1 .... 3.00

Vampfire: Erotic Echo

Brainstorm, 1997

1-2/Nude 3.00

Vampfire: Necromantique

Brainstorm, 1997

1-2 .... 3.00

Vampi

Harris, 2000

1 .... 3.00
1/A-1/C 5.00
1/D 6.00
1/E 8.00
1/F 15.00
2-5 .... 3.00
6-24 .... 4.00
25 .... 3.00
25/Ltd. 10.00
Ashcan 1 .... 4.00
Ashcan 1/A 10.00

Vampire Companion

Innovation

1-3 .... 3.00

Vampire Game

Tokyopop, 2003

1-13 .... 10.00

Vampire Girls: Bubble Gum & Blood

Angel

1-2 .... 3.00

Vampire Girls: California 1969

Angel Entertainment, 1996

0 .... 3.00
0/A-0/Nude 5.00
1 .... 3.00

Vampire Girls, Poets of Blood: San Francisco

Angel

1-2/Nude 5.00

Vampire Lestat (Anne Rice's...)

Innovation, 1990

1 .... 5.00
1/2nd-12 .... 3.00

Vampirella (Magazine)

Warren, 1969

1 .... 325.00
1/2nd 15.00
2 .... 125.00
3 .... 200.00
4-5 .... 75.00
6-9 .... 70.00
10 .... 30.00
11-15 .... 43.00
16-25 .... 30.00
26 .... 20.00
27 .... 30.00
28-36 .... 25.00
37-45 .... 20.00
46 .... 25.00
47-50 .... 20.00
51-70 .... 17.00
71-99 .... 16.00
100 .... 30.00
101-111 .... 16.00
112 .... 45.00
113 .... 195.00
Ann 1 .... 175.00
Special 1 .... 30.00

Vampirella

Harris, 1992

0-0/Silver 5.00
0/Gold-1 .... 15.00
1/2nd 5.00
2 .... 12.00
3 .... 10.00
4-5 .... 8.00

Tales of the Unexpected

Tales of the Witchblade

Tales Too Terrible to Tell

Tall Tails

Tangled Web

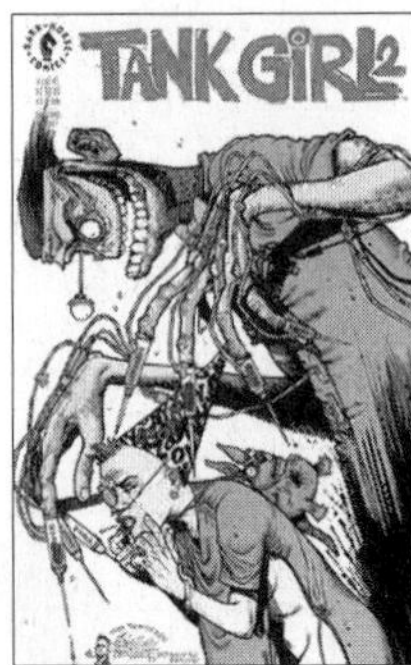

Tank Girl 2

Target Comics

Taskmaster

Vampirella & the Blood Red Queen of Hearts

Harris, 1996

1 ..... 10.00

Vampirella: Ascending Evil

Harris

1 ..... 3.00
2-4 ..... 3.00

Vampirella: Blood Lust

Harris, 1997

1-2 ..... 5.00

Vampirella Classic

Harris, 1995

1-5 ..... 3.00

Vampirella Commemorative Edition

Harris, 1996

1 ..... 3.00

Vampirella: Crossover Gallery

Harris, 1997

1 ..... 3.00

Vampirella: Death & Destruction

Harris, 1996

1-1/A 3.00
1/Ltd. 5.00
2-Ashcan 1 ..... 3.00

Vampirella/Dracula & Pantha Showcase

Harris, 1997

1-1/A 2.00

Vampirella/Dracula: The Centennial

Harris, 1997

1-2 ..... 6.00

Vampirella: Hell on Earth Battlebook

Harris, 1999

1 ..... 4.00

Vampirella: Julie Strain Special

Harris, 2000

1 ..... 4.00
1/A 15.00
1/B 25.00

Vampirella/Lady Death

Harris, 1999

1 ..... 4.00
1/A 5.00
1/Ltd. 10.00

Vampirella Lives

Harris, 1996

1-1/B 4.00
1/C 10.00
2-2/A 3.00
2/B 4.00
3 ..... 3.00
3/A 4.00

Vampirella Monthly

Harris, 1997

0-1 ..... 4.00
1/A-1/C 5.00
1/D 60.00
1/E 10.00
1/F 20.00
2 ..... 3.00
2/A 10.00
3 ..... 3.00
3/A 10.00
4 ..... 3.00
4/A 4.00
4/B-7 ..... 3.00
7/A 10.00
7/B 4.00
7/C 5.00
7/D 12.00
7/E 10.00
8-10 ..... 3.00
10/A 6.00
10/B 5.00
11-12/A 3.00
12/B 15.00
12/Variant 6.00
13-16/A 3.00
16/B 4.00
16/C 5.00
16/D 3.00
16/E-17 ..... 4.00
17/A 3.00
17/B-17/C 4.00
17/D 3.00
17/E 4.00
18 ..... 3.00
18/A-18/B 5.00
19 ..... 3.00
19/A 5.00
20 ..... 3.00
20/A 5.00
21 ..... 3.00
21/A 5.00
21/B-22 ..... 4.00
22/A 3.00
22/B 4.00
23 ..... 3.00
23/A 7.00
23/B 5.00
23/C 20.00
23/D 10.00
24-24/A 3.00
24/B 10.00
25-26/A 3.00
Ashcan 1-3 ..... 5.00
Ashcan 3/A 15.00
Ashcan 4-6 ..... 3.00

Vampirella: Morning in America

Harris, 1991

1-4 .... 4.00

Vampirella of Drakulon

Harris, 1994

0-3 .... 3.00

Vampirella/Painkiller Jane

Harris, 1998

1 .... 4.00
1/A 5.00
1/B-1/Gold 25.00
Ashcan 1 .... 3.00

Vampirella Pin-Up Special

Harris, 1995

1-1/A 3.00

Vampirella: Sad Wings of Destiny

Harris, 1996

1 .... 4.00
1/Gold 5.00

Vampirella/ShadowHawk: Creatures of the Night

Harris, 1995

1-2 .... 5.00

Vampirella/Shi

1 .... 3.00

Vampirella: Silver Anniversary Collection

Harris, 1997

1/A-4/B 3.00

Vampirella's Summer Nights

Harris, 1992

1 .... 4.00

Vampirella Strikes

Harris, 1995

1-1/C 3.00
1/Ltd. 10.00
2-Ann 1/B 3.00

Vampirella 30th Anniversary Celebration

Harris, 1999

1 .... 3.00

Vampirella 25th Anniversary Special

Harris, 1996

1-1/A 6.00

Vampirella vs. Hemorrhage

Harris, 1997

1-1/A 4.00
1/Ashcan 1.00
2-3 .... 4.00

Vampirella vs. Pantha

Harris, 1997

1/A-Ashcan 1 .... 4.00

Vampirella/Wetworks

Harris, 1997

1 .... 3.00

Vampire Miyu

Antarctic, 1995

1 .... 4.00
2-6 .... 3.00
Ashcan 1 .... 1.00

Vampires Lust

CFD, 1996

1 .... 3.00
1/Nude 4.00

Vampire's Prank

Acid Rain

1 .... 3.00

Vampire Tales

Marvel, 1973

1 .... 35.00
2-7 .... 18.00
8-10 .... 20.00
11 .... 25.00
☛Scarce
Ann 1 .... 30.00
☛Scarce

Vampire the Masquerade: Toreador

Moonstone, 2003

1 .... 6.00

Vampire Verses

CFD, 1995

1-1/3rd 3.00
1/Ltd. 5.00
2-2/3rd 3.00
2/Ltd. 5.00
3-3/2nd 3.00
3/Ltd. 5.00
4-4/2nd 3.00
4/Ltd. 5.00

Vampire Vixens

Acid Rain

1 .... 3.00

Vampire World

Acid Rain

1 .... 3.00

Vampire Yui

Ironcat, 2000

1 .... 3.00

Vampiric Jihad

Apple

1 .... 5.00

Vampornella

Adam Post

1 .... 3.00

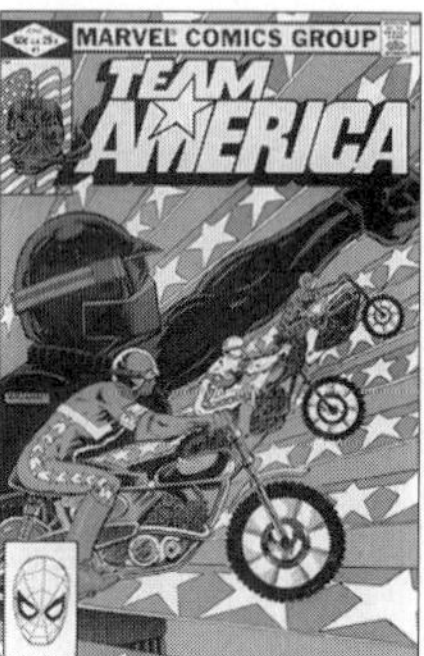

Team America

Team Youngblood

Tech Jacket

Teenage Hotrodders

Teenage Mutant Ninja Turtles Movie II

Teen Comics

Teen Confessions

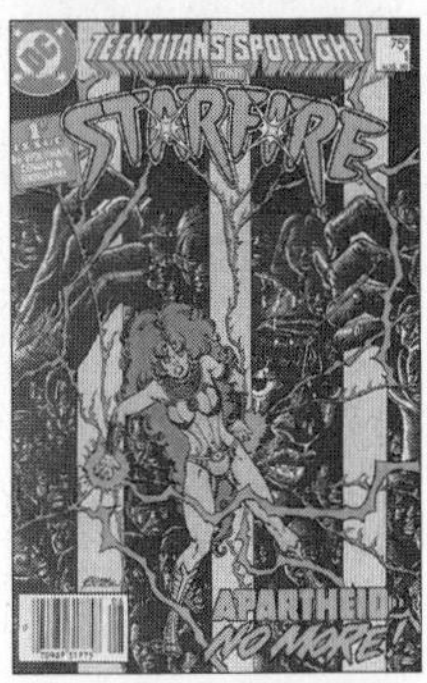

Teen Titans Spotlight

Vampress Luxura

Brainstorm, 1996

1 .... 3.00

1/Gold 8.00

Vamps

DC, 1994

1-6 .... 3.00

Vamps: Hollywood & Vein

DC, 1996

1-6 .... 3.00

Vamps: Pumpkin Time

DC, 1998

1-3 .... 3.00

Vampurada

Tavicat, 1995

1 .... 2.00

Vampyres

Eternity, 1989

1-4 .... 2.00

Vampyre's Kiss

Aircel, 1990

1-4 .... 3.00

Vampyre's Kiss, Book II

Aircel, 1990

1-4 .... 3.00

Vampyre's Kiss, Book III

Aircel, 1991

1-4 .... 3.00

Vandala

Chaos!, 2000

1 .... 3.00

Vanguard

Image, 1993

1-6 .... 2.00

Vanguard

Image, 1996

1-4 .... 3.00

Vanguard: Ethereal Warriors

Image, 2000

1 .... 6.00

Vanguard Illustrated

Pacific, 1983

1-6 .... 2.00

7 .... 4.00

Van Helsing One-Shot

Dark Horse, 2004

1 .... 3.00

Vanity

Pacific, 1984

1-2 .... 2.00

Vanity Angel

Antarctic, 1994

1-6 .... 4.00

Varcel's Vixens

Caliber, 1990

1-3 .... 3.00

Variations on the Theme

Scarlet Rose

1-4 .... 3.00

Varick: Chronicles of the Dark Prince

Q, 1999

1 .... 2.00

Variety Comics

Rural Home, 1944

1 .... 125.00

2 .... 65.00

3 .... 50.00

Variogenesis

Dagger, 1994

0 .... 4.00

Varla Vortex

Boneyard

1 .... 3.00

Varmints

Blue Comet

1 .... 2.00

Special 1 .... 3.00

Vast Knowledge of General Subjects, A

Fantagraphics, 1994

1 .... 5.00

Vault of Doomnation

B-Movie, 1986

1 .... 2.00

Vault of Evil

Marvel, 1973

1 .... 60.00

2-4 .... 25.00

5-10 .... 15.00

11-23 .... 12.00

Vault of Horror

E.C., 1950

12 .... 4,000.00

13 .... 800.00

14 .... 725.00

15 .... 600.00

16 .... 500.00

17-19 .... 360.00

20-25 .... 275.00

26-30 .... 225.00

31-40 .... 185.00

Vault of Horror

Gladstone, 1990

1-7 .... 3.00

Vault of Horror

Cochran, 1991

1-5 .... 2.00

Vault of Horror (RCP)
Gemstone, 1992
1-15 .... 2.00
16-29 .... 3.00
Ann 1 .... 9.00
Ann 2 .... 10.00
Ann 3 .... 11.00
Ann 4 .... 13.00
Ann 5 .... 14.00

Vault of Screaming Horror
Fantaco
1 .... 4.00

Vault of Whores
Fantagraphics
1 .... 3.00

V-Comics
Fox, 1942
1 .... 850.00
2 .... 600.00

VC's
Fleetway-Quality
1-5 .... 2.00

Vector
Now, 1986
1-4 .... 2.00

Vegas Knights
Pioneer
1 .... 2.00

Vegetable Lover
Fantagraphics, 1992
1 .... 3.00

Vegman
Checker, 1998
1-2 .... 3.00

Velocity
Image, 1995
1-3 .... 3.00

Velocity
Eclipse
5 .... 3.00

Velvet
Adventure, 1993
1-4 .... 3.00

Velvet Artichoke Theatre
Velvet Artichoke, 1998
1 .... 2.00

Velvet Touch
Antarctic, 1993
1-6 .... 4.00

Vendetta: Holy Vindicator
Red Bullet
1-4 .... 3.00

Vengeance of the Aztecs
Caliber
1-5 .... 3.00

Vengeance of Vampirella
Harris, 1994
0 .... 3.00
½-1 .... 4.00
1/A 3.00
1/Gold 10.00
1/2nd-6 .... 3.00
6/A 4.00
7-25/A 3.00
25/B-25/Gold 5.00
25/Platinum 6.00
25/Ashcan 5.00

Vengeance Squad
Charlton, 1975
1 .... 9.00
2-6 .... 5.00

Vengeful Skye
Davdez, 1998
1 .... 3.00

Venger Robo
Viz
1-7 .... 3.00

Venom
Marvel, 2003
1 .... 10.00
2 .... 3.00
3-7 .... 2.00
8 .... 3.00
9 .... 4.00
10-18 .... 3.00

Venom: Along Came a Spider
Marvel, 1996
1-4 .... 3.00

Venom: Carnage Unleashed
Marvel, 1995
1-4 .... 3.00

Venom: Deathtrap: The Vault
Marvel
1 .... 7.00

Venom: Finale
Marvel, 1997
1-3 .... 2.00

Venom: Funeral Pyre
Marvel, 1993
1-3 .... 3.00

Venom: Lethal Protector
Marvel, 1993
1 .... 3.00
1/Black 75.00
1/Gold 5.00
2-6 .... 3.00

Venom: License to Kill
Marvel, 1997
1-3 .... 2.00

Tekworld

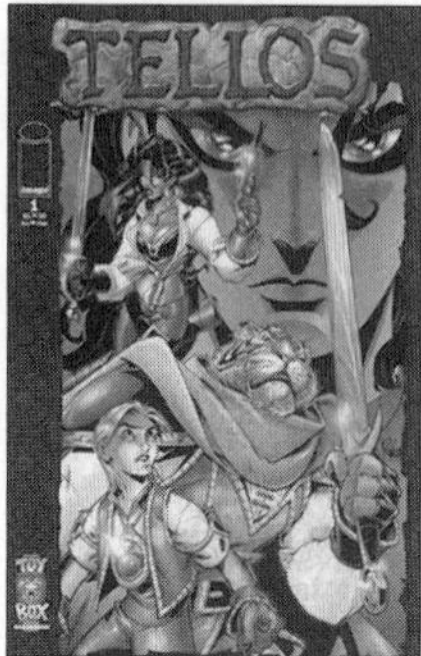

Tellos

Tempest

Terminal City

Terra Obscura

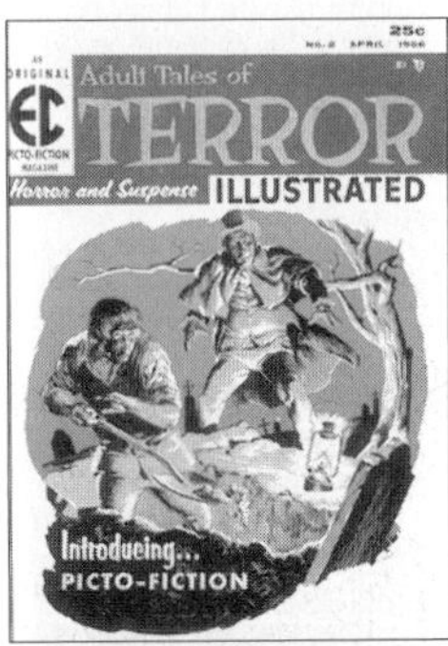

Terror Illustrated

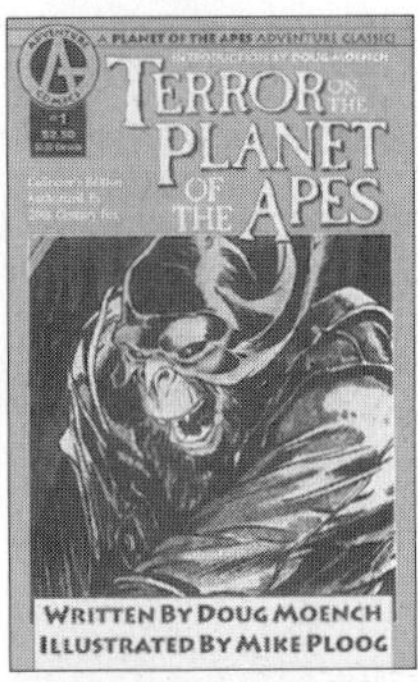

Terror on the Planet of the Apes

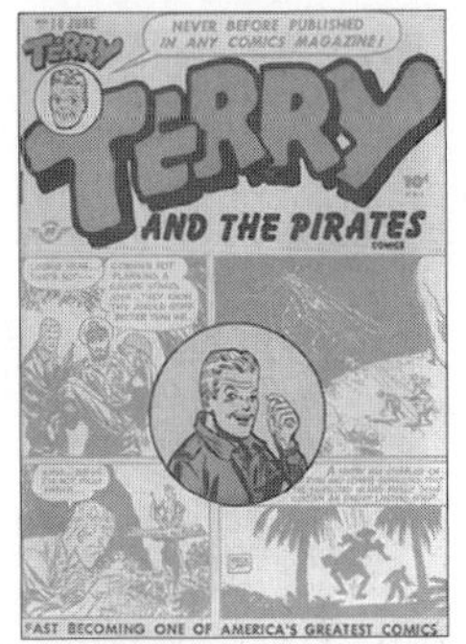

Terry and the Pirates Comics

Venom: Nights of Vengeance
Marvel, 1994
1-4 .... 3.00

Venom: On Trial
Marvel, 1997
1-3 .... 2.00

Venom: Seed of Darkness
Marvel, 1997
-1 .... 2.00

Venom: Separation Anxiety
Marvel, 1994
1-4 .... 3.00

Venom: Sign of the Boss
Marvel, 1997
1-2 .... 2.00

Venom: Sinner Takes All
Marvel, 1995
1-5 .... 3.00

Venom Super Special
Marvel, 1995
1 .... 4.00

Venom: The Enemy Within
Marvel, 1994
1-3 .... 3.00

Venom: The Hunger
Marvel, 1996
1-4 .... 2.00

Venom: The Hunted
Marvel, 1996
1-3 .... 3.00

Venom: The Mace
Marvel, 1994
1-3 .... 3.00

Venom: The Madness
Marvel, 1993
1-3 .... 3.00

Venom: Tooth and Claw
Marvel, 1996
1-3 .... 2.00

Venom vs. Carnage
Marvel, 2004
1 .... 6.00
2-4 .... 3.00

Venture
AC, 1986
1-3 .... 2.00

Venture
Image, 2003
1-4 .... 3.00

Venture San Diego Comic-Con Special Edition
Venture, 1994
1 .... 3.00

Venumb
Parody, 1993
1-1/Deluxe 3.00

Venus
Marvel, 1948
1 .... 1,425.00
2 .... 800.00
3 .... 675.00
4-5 .... 650.00
6-9 .... 640.00
10 .... 780.00
11 .... 800.00
12 .... 550.00
13-19 .... 820.00

Venus Domina
Verotik, 1997
1-3 .... 5.00

Venus Interface (Heavy Metal's...)
HM Communications
1 .... 6.00

Venus Wars
Dark Horse, 1991
1 .... 3.00
2-14 .... 2.00

Venus Wars II
Dark Horse, 1992
1-15 .... 3.00

Verbatim
Fantagraphics, 1993
1-2 .... 3.00

Verdict
Eternity, 1988
1-4 .... 2.00

Vermillion
DC, 1996
1-12 .... 2.00

Veronica
Archie, 1989
1-20 .... 2.00
21-35 .... 1.00
36-193 .... 2.00

Veronica's Digest Magazine
Archie, 1992
1-6 .... 2.00

Verotika
Verotik, 1994
1 .... 4.00
2-14 .... 3.00
15 .... 4.00

Verotik Illustrated
Verotik, 1997
1-3 .... 7.00

Verotik Rogues Gallery of Villains
Verotik, 1997
1 .... 4.00

Verotik World
Verotik, 2002
1 .... 4.00
1/Variant 5.00
2-3 .... 4.00
3/Variant 10.00

Version
Dark Horse, 1993
1.1-2.7 .... 3.00

Vertical
DC, 2004
1 .... 5.00

Vertigo Gallery: Dreams and Nightmares
DC
1 .... 4.00

Vertigo Jam
DC, 1993
1 .... 4.00

Vertigo Pop! Bangkok
DC, 2003
1-4 .... 3.00

Vertigo Pop! London
DC, 2002
1-4 .... 3.00

Vertigo Pop! Tokyo
DC, 2002
1-3 .... 3.00

Vertigo Preview
DC
1 .... 2.00

Vertigo Rave
DC, 1994
1 .... 2.00

Vertigo Secret Files & Origins: Swamp Thing
DC, 2000
1 .... 5.00

Vertigo Secret Files: Hellblazer
DC, 2000
1 .... 5.00

Vertigo Veritè: The Unseen Hand
DC, 1996
1-4 .... 3.00

Vertigo Visions: Doctor Occult
DC, 1994
1 .... 4.00

Vertigo Visions: Dr. Thirteen
DC, 1998
1 .... 6.00

Vertigo Visions: Prez
DC, 1995
1 .... 4.00

Vertigo Visions: The Geek
DC, 1993
1 .... 4.00

Vertigo Visions: The Phantom Stranger
DC, 1993
1 .... 4.00

Vertigo Visions: Tomahawk
DC, 1998
1 .... 5.00

Vertigo Voices: The Eaters
DC
1 .... 5.00

Vertigo: Winter's Edge
DC, 1998
1 .... 8.00
2-3 .... 7.00

Vertigo X Preview
DC, 2003
1 .... 1.00

Very Best of Dennis the Menace
Marvel, 1982
1 .... 3.00
2-3 .... 2.00

Very Mu Christmas, A
Mu, 1992
1 .... 3.00

Very Vicky
Iconografix, 1993
1-8 .... 3.00

Vespers
Mars Media Group, 1995
1 .... 3.00

Vext
DC, 1999
1-6 .... 3.00

V for Vendetta
DC, 1988
☛Alan Moore series
1-10 .... 3.00

Vibe
Young Gun, 1994
1 .... 2.00

Vic & Blood
Mad Dog, 1987
1-2 .... 2.00

Tessie the Typist

Texas Rangers in Action

Tex Ritter Western

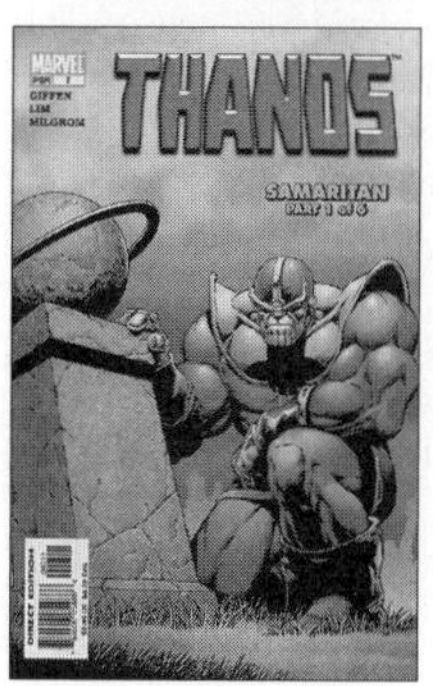

Thanos

That Wilkin Boy

THB

They Came from the 50S

Thirteen

V.I.C.E.
Image, 2005

1-5 .... 3.00

Vicious
Brainstorm

1 .... 3.00

Vic Jordan
Argo, 1945

1 .... 60.00

Vicki
Atlas-Seaboard, 1975

1 .... 28.00
2 .... 18.00
3-4 .... 12.00

Vicki Valentine
Renegade, 1985

1-4 .... 2.00

Victim
Silverwolf, 1987

1 .... 2.00

Victims
Eternity, 1983

1-6 .... 2.00

Victorian
Penny-Farthing, 1998

½ 1.00
1-25 .... 3.00

Victoria's Secret Service
Alias, 2005

0 .... 1.00

Vic Torry
Avalon

1 .... 3.00

Vic Torry and His Flying Saucer
Fawcett, 1950

1 .... 410.00

Victor Vector & Yondo
Fractal, 1994

1-3 .... 2.00

Victory (Topps)
Topps, 1994

1 .... 3.00

Victory
Image, 2003

1-4 .... 3.00

Victory Comics
Hillman, 1941

1 .... 1,875.00
2 .... 1,200.00
3 .... 850.00
4 .... 400.00

Victory
Image, 2004

1/A-4/C 3.00

Vic Verity
Verity, 1945

1 .... 100.00
2-4 .... 75.00
5-7 .... 50.00

Video Classics
Eternity

1-2 .... 4.00

Video Girl AI
Viz, 2003

1-5 .... 16.00
6-8 .... 13.00
9-13 .... 10.00

Video Hiroshima
Aeon, 1995

1 .... 3.00

Video Jack
Marvel, 1987

1-6 .... 1.00

Vietnam Journal
Apple, 1987

1-16 .... 2.00

Vietnam Journal: Bloodbath at Khe Sanh
Apple, 1993

1-4 .... 3.00

Vietnam Journal: Tet '68
Apple, 1992

1-6 .... 3.00

Vietnam Journal: Valley of Death
Apple, 1994

1 .... 3.00

Vigilante
DC, 1983

1-3 .... 2.00
4-23 .... 1.00
24 .... 2.00
25-50 .... 1.00
Ann 1-2 .... 2.00

Vigilante
DC, 2005

1-6 .... 3.00

Vigilante 8: Second Offense
Chaos, 1999

1 .... 3.00

Vigilante: City Lights, Prairie Justice
DC, 1995

1-4 .... 3.00

Vigil: Bloodline
Duality, 1998
1-8 .... 3.00

Vigil: Desert Foxes
Millennium, 1995
1-2 .... 4.00

Vigil: Eruption
Millennium, 1996
1-2 .... 3.00

Vigil: Fall from Grace
Innovation, 1992
1-2 .... 3.00

Vigil: Kukulkan
Innovation
1 .... 3.00

Vigil: Rebirth
Millennium, 1994
1-2 .... 3.00

Vigil: Scattershots
Duality, 1997
1-2 .... 4.00

Vigil: The Golden Parts
Innovation
1 .... 3.00

Vigil: Vamporum Animaturi
Millennium, 1994
1 .... 4.00

Vignette Comics
Harrier
1 .... 2.00

Viking Glory: The Viking Prince
DC
1 .... 15.00

Vile
Raging Rhino
1 .... 3.00

Villains & Vigilantes
Eclipse, 1986
1-4 .... 2.00

Villains United
DC, 2005
1 .... 12.00
1/2nd 8.00
1/3rd 3.00
2 .... 5.00
3-5 .... 3.00
6 .... 4.00

Villains United: Infinite Crisis Special
DC, 2006
1 .... 5.00

Villa of the Mysteries
Fantagraphics, 1998
1-3 .... 4.00

Vimanarama!
DC, 2005
1-3 .... 3.00

Vincent J. Mielcarek Jr. Memorial Comic
Cooper Union, 1993
1 .... 3.00

Vintage Comic Classics
Recollections, 1990
1 .... 2.00

Vintage Magnus Robot Fighter
Valiant, 1992
1-4 .... 5.00

Violator
Image, 1994
1-3 .... 3.00

Violator vs. Badrock
Image, 1995
1-4 .... 3.00

Violent Cases
Titan, 1992
1 .... 15.00
1/2nd 10.00
1/3rd 13.00

Violent Messiahs
Hurricane, 1997
1-3 .... 3.00

Violent Messiahs
Image, 2000
½/A-8 .... 3.00

Violent Messiahs: Genesis
Image, 2001
1 .... 6.00

Violent Messiahs: Lamenting Pain
Image, 2002
1-4 .... 3.00

Violent Tales
Death, 1997
1 .... 3.00

VIP
TV, 2000
1 .... 3.00

Viper
DC, 1994
1-4 .... 2.00

Viper Force
Acid Ram, 1995
1 .... 3.00

Thor

Thor Corps

Those Magnificent Men In Their Flying Machines

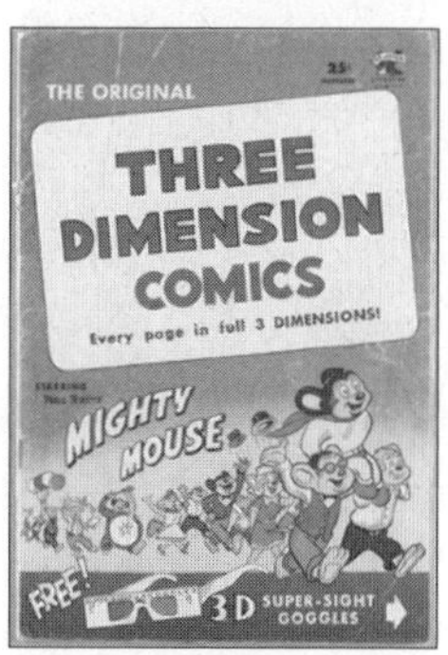

Three Dimension Comics

Three Mouseketeers

Thrilling Science Tales

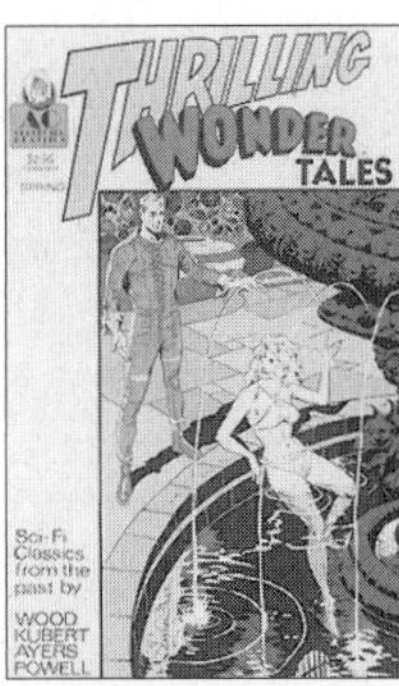

Thrilling Wonder Tales

T.H.U.N.D.E.R.

Virtex
Oktomica, 1998
0 .... 2.00
1-3 .... 3.00
Ashcan 1 .... 1.00

Virtua Fighter
Marvel, 1995
1 .... 3.00

Virtual Bang
Ironcat, 1998
1-2 .... 3.00

Virus
Dark Horse, 1993
1-4 .... 3.00

Visage Special Edition
Illusion, 1996
1 .... 2.00

Vision
Marvel, 1994
1-4 .... 2.00

Vision & Scarlet Witch
Marvel, 1982
1-4 .... 2.00

Vision & Scarlet Witch
Marvel, 1985
1 .... 2.00
2-12 .... 1.00

Visionaries
Marvel, 1988
1-6 .... 1.00

Visions
Caliber
1 .... 5.00

Visions: David Mack
Caliber
1 .... 6.00

Visions of Curves
Fantagraphics, 1994
1-3 .... 5.00

Visions: R.G. Taylor
Caliber
1 .... 3.00

Visitations
Image
1 .... 7.00

Visitor
Valiant, 1995
1-10 .... 2.00
11-12 .... 3.00
13 .... 5.00

Visitor vs. The Valiant Universe
Valiant, 1995
1 .... 3.00
1/$2.50 .... 10.00
2 .... 3.00
2/$2.50 .... 10.00

Visual Assault Omnibus
Visual Assault
1-3 .... 3.00

Vixen 9
Samson
1 .... 3.00

Vixen Warrior Diaries
Raging Rhino
1 .... 3.00

Vixen Wars
Raging Rhino
1-10 .... 3.00

Vogue
Image, 1995
1-4 .... 3.00

Void Indigo
Marvel, 1984
1-2 .... 2.00

Volcanic Nights
Palliard
1 .... 3.00

Volcanic Revolver
Oni, 1999
1-3 .... 3.00

Voltron
Solson
1-3 .... 1.00

Voltron: Defender of the Universe
Image, 2003
0-5 .... 3.00

Voltron: Defender of the Universe
Devil's Due, 2004
1-11 .... 3.00

Volunteer Comics Summer Line-Up '96
Volunteer, 1996
1 .... 3.00

Volunteer Comics Winter Line-Up '96
Volunteer, 1996
1 .... 3.00

Volunteers Quest for Dreams Lost
Literacy
1 .... 2.00

Von Fange Brothers: Green Hair and Red "S's"
Mikey-Sized Comics, 1996
1 .... 2.00

Von Fange Brothers: The Uncommons
Mikey-Sized Comics, 1996
1 .... 2.00

VonPyre
Eyeful
1 .... 3.00

Voodoo
Farrell, 1952
1 .... 350.00
2 .... 275.00
3-5 .... 225.00
6-10 .... 205.00
11-20 .... 170.00
Ann 1 .... 500.00

Voodoo
Image, 1997
1-4 .... 3.00

Voodoo Ink
Deja-Vu, 1989
0-5 .... 2.00

Voodoom
Oni, 2000
1 .... 5.00

Voodoo/Zealot: Skin Trade
Image, 1995
1 .... 5.00

Vortex
Vortex, 1982
1-15 .... 2.00

Vortex
Comico, 1991
1-4 .... 3.00

Vortex
Hall of Heroes, 1993
1-6 .... 3.00

Vortex
Entity, 1996
1 .... 3.00

Vortex the Wonder Mule
Cutting Edge
1-2 .... 3.00

Vox
Apple, 1989
1-7 .... 2.00

Voyage to the Bottom of the Sea
Gold Key, 1964
1 .... 60.00
2 .... 45.00
3-5 .... 35.00
6-10 .... 25.00
11-14 .... 18.00
15-16 .... 12.00

Voyage to the Deep
Dell, 1962
1 .... 28.00
2-4 .... 14.00

Voyeur
Aircel, 1991
1-4 .... 3.00

Vroom Socko
Slave Labor, 1993
1 .... 3.00

Vulgar Vince
Throb
1 .... 2.00

Vultures of Whapeton
Conquest
1 .... 3.00

W
Good, 1996
1 .... 3.00

Wabbit Wampage
Amazing, 1987
1 .... 2.00

Wacky Adventures of Cracky
Gold Key, 1972
1 .... 5.00
2-5 .... 3.00
6-12 .... 2.00

Wacky Duck
Timely, 1946
3-6 .... 125.00

Wacky Duck
Timely, 1948
1-2 .... 100.00

Wacky Races
Gold Key, 1969
1 .... 40.00
2 .... 26.00
3-7 .... 20.00

Wacky Squirrel
Dark Horse, 1987
1-Summer 1 .... 2.00

Wacky Witch
Gold Key, 1971
1 .... 12.00
2 .... 7.00
3-5 .... 5.00
6-10 .... 4.00
11-21 .... 3.00

Wagon Train
Dell, 1960
4-6 .... 38.00
7-9 .... 34.00
10-13 .... 25.00

THUNDER Agents

Thunderbolts

Thundercats

Thunderstrike

Tigra

Tilazeus Meets the Messiah

Timber Wolf

Time Breakers

Wagon Train

Gold Key, 1964

1 ....38.00
2-4 ....25.00

Wahh

Frank & Hank

1-2 ....3.00

Wahoo Morris

Too Hip Gotta Go Graphics, 2005

1 ....3.00

Wahoo Morris

Too Hip Gotat Go Graphics, 1988

1-3 ....3.00

Waiting for the End of the World

Rodent

1-3 ....1.00

Waiting Place

Slave Labor, 1997

1-6 ....3.00

Wake

NBM

1 ....10.00
2 ....9.00
3 ....10.00

Waldo World

Fantagraphics

1-2 ....3.00

Walking Dead

Image, 2003

1 ....45.00
2 ....32.00
3 ....15.00
4 ....12.00
4/A 6.00
5 ....4.00
6-33 ....3.00

Walking Dead

Aircel, 1989

1 ....5.00
2-4 ....3.00
Special 1 ....4.00

Walking Dead Script Book

Image, 2006

1 ....4.00

Walk Through October

Caliber, 1995

1 ....3.00

Wall of Flesh

AC

1 ....4.00

Wally

Gold Key, 1962

1 ....30.00
2-4 ....22.00

Wally the Wizard

Marvel, 1985

1-12 ....1.00

Walt Disney Comics Digest

Gold Key, 1968

1 ....60.00
2-5 ....40.00
6-13 ....25.00
14-20 ....20.00
21-43 ....15.00
44 ....40.00
45-50 ....15.00
51-57 ....10.00

Walt Disney Giant

Gladstone, 1995

1-7 ....2.00

Walt Disney Presents

Dell, 1958

2 ....50.00
3 ....45.00
4-6 ....35.00

Walt Disney's Autumn Adventures

Disney, 1991

1-2 ....3.00

Walt Disney's Christmas Parade

Dell, 1949

1 ....600.00
2 ....450.00
3 ....155.00
4 ....140.00
5 ....125.00
6 ....110.00
7 ....100.00
8-9 ....200.00

Walt Disney's Christmas Parade

Gold Key, 1962

1 ....75.00
2-8 ....50.00
9 ....20.00

Walt Disney's Christmas Parade

Gladstone, 1988

1-2 ....3.00

Walt Disney's Christmas Parade

Gemstone, 2003

1-3 ....9.00

Walt Disney's Comics and Stories

Dell, 1940

1 ....20,000.00
2 ....7,500.00
3 ....3,400.00
4 ....2,050.00

5 .... 1,250.00
6-7 .... 1,100.00
8-9 .... 900.00
10 .... 850.00
11-15 .... 750.00
16-17 .... 650.00
18 .... 625.00
19-30 .... 580.00
31 .... 3,700.00
☛Barks Donald starts
32 .... 2,000.00
33 .... 1,200.00
34 .... 950.00
35-36 .... 840.00
37 .... 435.00
38 .... 650.00
39-40 .... 580.00
41-46 .... 500.00
47-50 .... 475.00
51-60 .... 375.00
61-70 .... 305.00
71-80 .... 240.00
81-87 .... 215.00
88 .... 270.00
89-90 .... 210.00
91-97 .... 190.00
98 .... 365.00
☛Unc. Scrooge starts
99 .... 190.00
100 .... 200.00
101-112 .... 155.00
113-116 .... 90.00
117 .... 130.00
118-123 .... 85.00
124 .... 130.00
125 .... 190.00
126-129 .... 130.00
130-133 .... 125.00
134 .... 200.00
135-139 .... 105.00
140 .... 225.00
☛1st Barks Gyro
141-150 .... 94.00
151-170 .... 88.00
171-200 .... 80.00
201-240 .... 75.00
241-260 .... 60.00
261-283 .... 50.00
284-285 .... 25.00
286 .... 28.00
287 .... 25.00
288-289 .... 28.00
290 .... 25.00
291-293 .... 28.00
294-296 .... 25.00
297-308 .... 28.00
309-311 .... 25.00
312 .... 28.00
313-334 .... 14.00
335 .... 25.00
336-341 .... 14.00
342-351 .... 25.00
351/Poster 30.00
351/No poster 20.00
352 .... 25.00
352/Poster-352/No poster 30.00
353 .... 25.00
353/Poster 30.00
353/No poster 20.00
354 .... 25.00
354/Poster-354/No poster 30.00
355 .... 25.00
355/Poster-355/No poster 30.00
356 .... 25.00
356/Poster 30.00
356/No poster 20.00
357 .... 25.00
357/Poster-357/No poster 30.00
358 .... 25.00
358/Poster-358/No poster 30.00
359 .... 25.00
359/Poster 30.00
359/No poster 20.00
360 .... 25.00
360/Poster 30.00
360/No poster 20.00
361-400 .... 25.00
401-429 .... 14.00
430 .... 10.00
431-432 .... 12.00
433 .... 10.00
434-436 .... 12.00
437-438 .... 10.00
439-440 .... 12.00
441-443 .... 10.00
444-445 .... 6.00
446-465 .... 10.00
466 .... 6.00
467-478 .... 10.00
479 .... 30.00
480 .... 125.00
481-484 .... 30.00
485-510 .... 10.00
511 .... 15.00
512-513 .... 12.00
514-516 .... 8.00
517-518 .... 5.00
519 .... 14.00
520-549 .... 10.00
550 .... 6.00
551-554 .... 4.00
555-556 .... 3.00
557-573 .... 4.00
574-577 .... 5.00
578-579 .... 3.00
580 .... 5.00
581-584 .... 3.00
585 .... 5.00
586-597 .... 3.00
598-599 .... 4.00
600-611 .... 6.00
612-648 .... 7.00

Time Masters

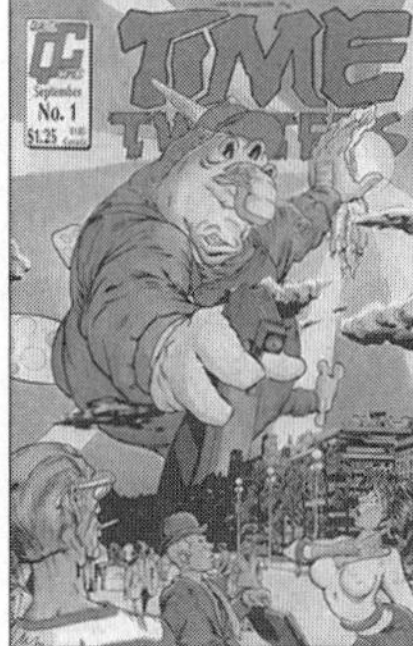

Time Twisters

Timewalker

Time Warp

Tim Holt Western Annual

To Be Announced

Tokyo Babylon

Tokyo Mew Mew

Walt Disney's Comics & Stories
Gemstone, 2003

634-661 ....7.00

Walt Disney's Comics and Stories Penny Pincher
Gladstone, 1997

1-4 ....1.00

Walt Disney's Comics Digest
Gladstone, 1986

1 ....6.00
2-7 ....4.00

Walt Disney's Holiday Parade
Disney, 1991

1-2 ....3.00

Walt Disney Showcase
Gold Key, 1970

1 ....16.00
2 ....10.00
3-4 ....9.00
5-6 ....12.00
7-8 ....9.00
9 ....10.00
10 ....12.00
11-13 ....8.00
14 ....12.00
15 ....8.00
16-18 ....12.00
19 ....10.00
20 ....9.00
21-23 ....8.00
24-29 ....7.00
30 ....15.00
☛Magica de Spell
31-32 ....9.00
33-39 ....7.00
40-41 ....8.00
42 ....7.00
43 ....9.00
44-48 ....10.00
49-54 ....7.00

Walt Disney's Spring Fever
Disney, 1991

1 ....3.00

Walt Disney's Summer Fun
Disney

1 ....3.00

Walt Disney's Three Musketeers
Gemstone, 2004

1 ....4.00

Walt Disney's Vacation Parade
Dell, 1950

1 ....550.00
2 ....160.00
3-5 ....90.00

Walt Disney's World of Adventure
Gold Key, 1963

1 ....8.00
2-3 ....5.00

Walter
Dark Horse, 1996

1-4 ....3.00

Walter Kitty in...the Hollow Earth
Vision, 1996

1-2 ....2.00

Walt The Wildcat
MotioN Comics, 1995

1 ....3.00

Wambi, Jungle Boy
Fiction House, 1942

1 ....500.00
2-3 ....300.00
4-5 ....175.00
6-10 ....150.00
11-14 ....125.00
15-18 ....100.00

Wanda Luwand & the Pirate Girls
Fantagraphics

1 ....3.00

Wanderers
DC, 1988

1-13 ....2.00

Wandering Star
Pen and Ink, 1993

1 ....8.00
1/2nd 4.00
1/3rd 3.00
2 ....5.00
2/2nd 2.00
3 ....4.00
3/2nd 2.00
4 ....4.00
4/2nd 2.00
5 ....4.00
5/2nd 2.00
6-21 ....3.00

Wandering Stars
Fantagraphics

1 ....2.00

Wanted
Celebrity, 1989

1-5 ....2.00

Wanted
Image, 2003

1 ....12.00
1/A 9.00
1/B 8.00

1/C 3.00
1/D 6.00
1/E 5.00
2 .... 3.00
2/B 4.00
2/C 5.00
3 .... 3.00
3/A 4.00
4-6 .... 3.00

Wanted Comics

Toytown, 1947

9 .... 120.00
10-11 .... 72.00
12 .... 105.00
13 .... 72.00
14-15 .... 65.00
16-17 .... 60.00
18 .... 140.00
19-22 .... 60.00
23-30 .... 48.00
31-34 .... 40.00
35 .... 65.00
36-38 .... 40.00
39 .... 105.00
40-49 .... 40.00
50-52 .... 65.00
53 .... 40.00

Wanted: Dossier One-Shot

Image, 2004

1 .... 3.00

Wanted Dossier One Shot

Image, 2004

1 .... 3.00

Wanted, the World's Most Dangerous Villains

DC, 1972

1 .... 10.00
2-3 .... 8.00
4-9 .... 6.00

War

Charlton, 1975

1 .... 8.00
2-10 .... 5.00
11-22 .... 3.00
23-49 .... 2.00

War

Marvel, 1989

1-4 .... 4.00

War Action

Atlas, 1952

1 .... 100.00
2 .... 60.00
3-10 .... 50.00
11-14 .... 60.00

War Adventures

Atlas, 1952

1 .... 100.00
2-13 .... 75.00

War Against Crime

E.C., 1948

1 .... 430.00
2-3 .... 250.00
4-5 .... 225.00
6-9 .... 210.00
10 .... 1,500.00
11 .... 775.00

War Against Crime

Gemstone, 2000

1-5 .... 3.00
Ann 1 .... 14.00

War and Attack

Charlton, 1964

1 .... 30.00
54-63 .... 10.00

War Angel: Book of Death (Brian Pulido's)

Avatar

1 .... 3.00
1/Platinum 15.00
1/Wraparound 3.00

Warblade: Endangered Species

Image, 1995

1-4 .... 3.00

Warcat

Coconut, 1997

Ashcan 1-Special 1 .... 3.00

Warchild

Maximum, 1994

1/A-4 .... 3.00

War Combat

Marvel, 1952

1 .... 60.00
2 .... 35.00
3-5 .... 22.00

War Comics

Dell, 1940

1 .... 350.00
2 .... 175.00
3-4 .... 125.00

War Comics

Atlas, 1950

1 .... 125.00
2 .... 75.00
3-10 .... 50.00
11 .... 60.00
12-20 .... 50.00
21-32 .... 45.00
33-49 .... 40.00

War Criminals

Comic Zone

1 .... 3.00

Warcry

Image

1 .... 3.00

Tomahawk

Tomb of Darkness

Tomb of Dracula

Tomoe

All comics prices listed are for NEAR MINT condition.

Tomorrow Stories

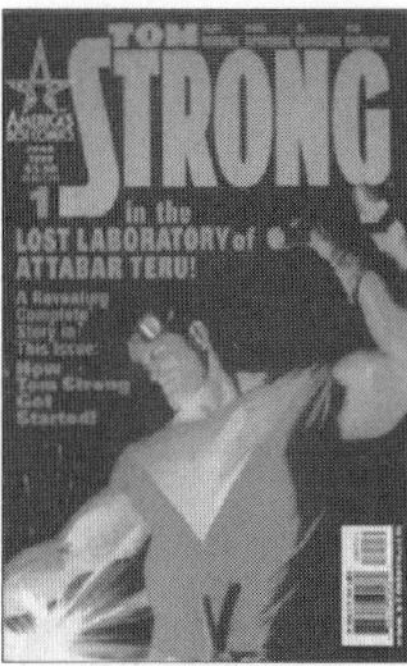

Tom Strong

Too Much Coffee Man

Top 10

War Dancer

Defiant, 1994

1-6 .... 3.00

Warfront

Harvey, 1951

1 .... 75.00
2 .... 45.00
3-5 .... 35.00
6-10 .... 32.00
11-20 .... 28.00
21-35 .... 24.00
36-39 .... 18.00

War Fury

Comic Media, 1952

1 .... 100.00
2-4 .... 75.00

Wargod

Speakeasy Comics, 2005

1 .... 5.00

Warhammer Monthly

Games Workshop, 1998

0 .... 1.00
1-51 .... 3.00
52-85 .... 4.00

Warhawks Comics Module

TSR, 1990

1-9 .... 3.00

Warheads

Marvel, 1992

1-14 .... 2.00

Warheads: Black Dawn

Marvel, 1993

1-2 .... 3.00

War Heroes

Dell, 1942

1 .... 120.00
2 .... 100.00
3-6 .... 80.00
7-11 .... 60.00

War Heroes

Ace, 1952

1 .... 50.00
2 .... 35.00
3-7 .... 30.00

War Heroes

Charlton, 1963

1-2 .... 25.00
3-5 .... 12.00
6-20 .... 8.00
21-27 .... 5.00

War Heroes Classics

Recollections, 1991

1 .... 2.00

War Is Hell

Marvel, 1973

1 .... 25.00
2 .... 18.00
3-5 .... 14.00
6-8 .... 10.00
9-15 .... 8.00

Warlands

Image, 1999

1-12 .... 3.00
Deluxe 1 .... 15.00

Warlands: Dark Tide Rising

Dreamwave, 2002

1-6 .... 3.00

Warlands Epilogue: Three Stories

Image, 2001

1 .... 6.00

Warlands: The Age of Ice

Dreamwave, 2001

0 .... 2.00
1-3 .... 3.00

Warlash

CFD, 1995

1 .... 3.00

Warlock

Marvel, 1972

1 .... 32.00
2-3 .... 15.00
4-5 .... 8.00
6-8 .... 7.00
9-11 .... 10.00
12 .... 8.00
12/30¢ 15.00
13 .... 8.00
13/30¢ 15.00
14 .... 8.00
14/30¢ 15.00
15 .... 8.00

Warlock

Marvel, 1982

1 .... 4.00
2-6 .... 3.00
Special 1 .... 2.00

Warlock

Marvel, 1992

1-6 .... 3.00

Warlock

Marvel, 1998

1-4 .... 3.00

Warlock

Marvel, 1999

1-4 .... 2.00

Warlock

Marvel, 2004

1-4 .... 3.00

Warlock and the Infinity Watch
Marvel, 1992
1 .... 3.00
2-24 .... 2.00
25 .... 3.00
26-42 .... 2.00

Warlock Chronicles
Marvel, 1993
1 .... 3.00
2-8 .... 2.00

Warlock 5
Aircel, 1986
1-22 .... 2.00

Warlock 5
Sirius, 1998
1-4 .... 3.00

Warlock 5 Book II
Aircel, 1989
1-7 .... 2.00

Warlocks
Aircel, 1988
1-Special 1 .... 2.00

Warlord
DC, 1976
1 .... 10.00
2 .... 4.00
3-6 .... 3.00
7-22 .... 2.00
22/Whitman 8.00
23-29 .... 2.00
30-47 .... 1.00
48 .... 2.00
49-130 .... 1.00
131 .... 2.00
132 .... 1.00
133 .... 2.00
Ann 1 .... 3.00
Ann 2-6 .... 1.00

Warlord
DC, 1992
1-6 .... 2.00

Warlord
DC, 2006
1-10 .... 3.00

War Machine
Marvel, 1994
1 .... 2.00
1/Variant 3.00
2-8 .... 2.00
8/CS 3.00
9-14 .... 2.00
15 .... 3.00
16-25 .... 2.00
Ashcan 1 .... 1.00

War Machine
Marvel, 2001
1-12 .... 2.00

War Man
Marvel, 1993
1-2 .... 3.00

War of the Gods
DC, 1991
1-4/Direct 2.00

War of the Worlds
Caliber, 1996
1-5 .... 3.00

War of the Worlds
Eternity, 1990
1-6 .... 2.00

War of the Worlds: The Memphis Front
Arrow, 1998
1-5 .... 3.00

Warp
First, 1983
1-7 .... 2.00
8-Special 3 .... 1.00

Warp-3
Equinox, 1990
1 .... 2.00

War Party
Lightning, 1994
1 .... 3.00

Warp Graphics Annual
Warp
1 .... 3.00

Warpwalking
Caliber
1-4 .... 3.00

War Report
Farrell, 1952
1 .... 50.00
2-5 .... 25.00

Warrior
Ultimate Creations, 1996
1-4 .... 3.00

Warrior Bugs
Artcoda, 2002
1 .... 3.00

Warrior Comics
Blackerby, 1945
1 .... 100.00

Warrior Nun Areala
Antarctic, 1994
1-1/Ltd. 5.00
1/2nd 3.00
2-3 .... 4.00
3/CS 8.00
3/Ltd. 5.00
Book 1 .... 10.00

Top Dog

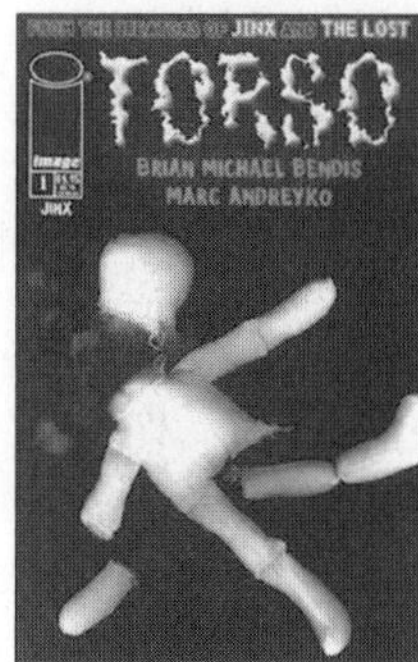

Torso

Total Eclipse

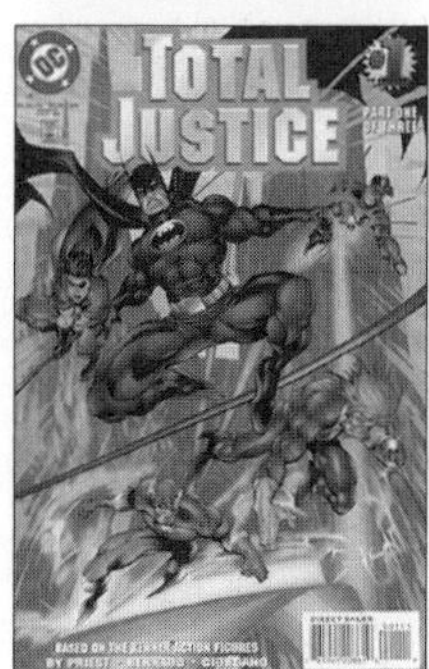

Total Justice

Total War

Toxic Avenger

Toxic Crusaders

Toyboy

Warrior Nun Areala
Antarctic, 1997

1 ..... 3.00
1/Variant 6.00
2-6 ..... 3.00

Warrior Nun Areala
Antarctic, 1999

1-2 ..... 3.00

Warrior Nun Areala and Avengelyne
Antarctic, 1996

1/A 3.00
1/B 6.00

Warrior Nun Areala and Glory
Antarctic, 1997

1 ..... 3.00
1/CS 6.00

Warrior Nun Areala/Razor: Revenge
Antarctic, 1999

1 ..... 3.00
1/Deluxe 6.00

Warrior Nun Areala: Resurrection
Antarctic, 1998

1-6 ..... 3.00
Ashcan 1 ..... 1.00

Warrior Nun Areala: Rheintchter
Antarctic, 1997

1-2 ..... 3.00

Warrior Nun Areala: Rituals
Antarctic, 1995

1 ..... 3.00
1/Variant 4.00
2-6 ..... 3.00

Warrior Nun: Black & White
Antarctic, 1997

1-21 ..... 3.00

Warrior Nun Brigantia
Antarctic, 2000

1-3 ..... 3.00

Warrior Nun Dei
Antarctic

1 ..... 6.00

Warrior Nun Dei: Aftertime
Antarctic, 1997

1-3 ..... 3.00

Warrior Nun: Frenzy
Antarctic, 1998

1-2 ..... 3.00

Warrior Nun: Scorpio Rose
Antarctic, 1996

1-4 ..... 3.00

Warrior Nun vs. Razor
Antarctic, 1996

1 ..... 4.00

Warrior of Waverly Street
Dark Horse, 1996

1-2 ..... 3.00

Warriors
Adventure, 1987

1-5 ..... 2.00

Warriors of Plasm
Defiant, 1993

1-13 ..... 3.00

Warriors of Plasm Graphic Novel
Defiant, 1993

1 ..... 7.00

Warrior's Way
Bench, 1998

1-3 ..... 3.00

War Sirens and Liberty Belles
Recollections

1 ..... 5.00

War Sluts
Pretty Graphic

1-2 ..... 4.00

War Stories
DC, 2004

1 ..... 20.00

War Story: Archangel
DC, 2003

1 ..... 5.00

War Story: D-Day Dodgers
DC, 2001

1 ..... 5.00

War Story: Johann's Tiger
DC, 2001

1 ..... 5.00

War Story: Nightingale
DC, 2002

1 ..... 5.00

War Story: Screaming Eagles
DC, 2002

1 ..... 5.00

Warstrike
Malibu, 1994

1-7 ..... 2.00
GS 1 ..... 3.00

Wartime Romances
St. John, 1951
1 .... 200.00
2-8 .... 100.00
9-13 .... 80.00
14-18 .... 60.00

War Victory Adventures
Harvey, 1942
1 .... 250.00
2 .... 175.00
3 .... 150.00

Warworld!
Dark Horse, 1989
1 .... 2.00

Warzone
Express, 1994
1-3 .... 3.00

Warzone 3719
Pocket Change
1 .... 2.00

Washmen
New York
1 .... 2.00

Washouts
Renaissance, 2002
1 .... 3.00

Wash Tubbs Quarterly
Dragon Lady
1 .... 5.00
2-5 .... 6.00

Waste L.A.: Descent
John Gaushell, 1996
1-3 .... 3.00

Wasteland
DC, 1987
1 .... 2.00
2-18 .... 2.00

Watchcats
Harrier
1 .... 2.00

Watchmen
DC, 1986
1 .... 8.00
☛Moore, Gibbons series
2-3 .... 5.00
4-12 .... 4.00

Waterloo Sunset
Image, 2004
1-4 .... 7.00

Waterworld: Children of Leviathan
Acclaim, 1997
1-4 .... 3.00

Wavemakers
Blind Bat, 1990
1 .... 3.00

Wave Warriors
Astroboys
1 .... 2.00

Waxwork
Blackthorne
1 .... 2.00
3D 1 .... 3.00

Way of the Rat
CrossGen, 2002
1-24 .... 3.00

Way Out Strips
Fantagraphics, 1994
1-3 .... 3.00

Way Out Strips
Tragedy Strikes, 1992
1-3 .... 3.00

Wayward Warrior
Alpha Productions, 1990
1-3 .... 2.00

WCW World Championship Wrestling
Marvel, 1992
1-12 .... 1.00

We 3
DC, 2004
1-3 .... 3.00

Weapons File
Antarctic, 2005
1-3 .... 5.00

Weapon X
Marvel, 1995
1-4 .... 2.00

Weapon X
Marvel, 2002
1-8 .... 2.00
9-28 .... 3.00

Weapon X: Days of Future Now
Marvel, 2005
1-5 .... 3.00

Weapon X: The Draft: Kane
Marvel, 2002
1 .... 2.00

Weapon XXX: Origin of the Implants
Friendly, 1992
1-3 .... 3.00

Weapon Zero
Image, 1995
1-5 .... 3.00

Weapon Zero
Image, 1996
1-14 .... 3.00
15 .... 4.00

Transmetropolitan

Triumph

Trouble

Troublemakers

True Comics

Trump

TV Western

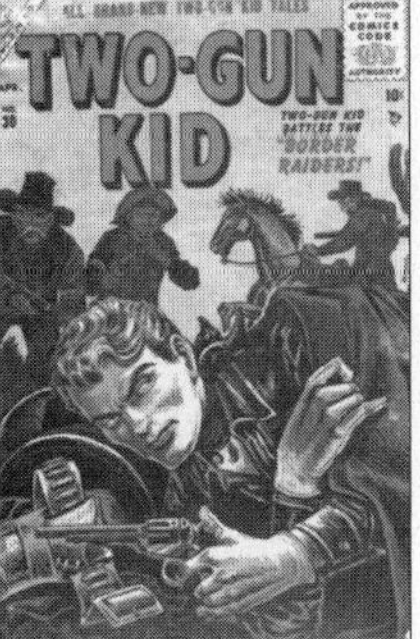

Two-Gun Kid

Weapon Zero/Silver Surfer
Top Cow, 1997
1-1/A 3.00

Weasel Guy: Road Trip
Image, 1999
1-1/A 3.00
2 .... 4.00

Weasel Patrol
Eclipse
1 .... 2.00

Weather Woman
CPM Manga, 2000
1-1/A 3.00

Weaveworld
Marvel, 1991
1-3 .... 5.00

Web
DC, 1991
1-14 .... 1.00
Ann 1 .... 3.00

Webber's World
Allstar
1 .... 5.00

Web-Man
Argosy
1 .... 3.00

Web of Evil
Quality, 1952
1 .... 550.00
2-7 .... 325.00
8-11 .... 250.00
12-21 .... 150.00

Web of Mystery
Ace, 1951
1 .... 325.00
2 .... 185.00
3-10 .... 155.00
11-26 .... 132.00
27 .... 116.00
28-29 .... 86.00

Web of Scarlet Spider
Marvel, 1995
1-4 .... 2.00

Web of Spider-Man
Marvel, 1985
1 .... 8.00
2 .... 6.00
3 .... 5.00
4-10 .... 4.00
11-28 .... 3.00
29 .... 5.00
30 .... 4.00
31-32 .... 5.00
33-35 .... 3.00
36 .... 4.00
37 .... 3.00
38 .... 5.00
39-47 .... 3.00
48 .... 8.00
☛1st Demogoblin
49 .... 2.00
50 .... 3.00
51-57 .... 2.00
58 .... 3.00
59 .... 8.00
60-61 .... 3.00
62-89 .... 2.00
90 .... 5.00
90/2nd 3.00
91-99 .... 2.00
100 .... 4.00
101-105 .... 2.00
106/CS 5.00
106 .... 1.00
107-113 .... 2.00
113/CS 4.00
114-116 .... 2.00
117 .... 3.00
117/Variant 5.00
118 .... 3.00
118/2nd-119 .... 2.00
119/CS 6.00
120 .... 4.00
121-124 .... 2.00
125 .... 3.00
125/Variant 4.00
126-129 .... 2.00
129/CS 5.00
Ann 1 .... 7.00
Ann 2 .... 6.00
Ann 3-10 .... 3.00
SS 1 .... 4.00

Webspinners: Tales of Spider-Man
Marvel, 1999
1-1/B 3.00
1/Sunburst 5.00
2/A-18 .... 3.00

Wedding Bells
Quality, 1954
1-12 .... 50.00

Wedding of Dracula
Marvel, 1993
1 .... 2.00

Wedding of Popeye and Olive
Ocean, 1998
1 .... 3.00

Weezul
Lightning, 1996
1/A-1/B 3.00

Weird
DC, 1988
1-4 .... 2.00

Weird (Magazine)

DC, 1997

1 .... 3.00

Weird

Avalon

1-4 .... 3.00

Weird Adventures

P.L., 1951

1 .... 325.00
2 .... 250.00
3 .... 225.00

Weird Adventures

Ziff-Davis, 1951

10 .... 225.00

Weird Business

Mojo

Ashcan 1 .... 1.00

Weird Chills

Key, 1954

1 .... 600.00
2 .... 450.00
3 .... 300.00

Weird Comics

Fox, 1940

1 .... 4,500.00
2 .... 2,000.00
3-5 .... 1,000.00
6-8 .... 925.00
9-10 .... 800.00
11-19 .... 600.00
20 .... 650.00

Weirdfall

Antarctic, 1995

1-3 .... 3.00

Weird Fantasy

E.C., 1950

1 .... 1,150.00
2 .... 500.00
3-4 .... 425.00
5 .... 335.00
6-10 .... 240.00
11-13 .... 180.00
14 .... 300.00
15 .... 200.00
16-19 .... 170.00
20 .... 200.00
21 .... 285.00
22 .... 140.00

Weird Fantasy

Gemstone, 1992

1 .... 3.00
2-10 .... 2.00
11-22 .... 3.00
Ann 1 .... 9.00
Ann 2 .... 10.00
Ann 3 .... 9.00
Ann 4 .... 10.00
Ann 5 .... 11.00

Weird Horrors

St. John, 1952

1 .... 300.00
2-3 .... 200.00
4-5 .... 160.00
6-7 .... 300.00
8-9 .... 225.00

Weird Melvin

Marc Hansen Stuff!, 1995

1-5 .... 3.00

Weird Mysteries

Gilmore, 1952

1 .... 600.00
2 .... 750.00
3 .... 550.00
4 .... 600.00
5 .... 625.00
6 .... 550.00
7 .... 450.00
8 .... 350.00
9 .... 300.00
10 .... 250.00
11 .... 225.00
12 .... 300.00

Weird Mystery Tales

DC, 1972

1 .... 30.00
2 .... 20.00
3 .... 15.00
4-10 .... 12.00
11-20 .... 10.00
21 .... 15.00
22-24 .... 10.00

Weirdo

Last Gasp, 1981

1 .... 15.00
2 .... 10.00
3 .... 8.00
4-10 .... 6.00
11-20 .... 5.00
21-26 .... 4.00

Weirdom Comix

Weirdom, 1968

1 .... 3.00
2-15 .... 2.00

Weird Romance

Eclipse, 1988

1 .... 2.00

Weird Science

E.C., 1950

1 .... 1,450.00
2 .... 625.00
3-4 .... 575.00
5-10 .... 360.00
11-14 .... 230.00
15-18 .... 260.00
19-22 .... 335.00

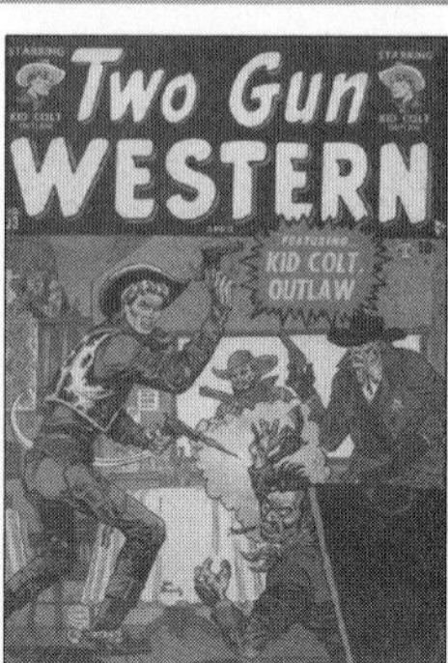

Two Gun Western

UFO Flying Saucers

Ultimate Adventures

Ultimate Fantastic Four

Ultimate Marvel Magazine

Ultimate Marvel Team-Up

Ultimate Nightmare

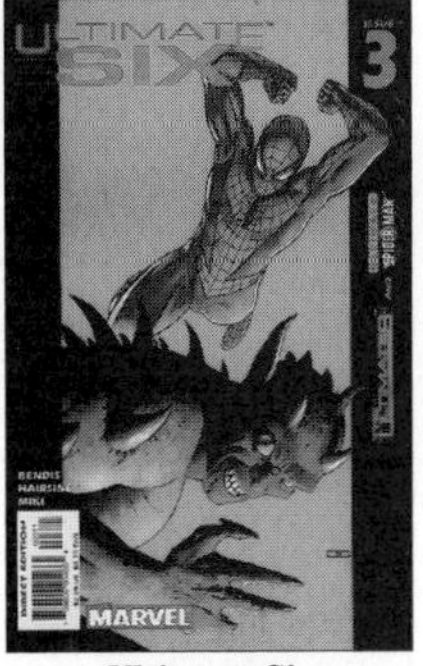

Ultimate Six

Weird Science
Gladstone, 1990

1-4 .... 2.00

Weird Science
Gemstone, 1992

1 .... 3.00
2-14 .... 2.00
15-22 .... 3.00
Ann 1 .... 9.00
Ann 2 .... 10.00
Ann 3 .... 11.00
Ann 4 .... 10.00
Ann 5 .... 11.00

Weird Science-Fantasy Annual
E.C., 1952

1 .... 2,000.00
2 .... 1,200.00

Weird Science-Fantasy
E.C., 1954

23-24 .... 235.00
25 .... 270.00
26 .... 220.00
27 .... 235.00
28 .... 260.00
29 .... 450.00

Weird Science-Fantasy
Gemstone, 1992

1-11 .... 2.00
Ann 1 .... 9.00
Ann 2 .... 13.00

Weird Secret Origins 80-Page Giant
DC, 2004

1 .... 6.00

Weird Sex
Fantagraphics, 1999

1 .... 3.00

Weird Space
Avalon

1-4 .... 3.00

Weird Suspense
Atlas-Seaboard, 1975

1 .... 12.00
2 .... 8.00
3 .... 7.00

Weird SuspenStories
Superior, 1951

1-3 .... 300.00

Weirdsville
Blindwolf, 1997

1-9 .... 3.00

Weird Tales Illustrated
Millennium

1 .... 3.00
1/Deluxe 5.00
2 .... 3.00

Weird Tales of the Future
Aragon, 1952

1 .... 600.00
2 .... 750.00
3-4 .... 600.00
5 .... 750.00
6 .... 350.00
7 .... 600.00
8 .... 425.00

Weird Tales of the Macabre
Atlas-Seaboard, 1975

1 .... 20.00
2 .... 30.00
☛Scarce

Weird Terror
Comic Media, 1952

1 .... 500.00
2-4 .... 300.00
5 .... 230.00
6 .... 260.00
7 .... 230.00
8 .... 260.00
9-10 .... 200.00
11 .... 260.00
12 .... 190.00
13 .... 200.00

Weird Thrillers
Ziff-Davis, 1951

1 .... 600.00
2 .... 450.00
3 .... 850.00
4 .... 400.00
5 .... 300.00

Weird Trips Magazine
Kitchen Sink

1 .... 4.00

Weird War Tales
DC, 1971

1 .... 125.00
2 .... 75.00
3 .... 45.00
4-5 .... 30.00
6-10 .... 20.00
11-20 .... 12.00
21-31 .... 8.00
32-50 .... 6.00
51-92 .... 5.00
93 .... 6.00
94-101 .... 5.00
102-124 .... 4.00

Weird War Tales
DC, 1997

1-4 .... 3.00
Special 1 .... 5.00

Weird West
Fantaco, 1992

1-3 .... 3.00

Weird Western Tales

DC, 1972

12 .... 45.00
13 .... 30.00
14-15 .... 20.00
16-28 .... 12.00
29 .... 16.00
30-42 .... 8.00
43-50 .... 6.00
51-70 .... 5.00

Weird Western Tales

DC, 2001

1-4 .... 3.00

Weird Wonder Tales

Marvel, 1973

1 .... 14.00
2-3 .... 7.00
4-7 .... 5.00
8-15 .... 4.00
15/30¢ 20.00
16 .... 4.00
16/30¢ 20.00
17 .... 4.00
17/30¢ 20.00
18-22 .... 4.00

Weird Worlds

DC, 1972

1 .... 12.00
2-5 .... 7.00
6 .... 8.00
7 .... 6.00
8-10 .... 5.00

Welcome Back, Kotter

DC, 1976

1 .... 10.00
2-10 .... 3.00

Welcome Back to the House of Mystery

DC, 1998

1 .... 6.00

Welcome to the Little Shop of Horrors

Roger Corman's Cosmic Comics, 1995

1-3 .... 3.00

Welcome to the Zone

Kitchen Sink

1 .... 10.00

Wendel

Kitchen Sink

1 .... 3.00

Wendy and the New Kids on the Block

Harvey, 1991

1-3 .... 2.00

Wendy Digest Magazine

Harvey, 1990

1-5 .... 2.00

Wendy, the Good Little Witch

Harvey, 1960

1 .... 60.00
2 .... 40.00
3-5 .... 28.00
6-10 .... 22.00
11-15 .... 14.00
16-20 .... 12.00
21-25 .... 8.00
26-30 .... 6.00
31-40 .... 5.00
41-50 .... 4.00
51-60 .... 3.00
61-93 .... 2.00
94-97 .... 1.00

Wendy the Good Little Witch

Harvey, 1991

1-15 .... 2.00

Wendy in 3-D

Blackthorne

1 .... 3.00

Wendy Whitebread, Undercover Slut

Fantagraphics, 1990

1-1/4th 3.00
1/5th 4.00
2 .... 3.00

Wendy Witch World

Harvey, 1961

1 .... 90.00
2-5 .... 50.00
6-10 .... 35.00
11-20 .... 26.00
21-30 .... 22.00
31-35 .... 18.00
36-44 .... 15.00
45-49 .... 12.00
50-53 .... 8.00

Werewolf

Dell, 1966

1 .... 8.00
2-3 .... 5.00

Werewolf

Blackthorne, 1988

1-4 .... 2.00

Werewolf at Large

Eternity, 1989

1-3 .... 2.00

Werewolf By Night

Marvel, 1972

1 .... 80.00
2 .... 30.00

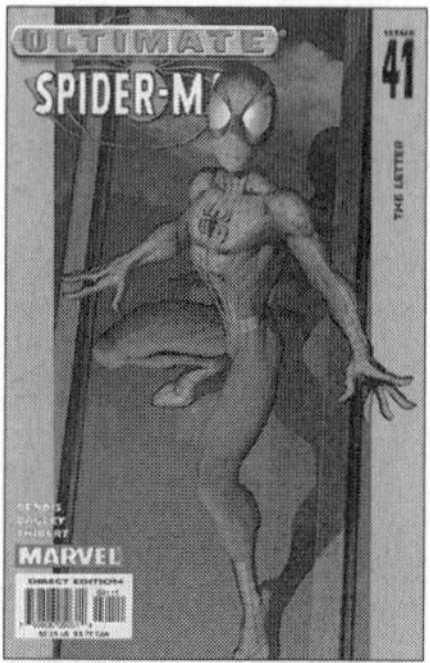

Ultimate Spider-Man

Ultimate X-Men

Ultraverse Origins

Ultraverse Premiere

Uncanny Origins

Uncle Scrooge and Donald Duck

Undersea Agent

Undertaker

3 .... 15.00
4 .... 18.00
5-10 .... 15.00
11-14 .... 12.00
15 .... 15.00
16-17 .... 12.00
18-20 .... 10.00
21-31 .... 8.00
32 .... 60.00
☛1st Moon Knight
33 .... 30.00
34 .... 8.00
35-36 .... 5.00
37 .... 10.00
38 .... 5.00
38/30¢ 15.00
39 .... 5.00
39/30¢ 15.00
40-41 .... 5.00
42 .... 12.00
43 .... 18.00

Werewolf By Night
Marvel, 1998
1-6 .... 3.00

Werewolf in 3-D
Blackthorne, 1988
1 .... 3.00

Werewolf the Apocalypse: Black Furies
Moonstone, 2003
1 .... 6.00

Werewolf the Apocalypse: Bone Gnawers
Moonstone, 2003
1 .... 6.00

West Coast Avengers
Marvel, 1984
1 .... 3.00
2-4 .... 2.00

West Coast Avengers
Marvel, 1985
1-3 .... 2.00
4 .... 3.00
5-46 .... 1.00
Ann 1-3 .... 2.00

Western Tales of Terror
Hoarse and Buggy, 2004
1-5 .... 4.00

Western Action
Atlas-Seaboard, 1975
1 .... 9.00

Western Adventure Comics
Ace, 1948
1 .... 135.00
2 .... 70.00
3 .... 75.00
4 .... 60.00

Western Comics
DC, 1948
1 .... 625.00
2 .... 300.00
3 .... 225.00
4-5 .... 200.00
6-7 .... 165.00
8 .... 200.00
9-10 .... 165.00
11-20 .... 110.00
21-30 .... 85.00
31-40 .... 60.00
41-50 .... 45.00
51-60 .... 38.00
61-85 .... 35.00

Western Crime Busters
Trojan, 1950
1 .... 175.00
2 .... 100.00
3-5 .... 85.00
6-7 .... 175.00
8 .... 85.00

Western Crime Cases
Star, 1951
9 .... 125.00

Westerner
Toytown, 1948
14 .... 75.00
15-25 .... 50.00
26 .... 75.00
27-30 .... 50.00
31-41 .... 40.00

Western Fighters (Vol. 1)
Hillman, 1948
1 .... 165.00
2-3 .... 48.00
4 .... 55.00
5-6 .... 32.00
7 .... 55.00
8-9 .... 32.00
10 .... 55.00
11 .... 125.00
12 .... 30.00

Western Fighters (Vol. 2)
Hillman, 1949
1 .... 45.00
2-12 .... 24.00

Western Fighters (Vol. 3)
Hillman, 1950
1-11 .... 20.00
12 .... 35.00

Western Fighters (Vol. 4)
Hillman, 1951
1-7 .... 30.00
3D 1 .... 160.00

Western Gunfighters (1st Series)

Atlas, 1956

20-21 .... 75.00
22 .... 100.00
23-24 .... 75.00
25-27 .... 55.00

Western Gunfighters (2nd Series)

Marvel, 1970

1 .... 28.00
2-3 .... 15.00
4 .... 18.00
5-7 .... 15.00
8-16 .... 7.00
17-33 .... 5.00

Western Hearts

Standard, 1949

1 .... 120.00
2-10 .... 80.00

Western Hero

Fawcett, 1949

76 .... 150.00
77-82 .... 100.00
83-95 .... 75.00
96-112 .... 60.00

Western Kid (2nd Series)

Marvel, 1971

1 .... 17.00
2-5 .... 8.00

Western Killers

Fox, 1948

60 .... 140.00
61-64 .... 110.00

Western Life Romances

Marvel, 1949

1 .... 125.00
2 .... 85.00

Western Love

Prize, 1949

1 .... 200.00
2 .... 150.00
3-4 .... 100.00
5 .... 150.00

Western Outlaws

Atlas, 1954

1 .... 150.00
2 .... 90.00
3-10 .... 60.00
11 .... 70.00
12-13 .... 60.00
14 .... 70.00
15-21 .... 60.00

Western Outlaws and Sheriffs

Marvel, 1949

60 .... 125.00
61-67 .... 100.00
68-72 .... 75.00
73 .... 80.00

Western Picture Stories

Comics Magazine, 1937

1 .... 1,100.00
2-4 .... 550.00

Western Roundup

Dell, 1952

1 .... 165.00
2 .... 120.00
3-5 .... 75.00
6-10 .... 65.00
11-17 .... 55.00
18 .... 65.00
19-23 .... 55.00
24 .... 60.00
25 .... 80.00

Western Team-Up

Marvel, 1973

1 .... 8.00

Western Thrillers

Fox, 1948

1 .... 275.00
2 .... 110.00
3-6 .... 100.00

Western Thrillers

Atlas, 1954

1 .... 100.00
2-4 .... 65.00

Western True Crime

Fox, 1949

4-6 .... 85.00

Western Winners

Marvel, 1949

5 .... 175.00
6-7 .... 150.00

West of the Dakotas

Comic Book Stories, 2002

1 .... 5.00

Westside

Antarctic, 2000

1 .... 3.00

West Street Stories

West Street, 1995

0-1 .... 3.00

Wetworks

Image, 1994

1 .... 3.00
1/3D 5.00
1/Ltd.-3 .... 2.00
4-24 .... 3.00
25-25/A 4.00

Union Jack

Unity

Universe X

Unknown Soldier

Unknown Worlds

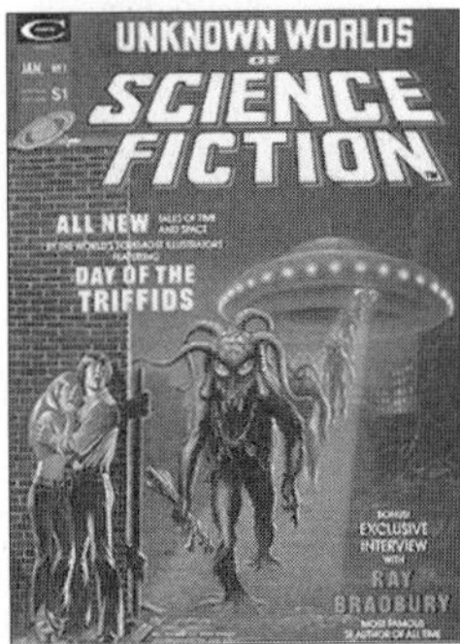

Unknown Worlds of Science Fiction

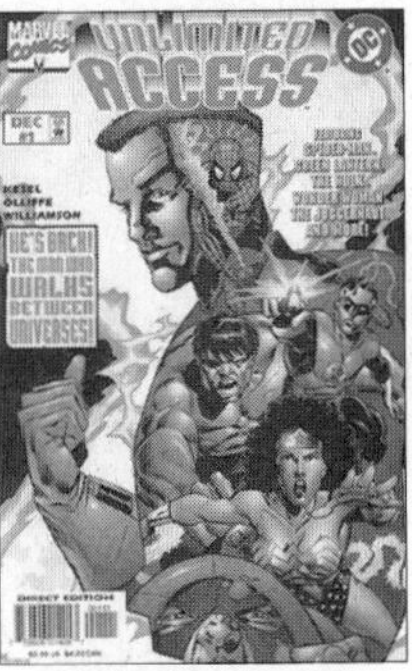

Unlimited Access

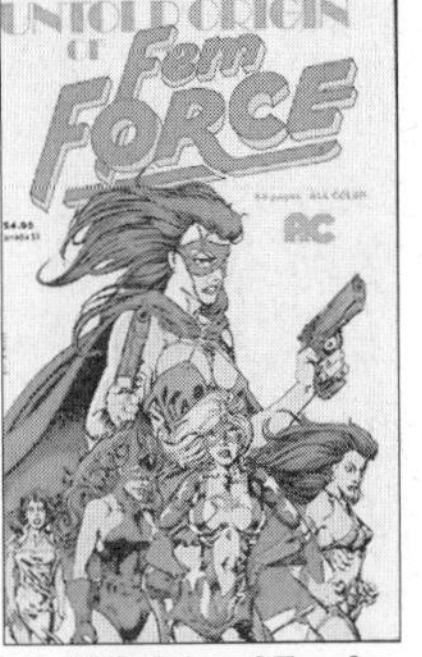

Untold Origin of Femforce

26-32 .... 3.00
32/A 4.00
33-43 .... 3.00
3D 1 .... 5.00

Wetworks Sourcebook

Image, 1994

1 .... 3.00

Wetworks/Vampirella

Image, 1997

1-1/A 3.00

Whack

St. John, 1953

1 .... 175.00
2-3 .... 85.00

Whacked!

River Group, 1994

1 .... 3.00

Wha... Huh?

Marvel, 2005

0 .... 4.00

Wham

Centaur, 1940

1 .... 1,000.00
2 .... 675.00

Wham-O Giant Comics

Wham-O, 1967

1 .... 100.00

What If...?

Marvel, 1977

1 .... 15.00
2 .... 10.00
3-5 .... 8.00
6-10 .... 5.00
11-12 .... 4.00
13 .... 5.00
14-15 .... 4.00
16 .... 3.00
17 .... 4.00
18-26 .... 3.00
27 .... 5.00
28 .... 8.00
29 .... 3.00
30-31 .... 8.00
32-34 .... 3.00
35 .... 5.00
36-45 .... 3.00
46 .... 4.00
47 .... 3.00
Special 1 .... 4.00

What If...?

Marvel, 1989

-1 .... 2.00
1 .... 4.00
2-20 .... 3.00
21-23 .... 2.00
24 .... 4.00
25 .... 3.00
26-49 .... 2.00
50 .... 3.00
51-104 .... 2.00
105 .... 12.00
106-113 .... 2.00
114 .... 3.00

What If ... Aunt May Had Died Instead of Uncle Ben?

Marvel, 2005

1 .... 3.00

What If: Avengers Disassembled

Marvel, 2007

1 .... 4.00

What If: Captain America

Marvel, 2006

1 .... 3.00

What If: Daredevil

Marvel, 2006

1 .... 3.00

What If ... Dr. Doom Had Become The Thing?

Marvel, 2005

1 .... 3.00

What If: Fantastic Four

Marvel, 2006

1 .... 3.00

What If ... General Ross Had Become The Hulk?

Marvel, 2005

1 .... 3.00

What If ... Jessica Jones Had Joined The Avengers?

Marvel, 2005

1 .... 3.00

What If ... Karen Page Had Lived?

Marvel, 2005

1 .... 3.00

What If ... Magneto Had Formed the X-Men with Professor X?

Marvel, 2005

1 .... 3.00

What If: Spider-Man – The Other

Marvel, 2007

1 .... 3.00

What If: Sub-Mariner

Marvel, 2006

1 .... 3.00

What If: Thor

Marvel, 2006

1 .... 3.00

What If: Wolverine
Marvel, 2006

1 .... 3.00

What If: Wolverine – Enemy of the State
Marvel, 2007

1 .... 3.00

What If: X-Men – Age of Apocalypse
Marvel, 2007

1 .... 3.00

What If: X-Men – Deadly Genesis
Marvel, 2007

1 .... 4.00

What Is...THE FACE?
Ace, 1986

1-3 .... 2.00

What's Michael: A Hard Day's Life
Dark Horse, 2002

1 .... 9.00

What's Michael: Fat Cat in the City
Dark Horse, 2003

1 .... 9.00

What's Michael: Living Together
Dark Horse, 1997

1 .... 6.00

What's Michael: Michael's Album
Dark Horse, 1997

1 .... 6.00

What's Michael: Michael's Favorite Spot
Dark Horse, 2002

1 .... 9.00

What's Michael: Michael's Mambo
Dark Horse, 1998

1 .... 6.00

What's Michael: Off the Deep End
Dark Horse, 1997

1 .... 6.00

What's Michael: Show Time
Dark Horse, 2003

1 .... 9.00

What's Michael: The Ideal Cat
Dark Horse, 2004

1 .... 9.00

What's New?- The Collected Adventures of Phil & Dixie
Palliard, 1991

1 .... 6.00
2 .... 8.00

What's New? With Phil and Dixie
Studio Foglio, 2000

1 .... 10.00
2 .... 9.00
3 .... 11.00

What The-?!
Marvel, 1988

1 .... 4.00
2-8 .... 3.00
9-24 .... 2.00
25-27 .... 3.00

Wheelie and the Chopper Bunch
Charlton, 1975

1 .... 20.00
☛Incl. Byrne art
2 .... 12.00
3-7 .... 10.00

Wheel of Worlds (Neil Gaiman's...)
Tekno, 1995

0-1 .... 3.00

When Beanies Attack
Blatant, 1999

1 .... 3.00
1/Variant 5.00

Where Creatures Roam
Marvel, 1970

1 .... 25.00
2-8 .... 10.00

Where in the World Is Carmen Sandiego?
DC, 1996

1-4 .... 2.00

Where Monsters Dwell
Marvel, 1970

1 .... 32.00
2-5 .... 10.00
6-11 .... 8.00
12 .... 10.00
13-31 .... 8.00
32-38 .... 7.00

While Fifty Million Died
Tome

1 .... 3.00

Whip Wilson
Bell Features, 1950

9 .... 350.00
10-11 .... 200.00

Untold Origin of Ms. Victory

Untold Tales of Spider-Man

Unusual Tales

U.S.Agent

U.S. Air Force

V

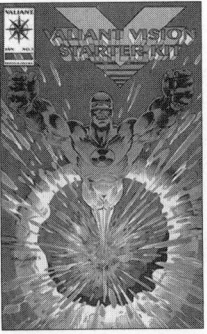

Valiant Vision Starter Kit

Vampirella Classic

Whirlwind Comics

Nita, 1940

1 .... 1,250.00
2-3 .... 850.00

Whispers and Shadows

Oasis, 1984

1-8 .... 2.00

Whisper

Capital, 1983

1 .... 3.00
2 .... 2.00

Whisper

First, 1985

1-37 .... 2.00
Special 1 .... 3.00

White Devil

Eternity, 1988

1-8 .... 3.00

White Fang

Disney, 1990

1 .... 3.00
1/Direct 6.00

White Like She

Dark Horse, 1994

1-4 .... 3.00

White Orchid

Atlantis

1 .... 3.00

Whiteout

Oni, 1998

1-4 .... 3.00

Whiteout: Melt

Oni, 1999

1-4 .... 3.00

White Princess of the Jungle

Avon, 1951

1-2 .... 400.00
3-4 .... 300.00
5 .... 350.00

White Raven

Visionary, 1995

1 .... 3.00

White Rider and Super Horse

Star, 1950

4 .... 100.00
5-6 .... 80.00

White Tiger

Marvel, 2007

1-2 .... 3.00

White Trash

Tundra

1-4 .... 4.00

Whiz Comics

Fawcett, 1940

1 .... 70,000.00
☛1st Captain Marvel
2 .... 5,200.00
3 .... 3,400.00
4 .... 2,800.00
5 .... 2,250.00
6 .... 1,650.00
7 .... 1,725.00
8-9 .... 1,650.00
10 .... 1,250.00
11-12 .... 1,100.00
13-14 .... 1,075.00
15 .... 1,250.00
16-18 .... 1,100.00
19-20 .... 750.00
21 .... 800.00
22-24 .... 600.00
25 .... 6,200.00
☛1st Capt. Marvel Jr.
26 .... 550.00
27-30 .... 525.00
31-32 .... 460.00
33 .... 525.00
34 .... 365.00
35 .... 410.00
36-40 .... 365.00
41-43 .... 260.00
44 .... 300.00
45-50 .... 260.00
51-60 .... 210.00
61-70 .... 175.00
71-82 .... 150.00
83-100 .... 130.00
101-120 .... 110.00
121-152 .... 100.00
153-155 .... 200.00

Whiz Kids

Image, 2003

1 .... 5.00

Whoa, Nellie!

Fantagraphics, 1996

1-3 .... 3.00

Whodunnit?

Eclipse, 1986

1-3 .... 2.00

Who Is Next?

Standard, 1953

5 .... 100.00

Who is the Crooked Man

Crusade, 1996

1 .... 4.00

Who Really Killed JFK

Revolutionary, 1993

1 .... 3.00

Who's Who in Star Trek

DC, 1987

1-2 .... 2.00

Who's Who in the DC Universe
DC, 1990
1-16 .... 5.00

Who's Who in the DC Universe Update 1993
DC, 1992
1-2 .... 6.00

Who's Who in the Impact Universe
DC, 1991
1-3 .... 5.00

Who's Who in the Legion of Super-Heroes
DC, 1988
1-7 .... 2.00

Who's Who: The Definitive Directory of the DC Universe
DC, 1985
1-26 .... 2.00

Who's Who Update '87
DC, 1987
1-5 .... 2.00

Who's Who Update '88
DC, 1988
1-4 .... 2.00

Whotnot
Fantagraphics
1-3 .... 3.00

Why I Hate Saturn
DC
1 .... 15.00

Wicked
Image, 1999
1-7 .... 3.00
Ashcan 1 .... 5.00

Wicked
Millennium, 1994
1-3 .... 3.00

Wicked: Medusa's Tale
Image, 2000
1 .... 4.00

Widow
Avatar, 2000
0 .... 4.00

Widow: Flesh and Blood
Ground Zero, 1992
1-3 .... 3.00

Widow: Metal Gypsies
London Night, 1995
1 .... 4.00

Wiindows
Cult, 1993
1 .... 4.00
2-17 .... 3.00

Wilbur
Archie, 1944
1 .... 260.00
2 .... 115.00
3-4 .... 85.00
5 .... 375.00
6-10 .... 85.00
11-21 .... 52.00
22-30 .... 36.00
31-50 .... 24.00
51-60 .... 15.00
61-70 .... 10.00
71-88 .... 8.00
89-90 .... 4.00

Wild
Atlas, 1954
1 .... 150.00
2 .... 85.00
3-5 .... 75.00

Wild
Eastern
1 .... 2.00

Wild!
Mu, 2003
1-14 .... 4.00

Wild Animals
Pacific, 1982
1 .... 2.00

Wild Bill Elliott
Dell, 1950
2-3 .... 75.00
4-10 .... 55.00
13-17 .... 40.00

Wild Bill Hickok
Avon, 1949
1 .... 165.00
2 .... 75.00
3-5 .... 60.00
6-9 .... 50.00
10-12 .... 60.00
13-14 .... 50.00
15-20 .... 40.00
21-28 .... 35.00

Wild Bill Hickok
Super, 1952
10-12 .... 60.00

Wild Bill Pecos
AC, 1989
1 .... 4.00

Wild Boy of the Congo
Ziff-Davis, 1951
10 (#1) 120.00
11 (#2) 100.00
12 (#3) 80.00

Vampire Tales

Vampire World

Vamps

Vanguard

Vanguard Illustrated

Vanity Angel

Velvet

Venom

4 .... 60.00
5-6 .... 50.00
7 .... 60.00
8-10 .... 50.00
11 .... 65.00
12-15 .... 50.00

WildB.R.A.T.s

Fantagraphics, 1992

1 .... 3.00

Wildcards

Marvel, 1990

1-4 .... 5.00

WildC.A.T.s

Image, 1992

0 .... 3.00
1 .... 4.00
1/3D 5.00
1/Gold 10.00
1/Variant 5.00
2 .... 4.00
3-10 .... 3.00
11 .... 15.00
11/Holofoil 22.00
12 .... 8.00
13 .... 6.00
14-24 .... 3.00
25 .... 5.00
26-49 .... 3.00
50 .... 4.00
50/Variant 5.00
Ann 1 .... 3.00
Special 1 .... 4.00

WildCats

DC, 1999

1-1/F 3.00
1/Sketch 10.00
2-28 .... 3.00
Ann 2000 .... 4.00

WildCats

DC, 2006

1-1/2nd variant 3.00

WildC.A.T.S Adventures

Image, 1994

1-3 .... 2.00
4-10 .... 3.00

WildC.A.T.S Adventures Sourcebook

Image, 1995

1 .... 3.00

WildC.A.T.S/Aliens

Image, 1998

1-1/A 5.00

WildCats/Cyberforce: Killer Instinct

DC, 2004

1 .... 15.00

WildC.A.T.S (Jim Lee's...)

Image, 1995

1 .... 2.00

WildCats: Ladytron

DC, 2000

1 .... 6.00

WildCats: Mosaic

DC, 2000

1 .... 4.00

WildCats: Nemesis

DC, 2005

1-9 .... 3.00

WildC.A.T.S Sourcebook

Image, 1993

1-2 .... 3.00

WildC.A.T.S Trilogy

Image, 1993

1 .... 3.00
2-3 .... 2.00

WildCats Version 3.0

DC, 2002

1-24 .... 3.00

WildC.A.T.s/X-Men: The Golden Age

Image, 1997

1-1/A 5.00
1/Scroll 8.00
1/C 5.00
1/w. glasses 7.00
1/F 5.00
1/Scroll w. gla 9.00

WildC.A.T.s/X-Men: The Modern Age

Image, 1997

1 .... 5.00
1/A 6.00
1/Nightcrawler 8.00
1/w. glasses 7.00
1/D 5.00
1/E 8.00

WildC.A.T.s/X-Men: The Silver Age

Image, 1997

1-1/B 5.00
1/3D-1/D 7.00
1/E 5.00

Wildcore

Image, 1997

1-1/A 3.00
1/B 5.00
2-Ashcan 1 .... 3.00

Wild Dog

DC, 1987

1-4 .... 2.00
Special 1 .... 3.00

Wilderness
4Winds
Deluxe 1 .... 25.00

Wildflower
Sirius, 1998
1-5 .... 3.00

Wild Frontier
Charlton, 1955
1 .... 60.00
2-6 .... 40.00
7 .... 50.00

Wild Frontier (Shanda)
Shanda, 1956
1 .... 60.00
2 .... 3.00

Wild Girl
DC, 2005
1-6 .... 3.00

Wildguard: Casting Call
Image, 2003
1-6 .... 3.00

Wildguard: Fire Power
Image, 2004
1/A-1/B 4.00

WildGuard: Fool's Gold
Image, 2005
1-2 .... 4.00

Wild Kingdom
Mu, 1991
1-7 .... 3.00
8-14 .... 4.00

Wild Knights
Eternity, 1988
1-10 .... 2.00

Wild Life
Antarctic, 1993
1-12 .... 3.00

Wild Life
Fantagraphics, 1994
1-2 .... 3.00

Wildlifers
Radio, 1999
1 .... 5.00

Wildman
Miller
1-11 .... 2.00

Wildman (Grass Green's...)
Megaton
1-2 .... 2.00

Wild Party
Kitchen Sink
1 .... 22.00

Wild Person in the Woods
G.T. Labs, 1999
1 .... 3.00

Wild Side
United, 1998
1-6 .... 4.00

Wildsiderz
DC, 2005
0 .... 2.00
0/Variant 3.00
1/A cover 4.00
1/B cover 5.00
1/Lenticular 6.00
2 .... 4.00

Wildstar
Image, 1995
1-4 .... 3.00

Wild Stars
Collector's, 1984
1 .... 1.00

Wild Stars
Collector's, 1988
1 .... 2.00

Wild Stars
Little Rocket, 2001
1-7 .... 3.00

Wildstar: Sky Zero
Image, 1993
1 .... 3.00
1/Gold 4.00
2 .... 2.00
3-4 .... 3.00

WildStorm!
Image, 1995
1-4 .... 3.00

WildStorm Annual
DC, 2000
2000 .... 4.00

WildStorm Chamber of Horrors
Image, 1995
1 .... 4.00

WildStorm Fine Art Spotlight: Jim Lee
DC, 2007
1 .... 4.00

WildStorm Halloween '97
Image, 1997
1 .... 3.00

WildStorm Rarities
Image, 1994
1 .... 5.00

Venture

Venus

Veronica

Vertigo Jam

V for Vendetta

Video Jack

Vintage Magnus Robot Fighter

Violator

WildStorm Rising
Image, 1995

1 ....3.00
2 ....2.00

WildStorm Sampler
Image

1 ....1.00

WildStorms Player's Guide
Image, 1996

1 ....2.00

WildStorm Spotlight
Image, 1997

1-4 ....3.00

Wildstorm Summer Special
DC, 2001

1 ....6.00

WildStorm Swimsuit Special
Image, 1994

1-1997 ....3.00

WildStorm Thunderbook
DC, 2000

1 ....7.00

Wildstorm Ultimate Sports Official Program
Image, 1997

1 ....3.00

WildStorm Universe '97
Image, 1996

1-3 ....3.00

WildStorm Universe Sourcebook
Image, 1995

1-2 ....3.00

Wildstorm Winter Special
DC, 2005

1 ....5.00

Wild Thing
Marvel, 1993

1 ....3.00
2-7 ....2.00

Wild Thing (2nd Series)
Marvel, 1999

1-5 ....2.00

Wild Things
Metro, 1986

1-3 ....2.00

Wild Thingz
ABC

0/A 3.00
0/B 6.00
0/Platinum 3.00

Wild Think
Wild Think, 1987

1 ....2.00

Wild Times: Deathblow
DC, 1999

1 ....3.00

Wild Times: DV8
DC, 1999

1 ....3.00

Wild Times: Gen13
DC, 1999

1 ....3.00

Wild Times: Grifter
DC, 1999

1 ....3.00

Wild Times: Wetworks
DC, 1999

1 ....3.00

Wild West
Marvel, 1948

1 ....200.00
2 ....125.00

Wild West
Charlton, 1966

58 ....10.00

Wild West C.O.W.-Boys of Moo Mesa
Archie, 1993

1-3 ....1.00

Wild Western
Atlas, 1948

3 ....160.00
4 ....110.00
5 ....125.00
6-8 ....75.00
9 ....100.00
10 ....110.00
11-19 ....75.00
20-30 ....55.00
31-40 ....45.00
41-47 ....40.00
48 ....50.00
49-51 ....40.00
52 ....50.00
53 ....40.00
54-55 ....50.00
56-57 ....40.00

Wild, Wild West
Gold Key, 1966

1 ....70.00
2 ....45.00
3-7 ....35.00

Wild, Wild West
Millennium, 1990

1-4 ....3.00

Wild Women
Paragon
1 .... 5.00

Wild Zoo
Radio, 2000
1-7 .... 3.00
8 .... 4.00

Will Eisner Presents
Eclipse, 1990
1-3 .... 3.00

Will Eisner Reader
DC, 2000
1 .... 10.00

Will Eisner's 3-D Classics: Spirit
Kitchen Sink, 1985
1 .... 2.00

Will Eisner's John Law: Angels and Ashes, Devils and Dust
Idea & Design Works, 2006
1 .... 4.00

Will Eisner's Quarterly
Kitchen Sink, 1983
1 .... 3.00
2 .... 4.00
3-8 .... 2.00

William Shatner
Celebrity
1 .... 6.00

Willie Comics
Marvel, 1946
5 .... 75.00
6-12 .... 50.00

Willow
Marvel, 1988
1-3 .... 2.00

Willow (Angel)
Angel, 1996
0 .... 3.00
0/Nude 10.00

Will Rogers
Fox, 1950
5 .... 175.00
2 .... 200.00

Will to Power
Dark Horse, 1994
1 .... 2.00
2-12 .... 1.00

Wimmen's Comix
Renegade, 1972
1 .... 10.00
2-4 .... 8.00
5-8 .... 5.00
9-10 .... 4.00
11-18 .... 3.00

Windburnt Plains of Wonder
Lohman Hills, 1996
1 .... 12.00

Wind in the Willows
NBM, 1999
1-2 .... 16.00

Windraven
Heroic
1 .... 3.00

Windraven Adventures
Blue Comet, 1993
1 .... 3.00

Winds of Winter
Antarctic, 2001
1 .... 5.00

Windsor
Win-Mil
1-2 .... 2.00

Windy and Willy
DC, 1969
1 .... 25.00
2-4 .... 15.00

Wingbird Akuma-She
Verotik, 1998
1 .... 4.00

Wingbird Returns
Verotik, 1997
1 .... 10.00

Wingding Orgy
Fantagraphics, 1997
1-2 .... 4.00

Winged Tiger
Cartoonists Across America, 1999
3 .... 3.00

Winging It
Solo
1 .... 2.00

Wings
Mu, 1992
1 .... 3.00

Wings Comics
Fiction House, 1940
1 .... 1,500.00
2 .... 800.00
3-5 .... 460.00
6-10 .... 365.00
11-15 .... 320.00
16-20 .... 275.00
21-30 .... 215.00
31-40 .... 175.00
41-50 .... 135.00
51-60 .... 110.00
61-80 .... 100.00
81-100 .... 90.00
101-124 .... 75.00

Violent Messiahs

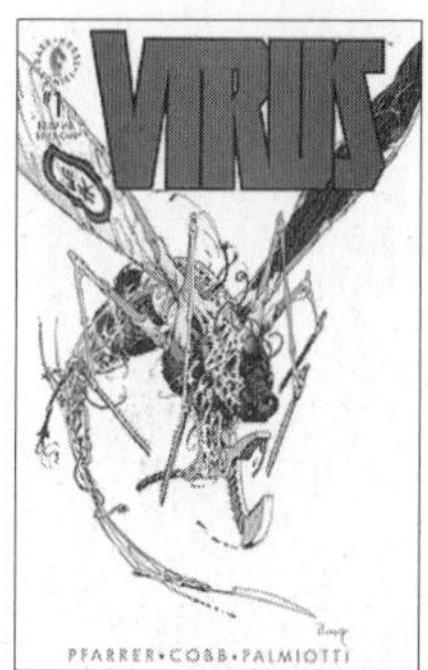

Virus

Void Indigo

Wacky Adventures of Cracky

All comics prices listed are for NEAR MINT condition.

Wacky Squirrel

Wacky Witch

Wally the Wizard

Walt Disney Showcase

Wings Comics (A-List)

A-List, 1997

1-4 .... 3.00

Winnie the Pooh

Gold Key, 1977

1 .... 20.00
2 .... 10.00
3-17 .... 7.00
18-19 .... 10.00
20 .... 125.00
21-28 .... 10.00
29-33 .... 20.00

Winnie Winkle

Dell, 1948

1 .... 50.00
2 .... 30.00
3-7 .... 25.00

Winning in the Desert

Apple

1-2 .... 3.00

Winter Men

DC, 2005

1-5 .... 3.00

Winter Soldier: Winter Kills

Marvel, 2007

1 .... 4.00

Winterstar

Echo, 1996

1 .... 3.00

Winterworld

Eclipse, 1987

1-3 .... 2.00

Wireheads

Fleetway-Quality

1-2 .... 3.00

Wisdom

Marvel, 2007

1 .... 4.00

Wisdom of the Gnomes

Celebrity, 1989

1-2 .... 3.00

Wise Son: The White Wolf

DC, 1996

1-4 .... 3.00

Wish

Tokyopop, 2002

1 .... 10.00

Wish Upon a Star

Warp, 1994

1 .... 1.00

Wisp

Oktomica, 1999

1 .... 3.00

Witch

Eternity

1 .... 2.00

Witchblade

Image, 1995

½ 15.00
1 .... 25.00
1/B 15.00
2 .... 18.00
2/A 15.00
2/2nd 4.00
3 .... 10.00
4-5 .... 8.00
6-7 .... 6.00
8-10 .... 5.00
11-14 .... 4.00
14/Gold 6.00
15 .... 4.00
16-18/A 3.00
19-24 .... 3.00
24/Variant 5.00
25 .... 3.00
25/A 4.00
25/B 8.00
25/C 15.00
26-29 .... 3.00
29/Variant 5.00
30-32 .... 3.00
32/Variant 15.00
33-41 .... 3.00
41/A 10.00
42-49 .... 3.00
50 .... 5.00
50/Silvestri-50/Turner 5.00
51-74 .... 3.00
75-75/Variant 5.00
76-80 .... 3.00
80/Holiday 5.00
80/Cho-80/Land 3.00
80/Conv 5.00
81-91 .... 3.00
92 .... 5.00
93-99 .... 3.00
100/Turner-100/Anime 5.00
101-102 .... 3.00
500 .... 5.00
Deluxe 1-3 .... 25.00

Witchblade/Dark Minds: Return of Paradox

Image, 2004

1 .... 10.00

Witchblade/Aliens/ The Darkness/Predator

Dark Horse, 2000

1-3 .... 3.00

Witchblade: Animated One Shot

Image, 2003

1 .... 3.00

Witchblade: Blood Oath
Image, 2004
1 .... 5.00

Witchblade/Darkchylde
Image, 2000
1 .... 3.00

Witchblade/Darkness Special
Image, 1999
½/Platinum 35.00
1 .... 4.00

Witchblade: Destiny's Child
Image, 2000
1-3 .... 3.00

Witchblade/Elektra
Marvel, 1997
1 .... 3.00

Witchblade Gallery
Image, 2000
1 .... 3.00

Witchblade Infinity
Image, 1999
1 .... 4.00

Witchblade/Lady Death
Image, 2001
1 .... 5.00

Witchblade: Movie Edition
Image, 2000
1-1/C 3.00

Witchblade: Nottingham
Image, 2003
1 .... 5.00

Witchblade: Obakemono
Image, 2002
1 .... 10.00

Witchblade 10th Anniversary Cover Gallery
Image, 2005
1 .... 3.00

Witchblade/Tomb Raider
Image, 1998
½ 5.00

Witchblade & Tomb Raider
Image, 2005
1 .... 3.00

Witchblade/Tomb Raider
Image, 1998
1/A 4.00
1/B 5.00
1/C 7.00

Witchblade/Wolverine
Image, 2004
1 .... 3.00

Witchcraft
Avon, 1952
1 .... 420.00
2 .... 315.00
3 .... 235.00
4 .... 265.00
5 .... 300.00
6 .... 235.00

Witchcraft
DC, 1994
1-3 .... 3.00

Witchcraft: La Terreur
DC, 1998
1-3 .... 3.00

Witches
Marvel, 2004
1-4 .... 3.00

Witches' Cauldron: The Battle of the Cherkassy Pocket
Heritage Collection
1 .... 4.00

Witches Tales
Harvey, 1951
1 .... 310.00
2 .... 260.00
3-10 .... 210.00
11-16 .... 190.00
17-19 .... 225.00
20-24 .... 190.00
25-28 .... 165.00

Witches' Western Tales
Harvey, 1955
29-30 .... 125.00

Witchfinder
Image, 1999
1-2 .... 3.00

Witch Hunter
Malibu, 1996
1 .... 3.00

Witching
DC, 2004
1-10 .... 3.00

Witching Hour
DC, 1969
1 .... 150.00
2 .... 70.00
3 .... 50.00
4-6 .... 25.00
7 .... 18.00
8-13 .... 15.00
14-51 .... 10.00
52-66 .... 8.00
67-85 .... 5.00

Witching Hour
DC, 2000
1-3 .... 6.00

Walter

Wandering Star

War

War Against Crime

War Dancer

Warfront

Warhammer Monthly

Warhawks Comics Module

Witching Hour (Anne Rice's...)
Millennium, 1992

1-13 .... 3.00

Within Our Reach
Star*Reach

1 .... 8.00

With the Marines on the Battlefronts of the World
Toby, 1953

1 .... 70.00
2 .... 40.00

Witness
Marvel, 1948

1 .... 1,250.00

Witty Comics
Chicago Nite Life News, 1945

1 .... 90.00
2 .... 55.00
3-7 .... 50.00

Wizard in Training
Upper Deck, 2002

0 .... 3.00

Wizard of 4th Street
Dark Horse, 1987

1-6 .... 2.00

Wizard of 4th Street
David P. House

1-3 .... 2.00

Wizard of Time
DPH, 1986

1-2 .... 2.00

Wizards of the Last Resort
Blackthorne, 1987

1-4 .... 2.00

Wizard Works
Fantasy General, 1986

1-4 .... 2.00

WJHC
Wilson Place, 1998

1 .... 2.00

Wogglebug
Arrow, 1988

1 .... 3.00

Wolf & Red
Dark Horse, 1995

1-3 .... 3.00

Wolff & Byrd, Counselors of the Macabre
Exhibit A, 1988

1 .... 4.00
2-23 .... 3.00

Wolff & Byrd, Counselors of the Macabre's Greatest Writs
Exhibit A

1 .... 3.00

Wolff & Byrd, Counselors of the Macabre's Secretary Mavis
Exhibit A, 1998

1-2 .... 3.00
3-4 .... 4.00

Wolff & Byrd: Supernatural Law
Exhibit A

1 .... 8.00

Wolf Gal (Al Capp's...)
Toby, 1951

1-2 .... 195.00

Wolfman
Dell, 1964

1 .... 24.00
1/2nd 20.00

Wolfpack
Marvel, 1988

1-12 .... 1.00

Wolf Run: A Known Associates Mystery
Known Associates

1 .... 3.00

Wolph
Blackthorne, 1987

1 .... 2.00

Wolverbroad vs. Hobo
Spoof, 1992

1 .... 3.00

Wolverine
Marvel, 1982

1 .... 25.00
2 .... 18.00
3 .... 17.00
4 .... 16.00

Wolverine
Marvel, 1988

-1 .... 2.00
½ 3.00
½/Ltd. 8.00
1 .... 10.00
2 .... 6.00
3-5 .... 5.00
6 .... 4.00
7-9 .... 5.00
10 .... 8.00
11-14 .... 4.00
15 .... 5.00
16-19 .... 4.00

20 .... 5.00
21-23 .... 4.00
24-40 .... 3.00
41 .... 4.00
41/2nd-42/2nd 2.00
43 .... 3.00
44 .... 2.00
45-49 .... 3.00
50 .... 4.00
51-56 .... 2.00
57 .... 3.00
58-74 .... 2.00
75 .... 4.00
76-79 .... 2.00
80 .... 8.00
81-84 .... 2.00
85 .... 3.00
85/Variant 4.00
86-87 .... 2.00
87/Deluxe 4.00
88 .... 2.00
88/Deluxe 4.00
89 .... 2.00
89/Deluxe 4.00
90 .... 2.00
90/Deluxe 4.00
91-98 .... 2.00
99 .... 4.00
100 .... 5.00
100/Variant 8.00
101-124 .... 2.00
125 .... 4.00
125/A-125/B 10.00
126-130 .... 2.00
131 .... 5.00
131/A 3.00
132-133 .... 2.00
133/Variant 4.00
134-144 .... 2.00
145 .... 4.00
145/Gold foil 25.00
145/Silver foil 30.00
145/Nabisco 400.00
146 .... 5.00
147-149 .... 2.00
150 .... 3.00
151-165 .... 2.00
166 .... 3.00
166/A 40.00
167-189 .... 2.00
Ann 1995 .... 4.00
Ann 1996-1997 .... 3.00
Ann 1999-2000 .... 4.00
Ann 2001 .... 3.00
Special 1 .... 4.00

Wolverine

Marvel, 2003

1 .... 7.00
2 .... 5.00
3 .... 4.00
4-9 .... 3.00
10 .... 2.00
11-15 .... 3.00
16 .... 2.00
17 .... 3.00
18-20 .... 2.00
20/Variant 90.00
☛Retailer incentive
20/Texas 20.00
☛Texas con premium
21-26 .... 2.00
26/Silvestri 15.00
27 .... 2.00
27/Quesada 25.00
28 .... 2.00
29-36 .... 3.00
36/Quesada 12.00
37-40 .... 3.00
41 .... 4.00
42-48 .... 3.00
49-50 .... 4.00

Wolverine and the Punisher: Damaging Evidence

Marvel, 1993

1-3 .... 2.00

Wolverine Battlebook

Battlebooks, 1998

1 .... 4.00
1/A 5.00

Wolverine Battles the Incredible Hulk

Marvel, 1989

1 .... 5.00

Wolverine: Black Rio

Marvel, 1998

1 .... 6.00

Wolverine: Blood Hungry!

Marvel, 1993

1-1/2nd 7.00

Wolverine: Bloodlust

Marvel, 1990

1 .... 5.00

Wolverine: Bloody Choices

Marvel, 1993

1 .... 8.00

Wolverine/Captain America

Marvel, 2004

1 .... 4.00
2-4 .... 3.00

Wolverine: Days of Future Past

Marvel, 1997

1-3 .... 3.00

Wolverine: Doombringer

Marvel, 1997

1 .... 6.00
1/Variant 15.00

Warheads

Warlands

Warlock and the Infinity Watch

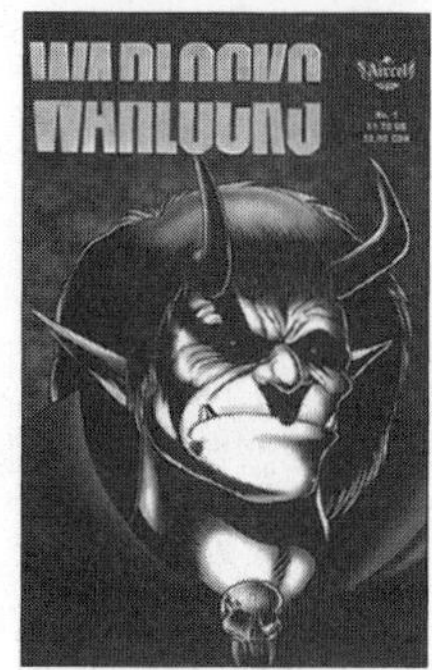

Warlocks

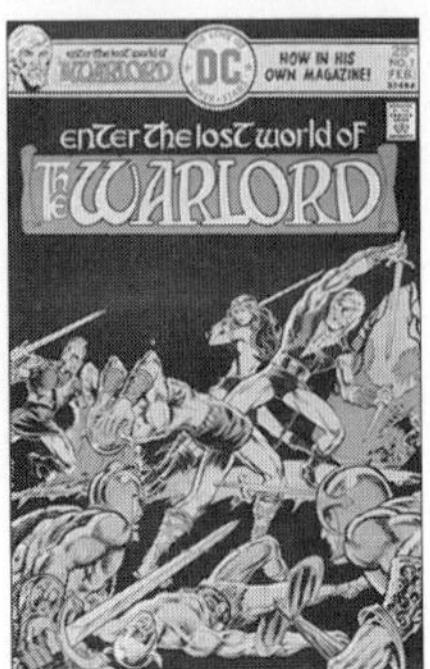

Warlord

War Machine

War of the Gods

Warp

Wolverine/Doop
Marvel, 2003

1-2 .... 3.00

Wolverine: Evilution
Marvel, 1994

1 .... 6.00

Wolverine/Gambit: Victims
Marvel, 1995

1-4 .... 3.00

Wolverine: Global Jeopardy
Marvel, 1993

1 .... 3.00

Wolverine/Hulk
Marvel, 2002

1-4 .... 4.00

Wolverine: Inner Fury
Marvel, 1992

1 .... 6.00

Wolverine: Killing
Marvel, 1993

1 .... 6.00

Wolverine: Knight of Terra
Marvel, 1995

1 .... 7.00

Wolverine: Netsuke
Marvel, 2002

1-4 .... 4.00

Wolverine and Nick Fury: Scorpio Rising
Marvel, 1994

1 .... 5.00

Wolverine/Nick Fury: The Scorpio Connection
Marvel

1 .... 13.00

Wolverine: Origins
Marvel, 2006

1-35 .... 3.00

Wolverine Poster Magazine
Marvel

1 .... 5.00

Wolverine/Punisher
Marvel, 2004

1-5 .... 3.00

Wolverine/Punisher Revelation
Marvel, 1999

1-4 .... 3.00

Wolverine: Rahne of Terra
Marvel, 1991

1 .... 6.00

Wolverine Saga
Marvel, 1989

1-4 .... 4.00

Wolverine: Save the Tiger!
Marvel, 1992

1 .... 3.00

Wolverine: Snikt!
Marvel, 2003

1-5 .... 3.00

Wolverine: Soultaker
Marvel, 2005

1-5 .... 3.00

Wolverine: The End
Marvel, 2004

1 .... 7.00
1/Texas 15.00
2 .... 6.00
3 .... 5.00
4 .... 4.00
5-6 .... 3.00

Wolverine: The Jungle Adventure
Marvel, 1990

1 .... 5.00

Wolverine: The Origin
Marvel, 2001

1 .... 25.00
2 .... 12.00
3 .... 8.00
4 .... 5.00
5 .... 4.00
6 .... 5.00

Wolverine Unleashed
Marvel, 2002

1 .... 5.00
2-10 .... 4.00
11-19 .... 3.00

Wolverine vs. Night Man
Marvel

0 .... 15.00

Wolverine vs. Spider-Man
Marvel, 1995

1 .... 3.00

Wolverine/Witchblade
Image, 1997

1 .... 5.00
1/A 3.00

Wolverine: Xisle
Marvel, 2003

1-5 .... 3.00

Wombles
Redan

1-2 .... 3.00

Women in Fur
Shanda Fantasy Arts

2 .... 5.00

Women in Love
Fox, 1949

1 ... 170.00
2 ... 140.00

Women in Rock Special
Revolutionary, 1993

1 ... 3.00

Women of Marvel Poster Book
Marvel, 2006

1 ... 5.00

Women on Top
Fantagraphics, 1991

1 ... 2.00

Women Outlaws
Fox, 1948

1 ... 450.00
2-3 ... 350.00
4-8 ... 275.00

Wonder Boy
Ajax, 1955

17 ... 275.00
18 ... 225.00

Wonder Comics (Fox)
Fox, 1939

1 ... 15,000.00
2 ... 5,000.00

Wonder Comics
Nedor, 1944

1 ... 1,100.00
2 ... 590.00
3-5 ... 540.00
6-10 ... 425.00
11-14 ... 500.00
15-20 ... 440.00

Wonderland
Arrow, 1985

1-3 ... 3.00

Wonderland
Wonderland Educational, 1962

1 ... 4.00
2-37 ... 3.00

Wonderlanders
Oktomica, 1999

1 ... 3.00

Wonder Man
Marvel, 1986

1 ... 2.00

Wonder Man
Marvel, 1991

1 ... 2.00
2-24 ... 1.00
25 ... 3.00
26-29 ... 1.00
Ann 1 ... 2.00
Ann 2 ... 3.00

Wonder Man
Marvel, 2007

1 ... 3.00

Wonders and Oddities (Rick Geary's...)
Dark Horse, 1988

1 ... 2.00

Wonder Wart-Hog, Hog of Steel
Rip Off

1-3 ... 3.00

Wonder Woman
DC, 1942

1 ... 17,000.00
2 ... 3,100.00
3 ... 1,900.00
4 ... 1,200.00
5 ... 1,050.00
6-10 ... 900.00
11-20 ... 650.00
21-23 ... 450.00
24 ... 600.00
25 ... 450.00
26-30 ... 425.00
31-40 ... 415.00
41-44 ... 400.00
45 ... 500.00
46-50 ... 400.00
51-60 ... 310.00
61-70 ... 240.00
71-79 ... 190.00
80-90 ... 155.00
91-100 ... 120.00
101-104 ... 90.00
105 ... 600.00
☛1st Wonder Girl
106-110 ... 80.00
111-130 ... 70.00
131-149 ... 56.00
150-159 ... 50.00
160-161 ... 30.00
162 ... 40.00
163-170 ... 30.00
171-180 ... 25.00
181-190 ... 33.00
191-200 ... 40.00
201-210 ... 14.00
211 ... 25.00
☛100-page issue
212-213 ... 11.00
214 ... 30.00
☛100-page issue
215-218 ... 11.00
219-236 ... 7.00
237-250 ... 6.00
250/Whitman ... 12.00
251 ... 6.00
251/Whitman ... 12.00
252 ... 6.00
252/Whitman ... 12.00

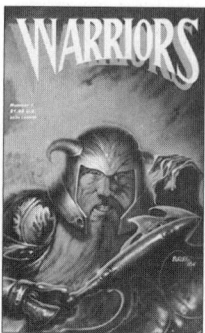

Warriors

Warriors of Plasm

Warstrike

Wasteland

Watchmen

Way of the Rat

WCW World Championship Wrestling

Weapon X

253-255 ....6.00
255/Whitman 12.00
256 ....6.00
256/Whitman 12.00
257 ....6.00
257/Whitman 12.00
258 ....6.00
258/Whitman 12.00
259 ....6.00
259/Whitman 12.00
260 ....6.00
260/Whitman 12.00
261 ....5.00
261/Whitman 15.00
262 ....5.00
262/Whitman 10.00
263 ....5.00
263/Whitman 15.00
264 ....5.00
264/Whitman 10.00
265-268 ....5.00
269-279 ....4.00
280 ....3.00
281-283 ....5.00
284-299 ....3.00
300 ....6.00
301-329 ....3.00

Wonder Woman

DC, 1987

0 ....6.00
1 ....4.00
2-10/A 3.00
11-84 ....2.00
85 ....10.00
☛1st Deodato art
86 ....4.00
87-93 ....3.00
94-99 ....2.00
100 ....3.00
100/Variant 4.00
101-119 ....2.00
120 ....3.00
121-199 ....2.00
200 ....4.00
201-213 ....2.00
214 ....25.00
☛Inf. Crisis tie
215 ....10.00
216 ....7.00
217 ....6.00
218 ....5.00
219 ....15.00
☛Max Lord dies
219/2nd 3.00
☛2nd print
220 ....12.00
220/2nd-1000000 ....3.00
Ann 1-2 ....2.00
Ann 3 ....3.00
Ann 4 ....4.00
Ann 5 ....3.00
Ann 6 ....4.00
Ann 7-8 ....3.00
Special 1 ....2.00

Wonder Woman

DC, 2006

1/A-Bk 4/HC 0.00
1 ....6.00
1/Variant-25 ....3.00

Wonder Woman: Amazonia

DC, 1998

1 ....8.00

Wonder Woman: Blue Amazon

DC, 2003

1 ....7.00

Wonder Woman: Donna Troy

DC, 1998

1 ....2.00

Wonder Woman Gallery

DC, 1996

1 ....4.00

Wonder Woman: Our Worlds At War

DC, 2001

1 ....3.00

Wonder Woman Plus

DC, 1997

1 ....3.00

Wonder Woman Secret Files

DC, 1998

1-3 ....5.00

Wonder Woman: Spirit of Truth

DC, 2000

1-1/2nd 10.00

Wonder Woman: The Once and Future Story

DC, 1998

1 ....5.00

Wonderworld Comics

Fox, 1939

3 ....5,000.00
4 ....3,000.00
5-6 ....1,600.00
7-8 ....2,000.00
9-10 ....1,600.00
11 ....1,200.00
12-15 ....1,000.00
16-20 ....750.00
21-28 ....500.00
29-33 ....350.00

Wonderworld Express

That Other Comix Co., 1984

1 ....2.00

Wonderworlds
Innovation, 1992
1 .... 4.00

Wood Boy (Raymond E. Feist's ...)
Image, 2005
1 .... 3.00

Woodstock: The Comic
Marvel
1 .... 6.00

Woodsy Owl
Gold Key, 1973
1 .... 8.00
2 .... 5.00
3-5 .... 4.00
6-10 .... 3.00

Woody Woodpecker (Walter Lantz...)
Dell, 1952
16-20 .... 14.00
21-50 .... 12.00
51-72 .... 9.00
73-75 .... 25.00
76-100 .... 15.00
101-120 .... 10.00
121-130 .... 6.00
131-170 .... 3.00
171-187 .... 2.00
188-189 .... 10.00
190-191 .... 25.00
193-201 .... 15.00

Woody Woodpecker
Harvey, 1991
1 .... 2.00
2-8 .... 1.00
9-12 .... 2.00

Woody Woodpecker 50th Anniversary Special
Harvey, 1991
1 .... 3.00

Woody Woodpecker Adventures
Harvey, 1992
1-3 .... 1.00

Woody Woodpecker and Friends
Harvey, 1991
1-4 .... 1.00

Woody Woodpecker Digest
Harvey, 1992
1 .... 2.00

Woody Woodpecker Giant Size
Harvey, 1992
1 .... 2.00

Woody Woodpecker's Back to School
Dell, 1952
1 .... 100.00
2-6 .... 75.00

Woody Woodpecker's Christmas Parade
Gold Key, 1968
1 .... 20.00

Woody Woodpecker's County Fair
Dell, 1956
5 .... 75.00
2 .... 60.00

Woody Woodpecker Summer Fun
Gold Key, 1966
1 .... 50.00

Woody Woodpecker Summer Special
Harvey, 1990
1 .... 2.00

Woofers and Hooters
Fantagraphics
1 .... 3.00

Woolworth's Happy Time Christmas Book
Whitman, 1952
1 .... 30.00

Words & Pictures
Maverick, 1994
1-2 .... 4.00

Wordsmith
Renegade, 1985
1-12 .... 2.00

Wordsmith
Caliber, 1996
1-6 .... 3.00

Word Warriors
Literacy Volunteers
1 .... 2.00

Worgard: Viking Berserkir
Stronghold, 1997
1 .... 3.00

Workshop
Blue Comet
1 .... 3.00

World Around Us
Gilberton, 1958
1 .... 35.00
2-12 .... 25.00
13 .... 40.00
14 .... 35.00
15-25 .... 25.00
26 .... 35.00

Weapon Zero

Weaveworld

Web of Mystery

Web of Scarlet Spider

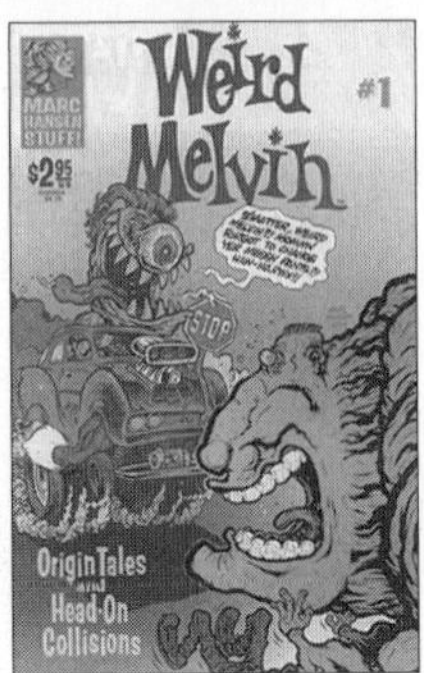

Weird Melvin

Weird Secret Origins 80-Page Giant

Weirdsville

Weird War Tales

27-33 .... 25.00
34 .... 35.00
35 .... 40.00
36 .... 25.00

World Bank
Public Services International
1 .... 3.00

World Below
Dark Horse, 1999
1-4 .... 3.00

World Below: Deeper and Stranger
Dark Horse, 1999
1-4 .... 3.00

World Class Comics
Image, 2002
1 .... 5.00

World Exists for Me
Tokyopop, 2005
1 .... 10.00

World Famous Heroes
Centaur, 1941
1 .... 750.00
2 .... 350.00
3-4 .... 275.00

World Hardball League
Titus, 1994
1-2 .... 3.00

World is His Parish: The Story of Pope Pius XII
George A. Pflaum, 1954
1 .... 100.00

World of Archie
Archie, 1992
1-22 .... 2.00

World of Fantasy
Atlas, 1956
1 .... 350.00
2 .... 300.00
3 .... 250.00
4 .... 200.00
5-6 .... 160.00
7-12 .... 150.00
13-15 .... 125.00
16-19 .... 100.00

World of Ginger Fox
Comico
1 .... 7.00

World of Hartz
Tokyopop, 2004
1 .... 10.00

World of Krypton
DC, 1979
1-3 .... 2.00

World of Krypton
DC, 1987
1-4 .... 2.00

World of Metropolis
DC, 1988
1-4 .... 2.00

World of Mystery
Atlas, 1956
1 .... 300.00
2 .... 100.00
3-4 .... 125.00
5-7 .... 100.00

World of Smallville
DC, 1988
1-4 .... 2.00

World of Suspense
Atlas, 1956
1 .... 225.00
2-3 .... 125.00
4-6 .... 100.00
7 .... 125.00
8 .... 100.00

World of Warcraft
DC, 2008
1-16 .... 3.00

World of Wheels
Charlton, 1967
17-20 .... 12.00
21-32 .... 8.00

World of Wood
Eclipse, 1986
1-5 .... 2.00

World of X-Ray
Pyramid
1 .... 2.00

World of Young Master
New Comics, 1989
1 .... 2.00

World's Best Comics
DC, 1941
1 .... 18,000.00

World's Best Comics: Silver Age DC Archive Sampler
DC, 2004
1 .... 1.00

Worlds Beyond
Fawcett, 1951
1 .... 250.00

Worlds Collide
DC, 1994
1 .... 3.00
1/CS-1/Platinum 4.00

World's Finest
DC, 1990
1-3 .... 5.00

World's Finest Comics

DC, 1941

2 .... 4,000.00
3 .... 2,900.00
4-5 .... 1,975.00
6-7 .... 1,450.00
8 .... 1,275.00
9 .... 1,300.00
10 .... 1,050.00
11-16 .... 895.00
17 .... 875.00
18-20 .... 805.00
21-30 .... 610.00
31-40 .... 530.00
41-60 .... 430.00
61-64 .... 320.00
65 .... 540.00
66-70 .... 370.00
71 .... 900.00
☛1st Superman/Batman team
72-73 .... 550.00
74-80 .... 375.00
81-90 .... 235.00
91-93 .... 175.00
94 .... 525.00
☛Superman/Batman team origin
95-99 .... 175.00
100 .... 260.00
101-110 .... 105.00
111-121 .... 85.00
122-142 .... 75.00
143-150 .... 52.00
151-152 .... 50.00
153-155 .... 45.00
156 .... 55.00
☛Bizarro, Joker app.
157-161 .... 45.00
162-177 .... 38.00
178-180 .... 30.00
181-190 .... 25.00
191-197 .... 20.00
☛Superman/Flash race
198-199 .... 80.00
☛Superman/Flash race
200-212 .... 16.00
213-228 .... 14.00
229-270 .... 6.00
271-300 .... 4.00
301-323 .... 3.00

World's Finest: Our Worlds at War

DC, 2001

1 .... 3.00

World's Funnest Comics

Moordam, 1998

1 .... 3.00

World's Greatest Songs

Atlas, 1954

1 .... 250.00

Worlds of Fear

Fawcett, 1952

2 .... 325.00
3 .... 250.00
4-9 .... 200.00
10 .... 475.00

Worlds of H.P. Lovecraft: Beyond The Wall of Sleep

Tome

1 .... 3.00

Worlds of H.P. Lovecraft: Dagon

Caliber

1 .... 3.00

Worlds of H.P. Lovecraft: The Alchemist

Tome

1 .... 3.00

Worlds of H.P. Lovecraft: The Music of Erich Zann

Caliber

1 .... 3.00

Worlds of H.P. Lovecraft: The Picture in the House

Caliber

1 .... 3.00

Worldstorm

DC, 2006

1 .... 3.00

Worlds Unknown

Marvel, 1973

1 .... 17.00
2 .... 10.00
3 .... 7.00
4-8 .... 5.00

World's Worst Comics Awards

Kitchen Sink, 1990

1-2 .... 3.00

World War II: 1946

Antarctic, 1999

1-12 .... 3.00

World War II: 1946/ Families of Altered Wars

Antarctic, 1998

1-2/2nd 4.00

World War III

Ace, 1953

1 .... 400.00
2 .... 350.00

World without End

DC, 1990

1-6 .... 3.00

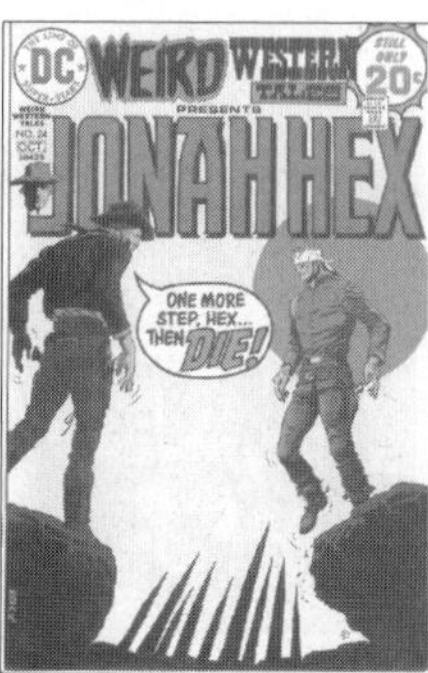

Weird Western Tales

Weird Worlds

Wendy Witch World

Werewolf By Night

Western Outlaws and Sheriffs

Western Roundup

Wetworks

Where Monsters Dwell

Wormwood Gentleman Corpse

Idea & Design Works, 2006

1-4 .... 4.00

Wormwood Gentleman Corpse: The Taster

Idea & Design Works, 2006

1 .... 4.00

Woron's Worlds

Illustration, 1993

1/A-3/B 3.00

Worst from Mad

E.C., 1958

nn 400.00
2 .... 300.00
3 .... 200.00
4 .... 175.00
5-6 .... 250.00
7-8 .... 175.00
9 .... 250.00
10-12 .... 175.00

Wow!

IPC, 1982

1-56 .... 0.00

Wow Comics

Fawcett, 1940

1 .... 13,800.00
2 .... 2,125.00
3 .... 1,200.00
4 .... 925.00
5 .... 560.00
6 .... 775.00
7-8 .... 610.00
9 .... 1,150.00
10 .... 610.00
11-15 .... 325.00
16-17 .... 260.00
18 .... 300.00
19-20 .... 260.00
21-30 .... 175.00
31-37 .... 115.00
38 .... 240.00
39-40 .... 115.00
41-50 .... 80.00
51-58 .... 66.00
59-60 .... 52.00
61-69 .... 42.00

W.O.W. The World of Ward

Allied American Artists

1 .... 4.00

Wraithborn

DC, 2005

1-5 .... 3.00
6 .... 4.00

Wraith

Outlander Comics Group, 1991

1-2 .... 2.00

Wrath

Malibu, 1994

1 .... 2.00
1/Ltd 3.00
2-9 .... 2.00
GS 1 .... 3.00

Wrath of the Spectre

DC, 1988

1-4 .... 3.00

Wretch

Caliber, 1997

1-4 .... 3.00

Wretch

Slave Labor, 1997

1-6 .... 3.00

Writers' Bloc Anthology

Writers' Bloc

1 .... 3.00

Wulf the Barbarian

Atlas-Seaboard, 1975

1 .... 12.00
2 .... 9.00
3-4 .... 8.00

Wu Wei

Angus

1-6 .... 3.00

WW 2

NEC, 2000

1-2 .... 4.00

WW2 Rommel

New England, 2005

1 .... 4.00

WWF: World Wrestling Foundation

Valiant

1-4 .... 3.00

WWW.

NBM

1 .... 11.00

Wyatt Earp

Marvel, 1955

1 .... 120.00
2 .... 70.00
3-10 .... 50.00
11-20 .... 42.00
21-29 .... 30.00
30-34 .... 5.00

Wyatt Earp

Dell, 1958

4-13 .... 30.00

Wyatt Earp: Dodge City

Moonstone, 2005

1-2 .... 3.00

Wyatt Earp, Frontier Marshal
Charlton, 1956
12 .... 35.00
13-18 .... 18.00
19 .... 40.00
☛Giant-sized
20-30 .... 14.00
31-40 .... 10.00
41-50 .... 8.00
51-72 .... 6.00

Wynonna Earp
Image, 1996
1-5 .... 3.00

Wyoming Territory
Ark, 1989
1 .... 2.00

Wyrd the Reluctant Warrior
Slave Labor, 1999
1-6 .... 3.00

X
Dark Horse, 1994
1-3 .... 3.00
4-7 .... 2.00
8-25 .... 3.00
Hero ed. 1 .... 1.00

X-Men: Colossus: Bloodline
Marvel, 2005
1-5 .... 3.00

X-Men: Kitty Pryde: Shadow & Flame
Marvel, 2005
1-5 .... 3.00

X-Men: The 198
Marvel, 2006
1-5 .... 3.00

Xanadu
Thoughts & Images, 1988
1-5 .... 2.00

Xanadu
3-D Zone, 1986
1-4 .... 2.00

Xanadu: Across Diamond Seas
Mu, 1994
1-5 .... 3.00

Xanadu Color Special
Eclipse, 1988
1 .... 2.00

Xander in Lost Universe (Gene Roddenberry's...)
Tekno, 1995
0-8 .... 2.00

Xanth Graphic Novel
Father Tree, 1990
1 .... 10.00

X-Babies: Murderama
Marvel, 1998
1 .... 3.00

X-Babies: Reborn
Marvel, 2000
1 .... 4.00

X-Calibre
Marvel, 1995
1-4 .... 2.00

Xena
Brainstorm, 1995
1 .... 3.00

Xena: Warrior Princess
Topps, 1997
0-1 .... 3.00
1/A 4.00
1/Variant 4.00
2 .... 3.00
2/Variant 4.00

Xena: Warrior Princess
Dark Horse, 1999
1-14/Variant 3.00

Xena: Warrior Princess: And the Original Olympics
Topps, 1998
1-3 .... 3.00

Xena: Warrior Princess: Bloodlines
Topps, 1998
1-2 .... 3.00

Xena: Warrior Princess/ Joxer: Warrior Prince
Topps, 1997
1-3/Variant 3.00

Xena: Warrior Princess: The Dragon's Teeth
Topps, 1997
1-3/Variant 3.00

Xena: Warrior Princess: The Orpheus Trilogy
Topps, 1998
1-3/Variant 3.00

Xena: Warrior Princess: The Warrior Way of Death
Dark Horse, 1999
1-2/Variant 3.00

Xena: Warrior Princess vs. Callisto
Topps, 1998
1 .... 3.00
1/A 5.00
1/Variant-3/Variant 3.00

Whiteout

Whiz Comics

Why I Hate Saturn

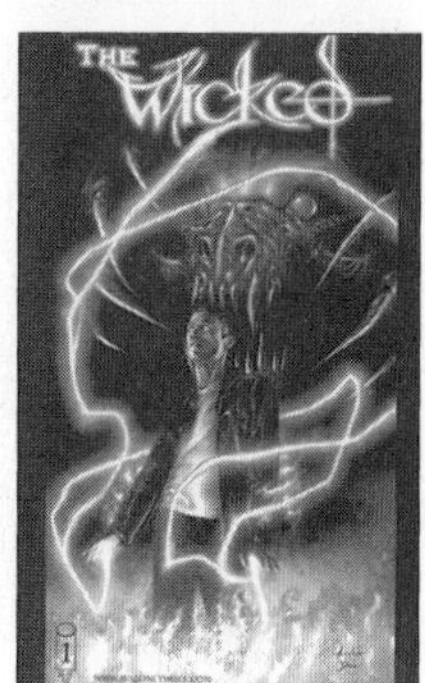

Wicked

Wilbur

Wild

Wild Bill Pecos

Wildcards

Xena, Warrior Princess: Wrath of Hera
Topps, 1998

1-2/Variant 3.00

Xena: Warrior Princess, Year One
Topps, 1998

1 .... 5.00
1/Gold 10.00

X-Men: Days of Future Past
Marvcl, 2004

1 .... 20.00

Xene
Eyeball Soup Designs, 1996

1-4 .... 5.00

Xenobrood
DC, 1994

0-6 .... 2.00

Xeno-Men
Blackthorne, 1987

1 .... 2.00

Xenon
Eclipse, 1987

1-23 .... 2.00

Xeno's Arrow
Cup o' Tea, 1999

1-4 .... 3.00

Xenotech
Mirage, 1994

1-3 .... 3.00

Xenozoic Tales
Kitchen Sink, 1987

1 .... 8.00
1/2nd 3.00
2-5 .... 6.00
6-10 .... 5.00
11-14 .... 4.00

Xenya
Sanctuary, 1994

1-3 .... 3.00

Xero
DC, 1997

1-12 .... 2.00

X-Factor
Marvel, 1986

25-2-86 .... 0.00
-1 .... 2.00
1 .... 3.00
2-4 .... 2.00
5 .... 3.00
6 .... 5.00
7 .... 3.00
8-22 .... 2.00
23 .... 5.00
24 .... 8.00
25-49 .... 2.00
50-53 .... 3.00
54-59 .... 2.00
60 .... 3.00
60/2nd 2.00
61-69 .... 3.00
70-91 .... 2.00
92 .... 4.00
93-100 .... 2.00
100/Variant 3.00
101-106 .... 2.00
106/Variant 3.00
107-124 .... 2.00
125 .... 3.00
126-129 .... 2.00
130 .... 3.00
131-149 .... 2.00
Ann 1-6 .... 3.00
Ann 7 .... 2.00
Ann 8-9 .... 3.00

X-Factor
Marvel, 2002

1-4 .... 3.00

X-Factor: Prisoner of Love
Marvel, 1990

1 .... 5.00

X-Factor
Marvel, 2006

1 .... 7.00
2-7 .... 3.00
8 .... 8.00
9-24 .... 3.00
25-26 .... 6.00
27-50 .... 3.00

X-Farce
Eclipse, 1992

1 .... 3.00

X-Farce vs. X-Cons: X-tinction
Parody, 1993

1-1.5 .... 3.00

X-51
Marvel, 1999

0 .... 1.00
1-12 .... 2.00

X-Files
Topps, 1995

-2–1 .... 10.00
0/A-0/C 4.00
½ 10.00
1 .... 8.00
1/2nd 3.00
2 .... 5.00
3 .... 4.00
3/2nd 3.00
4 .... 4.00
4/2nd-33 .... 3.00
33/Variant 5.00
34-41/Variant 3.00
Ann 1-Ashcan 1 .... 4.00
Special 1-5 .... 5.00

X-Files (Magazine)
Manga, 1996

1 .... 4.00
2-23 .... 3.00

X-Files Comics Digest
Topps, 1995

1-3 .... 4.00

X-Files Ground Zero
Topps, 1997

1-4 .... 3.00

X-Files: Season One
Topps, 1997

1-9 .... 5.00

X-Files: Afterflight
Topps, 1997

1 .... 6.00

X-Flies Bug Hunt
Twist and Shout, 1996

1-4 .... 3.00

X-Flies Conspiracy
Twist and Shout, 1996

1 .... 3.00

X-Flies Special
Twist and Shout, 1995

1 .... 3.00

X-Force
Marvel, 1991

-1-1/2nd 2.00
2 .... 3.00
3-24 .... 2.00
25 .... 3.00
26-30 .... 2.00
31-33 .... 1.00
34-38 .... 2.00
38/Variant 3.00
39-49/Deluxe 2.00
50 .... 3.00
50/A 4.00
50/Variant-98 .... 2.00
99 .... 3.00
100-129 .... 2.00
Ann 1-Ann 3 .... 3.00
Ann 1995 .... 4.00
Ann 1996-1997 .... 3.00
Ann 1998-1999 .... 4.00

X-Force
Marvel, 2004

1 .... 4.00
2-6 .... 3.00

X-Force: Shatterstar
Marvel, 2005

1-4 .... 3.00

X-Force/Youngblood
Marvel, 1996

1 .... 5.00

XIII
Alias, 2005

1 .... 1.00
2-5 .... 3.00

Ximos: Violent Past
Triumphant, 1994

1-2 .... 3.00

Xiola
Xero, 1994

0-3 .... 2.00
Ashcan 1 .... 1.00

XL
Blackthorne

1 .... 4.00

X-Lax
Thwack! Pow!

1 .... 1.00

X-Man
Marvel, 1995

-1 .... 2.00
1 .... 3.00
1/2nd 2.00
2-4 .... 3.00
5-14 .... 2.00
15 .... 3.00
16-24 .... 2.00
25 .... 3.00
26-74 .... 2.00
75 .... 3.00
Ann 1996-1998 .... 4.00

X-Man: All Saints' Day
Marvel, 1997

1 .... 6.00

Xmas Comics
Fawcett, 1941

1 .... 2,600.00
2 .... 1,100.00

Xmas Comics
Fawcett, 1949

4 .... 550.00
5-7 .... 375.00

X-Men
Marvel, 1963

1 .... 7,000.00
☛1st X-Men
2 .... 1,900.00
3 .... 1,030.00
4 .... 900.00
5 .... 550.00
6 .... 500.00
7 .... 475.00
8-10 .... 360.00
11 .... 300.00
12 .... 500.00
☛1st Juggernaut
13 .... 275.00
14 .... 250.00
15-16 .... 190.00

WildC.A.T.s

Wildcore

Wild Dog

Wild Frontier

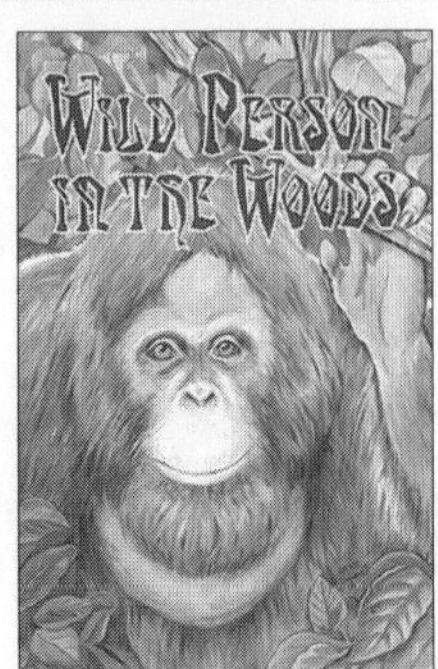

Wild Person in the Woods

Wildstar

WildStorm Rising

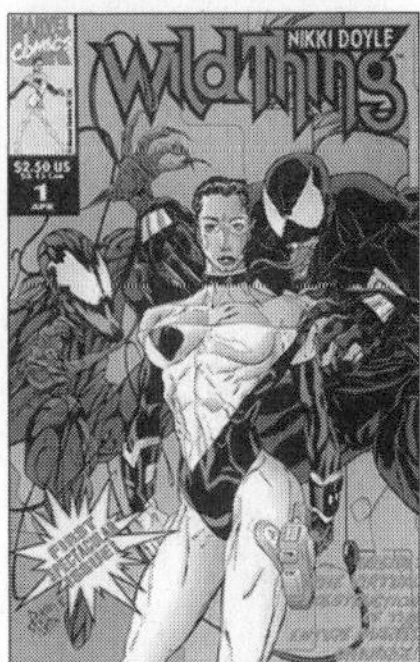

Wild Thing

17-20 .... 100.00
21-27 .... 90.00
28 .... 155.00
☛1st Banshee
28/2nd 2.00
29-34 .... 90.00
35 .... 150.00
☛Spider-Man appearance
36-37 .... 65.00
38 .... 80.00
39-40 .... 90.00
41-48 .... 65.00
49-51 .... 75.00
52 .... 65.00
53-57 .... 72.00
58 .... 100.00
☛1st Havok
59-62 .... 70.00
62/2nd 2.00
63 .... 70.00
63/2nd 2.00
64-65 .... 70.00
66 .... 80.00
☛Last new issue
67-80 .... 35.00
81-85 .... 40.00
86-93 .... 35.00
94 .... 500.00
☛2nd New X-Men
95 .... 85.00
☛Thunderbird dies
96 .... 55.00
97-98 .... 48.00
98/30¢ 125.00
99 .... 48.00
99/30¢ 125.00
100 .... 60.00
☛Phoenix origin starts
100/30¢ 135.00
101 .... 55.00
☛Phoenix origin
102-105 .... 28.00
105/35¢ 60.00
106 .... 28.00
106/35¢ 60.00
107 .... 28.00
107/35¢ 60.00
108 .... 35.00
☛1st Byrne X-Men
109 .... 30.00
☛1st Weapon alpha
110-115 .... 20.00
116-119 .... 16.00
☛1st Alpha Flight
120-121 .... 28.00
122-128 .... 12.00
129 .... 20.00
☛1st Kitty, Emma Frost
130-135 .... 12.00
136 .... 11.00
137 .... 14.00
☛Phoenix dies
138 .... 8.00
139-141 .... 11.00
☛Future Past

X-Men

Marvel, 1991

-1 .... 3.00
-1/A 4.00
1/Beast 5.00
1/Colossus 3.00
1/Cyclops 4.00
1/Magneto 3.00
1/Collector's 5.00
2 .... 4.00
3-20 .... 3.00
21-24 .... 2.00
25 .... 5.00
25/Gold 25.00
25/Ltd 30.00
26-29 .... 2.00
30 .... 3.00
31-49 .... 2.00
50 .... 3.00
50/Variant 4.00
51-54 .... 2.00
54/Silver 25.00
55-62 .... 2.00
62/A 3.00
63-79 .... 2.00
80 .... 3.00
80/Holofoil 10.00
80/DF 7.00
81-98 .... 2.00
99-100/G 3.00
101-104 .... 2.00
105 .... 3.00
106-113 .... 2.00
114 .... 5.00
115-144 .... 2.00
145-147 .... 3.00
148 .... 2.00
149 .... 3.00
150 .... 4.00
151 .... 3.00
152 .... 2.00
153-156 .... 3.00
157-158 .... 2.00
159 .... 3.00
160-164 .... 2.00
165 .... 3.00
166-169 .... 2.00
170-220 .... 3.00
Ann 11-3 .... 3.00
Ann 1995 .... 4.00
Ann 1996-1998 .... 3.00
Ann 1999-2001 .... 4.00
Ashcan 1 .... 1.00

X-Men Adventures

Marvel, 1992

1 .... 3.00
2-15 .... 2.00

X-Men Adventures
Marvel, 1994

1 ... 2.00
2-8 ... 1.00
9-13 ... 2.00

X-Men Adventures
Marvel, 1995

1-13 ... 2.00

X-Men: Age of Apocalypse
Marvel, 2005

0 ... 4.00

X-Men: Age of Apocalypse
Marvel, 2005

1 ... 4.00
2-6 ... 3.00

X-Men Alpha
Marvel, 1995

1 ... 3.00
1/Gold ... 20.00

X-Men/Alpha Flight
Marvel, 1985

1-2 ... 3.00

X-Men/Alpha Flight
Marvel, 1998

1-2 ... 3.00

X-Men/Alpha Flight: The Gift
Marvel, 1998

1 ... 4.00

X-Men and Power Pack
Marvel, 2005

1-4 ... 3.00

X-Men & The Micronauts
Marvel, 1984

1 ... 3.00
2-3 ... 2.00
4 ... 1.00

X-Men Animation Special: The Pryde of the X-Men
Marvel, 1990

1 ... 11.00

X-Men Anniversary Magazine
Marvel, 1993

1 ... 4.00

X-Men: Apocalypse vs. Dracula
Marvel, 2006

1-4 ... 3.00

X-Men Archives
Marvel, 1995

1-4 ... 3.00

X-Men Archives Featuring Captain Britain
Marvel, 1995

1-7 ... 3.00

X-Men Archives Sketchbook
Marvel, 2000

1 ... 3.00

X-Men at the State Fair
Marvel

1 ... 2.00

X-Men: Books of the Askani
Marvel, 1995

1 ... 3.00

X-Men: Children of the Atom
Marvel, 1999

1-6 ... 3.00

X-Men Chromium Classics: Days of Future Past
Marvel

1 ... 14.00

X-Men Chromium Classics: Death of the Phoenix
Marvel

1 ... 14.00
1/A ... 30.00

X-Men Chromium Classics: Origin of the X-Men
Marvel

1 ... 14.00

X-Men Chronicles
Fantaco, 1981

1 ... 2.00

X-Men Chronicles
Marvel, 1995

1-2 ... 4.00

X-Men: Clandestine
Marvel, 1996

1-2 ... 3.00

X-Men Classic
Marvel, 1990

46-110 ... 2.00

X-Men Classics
Marvel, 1983

1-3 ... 4.00

X-Men Collector's Edition
Marvel

2 ... 1.00

X-Men: Deadly Genesis
Marvel, 2006

1 ... 6.00
1/Quesada ... 14.00
1/Hairsine ... 7.00
2-6 ... 4.00

Will Eisner Presents

Will to Power

Wings Comics

Wish

Witchblade

Witches

Witching Hour

Witty Comics

X-Men: Declassified
Marvel, 2000
1 ....4.00

X-Men: Earthfall
Marvel, 1996
1 ....3.00

X-Men: Evolution
Marvel, 2002
1-9 ....2.00

X-Men: Fairy Tales
Marvel, 2006
1-4 ....3.00

X-Men/Fantastic Four
Marvel, 2005
1-5 ....4.00

X-Men: First Class
Marvel, 2006
1-4 ....3.00

X-Men Firsts
Marvel, 1996
1 ....5.00

X-Men Forever
Marvel, 2001
1/A 0.00
1-6 ....4.00

X-Men: God Loves, Man Kills – Special Edition
Marvel, 2003
1 ....5.00

X-Men: Hellfire Club
Marvel, 2000
1-4 ....3.00

X-Men in the Savage Land
Marvel
1 ....7.00

X-Men: Liberators
Marvel, 1998
1 ....3.00
1/Ltd. 20.00
2-4 ....3.00

X-Men: Lost Tales
Marvel, 1997
1-2 ....3.00

X-Men: Messiah Complex
Marvel, 2007
1 ....4.00

X-Men: Millennial Visions
Marvel, 2000
1-1/A 4.00

X-Men Movie Adaptation
Marvel, 2000
1 ....6.00

X-Men Movie Premiere Prequel Edition
Marvel, 2000
1 ....2.00

X-Men Movie Prequel: Magneto
Marvel, 2000
1 ....6.00

X-Men Movie Prequel: Rogue
Marvel, 2000
1-1/Variant 6.00

X-Men Movie Prequel: Wolverine
Marvel, 2000
1-1/Variant 6.00

X-Men Mutant Search R.U. 1?
Marvel, 1998
1 ....2.00

X-Men Omega
Marvel, 1995
1 ....6.00
1/Gold 25.00

X-Men: Phoenix
Marvel, 1999
1 ....4.00
2-3 ....3.00

X-Men: Phoenix – Endsong
Marvel, 2005
1 ....8.00
☛Green costume
1/Variant-2 ....6.00
2/Variant 5.00
☛Green costume
3 ....4.00
4-5 ....5.00

X-Men: Phoenix – Legacy of Fire
Marvel, 2003
1-3 ....3.00

X-Men: Phoenix – Warsong
Marvel, 2006
1-4 ....3.00

X-Men Poster Magazine
Marvel, 1994
1-4 ....5.00

X-Men Prime
Marvel, 1995
1 ....5.00

X-Men Rarities
Marvel, 1995
1 ....6.00

X-Men: Road to Onslaught
Marvel, 1996
1 .... 3.00

X-Men: Ronin
Marvel, 2003
1 .... 4.00
2-5 .... 3.00

X-Men Special Edition
Marvel, 1983
1 .... 5.00

X-Men Spotlight On... Starjammers
Marvel, 1990
1-2 .... 5.00

X-Men: Survival Guide to the Mansion
Marvel, 1993
1 .... 7.00

X-Men: The Early Years
Marvel, 1994
1 .... 3.00
2-16 .... 2.00
17 .... 3.00

X-Men: The End - Dreamers and Demons
Marvel, 2004
1 .... 4.00
2-6 .... 3.00

X-Men: The End - Heroes & Martyrs
Marvel, 2005
1-6 .... 3.00

X-Men: The End - Men and X-Men
Marvel, 2006
1-6 .... 3.00

X-Men: The Hidden Years
Marvel, 1999
1 .... 4.00
2-22 .... 3.00

X-Men: The Magneto War
Marvel, 1999
1 .... 3.00

X-Men: The Manga
Marvel, 1998
1-15 .... 3.00
16-26 .... 4.00

X-Men: The Movie Special
Marvel, 2000
1 .... 1.00

X-Men: The 198 Files
Marvel, 2006
1 .... 4.00

X-Men: The Search for Cyclops
Marvel, 2000
3/A-4 .... 3.00

X-Men: The Ultra Collection
Marvel, 1994
1-5 .... 3.00

X-Men: The Wedding Album
Marvel, 1994
1 .... 3.00

X-Men: True Friends
Marvel, 1999
1-3 .... 3.00

X-Men 2 Movie
Marvel, 2003
1 .... 4.00

X-Men 2 Movie Prequel: Nightcrawler
Marvel, 2003
1 .... 4.00

X-Men 2 Movie Prequel: Wolverine
Marvel, 2003
1 .... 4.00

X-Men 2099
Marvel, 1993
1 .... 2.00
1/Gold 3.00
1/2nd-5 .... 2.00
6-7 .... 1.00
8-24 .... 2.00
25 .... 3.00
25/Variant 4.00
26-35 .... 2.00
Special 1 .... 4.00

X-Men 2099: Oasis
Marvel, 1996
1 .... 6.00

X-Men Ultra III Preview
Marvel, 1995
1 .... 3.00

X-Men Universe
Marvel, 1999
1-11 .... 5.00
12-17 .... 4.00

X-Men Universe: Past, Present and Future
Marvel, 1999
1 .... 3.00

X-Men Unlimited
Marvel, 1993
1-31 .... 3.00
32-43 .... 4.00
44-50 .... 3.00

Wizard Works

Wolfpack

Wonderland

Woodsy Owl

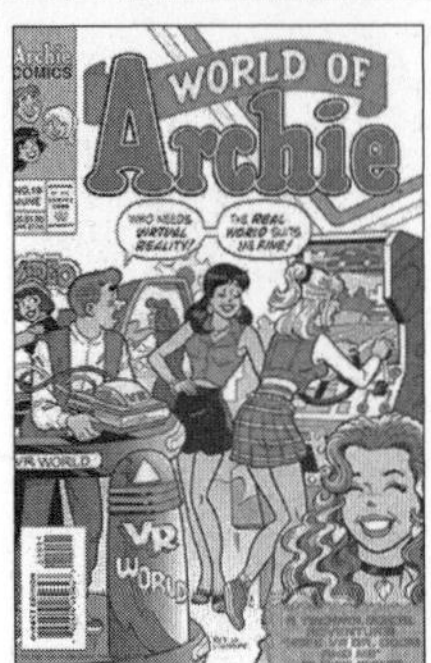

World of Archie

World of Smallville

World of Wheels

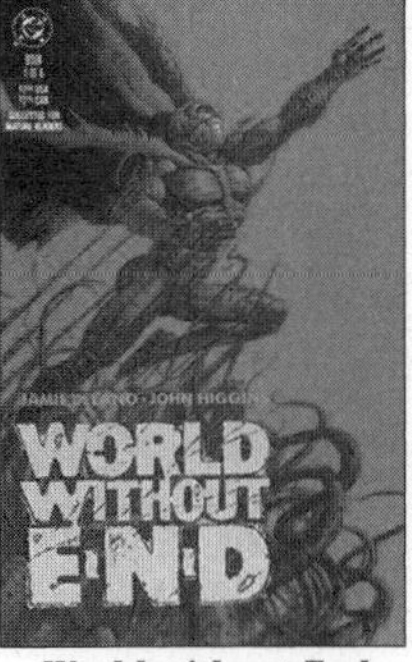

World without End

X-Men Unlimited

Marvel, 2004

1-14 .... 3.00

X-Men vs. Dracula

Marvel, 1993

1 .... 2.00

X-Men Vs. Exiles

Malibu, 1995

0 .... 3.00
0/Gold 5.00

X-Men vs. the Avengers

Marvel, 1987

1 .... 4.00
2-4 .... 3.00

X-Men vs. the Brood

Marvel, 1996

1-2 .... 3.00

X-Men/WildC.A.T.S: The Dark Age

Marvel, 1998

1/A-1/B 5.00

X-Men: Wrath of Apocalypse

Marvel, 1996

1 .... 5.00

X-Men: Year of the Mutants Collector's Preview

Marvel, 1995

1 .... 2.00

X-Nation 2099

Marvel, 1996

1 .... 4.00
2-6 .... 2.00

X/1999

Viz, 1996

1-6 .... 3.00

X-O Manowar

Valiant, 1992

0.5/GO-Dlx 1/HC 0.00
0 .... 2.00
0/Gold 35.00
½ 8.00
½/Gold 55.00
1 .... 7.00
2-4 .... 6.00
5 .... 5.00
6 .... 4.00
7-8 .... 3.00
9 .... 2.00
10-15 .... 1.00
15/Pink 8.00
16-27 .... 1.00
28 .... 2.00
29-35 .... 1.00
36 .... 2.00
37-41 .... 1.00
42-54 .... 2.00
55-62 .... 3.00
63-65 .... 4.00
66 .... 5.00
67 .... 7.00
68 .... 12.00
YB 1 .... 4.00

X-O Manowar

Acclaim, 1996

1-21 .... 3.00
Ashcan 1 .... 1.00

X-O Database

Valiant, 1993

1 .... 4.00
1/VVSS 30.00

X-O Manowar/Iron Man: In Heavy Metal

Acclaim, 1996

1 .... 3.00

Xombi

DC, 1994

0 .... 3.00
1 .... 2.00
1/Platinum 3.00
2-13 .... 2.00
14-16 .... 3.00
17 .... 1.00
18-20 .... 3.00
21 .... 4.00

X: One Shot to the Head

Dark Horse, 1994

1 .... 3.00

X-Patrol

Marvel, 1996

1 .... 2.00

X-Presidents

Random House, 2000

1 .... 13.00

X-Ray Comics

Slave Labor, 1998

1-3 .... 3.00

XSE

Marvel, 1996

1 .... 2.00
1/A 3.00
2-4 .... 2.00

Xstacy: The First Look Edition

Fresco

1 .... 3.00

Xstacy: The Libretto

Fresco

1 .... 3.00

X-Statix

Marvel, 2002

1 .... 3.00
2-7 .... 2.00
8-26 .... 3.00

X-Statix Presents Dead Girl
Marvel, 2006

1-5 .... 3.00

X-Terminators
Marvel, 1988

1-4 .... 2.00

X Man With X-Ray Eyes
Gold Key, 1963

1 .... 50.00

X-Treme X-Men
Marvel, 2001

1-35 .... 3.00
36-39 .... 4.00
40-46 .... 3.00
Ann 2001 .... 5.00

X-Treme X-Men: Savage Land
Marvel, 2001

1-4 .... 3.00

X-Treme X-Men X-pose
Marvel, 2003

1-2 .... 3.00

X-TV
Comic Zone, 1998

1-2 .... 3.00

X-23
Marvel, 2005

1 .... 7.00
1/Variant 3.00
2 .... 4.00
2/Variant 6.00
3 .... 5.00
4 .... 4.00
5 .... 3.00

X-23: Target X
Marvel, 2007

1-2 .... 3.00

X-Universe
Marvel, 1995

1-2 .... 4.00

X-Venture
Victory, 1947

1-2 .... 2.00

XXXenophile
Palliard, 1989

1 .... 8.00
1/2nd-1/3rd 3.00
2 .... 5.00
2/2nd 3.00
3 .... 4.00
3/2nd 3.00
4 .... 4.00
4/2nd-10 .... 3.00
11 .... 4.00

XXXenophile Presents
Palliard, 1992

1-4 .... 3.00

XXX Women
Fantagraphics

1-4 .... 3.00

XYZ Comics
Kitchen Sink, 1972

1 .... 25.00
1/2nd 12.00
1/3rd 8.00
1/4th-1/5th 6.00
1/6th 5.00
1/7th 3.00

Y2K: The Comic
NEC, 1999

1 .... 4.00

Yahoo
Fantagraphics, 1988

1 .... 3.00
2-3 .... 2.00
4-6 .... 3.00

Yakuza
Eternity, 1987

1-4 .... 2.00

Yamara
Steve Jackson Games

1 .... 10.00

Yang
Charlton, 1973

1 .... 9.00
2-13 .... 5.00
15-17 .... 3.00

Yankee Comics
Harry A. Chesler, 1941

1 .... 1,025.00
2 .... 570.00
3 .... 415.00
4 .... 310.00
4/A 55.00
5 .... 40.00

Yarn Man
Kitchen Sink, 1989

1 .... 2.00

Yattering and Jack
Eclipse

1 .... 10.00

Yawn
Parody, 1992

1-1/2nd 3.00

Yeah!
DC, 1999

1-8 .... 3.00

Year in Review: Spider-Man
Marvel, 2000

1 .... 3.00

Wrath

Wrath of the Spectre

Wulf the Barbarian

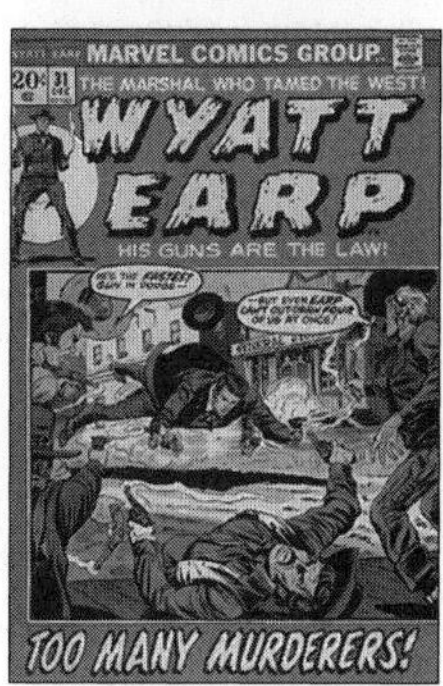

Wyatt Earp

X

X-Calibre

Xenon

Xenozoic Tales

Year of the Monkey (Aaron Warner's...)
Image, 1997

1-2 .... 3.00

Year One: Batman/Ra's al Ghul
DC, 2005

1-2 .... 6.00

Year One: Batman-Scarecrow
DC, 2005

1-2 .... 6.00

Yellow Claw
Atlas, 1956

1 .... 850.00
2 .... 675.00
3 .... 625.00
4 .... 550.00

Yellow Dog Comix
Print Mint, 1968

1 .... 50.00
2 .... 30.00
3-9/10 .... 25.00
11/12 .... 20.00
13/14 .... 30.00
15-25 .... 15.00

Yellowjacket Comics
Frank, 1944

1 .... 450.00
2 .... 350.00
3-5 .... 225.00
6 .... 300.00
7 .... 750.00
8-10 .... 250.00

Yellow Jar
NBM

1 .... 13.00

Yellow Submarine
Gold Key, 1969

1 .... 110.00

Yenny
Alias, 2005

1 .... 5.00
1/Variant 3.00

Yikes! (Weissman)
Weissman, 1995

1-5 .... 3.00

Yikes! (Alternative)
Alternative, 1997

1-2 .... 3.00

Yin Fei the Chinese Ninja
Dr. Leung's, 1988

1-8 .... 2.00

Yogi Bear
Dell, 1961

4-9 .... 40.00
10-11 .... 55.00
12 .... 30.00
13 .... 55.00
14-20 .... 30.00
21-31 .... 20.00
32-42 .... 15.00

Yogi Bear
Charlton, 1970

1 .... 22.00
2-3 .... 15.00
4-6 .... 12.00
7 .... 15.00
8-10 .... 12.00
11-20 .... 8.00
21-35 .... 6.00

Yogi Bear
Marvel, 1977

1 .... 6.00
2-5 .... 4.00
6-9 .... 3.00

Yogi Bear
Harvey, 1992

1 .... 2.00
2-6 .... 1.00

Yogi Bear
Archie, 1997

1 .... 2.00

Yogi Bear Big Book
Harvey, 1992

1-2 .... 2.00

Yogi Bear Giant Size
Harvey, 1992

1-2 .... 2.00

Yogi Berra Baseball Hero
Fawcett, 1951

1 .... 550.00

Yosemite Sam
Gold Key, 1970

1 .... 35.00
2-5 .... 20.00
6-10 .... 15.00
11-20 .... 10.00
21-50 .... 4.00
51-65 .... 3.00
66-67 .... 8.00
68 .... 20.00
69-70 .... 17.00
71-78 .... 10.00
79-81 .... 17.00

Yotsuba!
ADV Manga, 2005

1-3 .... 10.00

You and Your Big Mouth
Fantagraphics, 1993

1-4 .... 3.00

You Are Here
DC

1 ... 20.00

You Can Draw Manga
Antarctic, 2004

1-12 ... 5.00

Young Hearts
Marvel, 1949

1-2 ... 60.00

Young Allies Comics
Timely, 1941

1 ... 11,500.00
2 ... 3,000.00
3 ... 2,100.00
4 ... 3,000.00
5 ... 1,300.00
6-8 ... 875.00
9 ... 900.00
10 ... 875.00
11-14 ... 720.00
15-20 ... 615.00

Young All-Stars
DC, 1987

1-3 ... 3.00
4-31 ... 2.00
Ann 1 ... 3.00

Young Avengers
Marvel, 2005

1 ... 10.00
1/DirCut ... 6.00
1/Conv ... 15.00
2 ... 7.00
3 ... 4.00
4-12 ... 3.00

Young Avengers Special
Marvel, 2006

1 ... 3.00

Youngblood
Image, 1992

0 ... 2.00
0/Gold ... 4.00
1 ... 3.00
1/2nd ... 2.00
2-4 ... 3.00
5 ... 2.00
6 ... 4.00
7-10 ... 3.00
SS 1 ... 4.00
YB 1 ... 3.00

Youngblood
Image, 1995

1-15 ... 3.00

Youngblood
Awesome, 1998

1/A-1/L ... 3.00
1/M ... 4.00
1/N-2 ... 3.00

Youngblood Battlezone
Image, 1993

1 ... 2.00
2 ... 3.00

Youngblood: Bloodsport
Arcade, 2003

1 ... 4.00
1/Park-1/Variant ... 3.00

Youngblood: Strikefile
Image, 1993

1-11 ... 3.00

Youngblood/X-Force
Image, 1996

1/A-1/C ... 5.00

Young Brides
Prize, 1952

1 ... 175.00
2 ... 100.00
3-6 ... 90.00
7-18 ... 85.00
19-21 ... 25.00
22-25 ... 20.00
26 ... 75.00
27-28 ... 20.00
29-30 ... 30.00

Youngbroads: Stripfile
Parody, 1994

1 ... 3.00

Youngbrother
Multicultural, 1994

1 ... 2.00

Young Bug
Zoo Arsonist, 1996

1-3 ... 3.00

Young Cynics Club
Dark Horse, 1993

1 ... 3.00

Young Death
Fleetway-Quality, 1992

1-3 ... 3.00

Young Dracula
Caliber, 1993

1-3 ... 4.00

Young Dracula: Prayer of the Vampire
Boneyard, 1997

1-4 ... 3.00

Young Eagle
Fawcett, 1950

1 ... 105.00
2 ... 55.00
3-6 ... 50.00
7-10 ... 45.00

Young Eagle
Charlton, 1956

3-5 ... 40.00

Xero

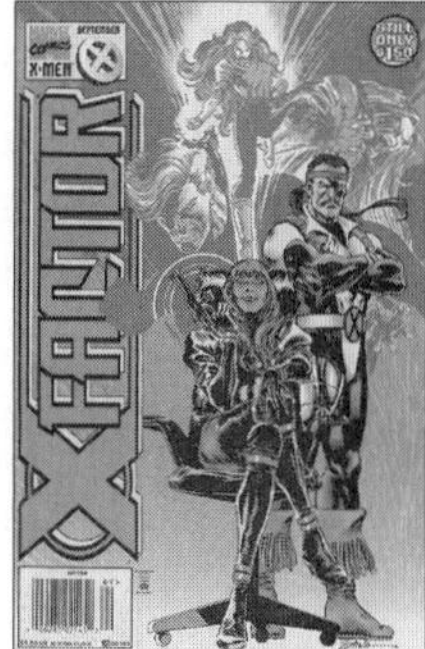

X-Factor

X-Farce

X-Force

X-Man

X-Men Alpha

X-Men Classic

X-Men Forever

Young Girl on Girl: Passion and Fashion

Angel

1 ....3.00
1/Nude 4.00

Young Gun

AC

1 ....3.00

Young Guns 2004 Sketch Book

Marvel, 2005

1 ....4.00

Young Guns Reloaded Sketchbook

Marvel, 2007

1 ....4.00

Young Hero

AC, 1989

1-2 ....3.00

Young Heroes in Love

DC, 1997

1 ....2.00
1/Ltd. 6.00
2-16 ....2.00
17-1000000 ....3.00

Young Indiana Jones Chronicles

Dark Horse, 1992

1-12 ....3.00

Young Indiana Jones Chronicles

Hollywood, 1992

1-3 ....3.00

Young Justice

DC, 1998

1 ....4.00
2-49 ....3.00
50 ....4.00
51-55 ....3.00
1000000 ....4.00
GS 1 ....5.00

Young Justice in No Man's Land

DC, 1999

1 ....4.00

Young Justice: Our Worlds At War

DC, 2001

1 ....3.00

Young Justice Secret Files

DC, 1999

1 ....5.00

Young Justice: Sins of Youth

DC, 2000

1-2 ....3.00

Young Justice: The Secret

DC, 1998

1 ....2.00

Young King Cole Vol. 1

Novelty, 1945

1 ....200.00
2-4 ....100.00

Young King Cole Vol. 2

Novelty, 1946

1 ....200.00
2-7 ....100.00

Young King Cole Vol. 3

Novelty, 1947

1 ....150.00
2-12 ....80.00

Young Lawyers

Dell, 1971

1-2 ....10.00

Young Love

Crestwood, 1949

1 ....200.00
2 ....100.00
3 ....80.00
4-5 ....65.00
6-10 ....52.00
11-20 ....45.00
21-30 ....36.00
31-40 ....26.00
41-50 ....20.00
51-60 ....18.00
61-70 ....14.00
71-73 ....12.00

Young Love

DC, 1963

39 ....30.00
40-50 ....24.00
51-70 ....20.00
71-90 ....14.00
91-100 ....10.00
101-106 ....7.00
107 ....25.00
108-114 ....20.00
115-126 ....12.00

Young Lovers

Charlton, 1957

16-17 ....80.00
18 ....400.00

Young Lovers

Avalon

1 ....3.00

Young Lust

Print Mint, 1970

1 .... 5.00
2-8 .... 3.00

Young Master

New Comics, 1987

1-9 .... 2.00

Young Men

Marvel, 1950

4 .... 120.00
5-10 .... 70.00
11-23 .... 52.00
24 .... 1,600.00
☛Cap, Namor origin
25 .... 775.00
25/2nd 2.00
26-28 .... 750.00

Young Rebels

Dell, 1971

1 .... 15.00

Young Romance

Prize, 1947

1 .... 325.00
2 .... 200.00
3-5 .... 150.00
6-10 .... 125.00
11-20 .... 95.00
21-30 .... 75.00
31-40 .... 60.00
41-48 .... 55.00
49-51 .... 24.00
52-60 .... 55.00
61-71 .... 45.00
72-77 .... 16.00
78-90 .... 40.00
91-92 .... 35.00
93-94 .... 15.00
95-97 .... 35.00
98 .... 15.00
99 .... 35.00
100 .... 15.00
101 .... 12.00
102-104 .... 30.00
105-124 .... 14.00

Young Romance

DC, 1963

125 .... 42.00
126-140 .... 18.00
141-150 .... 15.00
151-159 .... 12.00
160-170 .... 10.00
171-197 .... 9.00
198-201 .... 20.00
202-208 .... 8.00

Youngspud

Spoof, 1992

1 .... 3.00

Young Witches

Fantagraphics, 1991

1-4 .... 3.00

Young Witches III: Empire of Sin

Fantagraphics, 1993

1-3 .... 3.00

Young Witches VI: Wrath of Agatha

Fantagraphics

1-2 .... 4.00

Young Witches IV: The Eternal Dream

Fantagraphics, 1993

1-3 .... 3.00

Young Witches: London Babylon

Fantagraphics, 1992

1-6 .... 4.00

Young Zen: City of Death

Express

1 .... 3.00

Young Zen Intergalactic Ninja

Express

1 .... 4.00
2 .... 3.00

Your Big Book of Big Bang Comics

Image, 1998

1 .... 11.00

You're Under Arrest!

Dark Horse, 1995

1-8 .... 3.00

Your Hytone Comix

Apex Novelties, 1971

1 .... 8.00

Your United States

Lloyd Jacquet Studios, 1946

1 .... 25.00

Youthful Hearts

Youthful, 1952

1 .... 180.00
2-3 .... 150.00

Youthful Romances

Pix Parade, 1949

1 .... 150.00
2-6 .... 100.00
7-14 .... 80.00

Youthful Romances

Ribage, 1953

15-18 .... 70.00
5-8 .... 60.00

X-Men Omega

X-Men Prime

X-Men Special Edition

X-Men Universe

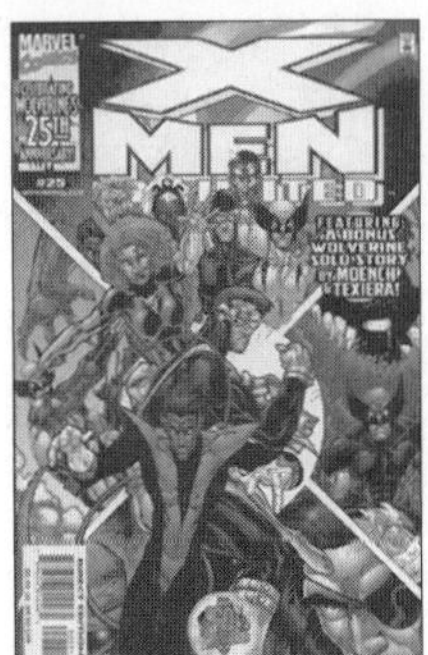
X-Men Unlimited

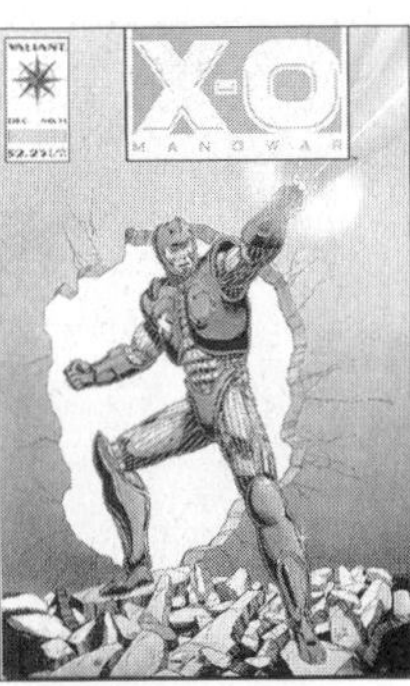
X-O Manowar

Xombi

X-Statix

Y's Guys
October, 1999

1 ....3.00

Y: The Last Man
DC, 2002

1 ....30.00
2 ....15.00
3 ....5.00
4-5 ....4.00
6-52 ....3.00

Yuggoth Cultures (Alan Moore's)
Avatar, 2003

1-3 ....4.00

Yu-Gi-Oh!
Viz, 2000

1 ....8.00

Yu-Gi-Oh!: Duelist
Viz, 2005

1-9 ....8.00

Yummy Fur
Vortex, 1986

1 ....6.00
2 ....5.00
3-5 ....4.00
6-32 ....3.00

Yuppies from Hell
Marvel

1 ....3.00

Yuppies, Rednecks and Lesbian Bitches From Mars
Fantagraphics, 1997

1-7 ....3.00

Yuri Monogatari
-Ism, 2005

1 ....15.00

YuYu Hakusho
Viz, 2003

1-8 ....8.00

Z
Keystone Graphics, 1994

1-3 ....3.00

Zago
Fox, 1948

1 ....525.00
2-3 ....410.00
4 ....305.00

Zaibatsu Tears
Limelight, 2000

1-3 ....3.00

Zane Grey's Stories of the West
Dell, 1955

27 ....50.00
28-35 ....45.00
36-39 ....40.00

Zap Comix
Last Gasp, 1967

0 ....300.00
0/2nd 110.00
0/3rd 45.00
0/4th 20.00
0/5th 12.00
0/6th 6.00
0/7th 4.00
0/8th-0/10th 3.00
1 ....3,000.00
1/2nd 110.00
1/3rd 70.00
1/4th 28.00
1/5th 8.00
1/6th 6.00
1/7th 4.00
1/8th 3.00
2 ....55.00
2/2nd 34.00
2/3rd 8.00
2/4th-2/5th 4.00
3 ....35.00
3/2nd 18.00
3/3rd 7.00
3/4th-3/5th 4.00
4 ....28.00
4/2nd 8.00
4/3rd-4/5th 4.00
5 ....28.00
5/2nd 8.00
5/3rd 4.00
5/4th 3.00
6 ....16.00
6/2nd 5.00
6/3rd-6/4th 4.00
7 ....10.00
7/2nd 4.00
7/3rd-7/4th 3.00
8 ....10.00
8/2nd-8/3rd 4.00
9 ....10.00
9/2nd-9/3rd 4.00
10 ....5.00
11 ....4.00
12-13 ....5.00
14 ....4.00

Zatanna
DC, 1993

1-4 ....2.00

Zatanna: Everyday Magic
DC, 2003

1 ....6.00

Zatanna Special
DC, 1987

1 ....2.00

Zatch Bell!
Viz, 2005

1-3 ....10.00

Zaza the Mystic (Avalon)

Avalon

1 .... 3.00

Zealot

Image, 1995

1-3 .... 3.00

Zegra, Jungle Empress

Fox, 1948

2 .... 525.00
3-5 .... 450.00

Zell Sworddancer

3-D Zone

1 .... 2.00

Zell, Sworddancer

Thoughts & Images, 1986

1 .... 2.00

Zendra

Penny-Farthing, 2000

1-4 .... 3.00

Zen Illustrated Novella

Entity

1-2 .... 3.00

Zen, Intergalactic Ninja

Zen, 1987

1 .... 3.00
1/2nd-6 .... 2.00

Zen, Intergalactic Ninja

Zen, 1990

1-4 .... 2.00

Zen, Intergalactic Ninja

Zen, 1992

1-5 .... 2.00
Holiday 1 .... 3.00

Zen Intergalactic Ninja

Archie, 1992

1-3 .... 1.00

Zen Intergalactic Ninja

Archie, 1992

1-7 .... 1.00

Zen Intergalactic Ninja

Express, 1993

0-0/A 3.00
0/B 4.00
0/Ltd.-1 .... 3.00
1/Variant 4.00
2-4 .... 3.00
Ashcan 1 .... 1.00
Spring 1 .... 3.00

Zen Intergalactic Ninja All-New Color Special

Express, 1994

0 .... 4.00

Zen Intergalactic Ninja Color

Express, 1994

1-3 .... 4.00
4-7 .... 3.00

Zen Intergalactic Ninja Color

Express, 1995

1-2 .... 3.00

Zen, Intergalactic Ninja Earth Day Annual

Zen, 1993

1 .... 3.00

Zen Intergalactic Ninja Milestone

Express, 1994

1 .... 3.00

Zen Intergalactic Ninja Starquest

Express, 1994

1-7 .... 3.00

Zen Intergalactic Ninja Summer Special: Video Warrior

Express, 1994

1 .... 3.00

Zen Intergalactic Ninja: Tour of the Universe Special, the Airbrush Art of Dan Cote

Express, 1995

1 .... 4.00

Zenith: Phase I

Fleetway-Quality

1-3 .... 2.00

Zenith: Phase II

Fleetway-Quality

1-2 .... 2.00

Zen: The New Adventures

Zen, 1997

1 .... 3.00

Zero

Zero Comics, 1975

1-3 .... 3.00

Zero Girl

Homage, 2001

1-5 .... 3.00

Zero Girl: Full Circle

DC, 2003

1-5 .... 3.00

Zero Hour

Dog Soup, 1995

1 .... 3.00

X-Treme X-Men

X-Universe

XYZ Comics

Yellow Dog Comix

Yellowjacket Comics

Yosemite Sam

Youngblood

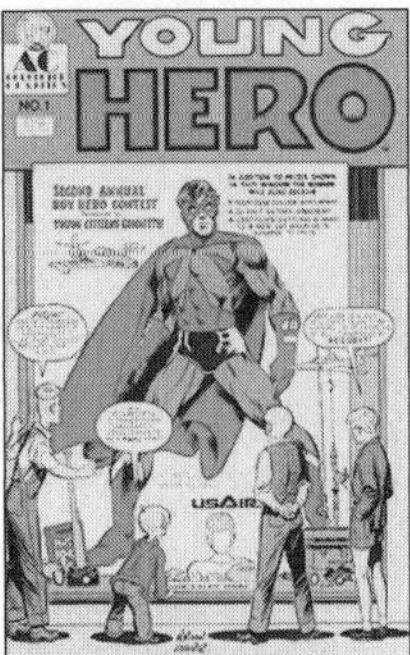

Young Hero

Zero Hour: Crisis in Time
DC, 1994
4-2 .... 2.00
1 .... 3.00
0 .... 2.00
Ashcan 1 .... 1.00

Zero Patrol
Continuity, 1984
1-2 .... 2.00

Zero Patrol
Continuity, 1987
1-5 .... 2.00

Zero Tolerance
First, 1990
1-4 .... 2.00

Zero Zero
Fantagraphics, 1995
1-7 .... 4.00
8 .... 6.00
9-26 .... 4.00

Zetraman
Antarctic, 1991
1-3 .... 2.00

Ziggy Pig & Silly Seal
Timely, 1944
1 .... 150.00
2-3 .... 80.00
4-6 .... 75.00

Zillion
Eternity, 1993
1-4 .... 3.00

Zip Comics
M.L.J., 1940
1 .... 3,500.00
2 .... 1,600.00
3 .... 1,250.00
4-5 .... 900.00
6-8 .... 750.00
9 .... 800.00
10 .... 750.00
11-17 .... 600.00
18 .... 625.00
19 .... 600.00
20 .... 900.00
21-26 .... 540.00
27 .... 800.00
28-30 .... 540.00
31-40 .... 375.00
41-47 .... 280.00

Zip Comics
Cozmic
1 .... 4.00

Zip Jet
St. John, 1953
1 .... 650.00
2 .... 450.00

Zippy Quarterly
Fantagraphics, 1993
1-2 .... 5.00
3-13 .... 4.00

Zoids: Chaotic Century
Viz, 2002
1-6 .... 7.00

Zolastraya and the Bard
Twilight Twins, 1987
1-5 .... 2.00

Zombie
Marvel, 2006
1-4 .... 4.00

Zombie 3-D
3-D Zone
1 .... 4.00

Zombie Boy
Antarctic, 1996
1-3 .... 3.00

Zombie King
Image, 2005
0 .... 3.00

Zombies!
Idea & Design Works, 2006
1-5 .... 4.00

Zombies: Eclipse of the Undead
Idea & Design Works, 2006
1-2 .... 4.00

Zombies vs. Robots
Idea & Design Works, 2006
1 .... 4.00

Zombie War
Tundra, 1992
1 .... 4.00

Zombie War
Fantaco, 1992
1-2 .... 4.00

Zombie W ar: Earth Must Be Destroyed
Fantaco, 1993
1-4 .... 3.00

ZombieWorld: Champion of the Worms
Dark Horse, 1997
1-3 .... 3.00

ZombieWorld: Dead End
Dark Horse, 1998
1-2 .... 3.00

ZombieWorld: Eat Your Heart Out
Dark Horse, 1998
1 .... 3.00

ZombieWorld: Home for the Holidays

Dark Horse, 1997

1 .... 3.00

ZombieWorld: Tree of Death

Dark Horse, 1999

1-4 .... 3.00

ZombieWorld: Winter's Dregs

Dark Horse, 1998

1-4 .... 3.00

Zomoid Illustories

3-D Zone

1 .... 3.00

Zone

Dark Horse

1 .... 2.00

Zone Continuum

Caliber, 1994

1 .... 3.00
1/A-1/B 2.00
2 .... 3.00

Zone Zero

Planet Boy

1 .... 3.00

Zoo Funnies

Children Comics, 1945

1 .... 120.00
2-3 .... 70.00
4-6 .... 60.00
7-9 .... 52.00
10-12 .... 40.00
13-15 .... 38.00

Zoo Funnies

Charlton, 1953

1 .... 42.00
2 .... 30.00
3 .... 24.00
4-7 .... 20.00
8-13 .... 32.00

Zoo Funnies

Charlton, 1984

1 .... 2.00

Zoom's Academy for the Super Gifted

Astonish, 2000

1-3 .... 4.00

Zooniverse

Eclipse, 1986

1-6 .... 2.00

Zoot!

Fantagraphics, 1992

1-6 .... 3.00

Zoot Comics

Fox, 1946

1 .... 175.00
2-5 .... 150.00
6-9 .... 125.00
10-11 .... 100.00
12-14 .... 90.00
13/A-14/A 425.00
15-16 .... 85.00

Zorann: Star-Warrior!

Blue Comet, 1994

0 .... 3.00
1 .... 2.00

Zori J's 3-D Bubble Bath

3-D Zone

1 .... 4.00

Zorro

Dell, 1959

8-9 .... 70.00
10-12 .... 68.00
13-15 .... 65.00

Zorro

Gold Key, 1966

1 .... 70.00
2-4 .... 38.00
5-7 .... 34.00
8-9 .... 28.00

Zorro

Marvel, 1990

1 .... 3.00
2-12 .... 2.00

Zorro

Topps, 1993

0 .... 3.00
1 .... 4.00
2 .... 8.00
3-11 .... 3.00

Zorro

NBM, 2005

1-6 .... 3.00

Zot!

Eclipse, 1984

1 .... 5.00
2-11 .... 3.00
12-35 .... 2.00
36 .... 3.00

Zu

Mu, 1992

1 .... 4.00

Zu

Mu, 1995

1-19 .... 3.00

ZZZ

Alan Bunce, 2000

1 .... 2.00

Young Justice

Young Men

Zatanna

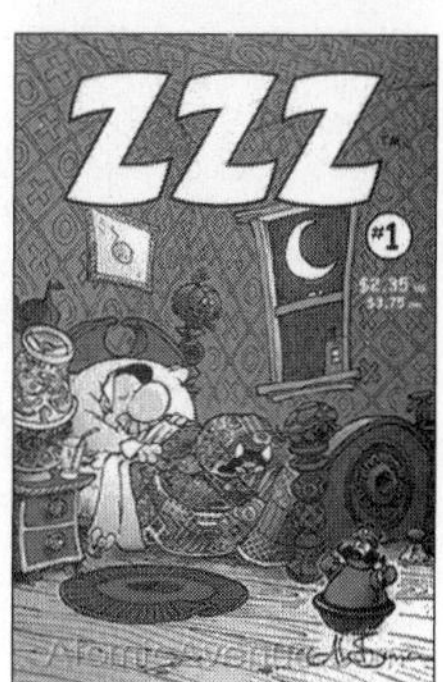

ZZZ

All comics prices listed are for NEAR MINT condition.

MORE ACTION - PACKED GUIDES

This easy-to-use and simple-to-search DVD contains 180,000 comic book listings, including comics from the Golden Age through the present. In addition to concise descriptions you'll also find thousands of color photos of covers, in a format which allows you to enlarge pages on your computer for closer inspection.
Item# Z3059 • $29.99

This PEZ-tastic book, by renowned PEZ-expert Shawn Peterson contains 1,200+ color photos, lists of rare variations, updated pricing and contacts for conventions and clubs.
Item# Z1843 • $24.99

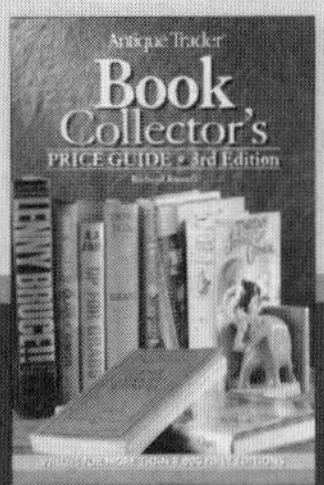

This new edition full-color guide to collectible books, the only one of its kind, features 14 categories of genres, 8,000 listings, 1,0a00 color photographs, and insider advice and a top ten list of rarities from each category.
Item# Z5019 • $24.99

The pioneers of scandalous and scintillating literature are celebrated and showcased in this extensive and thoroughly illustrated guide. By the founder of the NYC Collectible Paperback and Pulp Fiction Expo, this dynamic book delivers 700 pulp fiction covers with key details, including title, author, cover artist, publisher, number and pricing in three grades of condition.
Item #Z3823 • $24.99

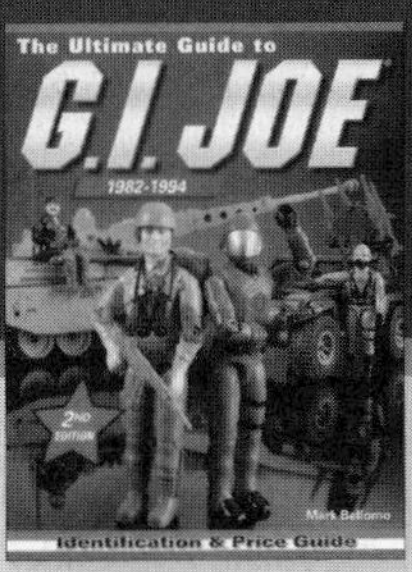

The G.I. Joe attitude is alive and well, and there's no better time to take a close look at the G.I. Joe action figures you may have tucked away. This new edition of the ULTIMATE guide to G.I. Joe is packed with photos, prices and key details to help you identify Joe and the team.

Item# Z3600 • $26.99

GET DISCOUNTS OF
10-30%
at shop.collect.com

Order Today at
shop.collect.com
or Call **800-726-9966**
(M-F 8 am-5 pm)

Use **Promo Code ACBA**
when ordering

COMING IN OCTOBER 2010

Order today for delivery after October 1, 2010

Shop.Collect.com or **Call 800-258-0929**

Promo Code
ACBA

COMICS BUYER'S GUIDE PRESENTS...

1000 COMIC BOOKS You Must Read

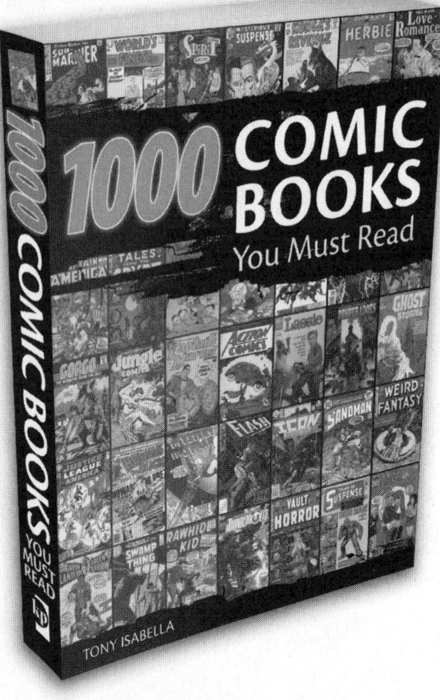

Hardcover • 10 x 10 • 272 p

Item #Z3599 • $29.99

Take a tour through comic book history that's unlike anything you've ever experienced! In this book you'll meet up with the famous and the infamous, including Superman, the Swamp Thing, The Fantastic Four, Iron Man, and the Crypt Keeper, among others. You'll also discover the reason why each one made Tony Isabella's must-read list, and you'll find the answers to comic book questions like:

- **Who became the Spectre in the 1940s?**
- **What super-power foursome fought a giant underwater gorilla in the 1960s?**
- **What's the name of Batman's "darker" mirror image?**
- **Which super-hero troupe (with a secret super-evil agenda) arrived on the scene in the 1990s?**

"...a glorious celebration of the whole comic-book industry."

~George Olshevsky, publisher of *"The Official Marvel Comics Index"*

Order online at

Shop.Collect.com

Call **800-258-0929**

Use Promo Code **ACBA** when ordering.